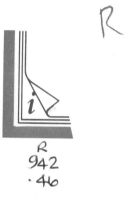

THE VICTORIA HISTORY
OF THE
COUNTIES OF ENGLAND

———

A HISTORY OF
STAFFORDSHIRE

VOLUME XVII

THE VICTORIA HISTORY
OF THE
COUNTIES OF ENGLAND

EDITED BY R. B. PUGH, D.LIT.

THE UNIVERSITY OF LONDON
INSTITUTE OF
HISTORICAL RESEARCH

Oxford University Press

OXFORD LONDON GLASGOW NEW YORK

TORONTO MELBOURNE WELLINGTON CAPE TOWN

IBADAN NAIROBI DAR ES SALAAM LUSAKA ADDIS ABABA

KUALA LUMPUR SINGAPORE JAKARTA HONG KONG TOKYO

DELHI BOMBAY CALCUTTA MADRAS KARACHI

© *University of London 1976*

ISBN 0 19 722743 0

*Printed in Great Britain
at the University Press, Oxford
by Vivian Ridler
Printer to the University*

INSCRIBED TO THE

MEMORY OF HER LATE MAJESTY

QUEEN VICTORIA

WHO GRACIOUSLY GAVE THE TITLE TO

AND ACCEPTED THE DEDICATION

OF THIS HISTORY

JRW 1836.

Smethwick Church.

SMETHWICK OLD CHURCH FROM THE SOUTH-EAST IN 1836

A HISTORY OF THE COUNTY OF

STAFFORD

EDITED BY M. W. GREENSLADE

VOLUME XVII

PUBLISHED FOR

THE INSTITUTE OF HISTORICAL RESEARCH

BY

OXFORD UNIVERSITY PRESS

1976

Distributed by Oxford University Press until 1 January 1979
thereafter by Dawsons of Pall Mall

CONTENTS OF VOLUME SEVENTEEN

LIST OF ILLUSTRATIONS

Grateful acknowledgement is made to the following for permission to use material: Aerofilms Ltd.; the *Birmingham Evening Mail*; the British Broadcasting Corporation; Sir Hugh Chance; Dorothy Parkes's Charity; Archibald Kenrick & Sons Ltd.; the National Portrait Gallery; the Borough Librarian, Metropolitan Borough of Sandwell; the Staffordshire Record Office; the Director of Walsall Libraries and Museum Services; the Trustees of the William Salt Library, Stafford; and the Curator of Wolverhampton Art Gallery. Unattributed photographs dated 1972 and 1975 are by A. P. Baggs.

LIST OF ILLUSTRATIONS

LIST OF MAPS AND PLANS

The maps of 1775 are from W. Yates, *A Map of the County of Stafford* (1775). The other maps were drawn by K. J. Wass of the Department of Geography, University College, London, from drafts prepared by M. W. Greenslade and D. A. Johnson; they are based on the Ordnance Survey with the sanction of the Controller of H.M. Stationery Office, Crown Copyright reserved, with the exception of the map of central Walsall in 1876 which is based on *Robinson's Map of Walsall published with the Walsall Red Book, 1876*. The plan of Walsall in 1679 is reproduced from the Isham (Lamport) MSS. in Northamptonshire Record Office (I.L. 3192). The other plans were drawn by A. P. Baggs. The plan of West Bromwich manor-house is based partly on drawings by J. A. Roberts, R.I.B.A. The plan of Sandwell Hall is based on a printed plan by T. Lightoler in Staffordshire Views, viii. 149, in the William Salt Library, Stafford. The plan of St. Matthew's Church, Walsall, is based partly on plans in the Lichfield Joint Record Office (B/C/5/1821, Walsall, and B/C/5/1877, Walsall). Thanks for permission to reproduce material are rendered to Sir Gyles Isham, Bt., Mr. Roberts, the Trustees of the William Salt Library, and the Diocesan Registrar.

EDITORIAL NOTE

THE present volume, the seventh to appear in the Staffordshire set, has, like its five immediate predecessors, been prepared under the auspices of the Staffordshire Victoria History Committee. The Committee, as explained in the Editorial Note to Volume IV, is the outcome of a partnership formed in 1950 between the University of London and a group of Staffordshire local authorities. The reorganization of local government in 1974 led to corresponding changes in the Committee, the new composition of which is set out on p. xvii. The University would like to express its thanks once more to the Staffordshire authorities for their continued support, especially as they have again generously increased the scale of their financial help.

A change in the local editorial staff occurred when Mr. G. C. Baugh, Assistant County Editor, left in 1971 to become County Editor of the Shropshire Victoria History. Mr. C. R. J. Currie was appointed in his place in 1972.

Many people have helped in the preparation of this volume. Several are acknowledged in the lists of illustrations and of maps and plans and in the footnotes to the articles on which their help was given. Thanks are also offered to Mr. S. Barton, Staffordshire County Librarian, and his staff, particularly Mr. D. Antill, formerly Assistant Information Officer; Mr. R. L. Ekin, Joint Registrar of Birmingham Diocese; Mr. M. B. S. Exham, Registrar of Lichfield Diocese; Miss Jane Isaac, assistant archivist at the Lichfield Joint Record Office; the Revd. J. D. McEvilly, archivist to the Archbishop of Birmingham; and Mr. F. B. Stitt, Staffordshire County Archivist and William Salt Librarian, and his staff.

The *General Introduction* to the *History* (1970) outlines the structure and aims of the series as a whole. The present volume relates to only three parishes in Offlow hundred: the account of the hundred itself and the history of the remaining parishes are reserved for future volumes.

STAFFORDSHIRE
VICTORIA COUNTY HISTORY COMMITTEE

as at 1 January 1975

Mr. G. C. W. Jones, Chairman   *Representing the Sandwell Metropolitan Borough Council*

Mr. H. Barks, o.b.e., Vice-Chairman   *Co-opted*

Mr. C. H. Stafford Northcote, Vice-Chairman
Mr. G. S. Angell
Mr. E. H. Beet
Dr. D. Ellis
Mr. J. Evans, m.b.e.
Mr. A. L. Garratt, m.b.e.   *Representing the Staffordshire County Council*
Mr. J. E. Roberts
Mr. F. W. Savill
Mr. S. O. Stewart
Mr. N. W. Tildesley

Mr. P. J. Bullock   *Representing the Dudley Metropolitan Borough Council*

Mrs. N. Daniel
Mr. F. H. Lamb   *Representing the Walsall Metropolitan Borough Council*

Mrs. E. D. Jevons
Mr. H. E. Lane   *Representing the Wolverhampton Metropolitan Borough Council*

Other Co-opted Members
Mr. F. B. Stitt   Mr. D. G. Stuart

Professor R. B. Pugh   Editor, *Victoria History of the Counties of England*

Mr. J. Blamire Brown   Honorary Secretary

Mr. G. Woodcock   Honorary Treasurer

Mr. M. W. Greenslade   County Editor

LIST OF CLASSES OF DOCUMENTS
IN THE PUBLIC RECORD OFFICE
USED IN THIS VOLUME
WITH THEIR CLASS NUMBERS

Clerks of Assize
  Assizes 4   Oxford Circuit, Miscellaneous Books

Chancery
          Proceedings
  C 1   Early
  C 2   Series I
  C 3   Series II
  C 5   Six Clerks Series, Bridges
          Enrolments
  C 54   Close Rolls
  C 60   Fine Rolls
  C 66   Patent Rolls
  C 78   Decree Rolls
  C 93   Proceedings of Commissioners for Charitable Uses, Inquisitions and Decrees
  C 103   Masters' Exhibits, Blunt
          Inquisitions post mortem Series I
  C 136   Richard II
  C 137   Henry IV
  C 139   Henry VI
  C 140   Edward IV
  C 142   Series II
  C 143   Inquisitions ad quod damnum

Court of Common Pleas
  C.P. 25(2) Feet of Fines, Series II
  C.P. 43   Recovery Rolls

Duchy of Lancaster
  D.L. 29   Ministers' Accounts

Exchequer, Treasury of the Receipt
  E 36   Books
  E 40   Deeds, Series A

Exchequer, King's Remembrancer
  E 101   Accounts, Various

E 133   Barons' Depositions
E 134   Depositions taken by Commission
E 150   Inquisitions post mortem, Series II
E 178   Special Commissions of Inquiry
E 210   Ancient Deeds, Series D

Exchequer, Augmentation Office
  E 326   Ancient Deeds, Series B

Ministry of Education
  Ed. 7   Elementary Education, Public Elementary Schools, Preliminary Statements

Home Office
  H.O. 107 Census Papers, Population Returns, 1841 and 1851
  H.O. 129 Census Papers, Ecclesiastical Returns

Prerogative Court of Canterbury
  Prob. 11 Registered Copies of Wills proved in P.C.C.

Registrar General
  R.G. 9   Census Returns, 1861
  R.G. 10 Census Returns, 1871

Court of Requests
  Req. 2   Proceedings

Special Collections
  S.C. 1   Ancient Correspondence
  S.C. 6   Ministers' Accounts

State Paper Office
  S.P. 23 Committee for Compounding with Delinquents

Court of Wards and Liveries
  Wards 7 Inquisitions post mortem
  Wards 9 Miscellaneous Books

LIST OF CLASSES OF OFFICIAL DOCUMENTS IN THE STAFFORDSHIRE RECORD OFFICE
USED IN THIS VOLUME

Records of the Court of Quarter Sessions

Administration

Q/ACp	police committee
Q/APr	police administration and returns to Chief Constable
Q/APs	police stations

Finance

Q/FAc	general accounts, constabulary
Q/FAm	general accounts, miscellaneous

Enrolment, Registration, and Deposit

Q/RDc	inclosure awards
Q/RHd	diversion, closing, and widening of highways
Q/RSc	charities
Q/RSe	scientific and literary societies
Q/RSf	friendly societies
Q/RTg	game duty (game certificates)
Q/RUm	public undertakings, plans of schemes
Q/RUo	public undertakings, Acts and Orders

The Court in Session

Q/SB	Sessions bundles
Q/SO	Sessions order books
Q/SR	Sessions rolls

Records of the County Council

C/C	County Clerk's Department
C/E	County Education Department
C/H	County Health Department
C/PC	County Police Committee

LIST OF CLASSES OF DOCUMENTS IN THE LICHFIELD JOINT RECORD OFFICE
USED IN THIS VOLUME

Archdeacons' Visitation Records

A/V/1	Visitation Books

Bishop's Administrative Records

B/A/1	Bishops' Registers (volumes 1 to 28)
B/A/2(i)	Bishops' Registers: Supplementary Series (volumes A to F)
B/A/3	Presentation Deeds and Grants of Advowson
B/A/12	Dissenters and Roman Catholics
B/A/15	Tithe Awards
B/A/27(i)	Volume relating to charitable endowments

Bishop's Court Records

B/C/5	Consistory Court Cause Papers
B/C/12	Faculties

Bishop's Visitation Records

B/V/1	Visitation Books
B/V/5	Primary Visitation Parish Returns and Churchwardens' Presentments to Articles of Inquiry
B/V/6	Glebe Terriers

LIST OF CLASSES OF DOCUMENTS IN THE LICHFIELD DIOCESAN REGISTRY
USED IN THIS VOLUME

Bishop's Administrative Records

B/A/1	Bishops' Registers (volumes 29 onwards)
B/A/2(i)	Bishops' Registers: Supplementary Series (volumes G onwards)

NOTE ON ABBREVIATIONS

Among the abbreviations and short titles used the following may require elucidation:

Allen, *Ind. Dev. Birm.*	G. C. Allen, *The Industrial Development of Birmingham and the Black Country 1860–1927* (1929)
B.A.A.	Birmingham Archdiocesan Archives, Archbishop's House, Birmingham
B.M.	British Museum (used in references to documents which in 1973 were transferred to the new British Library)
B.R.L.	Birmingham Central Library, Reference Library
Birm. and Mid. Hardware Dist.	*The Resources, Products, and Industrial History of Birmingham and the Midland Hardware District: Reports collected by the British Association in 1865*, ed. S. Timmins (1866)
Birm. Dioc. Regy.	Birmingham Diocesan Registry
Blay, 'Street Names of Walsall'	W. F. Blay, 'Street Names of Walsall' (typescript in Walsall Central Library)
Cason, *Blakenall Heath*	R. A. Cason, *Where Numbers Cease to Count: the Parish of Blakenall Heath 1872–1972* (Walsall, n. d. [1972])
Charter of Corp. of Walsall	*The Charter of the Corporation of Walsall: with an Account of the Estates thereto belonging* (facsimile of the 1774 edition, Walsall, 1925)
Ede, *Wednesbury*	J. R. Ede, *History of Wednesbury* (Wednesbury, 1962)
Erdeswick, *Staffs.*	S. Erdeswick, *A Survey of Staffordshire*, ed. T. Harwood (1844)
Fink, *Queen Mary's Grammar Sch.*	D. P. J. Fink, *Queen Mary's Grammar School 1554–1954* (Walsall, 1954)
Fowler, Map of West Bromwich (1856)	W. Fowler & Son, and Cooksey & Rollason, Map of the Parish of West Bromwich in the County of Stafford (1856) (in Sandwell Central Library)
Glew, *Walsall*	E. L. Glew, *History of the Borough and Foreign of Walsall* (Walsall, 1856)
Hackwood, *Smethwick*	F. W. Hackwood, *Some Records of Smethwick* (Smethwick, 1896)
Hackwood, *West Bromwich*	F. W. Hackwood, *A History of West Bromwich* (Birmingham, 1895)
Homeshaw, *Bloxwich*	E. J. Homeshaw, *The Story of Bloxwich* (Bloxwich, 1955)
Homeshaw, *Walsall*	E. J. Homeshaw, *The Corporation of the Borough and Foreign of Walsall* (Walsall, 1960)
L.J.R.O.	Lichfield Joint Record Office
Lee, *Walsall*	H. Lee, *A Short History of Walsall* (Walsall, 1927)
Lich. Dioc. Regy.	Lichfield Diocesan Registry
Mann, 'Smethwick'	Margaret B. Mann, 'Smethwick. A Geographical Study of Land Utilisation, 1800–1950' (Birmingham University B.A. Thesis, 1950) (copy in Smethwick District Library)
'Old Smethwick'	A series of articles under that general title by W. E. Jephcott in *Smethwick Telephone*
'Old West Bromwich'	A series of articles under that general title by W. E. Jephcott in *West Bromwich, Oldbury and Smethwick Midland Chronicle and Free Press*
Peacock & Cottrell, Map of West Bromwich (1857)	Map of the Parish of West Bromwich in the County of Stafford surveyed for the West Bromwich Improvement Commissioners by Peacock & Cottrell 1857 (in Sandwell Central Library)
Pearce, *Walsall*	T. Pearce, *The History and Directory of Walsall* (Walsall, 1813)
Pevsner, *Staffs.*	N. Pevsner, *The Buildings of England: Staffordshire* (1974)
Pevsner, *Worcs.*	N. Pevsner, *The Buildings of England: Worcestershire* (1969)
Pitt, *Staffs.*	W. Pitt, *A Topographical History of Staffordshire* (Newcastle-under-Lyme, 1817)
Plot, *Staffs.*	R. Plot, *The Natural History of Staffordshire* (Oxford, 1686)
Price, 'Smethwick'	G. L. A. Price, 'Smethwick: the Evolution and Modern Character of an Industrial County Borough' (Leicester University B.A. Thesis, 1963) (copy in Smethwick District Library)
Prince, *Old West Bromwich*	H. H. Prince, *Old West Bromwich or the Story of Long Ago* (West Bromwich, 1924)
Pye, *Modern Birmingham*	C. Pye, *A Description of Modern Birmingham; whereunto are annexed Observations made during an Excursion round the Town, in the Summer of 1818* (Birmingham, n. d. [1820])
Redhead, *Local Govt.*	S. C. Redhead, *County Borough of Smethwick: Notes on the History of Local Government in the Borough* (duplicated booklet, 1963) (copy in Smethwick District Library)
Reeves, *West Bromwich*	J. Reeves, *The History and Topography of West Bromwich and its Vicinity* (n. d. [1836])

Roper, Plan of Smethwick, 1858 — Plan of the Hamlet of Smethwick in the Parish of Harborne and County of Stafford. 1858. Surveyed for the purposes of the Public Health Act 1848. Henry C. Roper, Surveyor, Dudley (in Smethwick District Library)

Roper, Plans of Smethwick, 1857 — Plans of the Hamlet of Smethwick in the Parish of Harborne in the County of Stafford surveyed for the purposes of the Public Health Act 1848. 1857. Henry C. Roper, Engineering Surveyor (in Borough Surveyor's Department, Warley, in 1971)

S.H.C. — Staffordshire Record Society (formerly William Salt Archaeological Society), *Collections for a History of Staffordshire*

S.R.O. — Staffordshire Record Office

Shaw, *Staffs.* — Stebbing Shaw, *The History and Antiquities of Staffordshire* (2 vols., 1798, 1801)

Sims, *Cal. of Deeds* — R. Sims, *Calendar of the Deeds and Documents belonging to the Corporation of Walsall* (Walsall, 1882)

'Smethwick and Round About' — A series of articles under that general title by W. E. Jephcott in *Smethwick Telephone*

Snape, *Plan of Walsall* (1782) — J. Snape, Plan of the Town of Walsall: Taken in the Year 1782 (in Walsall Central Library); printed in Willmore, *Walsall* (see below)

Staffs. Cath. Hist. — *Staffordshire Catholic History* (the Journal of the Staffordshire Catholic History Society)

Statement of Accts. — *A Full Statement of Accounts of the Late Corporation of the Borough and Foreign of Walsall; from 1802 to 1835, being a period of Thirty-Three Years* (Walsall, n. d. [1836])

T.B.A.S. — Birmingham and Midland Institute: Birmingham Archaeological Society, *Transactions and Proceedings*

T.C.T. *Life's Realities* — [D. Plant], *Life's Realities* (Wolverhampton, n. d. [1922])

W.B.L. — West Bromwich Central Library (from 1974 Metropolitan Borough of Sandwell Central Library)

W.C.L. — Walsall Central Library

W.P.L. — Warley Public Libraries, Central Library, Smethwick (from 1974 Smethwick District Library, Metropolitan Borough of Sandwell)

W.S.L. — William Salt Library, Stafford

W.T.C. — Walsall Town Chest, Council House, Walsall

Walsall Records — *Walsall Records: Translations* [by R. W. Gillespie] *of Ancient Documents in the Walsall Chartulary in the British Museum* (Walsall, 1914)

West Bromwich Churchwardens' Bks. — Churchwardens' Books of the Parish Church of West Bromwich, transcribed by E. Lissimore, 1958, 1962 (typescript in Sandwell Central Library)

West Bromwich Ct. R. — Some Manorial Court Rolls of West Bromwich, transcribed and translated by E. Lissimore, 1965 (typescript in Sandwell Central Library)

West Bromwich Par. Bk. — Parish Book of West Bromwich 1735–1832 (in Sandwell Central Library)

West Bromwich Vestry Mins. — Minutes of vestry and various other meetings held in the parish of West Bromwich from September 1766 to August 1828, transcribed by E. Lissimore, 1960 (typescript in Sandwell Central Library)

West Bromwich Vestry Mins. (in burial reg.) — Minutes of vestry meetings held in the parish of West Bromwich between 1715 and 1745 (in the burial register 1753–77), transcribed by E. Lissimore, 1957 (typescript in Sandwell Central Library)

'West Bromwich 100 Years Ago' — A series of articles under that general title by S. Lees in *West Bromwich and Oldbury Chronicle*

Willett, *West Bromwich* — Mary Willett, *A History of West Bromwich* (West Bromwich, 1883)

Willmore, *Walsall* — F. W. Willmore, *A History of Walsall and its Neighbourhood* (Walsall, 1887)

Wood, *Plan of West Bromwich* (1837) — *Plan of West Bromwich from Actual Survey by John Wood 1837* (engraved by W. Murphy and J. Wood, Edinburgh)

Woodall, *Walsall Milestones* — R. D. Woodall, *Walsall Milestones* (Streetly, n. d. [1951])

Woodall, *West Bromwich Yesterdays* — R. D. Woodall, *West Bromwich Yesterdays* (Streetly, n. d. [1959])

Yates, *Map of Staffs.* (1775; 1799) — W. Yates, *A Map of the County of Stafford … Begun in the Year 1769 and Finished in 1775* (1775; revised edition by W. Faden, 1799)

ANALYSIS OF SOURCES
PRINTED IN
COLLECTIONS FOR A HISTORY OF STAFFORDSHIRE
(STAFFORDSHIRE RECORD SOCIETY)
AND USED IN THIS VOLUME

Vol.	*Pages*	*Subject-matter or title of article*
i	1–143	Pipe Rolls, 1130, 1155–89
	145–240	Liber Niger Scaccarii, 1166
	290–384	Manor and Parish of Blymhill
ii(1)	1–177	Pipe Rolls, 1189–1216
ii(2)	4–22	Obligatory Knighthood, *temp.* Chas. I
	24–65	Arms Recorded at the Visitation of Staffordshire, 1663–4
iii(1)	1–163	Plea Rolls, 1194–1215
	178–231	Staffordshire Chartulary, *c.* 1120–*c.* 1272
iii(2)		Visitation of Staffordshire, 1583
iv(1)	1–215	Plea Rolls, 1219–72
	218–63	Final Concords, 1218–72
v(1)	1–101	Burton Chartulary
	105–21	Staffordshire Hundred Rolls
	123–80	Pleas of the Forest, 1262–1300
v(2)		Visitations of Staffordshire, 1614 and 1663–4
vi(1)	29–36	Staffordshire Pleas, *temp.* Hen. III
	37–300	Plea Rolls, 1271–94
vii(1)	1–191	Plea Rolls, 1293–1307
	195–255	Subsidy Roll, 1327
ix(1)	3–118	Plea Rolls, 1308–26
ix(2)		The Barons of Dudley
x(1)	3–75	Plea Rolls, 1308–26
	79–132	Subsidy Roll, 1332–3
xi	3–123	Plea Rolls, 1327–41
	127–292	Final Concords, 1327–1546
xii(1)	3–173	Plea Rolls, 1341–59
	177–239	Final Concords, Hen. VII–Philip and Mary
xiii	3–204	Plea Rolls, 1360–87
	207–300	Final Concords, 1559–73
xiv(1)	3–162	Plea Rolls, 1327–83
	165–217	Final Concords, 1573–80
xv	3–126	Plea Rolls, 1387–1412
	129–98	Final Concords, 1580–9
	201–31	Staffordshire Muster of 1640
xvi	3–93	Plea Rolls, Edw. III–Hen. IV
	97–225	Final Concords, 1589–1603
xvii	3–153	Plea Rolls, 1413–35
	157–205	Poll Tax Returns, 1379–81
	209–36	Final Concords, 1558–88
xviii(1)	3–21	Final Concords, 1589–1602
	28–70	Final Concords, 1603–7
New Series ii		History of Weston-under-Lizard
New Series iii	3–70	Final Concords, 1607–12
	123–229	Plea Rolls, 1423–57, with 1392 and 1401
New Series iv	31–91	Final Concords, 1613–16
	95–212	Plea Rolls, 1456–74

ANALYSIS OF SOURCES

OFFLOW HUNDRED

(*part*)

WEST BROMWICH

WEST BROMWICH,[1] lying immediately north-west of Birmingham, was an ancient parish which became a borough in 1882 and a county borough in 1889. It was made part of the metropolitan borough of Sandwell in 1974.[2] The ancient parish and the original borough were 5,851 a. in area.[3] An adjustment of the boundary with Smethwick in 1897 added 8 a.[4] In 1928 645 a. at Hamstead were added from the urban district of Perry Barr. In 1931 332 a. at the Delves were added from the borough of Wednesbury and 727 a. from the civil parish of Great Barr; 371 a. were transferred to Wednesbury and a small area at Bescot to the borough of Walsall. The changes left West Bromwich with an increased area of 7,180 a.[5] In 1966 the borough was extended to 11,704 a. by the inclusion of most of the boroughs of Tipton and Wednesbury and by various boundary adjustments.[6] The present article is concerned primarily with the history of the area covered by the ancient parish of West Bromwich. Some account of the areas added before 1966 is given from the time of their addition. The earlier history of the Hamstead portion of Handsworth ancient parish added to West Bromwich in 1928 is narrated elsewhere;[7] otherwise the history of all new areas is reserved for treatment in future volumes of the Staffordshire *History*.

The ancient parish of West Bromwich has been described as 'a kind of peninsula' formed by a loop of the head-waters of the Tame.[8] The boundary was the Tame on the south-west, west, north, and north-east. On the south-east the boundary followed Park Lane and then Spon Brook to Bromford where

the brook enters the Tame.[9] The area lies at the northern end of the low plateau which itself forms part of the South Staffordshire Plateau and extends southwards to Birmingham and the Rea valley.[10] The central part of the town lies around the 525-foot contour, reaching 568 ft. at the junction of Beeches Road and Thynne Street. Two spurs run from this high ground, one northwards to All Saints' Church and Stone Cross, one north-westwards to Hill Top. Between the two ridges flows Hobnail Brook, which was called Hobbins Brook in the late 17th century;[11] it rises near Hall End and enters the Tame below Hydes Bridge. On the eastern side of the ancient parish the land slopes down to 348 ft. at Forge Mill Farm.[12] The landscape is now mainly urban, but the south-eastern part of the area remains open country, though crossed by the M5 motorway.

West Bromwich is situated on the Coal Measures and straddles the exposed and concealed sections of the South Staffordshire coalfield. The northern and western parts of the ancient parish consist of Carboniferous shales and marls respectively. The south-eastern part of the parish is beyond the coalfield's Eastern Boundary Fault, and there Carboniferous red sandstone overlies the Coal Measures. As a result it was the western part that became more heavily industrialized from the earlier 19th century.[13] Over the central high ground the drift consists of boulder clay, the western and eastern sides of the parish being largely shales and marls. There is sand and gravel around Greets Green and New Town. Along the Tame and Hobnail Brook the soil is alluvial.[14]

The settlement was originally known as Brom-

[1] This article was written mainly between 1968 and 1970; some material has been added up to 1974, the date to which the additional matter refers being indicated. Grateful acknowledgement of help is made to Mr. R. B. Ludgate, borough librarian, and his staff, especially Mrs. Madeline Reed. Thanks are also due to Mr. G. C. W. Jones, who made valuable comments on the article in draft, and others named in footnotes.

[2] See pp. 45–6.

[3] O.S. *Area Book: West Bromwich* (1889).

[4] Local Govt. Board Provisional Orders Conf. (No. 7) Act, 1897, 60 & 61 Vic. c. 72 (Local); S.R.O., L.G.O. 6/112.

[5] West Bromwich Corporation Act, 1927, 17 & 18 Geo. V, c. 86 (Local); West Bromwich Corporation Act, 1930, 20 & 21 Geo. V, c. 120 (Local); *Census*, 1931; Ede, *Wednesbury*, 385; S.R.O., L.G.O. 12/1 and 7.

[6] *County Boro. of West Bromwich: Council Diary and Municipal Yearbook 1966/67*, 7; below p. 46.

[7] In *V.C.H. Warws.* vii.

[8] Hackwood, *West Bromwich*, 46.

[9] See Yates, *Map of Staffs.* (1775), part of which is

reproduced on p. 2; Wood, *Plan of West Bromwich* (1837); Willett, *West Bromwich*, 247–8; E 134/27 and 28 Eliz. I Mich./2 m. 1; West Bromwich Ct. R. p. 81. For the various streams which form the head-waters of the Tame and have been called the Tame see T. Eastwood, T. H. Whitehead, and T. Robertson, *Memoirs of Geol. Surv.*, *Geol. of Country around Birmingham*, 2 n.; Reeves, *West Bromwich*, 5–6. Wood's *Plan* and B.R.L. 392629, p. 3 (1842), call the stream west of Bromford the Roway (or Row Hay) Brook. For Spon Brook see 'Old West Bromwich', 2 July, 24 Dec. 1943; 'Old Smethwick', 2 Apr. 1949; B.R.L. 392629, pp. 2–3. For the name Grete Brook see below p. 8.

[10] *Birmingham and its Regional Setting* (Brit. Assoc. 1950), 4–5, 8.

[11] West Bromwich Ct. R. p. 163.

[12] O.S. Map 1/2,500, Staffs. LXVIII. 7 (1947 edn.); West Bromwich Ref. Libr. *Short Hist. of West Bromwich* (1964), chap. 16; Hackwood, *West Bromwich*, 1.

[13] Geol. Surv. Map 1″, solid, sheet 168 (1924 edn.); below pp. 39–40.

[14] Geol. Surv. Map 1″, drift, sheet 168 (1924 edn.).

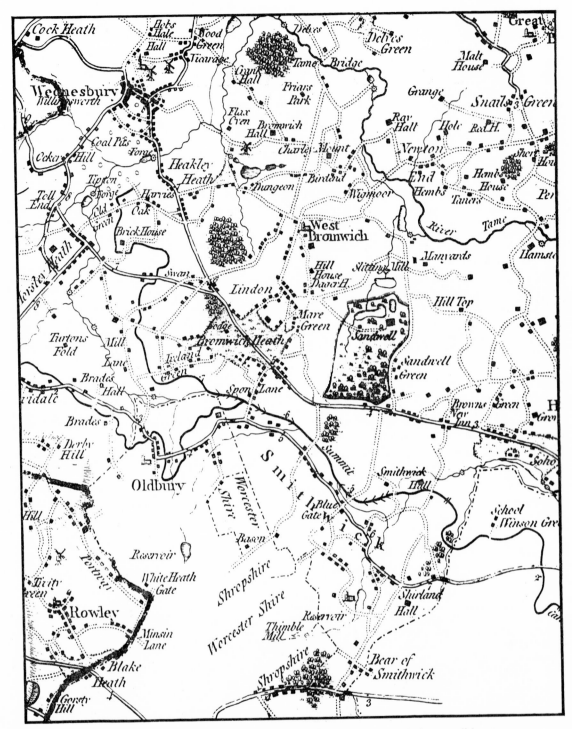

WEST BROMWICH AND SMETHWICK AREA, *c.* 1775 (scale about 1 inch to 1 mile)

wich, a name in use by the time of Domesday Book and suggesting a village where broom grew. It was becoming known as West Bromwich by the early 14th century, probably to distinguish it from Castle Bromwich and Little Bromwich, both in Aston (Warws.).[15] The inhabitants of West Bromwich are traditionally known as 'throstles'. The name is said to derive from the 'numberless donkeys who browsed upon the open common lands and whose discordant bray was thus satirically alluded to under the name of the sweet-voiced thrush'.[16]

Before the later 18th century West Bromwich was thinly populated and rural; from the 16th century the iron industry was developing, and domestic nailing in particular was added to agrarian pursuits. The main settlement was at Lyndon to the south of the parish church, although the manor-house stood about a mile north-west of the church. There was also a medieval settlement at Finchpath by the river-crossing into Wednesbury; this eventually

[15] E. Ekwall, *Concise Oxford Dict. of Eng. Place-Names* (4th edn.); *P.N. Warws.* (E.P.N.S.), 40; Reeves, *West Bromwich*, 156; *S.H.C.* v (1), 78; W.S.L., S. MS. 383, f. 209.   [16] Hackwood, *West Bromwich*, 115.

spread southwards up to Hill Top. Otherwise settlement in the parish consisted of small groups of cottages, or 'ends', around the Heath which extended south-west from Lyndon across the main Birmingham–Wolverhampton road; numerous cottages occur in 1723 as encroachments on the Heath.[17] There was also some settlement in the Charlemont–Wigmore area.[18] Sandwell in the south-east of the parish was the site of a small monastery in the Middle Ages and the home of the earls of Dartmouth in the 18th and earlier 19th centuries.[19] In the later 18th century the Heath, eventually the site of the new town, was still 'a warren full of rabbits and a long black common, intercepting the intercourse with Birmingham by a green sea of moor and barrenness'.[20] Nevertheless encroachment was continuing, notably on its eastern side.[21]

The population was small as well as scattered. In 1086 there were 10 villeins and 3 bordars.[22] There were 172 poll-tax payers in 1377[23] and 116 households in 1563.[24] The Protestation Returns of 1642 were signed by 398 men in West Bromwich.[25] In 1666 194 people were chargeable for hearth tax and 117 were exempt.[26] In the 18th century the growth of the iron industry caused a large rise in population.[27] By 1773 there were just under 1,200 houses in the parish,[28] and in 1801 the population numbered 5,687.[29]

The Heath was inclosed in 1804, and by about 1820 it was becoming the new centre of West Bromwich.[30] The population of the parish had risen to 9,505 by 1821,[31] and in the next few years the rapid growth of mining and the iron industry led to an even greater increase. It was estimated that by 1829 the population had increased some 50 per cent to over 14,000,[32] and it had reached 15,327 in 1831, 26,121 in 1841, and 34,591 in 1851.[33] 'What a town of a place this West Bromwich is!' wrote a visitor in 1828.[34] In fact he exaggerated the extent of the development. In the early 1840s an observer commented that a town of West Bromwich hardly existed since the population was distributed in groups over the western side of the parish.[35] David Christie Murray described West Bromwich about the time of his birth in 1847 as 'a rather doleful hybrid of a place—neither town nor country'.[36] Another writer, recalling the mid 1850s, stated that the population was 'sparingly and irregularly distributed, or grouped in certain areas into colonies or rookeries, without any sort of arrangement or sanitary consideration whatever'.[37] Nonetheless West

Bromwich in the mid 19th century was for many a very desirable place in which to live—'a West-end suburb' for 'the retired and thriven iron and coal masters, carriers, and factors of the Mining District which surrounds it'.[38] At the same time there was much poverty, and many small tenants were unable to pay rates.[39]

In 1901 the population of the borough numbered 65,175.[40] The enlarged borough had a population of 81,303 in 1931[41] and 96,041 in 1961.[42] From the later 1950s many immigrants, mainly Jamaicans and Indians, were settling in West Bromwich, particularly in the Beeches Road, Lodge Road, and Spon Lane areas in the south of the borough; in 1961 the population included 1,132 people born in Jamaica and 128 born in other Caribbean territories, 677 born in India, and 146 born in Pakistan.[43] The landscape has changed considerably in the 20th century, notably with the building of large housing estates since 1919 on derelict industrial land as well as in open country; the 1960s saw extensive redevelopment, old housing and factories giving way to new.

Notable people connected with the town include two holders of the manorial estate, Sir Richard Shelton, solicitor-general from 1625 to 1634, and Dr. Walter Needham, the 17th-century physician and anatomist.[44] Two of the incumbents, Edward Stillingfleet (1757–82) and William Jesse (1790–1814), were notable Evangelicals.[45] The Legge family was the leading local family for a century and a half after William Legge, Baron Dartmouth, bought the Sandwell estate in 1701. Lord Dartmouth, a Tory statesman during Queen Anne's reign who was created earl of Dartmouth in 1711, retired from political life after the accession of George I in 1714; he died in 1750.[46] His grandson the 2nd earl (d. 1801) was a prominent statesman under George III and was noted for his Evangelical piety.[47] Augustus Legge, the fifth son of the 4th earl of Dartmouth and bishop of Lichfield from 1891 to 1913, was born at Sandwell Hall in 1839. He left a request that if he was no longer bishop of Lichfield when he died, he should be buried at All Saints', West Bromwich. In the event he died as bishop and was buried in the Close at Lichfield.[48]

Other noteworthy natives of West Bromwich are Walter Parsons, the giant blacksmith who became porter to James I;[49] John Blackham (1834–1923), founder of the Pleasant Sunday Afternoon movement;[50] the brothers David Christie Murray (1847–

[17] See p. 28.
[18] Yates, *Map of Staffs.* (1775); below p. 6 and n.
[19] See p. 18.
[20] *Staffs. Advertiser*, 22 Dec. 1849. For the warren see below p. 23.
[21] See p. 28.   [22] *V.C.H. Staffs.* iv. 59, no. 299.
[23] *S.H.C.* 4th ser. vi. 1, 10.
[24] *S.H.C.* 1915, p. lxxii.
[25] House of Lords Rec. Office, HH. 4 (reference supplied by Dr. E. A. O. Whiteman).
[26] *S.H.C.* 1923, 246–52.   [27] Shaw, *Staffs.* ii. 134.
[28] L.J.R.O., B/V/5/1772–3.
[29] *V.C.H. Staffs.* i. 324.   [30] See pp. 4, 29.
[31] *V.C.H. Staffs.* i. 324.
[32] Pigot, *Com. Dir. Birm.* (1829), 101.
[33] *V.C.H. Staffs.* i. 324.
[34] *The Register: Literary, Scientific, and Sporting Jnl.* 22 Nov. 1828 (copy in W.S.L.).
[35] *1st Rep. Com. Midland Mining, S. Staffs.* [508], p. cxliv, H.C. (1843), xiii.
[36] D. C. Murray, *Recollections* (1908), 9.

[37] T. C. T. *Life's Realities*, 161.
[38] *Staffs. Advertiser*, 22 Dec. 1849.
[39] West Bromwich Rates Act, 1850, 13 & 14 Vic. c. 4 (Local and Personal).   [40] *Census*, 1901.
[41] *Census*, 1931. The population of the part of Perry Barr U.D. added in 1928 was 'treated as being 1,380': S.R.O., F. 1396, West Bromwich town clerk to county clerk, 29 June 1928. The areas added to and taken out of the borough in 1931 had had a population in 1921 of 198 and 83 respectively: *Census*, 1931.   [42] *Census*, 1961.
[43] Ibid.; ex inf. the boro. director of education (1969); below p. 5.
[44] See p. 16.   [45] See pp. 52, 63.
[46] *D.N.B.*; *Complete Peerage*, iv. 88.
[47] *D.N.B.*; B. D. Bargar, *Lord Dartmouth and the American Revolution* (Columbia, 1965); *V.C.H. Staffs.* iii. 65; below pp. 52, 63.
[48] *V.C.H. Staffs.* iii. 87; *Staffs. Advertiser*, 22 Mar. 1913.
[49] Plot, *Staffs.* 294; Hackwood, *West Bromwich*, 76–7.
[50] See p. 68.

1907) and Henry Murray (1859–1937), novelists;[51] and Madeleine Carroll (born 1906), film actress.[52] Francis Asbury (1745–1816), 'the John Wesley of the Western World',[53] was born at Hamstead in Handsworth but spent his early years at Newton; the cottage where he lived is preserved as a museum. He was a Methodist class leader in West Bromwich. He went to America in 1771 and in 1784 was made one of the two superintendents, or bishops, of the newly formed Methodist Episcopal Church of the United States of America.[54]

James Keir (1735–1820), chemist and industrialist, settled in the Midlands after serving in the army during the Seven Years War. He lived at Finchpath Hall at Hill Top from 1770 and was buried at All Saints' in 1820.[55] James Eaton (1785–1857) served in the *Téméraire* at the battle of Trafalgar and, as signal midshipman, repeated Nelson's message to the fleet. He had settled in West Bromwich by 1837, and by 1839 he was living at Hill House, where he died. For a few years in the early 1840s he owned an interest in the Heath Colliery Co.[56] John Bedford (1810–79), president (1867) of the Wesleyan Methodist Conference, was minister at the High Street chapel from 1846 to 1849.[57]

THE GROWTH OF THE TOWN. The chief settlement in the parish until the 19th century was Lyndon to the south of All Saints' Church. The church itself can be traced from the earlier 12th century[58] and the name Lyndon from the earlier 14th;[59] the name Lyne was also used.[60] The open fields lay in that part of the parish,[61] and a market was held there in the early 18th century.[62] By the later 18th century the main part of the village lay around the junction of the present Hargate Lane and the present Lyndon Street and extended south-

east to Mayer's Green.[63] East of the village there was a road running from the church to Mayer's Green via the present Church Vale (formerly Sot's Hole) and Dagger Lane.[64] At the north end of Dagger Lane stands Hill House, built in the earlier 16th century.[65] The avenue of trees along the east side of Dagger Lane was added from the Hill House estate when the road was widened in the late 19th century.[66] Dagger Hall at the junction of Dagger Lane and Salter's Lane occurs by 1667 but was demolished in 1894–5.[67] Hallam Street, now the main link from Church Vale to the Mayer's Green area, was originally a footpath running as far north as Little Lane; it was made into a road about the mid 1850s and had been extended to Church Vale by the 1880s.[68] There was settlement at Mayer's Green by the 1680s,[69] and by 1723 numerous cottages were being built as encroachments on the green.[70] Hall End west of the church was an inhabited area by the end of the 16th century.[71] Heath End south-east of the junction of the roads from Tipton and Wednesbury existed by 1723 when the Cross Guns inn there is mentioned.[72] To the south of Mayer's Green at Virgins End the Virgin inn is said to have been built in 1768,[73] while at Overend by the main road there was considerable settlement by the 1780s.[74]

As a result of the inclosure of the Heath in 1804, the centre of West Bromwich eventually shifted south-west from Lyndon to what became the High Street stretch of the Birmingham–Wolverhampton road. There was no immediate rush to take up building sites,[75] but by 1816 new streets had been laid out on the north-east side of the road—Lombard, New, and Bratt Streets.[76] Christ Church between High Street and Bratt Street was begun in 1821.[77] The development of High Street, however, was piecemeal. Although many houses had been built

[51] Woodall, *West Bromwich Yesterdays*, 76–83; *Midland Chron. & Free Press*, 7 Nov. 1969, p. 8. See also their autobiographical writings: D. C. Murray, *The Making of a Novelist* (1894) and *Recollections* (1908); H. Murray, *A Stepson of Fortune* (1909).
[52] Woodall, *West Bromwich Yesterdays*, 41; *Who's Who* (1970); *Midland Chron.* 23 Sept. 1927; *Civic Mag.* Jan. 1930, 16–17 (copy in W.B.L.); W.B.L., A. 199.
[53] The words of Bp. Hamilton in 1924: J. Lewis, *Francis Asbury*, 221.
[54] *D.N.B.*; *Jnl. and Letters of Francis Asbury* (3 vols., 1958), ed. E. T. Clark, J. M. Potts, and J. S. Payton; below p. 72.
[55] *D.N.B.*; N. G. Coley, 'James Keir', *West Midlands Studies*, iv; R. E. Schofield, *Lunar Society of Birmingham*; 'Smethwick and Round About', 3 Dec. 1954; 'Old West Bromwich', 2 Mar. 1945; Shaw, *Staffs*. ii. 134, 136–7; Hist. MSS. Com. 20, *15th Rep. I, Dartmouth*, iii, p. 273; C. J. L. Elwell, *The Iron Elwells* (Ilfracombe, 1964), 50; Hackwood, *West Bromwich*, 105.
[56] W. R. O'Byrne, *Naval Biog. Dict.* (1849), 323; S.R.O., D.(W.)633A(30); *Staffs. Advertiser*, 7 Mar. 1857; inscrip. on his gravestone in All Saints' churchyard; *Reg. of Electors within Southern Div. of County of Stafford . . . 1 Nov. 1839–1 Nov. 1840*, 63 (copy in W.S.L.); B.R.L. 459677.
[57] *D.N.B.*; *Hill's Alphabetical Arrangement of Wesleyan-Methodist Ministers*, ed. J. P. Haswell (7th edn., 1853), 15; *P.O. Dir. Staffs.* (1850).
[58] See p. 50.
[59] Willett, *West Bromwich*, 206, 208; *S.H.C.* 4th ser. vi. 10.
[60] E 134/27 and 28 Eliz. I Mich./2 m. 6 (1585); B.R.L. 456894 (1699); S.R.O., D.(W.)631A(30), J. Furneyhough, Plan of West Bromwich (c. 1820).
[61] See p. 27.   [62] Reeves, *West Bromwich*, 54–5.

[63] Yates, *Map of Staffs.* (1775).
[64] Willett, *West Bromwich*, 225–6 (1667); Yates, *Map of Staffs.* (1775); S.R.O., D.(W.)631A(30), J. Furneyhough, Plan of West Bromwich (c. 1820); *Short Hist. of West Bromwich*, chap. 13; 'Old West Bromwich', 17 Aug. 1945.
[65] See p. 23.
[66] 'Old West Bromwich', 31 Aug. 1945.
[67] See p. 21.
[68] 'Old West Bromwich', 17 Aug. 1945; S.R.O., Q/RDc 60, map (1804); Wood, *Plan of West Bromwich* (1837); O.S. Map 6″, Staffs. LXVIII. NW. (1891 edn.). It was described in 1851 as 'the intended new central road from Mayers Green towards the Old Church' ('Old West Bromwich', 28 May 1943) and was shown as far as Little Lane by Fowler, Map of West Bromwich (1856). Previously Walsall St. was called Hallam St.: Wood, *Plan of West Bromwich*.
[69] S.R.O., D. 564/3/1/18; West Bromwich Ct. R. p. 192. It was then known as Mares Green.
[70] See p. 28.
[71] Ct. R. pp. 13, 19, 76, 98, 105; B.R.L., Caddick and Yates 18; Yates, *Map of Staffs.* (1775).
[72] S.R.O., D.(W.)632A(30), name among list of essoins; Willett, *West Bromwich*, 257; Yates, *Map of Staffs.* (1775).
[73] 'Old West Bromwich', 31 Aug. 1945; S.R.O., Q/RDc 60, map.
[74] S.R.O., D.(W.)622A(30).
[75] S. Lees, 'Hist. of Ebenezer Chapel, West Bromwich' (1906; MS. at West Bromwich United Reformed Church), pp. 29–30.
[76] B.M., O.S.D. 212; C. and J. Greenwood, *Map of Staffs.* (1820); S.R.O., D.(W.)631A(30), J. Furneyhough, Plan of West Bromwich (c. 1820).
[77] See p. 55.

along the main road by 1818, building was still very scattered.[78] By 1834, however, High Street had 'many well-stocked shops . . . giving to the whole the air and bustle of a market town'.[79] There were also a house and foundry near Christ Church built some ten years before by James Roberts.[80] The southern end near the Bull's Head inn around what is now Dartmouth Square seems to have been one of the first main areas to develop, a process which had begun by 1818. The Bull's Head itself existed by the 1750s and was then called the Boot inn. In 1834 the Dartmouth Arms (by 1835 the Dartmouth Hotel) was opened on the site of the Bull's Head and became a centre for official, business, and social meetings; Dartmouth Square became the normal place for outdoor meetings.[81] By 1856 High Street was built up on both sides from Dartmouth Square to Christ Church and extensively so from Sandwell Road to Carter's Green. The area between New and Bull Streets had also been developed, but on the other side of High Street opposite Christ Church the area of the Lodge estate was developed only after 1867 when the estate was sold.[82] In 1868 High Street was a busy thoroughfare, broad, straight, well-paved, and flanked by stuccoed buildings. It had the appearance of 'some smart country town . . . But to dispel such bright imaginings, it is only needful to turn a few yards up any of the side streets . . . Painted stucco and elegant shop fronts give place to smoke-dried habitations, or dusty foundry walls, and parasols disappear in favour of huge fustian bonnets, in which the nymphs of the mine delight to deck themselves when clad in their work-a-day gear'.[83] With the opening of the town hall on part of the Lodge estate in 1875 the new centre of West Bromwich may be considered to have received official recognition.

The old centre too continued to expand. In particular the later 19th century saw the development of a residential area south of Mayer's Green in the south-western part of Sandwell Park.[84] When the 4th earl of Dartmouth left Sandwell for Patshull in 1853, there were already plans for developing the estate. Although Lord Dartmouth died later the same year, by 1854 a scheme had been prepared for the development of the south-west corner of the park down to the Birmingham road both for middle-class houses and for commercial purposes. Development did not in fact begin until the 1860s and was on a smaller scale. The main feature was the laying-out of the Beeches area as a residential district by G. B. Nichols, a West Bromwich architect and surveyor. In 1867 his plans were approved by the highway committee of the improvement commissioners and Lord Dartmouth sold him 21 freehold plots. Herbert Street was described as a new street in 1869, but Beeches Road was still being constructed in 1884, while houses in Legge Street are dated 1885 and 1887,[85] a terrace in Nicholls Street 1886, and a house in Herbert Street 1887. A well-to-do district resulted; its large houses have now been taken over by West Indians. In 1877 Lord Dartmouth gave 56 a. of the Sandwell estate in the area to the improvement commissioners for a public park; it was opened in 1878 as Dartmouth Park and extended eastwards by the gift of another 9½ a. in 1887. The land was at first held on a 99-year lease at a nominal rent, but in 1919 the 6th earl and his son Viscount Lewisham gave the freehold to the borough as a memorial to the local men who had served in the First World War.[86]

The first main development in the central part of the town in the 20th century was around Lyndon. The Tantany housing estate was begun by the corporation in 1920 with the laying-out of 95 a. on garden-city lines.[87] There is also extensive private housing of the period between the World Wars both to the south in the Cronehills area and eastward from there across Hallam Street to Dagger Lane. There is further private housing of the same period between All Saints Street and Vicarage Road and along Heath Lane; to the south of it is a council estate built since the Second World War. In 1969, after the clearance of the Pitt Street and Queen Street area, work was begun on a new town centre. The first section, the Sandwell Centre, was opened in 1971 and consists of a covered shopping precinct, a bus station, and a multi-storey car-park. The scheme is being carried out by the borough council and the National Coal Board Mineworkers' Pension Fund; the architects are the John Madin Design Group.[88] By 1970, when the stretch of the ring road from Birmingham Road to Carter's Green was begun, there had been extensive clearance along its route north-westward from the Mayer's Green area.[89]

The Sandwell area in the south-east corner of the borough is still open country. It was there that Sandwell priory was founded in the late 12th century on the site of a hermitage. A park was laid out,

[78] 'Old West Bromwich', 28 Dec. 1945; Pye, *Modern Birmingham*, 108.
[79] White, *Dir. Staffs.* (1834).
[80] 'Old West Bromwich', 10, 17, and 24 Nov. 1944.
[81] 'Old West Bromwich', 20 Aug. 1943, 28 Dec. 1945; 'West Bromwich 100 Years Ago', 10 May 1901; Reeves, *West Bromwich*, 52; Pigot, *Nat. Com. Dir.* (1835), 473; Wood, *Plan of West Bromwich* (1837).
[82] Fowler, Map of West Bromwich (1856); below p. 9.
[83] J. C. Tildesley, 'The Progress of the Black Country, No. VII: West Bromwich', *Birmingham Daily Gaz.* 1 June 1868 (cutting in W.B.L., Scrapbook 13, p. 15).
[84] *Staffs. Advertiser*, 24 June 1854; *Midland Counties Herald*, 24 Aug. 1854; 'Old West Bromwich', 21 Sept., 2 Nov. 1945; R. W. Sturgess, 'Landowners, Mining and Urban Development in Nineteenth-century Staffs.', *Land and Industry*, ed. J. T. Ward and R. G. Wilson, 175–6, 184–5, 188–9; conveyance by Lord Dartmouth and his trustees to G. B. Nichols, 21 Dec. 1867 (in possession of Mr. D. A. Dilworth of West Bromwich, 1970); S.R.O. 575; *P.O. Dir. Staffs.* (1868); S.R.O.,

D. 648/103/38; O.S. Map 6″, Staffs. LXVIII. SW. (edns. of 1890 and 1904); S.R.O., D. 564/8/1/21/July 1883, plan for construction of Beeches Rd.; ibid./July 1884, account of Alf. Palmer of Birmingham for making part of Beeches Rd. (drains, kerbs, etc.). For Herbert St. see trust deed of Spon Lane alms-houses, 1869, in Char. Com. files. For the Methodist chapel (1871–2) and St. Philip's Church (1892), both in Beeches Rd., see below pp. 59, 65.
[85] There are also two dates of 1896 and 1902 in Beeches Rd. and Nicholls St. respectively.
[86] *West Bromwich Official Handbook* [1963], 57; *Staffs. Advertiser*, 8 June 1878; *Kelly's Dir. Staffs.* (1892); S.R.O., D. 564/8/1/22/Dec. 1886.
[87] County Boro. of West Bromwich, *Representation to Minister of Health for Alteration of Boundary of County Boro.* (1921), 16 (copies in W.B.L. and in S.R.O., F. 1228); J. Richards, *West Bromwich and its Baptists 1796 to 1968*, 14 (copy in W.B.L.).
[88] *Evening Mail*, 5 Sept. 1969; *Express & Star*, 9 June 1971; plaques in the Sandwell Centre.
[89] *Evening Mail*, 26 Jan., 6 and 24 Mar. 1970.

probably in the mid 18th century when Sandwell Hall had become the Dartmouths' home.[90] In 1767 Richard Jago praised the beauty of the park in verse, contrasting it with 'the smoky scene',[91] and a century later it was thankfully commended as the 'one healthy lung of this great manufacturing parish'.[92] In 1947 the corporation bought the remaining 1,367 a. of the Sandwell estate, mainly to preserve it as open country.[93] Although the northern end of the M5 motorway, opened in 1970,[94] runs through it, much of it is occupied by the Sandwell Park and Dartmouth golf-courses, and the wild character of the part around the site of the hall is being preserved.[95]

The northern part of the parish remained open country until the 20th century; in 1970 a few farms still existed in the area extending northwards from Sandwell. At Hall Green stands the medieval manor-house. By the 13th century the area round it was known as Whisty. By at least the mid 16th century there was a house at Whisty which was evidently distinct from the manor-house; it was presumably the Whisty House at Hall Green which was stated in 1828 to have been recently demolished. There was still a field called Big Whisty on the south side of Hall Green in the mid 19th century.[96] The modern suburb of Stone Cross on the Walsall road east of Hall Green is named from a wayside cross which occurs in the early 17th century and still stood in the later 18th century; the base survived as part of a signpost until c. 1897.[97] Friar Park in the northern tip of the parish was an estate belonging to Halesowen abbey in the Middle Ages; its modern name was in use by the end of the 16th century.[98] In the later 18th century most of the settlement in the northern area of the parish lay around Charlemont, Bird End, and Wigmore.[99] On the Tame at Bustleholm the 17th-century ironworks was still in production.[1] Further south the 16th-century works known as Bromwich forge was also still working, and in 1784 seven people there owed suit at the manor court; the forge ceased to work c. 1830.[2]

In the 20th century housing estates have covered much of the northern area. In the Charlemont dis-

trict there is one of the earlier council estates in the town, 53 a. developed on garden-city lines in the 1920s.[3] There is also private housing of the period between the World Wars. The Charlemont Farm council estate, with multi-storey flats a prominent feature, and the private Bustleholm Mill estate date from the 1960s.[4] West of Walsall Road there are council estates of the period between the wars off Marsh Lane and on either side of Westminster Road.[5] The large Friar Park council estate is of the same period, and more recently some light industry has been established in Friar Park Road. The Crankhall Lane (West) estate to the north of Friar Park was built in the 1930s by Wednesbury borough council on part of the land acquired from West Bromwich in exchange for the Delves in 1931;[6] it has been extended since the Second World War. The Yew Tree council estate at the Delves was completed c. 1966.[7] Further east the parts of Hamstead and Great Barr added to West Bromwich in 1928 and 1931 have been developed with council and private estates dating from before and after the Second World War.[8] During the war a munitions factory was built on the east side of Walsall Road near the boundary; in the early 1970s the buildings were used partly as dwellings and partly for industrial purposes.[9] A recent feature of the Bustleholm area is the intersection of the M5 and M6 motorways with a striking system of fly-overs and sliproads.

Finchpath occurs in the 1420s as a hamlet on the West Bromwich bank of the Tame by the bridge into Wednesbury,[10] but the settlement apparently existed much earlier. The name Finchpath was already attached to the bridge in the earlier 13th century,[11] 'the mill of Finchespath' (apparently on the Wednesbury side of the river) occurs in 1255,[12] and there was coalmining there by 1309.[13] The Golde family was living there in 1332 and probably by the later 13th century.[14] The area called Finchpath originally extended as far south as Black Lake (Nether Finchpath) and west to Harvills Oak,[15] and in the 1780s a district still known as Finchpath was populous.[16] By the mid 18th century the area at the top of Holloway Bank (or Finchpath Hill)[17] was

[90] See pp. 18–20.
[91] R. Jago, Edge-Hill, or, The Rural Prospect Delineated and Moralized (1767), 111.
[92] West Bromwich Times, 20 June 1868 (cutting in W.B.L., Scrapbook 13, p. 7).
[93] West Bromwich Corp. deeds, no. 577A; West Bromwich Official Handbook [1963], 63. The area purchased consisted of 1,006 a. in West Bromwich and 361 a. in Handsworth.   [94] See p. 12.
[95] Express & Star, 12 Feb. 1970. For Sandwell Park Golf Club see Staffs. Life, Apr. 1951, 28–9.
[96] S.H.C. vi (1), 170; L.J.R.O., wills of Cecily Stanley (proved 5 Nov. 1552) and Francis Symcockes (proved 10 July 1610); West Bromwich Ct. R. pp. 11–12, 86; B.R.L. 297204; E 134/13 Geo. I. Mich./7 m. 1.; W.B.L., D. 57; deeds in possession of Mr. G. Harvey of Crankhall Lane, West Bromwich (1971), abstract of 1897 reciting will of Jas. Smith of 1828; L.J.R.O., B/A/15/West Bromwich, no. 3159; below p. 13.
[97] Willett, West Bromwich, 186, 191; L.J.R.O., will of Francis Symcockes; 'Old West Bromwich', 3 Aug. 1945; Evening Mail, 23 June 1969, reporting the discovery of stones from the cross in a rockery in Hall Green Rd.
[98] See p. 22.
[99] Yates, Map of Staffs. (1775); below pp. 20–1. Poplar Cottage in Charlemont Rd. at Bird End bears a tablet with the initials TCM and the date 1679. Wigmore gave its name to one of the open fields. For Wigmore Farm from 1746 see B.R.L., Caddick and Yates 33.

[1] See p. 32.
[2] See p. 33; S.R.O., D.(W.)622A(30).
[3] County Boro. of West Bromwich, Representation to Minister of Health for Alteration of Boundary of County Boro. (1921), 16 (copies in W.B.L. and in S.R.O., F. 1228).
[4] For details of the Charlemont Farm estate see West Bromwich Official Handbook (1966), 34; County Boro. of West Bromwich, Council Clarion, Oct. 1960, 13.
[5] For the Westminster Rd. estate see O.S. Map 1/2,500, Staffs. LXVIII. 2 (1943 edn.) and 6 (1946 edn.), revised 1938; Midland Chron. and Free Press, 28 July 1939.
[6] Ede, Wednesbury, 385, 401; above p. 1.
[7] West Bromwich Official Handbook (1966), 34; Council Clarion, Jan. 1961, 8; County Boro. of West Bromwich, Yew Tree Community Centre: Official Opening Thurs. 15th Nov. 1962 (copy in W.B.L.).
[8] See pp. 1, 47. For the Newton End part of Hamstead see V.C.H. Warws. vii. 24; Yates, Map of Staffs. (1775).
[9] Ex inf. the archivist, Walsall Central Library (1973).
[10] Ede, Wednesbury, 108 (no reference given).
[11] See pp. 12–13.
[12] Bk. of Fees, ii. 1291.
[13] See p. 39.
[14] S.H.C. vi (1), 50; vii (1), 229; xiii. 28.
[15] Hackwood, West Bromwich, 50; S.H.C. xiii. 294; Willett, West Bromwich, 216; below n. 41.
[16] S.R.O., D.(W.)622A(30); 'Old West Bromwich', 9 Feb. 1945.
[17] E 36/165 f. 136 (1526); below pp. 11, 26.

becoming known as Hill Top,[18] and at the end of the century it consisted of 'a large street' of small houses and also 'several good gentlemen's houses'.[19] One of these was Finchpath Hall opposite the end of Hawkes Lane, the home of James Keir; the house had been divided into two by 1901 and was demolished to make way for shops in 1938.[20] Another was Meyrick House, the home of Joseph Hateley, a solicitor, in the earlier 19th century. It was bought by the corporation in 1896, and in 1897–8 a police station and a reading room (now a branch library) were built on the site. The grounds were laid out as the 5-acre Hill Top Park, which was extended by another 4 a. c. 1960.[21] By the mid 19th century the area immediately west of the main road at Hill Top was developing,[22] and mining and especially iron-working had become established.[23] As early as 1799 Edward Elwell had converted a flour mill on the main road into a foundry, and he built up a successful hollow-ware business there; he lived at Five Ways House, Black Lake.[24]

The development of the area south and east of Hill Top dates mainly from the 19th and 20th centuries. Black Lake to the south was the name of a plot of land by the end of the 14th century (when it occurs with 'Whytelake')[25] and the name of a house or cottage by 1502.[26] Early in the 18th century the Presbyterians built the Old Meeting there.[27] By 1820 there was continuous settlement along the west side of the main road at Black Lake and more to the south in the Carter's Green area around the junction with the road from Tipton.[28] The name Carter's Green was in use by 1764.[29] Hateley Heath to the east of Hill Top occurs from the later 15th century as a piece of common land within the triangle formed by the present Wyntor, Allerton, and Jowett's Lanes, and a cottage there was mentioned at the end of the 16th century.[30] By the 1740s there was an iron-foundry there.[31] Ridgacre to the south, apparently an inhabited area in the earlier 14th century,[32] was densely wooded until the earlier 19th century.[33] In fact the new mines and ironworks of the whole district east of the main road and the canals serving them produced an industrial landscape which persisted into the 20th century.[34] The area is now occupied largely by council estates, notably one built between the World Wars on the triangle of the former Hateley Heath and two large estates to the north and south built since the Second World War. For the one on the north side of Witton Lane over 30 a. of derelict pit mounds were cleared in 1954–5.[35] There is also some private housing dating from the period between the wars in the Coles Lane area and at Black Lake and council housing built both before and after the Second World War to the east of Old Meeting Street. The small council estate on the west side of Old Meeting Street was completed in 1961.[36]

Golds Green in the north-west of the parish may take its name from the Golde family.[37] It was the scene of mining by the 1760s, and the Balls Hill branch of the Birmingham Canal was opened to serve the pits in 1769.[38] Since the late 18th century the district has also contained several ironworks, notably the Golds Hill works of John Bagnall & Sons; the closing of that works in 1882 caused a decline in the population of the district.[39] The area to the south-east known as Harvills Hawthorn was originally called Harvills Oak. The name Harvill is thought to be a corruption of Heronville, since the Heronvilles, lords of Wednesbury, acquired land in West Bromwich from the Goldes in the 14th century.[40] A tree called 'Harvyls Oke' is mentioned in 1531,[41] and Harvills Oak was the name of an inhabited district along the road from Hill Top to Golds Green by the mid 18th century.[42] That part of the road was coming to be known as Harvills Hawthorn by 1816,[43] although in the 1850s the northern stretch of Dial Lane was still called Harvills Oak.[44] By the 1830s the area was becoming industrialized, particularly with collieries and boiler factories,[45] and it was at the end of the Balls Hill branch canal that in 1897 John Brockhouse opened his spring and axle works, now the principal works of the Brockhouse Organization.[46] There is some council housing at Harvills Hawthorn built before the Second World War, but the main features of the area are the two large council estates built after the

[18] Hackwood, *West Bromwich*, 50; 'West Bromwich 100 Years Ago', 30 Aug. 1901.
[19] Shaw, *Staffs.* ii. 134.
[20] See p. 4; N. G. Coley, 'James Keir', *West Midlands Studies*, iv. 2.
[21] 'West Bromwich 100 Years Ago', 1 Feb. 1901; 'Old West Bromwich', 2 Mar. 1945; Hackwood, *West Bromwich*, 76; *West Bromwich Official Handbook* [1963], 62; inscription and plaque on present building.
[22] L.J.R.O., B/A/15/West Bromwich; Fowler, Map of West Bromwich (1856).
[23] 'Old West Bromwich', 11 and 25 May 1945; White, *Dir. Staffs.* (1851).
[24] 'Old West Bromwich', 23 Mar. 1945; C. J. L. Elwell, *The Iron Elwells* (Ilfracombe, 1964), 46–7, 51; Wood, *Plan of West Bromwich* (1837).
[25] Hackwood, *West Bromwich*, 50; Willett, *West Bromwich*, 209, 210. The early spelling is Blake, or Blak, Lake.
[26] Willett, *West Bromwich*, 211, 214–16, 218.
[27] See p. 67.
[28] Greenwood, *Map of Staffs.* (1820).
[29] S.R.O., D.(W.)579(30).
[30] W.S.L., S. D. Pearson 1461; Willett, *West Bromwich*, 217–18; Ct. R. p. 19; Yates, *Map of Staffs.* (1775).
[31] See p. 31.
[32] There are several references to Roger de Rugaker from 1327: Willett, *West Bromwich*, 193, 206; *S.H.C.* vii (1), 229; x (1), 103; xi. 100. Land called Ridgacres occurs in 1502: Willett, op. cit. 211.
[33] See p. 29. Church Lane was originally called Ridge-

acre Lane: Wood, *Plan of West Bromwich* (1837); Peacock & Cottrell, Map of West Bromwich (1857).
[34] See e.g. Wood, *Plan of West Bromwich* (1837); O.S. Map 6", Staffs. LXVIII. NW. (1921 edn.; provisional edn. with additions of 1938).
[35] County Boro. of West Bromwich, *Council Clarion*, Jan. 1959, 9.
[36] Ibid. Oct. 1958, 6–7; Apr. 1961, 4–5.
[37] See p. 6.
[38] See pp. 13, 40.
[39] A. C. Beardsmore, 'County Boro. of West Bromwich: Particulars of Schools . . .' (TS. in W.B.L.), Golds Hill Sch.; below p. 39.
[40] Ede, *Wednesbury*, 26. Land in Finchpath was held by the Heronvilles' successors in the 15th century: Shaw, *Staffs.* ii. 83–4. A Wm. de Hereville occurs in a lawsuit involving rent in West Bromwich in 1362, and a Ric. Hervill held land there in 1372: *S.H.C.* xi. 180; xiii. 28–9.
[41] Willett, *West Bromwich*, 164. It is described as in Finchpath in 1597: West Bromwich Ct. R. p. 15.
[42] S.R.O., D.(W.)629A(30); Yates, *Map of Staffs.* (1775).
[43] B.M., O.S.D. 212; S.R.O., D.(W.)631A(30), J. Furneyhough, Plan of West Bromwich (c. 1820); D.(W.) 626A(30). The name Harvills Oak was used in W.B.L., West Bromwich Highway Book 1819–20 and West Bromwich Highways Collecting Book 1826–7.
[44] W.B.L., Plan of West Bromwich (n.d.), sheet 10.
[45] Wood, *Plan of West Bromwich* (1837); 'Old West Bromwich', 11 May 1945.
[46] See p. 38.

war. The earlier was planned in the 1930s when 53 a. of derelict land were bought as the site, but the war delayed building. The first house was finished in 1946, and the estate was completed in 1948.[47]

Swan Village to the south, the area around the junction of Swan Lane, Phoenix Street, and the Tipton road, takes its name from the Swan inn. The inn occurs in 1655 when it was held by Richard Sterry,[48] but it probably existed by 1635.[49] Stabling and coach-houses were among the amenities which it advertised in 1801.[50] The present building dates only from c. 1860.[51] Mining and iron-working became established in the neighbourhood in the early 19th century,[52] and the Birmingham & Staffordshire Gas Light Company built its works at Swan Village in 1825.[53] A station on the new Birmingham–Wolverhampton railway was opened there in 1854.[54]

The south-western part of the parish was originally known as Greet, probably taking its name from the gravel of the area.[55] A mill at 'Grete' existed by the late 12th century,[56] and 'Grete' persisted as the name of part of the parish for at least another four centuries.[57] Great Bridge, where the main road crosses the Tame into Tipton, was originally Grete Bridge,[58] 'Great' being used by the end of the 17th century:[59] in the early 16th century the Tame in that area was known as Grete Brook.[60] There was settlement on the West Bromwich side of the bridge by the mid 16th century,[61] but much of the district now known as Great Bridge is in Tipton. Greets End near Great Bridge occurs in 1713.[62] Greets Green, the area around the junction of the roads from Great Bridge and Swan Village, is mentioned in the mid 16th century,[63] and in 1777 there was still a 'common or waste . . . commonly called Greets Green'.[64] Near by was the Dunkirk estate, the home of the Rider family by the late 16th century;[65] Ryders Green to the north-west[66] presumably took its name from the family. Another early estate was that held by the Hillary family in the 14th century, which later centred on Greet mill in what is now West Bromwich Street.[67] Cop Hall in the Sheepwash area south of Great Bridge existed by the early 17th century and was the home

of a John Turton in 1685.[68] Two cottages occur as encroachments on the waste at Sheepwash in 1723.[69]

Settlement in the south-western part of the parish was still scattered in the later 18th century,[70] but in the earlier 19th century extensive mining began there.[71] At Great Bridge there was iron-working by 1818;[72] by the middle of the century there were also several ironworks along the Birmingham Canal, notably the Union Furnaces established after Philip Williams & Co. bought the Union Farm estate in 1827.[73] From 1852 the ironworks were also served by the Stour Valley Railway running alongside the canal.[74] The extensive Crown Works of Braithwaite & Co. Structural Ltd. on the Balls Hill branch canal south of Ryder Street originated in the mid 19th century when Riley, Fleet & Newey started their structural engineering business there.[75] Tube-making had started at Great Bridge by 1861, and the first part of the large Wellington Tube Works was opened on the Broadwaters branch canal in 1872.[76] By the mid 19th century brickmaking became important in the Greets Green and Albion areas.[77] The industrial expansion was matched by a great increase of population. Greets Green and the Sheepwash area (including New Town) were developing by the 1830s,[78] and by the mid century Grout Street and adjoining streets had been built up.[79] In 1851 the population of the Greets Green area was given as 6,000.[80] The Dunkirk estate included several cottages, with adjoining brew-houses and piggeries, by 1853.[81] In that year part of the estate was put up for sale as building land, and the property was advertised as a good investment because of the fast increasing demand by miners and others for houses. It was also stated that more of the estate would soon be divided into small building plots by a Birmingham building society.[82] In 1853 and 1854 building land to the north of the main road between Swan Village and Great Bridge was advertised for sale by the society; mention was made of new streets there in 1854.[83] William Street to the south of the main road was described in 1855 as newly laid out,[84] and Fisher Street further west apparently dates from 1859.[85] Development continued; thus when

[47] *Official Opening of the Harvills Hawthorn No 1. Housing Estate* (copy in W.B.L.).
[48] *West Bromwich Par. Reg.* (Staffs. Par. Reg. Soc.), i. 81, 84, 95; Willett, *West Bromwich*, 204, 219; Ct. R. pp. 159–60; B.R.L., Caddick and Yates 17; S.R.O., D.(W.)627A(30)–629A(30), 632A(30).
[49] B.R.L., Caddick and Yates 18 (showing Wm. Sterrer of West Bromwich an innholder in 1635).
[50] 'West Bromwich 100 Years Ago', 5 Apr. 1901.
[51] Ibid.; *Short. Hist. of West Bromwich*, chap. 8.
[52] Wood, *Plan of West Bromwich* (1837); Reeves, *West Bromwich*, 51. For early chapels there see below pp. 65–6.
[53] See p. 49.   [54] See p. 14.
[55] *Eng. Place-name Elements* (E.P.N.S.), i. 209; above p. 1.
[56] See p. 31.
[57] *S.H.C.* N.S. iii. 154; Willett, *West Bromwich*, 214; E 40/14723; Ct. R. pp. 5, 13, 15. It appears in a rent-roll of the late 1740s: S.R.O., D.(W.)629A(30).
[58] See various spellings in 16th- and 17th-century references in Ct. R.
[59] S.R.O., Q/SO 10, Mich. 1699, E. 1702.
[60] E 36/165 f. 136v.
[61] *S.H.C.* 1926, 82–3; *S.H.C.* 1931, 155.
[62] W.S.L. 67/20/22, p. 1.
[63] See pp. 28–9.
[64] Willett, *West Bromwich*, 170.
[65] See p. 21.
[66] S.R.O., D.(W.)620A(30); Wood, *Plan of West Bromwich* (1837).

[67] See p. 24.
[68] Ct. R. p. 46; Willett, *West Bromwich*, 172; Wood, *Plan of West Bromwich* (1837); Pigot, *Nat. Com. Dir.* (1841), Staffs. p. 91, showing it as the home of Ric. Haines.
[69] S.R.O., D.(W.)632A(30).
[70] Yates, *Map of Staffs.* (1775).
[71] Wood, *Plan of West Bromwich* (1837).
[72] Parson and Bradshaw, *Dir. Staffs.* (1818); Wood, *Plan of West Bromwich* (1837).
[73] L.J.R.O., B/A/15/West Bromwich; 'Old West Bromwich', 14 and 21 July, 4 Aug. 1944; below p. 39. Greet mill had become part of a foundry in the 1780s: below p. 30.   [74] See p. 14.
[75] 'Old West Bromwich', 6 and 13 Oct. 1944.
[76] 'Old West Bromwich', 22 Dec. 1944.
[77] See p. 41.
[78] S.R.O., D.(W.)626A(30); 'Old West Bromwich', 13 Oct. 1944; Wood, *Plan of West Bromwich* (1837); L.J.R.O., B/A/15/West Bromwich; below pp. 57, 64, 66.
[79] L.J.R.O., B/A/15/West Bromwich.
[80] H.O. 129/381/3/1.
[81] *Aris's Birmingham Gaz.* 28 Feb. 1853.
[82] Ibid. 7, 14, 21, 28 Feb. 1853.
[83] *Midland Counties Herald*, 21 July 1853, 18 May, 1 June 1854.
[84] S.R.O., D. 1205, Sam. Banbrook and trustees of Victoria Permanent Building Investment and Land Soc. 5 Nov. 1855.
[85] *Staffs. Advertiser*, 16 July 1859; below p. 76.

St. Michael's mission church was opened in Bull Lane in 1881, in place of an earlier mission in Wood Lane, it was said to have been built for some 2,000 people, mainly brick-workers.[86] Farley Park in Whitehall Road was presented to the borough by Reuben Farley in 1891; it was extended from 5 to $8\frac{1}{2}$ a. in 1955.[87] Another open space is formed by the playing fields north of Greets Green Road. When the corporation bought the 58-acre site in 1922, it consisted of pit mounds; unemployed labour was used to level it, and it was opened as playing fields in 1926.[88] There is council and private housing off Oldbury Road dating from the period between the World Wars. The Cophall council estate west of Whitehall Road was begun in 1959 after the clearance of about 100 slum houses, some of them back-to-back.[89] A council estate was still being built in the Sheepwash area in 1970.

Much of the area eastward from Greets Green to the present town centre was still part of the Heath in the later 18th century.[90] A notable early building, however, is the Oak House in Oak Road, the nucleus of which dates from the later 16th century.[91] The Parliamentarians are said to have thrown up an encampment on the Heath near what is now Oak Lane during the siege of Dudley castle in 1644.[92] By the later 18th century there was some settlement at Ireland Green (the area around the present Gads Lane), Cutler's End (now Lambert's End), and Old End (the present Richard Street area).[93] To the east was the Lodge estate centring on a house that was originally a warrener's lodge. The estate was sold in 1867 and the house demolished in 1868. The District Hospital was built on part of the estate in 1869–71. The corporation bought another part and erected a group of public buildings there in 1874–5.[94] The rest of the estate was developed as a residential area; several new streets were laid out, including Lodge Road, but most of the development took place towards the end of the century.[95] The Guns Village area north of Dartmouth Street (a street formerly known as Danks Hill)[96] and the area between Oak Road and Moor Street had some buildings by the 1830s and were extensively built up by the 1880s.[97] The large Hambletts council estate to the north of Wood Lane dates mainly from the 1930s,[98] while the small council estate to the east at Lambert's End was completed in 1960.[99] The first

streets between Oak Road and Bromford Lane were appearing by the beginning of the 20th century,[1] and in the Westbourne Road and Margaret Street area there is some of the first council housing in the town, dating from the early 1920s.[2] Further west still, off Brandon Way, there is council housing built since the Second World War.

By 1775 there was settlement along the edge of the Heath around the present Moor Street, and the name Lyng was in use for the area. Sams Lane too was already in existence, linking the area with Spon Lane.[3] Further south in Bromford Lane is Lyttleton Hall Farm, where there was probably a house by the early 17th century.[4] By the mid 19th century several streets had been laid out in the Lyng area as far south as Sams Lane,[5] but most of the housing in Bromford Lane dates from the late 19th and early 20th centuries.[6] In the 1960s the Lyng was cleared by the council and redeveloped with houses, maisonettes, multi-storey flats, a shopping centre, and an old people's home; the parish church and the school were rebuilt. The first phase of the scheme won a Civic Trust commendation in 1967.[7] Immediately to the south is private and council housing of the period between the World Wars, and beyond is a council estate of the mid 1950s belonging to the borough of Warley.[8]

An area named Spon in the south of the parish existed by 1344 when William atte Sponne held land in West Bromwich.[9] Spon Brook is mentioned in 1585,[10] Spon Heath in 1633,[11] Spon Lane in 1694,[12] and Spon Coppice in 1695.[13] By the later 18th century the Spon Lane area was one of the more populous parts of the parish. There was much settlement along Spon Lane itself, particularly on the eastern side, and also eastwards along the Birmingham road; it was in the latter area that the Salters built their first works in the 1770s.[14] A number of foundries were built along the Birmingham Canal at the southern end of Spon Lane. In the early 1790s Archibald Kenrick built a foundry east of Spon Lane Bridge, leasing the site from John Houghton, clerk to the Birmingham Canal Co., who was building Houghton Street and a canal wharf. By 1798 there was a brassworks between Kenrick's foundry and Spon Lane. William Bullock established another foundry west of Spon Lane in 1805, and in 1830 Samuel Kenrick opened the Summit Foundry

---

[86] *Lich. Dioc. Yr. Bk.* 1881, 144. And see O.S. Map 6″, Staffs. LXVIII. SW. (edns. of 1890, 1904, 1921); datestones of 1897 and 1898 on housing in Whitehall Rd. near junction with Sheepwash Lane.
[87] *Staffs. Advertiser*, 2 Jan. 1892; *Kelly's Dir. Staffs.* (1896); *West Bromwich Official Handbook* [1963], 62.
[88] *West Bromwich Official Handbook* [1963], 62.
[89] County Boro. of West Bromwich, *Council Clarion*, Aug. 1959, 10; July 1960, 6.
[90] Yates, *Map of Staffs.* (1775).   [91] See p. 25.
[92] Reeves, *West Bromwich*, 156.
[93] Yates, *Map of Staffs.* (1775); 'West Bromwich 100 Years Ago', 12 Apr. 1901; L.J.R.O., B/A/15/West Bromwich. Richard St. West was formerly called Old End: O.S. Map 1/500, Staffs. LXVIII. 10. 23 (1886).
[94] See p. 23.
[95] O.S. Map 6″, Staffs. LXVIII. SW. (edns. of 1890 and 1904). Oxford Rd. was described as a proposed new road in 1900: Lich. Dioc. Regy., B/A/2(i)/U, p. 414.
[96] Wood, *Plan of West Bromwich* (1837).
[97] Ibid.; O.S. Map 6″, Staffs. LXVIII. SW. (1890 edn.).
[98] *Evening Mail*, 16 June 1970.
[99] County Boro. of West Bromwich, *Council Clarion*, Oct. 1960, 8–10.

[1] O.S. Map 6″, Staffs. LXVIII. SW. (1904 edn.).
[2] County Boro. of West Bromwich, *Representation to Minister of Health for Alteration of Boundary of County Boro.* (1921), 16 (copies in W.B.L. and in S.R.O., F. 1228).
[3] Yates, *Map of Staffs.* (1775); S.R.O., D.(W.)585(30); D.(W.)622A(30); D.(W.)631A(30), J. Furneyhough, Plan of West Bromwich (c. 1820).
[4] See p. 23.
[5] L.J.R.O., B/A/15/West Bromwich.
[6] Date-stones of 1888 and 1896; O.S. Map 6″, Staffs. LXVIII. SW. (edns. of 1890, 1904, 1921).
[7] *West Bromwich Official Handbook* (1966), 32–3; *Evening Mail*, 15 Jan., 18 Aug. 1965; *Birmingham Post*, 28 Nov. 1962, 29 Apr. 1967; *Council Clarion*, Dec. 1962, 8–10; below pp. 59, 80–1.
[8] *Smethwick Civic News*, Oct. 1954; *Smethwick Telephone*, 28 Dec. 1956; *Warley News Telephone*, 8 Feb. 1968.
[9] *S.H.C.* xii (i), 31.
[10] E 134/27 and 28 Eliz. I Mich./2 m. 1.
[11] West Bromwich Ct. R. p. 102.
[12] See p. 12.
[13] C 103/127/3c.
[14] Yates, *Map of Staffs.* (1775); S.R.O., D.(W.)620A(30); below pp. 35–6.

to the east of Archibald Kenrick's works.[15] By 1837 Kenrick's Village had been laid out around Glover Street to the north of the Kenrick foundries, and Trinity Road (then Garden Street) was being built.[16] The southern part of the Spon Lane area in fact developed as a very self-contained community.[17] The area around Glover Street became known locally as Monkey Green; its development was financed by a building society, and it has been suggested that this may account for the name, 'a monkey on the house' meaning a mortgage.[18] A new church was opened on part of Spon Coppice near the northern end of Trinity Road in 1841,[19] but most of the streets around it date from about the end of the century.[20] Kenrick Park east of Kenrick's Village originated in the gift of 19 a. to the borough in 1895 by J. A. and William Kenrick, part of it land transferred to the borough from Smethwick in 1897; by the early 1960s it was 25 a. in extent.[21] In his *English Journey* J. B. Priestley described a visit to Grice Street on the west side of Spon Lane in 1933 under the name 'Rusty Lane'; it presented 'a picture of grimy desolation' unparalleled in his experience.[22] There is private housing of the period between the World Wars at the southern end of Trinity Road, and the 1960s saw council redevelopment around Glover Street, notably with multistorey flats.[23] The ring road too has been built through that part, and the M5 motorway runs along the borough boundary.

Roebuck Lane in the south-east of the parish running into Smethwick from the Birmingham road existed by the later 18th century[24] and probably much earlier. A house called the Roebuck at the north end existed in 1684 and was demolished c. 1855.[25] Also at the top of Roebuck Lane, and on its western side, is the house called Springfields. By 1795 it was the home of Archibald Kenrick. After his death in 1835 his son Archibald lived there; it was rebuilt probably about that time. The younger Archibald was still living there in 1850, but it subsequently became the home of W. Bullock, an iron-founder like the Kenricks. By 1860 it had been bought by Thomas Bache Salter, who moved there from Spon House, and it remained the Salters' home until c. 1906.[26] In 1970 it was the social club of G. Salter & Co. Ltd. By 1836 there was a large

house to the south of Springfields called Oakley; it was owned by Timothy Kenrick, son of the elder Archibald Kenrick.[27] It was demolished c. 1960.[28] The western side of Roebuck Lane was occupied in 1970 by private housing built mainly in the period between the World Wars. The northern part of Roebuck Lane now ends at the M5 motorway on the borough boundary. Roebuck Street was laid out as Park Village in the 1850s;[29] by 1970, however, the street was given over to light industry. The area around Grove Crescent between Roebuck Lane and Roebuck Street was formerly occupied by the Grove and its 4-acre estate; the property was sold in 1892 and built over.[30]

The area east from Roebuck Lane to the borough boundary has been developed mainly in recent years and as an industrial estate. An ancient tree known as the Three Mile Oak formerly stood on the north side of the main road near the boundary; by the 1830s it had disappeared, but the name was preserved by the near-by inn and toll-gate.[31] Street House at the corner of Halford's Lane and the Birmingham road occurs from 1661. In 1818 it was the home of Joseph Halford, who later moved to Charlemont Hall. Between c. 1833 and c. 1846 Henry Halford, an iron merchant, was living there. It was rebuilt about that time and by the 1850s was known as the Hawthorns. It was made into the Hawthorns Hotel in 1903 to serve the patrons of the Hawthorns football ground on the opposite side of Halford's Lane.[32] The ground had become the home of West Bromwich Albion Football Club in 1900.[33] Halford's Lane takes its name from the Halford family, being earlier known variously as Street House Lane, Bowling Alley Lane, and Brasshouse Lane.[34] There is a motorway access point where the M5 passes under Birmingham Road; the classical stone gateway of Arch Lodge, formerly an entrance to Sandwell Park, has been preserved on the roundabout. A new road was opened from the roundabout to the southern part of Roebuck Lane in Smethwick as part of the southern ring road. The borough boundary with Smethwick was altered in 1966 when the Albion area on either side of Halford's Lane, until then in Smethwick, was taken into West Bromwich instead of becoming part of the new borough of Warley; the railway line then became

[15] R. A. Church, *Kenricks in Hardware* (Newton Abbot, 1969), 28, 39, 70; S.R.O., D. 613, bdle. 2; 'Old Smethwick', 19 Mar. 1949; S.R.O., D.(W.)631A(30), Furneyhough, Plan of West Bromwich (c. 1820); Wood, *Plan of West Bromwich* (1837).
[16] Wood, *Plan of West Bromwich* (1837); 'Old West Bromwich', 6 Aug. 1943.
[17] 'Old West Bromwich', 12 Nov. 1943, 11 Feb. 1944.
[18] 'Old Smethwick', 18 Sept. 1948; E. Partridge, *Dict. of Slang and Unconventional English* (5th edn.).
[19] Lich. Dioc. Regy., B/A/2(i)/L, pp. 246, 250–2; below p. 56.
[20] O.S. Map 6", Staffs. LXVIII. SW. (edns. of 1890 and 1904).
[21] *Staffs. Advertiser*, 28 Dec. 1895; *Kelly's Dir. Staffs.* (1896); *West Bromwich Official Handbook* [1963], 57; above p. 1.
[22] J. B. Priestley, *English Journey* (1948 edn.), 114; 'Old West Bromwich', 31 Dec. 1943.
[23] *Express & Star*, 30 July 1965.
[24] Yates, *Map of Staffs.* (1775).
[25] S.R.O., D. 564/3/1/19; ibid./3/2/7; Ct. R. p. 192; S.R.O., D. 742/VIII/3; 'West Bromwich 100 Years Ago', 10 May 1901; Reeves, *West Bromwich*, 157.
[26] 'Old West Bromwich', 16 July 1943; *P.O. Dir.*

Staffs. (1850); Mary Bache, *Salter, the Story of a Family Firm, 1760–1960* (West Bromwich, 1960), 22–3, 26–7, 40.
[27] Reeves, *West Bromwich*, 172; Wood, *Plan of West Bromwich* (1837); L.J.R.O., B/A/15/West Bromwich; Church, *Kenricks in Hardware*, 22, 41.
[28] Ex inf. Mr. G. C. W. Jones of West Bromwich (1974).
[29] Fowler, Map of West Bromwich (1856); E. Lissimore, 'Every Street has a Place in History', *West Bromwich News*, 25 Aug. 1966; below p. 65.
[30] 'Old West Bromwich', 16 July, 6 Aug. 1943.
[31] Reeves, *West Bromwich*, 159; 'West Bromwich 100 Years Ago', 11 Oct. 1901; Wood, *Plan of West Bromwich* (1837); below p. 11.
[32] S.R.O., D. 564/2/1; D. 564/3/1/13; Willett, *West Bromwich*, 248; 'Old West Bromwich', 2 July 1943; W.B.L., Plan of West Bromwich (n.d.), sheet 77. For the Halfords see Parson and Bradshaw, *Dir. Staffs.* (1818); Reeves, *West Bromwich*, 170; *Reg. of Electors within Southern Div. of County of Stafford . . . 1 Nov. 1833–1 Nov. 1834*, 59 (copy in W.S.L.); *Reg. of Persons entitled to vote . . . Southern Div. of County of Stafford . . . 30 Nov. 1846–1 Dec. 1847*, 253; *30 Nov. 1847–1 Dec. 1848*, 253; 'Old Smethwick', 2 Apr. 1949.
[33] See p. 74.
[34] See p. 92.

the boundary.[35] A small area including a stretch of the M5 motorway and a portion of the ring road around the junction with Roebuck Lane was transferred to Warley.[36]

COMMUNICATIONS. ROADS. West Bromwich is crossed by the ancient highway from Birmingham to Wolverhampton. By the beginning of the 16th century it was part of the route from London to Shrewsbury and ran from the south-eastern corner of the parish across the Heath and on to Great Bridge where it crossed the Tame.[37] In the late 17th century it was also being much used for carrying coal and was consequently in a poor state.[38] Perhaps for that reason an alternative route to Shrewsbury via Smethwick and Dudley was being favoured by long-distance traffic by 1675.[39] In 1699, however, the road through Great Bridge was described as the great road between London, Chester, and Shrewsbury, and it was the road's importance which caused the county to contribute towards rebuilding the bridge in that year.[40] By the 1720s it formed part of the post road between London and Shrewsbury and carried much iron, coal, and lime.[41]

The road which forks from the main road at Carter's Green and runs to Wednesbury and Wolverhampton was also an early one. It was mentioned as the road from Finchpath to Birmingham in the earlier 14th century,[42] and the bridge at Finchpath by which it crossed the Tame existed by 1225.[43] In 1685 there is a reference to the 'hollow way' down Finchpath Hill to Wednesbury Bridge;[44] it may have been cut to facilitate the transport of coal south from the area.[45] By the 1720s the road from Wednesbury to Carter's Green was in a dangerous state because of the great quantities of ironware and coal taken from Wednesbury to Birmingham.[46]

Both the main roads were turnpiked in 1727,[47] but real improvement came only when the coal traffic was transferred to the canal from 1769.[48] After the turnpiking of the Wednesbury–Bilston road in 1766 the Shrewsbury coaches began to use the shorter route via Wednesbury;[49] from 1808 this also became the main Holyhead mail route in preference

to the road via Coleshill and Lichfield.[50] There was a toll-gate at Three Mile Oak in the south-east of the parish by 1756.[51] By 1771 there were also toll-gates at Hill Top by the junction with New Street and Coles Lane; at the top of Holloway Bank by the junction with Witton Lane; and at Great Bridge by the junction with Whitehall Road.[52] By about 1820 there was also a gate by the junction with Sandwell Road.[53] The steepness of the hill at Holloway Bank was an obstacle. Coach passengers often alighted at the Fountain inn and walked up to ease the burden on the horses,[54] and in 1819 Thomas Telford described the road up the hill as 'inconveniently steep . . . crooked and much sunk into the ground'.[55] In 1821 the hill was lowered and the way raised.[56] Under the West Bromwich Improvement Act of 1854 most of the turnpiked road through the town—from Roebuck Lane to Hill Top and to the gas-works in Swan Village—was taken over from the turnpike trustees by the improvement commissioners.[57] The remainder was disturnpiked in 1870.[58]

Besides the two highways there are several ancient roads across the parish, notably those radiating from Lyndon and the area round All Saints' Church, the ancient centre of the parish. By the earlier 13th century there was a road to Wednesbury via Hydes Bridge; it apparently followed the line of Heath Lane to the Hateley Heath area and then ran along Rydding Lane to Hydes Road.[59] At Rydding Lane, presumably by an early period, the road was joined by another from Stone Cross and the manor-house, corresponding with the present Hall Green Road; its western stretch was straightened in 1817.[60] The road from the church to Finchpath, which occurs in 1336, presumably followed the Wednesbury road to Hateley Heath and from there ran to Holloway Bank along Jowett's Lane and Witton Lane.[61] By the end of the 13th century there was a road from the church to Greet mill, continuing thence to Oldbury. It must have followed approximately what are now Vicarage Road and Church Lane to Black Lake and continued either along Bilhay Lane, Claypit Lane, Bull Lane, Albion Road, and West Bromwich Street or along Swan Lane, Phoenix

[35] See p. 93.

[36] West Midlands Order 1965, S.I. 1965, no. 2139.

[37] *Birmingham and its Regional Setting* (Brit. Assoc. 1950), 146–7, 153; H. Owen and J. B. Blakeway, *Hist. of Shrewsbury* (1825), i. 279, 282; C 5/96/5 (citing a deed of 1619 which refers to it as the highway leading from Wolverhampton towards Birmingham).

[38] S.R.O., Q/SR M. 1699, no. 14.

[39] See p. 96.

[40] S.R.O., Q/SR M. 1699, no. 14; below p. 12.

[41] *V.C.H. Staffs.* ii. 278; *C.J.* xx. 741, 746.

[42] Willett, *West Bromwich*, 205–6; Hackwood, *West Bromwich*, 50.

[43] See pp. 12–13.

[44] West Bromwich Ct. R. pp. 145–6.

[45] Ede, *Wednesbury*, 117; below p. 39.

[46] *C.J.* xx. 746.

[47] 13 Geo. I, c. 14. *V.C.H. Staffs.* ii. 280, wrongly implies that the roads were turnpiked in 1726; also it mentions only the Wednesbury turnpike.

[48] *V.C.H. Warws.* vii. 27; *V.C.H. Staffs.* ii. 289; below p. 13.

[49] Ede, *Wednesbury*, 147. The Wednesbury road, and not the road via Great Bridge, is shown as the 'Turnpike Road to Birmingham' from Wolverhampton on a map in S.R.O., Q/SB A. 1781.

[50] Ede, *Wednesbury*, 223.

[51] S.R.O., D.(W.)571(30).

[52] B.R.L. 608107, Plan of Turnpike Road from Birmingham to Wednesbury, Dudley and Bilston 1771. The Holloway Bank toll-house, on the corner of Barrack St., still stood in 1945: 'Old West Bromwich', 16 Mar. 1945.

[53] C. and J. Greenwood, *Map of Staffs.* (1820). The toll-house was converted into a shop after the disturnpiking of 1870: 'Old West Bromwich', 28 Dec. 1945.

[54] 'Old West Bromwich', 16 Feb. 1945.

[55] *Rep. of Mr. Telford to Commissioners for Improvement of the Holyhead Road upon state of road between London and Shrewsbury*, H.C. 126, pp. 22–3 (1820), vi.

[56] *4th Rep. Sel. Cttee. on roads from London to Holyhead etc.* H.C. 343, p. 69 (1822), vi; W.B.L. 66/16150, chron. list of events.

[57] West Bromwich Improvement Act, 1854, 17 & 18 Vic. c. 163 (Local).

[58] Annual Turnpike Acts Continuance Act, 1870, 33 & 34 Vic. c. 73; S.R.O., D. 564/8/1/8/Aug. 1870 (plan); S.R.O., D. 742/Dartmouth Estates/II/9/703 and 704.

[59] See p. 13; Willett, *West Bromwich*, 203, 216; Yates, *Map of Staffs.* (1775).

[60] Yates, *Map of Staffs.* (1775); West Bromwich Vestry Mins. pp. 92–3 and plan facing p. 92.

[61] F. A. Homer, 'Collections for the Hist. of the Priory of Sandwell' (in W.S.L.), transcript of deed of 1336; Yates, *Map of Staffs.* (1775).

Street, Ryders Green Road, Oldbury Road, and West Bromwich Street.[62] The road from Lyndon to Walsall via Stone Cross and Tame Bridge was in use by the later Middle Ages;[63] the present line from Stone Cross to the borough boundary, with its dual carriageway, was opened in 1969.[64] The road from Lyndon to Birmingham ran south to Mayer's Green and thence south-east to the Birmingham road more or less along the line of the present Beeches Road, a stretch described in 1776 as 'an ancient horse road leading from Mares Green towards the Three Mile Oak Turnpike'. In the earlier 1770s, however, traffic was apparently taking a shorter route from Mayer's Green to the improved Birmingham road, along the present Reform and Bull Streets. The Beeches Road stretch became disused, and by 1776 Lord Dartmouth had taken it into his estate. It still existed as Holly Lane in 1804.[65] A road from Lyndon to Oldbury occurs in the early 17th century running over Bromwich Heath and along Bromford Lane.[66] Newton Road running east from the church is probably another old road; it was turnpiked in 1804 as part of the road from the Swan in West Bromwich to Sutton Coldfield, but there is no further record of the turnpike.[67] It was widened as far as Wigmore Lane in 1920-1 as an unemployment relief work.[68]

Salter's Lane, running westwards from Dagger Lane to the parish boundary at Park Lane, occurs by the later Middle Ages. It was originally known as Saltwell Lane but the modern name came into use in the 17th century. By the earlier 19th century the eastern half had become a footpath only and has so remained.[69] There was a road from Hateley Heath to Bird End and Newton by 1526, following the present Marsh Lane (so named by 1681) and Charlemont Road and crossing the Tame at Joan Bridge.[70] In 1526 there is also mention of the lane leading to Smethwick from the Birmingham–Wolverhampton road in West Bromwich; it was presumably Spon Lane, Roebuck Lane, or Halford's Lane.[71] Spon Lane occurs by name in 1694.[72] The highway from Greets Green to Dudley that occurs in the 16th century is presumably Whitehall Road,[73] and the lane from Great Bridge to Harvills Oak that occurs in 1616 is presumably Brickhouse Lane and Dial Lane.[74] Tinkers Lane, which ran from Greet mill to

Bromford Lane near Bromford Bridge, was mentioned in 1609 but had gone out of use by the 1720s.[75]

The chief addition to the roads in recent times is the stretch of the M5 motorway which runs on the west side of the town to link with the M6 at Bescot. It was opened in 1970, as was the extension of the M6 to Great Barr.[76] The stretch of the ring road between Greets Green Road and the roundabout where Birmingham Road crosses the M5 was completed in 1970; the stretch from the roundabout to Carter's Green, the Expressway, was opened in 1973.[77]

BRIDGES. With the Tame forming so much of the boundary West Bromwich possessed several bridges at an early date. The following account begins in the south of the parish and works downstream.

Bromford Bridge, which carries the road to Oldbury over the Tame, existed by 1617. It may have been only a footbridge for there was still a ford there in the earlier 19th century. It had become a county bridge by 1858.[78]

The bridge which carries Sheepwash Lane over the Tame existed by the earlier 19th century. It was maintained jointly by West Bromwich and Tipton.[79]

Great Bridge, originally 'Grete' Bridge,[80] takes the road to Tipton over the Tame. It existed by the 1550s,[81] and presumably much earlier in view of the importance of the road. It was maintained jointly by West Bromwich and Tipton, but because of the road's importance the county in 1699 assigned £50 towards the cost of its conversion from a horse bridge to a stone cart bridge.[82] West Bromwich refused to join Tipton in carrying out the work, and in 1702 quarter sessions ordered the justices concerned with the work to repay £20 and spend the remaining £30 on the Tipton half of the bridge and on the causeway leading to it on the Tipton side.[83] The rebuilding of the bridge had been completed by 1706. Tipton then claimed to be in debt as a result and was compensated by quarter sessions.[84] The bridge had become a county responsibility by 1780 when it was again rebuilt. It has subsequently been greatly widened, but the 18th-century structure forms the northern part of the present bridge.[85]

There was a bridge at Finchpath to the south of

[62] *Cat. Anct. D.* vi, C 4005; *Court Rolls of the Manor of Hales, 1270–1307* (Worcs. Hist. Soc.), ii. 428; W.S.L., S. D. Pearson 1459; Willett, *West Bromwich*, 203–4, 216, 221; West Bromwich Ct. R. p. 89; Yates, *Map of Staffs.* (1775).
[63] See p. 13.
[64] *Evening Mail*, 12 Sept. 1969.
[65] Yates, *Map of Staffs.* (1775); S.R.O., D.(W.)586(30); S.R.O., Q/RDc 60.
[66] Willett, *West Bromwich*, 164–5; see below.
[67] A. Cossons, 'Warwickshire Turnpikes', *T.B.A.S.* lxiv. 93. The Act was to last for 21 years 'and from thence to the then next session of Parliament'. The road is not shown as a turnpike road by J. Phillips and W. F. Hutchings, *Map of Staffs.* (1832).
[68] Ex inf. Mr. G. C. W. Jones of West Bromwich (1974); O.S. Map 6″, Staffs. LXVIII. NW., NE. (provisional edn., revision of 1913 with additions in 1938).
[69] S.R.O., D. 742/VIII/1/4, Jos. Cox to Lord Dartmouth; ibid. /VIII/3; D.(W.)1778/V/1222; E 134/27 and 28 Eliz. I Mich./2 m. 1; West Bromwich Ct. R. pp. 71, 81, 211; Yates, *Map of Staffs.* (1775); Greenwood, *Map of Staffs.* (1820); Wood, *Plan of West Bromwich* (1837); L.J.R.O., B/A/15/West Bromwich.
[70] See p. 13; Willett, *West Bromwich*, 217; B.R.L. 297303; Yates, *Map of Staffs.* (1775). This probably formed part of the road from Wednesbury to Joan mill

mentioned in 1501: W.C.L., box 46, no. 1. For the realignment of what is now Charlemont Rd. in 1804 see below p. 21.
[71] E 36/165 f. 136; Hackwood, *Smethwick*, 117.
[72] C 5/188/39.
[73] Willett, *West Bromwich*, 212, 214.
[74] *9th Rep. Com. Char.* H.C. 258, p. 538 (1823), ix; below p. 41.
[75] West Bromwich Ct. R. p. 61; Willett, *West Bromwich*, 164–5, 169; S.R.O., D.(W.)585(30).
[76] *Express & Star*, 13 and 15 May, 16 and 20 July 1970.
[77] *Evening Mail*, 4 Feb., 24 Mar., 13 May 1970, 7 May 1973; above p. 5.
[78] Willett, *West Bromwich*, 164, 247–8; West Bromwich Ct. R. p. 127; 'West Bromwich 100 Years Ago', 11 Oct. 1901; *Practice of Court of General Quarter Sessions of the Peace for the County of Stafford* (Stafford, 1858; copy in S.R.O.), 9, where it is called Bromwich Heath Bridge between Bromwich Heath and Oldbury.
[79] S.R.O., Q/SB, A. 1819.   [80] See p. 8.
[81] *S.H.C.* 1926, 82–3; *S.H.C.* 1931, 155.
[82] S.R.O., Q/SR, M. 1699, no. 14; Q/SO 10, M. 1699.
[83] Q/SO 10, E. 1702.
[84] Q/SO 10, M. 1706.
[85] Q/SO 17, f. 183; Q/SB, M. 1780 and A. 1781, map; *Aris's Birmingham Gaz.* 17 Apr. 1780; plate facing p. 33 below.

Wednesbury by 1225, carrying the main Birmingham–Wolverhampton road over the Tame.[86] The name Finchpath Bridge was still in use at the end of the 16th century,[87] but the bridge was being referred to as Wednesbury Bridge by 1620.[88] It was a county bridge by 1667 when quarter sessions ordered a levy for its repair.[89] It was rebuilt by Telford in 1826 as part of his improvements to the Holyhead road.[90] It has subsequently been rebuilt again and widened.

By 1858 there was a second Wednesbury Bridge on the Tame 'near Wednesbury'; it too was a county bridge.[91] It is probably identifiable with Hydes Bridge, which carries Hydes Road over the Tame and existed by 1804.[92] Hydes Bridge was evidently 'Wysti' Bridge, which occurs in the area in the earlier 13th century.[93] It is also presumably the bridge over 'Hides Brook' which was maintained jointly by West Bromwich and Wednesbury in the later 18th century; in 1785 the Wednesbury vestry authorized its rebuilding since it was 'insufficient to allow for a waggon'.[94] The present structure is modern.

Tame Bridge, which carries the road to Walsall over the Tame, probably existed by the later 15th century: by will proved in 1452 Thomas Mollesley of Walsall left 10 marks for building a 'new bridge of Tame'.[95] At the dissolution of the monasteries the bridge and a stretch of the road on the West Bromwich side were maintained with the profits from the adjoining Tame Bridge meadow, which an abbot of Halesowen had given for the purpose; by 1586 the land was owned by the town feoffees of Walsall, which was thus responsible for maintaining the bridge.[96] In 1781 the three-arched bridge was dangerous, and West Bromwich, Walsall, and some neighbouring parishes petitioned the county for help towards the cost of rebuilding it; it was rebuilt c. 1783.[97] In 1867 Walsall corporation sold the land, and in 1894 the owner transferred responsibility for the bridge to the county council with a payment of £100.[98] The bridge no longer exists, having disappeared in the late 1960s when the road and the river were re-aligned during the construction of the motorway interchange; the new line of the road crosses the Tame further downstream.

There have been two bridges near the site of Joan mill from an early date. Joan Mill Bridge occurs in 1401–2 and presumably carried what is now Charlemont Road over the mill-stream; its maintenance was the responsibility of Sandwell priory, the owner of the mill.[99] Joan Bridge, which carries the road over the Tame, occurs in 1526[1] but presumably existed by the earlier date. By 1549 it was the responsibility of West Bromwich and Great Barr,[2] and West Bromwich was still involved in its repair in 1767.[3] By 1831, however, it had become a county bridge.[4] In 1858 the two bridges, both county bridges, were known as Joan Upper Bridge and Joan Nether Bridge.[5]

CANALS. The canals of West Bromwich are concentrated in the western part of the parish where most of the collieries and ironworks developed in the later 18th and earlier 19th centuries. The Birmingham Canal built by James Brindley from Birmingham to Wolverhampton in 1768–72 runs along the boundary of West Bromwich for a short distance on either side of Spon Lane. Telford's new line through the south-west of the parish was built as far as the Albion area c. 1830 and was completed to Tipton in 1838 under an Act of 1835.[6] The Gower branch, opened in 1836, runs south from Telford's canal at Greets Green to Brindley's canal near Brades Village in Rowley Regis. There were two other branches from the West Bromwich stretch of Telford's canal, Dunkirk, opened in 1850 and abandoned in 1953, and Union (Roway), abandoned in 1954.[7]

The Balls Hill branch of the Birmingham Canal, built, like the main canal, under an Act of 1768, was opened from Spon Lane to 'Wednesbury Hollow-way' in 1769, three years before the completion of the main canal. It provided the pits of the Wednesbury area with an immediate outlet to Birmingham. The terminus was west of the main road at Hill Top near Golds Green, where coal was being raised at that time. It was described c. 1830 as of little use because a part of it had collapsed as a result of mining subsidence. Much of the canal was abandoned in stages between 1954 and 1960 and filled in.[8]

A local canal system soon developed, based on the Balls Hill branch. In 1786, under an Act of 1783, a branch was opened from Ryders Green through

[86] Ede, *Wednesbury*, 23, 103, 108; Ede, *Hist. of Wednesbury: Corrigenda and Addenda* (Tipton, 1969).
[87] West Bromwich Ct. R. p. 20.
[88] Willett, *West Bromwich*, 222, 224.
[89] S.R.O., Q/SO 7, f. 159; Q/SO 11, E. 1716; J. Potter, *List of Bridges which the Inhabitants of the County of Stafford are bound to repair* (Stafford, 1830), 6 (copy in W.S.L. Pamphs. *sub* Roads).
[90] Ede, *Wednesbury*, 224.
[91] *Practice of Court of General Quarter Sessions*, 18; S.R.O., Q/SB, M. 1862.
[92] S.R.O., Q/RDc 60, map. 'Hides' Bridge occurs as a county bridge in 1830: Q/SB, M. 1832. It does not, however, appear under that name in the 1858 list of county bridges in *Practice of Court of General Quarter Sessions*.
[93] Ede, *Wednesbury*, 103 and map on front end-paper; Ede, *Wednesbury: Corrigenda and Addenda*.
[94] Ede, *Wednesbury*, 182.
[95] W.T.C. I/54*; plate facing p. 33 below.
[96] S.R.O., Q/SR, T. 1608, no. 30; *S.H.C.* 1948–9, 82; C 93/2/25/4 and 5; Sims, *Cal. of Deeds*, p. 50; Homeshaw, *Walsall*, 63, 80, 114, 125, 133; S.R.O., Q/SB, E. 1862, M. 1862. For the feoffees see below p. 214.
[97] S.R.O., Q/SB, A. 1781 (with plans); W.B.L. 66/16150, chron. list of events.
[98] Walsall Council House, Misc. Docs. no. 13, inden-

ture between Staffs. County Council and Alf. Franks 16 Jan. 1894; Hackwood, *West Bromwich*, 47–8.
[99] S.R.O., D.(W.)1778/V/1222.
[1] E 36/165 f. 132.   [2] *S.H.C.* 1948–9, 81.
[3] West Bromwich Par. Bk., overseers' accts. 1756; Vestry Mins. 9 Mar. 1767.
[4] Q/SO 30, f. 298; Q/SB, T. 1834. What was called New Joan Bridge occurs as a county bridge in 1832: Q/SO 31, f. 65v.; Q/SB, M. 1832.
[5] *Practice of Court of General Quarter Sessions*, 14; Q/SB, M. 1862.
[6] C. Hadfield, *Canals of the West Midlands* (1969 edn.), 87–8; J. Phillips and W. F. Hutchings, *Map of Staffs.* (1832); Act to consolidate and extend the powers and provisions of the several Acts relating to the Birmingham Canal Navigations, 5 & 6 Wm. IV, c. 34 (Local and Personal).
[7] Hadfield, *Canals of W. Midlands*, 254–5, 320–1; Brit. Transport Com. Act, 1954, 2 & 3 Eliz. II, c. 55 (Local), 2nd sched.
[8] J. Priestley, *Hist. Account of the Navigable Rivers, Canals, and Railways throughout Gt. Brit.* (1831), 68, 77; J. Cary, *Inland Navigation* (1795), 35–6; Hadfield, *Canals of W. Midlands*, 318–19; Yates, *Map of Staffs.* (1775); J. Richards, 'West Bromwich and its Canals 1769–1969', 7 (TS. in W.B.L.); 2 & 3 Eliz. II, c. 55 (Local); below p. 40.

Great Bridge to Broadwaters in Wednesbury, with eight locks at Ryders Green; it was extended to Walsall in 1799.[9] Side canals were built from the branch. The Danks branch was built, apparently under the Act of 1783, from Toll End in Tipton through the Golds Green area; it was abandoned in stages between 1954 and 1960.[10] The Haines branch was opened from Great Bridge to the collieries in the south-west corner of the parish in 1833.[11] The industrial development of the earlier 19th century produced new branches from the Balls Hill branch. In 1826 the Ridgacre branch was opened from Swan Village to Ridgacre Lane (now Church Lane), and branches were soon built from it: Dartmouth, opened in 1828 to Hateley Heath and largely abandoned in 1947, Halford, also opened in 1828 and largely abandoned in 1947, and Jesson, opened in 1831 and abandoned in 1954. The Izon and Union branches from the Balls Hill branch served works in the south-west; the first was abandoned in 1954 and the second in stages between 1954 and 1965.[12]

The Tame Valley Canal, which crosses the north of the parish, was built under an Act of 1839 from the Walsall Canal near Ocker Hill in Tipton to the Birmingham and Fazeley Canal near Aston (Warws.). Opened in 1844, it provided a new outlet avoiding Birmingham.[13]

RAILWAYS. The first railway in West Bromwich, and also the first really national main line, was the Grand Junction Railway opened between Birmingham and Warrington in 1837. The line crosses the north-eastern part of the ancient parish, and a station was opened in 1837 on the north side of Newton Road.[14] A new station was opened in 1863 further north on the Great Barr side of the former boundary and was called West Bromwich for a few months before being renamed Newton Road.[15] A third station was opened to the south of Newton Road in 1902 and remained in use until 1945.[16] Bescot Junction station just inside the northern boundary of the parish was opened in 1847, with a branch linking the line from that point to the South Staffordshire Railway at Pleck in Walsall. Another link with the South Staffordshire Railway south of Pleck, known as Bescot Curve, was opened in 1850.[17] The up marshalling yard at Bescot was brought into use in 1881 and a new sorting siding in 1892.[18]

The opening of the Birmingham, Wolverhamp-

ton & Stour Valley Railway in 1852 with stations just over the parish boundary at Spon Lane in Smethwick and Bromford Lane in Oldbury brought the railway closer to the centre of West Bromwich; the station at Albion was opened in 1853.[19] The line also served the industrial area in the south-western part of the parish.[20] Spon Lane was closed in 1964; Albion was closed to passengers in 1960 and to freight in 1964.[21]

It was only in 1854 that the railway reached the centre of West Bromwich. In that year the Birmingham, Wolverhampton & Dudley Railway was opened from Birmingham to Wolverhampton with two stations in the town; West Bromwich station, off Paradise Street, served the centre of the town, and there was another station at Swan Village.[22] In 1866 the Great Bridge branch was opened from Swan Village junction to the South Staffordshire line near Great Bridge; the Swan Village Basin branch, apparently the line from Swan Village to the gas-works, was opened the same year.[23] In 1867 the main line of the Birmingham, Wolverhampton & Dudley Railway was joined by the Stourbridge Extension Railway near Halford's Lane.[24] Passenger services over the Great Bridge branch were suspended from 1915 to 1920,[25] and the line was closed in 1964.[26] Local passenger services along the main Birmingham–Wolverhampton line were much reduced in the late 1960s, and West Bromwich and Swan Village stations became unstaffed halts. The branch line from Swan Village to the gas-works was closed in 1967.[27] The passenger buildings at West Bromwich station were demolished in 1971, but a large brick goods shed, dating apparently from c. 1854,[28] was left standing. The South Staffordshire Railway, opened from Dudley to Wychnor in 1850, runs through the north-west of the parish. It has never had a station within the bounds of the pre-1966 borough.[29]

MANORS. In 1086 William fitz Ansculf, lord of Dudley, held three hides in *BROMWICH*; before the Conquest the land had been held by Brictuin.[30] The overlordship descended with the Dudley barony until the death without issue of John, Lord Somery, in 1322.[31] The barony was divided between his sisters in 1323, one knight's fee in West Bromwich being assigned to his younger sister Joan Botetourt.[32] The overlordship then descended with Weoley Castle in Northfield (Worcs.) until at

[9] Hadfield, *Canals of W. Midlands*, 71–2; *V.C.H. Staffs.* ii. 291–2; below p. 168.
[10] Hadfield, *Canals of W. Midlands*, 89, 254–5, 318–19; 2 & 3 Eliz. II, c. 55 (Local). It was probably one of the 6 collateral cuts authorized by the Act: Priestley, *Navigable Rivers, Canals, and Railways*, 70.
[11] Hadfield, *Canals of W. Midlands*, 254–5, 318–19; Wood, *Plan of West Bromwich* (1837).
[12] Hadfield, *Canals of W. Midlands*, 254–5, 318–19; 2 & 3 Eliz. II, c. 55 (Local).
[13] Hadfield, *Canals of W. Midlands*, 89, 320–1; *V.C.H. Staffs.* ii. 295–6.
[14] *V.C.H. Staffs.* ii. 305–7; J. Roscoe, *The Book of the Grand Junction Railway* (1839), 44–6; C. R. Clinker, *Railways of the West Midlands, a Chronology 1808–1954*, 10; L.J.R.O., B/A/15/West Bromwich.
[15] Clinker, *Railways of W. Midlands*, 29, 34; O.S. Map 6″, Staffs. LXVIII. NE. (1890 edn.).
[16] Clinker, *Railways of W. Midlands*, 50, 62; O.S. Map 6″, Staffs. LXVIII. NE. (1904 edn.).
[17] Clinker, *Railways of W. Midlands*, 18, 20, 34. For the

S. Staffs. Railway see below.
[18] Clinker, *Railways of W. Midlands*, 41, 47.
[19] Ibid. 21, 22, 45; below p. 98.
[20] For the industrial significance of the line see *V.C.H. Staffs.* ii. 296–8, 312.
[21] Ex inf. British Railways, London Midland Region (1970). [22] Clinker, *Railways of W. Midlands*, 24.
[23] Ibid. 32; *V.C.H. Staffs.* ii. 316.
[24] *V.C.H. Staffs.* ii. 316; S.R.O., Q/RUm 316; Clinker, *Railways of W. Midlands*, 32, 60.
[25] Clinker, *Railways of W. Midlands*, 56, 58.
[26] Ex inf. British Railways, London Midland Region; *V.C.H. Staffs.* ii. 333.
[27] *Express & Star*, 20 Apr. 1970; *Evening Mail*, 27 Nov. 1969; ex inf. British Railways, London Midland Region.
[28] It is shown by Fowler, Map of West Bromwich (1856). [29] *V.C.H. Staffs.* ii. 312.
[30] *V.C.H. Staffs.* iv. 59, no. 299.
[31] *S.H.C.* v (1), 108; ix (2), 34–5, 38, 42; *Complete Peerage*, xii (1), 114–15.
[32] *S.H.C.* ix (2), 45; Sanders, *Eng. Baronies*, 113–14.

least 1560, when it was held by Thomas Jervoise.[33] Gervase Paynel, lord of Dudley, confirmed the foundation of Sandwell priory by his under-tenant in West Bromwich c. 1190,[34] and it was as overlord of West Bromwich that Edward, Lord Dudley, consented to Cardinal Wolsey's dissolution of the priory in 1525.[35] It was presumably in error that the overlordship was said in 1432 to belong to the Sutton or Dudley family,[36] to whom the other half of the Dudley barony had passed in 1323.[37]

The three hides were held of William fitz Ansculf in 1086 by Ralph.[38] About 1140 Bromwich was in the hands of Guy de Offini,[39] who was still alive c. 1155.[40] In 1166 his son William held it.[41] Although there is evidence that he was alive in 1213,[42] his son Richard had succeeded him by 1212.[43] Richard died in 1222[44] and was succeeded by his brother William,[45] who himself died in 1224 with a son Richard, a minor, as his heir.[46] Still a minor in 1230, Richard was of age by 1242[47] but was dead by 1255, and possibly by 1248.[48] Bromwich was divided between his two daughters, Sarah, the wife of Walter Devereux, and Margaret, by 1275 the wife of Richard de Marnham of Bromwich.[49]

By 1293 Sarah's half share had passed to her son Walter Devereux, who held it as ½ knight's fee.[50] Walter was still alive in 1304,[51] but in 1322 and 1323 the ½ fee was held by Stephen Devereux,[52] who was still alive in 1336.[53] In 1356 this half of the manor was in the hands of William Devereux, and it may subsequently have passed to a John Devereux.[54] In 1381 it was apparently held by Roger Basset, and it later passed to the Vernon family of Nether Haddon (Derb.).[55] Sir William Vernon held it at

his death in 1467, and it then passed to his widow Margaret for life.[56] She was still alive in 1470,[57] but on her death the moiety passed to their son Sir Henry Vernon (d. 1515).[58] Sir Henry's sixth son, Sir John Vernon of Sudbury (Derb.), enjoyed a life interest in the moiety, and on his death in 1545 it passed to his nephew Sir George Vernon.[59] In 1560 Sir George sold his half of the manor to John Nall.[60] By 1566 it had been acquired by the Skeffington family of Fisherwick (in St. Michael's, Lichfield), who had owned other property in West Bromwich since 1520; it formed part of the marriage settlement of John Skeffington and his wife Alice in 1566.[61] In 1585 John included his share of the manor in the marriage settlement of his son William.[62] The subsequent history of this moiety of the manor is not known, but the rights belonging to it may have been lost as a result of William Skeffington's sales of land in West Bromwich in the late 1590s.[63]

The other half of the manor remained in the Marnham family until c. 1420. Richard de Marnham died between 1294 and 1296; his wife Margaret was still alive in 1298.[64] Their son Richard was holding this half share of the manor as ½ knight's fee in 1322 and 1323,[65] but he was dead by 1324.[66] A John de Marnham heads the tax roll for West Bromwich in 1327.[67] By 1329, however, William son of Richard de Marnham was lord of the moiety.[68] Still living in 1339,[69] he was dead by 1347 with a son John, a minor, as his heir.[70] John was still alive in 1397[71] but was dead by c. 1420.[72]

John's heirs were Nicholl Thorley, grandson of his sister Margery, and William Freeman, son of his

---

[33] S.H.C. xii (1), 101; C 139/82/46; C 142/97/70; C 142/114/28; below p. 16. For the descent of Weoley Castle see V.C.H. Worcs. iii. 194–6.

[34] V.C.H. Staffs. iii. 216.

[35] Ibid. 218; L. & P. Hen. VIII, iv (2), pp. 1594, 1711–12.

[36] Cal. Inq. p.m. (Rec. Com.), iv. 139; Cal. Fine R. 1430–7, 132–3.

[37] V.C.H. Worcs. iii. 92.

[38] V.C.H. Staffs. iv. 34, 59.

[39] See p. 50. His heir at that time was evidently his son Ric.

[40] S.H.C. i. 198.

[41] Ibid.

[42] Ibid. iii (1), 161. Between 1201 and 1210, however, there is a gap in the appearances of Wm. son of Guy in the Plea Rolls: ibid. 73, 149.

[43] Ibid. 153.

[44] He was still living in Jan. 1222, but his widow Geva was suing for dower in Jan. 1223: ibid. 24, 218–19. The account in S.H.C. i. 199, is wrong at this point.

[45] S.H.C. iv (1), 28–9.

[46] Ibid. 30–1, 33, 35.

[47] Ibid. 78, 94–5.

[48] S.H.C. v (1), 108. A fine of 1248 involving land in Bromwich is endorsed 'Sarra and Helis, daughters of Richard de Bromwyz, put in their claim': iv (1), 242–3. The family name of the holders of the manor was evidently de Bromwich by that time: ibid. 138.

[49] S.H.C. v (1), 108; vi (1), 56, 77, 224, 236. Margaret was still unmarried in 1258; she then accused a servant of Wal. Devereux of imprisoning her: iv (1), 138.

[50] S.H.C. vi (1), 224, 248; S.H.C. 1911, 206.

[51] S.H.C. vii (1), 124.

[52] S.H.C. ix (2), 45; S.H.C. 1911, 353.

[53] F. A. Homer, 'Collections for the Hist. of the Priory of Sandwell' (in W.S.L.), transcript of deed of 1336.

[54] The inq. post mortem of Sir Roger Hillary (d. 1356) shows that he held land in West Bromwich of Wm. Devereux: S.H.C. 1913, 169. Hillary's son, another Sir Roger (d. 1400), held land there of the heir of a John 'Deures': Willett, West Bromwich, 230–1.

[55] Basset is described as lord of the manor in the poll-tax

returns: S.H.C. xvii. 174. A Basset family had held land in West Bromwich in 1293: vi (1), 223. A family of Bassets, perhaps the same family, held half of Nether Haddon from c. 1170 until at least Edw. III's reign; from them it had passed by Hen. VI's reign to the Vernons: W. A. Carrington, 'Haddon: the Hall, the Manor, and its Lords', Jnl. Derb. Arch. & Nat. Hist. Soc. xxii. 3–5. Agnes Malley, described as lady of West Bromwich in 1456 (S.H.C. N.S. iii. 221; N.S. iv. 95), may have had a life interest in this moiety of the manor.

[56] C 140/24/24/10, stating that it was held of Sir Simon Mountfort. Mountfort has no apparent connexion with Weoley Castle (then belonging to Wm. Berkeley), to whose owners the overlordship had descended: J. C. Wedgwood and Anne D. Holt, Hist. of Parl.: Biogs. 1439–1509, 69, 603; and see above.

[57] Jnl. Derb. Arch. Soc. xxii. 12.

[58] C 142/41/43, which states that he held his moiety of the king as of the Duchy of Lancaster.

[59] Ibid.; Hist. MSS. Com. 24, 12th Rep. IV, Rutland, i, p. 22. John 'Vernam' was holding land in West Bromwich in 1526: E 36/165 f. 135v. For genealogical details see J. E. Auden, 'Documents relating to Tong College', Trans. Shropshire Arch. & Nat. Hist. Soc. 3rd ser. viii. 173–5; Shaw, Staffs. i. 396, 398.

[60] S.H.C. xiii. 209.

[61] S.H.C. xvii. 215; below pp. 24, 279.

[62] S.R.O., D. 260/M/T/2/7, marr. settlement of 17 Jan. 1585.

[63] S.H.C. xvi. 155, 166, 182.

[64] S.H.C. vii (1), 16, 35, 42, 48.

[65] S.H.C. ix (1), 64; ix (2), 45; S.H.C. 1911, 353.

[66] S.H.C. ix (1), 101.

[67] S.H.C. xii (1), 229.

[68] Willett, West Bromwich, 205–6; S.H.C. x (1), 103; xi. 130, 141.

[69] S.H.C. xi. 92–3.

[70] S.H.C. xii (1), 101.

[71] S.H.C. xiii. 18, 186, 189–90; xv. 5, 11, 15; xvii. 174; Shaw, Staffs. ii. 185; Willett, West Bromwich, 207–8 (wrongly dating a deed of 1397 to 1388).

[72] C 1/4/35.

sister Isabel. About 1420 they were disputing the moiety,[73] but in 1424 William Freeman settled it on his daughter Alice, widow of William Frebody of Dudley.[74] Freeman was dead by 1426,[75] and the next year Alice made a settlement of what was described as the manor of West Bromwich.[76] Her son William Frebody held the manor at his death in 1437 and was succeeded by his son William, who was then aged ten[77] and was still living in 1502.[78] By 1515 the manor was held by the younger William's granddaughter Cecily, the daughter of his son Richard; she was the wife of John Stanley.[79]

Cecily died at West Bromwich in 1552 and was succeeded by her son Francis Stanley.[80] He died in 1558 leaving a son George as his heir. George was a minor, and in 1560 the overlord, Thomas Jervoise, granted his wardship and marriage to John Littleton.[81] George made a settlement of the manor in 1572,[82] but Francis Stanley's widow Winifred held it in 1574.[83] She was still holding the manor court in 1580[84] and died in 1586 or 1587.[85] She was succeeded by her son Walter, who died in 1615.[86] His son William mortgaged the manor in 1622 to his cousin, Richard Shelton (knighted 1625), and Sir William Hewitt.[87]

In 1626 Sir Richard Shelton bought the manor with 1,599 a.[88] Sir Richard, a member of a prominent family of Birmingham merchants, was solicitor-general from 1625 until forced to resign in 1634. According to Clarendon he was dismissed because he was 'an old, useless, illiterate person'; more recently, however, it has been suggested that he may have made himself unacceptable to the government by expressing doubts about the legality of levying Ship Money in peacetime. He retired to West Bromwich where he died in 1647.[89] He left the manor to his sister Alice Lowe for life and then to his nephew John Shelton; it was conveyed to John by Alice and her husband Humphrey Lowe in

1648.[90] John died in 1665 and was succeeded by his son John, a minor, whose inheritance is said to have been wasted by his stepfather Dr. Walter Needham, the physician and anatomist.[91] John not only mortgaged the manor from 1681 but also sold several properties in West Bromwich in the early 18th century, and in 1713 the manor and estate were put up for sale under a Chancery decree.[92] John died in 1714, and his son Joseph inherited his embarrassments.[93] In 1715 the Sheltons were 'in very desperate circumstances and then absconding'; all or most of the demesne lands were 'neither set, mowed, nor grazed that year, but the product thereof rolled upon the ground'.[94] At a public meeting in 1716 it was resolved that the land-tax collectors and the parish officers should take legal advice how to collect the tax and rates due from Bromwich Hall and its demesne lands.[95] In 1720 the manor, with 1,596 a., was sold to Sir Samuel Clarke, a London merchant.[96]

Sir Samuel, who took an immediate interest in his new estate,[97] died in 1733.[98] He was succeeded by his son Samuel, whose wife, Mary Jervoise, was a descendant of the Jervoises who had held the overlordship in the 16th century.[99] Their son Jervoise succeeded on Samuel's death in 1767.[1] In 1777 he added Jervoise to the family name in compliance with the will of his maternal grandfather, Thomas Jervoise.[2] Jervoise Clarke Jervoise died in 1808 with his son Thomas as his heir.[3] The 3rd earl of Dartmouth was vainly trying to secure a lease of the manor at that time.[4] Thomas died mad in 1809,[5] and from 1822 or 1823 his property was sold under a Chancery order of 1819. The manorial rights with property worth some £580 a year were bought by the 4th earl of Dartmouth in 1823, and the manor then descended with Sandwell.[6]

There was a manor-house at West Bromwich by the early 1220s.[7] The oldest part of the present

73 Ibid.
74 C 139/82/46; C 142/97/70. In 1420 Wm. sued a Wm. Robyns of West Bromwich to render an account for the time when he was Freeman's bailiff at West Bromwich: S.H.C. xvii. 74.
75 S.H.C. xvii. 109.
76 Cal. Close, 1422–9, 378.
77 C 139/82/46.
78 Willett, West Bromwich, 210–11 (wrongly dating a deed of 1502 to 1501).
79 C 1/164/47; C 1/358/40. John Stanley died in 1534 holding land of his wife as of her manor of West Bromwich: C 142/156/31. Shaw, Staffs. ii, app. of additions and corrections to parochial hist. 16–17, is wrong in stating that John Stanley's marriage to Cecily was temp. Hen. VIII: their son and heir Francis was aged '30 and more' in 1534.
80 C 142/97/70; Willett, West Bromwich, 11.
81 C 142/114 no. 28; C 103/40.
82 S.H.C. xiii. 290–1.
83 West Bromwich Ct. R. p. 1. In 1574 the manor was settled on her and two of her sons-in-law by Ric. Smyth and his wife: S.H.C. xiv (1), 174–5. It was on Smyth that Geo. Stanley had settled the manor in 1572.
84 Willett, West Bromwich, 232–3.
85 Her will of 1586 was proved in Feb. 1587; S.H.C. 1928, 133–4.
86 W.S.L., S. MS. 336, f. 61; Willett, West Bromwich, 12; S.H.C. v (2), 277–8.
87 W.B.L., D. 47; Willett, West Bromwich, 12–14; S.H.C. n.s. x (1), 19; D.N.B. sub Shelton.
88 W.B.L., D. 47; C 103/127/3b.
89 D.N.B. (misquoting Clarendon); C. Gill, Hist. of Birmingham, i. 43–4; G. E. Aylmer, The King's Servants: the Civil Service of Charles I, 1625–1642, 112–13.
90 W.B.L., D. 47; C 103/40; P.R.O. Index 17238 f. 162v.

(the original fine is missing from C.P. 25(2)/486); S.R.O., D.(W.) 1817; Willett, West Bromwich, 14; S.H.C. 4th ser. ii. 30.
91 Willett, West Bromwich, 14, 16; S.H.C. 1923, 246; S.R.O., D. (W.) 1817. For Needham see D.N.B.; J. and J. A. Venn, Alumni Cantabrigienses . . . to 1751, iii. 239.
92 Willett, West Bromwich, 14–15, 201–4; C 103/40; W.B.L., D. 47; W.S.L., S. MS. 370/viii/II, pp. 455–6, 513, 556, 566; Notts. Rec. Office, DD. 4P/24/5.
93 Willett, West Bromwich, 15–16.
94 E 134/13 Geo. I Mich./7 m. 2.
95 West Bromwich Churchwardens' Bk. 1678–1787, p. 62.
96 Willett, West Bromwich, 15, 17; C 103/40; C 103/129/3; W. A. Shaw, Knights of Eng. ii. 277; Gent. Mag. iii. 662; List of Sheriffs (P.R.O. Lists and Indexes, ix), 207.
97 For his extensive planting of the gardens see below. For his dispute with Lord Dartmouth over the status of Sandwell in relation to West Bromwich manor see p. 44.
98 Gent. Mag. iii. 662.
99 Willett, West Bromwich, 19 and pedigree 3; V.C.H. Worcs. iii. 195.
1 Hist. of Parl.: House of Commons 1754–1790, ed. Sir Lewis Namier and J. Brooke, ii. 216–17.
2 17 Geo. III, c. 48 (Priv. Act).
3 Willett, West Bromwich, 19; C 103/129/1, deed of 25 Mar. 1823.
4 S.R.O., D.(W.)1778/I/ii/1718.
5 Willett, West Bromwich, 19; C 103/129/1, deed of 25 Mar. 1823.
6 Reeves, West Bromwich, 41; Willett, West Bromwich, 20; Hackwood, West Bromwich, 33; W.B.L., D. 53; C 103/41/3; Staffs. Advertiser, 8 Feb. 1823; S.R.O., D. 564/5/2/2; below pp. 18, 30, 43. The trustees of Thos. Clarke Jervoise still owned 415 a. in West Bromwich in 1845: L.J.R.O., B/A/15/West Bromwich.
7 S.H.C. iv (1), 29.

Oak House from the north-west in 1876

Sandwell Hall from the south-east *c.* 1810

WEST BROMWICH

View from the north-west, showing the hall and the kitchen

The interior of the hall during restoration

WEST BROMWICH MANOR-HOUSE

building, however, is the hall, which is thought to date from *c.* 1300, a time when the Marnhams had a house in West Bromwich.[8] It has two full bays and a short entry bay, marked by a spere truss, at the south end.[9] Presumably it originally extended further at each end to provide both service and private rooms, but they would have been removed in the earlier 15th century when the present cross wings were built. In the late 15th century a chapel, first referred to in 1552,[10] was added at the east end

On buying the hall in 1720 Sir Samuel Clarke immediately set about stocking the gardens with fruit, including grapes, nectarines, peaches, and figs.[13] Additions and alterations were made to the hall during the 18th century,[14] and in the 1790s it consisted 'of a large pile of irregular half-timbered building, black and white, and surrounded with numerous out-houses and lofty walls'.[15] In 1823 the hall, with a farm-house and 206 a., was sold to James Smith of the near-by Hall Green House. He

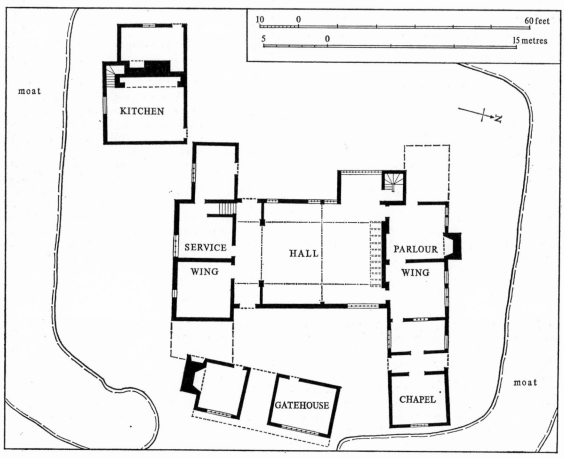

WEST BROMWICH MANOR-HOUSE

of the north cross wing. The west wall of the hall was rebuilt when the oriel was added at its north end in the 16th century, and the detached kitchen block to the south-west of the service wing is of about the same date. About 1600 a two-storeyed gatehouse range was built to the east of the hall and the service wing was extended to join it. The house occurs as Bromwich Hall in 1605,[11] and John Shelton was assessed for tax on 16 hearths there in 1666.[12]

died in 1829, and in 1845 the hall and 232 a. in West Bromwich were owned by his trustees.[16] In 1829 the hall was occupied by George Cooper,[17] but by 1836 three families were living there, including that of the assistant curate at All Saints'.[18] By the early 1880s the building had been converted into a number of tenements.[19] In 1950 the property, by then derelict, was bought by the corporation. After much controversy restoration was begun in 1957, and the additions of the 18th and 19th centuries were

[8] *S.H.C.* vi (1), 279.
[9] For the rest of this para. see, unless otherwise stated, J. A. Roberts and S. R. Jones, *West Bromwich Old Hall* (duplicated pamphlet, 1959; copy in W.S.L. Pamphs. *sub* West Bromwich); *The Manor House, West Bromwich* (brochure for the official opening, 1961). See also plate on facing page. Thanks for help are due to Mr. S. R. Jones, who is preparing an article on the house for the *Transactions* of the South Staffordshire Archaeological and Historical Society.
[10] L.J.R.O., will of Cecily Stanley (proved 5 Nov. 1552), inventory.
[11] *S.H.C.* 1940, 209.

[12] *S.H.C.* 1923, 246.
[13] Willett, *West Bromwich*, 248–58. There was further planting in the mid 18th century.
[14] *The Manor House, West Bromwich*, 10.
[15] Shaw, *Staffs.* ii. 128.
[16] W.B.L., D. 53, D. 55–7; Willett, *West Bromwich*, 19; Reeves, *West Bromwich*, 41; Parson and Bradshaw, *Dir. Staffs.* (1818); L.J.R.O., B/A/15/West Bromwich.
[17] Pigot, *Com. Dir. Birm.* (1829), 101.
[18] Reeves, *West Bromwich*, 41, 170, 174; Willett, *West Bromwich*, 20.
[19] Willett, *West Bromwich*, 20.

removed. In 1961 the building was opened as a restaurant by Ansells Brewery Ltd., the tenants of the corporation.[20]

The enclosing moat is probably contemporary with the hall. Most of it was filled in c. 1700, but the section in front of the gatehouse had been filled in earlier to make a forecourt.

SANDWELL presumably formed part of West Bromwich manor until William son of Guy de Offini founded a Benedictine priory c. 1190 on the site of a hermitage near the spring from which the area takes its name. The endowment included all the land around the hermitage, apparently a substantial block of property in the east of the parish adjacent to the Handsworth boundary. William also gave the priory some of his villein tenants in West Bromwich with their lands, rents, suits, and services.[21] The monks exercised a manorial jurisdiction over the estate.[22]

Sandwell priory was suppressed in 1525, and its property was granted to Cardinal Wolsey's college at Oxford; in 1530 on Wolsey's fall the property reverted to the Crown.[23] In 1531 the Crown conveyed to Dame Lucy Clifford various properties including what was called the manor of Sandwell. The grant was made in exchange for her share of a pension given by the Crown in 1339 to Sir Thomas de Bradeston in fee. Lucy's share of the pension had been settled on her at her first marriage to Sir John Cutte (d. 1528) of Horham Hall in Thaxted (Essex), by her aunt Elizabeth, Lady Scrope of Upsall, a daughter and heir of Isabel, marchioness of Montagu. Lucy died in 1557 and Sandwell passed to her grandson John Cutte.[24] In 1569 he sold the manor and lands formerly belonging to Sandwell priory to Robert Whorwood, a London mercer and a younger son of John Whorwood of Compton in Kinver.[25] Sandwell then descended in that branch of the Whorwood family, passing in 1590 to Robert's son William (knighted 1604), in 1614 to his grandson Thomas (knighted 1624), and in 1634 to his great-grandson Brome.[26] Brome's property was sequestrated by the Parliamentarians because of his royalist sympathies. In 1648, however, he compounded for his lands, stating that the annual value

of the Sandwell estate, including property in Handsworth and Barr, was £330 'before these times'.[27] He died in 1684 leaving no legitimate son, and Sandwell passed to his nephew Thomas Brome Whorwood.[28] Thomas mortgaged the estate several times between 1685 and 1697 for increasingly large sums[29] and finally in 1701 sold it to William, Baron Dartmouth (created earl of Dartmouth in 1711).[30] Sandwell remained with the Dartmouths, and in 1823 the 4th earl (d. 1853) became lord of West Bromwich manor also;[31] in 1845 he owned 2,012 a. in West Bromwich.[32] He moved to Patshull in 1853,[33] and in the later 19th century the south-western part of Sandwell Park was developed as a residential area.[34] The corporation bought 1,367 a. from the 7th earl in 1947 mainly in order to preserve Sandwell as open country,[35] and in 1968 the 9th earl owned no land in West Bromwich.[36]

The priory was ruinous at the time of its dissolution.[37] The 'priory house', however, was occupied successively by Humphrey Justice, Roger Green, and William Wyrley; Wyrley, farmer of the rectory by the dissolution, ceased to hold both house and rectory c. 1567.[38] Robert Whorwood lived at the house after acquiring the manor in 1569 and died at Sandwell in 1590.[39] His son William lived there, describing his house as Sandwell Hall in 1611.[40] After his death in 1614 the family normally lived at Holton (Oxon.),[41] but Brome Whorwood was evidently living at Sandwell in 1654 while he was sheriff.[42] He seems to have let the hall to Henry Freeth by 1659; Freeth was taxable on seven hearths in West Bromwich in 1666.[43] In 1697 Thomas Brome Whorwood gave Freeth a 21-year lease of part of the hall but reserved the house 'from the kitchen upwards', the garden adjoining the great parlour, the court before the house, two new stables adjoining the great barn, and housing in any of the barns for coach or coaches; he also reserved the right to build additions to the hall.[44] When Freeth died in May 1705[45] he was occupying the 'dwelling house', the 'dayhouse', the 'little dayhouse', and three chambers over the 'house', pantry, and entry; the cellars, pantry, brew-house, malt-rooms, cheese chamber, and cockloft; and the coach-house with

[20] *The Manor House, West Bromwich,* 11–15. The adjoining Moorlands Farm House, which also contains timber framing, was restored as the manager's house.
[21] *V.C.H. Staffs.* iii. 216–17; Dugdale, *Mon.* iv. 190. For the persistence of the place-name 'hermitage' in the area until at least the 18th century see E 36/165 f. 129; Willett, *West Bromwich,* 202.
[22] See p. 43. For more detailed descriptions of the bounds of Sandwell see S.R.O., D.(W.)1778/V/1222; D. 742/VIII/3. E 134/27 and 28 Eliz. I Mich./2 mm. 1–4, mentions a 'circuit or ring hedge' around the Sandwell demesnes.
[23] *V.C.H. Staffs.* iii. 219; *V.C.H. Salop.* ii. 44–5, which expands the account given in *V.C.H. Staffs.*
[24] Act of Exchange between the King's Highness and the heirs of the Lord Marquess Montagu, 22 Hen. VIII, c. 21; *Cal. Pat.* 1338–40, 395; C 142/124/179. For genealogical details see H. W. King, 'The Descent of the Manor of Horham, and of the Family of Cutts', *Trans. Essex Arch. Soc.* iv. 32–3 and pedigree by G. H. Rogers-Harrison facing p. 42 (where Lucy is confused with her mother, also Lucy, being called widow of Sir Anthony Browne instead of his daughter); W. H. St. John Hope, *Cowdray and Easebourne Priory in the County of Sussex* (1919), pedigree between pp. 26 and 27.
[25] *Cal. Pat.* 1566–9, 409; *S.H.C.* iii (2), 148–9; xiii. 274.
[26] C 142/232/61; C 142/367/101; C 142/505/135; W. A. Shaw, *Knights of Eng.* ii. 134, 185; Hackwood, *West Bromwich,* 54–5.

[27] S.P. 23/204 p. 781.
[28] *S.H.C.* v (2), 312 n.; *V.C.H. Oxon.* v. 172; Shaw, *Staffs.* ii. 129; S.R.O., D. 742/Dartmouth Estates/II/7/449–52.
[29] S.R.O., D. 1242/2.
[30] S.R.O., D. 742/Dartmouth Estates/II/7/453–5; D.(W.)1778/V/1260.
[31] See p. 16.
[32] L.J.R.O., B/A/15/West Bromwich.
[33] See p. 20.   [34] See p. 5.
[35] See p. 6.
[36] Ex inf. Lord Dartmouth (1968).
[37] *V.C.H. Staffs.* iii. 219.
[38] E 134/27 and 28 Eliz. I Mich./2 mm. 1–3. For Wyrley as farmer of the rectory see ibid. mm. 2–3; E 36/165 f. 127; *L. & P. Hen. VIII,* vi, p. 101; *Cal. Pat.* 1560–3, 516.
[39] E 134/27 and 28 Eliz. I Mich./2 mm. 1–3; C 142/232/61.
[40] Erdeswick, *Staffs.* 415 (describing the occupant as Thos. Whorwood); *S.H.C.* 1912, 286; 1940, 207; *Cal. S.P. Dom.* 1598–1601, 64; 1611–18, 32.
[41] *V.C.H. Oxon.* v. 161, 171–2.
[42] *S.H.C.* 1920 and 1922, 96.
[43] *West Bromwich Par. Reg.* (Staffs. Par. Reg. Soc.), i. 87; *S.H.C.* 1923, 248; West Bromwich Ct. R. pp. 133 (1685), 149 (1686).
[44] S.R.O., D. 564/3/1/2; *V.C.H. Bucks.* iv. 448.
[45] West Bromwich Par. Reg., burial 1 June 1705 (from transcript in W.S.L.).

the chamber over it.[46] In July two brothers were tenants at the hall, but by August the elder had left.[47]

Meanwhile Dartmouth had purchased Sandwell and decided to make it his Staffordshire seat. In 1703 William Smith of Tettenhall, the leading master-builder in the West Midlands, was engaged to 'mend the old house'.[48] The work, however, apparently turned into a thorough rebuilding. Smith's first contract, upon which he was working in 1704, included the reflooring and reroofing of part of the existing house as well as some new work.[49] Subsequently the remainder of the old building was

century building was discovered in 1928.[55] A plan of c. 1770[56] suggests that Smith's work may in part have followed the layout of the earlier house, which probably had three ranges surrounding a court open to the north; that arrangement presumably dated from the late 16th century. It seems that Smith rebuilt the east wing and extended it to include two parallel ranges of rooms. The new central range was also two rooms deep and contained the hall and chapel. The west wing followed the line of the earlier building, with an extension at the south-west corner. In the earlier 18th century the house had at least 66 rooms.[57] Views dating from the late 18th

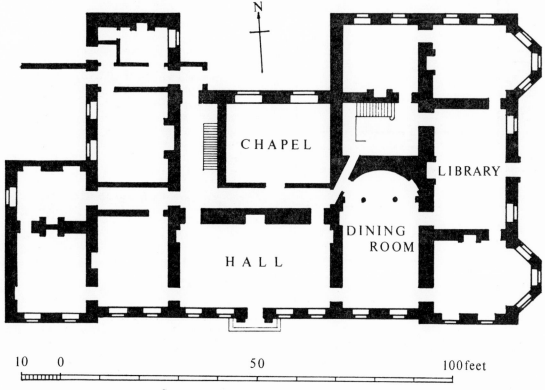

SANDWELL HALL: GROUND-FLOOR PLAN, c. 1770

pulled down, and in July 1705 the foundations of a new building were laid, evidently on the site of the old one.[50] It was then estimated that the work contracted for would take another five years.[51] Work was still in progress in the summer of 1708, by which time Smith had been paid over £1,750.[52] It was probably completed in or shortly after 1711: in May of that year all the offices were said to be finished and the foundations laid for the stables.[53]

The result of Smith's work was a new brick-built hall which he evidently designed himself.[54] There were, however, some survivals from earlier periods. Fragments of the priory buildings remained 'in the back part and offices'; part of a two-storeyed 14th-

century show symmetrical fronts on the south and east. There were two full storeys and an attic floor lit by dormer windows behind a balustrade. On the south-west, south-east, and north-east corners there were three-storeyed towers with hipped roofs. Two-storeyed window bays, facing east and surmounted by balustrades, projected from the two eastern towers.[58] The upper storeys of all three towers had probably been added in the mid 18th century; it seems that Smith's south front had twin gables.[59] By the end of the century the house had been 'neatly stuccoed white'.[60] The spring of Sandwell was close to the south front.[61]

Sandwell was the favourite residence of the 2nd

[46] L.J.R.O., will of Hen. Freeth (proved 28 Sept. 1705), inventory listing Freeth's goods in those rooms.
[47] S.R.O., D.(W.)1778/V/1325, Wm. James to Lord Dartmouth, 7 July and 4 Aug. 1705.
[48] D.(W.)1778/I/ii/58, Lord Digby to Lord Dartmouth, 22 Sept. 1703. For Smith see H. M. Colvin, *Biog. Dict. Eng. Architects, 1660–1840.*
[49] D.(W.)1778/V/1325, James to Dartmouth, 5 Aug. 1704, 4 June 1705.
[50] Ibid. 30 June, 7 and 11 July 1705.
[51] Ibid. 25 Aug. 1705.   [52] Ibid. 31 May 1708.
[53] D.(W.)1778/I/ii/256.

[54] See D.(W.)1778/V/1325, especially Smith's two letters to Dartmouth, 14 Aug. 1706 and 19 Mar. 1707.
[55] Shaw, *Staffs.* ii. 130; *Express & Star,* 16 Nov. 1928; F. A. Homer, 'Collections for the Hist. of the Priory of Sandwell' (in W.S.L.), photograph dated Nov. 1928.
[56] Reproduced above. For a plan and interior elevations of the chapel, unsigned and undated, see S.R.O., D. 564/12/10.   [57] S.R.O., D. 564/11/2.
[58] W.S.L., Staffs. Views, viii, pp. 146–7, 148a, 150b.
[59] S.R.O., D.(W.)1778/V/1325, James to Dartmouth, 26 Dec. 1705.   [60] Shaw, *Staffs.* ii. 130, 132.
[61] Willett, *West Bromwich,* 148.

earl of Dartmouth (succeeded 1750, d. 1801). A park was laid out probably in the mid 18th century, and Dartmouth's 'cultivated lawns' were praised in verse in 1767. In 1769 Lady Dartmouth had a menagerie there; it included specimens of North American fauna sent by Dartmouth's well-wishers

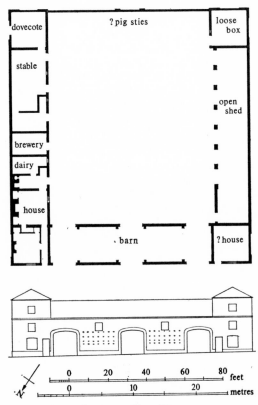

SANDWELL PARK FARM

after the repeal of the Stamp Act in 1766. In 1798 five turkeys were stolen from it.[62] By the beginning of the 19th century the park was well timbered, especially with oaks, and there were pools to the north of the hall; 'a lofty park wall and rich phalanx of plantations on rising ground to the south' ensured seclusion from the 'manufacturing country'.[63] Such seclusion was valued: in 1806 Lord Dartmouth's agent bought some land near Sandwell at a high price in order to prevent building on it.[64]

The hall was 'very much improved' c. 1805,[65] and by 1821 a portico had been added.[66] Yet when Lord Hatherton visited Sandwell in 1845 he found it 'a dull house in a very dull situation'; his room, indeed the whole house, was 'very dignified and dingy'.[67] In 1830 the 4th earl of Dartmouth was said to be planning 'a new mansion on a more elevated site'.[68] The house was in fact extended on the west side c. 1840.[69] Dartmouth, however, lived for some time at his Yorkshire seat, Woodsome Hall in Almondbury (Yorks. W.R.), and in 1848 he bought Patshull Hall on the Shropshire border. His heir, Viscount Lewisham, went to live there. Lord Dartmouth's own move to Patshull in 1853 may have been due in part to the deficiencies of Sandwell Hall, but the main cause was probably the rapid industrial development of West Bromwich; also his wife had died in 1849.[70]

After Dartmouth left, the hall was let for a time to G. F. Muntz, the metal manufacturer and political reformer.[71] Muntz, however, soon moved to Umberslade Hall in Tanworth (Warws.),[72] and Sandwell Hall then stood empty until 1857 when the 5th earl (d. 1891) gave it for use during his lifetime as an Anglican educational institution.[73] It was a lunatic asylum from 1897 to 1906, then a school for mental defectives,[74] and in the 1920s a boys' Borstal.[75] It was finally left empty and was demolished in 1928.[76] A fragment of the medieval building was then uncovered and left standing,[77] but little of it now remains.

Sandwell Park Farm, about a third of a mile north-west of the site of the hall on the opposite side of the former lake,[78] is an 18th-century rectangular planned farm of red brick. The symmetrical elevations with their corner towers are reminiscent of Sandwell Hall. The accommodation, which besides the disused farm-house includes a large barn, stables, a granary, and a long open shed, presumably for carts, suggests that the buildings were designed to serve a largely arable farm. There are additional cart-sheds on the west and kitchen gardens to the east.

OTHER ESTATES. Charlemont Hall stood on the west side of the present Charlemont Crescent. It was preceded by a house called Crump Hall,[79] probably the one at Crumpall Green which by 1732 belonged to Jesson Lowe, an ironmonger and a younger son of John Lowe of Lyndon.[80] Crump Hall was burnt down c. 1755.[81] Soon afterwards Jesson Lowe built himself a new house which he referred to in his will of 1758 as 'Charley Mount'; the surrounding area had already become known as

[62] B. D. Bargar, *Lord Dartmouth and the American Revolution* (Columbia, 1965), 7, 45–6, 176; S.R.O., D. 564/12/10 (plan and elevations of Sandwell menagerie); 'West Bromwich 100 Years Ago', 26 Apr. 1901; above p. 6.
[63] Shaw, *Staffs.* ii. 130, 132, and plate facing p. 128.
[64] R. W. Sturgess, 'Landowners, Mining and Development in Nineteenth-century Staffs.' *Land and Industry*, ed. J. T. Ward and R. G. Wilson, 174–5.
[65] Reeves, *West Bromwich*, 37. For a view c. 1810 see above, plate facing p. 16.
[66] S.R.O., D. 1501, portfolio.
[67] S.R.O., D. 260/M/F/5/26/37, 6 and 7 Nov. 1845.
[68] F. Calvert, *Picturesque Views . . . in Staffs. and Shropshire* (Birmingham, 1830), i. 66.
[69] Wood, *Plan of West Bromwich* (1837); L.J.R.O., B/A/15/West Bromwich.
[70] Hackwood, *West Bromwich*, 60, 62; *Gent. Mag.* N.S. xli (1), 190; *Complete Peerage*, iv. 91.

[71] 'Old Smethwick', 3 and 10 June 1950; below p. 88.
[72] 'Old Smethwick', 4 Feb. 1950; *V.C.H. Warws.* v. 168.
[73] L. F. Selwyn, *Chronicles of Sandwell* (Wolverhampton, 1875), 15 (copy in B.R.L.); below p. 83.
[74] Woodall, *West Bromwich Yesterdays*, 9; *V.C.H. Warws.* vii. 345; S.R.O., D. 564/8/1/30/Feb. 1897; Lich. Dioc. Regy., B/A/1/37, p. 81 (appointment of chaplain at Sandwell Institution for the care of the mentally defective, 1908). The last mention of a chaplain in *Lich. Dioc. Ch. Cal.* is in the edn. of 1921–2 (preface dated 1921).
[75] Local inf. (1969).
[76] Woodall, *West Bromwich Yesterdays*, 9; Homer, 'Sandwell', letters of 1928.   [77] See p. 19.
[78] O.S. Map 6", Staffs. LXVIII. SE. (1921 edn.).
[79] Reeves, *West Bromwich*, 50.
[80] S.R.O., D.(W.)627A(30)–629A(30); Willett, *West Bromwich*, 180, 184–5, and pedigree 8. For his father (d. 1740) see below p. 23.
[81] Reeves, *West Bromwich*, 50–1.

Charlemont by 1723. When Lowe died in 1758 his property also included a farm at Mount Ephraim to the north-west and another to the south-east near Bird End. The estate was then divided: the house passed to Lowe's sister Sarah on condition that she continued to live there, and the farms went to his brother Alexander.[82] In 1772, after Alexander's death, the farms also passed to Sarah.[83] She died in 1774, leaving the Charlemont estate to her elder sister Elizabeth.[84] Elizabeth was living at Charlemont in 1793, the year of her death; it then passed to her cousin John Hallam, dean of Bristol.[85] In 1806 he granted his West Bromwich property to his son Henry, the historian, but retained Charlemont Hall until his death in 1812.[86] In 1813 Henry sold the house to Thomas Jesson, who was living there in 1818.[87] In 1825 Jesson, who was then living at Westerham (Kent), sold Charlemont Hall with 41 a. to his brother-in-law Samuel James Dawes of the Leveretts, Handsworth.[88] In 1829 and between at least 1833 and 1841 it was let.[89] Dawes's son Henry was living at Charlemont by 1845, and father and son were both living there in 1851.[90]

After his purchase of the estate in 1825 S. J. Dawes bought more land in the area, 18 a. in 1830 and a further 12 a. in 1833. In 1851 he bought the remainder of Henry Hallam's property in the area, the 35-acre Stanton farm.[91] Dawes died in 1853 at his residence, Woodville in Handsworth, leaving his property in trust for his sons and their families.[92] His trustees sold Charlemont Hall in 1854 to J. N. Bagnall, who lived there until 1863 and then moved to Shenstone.[93] From 1871 the hall was let; the last occupants were Thomas Jones, town clerk of Wednesbury 1897–1921, and his widow.[94] The house was demolished in 1948,[95] and the site has since been covered by a housing estate. Almost 90 a. of land in the area continued to be held in trust for the Dawes family until 1916. The property consisted of two farms, Charlemont farm and Stanton

farm; both were bought in 1916 by two farmers, Frank and Harry Allen.[96]

Charlemont Hall was described c. 1800 as 'a lofty neat-looking house of brick, faced with stone, with iron palisades etc. in front'. An east wing was added in 1855.[97] At the inclosure of 1804 the two roads to the south and west were straightened to run further from the house; the southern half of the road running east of the house was taken into the grounds and planted.[98]

Dagger Hall at the junction of Dagger and Salter's Lanes occurs in 1667, when it was owned by William Turton of the Oak House.[99] In 1725 it was owned by his grandson, John Turton, also of the Oak House,[1] but by 1845 it was part of Lord Dartmouth's estate.[2] In the 19th century it was occupied as a farm by members of the Hall family. It was demolished between July 1894 and February 1895.[3]

The estate at Greets Green later known as Dunkirk was the home of the Rider family by the 16th century. Riders occur at West Bromwich in the 1380s.[4] Robert Rider held land in the Greets Green area in the 1520s[5] and may have had a house there.[6] He or another Robert died in 1561 or 1562 leaving his property in West Bromwich to a son, also Robert. The younger Robert left the estate to his son Simon in 1579, expressing the hope that 'he will keep it in the name wherein it hath remained many hundred years as by old and ancient deeds it doth and may appear'.[7]

In 1580 Simon, having succeeded to his father's property, came to West Bromwich from Oldbury;[8] he worked a mill on the estate and lived in a house near by.[9] He died apparently in 1640[10] and was succeeded by his grandson Robert (d. 1646).[11] Robert's son and heir Nicholas[12] got into financial difficulties: he was mortgaging land from the 1680s and was heavily in debt at his death in 1703.[13] The estate then consisted of a brick house, gardens, a windmill, a water-mill on the Tame, and arable,

[82] B.R.L. 456901 (will of Jesson Lowe dated Feb. 1758, proved July 1758). For the name Charlemont in 1723 see S.R.O., D.(W.)632A(30). Two fields in the area were known as Upper and Lower Charley in 1825: S.R.O., D. 1204, conveyance of 1825.
[83] B.R.L. 456901, 456904.
[84] B.R.L. 457167.
[85] B.R.L. 457171; Willett, West Bromwich, 181.
[86] B.R.L. 457173; D.N.B. sub Hallam, Hen.
[87] B.R.L. 457176; Parson and Bradshaw, Dir. Staffs. (1818). Thos. was the cousin of Thos. Jesson of Oakwood (d. 1837): Willett, West Bromwich, pedigree 7; below p. 26.
[88] Willett, West Bromwich, 182, and pedigree 7; S.R.O., D. 1204, conveyance of 1825 and abstract of title of trustee of will of Hen. Dawes.
[89] Pigot, Com. Dir. Birm. (1829), 101; Reeves, West Bromwich, 51, 61, 170; Reg. of Electors within Southern Div. of County of Stafford . . . 1 Nov. 1833–1 Nov. 1834, 59 (copy in W.S.L.); 1 Nov. 1841–1 Nov. 1842, 68.
[90] L.J.R.O., B/A/15/West Bromwich; White, Dir. Staffs. (1851).
[91] S.R.O., D. 1204, conveyances of 1830, 1833, and 1851; L.J.R.O., B/A/15/West Bromwich.
[92] S.R.O., D. 1204, abstract of title of trustee of will of Hen. Dawes; Staffs. Advertiser, 7 May 1853.
[93] Willett, West Bromwich, 182; Mary Willett, John Nock Bagnall (1885), 29, 32.
[94] E. Lissimore, 'The Oak House and other Old Buildings', West Bromwich News, 20 Oct. 1966; Kelly's Dir. Staffs. (1900); Ede, Wednesbury, 421, 423; 'Old West Bromwich', 10 Aug. 1945.
[95] West Bromwich News, 20 Oct. 1966.
[96] S.R.O., D. 1204, abstract of title of trustee of will of Hen. Dawes and conveyances of 1916.

[97] Shaw, Staffs. ii. 128; Hackwood, West Bromwich, 71. For a view of the house see West Bromwich Ref. Libr. Short Hist. of West Bromwich (1964).
[98] S.R.O., Q/RDc 60; B.R.L. 457176, 457177; S.R.O., D. 1204, plan on conveyance of 1825.
[99] C 103/40; Willett, West Bromwich, 225–6; S.R.O., D. 742/VIII/3.
[1] S.R.O., D. 1250/1.
[2] L.J.R.O., B/A/15/West Bromwich, no. 2539.
[3] White, Dir. Staffs. (1834; 1851); P.O. Dir. Staffs. (1860; 1872); Kelly's Dir. Staffs. (1892); S.R.O., D. 564/8/1/29/July 1894 and Feb. 1895.
[4] S.H.C. xv. 6; xvii. 174.
[5] Hackwood, West Bromwich, 71; C 1/933/29.
[6] Willett, West Bromwich, 212.
[7] L.J.R.O., wills of Rob. Rider (proved 18 Jan. 1561/2) and Rob. Rider (proved 13 Apr. 1580); W.S.L. 117/108/49.
[8] W.S.L., S. MS. 336, f. iv. His son Nic. was born at Oldbury in May 1579. He seems to have kept on a home there since several of his children were born there between 1581 and 1593; others were born at West Bromwich from 1585.
[9] For the mill see p. 31.
[10] He was still alive in 1636: Hackwood, West Bromwich, 72. A Simeon Rider was buried at West Bromwich in 1640: West Bromwich Par. Reg. (Staffs. Par. Reg. Soc.), i. 67.
[11] Hackwood, West Bromwich, 71–4; West Bromwich Par. Reg. i. 73.
[12] Hackwood, West Bromwich, 73–4.
[13] Ibid. 74–5; Willett, West Bromwich, 178; W.S.L. 117/21/49; 117/48/49; S.R.O., D. 590/42/1; West Bromwich Par. Reg., burial 18 Feb. 1702/3 (transcript in W.S.L.).

pasture, and meadow, all worth some £130 a year.[14] Nicholas's will directed that the estate should be sold to pay his debts and to provide portions for his children. In 1708 his creditors filed a bill in Chancery asking that his debts should be paid; his widow filed a cross bill to establish her dower.[15] The estate was in Chancery for over a century, but the house, like the mill, was occupied by Joseph Gutteridge between at least 1732 and 1760. James Gutteridge was killed at the mill in 1817, and Daniel Gutteridge, a farmer and miller, was apparently living there in 1818. The name Dunkirk was in use by 1748, and the mill became known as Gutteridge's Mill.[16]

In 1812 the estate was auctioned under a Chancery decree and most of it was bought jointly by Alexander Stansbie, Edward Blount of Bellamour in Colton, and Thomas Whitgreave of Moseley in Bushbury. In 1816 Stansbie went bankrupt, and his share of the property was sold to the Price family. In 1829 the estate was divided between Edward Blount, Thomas Whitgreave's son George, and the Prices.[17] The house was included in the Whitgreave share, and George owned it in 1845.[18] By 1881 it was owned by Reuben Farley (d. 1899).[19] By 1895 it consisted of two tenements, severally occupied by a dairyman and a smith and inn-keeper.[20] In 1900 Farley's executors sold it to Charles Darby, who built a brewery near by in 1902. The house passed to Darby's Brewery Ltd. and in 1970 was run as the Dunkirk inn by Mitchells & Butlers.[21]

In 1632 the house included a parlour surmounted by 'high chambers', a closet or study adjoining the parlour, and a 'long buttery' near by.[22] In the late 17th century[23] it was replaced by the present two-storey brick building with attic gables. The ground-floor has been greatly altered, both inside and out, but appears to have contained one room on each side of a central entrance hall and at the rear a stair with turned oak balusters. The surviving original windows have ovolo-moulded stone surrounds.

The estate in the north of the parish which became known as Friar Park belonged to Halesowen abbey in the Middle Ages. By 1223 the abbey had about 25 a. and a mill in West Bromwich, the gift of a lord of the manor.[24] By 1291 the abbey's West Bromwich property consisted of a carucate of land, meadow, rights of common pasture, the mill, and 2s. assized rent.[25] By 1500 it comprised pasture in Bromwich park and a tilehouse, both leased out.[26] At some unknown date an abbot of Halesowen gave part of the estate for the maintenance of Tame Bridge.[27]

Halesowen abbey was suppressed in 1538, and its estates, including the West Bromwich property, were granted to Sir John Dudley, later earl of Warwick and duke of Northumberland. After his attainder and forfeiture in 1553 the West Bromwich property remained with the Crown until granted in 1562 to his son Ambrose, earl of Warwick.[28] Warwick died without issue in 1590 and the estate again reverted to the Crown; by then it was known as Friar Park.[29] The property (c. 400 a.) was acquired by Sir William Whorwood, who held it at his death in 1614.[30] Thereafter Friar Park formed part of the Sandwell estate.[31] Friar Park House, in existence between at least 1634 and the mid 19th century,[32] may earlier have been the home of the Middlemores, who were living at Friar Park between at least 1602 and 1627.[33]

In 1845 Lord Dartmouth owned 385 a. at Friar Park; 330 a. were tithe-free and evidently represented the estate formerly owned by Halesowen abbey.[34] Parts of the estate were acquired by Sir Horace St. Paul in the mid 19th century[35] and by West Bromwich corporation about 1880.[36] It was the scene of small-scale mining and of brickmaking in the later 19th century,[37] and in the 20th century it has been almost completely built over.[38]

Hill House at the north end of Dagger Lane dates from the earlier 16th century, but the details of its history before the 19th century are obscure. It may have been held by the Grove family in the 17th century; if so, it would have passed by marriage from them to the Magenis family, who would have held it until about the mid 18th century.[39] By 1845 it was part of Lord Dartmouth's estate.[40] In the late 1820s it was occupied by Mary Jesse, the widow

[14] W.S.L., O.C. Newspaper Cuttings, West Bromwich, unidentified cutting of Aug. 1704.

[15] Willett, *West Bromwich*, 178–9; L.J.R.O., will of Nic. Rider (proved 15 Feb. 1704/5); W.S.L. 117/51/49; 117/84/49; 117/103/49; S.R.O., D. 707/17/4, deed of 16 May 1815.

[16] S.R.O., D.(W.)627A(30)–630A(30); Willett, *West Bromwich*, 174; W.B.L. 66/16150, chron. list of events; Parson and Bradshaw, *Dir. Staffs.* (1818); Reeves, *West Bromwich*, 50, stating that the Gutteridge family lived on the estate 'for upwards of 100 years'; below p. 31.

[17] Willett, *West Bromwich*, 179; *Lond. Gaz.* 4–8 Aug. 1812, p. 1511; S.R.O., D. 707/13/6; D. 707/17/4, deed of 16 May 1815; below p. 31.

[18] L.J.R.O., B/A/15/West Bromwich.

[19] Willett, *West Bromwich*, 176.

[20] Hackwood, *West Bromwich*, 74.

[21] 'Old West Bromwich', 15 Sept. 1944. For a photograph of the divided building in 1910 see W.B.L., Thompson Coll. no. 65.

[22] Willett, *West Bromwich*, 176; W.S.L. 117/32/49, which also corrects the transcript given by Willett (ibid.); 117/101/49.

[23] Hackwood, *West Bromwich*, 74; Reeves, *West Bromwich*, 50; above p. 21.

[24] *S.H.C.* iv (1), 24, 29, 94–5; below p. 31.

[25] *Tax. Eccl.* (Rec. Com.), 251. See also *S.H.C.* vi (1), 223.

[26] T. R. Nash, *Coll. for Hist. of Worcs.* ii (1782), App. p. xxxvi.

[27] See p. 13.

[28] *S.H.C.* xii (1), 186; *L. & P. Hen. VIII*, xiii (2), p. 191; B.R.L. 347137; *Complete Peerage*, ix. 722–6; *Cal. Pat.* 1560–3, 293.

[29] *Complete Peerage*, xii (2), 403; below p. 31.

[30] C 142/367/101; Erdeswick, *Staffs.* 377 n.

[31] Willett, *West Bromwich*, 190.

[32] S.R.O., D. 742/Dartmouth Estates/II/7/445; L.J.R.O., B/A/15/West Bromwich; S.R.O. 575.

[33] *S.H.C.* 1935, 437; S.R.O., D. 742/Dartmouth Estates/II/7/444; West Bromwich Ct. R. p. 85.

[34] L.J.R.O., B/A/15/West Bromwich.

[35] S.R.O. 575.

[36] *Midland Advertiser*, 15 May 1886.

[37] *Records of the School of Mines*, i (2), 271; S.R.O., D. 564/7/5; D. 564/8/111/Nov. 1873; S.R.O. 575.

[38] See p. 6.

[39] Hackwood, *West Bromwich*, 67–9. This associates the two families with the near-by Dagger Hall estate, which was in fact the property of the Turtons in the later 17th and earlier 18th centuries (see above p. 21). For Edw. Grove of West Bromwich at the beginning of the 17th century see *S.H.C.* 1940, 137, 153; 1948–9, 141. There was a Hill House in Handsworth, which was held by another branch of the Grove family and also passed to Lord Dartmouth, apparently c. 1771: S.R.O., D. 742/Dartmouth Estates/II/12/819–44; D. 742/VIII/9, letter from R. Holmes, 16 Nov. 1771.

[40] L.J.R.O., B/A/15/West Bromwich, no. 2544.

of William Jesse, minister of All Saints' (d. 1814); Elizabeth Jesse, presumably their daughter, was living there in the mid 1830s.[41] It then became the home of James Eaton, who died there in 1857.[42] The adjoining farm was occupied by Joseph Chambers in the mid 1830s and by Charles Cotterill in the mid 19th century.[43] Hill House was eventually bought by West Bromwich corporation.[44] Part of it was still tenanted in 1971.

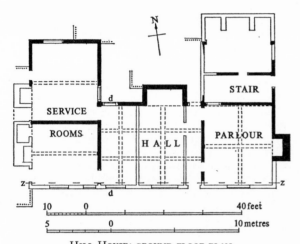

HILL HOUSE: GROUND-FLOOR PLAN
d d, former doorways; z–z, line of original wall. The surviving 16th-century walling is shown solid

Hill House is a timber-framed building of the earlier 16th century with brick additions of the 17th to 19th centuries. The original house had a central hall range flanked by cross-wings, that on the west containing the kitchen and service rooms, that on the east the parlour and principal staircase. The north front was jettied at the level of the first floor, and there were gables to the wings. The hall chimney-stack is probably original, and that to the parlour is an early addition. An early-17th-century carved overmantel and some panelling remain inside. At some time in the later 17th century the north front was built up in brick and the original timber wall was removed. The house was later subdivided, and brick additions were made which included an extension at the rear of the parlour range to form a kitchen (perhaps in the 18th century),

a pantry behind the hall chimney, and a 19th-century range of one storey on the west.

In 1699 John Lowe, an ironmonger, was living in a house known in the early 19th century as Line House, which he had bought from Josiah Simcox: it stood in Stoney Lane south of the present Lewisham Street.[45] He died in 1702 and was succeeded by his son John (d. 1740), who lived at Line House.[46] His son and heir Samuel[47] had let the house by 1748 to a Mr. Howell,[48] probably the William Howell who was keeping a boys' boarding school there by the 1760s.[49] Samuel was apparently living at the house in 1767; it was then described as having seven rooms on the first-floor, six on the second, and five on the third, with a large garden and land for cattle.[50] By 1793 the owner was Elizabeth Lowe of Charlemont, Samuel's sister;[51] the property had presumably passed to her on Samuel's death in 1783.[52] She died in 1793, and it passed with Charlemont to her cousin John Hallam.[53] He let it in 1803 and in 1806 conveyed the ownership to his son Henry,[54] who demolished it c. 1820 but still owned 20 a. in Lyndon in 1845.[55]

The 19th-century Lodge estate lay to the west of High Street with its main entrance opposite Christ Church. It centred on a warrener's lodge which existed by the early 1770s[56] and is probably identifiable with the warrener's lodge on the Heath mentioned in the 1650s.[57] In 1759 and 1792 the lord of the manor granted leases of the warren with a house.[58] William Izon the ironfounder became the tenant of the estate in 1815. In 1824 he bought what was described as Lodge Farm with some 55 a. and lived there until his death in 1867. The estate was then sold, and the house was demolished in 1868. The District Hospital was built on part of the land in 1869–71 and the town hall and other public buildings on another part in 1874–5. Houses were built over the rest.[59]

Lyttleton Hall Farm on the east side of Bromford Lane is probably the successor of a house in West Bromwich which was held by the Littleton family in 1609.[60] Littleton's Hall occurs in 1723, held of the lord of the manor by John Richards and his son John; it was held by Samuel Richards in the late 1750s.[61] In 1764 what was described as Littleton's Hall Farm was owned by Susannah Abney, who in 1770 inherited the near-by Mill estate.[62] The house

[41] Pigot, *Com. Dir. Birm.* (1829), 101; Pigot, *Nat. Com. Dir.* (1835), 472; White, *Dir. Staffs.* (1834); Reeves, *West Bromwich*, 172; *Express & Star*, 4 May 1967.
[42] See p. 4.
[43] White, *Dir. Staffs.* (1834; 1851); L.J.R.O., B/A/15/ West Bromwich.
[44] *Express & Star*, 4 May 1967.
[45] B.R.L. 456894, will of John Lowe. This also mentions other houses and lands in Lyndon which he had bought from his brother Paul. In 1666 a John Lowe was chargeable for tax on 6 hearths in West Bromwich and Paul Lowe on 3; a 'Mr. John Symcox' was chargeable on 5: *S.H.C.* 1923, 247. And see below p. 67. For the name and site see B.R.L. 457173, 457177.
[46] Willett, *West Bromwich*, 180, 182, and pedigree 8; S.R.O., D.(W.)627A(30), 628A(30); West Bromwich Par. Reg., burial 23 July 1740 (transcript in W.S.L.). Willett wrongly gives the younger John's date of death as 1729; the John who died in 1729 was presumably his eldest son.
[47] B.R.L. 456899, copy of will of 1740.
[48] S.R.O., D.(W.)629A(30). It must have been another Samuel Lowe who died in 1741: West Bromwich Par. Reg., burial 26 June 1741 (transcript in W.S.L.).
[49] Reeves, *West Bromwich*, 55–6.

[50] *Aris's Birmingham Gaz.* 9 Feb. 1767.
[51] S.R.O., D. 742/Dartmouth Estates/II/9/680.
[52] His will was proved Dec. 1783: B.R.L. 457169.
[53] See p. 21.
[54] B.R.L. 457172–3.
[55] Reeves, *West Bromwich*, 55–6; L.J.R.O., B/A/15/West Bromwich.
[56] B.R.L. 608107, Plan of Turnpike Road from Birmingham to Wednesbury, Dudley and Bilston 1771; Yates, *Map of Staffs.* (1775); Wood, *Plan of West Bromwich* (1837); W. E. Jephcott, *House of Izons* (London and Dudley, 1948), 28–9 and plate facing p. 28.
[57] S.R.O., D. 742/VIII/3. It was described as the ancient lodge in 1804: S.R.O., Q/RDc 60.
[58] B.R.L. 297309. Two houses were included in 1792.
[59] Jephcott, *Izons*, 26–9; W.B.L. 66/16151; 'Old West Bromwich', 2, 9, 16, and 23 June 1944; above p. 9 and below pp. 34, 46, 48, 72.
[60] *S.H.C.* n.s. iii. 35; Jephcott, *Izons*, 24; B.R.L. 378061, rent-roll (damaged, date missing).
[61] S.R.O., D.(W.)630A(30), 632A(30). It seems to have been held by Jas. Fenton in 1732 and 1733: ibid. 627A(30).
[62] S.R.O., D. 707/17/3, abstract of title, p. 19; below p. 24.

was apparently rebuilt about that time, being described in 1779 as newly built. It was then up for sale with some 163 a. of land,[63] but it was still owned in 1796 by the testamentary trustees of Susannah's husband, Roger Holmes.[64] By then it had become the home of John Izon the ironfounder, tenant of Greet mill from 1782.[65] About 1800 the property was apparently sold to Thomas Blakemore (d. 1808); it was held by the trustees of Mrs. Blakemore in 1837 and by Richard Blakemore and others in 1845.[66] Meanwhile John Izon's son William advertised the house for letting in 1816 with some 57 a., and it passed to the Dawes family, owners of the near-by Bromford Ironworks; they mined coal on the estate to supply the works.[67] John Dawes the elder (d. 1841) was living at Lyttleton Hall from at least 1834,[68] and in the later 1840s it was the home of John Broughall, the manager of Lyttleton Hall Colliery.[69] The house was used as an isolation hospital during the smallpox epidemic of the earlier 1880s, but in 1885 it returned to private occupation.[70] Early in the 20th century it was occupied by a Mr. Hennessy, who mortgaged it to Edward Caddick, a local lawyer, and absconded. Caddick foreclosed and became the owner. He leased the house in 1911 to Joseph Whitehouse, who in 1925 bought it with 361 a. and ran a dairy farm there until c. 1950. He continued to live at what was by then called Lyttleton Hall Farm until his death in 1970; it then passed to his daughter Edna Ridyard.[71] The house is a square three-storey brick building of the later 18th century.

The Mill estate centring on Greet mill in the south-west of the parish can be traced from 1320. Greet mill itself occurs by the 1290s.[72] The estate that was associated with it by the mid 16th century occurs in 1320 when it was settled on Roger Hillary (knighted 1337) and his wife Katherine by Robert Hillary, rector of Sutton Coldfield (Warws.).[73] When Sir Roger died in 1356 it was said to comprise 3 messuages, 39 a., and 10s. rent.[74] It then descended with the manor of Shelfield in Walsall until 1583.[75] In 1556 it consisted of 2 cottages, 24 a., and a water-mill.[76]

In 1583 John Skeffington sold the estate to William Turton and Thomas Cowper alias Piddocke with remainder to Turton's heirs; it was then said to comprise 52 a. and two water-mills.[77] Turton bought out Cowper's interest in the property in 1592;[78] he probably had a house near the mills,[79] but the house called the Mill is first mentioned by name in 1656.[80] On his death in 1628 Turton was succeeded by his grandson William.[81] William died in 1656,[82] and in 1666 his son William was chargeable for tax on nine hearths at the Mill.[83] He was succeeded in 1681 by his brother Richard Turton of Oldbury (Worcs.), who was living at the Mill in 1682.[84] Richard died in 1685 and left his property to his sister Eleanor, who was living there in 1687.[85] Eleanor died unmarried in 1701; she left the Mill estate, including some 12 a. in Oldbury, to her niece, Phoebe Freeth.[86] In 1703 Phoebe married her cousin Josiah Turton,[87] who was living at the Mill by 1708.[88]

Josiah died in 1735 leaving two unmarried daughters, Phoebe and Mary.[89] A few months after her father's death Mary married Robert Abney,[90] who was living at the Mill by 1736.[91] Mary survived her husband, and on her death in 1770[92] the whole of the property apparently passed to their daughter Susannah: in 1772 it was settled on Roger Holmes, town clerk of Walsall, on his marriage to Susannah.[93] Holmes died in 1778,[94] and the estate passed to his widow under the terms of the marriage settlement of 1772. She died in 1800 and was succeeded by two daughters, Ann (d. 1826) and Susannah (d. 1838).[95] On the younger Susannah's death her property was

[63] *Aris's Birmingham Gaz.* 22 Nov. 1779, 7 Aug. 1780.
[64] S.R.O., D. 707/17/3, abstract of title, pp. 38–41. It was again up for sale in 1795: Jephcott, *Izons*, 23.
[65] S.R.O., D. 707/17/3, abstract of title, p. 40; Jephcott, *Izons*, 23; below p. 30.
[66] W.B.L. 66/16151; Wood, *Plan of West Bromwich* (1837); L.J.R.O., B/A/15/West Bromwich, no. 1200.
[67] Jephcott, *Izons*, 24.
[68] White, *Dir. Staffs.* (1834); *Reg. of Electors within Southern Div. of County of Stafford . . . 1 Nov. 1835–1 Nov. 1836*, 65 (copy in W.S.L.); *1 Nov. 1840–1 Nov. 1841*, 64; Reeves, *West Bromwich*, 168; Wood, *Plan of West Bromwich* (1837); J. Foster, *Pedigrees of County Families of Eng.* i (1873), Dawes of Shawe Place.
[69] L.J.R.O., B/A/15/West Bromwich; *P.O. Dir. Staffs.* (1845; 1850).
[70] *Boro. of West Bromwich: Ann. Rep. of Medical Officer of Health for 1885*, 4 (copy in W.B.L.); 'Old West Bromwich', 10 Mar. 1944.
[71] 'Old West Bromwich', 10 Mar. 1944; *Evening Mail*, 19 June 1970; ex inf. Mrs. Edna Ridyard (1970).
[72] See p. 30.
[73] *S.H.C.* ix (1), 79; *S.H.C.* 1911, 94–5; *Cal. Pat. 1317–21*, 104; W. A. Shaw, *Knights of Eng.* ii. 5 (date corrected in *Complete Peerage*, iii. 435).
[74] *Cal. Inq. p.m.* x, p. 280.
[75] Willett, *West Bromwich*, 230–1; *Cal. Close, 1402–5*, 216; below p. 279 and references there cited.
[76] N.R.A., Chilham Castle, Kent, Massereene (Staffs.) deeds, 29.   [77] *S.H.C.* xv. 149.
[78] W.S.L., S. MS. 336, f. 26; Willett, *West Bromwich*, 163.   [79] Hackwood, *West Bromwich*, 63.
[80] *West Bromwich Par. Reg.* (Staffs. Par. Reg. Soc.), i. 93.
[81] Hackwood, *West Bromwich*, 63; C. S. James, 'The Turton Family', *T.B.A.S.* l. 8–9.
[82] *T.B.A.S.* l. 11; *West Bromwich Par. Reg.* i. 93.

Willett, *West Bromwich*, pedigree 6, and Hackwood, *West Bromwich*, 63, give the date of his death as 1663.
[83] *S.H.C.* 1923, 248.
[84] Hackwood, *West Bromwich*, 63; Willett, *West Bromwich*, 167; L.J.R.O., will of Ric. Turton (proved 17 July 1685).
[85] Hackwood, *West Bromwich*, 63; West Bromwich Ct. R. p. 170.
[86] Prob. 11/461 (P.C.C. 105 Dyer); S.R.O., D. 707/17/3, abstract of title, pp. 2–3. Eleanor left an annuity of 50s. out of the estate for the poor of West Bromwich: see below pp. 84–5.
[87] F. A. Homer and C. S. James, *Pedigree of Turton of Staffordshire &c.* (priv. print. 1924), 4 (copy in B.R.L.). Phoebe's maiden name is there given as Heath; it was in fact Freeth: B.R.L. 338279.
[88] Willett, *West Bromwich*, 201–2.
[89] *T.B.A.S.* l. 9.
[90] Willett, *West Bromwich*, 173; *T.B.A.S.* l. 9; J. Nichols, *Hist. and Antiquities of Town and County of Leicester*, iii (2), 1042 and pedigree facing p. 1032; S.R.O., D. 707/17/3, abstract of title, p. 19.
[91] S.R.O., D.(W.)628A(30).
[92] West Bromwich Par. Reg., burial 2 June 1770 (transcript in W.S.L.).
[93] S.R.O., D. 707/17/3, abstract of title, pp. 1–20; Par. Reg., marriage 29 Oct. 1772 (transcript in W.S.L.); Glew, *Walsall*, 125.
[94] S.R.O., D. 707/17/3, abstract of title, p. 32; Glew, *Walsall*, 125.
[95] S.R.O., D. 707/17/3, abstract of title, p. 43. According to Willett, *West Bromwich*, 162, Ann and Susannah Holmes were lunatics and died at Lichfield. Both sisters died intestate, but they seem to have moved from Lichfield to Brewood in the mid 1820s; both were buried at Brewood. See S.R.O., D. 707/17/3, abstract of title, p. 43; *9th Rep. Com. Char.* H.C. 258, p. 539 (1823), ix.

claimed by her cousin's son, Edward Holmes, a labourer in Plymouth dockyard. Doubt was cast on his legitimacy, however, and numerous other claims were made to the property. In 1848, after proceedings in Chancery, the estate was vested by agreement in trustees for the benefit of Edward Holmes and the other claimants.[96] In 1782 it had been let to John Izon and Thomas Whitehurst who built an iron-foundry there; in 1845 the tenant was John Izon's son William.[97]

By 1899 part of the Mill estate had been sold to the Hamblet Blue Brick Co. Ltd.[98] The other part, occupied by Izons & Co. Ltd., was owned by the Holmes trustees. By 1903, however, that part had been sold to Messrs. Marsh of Bromford Colliery, Oldbury. By 1904 it had apparently passed to J. H. Chesshire, head of Izons & Co. Ltd. The firm has owned it since at least 1909.

The house in Oak Road known as the Oak House by 1725[99] was occupied in 1634 by Thomas Turton, third son of the William Turton who had bought the Mill in the late 16th century. In 1634 Thomas conveyed it to his elder brother John. In 1636 John conveyed it to his second son John; it was to be held by the younger John for life and then by his son William in fee.[1] By 1654 William was living at what was then called the Oak.[2] William's father died in 1673 and William himself in 1682.[3] He was succeeded by his son John and he by his son, another John, in 1705. When John died in 1768 the property passed to William Whyley, his natural son by Ann Whyley of Charlemont.[4] William died in 1800 with a son William, a minor, as his heir. The younger William died in 1806, and the estate passed to his mother, Jane Whyley, who then leased it out and moved into a newly built house near by.[5] She died in 1837, and by 1845 the property had passed to John Edwards Piercy, probably her nephew.[6] Part of the estate was sold c. 1850 to Joseph Hamblet.[7] After Piercy's death in 1853 the rest, including the Oak House, descended to his daughter Grace (d. 1880), and then to J. H. W. Piercy, who sold it in lots in 1894. The house and 22 a. were bought by Reuben Farley, then mayor, who in 1895 gave the house and 1 a. adjoining to the corporation for use as a museum. The building was then restored by Wood & Kendrick and opened as a museum in 1898; gardens and a bowling green were also laid out. To mark the fiftieth anniversary of the gift the corporation decided to convert the Oak House into a period house with antique furnishings; the formal reopening took place in 1951.[8]

The house is a timber-framed building of the later 16th century with 17th-century brick additions.[9] The earliest part is the hall and the kitchen. The present kitchen seems originally to have been the parlour; the kitchen and service rooms would then have been to the right of the entrance on the site of a later range containing two parlours, which was built c. 1600. Presumably the old parlour was then turned into the kitchen and the brick chimney-

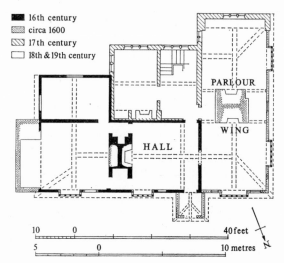

OAK HOUSE: GROUND-FLOOR PLAN

stack on the east gable built. The new parlours, although of similar construction to the older rooms, were on a more generous scale. Above them were principal bedrooms, in one of which part of a wall painting survives. A few years later a two-storeyed porch was built in front of the entrance and a belvedere or viewing tower was erected above the roof of the hall. Before the mid 17th century the southern end of the new parlour range was rebuilt in brick; at the same time the space between the two side ranges was filled in with a new block, also of brick, containing a room on each floor and a staircase with elaborately fretted balusters. The repairs and additions may have been made between 1634 and 1636 when the house seems nearly to have doubled in value.[10] William Turton was taxable on eleven hearths at the Oak in 1666.[11] There were minor alterations in the 18th and early 19th centuries, notably the insertion of several new fireplaces. Extensive restoration took place in the late 19th and the 20th centuries: many of the windows were

[96] S.R.O., D. 707/17/3, abstract of title; *T.B.A.S.* l. 9. Willett, *West Bromwich*, 162, refers to Holmes as a labourer at the dockyard. He was described as a ropemaker of Plymouth in 1839 and 1841, as a gentleman in 1841, and as a flax-dresser in 1848: S.R.O., D. 707/17/3, abstract of title, pp. 44, 61, 73, 127.

[97] See p. 30; L.J.R.O., B/A/15/West Bromwich, no. 535.

[98] For this para. see Char. Com. files.

[99] S.R.O., D. 1250/1.

[1] Willett, *West Bromwich*, 166–7 (wrongly giving the date of the second sale as 1635) and pedigree 6. Thos. was still living there in 1636. For the Mill see above p. 24.

[2] Willett, *West Bromwich*, 167, 171.

[3] Ibid. 167–8 and pedigree 6; C. S. James, 'The Turton Family', *T.B.A.S.* l. 5.

[4] Willett, *West Bromwich*, 168–9 and pedigree 6; Reeves, *West Bromwich*, 44.

[5] Reeves, *West Bromwich*, 43–5.

[6] Willett, *West Bromwich*, pedigree 6; F. A. Homer, 'Collections for the Hist. of the Priory of Sandwell'

(in W.S.L.), account of Mayer's Green chapel, p. 8; Reeves, *West Bromwich*, 182; Wood, *Plan of West Bromwich* (1837); L.J.R.O., B/A/15/West Bromwich, no. 559. Jane Whyley's sister, *née* Edwards, married into the Piercy family: Homer, loc. cit.

[7] See p. 41.

[8] 'Old West Bromwich', 7 July 1944; West Bromwich Corp. deeds, no. 33; *Oak House Souvenir Booklet* (2nd edn.), 20 sqq.; *Kelly's Dir. Staffs.* (1900); Hackwood, *West Bromwich*, 66; W. H. Kendrick, 'The Oak House, West Bromwich', *T.B.A.S.* xxxvi. 23–4; W. H. Kendrick, *Oak House, West Bromwich: Rep. to Town Council, Sept. 1895* (copy in W.S.L. Pamphs.); W.B.L., Scrapbook 13, p. 140.

[9] See *T.B.A.S.* xxxvi. 9 sqq.; ibid. l. 10; *The Building News*, 12 Oct. 1877; 'Oak House, West Bromwich, Staffs.', *Antique Collector*, April–May 1969; plate facing p. 16 above.

[10] Willett, *West Bromwich*, 166.

[11] *S.H.C.* 1923, 248.

renewed, some new ones were made, and much new panelling was added to that of the 17th century which had remained in the house.

The house is thought to have taken its name from an oak which stood on the green in front of it and was burnt down c. 1800. The estate was once full of oaks. The last John Turton advised William Whyley to fell them, and in 1768 many were used to make lock-gates for the Birmingham Canal, which was then being built through West Bromwich. Very few oaks remained in 1836.[12]

The house known as Oakwood stood on the east side of Old Meeting Street. It was built by Thomas Jesson (d. 1703) of Sutton Coldfield (Warws.), who had bought the site, known as Oakley's Croft, in 1679.[13] He was succeeded by his nephew Thomas (d. 1766), an ironmonger,[14] and he by his son Joseph (d. 1816); both lived at Oakwood.[15] Joseph's heir was his son Thomas (d. 1837), who was succeeded by his son, another Thomas.[16] Thomas owned a 43-acre estate in West Bromwich in 1845, mostly around Oakwood. The house, however, was then occupied by William Bagnall, and Jesson was living at Greswold Cottage on the corner of Bilhay Lane and Old Meeting Street.[17] Jesson died at Oakwood in 1873, and for a few months afterwards his son, the Revd. Thomas Jesson, lived there.[18] In 1912 he presented the house to the borough. The corporation demolished it in 1955, and the grounds have been laid out as a park.[19]

The central part of the house was of brick and had a symmetrical two-storey front of four bays with a heavy wooden cornice. There were dormer windows and shaped brick gables. The house was extended on either side in the 18th century.[20]

Another branch of the Jesson family had a house on Finchpath Hill called the Over House. It may be identifiable with the house at Finchpath which was conveyed in 1439 by John Hexton of Upper Arley (formerly Staffs., now Worcs.) to Thomas Swetcocke and his wife Sybil.[21] In 1446 Thomas conveyed land at Finchpath, including a croft called Black Lake, to Henry Jesson.[22] John Jesson of West Bromwich, who apparently held the house at Finchpath by 1597,[23] settled a house in West Bromwich and other property on his nephew John Jesson in 1610, retaining a life-interest.[24] He died in 1615 and the younger John in 1625. By 1635 Thomas Jesson, son of the younger John, held the property, which in 1670 included two houses in

West Bromwich in which he and his son Thomas lived. The elder Thomas was still alive in 1680. By 1693 or 1694, however, the younger Thomas held both houses, described as the Over House and the Lower House; he then settled the Lower House on his son John, retaining a life-interest in the Over House. By 1697 the estate, including both houses and a glass-house at Finchpath, had passed to John. He was succeeded between 1728 and 1732 by his son John, a Wednesbury baker, whose son, another John, held the property in 1756. In a settlement of that year the houses were called the Over House and the Lower Farm. John died between 1773 and 1775. In 1795 the Over House, described as on Finchpath Hill, and the Lower Farm passed under the 1756 settlement to Richard, the younger and survivor of John's two sons. The later history of the property is not known.

When Guy de Offini granted West Bromwich church to Worcester priory c. 1140–5 he included half a virgate and certain assarts in the grant,[25] but it is not known that the property subsequently formed part of the rectory. About 1230 the rectory passed to Sandwell priory which retained it until the dissolution in 1525. In 1526 the Crown granted Sandwell's property to Cardinal Wolsey, who in turn granted it to Cardinal College.[26] By then the tithes of corn and lambs with 'all quick mortuaries' were being farmed,[27] and after the property had passed back to the Crown in 1530 it continued to lease out the rectory.[28] In 1608 the Crown granted it to three men, presumably speculators,[29] who conveyed it in 1609 or 1610 to Sir William Whorwood of Sandwell.[30] The rectory then descended with Sandwell. It included both great and small tithes, which continued to be leased out.[31] They were commuted for £701 8s. 6d. in 1845.[32]

Sir Thomas Aston was licensed in 1404 to grant rent from a house and land at Finchpath to his chantry founded in 1390 in Walsall church, which still held it at the suppression.[33] In 1411 Thomas Thykness, Richard Snedde, John Westethorp, and Thomas Walton sought licence to give 24 a. of land, 2 a. of meadow, and rent in West Bromwich to a chantry in Walsall, apparently Sir Roger Hillary's second chantry, which held land in West Bromwich at the suppression.[34] A chantry founded at Walsall by the mayor and burgesses or St. John's guild held land in West Bromwich by 1527.[35] By 1535 too the college of vicars choral at Lichfield

[12] Reeves, *West Bromwich*, 42.

[13] Willett, *West Bromwich*, 173 and pedigree 7. There were Jessons living at West Bromwich from at least the 15th century: ibid. 209; *S.H.C.* xviii (1), 49; W.B.L., Jesson Deeds, no. 141, pedigree 2.

[14] Willett, *West Bromwich*, pedigree 7; Hackwood, *West Bromwich*, 67.

[15] Hackwood, *West Bromwich*, 67. Both are described as of Oakwood on their memorial tablet in All Saints' Church.

[16] Hackwood, *West Bromwich*, 67; W.B.L., Jesson Deeds, nos. 131–2.

[17] L.J.R.O., B/A/15/West Bromwich; J. Wood, *Plan of West Bromwich* (1837).

[18] Hackwood, *West Bromwich*, 67. *P.O. Dir. Staffs.* (1876), shows an Edw. Jones living there.

[19] West Bromwich Ref. Libr. *Short Hist. of West Bromwich* (1964), chap. 8; Woodall, *West Bromwich Yesterdays*, 12. Land immediately to the north was sold by Jesson in 1917 to Eliz. Akrill's executors and is now the site of the Akrill Homes: see below p. 84.

[20] Photographs in National Monuments Record.

[21] West Bromwich Ct. R. p. 14; *V.C.H. Worcs.* iii. 7.

[22] Willett, *West Bromwich*, 209.   [23] Ct. R. p. 14.

[24] For the rest of this para. see W.C.L., box 23, no. 8; W.B.L., Jesson Deeds, no. 141, pedigree 2.

[25] *Cartulary of Worcester Cathedral Priory* (Pipe R. Soc. N.S. xxxviii), pp. 101–2.

[26] See p. 18.   [27] E 36/165 f. 127.

[28] See p. 18 and n.; *Cal. Pat.* 1560–3, 516; C 66/1143 mm. 37–8; C 66/1283 mm. 13–15; E 134/27 and 28 Eliz. I Mich./2.

[29] C 66/1753 no. 18.

[30] Reeves, *West Bromwich*, 11, giving date as Feb. 6 Jas. I, 1609; S.R.O., D. 742/VIII/1/4, giving date as 7 Jas. I (i.e. Mar. 1609–Mar. 1610).

[31] C 2/Jas.I/C 26/29; S.P. 23/204 p. 781; E 134/13 Geo. I Mich./7 m. 3; S.R.O., D. 564/3/2/4; D. 742/Dartmouth Estates/II/7/453–5; D. 742/VIII/3; above p. 18.

[32] L.J.R.O., B/A/15/West Bromwich.

[33] *Walsall Records*, 16; *Cal. Pat.* 1401–5, 350; 1560–3, 406; below p. 228.

[34] C143/442 no. 22; *Cal. Pat.* 1549–51, 13; below p. 228.

[35] C 1/644 no. 43; below p. 228.

cathedral had lands in the parish given for the obits of William Heyworth, bishop of Coventry and Lichfield (d. 1447), John Ridell, prebendary of Ufton Decani and Pipa Minor in the 1450s, Thomas Reynold, a former Lichfield canon, and one Prior Richard.[36] This may have been the property which was said in 1564 to have belonged to the New College at Lichfield.[37] The chantry in Lichfield cathedral founded by Canon John de Kynardessey in the earlier 14th century owned a house in West Bromwich at the suppression,[38] and a chantry of St. Mary's guild in Wednesbury church also held land and rents there.[39]

ECONOMIC HISTORY. AGRICULTURE. In 1086 the manor was 3 hides in extent and had land for 3 ploughs. There were 3 teams worked by 10 villeins and 3 bordars and a fourth team in demesne. The value, 40s., was the same as it had been in 1066.[40]

During the Middle Ages the farming pattern was a mixture of open-field husbandry and farming in severalty. Three cases brought against the lords of the manor in 1293 suggest that by that date the demesne arable had been inclosed for 50 years or more and that others were following the lords' example and inclosing parts of the open fields.[41] Elsewhere in the parish the area of inclosed land was gradually increased by assarting. In the late 13th century lords and tenants reached a formal agreement on the payment of heriots for assarts and new lands, in which a distinction was drawn between those lands which had been built upon and those which had not.[42] The process of assarting and inclosure continued,[43] and manorial ordinances of 1606 accept the possibility of inclosure of strips in the open fields as a matter of course.[44]

The open fields in the parish lay around All Saints' Church on the ridge east of the Hobnail valley.[45] One, north-west of the church, was probably bounded by what are now Walsall Road, Marsh Lane, and Heath Lane. It occurs as Gnarpanell field in 1516,[46] as variations of Knapeney Hill field between at least 1526 and 1709,[47] and as Napney field from at least 1686;[48] Lydiate field occurs as an alternative name in 1610 and 1709 and Walsall Lane field in the 1780s.[49] Another field lay north and north-east of the church. If the small areas known in the early 19th century as Middle field and

Tenter House field originally formed part of it, it was probably bounded by the present Walsall Road, Charlemont Road to about Bird End, and, in the south, by the upper end of Water Lane, Newton Road, and Heath Lane. Its original name seems to have been Wigmore field, and it occurs as such between at least 1348 and 1709.[50] The name Church field occurs from 1531.[51] At first it may have been used for only part of Wigmore field: the mention in 1641 of an acre of arable lying in two fields called Church and Wigmore fields[52] suggests a division of the original Wigmore field. Church field was given as an alternative name for Wigmore field in 1709[53] and by the earlier 19th century was the name of what remained of the field. An open field in the Wigmore area known as the 'heyefeld' occurs in the 14th and 15th centuries;[54] it may have been Wigmore field under another name. Another field lay between the church and Lyndon; it included the triangle of land between the present Church Vale and Tenscore Street and extended a little to the east and west of those two roads. From at least the earlier 17th century it was called Lyndon field.[55] The south-eastern portion of the field was known as Stye Croft from at least 1531,[56] and its northern end Windmill field or Little Church field by the 1780s.[57]

Open-field husbandry appears to have continued in some form until 1804 when under an Act of 1801 the remaining fragments of the three fields were inclosed. Of the 387 a. inclosed by the Act only some 111 were described in the award as being part of the open fields, and those were scattered among areas of piecemeal inclosure.[58] The tenants' obligation to maintain gates and field hedges had been enforced until at least the early 18th century,[59] and overseers of the field hedges were regularly appointed in the manor court until 1804.[60] By the later 18th century, however, their duties may have become more formal as tenants continued to throw together and inclose acres in the fields.[61]

Three-course rotation was used in the parish by the late 13th century,[62] and farming in the open fields during the Middle Ages probably followed the course recorded several times in the 17th century: winter-sown rye, spring-sown oats, and fallow.[63] In at least the late 16th and early 17th centuries, however, wheat and barley were also being grown in the open fields, though in smaller quantities than rye and oats.[64] Other crops included

[36] Valor Eccl. (Rec. Com.), iii. 139. And see S.H.C. 1915, 167–8.
[37] Cal. Pat. 1563–6, p. 70.
[38] Ibid. 1549–51, 162; S.H.C. 1915, 158.
[39] Cal. Pat. 1563–6, p. 70; 1566–9, p. 348.
[40] V.C.H. Staffs. iv. 59, no. 299.
[41] S.H.C. vi (1), 233, 236.
[42] F. A. Homer, 'Collections for the Hist. of the Priory of Sandwell' (in W.S.L.), transcript of undated charter of Wal. Devereux and Ric. de Marnham.
[43] See e.g. S.H.C. xv. 27; ibid. N.S. iii. 140, 154; Willett, West Bromwich, 205–6.
[44] West Bromwich Ct. R. p. 43.
[45] For the following para. see, unless otherwise stated, D. A. Dilworth, 'The Field Pattern of West Bromwich', Proc. Birmingham Natural Hist. Soc. xxi. 169–71; C 103/129/3; S.R.O., Q/RDc 60.
[46] Willett, West Bromwich, 211. The spelling 'Guarpanell' given there is evidently a mistranscription.
[47] E 36/165 ff. 133v., 134; Willett, West Bromwich, 203.
[48] Ct. R. p. 165.
[49] Homer, 'Sandwell', transcript of lease 16 Oct. 1610; Willett, West Bromwich, 203; S.R.O., D. 564/1/1/3.

[50] W.C.L., box 46, no. 2; Willett, West Bromwich, 203.
[51] Willet, West Bromwich, 164.
[52] L.J.R.O., will of Geo. Partridge (proved 22 Feb. 1640/1).
[53] Willett, West Bromwich, 203.
[54] Homer, 'Sandwell', transcript of grant by Rob. son of Wm. Cocus to Nic. Golde, 1329; C 139/82/46.
[55] Ct. R. p. 88; Willett, West Bromwich, 186, 202; C 103/129/3.
[56] Willett, West Bromwich, 164.
[57] S.R.O., D. 564/1/1/3.
[58] West Bromwich Inclosure Act, 41 Geo. III, Sess. 2, c. 14 (Private and Personal, not printed); S.R.O., Q/RDc 60.
[59] Ct. R. pp. 5, 69, 77, 88, 124–5, 146, 179–80, 193–6, 229.
[60] See p. 43.
[61] For examples see C 103/127; C 103/129/3.
[62] S.H.C. vi (1), 236.
[63] Ct. R. pp. 43, 69, 124–5, 179–80, 193–4.
[64] L.J.R.O., will of Cecily Stanley (proved 5 Nov. 1552), inventory; will of Francis Symcockes (proved 10 July 1610), inventory.

dredge,[65] hemp and flax,[66] and a mixture of oats and peas.[67] Cottages with 'hemplecks' (small pieces of ground for growing hemp or flax) are found in surveys of 1630 and 1695,[68] and flax was grown in the parish until at least the later 18th century. Bustleholm mill was worked as an oil-mill between at least 1732 and 1758,[69] presumably producing linseed oil, and there was a flax-oven near West Bromwich Hall in the 1770s.[70] When Arthur Young visited the parish in 1776 he found both three-course and four-course rotation being employed.[71] In the former case the sequence was fallow, wheat, and barley or oats; in the latter it was turnips, barley, clover and rye-grass, and oats or wheat. For turnips lime was applied at the rate of 8 or 10 quarters an acre. Large quantities of potatoes had been planted in previous years; but there had been a glut of them in 1775, and fewer were being grown in 1776. Some farms were being let at from 15s. to 25s. an acre.

Pasture in the fields, in the meadows by the Tame, and on the waste was an important feature of the agricultural economy of the parish. In 1291 pasture and the sale of grazing rights (or perhaps of hay) accounted for almost half the value of the small Halesowen abbey estate, and a case of 1293 in which the abbot unsuccessfully claimed common of pasture for 600 sheep[72] may give some indication of the scale of live-stock farming in West Bromwich. At the end of the 15th century the abbey was drawing £6 13s. 4d. a year from pastures in Bromwich park.[73] Meadow, pasture, heath, and commoning rights feature prominently in a number of 16th-century land transactions.[74] Flocks of between 30 and 60 sheep were not uncommon in the late 16th and early 17th centuries;[75] no really large flocks have been found. Pasture was stinted by the early 17th century. Manorial ordinances of 1606 allowed one beast or five sheep for each acre in the fields and laid down that any tenant who inclosed land in the fields was to lose his pasture rights in them.[76] In 1591 Henry Partriche's small herd of cattle included 13 'fatting kine',[77] and by at least the late 17th century West Bromwich had probably become one of the areas in which animals were raised for the expanding Birmingham market. Land in the parish was being leased to outsiders who fattened beef cattle,[78] and in 1688 tenants of the manor were forbidden to pasture the sheep of 'foreigners' on the commons.[79]

Encroachment on the waste continued throughout the 17th and 18th centuries. Occasionally it was for industrial purposes: the construction of a saw-pit in 1634, for example, or, in the 1680s, the digging of sand; many cottagers built small workshops on to

their houses.[80] In general, however, most of the early encroachments appear to have been for cultivation or for the building of cottages. In 1630 17 cottagers, the more prosperous ones, paid rents of 2s. a year and upwards to the lord of the manor; at least 3 lived in cottages taken from the waste. Rent of a further 10s. 10d. a year covered the rest of the cottages upon the waste and some little parcels of waste ground which could not be improved because they were held by poor tenants.[81] In 1723 99 cottages in the manor were listed as encroachments on the waste; 54 were on Bromwich Heath, 20 at Mayer's Green, and the rest scattered throughout the parish.[82] Sporadic attempts were made to solve the problem by ejecting trespassers. In 1692, 1699, 1709, and 1718 the freeholders threw down illegal inclosures. In 1720 they decided at a public meeting to prosecute nine cottagers at quarter sessions, possibly as a test case; the grand jury found only three true bills, however, and there is no evidence that further action of that kind was taken.[83] The machinery of the manor court was also used, though with diminishing frequency and effect. In 1734, when the parish was 'abounding in cottages which frequently prove chargeable to it' and the number of them was increasing, the lord of the manor was asked by some leading parishioners to order that the court should actually collect the fines regularly imposed for encroachments on the waste. The intention was apparently not to demolish existing cottages but to prevent the erection of new ones. Although the cottagers paid, except for some at Mayer's Green,[84] the experiment was soon abandoned: in 1765 it was noted that, although the cottagers were still 'regularly amerced, fined, and called every court', no fine had been paid for 20 years.[85] In the later 1750s there were 129 long-standing encroachments on the waste (52 cottages on Bromwich Heath, 47 at Mayer's Green, and 30 others scattered elsewhere) and some 40 more recent inclosures. More were added every year, until by 1803 there were just over 200. About half of them were on the Heath and its fringes. Most consisted of gardens, privies, pigsties, or courtyards added to existing buildings; but about 50 were houses and cottages. A large-scale developer was Thomas Penn, who in the 1780s erected and leased out several houses on the eastern side of the Heath.[86]

The growth of settlement around the various hamlets in the parish meant that from an early date the waste was gradually dismembered. The spread of housing and cultivation led to the emergence of several distinct patches of waste: thus Hateley Heath occurs by 1485, Greets Green by

[65] See e.g. L.J.R.O., will of Rob. Ryder (proved 13 Apr. 1580), inventory.
[66] See e.g. L.J.R.O., will of Thomasine Wyly (proved 24 July 1638), inventory.
[67] W.S.L., S. MS. 336, f. 45v.
[68] C 103/127/3a and 3c.
[69] See p. 32.
[70] Yates, Map of Staffs. (1775).
[71] For the rest of this para. see Tours in Eng. and Wales by Arthur Young: Selected from the Annals of Agriculture (London Sch. of Economics, Reprints of Scarce Tracts in Economic and Political Science, no. 14, 1932), 141.
[72] Tax. Eccl. (Rec. Com.), 251; S.H.C. vi (1), 236.
[73] T. R. Nash, Coll. for Hist. of Worcs. ii (1782), App. p. xxxvi.
[74] See e.g. S.H.C. xii (1), 228; xiii. 209, 211, 221-2, 290; xiv (1), 195, 200, 212; xv. 146, 163, 185.

[75] See e.g. L.J.R.O., inventories of Phil. Orme (will proved 12 Feb. 1560/1) and Wm. Whyle (will proved 11 Jan. 1582/3); W.S.L., S. MS. 336, ff. 37-8.
[76] Ct. R. pp. 39-40, 42, 44.
[77] L.J.R.O., will proved 24 Nov. 1591, inventory.
[78] E 134/13 Geo. I Mich./7 m. 3.
[79] Ct. R. pp. 194-5.
[80] Ibid. pp. 120, 135-42, 145-6, 152-8, 171-9, 186-92, 194, 196.
[81] C 103/127/3a.
[82] S.R.O., D.(W.)632A(30).
[83] West Bromwich Churchwardens' Bk. 1678-1787, pp. 22-3, 34-5, 50-1, 66-7; S.R.O., Q/SO 12, f. 1v.
[84] S.R.O., D. 742/VIII/1/4.
[85] S.R.O., D.(W.)516(30).
[86] S.R.O., D.(W.)515(30) sqq.; ibid. 571(30) sqq. For Penn see ibid. 552(30)-557(30).

1556, and Mayer's Green by the 1660s.[87] These and other fragments (Ryders, Golds, Hall, Ireland, and Carter's Greens) have survived as modern place-names but were insignificant by the beginning of the 19th century; Bromwich Heath was then the only substantial area of waste left,[88] and it was inclosed in 1804 under the 1801 Act.[89] A few years later the Heath, like several other recently inclosed commons in south and east Staffordshire, was 'in part brought into cultivation, and covered with growing crops; and other parts preparing for turnips, or in fallow, and coming round in course'.[90] The high price fetched by some of the newly inclosed land, apparently sold for building, was noted in 1818.[91]

The spread of new streets and the industrialization of the parish became more marked in the course of the 19th century. Agriculture had long been, in economic terms, of secondary importance. Young had found it 'carried on so connectedly with manufactures that it is subservient to them'.[92] In 1801 only 245 of a population of 5,687 were farmers or farm workers,[93] and the percentage of those so employed continued to drop steadily. Large tracts of the parish, however, were still farmed. In 1845 the area of some 4,600 a. subject to tithe included 2,385 a. of arable and 1,190 a. of meadow and pasture.[94] In 1882 about half the parish remained agricultural.[95] Of this some two-thirds belonged to the Sandwell estate. By the later 19th century farming on the estate conformed to the pattern found elsewhere on the fringes of large towns. Farmers were permitted to abandon classical crop rotation and grew successive straw crops on part of their land for sale to urban horse-owners in West Bromwich and other neighbouring towns; the fertility of the ground was maintained by the use of night soil. Milk, potatoes, and pigmeat were produced for urban consumption.[96] Only 1,258 a. of farmland were left in the early 1950s,[97] and since then housing, industry, and new roads have reduced the total. By 1969 what remained lay in the east of the parish; five farms survived, all save one having lost land to development.[98]

In 1086 there was woodland 1 league in length and ½ league in breadth;[99] it may have lain in the northern part of the lordship which was bordered on the north-west by Cannock forest and on the north-east by Sutton Chase.[1] By the early 13th century there was a wooded park belonging to the manor.[2] The other most considerable area of woodland was on the

lands of Sandwell priory; in 1526 more than 145 a. were thickly wooded.[3]

The establishment of the iron industry in West Bromwich during the later 16th century must have led to the felling of much timber in the area. In the 1590s William Whorwood, owner of the Sandwell estate, became partner with Thomas Parkes in several Staffordshire ironworks. The partnership broke up, however, and it has been suggested that the long quarrel which followed was caused partly by the erstwhile partners' competition for charcoal supplies. Certainly when the quarrel was finally settled Whorwood sold Parkes all or most of his woods in West Bromwich to be felled, coaled, and carried away within the space of about ten or eleven years.[4] There was still timber on the Sandwell estate in Brome Whorwood's time (1634–84), for his steward was felling and coaling trees partly for Whorwood's own use and partly for sale to Bromwich forge.[5]

Friar Park, an estate belonging to the Whorwoods in the north of the parish, was being regularly coppiced during the 17th century. The property needed much supervision by the owner as the wood was evidently a profitable crop whose value was enhanced by the needs of the many local ironworks. For most of the century, when the Whorwoods were living at Holton (Oxon.), the tenants of their Balls Hill property had to promise to ensure that no damage was done to the growing timber in the coppices at Friar Park.[6] In the early 18th century William James, the Sandwell agent, took great pains to safeguard Lord Dartmouth's interests during the cutting, cording, and coaling of the wood each year.[7] When cutting began in December 1705 James had to recommend that a house be built for a watchman who could see that the next year's spring of wood was not damaged.[8] The need for vigilance was emphasized by James again in 1707 when he reported that the tenant farmer at Friar Park had allowed his cattle to damage the previous year's wood when it first sprang.[9] At that period Lord Dartmouth was selling the wood to the Mr. Downing who, from at least the spring of 1707, was trying to obtain a lease of Bromwich forge.[10]

At the end of the 18th century the most extensive areas of woodland were Friar Park, Sandwell Park, and Ridgacre Coppice to the south-east of Hill Top.[11] Ridgacre Coppice was cut down apparently in the 1820s to make way for the Ridgacre and

[87] W.S.L., S. D. Pearson 1461; Willett, *West Bromwich*, 214; S.R.O., D. 742/VIII/3.
[88] S.R.O., Q/RDc 60.
[89] See p. 27 n. 58.
[90] W. Pitt, *General View of Agric. of Staffs.* (1813 edn.), 147.
[91] Pye, *Modern Birmingham*, 109.
[92] *Tours in Eng. and Wales by Arthur Young: Selected from the Annals of Agriculture*, 141.
[93] *Census*, 1801.
[94] L.J.R.O., B/A/15/West Bromwich. An additional 711 a. in the parish were tithe-free.
[95] *Incorporation of West Bromwich: Full Rep. of Official Enquiry . . . 1882* (West Bromwich, n.d. but 1882), 16 (copy in W.B.L.).
[96] R. W. Sturgess, 'The Response of Agriculture in Staffs. to the Price Changes of the 19th Century' (Manchester Univ. Ph.D. thesis, 1965), chap. iv, esp. pp. 98 sqq.
[97] I. Davies, 'Agriculture of West Midland Conurbation' (Birmingham Univ. M.A. thesis, 1953), 188.
[98] *Evening Mail*, 12 Aug. 1969.

[99] *V.C.H. Staffs.* iv. 59, no. 299.
[1] For the bounds of Cannock forest see ibid. ii. 336. Sutton Chase was mainly in Warws. but extended over parts of SE. Staffs., including Great Barr (in Aldridge) to the NE. of West Bromwich: *V.C.H. Warws.* iv. 235–6; [L. Bracken], *Hist. of Forest and Chase of Sutton Coldfield* (1860), 135–68; J. T. Gould, *Men of Aldridge* (Walsall, 1957), 20.
[2] *S.H.C.* iv (1), 78, 85.
[3] E 36/165 ff. 129 sqq. And see *S.H.C.* 1928, 201.
[4] C 2/Jas.I/A5/37; Ede, *Wednesbury*, 124–5.
[5] S.R.O., D. 742/VIII/3.
[6] S.R.O., D. 564/3/1/4; W.B.L., Jesson Deeds, no. 23.
[7] S.R.O., D.(W.)1778/V/1325, Wm. James to Lord Dartmouth, 1 Dec. 1705, 15 May and 11 Dec. 1706, 3 Feb. and 3 Dec. 1707.
[8] Ibid. 19 Dec. 1705.
[9] Ibid. 3 Feb. 1707.
[10] Ibid. 15 June 1706; below p. 33.
[11] Yates, *Map of Staffs.* (edns. of 1775 and 1799); Willett, *West Bromwich*, 193.

Dartmouth branch canals.[12] At Friar Park Lord Dartmouth still owned 102 a. of woodland in 1845; in 1886, however, the area was said to be losing the seclusion which had made it attractive to wild birds, and most of the woodland disappeared soon afterwards.[13] By the beginning of the 19th century Sandwell Park had been planted with timber in such a way that it was secluded from the surrounding industrial landscape,[14] and although some ornamental plantations were felled after Lord Dartmouth moved to Patshull in 1853,[15] much timber remained there in 1970.

Free warren in his demesne lands at West Bromwich was successfully claimed in 1293 by Walter Devereux, one of the lords of the divided manor, who cited a charter granted by Henry III to Walter, his father. In 1294 Walter's coparceners, Richard de Marnham and his wife, renounced all claim to free warren in the manor.[16] In 1606 it was stated to be one of the rights of the lord of the manor,[17] and he retained it over Bromwich Heath until inclosure.[18] The warrener had a lodge on the Heath from at least the 1650s.[19] Fishing rights in the Tame presumably belonged to the lords of the manor in the Middle Ages and are mentioned as an appurtenance of the manor in 1560 and 1719.[20] They were reserved to the lord by the Inclosure Act of 1801 and in 1901 were held by Lord Dartmouth as lord.[21]

MILLS. The mill at Bromford stood on the Oldbury bank of the Tame, but in the mid 19th century at least the greater part of its pool was within West Bromwich.[22] The mill is probably the same as Oldbury mill, mentioned in 1306.[23] There was certainly a mill on the site by 1610 when William Turton the younger bought the manor of Oldbury and Wallexhall. Turton sold the manor in 1617 but retained a blade-mill with adjacent land. On his death in 1621 the mill passed to his son William.[24] The Turtons also owned Greet mill, the next mill downstream, and the flow of water powering the two mills was controlled under a family agreement. About 1690, however, the blade-mill was bought by Joseph Carles (or Careles); he pulled it down and built in its place 'an iron forge or flatting-mill'. The new forge required more power than the old blade-mill. Carles apparently enlarged the mill-

pool, and in 1694 it was alleged by Eleanor Turton, the owner of Greet mill, that two streams which should have powered her mill had been diverted by Carles.[25] The forge was owned by the Carles family for some seventy-five years. In the mid 18th century it was worked for a time as a plating forge by Edward Gibbons, and by the later 18th century it was variously known as Oldbury forge, Bromford forge, or Oldbury mill. In 1765, while it was untenanted, it was bought by Mary Abney, a descendant of the Turtons and owner of Greet mill. She immediately let it to William Taylor,[26] and it was described as a grinding-mill in 1772.[27] A few years later it was turned into a water-powered wireworks by Roger Holmes, Mary Abney's son-in-law.[28] The wireworks had presumably ceased operations by 1796 when the mill-pool was let to John Izon, who had an iron-foundry at Greet mill; the foundry seems thenceforward to have drawn on the pool.[29] Nonetheless a small grinding-mill evidently existed there until at least 1845.[30] The pool became almost entirely covered by spoil heaps in the later 19th century, and railway sidings were built over the rest in the early 1890s.[31]

The mill known as Greet mill by the 1290s stood on the Tame a little below Bromford mill where the road now called West Bromwich Street crosses the river. It occurs in the early 14th century, but the next known reference is in 1556.[32] In 1592 it comprised a corn-mill and a blade-mill;[33] by 1694 both were corn-mills.[34] They were occupied by Thomas Hawkes in 1782 as a set of overshot mills used for grinding corn and dressing leather. In October 1782 Izon & Whitehurst, an iron-founding firm of Aston (Warws.) in search of extra sources of power, took a lease of the mills and the adjacent estate. There the firm erected a new foundry and a row of workmen's cottages; John Izon moved into a house standing near the mill. During the 1780s Izon & Whitehurst abandoned water-power in favour of steam, but they remained at the mill, which was situated on the Birmingham Canal conveniently for the transport of the foundry's raw materials and finished products.[35] Nothing now remains of the mill buildings. Until 1906 or 1907 water from the mill-pool was used to cool the firm's beam-engine. The house in which John Izon lived was still used

[12] C. and J. Greenwood, *Map of Staffs.* (1820); Wood, *Plan of West Bromwich* (1837); C 103/41/5; above p. 14.
[13] L.J.R.O., B/A/15/West Bromwich, nos. 3452, 3477; *Midland Advertiser*, 15 May 1886; O.S. Map 6", Staffs. LXIII. SW. (edns. of 1889 and 1904).
[14] See p. 20.
[15] Sturgess, 'Response of Agric. in Staffs.', 83.
[16] *Plac. de Quo Warr.* (Rec. Com.), 715; *S.H.C.* vii (1), 16.   [17] Ct. R. p. 41.
[18] West Bromwich Inclosure Act, 41 Geo. III, Sess. 2, c. 14 (Private and Personal, not printed).
[19] See p. 23.   [20] *S.H.C.* xiii. 209; C 103/127/3d.
[21] 'West Bromwich 100 Years Ago', 20 Sept. 1901.
[22] Wood, *Plan of West Bromwich* (1837); Peacock & Cottrell, Map of West Bromwich (1857). Thanks are due to Mr. D. A. Dilworth of West Bromwich for help with this section.
[23] *Court Rolls of the Manor of Hales, 1270–1307* (Worcs. Hist. Soc.), ii. 548.
[24] C 142/390/153; Prob. 11/137 (P.C.C. 57 Dale).
[25] C 5/188/39.
[26] S.R.O., D. 707/17/3, abstract of title, pp. 19, 21, 32–3; S.R.O., Q/SB, A. 1781; R. Whitworth, *Plan of Intended Navigation from Birmingham to Canal at Aldersley near Wolverhampton survey'd 1767* (copy in W.S.L.); 'Old West Bromwich', 17 Mar. 1944; above p. 24.

[27] S.R.O., D. 707/17/3, abstract of title, pp. 15–16.
[28] 'Old West Bromwich', 17 Mar. 1944; Birmingham Assay Office, Boulton Papers, letter from Holmes to Boulton (with plan), 15 Sept. 1774 (reference supplied by Mr. D. A. Dilworth); S.R.O., D. 707/17/3, abstract of title, pp. 32–41.
[29] S.R.O., D. 707/17/3, abstract of title, p. 39. Wm. Izon was tenant of Bromford Pool in 1845: L.J.R.O., B/A/15/West Bromwich.
[30] Reeves, *West Bromwich*, 5–6; below p. 109.
[31] Peacock & Cottrell, Map of West Bromwich (1857); O.S. Map 6", Staffs. LXVIII. SW. (edns. of 1890 and 1904); C. R. Clinker, *Railways of the West Midlands, a Chronology 1808–1954*, 45.
[32] *Ct. R. of Manor of Hales*, ii. 428, 508, 548; *Cat. Anct. D.* vi, C 4005. For the descent from 1556 see above p. 24. *V.C.H. Worcs.* iii. 143, wrongly implies that the mill was in Oldbury.
[33] W.S.L., S. MS. 336, f. 26. Willett, *West Bromwich*, 161 (followed by later writers), identified the two mills as Greet mill and Bromford mill, but the Turtons did not acquire Bromford mill until 1610.
[34] C 5/188/39.
[35] W. E. Jephcott, *House of Izons* (London and Dudley, 1948), 11–15 and plate facing p. 35; *Aris's Birmingham Gaz.* 7 Oct. 1782.

as a storehouse in 1941 but has since disappeared; the workmen's cottages erected by Izon & White-hurst were demolished in 1901.[36]

There was a mill on Robert Rider's estate by 1554,[37] situated on the Tame about half a mile west of Greets Green. It remained with the Riders during the 17th century and became known as Rider's Mill.[38] In the 1650s and 1660s it was apparently worked by Nicholas Rider, a kinsman of the Nicholas Rider who owned the estate.[39] Between at least 1732 and 1818 the mill was occupied by the Gutteridge family[40] and became known as Gutteridge's Mill, a name still in occasional use in the later 19th century.[41] The estate was sold in 1812, most of it going to three joint purchasers, most of whom went bankrupt in 1816. Most of his interest was bought by Thomas Price of Bescot Hall in Walsall, a coalmaster and ironmaster, who in 1822 died at Charlemont Hall, West Bromwich.[42] In 1829 the jointly purchased estate was finally partitioned, and the mill, with its pool and adjacent land, passed to the Prices.[43] Meanwhile in 1828 the mill had been burnt down.[44] It was rebuilt and worked for many years as Dunkirk Forge.[45] The new line of the Birmingham Canal was carried across the southern part of the mill-pool c. 1835, and the Birmingham, Wolverhampton & Stour Valley Railway, opened in 1852, was carried along the same embankment.[46] In 1970 the culverted mill-stream could still be seen on both sides of the canal and railway embankment; most of the dry mill-pool on the north side of the embankment was also visible.

There was a mill at 'Grete' by the late 12th century, when it was given by the lord of West Bromwich manor as part of his endowment of Sandwell priory.[47] It may have stood on the Tame to the south of Great Bridge where the priory owned a meadow on either side of the river in the early 16th century.[48] It may also be the mill with ½ a. for which the prior sued Nicholas Comitassone in 1294.[49] It was not, however, one of the two West Bromwich mills owned by the monks in the early 16th century.[50] By the later 18th century there was a mill at Sheepwash south of Great Bridge but on the Tipton side of the Tame.[51]

The pair of water-mills known by the earlier 18th century as the Hall mills stood on Hobnail Brook near Hateley Heath.[52] They existed apparently by

the 1570s,[53] and they remained part of the manorial estate until the 19th century; they were retained by the Clarke Jervoise trustees when the manor was sold to Lord Dartmouth in the 1820s. They were leased to Jeremiah Parker in 1673 and Richard Dickenson in 1693[54] and by 1720 were held by William Webb who later renewed his lease for a further 18 years from 1733.[55] Webb worked at least one of them as an iron-foundry, for which Thomas Webb was buying iron in Worcestershire in the 1740s; Thomas's last purchases appear to have been made in 1748 and Webb may have given the foundry up shortly afterwards.[56] The mills then seem to have been held on separate tenancies. Bayly and William Brett, the sons of a West Bromwich ironmonger,[57] took a lease of the smaller mill for 21 years from 1751 and may have used it as a slitting-mill.[58] In 1752 the larger mill was taken by Harvey Walklate for 21 years, but he was soon succeeded by William Elwell of Walsall. William worked for a time in partnership with his brother Edward, and on the dissolution of their partnership c. 1762 Edward took over the West Bromwich concern, working it as a blade-mill and iron-foundry in 1781. He died in 1809, and either he or his son, another Edward, was succeeded by Edward Reddell, who was working the foundry in 1836.[59] By the mid 1840s the mills had ceased to exist; the site and adjacent land had been let by the trustees of Thomas Clarke Jervoise to the coal-mining firm of Thomas Botteley & Co.[60]

The mill which was known as Friar Park smithy by the later 16th century stood on the Tame in the northernmost part of the parish. It is almost certainly to be identified with the mill which Halesowen abbey owned in 1223 as part of the estate in West Bromwich given by a lord of the manor.[61] The mill had been leased out by the earlier 16th century. It occurs as Friar Park smithy in 1587, and in 1590 Laurence Thomson of Laleham (Mdx.) was working it. By 1592, however, it had ceased to be used as a smithy because the timber in the area had been used up, and it was ruinous.[62] By c. 1776 a mill on the site was being used as a tannery. In 1781 it was described as Friar Park blade- and corn-mill, but it seems to have been converted into a rolling-mill by one Leonard (probably Charles Leonard) about that time. It was subsequently worked as a

[36] Jephcott, *Izons*, 14–15.
[37] L.J.R.O., will of Rob. Rider (proved 18 Jan. 1561/2); above p. 21.
[38] W.S.L., S. MS. 336, ff. 35v., 73v.; West Bromwich Ct. R. p. 46; Willett, *West Bromwich*, 177.
[39] L.J.R.O., B/V/1/75; *West Bromwich Par. Reg.* (Staffs. Par. Reg. Soc.), i. 90.
[40] See p. 22.
[41] S.R.O., Q/SB, A. 1781; Wood, *Plan of West Bromwich* (1837); White, *Dir. Staffs.* (1851), calling it 'Good-ridge Mill'; Willett, *West Bromwich*, 174.
[42] See p. 22. For Price see Parson and Bradshaw, *Dir. Staffs.* (1818), 320; *Staffs. Advertiser*, 7 Dec. 1822.
[43] See p. 22. In 1845 the mill with 19 a. of land belonged to J. W. Turton and other trustees for the Price family: L.J.R.O., B/A/15/West Bromwich.
[44] W.B.L. 66/16150, chron. list of events.
[45] 'Old West Bromwich', 28 July 1944; B.R.L. 447845–8; Pigot, *Nat. Com. Dir.* (1835), 474; Reeves, *West Bromwich*, 114.
[46] O.S. Map 6", Staffs. LXVIII. SW. (1890 edn.); above pp. 13–14.
[47] *V.C.H. Staffs.* iii. 216–17.
[48] E 36/165 f. 136v.
[49] *S.H.C.* vii (1), 17–18.

[50] See pp. 32–3.
[51] Yates, *Map of Staffs.* (1775); S.R.O., Q/SB, A. 1781; Q/RDc 60, map.
[52] West Bromwich Ct. R. pp. 163–5; Yates, *Map of Staffs.* (1775); C 103/127/3e.
[53] *S.H.C.* xiii. 290–1; xiv (1), 174–5.
[54] B.R.L. 297302. [55] C 103/127/3c.
[56] C 103/127/3e; /129/3; ex inf. Mr. Dilworth (based on Knight MSS. in Kidderminster Public Libr.). Possibly, however, he continued some other kind of milling: *Aris's Birmingham Gaz.* 19 Jan. 1767, refers to a lately deceased West Bromwich miller called Wm. Webb.
[57] For the family see S.R.O., D.(W.)1753/15.
[58] C 103/127/3e, giving Bayly Brett as the tenant. Wm. Brett & Co. were buying iron in Worcs. in 1752–3: ex inf. Mr. Dilworth (based on Knight MSS.). Wm. Brett later occurs as a nail manufacturer: see p. 35.
[59] C 103/127/3e; C. J. L. Elwell, *The Iron Elwells* (Ilfracombe, 1964), 36–9, 46; Reeves, *West Bromwich*, 116; S.R.O., Q/SB, A. 1781.
[60] L.J.R.O., B/A/15/West Bromwich.
[61] See p. 22.
[62] S.R.O., D 260/M/T/1/13b; C 3/295/94; E 178/2099. In 1592 John Persehouse was said to be then or lately the tenant.

forge by Edward Elwell.[63] By 1836 it had been disused for some years.[64] The mill-stream and the dried-up pool still existed in the mid 1840s, but by the 1880s the whole site had been obliterated by railway sidings.[65]

Bustleholm mill on the Tame in the north-east of the parish seems originally to have belonged to Wednesbury manor: in 1595 William Comberford, lord of Wednesbury, sold it to Walter Stanley, lord of West Bromwich.[66] It was probably one of the mills that had been settled on William and his wife with Wednesbury manor in 1567.[67] In 1625 William Stanley leased it with some land to Hugh Woodman and John Reignolds; it then comprised two mills under one roof.[68] By 1630 Sir Richard Shelton had let the mills to Sir Edward Peyto of Chesterton (Warws.) and Roger Fowke of Wolverhampton, and they seem to have begun the conversion of one of the mills into a slitting-mill by then.[69] Bustleholm was certainly working as a slitting-mill by 1633 when Richard Foley of Stourbridge (Worcs.) undertook to supply it with six tons of iron a week.[70] Thomas Foley of Stourbridge and Gerard Fowke of Gunstone in Brewood were renting the mill from John Shelton in 1649, and in 1650 they took a lease of Bustleholm, which then consisted of a corn-mill and a slitting-mill. Foley worked the mill as part of an integrated system of ironworks, sending bars from his forges at Little Aston in Shenstone, West Bromwich, and Wednesbury to be slit into rods.[71] From 1667 the mill was worked by Thomas Foley's son Philip, and in 1669 his forge at Little Aston was sending about 100 tons of bar iron a year to Bustleholm to be slit. From c. 1676 Philip appears to have sub-let the mill to Humphrey Jennens of Erdington, Warws. (d. 1690). He took a new lease in 1692.[72] By c. 1700 the mill was in the hands of Humphrey Jennens's son John, a leading Birmingham ironmaster who also worked Bromwich forge about that time.[73] In 1709 John Shelton, lord of West Bromwich, sold Bustleholm mill to John Lowe, an ironmonger; it then comprised a slitting-mill and a corn-mill. Lowe's third son Jesson, also an ironmonger, was working Bustleholm as a

slitting- and oil-mill in 1732, and in 1742 as a forge also.[74] In 1758 he left his 'rod-mill and oil-mill or ironworks' to his brother Alexander, who was working it as a slitting-mill in 1765.[75] About 1775 Charles Leonard may have occupied the slitting-mill.[76] By 1818 Bustleholm, then belonging to James Smith of Hall Green House, was let to William Chapman, a farmer and bayonet-maker, who probably used it as a blade-mill. It was leased from 1820 to Thomas and William Morris, two Bradley ironmasters, who worked it as a rolling-mill. After they left the mill stood idle for some years. It may subsequently have been worked by G. B. Thorneycroft to produce sheet iron.[77] By the mid 1830s Bustleholm had been converted to agricultural milling; it then comprised three corn-mills and was being worked by George Smith Dorsett.[78] It remained the property of James Smith's trustees, who granted a series of leases.[79] By 1900 it was grinding iron-founders' blacking, coal slack being brought by barge on the Tame Valley Canal.[80] It ceased to work during the First World War; the machinery was dismantled some time shortly after 1947.[81] The building, erected probably in the early 19th century and housing an undershot wheel, was demolished in 1971.[82]

Joan mill stood about three-quarters of a mile south of Bustleholm either on the Tame or on a stream flowing through the Wigmore area and into the Tame. It existed by 1401–2[83] and was one of the two West Bromwich mills owned by Sandwell priory at its dissolution in 1525. In 1526 it was held by Ann Heles but was decayed 'for lack of timber'.[84]

The water-mill known as Bromwich forge stood on the Tame about a mile below Joan mill. It probably did not exist before 1586 when Walter Stanley, lord of West Bromwich, authorized Thomas Parkes of Wednesbury to make a watercourse as an extension of that which had formerly powered Joan mill.[85] The mill stood on property belonging to the lord of West Bromwich; the new watercourse, however, crossed the Whorwoods' property, and for over two centuries the lord of the manor's tenants

[63] Reeves, *West Bromwich*, 113; F. W. Hackwood, *Wednesbury Workshops* (Wednesbury, 1889), 24; S.R.O., Q/SB, A. 1781; Elwell, *The Iron Elwells*, 46. For Chas. Leonard see below and p. 33.

[64] Reeves, *West Bromwich*, 113.

[65] L.J.R.O., B/A/15/West Bromwich; O.S. Map 6″, Staffs. LXIII. SW. (1889 edn.); above p. 14.

[66] Willett, *West Bromwich*, 185–6; Hackwood, *West Bromwich*, 48; F. W. Hackwood, *The Wednesbury Papers* (Wednesbury, 1884), 101.

[67] *S.H.C.* xiii. 267; Ede, *Wednesbury*, 71.

[68] C 103/127/3b.

[69] Ibid. /3a. Bustleholm is said to have been a blade-mill before its conversion into a slitting-mill: Hackwood, *Wednesbury Workshops*, 50.

[70] *V.C.H. Staffs.* ii. 114–15; H. R. Schubert, *Hist. of the Brit. Iron and Steel Ind.* 310–11.

[71] B.R.L. 378062; C 5/482/60; Hackwood, *West Bromwich*, 53; *V.C.H. Staffs.* ii. 115. Bustleholm is said to have been worked as a blade-mill during the Civil War: Hackwood, op. cit. 31.

[72] *V.C.H. Staffs.* ii. 115; G. R. Morton and J. Gould, 'Little Aston Forge: 1574–1798', *Jnl. of Iron and Steel Inst.* ccv. 238; C 103/127/3c; Herefs. Rec. Office, F/VI/GAF/24, F/VI/KBF, F/VI/KG/3 and 8 (references supplied by Mr. D. A. Dilworth); *V.C.H. Warws.* vii. 64.

[73] *V.C.H. Staffs.* ii. 118; Ede, *Wednesbury*, 128; below p. 33. For Jennens see also B. L. C. Johnson, 'The Foley

Partnerships: the Iron Ind. at the end of the Charcoal Era', *Econ. Hist. Rev.* 2nd ser. iv. 330–1; B. L. C. Johnson, 'The Charcoal Iron Ind. in the Early Eighteenth Cent.' *Geog. Jnl.* cxvii. 177.

[74] Willett, *West Bromwich*, 187–9 and pedigree 8; Hackwood, *West Bromwich*, 48, 70; *Aris's Birmingham Gaz.* 29 Nov. 1742; above pp. 20, 23.

[75] B.R.L. 456901; *Aris's Birmingham Gaz.* 25 Nov. 1765.

[76] Reeves, *West Bromwich*, 113.

[77] W.B.L., D.58; Parson and Bradshaw, *Dir. Staffs.* (1818); Willett, *West Bromwich*, 185.

[78] White, *Dir. Staffs.* (1834); Pigot, *Nat. Com. Dir.* (1835), 474; W.B.L., D. 59.

[79] W.B.L., D. 59–61, 63, 74; *P.O. Dir. Staffs.* (1845; 1868; 1872); *Staffs. Advertiser*, 17 Mar. 1860 (advert.); *Kelly's Dir. Staffs.* (1904).

[80] *Kelly's Dir. Staffs.* (1900); ex inf. Mr. Dilworth.

[81] Ex inf. Mr. Dilworth.

[82] A. H. Price, 'Bustleholm Mill', *The Blackcountryman*, i (4), 26; ex inf. Mr. R. J. Sherlock, archaeological assistant to Staffs. County Planning and Development Officer (1970).

[83] See p. 13.

[84] E 36/165 f. 132; *V.C.H. Staffs.* iii. 219.

[85] J. Izon, 'A Handsworth Case in the Court of Star Chamber', *Birmingham Post*, 19 June 1952. F. W. Hackwood, *Handsworth Old and New* (Handsworth, 1908), 21, wrongly states that the mill belonged to Sandwell priory in 1525, confusing it with Joan mill.

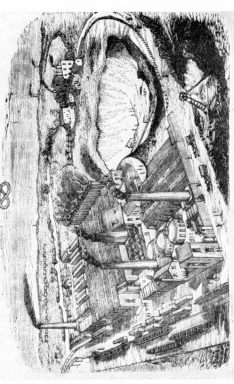

Advertisement of 1836

Advertisement of 1872

WEST BROMWICH

West Bromwich: Cemetery Chapels
opened in 1859

West Bromwich: Great Bridge from the north
rebuilt in 1780

West Bromwich: Tame Bridge in 1781

Smethwick: Regent Street Baptist Chapel
opened in 1879

of the forge had to take a separate lease of the watercourse from the owners of the Sandwell estate.[86] By c. 1590 Parkes had built a forge or hammer-mill, a furnace, and cottages for his workmen. The furnace evidently stood a little way south-west of the forge.[87] The ironworks was operated by Parkes until his death in 1602 and by his son Richard (d. 1618), but about six months after Richard's death his son Thomas, of Willingsworth Hall in Sedgley, sold his interest to John Middleton, Thomas Nye, and others.[88] The furnace was worked by Richard Foley probably from c. 1625,[89] and he seems to have occupied the forge from about the same time: in 1630 he was holding the furnace and forge on two separate leases from the lord of the manor, though by then the furnace had probably gone out of use.[90] Bromwich forge was one of three ironworks in the area which Foley was operating in 1633 and was one of the many works which were operated by his grandson Philip from 1667. It supplied bar-iron to be slit by the Foleys' mill at Bustleholm.[91] In 1676 Philip Foley assigned an interest in the works to Humphrey Jennens, and after Humphrey's death in 1690 the works passed to his son John, who apparently held it until 1708.[92] Probably from 1708 the forge was let to a Mr. Downing, apparently another ironmaster, who had been trying to secure a lease from at least the spring of 1707.[93] In 1714 John Shelton leased it to Richard Guest (or Geast) of Handsworth,[94] who seems earlier to have been in partnership with Downing.[95] In 1725 the forge was leased to Thomas Powell, a Dudley ironmaster who had apparently attempted to take a lease of it in 1706. Powell's lease was subsequently assigned to Edward Kendall.[96] In 1742, on Kendall's surrender of the lease, the forge was let to a partnership of four ironmasters—John Churchill of Hints forge, John Thompson of Abbots Bromley, James Bourne of Rushall furnace, and Henry Bourne of Abbots Bromley.[97] In 1762 the forge was let to John

Churchill,[98] but from 1766–7 it was worked by the iron-manufacturing partnership of John Wright and Richard Jesson as a rolling- and slitting-mill.[99] Joseph Jesson & Co. worked it c. 1800 but by 1804 had moved to Bromford Ironworks near the Oldbury boundary.[1] The mill was subsequently worked by Charles Bache, an ironmaster, who was still there in 1823. By then it was owned by Lord Dartmouth, the new lord of the manor.[2] The forge was said in 1836 to have 'lain in ruins several years'.[3] A flour-mill known as the Old Forge mill was built on the site soon afterwards.[4] It ground fodder for local farmers from the early 1890s until c. 1914; the pool was then emptied and converted to pasture and the mill was dismantled.[5] In 1970 the 19th-century corn-mill building was still standing and the position of the undershot wheel and sluice on its north side could still be seen. The 18th-century mill had two wheels and probably stood immediately to the north of the 19th-century building; in 1970 there were still traces of a second sluice a few yards to the north of the one in use in the 19th century.[6] A cottage, cart-shed, and stable, all of the 19th century, also remained.

Sandwell mill stood on the north side of what is now known as Swan Pool, about half a mile north of Sandwell priory. It was one of the two West Bromwich mills owned by the priory at its dissolution. In 1526 it was a substantial thatched wooden building but was not working.[7] If the mill was ever put into operation again it had fallen into disuse by 1639: one of Brome Whorwood's tenants then had to promise to grind his corn at the mill within the manor of Sandwell if such a mill should be built.[8] Nothing more is known of a mill on that site until 1775 when there seems to have been a slitting-mill there.[9] It is probably to be identified with a rolling- and slitting-mill which stood about half a mile from Sandwell and was owned by Charles Leonard in the late 18th century.[10] By 1851 the mill was working as a

[86] C 3/373/1; S.R.O., D. 564/3/1/23; D. 742/V/9; D.(W.)1778/V/1325.
[87] Birmingham Post, 19 June 1952; Schubert, Brit. Iron and Steel Ind. 180, 390; Reeves, West Bromwich, 112 n.
[88] C 3/373/1; S.H.C. 1932, 300. For the Parkes family see S.H.C. v (2), 231; F. W. Hackwood, Sedgley Researches (Dudley, 1898), 29–31.
[89] Schubert, Brit. Iron and Steel Ind. 390, states that Foley worked the furnace from 1624. Foley, however, is not given as a tenant of the manor in a 1625 list of rents (C 103/127/3b).
[90] C 103/127/3a. The annual rent for the forge or hammer-mill was £20; that for the furnace was 1s., though it was thought capable of improvement to £10. In 1692 and 1762 the furnace was 'decayed': S.R.O., D. 742/V/9; D. 564/3/2/6.
[91] V.C.H. Staffs. ii. 115; C 5/482/60; Jnl. of Iron and Steel Inst. ccv. 238; Herefs. Rec. Office, F/VI/KBF (reference supplied by Mr. Dilworth).
[92] Herefs. Rec. Office, F/VI/KG/1 sqq. (reference supplied by Mr. Dilworth); S.R.O., D. 742/V/9; S.R.O., D.(W.)1778/V/1325, Wm. James to Lord Dartmouth, 9 and 14 June, 19 Nov. 1707; V.C.H. Staffs. ii. 118; V.C.H. Warws. vii. 64, 83.
[93] S.R.O., D.(W.)1778/V/1325, James to Dartmouth, 31 Mar., 15 Oct., 19 Nov. 1707, 3 Apr., 3 and 17 May 1708. In Dec. 1707 he was coaling wood in Friar Park: ibid. 3 Dec. 1707.
[94] B.R.L., 378063; S.R.O., D.(W.)1778/I/ii/463.
[95] S.R.O., D.(W.)1778/V/1325, James to Dartmouth, 15 Oct. 1707, 3 Apr., 3 and 17 May 1708.

[96] S.R.O., D. 564/3/2/6; D. 742/VIII/3; D.(W.)1778/V/1325, James to Dartmouth, 6 May 1706. For Kendall see Econ. Hist. Rev. 2nd ser. iv. 329.
[97] S.R.O., D. 742/Dartmouth Estates/II/7/456.
[98] S.R.O., D. 564/3/2/6.
[99] Kidderminster Public Libr., Knight MSS., Stour Forge Acct. 1767–8; Birmingham Assay Office, Boulton Papers, notebook of Mat. Boulton recording a visit to Bromwich forge. Both references have been supplied by Mr. Dilworth.
[1] Shaw, Staffs. ii. 117; S.R.O., Q/RDc 60, map; below p. 38.
[2] Willett, West Bromwich, 191; Parson and Bradshaw, Dir. Staffs. (1818); S.R.O., D. 564/5/2/1.
[3] Reeves, West Bromwich, 112.
[4] P.O. Dir. Staffs. (1845); W. H. Dix & Co. Gen. Com. Dir. Birm. (1858); P.O. Dir Staffs. (1864); S.R.O., D. 564/8/1/12; Kelly's Dir. Staffs. (1884; 1892). L.J.R.O., B/A/15/West Bromwich, wrongly describes Old Forge mill as a saw-mill, confusing it with Sandwell mill.
[5] Ex inf. Mr. Dilworth.
[6] Ex inf. Mr. Dilworth; Birmingham Assay Office, Boulton Papers, Mat. Boulton's notebook.
[7] E 36/165 f. 128v.; V.C.H. Staffs. iii. 219. It was called Sandwell mill by the mid 19th century: L.J.R.O., B/A/15/ West Bromwich.
[8] S.R.O., D. 564/3/1/5 (lease of 1639); /8 (lease of 1651, repeating the condition).
[9] Yates, Map of Staffs. (1775).
[10] Univ. Brit. Dir. iv. 707. In 1828 the meadow north of Swan Pool was still known as Slitting Mill Meadow: S.R.O., Q/SB, A. 1828.

saw-mill on the Sandwell estate.[11] The site has been obliterated by the spoil heap of Jubilee Pit, sunk in 1897.[12]

The lord of West Bromwich owned a windmill in 1616 and 1622.[13] It stood on the south side of the present Hydes Road near the Hall mills,[14] and it was probably worked in conjunction with them, for all were in the hands of the lord in 1626 and all were leased to Jeremiah Parker in 1673.[15] The windmill still existed in 1822, but it had disappeared by the mid 1840s.[16] There was a windmill on the Riders' estate by 1694 about a quarter of a mile south of their water-mill on the Tame.[17] It still existed in 1767 but was apparently demolished soon afterwards.[18] There was a windmill on the north side of Mill Street at what is now the junction with Tantany Lane in 1837.[19] It was probably the mill which was being worked by Charles Higgins in 1834 and Richard Higgins in 1835.[20] It still existed in 1842.[21] There may have been a windmill a little to the north of Lyndon where land was still called Windmill field in the early 19th century.[22] It is also said that Crabb's Mill Farm, which stood on the east side of Holloway Bank by 1742, took its name from a windmill.[23]

MARKETS. A market house at Lyndon, implying the existence of a market there, belonged to the lord of the manor in 1725. It seems to have fallen into decay by c. 1740.[24] In 1824 the manor court urged the revival of the market,[25] and by 1840 a street market was being held in High Street.[26] In that year a market-place was opened on private ground between High Street and Paradise Street, and in 1970 markets were still being held in a hall on that site on Mondays, Fridays, and Saturdays. In at least the 1850s the triangular piece of land at the junction of Paradise Street and High Street was also used on Saturdays.[27] In 1874 a market hall designed by Weller & Proud of Wolverhampton was completed as part of the new public buildings in High Street, with an open-air cattle market behind it. The new market was not a success, partly because people preferred the older open market, partly because the market hall did not form a thoroughfare between two centres.[28] Under an Act of 1899 it was discontinued, the hall demolished, and the site used for the public library.[29]

THE IRON INDUSTRY. Since the 16th century the main industrial activity of West Bromwich has been concerned with iron—both with getting and smelting the ore and with working the iron into a wide range of manufactured articles. The second activity developed earlier. The iron-using and finished-metal trades were established by the early 16th century, depending on imported raw materials as they do again today. In 1970 they remained the town's most important industry. The primary iron industry flourished from the late 16th century and reached its greatest prosperity in the mid 19th century with the development of local mining. Unlike the secondary industry, however, it did not survive the exhaustion of the local coal and iron ore later in the century.

The metal trades. The first evidence of a local metal manufacture serving a more than local market comes from the early years of the 16th century when John Repton of West Bromwich was supplying buckles, rings, and bridle bits to the Crown.[30] When John Wilkes of West Bromwich died, probably in 1533, he was apparently engaged in metal trading at least as far afield as Uttoxeter.[31] By the end of the century nailing was probably the most widely practised of the West Bromwich iron trades. In the 1590s and the early years of the 17th century various West Bromwich husbandmen were accused of working as nailers without having been apprenticed.[32] Two West Bromwich nailers, Edward Ashmore and John Norris, were particularly active in bringing prosecutions against unapprenticed nailers. They became professional informers and their careers suggest that in West Bromwich and the surrounding parishes the nailing industry was growing rapidly.[33] Buckle-making too was practised,[34] and in 1601 Richard Hopkis, buckle-maker and blacksmith, informed against two men who had worked in West Bromwich as buckle-makers without having served apprenticeships.[35] In the early 17th century the manor court was attempting to enforce the apprenticeship laws and to regulate the employment of journeymen from outside the manor.[36] In 1606 it also forbade anyone employed as a smith, nailer, or buckle-maker to let any 'stall or stock' to anyone of the same trade.[37] The regulation must partly have aimed at limiting the number taking up those overcrowded trades, but it was

[11] H.O. 107/2026(3) f. 388v.
[12] See p. 41. It was, however, still shown as Sandwell saw mill on O.S. Map 6″, Staffs. LXVIII. SE. (1921 edn., revision of 1913).
[13] *S.H.C.* N.S. vi (1), 13; N.S. x (1), 19.
[14] West Bromwich Vestry Mins., plan facing p. 92.
[15] C 103/127/3b; B.R.L. 297302.
[16] C 103/41/3, particulars of sale of manor of West Bromwich. It is not shown on L.J.R.O., B/A/15/West Bromwich.
[17] S.R.O., D. 590/42/1; Willett, *West Bromwich*, 178; S.R.O., D. 707/17/4; above p. 31.
[18] It is shown by R. Whitworth, *Plan of Intended Navigation from Birmingham to Canal at Aldersley near Wolverhampton survey'd 1767* (copy in W.S.L.), but not by Yates, *Map of Staffs.* (1775).
[19] Wood, *Plan of West Bromwich* (1837).
[20] White, *Dir. Staffs.* (1834); Pigot, *Nat. Com. Dir.* (1835), 474.
[21] Willett, *West Bromwich*, 123.
[22] See p. 27; S.R.O., Q/RDc 60. It may be identifiable with the corn-mill at Churchfield in the mid 1830s: White, *Dir. Staffs.* (1834); Pigot, *Nat. Com. Dir.* (1835), 474.
[23] 'Old West Bromwich', 16 Feb. 1945.
[24] Reeves, *West Bromwich*, 54–5; C 103/127/3a.
[25] S.R.O., D.(W.)633A(30).

[26] 'Old West Bromwich', 12 Apr. 1946.
[27] Ibid.; T. C. T. *Life's Realities*, 176–81; Hackwood, *West Bromwich*, 106; West Bromwich Improvement Act, 1854, 17 & 18 Vic. c. 163 (Local and Personal); W.B.L., Scrapbook 12, p. 54; *Staffs. Advertiser* (S. Staffs. edn.), 11 July 1874; O.S. Map 1/500, Staffs. LXVIII. 10. 19; ibid. 10. 24; *Markets Year Book* (11th edn.), 199.
[28] *Staffs. Advertiser* (S. Staffs. edn.), 11 July 1874; Hackwood, *West Bromwich*, 106.
[29] Local Govt. Board's Provisional Orders Conf. (No. 11) Act, 1899, 62 & 63 Vic. c. 113 (Local); below p. 72.
[30] *L. & P. Hen. VIII*, i, pp. 1509, 1513 (receipts for payment dated Feb. and May 1514).
[31] L.J.R.O., will of John Wilkes (proved 12 July 1533), inventory.
[32] *S.H.C.* 1932, 105, 209; 1935, 291.
[33] Ibid. 1929, 30–1; 1930, 133, 139, 146, 217–18; 1932, 60–1, 205–6, 209; 1935, 45, 83, 123–4; 1940, 34; Margaret G. Davies, *Enforcement of English Apprenticeship* (Cambridge, Mass., 1956), 45–7; W. H. B. Court, *Rise of Midland Ind.* (1953 edn.), 57–9.
[34] W.S.L., S. MS. 336, f. 58v.; *S.H.C.* 1935, 100, 161; West Bromwich Ct. R. pp. 51–2; p. 35 n. 39 below.
[35] *S.H.C.* 1935, 292, 380–1, 403–4.
[36] Ct. R. pp. 44–5, 51–2, 55.
[37] Ibid. p. 45.

probably also intended to prevent the engrossing of the iron supplies for those trades by the capitalist chapmen and truckmasters whose increasing influence over the Black Country metal trades was arousing bitter complaint at that time.[38] In 1609 John White and William Jefferson were each fined for letting stalls in their workshops to a buckle-maker,[39] but in general such efforts to prevent the growth of capitalist power over those domestic industries must have been ineffective. John Partrydge, a West Bromwich ironmonger, was probably one such early capitalist: when he died in 1617 he was owed almost £60.[40]

Buckle-making gradually became concentrated in Walsall,[41] but the manufacture of hand-wrought nails continued to develop in West Bromwich. In the mid 17th century very many people were employed in it.[42] In the late 1690s John Lowe may have been engaged by the parish to employ the poor in nail-making, and in 1738–9 nails were apparently being made in the workhouse.[43] The hand-wrought nail trade reached its greatest prosperity in the later 18th century,[44] and by 1775 West Bromwich was one of the principal nail-manufacturing parishes in the Black Country. The trade was controlled by the 'nail ironmongers', merchant employers who gave out work to the nailers. In 1775 the nail ironmongers in West Bromwich were Turton & Co., Richard Jesson, and William Brett. Turton & Co. used 450 tons of iron a year in nail-making; only three other Black Country firms operated on a larger scale. Jesson and Brett used 350 tons and 260 tons a year respectively, and both were operating on a larger scale than the average Black Country firm.[45] The three firms were probably employing between 1,200 and 1,300 nailers.[46] Arthur Young, travelling from Birmingham through West Bromwich in 1776, found the road 'one continued village of nailers' for five or six miles.[47]

Nails formed an important part of the iron goods exported to America, and the industry suffered during the general decline in the iron trade brought about by the War of Independence. Early in 1775 Matthew Boulton, writing to Lord Dartmouth to warn him of the consequences of a long war against the American colonists, stressed the seriousness of the threat to the nailing industry of West Bromwich.[48] In 1776 Arthur Young noted the decline which the war had caused to the industry locally,[49] although the three West Bromwich nailmasters

mentioned in 1775 were still in business after the end of the war.[50] In addition the hand-wrought nail trade was beginning to feel the competition of cast nails by the 1780s, a point urged in 1783 by Richard Jesson, one of the partners producing wrought iron at Bromwich forge.[51]

The hand-wrought nail industry, however, continued to be of great importance in West Bromwich until the early 19th century. In 1812 William Whitehouse, a West Bromwich nail ironmonger, stated that nail-making was conducted on an 'immense' scale in the parish.[52] The industry was, however, entering on a long period of irreversible decline. It was badly affected by the Orders in Council of 1807 and the Anglo-American war of 1812, and the working nailers suffered depressed wages and unemployment. In 1812 Whitehouse stated that over the previous two years he had had to reduce the number of workers he employed by more than half. More serious for the industry in the long term was the new technique, developed by 1811, of cutting nails by machinery. In 1820 nail-making was still listed as a principal source of employment in West Bromwich,[53] but the competition of factory-made nails began to be felt from about 1830. Nevertheless the town's 'father trade'[54] lingered on until at least the 1880s as a domestic industry increasingly left to women workers.

In 1820 the making of gun and pistol locks was said to be a principal source of employment in West Bromwich.[55] Gun-lock filing and forging were established there, probably on a small scale, by the later 18th century.[56] They were skilled trades,[57] and that may be one reason why they never attracted so many workers as the more easily acquired craft of the nailer. More important, however, was the growing concentration of the gun-making trades elsewhere —in Birmingham, Wednesbury, and Darlaston. In 1809 the Committee of the Manufacturers of Arms and Materials for Arms offered rewards to those who would teach or learn gun-lock filing and forging. Out of 27 men who were qualified to give out work and instruction in those trades only three were West Bromwich men: James Negus, Michael Peters, and William Seddon.[58]

A West Bromwich industry associated with the gun trade was the manufacture of steel bayonets, which were made to the specifications of the gun-makers. The Salter family was making bayonets in West Bromwich from the 1770s in the area between

[38] V.C.H. Staffs. ii. 235–6, 239, 251; Court, Midland Ind. 60 sqq.; G. W. Hilton, Truck System, 70–1.
[39] Ct. R. pp. 52, 55. White is probably to be identified with the West Bromwich man of that name who was working as a buckle-maker in 1591: S.H.C. 1930, 172.
[40] L.J.R.O., inventory of John Partrydge (appraised 13 Jan. 1617/18).
[41] V.C.H. Staffs. ii. 235–6.
[42] See e.g. ibid. 239; S.H.C. 4th ser. ii. 88–9.
[43] West Bromwich Churchwardens' Bk. 1678–1787, pp. 33–4; Hackwood, West Bromwich, 69–70 (where the figures are printed inaccurately), 100; Par. Bk., p. 123.
[44] V.C.H. Staffs. ii. 240.
[45] Birmingham Assay Office, Boulton Papers, box labelled 'America', item 8 ('An Estimate of the Iron Supposed to be Manufactured into Nails Annually, by the under persons at the under places', compiled by Thos. Green, a Birmingham nail ironmonger). This document is discussed in Court, Midland Ind. 195–6, 198–9, 203–4, 207. For Green see V.C.H. Warws. vii. 72; Shaw, Staffs. ii. 124.
[46] Figures based on Green's method of calculating the

number of working nailers from the amount of iron used.
[47] V.C.H. Staffs. ii. 240; Court, Midland Ind. 195.
[48] S.R.O., D.(W.)1778/II/i/1104; R. A. Pelham, 'The West Midland Iron Ind. and the American Market in the 18th Cent.', Univ. of Birm. Hist. Jnl. ii. 161.
[49] V.C.H. Staffs. ii. 240.
[50] Bailey's Brit. Dir. (1784), ii. 482–3.
[51] S.R.O., D.(W.)1778/V/727, R. Jesson to Lord Dartmouth, 8 Jan. 1783.
[52] For this para. see Court, Midland Ind. 197, 209–12; V.C.H. Staffs. ii. 240–1.
[53] West Bromwich Vestry Mins. p. 111.
[54] Staffs. Advertiser, 22 Dec. 1849.
[55] Vestry Mins. p. 111.
[56] B.R.L., Caddick and Yates 18, deeds of 1770 and 1772.
[57] Allen, Ind. Dev. Birm. 116–20; Aris's Birmingham Gaz. 20 Oct. 1766.
[58] Swinney's Birmingham Chron. 26 Jan. 1769; V.C.H. Staffs. ii. 272. Of the other 24 men, 11 were of Birmingham, 8 of Wednesbury, and 5 of Darlaston.

Spon Lane and High Street where the works of George Salter & Co. Ltd. still stood in 1970, and the family became well known in the trade during the earlier 19th century. The Salters, however, chiefly made articles incorporating springs, notably the spring balances known as pocket steelyards. The family's bayonet manufacture was linked with spring manufacture because bayonet steel was the most suitable raw material for making light springs.[59]

In the 1780s William Bullock the elder, a West Bromwich toy-maker, was making various metal wares, some involving the use of steel: sword-hilts, buckles, buttons, watch-chains, and hat-pins.[60] Other references to steel-toy making in the later 18th and early 19th centuries[61] indicate that the trade was then carried on in West Bromwich, but it was not important. The Bullocks had turned to iron-founding by 1805.[62]

The foundry industry was well established in West Bromwich by the end of the 18th century. Before the development of a local iron-smelting industry in the 1820s the West Bromwich foundries must have depended on pig-iron brought in from other areas. Indeed the great increase in the production of pig-iron in the later 18th century and the improvement of transport enabled the iron-founder to set up his works where cheap power was most readily available. In West Bromwich the earliest foundries, opened before the advent of steam-power, were in converted water-mills. Edward Elwell (d. 1809) was operating such a foundry from c. 1762 at Hateley Heath where water-power was available; he later built a foundry at Hill Top where he produced cast-iron tinned hollow-ware with machinery driven by a Watt beam engine. By 1809 his son, another Edward, had built a foundry at Great Bridge.[63] In 1782 Izon & Whitehurst, of Aston (Warws.), opened a foundry at Greet mill near the Oldbury boundary and began to produce tinned hollow-ware. The availability of water-power had determined the firm's choice of the site, but within a few years a Boulton & Watt beam engine had been installed and the site's chief advantage thereafter was the cheap transport available on the Birmingham Canal.[64] By the early 1790s, when Archibald Kenrick, a Birmingham buckle-maker, began to manufacture cast ironmongery beside the canal off Spon Lane,[65] water-power had probably ceased to be of prime importance.

There were 14 iron-founding firms in 1834, probably employing over 1,500 workers,[66] and by 1851 there were about 20.[67] The oldest firms of founders in the town, Izons, Kenricks, and Bullocks, dominated the West Bromwich cast-iron hollow-ware industry by the mid 19th century. Izons and

Kenricks in particular had built up reputations in the industry based on many years' use of patent processes which they had bought or developed themselves.[68] Despite their dominant position in the local hollow-ware industry, however, all three firms continued to make a wide range of general cast-iron ware.[69]

By the mid 19th century the iron-founding industry was divided between firms which specialized respectively in light and heavy castings. As already seen, the leading producers of light castings were then the long-established firms which dominated the town's hollow-ware trade. At the same period the heavy founding trade in West Bromwich was led by more recently established firms:[70] James Roberts of Swan Village (c. 1824), Wathew & Siddons of Hateley Heath (1833), and Johnson & Cranage of the Ridgacre Foundry (c. 1840). The heavy iron-founders generally concentrated on large industrial castings and castings for the engineering trade. James Roberts began by producing the latter at a foundry in High Street adjacent to Christ Church. Later he concentrated on cast-iron gas- and water-pipes, and by 1836, probably as a consequence of that specialization, he had moved to a larger site in Swan Village. By 1845 Johnson & Cranage, iron- and brass-founders, were casting case-hardened chilled rolls for ironworks at the Ridgacre Foundry.

The growth of the heavy foundry trade in West Bromwich coincided with a growing use of wrought iron in smithies and forges. The mounting demand for wrought iron by the constructional and engineering trades and the railways was being met by the growing specialization of the general smiths and coach-iron smiths of the Black Country. Besides the specialized engineering firms great integrated iron-making companies like Bagnalls[71] were among the earliest firms to meet the demands of the railways for heavy ironwork.[72] Boiler-making and engine-making were established in West Bromwich by 1829, and by 1851 there were two boiler-making and five engine-making firms.[73] The manufacture of one important type of structural ironwork, corrugated sheets, had been improved by a West Bromwich ironmaster, John Spencer, the brother of Thomas Spencer of Dunkirk Forge and the Vulcan Works, Spon Lane. From c. 1833, when they were first produced, corrugated-iron sheets had been stamped. John Spencer, however, patented a method of hot and cold rolling in 1844, and on the Balls Hill branch canal between Swan Village and Greets Green he erected the Phoenix Ironworks. A great oversea market for corrugated sheets developed, especially during the Californian and Australian

[59] Mary Bache, *Salter, the Story of a Family Firm, 1760–1960* (West Bromwich, 1960), 14, 16–18, 23–6, 56–63; Allen, *Ind. Dev. Birm.* 92.
[60] *Bailey's Brit. Dir.* (1784), ii. 482; *S.H.C.* 1947, 96.
[61] B.R.L., Caddick and Yates 18, deed of 1770; B.R.L. 378066.
[62] See p. 9.
[63] C. J. L. Elwell, *The Iron Elwells* (Ilfracombe, 1964), 38, 46–7, 50; *S.H.C.* 1947, 96; Reeves, *West Bromwich*, 116; above p. 31.
[64] W. E. Jephcott, *House of Izons* (London and Dudley, 1948), 13–15.
[65] R. A. Church, *Kenricks in Hardware* (Newton Abbot, 1969), 19–38; *V.C.H. Staffs.* ii. 182.
[66] White, *Dir. Staffs.* (1834), including 2 ironmasters making castings; Reeves, *West Bromwich*, 116–17.

[67] White, *Dir. Staffs.* (1851).
[68] Church, *Kenricks in Hardware*, 31–8, 59–65, 70; Jephcott, *Izons*, 10–11; *Staffs. Advertiser*, 22 Dec. 1849; *V.C.H. Staffs.* ii. 182.
[69] Jephcott, *Izons*, 31–4; Archibald Kenrick & Sons, *Cat. of Manufactures* (1862; copy in W.B.L.); plate facing p. 32 above; J. M. Fletcher, 'Cast Iron from West Bromwich', *The Blackcountryman*, ii (1), 62–5 (discussing later-19th-cent. cat. of Bullocks).
[70] For these firms see *Staffs. Advertiser*, 22 Dec. 1849; Reeves, *West Bromwich*, 116; 'Old West Bromwich', 10 and 17 Nov. 1944; *P.O. Dir. Staffs.* (1845).
[71] See p. 39.
[72] Madeleine Elsas, *Iron in the Making: Dowlais Iron Company Letters 1782–1860*, 10–11.
[73] *V.C.H. Staffs.* ii. 167–8; White, *Dir. Staffs.* (1851).

gold rushes of 1849 and 1851–2. Spencer's sons, John and J. E. Spencer, continued in the heavy wrought-iron and engineering trade at the Vulcan Works (from 1874) and at the Globe Tube Works near Wednesbury Bridge (from 1882).[74]

By 1851 there were eighteen firms of coach-iron-work smiths in West Bromwich, five of them specialists in railway work.[75] Axles became a particular speciality of the town.[76] Some of the most notable West Bromwich producers of engineering wrought-ironwork began as coach-ironwork smiths. Richard Disturnal & Co. was making coach springs and axles near Wednesbury Bridge in 1851, and it was at Disturnals that John Brockhouse was apprenticed c. 1857; he was the son of a Wednesbury coach-ironwork maker and subsequently founded one of the largest engineering concerns in the Black Country.[77]

In response to the demand of the railways some concerns with small beginnings, like those of James Grice and Josiah Lane, expanded by specializing in the manufacture of particular products. Grice made screws and gun implements in Bull Street in 1851. He was the first to make screws in a 'clam' lathe, which was invented by one of his workmen, Josiah Lane. Lane set up his own works in Sams Lane to produce screw-making machinery, and Grice went into partnership with the son of a Bristol iron merchant called Weston. Weston & Grice concentrated on the production of railway accessories; the firm expanded, moved to the Stour Valley Works, and eventually amalgamated with a Smethwick firm, Watkins & Keen, to form the Patent Nut and Bolt Co. Ltd. in 1864.[78] Not all firms, however, grew by specializing. By 1861, for example, Fleet & Newey, of the Crown Works near Swan Village, was producing wrought-iron steam engines, boilers, gas-holders, purifiers, tanks, bridge and other girders, iron roofings, Thames and canal boats, evaporating and sugar pans, water-barrels, barrows, and miners' tools. They also advertised themselves as general smiths.[79]

By the 1860s the industrial prosperity of West Bromwich was linked not merely to the foundry and wrought-iron trades. It also depended on the few great integrated ironworks in the town which controlled the whole process of manufacture from the mining of coal and ironstone to the making of marked iron bars and many finished iron products. Their prosperity, however, did not outlast the 1860s and the exhaustion of the coal and ironstone of the South Staffordshire coalfield.[80] Nevertheless from the 1870s West Bromwich continued to be re-

latively properous as a result of the diversification of its iron products.[81]

The cast-iron hollow-ware trade continued to flourish until the end of the 19th century. From the 1890s until the First World War cheap stamped-steel and aluminium hollow-ware began to be imported from Germany. This may have affected the town's prosperity: the labour force of the many hollow-ware foundries probably declined in the early 1900s.[82] The decline in the founding trade, however, was partly compensated by the growth of a local manufacture of stamped-steel hollow-ware.[83] From the early 20th century the foundries sought to counteract the declining demand for their cast-iron hollow-ware by turning to new types of product, and by the 1960s most were producing castings in iron and non-ferrous metals for the motor-car, electrical, and aircraft industries.[84] Some, however, still made traditional cast-iron and steel products: hollow-ware, grates, baths, and box-, laundry, and sad-irons.[85]

The spring trade expanded greatly in the later 19th century. In 1850 light coiled steel springs had long been the speciality of Salters,[86] and some of the coach-ironwork smiths produced heavy laminated springs; but the trade was still very small.[87] Its expansion also resulted in its concentration in West Bromwich. By 1900 five of the six Staffordshire spring-making firms were working in West Bromwich; by 1916 fourteen out of the seventeen Staffordshire spring-makers were working there.[88] Salters extended its works several times in the later 19th century, while in 1936 and 1940 it built two large blocks on the north side of High Street opposite the existing works; the firm also acquired Bullocks' Spon Lane Ironfoundry in 1885.[89] West Bromwich remained a leading centre of spring manufacture in the 1960s. Springs had found a growing market in the motor-car and aircraft industries, but the town's products also ranged from 5-cwt. springs for railway rolling-stock to tiny springs for radio equipment. More than 30 firms were active in the early 1960s, and at least 24 remained in operation in 1971. George Salter & Co. Ltd. specialized in spring balances and weighing-machines of all sizes and types.[90]

The constructional engineering trades also prospered during the later 19th century,[91] and the fortunes of one outstandingly successful West Bromwich company illustrate this. In 1886 John Brockhouse started a coach-spring and axle business at Harvills Hawthorn and in 1888 built a small works in the same district with a wharf on the Balls

[74] J. C. Carr and W. Taplin, *Hist. of the British Steel Ind.* (Cambridge, Mass., 1962), 58; 'Old West Bromwich', 28 July 1944; Ede, *Wednesbury*, 275–6; C. Spencer, 'A Spencer Was There', *The Blackcountryman*, ii (1), 24; *Birmingham Post*, 11 Dec. 1965; B.R.L. 447845–8. *V.C.H. Staffs.* ii. 273, wrongly implies that the Globe Works is in Wednesbury.
[75] White, *Dir. Staffs.* (1851).
[76] Allen, *Ind. Dev. Birm.* 93.
[77] *V.C.H. Staffs.* ii. 139; 'Old West Bromwich', 1 June 1945.
[78] 'Old West Bromwich', 8 and 22 Oct., 31 Dec. 1943; *Griffiths' Guide to the Iron Trade of Gt. Britain* (new edn., Newton Abbot, 1967), 82–3; below p. 113.
[79] 'Old West Bromwich', 6 Oct. 1944; W. Cornish, *Corp. Dir. Birm.* (1861).
[80] Allen, *Ind. Dev. Birm.* 92–3, 184.
[81] Ibid. 98.

[82] Ibid. 262–3, 276.
[83] Ibid. 262, 330.
[84] *West Bromwich Official Handbook* [1963], 79–82, 88–9, 93–5, 102–7, 113–19; Allen, *Ind. Dev. Birm.* 299–300; *The Times*, 26 Nov. 1968, supplement; J. A. Wylde, 'Malleable Iron and the Black Country', *The Blackcountryman*, ii (1), 8–10; Joint Iron Council, *Guide to the Engineering Properties of Iron Castings* (1963), 36, 39, 41–2.
[85] *West Bromwich Official Handbook* [1963], 83, 101.
[86] See p. 36.
[87] Allen, *Ind. Dev. Birm.* 275–6, 299.
[88] *Kelly's Dir. Staffs.* (1900; 1916).
[89] Bache, *Salter*, 38, 59–60, 63, 67–8.
[90] Allen, *Ind. Dev. Birm.* 403, 419–20; *West Bromwich Official Handbook* [1963], 127, 131, 139–43; *P.O. Telephone Dir. Section 452: 1971.*
[91] Allen, *Ind. Dev. Birm.* 184.

Hill branch canal. In 1897 he opened the Victoria Works at the end of the Balls Hill branch west of Hill Top, and in 1898 the firm became a limited company. During the years before the First World War John Brockhouse & Co. Ltd. bought several firms in the Black Country and elsewhere and was thus able to meet the increased demand for its products during the war. The Victoria Works, greatly extended, remained in 1970 the principal works of the Brockhouse Organization.[92]

Since the end of the First World War the most rapidly expanding market for the products of the metal trades of the Black Country has been provided by the motor-car industry, which has stimulated the Black Country as railways did in the 19th century.[93] As already seen, cast motor-car components were being produced in the 1960s. Motor cars themselves have been made in West Bromwich since 1936 by Jensen Motors Ltd., which originated as a business carried on by W. J. Smith & Son Ltd. Smiths, a firm of motor-body builders and formerly coach-builders, had been established near the junction of High Street and Shaftesbury Street by 1904 and had been working for about twenty years before that in Spon Lane. At first Jensens' products consisted mainly of bodywork subcontracted by other motor-manufacturing concerns. In the later 1950s the firm began to build its own factory on 10 a. of the Lyttleton Hall estate. In 1968 Jensens was acquired by a merchant bank and a controlling interest subsequently passed to an American consortium. After various managerial changes the firm's subcontracted work was phased out and Jensens began to concentrate on its own luxury cars, the Interceptor and the Jensen FF, introduced in 1965–6. By 1968 the firm was making 700 cars a year.[94]

Office equipment has long been another important product. Metal safes were made in the town by 1860,[95] and the first wholly British typewriter was produced by George Salter & Co. c. 1890.[96] Safes, typewriters, and other office equipment were being made in the 1960s as well as much steel furniture for offices.[97]

The primary iron industry. By the later 16th century the primary iron industry had spread from its older centres to West Bromwich, probably because wood fuel and water-power were available there.[98] Friar Park mill was worked as a bloomsmithy for a time,[99] and the first recorded blast-furnace in the Black Country was built c. 1590 in West Bromwich near the Handsworth boundary by Thomas Parkes, who also built a forge near by on the Tame.[1] The local industry, however, remained on a small scale

until the 19th century, and smelting ceased when Parkes's furnace closed probably c. 1630. Nevertheless there were several forges and slitting-mills in the 17th and 18th centuries.[2]

Expansion began throughout the Black Country in the late 18th century, and a West Bromwich firm contributed to the first of the technological developments which made the expansion possible, the use of coal in the forge. The first commercially successful method of producing wrought iron with coke, patented in 1773, was employed by Joseph and Richard Jesson and John Wright, who became ironmasters in partnership in December 1775. The Jessons were brothers and members of a West Bromwich family many of whom since the 17th century had been iron merchants; Wright was their brother-in-law. In 1775 the partners leased several mills and ironworks in Shropshire and were also working Bromwich forge in West Bromwich; using coke for fuel, they were producing 3,000 cwt. of wrought iron a year at West Bromwich from pig-iron made in their Shropshire works. By 1784 the firm's patent process was being widely used in the Black Country.[3] The partners traded under the name Joseph Jesson & Co. and were evidently for many years the only iron-making firm of any size in West Bromwich: theirs was the only West Bromwich firm of ironmasters to be mentioned in national directories published in 1784 and 1798.[4] The partnership was reconstituted when Joseph Jesson retired at the end of 1808. Richard Jesson's son, Thomas, and son-in-law, Samuel James Dawes, came into the firm as managing partners, and the firm became known as Richard Jesson & Co.[5] The Dawes family eventually dominated the firm: by 1818 Samuel had been joined by his brother John and the firm was known as S. & J. Dawes. By the mid 19th century it was being run by John Dawes's sons, J. S. Dawes of Smethwick House and W. H. Dawes.[6] About the turn of the 18th century the firm moved from Bromwich forge to Bromford Ironworks in the south of the parish beside the Birmingham Canal.[7] The move may be taken to symbolize the beginning of a new period in the history of the iron industry in West Bromwich. Freed from its dependence on water-power, the industry moved to the western and southern parts of the parish where coal, ironstone, and cheap transport were all readily available.

Of the seven firms of ironmasters in West Bromwich listed in a directory of 1818,[8] only S. & J. Dawes is known to have been established for any length of time, and it was the only one which in fact

[92] *V.C.H. Staffs.* ii. 139–40; Allen, *Ind. Dev. Birm.* 375; O.S. Map 6″, Staffs. LXVIII. NW. (1904 and later edns.).
[93] Allen, *Ind. Dev. Birm.* 401–3.
[94] *West Bromwich Official Handbook* (8th edn.), 127–8; *Kelly's Dir. Staffs.* (1884; 1904; 1932); *Car,* Apr. 1967, 5, 10–29; *Midland Chron. & Free Press,* 12 Jan., 30 Aug. 1968; *Evening Mail,* 12 Aug., 3 and 30 Sept. 1969; *Birmingham Post,* 3 Apr., 23 June 1970; *V.C.H. Staffs.* ii. 153.
[95] Allen, *Ind. Dev. Birm.* 81, 98.
[96] Bache, *Salter,* 38, 41–2.
[97] *West Bromwich Official Handbook* [1963], 127, 131, 137, 139; (1966), 80–1, 85, 87.
[98] R. A. Pelham, 'The Migration of the Iron Ind. towards Birmingham during the Sixteenth Century', *T.B.A.S.* lxvi. 142–4, 148–9; *Birmingham and its Regional Setting* (Brit. Assoc. 1950), 147–9.
[99] See p. 31.
[1] H. R. Schubert, *Hist. of Brit. Iron and Steel Ind.* 180; above p. 33.

[2] See pp. 30–3.
[3] W. K. V. Gale, *The Black Country Iron Ind.* 23–6, 32–3; Allen, *Ind. Dev. Birm.* 21–2; S.R.O., D. 845/4; *V.C.H. Staffs.* ii. 121–2; Hackwood, *West Bromwich,* 67; Willett, *West Bromwich,* pedigree 7.
[4] *Bailey's Brit. Dir.* (1784), ii. 483; *Univ. Brit. Dir.* iv. 707.
[5] S.R.O., D. 845/4–5; Willett, *West Bromwich,* pedigree 7. John Wright's share in the firm had passed to his son Richard.
[6] Parson and Bradshaw, *Dir. Staffs.* (1818); 'Old West Bromwich', 24 Mar. 1944; 'Smethwick and Round About', 20 Oct. 1951; J. Foster, *Pedigrees of County Families of Eng.* i (1873), Dawes of Shawe Place; below p. 106.
[7] *Univ. Brit. Dir.* iv. 707; S.R.O., Q/RDc 60, map. Willett, *West Bromwich,* 191, states that the firm occupied the Old Forge 'sixty or seventy years ago', i.e. c. 1812–22.
[8] Parson and Bradshaw, *Dir. Staffs.* (1818).

endured, becoming John Dawes & Sons by 1829.[9] John and Edward Bagnall, the sons of a mining engineer of Broseley (Salop.), were not mentioned in the directory but had by that time been running the Golds Hill Ironworks for about thirty years.[10] The Dawes firm apparently still controlled all the processes of its iron manufacture for it retained its Shropshire works until 1821.[11]

The principal West Bromwich ironworks came into existence between 1820 and 1845. In 1820, at their Golds Hill Ironworks, the Bagnalls erected the first blast-furnace to be built in West Bromwich since Thomas Parkes's furnace of c. 1590.[12] In 1827 Philip Williams & Co. bought an estate in the south of the parish adjacent to the Birmingham Canal and with coal beneath it; there the firm erected two blast-furnaces, later known as the Union Furnaces.[13] By 1845 T. Davies & Son had established the Crookhay Ironworks near Hateley Heath and had long been involved in coalmining in the area. Within the next four years the firm had built three blast-furnaces at the Crookhay works.[14]

By 1861 there were ten blast-furnaces in West Bromwich: three at Golds Hill belonging to John Bagnall & Sons, the three Union furnaces of Philip Williams & Co., and four furnaces at the Crookhay Ironworks, then operated by G. Thompson & Co. Seven of the ten furnaces were in blast.[15] After 1870, however, in West Bromwich as in the Black Country generally, iron smelting began to decline. By 1873 only four and a half of the ten West Bromwich furnaces were in blast, and all had disappeared by the beginning of the 20th century.[16] The decline, caused by the exhaustion of the area's coal and iron-stone, meant that large integrated concerns like the smelting firms could not survive unchanged.

The Bagnall family sold its business before the beginning of the depression became evident. By the early 1870s most of the Bagnalls who had been concerned with the firm had retired, and the business was being run by John Bagnall's sixth son, James. He died in 1871, and in 1873 the business was sold to a public company, John Bagnall & Sons Ltd. The shares were over-subscribed, but irregularities in the floating of the new company and the almost immediate onset of the iron-trade depression meant that much of the capital had to be written off in 1878. The Golds Hill Ironworks was closed down in 1882.[17]

Philip Williams & Co. still worked the Union Furnaces in 1872, but in 1873 the Stour Valley Coal and Iron Co. acquired the ironworks. The new owners, however, could not run the business profitably and Philip Williams & Co. resumed possession. The furnaces were blown out in 1884.[18] Two of the four furnaces at Crookhay were in blast in 1873, but they seem to have been blown out by 1888.[19] John Dawes & Sons, despite a vast expansion of its interests outside Staffordshire, also failed to survive the 1880s. Many years of bad trade after the early 1870s led to its failure and the closure of the Bromford Ironworks in 1887.[20]

Thus the primary process of the iron industry ended in West Bromwich during the 1880s. In some cases, however, the works survived. Although the Union Furnaces were blown out in 1884, the foundry that Philip Williams & Co. had operated there continued to work for some years afterwards.[21] Similarly the Crookhay Ironworks continued for a few years after the blowing out of the furnaces, but by 1902 it had been demolished.[22] At Bromford the Dawes's failure and the closing of the works had a happier sequel. The Bromford Ironworks was re-started by a new company in 1888[23] and was still in production in 1970. By then, however, in West Bromwich as elsewhere in the Black Country the basic manufacture of iron had yielded to more finished processes such as the production of bright drawn and rolled steel; metal strips and sheets in iron, steel, zinc, brass, and copper; and iron and steel galvanized and corrugated sheets. The material for those products was imported into the area.[24]

COAL-MINING. West Bromwich straddles the Eastern Boundary Fault of the South Staffordshire coalfield and thus overlies the exposed and concealed sections of the field. The northern and western parts of the ancient parish are within the exposed section, while in the eastern and southern parts the coal lies below the Red Sandstone.[25] Thus in a pit at Hall End Colliery in the mid 1830s the coal lay at a depth of only 45 feet; but at Heath Colliery near Christ Church at the same period the first pit was being sunk to a depth of over 900 feet through 660 feet of sandstone.[26] The coal worked has been mainly the Thick Coal; ironstone and fireclay have also been mined.

Early mining in West Bromwich was naturally in the exposed field. By the early 14th century coal was taken from Finchpath to Northamptonshire and Oxfordshire.[27] There is mention of a 'coal carrier' in 1657.[28] In 1706 Lord Dartmouth began boring on his newly acquired West Bromwich estate, evidently near Balls Hill, and four pits were opened in 1707;

[9] Pigot, *Com. Dir. Birm.* (1829), 102.
[10] 'Old West Bromwich', 12 Jan. 1945.
[11] Salop. Rec. Office 1224, bdle. 190, Willey estate rent rolls 1821.
[12] *Staffs. Advertiser*, 22 Dec. 1849.
[13] 'Old West Bromwich', 14 July and 4 Aug. 1944.
[14] White, *Dir. Staffs.* (1834); Wood, *Plan of West Bromwich* (1837); *P.O. Dir. Staffs.* (1845).
[15] *Staffs. Advertiser*, 12 Jan. 1861.
[16] *Griffiths' Guide to the Iron Trade of Gt. Britain* (new edn., Newton Abbot, 1967), 254–5; Allen, *Ind. Dev. Birm.* 283.
[17] Mary Willett, *John Nock Bagnall* (London, 1885), 25; *Staffs. Advertiser*, 20 Jan. 1872, 17, 24, 31 Mar. and 28 Apr. 1877, 30 Dec. 1882; F. W. Hackwood, *Hist. of Tipton* (Dudley, 1891), 44–5; 'Old West Bromwich', 12 Jan. 1945.
[18] *P.O. Dir. Staffs.* (1872); 'Old West Bromwich', 14 July 1944.

[19] *Griffiths' Guide to Iron Trade of Gt. Brit.* 255. None was included in the lease: S.R.O., D. 695/4/31/2.
[20] 'Old West Bromwich', 24 and 31 Mar. 1944; 'Smethwick and Round About', 3 Nov. 1951; *Staffs. Advertiser*, 21 May, 31 Dec. 1887, 11 Feb., 29 Dec. 1888.
[21] 'Old West Bromwich', 14 July 1944.
[22] S.R.O., D. 695/4/31/2; O.S. Map 6", Staffs. LXVIII. NW. (1904 edn).
[23] *Staffs. Advertiser*, 31 Dec. 1887, 11 Feb. and 29 Dec. 1888.
[24] *West Bromwich Official Handbook* [1963], 83, 131; Allen, *Ind. Dev. Birm.* 289–90.
[25] *V.C.H. Staffs.* i. 16 and map preceding p. 1; ii. 68, 75; R. I. Murchison, *The Silurian System* (1839), ii. 58, 466, 476, 728–9, and plan between pp. 724 and 725.
[26] Reeves, *West Bromwich*, 105 n., 159; *1st Rep. Com. Midland Mining, S. Staffs.* [508], p. 23, H.C. (1843), xiii.
[27] Bodl. MS. DD. Ch. Ch. OR/96, /137.
[28] *West Bromwich Par. Reg.* (Staffs. Par. Reg. Soc.), i. 84.

two new pits were sunk in 1708.[29] By the end of 1707 the Sheltons, who owned the manor, had begun to mine near Dartmouth's workings, an operation which caused his agent some alarm,[30] and in 1719 the manorial estate was said to include a very good mine.[31] There was keen competition for custom between Dartmouth and the Sheltons,[32] but Dartmouth at least found himself hampered by poor transport[33] and by the irregular working habits of the colliers.[34]

The rapid growth of coal-mining in West Bromwich came with the development of local coal-consuming industries and the improvement of local transport. Nevertheless coal under 5 a. of land in the parish was advertised for letting or selling in 1764.[35] By the 1760s there was mining to the north of Golds Green, and the branch of the Birmingham Canal opened in 1769 was built to serve the pits there.[36]

The Act of 1801, under which the Heath was inclosed, recognized the lord of the manor's right to mine there; but it forbade him to do so within 40 yards of any house and required him to put the land back into its original state when operations were finished.[37] Inclosure, completed in 1804, was not followed by any great burst of activity on the Heath. Nevertheless surveys of Lord Dartmouth's estates were made the following winter by the new agent William James (1771–1837), who himself became a colliery owner and also a noted railway projector. The surveys held out the hope that the Ten Yard coal underlay much of the estate.[38] Work apparently went ahead. In 1808 James reported to Lord Dartmouth that pits were being sunk at Balls Hill and hoped that the next winter's coal supply for Sandwell would come from the estate.[39] By 1812 James & Co. was working Balls Hill Colliery on the east side of Holloway Bank; mining had also increased in the Golds Green area and had started in the southwest of the parish where Union Colliery was in operation.[40] Meetings of coalmasters were being held at West Bromwich by 1816, with James as chairman.[41] About that time mining was being developed around Swan Village by the Holloway

family.[42] Yet in 1821 three experienced coalmasters certified that there was no coal beneath the site of the proposed Christ Church, an area which was in fact above the concealed coal.[43]

Within the next few years, however, coal-mining became a major industry in West Bromwich, closely linked with the local iron industry.[44] The ironworks were great consumers of coal, and many ironmasters were coalmasters as well.[45] It was in fact stated in 1842 that nearly all the colliery owners had made their money first in the iron trade.[46] It was also stated that 'the iron trade rules the coal trade here, because if the price of iron is reduced, the ironmasters will not give the price for coal which they do now, and so that reduces it all over'.[47] By 1829 there were 18 coal-mining concerns operating in West Bromwich;[48] by 1835 there were 40, raising 'immense quantities' of coal and sending much of it to Birmingham, Oxford, and elsewhere.[49] By then work had started in the concealed coal in the southeastern part of the parish: in 1833 Lord Dartmouth began the sinkings for Heath Colliery near Christ Church. This was the first large-scale mining in West Bromwich and was undertaken on the advice of R. I. (later Sir Roderick) Murchison, the distinguished geologist. After seven years and the expenditure of some £30,000 coal was reached at a depth of over 900 feet. The colliery was then leased out to Salter & Raybould, and in July 1842 there were 35 men working below ground and 9 above.[50] By the mid 1850s there were some 60 collieries in West Bromwich, though several of them were evidently very small-scale; some were run in conjunction with ironworks. Most were in the western part of the parish on the exposed coal, close to the canals or linked to them by tramways.[51]

West Bromwich shared in the general decline of the South Staffordshire coalfield in the later 19th century. At Heath Colliery, for example, coal was becoming exhausted by the 1860s.[52] Of 65 collieries in existence in 1868, only 40 were being worked.[53] By 1873 the number worked was down to 36,[54] and by 1896 it had dropped to fourteen.[55] In 1873

[29] S.R.O., D.(W.)1778/V/1325, Wm. James to Lord Dartmouth, 6 May 1706, 12 and 31 Mar., 3 May, 3, 10, 17 Dec. 1707, 20 Mar. 1708.
[30] Ibid. 10 and 17 Dec. 1707.   [31] C 103/127/3d.
[32] S.R.O., D.(W.)1778/V/1325, 17 Dec. 1707, 10 Jan., 11 Feb. 1708.
[33] Ibid. 15 Oct., 10 Dec. 1707, 11 Feb., 20 Mar. 1708.
[34] Ibid. 28 May, 9 and 14 June, 15 Oct., 3 Dec. 1707, 5 Jan., 31 May 1708.
[35] Aris's Birmingham Gaz. 29 Oct. 1764.
[36] R. Whitworth, Plan of Intended Navigation from Birmingham to Canal at Aldersley survey'd 1767 (copy in W.S.L.); Yates, Map of Staffs. (1775); Reeves, West Bromwich, 129 n.; above p. 13.
[37] V.C.H. Staffs. ii. 96.
[38] R. W. Sturgess, 'Landowners, Mining and Urban Development in Nineteenth-century Staffs.', Land and Industry, ed. J. T. Ward and R. G. Wilson, 179. For James see D.N.B.
[39] S.R.O., D.(W.)1778/I/ii/1718.
[40] J. Sherriff, Plan of the Mines of Lord Dudley and Others (1812), reproduced as front end-paper in W. K. V. Gale, Black Country Iron Industry; E. M. S. P. The Two James's and the Two Stephensons (1861), 13, 95 (where Goldenhill Colliery, listed as one of James's interests in 1813, presumably means Golds Hill Colliery).
[41] V.C.H. Staffs. ii. 107; Woodall, West Bromwich Yesterdays, 66.
[42] Parson and Bradshaw, Dir. Staffs. (1818); S.R.O., D. 695/4/26/3; T. Smith, The Miner's Guide (1836), 194–5.

[43] 1st Rep. Com. Midland Mining, S. Staffs. p. cxliv; above p. 39.
[44] 1st Rep. Com. Midland Mining, S. Staffs. p. cxliv; Pigot, Com. Dir. Birm. (1829), 101–2.
[45] White, Dir. Staffs. (1834).
[46] 1st Rep. Com. Midland Mining, S. Staffs. 23.
[47] Ibid. 25.
[48] Pigot, Com. Dir. Birm. (1829), 101.
[49] Pigot, Nat. Com. Dir. (1835), 473; White, Dir. Staffs. (1834). And see J. Phillips and W. F. Hutchings, Map of Staffs. (1832); Wood, Plan of West Bromwich (1837).
[50] Hackwood, West Bromwich, 60; Reeves, West Bromwich, 159–60 (giving 1833 as the date when sinking began); H. Johnson, 'On the Mode of Working the Thick or Ten-Yard Coal of South Staffs.', Trans. North of England Inst. of Mining Engineers, x. 184 (giving 1832); Murchison, Silurian System, 58, 728; 1st Rep. Com. Midland Mining, S. Staffs. 21, 23, 25–6; Staffs. Advertiser, 14 Jan. 1871, p. 2; S.R.O., D. 761/3; B.R.L. 459677. For Murchison see D.N.B.
[51] R. Hunt, Memoirs of Geol. Surv., Mineral Statistics of U.K. for 1853 and 1854, 108–9 (listing 59 collieries); 1856, 175–6 (listing 61); L.J.R.O., B/A/15/West Bromwich.
[52] S.R.O., D. 564/7/4/9/Dec. 1862; /8/1/2/Feb. and Mar. 1863; /8/1/12/Apr. 1874.
[53] Hunt, Mineral Statistics 1868, 184–5.
[54] Reps. Inspectors of Mines 1873 [C. 1056], pp. 111–16, H.C. (1874), xiii. There was also a fireclay mine.
[55] Reps. Inspector of Mines for South Stafford District for 1896 [C. 8450], pp. 25–36, H.C. (1897), xx.

attempts to drain flooded collieries began: the West Bromwich Colliery Co., for example, was formed to drain and reopen Great Bridge Colliery and Brickhouse Colliery, which had been waterlogged for some thirty years.[56] The most notable venture of the period, however, was Sandwell Park Colliery, which worked the concealed part of the coalfield; the first shaft was sunk east of Roebuck Lane, just on the Smethwick side of the borough boundary, in 1870.[57] In 1897 the company began a new colliery to tap an area to the north, sinking the first pit, Jubilee Pit, at Warstone Fields in West Bromwich. The Thick Coal was reached in 1901, and by 1903 a second pit, Primrose Pit, was being sunk.[58] Sandwell Park (Jubilee) Colliery ceased production in 1960.[59]

The success of the Sandwell Park Colliery Co. led to the formation of the Hamstead Colliery Co. In 1875 sinkings began at Hamstead, on the Handsworth side of the boundary of the ancient parish but within the borough of West Bromwich from 1928.[60] Coal was reached in 1880 at a depth of 1,845 feet,[61] and in 1896 the colliery was employing 455 men below ground and 195 above.[62] The last remaining colliery within the pre-1966 borough, it ceased production in 1965.[63]

BRICK-MAKING. The beds of Etruria (Old Hill) marl used for brick-making form part of the Upper Coal Measures of the South Staffordshire coalfield and thus are terminated by the Eastern Boundary Fault.[64] As a result brick-making has been concentrated in the west and south-west of the parish. The road from Great Bridge to Harvills Hawthorn was evidently called Brickhouse Lane by c. 1600, and in 1635 property on the south-west of the Heath bought for the poor was known as the Brick-kiln Land.[65] Before the 19th century, however, brick-making was limited to particular building operations.[66] In 1818 there was apparently only 1 brickmaker in the parish; there were 4 in 1829, 5 in 1834, and 11 in 1851.[67]

The largest of the brickworks was started in 1851, after Joseph Hamblet had acquired part of J. E. Piercy's estate near Greets Green and Ireland Green. The Piercy Brickworks was run by Hamblet in partnership with one Parkes until at least the early 1860s.[68] Later, however, Hamblet became sole proprietor as well as manager,[69] and in the 1870s and 1880s Hamblet was making blue and red bricks,

flooring and roofing tiles, pavings, copings, kerbings, channel and sough bricks, and machine-made brindled bricks.[70] Blue bricks, however, were the firm's speciality. In 1898, four years after Hamblet's death, the business became a limited company as the Hamblet Blue Brick Co. Ltd.[71]

The industry reached its zenith in the 1880s and 1890s.[72] The mission church of St. Michael and All Angels, opened in Bull Lane in 1881, was built to serve some 2,000 people, chiefly brickworkers,[73] who apparently lived in the area between Swan Village and Ireland Green.[74] In the mid 1890s the two biggest brickworks in West Bromwich were on the edge of that area. At the Piercy Brickworks the Hamblet firm was producing between 400,000 and 500,000 bricks every week, while at the adjacent Albion Brickworks Wood & Ivery had a weekly make of between 200,000 and 300,000. There were then five other firms in West Bromwich; their weekly outputs varied from 50,000 to 70,000.[75]

The industry declined in West Bromwich during the earlier 20th century. The Hamblet Blue Brick Co. was forced by fuel and labour shortages to close its West Bromwich works in 1915, and the estate and plant were sold in 1919. By that time the firm had excavated three large marl holes, and the estate was eventually bought by the corporation, which used the holes first as municipal tips and later as building sites.[76] In 1921 there were only three brick-making firms in the town.[77] There were two by 1924, and by 1940 the only survivor was the Hall End Brick Co. Ltd. whose works was in Church Lane.[78] In the early 1960s bricks were still made on the outskirts of the town, and brick-making plant and machinery were also produced.[79]

BREWING. The first evidence of wholesale brewing, as opposed to brewing for domestic and retail purposes, is in 1777 when the justices licensed Joseph Bullevant to establish a wholesale brewery in West Bromwich. Bullevant promised to sell no smaller quantity than a gallon, not to permit drinking on his premises, and to brew for the sole purpose of 'serving housekeepers with beer and ale at a reasonable price'. He left his licence in the keeping of Lord Dartmouth's steward, who was to destroy it if Bullevant failed to observe the conditions.[80]

The evidence of directories suggests that in the

[56] *Staffs. Advertiser* (S. Staffs. edn.), 4 Oct., 1 Nov. 1873, 24 Oct. 1874.
[57] See p. 115.
[58] *Midland Advertiser*, 19 June 1897; *V.C.H. Staffs.* ii. 75, 86; *West Bromwich and Oldbury Chron.* 22 Nov. 1901; S.R.O., D. 564/7/4/57/Nov. and Dec. 1903; *Smethwick Telephone*, 10 Sept. 1910.
[59] Ex inf. N.C.B. (1969).
[60] *Trans. Federated Institution of Mining Engineers*, viii. 402–3.
[61] *V.C.H. Staffs.* ii. 81.
[62] *Reps. Inspector of Mines S. Stafford Dist. 1896*, 31.
[63] *Evening Mail*, 26 Mar. 1965.
[64] *V.C.H. Staffs.* i. 3, 17, and map preceding p. 1; ii. 255 (where Old Mill marl should read Old Hill marl); T. H. Whitehead and T. Eastwood, *Memoirs of Geol. Surv., Geol. of Southern Part of S. Staffs. Coalfield*, 88–9 and plate II; above p. 39.
[65] Hackwood, *West Bromwich*, 50; below p. 84.
[66] See e.g. *V.C.H. Staffs.* ii. 255; S.R.O., D. 742/VIII/3; S.R.O., D.(W.)1778/V/1325, Wm. James to Lord Dartmouth, 7 July 1705, Wm. Smith to Lord Dartmouth,

19 Mar. 1707; D.(W.)1778/I/ii/1718, Wm. James to Lord Dartmouth, 5 Feb. 1808.
[67] Parson and Bradshaw, *Dir. Staffs.* (1818); Pigot, *New Com. Dir.* [1829], 753; *V.C.H. Staffs.* ii. 256.
[68] 'Old West Bromwich', 7 July 1944.
[69] *Staffs. Advertiser*, 6 Jan. 1877.
[70] *P.O. Dir. Staffs.* (1872); *Kelly's Dir. Staffs.* (1880; 1884).
[71] 'Old West Bromwich', 7 July 1944; *Staffs. Advertiser*, 29 Dec. 1894; *V.C.H. Staffs.* ii. 256.
[72] 'Old West Bromwich', 7 July 1944.
[73] *Lich. Dioc. Yr. Bk.* 1881, 144; below p. 59.
[74] i.e. the area formally assigned to the church as a conventional district in 1903: Lich. Dioc. Regy., B/A/1/36, pp. 133–5.
[75] 'Old West Bromwich', 7 July 1944.
[76] Ibid.
[77] Cope, *Dir. Staffs.* (1921).
[78] *Kelly's Dir. Staffs.* (1924; 1940).
[79] *West Bromwich Official Handbook* [1963], 83.
[80] S.R.O., D.(W.)1778/V/721. See also P. Mathias, *Brewing Ind. in Eng. 1700–1830*, pp. xxv–xxvi.

earlier and mid 19th century there were normally two or three common brewers in West Bromwich.[81] They probably supplied a purely local market and were no doubt protected against competition from the large breweries of Burton-upon-Trent by the high cost of transport (including pilferage *en route*) and conservative local tastes. Those at any rate were some of the difficulties being experienced by Samuel Allsopp, the Burton brewer, in 1808, when he was forced to give up his short-lived sales agency in West Bromwich.[82]

The Fisher family were common brewers at Greets Green in 1835 and 1845, and John Chapman was running the West Bromwich Brewery at Churchfield between at least 1851 and 1860.[83] No other West Bromwich brewers in the earlier and mid 19th century, however, are known to have continued in business as long as the Fishers or Chapman. Between the 1860s and 1880s wholesale brewing seems virtually to have ceased in the town, though George and Elisha Whitehouse, brewers of Tipton, may have had a brewery in West Bromwich for a few years in the 1870s.[84]

By 1888 there were two wholesale brewers at work in the town once more, and the number continued to increase.[85] Many public houses served their own brews at that time,[86] and some brewing businesses doubtless developed out of the beer retail trade. One such was Darby's Brewery Ltd. Charles Darby and his son George were beer sellers in West Bromwich by the late 1860s. About 1895 George Darby's son Charles took over the Bush inn, Claypit Lane, from his father. In 1900 he bought Dunkirk Hall in Whitehall Road and ran the Dunkirk inn in part of it. In 1902 he began to build a brewery next to the hall.[87] By 1908 there were evidently eight breweries in West Bromwich, including Darby's newly built brewery in Whitehall Road.[88] In 1921 there were six breweries and two chemical manufacturers who apparently specialized in the production of brewers' finings.[89] There were only three breweries in the town by 1940.[90] The industry had ceased to exist by 1970, one of the last breweries to survive being that of Darby's Brewery Ltd. which apparently closed during the 1950s.[91]

CHEMICAL INDUSTRIES. John Nock was working as a soap-boiler at Hateley Heath in 1818,[92] and it seems likely that soap was being produced in the earlier 19th century by the various manufacturing chemists working in Swan Village and elsewhere in the parish.[93] Robert Boyle & Sons, for example, a Swan Village firm of the mid 1830s,[94] was probably connected with the Boyle who was then a partner in the Smethwick firm of Adkins, Nock & Boyle and had earlier developed an improved method of bleaching soap.[95]

Although by the mid 19th century soap-making was beginning to be concentrated in the seaport towns,[96] soap continued to be manufactured in West Bromwich. Robert Spear Hudson, the inventor of Hudson's Dry Soap Powder, was the son of John Hudson, minister of the Congregational chapel at Mayer's Green from 1801 to 1843. Robert founded his business in 1837, probably in High Street where he was trading as a chemist by 1845,[97] but the date when he invented his soap powder is unknown. In the 1850s the business began to expand, and by 1875, when he opened a works at Liverpool, his firm enjoyed a substantial export trade to Australia, New Zealand, and the Continent.[98] By 1900 the West Bromwich and Liverpool works were producing over 18,000 tons of soap powder a year and R. S. Hudson Ltd. dominated the market; during the next few years the firm overcame the challenge of a rival brand of soap powder introduced by Lever Bros. of Port Sunlight (Ches.). The Hudsons were, however, becoming more interested in politics than in soap, and in 1908 they sold the business to Levers (later Unilever Ltd.), who ran the firm as a subsidiary until the mid 1930s. The works at West Bromwich (the Royal Chemical Works in High Street) and Liverpool were then closed as part of Unilever's programme of rationalization.[99]

In 1851 there were three manufacturing chemists in West Bromwich, including Peter Ward of Paradise Street. William Ward was making washing crystals, soap, and washing-powder as well as baking- and egg-powder at the Victoria Chemical Works in New Street between at least 1860 and 1880.[1] By the early 1890s W. & A. Ward was making soap in High Street, and besides the Hudson and Ward firms there was a third soap manufacturer, Cornelius Walters of Brickhouse Lane. Wards continued in business until the early 20th century and Walters until the early 1920s.[2]

In the mid 1830s Isaac Hadley and John Riding were making iron-founders' charcoal blacking, and John Riding the younger was engaged in the manufacture in 1845.[3] The foundries of the town must have provided a steady market for the product, and by the late 1880s there were five West Bromwich firms making blacking—three of them expressly for iron-founders.[4] The manufacture of iron-founders' blacking declined during the 1890s; by 1900 it was being made only at Bustleholm mill.[5] While &

[81] See e.g. Pigot, *Nat. Com. Dir.* (1835), 472; *P.O. Dir. Staffs.* (1854).
[82] *V.C.H. Staffs.* ii. 244; Mathias, *Brewing Ind.* 183.
[83] Pigot, *Nat. Com. Dir.* (1835), 472; *P.O. Dir. Staffs.* (1845; 1860); White, *Dir. Staffs.* (1851).
[84] *P.O. Dir. Staffs.* (1872; 1876).
[85] *Kelly's Dir. Staffs.* (1888).
[86] Woodall, *West Bromwich Yesterdays*, 25.
[87] 'Old West Bromwich', 25 Aug., 15 Sept. 1944; *P.O. Dir. Staffs.* (1868); *Kelly's Dir. Staffs.* (1892; 1896).
[88] *Kelly's Dir. Staffs.* (1908). Darby's brewery was not listed in *Kelly's Dir.* until 1916.
[89] Cope, *Dir. Staffs.* (1921).
[90] *Kelly's Dir. Staffs.* (1940).
[91] W.B.L., Scrapbook 7, cutting from *Birmingham Weekly Post*, 5 Jan. 1951; Woodall, *West Bromwich Yesterdays*, 25.
[92] Parson and Bradshaw, *Dir. Staffs.* (1818).

[93] Pigot, *New Com. Dir.* [1829], 753; *P.O. Dir. Staffs.* (1845; 1850).
[94] White, *Dir. Staffs.* (1834); Reeves, *West Bromwich*, 166.
[95] *Birm. and Mid. Hardware Dist.* 168, 177–8.
[96] Ibid. 168; C. Wilson, *Hist. of Unilever*, i. 9–11.
[97] Wilson, *Unilever*, i. 12; *P.O. Dir. Staffs.* (1845); below p. 68 n. 46. [98] Wilson, *Unilever*, i. 12.
[99] Ibid. 57, 120–1; ii. 347; *D.N.B.* 1951–60, *sub* R. S. Hudson, Vct. Hudson.
[1] White, *Dir. Staffs.* (1851); *P.O. Dir. Staffs.* (1860); *Kelly's Dir. Staffs.* (1880).
[2] *Kelly's Dir. Staffs.* (1892; 1904); Cope, *Dir. Staffs.* (1921).
[3] Pigot, *Nat. Com. Dir.* (1835), 476; *P.O. Dir. Staffs.* (1845).
[4] *Kelly's Dir. Staffs.* (1888).
[5] Ibid. (1900); above p. 32.

Smallman of the Crown Works in Swan Village continued to make blacking until *c.* 1912.[6]

The development of West Bromwich's chemical industries since the later 19th century is difficult to summarize succinctly owing to changes in the ownership of individual firms and to the diversification of their products. The firm of Robinson Brothers Ltd., for example, founded in 1869, began as tar and ammonia distillers. It turned to horticultural products in the 1920s and in 1930 began to produce chemicals needed for rubber processing. Since the Second World War its greatly diversified range of products has included fungicides, chemicals for the plastics industry, and gas odorants.[7] Ramifying family interests often complicate the story further. The Keys family seems to have become involved in the chemical industry through an initial connexion with brewing. Samuel Keys was trading as a hop merchant in West Bromwich in the late 1860s.[8] Within a few years he had also turned to making brewers' finings,[9] and in the 1880s two Keys firms were working as manufacturing chemists in West Bromwich: Samuel Keys & Co. Ltd. by 1884 and W. H. Keys by 1888.[10] Keys & Co. Ltd., of Swan Village, continued in business until the early 20th century, when they were manufacturing cordials and British wines.[11] About 1900 the firm of W. H. Keys was making many products at its Hall End chemical works on the Halford branch of the Birmingham Canal: oil, grease, tar, varnish, carbolic acid, zathanite, boiler composition, and disinfectant.[12] Since then the manufacture of oils and greases has been a speciality of the firm.[13] In the early 1960s the manufacture of lubricants remained an important local industry, but many other chemical products were made: boiler compositions, fertilizers, paints, and plastics.[14]

LOCAL GOVERNMENT. MANORIAL GOVERNMENT. The lords of the divided manor held view of frankpledge by 1255,[15] and in the later 13th century the court leet, apparently held jointly for both parts, was meeting twice a year, at Michaelmas and Easter.[16] In 1293 the lords successfully maintained their claim to the view, infangthief, and gallows; although a jury also upheld their claim to waif, the Crown contested it but proceedings seem to have lapsed.[17] From at least the end of the 16th century[18] until the earlier 19th century there was only one meeting of the leet each year, in October.[19] In the

late 16th and earlier 17th centuries the court baron was meeting every three weeks.[20] Lord Dartmouth, having acquired the manor in 1823, held courts leet and baron in May 1824 and April 1837.[21] The meeting-place by the earlier 19th century was either the Bull's Head or the Swan.[22] The officers appointed by the court from at least the later 16th century included the constable, one or more deputy constables, and two tithingmen or thirdboroughs. Until at least 1634 the tithingmen were often described as ale-tasters as well. From at least 1685 until 1804 two overseers of the field hedges were elected. The election of a pinner is recorded in 1685.[23] The constable was presenting his accounts to the vestry by at least 1679.[24]

About 1830 a pound, stocks, and whipping-post stood at the corner of Hollyhedge Road and Heath Lane opposite All Saints' Church. All three were then moved to a site in front of the Ring of Bells at the junction of All Saints Street and Church Vale.[25] The stocks and whipping-post were apparently taken away when the police force was established in 1840.[26] In 1970 the pound still stood, and the stocks were preserved in the grounds of the Oak House. There seems to have been a lock-up at Lyndon in the 18th century.[27] The inhabitants were in trouble in 1633 when it was reported at the manor court that the parish had no tumbrel or cucking-stool.[28]

Sandwell priory exercised a separate manorial jurisdiction over its estate. According to a survey of 1526 the inclosed demesne lands surrounding the priory yielded the profits of leets 'that there shall happen and . . . like liberties from a place called Horeston unto a place called Brend Oke'. Anyone succeeding to or buying freehold property within the lordship had to pay the priory a fine. The survey mentions no copyholders, but most of the freeholders owed suit of court as well as rent; two of them were also subject to the incidents of wardship and marriage and had to pay heriot as well as relief.[29] The Whorwoods too regarded their Sandwell estate as a manor. In a lease of land in 1608 Sir William Whorwood reserved a twice-yearly suit to his manor of Sandwell,[30] and other leases between 1639 and 1659 mention suit of court, suit of mill, and heriots.[31] It seems unlikely, however, that suit was ever exacted,[32] and during the 17th century the status of Sandwell as a separate manor was apparently being questioned by the lords of West Bromwich. In 1617 and 1619 West Bromwich manor court stated that

[6] *Kelly's Dir Staffs.* (1912).
[7] *West Bromwich Official Handbook* [1970], 80.
[8] *P.O. Dir. Staffs.* (1868).
[9] Ibid. (1872; 1876); *Kelly's Dir. Staffs.* (1880).
[10] *Kelly's Dir. Staffs.* (1884; 1888).
[11] Ibid. (1900; 1904; 1908).
[12] Ibid. (1896; 1900; 1904).
[13] Ibid. (1908 and later edns.).
[14] *West Bromwich Official Handbook* [1963], 82–3, 89–93, 101, 119–20.
[15] Shaw, *Staffs.* i, App. to Gen. Hist. p. xvii.
[16] *S.H.C.* vi (1), 84; F. A. Homer, 'Collections for the Hist. of the Priory of Sandwell' (in W.S.L.), transcript of grant by Ric. de Marnham to Wm. the miller; *Cat. Anct. D.* vi, C 4005.
[17] *Plac. de Quo Warr.* (Rec. Com.), 715; *S.H.C.* vi (1), 248; vii (1), 16.
[18] The earliest extant roll is for Apr. 1574: West Bromwich Ct. R. p. 1. In 1723, however, the lord of the manor produced court rolls from at least 1401–2 onwards in his suit against Lord Dartmouth: S.R.O., D.(W.)1778/V/1222 (which includes extracts from the rolls); below p. 44.

[19] Ct. R.; Willett, *West Bromwich*, 232–3; S.R.O., D.(W.)549(30)–589(30), 632A(30), 633A(30); W.S.L., S. MS. 336, f. 74v.
[20] Ct. R. pp. 11–12, 30–1, 60; W.S.L., S. MS. 336, ff. 45, 47.
[21] S.R.O., D.(W.)633A(30).
[22] S.R.O., D.(W.)605(30); docs. at All Saints', West Bromwich, parcel 9, summons to Lord Dartmouth's 'court leet or law day and view of frankpledge, with the court baron' at the Bull's Head on 10 May 1824.
[23] Ct. R.; S.R.O., D.(W.)549(30)–589(30).
[24] West Bromwich Churchwardens' Bk. 1678–1787.
[25] Hackwood, *West Bromwich*, 33; Wood, *Plan of West Bromwich* (1837).
[26] Hackwood, *West Bromwich*, 33; below p. 48.
[27] Reeves, *West Bromwich*, 55.
[28] Ct. R. p. 105.
[29] E 36/165 ff. 128v., 130v., 134–135v., 138.
[30] S.R.O., D.564/3/1/3.
[31] Ibid. /3/1/5, 8, and 9.
[32] The owner of Sandwell could produce no court rolls in 1723: see below.

Sandwell was within the manor of West Bromwich.[33] In 1617, however, quarter sessions ordered that the occupants of Sandwell Hall should thenceforth be free from liability for parish office since it was a manor-house and once the 'mansion house' of the priory.[34] By the later 17th century the owners of Sandwell were having to defend the rights which they claimed as manorial lords. At that time Brome Whorwood's steward erected brick-kilns on the waste near Sandwell Gate to test the reaction of the lord of West Bromwich manor; the steward was also claiming a separate manorial pound and rights of warren on that part of the Heath which lay within the bounds of Sandwell.[35] The lords of West Bromwich continued to press their claims after Lord Dartmouth had bought Sandwell in 1701. Dartmouth in fact believed that Joseph Shelton was doing so in order to give him a greater inducement to buy West Bromwich manor.[36] Soon after Sir Samuel Clarke bought the manor in 1720 the issue was tested at law. At the spring assizes of 1723 a tenancy was disputed: the defendant claimed to hold the property from Dartmouth on whose waste it stood, but for the plaintiff, who was Clarke's tenant in the same property, it was argued that Sandwell was not a manor and that Dartmouth therefore held none of the waste. Dartmouth could not produce any court rolls, and the plaintiff won.[37] A few months later Dartmouth was summoned to Clarke's manor court as owing suit and service for his Sandwell property. He did not, however, appear,[38] and Sandwell was still referred to as a manor in family settlements of 1755 and 1786.[39]

PARISH GOVERNMENT. By the end of the 17th century the vestry had emerged as the main organ of local government.[40] Meetings were open to all ratepayers,[41] but attendances were usually small. Sixty-seven people are recorded attending a meeting held at the parish church in April 1735 and concerned with the provision of a workhouse. Fifty-three of those present opposed the use of a levy for any other purpose than direct relief of the poor, while fourteen supported its expenditure on a workhouse. Similar numbers attended further meetings on the same subject in June and July.[42] The figures are by far the highest for any meeting in the vestry records. The meeting-place was normally the church or the workhouse, but occasionally parishioners' houses, including the Swan, were used; in the later 1780s a vestry room was built at the church.[43] A

vestry clerk, whose duties included the keeping of the parish accounts, was appointed in 1823. In 1824 he was voted a salary.[44]

There were two churchwardens by the earlier 16th century.[45] In the late 17th and earlier 18th centuries both seem to have been chosen by the vestry at its meeting in Easter week; from 1736 the minister normally chose one and the inhabitants the other at the Easter vestry.[46] A paid parish clerk occurs by the late 16th century.[47] In 1800 he was appointed by the vestry,[48] but at a visitation 30 years later it was stated that the minister appointed him.[49] A beadle was appointed by the vestry by 1788.[50]

By the early 17th century there were two highway surveyors, apparently appointed by the parish but responsible to the manor court.[51] They were nominated by the constable at a December vestry meeting from at least 1679 until 1691.[52] In the 1820s the vestry appointed a salaried assistant surveyor.[53]

There were four overseers of the poor in 1599[54] but only two in the mid 17th century.[55] Two then remained the usual figure. By 1740 each overseer held office for six months, but this was stopped in 1780 when the vestry ruled that 'it will be better for the parish for the overseers to go hand in hand through the year and not divide the time'.[56] In 1708 a salaried overseer was appointed,[57] and the use of a paid official was repeated periodically during the 18th century, notably from 1718 to 1733 when there were apparently no other overseers.[58] In 1789, alarmed by the great increase in the rates, the vestry appointed a paid standing overseer to scrutinize strictly all applications for relief.[59] From at least 1772 the governor of the workhouse acted as an assistant to the overseers, particularly in the collection of the rates; a paid collector was appointed in 1788, but the governor was again acting as collector between at least 1803 and 1828.[60] By 1833 the poor-rate was being collected with the other parish rates by a salaried collector.[61]

The parish was stated in 1599 to be 'overcharged with poor to the number of threescore and more',[62] but it was in the later 18th century that the number of paupers increased sharply. In 1789 the vestry referred to 'the numerous increase of poor' in the parish,[63] and at the beginning of October 1798 there were 39 in the workhouse and 243 in receipt of outdoor relief. In June 1817 the numbers were 72 and 444, but in February 1820, during a period of great distress, 1,950 were receiving parish relief. In March 1832 there were 57 in the workhouse and 490 on

33 Ct. R. pp. 71–2, 81–2.
34 S.R.O., Q/SR, M. 1617, no. 32.
35 S.R.O., D. 742/VIII/3.   36 Ibid./VIII/1/4.
37 Ibid. /VIII/1, /3, and /4; D.(W.)1778/V/1216, /1221–2.
38 S.R.O., D.(W.)632A(30).
39 S.R.O., D. 612/1, abstract of title of Earl of Dartmouth and Trustees, pp. 4, 16.
40 Records survive from then: West Bromwich Churchwardens' Bks. 1678–1787, 1787–1832; West Bromwich Parish Bk. 1735–1832; West Bromwich Vestry Mins. 1715–45 (in burial reg.) and 1766–1828.
41 See e.g. Vestry Mins. pp. 37, 116.
42 Vestry Mins. (in burial reg.), pp. 57–62.
43 See p. 54.   44 Vestry Mins. pp. 122–3, 126, 129.
45 Willett, West Bromwich, 49. For the dating of the chapel mentioned there see below p. 54.
46 Churchwardens' Bks. 1678–1787, 1787–1832. For a list 1678–1771 see Willett, West Bromwich, 129–31.
47 E 134/27 and 28 Eliz. I Mich./2 m. 4; L.J.R.O., B/V/1/2 and 11; W.S.L., S. MS. 336, ff. 32v., 34, 41v. (references to his wages 1596–1600, 1613). For a list of

clerks from 1688 to the 1830s see Reeves, West Bromwich, 138.
48 Vestry Mins. p. 44. In at least the later 18th century the clerk acted as sexton also: ibid.; Par. Bk. 8 June 1759.
49 L.J.R.O., A/V/1/3/34. For the minister's appointment of the clerk in 1859 see Willett, West Bromwich, 126.
50 Willett, West Bromwich, 48, 109; W.B.L., A. 123; Vestry Mins. p. 128. For the 2 beadles at Christ Church in 1829 see Willett, op. cit. 119.   51 Ct. R. p. 37.
52 Churchwardens' Bk. 1678–1787, pp. 2–21.
53 Vestry Mins. pp. 118, 132–3, 135–6, 138–9, 145.
54 S.H.C. 1935, 189.
55 Hackwood, West Bromwich, 100.
56 Vestry Mins. (in burial reg.); Par. Bk.; Vestry Mins. pp. 2, 23.
57 Churchwardens' Bk. 1678–1787, p. 49.
58 Ibid. passim; Vestry Mins. pp. 16, 25.
59 Vestry Mins. p. 31.
60 Ibid. pp. 7–8, 17–18, 26–9, 54, 68, 71, 73–5, 100, 140.
61 Willett, West Bromwich, 122.
62 S.H.C. 1935, 189.   63 Vestry Mins. p. 31.

out-door relief.[64] Badging was resolved upon in 1766.[65] In 1772 the governor of the workhouse was given the duty of visiting families who became chargeable as a result of sickness 'so that the overseers may not be imposed upon'.[66] In 1775 attention was given to the removal of 'out-parishioners', and in 1780 and 1783 it was stressed that no money raised for poor relief was to be spent outside the parish.[67] It was also ordered in 1780 that no relief was to be given outside the workhouse except in cases of sickness, accident, or old age (70 and over). The aged, however, were not to receive more than 6d. a week unless they had been 'industrious and careful in their youth'; 'disordered incurable people' were to be taken into the workhouse.[68] From at least 1773, on the other hand, the vestry paid a doctor to attend the poor,[69] and in the early 1780s it agreed to subscribe to the newly built Birmingham General Hospital so that paupers could be sent there.[70] The arrangements of 1789 for scrutinizing all applications for relief have been mentioned above. In 1810 it was ordered that all receiving parish relief were, if capable, to attend at the workhouse with their children for inspection,[71] while in 1816 anyone keeping a dog was banned from parish relief; in fact all who kept a dog were to be compelled to pay parish rates.[72]

In the 1690s the poor may have been set to work making nails for the profit of the parish,[73] but there was then no workhouse. In 1716 the vestry agreed to build houses for the poor on land known as the Poors Land,[74] presumably for use as poor-houses. It established a workhouse in 1735, although there was strong opposition from one section of the inhabitants who even went to law on the matter.[75] The building was a former nail warehouse in the present St. Clement's Lane.[76] An extension was agreed to in 1768, and in 1771 the vestry ordered the conversion of the stables to provide more accommodation.[77] Further extensions were necessary in 1774,[78] and in 1777 the building was said to accommodate 100.[79] In 1791 the erection of a boundary wall with spikes on the top was ordered to prevent the inmates from getting out.[80] A committee set up in 1814 to consider the need for a new workhouse found the existing building completely unfit, but plans for a new building were not carried out, apparently for lack of money.[81]

The governor of the workhouse appointed in 1772 was paid a salary of £20,[82] but in 1784 the vestry decided instead 'to set the poor in the workhouse by the head by the week' at the rate of 2s. each.[83] In 1788 the governor complained that this was too low because of the number of inmates who were not well enough to work, and the sum was duly raised to 2s. 3d.[84] A new governor was appointed in 1789 at a salary of £15 with 'all reasonable maintenance, meat, drink, washing, and lodging' and maintenance for his young son if he wished.[85] The governor appointed in 1803 was given a salary of £40.[86]

The West Bromwich poor-law union was formed in 1836, from the Staffordshire parishes of West Bromwich, Wednesbury, and Handsworth and from Oldbury, Warley Salop, and Warley Wigorn in Halesowen (Worcs.).[87] The parish workhouses at West Bromwich and Wednesbury were retained and enlarged; the West Bromwich workhouse as a result had accommodation for 140 paupers.[88] In 1844 Lord Dartmouth described it as 'a disgrace to the place',[89] and there was an unsuccessful scheme for building a workhouse at the Cronehills in 1854.[90] In 1857, however, a new union workhouse was opened in Hallam Street; it was an extensive red-brick building designed by Briggs & Evoral.[91] The surviving buildings form part of Hallam Hospital.[92] In 1872 the Walsall and West Bromwich poor-law unions opened the Walsall and West Bromwich District Schools for pauper children, housed in an Elizabethan-style building at Wigmore designed by S. E. Bindley of Birmingham. It was closed in 1935.[93]

IMPROVEMENT COMMISSIONERS. With the rapid growth of the town in the 19th century the vestry was no longer able to provide adequate local government. In 1853 the vestry itself appointed a large committee to promote an Act establishing a local board of health for the town,[94] and in 1854 the West Bromwich Improvement Act set up a body of 16 improvement commissioners (13 elected members and 3 magistrates).[95] The commissioners' powers were extended by Acts of 1855 and 1865.[96]

THE BOROUGH. In 1882 the parish was granted a charter of incorporation as a borough. The council consisted of 6 aldermen and 18 councillors, and the borough was divided into six wards—Sandwell, Lyndon, Hill Top, Greets Green, Town Hall, and

[64] Reeves, *West Bromwich*, 126; Vestry Mins. p. 111.
[65] Vestry Mins. p. 1.   [66] Ibid. pp. 7–8.
[67] Ibid. pp. 19, 23, 25.   [68] Ibid. pp. 22–3.
[69] Ibid. pp. 12, 15, 67, 95–140 *passim*.
[70] Ibid. p. 24; *V.C.H. Warws.* vii. 339.
[71] Vestry Mins. p. 69.   [72] Ibid. p. 84.
[73] See p. 35.   [74] Willett, *West Bromwich*, 97.
[75] Ibid. 100–3; Par. Bk.; above p. 44.
[76] Reeves, *West Bromwich*, 125; B.R.L. 457177, plan of Line House estate 1808, showing the position of the workhouse.
[77] Willett, *West Bromwich*, 103; Vestry Mins. pp. 3–5.
[78] Willett, *West Bromwich*, 104.
[79] *Rep. Cttee. Returns made by Overseers of Poor, 1777*, H.C. ser. i, p. 458 (1803), ix.
[80] Vestry Mins. p. 34.   [81] Ibid. pp. 79–82.
[82] Ibid. pp. 7–8. The retiring governor was given a pension of 2s. 6d. a week for life: Churchwardens' Bk. 1678–1787, p. 121.
[83] Vestry Mins. pp. 26–7.   [84] Ibid. pp. 29–30.
[85] Ibid. p. 32.   [86] Ibid. p. 54.
[87] *3rd Ann. Rep. Poor Law Com.* H.C. 546–I, p. 164 (1837), xxxi.

[88] White, *Dir. Staffs.* (1851); W.B.L., mining etc. plans, no. 211.
[89] *Staffs. Advertiser*, 13 Apr. 1844.
[90] *The Cronehills Land in the Parish of West Bromwich: Rep. of the Clerk to the Guardians, presented to the Board of Guardians . . . 15th July, 1901*, 4 (copy in W.B.L.).
[91] Hackwood, *West Bromwich*, 102; *P.O. Dir. Staffs.* (1860); *Staffs. Advertiser*, 15 Mar. 1856; W.B.L., mining etc. plans, no. 211; 'Old West Bromwich', 3 Sept. 1943.
[92] See p. 48.
[93] For this para. see Hackwood, *West Bromwich*, 102; *Staffs. Advertiser*, 14 May 1870 (reporting laying of 'memorial stones' and incorrectly giving Bindley's initials as E. S.); W.C.L., Wigmore Schools box, town clerk of Walsall to district valuer, 6 Apr. 1935. For Bindley's initials see *Hulley's Birmingham Dir.* (1870), 14, 160.
[94] Willett, *West Bromwich*, 125.
[95] 17 & 18 Vic. c. 163 (Local and Personal); Hackwood, *West Bromwich*, 105. For local opposition to the Act see *Staffs. Advertiser*, 8 Apr., 24 June 1854, 13 Sept. 1856.
[96] 18 & 19 Vic. c. 138 (Local and Personal); 28 & 29 Vic. c. 160 (Local and Personal).

Spon Lane. West Bromwich became a county borough in 1889.[97] In 1918 two new wards were created, Lyng and Tantany, and the council was increased to 8 aldermen and 24 councillors.[98] A ninth ward, Barr, was created after the acquisition of part of the urban district of Perry Barr in 1928; it was represented by one councillor.[99] The number of wards was increased to 11 in 1952 when Lyndon was divided into three, Hateley Heath, Friar Park, and Charlemont; the number of aldermen was raised to 11 and the number of councillors to thirty-three.[1] The borough was granted a commission of the peace in 1888 and quarter sessions in 1890.[2]

THE BOROUGH OF WEST BROMWICH. *Azure, a stag's head caboshed argent between three fers-de-moline or, a bordure argent charged with four mullets and four fleurs-de-lis alternately azure.*

[Granted 1882]

In 1966, as part of the reorganization of local government in the West Midlands, the borough of West Bromwich was extended to include most of Tipton and Wednesbury with parts of Birmingham, Smethwick, Oldbury, Rowley Regis, Coseley, Bilston, Walsall, and Aldridge; parts were transferred to Birmingham and Walsall.[3] In 1974 West Bromwich became part of the metropolitan borough of Sandwell.[4]

The council had a majority of Conservatives, Liberals, and Independents until 1946.[5] The first Labour councillor, however, was elected before the First World War, for Spon Lane ward, and the first Labour mayor was chosen in 1934.[6] Labour took control in 1945 and retained it until 1961.[7] The Conservatives were then in control for two years, although from 1962 the two Independents on the council held the balance.[8] Labour regained control in 1963, retaining it until 1967.[9]

The town hall on the corner of High Street and Lodge Road was built in 1875. It is of brick and stone in an Italian Gothic style with a large tower and was designed by Alexander & Henman of Stockton-on-Tees (co. Dur.).[10] An organ was presented in 1878 by Alexander Brogden, the first M.P.

for Wednesbury, West Bromwich then being part of that constituency.[11] The town hall was altered in 1905 to provide more offices and a committee room,[12] and in 1924 the reading room of the former free library building next to the town hall was converted into a council chamber.[13] The law-courts in Lombard Street West were built in 1890–1 to the designs of Wood & Kendrick of West Bromwich.[14]

The insignia of the former borough include a gold mayoral chain presented by Lord Dartmouth in 1882 and a silver mace presented by Reuben Farley, the first mayor, also in 1882. The borough seal is circular, $2\frac{1}{2}$ in.; it is dated 1882 and depicts the arms of the borough. Legend, humanistic: THE SEAL OF THE MAYOR ALDERMEN & BURGESSES OF THE BOROUGH OF WEST BROMWICH.

A complete list of mayors is given in the *County Borough of West Bromwich Year Book 1971–72.*

PUBLIC SERVICES. Conditions in West Bromwich in the 19th century were not so insanitary as in many other towns, because much of it was situated on sloping ground and because the soil facilitated drainage.[15] None the less public health was a problem by then. West Bromwich suffered during the cholera epidemic of 1832. A temporary board of health was set up and a hospital opened in the former Revivalist chapel in Spon Lane.[16] The report of the commissioners inquiring into the state of large towns in the early 1840s[17] showed that at West Bromwich streets were on the whole wide and well laid out but drainage was often inadequate: stagnant pools and watercourses, accumulations of refuse, and blocked drains were common. The poorer houses were generally built in courts, with two to four rooms a house; some of the houses were back-to-back. Normally there was one privy to every five or six houses. There were no arrangements for cleansing the courts, but the privies were emptied by night-soil men. The prevalence of typhus and smallpox was reported in 1850 and ascribed to bad drainage and the poor water supply.[18] Widespread pig-keeping was noted in 1866 as another bad feature.[19]

The improvement commissioners established in 1854 did something to deal with problems of public health, and they quickly appointed a full-time surveyor and inspector of nuisances;[20] in 1868 they appointed a medical officer of health.[21] Yet the clerk

97 Hackwood, *West Bromwich*, 108; 51 & 52 Vic. c. 41.
98 West Bromwich Corporation Act, 1918, 8 & 9 Geo. V, c. 16 (Local).
99 West Bromwich Corporation Act, 1927, 17 & 18 Geo. V, c. 86 (Local).
1 Woodall, *West Bromwich Yesterdays*, 47; *West Bromwich Official Handbook* (8th edn.), 21–2.
2 *Kelly's Dir. Staffs.* (1892).
3 West Midlands Order 1965, S.I. 1965, no. 2139, pp. 5–6, 87, 120, and maps; *County Boro. of West Bromwich: Council Diary & Municipal Yearbook 1966/67.*
4 Local Govt. Act 1972, c. 70; The Metropolitan Districts (Names) Order 1973, S.I. 1973, no. 137; letters patent of 27 Feb. 1974 granting the district of Sandwell borough status (in possession of the chief executive).
5 Woodall, *West Bromwich Yesterdays*, 46.
6 Ibid. 39; *Midland Chron. & Free Press*, 9 and 16 Nov. 1934.
7 Woodall, *West Bromwich Yesterdays*, 46–7; *Midland Chron. & Free Press*, 2 Nov. 1945.
8 *Midland Chron. & Free Press*, 19 May 1961, 18 May 1962.

9 Ibid. 17 May 1963, 21 May 1965, 19 May 1967.
10 *P.O. Dir. Staffs.* (1876); W.B.L., Scrapbook 12, pp. 54–5; plate facing p. 97 below.
11 *Staffs. Advertiser*, 11 May 1878; Ede, *Wednesbury*, 360; below p. 50.
12 *Kelly's Dir. Staffs.* (1908).
13 Ibid. (1928).
14 *Staffs. Advertiser*, 3 Jan. 1891, p. 6; 2 Jan. 1892, p. 6; Hackwood, *West Bromwich*, 111.
15 *Birmingham Daily Post*, 19 June 1866.
16 Reeves, *West Bromwich*, 22, 124; Willett, *West Bromwich*, 121–2; below p. 69.
17 *2nd Rep. Com. State of Large Towns and Populous Districts* [602], App. p. 40, H.C. (1845), xviii.
18 *Staffs. Advertiser*, 17 Aug., 22 Nov. 1850.
19 *Birmingham Daily Post*, 19 June 1866.
20 West Bromwich Town Hall, Improvement Commissioners' Min. Bk. 1854–63, *passim* (pp. 13–14, 17–19, for the appointment of the surveyor and inspector).
21 *Staffs. Advertiser*, 10 Oct., 21 Nov. 1868; 'Old West Bromwich', 17 Nov. 1944.

to the commissioners in 1882 considered that it was only in the previous ten years that the board had wholeheartedly tackled its duties; as late as 1874 West Bromwich was a town 'having no proper public buildings, ill-lighted, totally unpaved, atrocious roads, undrained, and with a high death rate'.[22] About 1880 land was bought at Friar Park for a sewage farm, and by 1882 plans were well advanced for the first part of the works.[23] In 1886 the medical officer of health for the borough reported low mortality and good sanitary progress; the main needs were 'the completion of the sewerage and the satisfactory solution of the night soil difficulty'.[24] In 1890 the large-scale replacement of privies with water-closets was begun.[25] A new sewage works was built at Friar Park in 1903 and a small works in Newton Road in 1910.[26] The present sewage works at Ray Hall (in the part of the borough added from Great Barr in 1931) dates from the mid 1930s; control passed to the Upper Tame Main Drainage Authority in 1966.[27] In 1958 the council's first smoke control order came into force.[28]

Progress in housing and slum clearance was at first less satisfactory. In 1889 the medical officer of health recommended wholesale clearance in certain parts of the borough, observing that the continuance of back-to-back houses, unpaved yards, and open middens was a serious danger to health.[29] In 1890 he criticized the unwholesome effects of pig-keeping, and in 1891 he singled out Union and Glover Streets for their dilapidated wooden pigsties.[30] By 1896 he was able to report both clearance and the erection of improved housing.[31] Indeed there are still many working-class dwellings of the period c. 1880–1910, built to house the expanding population and to replace the insanitary dwellings of the earlier 19th century. Many of them are in a uniform style, red-brick, two-storeyed, and with moulded brick decoration above the windows and doorways and at the cornice. They are frequently in long terraces, each apparently the work of a single developer; each house has a short front garden and a larger plot behind.

Some clearance was carried out under the West Bromwich Corporation Act of 1913.[32] After the passing of the 1919 Housing Act the corporation scheduled nearly 2,900 houses as unfit, but by 1933 only 346 had been demolished, chiefly in Barton Street (in the former Old End area) and Swan Village. The pace quickened thereafter; yet, when a new clearance programme began in 1955, as many as 4,000 houses were considered unfit, and over the next ten years some 15 per cent of the town's population was rehoused.[33] The corporation has built several estates since 1919. After the Act of that year it prepared a comprehensive housing scheme, and work began at Tantany in 1920.[34] In the part of Hamstead added to the borough in 1928 over 100 dwellings had been built by 1930.[35] By 1939 the corporation had built over 5,000 houses and flats, and by the early 1960s it owned well over 12,000 dwellings, including multi-storey flats and old people's flatlets.[36]

Of the springs which supplied West Bromwich with water before the arrival of a piped supply in the later 19th century, the most used was apparently Lyne Purl in Stoney Lane. In 1606 the manor court forbade the washing of anything dirty like 'filthie clothes' or 'beastes bellies' in or near the spring.[37] Despite the condemnation of its water in the later 19th century after an analysis, an official attempt to stop access to the spring was fiercely resisted.[38] It was presented to the town in 1956 by J. J. Grant to commemorate his wife's term as mayor, and an ornamental surround was built. The spring still flows, but the pool was covered over in 1969.[39] Many of the springs were iron-impregnated, notably one at Wigmore, and in the mid 19th century one writer indulged the fancy that the town could become a Leamington or a Cheltenham.[40] Pumps were set up along the main road through the town in 1829,[41] and another source of domestic supply in the 1850s was the water pumped out of the coal pit in Pitt Street, which was widely used for making tea.[42] In 1866 the Hill Top area was found to be particularly badly off since most of the springs had been destroyed by mining; the little spring water available was largely polluted by drainage. Water from the pits was used, as was canal water until that too became polluted by factory refuse.[43] West Bromwich lies within the area supplied by the South Staffordshire Water Works Co., which opened its first works in 1858 at Lichfield.[44] In 1875, however, only 16 per cent of the houses in the town had a piped

[22] Incorporation of West Bromwich: Full Rep. of Official Enquiry ... 1882 (West Bromwich, 1882), 6 (copy in W.B.L.).   [23] Ibid. 11, 13.
[24] Boro. of West Bromwich: Ann. Rep. of Medical Officer of Health for 1886, 2 (copy in W.B.L.).
[25] Rep. on Health of County Boro. of West Bromwich for the year 1896, 7 (copy in W.B.L.).
[26] County Boro. of West Bromwich, Representation to Minister of Health for Alteration of Boundary of County Boro. (1921), 13–14 (copies in S.R.O., F. 1228, and in W.B.L.).
[27] Souvenir of West Bromwich Jubilee Week (1935), 7 (copy in W.B.L.); O.S. Map 1/2,500, Staffs. LXVIII. 3 (1947 edn., revised 1937); Express & Star, 9 Dec. 1965; West Midlands Order 1965, S.I. 1965, no. 2139, p. 44.
[28] County Boro. of West Bromwich, Council Clarion, Jan. 1959, 10–12.
[29] Boro. of West Bromwich: Ann. Rep. of Medical Officer of Health for 1889, 5.   [30] Ibid. 1890, 11; 1891, 14.
[31] Rep. on Health of County Boro. of West Bromwich for the year 1896, 6.
[32] Representation for Alteration of Boundary, 16; Woodall, West Bromwich Yesterdays, 36.
[33] Midland Chron. & Free Press, 4 Nov. 1938, p. 7; W.B.L., Scrapbook 11, pp. 26, 28; Woodall, West Bromwich Yesterdays, 36; West Bromwich Official Handbook

(9th edn.), 36; County Boro. of West Bromwich, Hygiene & Cleansing Dept. Ann. Rep. 1965, 6–7 (copy in possession of Chief Public Health Insp.).
[34] Representation for Alteration of Boundary, 16.
[35] Evening Despatch, 12 June 1930 (cutting in W.B.L., Scrapbook 11, p. 1).
[36] West Bromwich Official Handbook [1963], 35–6; County Borough of West Bromwich: Official Opening of the Harvills Hawthorn No. 1 Housing Estate (copy in W.B.L.); Woodall, West Bromwich Yesterdays, 36; Midland Chron. & Free Press, 28 July 1939 (opening of West Bromwich's 5,000th municipal house).
[37] West Bromwich Ct. R. p. 38.
[38] Hackwood, West Bromwich, 110. For the saving of the well in 1848 and repairs then carried out see loose cutting in West Bromwich Old Church Par. Mag. 1873–81 at All Saints' Church; plaque in situ.
[39] Evening Mail, 13 Nov. 1969.
[40] Staffs. Advertiser, 22 Dec. 1849, p. 7; Willett, West Bromwich, 192.   [41] Reeves, West Bromwich, 162.
[42] T.C.T. Life's Realities, 168.
[43] Birmingham Daily Post, 19 June 1866.
[44] A. Feeny, S. Staffs. Water Works Co.: Descriptive Sketch of the Company and Works (Birmingham, 1880), 18, 23 (copy in W.S.L. Pamphs.). The supply had reached Wednesbury by Feb. 1859: ibid. 24.

supply; the rest still depended on public and private wells, and in 1876 an analysis of the public wells at Spon Lane, Lyndon, and Mayer's Green (Messenger Street) showed the first two fairly pure but the third polluted.[45] By 1882 about half the houses were supplied by the waterworks company,[46] and by 1886 most had a piped supply.[47]

Public baths were built in Pitt Street by Lord Dartmouth in 1847.[48] New baths designed by Edward Pincher of West Bromwich were opened in Lombard Street West in 1874 and improved in 1897–8. The Gala Bath was completed in 1938, the last of several improvements begun in 1936.[49] The baths were damaged by enemy action in 1940, but rebuilding and extensions were carried out in 1959–62.[50] About 1880 there were privately owned baths at the corner of Union and Green Streets.[51]

The District Hospital, a plain red-brick building in Edward Street, was built in 1869–71 to the design of Martin & Chamberlain of Birmingham. It originated in the Provident Medical Dispensary in High Street opened in 1867.[52] Hallam Hospital in Hallam Street, another general hospital, originated in the infirmary added to the union workhouse in 1884. Improvements were begun in 1925, and the infirmary then became a separate institution named Hallam Hospital. The hospital includes surviving buildings of the former workhouse as well as more recent buildings.[53] Lyttleton Hall was used as an isolation hospital during the smallpox epidemic of the earlier 1880s.[54] It was replaced by a new infectious diseases hospital opened in Heath Lane in 1885; this has been used only for chest cases since c. 1952.[55] A smallpox hospital at Friar Park was opened in 1906 but closed in 1948.[56] A male sterilization clinic, the first in the country with its own operating unit, was opened in 1970 at Control House in Shaftesbury Street, the West Bromwich headquarters of the West Midlands Family Planning Association.[57]

The cemetery in Heath Lane was opened in 1859.[58] The chapels, of red brick with stone dressings, were designed by Edward Holmes of Birmingham in an early-Gothic style.[59] The crematorium in Forge Lane was opened in 1961.[60]

In 1765, after several robberies had been committed at West Bromwich, the inhabitants offered a 10-guinea reward for help in the conviction of anyone committing a robbery in the parish.[61] A West Bromwich Association for the Prosecution of Felons had been formed by 1773.[62] In the 1770s it was customary for the parish officers to inspect alehouses on Sunday afternoons during divine service, and in 1776 they proposed measures to suppress disorders in ale-houses and to limit their number.[63] Early in 1790, as a result of the number of highway robberies and cases of housebreaking, the vestry set up a committee to choose constables and others to inspect lodging and public houses and arrest rogues and vagabonds.[64] The vestry petitioned the justices in 1807 and 1814 against the granting of licences to new ale-houses in the parish.[65] In 1819 it appointed seven paid 'Sunday' constables to disperse disorderly crowds, close public houses during divine service and after 9 p.m. and shops after 9 a.m., prevent tippling in public houses, and expel loiterers from the churchyard during divine service.[66] Sabbath-breaking, however, continued, and in 1825 'Sunday' constables were reappointed especially to prevent tippling.[67] The vestry launched a new attack on Sunday trading, setting up a special committee and using 'Sunday' constables.[68] In 1831, in view of the increase of crime 'and the existence of a class . . . without any visible means of subsistence', it set up another committee to consider the better policing of the parish.[69] A county police force was established at West Bromwich in 1840.[70] The police station was apparently in rented premises in Seagar Street by at least the later 1840s,[71] but in 1851 a new station was built on the corner of High Street and Overend Street.[72] It was replaced in 1972 by the central police station built in New Street as part of the new town centre[73] and was demolished in 1973.

The manor court was taking precautions against fire by the early 17th century. In 1606 it ordered that no one was to carry fire from one house to another except in a lantern, a cup, or some safely covered container, and in 1609 a Richard Reeve was fined for carrying fire uncovered in the street.[74] By c. 1837 the Birmingham Fire Office Co. had a

[45] *Staffs. Advertiser* (S. Staffs. edn.), 4 Sept. 1875, 21 Oct. 1876; 'Old West Bromwich', 24 Dec. 1943.
[46] *Incorporation of West Bromwich*, 6.
[47] *Boro. of West Bromwich: Ann. Rep. of Medical Officer of Health for 1886*, 7.
[48] W.S.L., O.C. Newspaper Cuttings, West Bromwich, Nov. 1847; White, *Dir. Staffs.* (1851).
[49] *West Bromwich Corporation Baths: 1938 Extensions* (copy in W.B.L.); A. D. Greatorex, *Municipal Work in West Bromwich* (1903), 26–7, 34–5 (copy in W.B.L.); W.B.L., Scrapbook 12, p. 54.
[50] *West Bromwich Official Handbook* [1963], 29–31; *Midland Chron. & Free Press*, 5 Oct. 1962.
[51] 'Old West Bromwich', 24 Dec. 1943.
[52] Hackwood, *West Bromwich*, 102; *P.O. Dir. Staffs.* (1872); 'Old West Bromwich', 19 Apr. 1946 (giving 1866 as the date of the dispensary).
[53] *Kelly's Dir. Staffs.* (1884); ex inf. the hospital secretary (1970). [54] See p. 24.
[55] Hackwood, *West Bromwich*, 108; *Boro. of West Bromwich: Ann. Rep. of Medical Officer of Health for 1885*, 1, 4; ex inf. the secretary, West Bromwich and District Hospitals Group (1970).
[56] *Kelly's Dir. Staffs.* (1912); ex inf. the secretary, West Bromwich and District Hospitals Group (1970).
[57] *Birmingham Post*, 24 Feb. 1970.
[58] Lich. Dioc. Regy., B/A/2(i)/Q, pp. 263–7.
[59] *The Builder*, 22 Aug. 1857; plate facing p. 33 above.

[60] *West Bromwich Crematorium: Official Opening and Dedication* (copy in W.B.L.).
[61] *Aris's Birmingham Gaz.* 28 Jan. 1765.
[62] B.R.L., Caddick and Yates 84/2. It was still holding its anniversary dinner in 1810: *Aris's Birmingham Gaz.* 15 Jan. 1810.
[63] S.R.O., D.(W.)1778/V/720.
[64] Vestry Mins. p. 34.
[65] Willett, *West Bromwich*, 111–12.
[66] Vestry Mins. pp. 103–4; Willett, *West Bromwich*, 132–3. [67] Vestry Mins. pp. 127–9.
[68] Ibid. pp. 141–4. [69] Willett, *West Bromwich*, 121.
[70] S.R.O., Q/APr 2, rep. of supt. of police Apr. 1840; Willett, *West Bromwich*, 124. For the vestry's opposition to the new force see Willett, *West Bromwich*, 123–4; *Staffs. Advertiser*, 2 Sept., 21 Oct. 1843, 13 and 20 Apr. 1844.
[71] *P.O. Dir. Staffs.* (1845); Hackwood, *West Bromwich*, 33; S.R.O., Q/ACp 1/1, 16 Oct. 1848; Q/ACp 1/3, 10 and 17 Nov. 1848. For plans of 1841 of a proposed police station at Mayer's Green see Q/APs 4.
[72] White, *Dir. Staffs.* (1851); *P.O. Dir. Staffs.* (1860); 'Old West Bromwich', 27 Aug. 1943; S.R.O., Q/FAc 5/2, pp. 2–3, 23–4, 47; S.R.O., C/C/D/5/1; C/PC/VIII/6/1/1.
[73] *Evening Mail*, 9 Mar., 15 Sept. 1970, 8 Sept. 1972; *Express & Star*, 23 Feb. 1971.
[74] Ct. R. pp. 43, 52.

manual fire-engine at West Bromwich; it was manned by volunteers and kept at the premises of the company's agent in New Street. When William Burch became agent in 1854, the engine was moved to Hudson's Passage, behind his High Street chemist's shop; the Lancashire Insurance Co. of Birmingham, the successor of the Fire Office Co., still kept its engine there in 1884.[75] In the early 1840s the town had two small fire-engines but no practised firemen.[76] The fire at Holy Trinity Church in 1861 was fought by engines from Chance's works and the Birmingham Fire Office.[77] In 1878 the procession for the opening of Dartmouth Park was led by the engine of the Lancashire Insurance Co. and the engine from Chances.[78] In 1879 a second volunteer brigade was formed with an engine which was kept in Walsall Street.[79]

The improvement commissioners established a volunteer brigade in 1881 consisting of 12 officers and men; its steam fire-engine was kept in Paradise Street at the premises of an undertaker, who supplied the horses.[80] The brigade passed into the control of the new corporation in 1882.[81] By 1884 there were branch stations at Hill Top, Great Bridge, and Spon Lane;[82] the present station in Paradise Street dates from 1930.[83] In 1948 West Bromwich became a joint fire authority with Smethwick,[84] an arrangement which lasted until the local government reorganization of 1966. In 1969 the West Bromwich fire brigade had three stations, in Paradise Street and in Tipton and Wednesbury, with its headquarters in Pennyhill Lane, Wigmore.[85]

The Birmingham & Staffordshire Gas Light Co. was established by an Act of 1825 to supply gas to Birmingham and other places near by including West Bromwich; the lighting of the main road through the town was also mentioned in the Act.[86] In the same year the company opened its works at Swan Village, then the largest gas-works in the kingdom.[87] In 1875 Birmingham corporation bought up the undertakings supplying Birmingham with gas, and the West Bromwich commissioners decided to establish their own undertaking. An Act of 1876 empowered them to buy from Birmingham the right to do this. Birmingham retained the Swan Village works to supply Wednesbury and other outlying districts, and West Bromwich built a new works in Oldbury Road at Albion, close to the canal and the railway. The supply became available in 1880.[88] With nationalization in 1949 the undertaking came under the control of the West Midlands Gas Board.[89]

In 1883 the South Staffordshire Electric Lighting Co. Ltd. was authorized to supply electricity in West Bromwich, despite the opposition of the improvement commissioners the previous year.[90] In 1889 the corporation was planning its own undertaking, but the scheme was shelved largely because of the effect it would have on the gas undertaking.[91] The corporation finally established an electricity undertaking in 1898; a generating station was built at Black Lake, and the supply began in 1901.[92] In 1928 the Black Lake station was transferred to the West Midlands Joint Electricity Authority and the corporation became the distributing authority.[93] Nationalization came in 1948, and the supply is now under the control of the Midlands Electricity Board.

An omnibus service was begun between Birmingham and West Bromwich in 1835.[94] In 1872 a horse-drawn tramway service was started by the Birmingham and District Tramways Co. Ltd. from the Birmingham–Handsworth boundary at Hockley Brook through West Bromwich to Dudley Port in Tipton, and in 1873 it was extended to the centre of Birmingham.[95] In 1876 the firm was taken over by the Birmingham Tramways and Omnibus Co. Ltd. which restricted the trams to a service between Birmingham and Handsworth, thus discontinuing the service through West Bromwich. The South Staffordshire and Birmingham District Steam Tramways Co. Ltd. was formed in 1882; in 1883 it started a service through West Bromwich and Wednesbury to Darlaston, with a line to Great Bridge in 1884 and on to Dudley in 1885. Lines from West Smethwick along Spon Lane to Dartmouth Square and from Oldbury along Bromford Lane to St. Michael Street were opened by Birmingham and Midland Tramways Ltd. in 1885. The steam trams on those two routes ceased to operate in 1893, and the lines were then leased to B. Crowther, who ran a funeral service and a horse-vehicle hire business. He introduced horse trams, and a line was built along Paradise Street to connect the two routes with the stables and garage. The undertakings passed into the control of the British Electric Traction Co. Ltd. in 1897 and 1900. In 1901 West Bromwich corporation bought all the tramways in the borough; it introduced electric

[75] 'Old West Bromwich', 15 Mar. 1946. The Birmingham Fire Office Co. had been taken over by the Lancashire Insurance Co. in 1867.
[76] 2nd Rep. Com. State of Large Towns and Populous Districts [602], App. p. 41, H.C. (1845), xviii.
[77] Staffs. Advertiser, 12 Jan. 1861; below p. 56.
[78] Staffs. Advertiser, 8 June 1878.
[79] Weekly News, 10 Feb. 1879; Free Press, 15 Feb. 1879.
[80] Staffs. Advertiser, 7 Sept. 1878; Incorporation of West Bromwich: Full Rep. of Official Inquiry . . . 1882, 11; Express & Star, 10 Mar. 1970.
[81] Hackwood, West Bromwich, 111.
[82] Kelly's Dir. Staffs. (1884).
[83] West Bromwich Official Handbook (6th edn.), 55; S.R.O., D. 771/3/1/4/1 (plans of 1929); 'Old West Bromwich', 11 Aug. 1944.
[84] West Bromwich Official Handbook [1963], 52.
[85] Ex inf. the Chief Fire Officer (1969).
[86] Act to establish an additional company for more effectually lighting with gas the town of Birmingham and certain other parishes and places in the counties of Warwick and Stafford, 6 Geo. IV, c. 79 (Local and Personal).
[87] Ibid.; Reeves, West Bromwich, 122–3, 162.

[88] Hackwood, West Bromwich, 106–8; West Bromwich Improvement (Gas) Act, 1876, 39 & 40 Vic. c. 149 (Local); Midland Chron. 17 Oct. 1930.
[89] West Bromwich Official Handbook [1963], 64.
[90] S.R.O., Q/RUm 533; Q/RUo 5; Staffs. Advertiser (S. Staffs. edn.), 7 Oct., 4 Nov. 1882; Electric Lighting Orders Confirmation (No. 2) Act, 1883, 46 & 47 Vic. c. 214 (Local).
[91] S.R.O., Q/RUm 586; Staffs. Advertiser, 31 Dec. 1892, p. 6.
[92] S.R.O., Q/RUm 636; Electric Lighting Orders Confirmation (No. 10) Act, 1898, 61 & 62 Vic. c. 93 (Local); West Bromwich Official Handbook (5th edn.), 23.
[93] West Bromwich Official Handbook (5th edn.), 23.
[94] Reeves, West Bromwich, 162.
[95] For the rest of this para. and the following para. see J. S. Webb, Black Country Tramways, i (Bloxwich, priv. print. 1974), 1–3, 19, 22–3, 27, 64, 68–71, 105–6, 114, 123–8, 131–2, 179–84, 187–90, 192; A. J. Mason, Transport in West Bromwich (The Omnibus Society, 1963), 31–2 (copy in W.B.L.); County Boro. of West Bromwich: Transport Dept. Golden Jubilee 1964 (copy in W.B.L.); The West Midlands Passenger Transport Area (Transfer of Undertakings) Order 1969, S.I. 1969, no. 1175.

trams from the Handsworth boundary to Carter's Green at the end of 1902 and electrified the remaining routes in 1903–4. The tramways were then leased to operating companies. The portion of the Bromford Lane route in Oldbury was bought by Oldbury urban district council and the portion of the Spon Lane route in Smethwick by Smethwick corporation. Both were leased to Birmingham and Midland Tramways and in 1929 passed into the control of West Bromwich corporation.

In 1914 the corporation began to operate a motoromnibus service with a garage in Hardware Street, but the service was suspended later the same year when the War Office commandeered the chassis. In 1915 electric buses were introduced; they proved unreliable and were replaced in 1919. A bus service operated jointly by West Bromwich and Walsall corporations was begun in 1926, the first of several jointly run services in the borough. The trams along Spon Lane and Bromford Lane were replaced by buses in 1929, and in 1939 buses operated jointly by West Bromwich and Birmingham corporations replaced the trams running from Birmingham to Dudley and Wednesbury. A new garage and offices were built in Oak Lane in 1929 and extended in 1937–9. The transport undertaking passed to the West Midlands Passenger Transport Executive in 1969.

There was a postal service in West Bromwich by the 1720s: in 1809 Hannah Sutton was stated to have been 'the receiver and distributor of letters' in West Bromwich and Tipton for the previous 28 years like her parents and grandfather for 56 years before that.[96] The post office was then at Hill Top between the present New Street and Lakeside Road, but in 1828, with the growth of the new centre of population further south, it was moved to High Street.[97] The Suttons continued to run the post office until at least 1851.[98] There were also sub-offices at Hill Top, Spon Lane, and Great Bridge by the middle of the century.[99] In 1844 it was announced that the London day mail was to be extended to West Bromwich, Wednesbury, and Bilston 'in such a manner as will enable the inhabitants of those places to reply by the return night post to the letters conveyed by day mail'.[1] The post office moved into larger premises in different parts of High Street in 1868, 1872, and 1879. The present building in High Street was erected in 1918[2] and is of red brick and stone in a Georgian style.

Parks, libraries, and museums are treated elsewhere.[3]

PARLIAMENTARY HISTORY. Under the Reform Act of 1832 West Bromwich became part of the new southern division of the county, and under the Reform Act of 1867 it was transferred to the parliamentary borough of Wednesbury.[4] Under the Redistribution of Seats Act of 1885 the borough of West Bromwich became a parliamentary borough returning one member.[5] Although the boundaries of the county borough were subsequently altered, it was not until 1948 that the parliamentary borough was again made to coincide with the county borough.[6] In 1885 West Bromwich returned a Liberal, but from 1886 to 1918 it was held by the Conservatives, except for the period 1906–10 when it was again represented by a Liberal. From 1910 to 1918 the member was Viscount Lewisham (succeeded as 7th earl of Dartmouth in 1936). In 1918 it returned a Labour member, and, except for the period 1931–5 when the member was a National Unionist, it has remained a Labour seat.[7]

CHURCHES. Originally West Bromwich may have been part of Handsworth parish, but a church had been built by the 12th century and a parish established. The church of All Saints remained the only church in the parish until the 19th century. By then, however, the growth of population, particularly in the southern part of the parish, made a more centrally situated church an urgent need. One was opened in 1829, and others followed, notably in the later 19th century. The earls of Dartmouth, the patrons and lay rectors of the old parish church, generously supported church extension.

Guy de Offini, with the consent of his wife Christine and his son Richard, gave West Bromwich church to Worcester priory c. 1140–5, when his son Ralph became a monk there. The monks alone were to hold the rectory, and any vicar whom they appointed was to hold office at their pleasure.[8] The grant was apparently challenged by Handsworth church: a synod held at Lichfield by Bishop Clinton (1129–48) accepted that West Bromwich was a church in its own right and not subject to Handsworth. The decision was confirmed by Archbishop Theobald (1139–61).[9] Bishop Durdent (1149–59) confirmed Guy's grant, and the church was among the possessions confirmed to the monks by the bishop of Worcester in 1149 and by the pope at some time between 1159 and 1163; the pope also confirmed the freedom of West Bromwich from episcopal jurisdiction.[10]

Worcester soon became involved in further disputes over the church. At a synod held at Lichfield at some time between 1161 and 1182 a certain Hugh the priest acknowledged Worcester's right, and the prior granted him the church, apparently as vicar,

[96] Ex inf. Mr. J. Murt, citing G.P.O. records, Postmaster General's Rep. 17N, 1809.
[97] Reeves, *West Bromwich*, 162; Prince, *Old West Bromwich*, 119; West Bromwich Ref. Libr. *Short Hist. of West Bromwich* (1964), chap. 16; 'Old West Bromwich', 11 and 18 June 1943.
[98] Parson and Bradshaw, *Dir. Staffs.* 1818 (Hannah Sutton); Pigot, *Com. Dir. Birm.* (1829), 101 (Thos. Sutton); Reeves, *West Bromwich*, 164 (Thos. Sutton); White, *Dir. Staffs.* 1851 (Sam. Sutton).
[99] White, *Dir. Staffs.* (1851).
[1] *Staffs. Advertiser*, 12 Oct. 1844.
[2] Ibid. 29 Nov. 1879; 'Old West Bromwich', 18 June 1943.
[3] See pp. 5, 7, 9–10, 72.
[4] White, *Dir. Staffs.* (1834), 15; 30 & 31 Vic. c. 102. For

an attempt in 1859 to make West Bromwich a parliamentary borough see *Staffs. Advertiser*, 12 and 19 Feb., 5 Mar. 1859.
[5] *V.C.H. Staffs.* i. 273.
[6] Representation of the People Act, 1948, 11 & 12 Geo. VI, c. 65; Woodall, *West Bromwich Yesterdays*, 45.
[7] Woodall, *West Bromwich Yesterdays*, 44–6; *County Boro. of West Bromwich: Council Diary & Municipal Yearbook 1966/67*; Burke, *Peerage* (1967), 690.
[8] *Cartulary of Worcester Cathedral Priory* (Pipe R. Soc. N.S. xxxviii), pp. 101–2. For the Worcester tradition that the church was given to the priory by Hen. I see W. Thomas, *Survey of Cathedral Church of Worcester* (1737), 31.
[9] *Cart. of Worc. Cath. Priory*, p. 102.
[10] Ibid. pp. 42, 47–8, 103.

in return for an annual pension of ½ mark.[11] About the same time Henry, the priest at Handsworth, apparently revived his church's claim to West Bromwich. The matter was delegated by the pope to Bishop Foliot of London (1163–87) and was settled by 1181. Worcester granted the church to Henry's proctor for life in return for an annual pension of 5s. Hugh the priest, who was described as having served in the church in the prior's name, was admitted as vicar by the proctor in return for a pension of 1 mark.[12] A dispute also arose with Guy de Offini's grandson Richard who claimed the patronage, but he recognized Worcester's right in 1213–17.[13]

In 1217 or 1218 Bishop Cornhill gave Worcester permission to appropriate the church for the soul of King John and to the use of the sick, subject to the interest of Matthew de Cantilupe, presumably the vicar. The bishop repeated the licence, probably on Matthew's death or resignation. It was confirmed by the prior of Coventry and, in 1221, by the pope.[14]

About 1230 Worcester granted the church to Sandwell priory in return for an annual pension of 6 marks and an undertaking to maintain the church and provide books and ornaments. Bishop Stavensby confirmed the arrangement in 1230 and allowed the monks to serve the church by their own chaplain because of their poverty.[15] In 1585 an old parishioner stated that he had heard how the priors sometimes attended services at West Bromwich church and also sent straw there on Good Fridays 'to dress up the parishioners' seats against Easter'.[16]

In 1526 Sandwell's possessions were granted by the Crown to Cardinal Wolsey and by him to Cardinal College, Oxford.[17] Wolsey, however, seems to have retained some control over West Bromwich church. In 1528 Thomas Cromwell, then Wolsey's servant, ordered William Wyrley, the farmer of the West Bromwich tithes, to eject the curate, John Stylband, and to replace him by 'Sir William, the prior's monk that was'. Stylband refused to go, and there was a scene of some disorder in the church with the two priests competing to say mass. In 1529 Stylband brought an action against Wyrley and the rival priest.[18]

In 1530 on Wolsey's fall the Sandwell property passed back to the Crown.[19] The right of appointing to the curacy was still in the hands of the Crown in 1608 when it was reserved in a grant of the rectory,[20] but by 1680 it was in the hands of the lord of the

manor, who still held it in 1708.[21] By 1710 it had passed to Lord Dartmouth, who had bought Sandwell in 1701.[22] Thereafter it remained with the earls of Dartmouth until 1969 when it was transferred to the bishop of Lichfield.[23] The minister was described as a perpetual curate by 1752, and the living became a vicarage in 1868.[24] Under the terms of an Act of 1819 he must be an Oxford or Cambridge graduate.[25]

In 1526 it was stated that the priest, not being a vicar, took all the profits except those taken by the farmer of the tithes and accounted for them to 'the house of Sandwell or the officers now there, and they to pay him his wages'.[26] In 1604 his stipend was £6 and by the 1640s £14.[27] In 1657 'divers well-affected inhabitants' petitioned for an augmentation of £20 a year for their minister, and their request was granted by the Trustees for Maintenance of Ministers.[28] By the late 17th century the Whorwoods as impropriators allowed the curate a stipend of £20 and a house with c. ¼ a.; in addition there were surplice fees, which in 1705 were estimated at some £3 a year.[29] An assistant curate is recorded from the 1750s.[30] By 1773 the minister, Edward Stillingfleet, had fixed the assistant's stipend at £40 a year 'because the legal income of the living is small'; privately he agreed to pay £60.[31]

In 1614 Walter Stanley founded a lectureship to provide a lecturer who would preach every Sunday and on the principal feasts and also visit the sick. He was to be an Oxford or Cambridge graduate, single, and not beneficed elsewhere. Stanley endowed the lectureship with lands in Warwickshire; property in Wednesbury was added later with the proceeds from a sale of timber felled on the Warwickshire estate in 1662.[32] The income in 1698 was £32 13s. 4d., but it had risen to £132 1s. 6d. by 1800.[33] It was clearly intended that the lecturer should be a person other than the curate of All Saints', but from the later 17th century the trustees normally appointed the curate.[34] The practice was challenged in 1815,[35] and in 1819 the trust was reorganized by Act of Parliament. The curate of All Saints' was to act as lecturer and might be married. The income was to be divided equally between the curate of All Saints' and the minister of the proposed new church (Christ Church). Both ministers were to be Oxford or Cambridge graduates.[36] An Act of 1840 allowed the trustees to grant 99-year building leases of the property.[37] When the leases expired in the 1940s, it became possible to increase the income

[11] Ibid. p. 103.   [12] Ibid. p. 104.
[13] Ibid. pp. 104–5.
[14] Ibid. pp. 105–6. Cornhill's second licence mentioned the uses of hospitality as well as of the sick.
[15] Ibid. p. 107; V.C.H. Staffs. iii. 217; B.M. Harl. MS. 3868, f. 2v.
[16] E 134/27 and 28 Eliz. I Mich./2 m. 1.
[17] V.C.H. Staffs. iii. 218–19; S.H.C. xii (1), 183.
[18] L. & P. Hen. VIII, Addenda, i (1), pp. 202, 215–16. For Wyrley see above p. 18.
[19] V.C.H. Staffs. iii. 219.
[20] Cal. Pat. 1560–3, 516; C 66/1143 mm. 37–8; C 66/1283 mm. 13–15; C 66/1753 no. 18; E 134/27 and 28 Eliz. I Mich./2 mm. 1, 4; L.J.R.O., B/V/1/2–4.
[21] C.P. 43/391 rot. 8; C.P. 25(2)/966/7 Anne Trin. [no. 36].
[22] L.J.R.O., B/A/3/West Bromwich; above p. 18.
[23] Ex inf. the diocesan registrar (1970), citing conveyance of 20 Oct. 1969.
[24] L.J.R.O., B/A/1/21, p. 26; Willett, West Bromwich, 56–7.
[25] See below.   [26] E 36/165 f. 127.
[27] 'A Puritan Survey of the Church in Staffs. in 1604', ed. A. Peel, E.H.R. xxvi. 350; S.P. 23/204 p. 782.
[28] Cal. S.P. Dom. 1656–7, 283; S.H.C. 1915, 310.
[29] L.J.R.O., B/V/6/West Bromwich.
[30] Reeves, West Bromwich, 14; Willett, West Bromwich, 43, 52, 54.
[31] L.J.R.O., B/V/5/1772–3; B/A/1/23, p. 99.
[32] Willett, West Bromwich, 77–88 (wrongly giving the date of foundation as 1613 when it was Mar. 1613/14).
[33] L.J.R.O., B/V/6/West Bromwich.
[34] Willett, West Bromwich, 35, 39–43, 51, 87–90; S.R.O., D. 564/12/11, Edw. Stillingfleet to Lord Dartmouth, 5 Dec. 1789.
[35] Willett, West Bromwich, 90–1; Account of the Lectureship in the Parish of West Bromwich (Birmingham, 1815; copy in W.S.L.).
[36] 59 Geo. III, c. 87 (Private, not printed); Willett, West Bromwich, 92–3.
[37] Act to enable trustees of estates of Walter Stanley to grant building leases, 3 & 4 Vic. c. 21 (Private).

from rents. An Act of 1949 provided that the much-improved income should be divided among all the parishes within the bounds of the ancient parish after the payment of £600 to the vicar of All Saints' and £400 to the vicar of Christ Church.[38]

The income of the minister was improved in other ways during the 19th century. In 1829 Lord Dartmouth agreed to endow the living, by instalments, with £7,500 to replace the £20 a year which had previously been allowed out of the rectory; the process was completed in 1843.[39] In addition five augmentations totalling £3,000 were made from Queen Anne's Bounty in 1810, 1811 (two), 1812, and 1817.[40] In 1845 the minister's income consisted mainly of £345 from Queen Anne's Bounty and Lord Dartmouth's endowment and £151 from the Stanley Trust; there were also fees, which in 1838–41 had averaged £63 a year.[41]

Sandwell was providing a house for the chaplain of West Bromwich by 1336, apparently in the Hall End area west of All Saints'; the chaplain was still living in that area in 1526, but his house was then described as in decay.[42] It was in a house at Hall End that the minister and his wife were living in 1611.[43] About 1758 Lord Dartmouth built a new house for the incumbent, Churchfield House to the south-east of the church.[44] The old house, at Hall End on the north side of what is now Vicarage Road, became the assistant curate's residence and later the house of the teacher at the school established at Hall End in 1811. About 1843 Lord Dartmouth exchanged Church Farm, opposite the church at the junction of Heath Lane and All Saints Street, for the house at Hall End. Church Farm became the assistant curate's residence, but the incumbents have lived there since the appointment of Frederic Willett in 1865. The house, which may be partly of the 18th century, was enlarged and altered in 1868 and modernized in the early 1930s.[45] Churchfield House, which reverted to Lord Dartmouth, was derelict by 1945[46] and has been demolished.

About 1593 the minister was described as 'scholaris ruralis mediocriter doctus'.[47] A 1604 Puritan survey described the minister as a layman and no preacher.[48] It was doubtless to improve that state of affairs that Walter Stanley founded the lectureship in 1614. There is some evidence of Puritan influence in West Bromwich in the 17th century. In 1623 two men were accused of receiving communion seated.[49] Edward Lane, curate 1643–8, suffered at the hands of 'rebels': one Sunday they dragged him from the reading-desk and into the churchyard where they burnt the surplice and prayer-book in front of him.[50] In 1658 Moses Bennett of West Bromwich complained to quarter sessions that in July the minister and the inhabitants had broken the Sabbath and the Thanksgiving Day.[51] In 1668 he was accused of wearing his hat in church and of refusing to attend divine service, 'saying that he would not come whilst the minister has the devil's clothing, meaning the surplice'.[52]

In the later 18th century Evangelical influence was strong. The patron was William, earl of Dartmouth (d. 1801), one of the countess of Huntingdon's converts. The incumbents included Edward Stillingfleet (1757–82) and William Jesse (1790–1814), both notable Evangelicals.[53] In 1773 there were two services and two sermons every Sunday, with prayers on holy days and a sermon at 6 o'clock on Wednesday evenings. There was a communion service on the first Sunday of the month and on the great feasts, and the communicants numbered between 100 and 200. The children were catechized every Sunday in Lent in the presence of the congregation and privately on Wednesdays and Fridays during the summer. Stillingfleet reported a decline in the number of Roman Catholics and Protestant nonconformists, many of whom were attending the parish church regularly.[54] A Sunday school was established in 1788.[55] By 1830 the incumbent (Charles Townsend, 1815–36) was residing only half the year in the parish, being also rector of Calstone Wellington (Wilts.); there was, however, a resident assistant curate. There were still two Sunday services and a monthly communion but no weekday services; the number of communicants had dropped to 65.[56] In 1861 a group of laymen founded All Saints' Church Association and pressed for more frequent services; a Wednesday evening service was introduced and also a Sunday evensong at the Hallam Street school.[57]

With the coming of Frederic Willett, incumbent 1865–81, a revival began.[58] In January 1866 he introduced a fortnightly communion and daily even-

[38] Stanley's Charity (West Bromwich) Scheme Confirmation Act, 1949, 12, 13 & 14 Geo. VI, c. 58 (Local); ex inf. the clerk to the Stanley Trustees (1970).

[39] Willett, *West Bromwich*, 115; L.J.R.O., B/V/6/West Bromwich, 1824, 1845; docs. at All Saints', parcel 13; C. Hodgson, *Account of Augmentation of Small Livings by Governors of Bounty of Queen Anne: Supplement* (1864), p. lxxxviii.

[40] Hodgson, *Queen Anne's Bounty* (1845 edn.), p. ccxcviii; L.J.R.O., B/V/6/West Bromwich, 1824.

[41] L.J.R.O., B/V/6/West Bromwich, 1841, 1845.

[42] F. A. Homer, 'Collections for the Hist. of the Priory of Sandwell' (in W.S.L.), transcript of deed of 1336; Willett, *West Bromwich*, 211; E 36/165 f. 127.

[43] S.R.O., Q/SR, T. 1611, no. 45.

[44] S.R.O., D. 564/12/14/2, estimate of 1758 for a parsonage house of brick (£979 6s. 7d.); L.J.R.O., B/V/5/1772–3; B/A/15/West Bromwich; C. and J. Greenwood, *Map of Staffs.* (1820).

[45] L.J.R.O., B/V/5/1772–3; S.R.O., Q/RDc 60, map; S.R.O., D. 564/8/1/2/May 1863; Willett, *West Bromwich*, 55–6, 193; Wood, *Plan of West Bromwich* (1837); 'Old West Bromwich', 17 Aug. 1945; A. M. D. Ashley, *Joyful Servant: the Ministry of Percy Hartill* (Abingdon, c. 1967), 32, 38.

[46] 'Old West Bromwich', 17 Aug. 1945.

[47] *S.H.C.* 1915, 309–10, 398.

[48] *E.H.R.* xxvi. 350.

[49] A. G. Matthews, *Cong. Churches of Staffs.* 13.

[50] *Walker Revised*, ed. A. G. Matthews, 324.

[51] *Staffs. and the Great Rebellion*, ed. D. A. Johnson and D. G. Vaisey (Staffs. County Council Records Cttee.), 40–1. [52] Matthews, *Cong. Churches*, 56.

[53] *V.C.H. Staffs.* iii. 65; *Gent. Mag.* lxxxv (1), 87–8; below p. 63.

[54] L.J.R.O., B/V/5/1772–3. And see S.R.O., D.(W.) 1778/V/1238, for the return to the Anglican Church of Mary Abney, dau. of the Presbyterian Josiah Turton.

[55] Hackwood, *West Bromwich*, 92. The first Sunday school in West Bromwich was that established by the minister of the Old Meeting in 1786: see below p. 67.

[56] L.J.R.O., A/V/1/3, p. 34; *Rep. Com. Eccl. Revenues* [67], pp. 466–7, H.C. (1835), xxii; Willett, *West Bromwich*, 52–3.

[57] P. Hartill, *The Story of All Saints' Parish Church, West Bromwich*, 23 (copy in W.B.L.).

[58] For this para. see ibid. 23–5. For an obituary of Willett, who moved to Sussex in 1881 and died there in 1939 aged 100, see *Mid-Sussex Times*, 13 June 1939 (copy in W.S.L., Newspaper Cuttings).

song, in Advent the same year a weekly communion and daily matins, in 1867 celebrations on saints' days and holy days, in 1868 a celebration every Thursday, and in Advent 1871 a daily eucharist; services were also held in cottages and in the pits. The changes were accompanied by a rapid increase in the number of communicants. A surpliced choir was introduced in 1867, and eucharistic vestments were worn from 1872. In 1871–2 Willett rebuilt the church, considering the existing building totally unworthy. He also established a clergy house in Church Vale in 1871 where men could be trained for ordination.[59] A parochial council was formed in 1872. In 1866 a parish house was opened in Hargate Lane for the care of the sick and the poor.

Willett's ritualistic innovations and teachings provoked considerable opposition. Although the Easter Vestry of 1873 passed a resolution supporting him, the same year a petition against his practices was sent to the bishop. The 1,746 signatories included the vicar of St. James's, Hill Top, and (reluctantly, it seems) Lord Dartmouth. The bishop's reply did not satisfy the petitioners, and an appeal was made to the archbishop of Canterbury. The petitioners were even rumoured to be planning a citation in the ecclesiastical courts. In 1874 the board of guardians banned the parish magazine from the workhouse because the chaplain considered its contents to be against the spirit and teaching of the Church of England.[60] After Willett had retired for reasons of health in 1881[61] his successor, M. M. Connor, quickly discontinued the use of altar lights other than for lighting purposes and of vestments, wafer bread, the ceremonial mixing of the chalice, and obeisance to the altar. In 1883 he abandoned the daily eucharist on the ground that the parishioners were not yet ready 'for the exceptional spiritual advantages offered them in a daily celebration of holy communion'.[62]

Frederic Willett also established mission churches, believing that everyone should be within half a mile of the 'means of grace'.[63] The work had begun earlier, for All Saints' was badly situated to serve the new centre of population which developed in the southern part of the parish in the early 19th century. The first new church was Christ Church, opened in High Street in 1829.[64] Even so West Bromwich was declared by the archdeacon in 1839

to be ecclesiastically one of the worst provided places in the Black Country, with accommodation for less than a ninth of its population.[65] In 1841 he even urged the incumbent of All Saints' to consider rebuilding his church on a larger scale and in a more central district; the incumbent replied that Lord Dartmouth did not favour the idea.[66] New places of worship continued to be opened from All Saints' in the course of the 19th century. Holy Trinity was opened in 1841,[67] St. James's, Hill Top, in 1842,[68] St. Michael's, John Street, in 1866 (closed in 1868),[69] and St. Andrew's, Old Meeting Street, in 1867.[70] St. Michael's, Frederick Street, was opened in 1868 in a former nonconformist chapel; it was renamed St. Chad's in 1872, apparently when St. Michael's, Wood Lane, was opened, and was used until c. 1879.[71] St. Mary the Virgin, Hateley Heath, started in a disused public house in 1870; in 1871 it was replaced by a school-church in Jowett's Lane which c. 1881 became exclusively a mission church and so continued until c. 1888.[72] St. Mary Magdalene, Cottrell Street, was built in 1871, closed in 1965, and replaced by the church hall of St. Mary Magdalene in Beacon View Road on the Charlemont Farm housing estate in 1967.[73] The Friar Park area was transferred to St. Paul's, Wood Green, Wednesbury, in 1875, and when Friar Park itself became a conventional district in 1931, the Stone Cross portion of All Saints' parish was added to it.[74]

The 19th century saw several attempts to reach the people of the parish by means of the printed word. In 1819 the vestry was alarmed by 'blasphemous and seditious publications' calculated to turn the lower orders of the parish 'not only from obedience to the laws but also from that respect to the authority of divine revelation on which the laws must mainly depend'. It was resolved to launch a subscription so that 'tracts of a different and opposite tendency' could be bought and circulated.[75] A depot of the Society for Promoting Christian Knowledge was opened c. 1857.[76] The parish magazine was started by Frederic Willett in 1866.[77] By the mid 1880s there was a parochial library with 150 members.[78]

The present church of *ALL SAINTS* dates from 1871–2. The building which it replaced had been altered on several occasions, notably in the

---

[59] See also *Lich. Dioc. Ch. Cal.* (1872), 93; 'Old West Bromwich', 31 Aug. 1945.

[60] Hartill, *All Saints'*, 26; *Staffs. Advertiser*, 1 Nov. 1873; ibid. (S. Staffs. edn.), 11 Oct. 1873, 16 May 1874. For the accusation, brought against him in 1876–7 by a girl whose confessor he was, that he was the father of her illegitimate child see *Staffs. Advertiser*, 19 May, 29 Sept. 1877.

[61] *Lich. Dioc. Mag.* 1881, 158.

[62] *Staffs. Advertiser* (S. Staffs. edn.), 18 Mar., 13 May 1882; Hartill, *All Saints'*, 29.

[63] Hartill, *All Saints'*, 24.

[64] See p. 55.

[65] G. Hodson, *Charge delivered to the Clergy of the Archdeaconry of Stafford, 1839* (Rugeley, 1839), 47–8 (copy in W.S.L. Pamphs. *sub* Visitation Charges). Willenhall had accommodation for less than a tenth, Wednesfield for less than a twentieth.

[66] L.J.R.O., A/V/1/3/34.

[67] See p. 56.

[68] See p. 56.

[69] Hartill, *All Saints'*, 24.

[70] See p. 58.

[71] Hartill, *All Saints'*, 24; *Lich. Dioc. Ch. Cal.* (1869),

[76]; ibid. (1873, where it is listed under St. Peter's; 1874; 1880); below p. 58.

[72] Hartill, *All Saints'*, 24; Willett, *West Bromwich*, 73; *Lich. Dioc. Ch. Cal.* (1872), 93; ibid. (1889); Hackwood, *West Bromwich*, 96, mentioning its demolition; O.S. Map 6", Staffs. LXVIII. NW. (1890 edn.).

[73] *Lich. Dioc. Ch. Cal.* (1872), 93; docs. at All Saints', parcel 7; Lich. Dioc. Regy., B/A/1/33, p. 381; *The Old Church News, Centenary Number, 1866–1966* (copy in W.B.L.), mentioning also that, while the new hall was being built, house communions were held on the estate. A stone altar was found in the floor of the Cottrell St. chapel under the wooden altar in 1933. It has been suggested that it was taken there when All Saints' was rebuilt in 1871–2 and that it may be the medieval altar of that church, which could have been let into the floor or a wall at All Saints' at the Reformation. See Hartill, *All Saints'*, 16.

[74] See pp. 59–60.

[75] West Bromwich Vestry Mins. pp. 108–9. For the system of special constables established in 1819 to prevent profanation of the Sabbath see above p. 48.

[76] *Companion to Lich. Dioc. Ch. Cal.* (1858).

[77] *Old Church News, Centenary Number.*

[78] *Lich. Dioc. Mag.* 1886, 153.

late 18th century when a major reconstruction took place. The dedication was originally to St. Clement but was changed apparently in the 19th century.[79]

A baluster shaft possibly of the late 11th century, now reset in the tower, may come from the tower of an early church on the site. By the early 14th century there were a chancel and north aisle,[80] and the lower stages of the present tower were built or rebuilt in that century. A north chapel, the family chapel of the Stanleys, had probably been built by 1534, although described as new in 1552; it was apparently situated at the east end of the north aisle.[81] A south chapel, the family chapel of the Whorwoods and of their successors at Sandwell, the earls of Dartmouth, was built in 1619 under the terms of the will of Sir William Whorwood (d. 1614).[82] It seems that there was never a south aisle,[83] so that the south chapel must always have projected from the body of the church. A south porch, whose date of construction is not known, was repaired in 1706.[84] At a public meeting in 1713 it was agreed to have the church ceiled.[85] A north gallery existed by 1755 and a second was approved in that year; a gallery at the west end had probably been erected by then.[86]

In 1786 a major reconstruction was set in hand by the vestry.[87] The result was that the body of the church, consisting of chancel, nave, north aisle, and north chapel, was converted into 'one large space' 64 ft. by 41 ft.; the tower that had stood at the west end of the nave survived as a south-west tower, and the south chapel and apparently the south porch survived also. The side walls were raised, and the roof was completely renewed. Two rows of classical windows were inserted on the south side and presumably on the north as well. A projecting vestry was built at the east end with a window in the east wall on either side of it; that to the south was the east window of the former chancel and that to the north the east window of the former north chapel. Within the body of the church a sanctuary was defined by an elliptical arch on pilasters. North and south galleries were erected; the existing west gallery was evidently retained. Extensive use was made of brick in the new work.

The next major structural alteration was made in 1854 when a sanctuary with an east window was built in place of the vestry, at the expense of the 4th earl of Dartmouth (d. 1853); the two windows on either side were filled in. The 5th earl allowed the Whorwood chapel to be turned into a vestry.[88] A clock was installed in the tower in 1794, and a sundial was placed on the south face in the 1840s.[89] About 1862 the three-decker pulpit, dating apparently from the later 1780s, was replaced by a pulpit and reading-desk 'in a more suitable position'. At the same time the high pews were lowered and the square ones divided.[90]

The church was rebuilt on a larger scale in 1871–2, with the exception of the tower and the former Whorwood chapel.[91] Lord Dartmouth, Frederic Willett and his wife Mary, and J. N. Bagnall and his wife, the parents of Mary Willett, contributed towards the cost. The church is of sandstone and was designed in a mixture of Early English and Decorated styles by Somers Clarke the younger. It consists of chancel with north organ chamber and south vestry and chapel, nave, south aisle, and north and south porches; the medieval tower, which was restored in the course of the rebuilding, stands at the west end of the aisle. The former Whorwood chapel, which was apparently much restored,[92] leads off the aisle and is used as the choir vestry.

The 15th-century font[93] and the chest formed from a hollowed tree[94] presumably survive from the medieval church. The oak altar table in the chapel is dated 1626.[95] Two Whorwood effigies that had survived the reconstruction of the 1780s were placed between the chancel and the south aisle; they have been identified as probably those of Ann (d. 1599), wife of Sir William, and their fourth son Field (d. 1658).[96]

In 1553 the church goods included a silver chalice, parcel gilt, with a paten, and a pyx 'bound about with silver'.[97] The plate in 1830 consisted of two silver cups and patens, a pewter flagon, and two pewter dishes.[98] When the church was rebuilt in

[79] *Cartulary of Worcester Cathedral Priory* (Pipe R. Soc. N.S. xxxviii), p. 106; Willett, *West Bromwich*, 33; Hackwood, *West Bromwich*, 33–4; Shaw, *Staffs.* ii. 132; Pye, *Modern Birmingham*, 108. The dedication is given as All Saints by White, *Dir. Staffs.* (1834), and Reeves, *West Bromwich*, 7.

[80] See the style of the windows shown in *Gent. Mag.* lxvii (1), plate facing p. 185, and Reeves, *West Bromwich*, frontispiece.

[81] L.J.R.O., will of Cecily Stanley (proved 5 Nov. 1552); Willett, *West Bromwich*, 37–9, 48–50 (the latter including a transcript of W.S.L., S. MS. 336, f. 6.v); above p. 16 n. 79.

[82] Prob. 11/127 (P.C.C. 11 Cope); stone dated 1619 on E. face of chapel; Willett, *West Bromwich*, 36–8, 48, 95, 157; West Bromwich Churchwardens' Bk. 1678–1787, p. 39; S.R.O., D. 564/12/8; D.(W.)1778/V/1064–5 and 1267; L.J.R.O., B/C/5/West Bromwich, 1762.

[83] Willett, *West Bromwich*, 28. The mention of a middle aisle in the 18th century (ibid. 38) could refer to an arrangement of the seating.

[84] Shaw, *Staffs.* ii. 133.

[85] Churchwardens' Bk. 1678–1787, p. 57.

[86] L.J.R.O., B/C/5/West Bromwich, 1755; Willett, *West Bromwich*, 44, 104–5.

[87] For this para. see Willett, *West Bromwich*, 44–5, 48, 105–7, 109; Shaw, *Staffs.* ii. 132–3; Reeves, *West Bromwich*, frontispiece and p. 9; L.J.R.O., B/C/5/West Bromwich, 1786; W.B.L., A. 123; docs. at All Saints', parcel 3; S.R.O., D. 564/12/8; D.(W.)1778/I/ii/1358–9, J. Wright

to Lord Dartmouth, 13 and 20 Mar. 1786; plate facing p. 80 below.

[88] Willett, *West Bromwich*, 48.

[89] Ibid. 133; Vestry Mins. pp. 36, 125; Reeves, *West Bromwich*, 9; Hackwood, *West Bromwich*, 35; W.B.L., A. 123. The sun-dial bears the names of two churchwardens, Thos. Jesson and T. H. Beeson, who both held office 1842–9: *West Bromwich Old Church Par. Mag.* June 1880 (copy at All Saints').

[90] Willett, *West Bromwich*, 50, 54–5; Shaw, *Staffs.* ii. 132.

[91] Willett, *West Bromwich*, 60–71, 126–7; P. Hartill, *The Story of All Saints' Parish Church, West Bromwich*, 12, 25–6 (copy in W.B.L.); plate facing p. 80 below.

[92] It bears the date 1872 on its west face.

[93] S. A. Jeavons, 'The Fonts of Staffs.' *T.B.A.S.* lxviii. 20; Willett, *West Bromwich*, 68; Hackwood, *West Bromwich*, 34.

[94] In 1812 the vestry ordered the churchwardens to place 'a proper chest' for the parish documents in the church: Vestry Mins. p. 72. Hartill, *All Saints'*, 11, mentions that another medieval chest existed in 1836 but has since disappeared.

[95] Hartill, *All Saints'*, 16. For a theory about the survival of the medieval stone altar see above p. 53 n. 73.

[96] S. A. Jeavons, 'The Monumental Effigies of Staffs.', *T.B.A.S.* lxx. 35 and lxxi. 32; Willett, *West Bromwich*, 47; Shaw, *Staffs.* ii. 133.

[97] *S.H.C.* 1915, 309.

[98] L.J.R.O., A/V/1/3/34.

1871–2 a chalice in use in the previous church was reworked in parcel gilt and set with precious stones.[99]

In 1553 there were four 'great bells'.[1] The rebuilt church of 1872 had a ring of eight: (i) 1842; (ii), (iv), and (vi) 1711; (iii) and (vii) 1832; (v) recast 1872; (viii) 1848.[2] All the bells were recast in 1918, the cost being met with a legacy of £100 from George Salter.[3]

The registers date from 1608 and are substantially complete.[4]

The churchyard contains memorials from the late 17th century onwards. It has been steadily enlarged since the later 18th century.[5] A lich-gate was built at the main entrance in 1876 in memory of Thomas Jesson of Oakwood (d. 1873). Another, leading into the extension of the churchyard east of the church, was erected by Jesson's sons the Revd. Henry and the Revd. Thomas Jesson in memory of their sister Susan (d. 1878).[6]

The first new church in West Bromwich was *CHRIST CHURCH*, built in the 1820s in the present High Street, the new centre of the parish over a mile from All Saints' Church. The foundation-stone was laid in 1821, but work was delayed when the builder went bankrupt in 1822 and the church was not consecrated until January 1829. Nearly three-quarters of the cost was met by parliamentary grant and the rest by private subscribers.[7] Under an Act of 1819 the minister enjoyed half the income from the Stanley Trust.[8] Because of the grant from the Stanley Trust the appointment of the minister was shared between Lord Dartmouth, patron of All Saints', and the Stanley Trustees, Lord Dartmouth submitting the names of two Oxford or Cambridge graduates to the trustees.[9] In 1969 Lord Dartmouth transferred his interest to the bishop of Lichfield.[10] In 1837 a parish was formed covering the southern part of the ancient parish.[11] The living, at first a perpetual curacy, be-

came a vicarage in 1868.[12] A house on the Sandwell estate, Coopers Hill House, was originally provided for the minister by Lord Dartmouth.[13] The incumbents, however, had various residences[14] until the present vicarage in Bratt Street next to the church was built in 1891, to the designs of Wood & Kendrick of West Bromwich.[15]

The following churches and missions have been opened from Christ Church: Greets Green in 1851;[16] a mission in a house in Twenty House Row, Ault Street, by c. 1860;[17] St. John's in the 1860s;[18] St. Philip's in 1874;[19] St. Mark's in Duke Street, where an iron mission church was opened in 1892 and replaced in 1904 by a larger brick church used for services until 1933;[20] St. Stephen's (the former St. Philip's) c. 1892–3;[21] Christ Church Mission Room c. 1892–3;[22] and the Mission Hall at the Walsall Street schools c. 1910, continuing until the 1920s.[23]

Christ Church, of brick cased in Tixall stone, was designed by Francis Goodwin in a mixed Decorated and Perpendicular style.[24] The interior is in effect a single large space with a shallow chancel at the east end; there are galleries on three sides, and those on the north and south create aisles beneath them. There is a west tower. The window frames and tracery are of iron.[25] The design of the tracery of the east window had been used by Goodwin at St. Matthew's, Walsall.[26] The church was badly damaged by mining subsidence during the mid 1850s and was restored in 1858; the screen, which had darkened the interior, was replaced by 'a most elegant stone arch designed by Mr. Christian' (presumably Ewan Christian).[27] The three-decker pulpit at the east end of the nave was apparently then cut in half to form the pulpit and the minister's stall.[28] Further damage from subsidence led to another restoration in 1876.[29] At the same time there was a general reorganization of the interior. The small chancel was extended one bay into the nave and aisles, and choir stalls were introduced along with a

[99] Willett, *West Bromwich*, 71; S. A. Jeavons, 'Church Plate in the Archdeaconry of Stafford', *T.B.A.S.* lxxiii. 54–5. For the other plate, none of it pre-19th-century, see ibid. 1, 50–1, 54–5.
[1] *S.H.C.* 1915, 309.
[2] C. Lynam, *Church Bells of the County of Stafford* (1889), 33.
[3] *Kelly's Dir. Staffs.* (1924); A. E. Garbett, 'Church Bells of Staffs.', *Trans. Old Stafford Soc.* 1952–3, 15.
[4] They have been printed to 1659 by the Staffs. Par. Reg. Soc. (1909).
[5] Willett, *West Bromwich*, 74, 104, 117–18, 126–7; Lich. Dioc. Regy., B/A/2(i)/H, pp. 63–74, 86–97; /S, pp. 273–7; /V, pp. 85, 127–31; /W, pp. 540–1; docs. at All Saints', parcel 7; *Staffs. Advertiser*, 10 Sept. 1859; S.R.O., D. 564/8/1/13 and 14.
[6] *West Bromwich Old Church Par. Mag.* Jan. 1876 (copy at All Saints'), stating that the gate was being erected; Willett, *West Bromwich*, 73–5 (stating that it was erected in 1874) and pedigree 7; plaque on earlier gate.
[7] H. Baylis, *Christ Church, West Bromwich, 1829–1929* (West Bromwich, n.d. but published for centenary), 7 and plate facing p. 5; Reeves, *West Bromwich*, 14–15; Willett, *West Bromwich*, 113–16; Hackwood, *West Bromwich*, 94–5; White, *Dir. Staffs.* (1851); Lich. Dioc. Regy., B/A/2(i)/H, pp. 547–71; West Bromwich Vestry Mins. pp. 105–7.
[8] L.J.R.O., A/V/1/3/35; above p. 51.
[9] Willett, *West Bromwich*, 93, 132.
[10] Ex inf. the clerk to the Stanley Trustees (1970).
[11] *Lond. Gaz.* 24 Feb. 1837, pp. 450–1; Lich. Dioc. Regy., B/A/2(i)/K, pp. 401–2.
[12] *Lich. Dioc. Ch. Cal.* (1868; 1869).
[13] L.J.R.O., A/V/1/3/35; 'Old West Bromwich', 21 Sept., 2 Nov. 1945.

[14] White, *Dir. Staffs.* (1834; 1851); *Kelly's Dir. Staffs.* (1884; 1892).
[15] *Lich. Dioc. Mag.* 1890, 203; ibid. 1891, 14; *Lich. Dioc. Ch. Cal.* (1891), 160; Lich. Dioc. Regy., B/A/2(i)/T p. 479; Hackwood, *West Bromwich*, 95.
[16] See p. 57.
[17] 'Old West Bromwich', 12 Nov. 1943.
[18] See p. 58.   [19] See p. 59.
[20] Lich. Dioc. Regy., B/A/1/35, p. 251; /36, pp. 139–41; B/A/2(i)/U, pp. 288–94, 412–20; *Lich. Dioc. Ch. Cal.* (1893); *Lich. Dioc. Mag.* 1903, 38; ibid. 1904, 56; *Christ Church, West Bromwich: a history in picture, 1821–1909*, 15 (copy in W.B.L.); ex inf. the vicar of Christ Church (1969).
[21] *Lich. Dioc. Ch. Cal.* (1893; 1894); Baylis, *Christ Church*, 19.   [22] *Lich. Dioc. Ch. Cal.* (1893; 1894).
[23] Ibid. (1911); ex inf. the vicar of Christ Church (1968).
[24] Baylis, *Christ Church*, 7, 9–10; plate facing p. 81 below.
[25] Hackwood, *West Bromwich*, 95, notes this, with approval, as a 'novel feature'. A visitor to the town in 1828 thought that the frames, 'like those of St. George and another in Birmingham, will obscure the light': *The Register: Literary, Scientific, and Sporting Jnl.* (set in W.S.L.), 22 Nov. 1828.
[26] See p. 232.
[27] *Staffs. Advertiser*, 18 Dec. 1858; T.C.T. *Life's Realities*, 168.
[28] Baylis, *Christ Church*, 10, 13.
[29] For the changes of 1876 see ibid. 10, 16; *Staffs. Advertiser*, 3 May 1873, 24 Oct. 1874, 30 Dec. 1876; *Lich. Dioc. Ch. Cal.* (1878), 76. The old organ (for the purchase of which see Willett, *West Bromwich*, 118) was sold to St. Michael's R.C. Church: Baylis, *Christ Church*, 10.

surpliced choir. The original organ was replaced, and the position was changed from the west gallery to the north side of the chancel. The pews were reduced in height and their doors taken away. A new pulpit was installed in 1911.[30] The Lady chapel at the end of the north aisle was constructed in 1917.[31] The church originally had only two bells; eight more were added by public subscription in 1847 and two more as a tribute to William Gordon, the first minister, on his retirement in 1850.[32] The bells were recast and reduced to a ring of eight in 1954.[33] The lime trees along the churchyard walks were planted in 1880.[34]

The church of *HOLY TRINITY* was built by a committee in 1840–1 to serve the south-eastern part of the town. Subscribers included George Salter and William Chance, and the site was given by George Silvester.[35] An endowment of £1,000 was received from Thomas Hood and Edward Bullock, and in 1850 a grant of £200 was made from Queen Anne's Bounty.[36] The right of nominating the minister was granted by the bishop to trustees.[37] A parish was assigned out of Christ Church parish in 1842.[38] The living, at first a perpetual curacy and a vicarage from 1868, has remained in the gift of trustees (now the Peache Trustees).[39] A vicarage house was built on part of the site in 1844.[40]

In 1872 the schoolroom in Lower Trinity Street was licensed for divine service. It was used as a mission room until c. 1937.[41] Open-air services were held in the parish during Robert Thompson's time as vicar (1902–16); he was helped by Ethel Silvester, granddaughter of the donor of the site, who worked in the parish as a deaconess from 1906 to 1918.[42]

Holy Trinity Church is of brick and was designed by S. W. Dawkes in an Early English style.[43] It stands in a walled churchyard with streets on three sides and the vicarage house on the fourth. It consists of chancel, nave with galleries on three sides, and west tower; there is a small north porch near the east end, and the porches on either side of the tower were added c. 1872.[44] The chancel was burnt

down early in 1861 but was at once rebuilt.[45] The position of the organ was then changed from the chancel to the west gallery; soon after Robert Thompson's appointment as vicar in 1902 the organ was moved to the south side of the chancel, new stalls were provided, and a surpliced choir was introduced.[46] The pews, arranged in a large central block and two smaller blocks under the galleries, apparently date from 1884 when the existing 'close high-backed pews' were removed.[47]

Land for a church at Hill Top was given in 1840 by Joseph Hateley of Walsall, and the church of *ST. JAMES* there was licensed in 1842 and consecrated in 1844. Subscribers towards the cost included Lord Dartmouth and James Bagnall.[48] In 1844 a parish was formed covering the north-western part of the ancient parish.[49] The patronage of the living, at first a perpetual curacy and a vicarage from 1868, was held initially by the incumbent of All Saints', but in 1849 it was vested in the earls of Dartmouth.[50] In 1865 it was transferred to the bishop of Lichfield, who still holds it.[51] The living was endowed with £50 a year out of the impropriated tithes by Lord Dartmouth, who in 1845 also invested £300 for the insurance and repair of the church. In 1849 a further £50 a year was transferred to St. James's out of the endowment of All Saints'.[52] When the patronage was transferred to the bishop, the living was endowed with £102 a year out of the Common Fund.[53] In 1876 the benefice was endowed with £800 to provide a vicarage house.[54] A house on the corner of New Street, Hill Top, was acquired in 1891.[55] The present vicarage to the north-east of the church was built in 1963.[56]

St. Paul's, Golds Hill, which originated in a mission opened at the Golds Hill Ironworks in 1853, was in the parish of St. James until 1887.[57]

The church of St. James, designed by Robert Ebbles,[58] is of brick in a mainly Perpendicular style. There are two turrets at the west end and also a south-west tower added in 1890 to house the bell

---

[30] Baylis, *Christ Church*, 16.

[31] Ibid. 20–1.

[32] Lich. Dioc. Regy., B/A/2(i)/H, p. 560; C. Lynam, *Church Bells of the County of Stafford* (1889), 33–4; *Staffs. Advertiser*, 16 Nov. 1850. The font also was given in memory of Wm. Gordon by his daughter: inscription on font.

[33] A. E. Garbett, 'Church Bells of Staffs.' *Trans. Old Stafford Soc.* 1952–3, 11; *Christ Church, West Bromwich, Par. Mag.* May 1954 (copy in the W.B.L. copy of Baylis, *Christ Church*).

[34] Baylis, *Christ Church*, 17.

[35] *Holy Trinity Church Centenary Celebrations, 1841–1941*, 4 and loose printed sheet of building accounts (copy in W.B.L.); Lich. Dioc. Regy., B/A/2(i)/L, pp. 246–66; White, *Dir. Staffs.* (1851).

[36] Lich. Dioc. Regy., B/A/2(i)/L, pp. 244, 255; L.J.R.O., B/V/6/West Bromwich; White, *Dir. Staffs.* (1851); *Staffs. Advertiser*, 22 Dec. 1849; C. Hodgson, *Account of Augmentation of Small Livings by Governors of Bounty of Queen Anne: Supplement* (1864), pp. lxviii, lxxxvii.

[37] Lich. Dioc. Regy., B/A/2(i)/L, pp. 246–50.

[38] Ibid. pp. 382–3 (with plan); B/A/2(i)/P, pp. 166–7.

[39] White, *Dir. Staffs.* (1851); *Lich. Dioc. Ch. Cal.* (1869); *Lich. Dioc. Dir.* (1967). The trustees were first named as the Peache Trustees in *Lich. Dioc. Ch. Cal.* in 1913.

[40] White, *Dir. Staffs.* (1851); *Centenary Celebrations*, building accounts.

[41] Lich. Dioc. Regy., B/A/1/33, pp. 228–9; *Lich. Dioc. Mag.* 1884, 189; file at Holy Trinity.

[42] *Centenary Celebrations*, 5, 9, 15–16; 'Old West Bromwich', 6 Aug. 1943.

[43] *Midland Counties Herald*, 1 July 1841 (where the name is given as Dankes).

[44] *Centenary Celebrations*, 5, 12. For the bell of 1841 see ibid., building accounts; Lynam, *Church Bells of County of Stafford* (1889), 34; T. S. Jennings, *Hist. of Staffs. Bells* (priv. print. 1968), 99.

[45] *Staffs. Advertiser*, 12 Jan. 1861; *P.O. Dir. Staffs.* (1868); *Centenary Celebrations*, 4–5.

[46] *Centenary Celebrations*, 5, 15.

[47] *Lich. Dioc. Yr. Bk.* 1884, 71; *Lich. Dioc. Mag.* 1884, 189.

[48] Lich. Dioc. Regy., B/A/2(i)/N, pp. 102–8, 111–15; H.O. 129/381/4/1; White, *Dir. Staffs.* (1851); *St. James' Church, Hill Top, West Bromwich, Centenary 1942* (copy in W.B.L.).

[49] *Lond. Gaz.* 14 Sept. 1844, pp. 3221–2; docs. at All Saints', parcel 7.

[50] Lich. Dioc. Regy., B/A/1/31, pp. 14–15; B/A/2(i)/Q^A, pp. 68–71; *Lich. Dioc. Ch. Cal.* (1869).

[51] *Lond. Gaz.* 15 Sept. 1865, pp. 4461–2; *Lich. Dioc. Dir.* (1867).

[52] White, *Dir. Staffs.* (1851); Hackwood, *West Bromwich*, 95; Lich. Dioc. Regy., B/A/2(i)/Q^A, pp. 68–71; *Lond. Gaz.* 17 Aug. 1849, p. 2558; H.O. 129/381/4/1.

[53] *Lond. Gaz.* 15 Sept. 1865, pp. 4461–2.

[54] Lich. Dioc. Regy., B/A/2(i)/S, p. 117.

[55] *Lich. Dioc. Ch. Cal.* (1892), 174; Lich. Dioc. Regy., B/A/2(i)/T, p. 422.

[56] Ex inf. the vicar (1968).

[57] See p. 57.

[58] H. M. Colvin, *Biog. Dict. of Eng. Architects 1660–1840*, 188.

which had hung in a bellcot at the east end.[59] The interior is in effect a single space with a shallow sanctuary; aisles and a larger sanctuary have been created by the arrangement of the seating and other fittings. Originally there were galleries on three sides.[60] In 1890, in addition to the building of the tower, the façade was pointed in Portland cement and the vestry enlarged.[61] In 1892 the pews were replaced by chairs; sanctuary rails, a pulpit, an eagle lectern, and a font were presented; the organ was moved from the west gallery to the north side of the sanctuary; a surpliced choir was introduced and a choir vestry constructed; and generally 'the appointments of public worship' were made 'brighter and more reverent'.[62] The north and south galleries were removed in 1904, and the chairs were replaced by pews.[63] In the earlier 1960s the screen, erected in 1901, was moved to create a side chapel on the north and the sanctuary was refurnished.[64] By the late 1960s a modern organ had been installed.

By 1842, fifteen years before the building of the church of ST. PETER in Whitehall Road, there was a need for a church at Greets Green in Christ Church parish. John Bagnall & Sons had offered a site, but it proved impossible to raise enough money for building and endowment.[65] A room at Greets Green was hired for services in 1851.[66] St. Peter's, begun in 1857 on a site given by Sir Horace St. Paul, Bt., and Edward Jones, was consecrated in 1858. The living was granted a capital endowment of £1,000 from Queen Anne's Bounty.[67] A parish was assigned out of Christ Church parish in 1861.[68] The living, at first a perpetual curacy and a vicarage from 1868, has remained in the gift of the bishop of Lichfield.[69] Land given in 1856 as the site for the minister's house was used to extend the churchyard in 1882,[70] and the vicarage house was in fact in Old Meeting Street by the 1880s; the vicar was living in Fisher Street by the mid 1890s.[71] A new house in Whitehall Road north of the church was completed in 1898; it was largely paid for by Henry Jesson, vicar 1893–1910, who had served his first curacy in the parish.[72]

A mission of St. Matthew was being served from St. Peter's c. 1870.[73] It was apparently replaced by a mission room which was opened in 1885 'amid the poorest of the population' with the result that many were 'brought to church who had never previously attended any place of worship'; it was in turn replaced by a new room in 1886.[74] A mission chapel of St. Thomas was opened in 1874 in a former Methodist chapel and remained in use until c. 1885.[75]

The church of St. Peter, designed by Johnson & Son of Lichfield,[76] is of stone in a Decorated style and consists of chancel, aisled and clerestoried nave with south porch, and west tower. The churchyard was extended in 1881, 1882, and 1891.[77]

The church of ST. PAUL, Golds Hill, originated in a mission centre started at the Golds Hill Ironworks of John Bagnall & Sons in St. James's parish in 1853 and served by the firm's chaplain. It was replaced by the school which was opened at the works in 1855 and used as a chapel on Sundays 'for the working classes and others employed on the works'; the architect was S. W. Dawkes.[78] By 1868 the chapel was known as the Golds Hill Iron Works Episcopal Chapel.[79] It was replaced by St. Paul's Church which was built in Bagnall Street in 1881–2[80] and consecrated in 1886.[81] In 1887 a parish of St. Paul was assigned out of St. James's.[82] The patronage of the vicarage was vested in the vicar of St. James's,[83] but in 1923 he exchanged it for the patronage of St. John's, Tipton, with the vicar of St. Martin's, Tipton, in order to preserve the different ecclesiastical traditions of each church—'Reformed principles' in the case of St. Paul's.[84] The vicar of St. Martin's remains the patron.[85] With the building of St. Paul's the mission centre of 1853 was turned into a house for the curate-in-charge.[86] The present vicarage house to the east of the church dates from 1892.[87] The parish hall dates from 1898.[88]

A mission room was opened in Brickhouse Lane in 1889. At that time there was also a group of mission workers under a lay evangelist holding open-air and indoor services every night 'in a distant and

[59] Lich. Dioc. Mag. 1890, 148; Lich. Dioc. Ch. Cal. (1891), 160; Hackwood, West Bromwich, 95; Centenary 1942.   [60] Lich. Dioc. Regy., B/A/2(i)/N, p. 106.
[61] Lich. Dioc. Mag. 1890, 148; Lich. Dioc. Ch. Cal. (1891), 160; Hackwood, West Bromwich, 95.
[62] Lich. Dioc. Mag. 1893, 11; Hackwood, West Bromwich, 95–6.
[63] L.J.R.O., B/C/12, West Bromwich, St. James, 1903 and 1904; Lich. Dioc. Regy., B/A/1/36, pp. 143–4. For the interior of the church before the alterations see plan in B/C/12, West Bromwich, St. James, 1903, and a picture hanging at the back of the church (in 1968).
[64] B/C/12, West Bromwich, St. James, 1901, 1961; plate on screen; plate of 1965 on one of the reading desks.
[65] 1st Rep. Com. Midland Mining, S. Staffs. [508], p. 15, H.C. (1843), xiii.   [66] H.O. 129/381/3/1.
[67] Lich. Dioc. Regy. B/A/2(i)/Q, pp. 176–86; Staffs. Advertiser, 18 Apr. 1857; Annals of Dioc. of Lichfield: Supplement to Lich. Dioc. Ch. Cal. (1859), 65; C. Hodgson, Account of Augmentation of Small Livings by Governors of Bounty of Queen Anne: Supplement (1864), p. lxxxviii.
[68] Lond. Gaz. 3 May 1861, pp. 1892–3.
[69] Lich. Dioc. Ch. Cal. (1861); Lich. Dioc. Dir. (1967).
[70] Lich. Dioc. Regy., B/A/2(i)/S, p. 437. A new vicarage site was bought in 1882: Lich. Dioc. Ch. Cal. (1883), 74.
[71] Kelly's Dir. Staffs. (1884; 1892; 1896); O.S. Map 1/2,500, Staffs. LXVIII. 6 (1890 edn.).
[72] Lich. Dioc. Mag. 1898, 74–5; Kelly's Dir. Staffs. (1900); tablet in church.
[73] Lich. Dioc. Ch. Cal. (1871). It appears as St. Matthias in the edns. for 1871 and 1872.

[74] Ibid. (1886), 130; Lich. Dioc. Yr. Bk. 1885, 43, 101; Lich. Dioc. Mag. 1887, 35. St. Peter's parish mission room disappears from the Lich. Dioc. Dir. after the edn. of 1957.
[75] Lich. Dioc. Ch. Cal. (1875), 77; ibid. (1886); Lich. Dioc. Regy., B/A/1/33, p. 324.
[76] Staffs. Advertiser, 18 Apr. 1857.
[77] Lich. Dioc. Ch. Cal. (1882), 191; ibid. (1883), 74; Lich. Dioc. Regy., B/A/2(i)/T, pp. 408–26.
[78] St. Paul's Bapt. Reg. 1853–1950 (first entry July 1853 and note on fly-leaf stating that the first communion was held in Sept.); W.B.L., undated plan of West Bromwich, sheet 13; Staffs. Advertiser, 13 Jan. 1855; W. H. Dix & Co. Dir. of Birmingham and six miles round (1858); P.O. Dir. Staffs. (1860); Mary Willett, John Nock Bagnall (1885), 14, 24 (mentioning mealtime services); Lich. Dioc. Mag. 1899, 29; below p. 78.
[79] P.O. Dir. Staffs. (1868).
[80] St. Paul's Bapt. Reg. 1853–1950 (entries for 1882 and notes at end); Staffs. Advertiser (S. Staffs. edn.), 8 July 1882.
[81] Lich. Dioc. Mag. 1886, 172; Lich. Dioc. Ch. Cal. (1887), 144; Lich. Dioc. Regy., B/A/2(i)/T, p. 137.
[82] Lond. Gaz. 20 May 1887, p. 2780.
[83] Lich. Dioc. Regy., B/A/1/35, p. 114.
[84] Lond. Gaz. 2 Feb. 1923, pp. 773–4; 'Old West Bromwich', 2 and 9 Feb. 1945.   [85] Lich. Dioc. Dir. (1967).
[86] 'Old West Bromwich', 26 Jan. 1945.
[87] Lich. Dioc. Regy., B/A/2(i)/T, p. 478; foundation-stone dated 7 Oct. 1892.
[88] Foundation-stone dated 6 June 1898.

hitherto neglected part of the parish'.[89] A new mission room, dedicated to St. Mary, was built in Brickhouse Lane in 1892. It was leased to Steel Parts Ltd. in 1935 and sold to the firm in 1937.[90]

The church of St. Paul, which is not orientated,[91] is of brick with stone dressings. It consists of chancel with 'south' organ transept and 'north' vestry, and nave with 'south' porch; there is a bellcot with a bell over the junction of the chancel and nave. The furnishings and part of the structure were brought from Capponfields in Bilston. Bagnalls had built a chapel there for their workers in the 1850s; when that was closed the vicar of St. James's, West Bromwich, bought the building, and much of it was transported to Golds Hill for St. Paul's.[92]

The church of ST. JOHN THE EVANGELIST in Sams Lane originated in St. John's mission in Christ Church parish which was started in the 1860s at Newhall Street National School.[93] The church was built in 1876–8 on a site given by W. H. Dawes of the Bromford Ironworks.[94] A parish was assigned out of Christ Church parish in 1879,[95] and in 1880 the living was endowed with an income of £200 a year.[96] The first presentation to the vicarage was made by the vicar of Christ Church; the patronage then passed to the bishop of Lichfield.[97] The church ceased to be used in 1960 and was demolished in 1963.[98] In 1966 the parish was reorganized, the benefice being united with that of the Good Shepherd. A new church, dedicated to the Good Shepherd with St. John Evangelist, was opened in Lyttleton Street in 1968.[99] A vicarage house was built behind the church in 1882;[1] it too has been demolished.

A mission chapel dedicated to the Good Shepherd was opened in Ault Street in 1880.[2] Much was done for the mission by N. T. Langley, vicar of St. John's 1888–1900, who also enlarged St. John's.[3] In addition he was active in social work. In 1889 he opened the Young Men's Club and Gymnasium at the former Newhall Street school; despite its entirely working-class membership and the vicar's in-

sistence that there should be no subscription, the club was self-supporting. In 1893 Langley was also holding for the young men of the parish an institute on Wednesday nights, a social club on Saturdays, and a Bible class at the vicarage on Sunday afternoons.[4]

The former church of St. John the Evangelist, a brick building designed in the Early English style by E. J. Etwall of West Bromwich, at first consisted only of chancel, nave, and south aisle. A north aisle was built in 1892, and in 1903 transepts, a vestry, and an organ chamber were added.[5]

The church of ST. ANDREW in Old Meeting Street was built in 1867 on a site given by Thomas Jesson and was used both as a mission church served from All Saints' and as a National school.[6] In 1877 the building became a church only.[7] A new church in Dudley Street was consecrated in 1925.[8] In 1879 a parish was formed out of the parishes of All Saints, Christ Church, St. James, and St. Peter.[9] In 1880 it was endowed out of the Common Fund with an income of £200 a year.[10] The patronage of the vicarage has remained with the vicar of All Saints'.[11] The vicarage house in Old Meeting Street, replacing one to the north on the corner of Bilhay Lane, dates from 1894; it was designed by Wood & Kendrick of West Bromwich. The site was given by Henry Jesson, a former curate of St. Andrew's.[12] When the new parish was created the mission church of St. Michael in Wood Lane was included in it.[13]

The first church of St. Andrew was a plain brick building designed by Somers Clarke the younger.[14] The new church in Dudley Street was designed by Wood & Kendrick;[15] it is of brick and consists of nave and chancel. The orientation is reversed. Although it was consecrated in 1925, it was not completed until 1940.[16]

The church of ST. MICHAEL AND ALL ANGELS in Bull Lane originated in the wooden mission chapel of St. Michael erected in Wood Lane apparently in 1872.[17] It was served from All

[89] Lich. Dioc. Ch. Cal. (1890), 160.
[90] Ibid. (1893), 133, 195; file at St. Paul's; Staffs. Advertiser (S. Staffs. edn.), 4 June, 13 Aug. 1892. In 1968 the building still stood as part of the factory.
[91] Liturgical 'east' is in fact north-west.
[92] Staffs. Advertiser (S. Staffs. edn.), 8 July 1882; Lich. Dioc. Mag. 1882, 124.
[93] H. Baylis, Christ Church, West Bromwich, 1829–1929 (West Bromwich; n.d. but published for centenary), 15; Lich. Dioc. Ch. Cal. (1871); Lich. Dioc. Mag. 1896, 13.
[94] Staffs. Advertiser, 1 Jan. 1876; ibid. (S. Staffs. edn.), 27 Apr. 1878; Lich. Dioc. Regy., B/A/2(i)/S, pp. 175, 267–73; Lich. Dioc. Ch. Cal. (1878), 76; (1879), 75; Midland Chron. & Free Press, 17 May 1963.
[95] Lond. Gaz. 4 Mar. 1879, pp. 1870–1.
[96] Ibid. 11 June 1880, p. 3437.
[97] Lich. Dioc. Regy., B/A/2(i)/S, pp. 267–73; B/A/1/34, p. 90; B/A/1/35, p. 12.
[98] Midland Chron. & Free Press, 17 May 1963.
[99] See p. 59. The vicar of the Good Shepherd acted as priest-in-charge of St. John's from 1960: ex inf. the vicar of the Good Shepherd with St. John Evangelist (1968).
[1] Lich. Dioc. Ch. Cal. (1883), 74; Lich. Dioc. Regy., B/A/2(i)/S, pp. 563, 587; O.S. Map 1/500, Staffs. LXVIII. 10. 23.
[2] See p. 59.
[3] Lich. Dioc. Mag. 1900, 198; Lich. Dioc. Regy., B/A/1/35, p. 140; B/A/1/36, p. 251.
[4] Lich. Dioc. Mag. 1893, 45–6; 1896, 13; Lich. Dioc. Ch. Cal. (1890), 160; Hackwood, West Bromwich, 96.
[5] Kelly's Dir. Staffs. (1880; 1904); Lich. Dioc. Mag.

1890, 148–9; 1891, 161; 1892, 207; 1902, 90, 200, 222; Lich. Dioc. Ch. Cal. (1893), 195. The bell from St. John's has been rehung at the new church of the Good Shepherd with St. John: plaque in church; C. Lynam, Church Bells of the County of Stafford (1889), 34.
[6] Staffs. Advertiser, 7 Dec. 1867; Lich. Dioc. Ch. Cal. (1868), 96; (1869), 76; (1871), 156; Lich. Dioc. Regy., B/A/2(i)/S, pp. 255–60; West Bromwich Old Church Par. Mag. Apr. 1879; below p. 79.
[7] West Bromwich Old Church Par. Mag. Dec. 1876; ibid. May 1877.
[8] Lich. Dioc. Yr. Bk. 1912, 209; 1913, 217; 1914, 96; 1915, 129; Lich. Dioc. Regy., B/A/2(i)/W, pp. 200–3, 212.
[9] Lond. Gaz. 11 Mar. 1879, pp. 2044–5.
[10] Lich. Dioc. Regy., B/A/2(i)/S, p. 359.
[11] Ibid. B/A/1/34, pp. 89–90; Lich. Dioc. Dir. (1967).
[12] Lich. Dioc. Mag. 1894, 185; Lich. Dioc. Regy., B/A/2(i)/T, p. 519; Hackwood, West Bromwich, 96; O.S. Map 1/2,500, Staffs. LXVIII. 6 (1890 edn.). Jesson was then vicar of St. Peter's: see above p. 57.
[13] See p. 59.
[14] Staffs. Advertiser, 7 Dec. 1867.
[15] Inscription on foundation-stone.
[16] Inscription on Dudley St. front; list of vicars inside the church.
[17] West Bromwich Old Church Par. Mag. Aug. 1874; ibid. June 1879; Willett, West Bromwich, 76; Lich. Dioc. Mag. 1881, 47. It was evidently in 1872 that St. Michael's mission room in Frederick St. was renamed St. Chad's: see above p. 53, which also mentions an earlier St. Michael's mission in John St.

Saints' until its transfer to the new parish of St. Andrew in 1879.[18] The new church was opened in 1881. Designed by Wood & Kendrick of West Bromwich, it consisted of chancel, nave, sacristy, baptistery, and choir vestry; there was a school-room attached. Nearly the whole cost was met by Henry Jesson, who was working as curate-in-charge of that part of St. Andrew's parish without any stipend.[19] St. Michael's was assigned a conventional district in 1903, but in 1911 the district was abolished and the church again became the responsibility of St. Andrew's.[20] It was closed in 1953[21] and was demolished in the earlier 1970s.

The church of *ST. PHILIP* originated in St. Philip's Mission Room, a former oil warehouse in Pitt Street in Christ Church parish, licensed in 1874.[22] It was replaced in 1892 by St. Philip's Church on a site in Beeches Road given by Lord Dartmouth.[23] That building was in turn replaced by the present church, which was built to the east of it in 1898–9.[24] The 1892 church became a school and later the parish hall.[25] A new parish of St. Philip was assigned out of Christ Church parish in 1900.[26] The first nomination to the vicarage was made by the vicar of Christ Church, but the patronage has since been held by the bishop of Lichfield.[27] By 1967 the congregation was largely West Indian.[28] The vicarage house in Beeches Road was bought in 1939 to replace another house in the same road.[29]

St. Philip's Church is of red brick with terracotta dressings and was designed in a Gothic style by Wood & Kendrick. When opened in 1899 it consisted of nave, aisles, 'morning chapel', and vestries.[30] In 1913–14 the chancel, the Lady chapel, and new vestries were built.[31] The nave pillars have carvings on the capitals in memory of parishioners named on near-by wall plaques.

In 1880 a mission chapel dedicated to *THE GOOD SHEPHERD* was built in Ault Street in St. John's parish.[32] An endowment was established in 1898 to produce a stipend for a curate to serve the district,[33] and a new chapel in Spon Lane was licensed in 1902.[34] In 1908 a conventional district was formed.[35] A church was built on a site adjoining the chapel in 1908–9. Part of the cost was met by

£835 left by Mary Smith Dorsett (d. 1878) towards the building and endowing of a new evangelical church in West Bromwich; other contributors included Chance Brothers & Co. Ltd. and members of the Chance family.[36] The 1902 chapel then became the parish hall.[37]

A parish was formed in 1910 out of St. John's and Holy Trinity parishes.[38] The patronage of the vicarage was vested in the bishop of Lichfield and the patrons of Holy Trinity.[39] In 1966 the parish was reconstituted to include the whole of St. John's and that part of the Good Shepherd parish west of Spon Lane; the remainder of the Good Shepherd parish passed back to Holy Trinity parish. A new benefice of the Good Shepherd with St. John was created and is in the gift of the bishop.[40] A new parish church was consecrated in 1968,[41] and the church and parish hall in Spon Lane were subsequently demolished. The vicarage house in Johnston Street dating from 1955[42] was replaced in the early 1970s by a new house adjoining the church.

The church of the Good Shepherd was of brick with stone and terracotta dressings and was specially designed to withstand 'the fumes and smoke which are prevalent in the district'. It consisted of chancel with vestry and organ chamber, aisled and clerestoried nave, a south-east turret apparently with a bell, and porches facing Spon Lane on either side of a baptistery; the orientation was reversed. It was designed by Wood & Kendrick.[43] The church of the Good Shepherd with St. John Evangelist in Lyttleton Street was built in 1967–8 to the plans of the John Madin Design Group of Edgbaston. It is of blue brick in a modern style, and the orientation is reversed. A hall and other rooms form part of the same building.

A mission church of *ST. FRANCIS OF ASSISI* in Friar Park Road was licensed in 1931.[44] It was part of the parish of St. Paul, Wood Green, Wednesbury, to which the Friar Park area had been transferred from All Saints' parish in 1875.[45] The conventional district of St. Francis was formed in 1931 out of the parishes of All Saints, West Bromwich, and St. Paul, Wood Green, with a curate-in-charge appointed by the bishop.[46] The district became a

[18] *West Bromwich Old Church Par. Mag.* June 1879.
[19] Lich. Dioc. Regy., B/A/1/34, p. 180; *Lich. Dioc. Mag.* 1881, 47; *Lich. Dioc. Ch. Cal.* (1882), 81; *Lich. Dioc. Yr. Bk.* 1881, 144.
[20] Lich. Dioc. Regy., B/A/1/36, pp. 133–5; *Lich. Dioc. Ch. Cal.* (1904; 1910); ex inf. the vicar of St. Andrew's (1970).   [21] Ex inf. the vicar of St. Andrew's.
[22] Lich. Dioc. Regy., B/A/1/33, p. 312; *Lich. Dioc. Ch. Cal.* (1875); *Lich. Dioc. Mag.* 1883, 60. E. H. Daniels, *Short Hist. of St. Philip's Church, West Bromwich,* 1–2 (copy in W.B.L.), gives the date of establishment as 1872.
[23] Daniels, *St. Philip's Church,* 1–2; *Staffs. Advertiser,* 2 Jan. 1892; S.R.O., D.564/8/1/23/Feb. 1888. The Pitt St. church was renamed St. Stephen's: see above p. 55.
[24] Daniels, *St. Philip's Church,* 2; *Lich. Dioc. Mag.* 1898, 28–9, 75; Lich. Dioc. Regy., B/A/2(i)/U, pp. 389–95.
[25] *Lich. Dioc. Mag.* 1900, 168; Daniels, *St. Philip's Church,* 1.   [26] *Lond. Gaz.* 10 July 1900, pp. 4265–6.
[27] Lich. Dioc. Regy., B/A/1/36, pp. 195–204, 211; ibid./40, p. 304; *Lich. Dioc. Dir.* (1967).
[28] 'By 1967 the 11 a.m. congregation was two-thirds Caribbean and the Sunday School 80 per cent so': Daniels, *St. Philip's Church,* 2.
[29] Daniels, *St. Philip's Church,* 1; Lich. Dioc. Regy., B/A/2(i)/W, pp. 673–4. After Wm. Solly, vicar 1900–36, resigned, he continued to live in Beeches Rd. until his death in 1939; the new vicar lived in Nicholls St. until the purchase of the present vicarage.

[30] Daniels, *St. Philip's Church,* 3; Lich. Dioc. Regy., B/A/2(i)/U, pp. 389–95.
[31] Daniels, *St. Philip's Church,* 3; Lich. Dioc. Regy., B/A/1/37, p. 210; B/A/2(i)/V, pp. 446–9.
[32] Lich. Dioc. Regy., B/A/1/34, p. 137; *Lich. Dioc. Ch. Cal.* (1881), 72. For an earlier mission in Ault St. see above p. 55.
[33] *Lich. Dioc. Mag.* 1898, 61; 1900, 198.
[34] Lich. Dioc. Regy., B/A/1/36, p. 87; B/A/2(i)/U, p. 346; *Lich. Dioc. Mag.* 1900, 198. The foundation-stone was dated 1901.
[35] Lich. Dioc. Regy., B/A/1/37, pp. 68–70.
[36] *Free Press,* 10 Oct. 1909; foundation-stone dated 1908; Char. Com. files.
[37] Ex inf. the vicar of the Good Shepherd with St. John (1968).
[38] *Lond. Gaz.* 14 Oct. 1914, pp. 7228–9.
[39] Lich. Dioc. Regy., B/A/1/37, pp. 155–61; /38, p. 34.
[40] Ibid./42, p. 405.
[41] Lich. Dioc. Regy., B/A/2(i)/Y, pp. 73–7.
[42] Ex inf. the vicar (1968); Lich. Dioc. Regy., B/A/2(i)/Y, p. 74.
[43] *Free Press,* 10 Oct. 1909; *Midland Chron. & Free Press,* 3 Apr. 1964. A bell is mentioned in the consecration deed: L.J.R.O., B/A/2(i)/V, pp. 220–4.
[44] Lich. Dioc. Regy., B/A/1/39, pp. 367–8.
[45] *West Bromwich Old Church Par. Mag.* Apr. 1875.
[46] Lich. Dioc. Regy., B/A/1/39, pp. 369–71, 376–7.

parish in 1937 with the bishop as patron of the vicarage; the living was endowed out of bequests by Henry Marson and his sister Sarah Anne, both of Tettenhall.[47] A new church at the junction of Free-man and Keir Roads was licensed in 1940 and consecrated in 1941; it had accommodation for some 500 people. The cost was met from the Marson Bequest.[48] The vicarage house is in Freeman Road and adjoins the church.

The church of St. Francis of Assisi, designed in a Romanesque style by Harvey & Wicks of Birmingham,[49] is of brick faced with stone on the exterior. It consists of chancel with apsidal sanctuary, aisled nave, west tower, and north and south porches. A Lady chapel leads out of the north aisle, and there is a chapel at the east end of the south aisle furnished by the Friar Park British Legion in memory of those killed in the First World War.[50]

The mission church of THE ASCENSION in Walsall Road, Stone Cross, in the parish of St. Francis was built in 1938 on land given by Lord Dartmouth.[51] A conventional district was formed in 1942 under a curate-in-charge appointed by the bishop.[52] It lasted until 1958 when the building was found to be in a bad state and was given up.[53] The site reverted to Lord Dartmouth, who sold it in 1961 to the corporation.[54]

There are now two churches in those parts of Hamstead and the Delves which were added to the borough of West Bromwich in the 20th century. They are respectively the church of ST. BERNARD and the mission church of THE ANNUNCIATION. Hamstead has been in the diocese of Birmingham since 1905.

Hamstead was originally in Handsworth parish, and an iron mission church of St. Paul at the corner of Hamstead Lane and Spouthouse Lane (in that part of Hamstead now in the borough of West Bromwich) was opened from St. Mary's, Handsworth, c. 1870. It was replaced in 1892 by St. Paul's Church in Walsall Road (in that part of Hamstead now in the city of Birmingham). St. Paul's became a parish church in 1894 and eventually opened missions of its own.[55] The village institute in what is now the West Bromwich part of Hamstead was licensed for worship from c. 1919 to c. 1926.[56] In 1946 a site for a church was bought at the junction of Broome Avenue and Greenfield Road on the projected Tanhouse estate, but the

church of St. Bernard was not built there until 1961–2. Meanwhile services were held at the community centre on the Tanhouse estate from 1956. From 1958 the area was in the charge of a stipendiary curate, and since 1963 it has been the centre of a statutory district under a vicar collated by the bishop of Birmingham.[57] The church, which was also used as a hall, was incorporated in the new church and community centre designed by John Sharpe and dedicated in 1973.[58] The vicarage house is in Hamstead Road.

The part of the Delves formerly in Wednesbury and now in West Bromwich is in the parish of St. Gabriel, Fullbrook, in Walsall. The mission church of the Annunciation on the corner of Redwood Road and Thorncroft Way on the Yew Tree estate was dedicated in 1958. Designed by Hickton, Madeley & Salt,[59] it is of brick and consists of a hall, a sanctuary which can be shut off, and rooms along the north side. The priest-in-charge lives on the estate.

ROMAN CATHOLICISM. A Puritan survey of Staffordshire in 1604 reported 'many popish' in West Bromwich.[60] It was stated in 1607 that the wife of Sir William Whorwood of Sandwell and her daughters were 'notable recusants' and that Sir William's association with recusants led to his 'neither caring for his credit nor conscience'.[61] Thomas Brome Whorwood, who lived at Sandwell in the late 17th century, was married to a Roman Catholic, and their son Thomas was brought up in his mother's religion.[62] The Riders, however, were the main Roman Catholic family.[63] Simon Rider, who settled in West Bromwich in 1580, occurs as a recusant in 1593–4.[64] When in 1598 officers came to seize his forfeited goods, they were forcibly resisted by a crowd of 30.[65] Riders recur as papists until the later 18th century.[66] There is a tradition that an upper room at the back of the Riders' house, later known as Dunkirk Hall, was used as a chapel; there is also said to have been a priest's hiding hole, but it seems likely that the space was in fact made for a stairway.[67]

Five papists were reported in 1630[68] and 22 in 1657.[69] In 1705 the minister listed four families, all of them landless and 'of small ability'.[70] Only one papist registered an estate in 1715, a bridle-buckle maker with a freehold house.[71] The community

[47] B/A/1/40, pp. 374–5; Lond. Gaz. 11 June 1937, pp. 3744–5; Char. Com. files.
[48] B/A/1/41, pp. 12–13; B/A/2(i)/X, pp. 4, 7–11; inscription on font.
[49] Ex inf. the vicar (1968).   [50] Tablet in chapel.
[51] Lich. Dioc. Regy., B/A/1/40, pp. 387–8; Char. Com. files.
[52] B/A/1/41, pp. 103–5, 114–15.
[53] St. Francis of Assisi Par. Mag., autumn 1958.
[54] Char. Com. files.
[55] Lich. Dioc. Ch. Cal. (1871); ibid. (1875), the first edn. to call it St. Paul's; ex inf. the vicar of St. Bernard's (1970); V.C.H. Warws. vii. 394 (which begins its account only in 1886); Lich. Dioc. Regy., B/A/1/35, pp. 344–8.
[56] Birm. Dioc. Kal. (1919; 1926–7).
[57] Ex inf. the vicar (1970); Birm. Dioc. Regy., Bp.'s Act Bk. 2, pp. 251, 277, 279; Bp.'s Act Reg. 1960, pt. ii, pp. 38, 51–2; ibid. 1966, p. 197; Lond. Gaz. 25 Oct. 1963, p. 8769; Birm. Dioc. Dir. (1970–71).
[58] Evening Mail, 16 Apr. 1973.
[59] Inscription on west front.
[60] S.H.C. 1915, 309.   [61] C 2/Jas.I/A 5/37.

[62] V.C.H. Bucks. iii. 348; T. Fortescue, Lord Clermont, Sir John Fortescue, Knight, his Life, Works, and Family Hist. ii. (priv. print. 1869), 292–3; above p. 18. An early-18th-century reference to the Sheltons, lords of the manor, as 'Romanists' (S.R.O., D.(W.)1778/V/701, J. Meres to Lord Dartmouth, n.d.) may result from a confusion with the Whorwoods.
[63] See pp. 21–2.
[64] Cath. Rec. Soc. lvii. 150.   [65] S.H.C. 1935, 41.
[66] Cath. Rec. Soc. liii. 333; S.R.O., D. 1287/9/10, return of Staffs. papists 12 Mar. 1629/30; L.J.R.O., B/V/1/55, p. 33; S.H.C. 4th ser. ii. 88–9; Staffs. Cath. Hist. v. 23; vii. 29; xiii. 47–8.
[67] Reeves, West Bromwich, 49–50; A. Fea, Secret Chambers and Hiding Places, 289; 'Old West Bromwich', 15 Sept. 1944.
[68] S.R.O., D. 1287/9/10, return of Staffs. papists 12 Mar. 1629/30.
[69] S.H.C. 4th ser. ii. 88–9.
[70] Staffs. Cath. Hist. xiii. 47–8.
[71] E. E. Estcourt and J. O. Payne, Eng. Catholic Nonjurors of 1715, 247.

reported by the minister in 1767 consisted of two carpenters, a nailer, and two labourers; one of the latter was an Irish immigrant. Most of them were married to Protestants, and in one case the children were Protestants too. Five men and a woman, formerly papists, had conformed to the Church of England.[72]

In the early 19th century the few Catholics in West Bromwich were served from the mission at Bloxwich and later from that at Walsall.[73] After the opening of the church at Walsall in 1827 Francis Martyn, the priest who ran the Bloxwich and Walsall missions, was able to devote more attention to West Bromwich. He began to visit a house there every week to instruct the children of the family, but non-Catholics too proved eager to attend. He therefore started a regular course of instruction.[74] The congregation worshipped for a time in a Protestant nonconformist chapel which they rented.[75] A site for a church was bought in 1830[76] and the foundation-stone laid the same year.[77] The church was opened in 1832.[78] It was dedicated to St. Michael and the Holy Angels and stood in St. Michael Street. Designed by Joseph Ireland, it was in an Early English style with a turret at each corner.[79] Over a third of the cost was met by George Spencer, who became the first resident priest in 1832.[80] He was the youngest son of the 2nd Earl Spencer and was formerly in Anglican orders.[81]

The area for which Spencer was responsible included Oldbury, Tipton, and Dudley as well as West Bromwich, and numbers increased rapidly. In 1833 110 people were confirmed at St. Michael's, and 70 of them were converts. The number of communicants was given in 1834 as 120.[82] On Census Sunday 1851 500 people heard mass at St. Michael's.[83] There was a school in St. Michael Street by 1834.[84] From c. 1850 there was a convent of Sisters of Charity of St. Paul near the church. The nuns remained until c. 1853 and ran the church school and also a girls' boarding school.[85] In 1877 the mission was still large, extending 'from Handsworth to Dudley Port and from Spon Lane almost to Perry Barr'. The priest, J. J. Daly, reported a Roman Catholic population of 900, but attendance at mass was irregular, partly because of the size of the mission. Most of the congregation were poor and illiterate, and drunkenness was rife. Daly described 'the character of the place and the social tone of the whole district' as 'antagonistic to the Church'.[86]

Daly rebuilt the church in 1875–7 on the corner of High Street and St. Michael Street as a memorial to George Spencer. He raised a third of the cost in New York in 1873–4. Designed in an Early English style by Dunn & Hansom of Newcastle-upon-Tyne, the church is of Birmingham brick with Bath stone dressings.[87] It consists of sanctuary flanked by side chapels, aisled nave, and sacristy; there is an organ gallery at the west end. The south-west tower and spire, of Ruabon brick and Hollington stone, were added in 1911; the architect was Edmund Kirby.[88] The church was consecrated in 1917.[89] The presbytery, which seems to date from about the time of the rebuilding of the church,[90] adjoins it on the north.

The Roman Catholic population of St. Michael's parish in 1967 was 1,500,[91] but the parish no longer covered the whole of West Bromwich. A mass centre served from St. Michael's was started at the Stone Cross Hotel in 1948, and a church, used also as a hall, was opened in Hall Green Road in 1951.[92] A resident priest was appointed in 1953, and the parish of Holy Cross was formed the following year. The Roman Catholic population in 1967 was 1,740. The present church was opened in 1968. Designed by L. Brocki, it is a cruciform building of brick. The high altar is at the crossing, the sacristy in the eastern arm, and the seating for the congregation in the other three arms. There is an open-sided belfry over the crossing. The church stands in a large open space with the presbytery to the east.

A mass centre served from Stone Cross was started at the Delves Inn for the Delves and Yew Tree district in 1954. It was replaced in 1959 by the church of St. Joseph in Birchfield Way, a brick building designed by J. T. Lynch of Brierley Hill.[93]

PROTESTANT NONCONFORMITY. ASSEMBLIES OF GOD. Bethel temple in Gads Lane dates

[72] *Staffs. Cath. Hist.* vii. 29–30.
[73] B.A.A., R. 83 and 145, giving West Bromwich baptisms from 1822; *Laity's Dir.* (1832), 23.
[74] 'Catholic Chapels in Staffs.' *Cath. Mag.* v (1834; reprinted in *Staffs. Cath. Hist.* xiv), 312–13; *Laity's Dir.* (1832), 23.
[75] Hackwood, *West Bromwich*, 45; B. W. Kelly, *Historical Notes on Eng. Catholic Missions*, 422.
[76] *Cath. Mag.* v. 313; B.A.A. 12 July 1830, account book for West Bromwich Chapel 1830–3; Ed. 7/112/West Bromwich/19.
[77] B.A.A. 28 July 1830, copy of inscription on foundation stone.
[78] *Cath. Mag.* v. 313; Hackwood, *West Bromwich*, 45.
[79] *Cath. Mag.* v. 313; Hackwood, *West Bromwich*, 45; H. M. Colvin, *Biog. Dict. of Eng. Architects, 1660–1840*, 308; B.A.A. 12 July 1830, account book; White, *Dir. Staffs.* (1851). For the site of the church see 'Old West Bromwich', 12 Apr. 1946; Peacock & Cottrell, Map of West Bromwich (1857).
[80] B.A.A. 12 July 1830, account book; 7 Feb. 1831, statement of account; 9 Aug. 1832, accounts; *Cath. Mag.* v. 313; *Staffs. Advertiser*, 1 Dec. 1832.
[81] J. Gillow, *Bibliographical Dict. of Eng. Catholics*, v. 519; Hackwood, *West Bromwich*, 45.
[82] *Cath. Mag.* v. 313.
[83] H.O. 129/381/3/1. Dudley then had its own church, dating from 1835. [84] See p. 76.
[85] White, *Dir. Staffs.* (1851); G. V. Hudson, *Mother Geneviève Dupuis*, 150; 'Old West Bromwich', 12 Apr. 1946. The convent occurs in *Cath. Dir.* from 1851 to 1853.
[86] B.A.A. 12 Aug. 1877, visitation schedule and statistics.
[87] Hackwood, *West Bromwich*, 45–6; *Kelly's Dir. Staffs.* (1880); *Cath. Dir. of Province of Birm.* (1915), 62; *Staffs. Advertiser*, 9 Oct. 1875, 24 Mar. 1877; B.A.A. 12 Aug. 1877, visitation schedule and statistics. The organ was bought from Christ Church: see above p. 55 n. 29.
[88] *Kelly's Dir. Staffs.* (1912); ex inf. Mr. E. H. Hubbard (1970).
[89] *Cath. Dir. of Province of Birm.* (1918), 251–2.
[90] 'Old West Bromwich', 12 Apr. 1946. Dr. Edw. Gerrard, the last occupant of the house which preceded the presbytery, seems to have left it between 1872 and 1876: ibid.; *P.O. Dir. Staffs.* (1872) (1876).
[91] *Cath. Dir. of Archdioc. of Birm.* (1968).
[92] The rest of this para. is based on ibid. (1949); (1951), 191; (1953); (1954), 208–9; *West Bromwich News*, 4 Jan. 1968; plans at Archbishop's House, St. Chad's Cathedral, Birmingham; inf. from Mr. G. C. W. Jones of West Bromwich (1969).
[93] *Cath. Dir. of Archdioc. of Birm.* (1954), 209; (1960), 194–5.

from 1930.[94] Bethel church in Marsh Lane, Stone Cross, existed by the late 1960s.[95] By then there was also a Pentecostal church in Tanhouse Lane, Hamstead.[96]

BAPTISTS. The Baptist cause in West Bromwich was founded in 1796 to counter the Antinomians.[97] Providence chapel in Sandwell Road (also known as the Old Baptist Meeting) was opened in 1810.[98] By 1817 it was affiliated to the Midland Association of Baptist Churches, and had a membership of 43. The burial ground attached to it was presented by George Cutler, and the mortgage on the chapel was paid off by Mrs. Benjamin Cutler. There was already a Sunday school before the building of the chapel. The congregation at first belonged to the Particular Baptist Church, 'but it gradually sank into hyper-Calvinism and varied its course only to reach occasionally the lower and darker depth of Antinomianism'. On Census Sunday 1851 75 people attended the chapel in the morning and 150 in the evening.[99]

Meanwhile 'a few who mourned over the scene of disorder and decay', including the minister, seceded c. 1834. At first services were held in a private house, but in 1835 Bethel chapel was built at the west end of Danks Hill (the later Dartmouth Street). The members of the church numbered 25 at that time and 76 by 1843. A Sunday school was built behind the chapel for the growing number of children in 1855; it was also used as a day school. On Census Sunday 1851 the attendance at the chapel was 106 in the morning, 120 in the afternoon, and 146 in the evening.[1] William Stokes, minister from 1838 to 1843, supplemented his stipend with the income from his school in New Street.

The congregations of Bethel and Providence had united by 1853,[2] and in that year Providence chapel ceased to be used by the Baptists.[3] Despite the amalgamation membership was down to some 56 about 1855. Bethel continued in use until 1884, but by then it was suffering badly from mining subsidence and was closed. The congregation worshipped in the school for a short time and then met at Prince's Assembly Rooms on the corner of High Street and Lombard Street until a new Sunday school was opened for worship in 1886. A church was built in High Street in 1886–7. Designed by Ingall & Sons of Birmingham in a mixed Gothic style, it was of brick with Bath stone dressings. There was a tower, but the top was removed in 1967

because the stonework was in a dangerous state. The church was closed in 1971 and demolished in 1972; a new church in a modern style was opened in Tantany Lane in 1974, the congregation having in the meantime used the Unitarian church in Lodge Road.[4] The adult membership of the church at the beginning of 1969 was 98 and there were 88 children and young people.[5]

A chapel was built at Dunkirk in 1849. It still existed in 1851: on Census Sunday 30 people attended in the morning and 30 in the afternoon.[6]

In 1913 the High Street church took over a mission at the Lodge Estate school in Oak Lane. The mission had been started some years earlier in a house in Oak Road opposite the Oak House and was already in decline in 1913. It did not long survive the departure of many young men after the outbreak of the First World War.

BIBLE PATTERN CHURCH. The Bible Pattern Church registered a room in High Street in 1960.[7] By 1971 it was meeting in a room in Bull Street.

BRETHREN. The present Bethesda chapel in Witton Lane, Hill Top, belonging to the Brethren, originated in the work of Joseph Hewitt.[8] He was a shoemaker who came to Hill Top from Wednesbury in 1891. At first the mission consisted of cottage meetings and tent services, but in 1893 an iron mission room was opened at Holloway Bank. It was extended in 1922 and named Bethesda chapel. The present chapel in Witton Lane was opened in 1961.

In the late 1960s the Christian Brethren also opened Hargate chapel in Hargate Lane.[9]

CATHOLIC APOSTOLIC CHURCH. The Catholic Apostolic Church built a church in Victoria Street in 1869–70. It was taken over by the Elim Foursquare Gospel Alliance in 1945.[10]

CHRISTADELPHIANS. A Christadelphian group was formed at Greets Green in 1889. It moved into its first permanent hall in 1937 in Beeches Road. The building was compulsorily purchased by the corporation in 1968 as the site was needed for the northern loop road, and a new hall was opened in Seagar Street in 1969.[11]

CHRISTIAN SCIENTISTS. The Christian Scientists were meeting in Bull Street in the later 1920s but had moved to Barrows Street by 1932.[12] The church

[94] Date on building. It was registered in 1931: G.R.O., Worship Reg. no. 53494.
[95] Free Church Dir. (1968–69). It was registered in 1970: Worship Reg. 72021.   [96] Free Church Dir. (1968–69).
[97] Unless otherwise stated the following account is based on T. N. Honeybund, West Bromwich Baptist Church 1906: Bazaar Souvenir, 7–50 (copy in W.B.L.); J. Richards, West Bromwich and its Baptists 1796 to 1968 (copy in W.B.L.); Hackwood, West Bromwich, 83–4, 89; A. S. Langley, Birmingham Baptists Past and Present, 210–14; Records of an Old Association, ed. J. M. Gwynne Owen (Birmingham, 1905), 108–9; Reeves, West Bromwich, 21–2; Wood, Plan of West Bromwich (1837); below p. 78. The quotations are from W. Stokes, Hist. of the Midland Association of Baptist Churches (Birmingham, 1855), as given by Hackwood.
[98] W.S.L., O.C. Newspaper Cuttings, West Bromwich.
[99] H.O. 129/381/4/1.   [1] Ibid./3/1.
[2] There had been negotiations in 1843, but they were dropped because amalgamation would have involved Bethel in the heavy debt owed by Providence.

[3] It was used for baptisms 1884–6 when Prince's Assembly Rooms were being used for worship (see below): Richards, West Bromwich and its Baptists, 9. For its use by other groups see below pp. 67–8. It was demolished in the 1950s after standing empty for many years: Evening Mail, 3 June 1971.
[4] Midland Chron. & Free Press 3 Sept. 1971, 24 Jan. 1974.   [5] Baptist Handbook (1970), 180.
[6] H.O. 129/381/3/1.
[7] G.R.O., Worship Reg. 67929.
[8] This para. is based on information from the secretary of Bethesda chapel (1970) and Midland Chron. & Free Press, 28 July 1961.
[9] Free Church Dir. (1968–69); Worship Reg. no. 71638 (registration Jan. 1969).
[10] Hackwood, West Bromwich, 94; Staffs. Advertiser, 29 May 1869; Worship Reg. no. 19444; Kelly's Dir. Staffs. (1940); below p. 63.
[11] Evening Mail, 10 Dec. 1968; Express & Star, 19 Apr. 1969.
[12] Kelly's Dir. Staffs. (1928; 1932).

there was demolished in 1970 because the roof had become dangerous. A new church was opened in Walsall Street later the same year.[13]

CONGREGATIONALISTS, *see* PRESBYTERIANS AND CONGREGATIONALISTS.

ELIM FOURSQUARE GOSPEL ALLIANCE. The Elim Foursquare Gospel Alliance registered the People's Hall in High Street in 1936 and Ruskin Hall in Lombard Street instead in 1937; the People's Hall was registered again in 1939.[14] In 1945 the Alliance took over the former Catholic Apostolic Church in Victoria Street.[15] The church was extensively remodelled in 1971–2.[16]

FRIENDS. Two Quakers, John Edwards the elder and the younger, were reported in 1665.[17] In 1773 the minister at All Saints' stated that there were three Quakers in the parish.[18] There is, however, no record of any Quaker meeting-house.

GOSPEL BLUE RIBBON MISSION. In 1882 the Gospel Temperance Movement, also known as the Blue Ribbon Army, held a four-week mission in West Bromwich. The mission was followed by organized temperance work, and meetings were held in a house in Pitt Street and later in a building on the site formerly occupied by Hudson's soapworks, probably in High Street.[19] A corrugated-iron mission hall, capable of holding 800, was built in Pitt Street in 1892–3. The trustees included Charles Akrill, mayor in 1892–3 and 1896–7, and J. H. Blades, the borough's first M.P. (1885–6).[20] In 1968 there was an average Sunday congregation of 35.[21] The hall was demolished in 1969 after compulsory purchase by the corporation. The mission moved in 1969 to Grant Hall at the corner of Taylor's Lane and St. Clement's Lane as a temporary measure, and in 1972 the hall became its permanent centre.[22]

INDEPENDENTS, *see* PRESBYTERIANS.

JEHOVAH'S WITNESSES. A Kingdom Hall in High Street was registered in 1941.[23] By 1971 the Witnesses were meeting in the former adult-school building in Fisher Street.[24] A Kingdom Hall was opened in Jervoise Street in 1973.[25]

THE LABOUR CHURCH. There seems to have been a Labour Church in the town in the mid 1890s,[26] but the West Bromwich Labour Church held what was described as its inaugural service in 1899 in Grove's Assembly Room. There was a congregation of some 40, and the chairman was Henry Brockhouse, of John Brockhouse & Co. Ltd.[27] In 1901 the church opened its own premises, the People's Hall, a corrugated-iron building in High Street between Shaftesbury Street and Temple Street decorated to the design of Walter Crane.[28] A Sunday school was formed.[29] The church still existed in 1921 when a service there in memory of Henry Brockhouse was 'largely attended'.[30] It probably continued into the 1930s, but by 1936 the People's Hall was being used by the Elim Foursquare Gospel Alliance.[31]

LATTER-DAY SAINTS. A Mormon chapel was built in Temple Street in 1850. By 1851 it had an average Sunday attendance of 150 in the afternoon and 150 in the evening.[32] It still existed in 1854 but was no longer used in 1876.[33]

METHODISTS. *Wesleyan.* Charles Wesley preached at Holloway Bank in 1742 and made several converts. At his request his brother John preached there in January 1743, and the first Staffordshire society was then formed at Crabb's Mill Farm, the home of John Sheldon on Holloway Bank. In 1744 the society divided, the Wednesbury members moving to High Bullen and the West Bromwich members meeting in a cottage near Coles Lane.[34] Also in 1743 another group influenced by the Wesleys' preaching began to meet one evening a week in a house in the Mayer's Green area. At the end of the year George Whitefield 'broke up some fallow ground' at Mayer's Green. The groups at Holloway Bank and Mayer's Green suffered during the anti-Methodist riots in the district in 1743 and 1744.[35] Among those inciting hostility towards the Methodists was Richard Witton, the Presbyterian minister.[36] On the other hand the earl of Dartmouth (d. 1801), the patron of All Saints', was friendly towards Methodists, and there is evidence that Edward Stillingfleet, the Evangelical minister of All Saints' 1757–82, was also sympathetic.[37]

[13] *Evening Mail*, 20 Nov. 1970.
[14] Worship Reg. nos. 56557, 57452, 58532.
[15] Ibid. no. 61048; ex inf. the treasurer to the Elim trustees (1969).
[16] *Midland Chron. & Free Press*, 20 Oct. 1972; *Evening Mail*, 27 Nov. 1972.
[17] L.J.R.O., B/V/1/72.   [18] B/V/5/1772–3.
[19] *Staffs. Advertiser* (S. Staffs. edn.), 5 Aug., 9 Sept. 1882; *West Bromwich Mail*, 28 Nov. 1972; above p. 42.
[20] *Evening Mail*, 26 Nov. 1968, 19 June 1970; 'Old West Bromwich', 26 Mar. 1943; *Staffs. Advertiser*, 30 Dec. 1893, p. 6.
[21] *Evening Mail*, 26 Nov. 1968.
[22] Ibid. 7 and 13 Jan. 1969; *West Bromwich Mail*, 28 Nov. 1972.
[23] Worship Reg. no. 59724.
[24] The building was still an adult sch. in 1946: *Adult Sch. Year Book and Dir.* (1946–7).
[25] *Midland Chron. & Free Press*, 22 Nov. 1973.
[26] D. F. Summers, 'The Labour Church and Allied Movements of the late 19th and early 20th Centuries' (Edinburgh Univ. Ph.D. thesis, 1939), ii. 314 (reference supplied by Mr. D. G. Stuart of the Dept. of Adult Educ., Keele University).
[27] Ibid. ii. 467 sqq.; Woodall, *West Bromwich Yesterdays*, 70–1; *West Bromwich and Oldbury Chron.* 13 Jan. 1899;

K. S. Inglis, *Churches and the Working Classes in Victorian Eng.* 238; *Trans. West Bromwich Local Hist. Soc.* i (5) (copy in W.B.L.).
[28] *West Bromwich and Oldbury Chron.* 15 Nov. 1901; Summers, 'Labour Church', ii. 310; *Evening Mail*, 18 Mar. 1970. For Crane see *D.N.B.* 1912–21.
[29] *Trans. West Bromwich Local Hist. Soc.* i (5).
[30] *Midland Chron.* 4 Mar. 1921, p. 8.
[31] See above. The Labour Church is listed in *Kelly's Dir. Staffs.* (1932; 1940).
[32] H.O. 129/381/4/1. There were also 51 Sunday-school children in the morning.
[33] Worship Reg. no. 4497, giving the address as Frederick St., Temple St.
[34] Hackwood, *West Bromwich*, 84–5; Ede, *Wednesbury*, 204–5; *V.C.H. Staffs.* iii. 64, 124; 'Old West Bromwich', 16 Feb. and 6 Apr. 1945; H. H. Prince, *Romance of Early Methodism in and around West Bromwich and Wednesbury* (West Bromwich, 1925), 10–11, 35.
[35] Hackwood, *West Bromwich*, 85–8; G. Whitefield, *Works*, ii (Edinburgh, 1771), 47.
[36] A. G. Cumberland, 'Protestant Nonconformity in the Black Country 1662–1851' (Birmingham Univ. M.A. thesis, 1951), 49–50, citing Chas. Wesley.
[37] Hackwood, *West Bromwich*, 90, 92; *D.N.B. sub* Legge. Before appointing Stillingfleet Lord Dartmouth

Meetings continued in private houses, including the house of James Wheatley opposite Dagger Hall.[38] In 1751 Wheatley was expelled from the connexion by Wesley and was the first preacher to come under his ban. He began to build a meeting-room on the Heath on a site in what is now Paradise Street,[39] but he did not finish it. In 1764 it was bought by two members of a religious brotherhood of five young men. The brotherhood, formed c. 1760, was the origin of the West Bromwich Heath Society Class. At first the members had attended the Wednesbury meeting and also West Bromwich church. They now finished Wheatley's building and opened it as a Methodist preaching-room, though continuing to attend the parish church. One member of the group was Francis Asbury, who was to be a founder of the Methodist Episcopal Church of America;[40] in 1763 at the age of 18 he had been made leader of the West Bromwich Heath Society Class. Other members were James Bayley, Lord Dartmouth's park-keeper at Sandwell for 47 years, and Thomas Ault, who like Asbury came from Great Barr. Ault was leader from 1779 for over twenty years but left the society when the members stopped attending the parish church; he was the clerk at All Saints' from 1799 to 1825.[41]

The minister at All Saints' reported fewer than 20 Methodists in the parish in 1773, and the West Bromwich society remained small until the beginning of the 19th century.[42] Yet John Wesley attracted large numbers when he visited West Bromwich. On at least three of the four occasions that he preached there the crowds were far too large to fit into the meeting-room; on all four occasions in fact he preached in the open air—once, possibly twice, in the courtyard of the Oak House.[43] The small size of the society was probably due to the fact that Wednesbury was at first the main Methodist centre in the district.[44] Wesley visited Wednesbury over thirty times.[45] It was also the Wednesbury meeting that Lord Dartmouth attended on occasion.[46]

By the early 19th century, however, the West Bromwich congregation was growing.[47] In 1803 a Sunday school was opened at the preaching-room, and in 1806 a new chapel was built in Paradise Street. In 1811 West Bromwich became the head of a circuit. The size of the society fluctuated over the next twenty years, but in 1813 a new school was built and in 1821 the chapel was extended. By 1832

numbers had reached nearly 300 and the building was then enlarged again. Numbers continued to increase, and in 1835 a new chapel (Wesley) was opened in High Street; the architect was Joseph Cutts of Birmingham. The old chapel was opened as a Sunday school in 1836, with a day school from 1838, and remained in use until the opening of the school in Bratt Street in 1858; in 1859 it became a public hall. Sunday attendance at the chapel in 1850–1 averaged 1,000 in the morning, 351 in the afternoon, and 1,300 in the evening.[48] Wesley chapel was refronted in 1905–6 with an elaborate façade of terracotta and red brick.[49] It was demolished in 1972, and a new church was opened on the same site in 1974.[50]

At Hill Top, as already seen, meetings were held from 1744 in a cottage near the top of Coles Lane. From the early 19th century they were being held at Martin's Farm on the corner of Coles Lane. From 1820 a barn at Harvills Hawthorn was used which had been taken over from the Old Meeting; in 1821 the society numbered 22. A chapel was built at Harvills Hawthorn in 1830, and the barn was used as a Sunday school until 1834 when a new school was opened on the opposite side of the road. A new chapel was built at Harvills Hawthorn in 1850 and the old building was turned into a house for the minister. By c. 1940 numbers had declined and services were held in the Sunday school; the chapel had become a warehouse. The present church in New Street, Hill Top, was opened in 1955. A number of Warrenite seceders from the society opened a chapel on the main road in 1835, but it was closed in 1844.[51]

Another early chapel was the 'obscure apartment', formerly a baker's shop, near the end of Hargate Lane at Lyndon which was in use for meetings from the end of the 18th century; it became an official Wesleyan chapel in 1829. It was replaced in 1834 by a new chapel off Lyndon Street, which was in turn replaced by the present church in Hallam Street dated 1883.[52] A meeting was started at Ireland Green 'under Thomas Simcox's tree' in 1803 by a group of six men from Wednesbury.[53] There was a meeting at Greets Green by 1821, and a chapel was built on the corner of Ryders Green Road and Greets Green Road in 1835.[54] It was replaced by the present church on the same site in 1873.[55] The Sunday-school building to the east in Greets Green Road is dated 1856. A chapel was

had offered the living to Wm. Romaine, Lady Huntingdon's chaplain: V.C.H. Staffs. iii. 65.

[38] For this para., unless otherwise stated, see Hackwood, West Bromwich, 89–92.

[39] For the site, where part of the building stood until the early 20th century, see Free Press, 19 Sept. 1930.

[40] See p. 4.

[41] Reeves, West Bromwich, 138; 'West Bromwich 100 Years Ago', 12 Apr. 1901.

[42] L.J.R.O., B/V/5/1772–3; Hackwood, West Bromwich, 92.

[43] Hackwood, West Bromwich, 89. For the tradition that he also preached in the open at Ireland Green (an event not recorded in his journal) during a visit to the Oak House see 'Old West Bromwich', 4 Aug. 1944.

[44] V.C.H. Staffs. iii. 124–5.

[45] Ede, Wednesbury, 211.

[46] Hackwood, West Bromwich, 92.

[47] For the rest of this para., unless otherwise stated, see Hackwood, West Bromwich, 92–3; T. C. Ingle, 'Methodism in West Bromwich', Wesleyan Methodist Mag. lxx. 180; Centenary of Wesley Chapel, High Street, West

Bromwich (copy in W.B.L.); W.B.L. 66/16150; Prince, Early Methodism, 56; below pp. 71, 76.

[48] H.O. 129/381/4/1.

[49] Centenary of Wesley Chapel, 14.

[50] Express & Star, 18 Feb. 1974.

[51] Hackwood, West Bromwich, 93; Hill Top Wesleyan Church and Sunday Schools: Centenary Souvenir, 4–6 (copy in W.B.L.); 'Old West Bromwich', 6 Apr. 1945; Wood, Plan of West Bromwich (1837); Peacock & Cottrell, Map of West Bromwich (1857); ex inf. the secretary, Hill Top Methodist church (1971).

[52] Reeves, West Bromwich, 23; 'West Bromwich 100 Years Ago', 14 June 1901; 'Old West Bromwich', 28 May 1943; Prince, Early Methodism, 60–1; Wood, Plan of West Bromwich (1837); date on foundation-stones of Hallam Street church.

[53] Hackwood, West Bromwich, 92.

[54] W.B.L. 66/16150, giving 10 May 1835 as the date of opening of the chapel; Wood, Plan of West Bromwich (1837). H.O. 129/381/3/1 gives 1836 as the date of erection.

[55] Hackwood, West Bromwich, 93; date on foundation-stones.

built in Victoria Street, Swan Village, in 1831 and was replaced in 1865 by the present chapel in Dudley Street. The new chapel was designed in a Romanesque style by Loxton Brothers of Wednesbury and by 1972 had been reduced in height and reroofed.[56] By the 1830s there was a preaching-place 'at the wharf bottom of Spon Lane'. This was the origin of the chapel in Spon Lane built in 1841; by the mid 1850s there was a separate Sunday-school building to the west. The chapel was rebuilt in 1877–8 and closed in 1927 when the congregation transferred to the church at West Smethwick.[57] In 1970 the building was being used by the metal pressings branch of John Smith Ltd. The chapels at Lyndon, Hill Top, Swan Village, Greets Green, and Spon Lane made returns at the religious census of 1851 which show that their total attendances on Sundays averaged 1,150.[58]

By 1847 the Wesleyans were organizing open-air preaching during the summer at four places in West Bromwich.[59] Between 1861 and 1890 John Skidmore, a Wesleyan lay preacher and missioner to the canal boatmen, held open-air services on Sundays from May to August at Middle Lock between Spon Lane and Bromford Lane.[60] In the early 1840s Wesleyan influence was felt in the collieries. According to a local Wesleyan minister butties belonging to the connexion were free from the dishonesty for which other butties were notorious. At one colliery, through the influence of a Wesleyan ground bailiff, prayers and scripture readings were held during the dinner hour, and there were rules against drinking and swearing. A Wesleyan miner, however, stated that 'pits that have praying companies in them are as few as parish churches'.[61]

By the end of the century West Bromwich had ten Wesleyan chapels in three circuits.[62] West Bromwich Wesley circuit (so named from 1883)[63] consisted of seven chapels. High Street, Greets Green, and Hallam Street have been described above. Beeches Road chapel, built in 1871–2 to the design of Edward Pincher of West Bromwich, replaced the Park Village Sunday school and chapel opened about the end of 1855.[64] At Carter's Green a school-

chapel was opened in 1863 and was replaced by a chapel designed by Loxton Brothers in a Gothic style and built on the site of the Junction inn in 1875–6; it had been closed by 1949, and after being used for some years as a warehouse it was demolished in 1970.[65] At the Lyng a centre was opened in 1872 and a chapel was built in Lyng Lane in 1881; the church was closed in 1965.[66] At Overend a centre had been opened by January 1871; a school-chapel there was registered in 1877 and was replaced in 1878 by a mission church in Overend Street which seems to have continued until the early 1960s and was occupied by the Spring Dart Co. Ltd. in 1971.[67] The West Bromwich chapels in Hill Top circuit (formed in 1862 as Wednesbury Wesley circuit and renamed in 1883)[68] were Hill Top and Swan Village. Smethwick circuit (formed out of West Bromwich circuit in 1876)[69] included the chapel in Spon Lane. In 1963 Hill Top circuit was abolished, and its two churches in West Bromwich, those at Hill Top and Swan Village, were added to West Bromwich Wesley circuit.[70]

In 1969 there were thirteen Methodist churches in the area of the pre-1966 borough. Twelve were in West Bromwich Wesley circuit:[71] Wesley (High Street), Greets Green, Swan Village, Beeches Road, Hallam Street, Charlemont, where a wooden church was erected in 1926 and the present church in Charlemont Road, designed by C. E. M. Fillmore, was opened in 1930,[72] Hill Top, Moorlands in Hall Green Road (1959), replacing the Hall Green Mission, formerly Primitive Methodist,[73] Yew Tree, where services were held in Fir Tree school from c. 1957 and the present church on the corner of Greenside Way and Redwood Road, designed by A. J. Jesson, was built in 1967,[74] and the former Primitive Methodist churches at the Lyng, in Great Bridge Street, and at Hall End. The thirteenth church was the Woods Estate Methodist Church in Coronation Road in Wednesbury circuit; it was opened in 1966.[75]

The cottage at Newton where Francis Asbury grew up was used for services in the later 18th century, but it is not known whether they continued

[56] Hackwood, *West Bromwich*, 93; 'Old West Bromwich', 10, 17, and 24 Nov., 29 Dec. 1944; Wood, *Plan of West Bromwich* (1837); *Staffs. Advertiser*, 17 June 1865; inscription on foundation-stone of Dudley St. chapel; G.R.O., Worship Reg. no. 17583 (registration of Sept. 1866). The old chapel became part of the Swan Foundry.
[57] Reeves, *West Bromwich*, 24; Hackwood, *West Bromwich*, 93; Hackwood, *Smethwick*, 82 (stating that the chapel was enlarged in 1878); date (1877) on foundation-stones of later building; ex inf. Mr. G. Beard, Quarterly Meeting Secretary, Smethwick circuit; W.B.L., Plan of West Bromwich (n.d.), sheet 70; W.B.L., West Bromwich in 4 Plans (1856), no. 4; below p. 132. H.O. 129/381/3/1 gives 1840 for the first chapel.
[58] H.O. 129/381/3/1 and /4/1.
[59] W.B.L., Min. Bk. of Local Preachers' Quarterly Meetings, West Bromwich, ff. 2, 3, 5v., 10, 34, 39v.
[60] Ibid. f. 47; 'Old West Bromwich', 7 May, 23 and 30 July 1943; T.C.T. *Life's Realities*, 184; *Free Press*, 4 Feb. 1899 (obituary).
[61] *1st Rep. Com. Midland Mining, S. Staffs.* [508], pp. 16, 21, H.C. (1843), xiii.
[62] *Kelly's Dir. Staffs.* (1900).
[63] *Hall's Circuits and Ministers* (1897 edn.), 322.
[64] W.B.L., Min. Bk. of Local Preachers' Quarterly Meetings, West Bromwich, ff. 30, 39, 40, 43v.; *Staffs. Advertiser*, 26 Mar. 1870, 29 July 1871; *P.O. Dir. Staffs.* (1872); *Kelly's Dir. Staffs.* (1884); *Centenary of Wesley Chapel, High Street, West Bromwich*, 13.

[65] *Carters Green Wesleyan Church, 1907: Bazaar Souvenir* (copy in W.B.L.); *Evening Mail*, 22 and 27 May, 3 June 1970; plate facing p. 241 below; G.R.O., Worship Reg. no. 22794.
[66] T. W. Camm, 'Appointments to conduct services and preach in Wesley chapels and union, West Bromwich Circuit' (in W.B.L.), West Bromwich circuit plan Apr.–July 1872; Worship Reg. no. 25734 (registration of chapel Aug. 1881); *Kelly's Dir. Staffs.* (1884), giving 1881 as date of chapel; Hackwood, *West Bromwich*, 93 (giving 1880 as date of erection of chapel); ex inf. the supt. minister, West Bromwich Wesley circuit (1969).
[67] Camm, 'Appointments', West Bromwich circuit plan Jan.–Apr. 1871; Worship Reg. no. 23293 (cancelled 1962); Hackwood, *West Bromwich*, 93; *Kelly's Dir. Staffs.* (1940); O.S. Map 1/500, Staffs. LXVIII. 10. 25 (1886).
[68] *Hall's Circuits and Ministers* (1897 edn.), 320, 322.
[69] Camm, 'Appointments', f. 65.
[70] Ex inf. the supt. minister (1969). The remaining 4 churches in the circuit were added to Tipton circuit.
[71] *West Bromwich (Wesley) Circuit Plan and Dir. Jan.–Apr. 1969.*
[72] *Kelly's Dir. Staffs.* (1928); ex inf. the minister in charge of Charlemont, Moorlands, and Yew Tree churches (1970).   [73] See pp. 66–7.
[74] Ex inf. the minister (1970); date on foundation-stones; *Express & Star*, 23 Nov. 1967.
[75] Ex inf. the supt. minister, Wednesbury circuit (1970); Worship Reg. no. 70613.

after his mother's death in 1802. A small Methodist chapel was built on the corner of Newton and Hamstead Roads in 1803 or 1804, but it was sold to the Congregationalists in 1823.[76] The Wesleyans, however, seem to have been using a chapel on the site between at least the later 1860s and 1885.[77]

New Connexion. The first Methodist New Connexion chapel in West Bromwich was built in 1826 in Victoria Street, Swan Village. On Census Sunday 1851 it had attendances of 80 in the afternoon and 140 in the evening.[78] It was replaced the same year by the new Zion chapel near by in Dudley Street,[79] which seems to have continued until *c.* 1870; it was demolished *c.* 1914.[80] A chapel was opened at Hill Top in 1836,[81] but nothing further is known about it. Another chapel was built in Wood Lane in 1841. Average attendance in 1850–1 was 55 in the afternoon and 120 in the evening.[82] It apparently ceased to be used in the early 1890s.[83]

Primitive. In 1833 a Primitive Methodist chapel was opened in Sandwell Road near the junction with Stoney Lane. Another was built at Golds Green at the west end of Harvills Hawthorn in 1836, and by then there were also meetings in Victoria Street in Swan Village and in Rydding Square off Witton Lane.[84] In 1837 there was also a 'Christian Primitive Methodist meeting-house' between Newhall Street and Sams Lane.[85] A building in Queen Street, originally intended as a public hall, was completed as a Primitive Methodist chapel in 1847 largely with the help of the Spittle family, local coalmasters.[86] In 1849 the chapel became the head of West Bromwich circuit, created that year out of Darlaston circuit and covering mainly West Bromwich and Tipton.[87] There was a Primitive Methodist chapel in Union Street by 1851; it was evidently the former non-denominational meeting-house erected by John Glover in 1833.[88]

By 1851 there were eight chapels or meeting-places in West Bromwich. Three were identified as the chapels in Queen Street and Union Street and at Golds Green. On Census Sunday 1851 Queen

Street had attendances of 100 in the morning, 363 in the afternoon, and 440 in the evening; Union Street had 32 in the morning, 40 in the afternoon, and 70 in the evening; Golds Green had 185 in the morning, 88 in the afternoon, and 360 in the evening.[89] Of the five unidentified places of worship four were presumably those in Sandwell Road (which apparently survived until the 1870s),[90] Swan Village,[91] Witton Lane, and Whitehall Road, Greets Green (dating from 1848).[92] The fifth was probably one of the two Primitive Methodist chapels opened in West Bromwich in 1851. One was in Guns Village and the other at the Lyng, in Sams Lane.[93] There were also preaching-rooms at Hall End and New Town by at least the end of 1852.[94] On Census Sunday 1851 four of the five unidentified places of worship had total attendances of some 235 in the afternoon and 370 in the evening.[95]

Seven of the chapels and meeting-places in existence in the early 1850s still existed in the mid 1890s: Queen Street (closed 1966),[96] Union Street (rebuilt 1852, bought with the adjoining school building by Archibald Kenrick & Sons Ltd. in 1964 and incorporated into the firm's works),[97] Golds Green (rebuilt 1912, closed 1969),[98] Witton Lane (rebuilt 1862,[99] closed by 1969), Greets Green (closed by 1958),[1] Guns Village (closed by 1969), and the Lyng. The chapel at the Lyng was rebuilt in Moor Street in 1900, and the old chapel in Sams Lane became the school. The new chapel was destroyed during an air raid in 1940, and the school was then used for services. The chapel was rebuilt in 1951.[2] Other places of worship in the mid 1890s included an 'iron room' in Hall Green Road built about 1876 by Annie Lloyd,[3] a chapel in Great Bridge Street opened in 1883[4] and presumably replacing the Swan Village chapel, and a house in Cophall Street.[5]

All nine of the chapels, divided into two circuits, were still in use at the time of the union of the Primitive Methodists with the Wesleyans and United Methodists in 1932;[6] there was also a chapel in

[76] W.B.L., Scrapbook 1, p. 60; H.O. 129/381/1/2; above p. 4. Hackwood, *West Bromwich*, 92, mentions a Methodist chapel *c.* 1790 at Bromwich forge which was sold to the Congregationalists *c.* 1821. Bromwich forge was not far from Newton.
[77] See p. 69.
[78] H.O. 129/381/3/1. It may have been the chapel in Swan Village registered in 1827: *S.H.C.* 4th ser. iii. 70.
[79] H.O. 129/381/3/1; White, *Dir. Staffs.* (1851); *P.O. Dir. Staffs.* (1860); Peacock & Cottrell, Map of West Bromwich (1857).
[80] 'Old West Bromwich', 29 Dec. 1944. It was listed in *P.O. Dir. Staffs.* (1868) but not ibid. (1872).
[81] Reeves, *West Bromwich*, 23.
[82] H.O. 129/381/3/1.
[83] It ceases to be listed in *Kelly's Dir. Staffs.* after 1892. It is not mentioned in Hackwood, *West Bromwich*.
[84] Reeves, *West Bromwich*, 23–4; H.O. 129/381/4/1; Wood, *Plan of West Bromwich* (1837), which describes the Swan Village and Rydding Sq. chapels as Revivalist; Peacock & Cottrell, Map of West Bromwich (1857).
[85] Wood, *Plan of West Bromwich* (1837).
[86] Hackwood, *West Bromwich*, 94; 'Old West Bromwich', 17 Sept. 1943.
[87] Hackwood, *West Bromwich*, 94; J. Petty, *Hist. of Prim. Meth. Connexion* (1864 edn.), 409.
[88] H.O. 129/381/3/1; below p. 70.
[89] H.O. 129/381/3/1 and /4/1.
[90] It is shown by Peacock & Cottrell, Map of West Bromwich (1857), and still listed in *P.O. Dir. Staffs.* (1876).
[91] *P.O. Dir. Staffs.* (1860), dating it to 1851 and giving

the address as Phoenix St.; this may indicate a rebuilding.
[92] Hackwood, *West Bromwich*, 94; W.B.L., Plan of West Bromwich (n.d.), sheet 43 (also showing a schoolhouse behind the chapel).
[93] Hackwood, *West Bromwich*, 94; G.R.O., Worship Reg. nos. 398, 439.
[94] Worship Reg. nos. 493, 495.
[95] H.O. 129/381/3/1 and /4/1.
[96] Ex inf. the supt. minister of West Bromwich Wesley circuit (1969).
[97] 'Old West Bromwich', 24 Dec. 1943; ex inf. Mr. W. E. Kenrick (1971).
[98] Inscription on building; *Express & Star*, 6 June 1966; ex inf. the supt. minister (1969). It was bought by the Triumphant Church of God: see p. 70.
[99] Hackwood, *West Bromwich*, 94.
[1] Its registration of 1860 was cancelled in 1958: Worship Reg. no. 10150.
[2] Ibid. nos. 37955, 59725, 63599; *Midland Chron. & Free Press*, 22 Nov. 1946; date on foundation-stones of present chapel.
[3] Ex inf. the minister of Moorlands church (1970); *P.O. Dir. Staffs.* (1876); 'Old West Bromwich', 20 July 1945; O.S. Map 6", Staffs. LXVIII. NW. (edns. of 1890, 1904, and 1921).
[4] Hackwood, *West Bromwich*, 94; foundation-stones dated Oct. 1882.
[5] Hackwood, *West Bromwich*, 94.
[6] *Kelly's Dir. Staffs.* (1932). This omits the Hall Green Road mission, which still existed. The circuits are given in *Kelly's Dir.* from 1908.

Vicarage Road, Hall End, from 1902.[7] In 1940 the Hall Green Road mission was joined by a society which had met in a scout hut at the junction of Hall Green Road and Crankhall Lane. The mission was replaced in 1959 by Moorlands Church in Hall Green Road, designed by A. J. Jesson.[8] In 1969 the four surviving chapels, those at the Lyng, in Hall Green Road, in Great Bridge Street, and at Hall End, were part of the West Bromwich Wesley circuit.[9]

Other Methodist Groups. The Methodist Free Church was using St. George's Hall in Paradise Street in 1864 but had ceased to do so by 1876.[10] The Methodist Reform Union registered the Gospel Hall in Pitt Street in 1869 and was using the former Providence Baptist chapel in Sandwell Road by 1892, remaining there until the early 20th century.[11] The Wesleyan Reformers were meeting in Groves's Assembly Room in Paradise Street by 1871 but had ceased to do so by 1896.[12]

PRESBYTERIANS AND CONGREGATIONALISTS (INDEPENDENTS), LATER UNITED REFORMED CHURCH. *The Old Meeting, later Ebenezer Church.* When Richard Hilton was ejected from the curacy of West Bromwich in 1662 some of his parishioners also left the Established Church. Hilton, however, went to Prestwood in Kingswinford for a time as chaplain to Philip Foley, and it was Thomas Badland, the ejected curate of Willenhall, who was minister at West Bromwich until he moved to Worcester in 1663.[13] At that time the lord of the manor, John Shelton, was a Presbyterian.[14] In 1667 Richard Fisher and his son and Henry Free and his son, all of West Bromwich, were in trouble for attending a suspect sermon at Oldbury chapel.[15] The Fishers at least were probably Presbyterians, for in 1672 the house of a Richard Fisher at West Bromwich was licensed for Presbyterian worship. In the same year Thomas Creese and Richard Hilton, both described as Presbyterians, were licensed as 'teachers', the former in the house of John Lowe.[16] In 1693 Lowe's house at Lyndon and the houses of Thomas Jesson (probably Oakwood), William Turton of Hateley Heath, and Bayly Brett were licensed for nonconformist worship and were presumably Presbyterian centres.[17] Hilton, who lived at Walsall, was minister of the Presbyterian congregation in 1690 and may have so continued until his death in 1706.[18] In 1699 John Lowe of West Bromwich left 50s. a year for

the maintenance of the two fortnightly sermons then preached in West Bromwich by dissenting ministers.[19] By then there was apparently a chapel at Finchpath: in 1696 a building there which had recently been repaired and which was called the new chapel was leased by the Jessons to Moses Bird.[20] In 1702 a weaver's child was baptized 'by a Presbyterian minister at St. Margaret's Chapel alias a barn' in West Bromwich.[21]

A newly built meeting-house was registered for dissenting worship early in 1710 by Josiah Turton of the Mill.[22] It stood near Five Ways, the area around the junction of Swan Lane and Black Lake where five roads meet, and was presumably on or close to the site of the later church in Old Meeting Street. The land seems to have been given by Elizabeth Jesson, and the cost of building was met by subscription.[23] The first trust deed was drawn up in 1714, and the trustees included members of the Lowe, Turton, Brett, and Nock families.[24] In July 1715 the Presbyterians of West Bromwich, like others in Staffordshire, suffered at the hands of the mob. Early in the month the house of John Mayo, one of the trustees of the meeting-house, was broken into and damaged. From the 13th the meeting-house was repeatedly attacked, and it was finally burnt down on the 18th.[25] The Presbyterians received compensation from the government, and the meeting-house was rebuilt the following year.[26] In 1816 it was largely rebuilt on a bigger scale,[27] and in 1839 there was another rebuilding on an adjoining site to the north. The name was then changed from Old Meeting to Ebenezer.[28]

In the early 18th century the West Bromwich congregation was served from Birmingham and Walsall and also by an itinerant minister. In 1722, however, Richard Witton came as resident minister.[29] The congregation consisted of 350 'hearers' in 1717.[30] In 1773 the minister at All Saints' reported between 200 and 300 Presbyterians in the parish, some of them 'persons of property'.[31] The congregation was little affected by heterodoxy; only one of the ministers, Benjamin Carpenter (1776–8), held Unitarian views.[32] A Sunday school, the first in West Bromwich, was opened in 1786 by the minister, George Osborne, who was a pioneer of the Sunday-school movement. The school was first held in a barn on the opposite side of Old Meeting Street to the chapel, but by 1838 the school building was

---

[7] Date on building.

[8] Ex inf. the minister of Moorlands church (1970).

[9] See p. 65.   [10] Worship Reg. no. 16471.

[11] Ibid. no. 19037; Hackwood, *West Bromwich*, 84; *P.O. Dir. Staffs.* (1872; 1876); *Kelly's Dir. Staffs.* (1892 and later edns. to 1908). For the Hall in 1881 see p. 70.

[12] Worship Reg. no. 20252.

[13] Hackwood, *West Bromwich*, 78; *S.H.C.* 1915, 338, 353.   [14] *S.H.C.* 4th ser. ii. 30.

[15] *Cal. S.P. Dom.* 1667, 466–7. And see A. G. Cumberland, 'Protestant Nonconformity in the Black Country 1662–1851' (Birmingham Univ. M.A. thesis, 1951), 17–18, 22.

[16] A. G. Matthews, *Congregational Churches of Staffs.* 92–3, giving Lowe as Law.

[17] L.J.R.O., B/A/12(ii); above p. 26.

[18] Matthews, *Cong. Churches*, 264, 266; *Freedom after Ejection*, ed. A. Gordon, 96, 284; below p. 248.

[19] B.R.L. 456894.

[20] W.C.L., box 23, no. 8, p. 11.

[21] W.S.L., extracts from par. regs. of West Bromwich and Wednesbury, f. 48. The entry occurs in the Wednesbury reg.

[22] *S.H.C.* 4th ser. iii. 117; Trustees' Min. Bk. 1729–1832 (at West Bromwich United Reformed Church), loose sheet endorsed 'Meeting House Accounts'.

[23] Hackwood, *West Bromwich*, 78; W.B.L. 66/16151; C. J. L. Elwell, *The Iron Elwells* (Ilfracombe, 1964), 51.

[24] Hackwood, *West Bromwich*, 78; Trustees' Min. Bk. 1729–1832.

[25] Hackwood, *West Bromwich*, 80–1; W.S.L., S. MS. 370/viii/II, pp. 479–81, 485, 487–8 (transcript from *The Flying Post*); Cal. Treas. Bks. Jan.–Dec. 1717, 186; Assizes 4/18 pp. 222, 229, 236–7, 244–5, 247–9; Willett, *West Bromwich*, 181–2.

[26] Reeves, *West Bromwich*, 16; *V.C.H. Staffs.* iii. 122–3.

[27] Reeves, *West Bromwich*, 16; W.S.L., O.C. Newspaper Cuttings, West Bromwich.

[28] Hackwood *West Bromwich*, 79–80; Matthews, *Cong. Churches*, 218; Char. Com. files, deed of Dec. 1839; W.B.L., mining etc. plans, no. 268.

[29] Matthews, *Cong. Churches*, 90, 96, 264, 266.

[30] Ibid. 129.

[31] L.J.R.O., B/V/5/1772–3.

[32] Matthews, *Cong. Churches*, 111, 146–7.

on the corner of what is now Greswold Street. When the chapel was rebuilt in 1839, the former chapel was turned into premises for day and Sunday schools; it was rebuilt in 1906.[33]

By 1834 the Old Meeting had become Independent or Congregational.[34] Average Sunday attendance in 1850–1 was 450 in the morning and 400 in the evening.[35] It was at Ebenezer that John Blackham, a deacon of the church, started the first adult school outside Birmingham in 1870 and founded the Pleasant Sunday Afternoon movement in 1875.[36] The adult membership of the church at the beginning of 1969 was 68, and there were 106 children.[37] Ebenezer was closed in 1971 on the opening of the West Bromwich Congregational church and was later converted into a Hindu temple.[38]

Even in the 18th century the Old Meeting was not the only Presbyterian place of worship in West Bromwich. Of the five houses registered for non-conformist worship during the century three can be identified as Presbyterian, those of Anne Stampes (1720), of Richard Witton (1733), presumably the minister at the Old Meeting, and of Moses Lea (1763).[39] James Cooper, minister 1808–29, started services in a barn at Harvills Hawthorn; he met with little success, and in 1820 the barn was taken over by the Wesleyan Methodists.[40] The former Providence Baptist chapel in Sandwell Road was used as the Ebenezer Home Mission for a few years from c. 1869.[41]

The former Ebenezer church is of brick faced with stucco and was designed in a plain classical style by one Rogers, described in 1839 as late of Birmingham.[42] The Sunday school to the south was built in 1906 to the design of James Withers.[43] In the churchyard there are burials going back to the 18th century. Two silver cups were presented to the church by Elizabeth Brett in 1765 and two by William Whitehouse in 1841;[44] individual communion cups were introduced in 1906,[45] but the four silver cups were in the possession of West Bromwich Congregational Church in 1971.

Mayer's Green Church. In 1785 or 1786 a few members of the Wednesbury Independent congregation withdrew after a dispute over the choosing of the minister.[46] Most of them lived in West Bromwich, and with a few friends they at first held prayer meetings on Sunday evenings in a private house in Spon Lane.[47] Later they rented a barn at Virgins End. The group was served until 1787 mainly from the King Street chapel in Birmingham, which belonged to the Countess of Huntingdon's Connexion. The first regular minister, Hugh Williams, who took charge after his ordination in 1787, had served the congregation earlier while he was still a student at Trevecca College. The countess herself wrote to 'my well beloved congregation of the West Bromwich Chapel' in 1790, and Williams's successor, appointed in 1799, was recommended by her chaplain.[48] The new minister left in 1800 after failing to secure an increase in his stipend. The congregation then formed themselves into a Congregational church.

In 1787 Williams began building a small chapel in Messenger Lane, which was opened in 1788. It was lengthened in 1790 and a gallery was erected. Money was scarce at first, but help was given by William Whyley of the Oak House (d. 1800).[49] In 1805 side galleries were added to the chapel, but even so the accommodation remained inadequate. In 1807–8 a new chapel was built on the opposite side of the road, a brick building with a classical façade: even there side galleries had to be added in 1825–6. The materials from the old chapel were reused, and William Whyley's widow Jane provided a malt-house as a temporary meeting-place during the rebuilding. She also contributed towards the cost of the new chapel from the proceeds of a sale of timber on her Oak House estate. The site of the old chapel became a burial ground; it was bought by the corporation in 1914.[50] A Sunday school was established in 1804; a building was erected for it in 1807 and was extended to twice the original size in 1813.[51] Average Sunday attendance at the chapel in 1850–1 was 430 in the morning (evidently including some 190 Sunday-school children) and 340 in the evening; about 90 young children also attended a special service in the morning.[52] Adult membership at the beginning of 1968 was 63, and there were 35 children.[53] In 1968 the church was bought by the corporation under a compulsory purchase order; it was gutted by fire in 1969. The congregation was united with that of Ebenezer.[54]

[33] Hackwood, *West Bromwich*, 79–80, 92; Prince, *Old West Bromwich*, 102; W.B.L., mining etc. plans, no. 268; below p. 77.

[34] Trustees' Min. Bk. 1832–41, 11 Oct. 1834, articles of agreement between the new minister and the congregation, stating that the minister's profession and declaration were sufficient evidence that he was a dissenter 'of the Congregational order or persuasion'.

[35] H.O. 129/381/4/1.

[36] *Free Press*, 8 June 1923, obituary; *V.C.H. Staffs.* iii. 133–4.

[37] *Cong. Year Book* (1969–70), 259.

[38] See p. 70.

[39] *S.H.C.* 4th ser. iii. 119 (identified as Presbyterian in S.R.O., Q/SR, E. 1720, no. 26), 120, 122.

[40] Hackwood, *West Bromwich*, 93.

[41] G.R.O., Worship Reg. no. 19074 (registration of 1869, cancelled 1876); *P.O. Dir. Staffs.* (1872; 1876). It was used by the Wesleyan Methodists for a short time in 1873: W.B.L., Wesleyan Methodist Church Preaching Appointments 1866–82, Circuit Plan July–Oct. 1873.

[42] W.S.L., O.C. Newspaper Cuttings, West Bromwich.

[43] *Ebenezer Sunday School, West Bromwich: Building Jubilee* (1956), 11–12 (copy in W.S.L. Pamphs. *sub* West Bromwich).

[44] Inscriptions on the cups.

[45] Notes in book containing S. Lees, 'Hist. of Ebenezer Chapel, West Bromwich' (1906; MS. at West Bromwich United Reformed Church).

[46] Unless otherwise stated this account is based on Hackwood, *West Bromwich*, 81–2; F. A. Homer, 'Collections for the Hist. of the Priory of Sandwell' (in W.S.L.), account of Mayer's Green chapel abstracted from MS. history written by John Hudson, minister at Mayer's Green 1801–43; 'Hist. of Mayers Green Congregational Chapel and Schools etc., West Bromwich' (MS. at West Bromwich United Reformed Church copied from an original MS. written by Hudson); Reeves, *West Bromwich*, 20–1.

[47] Cumberland, 'Prot. Nonconformity in the Black Country', 76.

[48] Ibid. 115; Matthews, *Cong. Churches*, 143; Hackwood, *West Bromwich*, 81.   [49] For Whyley see p. 25.

[50] 'Hist. of Mayers Green Cong. Chapel', transcript of letters.

[51] Hackwood, *West Bromwich*, 81–2; 'Hist. of Mayers Green Chapel'.

[52] H.O. 129/381/4/1. In addition to 192 Sunday-school children present on the morning of Census Sunday 1851 there were 70 children at a separate service.

[53] *Cong. Year Book* (1968–69), 259.

[54] *Evening Mail*, 25 Nov. 1968, 18 June 1969.

A benefit club connected with the chapel was founded in 1808. About 1855 a Bible class was begun. It soon attracted men of different denominations and of none from all over the district, and particular attention was devoted to the study of the Bible in the light of contemporary criticism. In the 1880s women were admitted, despite much opposition. In the 1890s there were several clubs and societies, a library, and a gymnasium.

A mission chapel belonging to the church was built in Woodward Street in 1880–1.[55] It too was bought by the corporation under a compulsory purchase order in 1969.[56]

Salem Church, Great Bridge. A church at Great Bridge was formed by a small group who had previously worshipped at the Old Meeting and at Darkhouse Lane chapel, Coseley (in Sedgley).[57] In 1833 meetings were held in a room in Blades Street, which ran between Brickhouse Lane and Great Bridge Street, and at the beginning of 1834 a small preaching-house was opened in Sheepwash Lane. It was initially a branch of the Old Meeting, but in 1836 a separate church was formed. At first it consisted of eleven people, but numbers increased. Services were held in the infants' school which had been opened in Sheepwash Lane in 1835, and there was also a well-attended Sunday school. Salem chapel in Sheepwash Lane was opened in 1839. Attendance on Census Sunday 1851 was 130 in the morning, 178 in the afternoon, and 283 in the evening.[58] The adult membership at the beginning of 1969 was 47, and there were 35 children.[59] The church is of stuccoed brick and in a classical style similar to that of Ebenezer church; it is perhaps by the same architect. There are extensions at the rear in plain brick.

High Street Church. In 1873 a group seceded from Mayer's Green chapel after the minister had been accused of preaching someone else's sermon. For four years it worshipped at Prince's Assembly Rooms on the corner of High Street and Lombard Street. In 1877, when numbers became too large, the group moved to the town hall, and in 1878 the foundation-stone of a new church in High Street was laid. It was opened in 1879 and was a building of brick and stone in a Gothic style designed by John Sulman of Holborn, London.[60] It was bought in 1963 by Kenrick & Jefferson Ltd., who demolished it in order to extend their works.[61]

The West Bromwich Congregational Church. In 1967 the Ebenezer and Mayer's Green congregations came together as 'the Congregational Church in West Bromwich with a joint diaconate and a joint church meeting, worshipping for the present time in the two sets of premises and thereafter moving towards unity as speedily as may be pos-

sible'.[62] Later the same year, on the departure of the minister of Mayer's Green, the minister of Ebenezer took charge of Mayer's Green as well. As mentioned above, the Mayer's Green congregation shared Ebenezer church from 1968. A second minister was appointed in 1970.

A site in Hardware Street was given by the corporation in place of the compulsorily purchased Mayer's Green site, and in 1970 the building of the West Bromwich Congregational church was begun there as a replacement for Ebenezer. The foundation stone was laid 'on behalf of the Mayers Green, Ebenezer, High Street Churches and Woodward Street Mission'. The church was opened in 1971. It is a building of brick in a modern style, designed by Cecil E. M. Fillmore and Partners, and it includes a hall and meeting-rooms. The organ from Ebenezer was moved there, and stained-glass windows from Ebenezer and Mayer's Green were placed in the foyer.

Allen Memorial Church, Newton. The Methodist chapel on the corner of Newton and Hamstead Roads was sold to the Congregationalists in 1823.[63] In 1850–1 it had an average attendance of 35 adults, although there was seating for 125 people. It was then served from Birmingham.[64] It is said to have been rebuilt as a Wesleyan chapel in the later 1860s, and a building on the site is shown as such in 1885 on the Ordnance Survey map.[65] By the beginning of the 20th century, however, the building was owned by the trustees of the Carrs Lane Congregational church in Birmingham and was being used as an institute.[66] In 1917 it was reopened as a Congregational church by the efforts of a Miss Powell, who had recently come to live in the district. It was replaced in 1932 by a church on the opposite corner, built by Miss Powell's nephews, Frank, Tom, and Harry Allen, in memory of their mother, Elizabeth Mary Allen. It is a brick building designed by Albert Bye of West Bromwich.[67] The adult membership at the beginning of 1969 was 56, and there were 125 children.[68]

QUAKERS, *see* FRIENDS.

REVIVALISTS. Land in Spon Lane was bought in 1821 as the site of a chapel for 'Revivalists in connection with Robert Winfield'. The chapel was opened in 1823, with Winfield preaching. The property, however, had been mortgaged by then. In 1831 the building was sold to Lord Dartmouth, and it was converted into a cholera hospital in 1832.[69]

SALVATION ARMY. The West Bromwich corps of the Salvation Army was formed in May 1879 and

[55] *Kelly's Dir. Staffs.* (1884); 'Old West Bromwich', 24 Aug. 1945; W.B.L., P. 207.
[56] Ex inf. the minister, Ebenezer (1969).
[57] Unless otherwise stated this account is based on Matthews, *Cong. Churches*, 213–14; Reeves, *West Bromwich*, 17. [58] H.O. 129/381/3/1.
[59] *Cong. Year Book* (1969–70), 259.
[60] Hackwood, *West Bromwich*, 82; Matthews, *Cong. Churches*, 228, 233; G.R.O., Worship Reg. no. 21302; *Staffs. Advertiser*, 30 Sept. 1876; W.B.L., Scrapbook 12, p. 57.
[61] Ex inf. the minister, Ebenezer (1969).
[62] For this section see *West Bromwich Cong. Church 1971* (copy in W.S.L. Pamphs. *sub* West Bromwich).

[63] See p. 66.
[64] H.O. 129/381/1/2. It was registered for Independents in 1857: G.R.O., Worship Reg. no. 8160.
[65] W.B.L., Scrapbook 1, p. 60 (unidentified newspaper cutting apparently of 1930 or 1931); O.S. Map 6", Staffs. LXVIII. NE. (1890 edn., surveyed 1885).
[66] O.S. Map 6", Staffs. LXVIII. NE. (1904 edn.); *The Chronicle*, 26 June 1908.
[67] W.B.L., Scrapbook 1, pp. 60–1; *Free Press*, 23 Sept. 1932; tablet in church; inscription on foundation-stone.
[68] *Cong. Year Book* (1969–70), 258.
[69] Reeves, *West Bromwich*, 22; S.R.O., D. 742/Dartmouth Estates/II/7/508–17. For Winfield see J. Petty, *Hist. of Prim. Meth. Connexion* (1864 edn.), 83–4.

opened a large hall called Ebenezer chapel in August.[70] It registered the Gospel Hall in Pitt Street in 1881,[71] and a barracks was opened in the former theatre in Queen Street in 1883.[72] The barracks was replaced by another in New Street registered in 1901,[73] and that was itself replaced by a barracks in Walsall Street, which was registered in 1902 and apparently remained in use until c. 1912.[74] A new hall was opened in Spon Lane in 1925.[75] It remained in use until 1972 when it was demolished in the course of the redevelopment of the area. A new hall was opened near by in Spon Lane in 1973.[76]

The Salvation Army used part of Bethel chapel in Dartmouth Street as a citadel after the Baptists had left it in 1884.[77] A malt-house at Hill Top was registered in 1885 but had ceased to be used by 1896.[78] By the earlier 1930s the army was working from a converted railway coach at Hill Top, but in 1934 it moved into a reconditioned bungalow in New Street there.[79] There is a barracks in Crankhall Lane dated 1954.[80]

SEVENTH-DAY ADVENTISTS. The Seventh-day Adventists began meeting in the town c. 1950. Services were held in various places until a church was built in Dartmouth Street in 1970.[81]

SPIRITUALISTS. The Spiritualists' Society was meeting in a room in Spon Lane by 1921.[82] The United Spiritualist Church was meeting in Walsall Street in the early 1930s[83] and the West Bromwich National Spiritualist Church in Old Meeting Street in 1954.[84] After meeting for a short time in a room in Guns Lane, the Spiritualists moved in 1972 to the Dartmouth Park Social Centre in Dagger Lane, and in 1974 they began to hold meetings at the Unitarian Church in Lodge Road.[85] There was formerly a Christian Spiritualist church in Whitehall Road;[86] it was derelict in 1970 and was then demolished.

THEOSOPHICAL SOCIETY. The Theosophical Society was meeting in a room in Victoria Chambers, Victoria Street, by 1916. In 1925 it had a room in Bank Chambers, High Street, but had ceased to meet there by 1927.[87]

TRIUMPHANT CHURCH OF GOD. After meeting in a house and a school hall, the Triumphant Church of God bought the former Methodist chapel at Golds Green in 1969.[88]

UNITARIANS. A Unitarian meeting and a Sunday school were established in 1859 at the Summit Schools in Spon Lane, founded and owned by the Kenrick family, who were prominent Unitarians.[89] In 1868 the congregation moved to the Assembly Room in Lombard Street, but they had to abandon it in 1869. In 1874 the Midland Christian Union invited the Revd. John Harrison to re-establish services, and he used St. George's Hall for the purpose. The present chapel in Lodge Road was opened in 1875. The trust deed gave its purpose simply as the worship of God, and in the mid 1890s Harrison was described as being 'as unconventional and in outward appearance as unclerical as his flock are unfettered by creed'. The chapel is a building of brick and stone in the Early English style.

UNITED REFORMED CHURCH, see PRESBYTERIANS AND CONGREGATIONALISTS.

OTHER GROUPS. In 1833 John Glover opened a chapel in Spon Lane for all Christians. It seems to have been in Union Street and to have become a Primitive Methodist chapel.[90]

A Bethel Mission in Great Bridge Street was registered in 1933.[91]

The Gospel Hall in Price Road, Friar Park, was registered in 1951.[92]

HINDUS. Ebenezer Congregational chapel, closed in 1971, was registered as Shree Krishna Temple in 1973. The official opening and the installation of idols took place in 1974.[93]

SOCIAL LIFE. A wake of unknown origin was originally held on All Saints' Day (1 November). By the 1830s it usually began on the first Monday in November and by the 1850s often lasted a week. Stalls were set up in High Street and shows housed in a field in Lodge Road and on open ground at the corner of High Street and Paradise Street.[94] In 1875, inspired by the example of the Wednesbury board of health, the improvement commissioners began a campaign for the suppression of the wake by forbidding the erection of stalls in the streets.[95]

[70] Ex inf. the Salvation Army International Headquarters, London (1969), citing *The Salvationist* (Sept. 1879) for Ebenezer.

[71] G.R.O., Worship Reg. no. 25715; *Staffs. Advertiser* (S. Staffs. edn.), 29 Apr., 14 Oct. 1882.

[72] Worship Reg. no. 27407; *Staffs. Advertiser*, 29 Dec. 1883; O.S. Map 1/500, Staffs. LXVIII. 10. 19 (1886); 'Old West Bromwich', 21 Sept. 1945; below p. 71.

[73] Worship Reg. no. 38198.

[74] Ibid. no. 38998 (cancelled 1912).

[75] *Midland Chron.* 9 Oct. 1925.

[76] *Express & Star*, 24 Feb. 1972; *Evening Mail*, 5 Oct. 1973.

[77] J. Richards, *West Bromwich and its Baptists 1796 to 1968*, 8 (copy in W.B.L.). The building was demolished in 1936. [78] Worship Reg. no. 28734.

[79] *Midland Chron. & Free Press*, 28 Dec. 1934.

[80] It was registered in June 1955: Worship Reg. no. 65010.

[81] *Midland Chron. & Free Press*, 20 Feb. 1970.

[82] Worship Reg. no. 48365.

[83] *Kelly's Dir. Staffs.* (1932).

[84] Worship Reg. no. 64315.

[85] Ibid. no. 73058; *Midland Chron. & Free Press*, 31 Jan. 1974.

[86] Name on building.

[87] Worship Reg. nos. 46825, 49593.

[88] *Express & Star*, 3 Oct. 1969.

[89] For this para. see R. A. Church, *Kenricks in Hardware* (Newton Abbot, 1969), 19, 28, 42; Hackwood, *West Bromwich*, 84; G. E. Evans, *Midland Churches: a Hist. of the Congregations on the Roll of the Midland Christian Union* (Dudley, 1899), 230–1; below p. 68.

[90] Reeves, *West Bromwich*, 23; White, *Dir. Staffs.* (1834); 'Old West Bromwich', 24 Dec. 1943; above p. 66.

[91] Worship Reg. no. 54191. [92] Ibid. no. 62999.

[93] G.R.O., Worship Reg. no. 73524; *Express & Star*, 22 June 1974; official programme of opening (copy in W.B.L.); above p. 68.

[94] Reeves, *West Bromwich*, 140–1; *Staffs. Advertiser*, 6 Nov. 1858; T.C.T. *Life's Realities*, 181–3; 'Old West Bromwich', 8 Feb. 1946.

[95] *Staffs. Advertiser* (S. Staffs. edn.), 8 and 15 Nov. 1873, 9 Oct. 1875.

The wake, however, continued on other sites, and it even survived the Second World War, although 'in an emasculated form'.[96] Another wake, called the Gooseberry Wake and held at Cutler's End on the first Sunday in August, existed in the early 19th century.[97]

Bull-baiting was a feature of the November wake, although the baiting-grounds were usually on the outskirts of the parish.[98] Martin's Act of 1822,[99] intended to suppress the pastime, was supported by the vestry and the local clergy.[1] When a prosecution brought after the 1827 wake revealed that through faulty drafting the Act could not outlaw bull-baiting[2] local agitation in West Bromwich and neighbouring towns helped to secure its statutory prohibition in 1835.[3] A baiting at the 1835 wake is the last known;[4] the substitution from 1837 of gymnastics and 'rural' sports at the wake brought the pastime to an end.[5]

Cocking, first recorded in the parish in 1574, and dog-fighting were popular sports in the 1850s.[6] Some traditional festivities were still observed in the 1850s: Hallowe'en was celebrated and the custom of 'heaving' in Easter Week was popular in some districts.[7] May Day celebrations, with a maypole, were held in a field adjoining the Stone Cross inn until c. 1915.[8]

Samuel Adams, a music dealer, established the first public hall, St. George's Hall in Paradise Street, in 1859 in a building which had formerly been a Wesleyan chapel and then a school. The remodelled interior provided a much-needed room for concerts, lectures, and meetings.[9] Though replaced by the new town hall as the chief meeting-place in 1875, it seems to have been sometimes used for entertainments until 1891 when it was converted into a wire works. It became a cinema after the First World War and was still so used in the 1940s.[10] In the late 19th century the town hall was the main location for 're-spectable' entertainment.[11]

In the 1850s Charles Udall, a publican, added to his Royal Exchange inn in Walsall Street a hall designed for 'free and easies'. It was later improved and turned into a concert hall and by 1869 was licensed as Udall's Music Hall.[12] By 1879, when it became the property of Walter Showell of Oldbury, a brewer, it was known as the Royal Exchange Theatre and, after partial rebuilding to the designs of Edward Pincher of West Bromwich, was re-opened in that year as the Theatre Royal.[13] It was extended in 1890, burnt down in 1895, and rebuilt in 1896 to the designs of Owen & Ward of Birmingham.[14] It closed c. 1940.[15] Bennett's Theatre, Queen Street, a music hall, was open by 1869. It was designed to serve also as a Volunteers' drill hall and soon after was being used solely for that purpose. It later became a Salvation Army barracks and in 1903 the first factory of the Manifold Printing Co., subsequently Manifoldia Ltd.[16] The New Hippodrome (later the Hippodrome), at the Carter's Green end of High Street, was opened in 1906 as a music hall and from 1911 was being used for variety, plays, and pantomimes. After the First World War it became a cinema, though variety shows continued to be given. It was closed in 1922 and soon afterwards demolished.[17]

The first cinemas were opened in 1910: the Electric, with entrances in High Street and Paradise Street, in May,[18] and the Queen's, Queen Street, later in the year.[19] The Imperial, Spon Lane, designed by A. Bye, was established in 1912.[20] By 1928 there were seven,[21] and in the 1930s and 1940s as many as eight were in operation at times.[22] When the A.B.C., Carter's Green, closed in 1968 only two, the King's in Paradise Street and the Queen's, were left. The Queen's was demolished in 1969, after a period of several months during which it had catered for immigrants by showing Indian and Pakistani films. In the same year, however, the Imperial, which had been converted into a bingo hall

[96] 'Old West Bromwich', 16 Apr., 2 July 1943, 8 Feb. 1946.
[97] 'West Bromwich 100 Years Ago', 10 May 1901.
[98] Hackwood, *West Bromwich*, 115; W.B.L., Scrapbook 13, p. 10.
[99] Act to prevent cruel and improper treatment of animals, 3 Geo. IV, c. 71. For the background to the Act see e.g. E. S. Turner, *All Heaven in a Rage*, chaps. 9 and 10.
[1] West Bromwich Vestry Mins. pp. 120–2; F. W. Hackwood, *Wednesbury Notes & Queries* (Wednesbury, 1886), para. 154; *Staffs. Advertiser*, 8 Dec. 1827.
[2] Hackwood, *West Bromwich*, 115; *Short Authentic Account of the late decision on the Bull Baiting Question, in the case of the King against John Hill* (Dudley, 1827; copy in B.R.L.); 'Ex parte John Hill', *The English Reports*, clxxii (1928), 397–8.
[3] Vestry Mins. pp. 137–8; *C.J.* lxxxiii. 407; *Staffs. Advertiser*, 1 Mar. and 14 June 1828; Act to consolidate and amend the several laws relating to the cruel and improper treatment of animals, 5 & 6 Wm. IV, c. 59.
[4] *Staffs. Advertiser*, 21 Nov. 1835. Reeves, *West Bromwich*, 141, states: 'At this [November] wake . . . we have bull-baiting'. His preface is dated 1 Dec. 1836, but the book must have been virtually completed before that year's wake. No evidence of baiting at the 1836 wake has been found.
[5] *Staffs. Advertiser*, 18 Nov. 1837; *1st Rep. Com. Midland Mining, S. Staffs.* [508], App. p. 15, H.C. (1843), xiii.
[6] West Bromwich Ct. R. p. 2; T.C.T. *Life's Realities*, 210; W.B.L., Notebook belonging to Revd. S. Lees (66/16151).
[7] T.C.T. *Life's Realities*, 193–4, 196–201. For 'heaving' see e.g. Charlotte Sophia Burne, *Shropshire Folk-lore* (1883), 336–40.
[8] 'Old West Bromwich', 3 Aug. 1945.
[9] *Staffs. Advertiser*, 29 Oct. 1859; Harrison, Harrod &

Co. *Dir. Staffs.* (1861); 'Old West Bromwich', 21 and 28 Jan. 1944 (stating that it was described as St. George's Hall in 1836 when it was let for a meeting). For the previous history of the building see above p. 64.
[10] *Midland Chron. & Free Press*, 21 Jan. 1944; *P.O. Dir. Staffs.* (1876).
[11] *Midland Chron. & Free Press*, 30 Oct. 1942.
[12] *Free Press*, 13 Sept. 1895; White, *Dir. Birm.* (1869). Udall was at the Royal Exchange in 1858 and had a beer-house (probably the Royal Exchange) in Walsall St. in 1851: W. H. Dix & Co. *Dir. Birm.* (1858); White, *Dir. Staffs.* (1851).
[13] *Free Press*, 15 Feb. 1879; *West Bromwich Echo*, 29 Mar. and 6 Sept. 1879. Showell was presumably head of the firm that appears as Walter Showell & Son Ltd. at Walsall in *Kelly's Dir. Staffs.* (1884).
[14] *Free Press*, 2 Jan. 1891, 13 Sept. 1895, 21 and 28 Aug. 1896. Between 1890 and 1895 the building was known as the New Theatre Royal.
[15] *Midland Chron. & Free Press*, 31 May 1940, contains what appears to have been its last advertisement in the local press. It was referred to as closed ibid. 30 Oct. 1942.
[16] White, *Dir. Birm.* (1869), referring to 'a theatre'; *P.O. Dir. Staffs.* (1872); 'Old West Bromwich', 21 Sept. 1945; T.C.T. *Life's Realities*, 181; *Fifty Years of Achievement, 1903–53* (history of Manifoldia Ltd. print. and pub. by the firm; copy in W.B.L.).
[17] *Midland Chron. & Free Press*, 23 and 30 Oct. 1942.
[18] *Chron. for West Bromwich and Oldbury*, 20 May 1910, reporting opening.
[19] Ibid. 30 Dec. 1910.
[20] Ibid. 19 Apr. 1912.
[21] *Kelly's Dir. Staffs.* (1928).
[22] Ibid. (1932; 1940); *Midland Chron. & Free Press*, 22 Dec. 1939, 25 Oct. 1946.

in 1965, became a cinema once more. It and the King's remained open in 1970.[23]

A concert was held at the Bull's Head inn in 1819, and in 1836 it was claimed that music, 'chiefly cultivated in private families', was the principal amusement of the town.[24] There was a choral society in 1847,[25] and in the 1850s Concerts for the People were being given by amateurs under the patronage of James Bagnall. Most of the performers were local working people and large audiences were attracted.[26] A Philharmonic Society was established in 1869.[27] A new choral society which was formed in 1876, the earlier body apparently having lapsed, was disbanded in 1906.[28] In 1970 the town had an operatic society and a youth orchestra.

George Osborne, minister at the Old Meeting from 1785 to 1792, was connected with the foundation and maintenance of what has been claimed as the first public library in West Bromwich; the books were kept at the Swan inn.[29] In the late 1820s William Salter, a New Street bookseller and printer, kept a newsroom,[30] while from the 1830s several libraries and newsrooms were established.[31] The Free Libraries Acts were adopted in 1870,[32] and a library designed by Weller & Proud of Wolverhampton formed part of the group of public buildings erected in High Street in the 1870s. It was opened in stages in 1874–5.[33] A subscription library (which operated until 1934) was added to the existing public library departments in 1884.[34] In 1907 the library moved into its present home, erected at the expense of Andrew Carnegie in High Street on the site of the market hall and the Heath iron warehouse and adjoining the old library. It is of brick with stone dressings and has a façade with Ionic columns and an interior decorated with coloured tiles, stained glass, and murals; the architect was Stephen J. Holliday of West Bromwich. In 1924 the reading room of the old library became the borough's council chamber. A junior open-access library was opened in 1929, and in 1937 open access was introduced in the adult library.[35] The West Bromwich Technical Library, housed in the Technical College, High Street (now the Engineering Division of the West Bromwich College of Commerce and Technology), was established in 1960. It is open to the public.[36]

The Oak House, Oak Road, presented to the borough by Reuben Farley, was opened as a museum in 1898.[37] The cottage at Newton where Francis Asbury, the Methodist pioneer, spent his early years was acquired by the corporation in 1955 and opened to the public in 1959.[38]

A newspaper called the *West Bromwich Reporter* was being published weekly in 1869[39] and probably dated from 1863. No more is known of it. The *Wednesbury Advertiser*, founded in 1859, had by 1868 become the *Wednesbury and West Bromwich Advertiser*; but it was always published at Wednesbury, and in 1872 West Bromwich was dropped from the title.[40] In 1867 William Osborne established the weekly *West Bromwich Times*, which he printed and published at his office in High Street. It had ceased publication by 1872.[41] There was a *West Bromwich Weekly News* in 1878;[42] it had been published by William Britten in High Street since at least 1876 and had probably been founded in 1871.[43] By 1880 the publishers were the Midland Printing Co., also in High Street. It continued to be printed and published at West Bromwich until 1904 and thereafter at Oldbury, where the publishers merged it with an existing *Weekly News* to form the *West Bromwich, Smethwick and Oldbury Weekly News* (subsequently the *Oldbury Weekly News*). A short-lived *West Bromwich Echo*, printed and published in Paradise Street by Joseph Bates, appeared weekly in 1879.[44]

The weekly *Free Press*, a Liberal paper, was founded in 1875.[45] When its proprietors, the Free Press Co., went into liquidation in 1878 J. A. Kenrick, a leading West Bromwich Liberal and a member of a prominent local family of ironfounders, bought the concern and went into partnership with F. T. Jefferson, a lawyer who had been the secretary of the Free Press Co. In 1882 the business moved from Hudson's Passage to High Street. From 1886 to 1894 Jefferson also published *The Labour Tribune*, a Radical paper which described itself as 'the organ of the miners, ironworkers, nut and bolt forgers, &c., of Great Britain' and aimed at a national readership.[46]

In 1896 another Liberal weekly, the *West Bromwich and Oldbury Chronicle*, was established by Astbury & Jewell in Paradise Street. Its early years,

[23] *Evening Mail*, 6 Dec. 1968, 6 Jan., 6 Aug. 1969; *West Bromwich News*, 5 Feb. 1970.
[24] 'West Bromwich 100 Years Ago', 19 Apr. 1901; Reeves, *West Bromwich*, 61.
[25] *Staffs. Advertiser*, 10 Apr. 1847.
[26] Ibid. 29 Nov. 1856, 3 Jan. 1857.
[27] Ibid. 19 June 1869.
[28] Ibid. (S. Staffs. edn.), 4 Mar. 1876, 20 Oct. 1906.
[29] S. Lees, 'Hist. of Ebenezer Chapel, West Bromwich' (MS. at West Bromwich United Reformed Church), 27.
[30] Pigot, *Com. Dir. Birm.* (1829), 101.
[31] See pp. 81–2.
[32] R. B. Ludgate, 'Libraries and the Public', *The Old Church News, Centenary Number, 1866–1966* (copy in W.B.L.).
[33] *P.O. Dir. Staffs.* (1876); W.B.L., Scrapbook 12, p. 54.
[34] W.B.L., Scrapbook 12, pp. 179, 182.
[35] Ibid. p. 171; *Old Church News, Centenary Number*; *Staffs. Advertiser* (S. Staffs. edn.), 28 Apr. 1906, 15 June 1907; above p. 46 and plate facing p. 97.
[36] *West Bromwich Official Handbook* [1963], 53–4.
[37] See p. 25.
[38] *Midland Chron. & Free Press*, 4 Dec. 1959; *Procs. of Tenth World Methodist Conference, Oslo, Norway, 1961*, 6, 55, 63; *West Bromwich Official Handbook* [1970], 55; above p. 4.

[39] Duplicated handlist of Staffs. newspapers held by B.M. Newspaper Libr. in late 1950s (copy in W.S.L.).
[40] Ibid.; *P.O. Dir. Staffs.* (1868), Adverts. p. 105. The paper became the *South Staffs. Advertiser* in 1872 and the *Midland Advertiser* later the same year.
[41] Woodall, *West Bromwich Yesterdays*, 62; *P.O. Dir. Staffs.* (1868), p. 724 and Adverts. p. 89; ibid. (1872).
[42] For the rest of this para. see handlist of Staffs. newspapers held by B.M.; *P.O. Dir. Staffs.* (1876); *Kelly's Dir. Staffs.* (1880 and later edns. to 1904); *Kelly's Dir. Worcs.* (1908), Adverts. p. 3. The *Weekly News* at Oldbury dated from 1874: Woodall, *West Bromwich Yesterdays*, 63.
[43] But it is not mentioned in *P.O. Dir. Staffs.* (1872).
[44] Set of nos. 1–24 of the *West Bromwich Echo* in W.B.L.
[45] Handlist of Staffs. newspapers held by B.M. Its name for the first 3 issues (25 Sept.–9 Oct. 1875) was *Midland Free Press*. For the rest of this para. see, unless otherwise stated, *Free Press*, 23 June 1933; Woodall, *West Bromwich Yesterdays*, 62; R. A. Church, *Kenricks in Hardware* (Newton Abbot, 1969), 80 and n.; *P.O. Dir. Staffs.* (1876); *Kelly's Dir. Staffs.* (1880 and later edns. to 1924).
[46] Woodall, *West Bromwich Yesterdays*, 62; handlist of Staffs. newspapers held by B.M.; bound set of nos. 1–96 of *The Labour Tribune* in W.B.L.

PRINTING AND PUBLISHING OFFICES OF THE FREE PRESS CO., 1885 (later the offices of Kenrick & Jefferson Ltd.)

like those of the *Free Press*, were financially insecure, and there were several changes of ownership as well as several slight changes of name.[47] J. L. Astbury became the sole proprietor in 1903.[48] The South Staffordshire Newspaper and Printing Co. Ltd. was formed in 1905 to take over the *Chronicle* and some other local papers, but it went into voluntary liquidation in 1910 and from then until 1912 the *Chronicle* was run by its printer, Joseph Wones. In 1912 the paper was acquired by its present owners, the Dudley Herald Ltd., now Midland United Newspapers Ltd. Later the same year the paper became the *Midland Chronicle for West Bromwich and Oldbury*.[49] The *Chronicle*'s layout and appearance were from its early days more popular in design than those of the rival *Free Press*. Its acquisition by a publishing group gave it greater financial stability. Kenrick & Jefferson Ltd., on the other hand, gradually lost interest in the *Free Press* and in 1933 sold it to the proprietors of the *Chronicle*, who merged the papers to form what is now the

West Bromwich Midland Chronicle and Free Press.[50] The local government changes of 1966, by which Wednesbury became part of the county borough of West Bromwich, prompted the West Midlands Press Ltd., proprietors of the *Wednesbury Times*, to increase the coverage of their paper and to alter its title. The first issue of the *West Bromwich News and Wednesbury Times* appeared in April 1966.[51] Like the *Chronicle* the *News* has offices in West Bromwich but is not printed in the town.

A cricket club was formed in 1828.[52] No more is known of it, but it may have been an ancestor of the present West Bromwich Dartmouth Cricket Club. Dartmouth, established in 1834,[53] was for some years early in its life apparently known as the Victoria Cricket Club; the present name was subsequently adopted as a compliment to the earls of Dartmouth, who have always been the club's patrons.[54] From 1837 the club played on the Four Acres, part of the Dartmouth estate, and in 1920 Lord Dartmouth provided the present ground in Sandwell Park. The

[47] Woodall, *West Bromwich Yesterdays*, 62; files of the newspaper in W.B.L.

[48] *West Bromwich and Oldbury Chron.* 9 Jan. 1903.

[49] Woodall, *West Bromwich Yesterdays*, 62–3; *West Bromwich and Oldbury Chron.* 5 May 1905; *Chron. for West Bromwich, Oldbury and District*, 22 Apr. 1910; *Chron. for West Bromwich and Oldbury*, 19 July 1912; *Midland Chron. for West Bromwich and Oldbury*, 25 Oct. 1912.

[50] Woodall, *West Bromwich Yesterdays*, 62; *Willing's Press Guide* (1969). The title has varied slightly since the 1933 merger. With the first issue of the new paper on 7 July 1933 it became the *West Bromwich, Oldbury and Smethwick Midland Chronicle and Free Press*; from 2 Mar. 1962 the *West Bromwich and Oldbury Midland Chronicle, Free Press*; from 4 Feb. 1966 the *West Bromwich and Warley Midland Chronicle, Free Press*. The present title was adopted from the issue of 29 July 1966.

[51] *West Bromwich News and Wednesbury Times*, 28 Apr. 1966.

[52] *Worcester Herald*, 28 June 1828. This reference has been supplied by Mr. John Ford of Horsted Keynes (Suss.). For what appears to be the club's first set of rules and a list of its founder members see B.R.L., Caddick and Yates 18.

[53] *Dartmouth Cricket Club Bazaar, March 22nd, 23rd, 24th and 25th 1939* (West Bromwich, 1939; copy in W.B.L.). *V.C.H. Staffs.* ii. 368, following *Civic Mag.* Jan. 1930, 13 (copy in W.B.L.), gives the date of establishment as 1837; but since Reeves (*West Bromwich*, 62) states that 'the Cricket Club', apparently still in existence when he was writing (1836), was founded in 1834 the earlier date appears to be correct. And see following note.

[54] *Dartmouth C.C. Bazaar, 1939*; ex inf. Mr. G. C. W. Jones of West Bromwich (1970). The name Victoria may have been adopted in 1837, thus giving rise to the tradition that the club was founded in that year.

club plays in the Birmingham and District Cricket League.[55] There is a West Bromwich Cricket League, which in 1969 consisted of 14 teams playing in two divisions.[56]

West Bromwich Albion Football Club (the 'Throstles') was founded in 1879 as West Bromwich Strollers by a group of men from Salter's spring works.[57] Men from Salter's continued to be prominent in the club for many years. Several of the early players lived in the Albion district of West Bromwich, and within a year of its foundation the club adopted its present name. The club took its first enclosed ground, in Walsall Street, in 1881; in 1882 it moved to the Four Acres; and in 1885 it moved to a larger ground in Stoney Lane and became a professional club. It was a founder member of the Football League, established in 1888. In 1900 it moved to its present home, the Hawthorns, at the corner of Birmingham Road and Halford's Lane.

In 1803 there were 10 friendly societies in West Bromwich, with an estimated membership of 500.[58] By 1813 there were over 700 members of friendly societies;[59] the number of societies at that date is unknown, for registration was generally unpopular in the Black Country and those which registered represented only a fraction of those in existence.[60] About 1832 a writer estimated that there were at least 40 such groups in the parish, 'including sick clubs, money clubs, clothes clubs, and clubs for land or furniture'. The oldest society was then 56 years old, but most had been founded in the previous 20 years.[61] Many of the clubs were in fact *ad hoc* bodies which broke up after a year or two; money clubs, as a West Bromwich collier stated in 1843, were little more than attempts by butties to promote drinking in a particular public house.[62] There were, however, more permanent groups, and, despite the prejudice against it, registration increased in the 1830s and 1840s. Purely local clubs—such as Woodhall's Friendly Society (1812), which met fortnightly at the Red Lion, Thomas Woodhall's public house near All Saints' Church—were supplemented in the 1840s by local branches of national organizations—the West Bromwich Loyal Tenerife Lodge of Nelsonic Crimson Oaks (1846) and several lodges of Odd Fellows and Odd Women. In addition there was at least one occupational society, the West Bromwich Miners Friendly Society (1841).[63] By 1876 there were 70 registered societies, mostly dating from the 1860s and 1870s.[64] The growth of friendly societies and benefit clubs was encouraged by some employers. Archibald Kenrick (d. 1835),

for example, organized a benefit association among the workers at his Spon Lane foundry;[65] in 1812 Edward Elwell the younger, another iron-founder, was president of Woodhall's Friendly Society;[66] about 1854 John Bagnall & Sons set up a sick club and contributed largely to the funds;[67] and T. B. Salter (d. 1887), head of the spring-balance firm, started a sick and burial club for his employees. By the early 20th century George Salter & Co. operated schemes which anticipated subsequent national welfare and insurance legislation.[68]

In 1856 the West Bromwich Association for Working Men, a body modelled on the Wednesbury Recreation Society, was formed, with the strong support of industrialists and the gentry, to provide lectures, concerts, and social intercourse.[69] A working men's club and newsroom was established in a large house in High Street in 1876 largely through the efforts of the local branch of the Church of England Temperance Society. When the club's committee decided to allow the consumption of beer on the premises a total abstinence group split off and in 1878 opened a temperance coffee house in High Street, modelled on those already established in Birmingham.[70]

The Y.M.C.A., after working for four years in a coach house and stables in New Street, moved in 1888 to new premises in St. Michael Street. The building has an impressive façade, in a pointed Gothic style with moulded brick decoration. By the end of the 19th century it was a centre of both social and educational life in West Bromwich. In 1965 the Association moved to temporary premises elsewhere in the town and in 1970 to a new hostel in Carter's Green with accommodation for 70 residents and a large sports hall.[71]

EDUCATION. There was a school in West Bromwich by 1686, apparently a private academy,[72] and by then the parish was entitled to send two boys to Old Swinford Hospital School (Worcs.), established in 1670.[73] By the later 18th century there were schools for the poor[74] and several private academies,[75] and the first Sunday schools were opened in 1786 and 1788.[76] The Dartmouths, the Clarkes, and others paid for the education of many poor children.[77] In 1819 the minister of All Saints' stated that there were enough schools for most of the poor and that parents were normally eager to take advantage of them.[78]

An unofficial house-to-house survey of working-

[55] *Civic Mag.* Jan. 1930, 13; ex inf. Mr. Jones.
[56] *Express & Star*, 10 June 1969.
[57] For the following para. see P. Morris, *West Bromwich Albion*. There is a brief account of the club's history in *V.C.H. Staffs.* ii. 373.
[58] *Abstract of Returns relative to Expence and Maintenance of Poor*, H.C. 175, p. 469 (1803–4), xiii.
[59] *Abstract of Answers and Returns relating to Expense and Maintenance of Poor in Eng.* p. 419, H.C. (1818), xix.
[60] *1st Rep. Com. Midland Mining, S. Staffs.* [508], p. li, H.C. (1843), xiii. By 1813 only 2 West Bromwich societies had registered: S.R.O., Q/RSf.
[61] W.B.L., MS. Notes on West Bromwich Methodism.
[62] *1st Rep. Com. Midland Mining, S. Staffs.* pp. l–li, 31.
[63] S.R.O., Q/RSf. For the location of the Red Lion see Parson and Bradshaw, *Dir. Staffs.* (1818).
[64] *Rep. Chief Registrar of Friendly Societies, 1876, App. P*, H.C. 429–1, pp. 395–6 (1877), lxxvii.
[65] Church, *Kenricks in Hardware*, 42.
[66] *Articles of Agreement . . . of Woodhall's Friendly Society* (Birmingham, 1812), 16 (copy in S.R.O., Q/RSf).
[67] *Rep. Com. State of Population in Mining Districts, 1854* [1838], p. 14, H.C. (1854), xix.
[68] Mary Bache, *Salter, the Story of a Family Firm* (West Bromwich, 1960), 21–2, 28–9, 38, 83–4.
[69] *Staffs. Advertiser*, 22 Nov. 1856.
[70] Ibid. (S. Staffs. edn.), 3 Apr. 1875, 29 Apr., 3 June, 1 July 1876, 13 July 1878; *P.O. Dir. Staffs.* (1876); *Kelly's Dir. Staffs.* (1880).
[71] *Express & Star*, 1 and 23 Apr. 1970; inscription on St. Michael Street building; Hackwood, *West Bromwich*, 94.   [72] See p. 83.
[73] T. R. Nash, *Colls. for Hist. of Worcs.* ii (1782), 210–11; *V.C.H. Worcs.* iii. 202–3, 213–14; iv. 536.
[74] Reeves, *West Bromwich*, 54–5, 159; S. Lees, 'Hist. of Ebenezer Chapel, West Bromwich' (MS. at West Bromwich United Reformed Church), 26–7.   [75] See p. 83.
[76] See pp. 52, 67.   [77] L.J.R.O., B/V/5/1772–3.
[78] *Digest of Returns to Sel. Cttee. on Educ. of Poor*, H.C. 224, p. 855 (1819), ix (2).

class education was undertaken in 1837.[79] It revealed that there were 7,803 working-class children living at home: 1,428 over the age of 14, 5,805 of school age (considered by the investigators to be from 2 to 14), and 570 who were under two. Of the first group some 27 per cent could read and write and almost 40 per cent could read but not write. Almost 46 per cent of the second group went to school; only 11 per cent could both read and write, although a further 71 per cent could read but could not write. Parents relied overwhelmingly on Sunday schools and dame schools: of the children at school over 42 per cent attended Sunday schools and just under 42 per cent went to dame schools to learn the alphabet or to the cheapest private schools to be taught reading and sewing. The two National schools accounted for only about 9 per cent of the total, while 7 per cent were at infants' schools.

A school board was formed in 1871. It at once undertook an educational census, which revealed that there were 14 schools in receipt of government aid, with room for 6,414 children, and 6 more schools not under government, with room for 1,850 children. A further 421 children were at schools where fees were more than 9d. a week, and there were 5 cheaper private-adventure schools with accommodation for 429 children. Seven hundred extra school places were needed.[80] A by-law making school attendance compulsory was passed in 1871, and after some early difficulties West Bromwich established one of the best records of school attendance among the Black Country boroughs.[81] Between 1882 and 1886 the board organized weekly classes for pupil teachers and uncertificated assistant teachers, and in 1896 it established a pupil-teachers' centre.[82] From 1893 to the early 1920s the corporation was a partner in running an industrial school at Lichfield.[83]

In 1903 West Bromwich county borough became responsible for all stages of public education. Schools were reorganized in 1930-3 on the lines laid down in the Hadow Report.[84] In 1946 a joint development plan for education was published for West Bromwich and Smethwick, which were then discussing amalgamation. Although amalgamation did not take place the report's proposals were adopted by each borough individually. West Bromwich decided to build more primary schools and

to provide its first nursery schools. The tripartite system of secondary education was adopted.[85] Comprehensive secondary education was introduced in 1955 and became general in 1969.[86]

In 1961 the corporation purchased Ingestre Hall near Stafford and established there a residential arts centre for young people from West Bromwich.[87] The Plas Gwynant Adventure School at Nantgwynant (Caernarvons.) was opened in 1959. By 1966 the corporation had established three special schools for handicapped or maladjusted children: Millfield Day School in Westminster Road, opened in 1958, and residential schools at Shenstone (1954) and Whittington (1965).[88]

Since the later 19th century several trusts have been established to provide scholarships and prizes.[89] They include the George and Thomas Henry Salter Trust, the Akrill, Wilson, and Kenrick Foundations, and the West Bromwich Educational Foundation.

All Saints' Church of England Junior and Infants' School. In 1811, with the help of Lord Dartmouth, a girls' school was established by subscription at Hall End. It was united with the National Society in 1815, and in 1827 it benefited under the terms of the will of Joseph Barrs of West Bromwich.[90] Boys were admitted from the mid 1840s.[91] In 1851 Lord Dartmouth provided new buildings in All Saints Street, with accommodation for both girls and boys; by May 1853 there was an average attendance of 60 girls and 65 boys.[92] An infants' school, built by Thomas Jesson, was added in 1854-5 on a site provided by Lord Dartmouth to the north of the 1851 schools.[93] Average attendance rose from 293 in January 1871 to 416 in 1881.[94] The schools were enlarged several times in the 1880s and 1890s,[95] and in 1900-1 the average attendance was 606.[96] In 1915, after a further building had been added, the school was reorganized into boys', girls', and infants' departments; in 1934 a further reorganization led to the creation of senior mixed, junior mixed, and infants' departments.[97] The junior and infants' departments were granted voluntary aided status in 1954. The senior (secondary modern) department was subsequently given voluntary controlled status but was closed in 1969 as a result of the reorganization of secondary education in the borough.[98]

[79] 'Rep. on the State of Educ. among the Working Classes in the Parish of West Bromwich', *Jnl. Statistical Soc. of London*, ii.
[80] *Lond. Gaz.* 10 Feb. 1871, p. 486; A. C. Beardsmore, 'West Bromwich School Board: a concise chronological record, 1871-1903' (TS. in W.B.L.), 2.
[81] Beardsmore, 'School Board', 3; Hackwood, *West Bromwich*, 97; P. Liddle, 'Development of Elementary Education in Walsall between 1862 and 1902' (London Univ. M.A. (Educ.) thesis, 1967), 77-9, 89.
[82] Hackwood, *West Bromwich*, 98-9; Beardsmore, 'School Board', 8, 10, 14.   [83] See p. 254.
[84] L. G. Rose, 'County Boro. of West Bromwich Education Facilities', *County Boro. of West Bromwich Municipal Tenants' Handbook* [1939], 28 (copy in W.B.L.).
[85] *West Bromwich Official Handbook* (6th edn.), 56; below pp. 136-7.
[86] *West Bromwich Official Handbook* [1970], 27; ex inf. West Bromwich Educ. Dept. (1970).
[87] *The Times*, 10 July 1961; ex inf. the Principal, Ingestre Hall (1969).
[88] *West Bromwich Official Handbook* [1963], 45-6; ibid. (1966), 15; ex inf. Educ. Dept.
[89] For this para. see *West Bromwich Official Handbook* [1963], 66. For the Salter Trust see below p. 85.

[90] White, *Dir. Staffs.* (1834; 1851); Nat. Soc. files; Reeves, *West Bromwich*, 143.
[91] *P.O. Dir. Staffs.* (1845) mentions a mistress and states that the school is for girls; Nat. Soc. *Church Schools Enquiry, 1846-7* (priv. print. 1849), states that there are 45 boys and 72 girls under a master and a mistress.
[92] Ed. 7/112/West Bromwich/13; White, *Dir. Staffs.* (1851).
[93] Tablet on building giving date 1854; *P.O. Dir. Staffs.* (1860; 1868); S.R.O., D. 742/Dartmouth Estates/ II/9/702; Willett, *West Bromwich*, pedigree 7.
[94] Hackwood, *West Bromwich*, 97; *Incorporation of West Bromwich: Full Rep. of Official Enquiry . . . 1882* (West Bromwich, 1882), 27 (copy in W.B.L.).
[95] S.R.O., D. 564/8/1/20, rep. on All Saints' Sch., 1882; Lich. Dioc. Ch. Cal. (1888), 156; *Kelly's Dir. Staffs.* (1916); Nat. Soc. files.
[96] *List of Schs. under Admin. of Bd. 1901-2* [Cd. 1277], p. 218, H.C. (1902), lxxix.
[97] A. C. Beardsmore, 'County Borough of West Bromwich. Particulars of Schools acquired, or erected, by the School Board from 1871 to 1903, and the Local Education Authority from 1904 to 1950' (TS. in W.B.L.).
[98] Nat. Soc. files; West Bromwich Educ. Cttee.: List of Schools, 1969-70 (TS. in Educ. Dept.); ex inf. Educ. Dept.

Christ Church National School (Boys), later Christ Church Junior and Infants' School. A boys' school was established by subscription in New Street in 1811. Lord Dartmouth provided the site and was prominent in the work. The school was united with the National Society in 1815, and in 1827 it benefited under the terms of the will of Joseph Barrs of West Bromwich.[99] It became Christ Church National School on the formation of the new parish in 1837. In 1842 fees, 2*d.* a week, were charged only in the infants' department,[1] but by 1846–7 fees were charged throughout the school. There were then some 125 pupils.[2] The building had been enlarged by 1851, and there was an attendance of 200 in 1860.[3] In 1862 the 'small, old-fashioned, ill-convenienced, barn-like superstructure' was replaced by new schools for boys and infants on a site in Walsall Street given by Lord Dartmouth. He also gave the site and buildings of the old school to the parish, and the proceeds from their sale, with grants from government and the National Society, helped to pay for the new schools. They were completed in stages; the last part, the infants' school-room, was opened in 1863.[4] Average attendance in January 1871 was 305.[5] Robert Hodgson, vicar 1872–82, raised the numbers. The school was enlarged during his incumbency, and by 1881 the average attendance had risen to 448.[6] The school was transferred to the local authority in 1929. In 1932 it became a junior girls' and infants' school (the boys being transferred to Bratt Street), in 1934 a junior mixed school, and in 1948 a junior mixed and infants' school. It was closed in 1968, and the children were moved to the premises of the former Technical High School at the Cronehills.[7]

Great Bridge Wesleyan Methodist School, later Fisher Street Council School. A day school was built in 1826 at Great Bridge for the near-by Wesleyan Methodist chapel, which itself stood in Tipton parish.[8] By 1859 there was an attendance of some 120 and numbers were increasing. Since the building was due to be demolished to make way for a new street and was in any case regarded by the Wesleyans as 'totally inadequate for the improved system of instruction', larger buildings were erected the same year near by in Fisher Street.[9] The school reopened in 1860 with mixed and infants' departments,[10] and under Joseph Vincent, head teacher 1865–1909, it won a high reputation locally.[11] In 1907 it was transferred to the local authority. The senior pupils

were moved to the new George Salter School in 1932, and Fisher Street continued as a junior and infants' school until its closure in 1969.[12]

Lyndon Infants' School. An infants' school existed at Lyndon by 1834, when there was an attendance of about 100. It was organized from Ebenezer Congregational chapel by 1845 and had probably always been connected with it. No mention of it has been found after 1850, and it appears to have closed in that year.[13]

St. Michael's Roman Catholic School. A charity school in connexion with the Roman Catholic mission had been established in St. Michael Street by 1834. In the early 1850s it was run by the Sisters of Charity of St. Paul, who also kept a boarding-school for girls. A new school-house was built in 1870, and in January 1871 the average attendance was 75.[14] The infants' department was closed in 1910 because of lack of space, and infants were thenceforth taught at local authority schools.[15] The school itself was closed in 1962 and the pupils were transferred to the St. John Bosco Roman Catholic School.[16]

Great Bridge Congregational School. In 1835 an infants' school was opened in Sheepwash Lane, Great Bridge, by the Congregationalists, who in 1839 built Salem chapel there.[17] In 1851 there was a large British school attached to the chapel.[18] Day schools were still being conducted there in 1861,[19] but by 1868 the chapel maintained only Sunday schools.[20]

Paradise Street Wesleyan Methodist School, later Bratt Street Wesleyan Methodist School and Bratt Street Council School. In 1838 the Wesleyan Methodists opened day schools, including an infants' department, in their Sunday-school building in Paradise Street. In 1842 between 60 and 80 boys, a similar number of girls, and some 150 infants attended. The schools were replaced in 1858 by a new building in Bratt Street.[21] In 1911 the school was handed over to the local authority. Plans to replace it were halted by the First World War. From 1921 to 1925 the girls were housed in a block of Cronehills School, then not completed. In 1932 Bratt Street became a junior boys' and infants' school, the girls being transferred to Christ Church School. In 1934 the boys' department was converted into a special department for educationally sub-normal children, while the infants' department continued to function as a separate unit until it was closed in 1948, the pupils being transferred to Christ Church

[99] White, *Dir. Staffs.* (1834; 1851); Nat. Soc. files; Reeves, *West Bromwich*, 143.
[1] *1st Rep. Com. Midland Mining, S. Staffs.* [508], p. 15, H.C. (1843), xiii. The statement (p. cxlv) that Christ Church Sch. is for girls is apparently a confusion with All Saints' Sch.
[2] Nat. Soc. *Church Schs. Enquiry, 1846–7.*
[3] White, *Dir. Staffs.* (1851); *Staffs. Advertiser*, 26 May 1860.
[4] Ed. 7/112/West Bromwich/14; Nat. Soc. files; S.R.O., D. 812/7/West Bromwich, Christ Church Sch. (plans); *Lich. Dioc. Ch. Cal.* (1863), 145–6.
[5] Hackwood, *West Bromwich*, 97.
[6] *Lich. Dioc. Mag.* 1883, 60; *Incorp. of West Bromwich*, 27.
[7] Beardsmore, 'West Bromwich Schools'; *Express & Star*, 20 July 1968; ex inf. Educ. Dept.
[8] White, *Dir. Staffs.* (1851).
[9] *Staffs. Advertiser*, 18 June, 16 July 1859; J. Parkes, *Hist. of Tipton* (Tipton, 1915), 209.
[10] Beardsmore, 'West Bromwich Schools'.
[11] *Kelly's Dir. Staffs.* (1896); Parkes, *Tipton*, 209; Beardsmore, 'West Bromwich Schools'.

[12] Beardsmore, 'West Bromwich Schools', Fisher St. and Geo. Salter Schs.; List of Schools, 1968–9; ibid. 1969–70; ex inf. Educ. Dept.
[13] White, *Dir. Staffs.* (1834); *P.O. Dir. Staffs.* (1845; 1850). Its end may be connected with the alterations to the Ebenezer British Sch. in 1850: see below p. 77.
[14] Ed. 7/112/West Bromwich/19; White, *Dir. Staffs.* (1834); *P.O. Dir. Staffs.* (1860); Hackwood, *West Bromwich*, 97; above p. 61.
[15] Beardsmore, 'West Bromwich Schools'.
[16] Ex inf. Educ. Dept.
[17] A. G. Matthews, *Congregational Churches of Staffs.* 214.
[18] White, *Dir. Staffs.* (1851). Neither this school nor the infants' school is listed in *P.O. Dir. Staffs.* (1850) or in any earlier directory.
[19] Harrison, Harrod & Co. *Dir. Staffs.* (1861).
[20] *P.O. Dir. Staffs.* (1868).
[21] Hackwood, *West Bromwich*, 92–3; *1st Rep. Com. Midland Mining, S. Staffs.* 16; Prince, *Old West Bromwich*, 130; *P.O. Dir. Staffs.* (1860).

School and other schools near by. With the transfer of educationally sub-normal pupils to the new Millfield Day School, Westminster Road, in 1958, Bratt Street was closed completely.[22] The building, which was of red brick with stone dressings and in an early-Gothic style,[23] was demolished in 1971.

Ebenezer British School, later Ebenezer Board School. When the Congregationalists opened Ebenezer chapel in Old Meeting Street in 1839 the former chapel on an adjoining site was converted into premises for day and Sunday schools. The day school was united with the British Society by 1845. From 1850 the building consisted of a schoolroom and two classrooms. In October 1858 there were 70 on the books.[24] In January 1871 the school had an average attendance of 127.[25] From 1878 until the opening of Black Lake Board School in 1885 the premises were leased to the board as a mixed and infants' board school.[26]

Summit British School, later Summit Board School. By 1842 the Kenricks were running a school for boys, girls, and infants in Glover Street near their Summit Foundry. It was intended primarily for the education of the firm's workers and their children but was also open to outsiders. The two teachers in 1842 were, like the Kenricks themselves, nonconformists. In 1849 accommodation consisted of a schoolroom for boys and a schoolroom and classroom for girls. The school was united with the British Society by 1855, and in 1860 it had an attendance of about 100. A separate infants' schoolroom was built in 1861, and an infants' school was established in 1862 with 80 on the books.[27] From 1872 until the opening of Spon Lane Board School in 1889 the Kenricks leased their school premises to the board.[28]

Holy Trinity Church of England Junior and Infants' School, formerly Holy Trinity National School. In 1842 George Silvester, donor of the site of Holy Trinity Church and its vicarage, presented the minister and churchwardens with a further plot near the church for a school.[29] The school, in what is now Trinity Road, was built in a plain style to a design furnished by the Education Department, with the aid of grants from government, the National Society, and the Diocesan Schools Society,[30] and was opened in 1843 as a mixed National school.[31] By 1853 the average attendance had reached 180 on weekdays, with about 450 at the Sunday school.

In 1854 a new department for over 100 infants was built at the corner of the present Lower Trinity Street and Constance Avenue with a grant from the National Society. It was opened early in 1855 and remained in use until 1889, when Spon Lane Board School was opened.[32] Holy Trinity School itself became a voluntary controlled mixed and infants' school following the 1902 Act. The buildings were enlarged in 1910. The school ceased to take senior pupils in 1934, and since then it has remained a voluntary controlled junior and infants' school.[33]

Mayer's Green and Queen Street British School, later Mayer's Green and Queen Street Board School. A day school in connexion with Mayer's Green Congregational chapel was established in 1844 with the arrival of a new minister, B. H. Cooper. It was housed in a new two-storey building adjoining the chapel. An additional building was subsequently erected near by in Queen Street. By 1851 the school was united with the British Society.[34] The premises were leased to the board in 1871 and were reopened in 1872 as a mixed and infants' board school; the boys were housed in the Queen Street building and the girls and infants in the two-storey block by the chapel.[35] The school closed in 1893 with the opening of Beeches Road Board School.[36]

Hill Top Wesleyan Methodist School, later Hill Top Temporary Council School. A day school was built at Hill Top in 1844 by the trustees of the Wesleyan Methodist chapel there and was in use in 1845.[37] The average attendance in January 1871 was 241.[38] A new infants' school was added in 1873.[39] The school was transferred to the local authority in 1906 and continued as Hill Top Temporary Council School until 1911, when the pupils were transferred to the new Hill Top Council School.[40]

St. James's National School, Hill Top. A National school was opened next to St. James's Church, Hill Top, in 1845.[41] In 1846–7 there were 562 pupils, including 130 infants.[42] The school was improved and enlarged in 1871.[43] Average attendance was 314 in January 1871 and 543 in 1900–1.[44] It eventually proved too expensive to maintain the buildings in the required state, and the school closed in 1911. The pupils were transferred to Hill Top Council School.[45]

Christ Church National School (Girls), later St. John's National School. In 1846 the managers of

[22] Beardsmore, 'West Bromwich Schools', Bratt St. and Secondary Technical Schs.; ex inf. Educ. Dept.
[23] See plate facing p. 241.
[24] *P.O. Dir. Staffs.* (1845); Ed. 7/113/West Bromwich/ Ebenezer; above p. 68.
[25] Hackwood, *West Bromwich*, 97.
[26] Ed. 7/112/West Bromwich/2; Beardsmore, 'School Board', 6; Beardsmore, 'West Bromwich Schools', Black Lake Sch.
[27] *1st Rep. Com. Midland Mining, S. Staffs.* 16; Ed. 7/113/West Bromwich/Summit Foundry Sch.; ibid./ Summit Board Sch. (Infants); Hackwood, *West Bromwich*, 97; *P.O. Dir. Staffs.* (1860).
[28] Beardsmore, 'School Board', 2, 10; Hackwood, *West Bromwich*, 99.   [29] Nat. Soc. files; above p. 56.
[30] *Midland Counties Herald*, 30 June 1842; *Holy Trinity Church Centenary Celebrations, 1841–1941*, 6 and loose printed sheet of building accounts (copy in W.B.L.).
[31] White, *Dir. Staffs.* (1851); Nat. Soc. files.
[32] Nat. Soc. files; S.R.O., D. 812/7/West Bromwich, Holy Trinity Nat. Sch. (plans); *Lich. Dioc. Ch. Cal.* (1890), 161.
[33] *Holy Trinity Church Centenary Celebrations*, 7; *Lich.*

Dioc. Yr. Bk. 1910, 119; Nat. Soc. files; Beardsmore, 'West Bromwich Schools'; ex inf. Educ. Dept.
[34] Hackwood, *West Bromwich*, 82; Ed. 7/112/West Bromwich/1; White, *Dir. Staffs.* (1851).
[35] Beardsmore, 'School Board', 2; Beardsmore, 'West Bromwich Schools', Beeches Rd. Sch.; Ed. 7/112/West Bromwich/1.
[36] Beardsmore, 'West Bromwich Schools', Beeches Rd. Sch.; Beardsmore, 'School Board', 13.
[37] Ed. 7/112/West Bromwich/16; *P.O. Dir. Staffs.* (1845).
[38] Hackwood, *West Bromwich*, 97.
[39] *Kelly's Dir. Staffs.* (1884).
[40] Beardsmore, 'West Bromwich Schools'.
[41] Hackwood, *West Bromwich*, 95; *St. James' Church, Hill Top, West Bromwich, Centenary 1942* (copy in W.B.L.); S.R.O., D. 812/7/West Bromwich, St. James's Nat. Sch. (plans).
[42] Nat. Soc. *Church Schs. Enquiry, 1846–7.*
[43] *Lich. Dioc. Ch. Cal.* (1872), 93.
[44] Hackwood, *West Bromwich*, 97; *List of Schs. 1901–2*, 218.
[45] Beardsmore, 'West Bromwich Schools', Hill Top Sch.; Ed. 7/113/West Bromwich/18.

Christ Church National School for boys in New Street established a school for girls in a building in Newhall Street rented from Lord Dartmouth. In 1855 the average attendance was 65; there were 84 girls on the books, of whom 10 were taught free, 50 paid 2*d.* a week, and 24 3*d.* a week.[46] There was then accommodation for 160 children, and in 1856 alterations and repairs carried out with a small grant from the National Society raised this to 250.[47] In 1857 Lord Dartmouth gave the site and building to Christ Church.[48] By January 1871 the average attendance had risen to 143, and in that year a schoolroom for infants was erected next to the existing building.[49] The school became the responsibility of the new parish of St. John the Evangelist formed in 1879.[50] It lost pupils to Lyng Board School, opened in 1880–1, and was closed in 1884.[51]

Golds Hill School, later Golds Hill Council School. In March 1853 the Bagnalls began to run evening classes at three of their works, including the Golds Hill Ironworks in West Bromwich. The school there, which was for boys and young men employed at the works, was open four nights a week; it started at 7 p.m. and those who attended it thus had an hour's break after the day shift had ended. By the end of the year there were 227 on the books. Their ages ranged from 10 to 20; they were taught the elements and general knowledge; they were encouraged by the Bagnalls with gifts of books and preferential treatment when it came to membership of the works cricket teams.[52] In 1855 a school for boys, girls, and infants was opened at the works. It was intended primarily for the children of those connected with the firm but was also open to outsiders. There were 226 children on the books in April 1855, paying fees of between 2*d.* and 6*d.* a week. The evening school continued to be held in the building four nights a week, and in 1856 200 boys employed by the firm attended it.[53] In the late 1850s a report to the Newcastle Commission named the Bagnalls' school as one of those in the Black Country which deservedly had 'the highest reputation for efficiency'.[54] The average attendance in January 1871 was 277.[55]

The board purchased the site and buildings in 1878 and, after improving and enlarging the buildings, reopened the school as a board school for boys, girls, and infants.[56] In 1882, after the closure of the ironworks and the consequent drop in the population of the area, the boys' and girls' departments

were merged. The infants' and mixed departments were merged in 1911 to form a junior mixed and infants' school. The infants were transferred to a new school at Harvills Hawthorn in 1949, and when the junior pupils followed them in 1950 Golds Hill School was closed.

Dartmouth Street School, later Dartmouth Street Board School. A Baptist day school supported entirely by pence existed by 1833.[57] In the later 1850s a day school connected with Bethel Baptist chapel in Dartmouth Street was being conducted in a building erected behind the chapel in 1855.[58] In the early 1870s it was a mixed school with an average attendance, in January 1871, of 75. Numbers more than doubled over the next three years,[59] but in 1876 the managers leased the building to the board, which needed additional accommodation in the area.[60] It continued as a board school until 1886.[61]

St. Peter's National School, later St. Peter's Council School. A National school in connexion with St. Peter's, Greets Green, was set up in 1859, shortly after the building of the church. It was initially housed in a small corrugated-iron building adjoining the church. Within a few weeks there was an average daily attendance of over 100, and the need for additional accommodation was soon felt. A site for a new school to the south of the church was presented by W. Jones, and in 1866 a two-storeyed building in a Venetian Gothic style was opened for boys, girls, and infants.[62] In January 1871 there was an average attendance of 409.[63] By 1878 the school was in financial difficulties, and it was decided to hand it over to the board. The step was averted, apparently at the last moment, by the new incumbent, W. F. Bradley, and in 1881 the finances were on a sound footing, though the average attendance had fallen to 328.[64] The school was transferred to the local authority in 1910 and continued as a mixed and infants' council school until the opening in 1932 of George Salter School.[65]

Hallam Street Infants' School. An infants' school existed in Hallam Street by 1860. In 1870 it occupied a building leased from Lord Dartmouth and was run by a board of managers, who employed a mistress and two assistants. There were some 150 children on the books.[66] When the mission church of St. Mary Magdalene, Cottrell Street, was opened in 1871[67] the school was apparently attached to it. In January 1871 the average attendance had been

[46] Ed. 7/112/West Bromwich/14.   [47] Nat. Soc. files.
[48] Ed. 7/113/West Bromwich/14.
[49] Hackwood, *West Bromwich*, 97; Ed. 7/113/West Bromwich/14.   [50] *Kelly's Dir. Staffs.* (1880).
[51] Nat. Soc. files, West Bromwich, Christ Church, letter of 30 Oct. 1884, stating that the school is to be closed the following day; S.R.O., D. 564/8/1/29, letter of 6 June 1895, giving date of closure as 22 Feb. 1885 or 1886.
[52] *Rep. Com. State of Population in Mining Districts, 1854* [1838], pp. 10–13, H.C. (1854), xix.
[53] Ed. 7/112/West Bromwich/4; Mary Willett, *John Nock Bagnall* (1885), 24; *Midland Counties Herald*, 11 Jan. 1855; *Staffs. Advertiser*, 13 Jan. 1855, 27 Dec. 1856.
[54] *Rep. Com. State of Popular Educ. in Eng.* vol. ii [2794–II], p. 257, H.C. (1861), xxi (2).
[55] Hackwood, *West Bromwich*, 97.
[56] For this para. see Beardsmore, 'West Bromwich Schools'.
[57] *Educ. Enquiry Abstract*, H.C. 62, p. 891 (1835), xlii.
[58] T. N. Honeybund, *West Bromwich Baptist Church*

1906: Bazaar Souvenir (West Bromwich, 1906), 20 (copy in W.B.L.); A. S. Langley, *Birmingham Baptists Past and Present*, 211; *Kelly's Dir. Staffs.* (1884).
[59] *P.O. Dir. Staffs.* (1872); Hackwood, *West Bromwich*, 97.
[60] Beardsmore, 'West Bromwich Schools', Guns Village Sch.; Ed. 7/113/West Bromwich/Dartmouth Street Board Sch.   [61] See p. 80.
[62] Ed. 7/112/West Bromwich/20; *Staffs. Advertiser*, 14 Apr. 1866; *Lich. Dioc. Ch. Cal.* (1868), 96; S.R.O., D. 812/7/West Bromwich, St. Peter's Nat. Sch. (plans); O.S. Map 6″, Staffs. LXVIII. SW (1890 edn.).
[63] Hackwood, *West Bromwich*, 97.
[64] *Lich. Dioc. Rep. of Diocesan Institutions, 1878*, 49; *Lich. Dioc. Mag.* 1881, 94; *Incorp. of West Bromwich*, 27.
[65] *Lich. Dioc. Yr. Bk. 1910*, 122; *Kelly's Dir. Staffs.* (1912 and later edns. to 1924); Beardsmore, 'West Bromwich Schools', Geo. Salter Sch.
[66] *P.O. Dir. Staffs.* (1860; 1868); Ed. 7/113/West Bromwich/Hallam St. Infants' Sch.
[67] See p. 53.

79. The school closed at some date between 1876 and 1880.[68]

Moor Street Ragged School, later Moor Street Board School. A ragged school was opened by a body of trustees in a newly erected building in Moor Street in 1863. There was an infants' ragged school by 1868. In January 1871 the average attendance was 150.[69] In 1876 the premises and their fittings were sold to the board and the school re-opened as Moor Street Board School, taking girls and infants. Accommodation was increased,[70] and in 1881 the average attendance was 350. Moor Street became a mixed and infants' school in 1890 and closed in 1917 because a firm engaged in war work required the building. The pupils were dispersed.[71]

St. Andrew's National School. The school-church of St. Andrew, Old Meeting Street, was opened in November 1867 and a school was established in January 1868. It had accommodation for 300 children; boys were taught in the nave, girls in the transepts, and infants in the chancel.[72] In January 1871 the average attendance was 96.[73] Later in 1871 an infants' school for 200 children was opened, also in Old Meeting Street, and the chancel of St. Andrew's was thenceforth used solely for worship.[74] From 1877 the whole building was used exclusively as a church, and the infants' school became a mixed school, with an average attendance in 1881 of 134.[75] It closed in 1893.[76]

Spon Lane Wesleyan Methodist School, later Spon Lane Board School. In January 1871 a mixed and infants' day school was established in existing Sunday-school buildings behind the Wesleyan Methodist chapel in Spon Lane. Attendance the following month was estimated at 122.[77] In 1878 the buildings were leased to the board, and the school continued as a mixed board school. In 1889 it was superseded by the new board school in Spon Lane.[78]

Other public elementary schools in existence before 1871. These included an infants' school at Greets Green, mentioned about 1860;[79] another infants' school maintained for many years by William Bullock & Co. of the Spon Lane Foundry and held in a house in Twenty House Row, Ault Street, in 1861;[80] and a day school for boys and girls attached to one of the Primitive Methodist chapels in the late 1860s and early 1870s.[81] A Wesleyan Methodist school noted in Roebuck Street in 1868 may have been merely the Sunday school of c. 1855. In 1878 it became a board school.[82] A ragged school attached to St. Peter's was opened in 1866;[83] nothing more is known of this or of a ragged school in Newton Road noted in 1869.[84]

SCHOOLS OPENED SINCE 1871.[85] Beeches Junior and Infants' School, Beeches Road, was opened in 1893 as a board school for boys, girls, and infants (Beeches Road Board School) and replaced the Mayer's Green and Queen Street schoolrooms rented by the board since 1872. A separate building was erected as a cookery centre; but from 1896 to 1907 it was used as a pupil-teachers' centre, subsequently as classrooms, and then as a nursery annexe to the infants' department. In 1939, the number of pupils having fallen, Beeches Road was reorganized as a junior and infants' school.

Black Lake Junior and Infants' School, Swan Lane, was opened in 1885 as a mixed and infants' board school. In 1918 it was reorganized as a three-department school (boys, girls, and infants), and it functioned as such until 1943, when it reverted to two departments. It closed in 1969.

Bull Lane Board School, for infants and young children, was housed in rented premises in Bull Lane from 1890 until 1895. In 1895 it moved to new buildings, also in Bull Lane. The buildings were later affected by mining subsidence, and the school closed in 1932.[86]

Charlemont Junior and Infants' School, Willett Road, originated as an all-age school planned in the late 1920s to serve the new Charlemont housing estate. The first buildings were opened in 1929 as a temporary infants' department. Senior and junior departments were added in 1930 as new buildings were completed, and in 1931 further expansion made possible the division of the senior department into separate boys' and girls' departments. Following the acquisition in 1937 of an adjacent site in Hollyhedge Road two new assembly halls, a gymnasium, and other buildings were added. The senior departments became a secondary modern school in the reorganization after 1944 and were closed in 1967. The remaining departments continued as Charlemont Junior and Infants' School.

Churchfields High School, Church Vale, the borough's first comprehensive secondary school, was opened in 1955.

Cronehills Junior and Infants' School, Hardware Street, was designed as a replacement for Bratt Street School.[87] The school was to consist of two large classroom blocks and another block to house centres for subjects such as housewifery. Building

[68] *P.O. Dir. Staffs.* (1872; 1876); *Kelly's Dir. Staffs.* (1880); Hackwood, *West Bromwich*, 97.
[69] Ed. 7/113/West Bromwich/9; Hackwood, *West Bromwich*, 97; *P.O. Dir. Staffs.* (1868).
[70] Beardsmore, 'West Bromwich Schools'; Beardsmore, 'School Board', 5–6.
[71] *Incorp. of West Bromwich*, 26; Beardsmore, 'West Bromwich Schools'.
[72] Willett, *West Bromwich*, 55; *P.O. Dir. Staffs.* (1868); Ed. 7/113/West Bromwich/St. Andrew's Nat. Sch.
[73] Hackwood, *West Bromwich*, 97.
[74] *Lich. Dioc. Ch. Cal.* (1872), 93; *P.O. Dir. Staffs.* (1872).
[75] *Kelly's Dir. Staffs.* (1880; 1884; 1892); *Incorp. of West Bromwich*, 27; above p. 58.
[76] *Lich. Dioc. Ch. Cal.* (1893), 87; (1894), 89.
[77] Ed. 7/112/West Bromwich/11.
[78] Beardsmore, 'West Bromwich Schools'.
[79] *P.O. Dir. Staffs.* (1860); Harrison, Harrod & Co. *Dir. Staffs.* (1861).

[80] W. Cornish, *Corp. Dir. Birm.* (1861); 'Old West Bromwich', 12 Nov. 1943.
[81] *P.O. Dir. Staffs.* (1868; 1872).
[82] Ibid. (1868); above p. 65 and below p. 81. The school is not listed in *P.O. Dir. Staffs.* (1872), published in the year in which the Beeches Rd. chapel replaced the Roebuck St. (Park Village) building: above p. 65. There was a Wesleyan Methodist Sunday school in Roebuck St. in 1861: Cornish, *Corp. Dir. Birm.* (1861).
[83] *Lich. Dioc. Ch. Cal.* (1867), 90.
[84] White, *Dir. Birm.* (1869).
[85] Unless otherwise stated, this section is based on Beardsmore, 'West Bromwich Schools' and inf. from Educ. Dept. For Albion Junior Sch. and Sandwell Secondary Schs., situated in West Bromwich but established by Smethwick, see below pp. 139–40.
[86] For this school see also Ed. 7/112/West Bromwich/3.
[87] For this para. see also *West Bromwich Official Handbook* (6th edn.), 57; *Express & Star*, 20 July 1968.

began in 1915, but because of the war nothing was available for use until 1921, when the special-subject block was adapted as a temporary girls' school for pupils from Bratt Street. The completed school was opened in 1925 as a selective central school for boys and girls, and the girls who had been housed in the special-subject block returned to Bratt Street. In 1947 Cronehills became West Bromwich Secondary Technical School and in 1948 absorbed the junior technical school which had been carried on since 1930 at Kenrick Technical College. In 1952 the boys' and girls' departments were merged. In 1967–8 the technical school also occupied part of Charlemont School as an annexe for first-year pupils. In 1968 all pupils moved to the new Manor High School, Friar Park Road, and the Cronehills premises were occupied by children from the closed Christ Church Junior and Infants' School.

Cronehills Selective Central School, see Cronehills Junior and Infants' School.

Dartmouth High School, Wilderness Lane, a comprehensive secondary school, was opened in 1965.

Fir Tree Junior and Infants' Schools, Greenside Way, consist of a junior school opened as a junior and infants' school in 1956, and an infants' school added in 1959.

George Salter High School, Claypit Lane, was opened in 1932 as George Salter School, senior pupils being transferred to it from the Fisher Street and St. Peter's schools. As a result of the reorganization after 1944 a secondary modern school for boys and another for girls were housed in the buildings. In 1969 the two schools were amalgamated with the Spon Lane secondary modern school to form the comprehensive George Salter High School, with its main centre in Claypit Lane.

Gorse Farm Junior and Infants' School, Ferndale Avenue, was opened in stages, the infants' school in 1956 and the junior school in 1957.

Greets Green Junior and Infants' School, Whitgreave Street, began its life early in 1872, when the board hired rooms attached to the Greets Green Wesleyan and Primitive Methodist chapels as temporary accommodation for a new board school. Greets Green Board School, for boys, girls, and infants, was opened a few weeks later. By April 1872 there were some 140 pupils.[88] In 1876 the school moved into new buildings in Whitgreave Street. New classrooms were opened in 1890,[89] and the Primitive Methodist premises were hired again to provide yet more accommodation, an arrangement which continued until 1932. Because of declining numbers the boys' and girls' departments were merged into a mixed department in 1938.

Grove Vale Junior and Infants' School, Monksfield Avenue, was opened in 1963.

Guns Village Junior and Infants' School, Earl Street, was opened in 1879 as a board school. Previously the board had hired temporary premises for children from the area: rooms adjoining the Primitive Methodist chapel in Guns Lane in 1873 and the building which had been used by the day school attached to the Baptist chapel in Dartmouth Street in 1876. The new school originally housed older pupils only; the Dartmouth Street building

was retained as a school for infants and First Standard children. Dartmouth Street was closed in 1886; the pupils were transferred to Guns Village, which in turn lost its older pupils to Black Lake School. The school was extended in 1896.

Hall Green Junior and Infants' School, Westminster Road, was opened in 1940.

Hamstead Junior and Infants' School, Hamstead Road, was opened in 1937. It was extended in the late 1940s and early 1950s.

Hargate Junior and Infants' School, Hargate Lane, was opened in 1968.

Harvills Hawthorn Junior and Infants' School, Wolseley Road, was opened in 1949. The infants who had previously attended Golds Hill School were transferred to the new school, and in 1950 the juniors from Golds Hill were similarly transferred.

Hateley Heath Junior and Infants' School, Huntingdon Road, was opened in stages, the infants' school in 1950 and the junior school in 1952.

Hill Top High School, at the junction of Hill Top and Coles Lane, was opened in 1911 as a council school with four departments: senior boys', senior girls', junior mixed, and infants'. It replaced the two schools then existing at Hill Top, St. James's and that maintained by the Wesleyan chapel. In 1914 it was enlarged.[90] The assembly halls and two classrooms were destroyed by enemy action in 1940. The infants were transferred to Hateley Heath School in 1950 and the juniors in 1952, leaving Hill Top a secondary modern school. In 1969 it became the comprehensive Hill Top High School.

Hollyhedge Junior and Infants' School, Connor Road, was opened in 1964 in premises belonging to Charlemont School.

Joseph Edward Cox Junior and Infants' School, Dorset Road, was opened in 1930 in temporary premises adjoining the site of the present school, the junior department of which was opened in 1934 and the infants' department in 1936.

Kenrick Junior Technical School was established in 1930 as West Bromwich Junior Technical School in the buildings of Kenrick Technical College. In 1948 it was absorbed by the newly established West Bromwich Secondary Technical School.[91]

Kent Close Junior and Infants' School off Denbigh Drive, Hateley Heath, was opened in 1960.

Lodge Estate Junior and Infants' School, Lodge Road, was opened in 1904 as a three-department school for boys, girls, and infants. It was enlarged in 1911. In 1940 the senior pupils were transferred to George Salter and Spon Lane schools, and Lodge Estate continued as an infants' school. By 1970 it was a junior and infants' school.

Lyng Junior School, opposite Dora Road, originated in the Lyng Board School for boys and infants opened in 1877.[92] It was originally housed in temporary premises leased by the board, the Sunday-school building attached to Lyng Primitive Methodist chapel. Those premises were vacated in 1880 when the boys' and infants' departments of a new school in Sams Lane were opened. A girls' department was added in 1881, and the buildings were extended in 1883. Further extension followed in 1911. The school was demolished in 1966 during the re-

88 Ed. 7/112/West Bromwich/5.
89 Kelly's Dir. Staffs. (1892).   90 Ibid. (1916).
91 Midland Chron. & Free Press, 22 Oct. 1954.
92 Ed. 7/112/West Bromwich/8.

View from the south-west *c.* 1840

Interior in 1972

WEST BROMWICH: ALL SAINTS' CHURCH

WEST BROMWICH: CHRIST CHURCH IN 1841

WALSALL WOOD: ST. JOHN'S CHURCH c. 1840

BLOXWICH CHURCH IN 1845

development of the area. It was then a junior and infants' school, and the pupils were transferred to new schools a short distance away, the infants to Lyttleton Hall School and the juniors to a new Lyng School. The two schools form a single building opposite Dora Road and share certain facilities.

Lyttleton Hall Infants' School, opposite Dora Road, was opened in 1966, receiving initially the infants from Lyng School in Sams Lane.

Manor High School, a comprehensive secondary school in Friar Park Road, was opened in 1968.

Menzies High School, Clarkes Lane, originated as West Bromwich Municipal Secondary School, established in 1902 at the West Bromwich Institute, Lodge Road, at the expense of G. H. (later Sir George) Kenrick. The school premises were extended in 1907 and 1909. In December 1919 there were 470 pupils. In its early years the school took many children from outside the borough, chiefly from Wednesbury, Tipton, and Bilston, but by the early 1930s virtually all the pupils came from West Bromwich.[93] In the reorganization after 1944 the school remained the borough's only grammar school, and in 1964 it moved to new buildings in Clarkes Lane.[94] In 1969 it became the comprehensive Menzies High School.

Moorlands Junior and Infants' School, Winchester Road, was opened in 1960.

Park Village Board School, Roebuck Street, was opened in 1878 in premises leased from the trustees of Beeches Road Wesleyan Methodist chapel.[95] It took children up to the age of nine. In 1908, since there was then sufficient accommodation in near-by schools for children of five and over, it was closed.

Ryders Green Junior and Infants' Schools, Claypit Lane, were opened in 1969.

St. John Bosco Roman Catholic Junior and Infants' School, Monmouth Drive, Hateley Heath, was opened in 1962, replacing St. Michael's Roman Catholic School.

St. Mary's National School for Infants, Hateley Heath, was established in 1872 in the school-church of St. Mary the Virgin, Hateley Heath, erected in 1871. It was closed c. 1881 as a result of a decline in the population of the area.[96]

St. Paul's Church of England School, Hamstead, became a responsibility of the West Bromwich education department in 1928 as a result of that year's boundary changes. Its premises, built some time after 1874 and extended in 1894, had already been classified by the Board of Education as inadequate. Its senior pupils were transferred to Charlemont School in 1934, the younger ones to Hamstead Junior and Infants' School in 1937, and St. Paul's was then closed.

Spon Lane School, Parliament Street, was opened in 1889 as a board school to take pupils from the temporary board schools which had been established at Summit School and Spon Lane Wesleyan School. It was extended in 1911, 1927, and 1931, became a secondary modern school in the reorganization after 1944, and in 1969 was amalgamated with the George Salter Schools in Claypit Lane to form the new comprehensive George Salter High School. The buildings remained in use in 1970 as an annexe to the high school.

Tanhouse Junior and Infants' School, Hamstead Road, was opened in 1970.

West Bromwich Grammar School, see Menzies High School.

West Bromwich Junior Technical School, see Kenrick Junior Technical School.

West Bromwich Municipal Secondary School, see Menzies High School.

West Bromwich Secondary Technical School, see Cronehills Junior and Infants' School.

Yew Tree Junior and Infants' Schools, Birchfield Way, consist of an infants' school opened as a junior and infants' school in 1953, and a junior school added in 1954.

SCIENTIFIC AND LITERARY INSTITUTIONS. A small mechanics' institute was formed in 1829 by the manager of the Swan Village gas-works but was apparently short-lived.[97]

In 1836 the West Bromwich Institution for the Advancement of Knowledge was formed under the presidency of R. L. Chance.[98] The subscription was £1 a year; new members over the age of 21 also paid a 5s. entrance fee. In return members had the use of a library, which by 1849 contained some 1,600 volumes, and a reading room. Lectures were arranged and in 1844 there were classes for debating, mathematics, and English grammar; in 1837 there had been a short-lived weekly class in mechanical drawing, run by a local teacher. Despite the patronage of Chance and Samuel Kenrick the Institution never established itself firmly. Membership, which at one stage rose to about 120, had fallen to 70 by 1849, though it appears to have risen to 90 by 1851.[99] There were several financial crises. It still existed in 1856, with Chance as its president, but its later history is obscure.

The Institution was the only mechanics' or literary institute noted in West Bromwich in the 1851 Educational Census. Nevertheless by 1845 there appears also to have been a separate mechanics' institute, with its own library and reading room.[1] Little is known of it. It apparently lasted until at least 1861,[2] but like the Institution it seems to have had little influence.[3] Its president between at least 1845 and 1850 was Thomas Bagnall.[4] Possibly it is

[93] S.R.O., C/E/correspondence/West Bromwich.

[94] *Midland Chron. & Free Press*, 8 July 1964.

[95] For a Wesleyan Methodist school in Roebuck St. in 1868 see p. 79.

[96] Ed. 7/113/West Bromwich/St. Mary's Infant Nat. Sch.; above p. 53. *Kelly's Dir. Staffs.* (1884) lists a mixed school attached to St. Mary's, but neither this nor the infants' school is mentioned in any earlier or later directory.

[97] 'Old West Bromwich', 26 Apr. 1946; W.B.L. 66/16150, giving date of formation as 27 Jan. 1829.

[98] For the following para. see, unless otherwise stated, W.B.L., Min. Bk. of the West Bromwich Institution for the Advancement of Knowledge 1836–56.

[99] *Census*, 1851, *Tables relating to Schools &c.* 236.

[1] *P.O. Dir. Staffs.* (1845), listing both the mechanics' institute and the Institution.

[2] Harrison, Harrod & Co. *Dir. Staffs.* (1861).

[3] According to one authority there was in 1853 no library, reading room, or lecture hall for the working classes of West Bromwich save those at the Chances' works in Spon Lane, Smethwick: *West Bromwich Temperance and Educational Mission, Tract No. 10, Jan. 1853*, 1 (copy in W.S.L. Pamphs. *sub* West Bromwich); below p. 140.

[4] *P.O. Dir. Staffs.* (1845; 1850). Both give the president's surname as Ragnall, but Thos. Bagnall is evidently the man referred to.

to be identified with a branch of the Institution which was established at Hill Top in 1843 and seceded from the parent body in 1844.[5] In 1843 Reuben Farley proposed the establishment of a mechanics' institute at Greets Green; but the project failed to win Lord Dartmouth's support and Farley took it no further.[6]

In 1846 George Kenrick established a People's Library and Reading Room, apparently at Summit School. For 1d. a week working men had the use of a library which eventually amounted to some 300 volumes; newspapers, periodicals, and lectures were also provided. The establishment apparently came to an end on Kenrick's death in 1848.[7]

The West Bromwich Temperance and Educational Mission began work in the town in 1852, also under the patronage of the Kenricks. Its aim was the reform and education of the working classes. A missionary preached the evils of intoxicating drink and began to hold mutual improvement classes, in the form of discussion groups, at the school attached to Salem Chapel, Great Bridge, and at the reading rooms at the Chances' works in Spon Lane, Smethwick. In 1853 the mission opened an institute in a house on the corner of High Street and St. Michael Street. George Kenrick's brother Archibald, chairman of the managing committee, guaranteed the rent for a trial period and presented the books from the People's Library. The institute was to have a reading room and a circulating library, and activities were to include lectures, a Mutual Improvement and Discussion Society, meeting weekly, and evening classes to teach adults reading and writing. The yearly subscription was 6s. for the use of the reading room and the library and 4s. for the use of the library only.[8] By 1860 the library, known like George Kenrick's as the People's Library, contained nearly 1,000 volumes of standard and scientific works, the reading room was well supplied with newspapers and periodicals, and lectures were held during the winter.[9] Although the library had dropped to 600 volumes by 1869, the Mission was still in existence in 1872. It appears to have closed by 1876, possibly as a result of the opening of the free public library in 1874–5.[10]

The 1860s and 1870s saw the establishment of a number of groups concerned with adult and further education. In 1863 the Hill Top Adult School, which later claimed to have been the first such school in the Black Country, began with three or four people meeting in a small room; by 1886 there were 260 on the books, with an average attendance of 212.[11] The incumbent of St. Peter's was

running a night school for adults in 1863.[12] Another night school, established in 1869, met at the Holy Trinity National school and was attended largely by young people employed by the Salters. A mutual improvement class was meeting at the school in 1872.[13] The Adult-School movement also established schools giving instruction in the elements as an aid to Bible reading. The first outside Birmingham was that started at Ebenezer in 1870.[14] In the mid 1880s the Anglicans too had at least one Sunday-morning adult school giving instruction in the elements.[15] A West Bromwich Young Men's Literary Association met at the Bratt Street school in at least the late 1860s and early 1870s, and there were other self-improvement societies.[16]

In 1881 a few local industrialists began to press for the establishment of a literary and scientific institute. The model was to be the Birmingham and Midland Institute and the chief object the education of artisans in 'the principles and technicalities affecting their several pursuits'. Other social and educational activities were to be offered to make the proposed institute more widely attractive. A public meeting held in 1882 decided that a building should be erected; money was raised by subscription, and in 1886 the West Bromwich Institute in Lodge Road was opened, with a reading room, classrooms, laboratory, lecture theatre, and assembly hall.[17] Some 24 classes in art and the 'more severe branches of study' were begun as part of the Institute's activities;[18] in 1887 the art classes were organized into a school of art.[19] The management of the art school and science classes was handed over in 1891 to the town council's newly formed technical instruction committee,[20] and five years later the building in Lodge Road was itself transferred to the corporation, the conveyance reserving to the Institute the use of certain rooms for its own purposes.[21] The Institute continued as a voluntary body and still existed in 1970. The three-storeyed Institute building is of brick and terracotta and was designed by Wood & Kendrick of West Bromwich in the 'Tudor or late Gothic' style.[22]

In 1891 the town council adopted the Technical Instruction Act and took over the educational work then being organized by the Institute; later in 1891 the Institute's art school and science classes became the Municipal Art School and the Municipal Science and Technical School.[23] In 1896 the Institute building in Lodge Road was conveyed to the corporation,[24] which extended it in 1898.[25] The art school was transferred from the Institute in 1902 to the new Ryland Memorial School of Art, built on an

[5] W.B.L., Min. Bk. of West Bromwich Institution 1836–56, ff. 88–9, 92, 95.
[6] Hackwood, *West Bromwich*, 60, giving no date but stating that Farley was 17 at the time. He was born in 1826: W.B.L., Scrapbook 12, p. 63.
[7] *Staffs. Advertiser*, 25 Apr. 1846, 10 Apr. 1847; *West Bromwich Temperance and Educational Mission, Tract 10*, 4. Kenrick died 12 Dec. 1848: *Staffs. Advertiser*, 23 Dec. 1848.
[8] *Missionary's 1st Ann. Rep. to West Bromwich Temperance and Educational Mission, 28 Feb. 1853*, 5 (copy in W.S.L. Pamphs. *sub* West Bromwich); *To the Friends of the Mental, Moral, and Social Education of the People* (printed appeal issued by West Bromwich Temperance and Educational Mission, n.d. but 1853), 2–4 (copy in W.S.L. Pamphs. *sub* West Bromwich).
[9] *P.O. Dir. Staffs.* (1860).
[10] White, *Dir. Birm.* (1869); *P.O. Dir. Staffs.* (1872; 1876); above p. 72.

[11] *Free Press*, 2 Jan. 1886.
[12] *Lich. Dioc. Ch. Cal.* (1864), 148.
[13] *Holy Trinity Church Centenary Celebrations, 1841–1941*, 6 (copy in W.B.L.); *P.O. Dir. Staffs.* (1872).
[14] See p. 68.   [15] *Lich. Dioc. Mag.* 1884, 158.
[16] *P.O. Dir. Staffs.* (1868; 1872); White, *Dir. Birm.* (1869).
[17] *Free Press*, 8 May 1886.
[18] *Staffs. Advertiser* (S. Staffs. edn.), 8 May 1886.
[19] *Staffs. Advertiser*, 31 Dec. 1887.
[20] *Free Press*, 6 Mar. 1891.
[21] *Boro. of West Bromwich: Procs. of the Council 9 Nov. 1895 to 7 Oct. 1896*, 270, 271; *West Bromwich News & Wednesbury Times*, 9 Jan. 1969.
[22] *Free Press*, 8 May 1882.
[23] Ibid. 16 Jan., 7 Feb., 6 Mar. 1891; *Staffs. Advertiser*, 30 Dec. 1893; *Midland Chron. & Free Press*, 22 Oct. 1954.
[24] See above.
[25] *Kelly's Dir. Staffs.* (1904).

adjoining site at the expense of G. H. (later Sir George) Kenrick, who also paid for the conversion of part of the Institute building into a municipal secondary school.[26] Kenrick Technical College, a building to the design of T. Spencer Wood in High Street adjoining the Institute site, was officially opened in 1928 and replaced the Municipal Science and Technical School; there was still, however, some shortage of accommodation, and rooms in the Institute were also used for the college's work. From 1930 to 1948 the college included a junior technical school.[27] Work on a new West Bromwich Technical College in High Street, occupying part of the site of Kenrick Technical College, began in 1949 and the new college was officially opened in 1954; parts of it had been in use since 1951. The building, also to the design of T. Spencer Wood, consists of a large single-storey block with a seven-storey block at one end.[28] In 1969 the Technical College merged with Ryland Memorial School and two other colleges in the enlarged borough, the Wednesbury colleges of Commerce and Technology, to form the West Bromwich College of Commerce and Technology. The premises in High Street became the Engineering Division of the new college.[29]

PRIVATE SCHOOLS. A Job Wiggin was teaching in the parish by 1686;[30] later he was probably assisted by his son Job, described in 1726 as a writing-master.[31] The elder Wiggin was moderately wealthy,[32] and his prosperity suggests that his school was a private academy. Boarding-schools in the 1760s included a boys' school at Lyndon kept by William Howell,[33] a commercial academy, and a girls' school.[34] Richard Witton (d. 1765), minister of the Old Meeting, kept a school at his house in what is now Witton Lane.[35] Perhaps the best known of the 18th- and early-19th-century private schools was that run by Philemon Parkes from at least 1776 until his death in 1786; it was probably the school which Witton had owned, and it survived under various names until at least the mid 19th century.[36] Another school important locally was that run from at least 1807 until 1859 first by Joseph Jacques and then by his son Charles.[37] In 1829 there were at least 13 private schools, of which eight took boarders,[38] and directories show that private day

and boarding schools continued to flourish in the later 19th century.

From 1857 until his death in 1891 the 5th Lord Dartmouth housed an Anglican educational institution in Sandwell Hall rent free.[39] It was originally intended for the training of girls as domestic servants and boys as agricultural labourers. Under the direction of Laetitia Frances Selwyn, sister of the bishop of Lichfield, the house also became a ladies' home and a school for middle-class girls, many of whom were trained as governesses. In the 1880s, under Miss Selwyn's successor, Sandwell combined the functions of a girls' school, a college for the higher education of girls, and an industrial school for girls and boys.

CHARITIES FOR THE POOR. *The Spon Lane Trust Alms-houses.* By deed of 1869 Ann Murdock of West Bromwich settled in trust land south of Herbert Street where she had recently erected eleven alms-houses and a boardroom for trustees' meetings to be called the Spon Lane Trust Alms-houses. Each alms-house was to be occupied by a poor woman, though a husband and wife or two women could share one; no inmate was to be under sixty. A resident matron was to be appointed. The foundress also gave £100 for maintenance.[40] In 1888 a second block of alms-houses was built on an adjoining site with money given for the purpose by John Pugh.[41] The charity's endowment has been increased by several gifts. By deed of 1875 Maria Marshall Ely, the daughter of a foundation trustee, settled £1,000 in fulfilment of a gift which her father had intended to make. Thomas Henry Salter, of Prestwood House near Wordsley in Kingswinford, by will proved in 1915, left £500 to be invested. In 1956 a Mrs. Newey gave the trustees £3,000.[42] In the earlier 1960s over a quarter of the average annual income was derived from grants made by other charitable foundations including the George and Thomas Henry Salter Trust, Baron Davenport's Trust, and the West Bromwich Charity. In 1966 the income was £581, of which £100 was given by the Salter Trust and £50 by Davenport's Trust; £160 was derived from stock.[43] The foundation deed provided that future trustees

[26] Ibid.; *Who's Who* (1928), *sub* Kenrick, Sir Geo. Hamilton; plate facing p. 225 below.
[27] *Free Press*, 27 Jan., 3 Feb. 1928; *Midland Chron. & Free Press*, 22 Oct. 1954. For the building see also *Kenrick Technical College Prospectus, 1927–8* (copy in W.B.L.).
[28] *Midland Chron. & Free Press*, 22 Oct. 1954; ex inf. the Educ. Dept.
[29] *Express & Star*, 3 Sept. 1970; *West Bromwich Mail*, 15 Oct. 1970; ex inf. Educ. Dept.
[30] West Bromwich Ct. R. p. 148.
[31] E 134/13 Geo. I Mich./7 m. 4.
[32] S.R.O., D. 564/3/1/21; E 134/13 Geo. I Mich./7 m. 4; S.R.O., D. 742/VIII/3, lease of tithes formerly farmed by Job Wiggin of West Bromwich, schoolmaster, 23 Mar. 1741/2; West Bromwich Par. Reg.. burial 27 Mar. 1741 (transcript in W.S.L.).
[33] See p. 23.
[34] *Aris's Birmingham Gaz.* 24 Feb., 31 Mar. 1766.
[35] 'West Bromwich 100 Years Ago', 13 Sept. 1901; W.B.L., P. 248 (photograph of the house, which was demolished in 1966); E. Lissimore, 'Early Education in West Bromwich', *West Bromwich News*, 22 Sept. 1966.
[36] L.J.R.O., B/A/1/23, p. 98; S. Morse, *The Power of Grace: exemplified in the last illness and dying words of Mr. Philemon Parkes, of West Bromwich, Staffs.* (Birmingham, 1786; copy in W.S.L. Pamphs. *sub* West

Bromwich); 'West Bromwich 100 Years Ago', 13 Sept. 1901. For the syllabus see advert. in *Aris's Birmingham Gaz.* 10 Apr. 1780. Willett, *West Bromwich*, 199–200, wrongly states that T. W. Hill's Hill Top Sch., the precursor of his more famous Hazelwood Sch. (see *D.N.B.*), was in West Bromwich. It was in fact in Birmingham: J. L. Dobson, 'The Hill Family and Educational Change in the early 19th century, I: Thos. Wright Hill and the school at Hill Top, Birmingham', *Durham Research Review*, no. 10, 264.
[37] S.R.O., D. 564/6/1; D. 564/5/4/1–6; Hackwood, *West Bromwich*, 60; T.C.T. *Life's Realities*, 234 sqq.
[38] Pigot, *Com. Dir. Birm.* (1829), 101.
[39] For this para. see L. F. Selwyn, *Chronicles of Sandwell* (Wolverhampton, 1875; copy in B.R.L.); *Lich. Dioc. Ch. Cal.* (1858), 90, and reps. on Sandwell in later edns.; *Companion to Lich. Dioc. Ch. Cal. 1858* (Newcastle-under-Lyme, 1858), 46–8 (copy in W.S.L. Pamphs. *sub* Lichfield); Willett, *West Bromwich*, 158; *P.O. Dir. Staffs.* (1868; 1872; 1876); *Kelly's Dir. Staffs.* (1880); *D.N.B. sub* Selwyn, Wm.
[40] Char. Com. files.
[41] Ibid.; date on building.
[42] Char. Com. files.
[43] Ibid. For Davenport's Trust see *V.C.H. Warws.* vii. 558.

should always include representatives of the Methodist and Congregational churches and of Holy Trinity Church, and Wesleyan services were held at the alms-houses from the time of their foundation until at least 1918. Services were later held in the boardroom by the vicar of St. Philip's, a practice which had ceased by 1969.[44]

The alms-houses consist of two blocks of two storeys. The older block contains eleven dwellings and the boardroom; in the newer block are seven dwellings including the matron's quarters. Each dwelling has three rooms.

The Akrill Homes. By will proved in 1913 Elizabeth Akrill left £9,000 for the foundation of alms-houses in memory of her husband Charles.[45] Her executors were to invest up to £2,000 to endow the charity; the rest was to be used to buy a site and to build the alms-houses, a house for a matron, and a hall for religious services and social gatherings. In 1917 the executors acquired part of the Oakwood estate in Old Meeting Street. The homes were built in 1932, and in 1933 the executors settled the land and homes in trust for poor people of West Bromwich over 60 not receiving poor relief, who had lived in West Bromwich for at least five years.[46] Each home might be occupied by one or two people. A married couple might be given a home when only one of the partners was qualified, and at the trustees' discretion a widow or spinster might share one with an unqualified female relative or friend. In recent years, however, homes have been granted to married couples only. The trustees appoint a resident matron and a medical attendant and provide the alms-people with gifts of coal at Christmas.[47] The income in 1966–7 was £686 from stock.

The homes, the hall, and the matron's residence are of brick with stone dressings. They occupy three sides of a planted quadrangle lying open towards Old Meeting Street. Each of the twelve homes is a three-room semi-detached bungalow with its own back-garden.

Whorwood's Charity (The Tithe Dole and the Brick-kiln Dole). By will proved in 1615 Sir William Whorwood left a dole out of the West Bromwich tithes to 33 poor of the parish and 'such poor of Handsworth as dwell along the highway near Sandwell'. For ten years after his death the dole was to be £6 12s. a year and thereafter £10; it was to be paid twice yearly.[48] It was not, however, regularly paid until 1629, after legal proceedings.[49] In the early 19th century the money was distributed at Sandwell Hall and had become known as the Sandwell Dole.

From Christmas 1816, however, it was distributed at All Saints'. By the early 1820s it was paid twice a year to 100 West Bromwich poor in sixpences and to 50 Handsworth poor in shillings.[50] Later in the century it was paid in larger sums to fewer people.[51] In 1919 the charge was redeemed for £400 stock, which was invested for the benefit of West Bromwich and Handsworth in equal shares.[52] The West Bromwich half was then united with the Brick-kiln Dole.[53]

That charity had been founded with £62 arrears for the years during which payment of Whorwood's charity had been withheld. In 1635 2 a. in West Bromwich called the Brick-kiln Land was bought and settled on the poor of West Bromwich.[54] The annual income rose from £5 in 1786 to £12 in 1861. In 1862 the mineral rights under the property were sold for £600, which was invested. In 1919 the income was £6 5s. from rent and £27 16s. from investments. The land was sold in 1928 for £1,400, and that too was invested.[55] Under a decree of 1629 the income was to be spent like that of the Tithe Dole.[56] In the late 18th and early 19th centuries, however, it was distributed in sums varying from 1s. to 2s. 6d.[57] Later it was paid in single shillings, but in 1870 the trustees and the vicar and churchwardens of All Saints' agreed to use the money to buy blankets for the poor of the various West Bromwich parishes.[58]

The income of the two charities in 1968 was just over £84 from investments. In 1969, under Schemes of 1927 and 1964, the income was assigned in equal portions to the ten ecclesiastical parishes within the ancient parish of West Bromwich for distribution to the poor.[59]

William Turton's Charity. By deed of 1616 William Turton the elder, of the Mill, settled in trust an annual rent-charge of 40s. from land in West Bromwich to be paid twice yearly to deserving poor of the parish.[60] The rent-charge apparently came to fall solely on that part of the land called Puddings Land and the charity became known as the Pudding Land Dole.[61] In 1938 the rent-charge was redeemed for £80 stock; the income in 1968 was £2.[62] In 1667–8 the dole was distributed to 40 or more persons in sums of 1s. or less.[63] By 1823 it was normally given out in shillings to 20 poor who received the charity for life.[64] In 1969 the vicar of All Saints' used the income to help various deserving cases.[65]

Eleanor Turton's Charity. By will proved in 1701 Eleanor Turton gave an annuity of 50s. out of the

---

44 Char. Com. files; W.B.L., Wesleyan Methodist Church Preaching Appointments 1866–82, circuit plans from July 1869; ex inf. the trustees (1969).
45 The account of this charity is taken, unless otherwise stated, from Char. Com. files. For Chas. Akrill see below p. 86.
46 West Bromwich is defined in the regulations as the borough existing on 21 Aug. 1912 (the date of Eliz. Akrill's will).   47 Ex inf. the trustees (1969).
48 Prob. 11/127 (P.C.C. 11 Cope).
49 Shaw, *Staffs.* ii. 129; *V.C.H. Oxon.* v. 161.
50 *9th Rep. Com. Char.* H.C. 258, p. 537 (1823), ix; docs. at All Saints', Tithe (Sandwell) Dole Bk. of Payments 1816–77; *Free Press*, 29 Apr. 1910.
51 Docs. at All Saints', parcel 13, terrier of 1885.
52 *V.C.H. Warws.* vii. 567.
53 Char. Com. Scheme, 14 Nov. 1919.
54 C 93/11/19; B.R.L. 277339; *9th Rep. Com. Char.* 537–8; Hackwood, *West Bromwich*, 55; Char. Com. files.
55 *Abstract of Returns of Charitable Donations, 1786–8,*

H.C. 511, pp. 1134–5 (1816), xiv (2); *9th Rep. Com. Char.* 538; Willett, *West Bromwich*, 139; Char. Com. files.
56 B.R.L. 277339.   57 *9th Rep. Com. Char.* 538.
58 Willett, *West Bromwich*, 139.
59 Char. Com. files; Char. Com. Schemes, 7 Oct. 1927, 20 May 1964; ex inf. the vicar of All Saints' (1969); ex inf. the secretary to the trustees (1969).
60 Docs. at All Saints', parcel 4; *9th Rep. Com. Char.* 538. Willett, *West Bromwich*, 139, wrongly dates the gift to 10 May 1635. For the location of Puddings Land see S.R.O., D. 794/8; docs. at All Saints', parcel 13, letter from Thursfield, Messiter & Shirlaw to the vicar of All Saints', 1 Jan. 1931; L.J.R.O., B/A/15/West Bromwich (*sub* Elwell, Edw.).   61 Willett, *West Bromwich*, 139.
62 Docs. at All Saints', parcel 13; Char. Com. files; Char. Com. Scheme, 28 Oct. 1938; ex inf. the vicar of All Saints' (1969).
63 W.B.L., Jesson Deeds, nos. 57–8.
64 *9th Rep. Com. Char.* 538.
65 Char. Com. files; ex inf. the vicar of All Saints'.

Mill estate to be distributed yearly among the poor of the parish.[66] When the estate passed to the Abney family in 1735 the charity became known for a time as the Abney Dole.[67] By 1823 the money was distributed each year in shillings to 50 poor widows of West Bromwich; by 1885, however, it was customarily spent on blankets or flannel for 'deserving poor'.[68] The rent-charge was paid until at least 1948,[69] but by 1969 nothing was known of the charity.[70]

Moore's Charity. By will proved in 1761 Ralph Moore left to the poor of West Bromwich a house and land then let for £4 8s. a year. His gift was legally defective, but his widow Phoebe settled the property to fulfil her husband's intentions. The trustees were to distribute the rent twice yearly to poor of West Bromwich not receiving parish relief. The charity was distributed from 1763 until 1777 in sums of 1s., 1s. 6d., and 2s. In 1777, however, the trustees' title was apparently questioned. Phoebe (by then the wife of Richard Parker) made a new trust settlement, but it was not completed and the charity ceased.[71]

The West Bromwich Charity. The West Bromwich Improvement Amendment Act of 1865 provided that the income from land at the Cronehills or the proceeds from its sale were to be used for aged poor or poor children of West Bromwich in ways not covered by the poor-rates.[72] The charity did not take effect until the land was sold under the West Bromwich Corporation Act of 1903 for £2,000, which was to be held in trust for a charity to be known as the West Bromwich Charity; the income was to be applied to the poor of the parish but not in relief of the rates.[73] In the early 1960s the income was £71 a year, and the trustees used it to provide clothing, food, and money.[74] The West Bromwich Corporation Act of 1969 provided that the trustees should apply the income to the poor of the borough as constituted for the time being.[75]

Dunn's Charity. By will proved in 1876 Sarah Dunn left the residue of her estate to provide yearly doles to 'certain godly persons, aged widows or poor, residing at Golds Hill'. In the 1960s the annual income was just over £5 from stock, and in 1968 it was spent on Christmas food parcels.[76]

Broughall's Charity. By will proved in 1903 Eliza Jane Broughall left £400 for poor members of the congregations of Christ Church and St. Philip's. In the same year the legacy was divided, Christ Church receiving £250 and St. Philip's £150, and

in 1968 the income was £8 15s. and £5 respectively. In 1968 both churches combined their sums with other parochial funds to help their poor and sick members.[77]

Hunt's Charity. By will proved in 1904 Edwin Hunt, a Wednesbury chemical manufacturer, left the income from £1,000 to 'dissenting poor' attending the chapels of Hill Top Wesleyan Methodist circuit. In 1968 the income was about £34. It was divided equally among the six churches of the former circuit, which normally used their shares with any other funds at their disposal for the relief of poverty.[78]

The Spencer Trust. By will proved in 1911 John Spencer of Island Lodge, Handsworth, a Wednesbury tube manufacturer, left the income from £1,000 to help the poor of West Bromwich not relieved from the rates, or for any other benevolent charitable object connected with the borough. Spencer's estate, however, was insufficient to pay his legacies in full. By 1930 £800 had been paid towards the endowment of the charity, and the capital was later slightly increased. The income in 1969–70 was £43 and was used to relieve special cases of need in the pre-1966 borough.[79]

The Salter Trust. By will proved in 1917 George Salter of Prestwood House in Kingswinford, chairman and managing director of George Salter & Co. Ltd., left £10,000 stock in the firm to endow the George and Thomas Henry Salter Trust.[80] The trustees were to increase the capital of the trust by accumulating half the income from the endowment for as long as was legally possible. The other half (and the whole, after accumulation ceased) was to be divided between two funds. One was for education.[81] The other was to be used for pensions, for supporting charitable institutions, or otherwise at the trustees' discretion for individuals of good character and resident for at least two years in West Bromwich. The trustees accumulated half the income of the original endowment until 1959. In the earlier 1960s the average annual income was almost £3,000, which was divided each year between an Educational Fund and a Pensions and Assistance Fund. Both accumulated much of their income; by 1967 the Pensions and Assistance Fund had accumulated about £8,000. In 1968, therefore, the trustees secured a Scheme extending the beneficial area to the borough of West Bromwich as enlarged in 1966.[82]

The Susanah Langstone Blackham Memorial

[66] Prob. 11/461 (P.C.C. 105 Dyer).
[67] Willett, *West Bromwich*, 140.
[68] *9th Rep. Com. Char.* 538–9; docs. at All Saints', parcel 13, terrier of 1885.
[69] Char. Com. files; docs. at All Saints', parcel 13; W. E. Jephcott, *House of Izons* (London and Dudley, 1948), 13.
[70] Ex inf. the vicar of All Saints' (1969) and the managing director of Izons & Co. Ltd. (1969).
[71] *9th Rep. Com. Char.* 539–40; L.J.R.O., Moore's will proved 13 May 1761. According to Willett, *West Bromwich*, 141, and L.J.R.O., B/V/5/1772–3, the property was let for £4 10s. a year.
[72] 28 & 29 Vic. c. 160 (Local and Personal); *The Cronehills Land in the Parish of West Bromwich: Rep. of the Clerk to the Guardians, presented to the Board of Guardians at a meeting held on the 15th July, 1901,* 4–5 (copy in B.R.L.); *Staffs. Advertiser,* 13 Apr., 16 Nov. 1861; Willett, *West Bromwich*, 124.
[73] *The Cronehills Land,* 8–15; Char. Com. files; 3 Edw. VII, c. 203 (Local).

[74] *West Bromwich Official Handbook* [1963], 66.
[75] 17 & 18 Eliz. II, c. 69 (Local and Personal). s. 150.
[76] L.J.R.O., Copies of Wills, vol. xliii, ff. 155v.–156; Char. Com. files; Char. Com. Scheme, 21 Oct. 1924; ex inf. the vicar of St. Paul's (1968).
[77] L.J.R.O., Copies of Wills, vol. cxiv, ff. 239–40; *Free Press,* 10 July 1903; Char. Com. files; H. Baylis, *Christ Church, West Bromwich, 1829–1929* (West Bromwich, n.d. but published for centenary), 25; ex inf. the vicar of Christ Church (1968) and the vicar of St. Philip's (1969).
[78] Char. Com. files; ex inf. the supt. minister of West Bromwich Wesley circuit (1969).
[79] Char. Com. files; Ede, *Wednesbury,* 275–6; *West Bromwich Official Handbook* [1963], 66; ex inf. the borough treasurer (1970).
[80] The account of this charity is taken, unless otherwise stated, from Char. Com. files. For Salter see Bache, *Salter,* 43; *The Times,* 19 Nov. 1917. For the firm see above pp. 35–7.
[81] See p. 75.
[82] Char. Com. Scheme, 29 Mar. 1968; *Midland Chron. & Free Press,* 23 Feb. 1968 (advert.).

Fund. In 1927 Emily G. Bainton gave £100 in memory of her mother, wife of John Blackham, for distribution at Christmas to poor members of Ebenezer Congregational Church or in default to the poor of the community. In 1971 the income was distributed in 50p doles to seven poor members of the church.[83]

The Hammond Memorial Trust. In 1952 Charlotte Clarice Withers gave £250 for the aged poor of St. James's parish, the income to be distributed at Christmas. In 1968 the income was £10 from stock. The charity was named after the founder's parents.[84]

The Akrill Trust. Charles Akrill, a West Bromwich iron-founder twice mayor of the borough, built a house in Grange Road in 1901–2 and settled it as a home and a training and recreational centre for nurses engaged in home nursing.[85] The home was sold in 1952 to the corporation and the proceeds, with the funds accumulated by the West Bromwich District Nursing Association up to 1948, were invested. A Scheme of 1955 provided that the income should be spent on the sick poor of the borough. In 1966 it was £520, and £420 was distributed in money, clothing, and other comforts. The area of benefit is that of the pre-1966 borough.

[83] Ex inf. the minister of West Bromwich Congregational Church (1971).
[84] Char. Com. files; ex inf. the vicar of St. James's (1968).
[85] The account of this charity is taken from Char. Com.

files; Char. Com. Scheme, 28 Jan. 1955; *Staffs. Advertiser*, 31 May 1902. For Akrill see ibid. 22 June 1907. The Nursing Association's 47th ann. rep. was published in 1945; this suggests that it was founded in 1898.

SMETHWICK

SMETHWICK[1] was originally a township within the ancient parish of Harborne to the west of Birmingham. Harborne parish was shaped roughly like an hour-glass, with Smethwick forming the upper part and the neck and Harborne township the lower part. The boundary between the townships followed the Birmingham–Halesowen road.[2] Smethwick became an urban district in 1894, a borough in 1899, and a county borough in 1907. In 1966 it became part of the new Worcestershire county borough of Warley, which itself became part of the metropolitan borough of Sandwell in 1974.[3] There was a boundary adjustment in 1897 involving the transfer of 8 a. to West Bromwich,[4] and in 1901 the borough had an area of 1,929 a.[5] It was enlarged to 2,496 a. in 1928 by the transfer of Warley Woods from the urban district of Oldbury (Worcs.).[6] The present article is concerned primarily with the history of the area covered by the borough of 1899; some account is given of Warley Woods from 1928, but its earlier history has been treated under its parent parish of Halesowen (Worcs., formerly Salop. and Worcs.).[7]

Smethwick, a name which has been variously interpreted as meaning the smith's dwelling and the village on the plain,[8] is situated on the South Staffordshire Plateau. The geological formation is mainly sandstone with drifted boulder clay.[9] The higher ground is in the south and west, and a height of 753 feet is reached in Harborne Road on the former south-western boundary; the ground drops to 421 feet at Black Patch on the north-eastern boundary.[10] It is through the lower ground in the north that the canals and railways run, and the presence of those lines of communication led to the siting of the main industrial area in the north. There is some undulation of the ground, with several streams, now largely culverted, flowing through the valleys. Many of the streams helped to form the boundaries: Hockley Brook on the north-east; its tributary Shireland Brook (also known in the 1830s as Bear or Cape of Good Hope Stream), forming much of the eastern boundary; a stream rising in West Smethwick Park and forming the north-western boundary; and Spon Brook, forming much of the northern boundary.[11] Thimblemill Brook flows north-east through the town to join Hockley Brook but is culverted from Edmund Road.[12] A stream (known in the 1830s as Bluegate Stream) that rises to the south of Holly Lane flows through Smethwick Hall Park, part of the grounds of the former Smethwick Hall, where it has been dammed to create a pool; it is then culverted through the lower ground by Stony Lane and discharges into the Birmingham Canal and Hockley Brook.[13]

Before the 19th century Smethwick was a thinly populated rural area, and in 1675 it was described as 'a discontinued village' strung out along the Birmingham–Dudley road.[14] A rental of the manors of Smethwick and Harborne dating from *c.* 1275 lists 39 tenants in Smethwick.[15] In 1666 49 people in Smethwick township were assessed for hearth tax.[16] The first church was opened in 1732.[17] The cutting of the Birmingham Canal through the northern part of the township in 1768–9 brought some industrial development. As a result there was a sharp rise in the population of the township, which numbered 1,097 in 1801.[18] From the later 18th century too a number of Birmingham business and

---

[1] This article was written mainly in 1970 and 1971; some material has been added up to 1974, the date to which the additional matter refers being indicated. Grateful acknowledgement of help is made to Mr. A. H. Huskinson, former borough librarian of Warley, and his staff, especially Mr. K. W. Inskip, Miss R. J. Armstrong, and Mrs. O. T. Herbert, and to others named in footnotes.
[2] C. and J. Greenwood, *Map of Staffs.* (1820); Lich. Dioc. Regy., B/A/2(i)/L, map facing p. 142. For the history of Harborne township see *V.C.H. Warws.* vii.
[3] See pp. 119–20.   [4] See p. 1.
[5] *Census,* 1901. The area of the Smethwick local board of health district (the boundaries of which were the same as those of the 1899 borough), was given as 1,795 a. in the 1894 petition for incorporation and as 1,872 a. 'or thereabouts' in the charter of incorporation: Hackwood, *Smethwick,* 108; printed copy of charter in W.P.L.
[6] *Census,* 1931; S.R.O., L.G.O. 9/11; below p. 119.
[7] *V.C.H. Worcs.* iii.
[8] E. Ekwall, *Concise Oxford Dict. of Eng. Place-names* (4th edn.); *Eng. Place-name Elements, pt. II* (E.P.N.S.), 130–1; W. H. Duignan, *Notes on Staffs. Place Names* (1902), 139–40.
[9] Price, 'Smethwick', 1–5; Geol. Surv. Map 1″, solid and drift, sheet 168 (1924 edn.); Hackwood, *Smethwick,* 7.
[10] *Birmingham and its Regional Setting* (Brit. Assoc. 1950), 4–5, 8; Price, 'Smethwick', 5; O.S. Map 1/2,500, Staffs. SP 08 (1952 edn.).
[11] J. Ogilby, *Britannia* (1675), plate preceding p. 99; Yates, *Map of Staffs.* (1775), part of which is reproduced

above, p. 2; B.M., O.S.D. 256; Act to consolidate and extend powers and provisions of the several Acts relating to the Birmingham Canal Navigations, 5 & 6 Wm. IV, c. 34 (Local and Personal), p. 64; W.S.L., S. MS. 417/Harborne; Roper, Plan of Smethwick, 1858; Willett, *West Bromwich,* 248; 'Old West Bromwich', 24 Dec. 1943; Geol. Surv. Map 1″, solid, sheet 168 (1924 edn.); above p. 1. Shireland Brook is so named in the late 18th century: S.R.O., D. 1141/4/3/2, pp. 2, 33. For the Cape of Good Hope inn see below p. 94.
[12] *Smethwick Civic News,* Oct. 1958 (copy in W.P.L.); 'Smethwick and Round About', 25 Nov. 1955; B.M., O.S.D. 212, 219; J. C. Stuart, *Street Map of Smethwick, 1890* (copy in W.P.L.).
[13] Ogilby, *Britannia,* plate preceding p. 99; B.M., O.S.D. 212; Act to consolidate and extend powers and provisions of the several Acts relating to the Birmingham Canal Navigations, 5 & 6 Wm. IV, c. 34 (Local and Personal); Roper, Plan of Smethwick, 1858; O.S. Map 6″, Staffs. LXXII. NW., NE. (1890 edn.); Stuart, *Street Map of Smethwick, 1890; Smethwick Civic News,* Nov. 1959. For the suggestion that it may be the Stonnoss Brook of 1757 see below p. 97.
[14] Ogilby, *Britannia,* 99.
[15] *Court Rolls of the Manor of Hales, 1270–1307* (Worcs. Hist. Soc.), i. 21–3.
[16] *S.H.C.* 1923, 254–5.
[17] See p. 123.
[18] Shaw, *Staffs.* ii. 126; White, *Dir. Staffs.* (1834), 294; below pp. 97, 109–10.

professional men came to live in Smethwick.[19] In the early 19th century, however, settlement was still scattered.[20]

The number of industries continued to increase, above all with the opening of Telford's new canal in the later 1820s.[21] By 1831 the population had reached 2,676.[22] Development was very rapid in the 1830s, with the New Village growing up on either side of the Birmingham–Dudley road north of the old centre round Bearwood Hill. In 1842 the new parish of North Harborne was created, covering the northern half of Smethwick.[23] The first railway through the town was completed in 1852.[24] The population had reached 5,020 by 1841 and 8,379 by 1851. By 1871 it was 17,158, by 1891 36,170, and by 1901 54,539. Thereafter the increase slackened, and eventually there was a decline. The population of the enlarged borough was 84,406 in 1931, but by 1951 it had dropped to 76,407 and by 1961 to 68,390; in 1965 it was estimated as 67,370.[25] The drop is partly to be explained by the fact that the corporation had to build much of its housing outside the borough owing to the shortage of available land within its boundaries.[26] Nevertheless Smethwick was one of the most densely populated county boroughs in England: outside London it was exceeded only by Salford in 1951.[27] In the later 1940s only 21·2 per cent of its land was not built up, whereas the figure for the Black Country conurbation as a whole (including Birmingham) was 56·1 per cent.[28]

The French and Belgians whom R. L. Chance brought to the Spon Lane glass-works in 1832 provide an early example of immigration into the town from abroad. In 1837 there was a Belgium Street on the north side of Union Street (now part of the site of Kenrick Park and in West Bromwich). In 1851 there were several French and Belgian families living in Scotch Row adjoining the works and in the Smethwick part of Spon Lane. In spite of attempts to replace highly paid foreign workers with cheaper English labour, there was still a colony of French workers and their families in 1862 living in a row of houses adjoining the factory.[29] In the 1950s many immigrants settled in Smethwick, notably Sikhs from the Punjab.[30] There was a sufficiently large Indian community in Spon Lane ward by 1955 for the Conservative candidate in the council elections to send out a translation of his address. In 1961 the population included 1,219 people born in India, 209 in Pakistan, and 769 in Jamaica.

Among notable people with local connexions George Frederick Muntz (1794–1857), the political reformer who was M.P. for Birmingham from 1840 until his death, produced Muntz metal at the French Walls from 1842.[31] Charles Fox (1810–74), the engineer, knighted in 1851 for his work on the Crystal Palace, was a partner at the London Works from 1840 to 1856.[32] James Timmins Chance (1814–1902), created a baronet in 1900, was associated particularly with the development of lighthouse glass at the Spon Lane works of Chance Brothers & Co.; he was also prominent in local and county affairs and was made high sheriff of Staffordshire in 1868.[33] Edward Caswall (1814–78), divine and poet, was a founder of the Roman Catholic mission at Smethwick; ordained in the Church of England, he joined the Roman Catholic Church in 1847, and in 1850 he became a member of the Oratory at Edgbaston (Birmingham), where he remained until his death.[34] William Siemens (1823–83), the metallurgist and electrician, knighted in 1883, was as a young man employed by Fox, Henderson & Co. at the London Works.[35] Joseph Chamberlain (1836–1914), the statesman, was with the firm of Nettlefold & Chamberlain from 1854 to 1874 and became a partner in 1869.[36] George Newnes (1851–1910), created a baronet in 1895, the publisher who founded several magazines including *Tit-Bits*, *The Strand Magazine* and *Country Life*, attended Shireland Hall School *c.* 1865.[37] Alphonse Bertillon (1853–1914), who became well known for his application of scientific techniques such as finger-printing to police investigation, taught French at the Collegiate School in South Road in 1874.[38] S. F. Barnes (1873–1967), the England Test cricketer, outstanding as a bowler, was a native of Smethwick.[39]

THE GROWTH OF THE TOWN. Before the 19th century the main centre of population seems to have been Bearwood Hill at the junction of the Birmingham–Dudley road and the road from Harborne (now Bearwood Road).[40] It was an inhabited area by 1278,[41] and the name Bearwood Hill was in use by the early 18th century.[42] The name was also used for the adjoining stretch of the Birmingham–Dudley road, which was renamed High Street *c.* 1906.[43] Cottages which stood until *c.* 1906 at what is now the northern end of Cheshire Road dated from at least the early 18th century.[44] The earliest build-

[19] See pp. 94, 99–100, 104–6.
[20] C. Hicks, *A Walk through Smethwick* (Birmingham, 1850), 7 (copy in W.P.L.). And see 'Smethwick and Round About', 18 Nov. 1955.
[21] Hicks, *Walk through Smethwick*, 9; below pp. 97–8.
[22] White, *Dir. Staffs.* (1834), 294.
[23] See p. 125.   [24] See p. 98.
[25] For the population figures see White, *Dir. Staffs.* (1851); *Census* 1861–1961; K. W. Inskip, *Smethwick: from Hamlet to County Boro.* (1966), 14 (copy in W.P.L.).
[26] See p. 121.
[27] *Smethwick Civic News*, Apr. 1954.
[28] West Midland Group, *Conurbation* (1948), 89, 172–5.
[29] J. F. Chance, *Hist. of Firm of Chance Brothers & Co.* (priv. print. 1919), 6–9, 43–4, 49, 51–2, 56–7; 'Old West Bromwich', 4 Feb. 1944; Wood, *Plan of West Bromwich* (1837); H.O. 107/2050(2) ff. 203–8.
[30] For the rest of this para. see *Smethwick Civic News*, Apr. 1961; *Smethwick Telephone*, 13 May 1955; *Census, 1961*; below p. 134.
[31] *D.N.B.*; below p. 111.

[32] *D.N.B.*; below pp. 110–11.
[33] *D.N.B.*; below p. 116.
[34] J. Gillow, *Bibliographical Dict. of Eng. Catholics*, i. 429–31; *D.N.B.*; below p. 129.
[35] *D.N.B.*; below p. 111.
[36] 'Smethwick and Round About', 2, 9, 16 July 1954; below p. 113.
[37] Hulda Friederichs, *Life of Sir George Newnes, Bart.* 27–8; *D.N.B.*
[38] H. T. F. Rhodes, *Alphonse Bertillon*, 54–7, 220. For the Collegiate School see 'Smethwick and Round About', 12 Dec. 1952.
[39] L. Duckworth, *S. F. Barnes—Master Bowler*, 35–8, 146–8; article on Barnes in *Smethwick Telephone*, 10 Nov. 1934; obituary in *The Guardian*, 27 Dec. 1967.
[40] Yates, *Map of Staffs.* (1775).
[41] *S.H.C.* 1924, p. 82.
[42] 'Old Smethwick', 12 May 1951; S.R.O., D. 1141/4/3/2.
[43] 'Smethwick and Round About', 11 Aug., 1 Dec. 1951.
[44] See photographs in W.P.L., P. 1254–5.

ings surviving in 1971 were the two pairs of early-19th-century cottages on the north side of Firs Lane. The area in the fork between the two main roads, by 1971 cleared of buildings and planted as a public garden, was formerly known as Newlands Green, apparently after William Newland, a Congregationalist wheelwright who lived there and owned property there in the early 19th century;[45] the name is still used for the street linking the two roads. The Red Cow inn, dating from at least the 18th century, formerly stood at Newlands Green; it was rebuilt on its present site further north in High Street in 1936–7.[46] The Sow and Pigs, which existed by 1818,[47] stood to the south of the former site of the Red Cow. Smethwick Cross at Bearwood Hill is mentioned in the 17th and earlier 18th centuries; it may have been a wayside cross, or the name may simply refer to the road junction.[48] Waterloo Road to the south-east (formerly Shireland Lane) formed part of an old road leading to Handsworth; it was the scene of the final stages of the battle in 1643 which resulted in Prince Rupert's capture of Birmingham.[49] By 1771 there was settlement west of Bearwood Hill at Bosoms End (also called Blossoms End by 1839), which lay around the triangle formed by the streets now called the Uplands, Cemetery Road, and Parkes Street. A road ran south-east from the area across Bearwood Road to Waterloo Road—the line of the present Uplands, Church Road, and Grange Road.[50]

It was not until the end of the 19th century that extensive development began to take place around Bearwood Hill. By the beginning of the 20th century nearly all the streets of houses south-east from Bearwood Hill to Waterloo Road and on the south-west around Wellington Road had appeared, and in 1900 Cheshire Road was being built up, particularly on its eastern side. The block of streets to the north-east of the Bosoms End triangle had also appeared, and the terrace on the west side of Cemetery Road was built in 1900–1.[51] Victoria Park was laid out to the east of Bearwood Hill in 1887–8 on 35½ a. around Pool Farm (formerly Berwoods Hill Farm) bought by the local board from Major-general E. M. Studd; it was extended in 1894 when land near Crockett's Lane was added.[52] Harry Mitchell Park north of Parkes Street was laid out on

6 a. of the land which Henry Mitchell conveyed to the corporation in 1899 in memory of his son Harry.[53] The Council House was built in 1905–7 in High Street at the north-west corner of Victoria Park.[54] By 1914 the streets west of Cheshire Road and the streets between the Uplands and the cemetery had been built up; Capethorn Road, running from Waterloo Road to Bearwood Road, was built up after the demolition in 1908 of Capethorn, a house of c. 1800.[55] The council estate at the corner of Bearwood and Church Roads was built around 1950; it consists of four-storey blocks containing two-storey dwellings one above the other and two-storey blocks of old people's maisonettes.[56] The flats on the south side of Newlands Green are a little later.[57] Bearwood House, a 15-storey block of council flats at the north end of Bearwood Road, was opened in 1966.[58]

Until the period between the World Wars the district further west remained open country, with several farms and large houses.[59] Smethwick Old Church was built there in 1732 and its school about the same time. Old Chapel farm, part of the estate with which Dorothy Parkes (d. 1728) endowed the church, lay to the west.[60] The Old Chapel public house to the north of the church dates from c. 1800. Smethwick Hall (formerly Smethwick House), which stood at the west end of Stony Lane until 1937, is said to have been built in 1746, and Spout House to the south-east, also demolished in 1937, existed by the late 18th century.[61] Between the World Wars, however, the area, like the adjoining part of Oldbury which was added to Smethwick in 1928, was used for new council estates, with the earliest of the borough's council housing being built in Hales Lane. Over 42 a. south of Church Road and in Hales Lane, including Old Chapel Farm, were sold by the trustees of Dorothy Parkes in 1927 and laid out for housing. The footpath running from Cemetery Road to Londonderry Lane became Manor Road, and streets of houses were built on either side.[62] In 1928 the corporation acquired the Smethwick Hall estate and opened Smethwick Hall Park on part of it in 1930; in 1939 schools were opened on the site of the Hall.[63] The corporation continued to use the western district for new estates after the Second World War, but because of the

[45] 'Old Smethwick', 19 May 1951; 'Smethwick and Round About', 15 Sept. 1951; below p. 131.
[46] 'Old Smethwick', 12 and 19 May 1951; Parson and Bradshaw, Dir. Staffs. (1818),; W.S.L., S. MS. 417/Harborne, sub Smallwood, Wm., no. 1002; Smethwick Telephone, 31 Oct. 1936.
[47] Parson and Bradshaw, Dir. Staffs. (1818) W.S.L., S. MS. 417/Harborne, sub Horton, Jos., no. 998.
[48] W.P.L. 16334; B.R.L. 297360; B.R.L. 393642, f. 7; 'Smethwick and Round About', 29 June 1956. It was probably different from Lightwood Cross: B.R.L. 324232 and 324239.
[49] Hackwood, Smethwick, 40; below p. 97.
[50] Yates, Map of Staffs. (1775); S.R.O., D. 1141/4/3/1, pp. 47–8; D. 1141/4/3/2, pp. 12, 17, 21, 25, 29, 60; Lich. Dioc. Regy., B/A/2(i)/L, map facing p. 142.
[51] O.S. Map 6", Staffs. LXXII. NE. (1905 edn.); date-stones from 1884 to 1900 on houses in High St. opposite Victoria Park, of 1899 on terrace on N. side of Waterloo Rd., of 1899 and 1900 in Edgbaston Rd., of 1900 in Claremont Rd., of 1900 in Cheshire Rd., of 1900 and 1901 in Cemetery Rd., and of 1900 and 1902 at junction of Church Rd. and Wellington Rd.; plaque commemorating the 1897 Jubilee at corner of Park Hill and Westfield Rd.
[52] O.S. Map 6", Staffs. LXXII. NE. (1890 edn.); Kelly's Dir. Birm. (1890); Smethwick Annual (1903), 98 (copy in

W.P.L.); Smethwick Official Industrial Handbook [1959], 71; 'Smethwick and Round About', 21 Mar. 1952, 30 Dec. 1955.
[53] Smethwick Official Industrial Handbook [1959], 71; below p. 136.   [54] See p. 120.
[55] O.S. Map 6", Staffs. LXXII. NE. (1921 edn.); 'Smethwick and Round About', 19 Jan. 1952.
[56] Smethwick Telephone, 29 Jan. 1949; Smethwick Official Industrial Handbook [1959], 64; Mann, 'Smethwick', 45, 50; W.P.L., P. 2032.
[57] They are not shown on W.P.L., P. 1434–41 (photographs of the area in Jan. 1950).
[58] Plaque in entrance hall.
[59] Hackwood, Smethwick, 5.
[60] See pp. 123, 137; volume of estate maps (1815) in possession of the secretary to the trustees of Dorothy Parkes (Lee, Crowder & Co., Birmingham), whose help is gratefully acknowledged.
[61] See pp. 105–6; W.P.L., P. 1226, P. 2162, photographs of Spout House shortly before its demolition showing a late-18th-century building.
[62] O.S. Map 6", Staffs. LXXII. NW., NE. (edn. of 1921 and prov. edn. with addns. of 1938); 'Old Smethwick', 23 Dec. 1950; W.P.L., P. 93, P. 141, P. 208, P. 218, P. 359; below p. 96.
[63] See pp. 106, 140.

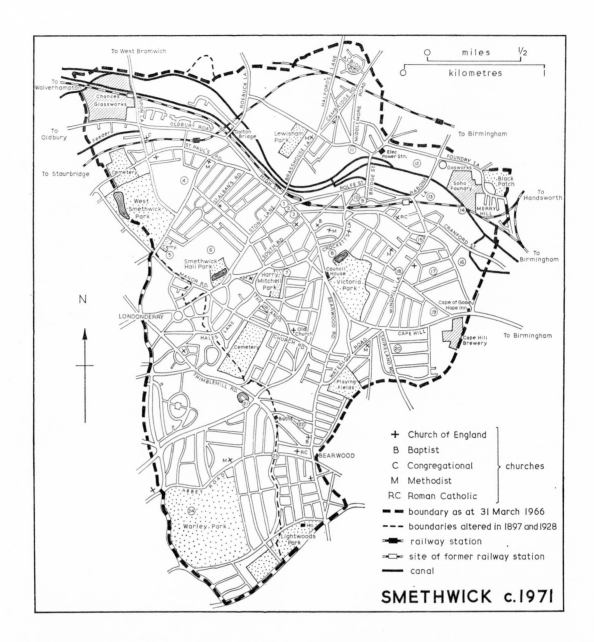

SMETHWICK c.1971

KEY

1. Site of former public library
2. Central library, formerly the public buildings
3. Sikh temple, formerly Congregational church
4. Former Holly Lodge
5. Midland Centre for Neurosurgery and Neurology, formerly infectious diseases hospital
6. Site of Smethwick House, later Smethwick Hall
7. Henry Mitchell Alms-houses
8. Chance Building, Warley College of Technology
9. Site of 1826 Wesleyan Methodist chapel
10. Site of 1856 Wesleyan Methodist chapel
11. Site of the Ruck of Stones
12. Site of Smethwick Hall
13. Site of the French Walls
14. Site of Piddocks (later Cranford) Farm
15. Site of Presbyterian church
16. Site of Smethwick Grove
17. Site of the Woodlands
18. Site of windmill
19. Site of the Coppice
20. Site of Shireland Hall
21. Site of Thimble Mill
22. Site of Beakes Farm
23. Site of Three Shires Oak
24. Site of Warley Abbey

shortage of land it built blocks of flats and maisonettes instead of houses. The blocks in Cemetery Road known as Thompson Gardens were erected in 1959–61 on the site of the Uplands, a villa built in 1847 by Samuel Thompson and demolished in 1958. The development includes a 15-storey block of flats, the first of several of that height in the town. Brookview at the junction of Stanhope Road and Beakes Road is a similar development of the same date and includes a 12-storey block.[64]

The district to the north of Bearwood Hill became the new centre of Smethwick in the 1830s. Earlier it consisted of scattered settlement along the Birmingham–Dudley road. The Blue Gates inn on the corner of Stony Lane probably existed by the 1770s.[65] There were then some buildings at the end of Crockett's Lane (which as late as 1868 was also known as Berwood Lane).[66] Building-plots at the corner of Stony Lane and apparently at the corner of Cross Street were offered for sale in 1824.[67] With the opening of the new line of the Birmingham Canal in the later 1820s the New Village grew up; it lay on the east side of the main road and was predominantly an area of factories and workers' houses.[68] By 1836 Cross, New, and Bridge Streets had been laid out and numerous houses had been built there.[69] Holy Trinity Church was being planned in 1835 and was built in 1837–8 on a site on the west side of the main road.[70] At that point the main road reaches the top of a slope, and the height of the summit was lowered at the time of the building of the church to ease the climb up from the Blue Gates.[71] Schools too were being opened in the area from 1836.[72] Rolfe Street existed by 1839, and by the middle of the century it had become the commercial centre of Smethwick, lined with shops, works, business premises, and numerous public houses. A railway station was opened there on the Birmingham, Wolverhampton & Stour Valley line in 1852. Rolfe Street retained its pre-eminence until the later part of the century when Soho Street became the shopping centre of the town; the decline was apparently caused by the closure of several works and also by the demolition of property in the late 1880s when a railway bridge replaced a level crossing.[73] Union Street was being built up by

1841.[74] Both it and Cross Street had apparently been laid out by one of the Downing family.[75] Regent Street was begun between 1868 and the late 1870s.[76] Piddock Road dates from c. 1907.[77] Most of the housing in the streets on the east side of the main road was demolished in 1970–1.

The area west of the main road developed at first as a middle-class district around Holy Trinity Church. J. W. Unett of the Woodlands laid out the streets flanking the churchyard on the north, west, and south in the later 1830s. Within the next decade he had also built Broomfield south-west from Queen Street, itself described as new in 1842. South Road was built up from the 1840s by John Harley, a Smethwick builder, who was later joined by his son James; by 1850 Belle Vue Terrace had been built there, with business and professional men as residents. As the development spread westwards the houses became larger; they are characterized by heavy stucco decoration. The district north-west to Holly Lane dates mainly from the late 19th and early 20th centuries.[78] Several of the streets between Stony Lane and Holly Lane have Devonshire names because Samuel Dibble, the founder of the firm that built them, and George Bowden, the architect, were natives of that county. Plans for making that part of the area into a separate parish were first mooted in 1899. By 1903 some 3,000 people were living there, and it continued to expand as a working-class district.[79] Most of the streets to the south-west of Devonshire Road were built up from the early 1930s.[80] There was rebuilding on the west and north sides of Holy Trinity Church in the 1950s and 1960s, with government offices on the site of the 1839 vicarage house and a post office on the site of the National school of 1840–1.[81] A council estate was being completed in 1971 between High Street and Holly Street, obliterating Queen and James Streets.

The area in the north-west of the former borough, known as West Smethwick by 1857,[82] developed in the 19th century as a distinct community focused on the Chance glass-works, with shops around the southern end of Spon Lane.[83] Spon Lane itself is mentioned in 1694.[84] In the later 18th century there were houses along the Birmingham–Dudley road

[64] *Smethwick Civic News*, May 1960, May, Sept. 1961 (copy in W.P.L.); County Boro. of Smethwick, *Opening of Brookview ... 19th May 1961* (copy in W.P.L.); 'Old Smethwick', 24 Dec. 1949, 7 Jan. 1950.
[65] Yates, *Map of Staffs.* (1775); J. Phillips and W. F. Hutchings, *Map of Staffs.* (1832); below p. 97.
[66] Yates, *Map of Staffs.* (1775); 'Old Smethwick', 13 Aug. 1949; 'Smethwick and Round About', 21 Mar. 1952; Hackwood, *Smethwick*, 117.
[67] 'Smethwick and Round About', 13 June 1952.
[68] W.P.L., D.R.O. 15/Misc. A/2, printed appeal; /Misc. A/4, Eccl. Commrs.' questionnaire.
[69] Redhead, *Local Govt.* 20; 'Smethwick and Round About', 19 June 1953.   [70] See p. 125.
[71] 'Smethwick and Round About', 3 Jan. 1958.
[72] See pp. 137–8.
[73] S.R.O., D. 610, bdle. 2, plan; 'Old Smethwick', 6 and 13 Aug., 3 Sept., 15 Oct. 1949; W.S.L., S. MS. 417/Harborne; Roper, Plans of Smethwick, 1857, nos. 14 and 15.
[74] Houses inscribed 'Union Cottages T.W. 1841' stood in Union St. until 1970–1.
[75] Docs. at St. Peter's, Harborne, 14, Vestry Mins. 1829–57, 2 Dec. 1842.
[76] 'Old Smethwick', 13 Aug. 1949; 'Smethwick and Round About', 28 July 1951; date-stone of 1881; below p. 130.

[77] *Staffs. Advertiser*, 31 Dec. 1904, p. 6; below p. 122.
[78] 'Smethwick and Round About', 11 Sept. 1953; Lich. Dioc. Regy., B/A/2(i)/L, p. 157; W.S.L., S. MS. 417/Harborne; S.R.O., Q/SB, A. 1849; docs. at St. Peter's, Harborne, 14, Vestry Mins. 1829–57, 2 Dec. 1842; H.O. 107/2050(2) ff. 266–9; Roper, Plans of Smethwick, 1857, nos. 22 and 23; O.S. Map 6″, Staffs. LXXII. NE. (edns. of 1890, 1905, 1921); below p. 106. Holly Place in Holly St. is dated 1854 and Broom Hill Place in Broomfield 1867.
[79] O.S. Map 6″, Staffs. LXXII. NE. (edns. of 1890, 1905, 1921); ibid. LXXII. NW. (edns. of 1890, 1904, 1921); 'Smethwick and Round About', 7 Aug. 1953; J. C. Stuart, *Street Map of Smethwick, 1890* (copy in W.P.L.); Lich. Dioc. Mag. 1903, 37; 1904, 89; 1905, 168; *Holy Trinity, Smethwick, Par. Mag.* July 1908 (copy in B.R.L.); *St. Alban the Martyr, Smethwick, 1906–1966*, 1.
[80] *St. Alban the Martyr*, 7–8; O.S. Map 6″, Staffs. LXXII. NW. (prov. edn. with addns. of 1938).
[81] Date-stones of 1953 and 1960 on the government offices; below p. 123.
[82] *Staffs. Advertiser*, 20 June 1857, 31 July 1858; *St. Paul's Church, West Smethwick, Staffs., 1858–1958* (copy in W.P.L.).
[83] 'Old Smethwick', 11 Dec. 1948.
[84] See p. 9.

(the present Oldbury Road) and several small farms, some of which survived until the later 19th century.[85] Blakeley Hall farm, said to have belonged to Halesowen abbey (Worcs.), lay on the north side of the main road, between Spon Lane and the Oldbury boundary, and in 1810 was 35 a. in extent.[86] Holt Hill farm, the home of the Birch family in the earlier 18th century, covered 79 a. in the Roebuck Lane area in 1780.[87] A farm on the west side of Holly Lane can also be traced from the earlier 18th century.[88] The Swan inn, which stands on the corner of Holly Lane and Oldbury Road, apparently existed by 1733,[89] although the present inn dates from the 20th century. The earliest surviving building is a late-18th-century house, no. 493 Oldbury Road, by 1971 used as commercial premises; near by on either side of the road there are some terraced cottages of the earlier 19th century. By 1810 part of Blakeley Hall farm had been divided into building plots, and several cottages were subsequently erected there.[90] The development of the area, however, began with the opening of Thomas Shutt's glass-works beside the Birmingham Canal on part of the farm apparently in 1815; the works was bought by R. L. Chance in 1822.[91] By the mid 1840s there were about 300 people living in Scotch Row in some 40 cottages belonging to the works.[92] George Street on the east side of Spon Lane existed by the mid 1840s, and by 1857 the area was built up as far as West Street.[93] With the completion of the Birmingham, Wolverhampton & Stour Valley railway through Smethwick in 1852 a station was provided in Spon Lane.[94] When St. Paul's Church was opened in 1858, it was stated to have been built for the needs of a population of over 2,700 in the Spon Lane area.[95]

The part of West Smethwick lying south of Oldbury Road developed later. The stretch of what is now St. Paul's Road from High Street to Holly Lane had been built by 1816,[96] but its continuation westwards was described as newly made in 1857.[97] In 1826 there were two newly built streets running south from Oldbury Road: Downing Street (the site of which is occupied by Smethwick West station of 1867) and Pleasant Street (the present Nine Leasowes).[98] Church Street West (now Mallin Street) and Church Street (now Marriott Street) were newly laid out in 1857 but were not then built up.[99] Much of the district had been developed by the later 1880s, but the area south-east of St. Paul's dates

from the late 19th and early 20th centuries and the Lonsdale Road area from the early 20th century.[1] West Smethwick Park was opened in 1895 on 43 a. given, laid out, and endowed by James Timmins Chance (later Sir James Chance, Bt.); he added more land in 1896, bringing the park to 50 a., a small part of it on the Oldbury side of the borough boundary. At first it was in the hands of trustees, but they conveyed it to Smethwick corporation in 1912. Chance also built Park Road (now West Park Road) and Victoria Road (in Oldbury) along the eastern and western boundaries of the park.[2]

An estate of prefabricated houses was built in Summit Crescent between the two levels of the Birmingham Canal west of Roebuck Lane in the later 1940s;[3] by 1971 they had been replaced by an industrial estate. The council estate on the north side of Oldbury Road, which has obliterated the 19th-century street pattern, dates from the late 1960s, and the multi-storey flats on the opposite site of the road are of the same period.[4] In 1971 further redevelopment was in progress on the south side of Oldbury Road to the east of Marriott Street. The small area of West Bromwich added in 1966[5] is occupied by a stretch of the M5 motorway and part of the West Bromwich ring road.

The district in the extreme north of the town beyond the Birmingham Canal developed as an industrial area mainly in the later 19th century and included the only colliery in Smethwick as well as numerous factories. It is crossed by an old road which joins the Birmingham–Wolverhampton road at the former Street House in the south-east of West Bromwich. The road has had several names, the oldest being Bowling Alley Lane and Street House Lane; land in Street House Lane variously called the Bowling Alley and the Bowling Green was owned by the Pope family in the earlier 19th century. The name Brasshouse Lane was also in use by the mid 1830s, and Halford's Lane was yet another version by 1851, deriving from the name of the family who had occupied Street House. By the later 1880s the southern part of the road, as far as the junction with Dartmouth Road, was called Brasshouse Lane and the rest Halford's Lane. A footbridge over the railway replaced a level crossing as part of the improvements in the area in 1888–90; the High Street end of Brasshouse Lane was thus blocked to vehicles, and North Western Road was built as a link to Rolfe Street.[6] Much of the area was

[85] Yates, *Map of Staffs.* (1775); 'Old Smethwick', 4 Sept., 9, 16, and 23 Oct., 25 Dec. 1948; below p. 107.

[86] 'Old Smethwick', 8 and 15 Jan. 1949.

[87] Docs. at St. Peter's, Harborne, 103 (1739), 151A (1711); *Aris's Birmingham Gaz.* 11 Dec. 1780; S.R.O., D. 1141/4/3/1 (showing Thos. Birch paying rent to the lords of the manor 1773–1804); R. Whitworth, *Plan of Intended Navigation from Birmingham to Canal at Aldersley near Wolverhampton survey'd 1767* (copy in W.S.L.).

[88] See p. 101. [89] See p. 107.

[90] 'Old Smethwick', 15 Jan. 1949; archives at Chance Brothers Ltd., plan of 1810. [91] See p. 115.

[92] R. Rawlinson, *Rep. to General Board of Health on a Preliminary Inquiry into . . . Smethwick* (1855), 12–14 and plan (copy in W.S.L.); 'Smethwick and Round About', 3 and 31 July 1953; Redhead, *Local Govt.* 21; Chance, *Chance Brothers*, 2, 23, 45, 49, 132.

[93] Rawlinson, *Smethwick*, 10, 12; Roper, *Plans of Smethwick*, 1857, no. 4. [94] See p. 98.

[95] L.J.R.O., B/A/2(i)/Q, p. 142.

[96] B.M., O.S.D. 212.

[97] 'Old Smethwick', 9 Oct. 1948.

[98] S.R.O., D. 707/12/3; 'Old Smethwick', 1 Jan. 1949; Roper, Plans of Smethwick, 1857, no. 4.

[99] Roper, Plans of Smethwick, 1857, no. 36; 'Old Smethwick', 9 Oct. 1948, 1 Jan. 1949.

[1] O.S. Map. 6", Staffs. LXVIII. SW., LXXII. NW. (edns. of 1890, 1904, 1921).

[2] Chance, *Chance Brothers*, 262–5; 'Old Smethwick', 9 Oct. 1948; Char. Com. files; *Smethwick Telephone*, 14 Apr. 1894.

[3] 'Old Smethwick', 23 Oct. 1948; *Express & Star*, 6 Mar. 1963.

[4] County Boro. of Warley, *4,000 Houses in 4 Years*, 7 (copy in W.P.L.); W.P.L., P. 5140.

[5] See p. 11.

[6] 'Old Smethwick', 19 and 26 Mar., 2 Apr., 3 Sept. 1949; 'Smethwick and Round About', 23 Jan., 31 July 1953; S.R.O., D. 613, bdle. 3, abstract of title, 1867; B.R.L. 445768, 445775; *Aris's Birmingham Gaz.* 15 Aug. 1836; Redhead, *Local Govt.* 20; Wood, *Plan of West Bromwich* (1837); White, *Dir. Staffs.* (1851); O.S. Map 6", Staffs. LXVIII. SE., LXXII. NE. (1890 edn.); above p. 10; below p. 98.

formerly occupied by the Ruck of Stones farm, which can be traced from the late 16th century.[7] Another farm, between Halford's Lane and Roebuck Lane, can be traced from the early 18th century.[8] Galton House between the two levels of the canal on the east side of Roebuck Lane existed by 1790. It was probably connected at one time with the Galton family, but it was owned by the Birmingham Canal Navigations by 1842 and was occupied by the company's agents for some years; it was demolished c. 1916.[9] Hadley House on the east side of Brasshouse Lane south of Lewisham Road existed by 1816. It was the home of Joseph Hadley, an ironmaster, in the mid 1830s and of T. R. B. Bindley, founder of a near-by glue factory, in 1851; it still stood in 1913 but has since been demolished.[10] A spring issuing from the side of the canal cutting near Roebuck Lane and known as the Sugar Well from the white deposit left by the water formerly attracted people from a considerable distance because the mineral content of the water was said to be good for eye complaints.[11]

The brasshouse from which the lane took its name existed by 1790; there were a steelworks and rolling-mills on the north bank of the canal east of Brasshouse Lane by 1842; drain-pipes were being made in Pottery Lane from c. 1850.[12] There were several houses in Brasshouse Lane and in Ruck of Stones Lane (now Lewisham Road) by the mid 1830s.[13] They included the block of twenty houses in Brasshouse Lane which evidently existed by 1816 and which was known by the 1850s as Twenty House Row.[14] About 1840 Daniel Holloway, a coal-dealer, built himself a house in Halford's Lane which c. 1860 became the public house called The Old House at Home; in 1855 he also built eight cottages on adjoining land.[15] What was called Arthur Street in 1851 and Great Arthur Street by the late 1880s existed by 1842, and houses had been built there by 1857; only the eastern part existed then, and it was extended to Roebuck Lane apparently in the 1940s.[16] By 1851 St. George Street (now Perry Street) was being built up.[17] There was also some building by 1852 at the east end of what was later called Dartmouth Road, but most of its course to Roebuck Lane was evidently still a track; the road was made c. 1865 and follows a more northerly line.[18] The Birmingham, Wolverhampton & Dudley Rail-

way was opened through the area in 1854.[19] In 1864 the Birmingham Wagon Co. (later the Birmingham Railway Carriage and Wagon Co.) built its works beside the railway off Middlemore Road;[20] the manager, Edmund Fowler, built himself a house, the Laurels, to the north-east and converted Middlemore Road from a bridlepath into a highway.[21] In 1874 the first sinking was completed at the Sandwell Park Colliery, also beside the railway.[22] By 1881 the area had a population of over 2,500 and was still expanding. Some 60 cottages were being built towards the end of that year, and a large number of building sites had been marked out.[23] By the later 1880s Mornington Road, Pope Street, and part of Middlemore Road had been built up, and the terraces known as Sandwell Place between Halford's Lane and Oxford Road had been erected. Oxford, Cambridge, and Sydenham Roads had been laid out, and they were built up soon afterwards. Mafeking and Kimberley Roads date from the early 20th century.[24] Lewisham Park on the south side of Dartmouth Road was leased to the town by Lord Dartmouth at a nominal rent and was opened in 1905; the area had been part of a bowling alley and later a football ground for the Birmingham Railway Carriage and Wagon Works.[25] Several factories have been built on either side of Dartmouth Road in the 20th century; the earliest was the 1905 portion of the works of Henry Hope & Sons on the corner of Halford's Lane.[26] Middlemore Industrial Estate was developed on the 56-acre site of the Birmingham Railway Carriage and Wagon Works after it had ceased production in 1963.[27] Extensive demolition of the 19th-century terraced housing was in progress in 1971. In 1966 the northern boundary was changed by the transfer to West Bromwich of the area on either side of Halford's Lane north of the railway, occupied largely by the Albion council estate built between the World Wars.[28]

The area in the north-east of the town became steadily industrialized from the late 18th century, with factories being built on either side of the Birmingham Canal. It is crossed by an old road to Handsworth, known in 1815 as New Inn Lane and by 1851 as Rabone Lane.[29] Bridge Street existed by the 1770s, running from Rabone Lane to the Ruck of Stones area.[30] Slough Lane (now Wellington Street) on the Birmingham boundary occurs

[7] See p. 103.

[8] See pp. 106–7.

[9] 'Old Smethwick', 12 Mar. 1949, 21 Oct. 1950; 'Smethwick and Round About', 4 Nov. 1955; W.S.L., S. MS. 417/Harborne, no. 1653; Hackwood, *Smethwick*, 125; *Evening Mail*, 9 Dec. 1970.

[10] B.M., O.S.D. 212; Redhead, *Local Govt.* 20; White, *Dir. Staffs.* (1834); 'Old Smethwick', 17 July 1948, 2 July 1949; O.S. Map 6″, Staffs. LXVIII. SE. (edns. of 1904 and 1921).

[11] 'Old Smethwick', 7 May 1949.

[12] See pp. 109, 118; W.S.L., S. MS. 417/Harborne, *sub* Hadley, Jos.

[13] Redhead, *Local Govt.* 20–1.

[14] B.M., O.S.D. 212; W.S.L., S. MS. 417/Harborne, *sub* Smith, John, and Thomson, Jas., nos. 1377–9; Roper, Plans of Smethwick, 1857, no. 7.

[15] S.R.O., D. 613, bdle. 3, abstract of title 1867, and agreement between Jas. Turner and Jas. Gregory 1871; W.S.L., S. MS. 417/Harborne, no. 1370.

[16] W.S.L., S. MS. 417/Harborne; H.O. 107/2050(2) ff. 230v.–234; Roper, Plans of Smethwick, 1857, no. 11; O.S. Map 6″, Staffs. LXVIII. SE., LXXII. NE. (1890 edn.). It is still shown as a short road ibid. LXVIII. SE. (prov. edn. with addns. of 1938), but as running to Roe-

buck Lane by R. Fletcher, Street Map of Boro. of Smethwick (1949; copy in W.P.L.).

[17] H.O. 107/2050(2) ff. 234–5; Roper, Plans of Smethwick, 1857, no. 11.

[18] Roper, Plans of Smethwick, 1857, nos. 6 and 7; S.R.O., Q/SB, T. 1865. It is shown as Dartmouth Rd. on O.S. Map 6″, Staffs. LXVIII. SE. (1890 edn.).

[19] See p. 98.   [20] See p. 112.

[21] 'Old Smethwick', 28 May 1949.

[22] See p. 115.   [23] *Lich. Dioc. Mag.* 1881, 174–5.

[24] O.S. Map. 6″, Staffs. LXVIII. SE. (edns. of 1890, 1904, 1921); 'Old Smethwick', 9 Apr. 1949; W.P.L., P. 259, showing Ethel Buildings in Mornington Rd. (now demolished) dated 1881.

[25] *Smethwick Annual* (1904), 77 (copy in W.P.L.); 'Old Smethwick', 4 June 1949; S.R.O., Q/SB, T. 1865.

[26] O.S. Map 6″, Staffs. LXVIII. SE. (1921 edn. and prov. edn. with addns. of 1938); 'Old Smethwick', 30 Apr. 1949; below p. 115.

[27] See p. 112.

[28] *Evening Mail*, 18 Nov. 1965; S.R.O., L.G.O. 29, boundary maps of West Midlands Order, 1965.

[29] B.R.L., j. 498, p. 6; White, *Dir. Staffs.* (1851); below pp. 97, 105.

[30] Yates, *Map of Staffs.* (1775).

from 1622 as Slowe or Sloe Lane; Slowe Moor too occurs in the area from that date.[31] The name may even have been in use *c.* 1275 when Agnes de Slouf occurs among the tenants of Smethwick manor.[32] It was stated in 1884 that the name derived from the sloes that had abounded in the area within living memory;[33] the earlier existence of Fenfield in the area[34] suggests 'slough' as an alternative derivation. A farm called the French Walls, Piddocks farm, and probably Smethwick Hall (later Rabone Hall) existed by the mid 17th century.[35] Soho Foundry was opened in 1796, and a gun-barrel factory was built at the French Walls about the same time.[36] A row of cottages off Foundry Lane, used in 1972 as offices by the Foundry, existed by 1814.[37] Part of the Merry Hill area, near the Birmingham boundary became known as the Soap Hole from the soap-works established there by 1818.[38] By the mid 1830s there were numerous houses as well as new factories.[39] The French Walls became the site of G. F. Muntz & Co.'s metal works in 1842 and Rabone Hall the site of Tangye Bros. & Price's Cornwall engineering works in 1864.[40] The area is crossed by the Birmingham, Wolverhampton & Stour Valley Railway, completed in 1852; a station was opened at Soho in 1853.[41] The gas-works in Rabone Lane dates from 1881 and the power station in Downing Street from *c.* 1900.[42] The area occupied by Black Patch Park in the north-east corner of Smethwick was originally part of a larger open space extending into Handsworth and Birmingham and used in the later 19th century as a gypsy encampment. The owners of the land evicted the gypsies in 1904, and the park was laid out by the city of Birmingham in 1910–11. In 1966 it was taken over by the new borough of Warley.[43] In the mid 1960s the Vittoria Street area was redeveloped with council housing, including a 15-storey block;[44] the street was divided into two separate parts, the northern half becoming Boulton Road. The north-eastern boundary was changed in 1966 by the addition of a small part of Birmingham.[45]

The Cape Hill, Windmill Lane, and Shireland Road areas to the south-west of this industrialized part of the town developed largely as a district of workers' houses, with factories on the eastern boundary and a new commercial centre along the Birmingham–Dudley road and part of Waterloo Road. Besides the main road two other old roads cross the area, running north to Handsworth along Grove Lane (formerly Cape Lane) and along Windmill Lane (taking its name from the windmill built at the beginning of the 19th century).[46] There were formerly several farms and extensive woodland; the area was also one where Birmingham business and professional men settled from the later 18th century.[47] In 1850, however, it was stated that anyone proceeding along Grove Lane to the New Village would see 'nothing but new-formed streets, and others staked out, and group after group of tenements'.[48]

The Cape Hill district takes its name from the Cape of Good Hope inn which stood by 1814 at the junction of Grove Lane and the main road. The present building, apparently the third on the site, was opened in 1925.[49] There was still little building in the area in 1842, although the present Raglan Road, Reynolds Street, and Wills Street were then described as 'intended new streets'; twelve houses were being built in Reynolds Street.[50] At the junction of Waterloo Road and the main road stood Berwood Cottage. It belonged to William Spurrier (d. 1848), a Birmingham lawyer, who owned 214 a. in Smethwick. He had lived in Smethwick earlier in the century, but by 1842 Berwood Cottage with 7 a. attached was occupied by William Mather. It was known locally as Blood Hall because Spurrier acted for the Crown in prosecutions for forgery and coining. The Elms was built on the site by Dr. William Sutton *c.* 1875 and was replaced by Lloyds Bank in 1907.[51] Cranford Street existed by 1847, presumably taking its name from Cranford farm,[52] and Poplar and Lower Cross Streets were built by J. W. Unett of the near-by Woodlands *c.* 1848.[53] The area east of Grove Lane had by then become industrialized.[54] In 1854 the site for St. Matthew's Church on the east side of Windmill Lane was conveyed by Unett; the conveyance mentioned land to the north-east and south-west belonging to Unett over which it was planned to make new streets.[55] By 1857 Upper Grove Street and London Street existed, both with some houses; there was also building around the Six Ways junction at the north end of Windmill Lane.[56] The failure in 1856 of Fox,

[31] B.R.L., 224613; A. L. Reade, *The Reades of Blackwood Hill* (priv. print. 1906), 204.
[32] *Court Rolls of the Manor of Hales, 1270–1307* (Worcs. Hist. Soc.), i. 22.
[33] *Midland Antiquary*, iii. 34. [34] See p. 107.
[35] See pp. 100, 102, 105. [36] See pp. 100, 110.
[37] B.M., O.S.D. 256. For workers' houses at the Foundry by 1800 see below p. 110.
[38] 'Old Smethwick', 23 Sept. 1950; below p. 116.
[39] Redhead, *Local Govt.* 20. [40] See pp. 111–12.
[41] See p. 98. [42] See p. 122.
[43] 'Old Smethwick', 30 Sept. 1950; 'Smethwick and Round About', 3, 10, 17 Sept. 1954; ex inf. the general manager, Warley Parks and Cemeteries Dept. (1973).
[44] County Boro. of Warley, *4,000 Houses in 4 Years*, 7; *Smethwick Civic News*, June 1962. The statement in 'Old Smethwick', 29 Apr. 1950, that Vittoria St. was renamed from Victoria St. after the opening of Victoria Park in 1888 is incorrect; the name Vittoria Street was in use by 1871: see below p. 121. On Roper, Plans of Smethwick, 1857, nos 17 and 18, however, it is shown as Victoria St.
[45] S.R.O., L.G.O. 29, boundary maps of West Midlands Order, 1965.
[46] See p. 109. Cape Lane occurs in 1846: 'Smethwick and Round About', 28 Aug. 1953. White, *Dir. Staffs.* (1851), lists Cape or Grove Lane.

[47] See pp. 100, 104, 106; Redhead, *Local Govt.* 20; 'Old Smethwick', 27 May 1950.
[48] C. Hicks, *A Walk through Smethwick* (Birmingham, 1850), 16 (copy in W.P.L.).
[49] B.M., O.S.D. 256; W.S.L., S. MS. 417/Harborne, *sub* Pennel, Wm., no. 842; 'Old Smethwick', 26 May 1951; Mitchells & Butlers Ltd. *Fifty Years of Brewing, 1879–1929*, 87–9 (copy in W.P.L.).
[50] W.S.L., S. MS. 417/Harborne, *sub* Mather, Wm., and Warden, Sam., nos. 850–1, 855, 873; 'Old Smethwick', 29 Apr. 1950.
[51] 'Old Smethwick', 24 June, 1 and 22 July 1950; 'Smethwick and Round About', 21 Mar. 1952, 31 July 1953, 4 Feb. 1955; Parson and Bradshaw, *Dir. Staffs.* (1818); Burke, *Land. Gent.* (1894), 1951; W.S.L., S. MS. 417/Harborne. The earliest dates on the family tomb in the churchyard of the Old Church (near the west door) are 1807 and 1808 when two of Spurrier's children were buried there; this suggests that the family was then living in Smethwick.
[52] S.R.O., D. 707/12/1, conveyance of Feb. 1847. For Cranford farm see below p. 103.
[53] S.R.O., Q/SB, E. 1848, A. 1849.
[54] 'Smethwick and Round About', 27 Mar. 1953.
[55] Lich. Dioc. Regy., B/A/2(i)/P, ff. 298v.–299.
[56] Roper, Plans of Smethwick, 1857, nos. 19 and 26.

Henderson & Co. of the London Works in Cranford Street caused a decline in the district for some years. Richard Tangye visited the area soon after the failure and later recalled the deserted and grass-grown streets and rotting doors and windows; the workers had left, and the small shopkeepers were ruined.[57] The first part of Cape Hill Brewery was built on the south side of the main road in 1878–9.[58] Further development took place in the 1880s after the break-up of the Coppice and Woodlands estates, and the whole triangle between Windmill Lane, Grove Lane, and the Cape Hill stretch of the main road was built up by the beginning of the 20th century.[59] The two-storeyed blocks on the south side of Cape Hill inscribed 'Smethwick Market' and 'Cape Hill Market' (now shops on the ground-floor and living accommodation on the first floor) had been built by the late 1880s and represent the beginning of the shopping centre which now extends part of the way along Shireland and Waterloo Roads.[60] Covered markets have been held in Windmill Lane since at least the later 1920s in place of earlier open-air markets.[61] Extensive redevelopment of the area between Raglan Road, Windmill Lane, and Grove Lane with council housing, including multi-storey flats, started in the earlier 1960s.[62]

The west side of Windmill Lane began to be developed about the mid 19th century. Earlier in the century there was only the windmill, Oakfield farm to the east, and a row of houses (called High Park Row and later Hill Row) on the west side of what is now Soho Street.[63] About 1850 the group of streets between the windmill and the main road were laid out—Ballot, Suffrage, Corbett, and Hume Streets. Building there, however, was piece-meal over the next half century.[64] By the mid 1850s Price Street and the streets north to Messenger Road (formerly part of High Park Road) had been laid out, but building there too was scattered.[65] High Park Road occurs by the mid 1850s and was then known also as Hyde Park Road; there was a Hyde Park Leasow on the east side of Soho Street in 1842.[66] The streets south from Price Street to Ballot Street were built in the earlier 1880s; nearly 70 years later an old man recalled the process:[67]

About 1882 a man named Mackey started to build in Exeter Road, about twelve houses near Corbett Schools . . . Then in '83 or '84 Dibble came on the scene, started to make streets, and Sewer started to build in Tiverton Road in blocks of eight. They flew up, not much foundations . . . Brickies first, then slaters, carpenters, doors and windows already made, and that is how Tiverton, Exeter, Bolham, and Bampton Roads were made.

Devonshire names were given to several of the streets because Samuel Dibble was a native of Devonshire.[68] The Windmill Brewery in Windmill Lane was built in 1886–7.[69] The Soho Street area became the shopping centre of Smethwick c. 1890 with the decline of Rolfe Street but was later superseded by Cape Hill.[70] The whole area between the main road and Messenger Road had been built up by the beginning of the 20th century; Victoria Park Road and Pool Road were also being built up by then.[71] The corporation began to redevelop the area north from Suffrage Street to Messenger Road in 1954, and building was still in progress in 1971. It consists almost entirely of blocks of maisonettes and flats, some of them 15 storeys high, and there is also a shopping precinct.[72] Council flats were also built to the north of Messenger Road in the mid 1960s.[73]

The Shireland Hall estate to the south of Cape Hill existed by the later 17th century.[74] The northern half of Montague Road had been built by 1854,[75] and in 1856 there were plans for developing part of the estate.[76] In fact it was some time before the new district began to be laid out. Shireland Road had been built apparently by 1877,[77] and in 1881 mention was made of the large and rapidly increasing population on the Shireland Hall estate, consisting mainly of workers who wanted to live nearer their place of work.[78] Houses were being erected in Florence Road in 1886 by Thomas Butler, a

57 'Old Smethwick', 15 July 1950.
58 See p. 117.
59 O.S. Map 6″, Staffs. LXXII. NE. (edns. of 1890 and 1905); B.R.L. 452905–6; date-stones of 1878 in Raglan Rd., 1882 and 1885 in Woodlands St., and 1901 in Salisbury Rd.; below pp. 100, 106.
60 O.S. Map 6″, Staffs. LXXII. NE. (1890 edn.); 'Old Smethwick', 22 July 1950.
61 Inf. from Miss Amy Hill, St. Philip's R.C. School (1971); Warley News Telephone, 17 July 1969, p. 9, stating that Smethwick market was burnt down in 1928; Smethwick Official Handbook (4th edn.), 24; O.S. Map 1/2,500, Staffs. LXXII. 3 (1948 edn., based on revision of 1938).
62 County Boro. of Warley, 4,000 Houses in 4 Years, 8–9.
63 J. Phillips and W. F. Hutchings, Map of Staffs. (1832); O.S. Map 1″, LXII. SW. (1834 edn.); Lich. Dioc. Regy., B/A/2(i)/L, map facing p. 142; W.S.L., S. MS. 417/Harborne, sub Watt, Jas., no. 1035 (giving 22 houses in the row); H.O. 107/2050(2) ff. 137–40 (giving 21 houses); O.S. Map 6″, Staffs. LXXII. NE. (1921 edn.), giving the name as Hill Row; below p. 109.
64 'Smethwick and Round About', 23 June 1951; S.R.O., D. 613, bdle. 3, indenture of 1850; R. Rawlinson, Rep. to General Board of Health on a Preliminary Inquiry into . . . Smethwick (1855), 16 (copy in W.S.L.); Roper, Plans of Smethwick, 1857, nos. 25 and 30 (giving Corbett St. as Cobbett St.); O.S. Map 6″, Staffs. LXXII. NE. (edns. of 1890 and 1905), NW. (edns. of 1890 and 1904); date-stones of 1876, 1877, and 1891 in Corbett St. and 1883 in Suffrage St. For Votingham as an address in or off

Windmill Lane see 'Smethwick and Round About', 23 June 1951; P.O. Dir. Staffs. (1868; 1872); White, Dir. Birm. (1869), sub Richardson.
65 Rawlinson, Smethwick, plan; Roper, Plans of Smethwick, 1857, nos. 20 and 25; S.R.O., Q/SB, E. 1857.
66 'Old Smethwick', 17 July 1948, 15 Apr. 1950, 27 Jan. 1951; F. White & Co., Dir. Birm. (1855), 538; S.R.O., Q/SB, E. 1857; Rawlinson, Smethwick, plan; Roper, Plans of Smethwick, 1857, no. 20; W. H. Dix & Co. Dir. Birm. (1858), 665–6, 669; S.R.O., D. 812/5/Smethwick R.C. School; W.S.L., S. MS. 417/Harborne, sub Watt, Jas., no. 945.
67 Smethwick Telephone, 13 Aug. 1949.
68 See p. 91.   69 See p. 118.
70 'Old Smethwick', 22 and 29 Apr., 20 and 27 May 1950; 'Smethwick and Round About', 4 Apr. 1952, 2 and 30 Jan. 1953.
71 O.S. Map 6″, Staffs. LXXII. NE. (edns. of 1890, 1905, 1921); date-stone of 1897 on Co-operative Soc. building in Messenger Rd.
72 Smethwick Civic News, Apr., Dec. 1954, Aug. 1955, Nov., Dec. 1957, Oct. 1960, June, July, Aug., Nov. 1962, Oct. 1963, May 1964; Smethwick Telephone and Warley Courier, 7 May 1965.
73 County Boro. of Warley, 4,000 Houses in 4 Years, 7.
74 See p. 103.
75 Rawlinson, Smethwick, plan.
76 See p. 104.
77 Date-stone of 1877 opposite end of Edith Rd.
78 Lich. Dioc. Mag. 1881, 93.

Handsworth builder.[79] Most of the streets between Montague and Waterloo Roads had been laid out by the later 1880s. An appeal in 1901 for the new church then being built in Shireland Road in place of a mission church of 1882 gave the population as over 7,000; it was still rapidly increasing and consisted entirely of workers in the factories of the district.[80] Hadley Playing Fields at the south end of Waterloo Road were opened in 1962; much of the site had long been used for recreation. The land was left to the corporation by Sarah Hadley (d. 1936) of the adjoining Bell House, which stood on the corner of Waterloo Road and Bearwood Road and was demolished in 1959 to allow for road widening and the laying-out of the playing fields.[81]

Bearwood, which forms the southern extremity of Smethwick, was in the later 18th century still an area of extensive woodland, a feature from which the 18th-century Lightwoods House takes its name.[82] A tree known as the Three Shires Oak stood at what is now the junction of Three Shires Oak Road, Thimblemill Road, Wigorn Road, and Abbey Road, where Staffordshire adjoined detached portions of Shropshire and Worcestershire; it was cut down in 1904.[83] A plot of arable on the south side of Three Shires Oak Road was known as the Bear Wood in the 1830s.[84] The Beakes, a moated farmhouse formerly standing west of Bearwood Road, existed by the late 17th century.[85] By 1775 there was some building at the cross-roads formed by the ancient road running from Harborne to Smethwick (the present Bearwood Road) and the road from Rowley Regis to Edgbaston (here following Three Shires Oak Road and Sandon Road, formerly Bear Lane). The buildings included the Bear inn, which may have existed by 1718; the present building dates from 1906–7.[86] The southern boundary of Smethwick was formed by the Birmingham–Halesowen road, and by 1775 there was some building where the Harborne–Smethwick road crosses it.[87] Bearwood remained rural until the late 19th century. By the later 1880s there was some building along the west side of Bearwood Road. Poplar Road, Warley Road (now the eastern part of Anderson Road), and Milton Street (now Rutland Road) had been built, and Ethel Street on the east side of Bearwood Road also existed.[88] A church was erected in 1887–8,[89] and in the 1890s the population

increased rapidly.[90] By 1903 new streets of houses had been built on the west side of Bearwood Road to the borough boundary as far north as Rawlings Road, and Reginald Road had been constructed, though it was not yet built up.[91] About that time the houses at the southern end of Bearwood Road began to be converted into shops.[92] By 1914 the built-up area had been extended further north to Beakes Road and also included new streets on the east between Bearwood and Merrivale Roads.[93] The Lightwoods estate became a public park in 1902.[94] In 1966 a small area of Birmingham was added to the new borough of Warley at Bearwood, the former Smethwick boundary being extended eastwards to run along Sandon Road to Barnsley Road.[95]

The Warley Woods portion of Oldbury, which was added to Smethwick in 1928, was then partly rural. By the early 20th century, however, the built-up area of Bearwood had spread over the Oldbury boundary as far as Warley Park and Rathbone Road, and by 1914 new streets were being laid out west of Rathbone Road.[96] In the 1920s, even before the extension of the boundary, Smethwick corporation had begun two estates in Warley Woods, one to the west of Rathbone Road and the other at Londonderry, and by 1938 nearly the whole area had been laid out with council housing.[97] The main exception was Warley Park, originally an estate centring on the 19th-century Warley Abbey. It became a public park in 1906 when Birmingham corporation acquired the estate. The Tudor-style mansion was used as a golf club-house until 1957 and was then demolished.[98] The Londonderry Playing Fields in Londonderry Lane were laid out on 13 a. of Queens Head farm, a property which Smethwick corporation bought in 1921.[99]

COMMUNICATIONS. Smethwick lies on the main road from Birmingham to Oldbury and Dudley. The Smethwick section was mentioned in 1278 as the highway from Smethwick to Birmingham.[1] It formed part of the main route from London to Shrewsbury by 1675, but by 1723 the older and better route through West Bromwich and Wolverhampton was again preferred.[2] In 1760 the road through Smethwick was turnpiked as part of

[79] B.R.L., Springthorpe, Holcroft & Bishop 86.
[80] O.S. Map 6″, Staffs. LXXII. NE. (edns. of 1890 and 1905); printed appeal for new church building fund (copy at Old Church vicarage); date-stones of 1888 and 1900 in Grantham Rd. A terrace in Sycamore Rd. carries the names Pretoria, Mafeking, Colenso, and Kimberley Villas.
[81] 'Old Smethwick', 27 Jan. 1951; W.P.L., P. 4004–6; O.S. Map 6″, Staffs. LXXII. NE. (1921 edn.); below p. 136.
[82] See pp. 101, 108.
[83] 'Smethwick and Round About', 5 Jan. 1952; N. & Q. clxxxiv. 164–5; St. Mary's Church, Bearwood, 1888–1968; O.S. Map 1″, LXII. SW. (1834 edn.); W.P.L., P. 428–9 (photographs of 1901 and 1892).
[84] B.R.L. 500281–2; W.S.L., S. MS. 417/Harborne, sub Robinson, Edw., no. 731.
[85] See p. 99.
[86] Yates, Map of Staffs. (1775); 'Old Smethwick', 26 May 1951; S.R.O., D. 1141/4/3/2; W.S.L., S. MS. 417/Harborne, sub Wright, E., J., and T., no. 733; below p. 97. For Sandon Rd. as Bear Lane see B.R.L. 662129–30.
[87] Yates, Map of Staffs. (1775); below p. 97.
[88] O.S. Map 6″, Staffs. LXXII. NE. (1890 edn.).
[89] See p. 128.   [90] Hackwood, Smethwick, 70.
[91] O.S. Map 6″, Staffs. LXXII. NE. (1905 edn.); B.R.L.,

Springthorpe, Holcroft & Bishop 84 (for new houses in Ethel St., 1891).   [92] W.P.L., P. 174–5, P. 1216.
[93] O.S. Map 6″, Staffs. LXXII. NE. (1921 edn.).
[94] See p. 102.
[95] S.R.O., L.G.O. 29, boundary maps of West Midlands Order, 1965.
[96] O.S. Map 6″, Staffs. LXXII. NE. (1921 edn.); Char. Com. files, papers relating to St. Hilda's Church, Warley Woods, describing Rathbone Rd. as 'proposed' in 1907; 'Smethwick and Round About', 8 Mar. 1957; below p. 119.
[97] S.R.O., L.G.O. 9/11, map of 1927 showing housing additional to that on O.S. Map 6″, Staffs. LXXII. NW., NE. (1921 edn.); O.S. Map 6″, Staffs. LXII. NW., NE. (prov. edn. with addns. of 1938); Census, 1931, 1961; W.P.L., P. 103–4, P. 129, P. 369, P. 417, P. 2668.
[98] 'Smethwick and Round About', 25 Jan., 15 Feb., 15 Mar. 1957; R. Lugar, Villa Architecture (1828), plates xxxii–xxxiv; C. A. Vince, Hist. of Corporation of Birmingham, iv (Birmingham, 1923), 234–5; photographs at W. P. L. and National Monuments Record.
[99] Smethwick Official Industrial Handbook [1959], 71; S.R.O., L.G.O. 9/11.
[1] S.H.C. 1924, p. 82.
[2] V.C.H. Staffs. ii. 278; J. Ogilby, Britannia (1675), 99 and plate preceding; above p. 11.

WEST BROMWICH: THE JUNCTION OF THE M5 AND THE M6 FROM THE WEST IN 1971
with Bescot sidings in the foreground

SMETHWICK FROM THE WEST IN 1962
showing, from left to right, the old and new lines of the Birmingham Canal and the Stour Valley railway
line; in the right foreground is Galton Bridge

WEST BROMWICH: THE TOWN HALL IN 1975 with the library on the left

WALSALL: THE COUNTY COURT AND THE COUNCIL HOUSE c. 1930

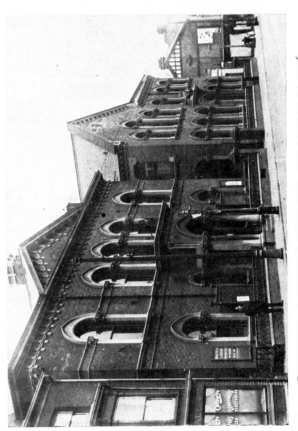

SMETHWICK: THE FORMER TOWN HALL AND LIBRARY IN 1926

the Birmingham, Dudley, and Wolverhampton turnpike.[3] A toll-gate on the Smethwick section existed by 1762.[4] It is probably to be identified with the 'Blugates' which a map made in 1767 shows as standing at the junction with what is now Brasshouse Lane.[5] The later Blue Gates hotel on the opposite side of the main road (opened in 1932) preserved the name of two earlier inns on the same site; the first existed by 1781 and probably 1773, and presumably took its name from the colour of the barrier.[6] There may have been a toll-gate at the junction of the main road with Holly Lane and Roebuck Lane in the early 19th century: what was probably an inn there was called the White Gates.[7] By 1857 there was also a toll-gate at the junction with Windmill Lane.[8] There was another gate at the junction with Grove Lane on the boundary with Birmingham, the toll-house being on the Birmingham side.[9] The road was disturnpiked in 1876.[10] The Blue Gates toll-house opposite the Blue Gates hotel has been converted into a shop. The toll-house at Windmill Lane was demolished in 1896[11] and that at Grove Lane c. 1925.[12]

The main road was crossed by other old roads running south-west towards Rowley Regis and Halesowen and north to West Bromwich. One road ran south-west along Stony Lane and Hales Lane and north along Brasshouse Lane and Halford's Lane; the other ran along Holly Lane and Roebuck Lane. The main road was also crossed by the road from Halesowen to Handsworth running from Hales Lane along Cooper's Lane, Crockett's Lane, and Rabone Lane (formerly New Inn Lane), and by the road from Harborne to Handsworth, which branched north-east from Bearwood Road to follow Waterloo Road, Windmill Lane, and Soho Street to Rabone Lane.[13]

Bearwood Road, which forks south from the Birmingham–Dudley road to run to Bearwood and Harborne, was mentioned as the highway from Smethwick to Harborne in 1278.[14] At Bearwood it meets the Birmingham–Halesowen road, which formed the boundary between the manors and townships of Smethwick and Harborne.[15] The Birmingham–Halesowen road was turnpiked in 1753, and by 1858 there was a toll-gate at the Two

Mile Stump at the junction with Bearwood Road; it replaced the toll-gate at the near-by junction with Sandon Road (in Edgbaston), in existence in 1814 and apparently still in use in 1842. The road was disturnpiked in 1877. Part of the toll-house was sold that year and the remainder demolished.[16]

In 1757 and 1760 the Smethwick highway surveyor paid for work on a bridge below Smethwick Chapel;[17] it presumably carried the present Church Road over Thimblemill Brook. In 1782 the surveyor paid for work on a bridge in Stony Lane over the stream flowing from the grounds of Smethwick Hall.[18] It may perhaps be the Stonnoss Brook bridge on which work had been carried out in 1757.[19] There was also a bridge on the Birmingham–Dudley road where it crossed Shireland Brook on the boundary between Birmingham and Smethwick;[20] it may have been Smethwick bridge, which occurs as a county bridge in 1858 and 1862.[21] The main road still forded Thimblemill Brook at Bearwood Hill in the early 19th century, but the brook had been culverted by 1842.[22]

The northern part of Smethwick is crossed by the stretch of the Birmingham Canal built by James Brindley in 1768–9. At first the plan was to tunnel through the high ground in the north-west, but Brindley encountered 'running sand and other bad materials' and instead used 'locks and fire-engines'.[23] In 1788–90 the number of locks at either end of the mile-long summit level was reduced by means of a new line through a cutting; Summit Bridge, which bears the date 1790, was built to carry Roebuck Lane across the cutting.[24] The line of the canal between Birmingham and Smethwick was straightened as part of Thomas Telford's improvements from 1824, that part of the work being completed in 1827. Telford also by-passed the summit by making a new line from a point east of Rolfe Street through a deep cutting south of the first canal; it was completed in 1829. To carry Roebuck Lane over the new cutting Telford built the cast-iron Galton Bridge in 1828–9, which with its span of 154 feet was the longest canal bridge in the world.[25] The new line passes under the old canal at the former Spon Lane basin on the north-

[3] V.C.H. Warws. vii. 27.

[4] B.R.L., Pickard 5618, appeal to quarter sessions Apr. 1762 over payment of toll.

[5] R. Whitworth, Plan of Intended Navigation from Birmingham to Canal at Aldersley near Wolverhampton survey'd 1767 (copy in W.S.L.).

[6] 'Old Smethwick', 7 Apr. 1951; 'Smethwick and Round About', 23 June, 6 and 20 July 1956; Smethwick Telephone, 23 Mar. 1929; S.R.O., D. 1141/4/3, pp. 41–2.

[7] B.M., O.S.D. 212 (1816); C. and J. Greenwood, Map of Staffs. (1820), which shows a toll-bar there but calls it Blue Gates; Parson and Bradshaw, Dir. Staffs. (1818).

[8] Roper, Plans of Smethwick, 1857, no. 30.

[9] 'Smethwick and Round About', 25 July 1952.

[10] 'Old Smethwick', 9 July 1949.

[11] Smethwick Annual (1903), 21.

[12] 'Smethwick and Round About', 25 July 1952.

[13] Hackwood, Smethwick, 117; J. Ogilby, Britannia (1675), plate preceding p. 99; Yates, Map of Staffs. (1775); 'Old Smethwick', 21 Aug. 1948, 14 Jan. 1950; above p. 92.

[14] S.H.C. 1924, p. 82.   [15] See pp. 88, 99.

[16] V.C.H. Warws. vii. 28; Roper, Plan of Smethwick, 1858; 'Smethwick and Round About', 1 Feb. 1952; T. Presterne, Harborne once upon a time (Birmingham, 1913), 47; B.M., O.S.D. 256; B.R.L. 662129–30; Town Clerk's Dept., Birmingham, deed packet no. 657, abstract of title

of trustees of G. C. Adkins 1902. The Bearwood Rd. toll-gate did not exist in 1842: W.S.L., S. MS. 417/Harborne, map.

[17] W.P.L. 17599, 17629.

[18] W.P.L. 17572.

[19] W.P.L. 17627.

[20] 'Old Smethwick', 22 Apr. 1950; 'Smethwick and Round About', 25 July 1952.

[21] Practice of Court of General Quarter Sessions of the Peace for the County of Stafford (Stafford, 1858), 17 (copy in S.R.O.); S.R.O., Q/SB E. 1862.

[22] 'Smethwick and Round About', 3 Jan. 1958; B.M., O.S.D. 212; W.S.L., S. MS. 417/Harborne. No ford is shown by C. and J. Greenwood, Map of Staffs. (1820), but the scale is small.

[23] V.C.H. Staffs. ii. 288–9; C. Hadfield, Canals of the West Midlands (1969 edn.), 65.

[24] Hadfield, Canals of W. Midlands, 67 (plan), 72; Hackwood, Smethwick, 87, 89.

[25] V.C.H. Staffs. ii. 294–5; Hadfield, Canals of W. Midlands, 87–8, 320; Staffs. Advertiser, 26 Dec. 1829; Reeves, West Bromwich, 59; Hackwood, Smethwick, 90; J. F. Chance, Hist. of Firm of Chance Brothers & Co. (priv. print. 1919), 19; C. Hicks, A Walk through Smethwick (Birmingham, 1850), 13 (copy in W.P.L.); inscription on the bridge 'Horseley Iron Works 1829'; plate facing p. 96 above. For the continuation of the new line through West Bromwich see above p. 13.

western boundary of Smethwick. There the old canal is joined by the Balls Hill branch canal opened in 1769 from the Hill Top area of West Bromwich. The amount of loading and unloading at Spon Lane basin began to decline in the 1920s, and the basin went out of use in 1954.[26] The site is now crossed by the M5 motorway.

A reservoir was made to the east of Smethwick Chapel c. 1769 by damming Thimblemill Brook.[27] It had gone out of use by 1842,[28] probably as a result of the opening of Rotton Park reservoir in Birmingham in 1826 and the construction by 1832 of the Titford feeder. The feeder runs from Rotton Park to Tat Bank in Oldbury where it joins the Titford branch canal, opened in 1837. It passes through Smethwick, but its course there has always been partly underground and is now almost completely culverted. It was originally carried across Stony Lane by an aqueduct; c. 1930 the aqueduct was removed and replaced by a siphon system.[29]

The Engine branch canal, which runs from Brindley's canal along the north side of Rolfe Street to Rabone Lane, was built in 1789–90 by making a feeder navigable so that coal could be brought to a pumping engine in Bridge Street.[30] It is carried over Telford's canal on an aqueduct built at the same time as that canal. Telford also extended the feeder eastwards to Rotton Park reservoir. The pumping engine, which was built by Boulton & Watt, had been erected in 1779 and was moved a short distance to Bridge Street when the new line of the main canal was cut in 1788–90. It remained in operation for over a century but was replaced by new pumping plant on a site west of Brasshouse Lane bridge in 1892. In 1897 it was removed to the canal maintenance depot at Ocker Hill in Tipton where it was preserved as a relic until 1959. It was then dismantled and taken to the Birmingham Museum of Science and Industry. It is thought to be the oldest condensing engine in existence.

The first railway through Smethwick was the Birmingham, Wolverhampton & Stour Valley Railway, opened in 1852 with stations in Rolfe Street and Spon Lane; the first locomotive ran through the area, however, in 1849. Soho station was opened in 1853. Rolfe Street station was rebuilt as part of the road improvement of 1888–90 when level crossings by the station and in Brasshouse Lane were replaced by bridges. The original station at Spon Lane was on the east side of the road, but by the later 1880s a new station had been built on the west side; it was closed in 1964 and has been demolished. Soho station was originally by Muntz's French Walls Works, but by the later 1880s it too had been rebuilt, to the west of Soho Street; it was closed for passengers in 1949 and demolished in 1953.[31] The Birmingham, Wolverhampton & Dudley Railway, which runs through the northern extremity of the town, was opened in 1854 with a station, Handsworth and Smethwick, just over the Handsworth boundary.[32] The Stourbridge Extension Railway, which runs through the north-west of the area, was opened in 1867, with a loop joining it to the Stour Valley Railway at Galton Junction; a station called Smethwick Junction (renamed Smethwick West in 1958) was opened south of Oldbury Road.[33] The Stourbridge Extension joined the Birmingham, Wolverhampton & Dudley Railway at Handsworth Junction near Halford's Lane. In 1931 the Hawthorns halt was opened there to serve the West Bromwich Albion football ground; it was closed in 1968.[34] The Soho, Handsworth & Perry Barr Junction Railway branching from the Stour Valley line in the north-east of the town was completed in 1889.[35]

MANOR. In 1086 *SMETHWICK* formed part of the episcopal manor of Lichfield. The overlordship remained with the bishops until 1546 and then passed to the Paget family.[36] In 1166 the bishop's tenant at Smethwick was Henry FitzGerold, who held it with Harborne as ½ knight's fee.[37] Thereafter it descended with Harborne until the early 18th century.[38] At some date before 1229 Henry's granddaughter Margaret de Breauté gave the manors of Harborne and Smethwick to Halesowen abbey (Worcs.), which held them until 1538. They were then granted to Sir John Dudley, later earl of Warwick and duke of Northumberland, were forfeited on his attainder in 1553, and were granted in 1554 to his relative Edward, Lord Dudley.[39] Edward's son Edward sold them in 1604 to Sir Charles Cornwallis, whose grandson, also Charles, sold them to Thomas Foley in 1661.

In 1709 Thomas Foley's son, Philip, of Prestwood in Kingswinford, sold the manors to George Birch of Harborne and Henry Hinckley of the Beakes, Smethwick.[40] In 1710 Birch and Hinckley divided

[26] *Express & Star*, 25 May 1963; O.S. Map 1/2,500, Staffs. LXVIII. 14 (1948 edn.); above p. 13.
[27] Hadfield, *Canals of W. Midlands*, 70; Yates, *Map of Staffs.* (1775); volume of estate maps (1815) in possession of the secretary to the trustees of Dorothy Parkes (Lee, Crowder & Co., Birmingham); Hackwood, *Smethwick*, 121. An Act of 1769 empowered the canal company to build reservoirs: *V.C.H. Staffs.* ii. 289.
[28] W.S.L., S. MS. 417/Harborne, no. 804.
[29] Hadfield, *Canals of W. Midlands*, 67 (plan), 70, 318–19; J. Phillips and W. F. Hutchings, *Map of Staffs.* (1832); W.S.L., S. MS. 417/Harborne; 'Old Smethwick', 7 Apr. 1951; 'Smethwick and Round About', 21 Mar. 1952; *Smethwick Telephone*, 16 Jan. 1953; W.P.L., P. 2649.
[30] For this para. see C. P. and C. R. Weaver, 'The Smethwick Pumping Engines', *Jnl. Railway and Canal Hist. Soc.* xvi. 57–61, which corrects some of the detail in *V.C.H. Staffs.* ii. 165–6; Hadfield, *Canals of W. Midlands*, 318–19; *Birmingham Canal Navigations* (working party rep. 1970), 18, 25 (copy in W.C.L.).
[31] C. R. Clinker, *Railways of the West Midlands, a Chronology 1808–1954*, 21–2, 32, 44, 46, 62; 'Old Smeth-

wick', 11 Sept. 1948, 20 and 27 Aug., 3 Sept. 1949, 28 Apr. 1950; 'Smethwick and Round About', 13 June 1952; Hackwood, *Smethwick*, 105; *Smethwick Telephone*, 10 Apr. 1953; O.S. Map 6″, Staffs. LXVIII. SW. (1890 edn.). For a view of the first Spon Lane station in the 1850s see below, plate facing p. 112.
[32] Clinker, *Railways of W. Midlands*, 24.
[33] Ibid. 32; *V.C.H. Staffs.* ii. 315–16; ex inf. British Railways, London Midland Region (1973).
[34] Clinker, *Railways of W. Midlands*, 60; *Express & Star*, 14 Aug. 1968; O.S. Map 1/2,500, Staffs. LXVIII. 15 (1947 edn.).
[35] *V.C.H. Staffs.* ii. 323.
[36] *V.C.H. Staffs.* iv. 43, no. 86 (where n. 45 wrongly describes Smethwick as in Birmingham); *V.C.H. Warws.* vii. 72.
[37] *S.H.C.* i. 155.
[38] For the rest of this para. see *V.C.H. Warws.* vii. 72.
[39] The statement ibid. that Edw. was Northumberland's nephew is incorrect; in fact he was the son of a cousin: *Complete Peerage*, iv. 480–1.
[40] B.R.L. 391781, 391783; Hackwood, *Smethwick*, 46; Shaw, *Staffs.* ii. 235.

the manors between them, Smethwick going to Hinckley. The Birmingham–Halesowen road was taken as the boundary, and all muniments transferred by Foley were to be kept in a box with two locks.[41] In 1718 Hinckley settled the manor on his son John at the time of John's marriage.[42] When John died in 1740 his property passed to his half-brother Henry Hinckley.[43] Henry, a physician, held the manor until 1766 when he sold it to John Baddeley of Birmingham.[44] In 1771 Baddeley was living in Holloway Head, Birmingham,[45] but by 1781 he had moved to Albrighton (Salop.) where he remained for the rest of his life, making clocks, watches, and telescopes.[46]

Baddeley was still sole lord in 1771,[47] but by 1781 he held the manor jointly with his brother George, a clock- and watch-maker of Newport (Salop.); George died in 1785.[48] Apparently in 1786 George's share was acquired by Samuel Smallwood and John Sillitoe,[49] who were joint lords with John Baddeley in 1787.[50] In 1790 John Reynolds bought the share belonging to Smallwood and Sillitoe.[51] Reynolds was described as a plater of Birmingham in 1792,[52] but within the next few years he retired, having made a considerable fortune in what his predecessor in the business had considered to be 'a worn out trade'. By 1796 he was living in Smethwick, presumably at Shireland Hall which was his home by c. 1800.[53] John Baddeley died in 1804,[54] leaving his half of the manor to his illegitimate son, John Baddeley, and to his married daughters, Martha Webster and Anne Underhill. In 1808 Baddeley and his sisters sold their moiety of the manor to John Reynolds.[55]

Reynolds evidently held the manor until his death in 1820, when he was living at the Coppice.[56] After his death his son, another John Reynolds, lived at the Coppice, and in the 1820s and early 1830s he was the largest landowner in Smethwick.[57] By 1830, however, he had begun to sell parts of the estate,[58] and in 1842 no one called Reynolds owned any property in Smethwick.[59]

OTHER ESTATES. The Beakes, a moated farm-house in the south of Smethwick, belonged to William Hunt of the Ruck of Stones in the late 17th century. He was dead by 1692, and the Beakes with its farm passed to his daughter Beata, who in 1692 married Henry Hinckley of Northfield (Worcs.). Hinckley came to live at the Beakes and began to buy more property in Smethwick. In 1710 he became lord of the manor of Smethwick, and the Beakes descended with the manor, remaining the home of the Hinckleys, until at least 1740.[60] In 1764–5 the Beakes with upwards of 60 a. was occupied by a Mrs. Turner, and John Turner, a Birmingham merchant, was living there in 1771.[61] By 1798,[62] perhaps in 1771,[63] the Beakes had been bought by Thomas Hanson of Smethwick House. The Hanson family still owned it in 1815.[64] The Stubbs family is said to have lived there, presumably in the early 19th century: Mary Stubbs (d. 1818) and her daughter Ann (d. 1821) were resident in Smethwick when they died.[65] By at least 1814, however, there were two houses at the Beakes; one was the old farm-house, while the other, immediately to the south, was presumably newer.[66] In 1818 one of them was the residence of William Wynne Smith.[67]

William Sprigg was living at the second house between at least 1830 and 1843. In 1842 he owned 57 a. around it between the Halesowen parish boundary and the present Bearwood Road; the house stood in 6 a. of garden and shrubbery with an orchard at the rear.[68] The rest was farmed by William Marshall, who had been tenant of the old farm-house by 1834 and was still living at what had become known as Beakes Farm in 1864.[69] The second house seems always to have been known as the Beakes.

[41] B.R.L. 391781.
[42] B.R.L. 297359, 324388–9, 445760; Hackwood, *Smethwick*, 46.
[43] Shaw, *Staffs.* ii. 126.
[44] B.R.L. 500271; C.P. 25(2)/1410/7 Geo. III Mich. no. 510; J. and J. A. Venn, *Alumni Cantabrigienses . . . to 1751*, ii. 376; W. Munk, *Roll of Royal Coll. of Physicians of London*, ii (1878 edn.), 198.
[45] B.R.L. 445765.
[46] B.R.L. 445774, 500276–7; S.R.O., D. 742/Dartmouth Estates/II/13/917; Shaw, *Staffs.* ii. 125.
[47] B.R.L. 445764–5.
[48] B.R.L. 445774; S.R.O., D. 1141/4/4, ct. book 27 Dec. 1784; *Shropshire Parish Registers* (Shrops. Par. Reg. Soc.), iv (4), 61, 63; Newport par. reg. (transcript in Shrewsbury Pub. Libr.), 16 Sept. 1785.
[49] B.R.L. 500271.
[50] B.R.L. 445766; S.R.O., D. 1141/4/4, ct. book 18 June 1787.
[51] B.R.L. 500271; C.P. 25(2)/1413/30 Geo. III Trin. no. 529.   [52] B.R.L. 500276–7.
[53] Pye, *Modern Birmingham*, 130; S.R.O., D. 742/Dartmouth Estates/II/13/917; Shaw, *Staffs.* ii. 125.
[54] J. B. Blakeway, 'Hist. of Albrighton, near Shifnal', *Trans. Shropshire Arch. and Nat. Hist. Soc.* 2nd ser. xi. 136.
[55] S.R.O., D. 742/Dartmouth Estates/II/13/907; S.R.O., D. 1141/4/4, ct. book, loose sheet giving valuation [1808].
[56] D. 742/Dartmouth Estates/II/13 /917, describing him as lord of the manor in 1814; D. 1141/4/4, loose rent accounts, showing chief rent due to him in 1815; B.R.L. 500272; memorial tablet in the Old Church, describing him as of the Coppice and of Bridgeford, Staffs.; below p. 100.

[57] B.R.L. 500272; 'Smethwick and Round About', 14 Mar. 1952, 30 Jan., 17 July 1953; White, *Dir. Staffs.* (1834); Pigot, *Nat. Com. Dir.* (1835), 472.
[58] S.R.O., D. 613, bdle. 3, abstract of title of Messrs. Taylor and Allbutt, 1856; B.R.L. 500269–72, 500278, 500281–2.
[59] W.S.L., S. MS. 417/Harborne.
[60] Shaw, *Staffs.* ii. 126; B.R.L. 297359, 374988, 374991; 'Smethwick and Round About', 2 June 1951, 11 Feb. 1955; Hackwood, *Smethwick*, 46; above pp. 98–9.
[61] *Aris's Birmingham Gaz.* 3 Dec. 1764, 7 Jan. 1765; below p. 100.
[62] Shaw, *Staffs.* ii. 126.
[63] B.R.L. 500271.
[64] Vol. of estate maps (1815) in possession of the secretary to the trustees of Dorothy Parkes (Lee, Crowder & Co., Birmingham).
[65] 'Old Smethwick', 16 Dec. 1950; Parson and Bradshaw, *Dir. Staffs.* (1818); Stubbs family memorial tablet in the Old Church; *Staffs. Advertiser*, 26 May 1821. In 1815 a Mrs. Stubbs is shown occupying a house near the junction of what are now the Uplands and Taylors Lane: see source cited in previous note.
[66] B.M., O.S.D. 219 (which calls it 'The Bakers'). The name is given correctly on O.S.D. 256.
[67] Pye, *Modern Birmingham*, 131.
[68] For this para. see 'Smethwick and Round About', 14 Mar. 1952; W.S.L., S. MS. 417/Harborne; *Reg. of persons entitled to vote . . . Southern Div. of County of Stafford . . . 30 Nov. 1843–1 Dec. 1844*, 27 (copy in W.S.L.).
[69] White, *Dir. Staffs.* (1834); W.S.L., S. MS. 417/Harborne; *Reg. of persons entitled to vote . . . Southern Div. of County of Stafford . . . 30 Nov. 1864–1 Dec. 1865*, 191 (copy in W.S.L.).

In 1845 and 1851 the house in which Sprigg had lived was occupied by William Fowler, a Birmingham solicitor and the third son of Thomas Leversage Fowler of Pendeford Hall in Tettenhall; in 1851 William's unmarried elder brother Thomas, the owner of Pendeford Hall, was living with him at the Beakes.[70] In the mid 1850s the house was occupied by George Vernon Blunt, a Birmingham merchant in the America trade,[71] and in the late 1850s Edmund Page, an ironmaster, was living there.[72] In the early 1860s it was the home of Thomas Astbury, an iron-founder.[73] It was occupied by a Mr. Smith in 1868,[74] by Joseph Stones in 1872,[75] by Edgerton Allcock in the 1880s,[76] and by a Mrs. Keeling in the 1890s.[77] The Beakes was probably demolished in 1897; certainly by 1903 its site, on the south side of the new Rawlings Road, had been built over.[78]

Beakes Farm was owned in the earlier 1860s by William Boycott of Hill Grove, Kidderminster (Worcs.).[79] It was occupied by the Powell family in the later 1860s and the 1870s,[80] by Joseph Vaughan in 1880,[81] by John Mould in 1888 and the earlier 1890s,[82] and by John Gosling from c. 1894 until c. 1902.[83] The house was then pulled down and the site built over.[84]

The house known as the Coppice stood on the north side of Cape Hill where Raglan Avenue was later built. It existed by 1814[85] and may have been built for John Reynolds, one of the lords of Smethwick manor from 1790. About 1800 Reynolds was living at Shireland Hall, but by 1818 he had moved to the Coppice[86] and is the first known occupant. He was living there when he died in 1820. His son John succeeded him and was still living there in 1839.[87] In 1842 the Coppice with 21 a. was owned and occupied by Samuel Warden.[88] In the early 1850s P. H. Muntz, then in partnership with his brother G. F. Muntz at a Birmingham metal works, was living there.[89] In 1853 the house and estate belonged to William Wills.[90] By 1856 the house was mortgaged to Thomas Gibson, and in that year Gibson and his mortgagee leased it for use as a girls' reformatory.[91] The house remained a reformatory until 1879, but soon after that it was demolished and the estate was built over.[92]

The Coppice was a three-storeyed brick building facing east. To the north was a walled courtyard containing the out-buildings, which in 1838 included a barn, cow-house, and granary. The house then stood in 15 a. of 'ornamental pasture ground' divided into several inclosures and studded with oaks and other trees. It was screened from the main road by a belt of shrubberies and plantations, and there are also said to have been fine gardens 'laid out in Italian style'.[93]

A small copyhold farm in the north-east of Smethwick called the French Walls belonged to the Piddock family in the mid 17th century.[94] In 1661 William Piddock sold it to John Pearsall of Hawne in Halesowen (Worcs.). It passed to John's son Thomas, who in 1709 purchased the freehold from Philip Foley, lord of the manors of Harborne and Smethwick. The farm then consisted of a house and 20 a. of land. Thomas died in 1714 and was succeeded by his son, another Thomas (d. 1759). The younger Thomas's son, the Revd. John Peshall, who had changed the spelling of his name in order to establish a claim to a baronetcy, sold the estate in 1771 to John Turner, a Birmingham merchant then living at the Beakes. Turner was still alive in 1776, but by 1786 he was dead and the estate had passed to his brother, William Turner of Birmingham. In 1791 William, then living at Shenstone Moss, sold the estate to John Whately (d. 1794), a Birmingham gunsmith,[95] who was succeeded by his son Henry Pyddocke Whately.[96] In 1815 a number of properties formerly part of the French Walls and including the house were offered for sale in separate lots,[97] and the estate may thus have been split up. Nevertheless H. P. Whately still owned at least part of it in 1818.[98]

The Birmingham Canal was cut through the estate in 1768–9, and thereafter the land was increasingly developed for industry. By c. 1800 on the south side of the canal opposite Soho Foundry there was 'a large manufactory of gun-barrels, which are forged and bored, &c. by the aid of the steam engine'. It belonged to H. P. Whately and had presumably been erected in the 1790s after his father's purchase of the estate.[99] By 1815 the manufactory had become the French Walls flour-mill, but the

[70] P.O. Dir. Staffs. (1845); H.O. 107/2050(1) f. 81; White, Dir. Staffs. (1851), 207. For genealogical details see Shaw, Staffs. ii. 202–3; J. P. Jones, Hist. of Parish of Tettenhall (1894), 97–100; Burke, Land. Gent. (1925), 254.
[71] Reg. of persons entitled to vote . . . Southern Div. of County of Stafford . . . 30 Nov. 1854–1 Dec. 1855, 61 (copy in W.S.L.); 30 Nov. 1855–1 Dec. 1856, 198. For Blunt see P.O. Dir. Birm., Staffs., and Worcs. (1850), 102; W. H. Dix & Co. Dir. Birm. (1858), 69.
[72] Reg. of persons entitled to vote . . . Southern Div. of County of Stafford . . . 30 Nov. 1859–1 Dec. 1860, 210. W. H. Dix & Co. Dir. Birm. (1858), gives a Geo. Page, ironmaster, at Beakes Hall.
[73] Reg. of persons entitled to vote . . . Southern Div. of County of Stafford . . . 30 Nov. 1860–1 Dec. 1861, 188; 30 Nov. 1861–1 Dec. 1862, 190.
[74] P.O. Dir. Staffs. (1868).   [75] Ibid. (1872).
[76] Kelly's Dir. Staffs. (1880); Kelly's Dir. Birm. (1890).
[77] Kelly's Dir. Birm. (1892; 1895).
[78] W. P. L., P. 1147 (stating that Beakes Farm was demolished in 1897, but probably confusing it with the Beakes); O.S. Map 6", Staffs. LXXII. NE. (1905 edn.).
[79] Reg. of persons entitled to vote . . . Southern Div. of County of Stafford . . . 30 Nov. 1860–1 Dec. 1861, 188; 30 Nov. 1865–1 Dec. 1866, 184.
[80] P.O. Dir. Staffs. (1868; 1876).
[81] Kelly's Dir. Staffs. (1880).

[82] Kelly's Dir. Birm. (1888; 1894).
[83] Ibid. (1895; 1902).
[84] O.S. Map 6", Staffs. LXXII. NE. (edns. of 1890, 1905, 1921); Kelly's Dir. Birm. (1903).
[85] B.M., O.S.D. 256.
[86] See p. 99; Pye, Modern Birmingham, 130.
[87] Reg. of electors within Southern Div. of County of Stafford . . . 1 Nov. 1838–1 Nov. 1839, 38 (copy in W.S.L.); 1 Nov. 1839–1 Nov. 1840, 38; Aris's Birmingham Gaz. 5 Mar. 1838, advert. for letting; above p. 99.
[88] W.S.L., S. MS. 417/Harborne.
[89] 'Old Smethwick', 4 Feb., 10 June 1950; 'Smethwick and Round About', 11 July 1952; P.O. Dir. Birm., Staffs., and Worcs. (1850), 141.
[90] B.R.L. 389363.   [91] B.R.L. 462097.
[92] 'Old Smethwick', 22 July 1950; 'Smethwick and Round About', 11 July 1952, 30 Jan. 1953; R.G. 9/2125 ff. 132v.–133v.
[93] Pye, Modern Birmingham, 130; B.R.L. 389363, 462097; 'Smethwick and Round About', 2 June 1951, 30 Jan. 1953; Aris's Birmingham Gaz. 5 Mar. 1838.
[94] For this para. see B.R.L., j. 335, j. 406, j. 409; S.R.O., D. 1141/4/3/1, pp. 10–11; G.E.C. Baronetage, i. 102.
[95] B.R.L., j. 335.
[96] B.R.L., j. 284–5, j. 295–6, j. 308–9, j. 334.
[97] B.R.L., j. 497–8.   [98] B.R.L., j. 342.
[99] Shaw, Staffs. ii. 126; above p. 97.

mill with its 12–horse-power Boulton & Watt engine was then said to be 'capable of being converted to almost any manufacturing purpose'. By that time there was also some workers' housing on the estate.[1] In 1816 James Watt the younger bought the mill and in 1820 agreed to lease it to Henry Downing for an ironworks. Downing went bankrupt in 1829.[2] In the mid 1830s the forge was in the hands of the Bordesley Steel Co., and the estate also included a house, a farm, and 46 houses.[3] About 1840 the former gun-manufactory, flour-mill, and forge formed Watt's French Walls iron and steel works, while George Downing occupied the house with 7 a. of garden and land, and there were some 40 workers' houses;[4] 7 a. of the estate on the north side of the canal between Soho Foundry and Rabone Lane were still undeveloped.[5] In 1842 the works passed to G. F. Muntz, who converted it for the production of non-ferrous metals.[6] Downing continued to live at the house until 1847 or 1848.[7] By the later 1880s the part of the estate on the south side of the canal was largely covered by Muntz's metal works and the Birmingham, Wolverhampton & Stour Valley Railway (opened in 1852); on the north side of the canal stood the local board's gas-works (opened in 1881).[8]

The Holly Lodge estate in north-west Smethwick was part of a larger one settled in 1710 on William Brearley of Handsworth at his marriage.[9] The property subsequently descended with estates elsewhere to his two daughters, Anna Maria who in 1743 married Charles Sacheverell (d. 1779) of New Hall in Sutton Coldfield (Warws.) and Mavesyn Ridware, and Jane who in 1758, as the widow of John Clopton, married Walter Gough of Perry Hall in Handsworth.[10] The sisters held the property as a joint inheritance which was preserved distinct from their husbands' estates, and in 1743 their Smethwick property consisted of a farm let to a tenant.[11] Both sisters subsequently purchased other estates in Smethwick which they owned separately from their joint property.[12] When Jane Gough died in 1781 she left her property to her sister for life. It was then to pass in tail male to Joseph Brearley, the son of her deceased cousin William Brearley of New Inn Hall in Handsworth, with remainders in tail to other members of the Brearley family.[13] Anna Maria Sacheverell died in 1795, having left all her real estate in tail male to Sir Robert Lawley, the 5th baronet, of Canwell Hall.[14] It thus became necessary to divide the estates which the sisters had held in

Smethwick and elsewhere as their joint property, and a division was made in 1797 between a Joseph Brearley and Sir Robert Lawley, the 6th baronet. The Smethwick estate, consisting of 65 a. on the west side of Holly Lane between Oldbury Road and the Halesowen boundary, passed to Sir Robert; it was then being farmed by John Downing, who had taken a 21-year lease in 1794.[15] Sir Robert sold the farm in 1802 to William Crockett, a Handsworth maltster and corn-factor.[16]

In 1816 Crockett's property was sold under a Chancery decree. The northern part of the farm, 30 a. surrounding the farmhouse at the corner of Oldbury Road and Holly Lane, was bought by Thomas Downing and his brother George; the remainder, 34 a. near the Halesowen boundary, was bought by William Spurrier, a Birmingham lawyer.[17] In 1848 Thomas Downing sold his share to his brother George, who died later the same year. George's widow and their son William continued to live at the farmhouse. The widow died in 1858, about the time that William was building Holly Lodge to the south-west of the farmhouse. In 1859 William sold the farmhouse, then known as Holly House, and moved into Holly Lodge. He continued to live there until his death in 1901. The house then seems to have been occupied by his widow and his son W. E. Downing and is said to have stood empty for a few years after the son's move to Hagley (Worcs.).[18]

In 1920 Holly Lodge and its land were bought by Smethwick corporation for housing development. In 1922, however, the corporation opened a school in the house, and it continued as a school until 1932. Subsequently it became an orthopaedic clinic,[19] and it was still so used in 1971. Most of the land was then used as school playing-fields.

Lightwoods House in the south of Smethwick near the Harborne boundary took its name from the tract of woodland in the area.[20] The house is said to have been built by Jonathan Grundy in 1791,[21] but a brick in the wall immediately east of the entrance porch is inscribed 'Jonathan Grundy, June 19, 1780'. Grundy, the eldest son of Jonathan Grundy of Wigston Parva (Leics.), is the first known occupant of Lightwoods House and lived there until his death in 1803. His widow Hannah lived there until her death in 1815, and their daughter, also Hannah, lived in the house until she died unmarried in 1829. The house and its land then passed to Jonathan Grundy's niece Eliza, the wife of Henry

[1] B.R.L., j. 497–8.
[2] W. K. V. Gale, *The Black Country Iron Industry*, 76, 78.
[3] Redhead, *Local Govt.* 20; White, *Dir. Staffs.* (1834); Pigot, *Nat. Com. Dir.* (1835), 474.
[4] S.R.O., D. 707/12/1, marr. settlement of J. Moilliet and L. H. Galton, 28 Mar. 1832 (plan); W.S.L., S. MS. 417/Harborne; Gale, *Black Country Iron Industry*, 78–80.
[5] W.S.L., S. MS. 417/Harborne, nos. 926 and 926a (corresponding to lots 47–8 in B.R.L., j. 498). The land included a small part of the former Piddocks farm: see B.R.L., j. 449.
[6] See p. 111.
[7] *Reg. of persons entitled to vote ... Southern Div. of County of Stafford ... 30 Nov. 1847–1 Dec. 1848*, 51 (copy in W.S.L.).
[8] O.S. Map 6″, Staffs. LXXII. NE. (1890 edn.); B.R.L., Lee Crowder 1004; above p. 98; below p. 122.
[9] B.R.L. 329077, ff. 3–4.
[10] Ibid. ff. 7–9; 329075, ff. 4–14; Shaw, *Staffs.* i. 184–5; ii. 114 and pedigree facing p. 188; *V.C.H. Warws.* iv. 240.

[11] B.R.L. 329075, ff. 7–8, 14, 18.
[12] Ibid. ff. 15, 18–19. For the Ruck of Stones farm bought by Jane Gough see below p. 103.
[13] B.R.L. 329075, ff. 14–18; 329077, ff. 9–10.
[14] *Gent. Mag.* lxv (1), 170; Shaw, *Staffs.* i. 184 n. 8; B.R.L. 276786; 329075, ff. 18–21; 329077, f. 10.
[15] B.R.L. 329075, f. 22; Act to confirm a partition of divers lands devised by Jane Gough and Anna Maria Sacheverell, 37 Geo. III, c. 82 (Priv. Act); 'Old Smethwick', 25 Dec. 1948; W.S.L., S. MS. 417/Harborne, *sub* Downing (Geo. and Thos.) and Spurrier (Wm.).
[16] B.R.L. 329075, ff. 22–6, 36.
[17] Ibid. ff. 39–43; 'Old Smethwick', 25 Dec. 1948; W.S.L., S. MS. 417/Harborne; above p. 94.
[18] 'Old Smethwick', 1 Jan. 1949; *Kelly's Dir. Birm.* (1902 and later edns. to 1921), giving occupant as Mrs. Downing.
[19] 'Old Smethwick', 1 Jan. 1949; 'Smethwick and Round About', 2 Dec. 1955; below p. 140.
[20] See p. 108.
[21] 'Smethwick and Round About', 1 Sept. 1951.

Goodrich Willett.[22] In 1842 Willett, whose wife had died in 1837,[23] owned 38 a. of land in Smethwick; most of his estate lay immediately around the house, but part was between the present Bearwood, Waterloo, and Grange Roads.[24] Willett lived at Lightwoods House until his death in 1857.[25] His nephew, Captain H. J. Willett, occupied the house for a few months after his uncle's death, but in 1858 it was leased to George Caleb Adkins, a local soap manufacturer. Adkins bought the house with some land from Willett's trustees in 1865 and lived there until his death in 1887.[26]

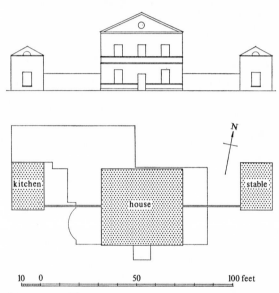

LIGHTWOODS HOUSE: RECONSTRUCTED ELEVATION AND PLAN, WITH THE AREA OF THE 18TH-CENTURY HOUSE STIPPLED

In 1902, on the death of Caleb Adkins, apparently his son, Lightwoods House with its 16-acre park was put up for sale, and it seemed likely that the house would be demolished and the land used for housing.[27] Mainly through the efforts of A. M. Chance, however, the house and park were bought for the public. In October 1902 the committee which had raised the purchase money handed over the property to Birmingham corporation as a public park. About the same time other land was added bringing the boundary to Adkins Lane and Galton Road, and further subscriptions enabled the committee to buy more land in 1905. A feature of the park is the garden, opened in 1915, which contains specimens of the plants mentioned by Shakespeare. Since the opening of Lightwoods Park the house has at various times accommodated a public library, public refreshment rooms, and rooms for the Sons of Rest. In 1971 it was being converted into studios

and offices by the lessees, John Hardman & Co. Ltd., stained-glass artists.

The original house was of brick with stone dressings and had a pedimented central block, with detached wings which housed the kitchen and stables. During the 19th century the symmetry of the original design was obscured by several extensions, the interior was remodelled, and the main front was enriched with stucco decoration in an early-18th-century style.

The estate which became known as Piddocks farm was situated in the north-east of Smethwick near the Handsworth boundary. The Piddock family, sometimes known as Cowper alias Piddock, was living in Smethwick by the 1470s,[28] and by the 1570s it owned property in the north-east of Smethwick.[29] A William Piddock of Smethwick occurs in the early 17th century,[30] and he is perhaps to be identified with the William Cowper who founded a charity in 1623 but was then no longer living in Smethwick.[31] In 1624 Thomas Piddock, brother and heir of William Piddock who had recently died, was admitted tenant of William's copyhold lands in the manor of Harborne and Smethwick.[32]

The family property in Smethwick was apparently sold in the earlier or mid 17th century. In 1661 the estate known as Piddocks farm, formerly belonging to William Piddock, was owned by Henry Ford, who lived near by at Winson Green (in Birmingham).[33] Ford was a lawyer and from c. 1672 steward of Brome Whorwood's Sandwell estate in West Bromwich. In 1683 he sold Piddocks farm, with property in Winson Green and Handsworth, to John Willes, vicar of Bishop's Itchington (Warws.).[34] In 1707 Willes's son John sold the estates to Henry Carver of Birmingham. In 1733 the Smethwick portion consisted of Piddocks farm, then tenanted, and a disused water-mill on Hockley Brook.[35] In that year Carver included the former Willes estates in the marriage settlement of his son Henry and Elizabeth Guest. They subsequently descended to the younger Henry's son Edward, but in 1793, after Edward's bankruptcy, his assignees sold the Smethwick property to George Kennedy, a Birmingham surgeon. It then consisted of a farm-house and 71 a. of land.

The Birmingham Canal was cut through the estate in 1768–9, and in 1795 Kennedy sold 18 a. on the east side of the canal; James Watt built Soho Foundry there in 1796. Watt convenanted with Kennedy not to erect on the property 'any brasshouse or other works which are prejudicial to vegetation ... except iron-foundries and steam-engines'; even his foundries and engines, however, had to be sited back from the western edge of his newly acquired property. The rest of the estate was

[22] 'Smethwick and Round About', 1 Sept. 1951, 17 July 1953; *Gent. Mag.* lxxiii (2), 1090; J. Nichols, *Hist. and Antiquities of County of Leic.* iv (1), 124; iv (2), 465; *Staffs. Advertiser*, 8 July 1815.   [23] B.R.L. 435534.
[24] W.S.L., S. MS. 417/Harborne. For a plan of the house and park c. 1820 see B.R.L. 454611.
[25] 'Smethwick and Round About', 15 Sept. 1951; H.O. 107/2050(1) f. 77v.
[26] B.R.L. 454635, 454644, 462242, 500268; R.G. 9/2125 f. 94; Town Clerk's Dept., Birmingham, deed packet no. 657; 'Smethwick and Round About', 15 Sept., 29 Dec. 1951, 25 Mar. 1955.
[27] For this para. see C. A. Vince, *Hist. of Corporation of Birmingham*, iv (Birmingham, 1923), 233–4; 'Smethwick and Round About', 8 and 15 Mar. 1957; *Kelly's Dir.*

Birm. (1915), 20; (1921), 20; (1970–71), 1712; Town Clerk's Dept., Birmingham, deed packet no. 657.
[28] B.R.L. 347166; below p. 141.
[29] C 3/146/15; *S.H.C.* 1938, 17–18; Req. 2/80/49.
[30] *S.H.C.* n.s. iv. 48; 1935, 379; 1940, 266; 1948–9, 153.
[31] See p. 141.   [32] B.R.L., j. 391.
[33] For this para. see, except where otherwise stated, B.R.L. 329279, 375015; A. L. Reade, *The Reades of Blackwood Hill* (priv. print. 1906), 128–32, 204–6. For Ford see A. L. Reade, *Johnsonian Gleanings* (priv. print.), i (1909), 5–7; iii (1922), 32–4; iv (1923), 42–5; x (1946), 170.
[34] E 134/6 Wm. and Mary East./1. For Willes see J. Foster, *Alumni Oxonienses ... 1500–1714*, iv. 1635; *V.C.H. Staffs.* iii. 178–9.
[35] See p. 108. For John Willes see *D.N.B.*

sold by Kennedy in 1796 to Alexander Walker, a Birmingham merchant. In 1816, after the bankruptcy of Walkers Sons & Co. and Alexander Walker's death, most of the property was bought by John Salter, the West Bromwich bayonet-maker. Salter immediately sold 6½ a. to J. L. Moilliet of Smethwick Grove. In 1825 Salter's executors sold the rest of the property to Moilliet, including the farm-house, which was known as Piddocks Farm or Cranford Farm by the 1790s.[36]

In 1835 Cranford farm was held by Joseph Eccles; between at least 1839 and 1853 the tenant was Charles Lutwyche.[37] No further reference to the farm has been found, and the house, which stood near Soho Bridge carrying the railway over the canal, was apparently demolished soon after the opening of the railway in 1852.[38]

The farm known as the Ruck of Stones in the northern extremity of Smethwick seems to have taken its name from a heap of stones which marked the parish boundary. The farm-house stood in Lewisham Road, formerly Ruck of Stones Lane.[39] By the later 16th century the farm seems to have belonged to the Hunt family. A William Hunt probably owned land in the north of Smethwick in 1575, and a William Hunt was apparently living at the Ruck of Stones in 1600, though he was no longer doing so in 1617; it is likely that he had been succeeded by a son of the same name. In 1630 William Hunt of Smethwick was fined £10 for not taking the order of knighthood, but in 1664 a William Hunt of Harborne parish was refused the right to a coat of arms.[40] William Hunt was assessed for tax on four hearths in 1666, and his house was one of the larger houses in Smethwick.[41] He was perhaps the William Hunt of the Ruck of Stones who was dead by 1692 and whose estate passed to his three daughters.[42] In the earlier 18th century the Ruck of Stones farm belonged to Margaret Hunt, one of the three. Under the terms of her will, proved in 1734, it passed to her cousin Elizabeth Hall for life and subsequently to Margaret's nephew Richard Grevis, son of Benjamin Grevis and Jane Hunt, and his son Henshaw.[43] Richard Grevis, who lived at Moseley Hall in King's Norton (Worcs.), died in 1759 having so encumbered the family estates with mortgages that they had to be sold during the 1760s.[44] Henshaw Grevis was offering the Ruck of Stones for sale in 1764; the estate

then consisted of 140 a. let at will to Walter Adams, who was still the tenant in 1785.[45] In 1765 it was sold to the trustees of Jane Gough, the wife of Walter Gough of Perry Hall in Handsworth.[46]

Jane Gough (née Brearley) died in 1781. Under the terms of her will the Ruck of Stones passed to her sister Anna Maria Sacheverell (d. 1795) for life; thereafter it was entailed on their Brearley relatives.[47] In 1820 a Joseph Brearley of Pen Moel in Tidenham (Glos.) sold the Ruck of Stones; 6 a. were bought by Luke Pope, and the remainder by Richard Fryer of the Wergs in Tettenhall.[48] In 1825 Fryer sold his part of the estate to J. W. Unett,[49] who in 1842 owned 65 a. with the farm-house; the tenant of the house was then Hannah Scott. Other outlying portions belonged to the Pope family in 1842.[50] By 1851 William Holloway was living at the Ruck of Stones and farming 56 a. there; he was still farming in Smethwick in 1861, and in the 1860s and 1870s his widow Martha was running the farm.[51] By 1881 houses had been built over the area.[52]

The farm-house, as it existed in 1842, seems to have been a long building set back from what is now Lewisham Road and lying at right angles to it.[53] It seems to have survived until the later 1880s, but by the beginning of the 20th century its site was covered by part of the Surrey Works of Evered & Co. Ltd.[54]

Land in the south-east of Smethwick adjoining the county boundary was known as Shireland by the mid 16th century. In 1546 John Fyld of King's Norton (Worcs.) sold to William Sparry various properties in Smethwick which included a pasture called Little Shireland; it was said to lie between land called Great Shireland, the highway from Birmingham to Smethwick, and Rotton Park (in Birmingham).[55] By the 1680s there was a house in the area occupied by a member of the Jennens (or Jennings) family.[56] This was probably Edward Jennens who was living in Harborne parish in the 1660s and 1670s and had extensive property there; he lived in one of the largest houses in Smethwick, being assessed for tax on five hearths in 1666.[57] He was the son of a Birmingham ironmonger and a kinsman of Dorothy Parkes, who endowed Smethwick Old Church; his nephew Charles Jennens of Gopsall (Leics.), the librettist of Handel's *Messiah*, was one of her trustees.[58] The house in which Jennens lived in the 1680s may have been that

[36] B.R.L. 374792, 375015; B.R.L., j. 449; V.C.H. Staffs. ii. 165; above p. 97.
[37] Reg. of electors within Southern Div. of County of Stafford . . . 1 Nov. 1835–1 Nov. 1836, 39 (copy in W.S.L.); 1 Nov. 1839–1 Nov. 1840, 38; Reg. of persons entitled to vote . . . Southern Div. of County of Stafford . . . 30 Nov. 1853–1 Dec. 1854, 59.
[38] See p. 98.
[39] 'Smethwick and Round About', 9 June 1951; Yates, Map of Staffs. (1799 edn.).
[40] Req. 2/80/49; S.H.C. ii (2), 21, 64; 1935, 268, 360, 438, 480; 1940, 5, 194; West Bromwich Ct. R. p. 71.
[41] S.H.C. 1923, 254.
[42] B.R.L. 374988; above p. 99.
[43] L.J.R.O., will of Marg. Hunt (proved 9 Nov. 1734); Shaw, Staffs. ii. 125; 'Smethwick and Round About', 21 Sept. 1956.
[44] 'Smethwick and Round About', 21 Sept. 1956; B.R.L. 374778, 375007; V.C.H. Worcs. iii. 185, 240; V.C.H. Warws. vii. 267.
[45] S.R.O., D. 564/12/14/5; Aris's Birmingham Gaz. 19 Nov., 17 Dec. 1764, 14 Nov. 1785.
[46] B.R.L. 329075, 375005; Shaw, Staffs. ii, pedigree facing p. 188.

[47] Shaw, Staffs. ii. 114; Gent. Mag. lxv (1), 170; B.R.L. 329075; S.R.O., D. 1141/4/3/1, p. 9.
[48] B.R.L. 445769, 445774.
[49] S.R.O., D. 613, bdle. 3, abstract of title 1867.
[50] W.S.L., S. MS. 417/Harborne.
[51] H.O. 107/2050 (2) f. 244v.; Harrison, Harrod & Co. Dir. Staffs. (1861); P.O. Dir. Staffs. (1868; 1872; 1876).
[52] See p. 93.
[53] W.S.L., S. MS. 417/Harborne.
[54] O.S. Map 6", Staffs. LXVIII. SE. (edns. of 1890 and 1904); Kelly's Dir. Birm. (1900), 741; (1904), 771. 'Old Smethwick', 9 Apr. 1949, shows a double-fronted two-storey house in Lewisham Rd. and calls it 'William Hunt's farmhouse as it exists today, although probably not the original building'.
[55] E 326/12160.
[56] Plot, Staffs. map dated 1682, marks a house at 'Shire lanes' in Smethwick and gives the arms of 'Jennens' who evidently lived there.
[57] J. Nichols, Hist. and Antiquities of County of Leic. iv (2), 859; S.H.C. 1923, 254.
[58] Hackwood, Smethwick, 51, 55; 'Old Smethwick', 9 Dec. 1950; D.N.B.; P. H. Lang, George Frideric Handel, 301 sqq.

which, under the name of Shireland Hall, was advertised for letting in 1765; described as 'fit for a genteel family', it had a 140-acre estate of arable, meadow, and pasture.[59] By 1767 the estate had passed to John Baddeley, lord of the manor, who then leased it out.[60] In 1791, after the expiry of the lease, the estate was split up. The greater part, 113 a., was taken by John Reynolds, who had recently acquired half the manor. Thomas Clift, who had been tenant of the Bear inn at Bearwood since 1776, took 26 a. and still occupied part of the estate in 1819.[61]

John Reynolds was living at Shireland Hall by c. 1800 and probably by 1796,[62] but it is uncertain whether the house he lived in was the Shireland Hall of the 1760s, for a new house, known like the old one as Shireland Hall, had by then been built on the estate.[63] It is possible that the old house survived as Shireland Hall Farm, which in 1814 stood some 30 yards south-west of the new hall.[64] The new hall, according to a newspaper advertisement of 1810, was built so as to make 'two good and complete houses', although it is clear that it then formed only one. It is variously said to have been rebuilt in the late 18th century by John Reynolds and to have been built in 1790 by Edward Cairns, a partner in Cairns, Frears, Carmichael, Halliday & Co., a Birmingham firm of merchants in the America trade. If the new hall was occupied as two residences from the time of its erection, it is possible that one of Cairns's partners lived in one of them: in 1792 'Mr. Edward Carnes & Freer' entered into possession of Shireland Hall and began to pay rent for it to the lords of the manor. Cairns lived at Shireland Hall until 1811.[65] It is possible that the Shireland Hall which was said to be John Reynolds's residence c. 1800 was the other half of the house built in 1790; in that case Freer, if he ever lived there at all, can have done so for only a few years. Reynolds was still living at Shireland Hall in 1803, but he had left by 1818.[66]

In 1810, presumably when Cairns was about to leave, the lease of Shireland Hall and a 56-acre farm was advertised for sale.[67] The freehold was apparently acquired by Richard Roberts, whose executor held the hall and 55 a. in 1842.[68] By 1818 the hall was occupied by a Miss Marmont, who conducted a girls' school there.[69] A few years later

Edward Bagnall, a West Bromwich ironmaster, moved to the hall, and after he left the house is said to have been occupied by a retired Birmingham draper called Lander. The sequence of occupiers, however, is uncertain since by 1830 the house again consisted of two separate residences.[70] Thomas Townsend, a civil engineer and railway contractor, was living there between at least 1833 and 1835,[71] and between at least 1839 and 1851 it was the home of William Beynon.[72] It then became a school once more. In 1852 T. H. Morgan, a Baptist minister, was the tenant, and he ran a school there for the sons of clergy of all denominations until at least 1865.[73] By 1868 the Misses Beynon were running a girls' school there; they had gone by 1876 and were the last residents. From 1878 to 1886 the schoolroom in the hall was used for Wesleyan services, but otherwise the house was unoccupied.[74]

By 1856 there were plans for developing the area, although building did not in fact take place for many years.[75] By the early 1880s, however, development had begun.[76] Shireland Hall itself had become unsafe. In 1887 it belonged to Edward Mullett, a West Bromwich farmer; part of the building fell down that year, and shortly afterwards the hall was demolished.[77]

The late-18th century house was situated to the east of the present Shireland Road on land sloping gently towards the south-east; its site is now occupied by the two terraces of houses on the south side of Florence Road called Poplar Grove and Lime Grove.[78] In the 1820s it was a plain three-storeyed Georgian house with a low-pitched roof. A plan of c. 1857 shows a square house standing in wooded grounds; stretching back from the rear corners of the house were two irregular ranges of buildings, one of which may have been one of the original self-contained residences. Between two driveways running north to Cape Hill was a pool surrounded by plantations.

The house called Smethwick Grove stood near the eastern boundary of Smethwick on the east side of what is now Grove Lane. In 1813 the house with 16 a. of land was bought by J. L. Moilliet, a Swiss merchant who had settled in Birmingham by 1801.[79] He may have been living at the Grove before buying it.[80] During the next few years he greatly increased the size of the estate and by 1828 owned 59 a. His

[59] Aris's Birmingham Gaz. 4 Mar. 1765.
[60] S.R.O., D. 1141/4/3/2, p. 14.
[61] Ibid. pp. 4, 26, 32; 'Smethwick and Round About', 3 July 1953.   [62] See p. 99.
[63] 'Old Smethwick', 29 July 1950.
[64] B.M., O.S.D. 256; W.S.L., S. MS. 417/Harborne.
[65] 'Old Smethwick', 29 July 1950; Shaw, Staffs. ii. 125; Aris's Birmingham Gaz. 30 July, 6 Aug. 1810; S.R.O., D. 1141/4/3/2, pp. 41, 72.
[66] 'Old Smethwick', 9 Sept. 1950; above p. 99.
[67] Aris's Birmingham Gaz. 30 July, 6 Aug., 3 Sept. 1810.
[68] W.S.L., S. MS. 417/Harborne.
[69] Pye, Modern Birmingham, 130-1.
[70] 'Old Smethwick', 29 July 1950; 'Smethwick and Round About', 14 Mar. 1952; 'Old West Bromwich', 12 Jan. 1945. Bagnall was described as 'of Smethwick' in 1850: B.R.L. 447347.
[71] Reg. of electors within Southern Div. of County of Stafford . . . 1 Nov. 1833–1 Nov. 1834, 41 (copy in W.S.L.); Pigot, Nat. Com. Dir. (1835), 476.
[72] Reg. of electors within Southern Div. of County of Stafford . . . 1 Nov. 1839–1 Nov. 1840, 36 (copy in W.S.L.); H.O. 107/2050 (1) f. 122.
[73] Reg. of persons entitled to vote . . . Southern Div. of County of Stafford . . . 30 Nov. 1852–1 Dec. 1853, 59

(copy in W.S.L.); 'Smethwick and Round About', 25 Oct. 1957; R.G. 9/2125 ff. 98v.–99v.; A. S. Langley, Birmingham Baptists Past and Present, 36, 248.
[74] P.O. Dir. Staffs. (1868); 'Old Smethwick', 29 July, 11 Nov. 1950; below p. 132. A gravestone near the west door of the Old Church records the death of Emma Beynon of Shireland Hall on 19 July 1874.
[75] 'Old Smethwick', 29 July, 28 Oct. 1950; S.R.O., D. 613, bdle. 3, supplemental abstract of title of Hen. Hallett 1880.
[76] Lich. Dioc. Mag. 1881, 93; 1882, 88; Smethwick Annual (1903), 33 (copy in W.P.L.); 'Old Smethwick', 22 July 1950; O.S. Map 6", Staffs. LXXII. NE. (1890 edn.); above p. 95; below p. 127.
[77] 'Old Smethwick', 29 July 1950.
[78] For this para. see 'Old Smethwick', 22 and 29 July 1950; W.P.L. 10592; O.S. Map 6" Staffs. LXXII. NE. (edns. of 1890 and 1905).
[79] S.R.O., D. 707/12/1, marriage settlement of Jas. Moilliet and Lucy Harriot Galton, 28 Mar. 1832; 'Smethwick and Round About', 20 Feb. 1953; Staffs. Advertiser, 23 May 1801.
[80] 'Smethwick and Round About', 20 Mar. 1953, 3 Dec. 1954, asserts that Moilliet lived there from 1801 and that his father-in-law Jas. Keir had lived there in the mid 1780s.

largest purchases, amounting to 30 a., were the southern and western portions of Piddocks (or Cranford) farm. In 1828 he bought the short stretch of the old line of the Birmingham Canal which ran through his estate; it had been rendered obsolete by Telford's improvements of 1824–7 and may have become an ornamental feature.[81]

Moilliet lived at Smethwick Grove until 1826. In 1801 he had married Amelia Keir, daughter of James Keir of West Bromwich, the chemist and industrialist, and the Moilliets were thus brought into contact with some of the leading intellectual figures of the time. Maria Edgeworth, the novelist, became a great friend of Amelia Moilliet and visited Smethwick Grove in 1819 and 1821. In 1826 Moilliet moved to Hamstead Hall in Handsworth and the Grove was let to George Bacchus, a partner in a Birmingham firm of flint-glass manufacturers. Bacchus left in 1830, and Moilliet's son James moved into the house after his marriage in 1832. He was still living there in 1837 but by 1838 had moved to Sutton Coldfield (Warws.). Thomas Atkins was living at the Grove in 1842. The house, with some adjacent land, was sold in 1846 to George Selby, a lawyer and partner in a tube-manufacturing concern. Soon afterwards Selby built a tube-works near by.[82] He still owned the house in 1855,[83] but the estate was by then losing its rural character: trees had been felled and various works built, while Shireland Brook, which bounded the estate to the east and divided Smethwick from Birmingham, had been culverted.[84] The house still stood in the earlier 1860s when Thomas Gibson lived there[85] but was probably demolished soon afterwards. Its site now forms part of the St. George's Works of Guest, Keen & Nettlefolds.

About 1830 Smethwick Grove was a plain two-storeyed Georgian house standing in well wooded grounds.[86] It overlooked lawns and a sheet of water—either a pool formed by damming Shireland Brook[87] or the old line of the Birmingham Canal.

A house known as Smethwick Hall existed by 1660 when Charles Lane lived there.[88] It probably stood in the north-eastern part of Smethwick where there was a house of that name by 1767.[89] The Lane family had lived in Smethwick from at least the early 16th century.[90] Charles Lane had moved to Harborne by 1666, presumably as a result of marriage with Mary Birch, the heir of Henry Birch of Harborne. In 1666 his assessment for tax on six hearths, the second largest assessment in the parish, was entered under the Harborne division of the parish,[91] and he is usually thereafter referred to as of Harborne. Plot mentions the house in the 1680s but does not name the owner or resident.[92] Lane seems to have been in continuous financial trouble, and by 1702 his affairs were apparently in the hands of his Birch relatives. In that year, when arranging for the enfranchisement of his copyhold estates, he recorded that several parts of his Smethwick estate had been sold.[93] He died in 1707.[94]

About 1780 Smethwick Hall seems to have been the home of the Rabone family, prominent Birmingham merchants. Richard Rabone was living there in 1834, and when he died in 1838 aged 85, he was said to have resided there for almost sixty years.[95] It is uncertain whether he died there as in 1835 Edward Rabone was said to be the occupant. He still lived there in 1850.[96] In 1851, however, the hall was occupied by a tenant, Samuel Clarke, who farmed 30 a.[97] He was still there in 1853 and was succeeded by John Howard Blackwell, tenant of an ironworks near Halford's Lane, who lived at the hall in at least 1854 and 1855.[98] By 1859 the Rabones had sold the hall to Joseph Gillott, a Birmingham steel-pen manufacturer. By then the house was known locally as Rabone Hall.[99] In 1862 the house and grounds were bought by a firm of hydraulic engineers, Tangye Bros. & Price of Clement Street, Birmingham. The house was demolished and the firm erected the Cornwall Works on the site.[1]

In the mid 19th century the hall, an irregular three-storeyed brick house, stood between the Birmingham Canal and the Handsworth boundary. A drive led south to what is now Rabone Lane, and the house was secluded from the road by trees. North of it there were pools and a wilderness.[2]

A house on the north-west side of Stony Lane near the western boundary of Smethwick was called Smethwick House by the early 1830s.[3] It was still

[81] S.R.O., D. 707/12/1, marr. settlement of J. Moilliet and L. H. Galton; above pp. 97, 103. W.P.L. 10592 has a view of the Grove across what seems to be the old line of the canal.

[82] 'Smethwick and Round About', 6, 13, 20, and 27 Mar., 28 Aug. 1953; R. E. Schofield, *The Lunar Society of Birmingham*, 432; *D.N.B.*; *Maria Edgeworth: Letters from England 1813–1844*, ed. Christina Colvin, pp. xviii, 172–3, 233, 243; *Reg. of electors within Southern Div. of County of Stafford . . . 1 Nov. 1837–1 Nov. 1838*, 39 (copy in W.S.L.); *1 Nov. 1838–1 Nov. 1839*, 37; W.S.L., S. MS. 417/Harborne; W.S.L. 847/36; F. W. Hackwood, *Wednesbury Workshops* (Wednesbury, 1889), 97–8.

[83] W.S.L. 846/36.

[84] 'Smethwick and Round About', 27 Mar., 28 Aug. 1953.

[85] *P.O. Dir. Birm.* (1860); *Reg. of persons entitled to vote . . . Southern Div. of County of Stafford . . . 30 Nov. 1865–1 Dec. 1866*, 186.   [86] See plate facing p. 128.

[87] B.M., O.S.D. 256; S.R.O., D. 707/12/1, marr. settlement of J. Moilliet and L. H. Galton (plan).

[88] B.R.L. 391076.

[89] R. Whitworth, *Plan of Intended Navigation from Birmingham to Canal at Aldersley near Wolverhampton survey'd 1767* (copy in W.S.L.); below p. 108.

[90] *S.H.C.* 1931, 188; 1935, 224, 247, 260, 378, 427; W.S.L. 82/17–18/43; B.R.L. 176962, 252294, 268869, 270056, 276782, 348011, 453640–1; B.R.L., j. 121; C 3/191/7.

[91] *S.H.C.* 1923, 252. For his marriage settlement of Dec. 1660 see B.R.L. 391076.

[92] Plot, *Staffs.* 207.

[93] B.R.L. 393642, ff. 3, 8–12; below p. 107.

[94] L.J.R.O., Peculiars, will of Chas. Lane (dated 22 Feb. 1705/6, proved 11 Apr. 1706).

[95] Docs. at St. Peter's, Harborne, 151B, Levy Book 1778; White, *Dir. Staffs.* (1834); *Staffs. Advertiser*, 10 Feb. 1838; 'Old Smethwick', 26 June 1948; B. Walker, 'Some Eighteenth-Century Birmingham Houses, and the Men who lived in them', *T.B.A.S.* lvi. 24–5.

[96] Pigot, *Nat. Com. Dir.* (1835), 472; *P.O. Dir. Staffs.* (1850).

[97] H.O. 107/2050(2) f. 250v.; 'Old Smethwick', 10 June 1950.

[98] *Reg. of persons entitled to vote . . . Southern Div. of County of Stafford . . . 30 Nov. 1853–1 Dec. 1854*, 95 (copy in W.S.L.); *30 Nov. 1854–1 Dec. 1855*, 61; *30 Nov. 1855–1 Dec. 1856*, 198.

[99] *Reg. of persons entitled to vote . . . 30 Nov. 1855–1 Dec. 1856*, 198; 'Old Smethwick', 11 Feb. 1950; *V.C.H. Warws.* vii. 98.

[1] R. Tangye, *One and All* (2nd edn.), 88–9, 103; 'Old Smethwick', 5 Nov. 1949, 11 Feb. 1950; *V.C.H. Staffs.* ii. 160.

[2] W.S.L., S. MS. 417/Harborne; W.P.L., P. 2619; Tangye, *One and All*, 13–14; 'Smethwick and Round About', 25 Nov. 1955, 3 Jan. 1958.

[3] J. Phillips and W. F. Hutchings, *Map of Staffs.* (1832).

so called in 1861[4] but in the later 19th century it became known as Smethwick Hall.[5] It is said to have been built in 1746 by Thomas Hanson. A Thomas Hanson was living there by 1818; he was probably the son of the Thomas Hanson who died in 1800 aged 76. In 1842 Hanson owned 65 a. in Smethwick; outlying portions of his estate were let to tenants, but he retained 29 a., mainly meadow and pasture, around his house. He was still living there in 1846.[6] The house and estate were subsequently acquired by Thomas Darby,[7] but by 1851 they had passed to John Samuel Dawes, a partner in John Dawes & Sons, a firm of ironmasters with works in West Bromwich and Oldbury. Dawes, who was one of the founders of the Birmingham and Midland Institute, retired from the family firm c. 1857 to pursue his interest in geology. He was still living at Smethwick House in 1861, but he subsequently left to live in Edgbaston, where he died in 1878.[8] The house apparently remained in the ownership of the Dawes family, but for a number of years it was used as a school. In 1872 it was occupied by Thomas Townsend, and Mrs. Eliza Townsend was keeping a school there. By 1875 the Revd. J. Dixon and his wife were conducting a day and boarding school in the house. The school was later sold to a Baptist minister called Munns, who carried it on until the 1880s.[9] In 1885 George Dawes, a younger brother of J. S. Dawes, came to live at Smethwick Hall. Until he retired to Smethwick he had been running the Milton and Elsecar Ironworks near Barnsley (Yorks. W.R.), but the depression in the iron trade had forced him to close the works. He died at Smethwick Hall in 1888, and it was subsequently bought by Sir Richard Tangye. Sir Richard's son H. L. Tangye lived there for a time but later moved to Maxstoke Castle (Warws.). John A. Thompson, a member of a local family of maltsters, later lived at the hall.[10]

Early in the First World War Belgian refugees were living at the hall, but from 1916 to 1925 it was the home of Benjamin Shakespeare, clerk to the Smethwick justices. Already, however, the Smethwick Hall Estate Co. Ltd. was developing the estate. Auckland Road had been laid out and partly built up along the north-east edge by 1902. In 1928 the hall and the remaining 28 a. were bought by Smethwick corporation, which in 1930 opened Smethwick Hall Park on 8 a. of the grounds beside Stony Lane. The hall still stood in June 1937 but was demolished soon afterwards to make way for council schools opened in 1939.[11]

The hall was of three storeys in a plain Georgian style. About 1840 there were stables, cowsheds, and a barn beside the main drive curving down to Stony Lane.[12] In front of the house the grounds sloped sharply to a pool formed by damming the brook which flows north-eastwards alongside Stony Lane. The pool remains a feature of Smethwick Hall Park.

The house known as the Woodlands was probably built in the early 19th century. It existed by 1814,[13] when it stood in open country north of Cape Hill. It may have been built for John Wilkes Unett, a Birmingham solicitor and the first known occupant. He lived in Birmingham until at least 1800, but by 1830, and probably much earlier, he was living in Smethwick, almost certainly at the Woodlands.[14] By 1842 he owned 128 a. of land in Smethwick; 32 a. lay around his house, and the other properties consisted of 65 a. of the Ruck of Stones farm and 31 a. in the Broomfield area.[15] Unett lived at the Woodlands until 1856, when he retired from practice and moved to Milverton (Warws.). He died later the same year, still owning the Smethwick properties. From the late 1830s he was laying out new streets over much of his land.[16] In 1861 Hannah Shelley was living at the Woodlands.[17] The Unett family's Smethwick estates were being broken up for sale and development in the 1870s and 1880s.[18] About 1912 J. W. Hinton founded the Smethwick Working Men's Club at the Woodlands, and in the early 1950s the house, then said to be much altered, was still occupied by the club.[19] It was subsequently demolished and new premises for the club were built on the site, on the north side of Woodlands Street.

When Philip Foley sold the manors of Harborne and Smethwick to George Birch and Henry Hinckley in 1709, he retained a house and over 50 a. in the Roebuck Lane area. The property was subsequently sold to Thomas Finch, a Dudley ironmonger, whose widow and son sold it to Lord Dartmouth in 1756.[20] By 1842 the 4th earl owned most of the land between the Birmingham Canal, the West Bromwich boundary, and Halford's Lane, amounting to 110 a.[21] In 1865 the 5th earl sold 5 a. to the Great Western Railway Co. for the Stourbridge Extension Railway, opened in 1867.[22] In the 1880s, however, he still owned 105 a. in the area; 16 a. were occupied by the Sandwell Park Colliery Co., which had sunk its first shaft there in 1870.[23] Part of the estate was

[4] R.G. 9/2126 f. 63.
[5] See e.g. *Staffs. Advertiser*, 25 Aug. 1888 (notice of death of Geo. Dawes at The Hall, Smethwick).
[6] 'Smethwick and Round About', 13 Oct. 1951; Parson and Bradshaw, *Dir. Staffs.* (1818); W.S.L., S. MS. 417/ Harborne; *Reg. of electors within Southern Div. of County of Stafford . . . 30 Nov. 1846–1 Dec. 1847*, 52 (copy in W.S.L.).
[7] 'Smethwick and Round About', 13 and 20 Oct. 1951, citing a plan which is evidently now B.R.L. 394239 and dating it 1840, although the plan itself is undated. B.R.L. 394258 (said to be c. 1840) gives T. Hanson as owner of the estate.
[8] H.O. 107/2050(3) ff. 264v.–265; R.G. 9/2126 ff. 76v.–77; 'Smethwick and Round About', 20 Oct. 1951; above p. 38.
[9] 'Smethwick and Round About', 27 Oct. 1951.
[10] Ibid. 3 Nov. 1951; *V.C.H. Warws.* ii. 391; above n. 5.
[11] 'Smethwick and Round About', 3 Nov. 1951; O.S. Map 6″, Staffs. LXXII. NW., NE. (1904–5 edn.); *Kelly's*

Dir. Birm. (1960); W.P.L., P. 1233–4, P. 1849; below p. 140. [12] B.R.L. 394239; W.P.L., P. 1224.
[13] B.M., O.S.D. 256.
[14] 'Smethwick and Round About', 14 Mar., 14 Nov.–19 Dec. 1952, 14 Aug. 1953.
[15] W.S.L., S. MS. 417/Harborne; above p. 103.
[16] *Staffs. Advertiser*, 22 Nov. 1856; 'Smethwick and Round About', 5 Dec. 1952; above pp. 91, 94. He also developed the resort at Filey (Yorks. E.R.) from 1835; *V.C.H. Yorks. East Riding*, ii. 134–6, 143, 149 n.
[17] R.G. 9/2126, f. 6v.
[18] 'Old Smethwick', 2 Apr. 1949; B.R.L. 452905–6; above p. 103.
[19] 'Old Smethwick', 29 Apr. 1950; *Kelly's Dir. Birm.* (1913); 'Smethwick and Round About', 21 Mar. 1952.
[20] S.R.O., D. 742/Dartmouth Estates/II/13/921; B.R.L. 391783.
[21] W.S.L., S. MS. 417/Harborne.
[22] S.R.O., D. 564/10/1/1; above p. 98.
[23] D. 564/8/1/23/Feb. 1887; /8/1/24/Dec. 1889; O.S. Map 6″, Staffs. LXVIII. SE. (1890 edn.); below p. 115.

opened as Lewisham Park in 1905.[24] The neighbouring portion was being used as allotment gardens by 1913.[25] By the late 1940s, however, much of the land had been developed by industry, notably by Birmid Ltd.[26] The area formerly occupied by the colliery was derelict in 1971.

ECONOMIC HISTORY. AGRICULTURE. In 1086 Smethwick had land for two ploughs as against Harborne with land for only one.[27] Although Harborne had emerged as the ecclesiastical centre by the early 13th century,[28] economically and administratively Smethwick seems to have remained at least as important even before the 19th century.[29] Mixed farming was the main occupation there until the 19th century, though it was often combined with other pursuits such as nailing and inn-keeping.[30] Crops mentioned in probate inventories between 1647 and 1698 were wheat, rye, barley, oats, and peas; several farmers were also engaged in cattle and sheep farming.[31]

There seems to have been a common field called Fenfield in the north-east of Smethwick. A furlong of land in Fenfield is mentioned in 1575, but by then other parts of it were inclosed pastures.[32]

Common rights in the wastes and woodland of Smethwick seem to have survived the abandonment of open-field cultivation. The lords of the manor were apparently inclosing the waste piecemeal from at least the 13th century: in 1278 Halesowen abbey granted a piece of the Smethwick waste to the rectors of Harborne.[33] Nevertheless there is some evidence to suggest that the freeholders' consent was occasionally necessary before inclosure could take place. In 1631 Christopher Lyddyat recalled that between thirty and forty years earlier Lord Dudley, on Lyddyat's petition 'and upon the suit of the freeholders of Smethwick', had granted him a plot of land on the waste on Smethwick Common as the site for a cottage.[34] Lyddyat's property, and therefore also that part of the waste known as Smethwick Common, probably lay in the north or north-east of Smethwick.[35] Parts of the waste were still uninclosed in the 18th century, but the sparse evidence suggests that they were small roadside areas. It also seems likely that by then such areas were at the disposal of the lord of the manor. 'A shop at the Swan' standing on the waste, apparently on the corner of Holly

Lane and the Birmingham–Dudley road, was leased out by the lord for 99 years from 1733.[36] In 1771 the lord leased a piece of common or waste, c. 1 a. in extent and taken from Ruck of Stones Lane (now Lewisham Road), to Luke Pope, a Smethwick nurseryman, for 99 years; Pope covenanted to keep the property fenced and to build a house there worth at least £30.[37] In 1781 he bought the property outright.[38]

Enfranchisement of copyhold land was in progress by the beginning of the 18th century. In 1702 Charles Lane authorized the payment of £10 10s. to the lord of Harborne and Smethwick for the enfranchisement of his Smethwick estate,[39] and in 1709 Thomas Pearsall paid £30 to enfranchise his French Walls estate. After enfranchisement the French Walls estate, formerly held for a chief rent of 3s. a year, suit of court, fine, heriot, and fealty, was to be held simply for the chief rent and suit and service once a year when the owner was summoned.[40] Copyhold land still existed in 1809 when the lord of Smethwick enfranchised Luke Pope's property for £75,[41] but there was none left at the end of the 19th century.[42]

There was still extensive agricultural land in the mid 19th century, but by the early 1880s much of it was being swallowed up in the development of the town. Thus housing was then being built over the Ruck of Stones farm in the north, and the site of the farm-house became part of the Surrey Works.[43] The Shireland area in the south-east was also being developed on farm-land.[44] The remaining agricultural land was concentrated on the higher ground in the south-west, with some also surviving in the north.[45] Even where land was not actually built over, urbanization affected farming in other ways. New roads split farms up. Canals, railways, and buildings often made agricultural land difficult of access. Crops were polluted by smoke.[46] By the early 20th century even the farm-land in the south-west had shrunk considerably, and there were more open spaces, such as parks, playing-fields, and allotments, than there was agricultural land. West Smethwick Park in fact had been laid out over farm-land.[47] The area added to Smethwick from Oldbury in 1928 was partly rural, but it was quickly used for housing.[48] A patch of farm-land survived in the northern extremity of the borough off Halford's Lane until c. 1950 when it was bought by the corporation as

24 See p. 93.
25 O.S. Map 6″, Staffs. LXVIII. SE. (1921 edn.).
26 R. Fletcher, Street Map of Boro. of Smethwick (1949; copy in W.P.L.).
27 V.C.H. Staffs. iv. 43, no. 86.
28 V.C.H. Warws. vii. 373.
29 Court Rolls of the Manor of Hales, 1270–1307 (Worcs. Hist. Soc.), i, pp. xx, 21–3; T. R. Nash, Colls. for Hist. of Worcs. ii (1782), App. p. xxxvi; Valor Eccl. (Rec. Com.), iii. 206; Dudley Central Libr. 7/13. For comparative population figures see S.H.C. 1923, 252–5; Census, 1801–31. For the administrative position see below pp. 118–19.
30 See L.J.R.O., Peculiars, wills of Wm. Walker, nailer (proved 16 June 1663), Wm. Smith, whitesmith (proved 18 May 1688), inventories; Mann, 'Smethwick', 16.
31 L.J.R.O., Peculiars, wills of Thos. Cowley alias Glover (proved 2 Oct. 1647), Thos. Cox (proved 7 Feb. 1667/8), Rog. Parkes (proved 6 Dec. 1677), John Guest (proved 7 May 1686), Ric. Ashford (proved 28 Aug. 1686), Geo. Birch (proved 18 May 1698), and Hen. Fryth (proved 30 July 1698). For mixed farming on the Downing family's farm in West Smethwick in the later 19th century see 'Old Smethwick', 23 Oct., 6 Nov. 1948, 1 Jan. 1949; 'Smethwick and Round About', 2 Sept. 1955.

32 Req. 2/80/49; C 3/146/15; S.H.C. 1938, 17–18; B.R.L., j. 406; S.R.O., D. 1141/4/4, ct. book 23 Nov. 1757.
33 S.H.C. 1924, p. 82.   34 C 3/399/93.
35 The evidence was given in the course of a series of actions concerning a large area in the north of Smethwick called Aspers Moor: C 3/339/4; C 3/341/3; 'Old Smethwick', 9 Apr. 1949; S.R.O., D 742/Dartmouth Estates/II/13/921. Lyddyat stated that the property lay near a forge; this may have been the Pig Mill (see below pp. 108–9).
36 S.R.O., D. 1141/4/3/2, p. 23; Roper, Plans of Smethwick, 1857, no. 12.   37 B.R.L. 445765.
38 B.R.L. 445774.   39 B.R.L. 393642, f. 12.
40 B.R.L., j. 409.
41 B.R.L. 445775.
42 See p. 118.
43 See p. 103.
44 O.S. Map 6″, Staffs. LXXII. NE. (1890 edn.); above p. 104.
45 I. Davies, 'Agriculture of W. Midland Conurbation' (Birm. Univ. M.A. thesis, 1953), 90–1 and map 20.
46 Ibid. 89–90, 93.
47 Ibid. 91 and map 20; 'Old Smethwick', 9 Oct. 1948; above p. 92.
48 See p. 96.

the site of Albion School.[49] Three plots of agricultural land, however, remained in the early 1950s, one in the south-west and two in the north-west; one was a small-holding, one supported a small dairy herd, and the third was used as a hospital vegetable garden.[50]

Smethwick once had several tracts of woodland, consisting mainly of oaks, birches, and beeches.[51] The two largest areas of woodland lay in the south and east of the township. In the south Lightwood, which lay on either side of the boundary with Harborne township, was held by the lord of the manor in the mid 16th century when it was also known as 'Yonge Wood'.[52] The Smethwick portion was acquired by the Lytteltons of Frankley and Hagley (Worcs.), probably in the later 16th century when Sir John Lyttelton was steward of the manor and a trustee of Edward, Lord Dudley (d. 1586);[53] by 1658 it was owned by Sir Henry Lyttelton,[54] and it was still an extensive area of woodland c. 1770.[55] The Harborne section was retained by the lord of the manor. By the early 18th century it was known as Great Lightwood or Lords Wood, and it was customary for it to be coppiced; the neighbouring inhabitants of Smethwick and Harborne, however, had common rights there. They appear to have surrendered those rights in 1709 to George Birch of Harborne, who had recently bought Great Lightwood from the lord of the manor.[56] Bearwood, the area immediately to the north of Lightwood, was a well wooded area during the 18th century. The Aston family of Aston in Runcorn (Ches.) owned woods and coppices there by 1712, and in 1792 Henry Hervey Aston sold c. 14 a. of coppices to the lords of Smethwick manor.[57] In the east of Smethwick land on both sides of the main road (now Cape Hill) was once well wooded. 'A little wood' on either side of the road was mentioned in 1675, and there was still extensive woodland to the north of the road a century later.[58] The memory at least of its former wooded character was preserved by the names of the houses which had been built there by the early 19th century: the Coppice, Smethwick Grove, and the Woodlands.[59] To the south of the main road in the Shireland area there was a coppice containing 236 oaks and 2 ashes in 1782,[60] and woodland survived there as late as the 1850s.[61] Until the 19th century there was also woodland in the Uplands and Broomfield districts and at West Smethwick.[62]

Felling was in progress in the later 18th century. A coppice near the Bear inn at Bearwood was cut in 1765 to create new arable.[63] In 1769 William Hutton, the historian of Birmingham, bought 13 a. of land in Smethwick from the lord of the manor and sold the timber for half the purchase price of the land.[64] By 1842 most of the timber in the Cape Hill area had evidently disappeared, although the Smethwick Grove estate still included 4 a. of woodland.[65] In the mid 19th century there was extensive felling, and oaks from the Uplands and Broomfield areas were sold to railway contractors.[66]

Luke Pope of Smethwick founded a notable firm of nurserymen specializing in tulips and later in North American shrubs and plants. He was successively described as gardener, seedsman, and nurseryman during the late 18th and early 19th centuries when he was buying up various small copyhold estates in Smethwick. By 1771 he had established nurseries in the north-east of Smethwick near the Ruck of Stones farm, and by the mid 19th century the firm, then known as John Pope & Sons, also had nurseries in the adjacent parts of Handsworth and West Bromwich.[67]

MILLS. Halesowen abbey had a mill at Smethwick in 1499; it was known as 'Briddismylne' and was held by Richard Piddock.[68] It may be identifiable with the mill which stood on Thimblemill Brook below the Old Church and which disappeared when the Birmingham Canal Co. built a reservoir there c. 1769; in 1778 the company was paying rates on the Old Pool and Mill Croft.[69] That mill may itself be identifiable with the walk-mill which stood in the area in the mid 17th century.[70]

By 1659 there was a mill on Hockley Brook where it formed the Smethwick–Handsworth boundary. The mill may at that time have stood on the Handsworth side of the boundary, but a map of 1831–2 shows a mill on the Smethwick side. In 1659 the mill belonged to a Mr. Lane, probably Charles Lane of Smethwick Hall; a blade-mill had then been newly erected beside Lane's old corn-mill. At the beginning of the 18th century the mill was part of the Smethwick estate sold by John Willes to Henry Carver.[71] It was apparently not in use in 1733,[72] but in the 1720s and 1750s it was shown on maps as the Pig Mill.[73] The name, which was in use apparently in the mid 17th century and probably by the late 16th century,[74] suggests that the mill

[49] Mann, 'Smethwick', 44, 50.
[50] Davies, 'Agric. of W. Midland Conurbation', 92–3 and map 20.
[51] 'Old Smethwick', 21 Aug. 1948; 'Smethwick and Round About', 3 Jan. 1958; Price, 'Smethwick', 8.
[52] Cal. Pat. 1554–5, 23.
[53] S.H.C. ix (2), 107, 111; B.R.L. 256393, 297360.
[54] B.R.L. 324134, 324239.
[55] Yates, Map of Staffs. (1775).
[56] B.R.L. 393642, f. 12.
[57] W.S.L. 11/475/2/50, p. 1; B.R.L. 500272, 500276–8, 500281–2.
[58] J. Ogilby, Britannia (1675), 99 and preceding plate; Yates, Map of Staffs. (1775).
[59] See pp. 100, 104, 106.
[60] S.R.O., D. 1141/4/3/1, note on back end-paper.
[61] 'Smethwick and Round About', 17 July 1953 (mentioning 'woodland, late Cairns and late Samuel Price'); above p. 104.
[62] 'Old Smethwick', 21 Aug. 1948; 'Smethwick and Round About', 3 Jan. 1958.
[63] Aris's Birmingham Gaz. 4 and 11 Mar. 1765.

[64] Life of William Hutton . . . written by himself (1817 edn.), 182.
[65] W.S.L., S. MS. 417/Harborne, no. 863.
[66] 'Old Smethwick', 21 Aug. 1948; 'Smethwick and Round About', 3 Jan. 1958.
[67] M. Hadfield, 'Camellias at the Hawthorns', Gardeners Chronicle Gardening Illustrated, 27 Jan. 1962; B.R.L. 445765–8; White, Dir. Staffs. (1851), 697 (stating that the firm was then over a century old); W.S.L., S. MS. 417/Harborne; ibid./West Bromwich (sub Dartmouth, earl of); B.R.L. 299997.
[68] T. R. Nash, Colls. for Hist. of Worcs. ii (1782), App. p. xxxvi.
[69] 'Old Smethwick', 21 Aug. 1948; docs. at St. Peter's, Harborne, 151B; above p. 98.   [70] W.P.L. 16334.
[71] Shaw, Staffs. ii. 108; J. Phillips and W. F. Hutchings, Map of Staffs. (1832); B.R.L. 329279, p. 2; above pp. 102, 104.   [72] B.R.L. 329279, p. 2.
[73] V.C.H. Warws. vii. 258.
[74] 9th Rep. Com. Char. H.C. 258, p. 552 (1823), ix, referring to Pig Hill Meadow, probably in error for Pig Mill Meadow.

had been used as an ironworks. In the 1760s and the early 19th century it seems to have been worked as a forge. Between 1821 and 1826 John Whitehead bought the mill with a farm called Pig Mill farm from A. S. Lillingston. It was probably dismantled in the early 1830s.[75]

The mill which gave Thimblemill Brook its name stood on the brook near what is now the junction of Thimblemill Road and Norman Road, in the part of Oldbury that was acquired by Smethwick in 1928.[76] It probably began as a corn-mill and was later converted to thimble-making. It was known as the Thimble Mill by 1775. By 1837, however, it was being used by W. W. Blyth for the cutting of files by machinery, a pioneer venture that resulted from the patent taken out in 1833 by William Shilton of Birmingham. William Summerton moved to the Thimble Mill from Oldbury mill in 1845 and used it as a corn-mill. He remained there about nine years and then moved to a new mill which he had built in Bearwood nearly opposite the Bear inn. The Thimble Mill was still standing in the late 1880s, and the pool survives as part of a recreation and sports ground for the employees of Guest, Keen & Nettlefolds.

William Croxall, a miller, bought land in what is now Windmill Lane in 1803 and built a windmill there.[77] His son Samuel had succeeded him by 1818 and was still working the windmill in 1838. By 1851 it was in the hands of Joseph and Frederick Lees. It continued as a corn-mill until the 1860s; it then went out of use, except for a few months c. 1873 when it was used to grind spice. When the site became part of the Windmill Brewery, built in 1886, the machinery was dismantled and the tower became a storehouse. It was demolished in 1949.

In 1949 an old man recalled the existence of a second windmill opposite the toll-house at the junction of Windmill Lane and Cape Hill. It may perhaps have been the mill in 'Cape Road' that occurs in 1836.[78]

THE METAL TRADES. It was the cutting of the Birmingham Canal in 1768–9 that eventually brought manufacturing industry to Smethwick; the firms which from the late 18th century set up works along its banks were concerned mainly with metalworking, which has ever since played a predominant role in the town's economy. The primary production of metals from ores has never been of any significance, but many forms of engineering have flourished. In the early 1870s Smethwick and Dudley Port, 'with a thousand swarming hives of metallurgical industries ... too numerous to mention', were contrasted with other Black Country towns which specialized in one or two specific types of metalware.[79] Such variety remains.

Nailers were working at Smethwick c. 1600[80] and are found regularly, though not in great numbers, in the later 17th century and throughout the 18th century.[81] As late as 1850 it was stated that the population included many nailers, 'working in their own houses',[82] but by then nailing was declining as a domestic industry. In 1851 only 37 people described themselves as nailers, and of those at least 12 were factory hands producing cut- or cast-nails.[83] Men and women who did not consider themselves nailers by trade may, however, have turned to nailing from time to time to supplement the family's income.[84] From the later 17th century other metalworkers appear. Samuel Jervase (d. 1675) worked as a whitesmith, but his probate inventory does not reveal what he made; another whitesmith, William Smith (d. 1687), made malt mills and, apparently, bellows, sending them as far as London. George Birch (d. 1698) was a yeoman whose will and probate inventory show that he possessed 'shop tools' to the value of £16 and that he was owed money by a Birmingham gunsmith. He may have been an early supplier of components to the Birmingham gun trade; he may also have been the George Birch who was described in 1691 as a nailer.[85] Smethwick was certainly connected with the gun trade, though apparently in a small way. A gunsmith, John Freeth, was at work there by 1706, and another, William Smith, occurs in 1729.[86] The first engineering works to be established after the cutting of the Birmingham Canal was probably the Whately family's gunbarrel factory, established by c. 1800.[87]

The first works of any kind, however, was the brasshouse from which Brasshouse Lane takes its name. It had been established near the canal by 1790 on a site occupied in 1972 by part of the works of the District Iron and Steel Co. Ltd.[88] Shares in Smethwick Brass Works were on sale in 1792 and 1795; in 1834 the proprietor was the Smethwick Brass Co., manufacturer of ingot brass.[89] The company was probably formed, like the Birmingham Metal Co. of 1781, by Birmingham brass users anxious to break the virtual monopoly of supply held by the Cheadle and Bristol brasshouses;[90] it is perhaps to be identified with the 'Brass Company'

[75] V.C.H. Warws. vii. 258 (where it is suggested that the Pig Mill may have been used by Wright and Jesson as a slitting-mill in the early 19th century; the source cited, however, refers to Bromwich forge, for which see above p. 33); Parson and Bradshaw, Dir. Staffs. (1818), 303; Prob. 11/1762 (P.C.C. 618 Liverpool, will of J. Whitehead).

[76] For this para. see 'Old Smethwick', 3 July, 21 Aug. 1948, 13, 20, and 27 Aug. 1949; 'Smethwick and Round About', 5 Sept. 1952 (illustration), 31 Dec. 1954; B. Woodcroft, Alphabetical Index of Patentees of Inventions, 1617–1852; Yates, Map of Staffs. (1775); O.S. Map 6", Staffs. LXXII. NE. (1890 edn.).

[77] For this para. see 'Old Smethwick', 9 and 16 Sept. 1950,; 'Smethwick and Round About', 21 Mar. 1952, 17 July 1953, 2 Dec. 1955; W.P.L. 16976, including cutting from Smethwick Telephone, 13 Aug. 1949; W.S.L., S. MS. 417/Harborne; White, Dir. Staffs. (1851); Smethwick Civic News, Jan. 1961 (copy in W.P.L.).

[78] 'Old Smethwick', 14 May 1949; Redhead, Local Govt. 20.

[79] S. Griffiths, Griffiths' Guide to the Iron Trade of Great Britain (1873), 46.

[80] S.H.C. 1935, 265; C 3/399/93.

[81] See e.g. B.R.L. 324374, 329261, 377485, 581536; S.R.O., D.(W.)1790/A/9/10; S.R.O., D. 1141/4/3/2, pp. 22, 35; D. 1141/4/4, ct. book 13 Mar. 1771, 18 June 1787.

[82] P.O. Dir Staffs. (1850).

[83] H.O. 107/2050(1) ff. 79, 80, 83v., 86v., 95v.; /2050(2) ff. 160v., 161v.,168, 182v., 209, 210, 211v., 216, 219v., 235, 246, 246v., 259, 275v., 314v.

[84] See e.g. 'Old Smethwick', 20 Aug. 1949.

[85] L.J.R.O., Peculiars, wills of Sam. Jervase (proved 20 Sept. 1675), Wm. Smith (proved 18 May 1688), and Geo. Birch (proved 18 May 1698); S.R.O., D.(W.)1790/A/9/10.

[86] 'Old Smethwick', 12 May 1951; B.R.L., Pickard 5618.   [87] See p. 100.

[88] 'Old Smethwick', 19 Mar. 1949.

[89] Ibid.; White, Dir. Staffs. (1834).

[90] V.C.H. Warws. vii. 124–5.

which paid rates on a house at Bearwood Hill in 1778.[91] Its later history is obscure, but it had apparently gone out of business by 1842, when the District Iron and Steel Co. held its former premises. The building was still standing in the 1860s.[92]

In 1795 Boulton, Watt & Sons, faced with difficulties in obtaining the components for their engines, decided to manufacture them themselves.[93] James Watt bought 18½ a. by the canal at Merry Hill, about a mile from the firm's Soho Manufactory in Handsworth; in 1796 the firm opened Soho Foundry there 'for the purpose of casting everything relating to our steam engines'.[94] Watt owned the land until 1801 but otherwise took no part in the new enterprise, its development being the work of Matthew Boulton's son M. R. Boulton and James Watt the younger. The site was carefully chosen, and the buildings were meticulously planned with the requirements of the various processes in mind. In 1799–1800 they comprised foundry stoves and furnaces, a boring mill, turning-, fitting-, carpenters', smiths', and pattern shops, a boiling-house, a magazine, a shed for sand, a drying-kiln, and 13 workers' houses.[95] Stebbing Shaw noted the extensive use of steam-power for 'whatever tends to abridge human labour and obtain accuracy' and was struck by 'the extraordinary regularity and neatness which pervades the whole'.[96] In 1800 the firm became Boulton, Watt & Co., with M. R. Boulton and James Watt the younger as the leading partners. In 1816 the latter bought the French Walls mill and in 1820 leased it to Henry Downing, lending him the money necessary to convert it into an ironworks. Downing went bankrupt in 1829. Watt then leased the property to the Bordesley Steel Co., which was still running it in the mid 1830s, but he evidently appreciated the potential advantages to his firm of an ironworks under his direct control. He took the French Walls Works into his own hands and ran it in conjunction with the Foundry, though as a separate concern, until old age forced him to give it up in 1842. The French Walls provided the Foundry with boiler plates and uses (semi-finished forgings for engines) as well as turning out merchant iron and steel. Scrap from the Foundry was returned to the French Walls for reworking.[97]

On the younger Watt's death in 1848 the Soho Manufactory and the mint which Matthew Boulton had established there were closed, and the firm, thenceforth known as James Watt & Co., carried on work only at Soho Foundry. By the 1860s the Foundry covered 10 a. and besides a variety of steam-engines its output included boilers, mill gearing, sugar mills, and machinery for pneumatic railways and sewage works. Perhaps the most notable product after the younger Watt's death was the 4-cylinder engine which powered the screw of Brunel's *Great Eastern*, launched in 1858.[98] In 1860 a former interest of the firm was revived when a mint was opened at the Foundry, and much of the country's new bronze coinage introduced in 1860 was struck by James Watt & Co. and the Birmingham firm of Ralph Heaton & Sons. In 1866 there were eleven screw coinage presses at the Foundry mint and the firm was striking copper and bronze coins, presumably for foreign governments since it appears to have done no work for the Royal Mint after 1863.[99]

Several firms engaged in engineering and metalworking were established in the town in the mid 19th century. The most important in the 1840s and early 1850s was Bramah, Fox & Co., later Fox, Henderson & Co., of the London Works in Cranford Street. The firm was established in 1839 by Charles Fox, an engineer who had acted as one of Robert Stephenson's principal assistants during the construction of the London and Birmingham Railway, and John Joseph Bramah, one of a notable family of engineers and iron-founders.[1] The partners acquired 5 a. of the Moilliets' Smethwick Grove estate and in 1840 began the erection of their works.[2] It was apparently in operation by 1841.[3] Fox, although initially the junior partner, was probably from the first its leading figure; it was he who designed the works and supervised its construction.[4] By 1845 Bramah had retired from the business, Fox had been joined by John Henderson, a Scottish engineer, and the firm had become Fox, Henderson & Co.[5] Fox's experience as a railway engineer led him to invent various improvements to railway permanent way, and his firm was the first to produce a virtually complete range of railway plant and stock. There was, however, much other business: products c. 1850 included wrought-iron pipes, steam-engines, boilers, gasometers, and tanks for ships.[6] Fox, Henderson & Co. became one of the

[91] Docs. at St. Peter's, Harborne, 151B, 29 Apr. 1778.
[92] W.S.L., S. MS. 417/Harborne, *sub* Steel Co.;' Old Smethwick', 19 Mar. 1949; *Birm. and Mid. Hardware Dist.* 255.
[93] For this para. see, unless otherwise stated, Sir Eric Roll, *An Early Experiment in Industrial Organisation* (1968 edn.), 149 sqq.; W. K. V. Gale, *Soho Foundry* (pamph. pub. by W. & T. Avery Ltd., 1948 edn.), 30 sqq. (copy in B.R.L.); H. W. Dickinson, *Matthew Boulton*, 167–73; H. W. Dickinson and R. Jenkins, *James Watt and the Steam Engine*, 268, 270–9, 346–7.
[94] Roll, *Early Experiment*, 162, quoting a letter from Boulton.
[95] Ibid. 260.   [96] Shaw, *Staffs*. ii. 119.
[97] Roll, *Early Experiment*, 163–4; Gale, *Soho Foundry*, 33; W. K. V. Gale, *Black Country Iron Industry*, 76, 78–80; above p. 101.
[98] Gale, *Soho Foundry*, 34; *Birm. and Mid. Hardware Dist.* 644–5; *D.N.B. sub* Brunel.
[99] Gale, *Soho Foundry*, 35; *Birm. and Mid. Hardware Dist.* 555–6, 558–9; C. Wilson Peck, *Eng. Copper, Tin, and Bronze Coins in the British Museum, 1558–1958*, 221, 416–17, giving firm's name in 1860 incorrectly as Boulton & Watt. *V.C.H. Warws*. vii. 107, wrongly states that minting began at the Foundry in 1848.

[1] *D.N.B.; sub* Fox; *Men of the Reign*, ed. T. H. Ward (1886 edn.), 333, stating that the partnership was established a year after the opening of the London & Birmingham Railway. The railway was completed in 1838: *V.C.H. Warws*. vii. 38. For Bramah's Christian names see W.S.L., S. MS. 417/Harborne, *sub* Bramah & Fox. He is not mentioned in I. McNeil, *Joseph Bramah: a Century of Invention, 1749–1851*, chap. 13, which gives some account of the family of Jos. Bramah, the inventor, but it has been suggested (Hermione Hobhouse, *Thomas Cubitt, Master Builder*, 517 n.) that he was probably one of Jos.'s grandsons.
[2] For the site see S.R.O., D. 707/12/1, plan of Smethwick Grove estate attached to marriage settlement of 28 Mar. 1832; W.S.L., S. MS. 417/Harborne, *sub* Bramah & Fox. In 1850 it was stated that the plan of the works was laid down 'ten years ago': *Staffs. Advertiser*, 9 Nov. 1850 (reprinting an article from the *Daily News*).
[3] Pigot, *Nat. Com. Dir.* (1841), Staffs. p. 93.
[4] *Staffs. Advertiser*, 9 Nov. 1850.
[5] *D.N.B.; P.O. Dir. Birm.* (1845), 133. The firm's style is incorrectly given as 'Henderson & Co.' ibid. 95. For Henderson see 'Old Smethwick', 8, 15, and 22 July 1950.
[6] *D.N.B.;* B. Woodcroft, *Alphabetical Index of Patentees of Inventions, 1617–1852*; 'Old Smethwick', 10 July 1948.

most celebrated firms of civil engineers in the country as a result of its work for Joseph Paxton's Crystal Palace. Fox produced the working drawings for Paxton, who also made a major addition to his original plan at Henderson's suggestion. The firm was the contractor for erecting the palace and made most of its iron work. Fox supervised the construction of the building and was knighted in 1851 for his contribution towards the Exhibition. He and Henderson were also the contractors for the removal of the palace to Sydenham.[7] Fox and Henderson's experience with William (later Sir William) Siemens, inventor of the regenerative furnace, was less satisfactory. In 1848 Siemens, then a young man, interested the partners in one of his early inventions, a regenerative steam-engine and condenser. The firm employed him and bought patent rights in the invention, and for some five years attempts were made to build engines to Siemens's specifications. None was successful. Siemens himself profited greatly from his years at the London Works; Fox and Henderson, however, began to recoup their losses only when he persuaded them to interest themselves in the electric-telegraph equipment patented by his brother Werner, thereby helping them to win large telegraph contracts.[8]

In 1850 the London Works was described as 'the finest and most compact range of [industrial] buildings in South Staffordshire'. It had been expanded to form a hollow square, in the centre of which stood the boiler-house with its two 75 h.p. engines. The smiths' shop contained 70 forges and was stated to be the largest in the world. The firm was then producing about 300 tons of castings a week and usually had between 800 and 1,200 men working at Smethwick. At the height of its success it was the town's principal employer of labour, and when it failed in 1856 some 2,000 people were thrown out of work.[9] The crash apparently came because it could not obtain payment for one of its numerous foreign contracts. Its creditors attempted to keep the works going but were unsuccessful.[10]

The French Walls Works was bought in 1842 by G. F. Muntz, notable as the inventor of the alloy of copper and zinc which came to be known as Muntz metal.[11] He moved to Smethwick because the demand for his product was outstripping the capacity of his works in Birmingham. The 4½-acre French Walls site soon became inadequate for his needs, and c. 1850 a further 6½ a. were acquired to the west, divided from the original site by the

Birmingham, Wolverhampton & Stour Valley Railway, authorized in 1846 and completed in 1852. A new works was built there and a private bridge over the railway linked the 'Old Side Works' and the 'New Side Works'. After Muntz's death in 1857 the business was carried on for several years by his eldest son, G. F. Muntz the younger, who in 1864 sold it to the newly formed Muntz's Metal Co. Ltd.

Tube-making was apparently brought to the town by George Selby, a lawyer and a partner in a tube-manufacturing concern, the Birmingham Patent Iron and Brass Tube Co., established in 1842. In 1846 he bought Smethwick Grove and some adjoining land and shortly afterwards erected a tube-works near the house for the company. It lay in the angle between the present London Street and Grove Lane and had a frontage on the Cape arm of the Birmingham Canal to the east.[12] The works was in production by 1851. The company was still in operation on the same site in the 1880s, when it was making lap-welded iron and steel boiler tubes, solid-drawn brass and copper tubes, tubes and fittings for gas, steam, and water purposes, and brass and copper sheets. The company probably ceased operations in the late 1880s, and by 1903 the works had become part of the St. George's Works of Guest, Keen & Nettlefolds.[13]

The tube-making firm of Richard Evered & Son (since 1874 Evered & Co. Ltd.) came to Smethwick in 1866.[14] It had been established in London in 1809 and had acquired a factory at Birmingham in 1860. When a third and larger works was needed, the firm took a three-storey factory in Smethwick known as the Manchester Works, which stood between Lewisham Road and the old Birmingham Canal on part of the former Ruck of Stones estate. The building was adapted and renamed the Surrey Works. Many types of brass tubes and fittings were produced, but brass bedsteads became the speciality. In 1885 the firm added more workshops for bedstead manufacture. A cot department was added in 1894. In 1908 Evereds were making gas, water, and electric fittings, brass and copper tubes, and 'general brass-foundry of every description' as well as cots and bedsteads.[15] Between the two World Wars the firm concentrated all its production at Smethwick and the Surrey Works was considerably extended. In the late 1960s the firm made non-ferrous tubes and strips, gas and water fittings, builders' hardware, plastic mouldings, and plumbers' brass-foundry. There were c. 1,000 employees.[16]

Several other firms in Smethwick were engaged

[7] C. Hobhouse, *1851 and the Crystal Palace* (1950 edn.), 38–40, 43–53, 73, 149, 154–6; C. R. Fay, *Palace of Industry, 1851*, 12–16, 70, 95; Yvonne ffrench, *The Great Exhibition, 1851*, 94, 96, 103–6, 108–9, 142–3, 167. The glass for the Crystal Palace was made by Chance Brothers: below p. 115. Simpson, Astbury & Co. (later Thos. Astbury & Co. and then Thos. Astbury & Son) of the Smethwick Foundry made ironwork for the Crystal Palace: 'Old Smethwick', 24 Sept. 1949.
[8] W. Pole, *Life of Sir William Siemens* (1888), 69–97; *D.N.B. sub* Siemens.
[9] *Staffs. Advertiser*, 9 Nov. 1850; 'Old Smethwick', 15 July 1950; above pp. 94–5.
[10] *Staffs. Advertiser*, 1 Nov. 1856; 'Old Smethwick', 8, 15, and 22 July 1950.
[11] For this para. see *Muntz's Metal Co. Ltd. . . . French Walls Works, nr. Birmingham* (illustrated pamph. c. 1907), 5–11 (copy in W.P.L.); 'Old Smethwick', 14, 21, and 28 Jan. 1950; B.R.L., Lee Crowder 1004; above p. 98. For G. F. Muntz see above pp. 20, 88.

[12] Above p. 105; F. W. Hackwood, *Wednesbury Workshops* (Wednesbury, 1889), 97–8; *Kelly's Dir. Staffs.* (1880), 251 and adverts. p. 48; O.S. Map 6″, Staffs. LXXII. NE. (edn. of 1890).
[13] White, *Dir. Staffs.* (1851); *Kelly's Dir. Staffs.* (1880), 251 and adverts. p. 48; Hackwood, *Wednesbury Workshops*, 98; O.S. Map 6″, Staffs. LXXII. NE. (edns. of 1890 and 1905). The works is shown on the 1890 edn. of the 6″ map (surveyed 1886–8) but the company is not listed in *Kelly's Dir. Birm.* (1890).
[14] For this para. see, unless otherwise stated, W. Ellery Jephcott, *Over a Century of Progress* (history of Evered & Co. Ltd. 1809–1949; copy in W.P.L.); 'Old Smethwick', 18 June 1949. The Manchester Works is shown on Roper, Plans of Smethwick, 1857, no. 10, as a works producing hooks and eyes. [15] *Kelly's Dir. Birm.* (1908), 833.
[16] *Warley Official Guide* [1968], 75; Dun & Bradstreet, *Guide to Key British Enterprises* (1969 edn.). Evered does not make the plastic for its mouldings but obtains it from outside suppliers: inf. from Evered & Co. (1972).

in the metal-bedstead trade, which had become a speciality of manufacturers in the Birmingham area by the 1840s. In 1869 two companies, Thomas and James Middleton of the Victoria Iron Foundry in Rolfe Street and Solomon Cross & Co. of High Street, specialized in iron bedsteads. By the mid 1900s at least four firms, including Evereds, were making them.[17] In the early 1920s three firms were manufacturing bedsteads, and Evereds were still producing them after the Second World War.[18] A number of other firms contributed to the trade by supplying components and material. Items such as tubes, angles, and brass mounts were generally bought by bedstead firms from specialist suppliers such as the District Iron and Steel Co., which until c. 1930 made tubes for bedsteads and was still a prominent supplier of light angles for the bedstead trade in the late 1960s. Earlier another Smethwick manufacturer, H. S. Richards, had made black enamel for bedsteads.[19]

Railway engineering continued to play an important part in the industrial life of the town after the collapse of Fox, Henderson & Co. A number of firms produced components for locomotives, rolling-stock, and permanent way. In 1869, for example, the output of the Birmingham Patent Iron and Brass Tube Co. of London Street included tubes for locomotive boilers; T. F. Griffiths, Son & Co. of the Midland Nut and Bolt Works, Soho, advertised railway fish and fang bolts; the Patent Rivet Co. of Rolfe Street made nuts, bolts, screws, rivets, and pins for railway use; and William Baines & Co. of Soho made turntables and other railway plant.[20] An important supplier of railway ironwork was the firm established in Rolfe Street in 1870 as Lones, Raybould & Vernon. By 1872 it had become Lones, Vernon & Holden, and by 1876 it had opened its Sandwell Works on the Birmingham Canal off Lewisham Road, to which all its business had been transferred by 1880. Its speciality was axles.[21] It was taken over by John Brockhouse & Co. Ltd. of West Bromwich in 1919 and at the end of the Second World War was producing annually some 60,000 buffers and other carriage and wagon ironwork. It ceased production in 1958.[22]

The Birmingham Wagon Co. Ltd., which came to Smethwick in 1864 and became one of the most important employers in the town, was, unlike the firms already mentioned, completely dependent on the railways.[23] It had been launched ten years earlier by a group of Birmingham businessmen who were the first people to appreciate the potential market open to a company offering railway wagons for hire as well as for sale. At first the company had its wagons built and maintained for it at Saltley, in Aston (Warws., now Birmingham). The success of its scheme eventually prompted it to build its own wagons. A 10-acre site was purchased in Smethwick on the south side of the Birmingham, Wolverhampton & Dudley Railway, adjoining the Handsworth boundary, and in 1864 a small works was built. The business expanded rapidly. Railway carriages too were made from 1876 and tram-cars from about the same date; the company therefore changed its name in 1878 to the Birmingham Railway Carriage and Wagon Co. Ltd. Between the later 1880s and 1902 the works was extended over the Handsworth boundary; later it filled the area between the railway, and Middlemore, Mornington, and Wattville Roads.[24] By the last decades of the 19th century the firm had become one of the country's leading manufacturers of rolling-stock, a position that it maintained until after the Second World War. In 1963 the works, which covered 56 a., was closed. The site was redeveloped as the Middlemore Industrial Estate, opened in 1966; the parent company became the First National Finance Corporation Ltd. in 1965.

Another substantial concern which moved to the town in the mid 19th century was the Birmingham firm of Tangye Bros. & Price, which made hydraulic presses and jacks. In 1862 it purchased Rabone Hall and its grounds, which lay on the north side of the Birmingham Canal. The company demolished the house and built the Cornwall Works, initially covering some 3 a.[25] It was opened in 1864 and most of the company's production was immediately transferred there.[26] The firm became Tangye Bros. in 1871 and Tangyes Ltd. in 1881.[27] It retained and extended its interest in hydraulic engineering, for which it was always best known, but it later entered other fields, including the manufacture of steam, gas, petrol, and oil engines.[28] The works was gradually enlarged until by 1950 it covered 20 a.[29] In 1966 the firm became a subsidiary of the Central Wagon Co. Ltd. of Wigan (Lancs.), and in 1969 it moved to Greet, in Birmingham (formerly in Yardley, Worcs.). The Cornwall Works was taken over by the steel-stockholding firm of R. G. Brown & Co. Ltd., another subsidiary of the Central Wagon Co.[30]

During the later 19th century the manufacture of nuts, bolts, and screws became the town's most important industry and Smethwick emerged as one

[17] Birm. and Mid. Hardware Dist. 624–7; White, Dir. Birm. (1869); 'Borough' Pocket Guide to Smethwick (n.d. but c. 1908), 22 (copy in W.P.L.).
[18] Smethwick Official Handbook [1922], 23–4 (copy in W.P.L.); Smethwick Official Industrial Handbook [1959], 9, 11.
[19] Smethwick Official Handbook [1922], 23; 'Old Smethwick', 16 Apr. 1949; Smethwick Official Industrial Handbook [1959], 9; Warley Official Guide [1968], 2; below p. 117.
[20] White, Dir. Birm. (1869). For advertisements by the 3 last-named firms see ibid. adverts. pp. 29a, 53, 71.
[21] 'Old Smethwick', 18 and 25 Sept. 1948; 'Old West Bromwich', 21 July 1944; Hulley's Birm. Dir. (1870); P.O. Dir. Staffs. (1872; 1876); Kelly's Dir. Staffs. (1880); 'Borough' Pocket Guide to Smethwick, 20; O.S. Map 6", Staffs. LXXII. NE. (1890 edn.); plate facing p. 113 below.
[22] Compton Mackenzie, Brockhouse (West Bromwich, 1945), 18, 35, 46; ex inf. John Brockhouse & Co. Ltd. (1972).

[23] For this para. see, unless otherwise stated, 'Old Smethwick', 21 and 28 May, 4 June 1949; 'Borough' Pocket Guide to Smethwick, 20; Birmingham Post, 27 June 1966. The Birmingham Railway Carriage and Wagon Co. Ltd.'s archives are in S.R.O.
[24] O.S. Map 6", Staffs. LXVIII. SE. (edns. of 1890 and 1904, and prov. edn. with addns. of 1938).
[25] Above p. 105; 'Old Smethwick', 11 Feb. 1950.
[26] Rachel E. Waterhouse, A Hundred Years of Engineering Craftsmanship, Tangyes Ltd. 1857–1957, 29; V.C.H. Staffs. ii. 160.
[27] 1856–1950: a Brief History of Cornwall Works . . . (priv. print. 1950), 9 (copy in W.P.L.); Waterhouse, Tangyes, 53.
[28] See e.g. V.C.H. Staffs. ii. 160–1, 168, 172.
[29] Waterhouse, Tangyes, 51; 'Old Smethwick', 11 and 18 Feb. 1950.
[30] Warley News Telephone, 18 Jan. 1968; Warley Official Guide [1968], 73; inf. from Tangye Epco Ltd. and from R. G. Brown & Co. Ltd. (1972).

SMETHWICK: CHANCE'S GLASS-WORKS IN 1851
from the south-east

WEST BROMWICH: THE WORKS OF ARCHIBALD KENRICK & SONS LTD. IN 1887
from the south-west

Mitchells & Butlers' Cape Hill Brewery from the north-east *c.* 1955

Lones, Vernon & Holden's Sandwell Works from the south *c.* 1930, with the Birmingham Canal in the foreground

SMETHWICK

of the country's leading centres of the trade. The development was due almost entirely to the work of two firms, Watkins & Keen and Nettlefold & Chamberlain, ancestors of the present G.K.N. group of companies.

In the mid 1850s[31] Frederick Watkins and Arthur Keen entered into partnership as nut and bolt manufacturers. Watkins was working for Thomas Astbury of the Smethwick Foundry in Rolfe Street, a prominent iron-founder and ordnance manufacturer. He had designed a machine for making nuts and bolts but lacked the capital to establish himself in business. Astbury was Keen's father-in-law; he negotiated the partnership and provided capital and premises.[32] The new firm, Watkins & Keen, apparently began business in Astbury's Victoria Works in Rolfe Street adjoining his Smethwick Foundry.[33] By 1860, however, it appears to have been jointly occupying the London Works with Thomas Astbury & Co.;[34] by 1869 it occupied the whole works.[35] By the early 1860s Watkins & Keen produced about a third of the nuts and bolts made in the Midlands, itself the country's main area of manufacture. The company's chief competitor was probably Weston & Grice of West Bromwich, but in 1864 the two companies merged as the Patent Nut and Bolt Co. Ltd., the first public company in the industry; its headquarters was at Smethwick, and Keen became its first chairman. At the same time the company acquired an ironworks at Cwmbran (Mon.) and was thus able to produce its own iron. In 1900 it amalgamated with a large iron-founding company, Guest & Co. of the Dowlais Iron Works, Dowlais (Glam.), to form Guest, Keen & Co. Ltd.[36]

From 1870 Keen had made attempts to acquire another Smethwick firm.[37] In 1854 J. S. Nettlefold, a Birmingham screw manufacturer, had revolutionized his industry by introducing automated American machinery. Room was needed to house this; Nettlefold, joined by his brother-in-law Joseph Chamberlain, father of the statesman, established the Heath Street Works in Cranford Street, Smethwick.[38] The firm (until 1874 Nettlefold & Chamberlain and then Nettlefolds Ltd.) dominated the market by the mid 1860s.[39] Among those prominent in its development was the younger Joseph Chamberlain, who joined it in 1854 and soon afterwards took charge of the commercial side of the organization. He became a partner in 1869 and remained

with the firm until 1874, when he retired to devote himself to politics.[40] The firm had by then begun to acquire additional premises. In 1869 it bought the Imperial Mills, which stood on the north side of Cranford Street, opposite the Heath Street Works. The mills were converted for the manufacture of nuts and bolts, and a wire-drawing mill, a bar shop, and a nail-making shop were built.[41] In 1880, the year in which it became a limited company, Nettlefolds took over one of its local rivals, the Birmingham Screw Co., which had set up its St. George's Works in Grove Lane in 1868. The newly acquired works was almost as large as the Heath Street Works and faced it from the opposite bank of the Birmingham Canal.[42]

Although the firm continued to expand, its profits fluctuated considerably during the last twenty years of the 19th century, and in 1902 the merger for which Arthur Keen had been working took place: Nettlefolds joined Guest, Keen & Co. to form Guest, Keen & Nettlefolds Ltd. By the outbreak of the First World War the new company produced over half the screws and about a quarter of the nuts and bolts made in the country.[43] The amalgamation made the firm the largest employer in the town.[44] In the late 1960s the headquarters of Guest, Keen & Nettlefolds Ltd., by then an investment company, adjoined the Heath Street Works, a 50-acre complex run by G.K.N. Screws and Fasteners Ltd. and employing some 4,500 people. G.K.N. had several other subsidiaries in Smethwick. G.K.N. Distributors Ltd. had its headquarters at the London Works, while G.K.N. Group Services Ltd. was in Cranford Street, G.K.N. Reinforcements Ltd. in Alma Street, and G.K.N. Fasteners Corrosion Laboratory in Abberley Street.[45] Smethwick Drop Forgings Ltd. of Rolfe Street, acquired by G.K.N. in 1963, was run as a subsidiary of G.K.N. Forgings Ltd.[46]

Since the 1890s much of Smethwick's industry has changed to adapt to new needs and developments, and a few prominent names have disappeared. The most notable name to be lost was that of James Watt & Co. of Soho Foundry. By the 1890s the few remaining partners in the firm were old, and they decided to sell the business. It was bought in 1895 by W. & T. Avery Ltd., a Birmingham firm which made weighing-machinery. Watt's steam-engine business was gradually discontinued

[31] *Guest, Keen & Nettlefolds Ltd.: an Outline History* (n.d. but *c.* 1922), 17 (copy in W.P.L.), giving 1853 (and wrongly stating that the firm began its life at the London Works); 'Old Smethwick', 5 Aug. 1950, suggesting 1853; J. A. C. Baker, 'Hist. of Nut and Bolt Industry in the West Midlands' (Birm. Univ. M. Com. thesis, 1965), 15 (giving 1855), 122 (giving 1854).

[32] 'Old Smethwick', 1 Oct. 1949, 5 Aug. 1950; Baker, 'Nut and Bolt Ind.' 3–4, 14–15, stating that Keen's father-in-law was G. A. Astbury, owner of 'a small iron foundry'.

[33] 'Old Smethwick', 24 Sept. and 1 Oct. 1949, 5 Aug. 1950. See also the account in *Birm. and Mid. Hardware Dist.* 609.

[34] *P.O. Dir. Staffs.* (1860) gives the London Works as the address of both firms.

[35] White, *Dir. Birm.* (1869).

[36] Baker, 'Nut and Bolt Ind.' 16–24, 28, 52, 60–1; *Guest, Keen & Nettlefolds Ltd.* 31. For Weston & Grice see above p. 37.

[37] Baker, 'Nut and Bolt Ind.' 23.

[38] *Guest, Keen & Nettlefolds Ltd.* 21–2; *Birm. and Mid. Hardware Dist.* 604–8. The postal address of the works

appears generally to have been Heath St., which is the name given to Cranford St. when it crosses the boundary into Birmingham; but Roper, Plan of Smethwick, 1858, and O.S. Map 6″, Staffs. LXXII. NE. show it in Smethwick.

[39] *Guest, Keen & Nettlefolds Ltd.* 21; *Birm. and Mid. Hardware Dist.* 609.

[40] J. L. Garvin, *Life of Joseph Chamberlain*, i. 53–7, 170–5.

[41] *Guest, Keen & Nettlefolds Ltd.* 27; O.S. Map 6″, Staffs. LXXII. NE. (1890 edn.). Baker, 'Nut and Bolt Ind.' 123, gives the date of purchase as 1867.

[42] *Guest, Keen & Nettlefolds Ltd.* 25; *Smethwick Official Industrial Handbook* [1959], 47; O.S. Map 6″, Staffs. LXXII. NE. (1905 edn.).

[43] Baker, 'Nut and Bolt Ind.' 123–5.

[44] 'Borough' Pocket Guide to Smethwick, 20.

[45] *Smethwick Official Industrial Handbook* [1959], 43, 45, 47; *Warley Official Guide* [1968], 71; *P.O. Telephone Dir. Sect. 211: 1971*.

[46] *Who Owns Whom 1971 (U.K. Edition)*; ex inf. G.K.N. Ltd. (1972). For the earlier history of Smethwick Drop Forgings see below p. 114.

and Averys converted the works to their own manufacture. An extensive building programme was also begun. By 1914 Averys had more than doubled the size of the works, and between the two World Wars there was extensive redevelopment. In the late 1960s W. & T. Avery Ltd. was the largest manufacturer of weighing, counting, measuring, and testing machines in the world; its products ranged from shop scales to weighbridges. The Foundry was also the headquarters of Averys Ltd., a holding company of which W. & T. Avery Ltd. was a subsidiary.[47] Muntz's has also disappeared. In 1921 the firm was taken over by a Birmingham non-ferrous metal company which in its turn became part of Imperial Chemical Industries Ltd. in 1928. The manufacture of non-ferrous metals at the French Walls Works ceased in 1932. In 1950 I.C.I.'s Paints Division occupied the 'New Side Works'. The 'Old Side Works' had been sold to a firm of tube manufacturers, George Burn Ltd.[48]

George Burn Ltd. was one of several tube-making firms which had come to the town since the 1880s. In 1889 the newly formed Credenda Seamless Tube Co. Ltd. bought the Bridge Street factory of the former Birmingham Plate Glass Co. and converted it into a tube mill, the Credenda Works. The business was bought in 1896 by a Birmingham firm, the Star Tube Co., which in 1897 became part of the combine known as Weldless Tubes Ltd. (later Tubes Ltd.). The works was closed in 1906.[49] Allen Everitt & Sons Ltd., a firm which specialized in the manufacture of condenser tubes, moved in stages from Birmingham to the Kingston Works in Bridge Street between the early 1890s and 1902. It was acquired in 1929 by I.C.I. and remained in business until 1958. Another I.C.I. subsidiary, Yorkshire Imperial Metals Ltd., was then formed to take in the Yorkshire Copper Works Ltd. of Leeds and the plate, tube, and fittings interests of I.C.I.; it was making non-ferrous tubes, fittings, and plates at the Kingston Works (renamed the Allen Everitt Works) in 1971.[50] The Smethwick Tube Co. was set up in Rolfe Street in 1920 and became part of George Burn Ltd., a Birmingham tube-making concern, in 1921. During the twenties and thirties Burns acquired a number of other premises in Rolfe Street, including the soap works of William Cliff & Sons, and replaced them by tube mills. Finally in 1937 the firm opened the City Tube and Conduit Mills in Rabone Lane on the site of Muntz's 'Old Side Works'. It became Burns's headquarters and main works; the Birmingham works was sold and the company concentrated all its activities in Smethwick. It remained there until 1971, when it moved to Shirley (Warws.).[51]

In 1908 the Birmingham firm of J. A. Phillips & Co. Ltd., manufacturer of bicycles and bicycle components, bought the Credenda Works and gave up its Birmingham premises. In 1949 the firm, by then a subsidiary of Tube Investments Ltd., employed some 2,000 people at the greatly enlarged Credenda Works, producing and distributing bicycle components. It was still at the works in 1971.[52] Another cycle firm, the Coventry-Eagle Cycle and Motor Co. Ltd., moved from Coventry to the Grove Lane Works in Wills Street in 1959 and remained in business in the town until 1968, when it moved to Barton-upon-Humber (Lincs.).[53]

Smethwick has had only one motor-car manufacturer, the short-lived Crescent Motors Ltd., maker of Crescent cars and cycle-cars; it moved from Walsall shortly before the First World War and ceased production in 1914 or 1915.[54] The town's contribution to the motor industry has been rather as a supplier of components. From c. 1900 Muntz's produced aluminium gear- and crank-cases and cover plates; William Mills Ltd., a Sunderland firm which moved to Grove Street in 1903, made iron and aluminium castings there for the motor industry.[55] In the 1920s the firm now known as Smethwick Drop Forgings Ltd., established in 1912 by A. Harper, Sons & Bean Ltd. of Dudley, made forgings for the Bean car.[56] Three Smethwick members of the large Smethwick-based foundry group, Birmid Qualcast Ltd., formed in 1967, have been substantial manufacturers of components. All have their works in Dartmouth Road. The Midland Motor Cylinder Co. Ltd. was set up in 1914 in Fawdry Street, where it made air-cooled cylinders for motor bicycles. It moved to Rolfe Street in 1916 and to its present site shortly after the First World War. In the late 1960s it specialized in the manufacture of grey-iron camshafts, cylinder blocks and heads, and brake drums. The Birmingham Aluminium Casting (1903) Co. Ltd. moved to Dartmouth Road from Birmingham at about the same date as Midland Motor Cylinder. In 1927 its 7-acre factory was described as one of the largest of its kind in Europe and the 2,000 workers were almost entirely engaged in the manufacture of castings for the motor-vehicle industry. In the late 1960s it produced pistons, gear-boxes, cylinder blocks, and steering-boxes. Dartmouth Auto Castings Ltd., which established its first foundry in 1933, was in the late 1960s using one of its two Smethwick foundries to make camshafts.[57] Another firm produc-

[47] Gale, *Soho Foundry*, 35 sqq.; *V.C.H. Staffs.* ii. 171; *Warley Official Guide* [1968], 69; Dun & Bradstreet, *Guide to Key British Enterprises* (1969 edn.).

[48] 'Old Smethwick', 28 Jan. 1950.

[49] Ibid. 12 Nov. 1949.

[50] Ibid. 26 Nov., 3 and 10 Dec. 1949; ex inf. Yorkshire Imperial Metals Ltd. (1972).

[51] 'Old Smethwick', 4 Feb. 1950; *Smethwick Official Industrial Handbook* [1959], 36–9; ex inf. Burns Tubes Ltd. (1972); below p. 117.

[52] 'Old Smethwick', 12 Nov. 1949; *Birmingham Area P.O. Telephone Dir.* (1971).

[53] *V.C.H. Warws.* viii. 175; *Kelly's Dir. Birm.* (1959; 1966–7); inf. from Coventry-Eagle Cycle and Motor Co. Ltd. (1972).

[54] G. R. Doyle, *The World's Automobiles* (1959 edn.), 57; G. R. Doyle and G. N. Georgano, *The World's Automo-*

biles, 1862–1962, 56; E. F. Carter, *Edwardian Cars*, 177, 239; D. Scott-Moncrieff, *Veteran and Edwardian Motor-cars*, 113.

[55] *Muntz's Metal Co. Ltd.* 11; *V.C.H. Staffs.* ii. 153–4.

[56] 'Old Smethwick', 10 Dec. 1949; *Express & Star*, 15 Oct. 1971; *V.C.H. Staffs.* ii. 153; Doyle and Georgano, *World's Automobiles*, 38.

[57] *This is Birmid Qualcast* (brochure pub. by Birmid Qualcast Ltd., 1967; copy in W.P.L.); *Proc. Inst. Mech. Eng.* (June 1927), 661; Dun & Bradstreet, *Guide to Key British Enterprises* (1969 edn.). For the Midland Motor Cylinder Co. Ltd. see also *Midcyl Golden Jubilee* (brochure pub. by the firm in 1965 to celebrate the 50th anniversary of its incorporation as a private company; copy in W.S.L. Pamphs.). In *V.C.H. Staffs.* ii. 154, the Birmingham Aluminium Casting Co. is wrongly named the British Aluminium Casting Co.

ing components for the motor industry in the late 1960s was the United Spring Co. Ltd., incorporated in 1932 to acquire a spring-making firm founded in 1912; it made springs for the motor-car, aircraft, and other industries at its Hawthorn Works in Oldbury Road.[58]

In 1904 Henry Hope & Sons Ltd., a Birmingham firm which specialized in making metal windows, roof glazing, and central heating, purchased some land at the corner of Dartmouth Road and Halford's Lane, upon which it built its Halford Works in 1905.[59] The works was gradually extended, and in 1919 all business was transferred to Smethwick. By the late 1950s the factory covered 10 a. In 1965 the firm merged with Crittall Manufacturing Co. Ltd. of Braintree (Essex), another firm which made metal windows, doors, and casements, to form Crittall-Hope Ltd. Braintree became the new company's headquarters and the Halford Works its Smethwick Division.

COAL-MINING. Although the Thick Coal underlies Smethwick, the district is situated beyond the fault which formed the eastern limit of early working in the South Staffordshire coalfield.[60] There was no mining in Smethwick until the 1870s, and it remained confined to a single colliery in the extreme north of the borough. During the previous half-century, however, there had been hopes of reaching coal in Smethwick,[61] and in fact the first boring east of the boundary fault is said to have been made at Smethwick on land belonging to James Horton; it reached 563 feet without finding coal or ironstone.[62]

In 1870 the Sandwell Park Colliery Co. was formed and sank a shaft east of Roebuck Lane on land belonging to Lord Dartmouth close to the junction of the Birmingham–Wolverhampton railway and the Stourbridge Extension line. The Thick Coal was reached in 1874 at a depth of 1,254 feet, and the news caused great excitement in Smethwick, West Bromwich, and Handsworth.[63] A second shaft was sunk in 1874–6; a third, begun in 1882, reached the coal at 1,263 feet in 1883.[64] The undertaking, later hailed as having 'put new life into the almost exhausted coalfield',[65] was the high point in the career of Henry Johnson, the mining engineer

(1823–85). It was through his exertions that the company was launched, and the directors appointed him engineer and secretary. To make the sinking he used dynamite, then still in a pioneer stage for industrial purposes.[66] In 1896 483 men were employed below ground at the colliery and 162 above.[67] The workings were mainly towards Handsworth, and none extended under the Birmingham Canal.[68] Production ceased in 1914, the company having by then opened a new colliery in West Bromwich to tap the area to the north of the first workings.[69]

GLASS. The history of the glass industry in Smethwick is largely that of Chance Brothers.[70] Glassmaking was introduced by Thomas Shutt, who began building a works on part of Blakeley Hall farm beside the Birmingham Canal west of Spon Lane apparently in 1814 and started making crown window-glass there apparently in 1815. Shutt worked in partnership,[71] and from 1816 until his death in 1822 the business was carried on as the British Crown Glass Co. The works was sold in 1822 by Joseph Stock and Thomas and Philip Palmer, two of the original partners, to Robert Lucas Chance.[72] From 1828 Chance was in partnership with John Hartley, and in 1832 Chance's brother William also became a partner. The firm, however, continued to operate as the British Crown Glass Co. On John Hartley's death in 1833 his sons James and John became partners, and the firm was renamed Chances & Hartleys. When the Hartleys left the partnership in 1836 the firm became Chance Brothers & Co.

On acquiring the works R. L. Chance immediately built a second glass-house and in 1828 a third. His most notable achievement was the introduction into England of the regular manufacture of sheet glass as an alternative to crown-glass. He began its production in 1832 with the aid of French and Belgian workers.[73] Chance's sheet glass was used for Joseph Paxton's Crystal Palace in 1851, the firm having already supplied glass for Paxton's experiments in glass building at Chatsworth (Derb.).[74] The site was enlarged in 1844 and schools were built on part of the new land, primarily for the children of employees.[75] By 1845 there were six glass-houses, four

[58] *Warley Official Guide* [1968], 77, 79; *Kelly's Dir. Birm.* (1965).
[59] For this para. see *Hope's Windows: a Short History of Henry Hope & Sons Ltd. 1818–1958* (pamph. pub. by Hopes, 1958; copy in W.P.L.); 'Old Smethwick', 30 Apr. 1949; *Smethwick Official Industrial Handbook* [1959], 47–9; inf. from Crittall-Hope (Smethwick Division) Ltd. (1972).
[60] *V.C.H. Staffs.* i. 16 and map preceding p. 1; ii. 68.
[61] S.R.O., D. 695/1/1/13; 'Smethwick and Round About', 14 Mar., 20 June 1952; C. Hicks, *A Walk through Smethwick* (Birmingham, 1850), 31–2 (copy in W.P.L.).
[62] T. Smith, *The Miner's Guide* (1836), 24, 196–9; F. G. Meachem, 'The Search for Coal over the Eastern Boundary Fault of the South Staffs. Coalfield', *Trans. Federated Institution of Mining Engineers*, viii. 401.
[63] *Staffs. Advertiser*, 14 Jan. 1871; ibid. (S. Staffs. edn.), 11 July 1874; Hackwood, *Smethwick*, 101, citing *Colliery Guardian*, 5 June 1874; S.R.O., D. 648/103/38 (plan of 1870); O.S. Map 6", Staffs. LXVIII. SE. (1890 edn.); above p. 106.
[64] Ex inf. National Coal Board, Stoke-on-Trent (1969).
[65] Hackwood, *Smethwick*, 101.
[66] Ibid.; *Dudley Herald*, 11 July 1885 (Johnson's obituary notice, a copy of which is in S.R.O., D. 564/8/1/22/July 1885); *V.C.H. Staffs.* ii. 81, 101.
[67] *Reps. of Inspector of Mines for South Stafford District or 1896* [C. 8450], p. 35, H.C. (1897), xx.

[68] W.P.L. 16960.
[69] Ibid.; Price, 'Smethwick', 49; S.R.O., D. 876/132; below p. 41.
[70] For the following account of Chances see, unless otherwise stated, J. F. Chance, *Hist. of Firm of Chance Brothers & Co.* (priv. print. 1919); *V.C.H. Staffs.* ii. 229. Further information has been supplied by Sir Hugh Chance, C.B.E., and Mr. N. K. Hadley of the Spon Lane Works, and their help is gratefully acknowledged.
[71] Information on the partnership has been supplied by Sir Hugh Chance from MS. notes in J. F. Chance's own copy of his *Chance of Bromsgrove and Birmingham* (priv. print. 1892).
[72] Birm. Univ. Libr., acct. book of R. L. Chance 1821–31, ff. 15–17, 19, 60–1, and accompanying notes by Sir Hugh Chance; archives at Chance Brothers Ltd., R. L. Chance's MS. of his speech of thanks for a testimonial, Sept. 1860. The hitherto accepted date of the sale has been 1824. The writer's attention was drawn to the new date and the sources for it by Sir Hugh Chance.
[73] See also p. 88.
[74] For the work at Chatsworth see C. R. Fay, *Palace of Industry, 1851*, 15–16. Most of the ironwork for the Crystal Palace was made by Fox, Henderson & Co: see above p. 111.
[75] For the schools see p. 138.

of them producing sheet, and to make room for a seventh it was decided to move the acid works[76] to Oldbury, in Halesowen (Worcs.), where the firm had had a chemical works since 1835. In 1851 the factory, with c. 1,200 employees, was said to be the largest crown and sheet glass-works in England.[77] Five new glass-houses were built in the earlier 1850s. From the 1850s the making of lighthouse glass was developed under the direction of James Timmins Chance (later Sir James Chance, Bt.). An 80-foot brick tower was built where the lights could be tested, and from 1859 land was bought for the extension of the lighthouse works, notably in 1867 when the site of the lighthouse erecting room was acquired. The firm produced not only the optical apparatus but also such lighthouse components as burners, lanterns, cast-iron towers, and revolving carriages and their clockwork. In 1898 a substantial government contract initiated a period of expansion and the rebuilding of the lighthouse works. In 1889 Chance Brothers & Co. became a private limited company. In 1935 the company issued preference shares and changed its style to Chance Brothers Ltd.[78] Pilkington Brothers of St. Helens (Lancs.) acquired a large interest in 1936 and in 1955 took over the company. In 1971 the Spon Lane works, occupying a 64-a. site, was producing rolled plate (including figured glass), tubing for fluorescent and incandescent lighting, microscope glass and slides, protective glass for welders, and decorative glass tableware. Among the older buildings which then survived were a house, then used as offices and apparently built by R. L. Chance in 1822, and a seven-storeyed building of 1847.

Chances also became involved with the Birmingham Plate Glass Co., which was formed in 1836 and built a works in Bridge Street.[79] An attempted merger with Chances & Hartleys that year was unsuccessful. The works was producing crown and sheet as well as plate by the mid 1840s and by 1867 had six glass-houses. There were further attempts at mergers with or sales to Chance Brothers in 1845, 1846, and 1867, but it was only in 1873 that Chances bought the works. Production was stopped in 1874 because of the poor quality of the glass and the difficulty of selling it. Operations began again in 1875 but ceased finally in 1877. As during the closure of 1874–5, business was then limited to the purchase and resale of glass made elsewhere. James

Chance acquired the interests of the other members of his family and in 1889 sold the works to the Credenda Seamless Tube Co. Ltd.

Chance Brothers developed the production of coloured glass from the later 1830s[80] but gave up making stained glass in 1867. Several of the principal artists then set up on their own.[81] Samuel Evans started in a small way at West Smethwick and then built a works in Oldbury Road, in part of which Evans & Co. Ltd. still produced decorative glass until 1971.[82] Thomas William Camm started making stained glass in Brewery Street before moving to larger premises, presumably the purpose-built studios still standing on the corner of High Street and Regent Street; with two breaks he continued to work in Smethwick until his death in 1912, and the business was then carried on by his daughter and two sons. The works was closed c. 1963.[83] Camm's three brothers, who had originally been associated with him, returned to Smethwick from Birmingham in 1893, and started a business in High Street as Camm Brothers; as Camm & Co. the business produced stained-glass windows and other decorative glass until c. 1966.[84]

CHEMICALS. In 1818 Thomas Adkins and John Nock owned 'an extensive soap work' on the north bank of the Birmingham Canal at Merry Hill. Soon afterwards the partners were joined by a Mr. Boyle, the inventor of a new method of bleaching soap. Boyle had been the works manager of Blair & Stephenson of Tipton, the country's leading producer of red lead; the new firm of Adkins, Nock & Boyle took advantage of his experience and began to make red lead as well as soap.[85] About 1836 the firm became Thomas Adkins & Co.[86] During the late 1830s or early 1840s the Tipton concern for which Boyle had worked was wound up, and for several years Adkins & Co. was the country's main supplier of red lead.[87] By the mid 1860s the principal makers of the best-quality red lead were Midland manufacturers and Adkins & Co. was one of the three leading firms in the area.[88] It also retained a prominent place among local soap-makers.[89] That side of the business appears to have been subsequently run down, and by the later 1880s the firm was concentrating on the manufacture of red lead.[90] After the death of G. C. Adkins, Thomas's son, in 1887 the business was bought by the Birmingham

[76] See p. 117.
[77] White, *Dir. Staffs.* (1851); plate facing p. 112 above.
[78] 'Old Smethwick', 29 Jan. 1949.
[79] For this para. see Chance, *Chance Brothers*, 21–5, 61–4, 108–10; 'Old Smethwick', 5 Nov. 1949. For an account of a visit to the works see W. White, *All Round the Wrekin* (1860), chap. xxiii.
[80] Chance, *Chance Brothers*, 14, 19, 35. *V.C.H. Staffs.* ii. 229, wrongly states in this connexion that Georges Bontemps, the French expert in the manufacture of coloured glass, was installed at Spon Lane in the late 1830s; he in fact came there in 1848 (Chance, *Chance Brothers*, 50–1, 189).
[81] Chance, *Chance Brothers*, 194–6.
[82] 'Smethwick and Round About', 21 July 1951, 21 and 28 Dec. 1956; local inf. (1971).
[83] 'Smethwick and Round About', 28 July, 6 Oct. 1951; ex inf. Miss Ethel Squires of Smethwick (1972). It last appears in *Kelly's Dir. Birm.* in 1962. The firm's archives are in W.P.L.
[84] 'Smethwick and Round About', 6 Oct. 1951; ex inf. W.P.L., which possesses the firm's archives.
[85] Pye, *Modern Birmingham*, 131, noting existence in summer 1818 of a Smethwick soapworks owned by

Adkins and Nock; *Birm. and Mid. Hardware Dist.* 168, 177, stating that Boyle joined the 2 Smethwick men c. 1817. For the Christian names of Adkins and Nock see W.S.L., S. MS. 417/Harborne. For the location of the factory: ibid.; O.S. Map 6", Staffs. LXXII. NE. (edns. of 1890 and 1905).
[86] Pigot, *Nat. Com. Dir.* (1835), 476, giving firm as Adkins, Nock & Boyle; (1841), Staffs. p. 95, giving it as Thos. Adkins & Co.; *Aris's Birmingham Gazette*, 15 Aug. 1836, advert. referring to property bounded on one side by the works of Messrs. Atkins (*sic*) & Co.
[87] *Birm. and Mid. Hardware Dist.* 177–8, noting Adkins's rise 'on the retirement of Messrs. Stephenson and Co. from the trade'. John Stephenson & Co. occurs in Pigot, *Nat. Com. Dir.* (1835), 455, but not ibid. (1841).
[88] *Birm. and Mid. Hardware Dist.* 178, noting as another of the 3 leading Midland firms 'Messrs. Lloyd & Co., Smethwick'. Lloyds' works was in fact in Downing St., Handsworth: see e.g. *P.O. Dir. Staffs.* (1860).
[89] *Birm. and Mid. Hardware Dist.* 176.
[90] In *Kelly's Dir. Birm.* (1888) the firm is listed among red-lead manufacturers but not among soap manufacturers. O.S. Map 6", Staffs. LXXII. NE. (1890 edn.), shows the building as 'Chemical Works'.

firm of Henry Wiggin & Co. Ltd., one of the most important in the nickel industry. Wiggins continued make red lead but used part of the site to build a cupola and reverberatory furnaces for smelting nickel and cobalt ores. In 1892 Dr. Ludwig Mond, with the co-operation of the firm, built on another part of the site the experimental plant at which he produced the first carbonyl-refined nickel made on an industrial scale.[91] In 1896 Wiggins began to make tin oxide at Smethwick. It was the first time it had been manufactured in Great Britain, and the plant had to be imported from Germany, previously the sole source of supply; it was also manned at first by German workers. Production continued until 1931. Shortly after the First World War Wiggins was taken over by the Mond Nickel Co. Ltd., which was in turn taken over in 1929 by the International Nickel Co. of Canada Ltd.[92]

A soap factory was established in Rolfe Street in 1845 by a Mr. Johnson.[93] The business passed through several hands in its early years. By 1866, when it was owned by J. P. Harvey, it was one of the leading soap firms in the Birmingham area. Its specialities were 'curd', a very hard soap extensively used in laundries and in blanket and carpet mills, and 'grey mottled', a household soap. The firm, which in 1887 became William Cliff & Sons, was one of the few small provincial concerns to remain independent of the great soap combines which were formed in the late 19th and early 20th centuries, and it remained a family business until it closed after the First World War. The works was sold to George Burn Ltd., which in 1931 demolished it to make way for a tube mill.

From its early days Chances made alkali for glass manufacture, as well as the glass itself, at Spon Lane. Bought sulphate of soda was at first used, but in 1834 the firm built its own vitriol chamber and salt-cake furnaces as part of the works. They continued in operation until 1845, when the whole of the chemical manufacturing side of the business was transferred to the chemical works which the firm had established at Oldbury in Halesowen (Worcs.) in 1835.[94]

H. S. Richards, an oil and colour merchant and an importer and refiner of oil and tallow, was manufacturing tannate of soda (used to remove scale from boilers), locomotive and colliery greases, lubricating oils, paints, varnishes, and liquid enamels at his Brook Street works by the 1880s. Alterations in the pattern of local industry led to changes in the firm's range of products: thus when the demand for black stoving enamels for iron bedsteads began to decline there was a growing market for similar enamels for use on vehicle chassis and springs. In the early 1970s H. S. Richards Ltd. was making paints, varnishes, japans, and enamels for industrial uses.[95]

BREWING. By 1834 there was a brewery on the corner of High Street and Brewery Street where the Midland Bank now stands. It was run by Thomas Robinson. In 1841 he was licensee of the Old Talbot near by on the corner of Trinity Street and apparently still occupied the brewery. By 1851 he had been succeeded at the Old Talbot by Sarah Robinson, evidently his widow; she was also a brewer, but it is not clear whether she brewed on the premises or continued at the near-by brewery. Her son Thomas too was a brewer in the 1850s.[96] Old Smethwick Brewery in Oldbury Road a little to the south of the Swan inn existed by the early 1840s when it was run by Joseph Morris.[97]

There were several brewers in Smethwick by 1851,[98] but the expansion of the industry dates from 1861 when Henry Mitchell (1837–1914) took over the Crown inn in Oldbury Road from his father.[99] Until then beer brewed at the Crown had been intended for consumption on the premises, but Henry proceeded to build up a wider retail trade. In 1866 he built the Crown Brewery on an adjoining site and by 1872 was trading as Henry Mitchell & Co. In 1878 he bought a 14-acre site on the south side of Cape Hill and began to build a new Crown Brewery there; brewing started in 1879. In 1888 he took a partner, H. G. Bainbridge, and in the same year the firm became a private limited company. In 1898 the business was amalgamated with that of William Butler of the Crown Brewery, Broad Street, Birmingham, and the new firm was styled Mitchells & Butlers Ltd.; Butler himself had been licensee of the London Works Tavern in Smethwick from 1866 to 1876. Because of the large area available at Cape Hill and the good supply of water from artesian wells the Birmingham business was moved there, and the brewery was renamed the Cape Hill Brewery. The site was enlarged to 60 a. in 1900 and to 90 a. in 1914. The No. 2 brewery built in 1912 more than doubled the size of the plant. A high red-brick wall dominates the lower end of Cape Hill; an ornamental gateway was demolished in 1974. Since 1967 Mitchells & Butlers Ltd. has been a marketing company within Bass Charrington Ltd.

In 1913 Mitchells & Butlers bought the Windmill Brewery which had been founded by Edward Cheshire. He had acquired several public houses and found his brewing facilities inadequate. He

[91] 'Old Smethwick', 23 and 30 Sept. 1950; A. C. Sturney, Story of Mond Nickel (priv. print. 1951), 7–11, 13–15 (copy in W.P.L.).

[92] 'Old Smethwick', 30 Sept. 1950; Sturney, Mond Nickel, 37, 44; J. F. Thompson and N. Beasley, For the Years to Come: a Story of International Nickel of Canada (New York and Toronto, 1960), 195, 206.

[93] For this para. see 'Old Smethwick', 19 Nov. 1949, 4 Feb. 1950; Birm. and Mid. Hardware Dist. 169, 176.

[94] J. F. Chance, Hist. of Firm of Chance Brothers & Co. (priv. print. 1919), 18–19, 23, 35. For an account of the firm see above pp. 115–16.

[95] Kelly's Dir. Birm. (1888), 528 and adverts. p. 62; Smethwick Official Industrial Handbook [1959], 32–3, giving the date of the firm's foundation as 1839; P.O. Telephone Dir. Sect 211: 1971.

[96] 'Old Smethwick', 23 July 1949; White, Dir. Staffs.

(1834), which, however, gives Robinson's address as near the Summit Bridge (i.e. near Roebuck Lane); Pigot, Nat. Com. Dir. (1835), 472; (1841), Staffs. p. 92; W.S.L., S. MS. 417/Harborne, no. 1491; Pigot, Dir. Birm. (1845), 94; H.O. 107/2050(2) f. 260; Slater, Dir. Staffs. (1859), 121.

[97] 'Old Smethwick', 23 July 1949; Harborne Tithe Appt., nos. 1623 and 1635a (copy in W.P.L.); White, Dir. Staffs. (1851); Pigot, Dir. Birm. (1845), 94; Slater, Dir. Staffs. (1859), 121.

[98] H.O. 107/2050(2).

[99] For the rest of this para. see Mitchells & Butlers Ltd. Fifty Years of Brewing, 1879–1929 (copy in W.P.L.); 'Old Smethwick', 14 Oct.–2 Dec. 1950; P.O. Dir. Staffs. (1872); Brewery Manual, 1971, 108; plate facing p. 113 above. For a description of processes at the Cape Hill Brewery in 1903 see V.C.H. Warws. ii. 268.

therefore began building a brewery near the windmill in Windmill Lane in 1886, and brewing started there at the end of 1887. The business became a private limited company in 1896. Having been acquired by Mitchells & Butlers, the brewery was closed in 1914, and Cape Hill remains the only brewery in Smethwick.[1]

OTHER INDUSTRIES. In 1850 the Lambeth firm of Henry Doulton & Co., which made drain-pipes and conduits, built a pipe-works at Smethwick.[2] It stood on the north bank of the Birmingham Canal and was approached from Brasshouse Lane by what is now Pottery Road. The firm (from 1854 Doulton & Co. and from 1899 Doulton & Co. Ltd.) probably opened the works because an official report on the sanitary condition of Birmingham published in 1849 stressed the need for improved drainage there.[3] Doultons, which already had a pipe-works at Rowley Regis, was thus offered the prospect of an enlarged market for its products. The works remained in operation until 1913, when transport costs led to its closure. It was used again intermittently during the First World War but was finally closed in 1919.

In 1898 the Birmingham Tile and Pottery Works, a small potworks later known as the Ruskin Pottery, was established in Oldbury Road, West Smethwick, by William Howson Taylor (1876–1935) and his father, Edward Richard Taylor (d. 1912). They produced fine art pottery, which was first called Taylor ware; from 1904, the year in which they won their first international award, it was known as Ruskin pottery. The works closed in 1935, shortly before Howson Taylor's death. There is a representative collection of Ruskin pottery, presented by Howson Taylor, at the public library in High Street.[4]

Among several firms making soft drinks in the town the oldest is T. Mason & Sons Ltd.[5] The business was started by Titus Mason, who in 1895 arranged for his soft drinks to be sold at an off-licence in Cape Hill. The specially designed factory in Grantham Road is one of the largest units of its kind in England.

In 1972 British Pens Ltd., of the Pedigree Works, Bearwood Road, was the only British firm still extensively engaged in the manufacture of steel pen-nibs.[6] A Birmingham firm, William Mitchell (Pens) Ltd., built the Pedigree Works in 1909[7] and transferred its business there. In 1920 Mitchells amalgamated with Hinks, Wells & Co., a Birmingham

pen-making firm, to form British Pens Ltd. Despite the decline of the steel pen after the Second World War the firm survived, acquiring the pen interests of other firms in the Birmingham area in the 1960s. By 1972 its pen production, almost wholly limited to the manufacture of lithographic, mapping, and lettering pens, was concentrated at the Bearwood Road factory, where presswork parts for machinery in steel and non-ferrous metals were also made.

LOCAL GOVERNMENT. There was a single court baron for the jointly held manors of Harborne and Smethwick probably by the late 13th century,[8] although by c. 1275 each manor had its own reeve.[9] It seems likely that the court had ceased to meet regularly by 1535.[10] That was certainly so by 1575 when the lord of Harborne and Smethwick held 'scantly one court in a whole year'.[11] It is not known where the court normally met, but in 1628 there is record of its meeting at Smethwick.[12] A court baron was held for Smethwick after the two manors were separated in 1710. Between at least 1757 and 1802 it met at irregular intervals, apparently when specially summoned to deal with conveyances of copyhold land.[13] In the 1890s it was stated that no manorial court or customs had existed within living memory and that there was no copyhold land in Smethwick.[14]

In the late 13th century Smethwick was doing suit with Harborne at the bishop's view of frankpledge at Lichfield.[15] Harborne and Smethwick were presenting jointly by three frankpledges at the bishop's view at Longdon by 1327; by 1640 a constable and a thirdborough were presenting.[16] Expenses for attendance at Longdon court still appear in the constable's accounts in 1780.[17]

Although part of Harborne parish Smethwick was recognized as a distinct township by the 14th century.[18] In 1668 'the parish of Harborne and Smethwick' is mentioned, and the usage occurs regularly in parish documents of the earlier 18th century.[19] In 1733 it was decided that parish meetings should be held alternately at Harborne and Smethwick 'for the ease of the said parish'.[20]

By the early 18th century, even before the building of the chapel, a churchwarden was being appointed for Smethwick by the Harborne vestry. The system remained in force until 1834, but after that year the vestry minutes simply record the appointment of two churchwardens for Harborne parish. In 1845 a chapelwarden for Smethwick was also

[1] 'Old Smethwick', 2 Dec. 1950, 27 Jan. 1951; Smethwick Civic News, Jan. 1961.
[2] For this para. see 'Old Smethwick', 7 May 1949; D. Eyles, Royal Doulton, 1815–1965, 44–8, 58, 108, 129.
[3] For the report see V.C.H. Warws. vii. 340.
[4] L. B. Powell, Howson Taylor: Master Potter (Birmingham, 1936; copy in W.P.L.); 'Smethwick and Round About', 20 and 27 May, 10 June, 8 July 1955; Ruskin Pottery (illustrated brochure, n.d.; copy in W.P.L.).
[5] For this para. see Warley Official Guide [1968], 83.
[6] Unless otherwise stated, this para. is based on inf. from British Pens Ltd. (1972).
[7] Date on façade of works.
[8] Tax. Eccl. (Rec. Com.), 251; B.R.L. 347166. In the latter the court is referred to as curia magna, but the word magna, though inserted as an afterthought, is incorrect.
[9] Court Rolls of the Manor of Hales, 1270–1307 (Worcs. Hist. Soc.), i. 21, 23.
[10] Profits of court then averaged only 1s. 8d. a year: Valor Eccl. (Rec. Com.), iii. 206.
[11] Req. 2/80/49.
[12] W.S.L. 82/17/43; 82/18/43.
[13] S.R.O., D. 1141/4/4, ct. bk. 1757–87; B.R.L. 445767–8. The court book is the only known set of court rolls for Smethwick manor.
[14] Hackwood, Smethwick, 48.
[15] Plac. de Quo Warr. (Rec. Com.), 711.
[16] S.R.O., D.(W.)1734/2/1/598, mm. 2d., 4; D.(W.) 1734/2/1/615.
[17] For these expenses in the 18th century see docs. at St. Peter's, Harborne, 151A (1704–5); ibid., 151D, ff. 169v., 219v., 220; W.P.L. 17628; B.R.L., Pickard 5618.
[18] See e.g. S.H.C. vii (1), 234; x (1), 102; 1923, 252–5; 1929, 297; 4th ser. vi. 11.
[19] B.R.L. 449574, ff. 12, 18; Redhead, Local Govt. 2; B.R.L., Pickard 5618; docs. at St. Peter's, Harborne, 151D, f. 230v. In 1341 there is reference to the church of Harborne and Smethwick: Inq. Non. (Rec. Com.), 131.
[20] Docs. at St. Peter's, Harborne, 151D, f. 227v.

appointed.[21] There was a beadle for Smethwick by 1816.[22]

It was the vestry's practice by the earlier 18th century to appoint a constable for the Smethwick side of the parish and a thirdborough for the Harborne side in one year, and vice versa the next year.[23] By 1830 there was simply a constable for each.[24] Under the Lighting and Watching Act of 1830 the vestry made various attempts to improve policing: it established a body of 'inspectors' for Harborne in 1830 and another for Smethwick in 1836, increased the number of parish constables, and paid some of them.[25]

The vestry was appointing two overseers of the poor for each side of the parish by the earlier 18th century, and separate accounts were kept.[26] By 1830 there was a single overseer for each side, but there was also a salaried assistant overseer for the whole parish.[27] In addition the parish had adopted Gilbert's Act of 1782 by 1796, when two guardians and a visitor of the workhouse occur.[28] From 1830, after the vestry had examined the provisions of the Act, five guardians for each side and a visitor were appointed; one of the ten guardians assumed chief responsibility and was paid a salary.[29] A parish workhouse had been built by 1785. About 1796, under the terms of Gilbert's Act, either this or a new house was fitted out for the reception and employment of the poor; it stood on part of the Parish Lands at the junction of the present Lordswood and Gillhurst Roads in Harborne.[30] In 1836 Smethwick passed with the rest of Harborne into the King's Norton poor-law union.[31]

A surveyor of the highways was appointed for each side by the vestry by the earlier 18th century.[32] From 1836 the vestry tried various new ways of managing the roads of the parish. In Smethwick the experiments included the appointment of a second surveyor, of a salaried assistant, and of a board of surveyors.[33]

A parish pound occurs in 1776.[34] By 1829 the vestry was appointing the pinner, but the lord of Harborne manor was responsible for the upkeep of the pound.[35] It is presumably to be identified with the pound that stood next to the toll-house at the junction of Bearwood Road and the Birmingham–Halesowen road in 1877.[36] There was also a Smethwich pound in Oldbury Road, a smithy being built on the site of it c. 1878.[37]

In 1853 a movement was started for the establishment of a local board of health for Smethwick, and a board with 12 elected members was set up in 1856.[38] In 1888 a proposal that Smethwick should become part of Birmingham was defeated at a meeting of the board only by the chairman's casting vote.[39] In 1890 the membership of the board was increased to 15, divided between five wards.[40] The board became an urban district council in 1894.[41] The local board held its first meeting at the Star in Rolfe Street and later met at the office, also in Rolfe Street, of Ralph Docker, a solicitor and part-time clerk to the board.[42] Public buildings were erected in High Street in 1866–7, designed in a Gothic style by Yeoville Thomason.[43] A building to the north, dating from 1880, housed the free library and the offices of the gas undertaking; it was also used by the magistrates of the West Bromwich petty sessional division who held fortnightly sessions at Smethwick from 1882.[44]

Smethwick became a borough in 1899[45] and a county borough in 1907.[46] The council consisted of 6 aldermen and 18 councillors representing six wards: Bearwood, Sandwell, Soho, Spon Lane, Uplands, and Victoria.[47] Smethwick put forward a proposal in 1920 for the extension of its boundary to include Oldbury urban district (Worcs.); shortage of space at that time was forcing the council to acquire land in Oldbury for housing.[48] The proposal achieved partial success when in 1928 the Warley Woods area of Oldbury was added to Smethwick. The number of wards was increased to eight: the new area became Warley Woods ward, and Cape ward was formed out of Bearwood ward. An alderman and three councillors were assigned to each of the new wards.[49] The borough was granted a commission of the peace in 1901 and a court of quarter sessions in 1919.[50] In 1945 Smethwick and West Bromwich were planning to amalgamate, but

[21] B.R.L., Pickard 5618; docs. at St. Peter's, Harborne, 14, Vestry Mins. 1829–57; ibid. 151A, 151D.
[22] Docs. at St. Peter's, Harborne, 14, Churchwardens' Bk. 1813–32, 11 Apr. 1816.
[23] B.R.L., Pickard 5618; docs. at St. Peter's, Harborne, 151D.
[24] Docs. at St. Peter's, Harborne, 14, Vestry Mins. 1829–57.
[25] Ibid. ff. 43–5, 107–8, 136–7, 149–50, and 27 Sept. 1842 sqq.; S.R.O., Q/APr 3; 11 Geo IV, c. 27.
[26] B.R.L., Pickard 5618; docs. at St. Peter's, Harborne, 151D.　　　　[27] Vestry Mins. 1829–57.
[28] Docs. at St. Peter's, Harborne, 151C.
[29] Vestry Mins. 1829–57.
[30] V.C.H. Warws. vii. 335; W.S.L., S. MS. 417/Harborne; 'Smethwick and Round About', 1 Feb. 1952. For the Parish Lands see below pp. 141–2.
[31] 3rd Ann. Rep. Poor Law Com. H.C. 546–I, p. 167 (1837), xxxi.
[32] B.R.L., Pickard 5618; docs. at St. Peter's, Harborne, 151D.　　　　[33] Vestry Mins. 1829–57.
[34] Redhead, Local Govt. 6.
[35] Vestry Mins. 1829–57, 22 Sept. 1829, 2 Apr. 1841, 31 Mar. 1847, 17 Aug. 1855.
[36] Town Clerk's Dept., Birmingham, deed packet no. 657, abstract of title of trustees of G. C. Adkins 1902; 'Smethwick and Round About', 1 Feb. 1952; above p. 97.　　　　[37] 'Old Smethwick', 18 Dec. 1948.
[38] Redhead, Local Govt. 25–9; Lond. Gaz. 25 Apr. 1856, pp. 1538–40.

[39] 'Old Smethwick', 26 Aug. 1950.
[40] Hackwood, Smethwick, 106; Smethwick Local Board of Health 1891–2 Members, Meetings, etc. (copy in W.P.L.).
[41] Hackwood, Smethwick, 106; W.P.L., Min. Bk. 15, pp. 228, 240, 246.
[42] W.P.L., Min. Bk. 1, pp. 1, 5, 7, 9, 30.
[43] Hackwood, Smethwick, 103; 'Smethwick and Round About', 20 Sept. 1957; Pevsner, Worcs. 91; plate facing p. 97 above.
[44] S.R.O., Q/SOp 3, 17 Oct. 1881; Staffs. Advertiser (S. Staffs. edn.), 20 May 1882; Kelly's Dir. Birm. (1882); 'Smethwick and Round About', 20 July 1956; below p. 135.
[45] Hackwood, Smethwick, 107–9; K. W. Inskip, Smethwick: from Hamlet to County Borough (Smethwick, 1966), 10 (copy in W.P.L.); 'Old Smethwick', 31 Dec. 1949; Lond. Gaz. 18 Apr. 1899, pp. 2461–6; printed copy of charter of incorporation in W.P.L.
[46] Local Govt. Board's Provisional Order Confirmation (No. 6) Act, 1906, 6 Edw. VII, c. 105 (Local).
[47] Boro. of Smethwick Municipal Diary 1900–1 (copy in W.P.L.).
[48] County Boro. of Smethwick, Representation to Minister of Health for Alteration of Boundary of Boro. (1920; copy in W.P.L.); W.P.L. 3017; below p. 121.
[49] Smethwick Corp. Act, 1927, 17 & 18 Geo. V, c. 65 (Local).
[50] County Boro. of Smethwick, Representation to Minister of Health (1920), 3; Smethwick Telephone, 4 Jan. 1902.

in the event the only amalgamation was that of the two fire brigades in 1948.[51] In 1966, as part of the reorganization of local government in the West Midlands, Smethwick county borough became part of the new Worcestershire county borough of Warley,[52] which in 1974 became part of the metropolitan borough of Sandwell.[53]

The Labour party secured a majority on the borough council in 1926. In 1928, after the creation of the two new wards, the Unionists and Independents combined had as many seats as Labour, but the Labour party again secured a majority in 1929. Between 1930 and 1933 there seems to have been some fluctuation in control, but in 1934 the Conservatives had an over-all majority. They kept it until 1945 when the Labour party won control, retaining it until 1964. Racial matters had by then become an issue. The Conservatives took control in 1964 and kept it for the rest of the existence of the borough.[54]

The public buildings in High Street were replaced by the Council House, also in High Street, which was built in 1905–7. It was designed by F. J. Gill of Smethwick in a style that has been described as 'a free, somewhat Baroque William and Mary'; of brick and Bath stone, it consists of two storeys with a central portico and a cupola.[55] An extension, linked to the main building by a bridge, was opened in 1957.[56] The first public buildings, after being used as an employment exchange, were converted into the central library in 1927–8.[57] The court-house on the corner of Crockett's Lane and Piddock Street was built in 1931.[58]

The insignia of the former borough include a gold mayoral chain presented in 1899 by Jabez Lones, the first mayor (1899–1901), and his business partner Edward Holden, and a silver mace given by Samuel Smith, mayor in 1901–2.[59] The seal of the borough in use from 1899 to 1907 depicted the unregistered arms. That in use from 1907 to 1966 depicted the arms granted in 1907 but was otherwise similar.[60] It was circular, 2½"; legend, humanistic: COMMON SEAL OF THE MAYOR ALDERMEN AND BURGESSES OF THE BOROUGH OF SMETHWICK.

The arms of the borough from 1899 to 1907 were quartered to represent various industries of the town and showed a pumping engine, a lighthouse, a gasholder, and a worker at an anvil; the motto was 'Orbis terrarum officina'.[61] New arms were granted in 1907 which were derived partly from those of James Watt, Matthew Boulton, and Sir James Timmins Chance and also contained emblems representing various industries of the town; the motto,

'labore et ingenio', was that of James Watt reversed.[62]

THE BOROUGH OF SMETHWICK. *Or, a club in bend sinister surmounted by a caduceus in bend dexter, both proper; on a chief azure a beacon fired, between two symbols of the planet Mars or.* [Granted 1907]

A complete list of mayors is given in the *County Borough of Smethwick Municipal Year Book 1965–1966*.

PUBLIC SERVICES. By the mid 19th century Smethwick had the usual sanitary problems of a growing town.[63] There was no system of drains, and refuse collected in stagnant cesspools or on the roads. There was a surface drain in Rolfe Street, but in 1854 the district medical officer of the poor-law union reported that it was blocked up and that as a result his cellar was full of water. Refuse was collected by farmers, but only when convenient to themselves. Such conditions meant that the town was never free from fever, and epidemics were not uncommon. Chances' workers who lived in Scotch Row near the glass-works were constantly ill until R. L. Chance had drains and paving laid down in the earlier 1840s; at once there was a remarkable improvement in health. One of the duties of the doctor engaged by Chances from 1843 was to inspect the state of workers' houses. The Spon Lane area, Rolfe Street, Cross Street, and Windmill Street (presumably Windmill Lane) were described in 1854 as particularly insanitary. Cottages in the town were small, overcrowded, and badly ventilated. In 1862 twelve houses in Slough Lane (now Wellington Street) had only two privies between them; in 1871 the 40 houses in the same road had one privy to every three houses, and both houses and privies were dirty. The 28 houses in the court off Bridge Street known as Kingston Square (demolished in 1933),[64] had only eight privies between them, two in each corner of the square; in 1871 all the privies were found to be filthy and badly constructed. The numerous pigsties were another nuisance; it was stated in 1850 that 'the effluvia, nastiness, and dirt incident thereto are most injurious to the health of

[51] See pp. 122, 136–7.
[52] West Midlands Order 1965, S.I. 1965, no. 2139, pp. 5–7, 85–6, 120, 122–3.
[53] Local Govt. Act 1972, c. 70; The Metropolitan Districts (Names) Order 1973, S.I. 1973, no. 137; letters patent of 27 Feb. 1974 granting the district of Sandwell borough status (in possession of the chief executive).
[54] *Smethwick Telephone*, 6 Nov. 1926, 24 Mar. 1928, 9 Nov. 1929, 7 Nov. 1931, 5 Nov. 1932, 4 Nov. 1933, 3 Nov. 1934, 9 Nov. 1935, 5 Nov. 1938, 10 Nov. 1945, 18 May 1962, 15 May and 3 July 1964, 21 May 1965; *Birmingham Post*, 3 Nov. 1930; below p. 123.
[55] Pevsner, *Worcs.* 91; inscription on foundation-stone and plaque at entrance.
[56] County Boro. of Smethwick, *Formal Opening of First Phase of the Council House Extension . . . 22nd May 1957* (copy in W.P.L.).
[57] *Smethwick Official Handbook* [1959], 53; below p. 135.

[58] *Smethwick Telephone*, 7 Nov. 1931; *Kelly's Dir. Birm.* (1932).
[59] Inscriptions on chain and mace; 'Old Smethwick', 25 Sept. 1948; Inskip, *Smethwick*, 12.
[60] Ex inf. Mr. D. B. J. Hodgetts, Town Clerk's Dept., Warley (1971); die of 1907 seal in possession of the town clerk of Warley (1971).
[61] To be found e.g. on the mace.
[62] W.P.L. 501; Inskip, *Smethwick*, inside front cover.
[63] For this para. see Redhead, *Local Govt.* 25–7, 33–4; C. Hicks, *A Walk through Smethwick* (Birmingham, 1850), 18–19, 29 (copy in W.P.L.); R. Rawlinson, *Rep. to General Board of Health on a Preliminary Inquiry into . . . Smethwick* (1855; copy in W.S.L.); J. F. Chance, *Hist. of Firm of Chance Brothers & Co.* (priv. print. 1919), 248; W.P.L., Min. Bk. 4, pp. 68–70.
[64] 'Smethwick and Round About', 30 Nov. 1956. For 15 houses in Kingston Square in 1851 see H.O. 107/2050(2) ff. 288v.–290v.

families, which your dried flitch and cured ham strung up in your kitchens by no means compensate'. In 1871 a pigsty built against a house in Vittoria Street was causing a stench which was 'very detrimental' to the occupants. Smoke nuisance too was prevalent by the 1850s. In 1854 a surgeon stated that when the wind blew from the south-west the smoke from a chemical works took the bark off the trees and killed the leaves; he did not, however, know whether the smoke was prejudicial to human life. All the same it was claimed in 1854 that Smethwick's sanitary condition compared favourably with that of Oldbury, West Bromwich, and Bilston and that as far as buildings went the town was not yet overcrowded.

The local board of health established in 1856 soon appointed a surveyor and an inspector of nuisances.[65] In 1871, after receiving a report on the insanitary state of Kingston Square, Slough Lane, and Vittoria Street, the board appointed a medical officer of health.[66] The board turned its attention to smoke nuisance but apparently without effect; indeed in 1858 a motion to enforce the provision of the Local Government Act of that year requiring factories to consume their own smoke was defeated by five votes to three.[67] In 1859 the board made a by-law forbidding the erection of back-to-back houses.[68] In 1877 the Tame and Rea Drainage Board was formed to deal with the drainage and sewage of a large area including Smethwick.[69] Sewers were being laid from 1888, and the system was completed in 1895. The conversion of privies into water-closets and the abolition of middens was then undertaken by the urban district council, and by 1907 nearly 4,500 water-closets had been provided and nearly 3,000 middens removed.[70] A refuse destructor was built in Rolfe Street in 1908.[71] In 1949 the corporation began a series of measures to combat smoke nuisance.[72]

In 1920 the corporation was arranging the erection of 600 houses, although lack of space forced it to site well over half of them within the urban district of Oldbury (Worcs.). Indeed, when the Warley Woods area of Oldbury was added to Smethwick in 1928, housing was quickly built there.[73] In 1933 the corporation began a two-year drive to deal with unfit property, including the demolition or conversion of the 314 back-to-back houses in the borough.[74] By 1939 it had built 4,759 houses; 1,178 of them were then within the borough of Oldbury.[75] The

outbreak of war halted slum clearance, and in 1945 6,000 of Smethwick's 21,400 houses were substandard. It was not until 1958 that the corporation began a full attack on substandard housing, starting with the Windmill Lane area.[76] Extensive clearance was still in progress in 1971. Scarcity of land for new houses remained a problem after the war, and by 1959 the corporation had built 252 houses in West Bromwich as well as more in Oldbury.[77] The last major development of land owned by the corporation outside the borough was the Kingsway estate in the Quinton part of Oldbury, which was being built in 1962.[78] By 1966 the corporation had built some 8,400 dwellings, many of them in multi-storey blocks to make the most of the land available.[79]

In 1857 the South Staffordshire Water Works Co. promoted a Bill to extend its area of supply to Smethwick. The local board opposed the Bill with the claim that Smethwick had streams of good-quality water flowing through the parish sufficient for double the population. The board also hoped that a supply would come from the Birmingham Waterworks Co. whose rates were lower. The board withdrew its opposition when a clause was inserted in the Bill making the South Staffordshire company's power to supply Smethwick dependent on a request from the board. The company began laying mains in the district in 1862.[80] Even so in 1871 the 28 houses in Kingston Square were still dependent on a pump in the centre of the square; in Vittoria Street 20 houses were without water, although the near-by Slough Lane on the eastern boundary was supplied by the Birmingham company.[81]

The public baths in Rolfe Street were built in 1888 to the designs of Harris, Martin & Harris of Birmingham. Those at the Bearwood end of Thimblemill Road, the main baths for the area, were opened in 1933 and extended in 1966. The slipper baths in Malkin Street, West Smethwick, date from 1929 and those at Cape Hill from 1954.[82]

A smallpox epidemic in 1883–4 led to the building of an infectious diseases hospital in Holly Lane.[83] It was closed after Smethwick became a member of the South Staffordshire Joint Smallpox Hospital Board in 1904 and a hospital had been built at Moxley in Wednesbury. In 1906–7 Oldbury urban district council and Smethwick built an infectious diseases hospital to serve both places on the site of the Holly Lane hospital.[84] Since 1954 it has been

[65] W.P.L., Min. Bk. 1, pp. 28, 31.
[66] Min. Bk. 4, pp. 68–71, 83–4.
[67] Redhead, *Local Govt.* 33–4; 'Smethwick and Round About', 18 Apr. 1952.
[68] H. Paul, 'Back-to-back Houses' (copy in W.P.L. of article in unident. jnl. of 1935), 64.
[69] Hackwood, *Smethwick*, 104; Local Govt. Board's Provisional Orders Confirmation (Joint Boards) Act, 1877, 40 & 41 Vic. c. 229 (Local).
[70] Hackwood, *Smethwick*, 104; *County Boro. of Smethwick: Ann. Rep. for 1907 of M.O.H.* 40 (copy in S.R.O., C/H/1/2/2/39).
[71] County Boro. of Smethwick, *Official Opening of New Refuse Disposal Plant, Rolfe St., Smethwick . . . 29th Aug. 1956* (copy in W.P.L.).
[72] *Smethwick Civic News*, May 1954, Nov. 1961 (copy in W.P.L.).
[73] County Boro. of Smethwick, *Representation to Minister of Health for Alteration of Boundary of Boro.* (1920), 6 (copy in W.P.L.); above p. 96.
[74] Paul, 'Back-to-back Houses', 64–5, 68; *Smethwick Telephone*, 4 Nov. 1933.

[75] *Smethwick Official Handbook* (7th edn.), 35.
[76] West Midland Group, *Conurbation*, 91–2, 94.
[77] *Smethwick Official Handbook* [1959], 64; above p. 9.
[78] *Smethwick Civic News*, Oct. 1962.
[79] K. W. Inskip, *Smethwick: from Hamlet to County Borough* (Smethwick, 1966), 11 (copy in W.P.L.); Mann, 'Smethwick', 50; *Smethwick Official Industrial Handbook* (1959), 64.
[80] Redhead, *Local Govt.* 30–1; *Smethwick Civic News*, Oct. 1954.
[81] W.P.L., Min. Bk. 4, pp. 68–9.
[82] 'Smethwick and Round About', 5 Aug. 1955; *Kelly's Dir. Birm.* (1890); County Boro. of Smethwick, *Opening of Smethwick Baths, Thimblemill Rd., Smethwick, Mar. 30th, 1933* (copy in W.P.L.); County Boro. of Smethwick, *Formal Opening of Slipper Baths, Cape Hill . . . 1st Oct. 1954* (copy in W.P.L.).
[83] Hackwood, *Smethwick*, 104.
[84] *Representation to Minister of Health* (1920), 8, 14–16; *Smethwick and Oldbury Joint Isolation Hospital: Souvenir and Programme of Opening Ceremony 12th Sept. 1907* (copy in W.P.L.); *Ann. Rep. for 1907 of M.O.H.* 29.

the Midland Centre for Neurosurgery and Neurology.[85] In 1934–5 Smethwick corporation bought and extended St. Chad's Hospital in Hagley Road, Birmingham, built some 20 years before by the Edgbaston Private Nursing Home Ltd.[86]

The first cemetery in Smethwick was that at West Smethwick which was opened in 1857; it belonged, however, to the Oldbury burial board.[87] The architect of the chapels was W. Wigginton.[88] Holy Trinity churchyard was then the main burial ground for Smethwick. Its closure had become necessary for sanitary reasons by 1885 but was postponed until the local board should open a cemetery.[89] The board had been constituted a burial board in 1884, but the provision of a cemetery was delayed by the decision of the nonconformist majority on the board not to allow any part of a new cemetery to be consecrated. Their aim was to prevent the Anglican clergy from enjoying an advantage over the nonconformist ministers in the matter of fees. The four vicars of the town waived all such financial privileges, but the cemetery opened in Holly Lane in 1886 was never consecrated.[90] In 1890, however, Uplands cemetery was opened with a consecrated section.[91]

A county police force was established in Harborne parish in 1840.[92] A police station was built in High Street, Smethwick, a little to the south of Queen Street in 1860;[93] it was replaced by the station in Piddock Road in 1907.[94]

In the 19th century several firms formed their own fire brigades—Chances in 1843, Mitchells in 1882, Tangyes by 1885, and the Credenda Seamless Tube Co. c. 1890; the Birmingham Railway Carriage and Wagon Co. also had a brigade. A volunteer brigade was formed for the area in 1878 with an engine housed at the depot of the local board's highway department behind the public buildings. The fire station in Rolfe Street was opened in 1910; the adjoining block of twelve flats for married firemen dates from 1933.[95] In 1948 Smethwick became a joint fire authority with West Bromwich, and the arrangement lasted until the local government reorganization of 1966.[96] The new county borough of Warley then formed its own brigade with headquarters in Rolfe Street.[97]

From the beginning of 1857 the Birmingham and Staffordshire Gas Light Co. provided gas for 112 street lamps. The main road through the town, however, was not included since it was the responsibility of the turnpike trustees. Agreement was reached between the local board and the trustees for the lighting of the section of the road northwards from Watery Lane at the end of 1858, but it was not until 1863 that arrangements were agreed for the remainder.[98] In 1876 an Act empowered the board to establish its own gas undertaking,[99] and the works in Rabone Lane was opened in 1881. With nationalization in 1949 the undertaking passed from Smethwick corporation to the West Midlands Gas Board.[1]

In 1898 the urban district council was empowered by Act to supply electricity in its area,[2] and a generating station was built in Downing Street.[3] In 1907 the corporation transferred its undertaking to the Birmingham and Midland Tramways Ltd. (renamed the Birmingham District Power and Traction Co. Ltd. in 1912), which under an Act of 1913 transferred its rights to the Shropshire, Worcestershire and Staffordshire Electric Power Co.[4] With nationalization in 1948 the undertaking passed to the Midlands Electricity Board.[5]

A steam tramway from Birmingham to Dudley via Smethwick was opened by Birmingham and Midland Tramways Ltd. in 1885, with a branch from West Smethwick along Spon Lane to West Bromwich.[6] The depot was at West Smethwick. In 1902 Smethwick corporation bought the tramways in the borough but leased them to Birmingham and Midland Tramways, which had passed under the control of the British Electric Traction Co. Ltd. in 1900. Electric trams began operating on the Birmingham–Dudley line in 1904. New electrified branches were opened to Bearwood and along Waterloo Road in 1904 and to Soho station along Heath and Cranford Streets in 1905. In 1906 Birmingham corporation took over some of the shorter routes. All the Smethwick trams were replaced by buses in 1939, with Birmingham corporation working the Soho and Bearwood routes and the Birmingham and Midland Motor Omnibus Co. ('Midland Red') working the route to Dudley. There is a large bus garage in Bearwood Road, Bearwood, dating from 1914.[7]

Until 1837 the inhabitants of Smethwick had to go to Birmingham to send and collect mail.[8] In

[85] Express & Star, 12 Oct. 1971.
[86] St. Chad's Hospital: Opening Ceremony June 27th 1935 (copy in W.P.L.).
[87] 'Old Smethwick', 9 Oct. 1948; Kelly's Dir. Worcs. (1888), sub Oldbury.
[88] The Builder, 30 May 1857, p. 312.
[89] W.P.L., D.R.O. 15/Misc. A/22; Lich. Dioc. Mag. 1885, 136.
[90] Lich. Dioc. Mag. 1885, 136; Hackwood, Smethwick, 105; 'Old Smethwick', 16 July 1949.
[91] Hackwood, Smethwick, 105; Lich. Dioc. Regy., B/A/2(i)/T, pp. 297–300, 346–9.
[92] Docs. at St. Peter's, Harborne, 14, Vestry Mins. 1829–57, 27 Mar. 1840; S.R.O., Q/APr 2, rep. of supt. of police Apr. 1840.
[93] S.R.O., C/C/D/16/1; C/PC/VIII/6/1/1; O.S. Map 6″, Staffs. LXXII. NE. (1890 edn.).
[94] Smethwick Almanack (1911), 33. The building carries the date 1906.
[95] 'Smethwick and Round About', 24 Sept.–12 Nov. 1954; Smethwick Telephone, 17 June 1933; Mitchells & Butlers Ltd. Fifty Years of Brewing, 1879–1929, 102–3, 108 (copy in W.P.L.); 'Old Smethwick', 12 Nov. 1949.
[96] See p. 49.
[97] Warley Official Guide [1968], 45.

[98] Smethwick Civic News, Sept. 1954; Redhead, Local Govt. 30; Hackwood, Smethwick, 103.
[99] Smethwick Local Board (Gas) Act, 1876, 39 & 40 Vic. c. 171 (Local). And see above p. 49 for the general background.
[1] Staffs. Advertiser, 8 Oct. 1881, p. 7; W. Midlands Gas Board, Smethwick Gas Works 1955 (copy in W.P.L.).
[2] Electric Lighting Orders Confirmation (No. 10) Act, 1898, 61 & 62 Vic. c. 93 (Local).
[3] Smethwick Almanack (1911), 13.
[4] Electric Lighting Orders Confirmation (No. 1) Act, 1910, 10 Edw. VII & 1 Geo. V, c. 75 (Local); Electric Lighting Orders Confirmation (No. 5) Act, 1913, 3 & 4 Geo. V, c. 153 (Local); Smethwick Official Handbook [c. 1922], 40.
[5] Smethwick Official Guide (7th edn.), 25; (8th edn.), 83.
[6] For this para. see, except where otherwise stated, J. S. Webb, Black Country Tramways, i (Bloxwich, priv. print. 1974), 64, 179–80, 191–4, 199; J. S. Webb, Tramways of the Black Country (Bloxwich, 1954), 33 (copy in W.P.L.). For the Spon Lane route see above pp. 49–50.
[7] The façade carries the dates 1914 and 1925.
[8] For this para. see 'Old Smethwick', 17 and 24 Feb., 23 July, 6 Aug. 1949; 'Smethwick and Round About', 3 June 1955; Smethwick Telephone, 3 Oct. 1968.

that year a post office was opened in a small house in what is now High Street. The first postmaster was Joseph Vernon, a coal dealer and owner of a general store, who had led the agitation for a local post office. The office was managed by his daughter, and his sons acted as the postmen. Vernon remained postmaster until his death in 1866 when his daughter succeeded him. On her marriage her husband became postmaster, but she retained the management of the High Street office until her retirement in 1884. In 1890 a new head post office was opened in Rolfe Street. It was replaced by the office in Trinity Street in 1968.

Parks and libraries are treated elsewhere.[9]

PARLIAMENTARY HISTORY. In 1918 the borough of Smethwick, formerly included in the Handsworth division of the county, became a separate constituency.[10] At the election of that year the Labour candidate won against Christabel Pankhurst, the Coalition candidate, and Labour held the seat until 1931.[11] The member from 1926 to 1931 was O. E. Mosley (from 1928 Sir Oswald Mosley, Bt.), Chancellor of the Duchy of Lancaster 1929–30. In March 1931, after his resignation from the Labour Party, Sir Oswald formed the New Party, but he continued to represent Smethwick until the dissolution of Parliament later the same year.[12] From 1931 until 1945 Smethwick had a Conservative member, but Labour recaptured the seat at the general election of July 1945.[13] From October 1945 until 1964 the member was P. C. Gordon Walker, Secretary of State for Commonwealth Relations 1950–1 and Secretary of State for Foreign Affairs 1964–5.[14] In 1964 a Conservative, Alderman P. H. S. Griffiths, was elected. By that time the question of coloured immigrants had become an issue in both the parliamentary and the municipal politics of Smethwick. Since 1966 the seat has been held by a Labour member.[15]

CHURCHES. Until the 19th century Smethwick lay within the parish of St. Peter, Harborne. A chapel was consecrated at Smethwick in 1732, but it was not until 1842 that it was assigned a district. A second church was consecrated in 1838 and was assigned a parish in 1842. By 1905 there were eight independent churches in Smethwick and several mission centres. In that year all were transferred from Lichfield diocese to the new diocese of Birmingham.[16]

The first church in Smethwick was founded by Dorothy Parkes of Birmingham, daughter of Thomas Parkes of Smethwick. In 1719 she settled lands in Smethwick and in Halesowen (Worcs.) on trustees who were to build and furnish a chapel on part of the Smethwick property within three years of her death; if possible, the cost was not to exceed £800. The trustees were to provide bread and wine for communion, appoint a paid clerk or sexton, and lay out and maintain the chapelyard. They were to appoint the minister, who was to be a graduate and was not to hold any other ecclesiastical or teaching post; his stipend was to be the residue of the income from the property after the payment of £10 in charitable doles.[17] By her will of 1723[18] Dorothy confirmed the settlement of 1719 and gave a further £800 which, with any interest accruing, was to be used to build the chapel. She also left her 'divinity books and other books' for the use of the ministers of Harborne and Smethwick in accordance with the Parochial Libraries Act of 1708.[19] She left the residue of her personal estate for the building of a house near the chapel for the minister. By a codicil of 1725 she nominated John Williams, curate of St. Martin's, Birmingham, as the first minister. Robert Boyse, who was related to at least three of the trustees, was to be Williams's successor or the first minister if Williams declined the appointment. Dorothy also stipulated that her godson Thomas Bradburne should be offered the curacy after Boyse's death or resignation, but in fact he never held it.[20]

Dorothy died in 1728.[21] The new chapel was consecrated in September 1732, and Robert Boyse became the first perpetual curate in October.[22] A house was built opposite the church in what is now Church Road apparently in the mid 1730s.[23] By 1739 the trustees' annual income was £84, of which £10 was kept for the charitable doles; the remainder was paid to the minister, who had to provide bread and wine for communion out of it and pay for repairs to the church. Boyse also took fees for burials, which should have gone to the vicar of Harborne. His right to do so was challenged by the parish vestry in 1738, and in 1739 he agreed to desist.[24] At first marriages as well as baptisms and burials were conducted at Smethwick. After 1743, however, marriages by banns, and after 1758 even marriages by licence, ceased officially; it was not until 1839 that the chapel was licensed for marriages. It appears that in fact marriages continued unofficially at Smethwick, although they were recorded in the Harborne registers.[25] Harborne lay

[9] See pp. 89, 92–4, 96, 135.

[10] Representation of the People Act, 1918, 7 & 8 Geo. V, c. 64; *V.C.H. Staffs.* i. 273.

[11] 'Old Smethwick', 7 Jan. 1950; F. W. S. Craig, *British Parliamentary Election Results, 1918–1949* (Glasgow, 1969), 241.

[12] Sir Oswald Mosley, *My Life*, 17, 190–2, 230, 237, 247–50, 283; *Staffs. Advertiser*, 10 Oct. 1931, p. 7.

[13] Craig, *Parl. Election Results*, 241.

[14] *Dod's Parl. Companion* (1946); *Whitaker's Almanack* (1946 and later edns. to 1965).

[15] *Whitaker's Almanack* (1965 and later edns. to 1971); P. Foot, *Immigration and Race in British Politics*; *The Guardian*, 6 Feb. 1970.

[16] *V.C.H. Staffs.* iii. 89–90 and n., 95, 98.

[17] Hackwood, *Smethwick*, 51–5; volume of estate maps (1815) in possession of the secretary to the trustees of Dorothy Parkes (Lee, Crowder & Co., Birmingham). For the doles see below p. 142.

[18] Hackwood, *Smethwick*, 55–8; B.R.L., Lee Crowder 346 (including codicils omitted by Hackwood).

[19] 7 Anne, c. 14.

[20] B.R.L., Lee Crowder 346. For Boyse see A. L. Reade, *Johnsonian Gleanings* (priv. print.), v (1928), 100–1; x (1936), 99; Shaw, *Staffs.* ii. 126; 'Smethwick and Round About', 9 June 1951. Randall Bradburne, a Birmingham ironmonger, was one of the 1719 trustees.

[21] L.J.R.O., B/V/7/Harborne.

[22] Dean and Chapter Libr., Lichfield, 2/2/Smethwick. The faculty was granted in 1730 and described the chapel as 'jamjam extructam et edificatam'.

[23] Shaw, *Staffs.* ii. 126; B.R.L., Lee Crowder 346, acct. book of Sir Thos. Birch, pp. 3, 5; ibid., ground-plan of the house; volume of estate maps (1815).

[24] Docs. at St. Peter's, Harborne, 103; ibid., 151D, f. 226.

[25] Hackwood, *Smethwick*, 49, 61; Lich. Dioc. Regy., B/A/1/30, p. 142; B/A/2(i)/L, pp. 142–3.

within the peculiar jurisdiction of the dean and chapter of Lichfield, and in 1807 a dispute arose when the dean attempted a visitation of Smethwick. The curate refused to admit him, and the trustees supported the curate. In the course of the dispute it emerged that only the second of the three curates who had so far held office had been licensed by the chapter. In 1808 the trustees submitted and recognized the chapter's jurisdiction.[26] In the early 1820s the endowments, c. 75 a. in Smethwick and c. 33 a. in Halesowen, were bringing in £250 a year. The whole sum was paid to the minister, who met the

churches were opened in the chapelry, St. Matthew's in 1855 and St. Chad's in 1882; a third, St. Mary's, was opened in 1888.[33]

The church has no dedication. Originally it was called Parkes's Chapel,[34] but it was more usually known as Smethwick Chapel.[35] With the building of Holy Trinity Church in 1837–8 it became known as the Old Chapel,[36] and it is now called *SMETH-WICK OLD CHURCH*, the name which came into general use in the later 19th century.[37] It is a classical building of brick with stone dressings. There is a west tower, with a clock given in 1932

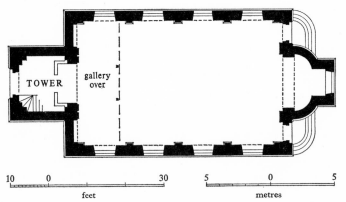

SMETHWICK OLD CHURCH: PLAN OF THE 18TH-CENTURY BUILDING

£10 due in doles.[27] The house, which was enlarged at some time, was demolished in 1929 as part of the development of the area and was replaced by a new house on the corner of Church and Old Chapel Roads.[28]

In 1842 the area served by the chapel, covering the southern half of Smethwick, was made into a district chapelry.[29] Fees were reserved to the vicar of Harborne until the first voidance of that vicarage, but it was not until 1892, after the fourth voidance, that they were transferred to Smethwick.[30] The district thereupon became the parish of Smethwick under the terms of the New Parishes Act of 1856.[31] The living, at first a perpetual curacy and a vicarage from 1868, has remained in the gift of the founder's trustees.[32]

Several changes were made by Edward Addenbrooke, incumbent 1850–83. He introduced a daily service in 1867. He removed the high-backed pews and three-decker pulpit and built a vestry. He provided a new organ in place of a small instrument of 1836, which had itself replaced a barrel-organ; he also organized a choir. During his time two new

by Sir John Mitchell.[38] The vestry, on the north-east, was built in 1963 to replace a smaller one burnt down in 1962,[39] presumably the one built by Addenbrooke. The interior is an undivided space with a shallow apse. It has a west gallery, erected in 1759; the rents from the seats in it were then assigned for 'repairs and beautifying the church',[40] but it now contains the organ. Dorothy Parkes was buried at Harborne in 1728, but her body was moved to Smethwick in 1735. The marble tablet commemorating her on the south wall of the chancel near the spot where she is buried was erected in 1736 under the terms of her will.[41]

The plate includes a silver chalice and paten inscribed 'Smethwick Chapel 1732'; a silver chalice and paten given in 1697 to Harborne church by Beata, the widow of William Hunt of the Ruck of Stones, and presented by Harborne parish to Smethwick township in 1828, the chalice being remade in 1842; and a silver flagon given in 1842 by 'a lady sincerely attached to the Church of England'.[42] Originally there was a single bell dated 1732 and given under the terms of Dorothy Parkes's

[26] Dean and Chapter Libr., Lichfield, 2/2/Smethwick; B.R.L., Lee Crowder 346, case respecting Smethwick Chapel.
[27] 9th Rep. Com. Char. H.C. 258, pp. 556–7 (1823), ix.
[28] 'Old Smethwick', 23 Dec. 1950; Char. Com. files; O.S. Map 1/2,500, Staffs. LXXII. 3 (1918 edn.); W.P.L., P. 519, P. 936.
[29] Lond. Gaz. 28 Oct. 1842, pp. 2969–72; Lich. Dioc. Regy., B/A/2(i)/L, plan facing p. 142.
[30] Lich. Dioc. Regy., B/A/2(i)/T, pp. 427, 435–6.
[31] 19 & 20 Vic. c. 104, s. 14. And see e.g. Lich. Dioc. Regy., B/A/2(i)/T, p. 456; Lond. Gaz. 1 July 1892, pp. 3800–1. For disputes between the vicars of the Old Church and of Holy Trinity in 1903 and 1942 over which church had the right to be called Smethwick parish church and also over the parochial status of the Old Church after 1842 see W.P.L., D.R.O. 15/Misc. A/23.
[32] Lich. Dioc. Ch. Cal. (1869); Birm. Dioc. Dir. (1970–71).
[33] 'Old Smethwick', 23 and 30 Dec. 1950, 6 and 13 Jan.

1951; Lich. Dioc. Ch. Cal. (1868), 95; below pp. 126–8.
[34] Shaw, Staffs. ii. 126. In the sentence of consecration the dedication is left blank: Dean and Chapter Libr., Lichfield, 2/2/Smethwick.
[35] See e.g. docs. at St. Peter's, Harborne, 103.
[36] Lich. Dioc. Regy., B/A/1/30, p. 142; B/A/2(i)/L, pp. 142–3.
[37] Lich. Dioc. Ch. Cal. (1868), 95; (1872), 92; Lich. Dioc. Regy., B/A/2(i)/T, p. 427 (1892).
[38] See frontispiece. For the clock see Kelly's Dir. Birm. (1932).
[39] Ex inf. the vicar (1971).
[40] Hackwood, Smethwick, 59.
[41] Ibid. 51, 56, 59–60; B.R.L., Lee Crowder 346, acct. book of Sir Thos. Birch, pp. 3, 5.
[42] S. A. Jeavons, 'Church Plate of the Diocese of Birmingham', T.B.A.S. lxxxi. 4, 6, 11, 36–7, 45. This dates the paten inscribed with the date 1732 as 1727 but the accompanying chalice as 1732. For Beata Hunt see Shaw, Staffs. ii. 125; above p. 99.

settlement. A peal of eight was installed to celebrate Queen Victoria's jubilee of 1897, but it was removed c. 1963 after being found unsafe. There are now two bells, that of 1732 and the tenor from the 1897 ring.[43]

The registers date from 1732 and are complete.

The chapelyard was enlarged by the addition of the site of the first charity school when it was demolished in 1855. There were further extensions in 1872 and 1909. A lich-gate was erected c. 1890.[44]

The church of *HOLY TRINITY* was already being planned in 1835 to meet the needs of the rapidly growing northern part of Smethwick. Progress was delayed mainly by the difficulty of finding a site, but eventually land on the west side of the main road was given by J. W. Unett of the Woodlands. Building was begun in 1837, and the church was consecrated in 1838. Much of the cost of building was met by the Revd. Thomas Green Simcox, lord of Harborne manor and the first incumbent of the new church.[45] In 1842 the parish of North Harborne was formed out of Harborne parish, with tithes which by 1851 were leased out for £100.[46] The living, a vicarage, was at first in the gift of Lichfield chapter, patrons of Harborne,[47] although it had originally been intended to grant the patronage to T. G. Simcox and his heirs in return for his benefactions to the new church.[48] In 1883 the patronage was transferred to the bishop of Lichfield with that of Harborne in exchange for the patronage of three Derbyshire parishes,[49] and since 1905 it has been held by the bishop of Birmingham.[50] A house for the minister was built to the west of the church in 1838–9 at Simcox's expense on a site given by Unett and was enlarged by J. H. Crump, vicar 1884–92.[51] It had been abandoned by 1940 when the vicar was living in private accommodation. In 1944 a house in South Road, bequeathed as a curate's residence by A. Prince (d. 1943), became the vicarage. In 1949 the 1839 house was sold with half the ground attached, and in 1952 a new vicarage facing into South Road was built on the remaining ground; it was extended in 1963.[52]

The following churches and mission centres have been opened in the parish: Chance's schoolroom in 1850, replaced by St. Paul's in 1858;[53] St. Stephen's in 1882;[54] Bridge Street, opened by 1883[55] and apparently replaced by Hill Street, in existence from c. 1886 until c. 1890,[56] St. Michael's in 1886;[57] St. Luke's apparently for a short time c. 1887;[58] and St. Alban's in 1904.[59]

Holy Trinity Church stands within a spacious churchyard bounded by High Street, Trinity Street, Church Hill, and South Road. The original church, designed in the Early English style by Thomas Johnson of Lichfield,[60] was built of Tixall stone and was cruciform, with a west tower and spire and one bell; there was a west gallery.[61] In 1877 a clock, given under the will of T. G. Simcox, was placed in the tower.[62] Thomas Roper, vicar 1871–84, removed the three-decker pulpit and high-backed pews and moved the organ and choir out of the west gallery. He also installed a new organ as part of his improvement of the musical side of the services.[63] The church, except for the tower and spire, was rebuilt on a larger scale in 1887–9 to the designs of Francis Bacon of Newbury (Berks.), mainly in the Early English style; much of the stone from the earlier church was reused.[64] In addition to the tower and spire, it consists of chancel with north vestry, nave with aisles under separate roofs, and south porch; the eight dormer windows which light the nave were added in 1934 as a memorial to Laura Hewitson (d. 1934).[65]

The pulpit in the churchyard in the angle between the chancel and the south aisle dates from 1913. It was erected by the Brotherhood, a men's organization founded by J. H. Newsham, vicar 1912–14, for its open-air services. The lich-gate was built by the Brotherhood in 1914.[66]

Before the building of the church of *ST. PAUL*, West Smethwick, the schoolroom at Chance Brothers' glass-works in Spon Lane was used for church services. It was licensed in 1850 and had its own curate-in-charge; it served part of Christ Church parish, West Bromwich, as well as the West Smethwick part of North Harborne parish.[67] Its congregation on Census Sunday 1851 was estimated at 20 in the morning and 50 in the evening.[68] Numbers increased rapidly, and St. Paul's Church in St. Paul's Road was begun in 1857 and consecrated in 1858. The cost was met entirely by

[43] T. S. Jennings, *Hist. of Staffs. Bells* (priv. print. 1968), 36, 91–2; Hackwood, *Smethwick*, 53; 'Smethwick and Round About', 23 June 1951; ex inf. the vicar.

[44] Hackwood, *Smethwick*, 60; *Staffs. Advertiser*, 4 Aug. 1855; Lich. Dioc. Regy., B/A/2(i)/P, ff. 332–3; B/A/2(i)/R, p. 565; Birm. Dioc. Regy., Act Book 1, p. 55; 'Old Smethwick', 2 Dec. 1950.

[45] W.P.L., D.R.O. 15/Misc. A/2, printed appeal; Lich. Dioc. Regy., B/A/1/30, pp. 142–3; B/A/2(i)/L, pp. 137–8, 157–66; H.O. 129/393/3/2. For Simcox see 'Smethwick and Round About', 11 and 25 Apr. 1952; *V.C.H. Warws.* vii. 72.

[46] *Lond. Gaz.* 28 Oct. 1842, pp. 2969–72; H.O. 129/393/3/2.

[47] White, *Dir. Staffs.* (1851); Lich. Dioc. Regy., B/A/1/33, p. 173.

[48] W.P.L., D.R.O. 15/Misc. A/2, printed appeal; Lich. Dioc. Regy., B/A/2(i)/L, p. 160.

[49] *Lond. Gaz.* 29 May 1883, pp. 2794–5.

[50] *Birm. Dioc. Cal.* (1906); *Birm. Dioc. Dir.* (1970–71).

[51] *Lich. Dioc. Ch. Cal.* (1864), 148 and plate facing; 'Smethwick and Round About', 11 Apr. 1952; Lich. Dioc. Regy., B/A/2(i)/L, p. 160; Hackwood, *Smethwick*, 68; O.S. Map 6", Staffs. LXXII. NE. (1890 edn.). For Crump see 'Smethwick and Round About', 2 May 1952.

[52] Char. Com. files; ex inf. the vicar (1970). For Prince, organist and choirmaster 1901–42, see 'Smethwick and

Round About', 11 Apr. 1952; plaques on organ and piano in the church.

[53] See below.   [54] See p. 127.

[55] *Kelly's Dir. Birm.* (1883; 1886).

[56] It first appears in *Lich. Dioc. Ch. Cal.* (1887) and disappears after the 1891 edn.

[57] See p. 127.

[58] It appears only in *Lich. Dioc. Ch. Cal.* (1888).

[59] See p. 128.

[60] Docs. at St. Peter's, Harborne, 14, vestry mins. 1829–57, f. 138 (acceptance of Johnson's plans Sept. 1835); White, *Dir. Staffs.* (1834), 156.

[61] *Lich. Dioc. Ch. Cal.* (1864), plate facing p. 148; White, *Dir. Staffs.* (1851); Lich. Dioc. Regy., B/A/2(i)/L, p. 158; 'Smethwick and Round About', 2 May 1952.

[62] *Lich. Dioc. Ch. Cal.* (1878), 75.

[63] 'Smethwick and Round About', 25 Apr. 1952.

[64] S.R.O., D. 564/8/1/23/Jan. 1888; Lich. Dioc. Regy., B/A/2(i)/T, pp. 227–30 (including details of faculty of 2 Aug. 1887); *Lich. Dioc. Ch. Cal.* (1888), 154; (1889), 159; Pevsner, *Worcs.* 89; tablet in church; 'Smethwick and Round About', 2 May 1952.

[65] *Smethwick Telephone*, 10 Nov. 1934.

[66] 'Smethwick and Round About', 8 Feb., 16 May 1952.

[67] W.P.L., D.R.O. 5/Baptisms 1, note on fly-leaf; H.O. 129/393/3/2; *Staffs. Advertiser*, 20 June 1857.

[68] H.O. 129/393/3/2.

private subscriptions, notably from Chances and the workers of the area; contributions were also received from Lord Dartmouth and 'the neighbouring gentry'. The site was given by John Silvester of Birmingham.[69] In 1860 a parish was formed out of North Harborne.[70] The living, at first a perpetual curacy and a vicarage from 1868,[71] was originally in the gift of five trustees. In 1858 it had been agreed that the first trustees should be the people who had contributed the greater part of the cost of building the church, and most of the trustees were members of the Chance family until 1955.[72] In that year the patronage was transferred to the bishop of Birmingham, who still holds it.[73] A house for the minister (now no. 109 St. Paul's Road) was built at the same time as the church at the expense of T. G. Simcox, the vicar of North Harborne.[74] A new house was built in West Park Road in 1905, with the Chances meeting much of the cost.[75] The adjoining Milverton Grange was bought as the vicarage house in 1968.[76]

The board school in Oldbury Road was used as a mission centre c. 1892–4.[77] St. Andrew's mission church on the corner of Oldbury Road and Bridge Street West (later West Street) was licensed in 1898. Formerly a Separatist chapel, it was bought in that year from the trustees of R. L. Chance, most of the cost being met by the Chances. It was closed in 1928.[78]

The original St. Paul's was a building of white Stourbridge brick with stone dressings. Designed in the Early English style by G. B. Nichols of West Bromwich, it consisted of apsidal chancel, nave, transepts, and north-west tower and spire; there were also north-east and south-east turrets containing spiral staircases giving access to galleries in the transepts. A west gallery contained the organ, but in 1891 a new organ was installed in the north transept; in 1919–20 a choir vestry was created in the transept and the organ placed above it.[79] Also in 1919–20 a Lady chapel was made in the south transept in memory of Louisa Jane Downing.[80] A new fibre-glass spire was erected in 1961.[81] There

were originally three bells.[82] A peal of eight was installed in 1924 in memory of Isaac Pitt, who had practised as a doctor in the parish for nearly sixty years.[83]

The church was burnt down in 1963. A new church, designed in a modern style by Denys Hinton & Associates and built over the east end of the former church, was consecrated in 1966; it is not orientated, the 'east' end being on the north. It incorporates the south-east turret of the former church, while the old tower and part of the old north wall form a screen between the street and the forecourt of the new church. It received a Civic Trust commendation in 1969.[84]

The church of *ST. MATTHEW* on a site in Windmill Lane given by J. W. Unett of the near-by Woodlands was consecrated in 1855.[85] In 1856 a parish was formed out of Smethwick chapelry.[86] The living, at first a perpetual curacy and a vicarage from 1868, was in the patronage of the incumbent of the Old Church.[87] In 1857 the benefice received a grant of £100 from Queen Anne's Bounty.[88] A vicarage house designed by Joseph James was built in Windmill Lane to the south-west of the church in 1856–7. It was given up in 1956 and demolished in 1958. The vicar then lived in Raglan Road in a house bought by the church some years before.[89] The vicarage in St. Matthew's Road was completed in 1969.[90] In 1970, after the closing of St. Chad's Church in Shireland Road, the parish of St. Matthew was united with that of St. Chad and the patronage vested in the bishop of Birmingham and the vicar of Smethwick alternately.[91]

St. Matthew's is built of stone in the Decorated style and consists of chancel, north vestry, aisled nave with north and south porches, and west bellcot with space for two bells; the architect was Joseph James.[92] The vestry was added in 1892.[93] In 1895 several memorials were erected to Harry Mitchell (d. 1894): a chancel window and reredos, presented by public subscription, and a pulpit, a font, and chancel rails, steps, pavement, and furnishings, given by the Mitchells.[94] The original bell was sold

[69] Lich. Dioc. Regy., B/A/2(i)/Q, pp. 142–53; *Staffs. Advertiser*, 27 Dec. 1856, 20 June 1857, 31 July 1858; *St. Paul's Church, West Smethwick, Staffs., 1858–1958* (copy in W.P.L.); J. F. Chance, *Hist. of Firm of Chance Brothers & Co.* (priv. print. 1919), 261.
[70] *Lond. Gaz.* 25 Jan. 1860, p. 298.
[71] *Lich. Dioc. Ch. Cal.* (1868; 1869).
[72] *St. Paul's Church, 1858–1958*; Hackwood, *Smethwick*, 69; Lich. Dioc. Regy., B/A/1/36, p. 268; B/A/2(i)/Q, p. 146; Birm. Dioc. Regy., Bp.'s Act Book 1, p. 174; Act Book 2, pp. 128, 193.
[73] *Lond. Gaz.* 5 Aug. 1955, p. 4487; *Birm. Dioc. Dir.* (1970–71).
[74] *Staffs. Advertiser*, 31 July 1858; Hackwood, *Smethwick*, 70; *St. Paul's Church, 1858–1958*; Roper, Plans of Smethwick, 1857, no. 36.
[75] Lich. Dioc. Regy., B/A/2(i)/U, pp. 640, 657; Chance, *Chance Brothers*, 261.
[76] Ex inf. the vicar (1970).
[77] *Lich. Dioc. Ch. Cal.* (1893), where it is listed under the Old Church missions as St. Paul's Board School; ibid. (1894), where it is listed under St. Paul's. It last appears in the 1895 edn.
[78] Lich. Dioc. Regy., B/A/1/35, p. 484; Chance, *Chance Brothers*, 261; *St. Paul's Church, 1858–1958*; *Smethwick Telephone*, 18 Aug. 1928, 11 Jan. 1930.
[79] *St. Paul's Church, 1858–1958*, including a view of the exterior of the church reproduced from the *Illustrated London News*, 16 Oct. 1858; *Staffs. Advertiser*, 20 June 1857, 31 July 1858; Hackwood, *Smethwick*, 69; Chance, *Chance Brothers*, 260.

[80] *St. Paul's Church, 1858–1958*; 'Old Smethwick', 1 Jan. 1949.   [81] *Smethwick Telephone*, 1 Dec. 1961.
[82] Lich. Dioc. Regy., B/A/2(i)/Q, p. 145.
[83] T. S. Jennings, *Hist. of Staffs. Bells* (priv. print. 1968), 96; tablet in tower; Birm. Dioc. Regy., Bp.'s Reg. 1, p. 472; 'Old Smethwick', 30 Oct. 1948.
[84] Tablet at entrance; Birm. Dioc. Regy., Bp.'s Act Reg. 1966, pp. 36–7; Pevsner, *Worcs.* 89; *Parish News of St. Paul's, West Smethwick*, Mar. 1963, 6–7 (copy in W.P.L.); *Civic Trust Awards 1969*, 64.
[85] Lich. Dioc. Regy., B/A/2(i)/P, ff. 298–300v. For Unett see above p. 106.   [86] *Lond. Gaz.* 25 July 1856, p. 2552.
[87] Lich. Dioc. Regy., B/A/2(i)/P, ff. 299v., 380v.–381; *Lich. Dioc. Ch. Cal.* (1869); *Birm. Dioc. Dir.* (1970–71). For proceedings in the 1870s against the vicar, Herbert Gardner, for ritualistic practices see *Staffs. Advertiser*, 27 Sept. 1873; ibid. (S. Staffs. edn.), 22 Apr. 1876; *V.C.H. Staffs.* ii. 83.
[88] C. Hodgson, *Account of Augmentation of Small Livings by Governors of Bounty of Queen Anne: Supplement* (1864), p. lxvii.
[89] W.B.L., Scrapbook 1, p. 50; *The Builder*, 14 Feb. 1857; O.S. Map 6", Staffs. LXXII. NE. (1890 edn.); Birm. Dioc. Regy., Misc. Reg. 1960, p. 39 (conveyance of site to mayor and corp. of Smethwick 1963).
[90] Ex inf. the vicar (1970).
[91] *Lond. Gaz.* 2 Oct. 1970, p. 10764; ex inf. the vicar.
[92] Pevsner, *Worcs.* 89; 'Old Smethwick', 17 June 1950.
[93] *Lich. Dioc. Mag.* 1893, 10.
[94] Hackwood, *Smethwick*, 68–9; inscription on east window.

in 1891 and replaced by one given in memory of Charles Carr, a bell-founder.[95] The churchyard was enlarged in 1870, but both it and the church were closed for burials in 1881.[96]

The mission district of *ST. STEPHEN* in North Harborne parish was formed in 1881. It was placed in the care of J. H. Crump, until then curate of St. Matthew's, who took charge of the district without stipend. He began work in a cottage in St. George Street (now Perry Street), but in 1882 a brick mission church dedicated to St. Stephen was opened in Cambridge Road. Crump erected a wooden Sunday-school building and meeting-room at his own cost a few months later so that the church could be kept for services and instruction classes.[97] A new church at the junction of Cambridge and Sydenham Roads was begun in 1901 and consecrated in 1902.[98] The mission church became the parish hall; it was demolished in 1932 after being condemned a few years before as unsafe.[99] A parish was formed out of North Harborne parish in 1903.[1] The vicarage was in the gift of the bishop of Lichfield until 1905, when the patronage passed to the bishop of Birmingham, the present patron.[2] The vicarage house adjoining the church in Sydenham Road dates from 1904–5.[3] St. Stephen's Church is a red-brick building designed in a Gothic style by F. T. Beck of Wolverhampton.[4] It consists of chancel, aisled nave, and narthex; there is a bellcot with a bell over the junction of the chancel and nave.

An iron mission church dedicated to *ST. CHAD* and situated on the corner of Shireland and Edith Roads on part of Shireland Hall farm was opened from the Old Church in 1882; it had its own curate-in-charge.[5] A new church on the same site was begun in 1900 and consecrated in 1901. The largest private subscriber towards the cost was Mitchells & Butlers Ltd. of the near-by Cape Hill Brewery.[6] A parish was formed out of Smethwick parish in 1902.[7] The vicarage was in the gift of the

bishop of Lichfield until 1905, when it passed to the bishop of Birmingham.[8] A house in Edgbaston Road was acquired as the vicarage house in 1929; it was replaced by a house in Portland Road, Edgbaston (in Birmingham) in 1961.[9] The church was closed at the end of 1968[10] and demolished in 1971. In 1970 the parish was united with that of St. Matthew.[11] The church was a building of red brick with stone dressings, designed in a Gothic style by F. J. Gill of Smethwick.[12] It consisted of chancel with north vestry and organ chamber, aisled nave with north porch, and north-east bellcot and bell.[13]

In 1886 a mission district was formed centring on the church of *ST. MICHAEL AND ALL ANGELS* in North Harborne parish; the district also included parts of the Old Church district and of St. Matthew's parish. The church occupied a converted warehouse in Brook Street which had been part of James Middleton's Britannia Bedstead Works. It had its own curate-in-charge, also living in Brook Street.[14] A new church in Crockett's Lane in the Old Church district was begun in 1891 and consecrated in 1892. Much of the cost was met by J. H. Chance.[15] A parish was formed in 1893 out of the three parishes in which the district lay.[16] The vicarage was in the gift of the bishop of Lichfield until 1905, when the patronage passed to the bishop of Birmingham, the present patron.[17] A vicarage house in Crockett's Lane was dedicated in 1896. In 1940, with the acquisition of the house for the extension of the municipal technical college, the corporation provided a house in Regent Street; this was rebuilt in 1958.[18]

About 1894 St. John's mission room was opened in a disused factory, formerly a non-denominational mission room, in Slough Lane (now Wellington Street). It continued in use until *c.* 1903.[19] The mission room of St. John the Evangelist was opened in Foundry Lane in 1910 and remained in use until 1967.[20]

The church of St. Michael and All Angels is a

[95] Lich. Dioc. Regy., B/A/2(i)/P, f. 299v.; T. S. Jennings, *Hist. of Staffs. Bells* (priv. print. 1968), 95; 'Old Smethwick', 17 June 1950, which states that it is uncertain whether there was ever more than one bell at any one time. In *Smethwick Telephone*, 28 Jan. 1950, however, it is stated that older residents may recall that there were once 2 bells but one was taken away because their combined weight was dangerous.

[96] Lich. Dioc. Regy., B/A/2(i)/R, pp. 372, 426, 443; *Lich. Dioc. Ch. Cal.* (1871), 75; *Lond. Gaz.* 11 Mar. 1881, p. 1144.

[97] *Lich. Dioc. Mag.* 1881, 174–5; 1882, 88; *Staffs. Advertiser*, 25 Feb. 1882; 'Smethwick and Round About', 2 May 1952; O.S. Map 6", Staffs. LXVIII. SE. (1890 edn.). The first entry in the registers is for 17 Oct. 1881: W.P.L., D.R.O. 14/Baptisms 1.

[98] Date on foundation-stone; Lich. Dioc. Regy., B/A/2(i)/U, pp. 522–7.

[99] Printed appeal for new hall 1932, with picture of old hall (copy in W.P.L.).

[1] *Lond. Gaz.* 17 Feb. 1903, pp. 1026–7.

[2] Ibid.; Lich. Dioc. Regy., B/A/1/36, pp. 288–93, 319; *Birm. Dioc. Cal.* (1906); *Birm. Dioc. Dir.* (1970–71).

[3] Lich. Dioc. Regy., B/A/2(i)/U, p. 636; *Lich. Dioc. Mag.* 1904, 180; *Birm. Dioc. Cal.* (1906), 191.

[4] Inscription on foundation-stone. For Beck see *Kelly's Dir. Staffs.* (1900), *sub* Wolverhampton.

[5] *Staffs. Advertiser* (S. Staffs. edn.), 13 May 1882; *Lich. Dioc. Mag.* 1882, 88; *Smethwick Annual* (1903), 33; O.S. Map 6", Staffs. LXXII. NE. (1890 edn.).

[6] *St. Chad's Church, Smethwick, Jubilee Souvenir Booklet, 1901–1951* (copy in W.P.L.); printed appeal for new church building fund (copy at Old Church Vicarage);

Lich. Dioc. Regy., B/A/2(i)/U, pp. 463–8.

[7] *Lond. Gaz.* 14 Jan. 1902, p. 286.

[8] Lich. Dioc. Regy., B/A/1/36, pp. 253–62, 279; *Lich. Dioc. Ch. Cal.* (1903); *Birm. Dioc. Cal.* (1906).

[9] Char. Com. files; Birm. Dioc. Regy., Misc. Reg. 1960, pp. 12, 16.

[10] Ex inf. the vicar of St. Matthew's (1970).

[11] See p. 126.

[12] *St. Chad's Church, 1901–1951*.

[13] For exterior and interior views see W.P.L., P. 4120–6.

[14] Hackwood, *Smethwick*, 70; *Lich. Dioc. Mag.* 1886, 192; 1887, 18; 'Smethwick and Round About', 9 May 1952; S.R.O., D. 564/8/1/22/Nov. 1886; Lich. Dioc. Regy., B/A/1/35, p. 85.

[15] Hackwood, *Smethwick*, 71; Lich. Dioc. Regy., B/A/2(i)/T, pp. 345, 456, 464–8; memorial tablet in chancel to J. H. Chance.

[16] *Lond. Gaz.* 17 Mar. 1893, pp. 1687–8.

[17] Ibid.; Lich. Dioc. Regy., B/A/2(i)/T, pp. 454–8; B/A/1/35, pp. 328–9; *Birm. Dioc. Cal.* (1906); *Birm. Dioc. Dir.* (1970–71).

[18] *Lich. Dioc. Mag.* 1896, 91; O.S. Map 6", Staffs. LXXII. NE. (1905 edn.); *Smethwick Civic News*, Jan. 1957; ex inf. the Birmingham diocesan joint registrar and the vicar (1973).

[19] *Lich. Dioc. Ch. Cal.* (1895); Hackwood, *Smethwick*, 71. It appears in *Smethwick Annual* (1903), 100, but not in the 1904 edn.

[20] Birm. Dioc. Regy., Bp.'s Act Book 1, p. 73; *Birm. Dioc. Cal.* (1911), 204; R. Fletcher, Street Map of Boro. of Smethwick (1949; copy in W.P.L.); ex inf. the vicar.

red-brick building designed by A. E. Street of London in an Early English style. It consists of chancel, north transept, aisled and clerestoried nave, and west baptistery flanked by porches; the interior brickwork is exposed. The chancel and transept were built as a raised platform to provide space for a parish room and a vestry beneath.[21] About 1922 the organ was moved from the transept to the south side of the chancel, apparently in place of a Lady chapel, and a vestry and a chapel were formed in the transept.[22] About 1933 the organ was moved to a platform above the vestry, and a Lady chapel was formed on the south side of the chancel as a memorial to Charlotte Louisa Evans (d. 1932), caretaker for twenty-five years.[23]

The church of *ST. MARY* at Bearwood, on the corner of Bearwood and St. Mary's Roads, was begun in 1887 and consecrated in 1888. Most of the cost was met by T. R. Tilley of Edgbaston (in Birmingham), father of the first priest-in-charge, and the site given by G. C. Adkins of Lightwoods House.[24] A parish was formed out of Smethwick parish in 1892, and the vicarage has remained in the gift of the vicar of the Old Church.[25] At first the vicarage house was in Bearwood Road. A new house was built in Poplar Avenue in Edgbaston *c.* 1907 to the designs of S. N. Cooke of Birmingham.[26]

The mission church of St. Dunstan in Marlborough Road, a brick building with a bell in a bellcot, was erected in 1911 to the designs of S. N. Cooke. It was intended to become the centre of a new ecclesiastical district, but the residential area expected there did not develop. The church was closed in the later 1920s and sold in 1936.[27] In 1971 it was used by a furniture-removal firm.

St. Mary's is a red-brick building with Bath stone dressings and was designed in an Early English style by J. A. Chatwin of Birmingham.[28] It consists of chancel with north and south vestries, aisled nave with north and south porches, and projecting western baptistery. In the interior the brick is left exposed, and the nave arcade is supported on short stone columns. There is a bell in a bellcot over the south vestry. The north vestry was added in 1939 to serve as both vestry and parish room; in 1971 it was converted into a chapel for weekday services.[29] An organ was installed apparently in

1892; it was replaced in 1952 by one given by the congregation as a memorial to J. G. Roberts, vicar 1935–48.[30]

A room, formerly a printing office, in Dibble Road in North Harborne parish was used for services from 1903[31] and was replaced in 1904 by the mission room of *ST. ALBAN* on a site in Silverton Road given anonymously by G. F. Chance.[32] This in turn was replaced by the church of St. Alban the Martyr on the corner of Devonshire and St. Alban's Roads, begun in 1905 and consecrated in 1906.[33] The 1904 building was used as the church hall until 1932; from 1960 it was used by Smethwick Repertory Company.[34] A parish was formed out of North Harborne parish in 1909, and the vicarage has remained in the gift of the bishop of Birmingham.[35] The vicarage house next to the church was built in 1910–11 on a site given by G. F. Chance.[36] The church is of red brick with stone dressings and was designed in a Tudor style by F. T. Beck of Wolverhampton.[37] It consists of chancel, aisled nave, and projecting western baptistery; there is a bell in a bellcot over the west end. A vestry was added in 1958 as a memorial to E. Edmonds-Smith, vicar 1934–55.[38]

The parochial hall of *ST. HILDA* in Rathbone Road, Warley Woods, was licensed for divine service in 1907 and a conventional district assigned to it. The area lay within the parish of Christ Church, the Quinton (formerly in Halesowen, Worcs., now in Birmingham).[39] In 1930 a statutory district was formed. The patronage of the perpetual curacy was vested in the Crown and the bishop of Birmingham alternately under the terms of the New Parishes Act of 1843; in 1934 it passed by exchange entirely to the bishop.[40] Also in 1934 part of the endowment of Harborne benefice was transferred to St. Hilda's.[41] Under the Act of 1843 the district was made a parish on the consecration of a new church in 1940.[42] The living became a vicarage and has remained in the patronage of the bishop.[43] A house in Abbey Road was bought in 1929 as a temporary residence for the minister, and in 1939 a house in Lightwoods Hill was rented. In 1959 a house was bought in Pitcairn Road pending the erection of a vicarage house, which was built beside the new church in 1960.[44] The church of St. Hilda was built in 1938–40

[21] Hackwood, *Smethwick*, 71; Pevsner, *Worcs.* 89; *Kelly's Dir. Birm.* (1894).
[22] Birm. Dioc. Regy., Bp.'s Reg. 1, pp. 421–2.
[23] Ibid. p. 756; memorial tablet in chapel.
[24] Lich. Dioc. Regy., B/A/2(i)/T, pp. 168, 219–22, 225; Hackwood, *Smethwick*, 70; *St. Mary's Church, Bearwood, 1888–1968*; 'Smethwick and Round About', 18 and 25 Mar., 1 Apr. 1955.
[25] *Lond. Gaz.* 1 July 1892, pp. 3800–1; Lich. Dioc. Regy., B/A/1/35, p. 281; *Birm. Dioc. Dir.* (1970–71). In 1902 and 1903, however, the bishop of Lichfield acted as patron: B/A/1/36, pp. 297, 336.
[26] *St. Mary's, Bearwood*; Birm. Dioc. Regy., Bp.'s Reg. 1, p. 77 (conveyance of site July 1907); *Smethwick Telephone*, 14 Jan. 1911.
[27] Birm. Dioc. Regy., Bp.'s Act Book 1, p. 84; *Smethwick Telephone*, 14 Jan. 1911; Char. Com. files. It appears for the last time in *Birm. Dioc. Kal.* in the 1926–7 edn.
[28] Pevsner, *Worcs.* 88; *Kelly's Dir. Birm.* (1892).
[29] Birm. Dioc. Regy., Bp.'s Reg. 2, p. 133; Char. Com. files; ex inf. the vicar (1971).
[30] *St. Mary's, Bearwood.*
[31] *St. Alban the Martyr, Smethwick, 1906–1966*, 5–6.
[32] Ibid. 6; Lich. Dioc. Regy., B/A/1/36, pp. 360–1; W.P.L., D.R.O. 4/Misc. 4.
[33] *Lich. Dioc. Mag.* 1903, 37; 1904, 89; 1905, 168; 1906,

118–19; *Birm. Dioc. Cal.* (1906), 190; Lich. Dioc. Regy., B/A/2(i)/U, p. 595; Birm. Dioc. Regy., Bp.'s Act Book 1, p. 15.
[34] *St. Alban the Martyr*, 7, 9.
[35] *Lond. Gaz.* 21 May 1909, pp. 3857–8; Birm. Dioc. Regy., Bp.'s Reg. 1, p. 125; Bp.'s Act Book 1, p. 55; *Birm. Dioc. Dir.* (1970–71).
[36] Birm. Dioc. Regy., Bp.'s Reg. 1, p. 157; *Birm. Dioc. Cal.* (1910), 198; (1911), 204; (1912), 199; *St. Alban the Martyr*, 6.
[37] Inscription on foundation-stone.
[38] *St. Alban the Martyr*, 8–10.
[39] Birm. Dioc. Regy., Bp.'s Act Book 1, pp. 20–1; *Birm. Dioc. Cal.* (1908). The district is first mentioned in the Cal. in 1916; until then St. Hilda's is listed among the missions. *V.C.H. Worcs.* iii (1913), 151, states that the new ecclesiastical district was formed in 1906. The first entry in the registers is for 17 Feb. 1907: W.P.L., D.R.O. 13/Baptisms 1.
[40] *Lond. Gaz.* 28 Feb. 1930, pp. 1295–6; 27 Mar. 1934, pp. 2030–1; 6 & 7 Vic. c. 37; Char. Com. files.
[41] Birm. Dioc. Regy., Bp.'s Reg. 2, pp. 9–12.
[42] Char. Com. files; Birm. Dioc. Regy., Act Book 2, pp. 73, 160.
[43] *Birm. Dioc. Dir.* (1941; 1970–71).
[44] Char. Com. files; Birm. Dioc. Regy., Misc. Reg. 1960, pp. 3, 7.

Smethwick Grove from the south-east *c.* 1830

The Bear at Bearwood *c.* 1825

SMETHWICK

DOROTHY PARKES, 1644–1728   WILLIAM LEGGE, 1ST EARL OF DARTMOUTH (d. 1750)

THE OPENING OF THE SIKH TEMPLE, SMETHWICK, IN 1961

The guests on the speaker's right are the mayor and mayoress of Smethwick (Councillor and Mrs. R. L. Pritchard) and Mr. P. C. Gordon Walker, M.P.

in Abbey Road on the Oldbury side of the boundary.[45] Designed by E. F. Reynolds,[46] it is a brick building with Byzantine features, notably a plan which suggests a Greek cross; there is a shallow tower over the entrance. With the opening of the new St. Hilda's the former church became the parish hall but was sold in 1961.[47]

A mission church of *ST. MARK* in Hales Lane, Londonderry, in the parish of Christ Church, the Quinton, was licensed in 1928.[48] A Peel district of St. Mark was formed in 1929 out of the parishes of the Quinton, Smethwick, Smethwick St. Alban, and Oldbury (Worcs.). The patronage of the perpetual curacy was vested in the Crown and the bishop of Birmingham alternately under the terms of the New Parishes Act of 1843, but in 1934 it passed by exchange entirely to the bishop.[49] Also in 1934 part of the endowment of Harborne benefice was assigned to St. Mark's.[50] A new church, a brick building designed by Frederick Randle, was built in 1935–6 on a site to the west of the first church.[51] On its consecration in 1936 the district was made a parish under the Act of 1843.[52] The living became a vicarage in the patronage of the bishop.[53] The vicarage house is in St. Mark's Road.

ROMAN CATHOLICISM. The first mission in Smethwick was founded by members of the Oratory in Hagley Road, Edgbaston (in Birmingham), a fact which accounts for the dedication of the church in Smethwick to St. Philip Neri, founder of the Congregation of the Oratory.[54] Edward Caswall, a member of the Oratory, was organizing the building of a school-chapel and a presbytery at his own expense from 1858, and the first resident priest, J. S. Flanagan, was also a member of the Oratory, although he left it a few months after coming to Smethwick in 1862. He lived in a house in Brook Street, which was at first also used as a mass-centre. By 1863 the school, in Watt Street, was being used for worship; part of the building (later the infants' school) was kept permanently as a chapel, and the rest was thrown open for services on Sundays. The presbytery, built on to the school, was completed in 1863. Caswall sold the school-chapel to the diocese of Birmingham for a nominal sum in 1876, but the Oratorians retained the ownership of the rest of the property until 1912.

The church of St. Philip Neri in what is now the Messenger Road section of High Park Road was built by C. E. Ryder, priest at Smethwick from 1882 to 1912 and grandson of Henry Ryder, bishop

of Lichfield and Coventry (1824–36); he paid for much of it himself. The nave was opened in 1893. Over the next nine years Ryder added the west porch flanked by the baptistery and a chapel; he also improved the site and bought an organ. In 1904 he built the sacristies and the south transept containing the Lady Chapel and in 1908 completed the work by adding the choir and the north transept containing the Sacred Heart Chapel. The church is a building of brick and terracotta designed in a mixed Romanesque and Gothic style by Alfred Pilkington of London. A marble high altar and sanctuary were installed as a memorial to Ryder in 1926; the altar was moved forward to the front of the sanctuary in 1969. The church was consecrated in 1936. A new presbytery was built south of the church c. 1960. The Roman Catholic population of St. Philip's parish was some 1,500 in 1936 and 2,250 in the late 1960s.

A mission dedicated to St. Gregory the Great was started at Bearwood in 1899 in a converted stable and coach-house in Three Shires Oak Road. It had a congregation of c. 20. A priest from the Oratory was in charge until 1909. The building was extended in that year to hold 200. In 1933–4 the church of Our Lady of Good Counsel and St. Gregory was built in Three Shires Oak Road; it was consecrated in 1961. Designed by P. B. Chatwin of Birmingham, it is a brick building with classical features. The Roman Catholic population of the parish in the late 1960s was 2,000.[55]

In 1924 a chapel dedicated to St. Teresa and served from St. Philip's was opened at Londonderry in a converted stable on the Oldbury side of Queen's Road. In 1932 the owner of the property required a price for it which was beyond the means available, and the chapel was closed.[56]

PROTESTANT NONCONFORMITY. APOS-TOLIC CHURCH. An unsectarian mission hall in Rolfe Street was registered in 1906. It was apparently the forerunner of the Rolfe Street Pentecostal Mission in existence by 1918 and known as Rolfe Street Apostolic Church by 1929. It was replaced by the Apostolic Church in Queen Street, registered in 1935. In 1972, after the demolition of the church during the redevelopment of the area, a new church was opened on the corner of Broomfield and Holly Street.[57]

ASSEMBLIES OF GOD. The New Covenant Pentecostal Church in Pargeter Road, Bearwood, was registered by the Assemblies of God in 1955.[58]

[45] Date on foundation-stone; Birm. Dioc. Regy., Bp.'s Reg. 2, pp. 132, 164, 166; *Weekly News*, 5 July 1940.
[46] At the consecration the bishop congratulated Edwin Reynolds as architect: *Weekly News*, 5 July 1940. The plans in W.P.L., D.R.O. 13/Misc. 1, are signed by Wood & Kendrick and Edwin F. Reynolds, architects, of Colmore Row, Birmingham.
[47] Char. Com. files; below p. 130.
[48] Birm. Dioc. Regy., Act Book 1, pp. 305–6.
[49] *Lond. Gaz.* 5 Mar. 1929, pp. 1562–4; 27 Mar. 1934, pp. 2030–1; 6 & 7 Vic. c. 37; Birm. Dioc. Regy., Act Book 1, pp. 319, 358, 388.
[50] Birm. Dioc. Regy., Bp.'s Reg. 2, pp. 9–12.
[51] Date on foundation-stone; Bp.'s Reg. 2, pp. 58–9, 72–3.
[52] Bp.'s Reg. 2, pp. 73, 160.
[53] *Birm. Dioc. Dir.* (1936–7; 1970–71).
[54] This and the following para. are based on T. E. Bird, *Church of St. Philip Neri, Smethwick* (copy in W.P.L.); *Cath. Dir. of Province of Birm.* (1914), 93–4; *Cath.*

Dir. of Archdioc. of Birm. (1970); O.S. Map 1/2,500, Staffs. LXXII. 3 (1948 edn.); inf. from the parish priest and Miss Amy Hill, St. Philip's School (1971). The size of the 1936 population is taken from a scrapbook at St. Philip's presbytery. For Caswall see above p. 88.
[55] *Cath. Dir. of Dioc. of Birm.* (1900), 42, 101; (1910), 80; *Cath. Dir. of Archdioc. of Birm.* (1934), 158; (1935), 170; (1970), 48; *Smethwick Telephone*, 29 Dec. 1961, p. 5; A. B. Chatwin, 'Architectural Work of Philip B. Chatwin', *T.B.A.S.* lxxviii. 3; W.P.L., P. 4500 (view of converted stable and coach-house). The baptismal reg. dates from 1900. The 1910 *Dir.* states that the site for a permanent church and a presbytery had been given by the Galton family.
[56] Bird, *Church of St. Philip Neri*, 27, 29; ex inf. Miss Amy Hill.
[57] G.R.O., Worship Reg. nos. 41597, 56185; *Kelly's Dir. Birm.* (1918, 1929); local inf. (1973).
[58] Worship Reg. no. 65038; *Free Church Dir.* (1968–69).

BAPTISTS. The Baptist cause in Smethwick was founded in 1839 when the minister from Bethel chapel in West Bromwich started regular preaching in a private house in Oldbury Road. Numbers grew, and the house of Joseph Vernon, the postmaster, was used instead. In 1842 a chapel with accommodation for some 200 was opened in Cross Street, although there was no resident minister until 1851; the first baptism there was performed by Arthur O'Neill, the Christian Chartist. In 1847 the church became independent of West Bromwich and in 1848 joined the Midland Baptist Association. There being no resident minister, numbers declined. Average attendance at services in 1850–1 was 50 in the afternoon and 40 in the evening; there was also a Sunday school. The chapel was given up in 1853 and sold to the Temperance Society, which rebuilt it in 1876.[59]

In 1866 an evangelist was sent to Smethwick by the Midland Baptist Association. At first he preached out of doors. Services were next held in the mess-room at the Patent Nut and Bolt Co.'s works, and later a shed was taken in Union Street where both services and a Sunday school were held. A chapel was built in Cross Street in 1869. Numbers increased, and a new chapel was built in Regent Street in 1877–9; it is a building of brick and stone in a baroque style. The adjoining Sunday school was built in 1908–9. At the beginning of 1969 the church's adult membership was 110, and there were 220 children and young people. In the later 1880s the Cross Street chapel had passed to the Salvation Army and in 1970 formed part of the works of James C. Nicklin Ltd.[60]

Services were held at the board school in Bearwood Road from 1898 by the minister at the Regent Street chapel. A branch church was formed in 1899. A school-chapel designed by George Bowden & Son was opened in Rawlings Road in 1903, and Bearwood became a separate church in 1915. A new church, designed by E. S. Mitton, was built in Bearwood Road adjoining the first church in 1921 and was itself replaced by another church on the same site in 1965. The 1903 building still stands. At the beginning of 1969 the adult membership was 118, and there were 134 children and young people.[61]

In 1882 a few people who had left the Regent Street church formed a church of Baptist Brethren. They leased the Temperance Hall in Cross Street and bought it in 1897. By the early 20th century a Baptist Gospel Temperance Mission was being carried on there. The cause joined the West Midland Baptist Association in 1920, and the chapel continued as the Central Baptist Mission until it was closed in the late 1960s.[62] It was demolished in the winter of 1970–1.

The institute in Mornington Road was registered for Baptists in 1910.[63] Nothing further is known about its use as a Baptist centre.

BRETHREN. A meeting-room was built at Bearwood in 1880, the first place of worship in that district. It was registered in 1881 simply for Christians but may have been the predecessor of the present Gospel Hall in Bearwood Road opened for the Brethren in 1896. Designed by G. F. Hawkes, the new meeting-room was built at the expense of Swaine Bourne. On his death in 1923 it passed to trustees under the terms of his will, with the stipulation that if it ceased to be used by the Open Brethren it should be conveyed to the Salvation Army.[64]

A meeting-room on the corner of Hume Street and Cape Hill was registered for 'believers' in 1900. It was replaced by the Gospel Hall in Hume Street, a brick building in an Early English style, dated 1901; there is a Sunday-school building attached. The new hall too was registered for 'believers', though not until 1916. By the later 1960s it was occupied by the Christian Brethren under the title of the Cape Hill Assembly.[65]

The Sandwell Gospel Hall above the canal off Brasshouse Lane was registered for the Plymouth Brethren in 1930. It was closed in 1969.[66]

The meeting-room in the former St. Hilda's Church in Rathbone Road was registered for the Plymouth Brethren in 1962.[67]

CATHOLIC APOSTOLIC CHURCH. The Catholic Apostolic Church had a meeting in Bridge Street in 1869, but it had ceased by 1896.[68]

CHRISTADELPHIANS. There was a Christadelphian meeting-room in Waterloo Road for some years from 1937. Another was opened in Hurst Road about the same time, and Warley Christadelphian Ecclesia was meeting in the community centre there in 1971.[69]

CONGREGATIONALISTS (INDEPENDENTS), LATER UNITED REFORMED CHURCH. In 1810 a preaching-station and a Sunday school were started in a room

[59] Hackwood, *Smethwick*, 78; A. S. Langley, *Birmingham Baptists Past and Present*, 199–200; 'Old Smethwick', 24 Feb. 1951; *Regent St. Baptist Church, Smethwick, Church Manual No. 4* (1892), 9 (copy in W.P.L.); H.O. 129/393/3/2 (giving 1840 as the date of the chapel); date on Temperance Hall (demolished 1970–1); above p. 123.
[60] Hackwood, *Smethwick*, 78–80; Langley, *Birmingham Baptists*, 200; Pevsner, *Worcs.* 90; *The Dickensland Bazaar, Baptist Church, Regent St., Smethwick* (1911), 11 (copy in W.P.L.); *Baptist Handbook* (1970), 193; dates on Regent St. buildings; below p. 133. For a view of Regent St. see plate facing p. 33 above.
[61] Langley, *Birmingham Baptists*, 189–90; *Dickensland Bazaar*, 9, 11; G.R.O., Worship Reg. nos. 41978, 48308, 70293; O.S. Map 6″, Staffs. LXXII. NE. (provisional edn. with additions of 1938); foundation-stone of present church dated Feb. 1965; W.P.L., P. 4677, 4686; *Baptist Handbook* (1970), 193. For interior and exterior views of the 1921 church see W.P.L., P. 4503–4.
[62] Hackwood, *Smethwick*, 81; Langley, *Birmingham Baptists*, 204; Char. Com. files; Worship Reg. no. 36958

(registration for Baptist Brethren 1899). It is listed in *Free Church Dir.* (1968–69), 171, but the registration was cancelled Mar. 1969.
[63] Worship Reg. no. 44105; below p. 134.
[64] Hackwood, *Smethwick*, 81; Worship Reg. nos. 25606, 35606; Char. Com. files; date on building. Hackwood seems to imply that the 1880 room was the predecessor.
[65] Worship Reg. nos. 38007, 46725; *Free Church Dir.* (1968–69), 216; O.S. Map 1/2,500, Staffs. LXXII. 3 (1918 edn., revision of 1913), showing both hall and school.
[66] Worship Reg. no. 52332 (registration of Feb. 1930, cancelled July 1969). It is listed in *Free Church Dir.* (1968–69), 216.
[67] Worship Reg. no. 68663.
[68] Worship Reg. no. 18902 (cancelled 1896 on revision of official list).
[69] *Kelly's Dir. Birm.* (1937) shows both. The Waterloo Rd. meeting-room was registered in 1937 (Worship Reg. no. 57337) and is still shown in *Kelly's Dir. Birm.* (1960); the registration, however, was cancelled in 1954.

on the Birmingham road in the Cape Hill area by members of the Carrs Lane Congregational church in Birmingham. In 1813 the congregation moved to the house of William Newland at Bearwood Hill at the junction of what are now Bearwood Road and High Street. A chapel, used also as a Sunday school, was built on the corner of Crockett's Lane in 1823–4 and registered as an Independent place of worship; it was later enlarged and a gallery added. For many years there was no resident minister, and the congregation regarded Carrs Lane as their church, going there to receive the sacrament. In 1837 a church was formed in Smethwick and a resident minister appointed. Average attendance at the chapel in 1850–1 was given as 140 morning and evening with 140 Sunday-school children in the morning.[70] A new chapel was built in High Street in 1853–4, a building of blue brick and stucco with a pedimented classical façade; it was opened in 1855.[71] The old chapel was used as a Sunday school until a school was built behind the new chapel in 1871.[72] The High Street church was closed in 1961 since the congregation could no longer afford to maintain the building or support a minister. It was then sold and converted into a Sikh temple.[73]

Cottage services were held in Victoria Street West in West Smethwick by members of the Smethwick and Oldbury churches, apparently by the 1860s. A church was formed in 1870 and placed in the care of those two churches. A school-chapel was built in Oldbury Road in 1872–3, and in 1877 average attendance on Sunday evenings was 100, with an average of 176 at the Sunday school. The mission had no resident minister until 1885. By 1896 Smethwick alone was responsible for the chapel, and by the later 1960s it was in the care of the church at Sedgley.[74] It was demolished in 1970 in the course of the redevelopment of the area, and a new church was opened in Mallin Street in 1971.[75]

In 1859 the Revd. Robert Ann of Graham Street chapel in Birmingham started meetings in Slough Lane and open-air services at Merry Hill. A mission hall was built in Slough Lane in 1870. It was bought by the Harborne school board for a school in 1875 but was used as a chapel as well until the building of

Winson Green Road chapel in Birmingham in 1882.[76]

ELIM FOURSQUARE GOSPEL ALLIANCE. Elim Tabernacle on the corner of Oldbury Road and West Street was registered in 1930. It was replaced by Elim Pentecostal Church in Woodlands Drive in 1967.[77]

LATTER-DAY SAINTS. Mormons were meeting in Cross Street in 1857.[78]

METHODISTS. *Wesleyan.* By 1821 there was a Wesleyan chapel at the French Walls; meetings had been held earlier at the house of a Mr. Grant in Harding Street.[79] A chapel was built near by in Rabone Lane close to the corner of Bridge Street in 1826. It had sittings for over 500 people in 1851, and attendances on Census Sunday were estimated as 245 in the morning, 211 in the afternoon, and 317 in the evening, numbers which were said to be lower than usual because it was Mothering Sunday.[80] The chapel was replaced by one in New Street built in 1855–6 with sittings for 829 people; a building of brick in a classical style, it was designed by G. B. Nichols of West Bromwich.[81] In 1880 there was a church membership of 168.[82] By 1921 the fabric was being weakened as a result of vibration caused by the hammers of Harper, Sons & Bean's stamping works in Rolfe Street. Also most of the congregation then lived at some distance from New Street. It was therefore decided to rebuild on a site which would serve one of the new centres of population, and Broomfield House and adjoining land in the Uplands area were bought. The Akrill Memorial Church was built there in 1928–31, mainly with money left by Elizabeth Akrill of Edgbaston (in Birmingham), by will proved in 1913. The church, designed in a Gothic style by Alfred Long,[83] is a brick building with a tower. The Akrill Memorial Sunday School and Institute in Queen Street was opened in 1931 and used as a Sunday school until the opening of the Sunday school adjoining the Akrill Church in 1932.[84] The New Street chapel was closed in 1931; the building then became a sweet factory[85] and by 1970 was part of the works of Smethwick Drop Forgings Ltd.

[70] Hackwood, *Smethwick*, 74–5 (based on a history of Smethwick Congregational church produced by the minister in 1887); A. G. Matthews, *Cong. Churches of Staffs.* 214–15 (giving 1813 as the date of the first preaching-station); 'Smethwick and Round About', 15 Sept. 1951; *S.H.C.* 4th ser. iii. 60; H.O. 129/393/3/2; W.S.L., S. MS. 417/Harborne. For an account of the formation of the church in 1837 see copy of memo. at beginning of W.P.L. 16370.
[71] Hackwood, *Smethwick*, 76–7; Pevsner, *Worcs.* 90.
[72] Hackwood, *Smethwick*, 77; *Staffs. Advertiser*, 20 May 1871.
[73] Char. Com. files; G.R.O., Worship Reg. no. 7529; W.P.L. 19281, pp. 222, 254–5; 19283, stencilled sheet facing p. 131, and pp. 132, 136, 142–3; *Smethwick Telephone*, 20 Nov. 1959.
[74] Matthews, *Cong. Churches*, 233; Hackwood, *Smethwick*, 77; *Staffs. Advertiser*, 21 Apr. 1877; Char. Com. files; *Cong. Year Book* (1969–70), 258; W.P.L., P. 103.
[75] *Express & Star*, 23 Aug. 1971; stone on Mallin St. church.
[76] *V.C.H. Warws.* vii. 454; W.P.L., Harborne School Board Min. Bk. A, pp. 154–5, 300; below p. 140.
[77] Worship Reg. nos. 52642, 71113; date on foundation-stone of new church. For exterior and interior views of the first church see W.P.L., P. 4046, P. 4048, P. 5066.
[78] Worship Reg. no. 8088 (cancelled 1896 on revision of official list).

[79] Hackwood, *West Bromwich*, 92; *Wesley Church, New Street, Smethwick: Souvenir of Jubilee Bazaar*, 5 (copy in W.P.L.).
[80] Hackwood, *Smethwick*, 82; H.O. 129/393/3/2; 'Smethwick and Round About', 5 Oct. 1956 (with photograph showing it still standing and used as offices), 16 and 23 Nov. 1956; W.S.L. S. MS. 417/Harborne; ex inf. Mr. G. Beard, Quarterly Meeting Secretary, Smethwick circuit (1971), citing a register of deeds which shows that the land was bought in 1826. Mid-Lent or Mothering Sunday was 'a day much observed in this district by parents having their children and friends around their tables': H.O. 129/382/2.
[81] 'Smethwick and Round About', 19 Oct.–9 Nov., 30 Nov. 1956; Hackwood, *Smethwick*, 82; W.B.L., MS. Notes on West Bromwich Methodism; G.R.O., Worship Reg. no. 7227; Pevsner, *Worcs.* 90. For the later use of the Rabone Lane chapel as an undenominational mission centre see below p. 134.
[82] T. W. Camm, 'Appointments to conduct services and preach in Wesley chapels and union, West Bromwich Circuit', Smethwick circuit plan July–Oct. 1880 (in W.B.L.).
[83] 'Smethwick and Round About', 14 Dec. 1956; inscription on foundation-stone of Akrill Memorial Church.
[84] Worship Reg. no. 53329; ex inf. Mr. G. Beard; date on Sunday-school building adjoining Akrill Memorial Church.
[85] 'Smethwick and Round About', 19 Oct. and 14 Dec. 1956.

Several new centres were opened from the mid 19th century. A meeting was apparently started at the soap works at Merry Hill in the north-east of the town in 1849, and by the late 1850s there was a prayer-meeting in a room near the London Works on the opposite side of the canal.[86] A school-chapel was built in Upper Grove Street in 1864 and replaced by a new chapel built in front of it in 1875. There was a membership of 47 in 1880. After the closing of Baldwin Street church (formerly New Connexion Methodist) in 1957 its congregation united with that of the Grove. The church in Upper Grove Street was replaced by St. John's Methodist Church in Price Street, a brick building in a modern style opened in 1963.[87] Halford Lane chapel in Brasshouse Lane existed by 1866, and there was a membership of 49 in 1880. A new chapel was built on an adjoining site to the north in 1882; the old chapel apparently survived as the school. The building was closed in 1970 and demolished in 1971.[88] There was a centre in Bearwood Road (then Bearwood Lane) by 1876, but it disappears from the circuit plan in 1878.[89] A mission centre in Bearwood Road is recorded from 1884 until 1904.[90] A mission centre was started in a cottage in Slough Lane (later Wellington Street) in 1878. When this became too small for the growing numbers a bakehouse in Slough Lane was used instead. A mission chapel was built on the site of the bakehouse in 1889 and continued in use until 1939.[91] A mission was begun in the schoolroom at Shireland Hall in 1878 and had a membership of 14 in 1880.[92] The centre was replaced by a school-chapel in Waterloo Road built in 1886 to the designs of Edward Pincher of West Bromwich. This was itself replaced in 1896 by the chapel on an adjoining site at the corner of Waterloo and Sycamore Roads. Designed by Ewen Harper in a Gothic style, it is of brick with stone dressings and has a tower and spire by the main entrance. The adjoining Sunday school was rebuilt in 1907.[93]

At the end of 1862 there was a plan for opening a centre at West Smethwick if a suitable place could be found, but the scheme was dropped in 1864.[94] A mission was started in 1902 at a shop in St. Paul's Road. A site was bought on the corner

of St. Paul's Road and Holly Lane, and in 1904 an iron chapel was erected there. A schoolroom was bought from Messrs. Cadbury in 1910. In 1927 the society amalgamated with the society from Spon Lane, and the following year a church was built on the Smethwick site. Designed by Webb & Gray, it is a brick building in a Romanesque style. The Avery organ from Spon Lane, dating from 1799, was installed in the new church.[95] The iron building was then used as the Sunday school until 1943 when it was demolished.[96] There was also a Methodist church (formerly Primitive Methodist) in Corser Street near Smethwick West station until the mid 1950s.[97]

A church was built in Abbey Road for the growing Warley Woods area in 1928. It is a brick building in a Gothic style with a tower and was designed by Moss (probably A. W. Moss) of Crouch, Butler & Savage of Birmingham. A new Sunday school replacing an earlier school was opened to the west in 1938.[98]

In 1970 there were six Methodist churches in the area of the former borough. Five were in Birmingham (Smethwick) circuit (formed out of West Bromwich circuit in 1876): St. John's, Price Street (65 members), Waterloo Road (107 members), West Smethwick (122 members), Akrill Memorial (173 members), and the former Primitive Methodist church in Regent Street (52 members).[99] The sixth, Warley Woods, was in Islington–Quinton circuit.

New Connexion. After meeting in a house in Brasshouse Lane and later at the Temperance Hall in Cross Street, members of the Methodist New Connexion built Mount Zion chapel in Baldwin Street, which was registered in 1865. In 1885 a new chapel was built in front of the old, designed in a debased Italian Gothic style by J. H. Burton of Ashton-under-Lyne (Lancs.); the first building then became the Sunday school. The church was United Methodist from 1907 and Methodist from 1932. The school building again became the church in 1952. It was closed in 1957 and the congregation moved to Upper Grove Street. By 1962 the site was occupied by James Watt House, a multi-storey block of flats.[1]

Primitive. The Primitive Methodists, after meet-

[86] Smethwick circuit records, Bridge St./New St. Society Stewards' Accts. 1848–95 and Leaders' Meeting Mins. 1849–66, 5 and 14 Feb., 18 Apr. 1849, 22 Sept. 1858, 19 Jan. 1859 (in custody of Mr. G. Beard, 1971).
[87] Hackwood, *Smethwick*, 82; *Staff. Advertiser* (S. Staffs. edn.), 3 Apr. 1875; Camm, 'Appointments', Smethwick circuit plan July–Oct. 1880; Worship Reg. nos. 22560, 41688; O.S. Map 6″, Staffs. LXXII. NE. (edns. of 1890 and 1905); ex inf. Mr. G. Beard; inscriptions on stones at St. John's. For views of the 1875 chapel see W.P.L., P. 938, P. 3984–7.
[88] Camm, 'Appointments', West Bromwich circuit plan 1866 and Smethwick circuit plan July–Oct. 1880; Worship Reg. nos. 19936, 26855, 47528, 59697; date on foundation-stones of 1882 building; ex inf. the supt. minister, Birmingham (Smethwick) circuit (1970). For views of the 1882 chapel and of the schoolroom see W.P.L., P. 2187–93.
[89] Camm, 'Appointments', Smethwick circuit plans 1876–8; 'Smethwick and Round About', 2 June 1951.
[90] *Kelly's Dir. Birm.* (1884; 1904).
[91] 'Old Smethwick', 27 May 1950; Camm, 'Appointments', Smethwick circuit plans, showing the mission centre from 1878 to 1880 only; Worship Reg. no. 31649; ex inf. Mr. G. Beard.
[92] Camm, 'Appointments', Smethwick circuit plan Oct. 1878–Jan. 1879 (with f. 69 giving Nov. 1868, clearly in error for Nov. 1878); ibid., Smethwick circuit plan

July–Oct. 1880; *Shireland Hall Mission and Sunday School Accounts 1878–9* (copy in W.P.L. 16952); *Free Press*, 27 Mar. 1886; 'Old Smethwick', 29 July 1950.
[93] *Free Press*, 27 Mar. 1886; Hackwood, *Smethwick*, 82; Pevsner, *Worcs.* 90; dates on foundation-stones of present Waterloo Rd. buildings; Worship Reg. no. 36001 (registration of Apr. 1897).
[94] W.B.L., Min. Bk. of Local Preachers' Quarterly Meetings, West Bromwich, ff. 46v., 49.
[95] *West Smethwick Methodist Church Silver Jubilee 1928–1953*, 2–3 (copy in W.P.L.); *Staffs. Advertiser*, 31 Dec. 1904, p. 6.
[96] W.P.L., P. 2194–5, P. 2199.
[97] See p. 133.
[98] Worship Reg. nos. 51903, 56671; Pevsner, *Worcs.* 90, 367; W.P.L., P. 943–5, P. 1308, P. 3401.
[99] *Birmingham (Smethwick) Circuit Plan and Dir. Oct. 1970–Jan. 1971*. The sixth church in the circuit was Cape in Dudley Rd. on the Birmingham side of the boundary. The circuit was renamed Smethwick Broomfield at the Methodist union of 1932 and became Birmingham (Smethwick) again in 1954: ex inf. Mr. G. Beard; below p. 133.
[1] Hackwood, *Smethwick*, 82; W.P.L. 16952; Worship Reg. nos. 16757, 31692, 63320; *Kelly's Dir. Birm.* (1908), giving 1884 as the date of the second chapel; W.P.L., P. 2937; ex inf. Mr. G. Beard; *Smethwick Civic News*, June 1962.

ing in a house in Bridge Street, built a chapel in Rolfe Street on the site of the later railway station; the materials were rough stone and cinders and it was known as the Cinder Chapel.[2] A new chapel with sittings for 100 people was built on the opposite side of the road in 1849. On Census Sunday 1851 it had attendances of 20 in the morning, 30 in the afternoon, and 50 in the evening; there was also a Sunday school.[3] Numbers increased and a gallery was erected; but the chapel proved too small for special occasions, and for those the railway goods shed was used. A large chapel with galleries all round was built on an adjoining site in 1873, and the 1849 building became the Sunday school.[4] By 1886 there were plans for widening Rolfe Street, and the chapel was sold. A chapel was opened in Regent Street in 1887; it is a building of brick, stone, and stucco in a debased Italian Romanesque style.[5] It had a membership of 52 in 1970.[6]

A chapel was built in Corser Street, West Smethwick, in 1878; it was a Methodist church from 1932 until c. 1955. It was then used as a factory and demolished in 1965.[7] A mission centre was opened in Pope Street from the Rolfe Street chapel in 1885 or 1886. It was replaced by a chapel built in Middlemore Road in 1901, which was closed in 1965.[8] In 1971 it was being used by City Electrical Factors (Midlands) Ltd.

Rolfe Street chapel became the head of the Birmingham Third Circuit when it was formed in 1881 out of Birmingham First Circuit. At the Methodist union of 1932 the name was changed to Smethwick Regent Street circuit. It was united with Smethwick Broomfield circuit to form Birmingham (Smethwick) circuit in 1954.[9]

Wesleyan Reform Association. From about the end of 1854 a class meeting was held at the house of its leader, Charles Richardson. In 1857 the group united with the New Street Wesleyans.[10]

PLYMOUTH BRETHREN, *see* BRETHREN.

PRESBYTERIANS. By 1851 a group belonging to the Presbyterian Church in England was worshipping on Thursday evenings at the Cape Hill school, built in 1846 by John Henderson of Fox, Henderson & Co.[11] The estimated attendance on 27 March 1851 was 27. Smethwick was recognized as a preaching-station in 1853. The school was apparently rebuilt by Henderson in 1854, and Sunday services began.

The group was recognized as a regular congregation in 1855, and in 1856 a resident minister was appointed. Fox, Henderson & Co. failed in 1856, and most of its workers left the area. The congregation dwindled, and by 1866 the remaining few had had to leave the Cape Hill premises. They built a hall in Helena Street off Windmill Lane; they also left the Presbyterian Church in England and joined the English Congregations of the United Presbyterian Church of Scotland. A church was opened on the corner of Helena Street and Windmill Lane in 1875, a building in a plain Byzantine style; the hall became the Sunday school. When the English Congregations and the Presbyterian Church in England united to form the Presbyterian Church of England in 1876, the Smethwick congregation became a member of the new body. The church in Windmill Lane was closed c. 1965 and subsequently demolished.

PROTESTANT EVANGELICAL CHURCH. The Protestant Evangelical Church was meeting at the Hope Mission Hall in Bridge Street in 1912.[12]

PROVIDENCE YOUNG MEN'S BIBLE CLASS. The Providence Young Men's Bible Class was founded in 1878, and by 1903 it met in the dining-hall at the Cornwall Works of Tangyes Ltd. In 1904 it opened a hall in Mafeking Road, where in 1971 Providence Mission was holding services.[13]

SALVATION ARMY. The Salvation Army 'opened fire' in Smethwick in 1881, meeting at first in the wooden theatre building in Grove Lane. In the later 1880s the former Baptist chapel of 1869 in Cross Street had become the Salvation Army barracks. It was replaced by a hall in Windmill Lane, registered in 1908; the registration was cancelled in 1918.[14]

SEPARATISTS. The Separatists met first at the house of R. L. Chance and later at the glass-works of Chance Brothers & Co. in Spon Lane. About 1862 Chance built a meeting-house on the corner of Oldbury Road and Bridge Street West (later West Street). After his death in 1865 his son, also R. L. Chance, continued to maintain the meeting-house. He died in 1897, and in 1898 the building was bought from his trustees and opened as an Anglican mission church.[15]

[2] Hackwood, *Smethwick*, 82–3. No date is given.
[3] Ibid. 83; H.O. 129/393/3/2.
[4] *Staffs. Advertiser* (S. Staffs. edn.), 19 Apr. 1873 (laying of foundation-stone); Worship Reg. 21634 (registration of Jan. 1874); Hackwood, *Smethwick*, 83.
[5] Hackwood, *Smethwick*, 83, 105; Char. Com. files; Pevsner, *Worcs.* 90; above p. 91. [6] See p. 132.
[7] Hackwood, *West Bromwich*, 93; *Kelly's Dir. Birm.* (1888), 812; Worship Reg. no. 58164 (registration of 1938, cancelled 1956); W.P.L., P. 3021 (showing it closed by Feb. 1956), P. 4722. It disappears from *Kelly's Dir. Birm.* after the 1956 edn.
[8] Hackwood, *Smethwick*, 83; Worship Reg. no. 38618; date on foundation-stone of Middlemore Rd. chapel; ex inf. Mr. G. Beard. [9] Ex inf. Mr. Beard.
[10] Smethwick circuit records, Bridge St./New St. Society Stewards' Accts. 1848–95 and Leaders' Meeting Mins. 1849–66, 14 Oct. 1857; W.B.L., Min. Bk. of Local Preachers' Quarterly Meetings, West Bromwich, 22 Dec. 1854.
[11] For this section see H.O. 129/393/3/1; Hackwood, *Smethwick*, 73–4, giving the history of the building only

from 1854 and describing it as built that year; Worship Reg. nos. 934 (registration of 1853, cancelled 1855), 6632 (registration of 1855, cancelled 1866), 22406 (registration of 1875, cancelled Feb. 1966); *Staffs. Advertiser* (S. Staffs. edn.), 19 June 1875; *Presbyterian Church of England, Windmill Lane, Smethwick: News Sheet* (June 1926; copy in W.P.L.); below p. 138. The Windmill Lane church disappears from *Kelly's Dir. Birm.* after the 1965 edn. For exterior and interior views see W.P.L., P. 2018–19.
[12] Worship Reg. no. 45281 (cancelled 1954 on revision of official list).
[13] Inscription on Mafeking Rd. hall; notice-board outside hall; *Smethwick Annual* (1903), 100; (1904), 85; Worship Reg. no. 40694.
[14] Hackwood, *Smethwick*, 84; G.R.O., Worship Reg. nos. 25924, 39223, 43195; *Kelly's Dir. Birm* (1890); *Smethwick Almanack* (1910), 37; (1911), 55; 'Old Smethwick', 27 May 1950.
[15] J. F. Chance, *Hist. of Firm of Chance Brothers & Co.* (priv. print. 1919), 95, 123, 260; Hackwood, *Smethwick* 83–4; Worship Reg. no. 15216; above p. 126.

SPIRITUALISTS. The Smethwick Spiritualists' Society met in a house in Hume Street from 1889. The accommodation became too small for the growing numbers, and from 1894 meetings were held at the Central Hall on the corner of Cape Hill and Shireland Road. In 1930 a church was opened in Church Lane near the Council House (apparently the northern part of the present Arden Road), and in 1936 it was registered as the Smethwick National Spiritualist Church. The group moved to Crockett's Lane, apparently in 1937, and in 1938 to Thimblemill Road, where, on the corner of Katherine Road, the Smethwick National Spiritualist Church and Healing Sanctuary stood in 1971.[16] The Christian Spiritualists registered the Sanctuary of Light and Healing Centre in Wellington Road in 1951; the registration was cancelled in 1956.[17]

SWEDENBORGIANS (NEW CHURCH). The Swedenborgians were meeting at a house in Bampton Road by 1896. By 1903 they had a meeting-room in Windmill Lane, where they continued until c. 1910.[18]

UNITED REFORMED CHURCH, see CONGREGATIONALISTS.

OTHER GROUPS. There was an undesignated religious group meeting at the Old Library (formerly the Stour Valley inn) in 1874; it had ceased to meet there by 1896.[19]

The Wattville Road undenominational chapel in Handsworth was running a mission centre in Mornington Road in 1892. It also ran the Young Men's Institute in Mornington Road, opened in a former coffee-house in 1900 by D. P. Wright and closed in 1969, and a mission in the former Rabone Lane Wesleyan chapel in the early 20th century.[20]

There was an undenominational mission room in Slough Lane (now Wellington Street) which was later used as a factory and c. 1894 became an Anglican mission room.[21]

SIKHS. Most of the Indians who settled in Smethwick in the 1950s were Sikhs from the Punjab. Many held religious services in their homes, but what was thought to be the first organized Sikh service in the Midlands was held at the Institute for Overseas Peoples in Brasshouse Lane in 1957.[22] In 1961 the Sikh community bought the Congregational chapel in High Street and converted it into

a temple, the Guru Nanak Gurdwara. It was then said to be the largest Sikh temple in Europe.[23]

SOCIAL LIFE. A wake, held in mid October, existed by 1826.[24] Its origin is not known; Harborne, Smethwick's mother parish, held its wake in September.[25] In the 1870s wake fêtes were held on the Galton Grounds, a piece of open land behind the Swan in Oldbury Road.[26] By 1908 land adjoining the Moilliet Arms at Six Ways was used for a wake fun-fair.[27] In its heyday the wake lasted two days or more; by 1950, however, it had become 'a rather emasculated survival'.[28] By the 1860s there was also an annual Cape Fair, held on the first or second Monday in September.[29]

There was bull-baiting at the 1826 wake.[30] In 1835 it was expected that the chief attractions at that year's wake would be bull-baiting and prize-fighting;[31] about that time a newcomer to Smethwick found that the only pastimes were bull- and bear-baiting, dog- and cock-fighting, 'and other low games'.[32] Bull-baiting and cock-fighting were held on open ground at Bearwood Hill between the Red Cow and the Sow and Pigs.[33]

A wooden theatre in Grove Lane, visited by itinerant companies of actors, was converted into a Salvation Army barracks in 1881. Nothing more appears to be known of it or of another makeshift theatre which about then stood at one end of Windmill Lane.[34] The Theatre Royal in Rolfe Street, built to the designs of Owen & Ward of Birmingham, was opened in 1897; it seated almost 3,000 and was claimed to be one of the largest theatres in the country.[35] It was closed in 1932 when its proprietors went bankrupt, was subsequently reopened for a few months for boxing matches, and was eventually demolished.[36] The Smethwick Empire in St. Paul's Road, built in 1910 to the designs of George Bowden & Son of Smethwick, was intended for use both as a theatre and as a cinema.[37] By 1930 it was being used solely as a cinema. It was closed in 1957[38] and by 1971 had been converted into shops. The Windsor in Bearwood Road, built in 1930 to the designs of H. G. Bradley of Birmingham, had a stage; but it was designed primarily as a cinema and was opened as such.[39] For 16 years stage performances were rare. In the winter of 1946–7, however, there was a season of pantomime followed by several weeks of variety, and from the autumn of

[16] Hackwood, *Smethwick*, 84; *Smethwick Telephone*, 8 Nov. 1930, 3 Jan. 1931; Worship Reg. nos. 34963, 57010, 58443; W.P.L., Smethwick Educ. Cttee. Min. Bk. V i, p. 350; *Kelly's Dir. Birm.* (1938).
[17] Worship Reg. no. 62896.
[18] Hackwood, *Smethwick*, 84; *Smethwick Annual* (1903), 100; *Kelly's Dir. Birm.* (1910), 1155.
[19] Worship Reg. no. 21900 (cancelled 1896 on revision of official list).
[20] *V.C.H. Warws.* vii. 482; 'Smethwick and Round About', 5 Oct. 1956; *Smethwick Annual* (1904), 40, 86; *Warley News Telephone*, 10 July 1969, p. 36. For the use of the Institute by the Baptists see above p. 130.
[21] See p. 127.
[22] *Smethwick Telephone*, 29 Nov. 1957.
[23] G.R.O., Worship Reg. no. 68359; Price, 'Smethwick', 84, citing *The Times*, 31 July 1962; above p. 131.
[24] *Staffs. Advertiser*, 21 Oct. 1826.
[25] T. Presterne, *Harborne once upon a time* (1913), 76.
[26] 'Old Smethwick', 27 Nov. 1948.
[27] Ibid. 27 May 1950; *Smethwick Telephone*, 24 Oct. 1908.

[28] W.P.L., log-book of St. Philip's R.C. School, pp. 4–5, 40; 'Old Smethwick', 27 Nov. 1948, 27 May 1950.
[29] W.P.L., log-book of St. Philip's R.C. School, pp. 2, 21.
[30] *Staffs. Advertiser*, 21 Oct. 1826.
[31] Docs. at St. Peter's, Harborne, 14, Vestry Mins. 1829–57, f. 138.
[32] 'Smethwick and Round About', 16 June 1951.
[33] Ibid. 2 Dec. 1955.
[34] 'Old Smethwick', 27 May 1950; 'Smethwick and Round About', 23 Oct. 1953; above p. 133.
[35] *Weekly News*, 18 and 25 Sept. 1897. For Owen & Ward see *Kelly's Dir. Birm.* (1897).
[36] 'Smethwick and Round About', 23 and 30 Oct. 1953.
[37] *Smethwick Telephone*, 10 Sept. 1910. For Geo. Bowden & Son see *Kelly's Dir. Birm.* (1910).
[38] *Smethwick Telephone*, 4 Jan. 1930; ibid. 5 Apr. 1957, carrying its last advertisement and news that it is to close 'in the very near future'.
[39] Ibid. 4 Oct. 1930. For Bradley see also ibid. 27 Dec. 1930.

1947 until 1957 the Windsor was run as a variety theatre. It then housed a professional repertory company until 1960. The building subsequently became an ice-skating rink and was still in use as such in 1971.[40]

The first purpose-built cinema was the New Cape Electric Theatre (later the Cape Electric Cinema), Cape Hill, built in 1911 to the designs of Oakley & Coulson of Dudley.[41] By 1917 the town had six cinemas (or seven if the Empire be included). By the early 1930s there were eight, five of them owned by a local man, Edward Hewitson (d. 1936), whose family retained its connexion with the cinema industry in Smethwick until 1970.[42] Seven cinemas were open in 1940 and six in January 1956.[43] By 1964, however, the Princes in High Street, a Hewitson cinema of 1930 designed in a derived art-nouveau style by H. G. Bradley, was the only English-language cinema still open.[44] It was closed in 1970.[45] In 1971 there was no commercial cinema showing English-language films within the area of the pre-1966 borough; at the reopened Princes and the Beacon, Brasshouse Lane, Indian and Pakistani films were shown.

A subscription library and literary institute was maintained at Cape Hill by the mid 1850s. Its leading patron was John Henderson of the London Works, and his bankruptcy in 1856 left it in debt. A public appeal in 1858, however, enabled it to re-establish itself in a room at the Greyhound, Rolfe Street, where it reopened in 1859 as Smethwick Library and Literary Institute. It moved in 1862 to premises at the corner of Union and Cross Streets, and in 1871 to some rooms in the local board's public buildings. The town adopted the Public Libraries Acts in 1876, and a public library was formed in 1877 when the Institute transferred its books and other property to the local board. The library remained in the public buildings until 1880, when a free library and reading room was erected on an adjoining site to the designs of Yeoville Thomason of Birmingham. Before the First World War a reference library and a junior library were established. Open access was introduced in 1922–3; as a result more people used the library and a larger building was needed. The public buildings were no longer used by the council, and in 1928, after extensive alterations, they were reopened as the public library.[46] In 1966 the building became the central public library for the county borough of Warley.[47]

The *Smethwick Telephone* was founded in 1884 by a group of Smethwick men who formed the Telephone Newspaper Co. Ltd.; several were active members of the local ratepayers' association, and it has been suggested that the *Telephone* may have been established to propagate the association's views. In 1886 or 1887 the *Telephone*'s proprietors sold it to F. D. Perrot, curate of Holy Trinity Church. The newspaper had originally been printed in Birmingham, but by 1887 it had a Smethwick printer and in 1888 Perrot opened offices and a printing shop in Rolfe Street. When he left Smethwick later in 1888 he sold the *Telephone* to James Billingsley, at that time the only reporter employed by the newspaper. Billingsley, who moved the *Telephone* to larger premises in Regent Street in 1890, then to new offices in the same road, and finally, in 1908, to offices in Hume Street, remained proprietor and editor until his death in 1943.[48] His daughter, Kathleen M. J. Billingsley, then became one of the few women newspaper proprietors in the country and was managing director and editor at the time of her death in 1962.[49] In 1963 the *Telephone* became the *Smethwick Telephone and Warley Courier* and in April 1966 the *Warley Courier and Smethwick Telephone*. It was subsequently acquired by the West Midlands Press Ltd. and in October 1966 merged with that firm's *Warley News* to form the *Warley News Telephone*.[50]

From 1890 to 1895 and again from 1906 to 1949 the proprietors of the *Weekly News*, an Oldbury newspaper, published a Smethwick edition entitled *Smethwick Weekly News*, printed on the *Weekly News* presses.[51] Seven issues of a weekly *Smethwick Globe* appeared in 1895 before it was incorporated with the *Midland Sun*, a Birmingham newspaper.[52] Another weekly, the *Smethwick Advertiser and Three Shires Indicator*, was published for a few months in 1909 from an office in Hume Street.[53]

Smethwick Cricket and Athletic Club may date from 1835 and certainly existed in 1840. By the mid 1870s, as Smethwick Cricket and Quoit Club, it was playing on the Broomfield ground, which was still its home in 1971.[54] Cricket and football were marked by the influence of local employers. Thus in the 1880s Harry Mitchell formed a cricket team at the family brewery at Cape Hill[55] and helped to promote a football club there (Mitchells St. George's),[56] while Nettlefolds raised a works football club and organized sports meetings.[57] From 1894 Mitchells also held annual athletic sports at Cape Hill, with open events as well as races for its employees. They

[40] Ibid. 21 Dec. 1946–22, Feb. 1947, 6 Sept. 1947, 30 Dec. 1960, 4 Jan. 1963; *Warley News Telephone*, 25 June 1970. [41] *Smethwick Telephone*, 17 June 1911.
[42] Ibid. 6 Jan. 1917, 4 Jan. 1930, 3 Jan. 1931; *Kelly's Dir. Birm.* (1931; 1932; 1933), *sub* Cinemas; *Warley News Telephone*, 25 June 1970.
[43] *Kelly's Dir. Birm.* (1940), *sub* Cinemas; *Smethwick Telephone*, 6 Jan. 1956.
[44] *Kelly's Dir. Birm.* (1964), *sub* Cinemas; *Smethwick Telephone*, 27 Dec. 1930.
[45] *Warley News Telephone*, 25 June 1970.
[46] [H. P. Marshall], *Smethwick Public Library, 1877–1927*, 6–7, 9–20 (copy in W.P.L.); W.P.L., Smethwick Library, Reading Room, and Literary Institute cttee. min. bks. 1855–77; *Staffs. Advertiser*, 21 Aug. 1880; W.P.L., invitation to opening of new public library, High Street, Smethwick, 23 Feb. 1928; above pp. 110–11.
[47] *Express & Star*, 29 Mar. 1966.
[48] *Warley News Telephone*, 13, 20, 27 Oct., 3 and 10 Nov. 1966. There are files of the *Telephone* from 1887 onwards at W.P.L.

[49] Obituary in *Smethwick Telephone*, 7 Dec. 1962.
[50] *Benn's Newspaper Press Dir.* (1971); newspaper files in W.P.L.
[51] *Warley News Telephone*, 6 Oct. 1966; files of the *Weekly News* (from 1881 onwards) at W.P.L. The *Weekly News* became the *Warley Weekly News* in 1963 and the *Warley News* in 1966.
[52] *The Times Tercentenary Handlist of English and Welsh Newspapers, Magazines and Reviews*, 292, 296, recording holdings of B.M. Newspaper Library. Neither W.P.L. nor B.R.L. has copies of the *Globe*.
[53] File of the *Advertiser* in W.P.L. The B.M. Newspaper Library has the first 5 issues only: *Times Tercentenary Handlist*, 316.
[54] 'Smethwick and Round About', 3 Apr.–5 June 1953. For the date 1840 see *V.C.H. Salop.* ii. 195.
[55] *V.C.H. Warws.* ii. 404; *V.C.H. Staffs.* ii. 370.
[56] 'Smethwick and Round About', 3 Nov. 1951, 14 Mar. 1952.
[57] Ibid. 27 Aug. 1954.

proved to be highly popular and still drew a crowd of 2,500 in 1908, even though several years of campaigning against 'the gambling element' had reduced attendances sharply.[58]

In 1899 Henry Mitchell presented the local Volunteers and the town with a drill hall, the adjacent Broomfield cricket ground, and a small park (now Harry Mitchell Park) as a memorial to his son Harry (d. 1894). After a public meeting in 1900 to discuss methods of making use of the gift the Smethwick Recreative and Amateur Athletic and Gymnastic Association was formed to promote and organize sport and leisure activities in the borough. Mitchell laid out the park as a recreation ground and provided gymnastic equipment for use in the drill hall. The hall was used by the Volunteers and subsequently by the Territorial Army until 1967 when, with some adjoining buildings erected by the army during the Second World War, it was handed over to the borough. Since then it has been developed as the Harry Mitchell Recreational Centre, which provides indoor sports facilities.[59] Hadley Playing Fields, Waterloo Road, were opened in 1962; they include a stadium which has been used for Midland athletic championships and is the annual venue of a large Sikh sports festival.[60] Thimblemill Baths in Thimblemill Road are among the largest in the Midlands and in the 1950s were used for international swimming matches.[61]

The first friendly society to be registered (though not necessarily the first to be formed) was the Smethwick Union Society, registered in 1836. The first societies were without national affiliations; but there was a lodge of the Manchester Unity of Odd Fellows by 1841, and a lodge of the Loyal Wolverhampton Order of Odd Fellows was registered in 1845.[62] In 1876 there were 27 registered friendly societies, including several lodges of Odd Fellows, two lodges of Free Gardeners, a lodge of Modern Masons, and nine courts of the Ancient Order of Foresters.[63] William Caldow (d. 1892), a Scot who moved to Smethwick in 1841, became known as the 'Father of Forestry' in the Midlands for his work on behalf of the Order of Foresters in south Staffordshire and north Worcestershire.[64]

EDUCATION. From 1670 Harborne was entitled to send two boys to the Old Swinford Hospital School (Worcs.); by 1834 it was customary to choose them alternately from Harborne and Smethwick.[65] Smethwick was later given three places at the school and is still entitled to send boys to it.[66] In 1730 Smethwick children were attending a recently founded charity school at Harborne.[67] In 1734 a charity school was established in Smethwick,[68] and by 1819 there were also two Sunday schools. Fifty-four children then attended the three schools, and the minister of Smethwick chapel considered that there was insufficient provision for the education of the poor.[69]

Smethwick and Harborne were formed into a school district under the 1870 Education Act. In 1871 a public meeting rejected proposals for the establishment of a school board; at the meeting one of the warmest advocates of a board was Joseph Chamberlain, then a partner in Nettlefold & Chamberlain. By then Smethwick had 2,900 school places, about the number officially judged adequate. There was, however, an average attendance of only 1,580, and it was generally agreed that three more free schools were needed; it was claimed that these could be provided by voluntary effort.[70] A board was eventually formed in 1873 on the orders of the Education Department. It was known as the Harborne School Board and remained in existence until 1891, when Harborne became part of Birmingham and the school district was broken up. What remained became a new district under a board originally called the School Board for the Extra-Municipal Part of the Parish of Harborne and from 1896 the Smethwick School Board.[71]

Under the terms of the 1902 Education Act Smethwick became a Part III authority responsible for elementary education, while Staffordshire county council, the authority responsible for higher education, delegated to it control of technical instruction and evening continuation schools.[72] When Smethwick became a county borough in 1907 it automatically assumed responsibility for higher education.

Between 1932 and 1939 there was an extensive reorganization of the borough's schools as a consequence of the Hadow Report.[73] In 1946 Smethwick and West Bromwich published a joint development plan for education. They had met the Ministry of Education's proposal in 1944 to create a Joint Education Board for the two boroughs by pointing out that they were already considering a complete merger to form one new borough. Although the

[58] Smethwick Telephone, 12 and 19 Sept. 1908.
[59] Char. Com. files; 'Old Smethwick', 4 Nov. 1950; County Borough of Warley Sports Facilities Handbook [1969], 13 (copy in W.P.L.); 1st Ann. Rep. of Smethwick Recreative and Amateur Athletic and Gymnastic Association, 1900–1901 (Birmingham, 1901; copy in W.P.L.).
[60] Warley Sports Facilities Handbook [1969], 13–14.
[61] Souvenir programmes (copies in W.P.L.) of swimming matches between Gt. Britain and France (1956), Sweden (1957), and East Germany (1959).
[62] S.R.O., Q/RSf; 'Smethwick and Round About', 24 Nov. 1951.
[63] Rep. Chief Registrar of Friendly Societies, 1876, App. P, H.C. 429-1, pp. 407–8 (1877), lxxvii.
[64] 'Smethwick and Round About', 10, 17, 24 Nov. 1951.
[65] T. R. Nash, Colls. for Hist. of Worcs. ii (1782), 210–11; docs. at St. Peter's, Harborne, 14, Vestry Min. Bk. 1829–57, f. 123. For the school see also V.C.H. Worcs. iii. 202–3, 213–14; iv. 536.
[66] 'Smethwick and Round About', 7 Mar. 1952; ex inf. the bursar, Old Swinford Hospital School (1972).
[67] Magna Britannia et Hibernia [ed. T. Cox], v (1730),

19, based on inf. from Hen. Hinckley, father of the lord of the manor of Smethwick, who stated that among those who contributed to the establishment of the school were 'the family of George Birch'. This would appear to place the foundation after Birch's death, which occurred in 1721: V.C.H. Warws. vii. 72. For the school's later history see ibid. 535–6.   [68] See p. 137.
[69] Digest of Returns to Sel. Cttee. on Educ. of Poor, H.C. 224, p. 861 (1819), ix (2).
[70] Birmingham Daily Gaz. 21 Feb. 1871; above p. 113.
[71] [A. H. Sears], Fifty Years of Education in Smethwick, 1873–1923 (pamph. compiled for Smethwick Educ. Cttee., 1923), 3–6, 43–6 (copy in W.P.L.); Hackwood, Smethwick, 113. The board referred to itself in its minutes as 'Smethwick School Board' from Aug. 1895 (W.P.L., Smethwick School Board Min. Bk. J, p. 521), but its legal name was not changed until Mar. 1896.
[72] Smethwick Educ. Cttee. Memorandum from the Organizer of Higher Education on the Educational Position in Smethwick (1904; copy in W.P.L.).
[73] Smethwick Educ. Cttee. Education in Smethwick, 1932–1938, 5–7 (copy in W.P.L.).

amalgamation did not take place and both boroughs retained their autonomy in educational matters, the plan remained the pattern for education. A tripartite system of secondary education was adopted; in 1970 Smethwick had grammar and secondary modern schools but had closed its technical school.[74]

A pupil-teacher centre was opened in 1894.[75] Special education for handicapped children also began in 1894 when, under the 1893 Elementary Education (Blind and Deaf Children) Act,[76] the school board first sent a child to a school for the blind. In 1907 the borough obtained permission to build Victoria Special School for the educationally subnormal;[77] it was replaced in 1959 by Highfield (now Arden) School.[78] The Firs Open Air School for delicate and physically handicapped children was opened in 1929; the building was completely remodelled in 1964–5.[79] The Edith Sands Nursery School, opened in 1938, remained the only nursery school run by the local authority in 1970.[80] Since 1928 parties of Smethwick schoolchildren have been sent during the summer to a school camp site at Ribbesford (Worcs.), presented to the borough by Frank Chapman and his wife.[81]

Smethwick Old Church Church of England School. Dorothy Parkes (d. 1728), founder of Smethwick Old Church, bequeathed £200 for the building and endowment of a charity school on a site on her estate at Smethwick and made the trustees for building her church responsible for its establishment. The schoolmistress, a single woman chosen by the trustees, was to teach reading, sewing, knitting, and the Catechism, without charge, to poor children chosen by the minister of the church, who was also to be responsible for the day-to-day management of the school.[82] A house with a schoolroom was completed in 1734 adjoining the east end of the Old Church graveyard. The first mistress had been appointed by Lady day 1734.[83] What remained of Dorothy Parkes's bequest, £136, was invested.[84] The school-house was later allowed to fall into disrepair, and by the early 1780s the school had apparently been discontinued for several years. A group of inhabitants then repaired the building with help from neighbouring parishes and petitioned the trustees for further action. They asked that a master to teach writing and accounts should be appointed as well as a mistress, and that some local people

should be nominated by the trustees to supervise the school's affairs. No mention was made of the responsibilities which Dorothy Parkes's will had laid upon the minister.[85] The school was revived, but there is no evidence to suggest that a local committee of management was set up, and in 1823 there was still only a mistress who taught the original curriculum to between 12 and 20 poor girls recommended by the trustees.[86] In 1846–7 the school was attended by 35 girls; there was also a Sunday school attended by the girls and 30 boys. Some of the children were then paying fees, and the school had received a grant from the National Society.[87]

In 1855 new schools with a separate house for the mistress were built on the corner of what are now Church Road and the Uplands; the former schoolhouse was demolished and the site added to the graveyard. In 1864 there were on the books 72 fee-paying pupils (26 boys, 36 girls, and 10 infants) and 15 children taught free. The school was managed by the minister of the church.[88] After the 1902 Education Act the school continued as a non-provided school with some local authority representation on its committee of managers. In 1904 the older boys were transferred to Bearwood Road Council school, leaving departments for girls and infants. In 1905 there was an average attendance of about 164. Numbers declined as additional council schools were built, and the school was closed in 1932.[89] Part of the building is incorporated in the church hall built in the early 1950s.[90]

Hill Street Infants' National School, later Hill Street Board School. An infants' National school was established in 1836 by James Moilliet of the Grove and his wife; the initiative may have come from Mrs. Moilliet, who took an interest in the education of poor children.[91] In 1840 there were 80 children.[92] In 1846–7 there were 43, taught by a mistress who received a salary of £10 and the children's pence and was provided with a house.[93] Although the incumbent of Holy Trinity stated in 1847 that it was a separate foundation and not part of his National school,[94] it was in his parish, its management was apparently in his hands, and by 1850 it was acting in effect as the infants' department of Holy Trinity School. It was then stated to be off Rolfe Street,[95] presumably in Hill Street, where it stood in 1860.[96] When Holy Trinity School built its own infants' department in 1880, Hill Street

[74] *County Boroughs of Smethwick and West Bromwich Joint Development Plan. Prepared in accordance with Section 11 of the Education Act, 1944* (Smethwick, 1946; copy in W.P.L.); Warley Educ. Cttee., TS. List of Schools, Aug. 1970 (copy in W.P.L.).
[75] W.P.L., Smethwick School Board Min. Bk. J, pp. 149–53.
[76] 56 & 57 Vic. c. 42.
[77] *Fifty Years of Educ. in Smethwick*, 16–19.
[78] *Smethwick Civic News*, Dec. 1958, Feb. 1960 (copy in W.P.L.); List of Schools, Aug. 1970.
[79] *Educ. in Smethwick, 1932–1938*, 10; *Smethwick Civic News*, July 1964.
[80] *Fifty Years of Educ. in Smethwick*, 12–13; *Educ. in Smethwick, 1932–1938*, 11; List of Schools, Aug. 1970.
[81] *Educ. in Smethwick, 1932–1938*, 10; *Smethwick Civic News*, July 1956.
[82] *9th Rep. Com. Char.* H.C. 258, p. 557 (1823), ix; Hackwood, *Smethwick*, 56.
[83] B.R.L., Lee Crowder 346, 'Book of receipts no. 1, Smethwick School, 1734'; volume of estate maps (1815) in possession of the secretary to the trustees of Dorothy Parkes (Lee, Crowder & Co., Birmingham).
[84] *9th Rep. Com. Char.* 557.
[85] B.R.L., Lee Crowder 346, petition to Smethwick

Chapel trustees from inhabitants of Smethwick. It is undated, but the local men suggested as suitable supervisors of the school's affairs Ric. Rabone probably came to Smethwick Hall *c.* 1780 and John Turner of the Beakes was dead by 1786: above pp. 100, 105.
[86] *9th Rep. Com. Char.* 557.
[87] National Society, *Church Schools Enquiry, 1846–7* (priv. print. 1849).
[88] Ed. 7/112/Smethwick/7; Char. Com. files.
[89] Old Church School, Smethwick, Managers' Min. Bk. 1902–32 (in possession of the vicar of Smethwick Old Church, 1971).
[90] *Smethwick Telephone*, 29 Sept. 1951.
[91] White, *Dir. Staffs.* (1851); 'Old Smethwick', 28 Aug. 1948; above pp. 104–5.
[92] *Mins. of Educ. Cttee. of Council, 1840–1* [317], pp. 40–1, H.C. (1841), xx.
[93] Nat. Soc. *Church Schs. Enquiry, 1846–7.*
[94] Ed. 7/112/Smethwick/6.
[95] C. Hicks, *A Walk through Smethwick* (Birmingham, 1850), 17 (copy in W.P.L.).
[96] *P.O. Dir. Staffs.* (1860). The only school in Hill St. in 1842 was owned and occupied by the Wesleyans: W.S.L., S. MS. 417/Harborne.

School became once more fully independent as a Church of England infants' school. In November 1880 there were 143 children on the books, and the average attendance was 98. It was transferred to the school board in 1883 and replaced in 1885 by a new board school for infants in Crockett's Lane.[97]

Smethwick National School or North Harborne Parish School, later Holy Trinity Church of England Schools. A National school for 400 children was built in 1840–1 in Trinity Street with the aid of grants from government and the National Society. In 1846–7 there were weekday, evening, and Sunday schools with 289 pupils under a master and a mistress.[98] The girls' department was put under government grant *c.* 1850 and the rest of the school later.[99] Classrooms and a master's house were added in the 1860s. Further extensions in 1880 included an infants' department. In September 1880, after the building of the extensions, there were 224 boys, 210 girls, and 76 infants.[1] The buildings were again extended and remodelled in the 1890s.[2] The schools were finally closed in 1939, and the buildings were destroyed by enemy action in 1940. Smethwick post office stands on the site.[3]

Crockett's Lane British School. A British school for boys and girls was opened *c.* 1840 in newly built schoolrooms in Crockett's Lane behind the Congregational chapel. It still existed in 1851.[4]

Chance's Schools. In 1845–6 Chance Brothers & Co. built British schools at its Spon Lane glassworks, with accommodation for 200 boys, 150 girls, and 100 infants.[5] The buildings, which included three schoolrooms, two classrooms, and houses for the teachers, were designed in a simple Gothic style and were opened in stages, the boys' school in 1845 and the girls' and infants' schools in 1846. They were intended primarily for the children of Chance's workpeople; the firm's decision in 1846 not to employ children under 12 was an attempt to persuade its workers to send their children to school. Outsiders' children, however, were also admitted, and the schools gradually became those for the Spon Lane area in general. The Chances engaged a master, a mistress, and an infants' mistress.[6] Frederick Talbot, master from 1845 to 1892, was a notable teacher and under him the schools gained a high reputation. The buildings were extensive, and there was a good supply of books and apparatus. A playground and a gymnasium were provided in 1858. The curriculum included the elements, grammar, geography, mechanics, and, from 1848, free-hand

drawing. In 1858 a special class for drawing was organized in connexion with Birmingham School of Art. An evening school for older boys, teaching the elements and other subjects, was maintained from 1846. A Sunday school was also held: 30 of the 299 children attending Chance's schools in 1846–7 were Sunday-school children only.[7]

In 1887 the schools were transferred to the school board. Average attendance in May–November 1887 was 352 (185 boys, 170 girls, and 97 infants).[8] Accommodation for girls was increased in 1900; in 1900–1 there was accommodation for 702 children and an average attendance of 633.[9] The schools were closed in 1914 on the opening of Smethwick Hall Council School (now Devonshire Road School).[10] The buildings were sold back to the firm and in 1971 were used as a canteen and social centre.

Cape Hill School, or Henderson's School. In 1846 John Henderson of the London Works built a day and Sunday school in the Cape Hill district. It was apparently rebuilt in 1854. It was still standing in 1857 off what is now Montague Road, but it probably did not long survive Henderson's bankruptcy in 1856.[11]

St. Matthew's Church of England Primary School. A school in connexion with St. Matthew's Church was established in temporary premises in 1859. After six months there were 85 pupils on the books. In 1861 the temporary accommodation was replaced by a National school for 300 children in Windmill Lane; three certificated teachers were engaged. In the early months of 1862 there was an average attendance of 185.[12] The buildings were extended in 1872.[13] The older children were transferred to council schools in 1935.[14] The school was moved to new buildings on the site of the former vicarage in 1966, and in 1971 it was a one-form-entry primary school.[15]

St. Philip Neri Roman Catholic Primary School. A Roman Catholic mixed and infants' school was built in 1860 on the site of the present church hall in Watt Street. Roman Catholic children had for some years previously been taught at 'Catten's School' in Cranford Street, so called from the name of the woman who ran it. The new school, which had a schoolroom for boys and girls, another for infants, and a classroom, was run by two mistresses on National-school lines. In February–March 1861 there was an average attendance of 103, of whom 38 were infants. Of the children 91 paid fees, while the others, whose parents were out of work, were taught

[97] Ed. 7/112/Smethwick/3; W.P.L., Harborne School Board Min. Bk. C, pp. 252, 484; Hackwood, *Smethwick*, 111.

[98] Ed. 7/112/Smethwick/6; S.R.O., D. 812/Smethwick National School; White, *Dir. Staffs.* (1851); *Mins. of Educ. Cttee. of Council, 1840–1,* 88–91; Nat. Soc. *Church Schs. Enquiry, 1846–7.* For a view of the schools in 1845 see *Lich. Dioc. Ch. Cal.* (1864), plate facing p. 148.

[99] 'Smethwick and Round About', 4 Apr. 1952.

[1] Ed. 7/112/Smethwick/3; *Lich. Dioc. Ch. Cal.* (1881), 71.

[2] 'Smethwick and Round About', 9 May 1952.

[3] W.P.L., Smethwick Educ. Cttee. Min. Bk. Y1, p. 13; *Smethwick Telephone,* 3 May 1963; inscription on E. window of S. aisle of Holy Trinity Church; local inf. (1970).

[4] Hackwood, *Smethwick,* 76, 110; H.O. 107/2050(2) f. 320v.

[5] For the following paras. see, unless otherwise stated, J. F. Chance, *Hist. of Firm of Chance Brothers & Co.*

(priv. print. 1919), 222–44. The architects' plans and elevations are among the archives at Chance's (1972).

[6] Ed. 7/112/Smethwick/4.

[7] Nat. Soc. *Church Schs. Enquiry, 1846–7.*

[8] Ed. 7/112/Smethwick/4; *Harborne School Board Year Book* (1887).

[9] *List of Schs. under Admin. of Bd. 1901–2* [Cd. 1277], p. 224, H.C. (1902), lxxix.

[10] Ed. 7/112/Smethwick/5A.

[11] H.O. 129/393/3; Roper, Plans of Smethwick, 1857, no. 34; 'Old Smethwick', 10 July 1948; above pp. 110–11.

[12] Ed. 7/112/Smethwick/9; S.R.O., D. 812/St. Matthew's National School, Smethwick; *Staffs. Advertiser,* 16 Nov. 1861; *P.O. Dir. Staffs.* (1868).

[13] *Lich. Dioc. Ch. Cal.* (1873), 93.

[14] W.P.L., Smethwick Educ. Cttee. Min. Bk. U1, p. 131.

[15] *Smethwick Telephone,* 17 Nov. 1961; *Smethwick Telephone & Warley Courier,* 19 Nov. 1965; *Express & Star,* 18 Mar. 1971.

free.[16] From at least 1863 until 1893 the building was also used as a church.[17] The school continued to cater for all Roman Catholic children of school age until the opening of Cardinal Newman Roman Catholic Secondary School in Edgbaston (Birmingham) in 1959. This took children from both Birmingham and Smethwick, and Smethwick corporation contributed towards its cost. The first part of a new St. Philip's School in Messenger Road was opened in 1959, and when the second part was opened in 1965 the old school was demolished.[18]

Smethwick Wesleyan School, later Rabone Lane Board School. In 1861 a Wesleyan Methodist day school was opened in the former chapel in Rabone Lane under a certificated teacher. There was a schoolroom for boys and girls and three classrooms. After a month 60 children were attending.[19] A new school was built in Rabone Lane in 1866.[20] It was subsequently enlarged and in 1888 was a mixed and infants' school with accommodation for 522 and an average attendance of 410.[21] It was handed over to the school board in 1894 and was closed in 1914 on the opening of Smethwick Hall Council School (now Devonshire Road School).[22]

SCHOOLS OPENED SINCE 1873.

Abbey Infants' School, Maurice Road, was opened in 1952.[23]

Abbey Road Junior School, built in 1909 by Oldbury urban district council and officially opened in 1910, stands in the area added to Smethwick borough in 1928. It was then a school for boys, girls, and infants but became a junior and infants' school in 1932 and a junior school in 1958.[24]

Albion Junior School, Halford's Lane, was opened in 1954. Since the 1966 boundary changes the building has stood in West Bromwich.[25]

Annie Lennard Infants' School, the Oval, was opened in 1954.[26]

Bearwood Road Junior and Infants' School, opened in 1882 as a board school for boys, girls, and infants, was considerably extended in the 1880s and 1890s. It became a junior and infants' school in 1932.[27]

Brasshouse Lane Infants' School was opened in 1876 as a mixed and infants' board school. In 1878 the mixed department was divided into separate boys' and girls' departments. The buildings were later enlarged several times.[28] From 1923, after another building had been added, Brasshouse Lane was a five-department school (senior boys, senior girls, junior boys, junior girls, and infants). It became a junior mixed and infants' school in 1935[29] and an infants' school in 1962.[30]

Cape Infants' School, Cape Hill, was opened in 1888 as a board school for boys, girls, and infants and was enlarged in 1894 and 1901.[31] It became a junior and infants' school in 1935[32] and was an infants' school by 1950.[33]

Central Board Schools, *see* Crockett's Lane Schools.

Corbett Street Infants' School, opened in 1879 as a board school for boys, girls, and infants, became a junior and infants' school in 1935 and an infants' school in 1965.[34]

Crockett's Lane Junior and Infants' Schools are the sole remnants of the former Central Board Schools, opened in stages on adjoining sites. An infants' school and a higher grade school for boys and girls were opened in 1885, an infants' school for boys was built in 1892, and a separate girls' school was added in 1898. The higher grade school took almost all the standard VI and standard VII children transferred from other schools, and subjects taught included chemistry and mechanics.[35] In 1935 the boys' school became a senior boys' school, the girls' school a senior girls' school, the infant boys' school a junior mixed school, and the infant girls' school a mixed infants' school.[36] In 1947 the senior girls' school became Park Secondary School for Girls and the senior boys' school was closed, its premises being taken over by James Watt Technical School.[37] Park School closed in 1957; Crockett's Lane Junior School moved into the vacated building, and James Watt School took over what had been the premises of the junior school as additional accommodation.[38]

Devonshire Road Junior and Infants' School was opened in 1914 as Smethwick Hall School, taking the pupils from Chance's and Rabone Lane schools and many pupils from Oldbury Road School. When Smethwick Hall Senior Schools were opened in 1939 the existing school became a junior and infants' school and was renamed.[39]

George Betts Junior and Infants' School, West End Avenue, was opened in 1954 as a junior school.

[16] Ed. 7/112/Smethwick/10; S.R.O., D. 812/Smethwick R.C. Schools; T. E. Bird, *Church of St. Philip Neri, Smethwick,* 9 (copy in W.P.L.).
[17] See p. 129.
[18] *Smethwick Civic News,* Aug. 1957, Aug. 1958; *V.C.H. Warws.* vii. 508; ex inf. Miss Amy Hill, St. Philip's School (1971).
[19] Ed. 7/112/Smethwick/8.
[20] 'Smethwick and Round About', 16 Nov., 7 Dec. 1956; S.R.O., D. 812/Smethwick Wesleyan School.
[21] 'Smethwick and Round About', 7 Dec. 1956; *Kelly's Dir. Birm.* (1888).
[22] W.P.L., Smethwick School Board Min. Bk. J, pp. 98–100, 291–2, 299–300, 344, 429; Min. Bk. K, pp. 35, 106, 294; Ed. 7/112/Smethwick/5A.
[23] *Smethwick Civic News,* Oct. 1954.
[24] Inscription on building; *Smethwick Weekly News,* 9 Apr. 1910; W.P.L., Smethwick Educ. Cttee. Min. Bk. R1, p. 18; *Smethwick Municipal Year Book 1958–1959.*
[25] *Smethwick Civic News,* July and Oct. 1954; above p. 93.
[26] *Smethwick Civic News,* July and Oct. 1954.
[27] Ed. 7/112/Smethwick/1; Hackwood, *Smethwick,* 111; W.P.L., Smethwick Educ. Cttee. Min. Bk. R1, p. 18.

[28] Ed. 7/112/Smethwick/2; W.P.L., Harborne School Board Min. Bk. A, p. 280; Min. Bk. B, pp. 14, 74–5; *Fifty Years of Educ. in Smethwick,* 7.
[29] Ed. 7/112/Smethwick/2; *Educ. in Smethwick, 1932–1938,* 21; W.P.L., Smethwick Educ. Cttee. Min. Bk. H1, p. 8; W.P.L., Brasshouse Lane School log-books.
[30] *Smethwick Municipal Year Book 1962–1963.*
[31] Ed. 7/112/Smethwick/12; Hackwood, *Smethwick,* 111, calling it Cape Hill Schools; *Fifty Years of Educ. in Smethwick,* 7.
[32] W.P.L., Smethwick Educ. Cttee. Min. Bk. U1, pp. 17, 297.
[33] *Smethwick Municipal Year Book 1950–1951.*
[34] Ed. 7/112/Smethwick/5; W.P.L., Smethwick Educ. Cttee. Min. Bk. U1, pp. 17, 297; *Educ. in Smethwick, 1932–1938,* 21; *Smethwick Municipal Year Book 1965–1966.*
[35] Ed. 7/112/Smethwick/3; *Fifty Years of Educ. in Smethwick,* 7, 19–20.
[36] W.P.L., Smethwick Educ. Cttee. Min. Bk. U1, pp. 91, 314; *Educ. in Smethwick, 1932–1938,* 21.
[37] *Smethwick Civic News,* June 1957; below p. 140.
[38] *Smethwick Civic News,* June and Nov. 1957.
[39] Ed. 7/112/Smethwick/5A; W.P.L., Smethwick Educ. Cttee. Min. Bk. V1, p. 56; Y1, pp. 232, 291; Z1, p. 67.

It was extended in 1970 and has since taken infants also.[40]

Holly Lodge Grammar Schools, Holly Lane, originated in 1922, when a high school for girls was opened in Holly Lodge, formerly the home of the Downing family. It moved to a new building near by in 1927, and a boys' high school was then opened in Holly Lodge, moving in its turn in 1932 to a new building adjoining that of the girls' high school.[41] The schools became the borough's two grammar schools in the reorganization after 1944. After the boys' grammar school had absorbed James Watt Technical School in 1967 its buildings were extended.[42]

James Watt Technical School, Crockett's Lane, was established in 1914 as Smethwick Junior Technical School. It took boys aged between 12 and 15 and was housed in the buildings of the Municipal Technical School. Until the Second World War girls were admitted also. In 1947 the age of entrance was lowered to 11, no more girls were admitted, and the school, renamed, moved to the premises formerly occupied by Crockett's Lane Senior Boys' School. In 1967 it was absorbed by Holly Lodge Boys' Grammar School.[43]

Merry Hill Infants' School, Foundry Lane, was opened in 1969.[44]

Oldbury Road Infants' School was opened in 1875 as a mixed and infants' board school, sometimes known as West Smethwick Board School. The mixed department was divided into separate boys' and girls' departments in 1878, and the school was subsequently extended several times.[45] It became a junior and infants' school in 1939 and an infants' school in 1959.[46]

Park Secondary School, see Crockett's Lane Schools.

St. Gregory's Roman Catholic Primary School, off Park Road, was opened in 1968. It has an annexe for infants, attached to the near-by Abbey Infants' School.[47]

Sandwell Schools, Halford's Lane, were opened in 1957. They are separate boys' and girls' secondary schools in a single building, which has always stood in West Bromwich.[48] They had been preceded during the school year 1956–7 by Sandwell 'Nucleus' School, which consisted of children moving up from Albion Junior School and was held in part of the Brasshouse Lane Junior School building.[49]

Shireland Secondary Schools, see Waterloo Road School.

Slough Lane School was opened in 1875 as a mixed and infants' board school. It was originally housed in the Congregational chapel but moved to new buildings in the same road in 1882. It was closed in 1937.[50]

Smethwick Hall Schools, Stony Lane, consisting of separate secondary schools for boys and girls, were opened in 1939 as senior schools and became secondary schools in the reorganization after 1944.[51] See also Devonshire Road School.

Smethwick Junior Technical School, see James Watt Technical School.

Uplands Secondary, Junior, and Infants' Schools, Thompson and Addenbrooke Roads, were opened in 1932 with senior boys', senior girls', junior, and infants' departments. The senior departments became boys' and girls' secondary schools in the reorganization after 1944. The secondary school for girls was closed in 1962, the premises being taken over by the boys' secondary school.[52]

Waterloo Road School was opened in 1907 (the boys' and girls' departments) and 1908 (the infants' department). In 1932 the boys' and girls' departments became senior departments. In the reorganization after 1944 they became Shireland Secondary School for Boys and Shireland Secondary School for Girls, the rest of the school becoming Waterloo Road Junior and Infants' School. The boys' school was closed in 1960, the girls' school taking over its premises.[53]

West Smethwick Board School, see Oldbury Road School.

FURTHER EDUCATION. Evening classes in science and art were established in 1846 by the Chance family at the schools attached to their Spon Lane glass-works. An institute formed at the works in 1852 flourished for almost twenty years.[54] John Henderson of the London Works formed a library and reading room in the Cape Hill district and was patron of an institute which met there in the mid 1850s,[55] while a few years later Joseph Chamberlain was fostering adult education at Nettlefold & Chamberlain's Smethwick works.[56] St. Matthew's Church had some 140 pupils at an evening school in 1870,[57] and Holy Trinity Church organized evening classes about the same date.[58] Smethwick Institute,

[40] Smethwick Civic News, July and Oct. 1954; W.P.L., programme of official opening of extensions to Geo. Betts Junior and Infant School, 25 Nov. 1970.
[41] Fifty Years of Educ. in Smethwick, 21–2; Educ. in Smethwick, 1932–1938, 13; above p. 101.
[42] Smethwick and West Bromwich Joint Development Plan (1946; copy in W.P.L.); Warley News Telephone, 10 Aug. 1967.
[43] Fifty Years of Educ. in Smethwick, 22; County Boro. of Smethwick, Scheme for Further Education and Plan for County Colleges . . . (1954; copy in W.P.L.); Smethwick Civic News, Apr. 1956, June 1957, Mar. 1958; Warley News Telephone, 29 Dec. 1966, 10 Aug. 1967.
[44] Warley News Telephone, 18 Sept. 1969.
[45] Ed. 7/112/Smethwick/6A; W.P.L., Harborne School Board Min. Bk. B, pp. 14, 74; Fifty Years of Educ. in Smethwick, 7.
[46] W.P.L., Smethwick Educ. Cttee. Min. Bk. X1, p. 361; Y1, p. 141; Smethwick Municipal Year Book 1959–1960.
[47] Warley News Telephone, 18 July 1968; County Boro. of Warley Year Book 1970–1971.
[48] Smethwick Civic News, Nov. 1957, Apr. 1958; Smethwick Telephone, 2 May 1958.
[49] Smethwick Civic News, June 1956, Aug. 1957.

[50] Fifty Years of Educ. in Smethwick, 7; W.P.L., Harborne School Board Min. Bk. C, p. 210; Educ. in Smethwick, 1932–1938, 7; O.S. Map 6″, Staffs. LXXII. NE. (1890 edn.); above p. 131.
[51] 'Smethwick and Round About', 3 Nov. 1951; Smethwick and West Bromwich Joint Development Plan (1946).
[52] Educ. in Smethwick, 1932–1938, 5, 21; Smethwick and West Bromwich Joint Development Plan (1946); Smethwick Civic News, July 1962.
[53] Ed. 7/112/Smethwick/14; W.P.L., Smethwick Educ. Cttee. Min. Bk. R1, p. 18; Smethwick and West Bromwich Joint Development Plan (1946); Smethwick Civic News, Sept. 1960.
[54] J. F. Chance, Hist. of Firm of Chance Brothers & Co. (priv. print. 1919), 228 sqq., 254.
[55] 'Smethwick and Round About', 26 Dec. 1952.
[56] J. L. Garvin, Life of Joseph Chamberlain, i. 65–6. Chamberlain was with the firm 1854–74: above p. 113.
[57] Birmingham Daily Gaz. 11 Oct. 1870, reporting inf. about his (unnamed) evening school given by the Revd. R. W. Ferguson to A.G.M. of South Staffs. Association for the Promotion of Adult Education and Evening Schools. Ferguson was vicar of St. Matthew's, Smethwick: Lich. Dioc. Ch. Cal. (1870).
[58] Fifty Years of Educ. in Smethwick, 19.

formed in 1887, met at the higher grade school in Crockett's Lane. For a few years after its foundation its activities included evening classes. It closed in the later 1920s.[59] Another institute was meeting at Bearwood in the 1880s.[60]

The school board constituted itself a local committee of the Science and Art Department in 1885 and organized evening classes in science and art at the higher grade school in Crockett's Lane.[61] In 1892 a technical instruction committee was set up consisting of members of the local board and the school board. It took over the management of the science and art classes, forming them into a municipal technical school.[62] The school board members withdrew from the committee in 1898, and from 1899 the whole committee was appointed by the town council.[63]

The technical school continued to meet in the evenings in the higher grade school until 1910, when a technical school building was opened in Crockett's Lane.[64] By 1913 there was an attendance of nearly 4,000.[65] From 1914 until 1947[66] the buildings also housed a secondary technical school, and pupils from it continued to use classrooms and laboratories until 1956. Evening classes were still the most important part of the institution's work in the late 1920s, although after the 1918 Education Act the first day-release students were enrolled, with originally five firms sending workers. The school became Smethwick Municipal College in 1927 and was renamed Chance Technical College in 1945. A block of engineering and building workshops was opened in 1950. Between 1952 and 1966 major extensions were built on an adjoining site in Crockett's Lane; they enabled the college to accommodate some 3,500 students by 1966, two-thirds of whom attended courses during the day. In 1968 the college was merged with Oldbury College of Further Education to form Warley College of Technology, with the buildings in Crockett's Lane (Chance Building) housing the main administrative centre of the new college and six of its eight departments.[67]

The original building, extensively renovated, is of brick with grey terracotta dressings, and was designed in a 'free Renaissance style' by F. J. Gill.[68] The extensions of 1952–66, designed by W. W. Atkinson and Partners, consist of five main blocks faced with Portland stone and coloured brick. They house workshops, classrooms, laboratories, assembly and recreation halls, and administrative offices.

PRIVATE SCHOOLS. Smethwick never maintained many private schools, and only a few are known to have survived for any length of time. Directories listed three private academies in 1835 and nine in 1872.[69] Both lists are evidently incomplete, but it is difficult to assess how many schools were omitted. In 1875 there were 30 private schools in Harborne School Board district, most of them dame schools; according to a census taken by the board in that year only some 38 per cent of the pupils were being efficiently taught.[70] Shireland Hall housed a succession of schools for middle-class children: a girls' school in 1818, a school for the sons of clergy of all denominations from the earlier 1850s until at least 1865, and another girls' school from later in the 1860s until the mid 1870s.[71] Smethwick Hall off Stony Lane was used as a school from at least 1872 until c. 1885.[72] A favoured area for genteel private schools was that around South Street (later South Road), where a number of such schools flourished between at least 1851 and the early 20th century.[73]

CHARITIES FOR THE POOR. *The Harborne Parish Lands Charity.* Smethwick enjoys a share of the charity which existed by 1640 when a body of trustees was administering lands granted for charitable uses in Harborne parish.[74] The trustees subsequently obtained the endowments of two other charities, both founded by members of the Smethwick family of Cowper alias Piddock. Elizabeth Cowper, by will dated 1576, left £40 to buy land, the rent from which was to be distributed as charity twice a year; 20s. was to go to the poor of Harborne parish, while the remainder[75] was apparently to be distributed without restriction of place. The land so bought was settled in trust in 1591.[76] About 1786 it was acquired by the parish, and by 1823 the rent was being applied in charitable relief with that of the other parish lands. In 1623 William Cowper, formerly of Smethwick, settled a cottage and ½ a. near Rood End, Oldbury, in Halesowen (Worcs.), in trust for the poor; 6s. 8d. of the income was to be distributed yearly to the poor of the adjacent part of Handsworth parish, and the rest twice yearly to those of Harborne parish, with at least half going to the poor of Smethwick. By c. 1765 the property had apparently passed to the parish lands trustees.

Trust deeds of 1640 and 1668 stipulated that the income of the parish lands was to be used for the relief of the aged or infirm poor of Harborne and Smethwick.[77] By 1723 the trustees were setting aside £10 a year to apprentice four poor children, two from Smethwick and two from Harborne.[78] By 1786 they were also maintaining what were in effect

[59] 'Smethwick and Round About', 24 June, 1 July 1955.
[60] 'Smethwick and Round About', 24 June 1955; programme of Bearwood Institute, 1887–8 (copy in W.P.L.).
[61] W.P.L., Harborne School Board Min. Bk. E, pp. 559 sqq.; Min. Bk. F, pp. 88, 300.
[62] Ibid. Min. Bk. I, pp. 83, 139–40; *Smethwick Telephone,* 6 Feb. 1892.
[63] *Smethwick Telephone,* 1 Oct. 1910.   [64] Ibid.
[65] Unless otherwise stated, the following account is based on that given in *The Chance Technical College* (programme of official opening of major extensions 23 May 1966; copy in W.P.L.).
[66] *Fifty Years of Educ. in Smethwick,* 22; County Boro. of Smethwick, *Scheme for Further Education and Plan for County Colleges.*
[67] *Warley News Telephone,* 4 Apr. 1968; County Boro. of Warley Educ. Cttee. *Warley College of Technology: widening horizons in further education and industrial training* (n.d. but 1968; copy in W.P.L.).

[68] *Smethwick Telephone,* 13 and 20 Aug. 1910.
[69] Pigot, *Nat. Com. Dir.* (1835), 472; *P.O. Dir. Staffs.* (1872).
[70] *Fifty Years of Educ. in Smethwick,* 8.
[71] See p. 104.   [72] See p. 106.
[73] H.O. 107/2050(2) f. 259v.; 'Smethwick and Round About', 12 Dec. 1952, 18 and 25 Sept. 1953.
[74] For this para. see, except where otherwise stated, *9th Rep. Com. Char.* H.C. 258, pp. 552–6 (1823), ix; *V.C.H. Warws.* vii. 560–1; B.R.L. 391003; B.R.L. 449574, ff. 39–48.
[75] It has apparently been distributed at various times in Handsworth and Birmingham parishes: *Gent. Mag.* lxiv (2), 713; B.R.L. 449574, f. 80; *V.C.H. Warws.* vii. 561.
[76] *Abstract of Returns of Charitable Donations, 1786–8,* H.C. 511, pp. 1128–9 (1816), xvi (2).
[77] B.R.L. 391003; B.R.L. 449574, ff. 18, 29–30.
[78] *9th Rep. Com. Char.* 553.

alms-houses, as cottage property which they owned was occupied rent-free by paupers; they drew £57 6s. from the rest of the property.[79] In 1823 there were thirteen cottages used as alms-houses, four in Smethwick and nine in Harborne. Smethwick received £75 14s. from the trustees, and Harborne £67 15s. Out of these sums the cottages were kept in repair and the two poor children of each township were apprenticed. In both places the remainder of the income was given to 'the more respectable description of poor, to whom it would be hurtful to apply for relief at the workhouse', either in weekly payments of 2s. or 3s. or in occasional payments of £1–£4.[80]

The income of the parish lands was £420 in 1872, £525 in 1895, and £820 in 1914.[81] In 1872, out of a total expenditure of £344 in Harborne and Smethwick, £270 was given in food or cash. The alms-people seem to have received no relief except rent-free accommodation. A Scheme of 1885, however, authorized payment of stipends to them; thereafter more and more of the charity's income went to support them, while less and less was spent on doles. In 1914, for example, the stipends, fuel, and medical attendance for the alms-people of both townships cost over £200 while only £3 5s. was distributed casually. The system of allowing the trust's cottages to be occupied as alms-houses meant that the number of alms-houses fluctuated. In Smethwick, as already seen, there were four in 1823. In 1842 there were six, in Crockett's Lane;[82] there were five there in 1851,[83] four in 1886, and six in 1890.[84] In 1912 the Smethwick alms-people were moved to new alms-houses in Harborne.[85]

In 1927 ten alms-houses and a matron's house were built in Cooper's Lane, Smethwick, by members of the Mitchell family in memory of Henry Mitchell; known as the Henry Mitchell Alms-houses, they were given to the Harborne Parish Lands Charity.[86] A Scheme of 1928 required candidates to have lived in the borough for three years or more; they were to be nominated to the parish lands trustees by a descendant of Henry Mitchell, in the first instance by J. E. Mitchell and subsequently by a descendant chosen by Mitchells & Butlers Ltd. By 1930 six more alms-houses had been built for the charity at the expense of five members of the Mitchell family. Under a Scheme of that year the five benefactors and successors appointed by them were empowered to nominate alms-people for the new houses. Under the Schemes of 1928 and 1930 residents of the Mitchell Alms-houses receive the same stipends as residents of the alms-houses in Harborne belonging to the Parish Lands Charity. They also benefit from £900 stock left by Mary Ann Penny, by will proved in 1969, to the parish lands trustees in memory of her husband Joseph. The

income was to provide excursions with teas for the residents, matron, and assistant matron of the Mitchell Alms-houses. Any resident unable to join an excursion was to receive a treat of equal value.

The sixteen alms-houses and the matron's house form a rectangle of brick-built bungalows enclosing a lawn. The entrance from Cooper's Lane to the north is by a covered passage between the matron's house and one of the alms-houses; there is a south range of three alms-houses while along the east and west sides are twelve semi-detached alms-houses.

Parkes's Charity. By deed of 1719 Dorothy Parkes charged her trustees with the payment of £10 a year out of the income from the lands which she gave for the foundation of Smethwick chapel. Payment was not to begin before they had built and furnished the chapel and appointed a minister or before the death of Mary Halfpenny, her servant. Of the £10, 52s. was for a weekly dole of penny-loaves to twelve poor inhabitants of Smethwick attending divine service in the chapel, and 52s. for a similar distribution at Harborne church; £4 10s. was to buy six coats or other garments to be given each year to three poor women from Smethwick and three from Harborne; and 6s. to buy bibles to be given yearly to poor inhabitants of Smethwick chosen by the minister of Smethwick. Any person who had received parish relief within the previous twelve months was disqualified from receiving the bread or garments.[87] The payments had begun by 1739.[88] By 1970 the trustees of Dorothy Parkes were paying £5 3s. a year to the parochial church council of Smethwick Old Church and £4 17s. a year to that of St. Peter's, Harborne.[89]

Dandy's Charity. By will proved in 1910 James Dandy of Bromsgrove (Worcs.) left £1,000 for the poor of Smethwick.[90] After the deduction of £2 a year for the upkeep of his tomb, the income was to be spent on warm clothes or bedding to be distributed yearly to poor people who had lived in Smethwick for at least six months; anyone who sold or pawned a gift was disqualified for the future. The trust's income in 1964 was £30; £40 was spent on gifts of bedding and clothing.

Hill Crest Home for the Aged. By deed of 1946 Arthur Mitchell, a director of Mitchells & Butlers, gave Smethwick corporation £5,000 to buy Hill Crest, a large Victorian house on the corner of Little Moor Hill and South Road, as a home for aged poor who had lived in Smethwick for at least ten years.[91] In 1948 Mitchell gave the corporation £250 Mitchells & Butlers stock to provide comforts for the residents of Hill Crest. The annual income from the endowment in 1963–4 was £95. In 1958 it was decided that the qualifying period of residence in the borough should be reduced from ten to three years.

[79] *Char. Donations, 1786–8,* 1128–9.
[80] *9th Rep. Com. Char.* 554–5.
[81] For this para. see, except where otherwise stated, *V.C.H. Warws.* vii. 561; docs. at St. Peter's, Harborne, 121A.
[82] W.S.L., S. MS. 417/Harborne.
[83] H.O. 107/2050 ff. 317v.–318.
[84] *Kelly's Dir. Birm.* (1886; 1890).
[85] *V.C.H. Warws.* vii. 561.

[86] For this para. see Char. Com. files; W.P.L. 12727–8, 19248; Char. Com. Schemes, 13 Jan. 1928, 1 Apr. 1930.
[87] Hackwood, *Smethwick,* 53.   [88] See p. 123.
[89] Ex inf. the secretary to the trustees of Dorothy Parkes (1971).
[90] The account of this charity is based on Char. Com. files.
[91] The account of this charity is based on Char. Com. files; 'Old Smethwick', 11 Nov. 1950.

WALSALL

THE ANCIENT parish of Walsall[1] consisted of a borough and a foreign. The two parts were incorporated as the borough and foreign of Walsall in 1627. A new borough of Walsall was created in 1835. It became a county borough in 1889 and part of a new metropolitan borough of Walsall in 1974.[2] The area known as Walsall Wood was a detached part of the foreign but was not included in the 1835 borough; in 1894 it became part of the urban district of Brownhills.[3] The ancient parish (including the 1,551 a. of Walsall Wood) comprised 8,324 a. The 1835 borough was 6,683 a. in area and was extended to 6,763 a. in 1876 and 7,480 a. in 1890 by the addition of parts of Rushall.[4] It was increased to 8,782 a. in 1931 by additions from the boroughs of Wednesbury and West Bromwich and the civil parishes of Bentley, Great Barr, and Rushall;[5] it was reduced to 8,780 a. in 1934 by an adjustment of the boundary with the urban district of Darlaston.[6] In 1966 it was extended to 12,990 a. by the addition of most of the urban districts of Darlaston and Willenhall and various boundary adjustments.[7] The present article is concerned primarily with the history of the area covered by the ancient parish, except Walsall Wood which is treated in a separate article. Some account of the areas added to the borough before 1966 is given from the time of their addition, but their earlier history is reserved for treatment in future volumes.

Walsall lies on the South Staffordshire Plateau on undulating ground that drops to 370 ft. in the south-west at Broadway West and rises to 539 ft. to the north of Bloxwich.[8] The limestone hill in the centre of the town, on which St. Matthew's Church stands at 491 ft., rises to 511 ft. at the junction of Sandwell and Windmill Streets south of the church; the ground falls away on all other sides of the church but rises again east of Ablewell Street to 497 ft. at the junction of Holtshill Lane and Charlotte Street.[9] Most of the parish is situated on the Coal Measures, but an inlier of Silurian limestones and shales runs east and south-east from the town centre. The drift is mainly boulder clay, but there is sand and gravel east of Bloxwich and in the south-west of the parish.[10]

Several streams flow through the area, and some of them formed the boundaries of the parish.[11] On the north-west the boundary followed Sneyd Brook, the lower part of which was known as Bentley Brook in the late 14th century and as both Bentley Brook and Park Brook in the 18th century.[12] It meets a stream flowing from the west in Bentley Mill Lane, and the united stream, known as Bescot Brook in the 18th century,[13] formed the south-western boundary down to its confluence with the Tame near Bescot. The Tame and its tributary Full Brook formed the southern boundary and a stream called Scottes Brook the south-eastern boundary. The Holbrook formed the pre-1890 boundary with Rushall in the present Arboretum area. Clock Mill Brook formed the north-eastern boundary at Goscote and Essington Wood Brook the northern boundary by Yieldfields Hall. The Holbrook joins Ford Brook[14] under the site between Lichfield and Darwall Streets occupied by the central library and the Gala Baths. As Walsall Brook the united stream flows under the centre of the town and joins Bescot Brook close to its confluence with the Tame; a mill

---

[1] This article was written between 1972 and 1974. The help of the following is gratefully acknowledged: Mr. J. A. Galloway, chief executive and town clerk, and his staff, especially Miss Olive Brookes; Mr. F. N. Bowler and Mr. F. H. Lamb, successive directors of the libraries and museum services, and their staff, especially Mr. A. J. Mealey, Mr. M. A. Mosesson, and Mr. K. F. Brown; and Mr. L. Harper, churchwarden of St. Matthew's, and others named in footnotes. Thanks are also due to the Earl of Bradford for making his archives readily available.

[2] See pp. 209–11, 215, 217.

[3] See p. 275.

[4] O.S. Area Book: Walsall (1886); Walsall Red Book (1877), 77; Census, 1911; below p. 217. The area of the borough is given as 7,480 a. in Census, 1891, 1901.

[5] Census, 1931; Walsall Corp. Act, 1930, 20 & 21 Geo. V, c. 170 (Local).

[6] Census, 1931.

[7] County Boro. of Walsall: Council Year Book 1966–7; below p. 217.

[8] O.S. Map 6″, Staffs. LVII. SW. (1887 edn.), LXIII. SW. (1889 edn.).

[9] Ibid. LXIII. SE. (edns. of 1890 and 1903).

[10] Geol. Surv. Map 1″, drift and solid, sheets 154 and 168 (3rd edn.).

[11] For the boundaries see S.R.O., D. 1287/1/2, survey of Walsall manor, 1576, mm. 11–13; ibid., ct. of recog. and survey, 1617, p. 18 (printed by Willmore, Walsall, 439–41); Pearce, Walsall, 223–6; L.J.R.O., B/A/15/Walsall, map; O.S. Map 6″, Staffs. LVII. SW., SE., LXIII.

[12] S.R.O., D. 641/1/2/32; B.M. Eg. Roll 8472; Act for repairing roads leading from Sutton Colefield Common to town of Walsall . . ., 21 Geo. II, c. 25; Pearce, Walsall, 223.

[13] Act for repairing and widening road from Muckley Corner to Walsall and Wednesbury . . ., 6 Geo. III, c. 99; Pearce, Walsall, 221; S.R.O., Q/SB, A. 1781. The stream flowing from the west and Bescot Brook are among several streams which have been called the Tame: see above p. 1 n. 9.

[14] Erdeswick Staffs. 399–412, calls Clock Mill and Ford Brooks Walsall Water. The lower part of Ford Brook was also called Hammerwich or Hambridge Forge Brook: Pearce, Walsall, 223; H. Jacob, Plan of Boundary Line between Township of Boro. and Township of Foreign of Walsall (Birmingham, 1816; copy in W.C.L.). Part at least of Butts Rd. was formerly called Homebridge (or Hambridge or Hammerwich) Forge Lane or Homebridge Lane: W.C.L., QSM 1/322; W.S.L., D. 1798/551, e.g. nos. 14, 61, 195, 485; S.R.O., D. 351/M/B/207.

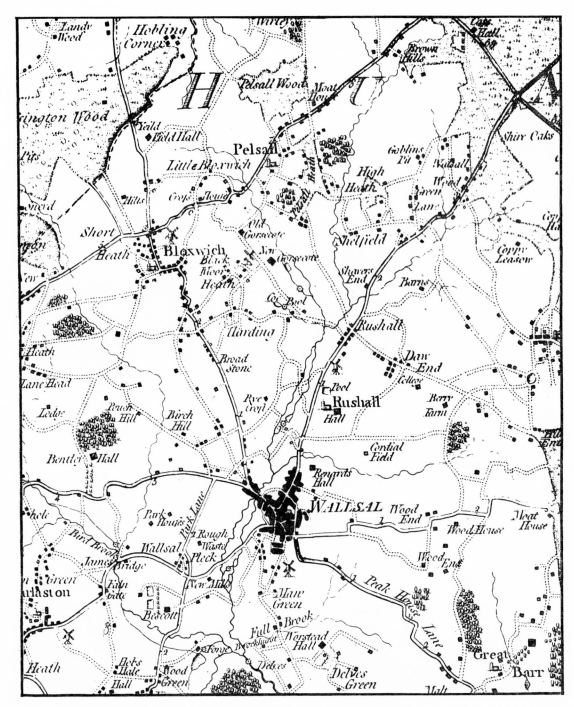

WALSALL AREA, *c.* 1775 (scale about 1 inch to 1 mile)

fleam runs off it near the Bridge and rejoins it below the site of the New Mills south of Wednesbury Road.[15]

The name Walsall suggests a settlement of foreigners, that is Britons, or of serfs.[16] The 'Walesho' of Wulfric Spot's will in the early 11th century may be Walsall; otherwise the first known mention of a settlement is in 1159, when it was presumably on the hill by the parish church.[17] A borough had been created by the earlier 13th century.[18] There is also evidence of early cultivation about a mile to the west on the sandy soil in the area

[15] S.R.O., D. 351/M/B/207; O.S. Map 6″, Staffs. LXIII. SE. (1890 edn.); *Walsall Observer*, 13 Sept. 1957; below p. 185. The united stream was called the Holbrook in the 1286 description of the bounds of Cannock forest (*S.H.C.* v (1), 166–7), the brook of Walsall in 1310 (*Walsall Records*, 31), and the town brook in the 16th and 17th centuries (S.R.O., D. 260/M/T/1/1a, deed of 10 Nov. 1513; Glew, *Walsall*, 121). It is given as Ford Brook by O.S. Map 1/10,000, SP 09 NW. (1972 edn.). The name Walsall

Brook was in use by the late 18th century: *Aris's Birmingham Gaz.* 1 Sept. 1766; S.R.O., Q/SB, A. 1781.
[16] *Eng. Place-name Elements* (E.P.N.S.), ii. 242. This also suggests (p. 243) that the second element is *hall*, 'a hall' or 'a farm-house'. E. Ekwall, *Concise Oxford Dict. of Eng. Place-names* (4th edn.), gives the derivation of the name as 'W(e)alh's *halh* or valley'.
[17] See p. 169.
[18] See p. 212.

occupied by the 13th-century park and the manor-house.[19] The other main settlement in the parish was at Bloxwich, a name suggesting a pre-Conquest origin.[20] Most of the parish lay within Cannock forest, a fact which influenced its early agrarian development.[21] Industrial activity was in progress by the 14th century when there is evidence of mining and iron-working.[22] Leland c. 1540 described Walsall as a little market town with a park, many smiths and bit-makers, and pits of coal, lime, and ironstone.[23] Much of Walsall's industry developed out of the requirements of horse transport, the production of horse furniture being followed by leather-working and rope-making.

There were 367 poll-tax payers in 1377.[24] In 1563 there were said to be 290 households.[25] In 1619 the number of recipients of Mollesley's Dole, by which everyone in Walsall on Twelfth Night received 1d., was 2,861 (1,622 of them in the borough) and in 1661 4,213 (2,241 in the borough); visitors, however, as well as inhabitants, were eligible.[26] The Compton Census of 1676 gives 1,360 adult conformists, 40 papists, and 200 Protestant non-conformists.[27] In 1773 the vicar reported some 1,500 houses in the parish, adding that there were 'no families of distinction but some gentlemen and several capital traders'.[28] The population in 1801 was 10,399 (5,222 of them in the foreign).[29]

Many changes were made in the central part of Walsall from the 1820s, with Lord Bradford, John Walhouse, and their successors acting as urban developers. It was stated in 1834 that Walsall 'ranks as the second manufacturing town in the county, as regards its population, and yields to none of them in beauty and elegance'.[30] In 1845 Lord Bradford's agent Peter Potter noted that the wealthier inhabitants were living in the central parts of the town but that in the area to the north-west the 'inhabitants are nearly all poor, being for the most part miners and mechanics'.[31] The population rose sharply from the 1820s, from 11,914 in 1821 to 26,822 in 1851; the large increase to 39,690 in 1861 was the result of the extension of mining and iron-working in the foreign. By 1901 the population of the county borough was 87,464. Growth was particularly marked in the foreign; in the borough township there was a decline in the later 19th century.[32] By the mid 19th century the population included an Irish element, concentrated in the Blue Lane area; by the early 20th century there was an Irish settlement at Coal Pool.[33] It has been noted

that 'the Irish have been the traditional scapegoats on whom Walsall projects its fears and frustrations'.[34]

Between the World Wars council estates became a feature of the landscape particularly in the north-eastern part of the borough, and after the Second World War in the north-western part.[35] In the centre of the town there was extensive clearance in the later 1930s and after the war and redevelopment in the 1950s and 1960s.[36] In addition reclamation of derelict land in the borough, largely for building, began after the war.[37] The population of the enlarged borough was 103,059 in 1931 and 118,498 in 1961.[38] By 1961 it included a number of immigrants, largely in the Caldmore and Palfrey areas; there were 625 born in India, 353 in Pakistan, and 478 in Jamaica.[39]

Notable natives of Walsall include John Edward Gray (1800–75), naturalist; Sir Harry Smith Parkes (1828–85), diplomatist, who was born at Birchills Hall; and Jerome Klapka Jerome (1859–1927), novelist and playwright, who was born in a house on the corner of Bradford Street and Caldmore Road.[40] Among other local worthies John Reynolds (1667–1727), writer of tracts and hymns, was assistant minister at the Presbyterian meeting-house from 1721 until his death; he was buried at West Bromwich. Josiah Owen (1711–55), author of sermons and anti-Jacobite tracts, was minister of the chapel in the late 1730s.[41] Dorothy Wyndlow Pattison (1832–78), otherwise known as Sister Dora, was noted for her work as nursing sister at the Cottage Hospital from 1865 to 1878.[42] Patrick Collins (1859–1943), amusement caterer, settled in Walsall in 1882 and later lived at Lime Tree House, Bloxwich; he was M.P. for Walsall from 1922 to 1924 and mayor in 1938–9.[43] Sir Henry Newbolt (1862–1938), poet and man of letters, was the grandson of G. B. Stubbs, a town clerk; he lived from 1866 to 1869 in Doveridge Place and from 1869 to 1873 in Birmingham Road, and attended the grammar school from 1870 to 1872.[44]

The inhabitants of Walsall were described in the mid 1520s by one of the lessees of the manor as 'light persons suddenly moved to affrays and insurrections'. He accused three townsmen of threatening to set 400 men on him armed with clubs known as 'Bayard and his thousand colts' and to rouse the townsmen by ringing Bayard's bell.[45] During the Civil War and Interregnum the corporation tended to support the Parliamentarians.[46] Henry Stone, mayor in 1638–9, was active in the county on the parliamentarian side and was governor of Stafford

---

[19] Ex inf. (1974) Mr. and Mrs. S. Wrathmell, who have excavated the manor-house site for Walsall Local Hist. Soc.

[20] See p. 161.

[21] See p. 180.

[22] See pp. 189, 192, 194.

[23] Leland, Itin. ed. Toulmin Smith, v. 23.

[24] S.H.C. 4th ser. vi. 1, 10.

[25] S.H.C. 1915, p. lxxii.

[26] W.T.C. II/31/1; II/13/49; below pp. 266–7. Not all the figures given in Homeshaw, Walsall, 4–6, are correct.

[27] W.S.L., S. MS. 330, p. [371].

[28] L.J.R.O., B/V/5/1772–3.

[29] V.C.H. Staffs. i. 324.

[30] White, Dir. Staffs. (1834).

[31] S.R.O., D. 1287/12/3, P. Potter to Lord Bradford, 1 Dec. 1845.

[32] V.C.H. Staffs. i. 324; Census, 1861; below p. 149. The details given here from 1881 are taken from the Censuses; they exclude Walsall Wood and cover the twice-enlarged borough.

[33] See pp. 161, 241; W.T.C., Street Cttee. Mins. 1849–51, 1 Dec. 1849; Cason, Blakenall Heath, 42.

[34] Cason, Blakenall Heath, 42.

[35] See pp. 163–5.

[36] See pp. 149, 161.

[37] See pp. 164–5, 221.

[38] Census, 1931, 1961.

[39] Ibid. 1961; below pp. 156–7, 249.

[40] D.N.B.; S. Lane-Poole, Sir Harry Parkes in China (1901), 3; J. K. Jerome, My Life and Times, 10–12.

[41] D.N.B.; A. G. Matthews, Cong. Churches of Staffs. 121.

[42] Jo Manton, Sister Dora; below p. 222.

[43] The Times, 9 Dec. 1943; Walsall Observer, 26 Feb. 1971; Express & Star, 1 Feb. 1971.

[44] My World as in My Time: Memoirs of Sir Henry Newbolt, 10–28; Woodall, Walsall Milestones, 65.

[45] Willmore, Walsall, 90; below pp. 214, 220.

[46] For this period see Homeshaw, Walsall, 34 sqq.; Willmore, Walsall, 304 sqq.; S.H.C. 4th ser. i, p. xxii; Cal. Cttee. for Money, iii. 1415; Cal. S.P. Dom. 1644, 177–8, 235.

from 1644 until at least 1651. The gentry of the foreign were royalist in sympathy, but they retained some influence on the town council, while Mark Antony Caesar Galliardello, who was employed by Henry Stone in 1651 and became town clerk in 1657, had been a royalist in 1643. The town was not garrisoned for either side during the war. In July 1643 Henrietta Maria passed through Walsall on her way from Lichfield to King's Norton (Worcs.)

easterly expansion into the foreign, works clock-wise area by area round the central district. Next the growth of Bloxwich is traced, and finally there is a clock-wise survey of each area round Bloxwich.

The street-plan of the early borough has been described as a cross with its head at St. Matthew's Church, its shaft continuing along High Street, Digbeth, and Park Street, its foot lying at Townend, and its arms formed by Rushall and Peal

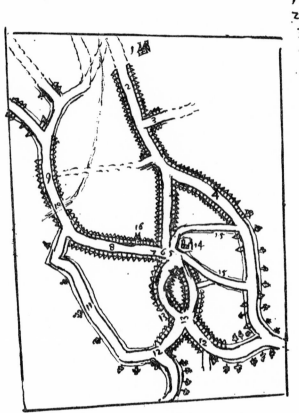

PLAN OF WALSALL, 1679

and is said to have stayed at George Hawe's house in Caldmore. In May 1644 the parliamentarian army under the earl of Denbigh stopped at Bloxwich on its way to besiege Rushall Hall and was quartered in Walsall during the siege. Denbigh returned for a time to Walsall after the indecisive fight at Dudley on 11 June 1644. Riots were frequent in the 18th century, and during a riot in 1750 George II was hanged in effigy on Church Hill. There was further rioting during the reform crisis of 1832.[47]

THE GROWTH OF THE TOWN. The following survey begins with the area covered by the pre-1835 borough and then, starting with its north-

Streets. That basic plan had evolved by the beginning of the 14th century. Open fields lay in three of the four spaces between the shaft and the arms, and meadow land occupied the fourth.[48] The settlement, in existence by the mid 12th century when Walsall is first mentioned, was presumably on the top of the limestone hill where the church stood by 1200.[49] Settlement spread westwards down High Street, the 'alta via' with its market-place of the 1309 borough charter,[50] and Digbeth, so named by 1583,[51] to the bridge over Walsall Brook, in existence c. 1300.[52] There was a mill to the north of the crossing by the mid 13th century, with a large pool fed by the Holbrook and Ford Brook.[53] Park Street continues west from the bridge to Townend, and there was evidently settlement in it by the end of the

[47] Below pp. 223–4; *Walsall Records*, 8–29 (2nd nos.).
[48] Homeshaw, *Walsall*, 1; W.T.C. I/9; below pp. 180–2.
[49] See pp. 144, 226.
[50] W.T.C. I/9.
[51] *S.H.C.* 1910, 168.

[52] See p. 167.
[53] See pp. 184–5. The pool may be the Broad Water mentioned in the later 16th and early 17th centuries: S.R.O., D. 260/M/T/1/1b and 49; D. 1287/1/2, survey of Walsall manor, 1576, m. 12; Willmore, *Walsall*, 440.

14th century;[54] the earliest known mention of it by name, however, is in 1462.[55] Townend occurs by name in 1557,[56] but it may be the 'head of the town' mentioned in the 1309 charter.[57] At Townend the road divided into three, one branch running to the manor-house and Wolverhampton, one to Birchills, and one to Bloxwich.

Rushall Street running north from the top of High Street existed as the road to Lichfield probably by the earlier 13th century and is named in 1339.[58] By the mid 15th century buildings there included one called 'my lord's inn', then in the hands of a tenant.[59] Peal Street running south from High Street is apparently the Hole End of 1380 and the Newgate Street of 1385–6; both names were in use in the 16th and 17th centuries, with Hall End as another variant. The name Peal Street was in use by 1763.[60] Until 1831 it was the first part of the road to Wednesbury and Darlaston, which continued along Dudley Street.[61] Steps ran up to the church from the top of High Street by the mid 16th century, and by the late 18th century they were flanked by buildings all the way up, although some old ones were then removed.[62] Church Street leading up from Peal Street apparently existed by the later 17th century.[63] Ablewell Street, running from Rushall Street below the east side of the church hill, occurs in 1403 and was one of the roads out of the town to Birmingham and London; the area occurs as 'Abelwellsych' in 1309.[64] Two roads led up to the church from Ablewell Street by the later 17th century, the Ditch and Hill Street; by the later 18th century they were linked below the church by Bullock's Row (or Road), while Pain's Yard, mentioned in 1733, ran between the top of the Ditch and Rushall Street.[65] Birmingham Street, running up from the southern end of Ablewell Street to New Street, is mentioned in 1535. New Street links it with Peal Street so that there was a second route out of the town to Birmingham and London.[66] In 1914 Springhill Road was built to bypass the curve on the southern end of Ablewell Street; in 1964 that part of Able-

well Street was closed and absorbed into the site of the new Blue Coat School.[67] By the later 18th century Gorton's Yard ran from the junction of Birmingham Street and New Street over the top of the hill to St. Matthew's.[68] Hall (or Haw) Lane ran from Digbeth to Dudley Street round the south-west of the town by the later 17th century;[69] George Street (formerly Castle Lane and also called New Row and St. George Street until the earlier 19th century) linked it with High Street by the later 18th century.[70]

The inner streets of the borough were densely built up by the later 17th century.[71] The recipients of Mollesley's Dole on Church Hill and in Hole End numbered 526 in 1619 and 746 in 1661, those in High Street, Park Street, and Townend 516 in 1619 and 711 in 1661, and those in Rushall Street 580 and 784.[72] The borough had a population of 5,177 in 1801.[73] The area of the borough township as defined in 1814 was 95 a.[74]

In the later 18th century there came the first in a succession of major changes in the street plan of the borough when under an Act of 1766 Bridge Street was built from the bridge east to Ablewell Street as a bypass to the town centre with its steep and narrow streets.[75] In the mid 1820s St. Paul's Street was built from Bridge Street to the new St. Paul's Church and continued to Townend parallel with Park Street.[76] Lord Bradford, having succeeded in 1825, began developing his land to the south-west of the town in the later 1820s, with his agent Peter Potter directing the operation. The old route to Wednesbury and Darlaston was bypassed in 1831 when Bradford Street was opened from the bridge to Vicarage Place.[77] In 1832 John Eglington, a Walsall builder, took a lease from Lord Bradford of land on the east side of Bradford Street. He laid out Newport and Little Newport Streets, named after Viscount Newport, Lord Bradford's eldest son, and built 28 houses there. In Bradford Street, between Newport Street and Cross Street (now the lower end of Caldmore Road), he built a classical terrace of houses which Potter described in 1837 as

[54] John Taylor 'ultra ponte' occurs in 1399: W.T.C. II/238, m. 1. A Ric. Bruggende occurs in 1377 but in 1399 was living in Rushall St.: ibid.
[55] S.H.C. 1928, 189.
[56] 'A little close lying at Walsall Townsinde in the highway towards the park' is mentioned then: Fink, Queen Mary's Grammar Sch. 132 and plate facing p. 145.
[57] W.T.C. I/9.
[58] S.R.O., D. 260/M/T/7/1, deed of 2 July 1339; below p. 165.
[59] B.M. Eg. Rolls 8529, 8539, 8542.
[60] S.R.O., D. 641/1/2/32; D. 1287/1/2, survey of Walsall manor, 1576, m. 6; D. 1287/8/2, p. 9; D. 260/M/F/1/8, ct. of recog. and survey, 1617, p. 12; /M/T/1/56 and 68; D. 593/A/2/20/26, 31, 43, 46; D. 593/A/2/22/31; W.T.C. II/13/42; S.H.C. 1931, 113; J. Snape, Plan of Town of Walsall (1782); Blay, Street Names of Walsall', 105.
[61] See p. 166. For a mid-19th-cent. description of its narrowness see Glew, Walsall, 32.
[62] S.R.O., D. 260/M/F/1/5, f. 72v.; Gent. Mag. lxix (2), 763; Snape, Plan of Walsall (1782); below p. 267.
[63] It seems to be shown on a plan of 1679: Northants. R.O., I.L. 3192 (reproduced on p. 146). It is shown by Snape, Plan of Walsall (1782).
[64] Sims, Cal. of Deeds, p. 12; W.T.C. I/9; below p. 165. For 17th-cent. variants of the name see W.T.C. II/13/39 (Amblere) and /13/51 (Ambelers); Northants. R.O., I.L. 3192 (Aumblers). For 'Ambling otherwise Ablewell Street' in 1791 see W.C.L., ACJ XII/14.
[65] Northants. R.O., I.L. 3192; Snape, Plan of Walsall (1782); W.S.L., S. D. Pearson 917; Blay, 'Street Names of Walsall', 35.

[66] S.R.O., D. 593/A/2/20/16; Northants. R.O., I.L. 3192; Snape, Plan of Walsall (1782).
[67] Lee, Walsall, 27; Walsall Corp. Act, 1914, 4 & 5 Geo. V, c. 160 (Local); Walsall Observer, 6 Dec. 1963, 3 Jan. 1964.
[68] Sketchley's and Adams's ... Univ. Dir. Birmingham ... (1770); Snape, Plan of Walsall (1782).
[69] Northants. R.O., I.L. 3192; Snape, Plan of Walsall (1782).
[70] Blay, 'Street Names of Walsall', 80, 154; Sketchley's and Adams's ... Univ. Dir. Birmingham ... (1770); Snape, Plan of Walsall (1782); Pearce, Walsall, 150 sqq.; T. Mason, Plan of Part of High Street, Walsall (1817; copy in W.C.L.); docs. at St. Matthew's, church rate 31 Mar. 1829; White, Dir. Staffs. (1834); below p. 244.
[71] Northants. R.O., I.L. 3192.
[72] W.T.C. II/31/1; II/13/49; above p. 145.
[73] V.C.H. Staffs. i. 324; White, Dir. Staffs. (1851).
[74] O.S. Area Book: Walsall (1886).
[75] Homeshaw, Walsall, 102–3; Willmore, Walsall, 376–7; 6 Geo. III, c. 99; W.T.C. 13/86; S.R.O., D. 1287/1/8, Holmes's acct. 1766–71; D. 1287/6/14, plan of part of Lord Mountrath's estate; D. 1287/15/1; Snape, Plan of Walsall (1782).
[76] Lich. Dioc. Regy., B/A/2(i)/H, p. 115; W.C.L., A.G. 138; below p. 236.
[77] Willmore, Walsall, 404; Act for improving and maintaining the road leading from Walsall to Muckley Corner near Lichfield and other roads in the county of Stafford, 11 Geo. IV and 1 Wm. IV, c. 11 (Local and Personal); S.R.O., D. 1287/18/25, business corresp. 1812–32, P. Potter to Lord Bradford, 24 Jan. 1827.

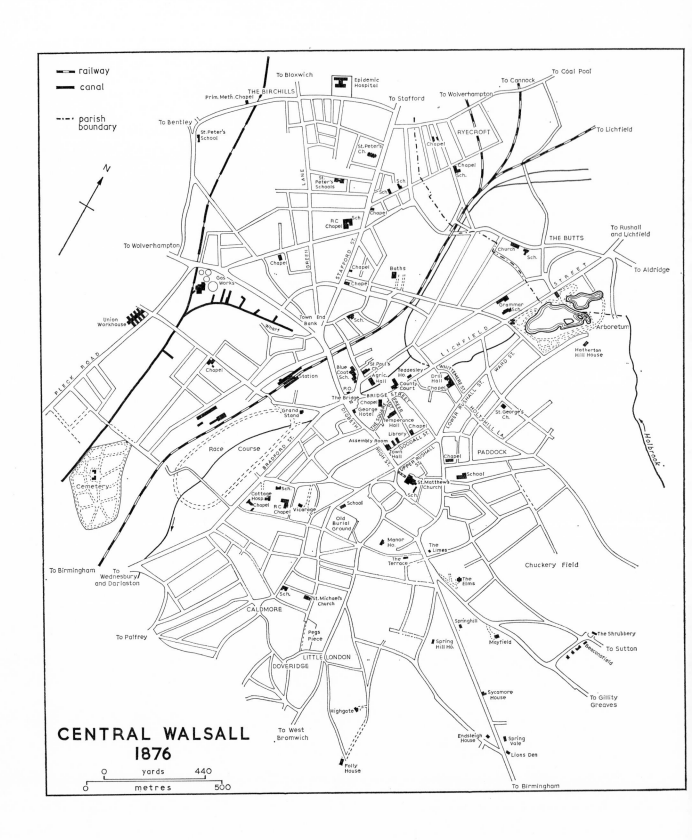

railway
canal
parish boundary

N

To Bloxwich
THE BIRCHILLS
Prim. Meth. Chapel
To Bentley
St. Peter's School
To Wolverhampton
GREEN LANE
St. Peter's Schools
Gas Works
Union Workhouse
Town End Bank
Wharf
Chapel
PLECK ROAD
Chapel
Station
The Bridge
BRIDGE STREET
Grand Stand
DIGBETH
BRADFORD ST.
Race Course
Cemetery
To Birmingham
To Wednesbury and Darlaston
To Palfrey
CALDMORE
Sch.
St. Michael's Church
Pegs Piece
LITTLE LONDON
DOVERIDGE
To West Bromwich
Highgate
Folly House

Epidemic Hospital
To Stafford
St. Peter's Ch.
St. Peter's Sch.
Sch.
Sch.
Chapel
R.C. Chapel
Sch.
STAFFORD ST.
Chapel
Chapel
Baths
Sch.
Blue Coat Sch.
P.O.
Chapel
George Hotel
THE SQUARE
Temperance Hall
Library
Assembly Room
HIGH ST.
Town Hall
GOODALL ST.
Cottage Hosp.
R.C. Chapel
Chapel
Vicarage
School
Old Burial Ground
Manor Ho.
The Terrace
St. Paul's Ch.
Agric. Hall
Teddesley Ho.
County Court
Drill Hall
Chapel
UPPER RUSHALL ST.
St. Matthew's Church
Sch.

To Wolverhampton
To Cannock
To Coal Pool
RYECROFT
Chapel
Chapel
Sch.
To Lichfield
Church
Sch.
THE BUTTS
To Rushall and Lichfield
To Aldridge
STREET
Grammar Sch.
Arboretum
Hatherton Hill House
LICHFIELD
WHITTIMERE ST.
WARD ST.
LOWER RUSHALL ST.
HOLTSHILL LA.
St. George's Ch.
Chapel
PADDOCK
School
The Limes
Chuckery Field
The Elms
Springhill
Spring Hill Ho.
Mayfield
The Shrubbery
Beaconsfield
To Sutton
To Gillity Greaves
Sycamore House
Endsleigh House
Spring Vale
Lions Den
To Birmingham
Holbrook

CENTRAL WALSALL 1876

0 yards 440
0 metres 500

'very magnificent'. It is a long symmetrical range with emphasized centre and end blocks. By 1974 it had been much altered, notably by the removal of the stucco ornament, and was occupied as shops and offices. Other terraces of about the same date survive to the south. Cross and Mountrath Streets are of the same period.[78] The new area was described in 1834 as forming a 'handsome and commodious' approach to the town.[79] Lord Bradford continued to grant leases in the area until the 1850s,[80] and a further improvement came in 1886 when Bradford Place was completed at the junction of Bradford and Bridgeman Streets; the cenotaph there was unveiled in 1922.[81] Also in the early 1830s Goodall Street was built between High Street and Bridge Street, with Freer Street running off it.[82] There was subsequently some development on the hill-top by St. Matthew's. Temple Street was built through to New Street in place of a winding alley apparently c. 1835.[83] In 1852 and 1853 dilapidated houses which closed the church in on the south were cleared away and the former grammar-school building was also demolished. Little Hill, the narrow foot-way leading to the church from the top of High Street, was widened into what is now Church Hill, and the market house at the foot of it was pulled down.[84]

In the mid 19th century the town centre shifted westwards to the bridge and Park Street. Part of the water-course by the bridge had been covered over c. 1815, and in 1851 the open space there was enlarged by further culverting. Houses and shops were then built, and in 1855 Bridge Square (soon called simply the Bridge) was described as 'the centre and most strikingly beautiful portion of the town'.[85] About 1851 too the level of Digbeth and Park Street was considerably raised.[86] In the late 1850s two Russian cannons captured during the Crimean War, a clock on a pillar, and a drinking fountain presented by F. B. Oerton, mayor 1854-5, were placed in the centre of the Bridge. In 1879 the cannons were sent to Woolwich Arsenal, and in 1886 the clock and fountain were replaced by a statue of Sister Dora.[87] The railway, opened in 1847, helped to establish the new centre. The first station, off Bridgeman Street, was replaced in 1849

by one in Station Street off Park Street. Station Street was described in 1855 as comprising 'a long range of neat, uniform buildings', mainly private houses but including the large Railway Commercial inn; a second hotel was being built. Although it is now largely a commercial street, many original red-brick houses survive.[88] In 1856 Lord Bradford's agent noted the decline in the value of property in the higher part of the town 'as the trade of the place has a tendency to follow in the direction of the railway'.[89] Upper Rushall Street had been described in 1847 as 'a third-rate street' where it was difficult to let houses as shops.[90] In 1855, however, it was described as 'composed of some good old-fashioned houses and shops and may be considered a fair business street'; Lower Rushall Street, on the other hand, contained 'some spacious dwellings, most of which, however, exhibit unmistakable signs of broken-down pride'.[91] The population of the borough township, which had risen to 8,761 by 1851, then fell and had dropped to 5,729 by 1901.[92]

In the later 1930s there was extensive slum clearance in Lower and Upper Rushall Streets, Peal Street, Dudley Street, Hill Street, the Ditch, and Bullock's Row, but there has been little re-building.[93] An exception is Warewell Close in Lower Rushall Street, council flats dating from the mid 1950s.[94] Slum clearance began by St. Matthew's in 1948, and by 1953 Temple Street had disappeared and there was an open space south of the church named St. Matthew's Close. The Memorial Gardens to the west were opened in 1952. Clearance continued, and flats were built along the south side of St. Matthew's Close in the mid 1950s.[95] In the 1960s a new shopping precinct was created in the upper part of Digbeth and in the Old Square running north from Digbeth to Freer Street. The Digbeth portion was completed in 1966 and was largely the work of a consortium of local traders, Digbeth (Walsall) Development Ltd.[96] The Old Square precinct, designed by Birch & Caulfield of Walsall, was completed in 1969.[97] Townend Square, a two-level shopping precinct at the north end of Park Street and St. Paul's Street, was opened in 1971.[98]

[78] S.R.O., D. 1287/box 6, valuation of Walsall estate, 1915; /box 7, abstract of title 1923; D. 1287/18/25, business corresp. 1812-32, Potter to Bradford, 3 Oct. 1831; D. 1287/Colliery Box no. 2, estate corresp. 1827-65, copy plan of part of Walsall estate, n.d. but probably 1831, Potter to H. Cory, 10 May 1832, and Potter to Bailey, Shaw, & Smith, 16 May 1837; S.R.O., D. 1362/57, pp. 5-6, 11-12; Blay, 'Street Names of Walsall', 132; W.C.L., A.G. 146; plate facing p. 161 below. Eglington, who also built a chapel (below p. 246), was living in Mountrath St. by 1834: White, Dir. Staffs. (1834).
[79] White, Dir. Staffs. (1834).
[80] S.R.O., D. 1362/57, pp. 16, 18, 24, 32, 43, 61, 101.
[81] Walsall Red Book (1887), 60; (1922), 97.
[82] Blay, 'Street Names of Walsall', 77, 83; White, Dir. Staffs. (1834); Willmore, Walsall, 404.
[83] Blay, 'Street Names of Walsall', 175; Snape, Plan of Walsall (1782); Map of Boro. of Walsall (1836; copy in W.C.L.); S.R.O., D. 351/M/B/207; White, Dir. Staffs. (1851), which mentions the street.
[84] Willmore, Walsall, 427; W.T.C., Street Cttee. Mins. 1849-51, 26 Apr. 1851 sqq.; below pp. 187, 255.
[85] Glew, Walsall, 47-9.
[86] Willmore, Walsall, 398.
[87] Walsall Observer, 12 Oct. 1973; W.C.L., box 36, no. 1; W.C.L., Meikle Coll., 'Middle of the Midlands', chap. 6; W.C.L. photograph 6; inscrip. on fountain; Walsall Red Book (1880), 109; Jo Manton, Sister Dora,

344-9 and plates facing pp. 225, 288, 289. The clock was re-erected in Park St. and the fountain removed to Queen St. cemetery: Walsall Red Book (1887), 61; Meikle Coll., op. cit. The original statue, of marble, was replaced by one of bronze in 1957.
[88] Glew, Walsall, 61; below p. 168.
[89] S.R.O., D. 1287/18/28, business corresp. 1856, Potter to Bradford, 1 Feb. 1856.
[90] D. 1287/Colliery Box no. 2, estate corresp. 1843-53, P. and J. Potter to J. Simpson, 23 Apr. 1847.
[91] Glew, Walsall, 34-5. And see Staffs. Advertiser, 3 Nov. 1849, p. 8. [92] V.C.H. Staffs. i. 324.
[93] W.C.L., slides G6, G11A, G20, G22, G40B, C, D, and photographs 289, 295, 299; W.C.L., Meikle Coll., 'Middle of the Midlands', chap. 19; T. N. Hulme, 'S. George's Par.: Street & Place Names' (in W.C.L.); Cason, Blakenall Heath, 41. For an artist's impression of 1936 showing the proposed redevelopment east of St. Matthew's see Walsall Red Book (1937), 9.
[94] Ex inf. the boro. housing manager (1974).
[95] Walsall Observer, 3 May 1952, 17 Apr., 15 May 1953, 6 May 1955, 30 Aug. 1957, 3 Jan. 1958.
[96] Ibid. 22 Nov., 19 Dec. 1963, 3 Jan. 1964, 27 Aug. 1965, 30 Mar. 1966, 24 Oct. 1969; Express & Star, 27 Aug. 1966.
[97] Walsall Observer, 5 and 26 Aug., 29 Nov., 16 Dec. 1966, 24 Oct. 1969.
[98] Ibid. 24 Oct. 1969; Evening Mail, 10 Sept. 1971.

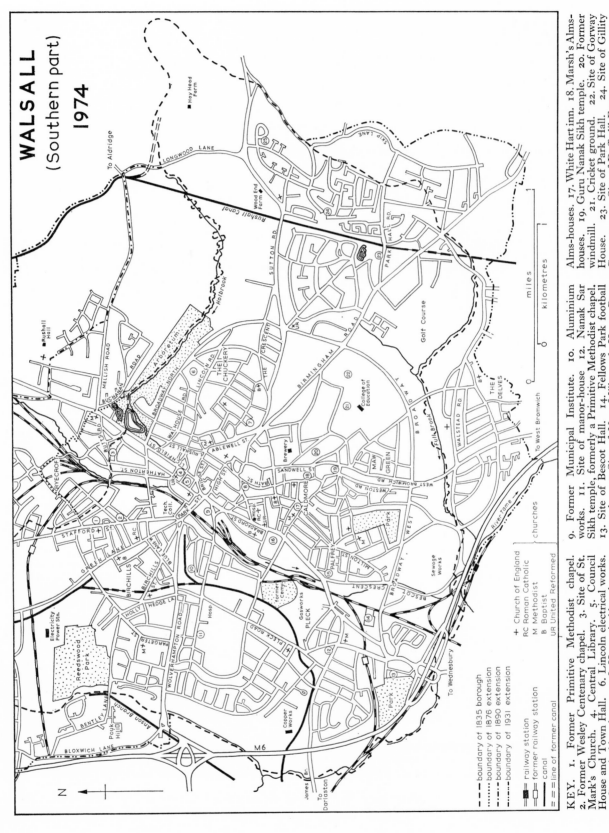

WALSALL
(Southern part)
1974

KEY. 1. Former Primitive Methodist chapel. 2. Former Wesley Centenary chapel. 3. Site of St. Mark's Church. 4. Central Library. 5. Council House and Town Hall. 6. Lincoln electrical works. 7. Crump's Alms-houses. 8. Harper's Alms-houses. 9. Former Municipal Institute. 10. Aluminium works. 11. Site of manor-house. 12. Nanak Sar Sikh temple, formerly a Primitive Methodist chapel. 13. Site of Bescot Hall. 14. Fellows Park football ground. 15. Site of New Mills. 16. Henry Boys Alms-houses. 17. White Hart inn. 18. Marsh's Alms-houses. 19. Guru Nanak Sikh temple. 20. Former windmill. 21. Cricket ground. 22. Site of Gorway House. 23. Site of Park Hall. 24. Site of Gillity Greaves. 25. Site of Daffodil Farm.

boundary of 1835 borough
boundary of 1876 extension
boundary of 1890 extension
boundary of 1931 extension

railway station
former railway station
canal
line of former canal

+ Church of England
RC Roman Catholic
M Methodist   churches
B Baptist
UR United Reformed

The area to the north-east of the town centre was developed in the 19th century mainly by John Walhouse and his successors the barons Hatherton, who owned most of the land.[99] Indeed Peter Potter, while developing the Bradford Street area for Lord Bradford, saw Walhouse as a competitor for 'the benefit of the increase of this town'.[1] The district is in the main residential, with houses ranging from large villas to working-class cottages. Much of the smaller property, however, has been replaced by council houses and flats, while many of the villas have been turned into offices.

The chief building before the 19th century was Reynold's Hall, near the present Arboretum Road. It was the house on which the Walhouse estate centred until John Walhouse demolished it in the late 18th century as limestone working developed in the area. The home farm survived until 1897.[2] The side road now called Intown Row existed by the later 17th century as part of a way leading from Rushall Street to Park Street. That way was presumably one leading from Rushall Street to Walsall field mentioned in the 15th century; it seems to have crossed the Holbrook by a stone bridge by the later 16th century.[3] Holtshill Lane, running up the hill to the east of Rushall Street, existed as Holt Lane in 1367.[4] The Holtshill area occurs as the Holt in the 14th century; the name Holtshill was in use by 1440, and Holtshill Top occurs in 1512.[5]

Lichfield Street was built from Bridge Street under an Act of 1830 and replaced Rushall Street and Dovegrove Street (renamed Ward Street c. 1864 in honour of Alderman William Ward) as the main road to Rushall and Lichfield.[6] In 1831 John Walhouse began to grant building-leases in Lichfield Street,[7] and by the 1850s the resulting villas had made it 'a street of remarkable beauty and not only the most picturesque but the most fashionable portion of the town'.[8] By the 1880s villas had been built along it to a point beyond Mellish Road and by the beginning of the 20th century nearly as far as the borough boundary.[9] A library was opened at the southern end in 1831. The Council House to the north was built on the site of Teddesley House in 1902–5; the central library further north on the

other side of the new Tower Street was opened in 1906. Public baths had been opened behind the library site in 1896.[10]

On the western side of Lichfield Street Hatherton Place, now the eastern end of Hatherton Road, existed by 1832; it was originally known as Littleton Place, a name in use by 1834 when a building-lease was granted there. Hatherton Street had been built north from it by 1836, and part of Littleton Road, now Littleton Street West, existed by then; Lower Forster Street was being planned. It had been built by 1843, and Littleton Road had then been extended east to Lichfield Street. Brook, later Albert, Street existed by 1839.[11] In 1855 Hatherton Place was described as a pleasant little street with particularly beautiful houses, while the Littleton Street area was one 'where streets and habitations are daily springing up on every side'.[12] Upper Forster Street was being planned in 1844, and by 1857 it was linked by Warwick Street with Teddesley Street, both of which were built up in the later 1850s and earlier 1860s;[13] the area consists mainly of terraced houses. Darwall Street was built in the late 1870s by the trustees of C. F. Darwall, and Leicester Street linking it with Bridge Street dates from the same time.[14] Hatherton Road running from Lichfield Street to St. Paul's Road dates from c. 1933.[15] By 1883 several factories, mainly tanneries and sawmills, had been built between Hatherton Street and Ford Brook.[16] Hatherton, Teddesley, and Upper Forster Streets run into the area known as the Butts, which was added to Walsall from Rushall in 1876 but had been part of the Walsall improvement commissioners' district from 1848.[17] Lord Hatherton granted leases in the area from 1840, and a working-class district grew up.[18] A school was opened in 1868 and a mission chapel in 1871.[19] Two new streets, William and Cecil Streets, were laid out over Lord Hatherton's land in the later 1870s.[20] The area to the north around Westbourne Road, a street existing by 1880, dates mainly from the late 19th and early 20th centuries; it consists largely of better-class terraces built on land belonging to Lord Hatherton and William Guy, a retired currier.[21] In 1974 much of the district was being

[99] For the estate see p. 177.
[1] S.R.O., D. 1287/18/25, business corresp. 1812–32, Potter to Bradford, 3 Oct. 1831.
[2] See pp. 152, 177, 191.
[3] Northants. R.O., I.L. 3192; Sims, *Cal. of Deeds*, pp. 11, 23–4; S.R.O., D. 260/M/T/1/1b, deed of 24 Nov. 1567; /49, deed of 24 June 1587.
[4] S.R.O., D. 260/M/T/7/1, deed of 24 June 1367. It is given as Heyrif Lane by Northants. R.O., I.L. 3192.
[5] *Walsall Records*, 48; W.S.L., D. 1798/83, deed of 12 June 1376; /100, deed of 2 Feb. 1439/40; S.R.O., D. 260/M/T/7/4, deed of 5 Dec. 1512.
[6] Act for improving and maintaining the road leading from Walsall to Muckley Corner . . ., 11 Geo. IV and 1 Wm. IV, c. 11 (Local and Personal); below p. 165. For the proposal to rename Dovegrove St. as Ward St. see S.R.O., D. 260/M/E/174, 27 Sept. 1864; for Wm. Ward see T. N. Hulme, 'S. George's Par.: Street & Place Names' (in W.C.L.). Dovegrove was probably derived from land in the area variously called Dovysgreven (or Donysgreven) and Dosegreaves: W.S.L., D. 1798/83, deed of 5 June 1448 (endorsement of 1615); ibid./84, deed of 2 Oct. 1346.
[7] S.R.O., D. 260/M/E/173, Walsall rental 1864; W.S.L., D. 1798/551; W.C.L., A.G. 146.
[8] Glew, *Walsall*, 51.
[9] O.S. Map 6", Staffs. LXIII. NE. (edns. of 1889 and 1903); date-stone of 1899 on W. side near boundary; W.S.L., D. 1798/551, nos. 565–6, 591.
[10] O.S. Map 6", Staffs. LXIII. NE. (edns. of 1889 and 1903); below pp. 218, 222, 251–2.
[11] W.S.L., D. 1798/551; *Map of Boro. of Walsall* (1836; copy in W.C.L.); W.S.L., S. MS. 417/Walsall. Hatherton Place was shown as a stretch of Lichfield St. in 1831: D. 1798/551, no. 5.
[12] Glew, *Walsall*, 52, 57.
[13] W.S.L., D. 1798/551; S.R.O., D. 260/M/E/174, 10 May 1864.
[14] S.R.O., D. 260/M/E/174, 9 Jan., 6 Feb., 11 Sept., 13 Nov. 1877; *Staffs. Advertiser* (S. Staffs. edn.), 6 Sept. 1879; Blay, 'Street Names of Walsall', 59.
[15] It first appears in *Walsall Red Book* in the edn. of 1934.
[16] O.S. Map 1/500, Staffs. LXIII. 7. 16 and 21 (1885 edn., surv. 1883). There was also a buckle works.
[17] See p. 217. Its earlier history is reserved for treatment under Rushall in a future volume of the Staffordshire *History*.
[18] W.S.L., D. 1798/551; date-stones of 1869 and 1878 in Mill Lane; O.S. Map 6", Staffs. LXIII. NE. (1889 edn.).
[19] See pp. 238, 261.
[20] W.S.L., D. 1798/551; date-stones of 1877 and 1880; O.S. Map 6", Staffs. LXIII. NE. (1889 edn.).
[21] O.S. Map 6", Staffs. LXIII. NE. (edns. of 1889, 1903, 1920); *Walsall Red Book* (1880); W.C.L., Town Clerk's Misc., box 5; W.S.L., D. 1798/551, for Lord Hatherton's building-leases in Borneo St. 1894–1902; date-stones of 1899 and 1900 in Borneo St.; Blay, 'Street Names of Walsall', 25, 67, 188.

redeveloped by the council, notably the area between Littleton Street East and Butts Road; several blocks of multi-storey flats had been built in the 1960s.[22]

To the east of Lichfield Street is a district mainly of villas and better-class terraces. Walhouse Street was built as far as Lower Rushall Street at the same time as Lichfield Street; the first lease was granted in 1831.[23] Persehouse Street, the southern end of which existed by the early 19th century, was laid out in the early 1850s.[24] Walhouse Street had been extended to meet it by 1856 and was renamed Lower and Upper Walhouse Streets.[25] A building-lease was granted in Holtshill Lane in 1828 and others from the 1840s; the 1860s, however, were the time when extensive building of terraces was carried out there, some of them with long front gardens.[26] The west end of Denmark Road, now part of Broadway North, existed as Littleton Place by 1857; it was extended c. 1865 and renamed in honour of the Princess of Wales.[27] Persehouse Street was extended north of Denmark Road in 1867 to accommodate 'buildings of good style and some pretension'; a building-lease was granted to Henry Farrington, who himself lived in one of the villas, Hatherton Hill House (now St. Patrick's Convent).[28] The extension is now called Arboretum Road. Rowley and Charlotte Streets were built in the later 1860s, being named after Charlotte Rowley, who married Lord Hatherton's eldest son in 1867; Upper Walhouse Street was extended to Charlotte Street at the same time.[29] St. George's Church was built at the corner of Persehouse and Upper Walhouse Streets in 1873–5, and many 'superior' houses were being built round it in 1874.[30] In the late 1890s Denmark Road was extended east, Reynold's Hall Farm being demolished to make way for it in 1897; the extension was named Foden Road after E. A. Foden, who as Lord Hatherton's agent was involved in the development of the area from 1867.[31] Both Denmark and Foden Roads became part of the ring road completed in 1929 and had been renamed Broadway North by 1934.[32] In 1925 Lower and Upper Walhouse Streets were renamed Walhouse Road, which in the years immediately following was extended to the ring road; Calder Avenue was built across the

extension.[33] The first stage of the flats called St. George's Place in Persehouse Street was completed in 1955; houses have been built opposite on the site of St. George's Church, demolished in the mid 1960s.[34]

The area to the north which is now occupied by the Arboretum was partly in Rushall until 1876. Limestone was being quarried there by the late 18th century. Operations had ceased by the earlier 1840s, leaving two flooded pits, the larger of which was known as Hatherton Lake by 1845. Victoria Terrace to the north was built as Hatherton Lake Villas by Henry Farrington in the earlier 1850s.[35] In 1858 it was suggested that a public park should be made in the area,[36] and from 1868 Lord Hatherton's agent was supporting the idea as a means of improving the locality and encouraging development.[37] The Walsall Arboretum and Lake Co. Ltd. was formed in 1870, and in 1873 it took a lease from Lord Hatherton and Sir George Mellish[38] of the two lakes and 7 a.; the land was to be laid out as 'an arboretum or pleasure grounds and gardens'. The park was opened in 1874, with lodges and boundary wall designed by Robert Griffiths of Stafford, the county surveyor.[39] It failed to pay its way, and in 1877 it was taken over by a committee, which made it a commercial success with such attractions as an aquatic fête featuring Captain Matthew Webb, the Channel swimmer, a steam launch, and a band of Zulu warriors. In 1881 the borough council, after much pressure, took a three-year lease of the Arboretum and opened it as a public park; it bought the freehold in 1884. The Arboretum was extended south-eastwards several times between 1891 and 1952 and now covers 145 a., of which 69 a. are playing-fields and over 40 a. free-play areas.

The district north-east of the Arboretum, which was part of Rushall until 1890, is a middle-class residential area with open country around Calderfields Farm.[40] The road running from the Butts to Aldridge is an old way; in 1869 the western end was straightened across the Moss Close area as Mellish Road, which takes its name from the Mellish family, owners of the estate centring on Rushall Hall.[41] Buchanan Road existed by 1874 and was

[22] For the flats see e.g. *Walsall Observer*, 10 Feb., 2 June 1967; *County Boro. of Walsall: Council Mins. 1972–3*, 669.
[23] Willmore, *Walsall*, 404; S.R.O., D. 260/M/E/173, rental 1864, p. 4.
[24] S.R.O., D. 351/M/B/209; W.S.L., D. 1798/551 (no. 92 of which describes it as an intended street in 1850); Glew, *Walsall*, 34.
[25] W.S.L., D. 1798/551, no. 229. The new names occur ibid. nos. 349–50 (1868), but Upper Walhouse St. occurs in R.G. 9/2016 no. 106 (1861).
[26] W.S.L., D. 1798/551; date-stones of 1865 and 1870. One of the houses on the N. side is inscribed 'The Hands of Industry Rewarded I.J.O.' A group of cottages on the S. side, dated 1865, was derelict in 1974.
[27] W.S.L., D. 1798/551, no. 213; S.R.O., D. 260/M/E/174, 24 Oct. 1865, 15 and 29 May, 12 June, 31 July 1866; Blay, 'Street Names of Walsall', 62.
[28] D. 260/M/E/174, 12 Feb., 12 Nov., 24 Dec. 1867; *Walsall Red Book* (1876); *Robinson's Map of Walsall* (pub. with *Walsall Red Book*, 1876).
[29] D. 260/M/E/174, 10 and 31 Dec. 1867, 21 and 28 Jan., 18 Feb., 3 Mar., 7 July, 22 Sept. 1868, 16–23 Mar., 13–20 Apr., 12 Oct. 1869; T. N. Hulme, 'S. George's Par.: Street & Place Names' (in W.C.L.).
[30] D. 260/M/E/174, 8 Sept. 1874; below p. 239.
[31] Hulme, 'Street & Place Names'. The first building-lease was in 1898: W.S.L., D. 1798/551, no. 562. For Foden see D. 260/M/E/174, 24 Sept. 1867 sqq.

[32] *Walsall Red Book* (1934), 139; below p. 166.
[33] Hulme, 'Street & Place Names'; *Walsall Red Book* (1926; 1927; 1929).
[34] *Walsall Observer*, 29 Apr. 1955; below p. 239.
[35] See p. 191; Glew, *Walsall*, 56–7; Blay, 'Street Names of Walsall', 92.
[36] *Walsall Observer*, 3 Aug. 1973. This is the first of 4 articles on the Arboretum, which were published 3–24 Aug. and on which the rest of this para. is based, unless otherwise stated. The articles are based on an unpublished history of the Arboretum by Mr. W. R. Foster of Walsall.
[37] S.R.O., D. 260/M/E/174, 17 Mar. 1868, 19–26 Apr. 1870.
[38] For the inclusion of Mellish see *Walsall Observer*, 10 Aug. 1872. For the family see below.
[39] *Walsall Observer*, 10 Aug. 1872; D. 260/M/E/174, [25 June], 2 and 9–16 July 1872; below p. 238. And see plate facing p. 160 below.
[40] Its earlier history is reserved for treatment under Rushall in a future volume of the Staffordshire *History*.
[41] Yates, *Map of Staffs.* (1775), showing it as straighter than it in fact was; B.M. O.S.D. 212; F. W. Willmore, *Records of Rushall* (Walsall, 1892), 85–8, 117; S.R.O., D. 260/M/E/174, 20 June, 24 Sept., 10 Oct. 1867. For Moss Close see Plot, *Staffs.* 159; Shaw, *Staffs.* ii. 66; W.S.L., S. MS. 417/Rushall, *sub* Mellish, nos. 277–8, 281, 289–92.

named after the family into which Frances Mellish had married in 1839.[42] The area contains houses of the late 19th and earlier 20th centuries, but the most extensive development has been since the Second World War, some of it over the site of earlier industrial working.

Of the streets on the east side of Ablewell Street Bott Lane existed by 1501.[43] A lane called Brygens Lane leading from Ablewell Street to land called Paddoke was mentioned in 1567 and was presumably Paddock Lane, which existed by 1782.[44] Lime Pit Bank (now Bank Street) was an area of metal-working by 1767.[45] What is now Pool Street existed by 1782.[46] An early lane ran along what are now Balls Street, Balls Hill, and Dog Kennel Lane.[47] The western end of Tantarra Street was built c. 1830, taking its name from the plot of land which it crossed.[48] Union Street, linking Paddock Lane and Holtshill Lane, existed by the mid 1840s and was so named by 1855.[49] The systematic building up of the area, with workshops, factories, and houses, began in the 1850s, Lord Bradford and Lord Hatherton both granting leases.[50] Tantarra Street had been extended eastwards by 1857 and was continued to Dark Lane in the early 1870s.[51] Ware-well Street apparently dates from the later 1850s.[52] Pasture in Bott Lane was offered for sale in 1860 as building land for houses and factories 'in this extending part of the town'.[53] Box Street was built in the late 1860s.[54] Selborne, Eldon, Burleigh, and Walsingham Streets were laid out by John Far-rington Crump, a solicitor, on land which he bought from Lord Hatherton in 1872.[55] Bernard Street was named in 1874,[56] and Lime and Richmond Streets apparently date from about the same time.[57] Pad-dock Lane and Tantarra Street were cut in two in the 1960s when five multi-storey blocks of council flats were built across them.[58] The main industries of the area in 1974 were metal- and leather-working.

The streets in the mainly residential area to the east known as the Chuckery date largely from the turn of the 19th century. The name may be derived from Churchgreave, the name of one of the common fields; the boundaries of the field seem to have followed the line of several of the present streets in the area.[59] A track ran from Holtshill Lane to the Sutton road by 1763; called Dark Lane until the 20th century, it followed more or less the line of the present Lincoln Road (named after the Lincoln electrical works opened there in the 1920s) and Prince's Avenue.[60] Lord Hatherton granted building-leases in the northern part in 1869 and 1870.[61] The main development in the area, however, was on land belonging to Lord Bradford, who granted leases in Lumley Road and Kinnerley, Florence, Moncrieffe, and Tong Streets between 1898 and 1903. The southern end of Beacon Street too dates from about that time.[62] Although Sutton Crescent (that part of the street now called the Crescent west of Broadway North) existed by the 1870s, houses were not built there until the early 20th century.[63] Some of the large houses to the south in Prince's Avenue are of the later 19th century, but those to the north of the Crescent, built on Lord Bradford's land, date mainly from the early 20th century.[64] The residential area was further extended between the World Wars. In the same period the Sutton road, which at least until the building of Sutton Crescent ran along Prince's Avenue and the Crescent, was realigned to run south of the Crescent.[65]

The district to the east contains an area of early settlement at Wood End, which straddled the Sutton road near the parish boundary and was inhabited by 1317.[66] There were around 30 recipients of Mol-lesley's Dole in the earlier 17th century.[67] The main road there was known as Wood End Lane in the 18th century, and at the point where it crossed the boundary the Epistle and Gospel were read during perambulations of the parish and manor.[68] Skip Lane, which runs from Great Barr in Aldridge to

[42] D. 260/M/E/174, 10 Nov. 1874; Blay, 'Street Names of Walsall', 34; Willmore, *Rushall*, 88.
[43] S.R.O., D. 593/A/2/22/20, calling it 'Battelone'; Yates, *Map of Staffs.* (1775), part of which is reproduced above, p. 144, shows buildings at its E. end.
[44] S.R.O., D. 260/M/T/1/49, deed of 20 Aug. 1567; Snape, *Plan of Walsall* (1782).
[45] *Sketchley's Birmingham . . . Dir.* (1767); W.C.L., C. 4.
[46] Snape, *Plan of Walsall* (1782).
[47] H. Jacob, *Plan of Boundary Line between Township of Boro. and Township of Foreign of Walsall* (Birmingham, 1816; copy in W.C.L.).
[48] It is shown on W.C.L., A.G. 146 (1832), but not on W.C.L., C. 4 (1824). The land was so named by 1763; S.R.O., D. 1287/8/2, survey, pp. 6, 8.
[49] S.R.O., D. 351/M/B/207; W.T.C., Street Cttee. Mins. 1849–51, 6 Aug. 1850.
[50] Glew, *Walsall*, 34; S.R.O., D. 1287/box 6, valuation of Walsall estate, 1915 (keyed with unnumbered plans); S.R.O., D. 1362/57; W.S.L., D. 1798/551.
[51] W.T.C., Street Cttee. Mins. 1849–51, 21 Feb. 1851; S.R.O., D. 260/M/E/174, 14–21 Sept. 1869, 23 May, 4–18 July 1871, 12 Nov. 1872; W. J. Boys, *Plan of Boro. of Walsall* (1875; copy in W.C.L.).
[52] W.S.L., D. 1798/551, no. 214.
[53] *Staffs. Advertiser*, 16 June 1860, p. 8.
[54] W.S.L., D. 1798/551, nos. 346, 379.
[55] W.C.L., ACJ 3/2 and 3/3; W.S.L., D. 1798/551, nos. 393, 411; W.C.L., Town Clerk's Misc., boxes 75 and 158; W.C.L., Fire Brigade papers, boro. surveyor to street cttee., 2 Oct. 1879; Boys, *Plan of Walsall* (1875); *Robinson's Map of Walsall* (pub. with *Walsall Red Book*, 1876); Blay, 'Street Names of Walsall', 69. For Crump's alms-houses in an extension of Eldon St. see below p. 268.
[56] *Robinson's Map of Walsall* (1876).

[57] Blay, 'Street Names of Walsall', 19.
[58] *Walsall Observer*, 19 May 1967; *Express & Star*, 8 Nov. 1969; ex inf. the boro. housing manager (1974).
[59] See p. 180. For the legend that the parish church was begun in the area but was removed to its present site by witches in the shape of white pigs see *N. & Q.* 4th ser. xii. 245.
[60] S.R.O., D. 1287/8/2, map; Yates, *Map of Staffs.* (1775); Blay, 'Street Names of Walsall', 58, 119; below p. 208. The name Dark Lane occurs in 1837: W.C.L., QSM 1/310.
[61] S.R.O., D. 260/M/E/174, 25–31 May, 14–21 Sept. 1869, 8 Mar. 1870, 23 Nov. 1871, 12 Nov. 1872.
[62] D. 1287/box 6, valuation of Walsall estate, 1915 (keyed with unnumbered plans); /box 7, contract 14 Aug. 1903; Blay, 'Street Names of Walsall', 73, 113, 122; O.S. Map 6″, Staffs. LXIII. SE. (1903 edn., revised 1901; 1920 edn., revised 1912–13).
[63] O.S. Map 6″, Staffs. LXIII. SE. (1920 edn., revised 1912–13). Sutton Crescent is shown on *Robinson's Map of Walsall* (1876). For a scheme in 1869 for villa development on Lord Hatherton's land in the Sutton road area see S.R.O., D. 260/M/E/174, 7–13 Dec. 1869.
[64] D. 1287/box 6, valuation of Walsall estate, 1915 (keyed with unnumbered plans); O.S. Map 6″, Staffs. LXIII. SE. (1920 edn., revised 1912–13).
[65] D. 1287/8/2, map; O.S. Map 6″, Staffs. LXIII. SE. (prov. edn. with addns. of 1938).
[66] B.M. Cott. MS. Nero C. xii, f. 145; below pp. 175, 179.
[67] Homeshaw, *Walsall*, 5; above p. 145.
[68] Act for repairing roads leading from Sutton Colefield Common to town of Walsall and from Sneals Green to Walsall . . ., 21 Geo. II, c. 25; S.R.O., D. 1287/1/8, rental of Walsall demesnes 1771–6, workmen's bills, 13 Feb. 1775; Pearce, *Walsall*, 222, 226.

the Sutton road and follows the boundary for a short distance, occurs as Hogfield Lane in 1479.[69] Longwood Lane running north to Aldridge Road may be the lane leading to Caldwell Wood mentioned in 1630.[70] There was limestone quarrying at Wood End by the later Middle Ages and at Hay Head to the north by the late 16th century.[71] Both sides of Sutton Road are lined with privately built houses mainly of the period between the two World Wars; the road was realigned at Wood End Farm as part of its general improvement at that time. The area to the north of the road is open country. The area to the south is also occupied by middle-class housing; a few of the roads had been laid out by 1938, but most of them date from the 1950s and 1960s.[72]

The area along Birmingham Road in the south-east of the borough has developed as a middle-class suburb. Until the late 18th century the road to Birmingham, known as Peakhouse Lane, followed a winding course along the present Jesson Road and through Five Ways along Park Hall and Lonsdale Roads, but it was straightened to its present course apparently c. 1788.[73] In the earlier 17th century Five Ways, then called Five Lanes End, had about 20 recipients of Mollesley's Dole.[74] Five Lane End farm occurs in 1696 and was also known as Sergeant's Coppice farm in the earlier 19th century.[75] By 1763 there were a few houses along and near the Birmingham road, including what was later called Gorway Farm.[76] The northern end of the road, known as King Street in the earlier 19th century, contained commercial premises by 1813, and although it was outside the borough it was populous enough to be included in the improvement commissioners' district in 1824.[77] Spring Hill House, in the part of Jesson Road now occupied by St. Mary's Roman Catholic school, existed by 1813 as Springfield, the home of Richard Jesson, an attorney.[78] Gorway House was built in the later 1820s by Peter Potter, Lord Bradford's agent.[79] The Terrace in Dandy's Walk off King Street (now part of the Blue Coat School) had been built by John Forster by 1834.[80] By then in fact the area was noted for its 'several neat villas'.[81]

In the 1860s a suburb of 'villas and terraces of villettes' developed around the northern part of the Birmingham road. It was considered by one writer to be the most attractive part of Walsall: 'above the lamplights and level pavement the branching trees spread their network of interchanging leaves after the manner of Parisian boulevards . . . and the denizens have had to consult horticultural encyclopaedias to find euphonious titles for their trim villas.'[82] Belvidere Road existed by 1860 when Lord Bradford began to grant building-leases there.[83] Lysways Street was described as a new road in 1866; it consists largely of better-class terraces and pairs of houses built by 1885. Emery Street, linking it with Lodge Street (now Sandymount Road) and containing smaller terraces, existed by 1885, but only the northern end had then been built up.[84] Highgate Brewery at the west end of Sandymount Road was opened in 1898.[85] The Highgate area further south contains many later-19th-century villas and some smaller houses of that period and the early 20th century. Highgate House was built in the mid 1850s by F. B. Oerton, a saddlers' ironmonger who had lived in a house by his works in Bath Street; he was mayor in 1854-5. Gorway Road linking Highgate Road with Birmingham Road dates from the late 19th century.[86] Park Hall was built in 1863 and from c. 1897 was the home of W. J. (later Sir William) Pearman Smith (d. 1939), a Walsall solicitor who was mayor 1899-1902.[87] By the mid 1880s roads had been laid out west of Birmingham Road at Sargent's Hill and on either side of the south-eastern boundary; the latter at least seem to have been connected with a private scheme which was promoted in 1871-2 by Samuel Wilkinson, the town clerk, for developing the 60-acre Park Lodge estate. In fact most of the houses there and at Sargent's Hill were not built until the years between the two World Wars and after.[88] The course belonging to Walsall Golf Club to the west of Sargent's Hill was opened in 1906.[89] A municipal golf-course was opened in the Gorway area on the north side of Broadway in 1930; it was ploughed up during the Second World War and is now part of the site of the West Midlands College of Educa-

[69] Sims, *Cal. of Deeds*, p. 22; Daffodil Farm deeds in poss. of Pearman Smith & Sons, Walsall, letter of 25 June 1952 referring to Skip Lane, otherwise Hodgfield Lane.
[70] W.S.L., S.D. Beck 129. It may be the lane in that area which occurs in 1603: W.S.L., S. D. Pearson 335*.
[71] See p. 191.
[72] O.S. Map 1/2,500, Staffs. LXIII. 11 (1946 edn., revised 1938), 12 (1947 edn., revised 1938); Fink, *Queen Mary's Grammar Sch.* 250; below pp. 175, 183-4.
[73] Act for repairing roads leading from Sutton Colefield Common to town of Walsall and from Sneals Green to Walsall . . ., 21 Geo. II, c. 25; Yates, *Map of Staffs.* (1775); S.R.O., Q/SO 11, T. 1708, calling it Peakers Lane; below p. 165.
[74] W.T.C. II/31/1, 5, and 6; II/13/49; above p. 145.
[75] S.R.O., D. 260/M/T/1/120b; D. 364/M/2; W.S.L., D. 1798/551, p. 7a; W.S.L., S. MS. 417/Walsall, *sub* Hatherton.
[76] S.R.O., D. 1287/8/2. Gorway Farm is named on O.S. Map 6", Staffs. LXIII. SE. (1903 edn.).
[77] Pearce, *Walsall*, 149, 157, 168; S.R.O., D. 351/M/B/207; Homeshaw, *Walsall*, 134. For a chape-maker in Peakhouse Lane in the 1760s see *Sketchley's Birmingham . . . Dir.* (1767).
[78] Pearce, *Walsall*, 159; Pigot, *Com. Dir. Birm* (1829), 90; White, *Dir. Staffs.* (1834).
[79] S.R.O., D. 1287/18/25, business corresp. 1820-9, P. Potter to Lord Bradford, 19 Aug. 1826; 1812-32,

envelope dated 15 May 1828 containing undated plan showing house, and Potter to Bradford, 30 Aug. 1830, dated from Gorway House.
[80] Deeds in poss. of trustees of Blue Coat School, abstract of title of Sir Chas. Forster; White, *Dir. Staffs.* (1834); W.S.L., S. MS. 417/Walsall, *sub* Forster; below pp. 227, 257, and plate facing p. 176.
[81] White, *Dir. Staffs.* (1834), 428, calling the area Wood End.
[82] W.C.L., Newscuttings 1A, pp. 73, 81.
[83] S.R.O., D. 1362/57; D. 1287/box 6, valuation of Walsall estate, 1915 (keyed with unnumbered plans); O.S. Map 6", Staffs. LXIII. SE. (1890 edn.).
[84] S.R.O., D. 1362/57, p. 156; O.S. Map 6", Staffs. LXIII. SE. (1890 edn., surv. 1882-5). Malvern Place at the W. end of Lysways St. is dated 1889.
[85] See p. 206.
[86] O.S. Map 6", Staffs. LXIII. SE. (edns. of 1890, 1903, 1920); date-stone of 1883 on terrace in Highgate Rd. For Oerton see Glew, *Walsall*, 32; White, *Dir. Staffs.* (1851); *P.O. Dir. Staffs.* (1860); above p. 149.
[87] W.C.L., Newscuttings 8, p. 147; *Walsall Red Book* (1898), 107; *County Boro. of Walsall: Council Year Book 1973-74*, 181.
[88] O.S. Map 6", Staffs. LXIII. SE. (1890 edn. and prov. edn. with addns. of 1938); *Staffs. Advertiser*, 20 July 1872, p. 7; *Walsall Free Press*, 20 July 1872.
[89] *Walsall Red Book* (1907), 250. The club's *Rules* (copy in W.C.L.) state that it was founded in 1907.

tion, opened in 1963.[90] The college also took over Gorway House and 7 a. in 1966 and built college extensions there in 1970–2 after demolishing the house.[91] The building of houses and flats has continued throughout the area, some on the sites of demolished villas. Broadway, built in the 1920s, is lined with houses of the period between the two World Wars.[92] In the south-east of the area there are many houses built privately since the Second World War over Brookhouse farm and much of the Park Hall estate.[93] Park Hall itself was demolished in the 1950s and a primary school opened on the site in 1970.[94]

Maw Green around what is now the junction of West Bromwich Road, Delves Road, and Highgate Road was an inhabited area by the 18th century.[95] Maw Green Farm to the south-east, which existed by the early 19th century, may have been there by 1747.[96] Collins Farm to the south at what is now the junction of West Bromwich Road and Tame Street occurs as the property of John Persehouse in 1608.[97] It may be identifiable with Cannock Farm at Caldmore which was held of the Crown by the Collins family in the earlier 1590s.[98] Folly House in Folly House Lane to the east of Maw Green existed by the early 19th century and was described in 1855 as an ancient habitation; later known as Rock's Cottage, it was demolished in 1931.[99] There was settlement by the 18th century at Fullbrook where the West Bromwich road crosses the former southern boundary.[1] It was not until the late 1890s that the Maw Green area began to be built over. Terraces were then built on Lord Bradford's land at the northern end of West Bromwich Road and in the new Weston Road; more were built in the early 20th century.[2] Council houses were built over much of the area in the later 1920s; Collins Farm was demolished in 1928 and Maw Green Farm in the 1930s. Broadway was built across the area in the 1920s, and privately owned houses had been built along it by 1938. Houses were built both by the council and privately along West Bromwich Road south of Broadway in the same period.[3]

On either side of West Bromwich Road south of

the old boundary is the portion of the Delves that was transferred from Wednesbury in 1931. The purpose of the transfer was to provide Walsall with land for houses, and most of the housing, both council and privately built, dates from the 1930s.[4] From the 1930s factories were built in the west of the area.[5] Houses were built south of Brockhurst Crescent c. 1970, and the M6 motorway, opened in 1970,[6] crosses that area. In the centre of the Delves is Delves Green, a 19-acre open space maintained by the corporation.[7]

The Caldmore area lies between the old roads to West Bromwich and Wednesbury. The West Bromwich road[8] ran along New Street, the southern part of which was formerly called Fieldgate,[9] and Sandwell Street, formerly called Windmill.[10] The Wednesbury road ran along Dudley Street and Vicarage Place until the opening of Bradford Street in 1831.[11] Though mainly common arable,[12] Caldmore was an inhabited area by the early 14th century. Thomas Faukes of Caldmore occurs in 1307,[13] and in 1317 a house there formerly held by William the reeve was in the hands of Richard Paynel.[14] The vicarage house of St. Matthew's stood to the south of Vicarage Place until the 19th century, probably occupying the same site from the Middle Ages.[15]

The main settlement was round Caldmore Green, where several old ways meet: Caldmore Road (formerly Caldmore Lane), Corporation Street (formerly Coal Pit Lane), West Bromwich Street, and Watery Lane.[16] Caldmore Lane ran into Bath Street along what is now Little Caldmore, and those roads presumably formed the highway from Walsall to Caldmore, mentioned in 1693.[17] Bath Street occurs as Prospect Row in the early 19th century and was renamed when the baths in Dudley Street were opened in 1850.[18] A house called Shur Hall stood at the southern end of Spout Lane by the early 19th century; by 1974 it was used as commercial premises.[19] Little London at the southern end of Sandwell Street was an inhabited area by the later 17th century.[20] There were 102 recipients of Mollesley's Dole in Caldmore in 1619 and 219 in 1661;

[90] *Walsall Red Book* (1931), 64; *Walsall Official Town Guide* (1952), 43, 60; *Walsall Observer*, 18 Jan. 1953; below p. 266.
[91] *Evening Mail*, 12 Apr. 1967; *66th Ann. Rep. Walsall Educ. Cttee.* (1969–70), 41; *68th Ann. Rep.* (1971–2), 47; ex inf. the deputy principal, West Midlands College of Education (1974).
[92] O.S. Map 6″, Staffs. LXIII. SE. (prov. edn. with addns. of 1938); below p. 166.
[93] Walsall Council House, deeds bdle. 1298.
[94] W.C.L., Newscuttings 8, p. 147; below p. 262.
[95] Yates, *Map of Staffs.* (1775).
[96] J. Smith, *New Map of Staffs.* (1747), showing a large house in the Maw Green area; B.M. O.S.D. 212; S.R.O., D. 351/M/B/209.
[97] S.R.O., D. 260/M/F/1/5, f. 120; W.S.L., S. MS. 417/ Walsall, *sub* Hatherton, no. 1584.
[98] E 134/35 and 36 Eliz. I Mich./19.
[99] B.M. O.S.D. 212; S.R.O., D. 351/M/B/209; Glew, *Walsall*, 32 n.; Blay, 'Street Names of Walsall', 73–4.
[1] Smith, *New Map of Staffs.* (1747); Yates, *Map of Staffs.* (1775).
[2] S.R.O., D. 1287/box 6, valuation of Walsall estate, 1915 (keyed with unnumbered plans); O.S. Map 6″, Staffs. LXIII. SE. (edns. of 1903 and 1920).
[3] Blay, 'Street Names of Walsall', 51, 173; Lee, *Walsall*, 55; O.S. Map 6″, Staffs. LXIII. SE. (prov. edn. with addns. of 1938); below p. 166.
[4] O.S. Map 6″, Staffs. LXIII. SE. (prov. edn. with addns. of 1938); Ede, *Wednesbury*, 385. The rest of the

Delves was added to West Bromwich: above p. 1. The earlier history of the Delves is reserved for treatment under Wednesbury in a future volume of the Staffordshire History.
[5] Ex inf. S.B. & N. Ltd. (1974).
[6] See p. 167.
[7] *County Boro. of Walsall: Council Year Book 1973–74*, 187.
[8] See p. 166.
[9] B.R.L. 292270 (1559); Snape, *Plan of Walsall* (1782).
[10] Pearce, *Walsall*, 152, 154, 156; W.C.L., C. 4 and A.G. 146; S.R.O., D. 1362/57, pp. 1, 8, 21, 26; Pigot, *Nat. Com. Dir.* (1841), Staffs. p. 80; S.R.O., D. 351/M/B/ 207 (showing Fieldgate, however, as Sandwell St.).
[11] See p. 166.
[12] See p. 181.
[13] *S.H.C.* 1911, 288.
[14] *Walsall Records*, 41–2.
[15] See p. 227.
[16] Yates, *Map of Staffs.* (1775); B.M. O.S.D. 212; S.R.O., D. 351/M/B/209; below pp. 178, 189.
[17] Yates, *Map of Staffs.* (1775); *Robinson's Map of Walsall* (pub. with *Walsall Red Book*, 1876); L.J.R.O., B/V/6/Walsall, 1693.
[18] Parson and Bradshaw, *Dir. Staffs.* (1818), 318, 334; W.C.L., C. 4; below p. 222.
[19] B.M. O.S.D. 212; L.J.R.O., B/A/15/Walsall, *sub* Steward (calling it Shur Hall); Blay, 'Street Names of Walsall', 161 (calling it Shut Hall).
[20] W.S.L., S. MS. 333/32, p. 3.

the second figure, however, and probably the first also, included Pleck.[21]

There was development in patches throughout the area by the 18th century. At Little London there was spur-making by the earlier 18th century.[22] By the 1760s an industrial suburb of metal-workers had developed along Fieldgate and in Windmill Street between Sandwell and Bath Streets, and there were also metal-workers at Caldmore itself. Doveridge along West Bromwich Street south-east of Caldmore included four metal-workers in 1770 as well as two farmers.[23] The Roman Catholic church of St. Mary was opened in 1827 on St. Mary's Mount above the vicarage,[24] and near by St. Mary's Row was built in the later 1840s, 'a neat row' consisting of the works and houses of Messrs. Harvey & Buffery, platers and harness-makers.[25] The Windmill area was further developed in the 1830s and early 1840s when Lord Bradford granted building-leases in Orlando Street and the north end of Sandwell Street. He granted further leases in the same area and in Cemetery Road (now Barleyfields Row) in the 1850s.[26] Newhall Street existed by 1843 and was so named by 1851.[27] The Walsall Freehold Land Society, established in 1851, bought nearly 3 a. for development in Caldmore Lane in 1855.[28] The streets on either side of Corporation Street were laid out in the 1860s and 1870s.[29] Lord Bradford granted several building-leases on the west side of Wednesbury Road in the 1870s, but the houses in that road date largely from the later years of the century.[30] An Anglican mission was established at Caldmore in 1866 and a school opened in 1867; St. Michael's Church in Bath Road was opened in 1871, and St. Michael Street (called Stratford Street until 1925) dates from about then.[31] Hope Street to the north was built c. 1876.[32] Oxford Street to the south of St. Michael's was renamed Carless Street in 1923 in memory of Seaman J. H. Carless, V.C., a native of Walsall who was killed in action in 1917.[33] The glebe land in the north of the area was built over in the 1880s and 1890s when Vicarage Street and Glebe Street were laid out along two

lanes called Vicarage Walk and were built up with terraces; Vicarage Terrace, however, in the southern part of Vicarage Street had been built in 1868 and the near-by Prospect House in 1872.[34] Vicarage Street was extended to Bradford Street via Cross Street in the mid 1930s and the whole became part of Caldmore Road.[35] Bath Street was extended south across Peg's Piece as Bath Road c. 1885 to join the street now called Little London, and the new road was built up during the next few years.[36] Arundel, Windsor, and Cambridge Streets on the south side of West Bromwich Street were laid out by 1875, but most of the terraces date from the late 1880s and the 1890s; Thorpe Road too was added then.[37]

There has been some redevelopment of Caldmore since the 1950s. The council houses and flats in Orlando Street replaced 100 slum properties; work began in the late 1950s and the first new dwelling was let in 1961. The multi-storey flats in Little London were first occupied in 1967.[38] An area in Spout Lane was cleared in 1962, but no rebuilding took place and the site became infested with rats and mice.[39] As a result the Caldmore Residents Action Group was formed in 1970, and in 1971 the council began rebuilding the area with flats and houses. The action group established a housing association in 1972, with offices and an aid centre in a converted shop on Caldmore Green. The council declared part of Caldmore a general improvement area in 1971, the first in Walsall. In 1973 several of the streets south from West Bromwich Street were planted with shrubs and plants. Some restrictions have also been placed on motor traffic. The Caldmore district (including much of Palfrey to the south) remains a working-class community; in 1974, however, 60 per cent of the population were owner-occupiers. Thirty per cent of the community were immigrants and their families, mainly of Asiatic origin.

Palfrey is continuous with Caldmore and has its centre upon Milton Street. Before the later 19th century, however, there was little settlement in the

[21] W.T.C. II/31/1; II/13/49; above p. 145.
[22] W.S.L., S. MS. 333/32, p. 5.
[23] Sketchley's Birmingham ... Dir. (1767); Sketchley's and Adams's ... Univ. Dir. Birmingham ... (1770); Yates, Map of Staffs. (1775); S.R.O., D. 351/M/B/209; below p. 195. The name Windmill St. is used in 1813: Pearce, Walsall, 152.
[24] See p. 240.
[25] Glew, Walsall, 30; P.O. Dir. Staffs. (1850), 353. The name St. Mary's Row was in use by 1834, apparently for what is now Glebe St.: White, Dir. Staffs. (1834); Map of Boro. of Walsall (1836; copy in W.C.L.).
[26] W.C.L., A.G. 146; S.R.O., D. 1287/Colliery Box no. 2/estate corresp. 1850–60, J. Potter to Bailey, Shaw, Smith & Bailey, 23 Apr., 15 Sept. 1851; D. 1362/57.
[27] W.S.L., S. MS. 417/Walsall, map; White, Dir. Staffs. (1851). [28] Glew, Walsall, 68.
[29] W.T.C., Council Mins. 1848–66, 29 Nov. 1860; date-stones of 1864 in South St., 1865 in Mount St., 1867 in Victor St., 1868 in Camden St., 1872–91 in Rutter St. (which occurs in 1871: R.G. 10/2965 no. 129), and 1878 in Bescot St.; deeds at Ansells Brewery, Aston Cross, Birmingham, abstract of title of Hannah and Hen. Owen and Sarah and Edw. Winkle to White Hart inn, 1882, with plan of 1870 showing Brace St. (which occurs in 1871: R.G. 10/2965 no. 125) as a proposed street; Robinson's Map of Walsall (1876); W.C.L., Town Clerk's Misc., box 158. For Victor St. alms-houses of c. 1868 see below p. 267.
[30] S.R.O., D. 1362/57; date-stones of 1874–1905; O.S. Map 6″, Staffs. LXIII. SW. (edns. of 1889, 1904, 1920).

[31] See pp. 238, 260. For St. Michael St. see Lich. Dioc. Regy., B/A/2(i)/R, p. 530; Blay, 'Street Names of Walsall', 155.
[32] W.C.L., Town Clerk's Misc., box 4/9.
[33] Walsall Red Book (1924), 86; memorial outside Walsall Central Libr.
[34] S.R.O., D. 1287/1/47, Walsall accts. 1881–2, p. 27; 1883–5, p. 24; 1884–5, p. 25; S.R.O., Q/RHd 39; Walsall Red Book (1887; 1888; 1889; 1895; 1897); Blay, 'Street Names of Walsall', 179; O.S. Map 6″, Staffs. LXIII. SE. (edns. of 1890 and 1903); date-stones of 1868 on Vicarage Terrace and 1872 on Providence House.
[35] Walsall Red Book (1935; 1936); O.S. Map 6″, Staffs. LXIII. SW. (1920 edn. and prov. edn. with addns. of 1938).
[36] S.R.O., Q/RHd 40; date-stones 1888–93; Robinson's Map of Walsall (1876); O.S. Map 6″, Staffs. LXIII. SE. (edns. of 1890 and 1903); Blay, 'Street Names of Walsall', 12–13; below p. 268. It first appears in Walsall Red Book in the 1893 edn. Peg's Piece, which formed part of the endowment of Harper's alms-houses, was sold in 1876: Char. Com. files.
[37] W. J. Boys, Plan of Boro. of Walsall (1875; copy in W.C.L.); O.S. Map 6″, Staffs. LXIII. SE. (edns. of 1890 and 1903); date-stones of 1889 and 1891 in Arundel St., 1889 in Thorpe Rd. and on corner of Windsor and Cambridge Streets, and 1892 in Cambridge St.; W.C.L., Town Clerk's Misc., boxes 84, 151.
[38] Ex inf. the boro. housing manager (1973).
[39] The rest of this para. is based on information supplied in 1974 by Mr. B. Blower of the Caldmore Housing Advice Centre.

area. Palfrey Green occurs in 1386 as demesne pasture and lay at the southern end of what is now Lord Street.[40] Other early lanes included one mentioned in 1587 running from Palfrey Green to Friar Park smithy in West Bromwich[41] and one which followed the lower part of the present Alexandra Road and part of the present Weston Street to the West Bromwich road in the Redhouse Farm area.[42] Milton Street is part of an early way running from Caldmore (along Watery Lane) and continuing to Bescot (along Wallows Lane).[43] The northern end of Milton Street ran by the pool of the early-17th-century New Mills and was formerly called Stank Lane.[44] There was evidently ironworking near Palfrey Green in the later Middle Ages.[45] In 1770 an awl-blade maker and a spurmaker were recorded at Whitehall between Palfrey and Caldmore.[46] This suggests the existence by then of the house called White Hall which still stood in 1843 at what is now the junction of Dale Street and Alexandra Road. Old cottages there were demolished in 1928.[47] Palfrey Farm in the area between Dale and King Streets existed by the early 19th century.[48]

Development began when the Walsall Freehold Land Society acquired a 22-acre estate at Palfrey in 1852. The land was divided into 145 lots and distributed among 78 people. Building had started by 1853.[49] This was the beginning of Cobden Street and its side streets, Queen Street (renamed Queen Mary Street in the later 1920s), King Street, and the west end of Dale Street, all of which contained houses by 1861. Whitehall Road, cut in the later 1860s, was built up by the mid 1870s, and Tennyson Street (now the east end of Dale Street), Alexandra Street (the north end of Alexandra Road), and Villiers Street existed by then. There were also buildings on the corner of Milton and Lord Streets.[50] The north end of Sun Street was described as a new street in 1881, and schools were built there in 1884; it had been extended to Dale Street by 1893.[51] Palfrey Park was opened in 1886 on 8 a. to the south of Dale Street, the two ends of which were presumably linked about that time; the park was extended to its present 16 a. c. 1935.[52] From the mid

1880s Lord Bradford was developing the area to the north of New Mills between Milton Street and Wednesbury Road. Several building-leases were granted in Stank Lane and Milton Street between 1885 and 1888. Earl Street and Countess Street were laid out in the early 1890s and building-leases granted in 1893, 1894, and 1899.[53] The streets to the south date from about the same time, and much of the building in Lord Street is of the late 19th and early 20th centuries.[54]

Building spread southwards to the borough boundary between the World Wars, with both council and privately built estates. Alexandra Street was extended south to Lord Street along Love Lane as part of the Palfrey council estate and renamed Alexandra Road. Broadway West was built across the southern area in the 1920s and is lined with privately built houses of the inter-war years. Bescot Crescent, dating from the same period, contains much light industry.[55] Many immigrants have settled in the old part of Palfrey. The Whitehall Road area has been included in the Caldmore improvement scheme. Demolition of several of the terraces was in progress in 1974, and there had been some rebuilding on cleared sites.

The Pleck, a name meaning a small plot of ground, occurs as a small area of waste in 1576 and 1617.[56] In the later 18th century at least it lay at the junction of Darlaston Road (then called Pleck Lane) and Old Pleck Road.[57] The oldest settlement in the vicinity was Bescot. The name suggests Saxon occupation ('Beorhtmund's cottage'),[58] and the place is mentioned in Domesday Book as a waste carucate.[59] It occurs as an inhabited area in the earlier 13th century[60] and contained a manor-house by the early fourteenth.[61] The area to the north between Darlaston Road, Pleck Road (formerly Park Lane), and Wolverhampton Road was occupied in the Middle Ages by the park and Walsall manor-house.[62] The Pleck itself was an inhabited area by the 17th century.[63] In 1619 there were 16 recipients of Mollesley's Dole at Bescot and 4 at the Park.[64] The area to the north-east between Pleck Road, Wednesbury Road, and Bradford Street remained undeveloped until the 19th century, except for the

[40] S.R.O., D. 641/1/2/32; W.S.L., S. MS. 417/Walsall.
[41] S.R.O., D. 260/M/T/1/13b. For Fishpool Lane near Palfrey Green in 1513 see ibid./1a, deed of 28 Mar. 1513.
[42] S.R.O., D. 351/M/B/209; O.S. Map 6″, Staffs. LXIII. SW. (1890 edn.), SE. (1890 edn.).
[43] Yates, *Map of Staffs.* (1775); S.R.O., D. 351/M/B/209.
[44] Yates, *Map of Staffs.* (1775); *Robinson's Map of Walsall* (1876); Blay, 'Street Names of Walsall', 127; below p. 185. The site of the mills was described as in Caldmore in 1618: S.R.O., D. 1287/6/14, deed of 19 Oct. 1618.   [45] See p. 192.
[46] *Sketchley's and Adams's . . . Univ. Dir. Birmingham . . .* (1770). Pearce, *Walsall*, 159, 164, records 2 platers and an awl-blade maker in 1813.
[47] B.M. O.S.D. 212; W.S.L., S. MS. 417/Walsall, sub Marlow; Blay, 'Street Names of Walsall', 58.
[48] B.M. O.S.D. 212; S.R.O., D. 351/M/B/209; W.S.L., S. MS. 417/Walsall, sub Oerton.
[49] Glew, *Walsall*, 68; *Staffs. Advertiser*, 20 Aug. 1853.
[50] R.G. 9/2017 nos. 93–4, 96; Boys, *Plan of Boro. of Walsall* (1875); Blay, 'Street Names of Walsall', 148, 192; date-stones of 1874–91 in Whitehall Rd.
[51] S.R.O., Q/SB, M. 1881; O.S. Map 6″, Staffs. LXIII. SW. (edns. of 1889 and 1904); date-stone of 1891 on corner of Sun and Dale Streets; below p. 262.
[52] *Walsall Red Book* (1886), 30; (1887), 59; *Kelly's Dir. Staffs.* (1936); *County Boro. of Walsall: Council Year Book 1973–74*, 187.

[53] S.R.O., D. 1287/1/47, Walsall accts. 1888–9, p. 23; D. 1287/box 6, valuation of Walsall estate, 1915 (keyed with unnumbered plans); /box 7, contracts 1892–3; date-stones of 1887 and 1888 in Milton St. (with one of 1885 on the eastern side also).
[54] O.S. Map 6″, Staffs. LXIII. SW. (edns. of 1904 and 1920); W.C.L., Town Clerk's Misc., box 145; Blay, 'Street Names of Walsall', 192; date-stone of 1888 in Lord St.
[55] Blay, 'Street Names of Walsall', 5; O.S. Map 6″, Staffs. LXIII. SW. (1889 edn. and prov. edn. with addns. of 1938); Lee, *Walsall*, 56; *31st Ann. Rep. Walsall Educ. Cttee.* (1934–5), 9 (copy in W.C.L.).
[56] *Eng. Place-name Elements* (E.P.N.S.), ii. 67; S.R.O., D. 1287/1/2, survey of Walsall manor, 1576, m. 13; D. 260/M/F/1/8, ct. of recog. and survey, 1617, p. 34.
[57] S.R.O., D. 1287/8/2; Pearce, *Walsall*, 221.
[58] E. Ekwall, *Concise Oxford Dict. of Eng. Place-names* (4th edn.).
[59] See p. 171.
[60] *Walsall Records*, 24.
[61] See p. 172.
[62] See pp. 170, 184. For Park Lane see Pearce, *Walsall*, 221; it is given as Pleck Lane or Park Lane in Act for repairing and widening the road from Muckley Corner to Walsall and Wednesbury . . ., 6 Geo. III, c. 99.
[63] See pp. 155–6.
[64] W.T.C. II/31/1; above p. 145.

race-course of the 1770s.[65] Several cottages had been built over the Pleck by 1763, when it was crossed by what are now Narrow Lane and Wellington Street (formerly Horseshoes Lane). There were also a few houses to the east along Wednesbury Road and Wallows Lane and to the west along Darlaston Road, including one on the boundary at James Bridge. There were several houses in the area of the former park; they included one with an 84-acre holding attached, known as Park House and the forerunner of what was called Parks Farm in the early 19th century. Bescot Farm at the end of what is now Slater's Lane also existed by the later 18th century.[66] The Walsall Canal was built through the district in the later 1790s.[67]

Extensive growth came in the later 19th century, but there had been some building earlier in the century. At Pleck itself a National school was opened in 1825 and a Wesleyan meeting was started c. 1827.[68] Chapel, Regent, and Oxford Streets had been laid out by 1843 in the angle of Old Pleck and Wednesbury Roads. Chapel Street took its name from the Wesleyan chapel opened there in 1840; it was renamed St. Quentin Street to commemorate the storming of the Hindenburg Line at the St. Quentin Canal in 1918, an operation in which Walsall men took part. Regent Street was renamed Caledon Street after the ship in which J. H. Carless, V.C., served.[69] In the area south of Wolverhampton Street there was limestone working by 1813.[70] It was there too that Bridgeman Street was built from Bradford Street to Pleck Road by Lord Bradford c. 1836. Two houses were being built near the bridge over Walsall Brook early in 1838, and Bridgeman Place near by existed then; as Bridgeman Terrace it was described in 1855 as 'a handsome row of fashionable houses with stucco fronts', one of them the home of Charles (later Sir Charles) Forster, M.P. for Walsall.[71] By 1843 Navigation Street had been built north from Bridgeman Street, and a road (now the eastern end of Moat Road) continued Bridgeman Street over Pleck Road beside the union workhouse of 1838.[72] There were brickworks at James Bridge and in the Park area by 1834, and James Bridge Colliery was working by 1843.[73]

The extension of mining and the building of iron-works from c. 1850 led to a great increase in the population of the Pleck area, said to be over 2,500 in 1858 when St. John's Church was opened in Pleck Road.[74] Most of the growth was east of Pleck Road where from the 1850s factories and streets of workers' cottages were built over Lord Bradford's land. The railway had been opened through that part in 1847, with a station first in Bridgeman Place and from 1849 in the new Station Street.[75] In the 1850s building-leases were granted not only in Bridgeman Street, Navigation Street, and Pleck Road but also in the new Rollingmill, Long (at first George), Queen (at first Earl), Frederick, Augustus, Henry, Weston, Brineton, and Wharf Streets. A cemetery was opened at the southern end of Queen Street in 1857. Development continued throughout the area in the 1860s and 1870s, and Short, Brook, and Brockhurst Streets and part of Charles Street were built.[76] Corporation Street West, continuing Queen Street to Wednesbury Road, dates from c. 1880.[77] By the 1880s there were works along both sides of the canal, mainly ironworks and tube works; Henry Boys's Waterloo Colliery and Brickworks had been opened by 1868, and the corporation's gasworks dates from 1877.[78] By the 1880s too development was extending eastwards over the race-course. Midland Road had been laid out by 1885,[79] and Tasker Street, which occurs as Tasker's Lane from 1587, was being built up by 1889.[80] Meadow Street dates from c. 1892.[81] In 1904 it was stated that upwards of 3,000 people lived close to the mission church in Rollingmill Street.[82] By 1974 the area was mainly industrial, and many of the factories were new. Some houses still stood in Queen Street, but few were occupied.[83]

The rest of the Pleck district also developed from the later 19th century, mainly as a residential area.[84] There was then, however, extensive coal-mining between Wolverhampton and Darlaston Roads and at Bescot. The last colliery, James Bridge, was abandoned in 1901. Brick-making apparently ceased c. 1897, but sand and gravel were still worked on both sides of Darlaston Road in 1916. James Bridge remains an industrial area.

In Pleck itself Lord Bradford granted building-leases round St. John's Church in the late 1850s, and terraces were built along the west side of Pleck

[65] See p. 250.
[66] S.R.O., D. 1287/8/2; Yates, *Map of Staffs.* (1775). For Horseshoes Lane see O.S. Map 1/2,500, Staffs. LXIII. 10 (1887 edn.).
[67] See p. 168.   [68] See pp. 245, 257.
[69] W.S.L., S. MS. 417/Walsall, map (where they are not named); Blay, 'Street Names of Walsall', 40, 157; above p. 156; below p. 245.
[70] See p. 191.
[71] *Map of Boro. of Walsall* (1836; copy in W.C.L.); S.R.O., D. 1287/18/26, business corresp. 1838–9, P. Potter to Lord Bradford, 10 Apr. 1838; W.C.L., QSM 1/359; W.S.L., S. MS. 417/Walsall, map; Glew, *Walsall*, 61.
[72] W.S.L., S. MS. 417/Walsall, map; S.R.O., D. 1287/18/26, business corresp. 1835–7, Potter to Bradford, 6 Mar. 1837; below p. 212.
[73] See pp. 189, 192.
[74] Nat. Soc. files/Walsall/Pleck and Bescot, 4 Apr. 1855; *Staffs. Advertiser*, 18 Apr. 1857; L.J.R.O., B/A/2(i)/Q, pp. 163–8.
[75] See p. 168.
[76] W.C.L., box 22, nos. 14 and 17; S.R.O., D. 1287/box 6, valuation of Walsall estate, 1915 (keyed with un-numbered plans); /Colliery Box no. 2, estate corresp. 1827–65, J. Potter to Bailey, Shaw, Smith & Bailey,

25 July 1855; P. Potter to same, 4 Dec. 1855, 24 Jan. and 1 Feb. 1856; P. and J. Potter to same, 22 Feb. 1856; J. Tute to Lord Bradford, 26 Nov. 1856; D. 1362/57; below p. 223.
[77] Not shown on *Robinson's Map of Walsall* (pub. with *Walsall Red Book*, 1876), it appears on O.S. Map 6", Staffs. LXIII. SW. (1889 edn., surv. 1885).
[78] O.S. Map 6", Staffs. LXIII. SW. (1889 edn.); *P.O. Dir. Staffs.* (1868); below pp. 193, 197, 200–1, 224.
[79] O.S. Map 6", Staffs. LXIII. SW. (1889 edn.).
[80] S.R.O., D. 260/M/T/1/13a, deed of 20 May 1587; date-stone of 1889. *Robinson's Map of Walsall* (1876), shows it as Tasker's Lane.
[81] W.C.L., Town Clerk's Misc., box 5; Blay, 'Street Names of Walsall', 125.
[82] Lich. Dioc. Regy., B/A/1/36, pp. 234–5.
[83] *Express & Star*, 12 June 1974.
[84] For this para. see O.S. Map 6", Staffs. LXIII. SW. (edns. of 1889, 1904, 1920); R. Hunt, *Memoirs of Geol. Surv., Mineral Statistics of U.K. for 1860*, 190; ibid. *1861*, app. p. 40; *Summaries of Reps. Inspectors of Mines and Mineral Statistics for 1883* [C. 4058], pp. 259, 265–6, H.C. (1884), xix; *Rep. H.M. Inspector of Mines for Stafford Dist. for 1901* [Cd. 1062], p. 29, H.C. (1902), xviii; *Walsall Red Book* (1888), adverts. p. xxiv; (1898), 58; *List of Quarries ... for 1916* (H.M.S.O. 1917), 525; below p. 194.

Road, also on the Bradford estate, shortly afterwards and in the early 1880s.[85] Houses were built at the Pleck end of Darlaston Road in 1867 and 1871.[86] Several villas had been built in Bescot Road by 1875, and a station was opened there in 1881; Slaney Road, though largely occupied by houses and flats built privately after the Second World War, dates from the late 19th century.[87] The development around the Pleck end of Wednesbury Road, now the shopping centre of the area, took place in the 1890s and the early 20th century.[88] Prince Street was laid out c. 1893.[89] The southern end of Scarborough Road and the terraces along the south side of Darlaston Road date from c. 1900.[90] The streets between Darlaston Road and Slater's Lane date mainly from the early 20th century.[91] Some terraces were built on Lord Bradford's land at the north end of Pleck Road in the later 1850s, and Moat Street (now Road) existed by 1860. Most houses in that area, however, date from the end of the century. Checketts Street was built by Walter Checketts on land leased from Lord Bradford in 1891 and 1893, and Forrester Street was being built up throughout the 1890s. The east end of Ida Road dates from the late 19th and early 20th centuries.[92]

In the 20th century much of the area has been used for council housing. The estate around Ida and Alumwell Roads dates from the later 1920s and the 1930s, and it was continued west to Primley Avenue from the later 1940s.[93] There is also an estate at the end of Slater's Lane, built both before and after the Second World War. Another, which includes several multi-storey blocks of flats, was laid out in the cleared Oxford Street area in the later 1960s.[94] Rebuilding in the Wolverhampton Road area was still in progress in 1974. The streets of privately built houses on either side of Bescot Road date from the years between the two World Wars; those on the west were laid out over part of the grounds of Bescot Hall after its demolition in 1929–30.[95] The 28-acre Pleck Park covers more of the grounds; the first portion was opened as a war-memorial playing-field in 1926, and the corporation bought more land in 1938.[96] The M6 motorway was opened through the west of the area as far as Bescot in 1968.[97]

Birchills occurs as an area of wood and waste in the earlier 14th century.[98] About 1540 40 trees were felled there,[99] and Birchills was described as 30 a. of common waste in surveys of 1576 and 1617.[1] Deadman's Lane, renamed Hospital Street c. 1872, existed by 1545.[2] Birchills Lane, running between Walsall and Birchills and also known as Green Lane by 1763, is mentioned in 1559, and there was a cottage beside it in 1587.[3] Coal was mined at Birchills by the early 17th century,[4] and there were about 20 recipients of Mollesley's Dole in the middle of the century.[5] The lane leading from Birchills to Bentley Hay, mentioned in 1729,[6] was presumably Bentley Lane, which existed by 1763. The roads now known as Birchills Street, Hollyhedge Lane, and Old Birchills also existed in 1763, and there was then settlement along all the roads in the area, including the present Wolverhampton Road.[7] Birchills Hall east of Green Lane apparently existed by the late 18th century; although part of it survived into the 20th century, by 1850 it was surrounded by pits and ironworks and much of it had then recently been demolished.[8]

By 1770 there were many metal-workers at Birchills.[9] The Wyrley and Essington Canal was built through the district at the end of the 18th century, and Birchills was the principal area of coal-mining in Walsall in the earlier 19th century. There was also iron-working and limestone mining.[10] A large population had grown up by the 1850s,[11] concentrated north of Blue Lane West. Burrowes Street existed by 1851. Regent Street and the eastern end of Farringdon Street were being built up in the 1850s on Lord Bradford's land, and the block of streets between Birchills Street and Wolverhampton Road dates from then. A Primitive Methodist centre was opened in 1850 in a schoolroom in

[85] S.R.O., D. 1287/box 6, valuation of Walsall estate, 1915 (keyed with unnumbered plans); D. 1362/57; W. J. Boys, *Plan of Boro. of Walsall* (1875; copy in W.C.L.); O.S. Map 6″, Staffs. LXIII. SW. (1889 edn.). Oxford Terrace in Old Pleck Rd. is dated 1879.
[86] Date-stones on N. side of Darlaston Rd.
[87] Boys, *Plan of Walsall*; date-stone of 1898 in Slaney Rd.; below p. 168.
[88] O.S. Map 6″, Staffs. LXIII. SW. (1904 edn.); Blay, 'Street Names of Walsall', 75; date-stones of 1890 and 1892 in Wednesbury Rd., 1890, 1901, and 1902 in Hillary St., and 1892 in Ford St.
[89] W.C.L., Town Clerk's Misc., box 147.
[90] S.R.O., D. 1287/box 6, valuation of Walsall estate, 1915 (keyed with unnumbered plans); O.S. Map 6″, Staffs. LXIII. SW. (1904 edn.); date-stone of 1901 on Osborne House at James Bridge. Globe Terrace on the N. side of Darlaston Rd. at James Bridge is dated 1900.
[91] O.S. Map 6″, Staffs. LXIII. SW. (1920 edn., revised 1912–13).
[92] S.R.O., D. 1287/box 6, valuation of Walsall estate, 1915 (keyed with unnumbered plans); D. 1362/57; O.S. Map 6″, Staffs. LXIII. NW. (edns. of 1889 and 1903), SW. (edns. of 1889 and 1904); date-stones of 1893 in Ida Rd., 1894 in Forrester St., and 1898 in Pleck Rd.; Blay, 'Street Names of Walsall', 46.
[93] O.S. Map 6″, Staffs. LXIII. NW., SW. (prov. edn. with addns. of 1938); Lee, *Walsall*, 56; *3rd Ann. Rep. Walsall Educ. Cttee.* (1936–7), 7 (copy in W.C.L.); ex inf. the boro. housing manager (1974).
[94] Ex inf. the boro. housing manager (1974); *Express & Star*, 5 Feb. 1970.
[95] O.S. Map 6″, Staffs. LXIII. SW. (prov. edn. with addns. of 1938); Walsall Council House, Bescot deeds,

abstract of title 1938; Blay, 'Street Names of Walsall', 104.
[96] *Metropolitan Boro. of Walsall Official Town Guide* [1974], 67; Walsall Council House, Bescot deeds, abstract of title 1964 and conveyance July 1938; *Walsall Red Book* (1927), 65 and photograph on p. 31; *County Boro. of Walsall: Council Year Book 1973–74*, 187.
[97] See p. 167.
[98] *S.H.C.* 1910, 199; *Walsall Records*, 49.
[99] C 1/1076/68–70.
[1] S.R.O., D. 1287/1/2, survey of Walsall manor, 1576, m. 13; D. 260/M/F/1/8, ct. of recog. and survey, 1617, p. 34.
[2] Sims, *Cal. of Deeds*, p. 31; S.R.O., D. 1287/8/2, map.
[3] Sims, *Cal. of Deeds*, p. 38; S.R.O., D. 260/M/T/1/12, deed of 29 Mar. 1587; D. 1287/8/2, map. The name Birchills Lane was still used in 1855: S.R.O., D. 1362/57, p. 100.
[4] See p. 189.
[5] Homeshaw, *Walsall*, 5; above p. 145.
[6] S.R.O., Q/SO 12, f. 198.
[7] S.R.O., D. 1287/8/2.
[8] S.R.O., Q/RTg/1/1, 1784, no. 170; 1790–1, no. 274; Homeshaw, *Bloxwich*, 103; Pearce, *Walsall*, 168; Willmore, *Walsall*, 436; S. Lane-Poole, *Sir Harry Parkes in China* (1901), 3, 104; *Kelly's Dir. Staffs.* (1904), 428; W.S.L., S. MS. 417/Walsall, map; O.S. Map 6″, Staffs. LXIII. NW. (1920 edn.).
[9] *Sketchley's and Adams's ... Univ. Dir. Birmingham ...* (1770).
[10] See pp. 168, 189, 192–3, 196, 198, 200.
[11] Nat. Soc. files/Walsall/St. Peter (Birchills), 1 July 1854.

Old Birchills, and a National school and Anglican mission were started in a building in Hollyhedge Lane in 1855. Building-leases on the Bradford estate in that area were granted in 1857, the later 1860s, and 1873, and also on the east side of Green Lane between Upper and Lower Union Streets (now Croft and Mary Streets) in the mid 1850s and mid 1860s.[12] Newland Street off Blue Lane West was built to provide new working-class houses in conjunction with the corporation's clearance of the adjoining Townend Bank area in the later 1870s.[13]

Birchills was a poor locality. In arguing the case for converting the derelict mining ground at Reedswood north of Bentley Lane into a park in 1879, the vicar of St. Peter's, Stafford Street, spoke of the pale and haggard looks of the inhabitants and the 'shoals of little ones at the entrance of court after court, making mud pies in the gutters or prying down the gullies of the common sewers in the streets'.[14] In 1886 the Anglican mission district was described as 'the poorest part of the poorest parish in Walsall'; out of a population of 5,000 or more there were only five households that kept a servant.[15] Although there was strong opposition in the town to the idea of reclaiming the ground at Reedswood, Lord Bradford conveyed 46 a. there to the corporation in 1885 for a nominal sum, and it was laid out as a park.[16]

By then building was spreading westwards. Raleigh Street was laid out c. 1882 by J. F. Crump and P. Pargeter, and Jessel Road and the north end of Pargeter Street were built about the same time.[17] The terraces at the east end of Bentley Lane were also begun,[18] and those in Dalkeith Street were built in the 1890s on land leased from Lord Bradford.[19] Neale Street was built in the early 1890s with the factory of Walsall Locks and Cart Gear Ltd. at the end of it.[20] Edward Street was built at the beginning of the 20th century.[21] More houses were built along Green Lane; Farringdon Street was extended and terraces were built there. The area around Lewis Street south of Hospital Street was built up c. 1892.[22] The houses at Bentley Moor, both council and privately built, date mostly from the years between the two World Wars.[23] The area lying north of Blue Lane includes maisonettes which were built in the earlier 1950s in Green

Lane and multi-storey blocks of flats of the later 1950s in Burrowes Street.[24] The council was still rebuilding the rest of it in 1974. The part of Green Lane north of Hospital Street remains industrial, with engineering works, tubeworks, and a power station; in 1973 derelict land by the canal to the north of Stephenson Avenue was reclaimed and landscaped.[25]

The area on either side of Bentley Lane added to the borough in 1931 includes the Pouk Hill quarry. The dolerite deposit there was worked in the later 17th century and was largely exhausted by the 1880s. Some quarrying, however, continued until the Second World War.[26] By 1974 much of the neighbouring area was covered with new streets of privately built houses. It also contained cash-and-carry warehouses and some light industry.

The Townend Bank area in the north-west of the town is an inverted triangle, with its base on Blue Lane (so named by 1768), its sides along Wolverhampton Street (formerly Hampton Lane) and the southern end of Stafford Street (formerly Bloxwich Lane), and its apex at Townend Bank itself at the end of Park Street. Six newly built cottages on the waste at Townend were mentioned in 1617, and by 1763 there were many more cottages there, mainly towards the apex. There were also several cottages in the stretch of Bloxwich Lane north of the area. Metal-working was being carried on in the area by 1767.[27] The Walsall Canal, opened in 1799, ended at a wharf in Marsh Lane to the south-west of Townend Bank.[28] By the early 19th century buildings had appeared along the southern end of what was by then called Stafford Street, and there were also some at the western end of Blue Lane.[29] By the 1830s Wisemore to the east of Townend Bank was densely built up, and Blue Lane and Portland Street were becoming so. The streets immediately north on either side of Stafford Street were laid out c. 1840.[30] In one of them was a school dating from 1840, and in Stafford Street a Wesleyan chapel was opened in 1840 and St. Peter's Church in 1841.[31] Littleton Street West dates from about that time.[32] Lord Hatherton granted leases in Stafford Street in the later 1840s and early 1850s, and in 1855 it was stated that the Stafford Street area had grown remarkably in the previous five years.[33] In the Town-

[12] H.O. 107/2023 no. 229; R.G. 9/2015 nos. 16–23, 28, 31–3; S.R.O., D. 1287/box 6, valuation of Walsall estate, 1915 (keyed with unnumbered plans); S.R.O., D. 1367/57; below pp. 247, 259. Francis St. was approved by the council's street cttee. in 1851: W.T.C., Street Cttee. Mins. 1849–51, loose sheet dated 8 Apr. 1851.
[13] *1st Rep. Com. Housing of Working Classes* [C. 4402–I], p. 703, H.C. (1884–5), xiii; below p. 221. The land was called Newlands by 1763: S.R.O., D. 1287/8/2.
[14] *Walsall Observer*, 23 Jan. 1953, p. 6.
[15] *Lich. Dioc. Mag.* 1886, 130, appeal by working men for the new church, giving the population as over 6,000. It is given variously as 4,000 and 4,500 ibid. 1885, 138.
[16] *Walsall Observer*, 23 Jan. 1953, p. 6; *Walsall Red Book* (1886), 30; Walsall Corp. Act, 1925, 15 & 16 Geo. V, c. 122 (Local), s. 57. The area is given as 53 a. in *County Boro. of Walsall: Council Year Book 1973–74*, 187.
[17] W.C.L., ACJ Acc. 48/VII/112; W.C.L., Town Clerk's Misc., box 147; date-stones of 1890 and 1892 in Raleigh St.; O.S. Map 6", Staffs. LXIII. NW. (1889 edn.).
[18] Date-stone of 1885; O.S. Map 6", Staffs. LXIII. NW. (1903 edn., revised 1900–1).
[19] S.R.O., D. 1287/box 6, valuation of Walsall estate, 1915 (keyed with unnumbered plans).
[20] Blay, 'Street Names of Walsall', 130. A terrace there is dated 1899.

[21] Date-stone of 1903; below p. 246. It is not shown on O.S. Map 6", Staffs. LXIII. NW. (1903 edn.).
[22] O.S. Map 6", Staffs. LXIII. NW. (1903 edn.); S.R.O., D. 1287/box 6, valuation of Walsall estate, 1915 (keyed with unnumbered plans); date-stone of 1893 in Farringon St.; W.C.L., Town Clerk's Misc., box 147; Blay, 'Street Names of Walsall', 117, 124; Fink, *Queen Mary's Grammar Sch.* 245 n.
[23] O.S. Map 6", Staffs. LXIII. NW. (prov. edn. with addns. of 1938).
[24] Ex inf. the boro. housing manager (1974).
[25] *Walsall Observer*, 8 June 1973.
[26] *V.C.H. Staffs.* ii. 203–4.
[27] S.R.O., D. 1287/8/2; *Sketchley's Birmingham . . . Dir.* (1767); *Sketchley's and Adams's . . . Univ. Dir. Birmingham . . .* (1770); Pearce, *Walsall*, 223; below p. 183.
[28] See p. 168.
[29] B.M. O.S.D. 212; S.R.O., D. 351/M/B/209; Pearce, *Walsall*, 152.
[30] W.C.L., A.G. 146; *Map of Boro. of Walsall* (1836; copy in W.C.L.); W.S.L., S. MS. 417/Walsall, map; S.R.O., D. 1287/18/26, business corresp. 1835–7, P. Potter to Lord Bradford, 3 May 1836.
[31] See pp. 236, 245, 258.   [32] See p. 151.
[33] S.R.O., D. 260/M/E/173, rental 1864; Glew, *Walsall*, 57; Blay, 'Street Names of Walsall', 132–3.

Design for the Arboretum *c.* 1872, with Lichfield Street in the foregound

The town from the north-west *c.* 1800

WALSALL

The Paddock from St. Matthew's churchyard

Bradford Street, with terraces of the 1830s

WALSALL

end Bank part of Green Lane Lord Hatherton granted several building leases between 1849 and 1861.[34] Houses and commercial property still standing on the north side of Wolverhampton Street in 1974 probably date from the earlier 19th century. North Walsall station was opened in 1872.[35] Terraces were built northwards up both sides of Stafford Street and its continuation Bloxwich Road as far as the canal during the later 19th century. Northcote Street on the west side existed by the beginning of the 20th century and Gladstone Street linking it with Hospital Street by 1913.[36]

The western end of the town was described in 1867 as one 'of smoke and lime-kilns, gasworks, and Irish hordes', and in 1886 St. Peter's parish was said to be the poorest in Walsall.[37] Improvements were carried out at Townend Bank in the 1870s and earlier 1880s by Lord Hatherton and by the corporation. Margaret Street was built in the earlier 1870s. From 1876 the slums of Townend Bank were cleared. Marsh Street, consisting largely of commercial buildings, was laid out, and some of the properties remaining in 1974 are early examples of the use of moulded-brick ornament in Walsall. The south-eastern end of Shaw Street was also built as part of the improvements; it was continued north-westward to Blue Lane West along the line of an existing footpath in the early 20th century. Algernon Street was laid out partly on the line of an old tramway.[38] Slums were cleared in Wisemore and in Short Acre and Long Acre Streets west of Stafford Street in the 1930s.[39] Part of the Townend Bank area had been demolished by 1974, and there had been some rebuilding. Most of Wisemore was obliterated by the technical college, built in stages from 1949 to 1969.[40] By 1971 competition from the new shopping areas in the town centre and uncertainty about the course of the projected ring road had led to the decay of the shops in Stafford Street.[41]

Ryecroft to the east of Stafford Street was in Rushall parish until the 19th century when it became an extension of Walsall's urban area and was taken into the borough.[42] By 1834 it was noted for its sand quarries.[43] Proffitt Street, part of an old road, was known as Sandwell Street in the earlier 19th century;[44] the streets on the south side were being built up by the early 1840s.[45] A Primitive Methodist chapel was opened in North Street in 1845.[46] Marlow Street on the Walsall side of the boundary was built about the late 1850s.[47] Twenty-five houses

were built in Long Ann Street c. 1855, nine of them fronting the street and the rest in 'a roomy court'.[48] The urban part of Ryecroft, having been included in the improvement commissioners' district in 1848, was added to the borough in 1876; a further part was added in 1890.[49] The cemetery in Coal Pool Lane was opened in 1894.[50] At the beginning of the 20th century a small estate was built on the north side of the railway on the site of the North Walsall Brickworks.[51] A council estate extended it northwards to Forest Lane in the later 1920s. Another council estate was built in the years between the two World Wars to the west off Coal Pool Lane, where the corporation bought Ryecroft farm in 1919. It also laid out 19 cottage holdings of 1 a. each on part of the farm for ex-servicemen. A council estate was built to the north of Proffitt Street, and in the 1930s the corporation rebuilt the slums in the old streets to the south.[52]

The name Bloxwich ('Blocc's dwelling') suggests Anglo-Saxon settlement,[53] but the place occurs in Domesday Book only as an area of woodland.[54] A distinction was drawn between Bloxwich and Great Bloxwich in 1300;[55] the first was presumably Little Bloxwich, a name in use in 1307.[56]

Great Bloxwich was the main settlement. A chapel of ease, the first in the parish, was built there apparently in the early 15th century.[57] The original centre was probably at the southern end of the present High Street in the Pinfold area, with building spreading north as encroachment on the waste. There was metal-working by the early 17th century, and probably earlier, and coal-mining c. 1597.[58] There were 419 recipients of Mollesley's Dole in 1619 and 611 in 1652.[59] By the later 18th century there was settlement not only in the Pinfold area but also around Chapel (later Elmore) Green where the church stands and round Short Heath to the north, approximately along the line of the present Wolverhampton Road, Sandbank, Bell Lane, Lichfield Road, and Park Road. There was also settlement at Wallington Heath further north round the junction of the Stafford road and Stoney Lane.[60] That was still the basic pattern in the early 1840s; there were also 11 new houses dating from c. 1840 along what is now Field Road.[61] New Street and Church Street date from 1850,[62] and the railway station to the south-west was opened in 1858.[63] By that time Bloxwich was becoming the chief coal-

[34] W.S.L., D. 1798/551. [35] See p. 169.
[36] O.S. Map 6″, Staffs. LXIII. NW. (edns. of 1889 and 1903); date-stones of 1886–98 in Stafford Street.
[37] W.C.L., Newscuttings 1A, p. 73; above p. 160.
[38] W.S.L., D. 1798/551; S.R.O., D. 260/M/E/174, 31 May 1870, 9–16 May 1871, 3 Sept. 1872 sqq.; W.C.L., box 50, no. 1; W.T.C., Council Mins. 1884–8, p. 132; date-stones of 1883 in Marsh St.; O.S. Map 6″, Staffs. LXIII. NW. (edns. of 1889 and 1903); below pp. 191, 221.
[39] Cason, Blakenall Heath, 41; Woodall, Walsall Milestones, 41. [40] See p. 265.
[41] Walsall Observer, 12 Feb. 1971.
[42] Its earlier history is reserved for treatment under Rushall in a future volume of the Staffordshire History.
[43] White, Dir. Staffs. (1834).
[44] S.R.O., D. 1287/8/2, map; Yates, Map of Staffs. (1775); S.R.O., D. 351/M/B/207.
[45] W.S.L., S. MS. 417/Rushall; S.R.O., D. 1287/box 6, valuation of Walsall estate, 1915.
[46] See p. 247.
[47] W.C.L., Town Clerk's Misc., box 151.
[48] Staffs. Advertiser, 22 Oct. 1859, p. 8.

[49] See p. 217. [50] See p. 223.
[51] O.S. Map 6″, Staffs. LXIII. NW. (edns. of 1903 and 1920); date-stone of 1906 in Essex St.; Blay, 'Street Names of Walsall', 111–12.
[52] O.S. Map 6″, Staffs. LXIII. NW. (prov. edn. with addns. of 1938); Staffs. Advertiser, 16 Apr. 1927, p. 8; Lee, Walsall, 54; Blay, 'Street Names of Walsall', 7; Woodall, Walsall Milestones, 41.
[53] E. Ekwall, Concise Oxford Dict. of Eng. Place-names; Homeshaw, Bloxwich, 9–10.
[54] See p. 184. [55] S.H.C. v (1), 178.
[56] S.H.C. vii (1), 186. [57] See p. 233.
[58] See pp. 189, 194–5.
[59] W.T.C. II/31/1; II/13/40; above p. 145. The 1661 figure, 763, was stated to cover Bloxwich, Marlpit House, some houses at the bottom of Bentley Hay, and one in Cornwall Field: W.T.C. II/13/49.
[60] S.R.O., D. 1287/8/2; Yates, Map of Staffs. (1775).
[61] W.S.L., S. MS. 417/Walsall; Midland Counties Herald, 18 Feb. 1841.
[62] Homeshaw, Bloxwich, 169.
[63] See pp. 168–9.

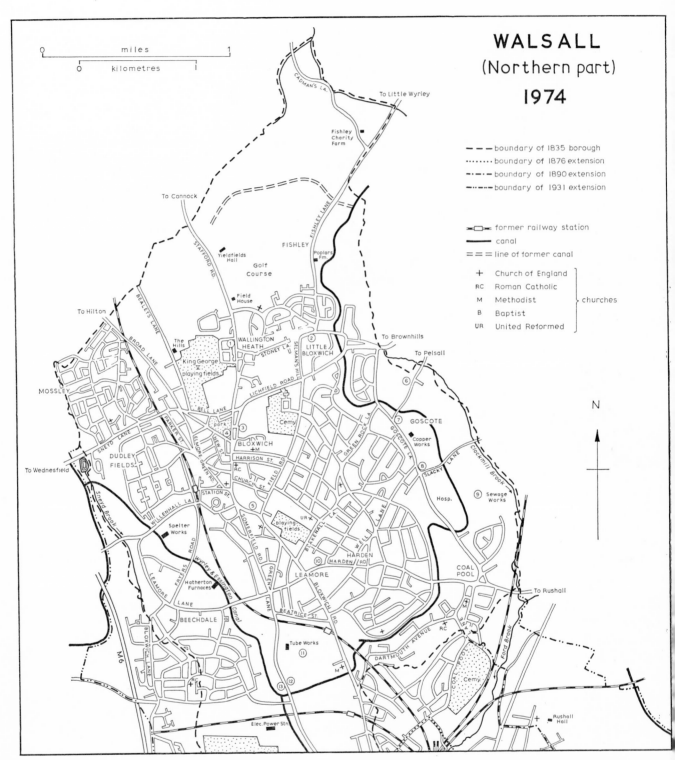

WALSALL
(Northern part)
1974

KEY

1. Site of Wallington House
2. Site of Lower farm
3. Former Wesleyan chapel
4. Former Bloxwich Music Hall
5. Site of Primitive Methodist chapel
6. Site of Goscote foundry
7. Site of Goscote manor-house
8. Site of Goscote Hall
9. Site of Goscote Lodge
10. Former R.C. chapel
11. Site of Birchills Hall
12. Site of New Birchills furnaces
13. Site of Green Lanes Furnaces

mining area in the parish.[64] Reeves Street existed by 1861 and Harrison Street by 1870.[65] The streets between Elmore Green Road and New Street apparently date from the later 1870s.[66] Wolverhampton Street had been cut by 1879 when the first of several terraces was built there; it was renamed Parker Street in 1890.[67]

To commemorate Queen Victoria's golden jubilee the council acquired 13 a. of the manorial waste in 1888 and laid out a 10-acre park on Bloxwich Green (the remains of Short Heath), opening it in 1890.[68] Houses were built on Lord Hatherton's land at the southern end of Field Road at the end of the century.[69] Some larger houses were built along the main road towards Wallington Heath about the same time.[70]

Between the World Wars council houses were built on the south side of Bloxwich and in Field Road and Broad Lane. The main areas of privately built houses were Victoria Street, Lichfield Road, Field Road, and Wallington Heath. The playing-fields on the west side of Blakenall Lane originated as a war-memorial playing-field bought in 1925; it was laid out by the Miners' Welfare Committee in the early 1930s. The King George V Playing-fields west of Wallington Heath date from the later 1930s.[71] Since the Second World War several more council estates have been built. They include one south of Lichfield Road and another at Dudley Fields south of Sneyd Lane, both dating from the later 1940s, and the Mossley estate north of Sneyd Lane dating from the later 1950s.[72] At Dudley Fields there is also an industrial estate of the later 1960s.[73] There are several estates of council flats. Those on cleared ground on either side of Alfred Street date from 1957 and the multi-storey blocks at the south end of High Street from the 1960s.[74] The Sandbank estate, consisting of three 12-storey blocks and one of 16 storeys, was begun in 1962 on a cleared site of 6 a.[75] Private building of houses has continued in the Wallington Heath area, including an estate laid out over the grounds of Wallington House after it had ceased to be a convent in the mid 1960s.[76] The area north of Wallington Heath to the boundary remains open country, occupied as farm-land[77] and by Bloxwich golf-course which dates from 1923 and has the 19th-century Field House as the club-house.[78]

By the later 18th century Little Bloxwich lay in the area formed by Little Bloxwich Lane (now Lichfield Road), Stoney Lane, and Selman's Hill.[79] It may originally have centred on the stretch of Stoney Lane between Fishley Lane and Selman's Hill where Little Bloxwich Green lay in the later 18th century.[80] Lower Farm, a late-medieval cruck-trussed house, stood in that part of Stoney Lane until its demolition in 1963.[81] The site of Poplar Farm in Fishley Lane was formerly moated.[82] Little Bloxwich had its own common fields.[83] It also lay on the Walsall–Stafford road until 1766, when the route was diverted to run through Great Bloxwich, and it had a coaching-inn.[84] There were 182 recipients of Mollesley's Dole in 1619 and 259 in 1661.[85] The Wyrley and Essington Canal runs through the area, and by the 1880s there was a canal basin off Fishley Lane. In the later 19th and early 20th centuries there was coal-mining in the Fishley area to the north of Little Bloxwich, and there was a steam mill near the basin in the earlier 20th century.[86] Selman's Hill and Sanstone Road contain privately built houses of the period between the World Wars, and after the Second World War Little Bloxwich became an area of mixed council and private housing. The first council houses date from the late 1940s, and by the early 1960s there were 270 of them.[87] The Lower Farm estate centres on nine blocks of council flats completed in 1963, eight of three storeys and one of six; a block of shops and maisonettes was built at the same time.[88] Fishley is an area of farm-land.

Blakenall was mentioned c. 1300 when it was crossed by the road from Leamore to Goscote, the present Blakenall Lane and Green Rock Lane.[89] It was described as a heath in 1544.[90] By 1763 a settlement of cottages had grown up round the common on the triangle now formed by the streets called Blakenall Lane, Blakenall Heath, and Ingram Road,[91] and there were several metal-workers there by the early 19th century.[92] A school and mission centre was opened on the heath in 1843.[93] By 1843 houses had been built to the south-east of the heath along Harden Lane (now Walker Road) and Barracks Lane (so called by the 1880s).[94] By 1859 houses were being built to the south-west of the heath along Blakenall Lane; Foster Street existed then, and the district was described as 'thriving and

[64] See p. 189.
[65] R.G. 9/2012 no. 70; R.G. 10/2958 no. 94; below p. 258.
[66] W.C.L., box 36, no. 1; O.S. Map 6″, Staffs. LVII. SW. (1887 edn.).
[67] Inscription 'Providence Place 1879'; Homeshaw, *Bloxwich*, 169.
[68] *Walsall Red Book* (1891), 26, 68.
[69] W.S.L., D. 1798/551; O.S. Map 6″, Staffs. LVII. SW. and LXIII. NW. (1903 edn., revised 1900–1).
[70] O.S. Map 6″, Staffs. LVII. SW. (1903 edn.).
[71] Homeshaw, *Bloxwich*, 206–7; *Metropolitan Boro. of Walsall Official Town Guide* [1974], 66–7.
[72] Ex inf. the boro. housing manager (1974); *Walsall: the Town of a Hundred Trades* (1949), 48 (copy in W.C.L.).
[73] Local inf. (1974).
[74] Ex inf. the boro. housing manager (1974).
[75] *Architects' Jnl. Inf. Libr.* 3 Sept. 1969, p. 570 (copy in W.C.L.); *Walsall Observer*, 3 Jan. 1964.
[76] See p. 241.
[77] For two of the farms see pp. 176, 179.
[78] Homeshaw, *Bloxwich*, 225.
[79] S.R.O., D. 1287/8/2; Yates, *Map of Staffs.* (1775). 'Stonie Way' occurs in 1576: S.R.O., D. 1287/1/2, survey of Walsall manor, 1576, m. 3. For Little Bloxwich Lane

see O.S. Map 6″, Staffs. LVII. SW. (edns. of 1887 and 1903).
[80] S.R.O., Q/SB, A. 1777.
[81] V. F. Penn, 'Lower Farm, Bloxwich', *Trans. Lichfield and S. Staffs. Arch. and Hist. Soc.* v. 69–73; J. T. Smith, 'The Evolution of the Eng. Peasant House to the late Seventeenth Century', *Jnl. Brit. Arch. Assoc.* 3rd ser. xxxiii. 130; Homeshaw, *Bloxwich*, plate facing p. 128.
[82] *V.C.H. Staffs.* i. 368.   [83] See p. 181.
[84] See pp. 166–7.
[85] W.T.C. II/31/1; II/13/49; above p. 145. The second figure at least includes Yieldfields.
[86] O.S. Map 6″, Staffs. LVII. SW. (edns. of 1887 and 1921); below p. 189.
[87] Ex inf. the boro. housing manager (1974); *Evening Mail*, 29 Nov. 1963.
[88] County Boro. of Walsall, *Lower Farm, Bloxwich, Development: Central Area Flats, Nov. 1963* (copy in W.C.L.); *Evening Mail*, 29 Nov. 1963.
[89] S.R.O., D. 593/A/2/22/35; below p. 166.
[90] See p. 182.   [91] S.R.O., D. 1287/8/2.
[92] Pearce, *Walsall*, 153 sqq.   [93] See pp. 237, 258.
[94] W.S.L., S. MS. 417/Walsall. In the 1880s there was a building called the Barracks in Well Lane at its junction with Barracks Lane: O.S. Map 6″, Staffs. LXIII. NW. (1889 edn.). Part of it existed as houses in 1843.

rapidly improving'.[95] A Primitive Methodist chapel was built c. 1866 in Chapel Street.[96] The first part of Booth Street was built in 1871 on Lord Hatherton's land.[97] Between the two World Wars streets of council houses were built round the settlement and some privately built houses were also erected.[98] It was in Blakenall Lane in 1920 that the first council house in the borough was completed,[99] and by 1927 450 houses had been built on the Blakenall estate.[1] Houses, maisonettes, and multi-storey flats have been built since the Second World War, including an estate in Green Rock Lane dating from the later 1940s.[2]

The hamlet of Goscote, a name meaning a hut in the gorse,[3] existed by the end of the 13th century and apparently lay towards the north end of Goscote Lane.[4] There were 54 recipients of Mollesley's Dole in Goscote and Coal Pool in 1619 and 68 in Goscote alone in 1661.[5] Goscote Hall on the corner of Goscote and Slacky Lanes existed by the mid 18th century, and Goscote Lodge Farm between Slacky Lane and the present Hildicks Crescent by the early 19th century.[6] The Wyrley and Essington Canal was built through the area in the 1790s.[7] Mining of coal and ironstone started then, and there was a foundry by the early 1800s.[8] By 1834 there were four lock-makers.[9] There were two brickworks by 1858.[10] An isolation hospital was opened in Goscote Lane in 1930 and a sanatorium was added in 1933.[11] Council estates were built west of Goscote Lane and Livingstone Road in the later 1930s and after the Second World War; they included 50 houses on 6 a. previously occupied by pit mounds.[12] Also in Goscote Lane are an electro-plating works and a copper refinery dating from the later 1940s.[13]

Coal Pool, at the junction of Harden, Goscote, and Coal Pool Lanes, was an inhabited area by the 1540s when the Stone family held Coal Pool House.[14] There was a water-mill there by the late 17th century.[15] Land near the boundary called Far and Near Coal Pit Pieces in 1843[16] suggests mining at some period. In the later 19th and earlier 20th centuries the main part of Coal Pool consisted of three rows of terraced houses east of Coal Pool Lane built evidently in the 1850s and occupied in 1861 mostly by coal-miners; they were demolished between the World Wars. A Wesleyan chapel was opened near by in 1852.[17] In the later 1930s a council estate was built at the south end of Goscote Lane, and a private estate had been built in Dartmouth Avenue by 1938.[18] The first council housing in Walsall after the Second World War was built at Coal Pool in the later 1940s, and more has been built there since.[19] In 1974 there was still some open ground along the canal north of Harden Road.

Harden, a hamlet lying around the junction of Harden Road, Broadstone Avenue, and Well Lane, existed by the late 13th century.[20] It had its own common fields.[21] There were 120 recipients of Mollesley's Dole in 1619 and 166 in 1652, figures which probably include Blakenall also; the combined recipients in Harden, Blakenall, and Coal Pool in 1661 numbered 171.[22] Coal was mined at Harden by the earlier 1850s, and mining continued in the vicinity until 1905.[23] The area now consists mainly of council estates, dating from the 1930s and the later 1940s;[24] there are also some privately built houses erected between the World Wars.

There was settlement in the Leamore area around Leamore Lane, Broadstone (now Bloxwich Road), and the northern end of Green Lane by 1775.[25] By the early 1840s there had been development on the south side of Leamore Lane, and Comwall Street, Portland (later Portsea) Street, and Providence Lane there were being built up by the 1880s.[26] Mining was in progress at Leamore in the 1850s and 1860s.[27] A Wesleyan chapel was opened in 1863, a board school in 1873, and an Anglican mission

[95] Staffs. Advertiser, 24 Dec. 1859, p. 8.
[96] See p. 247.
[97] S.R.O., D. 260/M/E/174, 10–17 Oct., 19 Dec. 1871; W.S.L., D. 1798/551 nos. 383–6, 623–4; W. J. Boys, Plan of Boro. of Walsall (1875; copy in W.C.L.); O.S. Map 6", Staffs. LXIII. NW. (1889 edn.).
[98] O.S. Map 6", Staffs. LVII. SW. and LXIII. NW. (prov. edn. with addns. of 1938).
[99] See p. 221.
[1] 23rd Ann. Rep. Walsall Educ. Cttee. (1926–7), 8 (copy in W.C.L.).
[2] Cason, Blakenall Heath, 50; Walsall: the Town of a Hundred Trades (1949), 48 (copy in W.C.L.); 46th Ann. Rep. Walsall Educ. Cttee. (1949–50), 7.
[3] Ekwall, Eng. Place-names.
[4] S.H.C. 1911, 232; below pp. 166, 174. The area is shown as Old Goscote by Yates, Map of Staffs. (1775).
[5] W.T.C. II/31/1; II/13/49; above p. 145.
[6] See pp. 174, 176. The area round the hall is shown as New Goscote by Yates, Map of Staffs. (1775).
[7] See p. 168.
[8] See pp. 189, 202.
[9] White, Dir. Staffs. (1834).
[10] R. Hunt, Memoirs of Geol. Surv., Mineral Statistics of U.K. for 1858, ii. 81; below p. 192.
[11] See p. 223.
[12] Ex inf. the boro. housing manager (1974); Homeshaw, Bloxwich, 203.
[13] Elkington: the First Name in Electro Plate (copy in W.C.L.); below p. 194.
[14] S.R.O., D. 260/M/F/1/5, f. 53; Yates, Map of Staffs. (1775).
[15] See p. 185.
[16] W.S.L., S. MS. 417/Walsall, sub Bradford, nos. 712–13.

[17] R.G. 9/2011 nos. 81–4; O.S. Map 6", Staffs. LXIII. NE. (edns. of 1889 and 1920 and prov. edn. with addns. of 1938); Cason, Blakenall Heath, 35; below p. 246.
[18] Ex inf. the boro. housing manager (1974); O.S. Map 6", Staffs. LXIII. NE. (prov. edn. with addns. of 1938).
[19] Cason, Blakenall Heath, 50, 69; Walsall: the Town of a Hundred Trades (1949), 48 (copy in W.C.L.).
[20] S.H.C. xv. 40; S.H.C. 1911, 187; Yates, Map of Staffs. (1775); below p. 166.
[21] See p. 181.
[22] W.T.C. II/31/1; II/13/40 and 49; above p. 145.
[23] R. Hunt, Memoirs of Geol. Surv., Mineral Statistics of U.K. for 1853 and 1854, 104 (Harden Colliery). The Forest Colliery was in operation by 1881: ibid. 1881, 222. It ceased operations in 1900 and Harden Colliery in 1905: Rep. H.M. Inspector of Mines for Stafford Dist. for 1903 [Cd. 2119–VIII], p. 64, H.C. (1904), xiii; ibid. 1905 [Cd. 2910–VIII], p. 56, H.C. (1906), xix.
[24] Ex inf. the boro. housing manager (1974); O.S. Map 6", Staffs. LXIII. NW. (prov. edn. with addns. of 1938); Cason, Blakenall Heath, 44, 50; Homeshaw, Bloxwich, 204; Walsall: the Town of a Hundred Trades (1949), 48.
[25] Yates, Map of Staffs. (1775). That stretch of Bloxwich Rd. is shown as Broadstone on O.S. Map 6", Staffs. LXIII. NW. (1889 edn.). For meadow in 'Leymore' in 1420 see Sims, Cal. of Deeds, p. 14.
[26] W.S.L., S. MS. 417/Walsall; O.S. Map 6", Staffs. LXIII. NW. (1889 edn., surv. 1884–5), naming only Portland St. (which existed by 1871: R.G. 10/2958/7). They all existed by 1875: W. J. Boys, Plan of Boro. of Walsall (1875; copy in W.C.L.).
[27] Hunt, Mineral Statistics 1853 and 1854, 104; ibid. 1868, 181; O.S. Map 6", Staffs. LXIII. NW. (1889 edn.).

chapel in 1883.[28] The area was described by the vicar of Blakenall in the early 1880s as 'populous yet poor'.[29] By the beginning of the 20th century West Street on the north side of Leamore Lane had been laid out, and houses had been built along the east side of Bloxwich Road and on the south side of Hope Street. To the south of the railway two brickworks had been opened, and Carl Street, dating from 1895, had been built on the west side of Bloxwich Road.[30] May and Beatrice Streets, named after the daughters of the builder, John Wilkes, were laid out c. 1904.[31] A council estate, including flats, was built in the later 1920s; some of the houses were built on empty sites in existing streets, and the estate also included the new Somerfield Road, which runs from Green Lane directly to Bloxwich.[32] In 1959 the corporation began clearing 8½ a. south of Leamore Lane in order to replace 180 slum properties with a multi-storey estate of 280 dwellings. The work was completed in 1964.[33]

The area to the west and north-west (including part of Bentley transferred to Walsall in 1931)[34] consisted by the 1880s mainly of derelict ground covered with old mine shafts; the Hatherton Brickworks, the Hatherton Furnaces, and the Walsall Glue Works had been built along the Wyrley and Essington Canal.[35] That stretch of the canal remains industrialized,[36] and an industrial estate has been built in Leamore Lane since the Second World War. The large Beechdale (formerly Gipsy Lane) housing estate was built by the council in the early 1950s.[37]

COMMUNICATIONS. ROADS. Walsall early became the meeting point of several roads—from Lichfield, Sutton Coldfield (Warws.), Birmingham, West Bromwich, Wednesbury, Darlaston, Wolverhampton, and Stafford via Bloxwich. Until the 18th century, however, national traffic routes avoided the area. By the 1740s Walsall's importance as a manufacturing centre, the fact that heavy traffic was making local roads ruinous and dangerous, and the rise in the cost of carriage of goods all led to a demand for improved roads. In 1748, in response to a petition from Wolverhampton 'and places adjacent', the first turnpike Act affecting Walsall was passed, dealing with part of the road to Birmingham and with the roads to Sutton Coldfield and to Wolverhampton and beyond.[38] Nearly all the main roads were turnpiked before the end of the century; they were disturnpiked in 1870.[39]

The road from Walsall to Rushall, Walsall Wood, and Lichfield probably existed by the earlier 13th century; it was mentioned by name in the early 14th century.[40] Until the construction of Lichfield Street in the early 1830s the road left the town along Rushall Street and what is now Ward Street.[41] It was turnpiked in 1766 as far as Muckley Corner (in Pipehill, in St. Michael's, Lichfield) on Watling Street.[42] By the early 19th century there was a toll-gate (Butts gate) at the junction with Butts Street, but it was moved c. 1840 to the bigger road junction to the north-east.[43]

The road to Sutton Coldfield, which occurs in 1349, linked the town with the London–Chester road on Sutton Coldfield Common and so was the way from Walsall to London.[44] The causeway from Wood End to the church, on which work was carried out in 1692, was presumably part of the road; the work included the setting up of posts, rails, and turnstiles to keep horses off.[45] The stretch from Walsall to Sutton Coldfield Common was turnpiked in 1748. Turnpiking was discontinued in 1772, but the road was again turnpiked in 1788.[46] A toll-gate was erected at the junction with the Birmingham road under the Act of 1748, the only gate which the Act allowed in the parishes of Walsall and Aldridge. Known as the Birmingham gate by 1824, it was still in use in the earlier 1840s but was subsequently replaced by gates further along the two roads.[47] The course of the Sutton road was realigned between the World Wars.[48]

The road to Birmingham occurs in the early 14th century and was probably in use by the mid 13th century.[49] It ran to Great Barr in Aldridge and then continued via Hamstead and Handsworth to the Birmingham–Wolverhampton road at Soho Hill.[50] The stretch to Great Barr was turnpiked from 1748 to 1772.[51] The stretch to Hamstead was turnpiked in 1788, and the straight course along Birmingham Road replacing the curving line along Jesson Road and along Park Hall and Lonsdale Roads apparently dates from about that time.[52] The continuation to

[28] See pp. 237, 246, 262.

[29] Cason, *Blakenall Heath*, 21.

[30] O.S. Map 6", Staffs. LXIII. NW. (1903 edn., revised 1900–1); terrace in Bloxwich Rd. inscribed 'Jubilee Cottages 1897'; Blay, 'Street Names of Walsall', 42.

[31] Date-stones of 1904, 1907, and 1911 in Beatrice St.; Stephens & Mackintosh, *Business Street Map of Walsall* [1906]; Blay, 'Street Names of Walsall', 14.

[32] Lee, *Walsall*, 56; *23rd Ann. Rep. Walsall Educ. Cttee.* (1926–7), 8 (copy in W.C.L.); *Staffs. Advertiser*, 16 Apr. 1927, p. 8; ex inf. the boro. housing manager (1973); below p. 166.

[33] *Walsall Observer*, 13 Mar. 1964.

[34] See p. 143.

[35] O.S. Map 6", Staffs. LXIII. NW. (1889 edn.); below pp. 193, 207.

[36] For an aerial view c. 1950 see Homeshaw, *Bloxwich*, plate facing p. 224.

[37] Cason, *Blakenall Heath*, 50; ex inf. the boro. housing manager (1974).

[38] Homeshaw, *Walsall*, 100; *V.C.H. Staffs.* ii. 281.

[39] Annual Turnpike Acts Continuance Act, 1869, 32 and 33 Vic. c. 90, 2nd sched., nos. 36 and 38.

[40] *Walsall Records*, 28; Sims, *Cal. of Deeds*, p. 7; W.S.L., D. 1798/84, deeds of 2 Apr. 1319, 27 Nov. 1323.

[41] See p. 151.   [42] 6 Geo. III, c. 99.

[43] W. F. Blay, *Story of Walsall Turnpike Roads and Tollgates* (Walsall, 1932), 11 (copy in W.C.L.); Willmore, *Walsall*, 374; B.M. O.S.D. 212. It is shown on the earlier site on *Map of Boro. of Walsall* (1836) and on the new site by W.S.L., S. MS. 417/Rushall, no. 274a (1843).

[44] S.R.O., D.(W.)1790/A/10/7; W.S.L., D. 1798/100, deed of 6 Dec. 1476; Yates, *Map of Staffs.* (1775); *V.C.H. Staffs.* ii. 277; S.R.O., D. 1287/8/2, map, showing it as London Road in 1763. In 1571 the road from Walsall to London is mentioned as passing through Rushall (*Cal. Pat. 1569–72*, 398); either the reference to Rushall is an error or a more northerly route is meant.

[45] W.T.C. II/13/66.

[46] 21 Geo. II, c. 25; 12 Geo. III, c. 101; 28 Geo. III, c. 98.

[47] Blay, *Walsall Turnpike Roads*, 6, 13–15; S.R.O., D. 1287/8/2, survey, p. 36; Walsall Improvement Act, 1824, 5 Geo. IV, c. 68 (Local and Personal); L.J.R.O., B/A/15/Walsall, map.

[48] See p. 153.

[49] *Walsall Records*, 48; *V.C.H. Warws.* vii. 26.

[50] Yates, *Map of Staffs.* (1775); S.R.O., Q/SO 10, T. 1698.

[51] 21 Geo. II, c. 25; 12 Geo. III, c. 101.

[52] 28 Geo. III, c. 98; Yates, *Map of Staffs.* (edns. of 1775 and 1799).

Soho Hill was turnpiked in 1809.[53] As mentioned above, there were successive toll-gates at the junction with the Sutton road and near the present junction with Broadway.

The road to West Bromwich via Fullbrook apparently existed in the later Middle Ages since Tame Bridge carrying it over the West Bromwich boundary existed then; and it was a Walsall man, Thomas Mollesley, who left money for building a new bridge there in 1452.[54] The road left Walsall along New Street, Sandwell Street, and West Bromwich Road.[55] The present route via Caldmore along Corporation Street West and West Bromwich Street was in use by the 1880s.[56]

The roads to Wednesbury and Darlaston, which follow the same route as far as Pleck, were sufficiently important in the Middle Ages to have bridges carrying them over Park Brook.[57] Until the opening of Bradford Street in 1831 the route from the town centre was along Peal Street, Dudley Street, and Vicarage Place,[58] and it was presumably that road which occurs in 1355 as the highway running through Caldmore to the walk-mill.[59] The Wednesbury and Darlaston roads were turnpiked in 1766 along with the present Pleck Road, which runs from the point where the two roads diverge north to the Wolverhampton road.[60]

The road to Wolverhampton, which occurs as the road to Bentley in 1323,[61] was turnpiked in 1748.[62]

The road from Walsall to Stafford, crossing Watling Street at Churchbridge in Cannock, originally ran through Little Bloxwich. It is said to have continued via Fishley to Great Wyrley, but there is evidence of a route via Yieldfields, where a road called Stafford way is mentioned in 1576 and 1617.[63] The road was turnpiked in 1766, and its course was then altered to run through Great Bloxwich.[64] By the early 19th century there was a toll-gate at the junction with what are now Blue Lane East and Portland Street; it was known as the Flax-oven Gate by 1824. About the mid 1840s it was moved north to cover the junction with Deadman's Lane (now Hospital Street) and Proffitt Street but continued to be known as the Flax-oven Gate. A second gate had been erected by 1816 on the Bloxwich side

of the junction of Green Lane and Bloxwich Road.[65] Green Lane forms an alternative route to Bloxwich via Birchills; Somerfield Road, which forms the direct route into Bloxwich from the cross-roads at Leamore Lane, dates from the later 1920s.[66]

Other old roads crossed the parish missing the town centre. One, which occurs in 1591, ran north of the town to Rushall mill, from the Wolverhampton road along Blue Lane, Portland Street, Butts Road, and Mill Lane. In 1593 the stretch between Walsall Park and Wombridge Ford was declared to be impassable in winter and the inhabitants of the foreign were ordered by quarter sessions to repair it.[67] Another road ran north from the Darlaston road at James Bridge and over the Wolverhampton road to Bloxwich, following approximately the line of the present Bentley Mill Lane, Bloxwich Lane, and Fryer's Road;[68] the road to Harden that runs from Bloxwich Lane along Leamore Lane and Harden Road evidently existed by the later 16th century.[69] The road from Leamore to Goscote via Blakenall Heath, along the present Blakenall Lane and Green Rock Lane, occurs c. 1300.[70] The lane running from Harden to Goscote (now Well Lane) occurs in 1544.[71] It was presumably part of the high road from Harden to Pelsall mentioned in 1509.[72] The road from Wolverhampton to Lichfield via Wednesfield and Brownhills runs through Bloxwich, crossing Sneyd Brook at Sneyd bridge, which existed by the later 16th century; it was presumably the 'Wulvernewey' which occurs in the northwestern part of Bloxwich c. 1300. The section east from Little Bloxwich was mentioned in 1634. The road was turnpiked in 1748 and disturnpiked in 1772.[73] The road from Great Bloxwich to Hilton via Essington Wood occurs in 1576 and was presumably the present Broad Lane;[74] it was turnpiked in 1766 and disturnpiked in 1830.[75]

Several road improvements were carried out in the 1920s, largely to provide work for the unemployed.[76] The most important was the construction of the Broadway ring-road to the east and south of the town centre, incorporating Denmark and Foden Roads by the Arboretum and continuing to Wallows Lane at Bescot. It was completed in 1929.

[53] 49 Geo. III, c. 147 (Local and Personal). For the new Walsall Road of 1831 forking from the old road south of Great Barr and running to Birmingham via Perry Barr (in Handsworth), see *V.C.H. Warws.* vii. 27; W.C.L., box 43, nos. 1–5; S.R.O., D. 1287/15/1.
[54] See p. 13.
[55] Yates, *Map of Staffs.* (1775); W.C.L., C. 4.
[56] S.R.O., Q/RHd 40/1–15.
[57] See p. 168.
[58] W.C.L., C. 4; C. and J. Greenwood, *Map of Staffs.* (1820); above p. 147.
[59] W.S.L., D. 1798/92, deed of 24 Apr. 1355.
[60] 6 Geo. III, c. 99; Yates, *Map of Staffs.* (1775).
[61] S.R.O., D. 1287/6/14, deeds relating to mill fleam, 9 Jan. 1322/3.
[62] 12 Geo. III, c. 25. Blay, 'Street Names of Walsall', 177, mentions a toll-gate at Townend at the junction of Wolverhampton St. and Green Lane.
[63] Willmore, *Walsall*, 377, 441; Homeshaw, *Bloxwich*, 118; Sims, *Cal. of Deeds*, p. 29; Yates, *Map of Staffs.* (1775); S.R.O., D. 1287/1/2, survey of Walsall manor, 1576, m. 13, which also mentions Fishley Lane as the road from Little Bloxwich to Little Wyrley.
[64] 6 Geo. III, c. 99; Homeshaw, *Bloxwich*, 121.
[65] Pearce, *Walsall*, 154; B.M. O.S.D. 212; Blay, *Walsall Turnpike Roads*, 11, 13; Glew, *Walsall*, 57; Walsall Improvement Act, 1824, 5 Geo. IV, c. 68 (Local and Personal); Walsall Improvement and Market Act, 1848, 11 & 12 Vic. c. 161 (Local and Personal), s. 20; L.J.R.O.,

B/A/15/Walsall, map; W.T.C., Street Cttee. Mins. 1849–51, loose sheet 29 Oct. 1852.
[66] S.R.O., D. 1287/8/2, map; Yates, *Map of Staffs.* (1775); Lee, *Walsall*, 28.
[67] *S.H.C.* 1930, 116–17, 353; Yates, *Map of Staffs.* (1775); F. W. Willmore, *Records of Rushall* (Walsall, 1892), 110.
[68] Yates, *Map of Staffs.* (1775); S.R.O., Q/SO 13, f. 161.
[69] Homeshaw, *Bloxwich*, 57; L.J.R.O., B/V/6/Bloxwich, 1694; Yates, *Map of Staffs.* (1775).
[70] S.R.O., D. 593/A/2/22/35; D. 1287/8/2, map.
[71] W.C.L., box 25, no. 22.
[72] Ibid. no. 29.
[73] B.M. Harl. MS. 2131, f. 12v.; Wolverhampton Churchwardens' Accts. 1520–1634, transcript of 1634 perambulation (in possession of Miss Dorothy Shaw-Helier, the Wodehouse, Wombourn); 21 Geo. II, c. 25; 12 Geo. III, c. 101; below p. 167. The 1748 turnpike road ran from Wolverhampton 'to a place called Cannock Wood in the road to Lichfield'.
[74] B.M. Harl. MS. 2131, f. 12v.; S.R.O., D. 1287/1/2, survey of Walsall manor, 1576, m. 8, where it is given as Clitchkyn Lane; Yates, *Map of Staffs.* (1775). It is presumably part of the lane from Great Saredon (in Shareshill) to Walsall mentioned in 1609: *S.H.C.* 1948–9, 37.
[75] 6 Geo. III, c. 99; 11 Geo. IV and 1 Wm. IV, c. 106 (Local and Personal).
[76] Lee, *Walsall*, 27–8.

It was originally called the Ring Road, but with the extension of the borough in 1931 that name was felt to be inappropriate and it was changed to Broadway.[77]

The south-western part of the pre-1966 borough is crossed by the M6 motorway. The stretch as far south as Bescot was opened in 1968 as part of the extension of the motorway south from Dunston. Its continuation into West Bromwich where it joins the M5 was opened in 1970.[78]

During the later 18th century the improvement of the roads brought a great increase in traffic, and several coaching inns were opened. By 1754 a coach between Wolverhampton and London passed through Walsall, leaving Wolverhampton on Mondays and London on Thursdays; it called at the Three Swans in Walsall.[79] At the end of 1757 it was announced that the post would pass through the town three times a week.[80] The Shrewsbury Machine between Shrewsbury and London called at Walsall by 1769,[81] and two years later a wagon plying between Shrewsbury and Coventry and taking passengers as well as parcels was calling at the Angel in Park Street.[82] From 1771 there was also a fly between Shrewsbury and Birmingham which called at the Castle.[83] The New Inn in Park Street just north of the Bridge was advertised for letting in 1774; 'newly erected and complete', it was described as 'conveniently situated for the reception of noblemen and gentlemen travelling through Walsall', and its business was increasing daily now that various turnpike roads had been 'made exceeding good'.[84] By 1780 Walsall was on the route of a London–Birmingham–Holyhead coach.[85] The George at the junction of Digbeth and Bridge Street was built in 1781 by Thomas Fletcher, who until then had been at the Dragon in High Street. It became the main coaching inn of the town, and in 1834 it was claimed that 'its internal arrangements and its external appearance rank second to none in the county'. It was particularly distinguished by its pillared portico, which was erected in 1823; this was brought from Fisherwick Hall, demolished some years before. An assembly-room had been added in 1793.[86] The building was bought by the corporation in 1927 and demolished in 1934. A new George hotel was opened on the same site in 1935 and closed in the early 1970s.[87] In Bloxwich, with

the diversion of the road north to run through Great Bloxwich instead of Little Bloxwich after its turnpiking in 1766, the coaching trade enjoyed by the King William inn at Little Bloxwich passed to the King's Arms at Wallington Heath (later the convent of St. Paul of Chartres).[88] The coming of the railway to Bescot in 1837 killed most of Walsall's coaching trade. In 1841, however, there were still coaches to Birmingham from the George, while omnibuses ran to Birmingham and Wolverhampton from the George and the Three Cups.[89]

BRIDGES. The bridge carrying the thoroughfare between Digbeth and Park Street over Walsall Brook occurs c. 1300 as the bridge of the town of Walsall.[90] It was described as a stone bridge in 1618,[91] but in 1724 over 3,000 bricks were bought for it.[92] A map of 1763 shows eight arches.[93] Although the corporation was still paying for its repair in 1824,[94] it had become a county responsibility by 1830 when Lord Bradford was given permission by the county quarter sessions to alter it at his own expense under the direction of the county surveyor as part of the improvements then being carried out in the area.[95] Although the structure still exists, it had been covered over by the 1870s.[96] It may be identifiable with Old Mill bridge which also occurs as a corporation responsibility in the 17th and early 18th centuries.[97] Another bridge was built to the north in the mid 1820s, a balustraded structure carrying the new St. Paul's Street over the brook.[98] It too disappeared with the building up of the area.[99]

There were two bridges carrying the road to Wednesbury and Darlaston over Walsall Brook and the mill fleam near the New Mills. Walk Mill bridge, apparently on Walsall Brook, occurs between 1603 and 1677 and was a corporation responsibility.[1] New Mill bridge occurs regularly in the corporation accounts from 1641 until the beginning of the 18th century, but it was subsequently rebuilt by either the county or the turnpike trustees and ceased to be a corporation responsibility.[2]

There were several early bridges over Sneyd (or Bentley) Brook on the western boundary. Sneyd bridge on the Wolverhampton–Lichfield road occurs in 1576 and 1617.[3] Park bridge on the Walsall–Wolverhampton road occurs in the early 19th century;[4] the site is now covered by a motorway access

[77] Ibid. 28, 35; Blay, 'Street Names of Walsall', 151; *Walsall Observer*, 16 June 1923; Woodall, *Walsall Milestones*, 41; 15 & 16 Geo. V, c. 122 (Local), s. 30; *Walsall Red Book* (1927), map facing p. 149.

[78] *Express & Star*, 13 May 1970.

[79] *Aris's Birmingham Gaz.* 4 Nov. 1754.

[80] Ibid. 2 Jan. 1758.   [81] Ibid. 22 May 1769.

[82] Ibid. 15 July 1771.

[83] Ibid. 23 Sept. 1771, 6 Jan. 1772. And see ibid. 15 Apr. 1771; Willmore, *Walsall*, 378.

[84] Willmore, *Walsall*, 378 and map facing p. 380.

[85] Ibid. 378.

[86] Ibid. 355, 378–81 and map facing p. 380, 400–1; W. H. Duignan, *The George Hotel, Walsall* (offprint in W.C.L. from *Walsall Observer*, Feb. 1878); White, *Dir. Staffs.* (1834), 106, 416, 446; Glew, *Walsall*, 49.

[87] *Walsall Official Handbook* [1936], 62; *Walsall Observer*, 20 Aug. 1971; W.C.L., Newscuttings 9, p. 116.

[88] Homeshaw, *Bloxwich*, 121, 154–5.

[89] Pigot, *Nat. Com. Dir.* (1841), Staffs. p. 87.

[90] *Walsall Records*, 35.

[91] S.R.O., D. 1287/6/14, deeds relating to mill fleam, 19 Oct. 1618. For a stone bridge on the Holbrook see above p. 151.

[92] W.T.C. II/13/83.   [93] S.R.O., D. 1287/8/2.

[94] Homeshaw, *Walsall*, 133.

[95] J. Potter, *List of Bridges which the Inhabitants of the County of Stafford are bound to repair* (Stafford, 1830), 6 (copy in W.S.L. Pamphs. *sub* Roads); S.R.O., Q/SO 30, f. 258v.; S.R.O., D. 1287/18/25/business corresp. 1812–32, P. Potter to Lord Bradford, 17 Sept. 1830; above p. 147.

[96] *Robinson's Map of Walsall* (pub. with *Walsall Red Book*, 1876). For an underground view early in the 20th cent. see *Walsall Red Book* (1905).

[97] W.T.C. II/31/6; II/13/40 sqq.; below p. 185.

[98] S.R.O., D. 1287/18/25, business corresp. 1820–9, Potter to Bradford, 21 Oct. 1826; W.C.L., A.G. 138.

[99] W.T.C., Street Cttee. Mins. 1849–51, 17 Oct., 4 Nov. 1851; *Robinson's Map of Walsall* (1876); O.S. Map 6", Staffs. LXIII. SE. (1890 edn.).

[1] S.R.O., D. 260/M/F/1/5, ff. 75, 91v.; W.T.C. II/13/16; II/31/9; S.R.O., D. 1287/1/8, Walsall rent roll, 1677; below p. 185.

[2] W.T.C. II/13/30, 43, 47 sqq.; II/31/13, 15, 17; II/50/37, stating that it was usually repaired by the inhabitants of the borough until its rebuilding; II/83/2; below p. 185.

[3] S.R.O., D. 1287/1/2, survey of Walsall manor, 1576, m. 6; Willmore, *Walsall*, 441.

[4] B.M. O.S.D. 212.

point. James Bridge on the Walsall–Darlaston road existed by the 1330s, and an abbot of Halesowen gave land in West Bromwich for its maintenance.[5] By 1625 it was a stone bridge maintained by the corporation, but by 1825 it was a county responsibility.[6] The lower part of the north side of the present structure probably dates from the early 19th century; it was widened southwards early in the 20th century.[7] Bescot bridge on the Walsall–Wednesbury road occurs c. 1300.[8] By 1825 it too was a county responsibility.[9] The site is now covered by a motorway access point. It may be identifiable with the Wednesbury bridge for which the corporation was responsible by 1657.[10]

Fullbrook bridge which carries the road from Walsall to West Bromwich over Full Brook on the southern boundary existed by the earlier 19th century and was then maintained by the corporation. In 1863 the county quarter sessions ordered that it should be repaired and added to the list of county bridges.[11]

The place-name 'Yolebruge' which occurs in the earlier 13th century may refer to a bridge carrying the old road to Lichfield over the Holbrook near what is now the centre of the Arboretum.[12] A bridge there was evidently maintained by the borough in the early 19th century.[13]

CANALS. After the failure of plans to build a canal to Walsall in the 1770s and 1780s[14] the branch of the Birmingham Canal between Ryders Green in West Bromwich and Broadwaters in Wednesbury was extended to Walsall in 1799 under an Act of 1794. It ended at a wharf in Marsh Lane near Townend Bank.[15] A tramway between the wharf and John Walhouse's limestone quarries on the Rushall boundary was built in 1823; by at least 1832 it also served the quarries at Daw End in Rushall.[16]

The 1790s also saw the building of the Wyrley and Essington Canal, opened in 1797 from the Birmingham Canal at Wolverhampton to the Trent and Mersey Canal near Lichfield under Acts of 1792 and 1794.[17] It loops through the Bloxwich area. A branch to Birchills was built about the same time. It was little used after the opening of the Walsall branch of the Birmingham Canal in 1799, and c. 1800 it was dammed off and left dry.[18] It was evidently in use again by 1819,[19] and by 1832 it was

linked to a limeworks at Shaw's Leasowes by a tramway. There were also tramways between local works and the Wyrley and Essington Canal in the Birchills area.[20] From 1825 there were various schemes for a junction between the Birchills branch and the Walsall branch of the Birmingham Canal, and a link was built in 1840–1 consisting of a flight of eight locks.[21]

Two other branches of the Wyrley and Essington Canal were built c. 1800, the so-called Lord Hay's branch from Fishley to the Lords Hay coal pits in Essington and the Daw End branch from Catshill Junction in Walsall Wood to the Hay Head limestone quarries. The Lord Hay's branch was abandoned in 1930, and the Hay Head end of the Daw End branch had become disused by 1939; both were filled in under an Act of 1954.[22] In 1847 the Rushall Canal was opened from the Daw End branch at Longwood Junction south to the Tame Valley Canal, completing Walsall's canal system.[23]

RAILWAYS. When the Grand Junction Railway between Birmingham and Warrington was opened in 1837 a station was provided at Bescot Bridge (also known as Walsall station) on the Wednesbury road near the borough boundary. A branch to Walsall had been planned but was not built; instead a 'light van' conveyed passengers between the station and the George hotel in the centre of the town. Bescot Bridge was closed in 1850, but in 1881 Wood Green station was opened on the site; it was closed in 1941.[24]

The railway came to the centre of Walsall in 1847 when the first part of the South Staffordshire Railway was opened from Bescot. A station was opened in Bridgeman Place but was replaced in 1849 by a new one in Station Street. The 1849 building, which is in a Jacobean style, still forms part of Walsall station, but a booking hall was opened in Park Street in 1884. It was burnt down in 1916, rebuilt, and reopened in 1923.[25]

New lines and new stations continued to be built until the 1880s. In 1849 the South Staffordshire line was extended north-east to the Midland Railway at Wychnor, and Rushall station was opened on the Walsall boundary in Station Road; it was closed in 1909.[26] A branch was opened from Ryecroft Junction to Cannock in 1858 and extended to Rugeley in 1859; in 1858 stations were opened at

[5] B.M. Harl. MS. 2131, ff. 12v., 19v.; *S.H.C.* 1948–9, 82.

[6] W.T.C. II/31/3; S.R.O., Q/SO 29, f. 83.

[7] O.S. Map 6", Staffs. LXIII. SW. (edns. of 1904 and 1920).

[8] B.M. Harl. MS. 2131, f. 11v.

[9] S.R.O., Q/SO 29, f. 83.

[10] W.T.C. II/31/15; II/83/1.

[11] Homeshaw, *Walsall*, 133; S.R.O., Q/SO 43, p. 369.

[12] For the name see W.S.L., D. 1798/83–4, 86. For the site see L.J.R.O., B/A/15/Walsall, map.

[13] W.T.C. II/50/37.

[14] C. Hadfield, *Canals of the West Midlands* (1969 edn.), 70–1; *V.C.H. Staffs.* ii. 292 n.; W.S.L., S. MS. 478/W.

[15] Hadfield, *Canals of W. Midlands*, 71, 85; Homeshaw, *Walsall*, 111; Pearce, *Walsall*, 180; above pp. 13–14.

[16] See p. 191; J. Phillips and W. F. Hutchings, *Map of Staffs.* (1832).

[17] *V.C.H. Staffs.* ii. 292–3; Hadfield, *Canals of W. Midlands*, 94–6.

[18] Hadfield, *Canals of W. Midlands*, 96; C. J. Gilson, 'The Wyrley and Essington Canal', *Trans. Lichfield Arch. and Hist. Soc.* i. 31; S.R.O., D. 1287/15/1.

[19] S.R.O., D. 351/M/B/209; C. and J. Greenwood, *Map of Staffs.* (1820).

[20] Phillips and Hutchings, *Map of Staffs.* (1832); below p. 191. For two tramways existing in the early 19th cent. see J. Farey, *General View of Agric. of Derbs.* iii. (1817), 453.

[21] Hadfield, *Canals of W. Midlands*, 98–9, 318–19; *Trans. Lichfield Arch. and Hist. Soc.* i. 34. *V.C.H. Staffs.* ii. 296, gives the date of building as 1839–40.

[22] Hadfield, *Canals of W. Midlands*, 95, 97–8, 263, 328–9; *V.C.H. Staffs.* ii. 293; *Trans. Lichfield Arch. and Hist. Soc.* i. 31; Phillips and Hutchings, *Map of Staffs.* (1832); Walsall Corp. Act, 1939, 2 & 3 Geo. VI, c. 82 (Local), s. 24; Brit. Transport Act, 1954, 2 & 3 Eliz. II, c. 55 (Local), 2nd sched.

[23] Hadfield, *Canals of W. Midlands*, 89–90, 99, 252, 261, 328–9. *V.C.H. Staffs.* ii. 296, gives the date of building as 1840–3.

[24] *V.C.H. Staffs.* ii. 306; C. R. Clinker, *Railways of the West Midlands, a Chronology 1808–1954*, 10, 19, 41, 62; Willmore, *Walsall*, 426; O.S. Map 6", Staffs. LXIII. SW. (1889 edn.).

[25] *V.C.H. Staffs.* ii. 312; Clinker, *Railways of W. Midlands*, 18, 19, 43; *Walsall Red Book* (1885), 54; (1917), 44; (1924), 86.

[26] Clinker, *Railways of W. Midlands*, 19, 53; O.S. Map 6", Staffs. LXIII. NE. (1889 edn.).

Birchills and Bloxwich. Birchills became a halt in 1909 and was closed in 1916; Bloxwich was closed in 1965.[27] The Wolverhampton & Walsall Railway was opened in 1872 with a station, North Walsall, in Bloxwich Road and was extended east as the Wolverhampton, Walsall & Midland Junction Railway in 1879. North Walsall was closed in 1925.[28] As a result of the extension Cooks opened an office in Walsall in 1879 to provide excursions.[29] In 1881 a loop was opened from the South Staffordshire line at Pleck Junction to the Grand Junction line at James Bridge with a station, Pleck, in Bescot Road. Pleck was closed from 1917 to 1924 and again for passengers in 1958.[30] The closing of Bloxwich in 1965 left Walsall station as the only one in the borough, and by then, as a result of the Beeching Report of 1963, there were passenger services to Birmingham only.[31]

AIRFIELD. The corporation established a municipal airfield in 1935 just beyond the borough boundary in Rushall and Aldridge.[32] It was licensed for public use the following year. In 1938 a newly built factory on part of the airfield was leased to Helliwells Ltd., a firm making aircraft components, and an additional lease was granted to Helliwells School of Flying Ltd. in 1943. The airfield was closed in the late 1940s.

MANORS. *WALSALL* may be the 'Walesho' which Wulfric Spot left to Morcar in his will of 1002–4.[33] It does not appear in Domesday Book, but it seems to have been a royal manor by then and was probably omitted in error.[34] Certainly it was accepted as ancient demesne from 1373, when the men of the manor were granted quittance of toll throughout the realm.[35] In 1159 Henry II granted it to Herbert le Rous (or Ruffus) in fee farm for £4 a year.[36] Herbert, described by the king in his grant as *serviens meus*, was almost certainly a member of the royal household[37] and was probably a kinsman of one or more of Henry II's household officials surnamed le Rous;[38] his son Richard later became

chamberlain to the king's son-in-law the duke of Saxony.[39] Herbert was still alive in 1166.[40]

Herbert or his son William died c. 1177 with William's son William, a minor, as heir. The boy was not at first put in ward, perhaps because his uncle Richard was abroad; instead the sheriff managed the estate from 1177 until 1189. Richard then became guardian. The fee-farm rent paid by the sheriff was raised twice, to £5 3s. in 1179 and £6 from 1180, apparently because the manor had been restocked.[41] William came of age in 1197–8[42] and was holding the manor at the old rent of £4 in 1212.[43] Henry II's grant was confirmed to him in 1227.[44] He was described as a knight in 1235.[45] He died in 1247,[46] and the manor was divided between his daughters Emecina and Margery.

By 1247 Emecina had married Geoffrey de Bakepuse.[47] He was still alive in 1255,[48] but by 1262 she was the wife of William de Morteyn.[49] She was still living in 1275,[50] but about then her son Sir William de Morteyn succeeded to her share of the manor.[51] He died in 1283, holding the moiety from the Crown in fee farm, and was succeeded by his nephew Roger de Morteyn.[52] Roger, who had been knighted by 1298,[53] mortgaged his moiety to John, Lord Somery, in 1311, with reversion to Ralph, Lord Basset of Drayton.[54] He seems not to have redeemed the mortgage, and between November 1313 and January 1314 Somery conveyed the manor to Basset.[55]

In 1338 Basset also acquired Margery's moiety. In 1247 she was still under age, and she was put into the guardianship of her brother-in-law Geoffrey.[56] A few years later she married Richard de Alazun, but at the beginning of the civil war, after some eight years of married life at Walsall, she was abducted by John de Lay. Richard fled and for long did not return to Walsall.[57] He was still living in 1289, but in the earlier 1280s Margery appears as the wife of John Paynel.[58] John was killed at Walsall in 1298; Margery was accused of murdering him and was acquitted only in 1302.[59] In 1293 she had to vindicate her right to the moiety against her daughter Alice and Alice's husband Nicholas

[27] *V.C.H. Staffs.* ii. 317; Clinker, *Railways of W. Midlands*, 26, 53, 56; O.S. Map 6″, Staffs. LXIII. NW. (1889 edn.); ex inf. British Railways, London Midland Region (1972).
[28] *V.C.H. Staffs.* ii. 317, 320; Clinker, *Railways of W. Midlands*, 35, 59; O.S. Map 6″, Staffs. LXIII. NW. (1889 edn.).
[29] *Walsall Observer*, 28 June 1879.
[30] *V.C.H. Staffs.* ii. 320; Clinker, *Railways of W. Midlands*, 41, 57, 59; O.S. Map 6″, Staffs. LXIII. SW. (1889 edn.); ex inf. British Railways, London Midland Region.
[31] *V.C.H. Staffs.* ii. 329, 333.
[32] For this para. see *Walsall Observer*, 13 July 1935, 31 Aug. 1973; *Boro. of Walsall: Council Year Book 1951–1952*, 154; *Walsall Red Book* (1939), 599; Walsall Council House, Aerodrome Cttee. Mins.
[33] Dorothy Whitelock, *Anglo-Saxon Wills*, 48–9, 155; *P.N. West Yorks.* (E.P.N.S.), i. 155–6.
[34] Homeshaw, *Walsall*, 7.
[35] *Cal. Pat.* 1370–4, 322; *Cal. Close*, 1396–9, 251; 1399–1402, 2.
[36] *Cartae Antiquae R.* (P.R.S. N.S. xxxiii), p. 105.
[37] Thus in 1160–1 the king paid him £8 for the purchase of horses: *S.H.C.* i. 32.
[38] T. F. Tout, *Chapters in Admin. Hist. of Med. Eng.* i. 109, 113–15; R. W. Eyton, *Court, Household, and Itinerary of King Henry II, passim*.
[39] *S.H.C.* ii (1), 4.   [40] *S.H.C.* i. 156.

[41] Ibid. 89 sqq.; ii (1), 4; *Curia Regis R.* i. 413, 419.
[42] *S.H.C.* ii (1), 74, 81.
[43] *Bk. of Fees*, i. 142. It was stated c. 1200 that he held by archer-service: ibid. 348.
[44] *Cal. Chart. R.* 1226–57, 32; *Ex. e Rot. Fin.* (Rec. Com.), i. 157.
[45] *Cal. Papal L.* i. 147.
[46] Homage had been taken from the husband of one of the coheirs by 31 Oct.: *Ex. e Rot. Fin.* ii. 22.
[47] Ibid.
[48] Shaw, *Staffs.* i, app. to Gen. Hist. p. xvii; *S.H.C.* v (1), 105–6.
[49] C 66/77 m. 12d. Several earlier writers give this husband as Eustace de Morteyn, who was in fact William's father.
[50] *S.H.C.* vi (1), 67–8.
[51] Ibid. 123; *Cal. Close*, 1272–9, 339.
[52] *S.H.C.* 1911, 187–8; *V.C.H. Warws.* iv. 40.
[53] *Knights of Edward I*, iii (Harl. Soc. lxxxii), 204.
[54] *Walsall Records*, 76–7; *Cal. Pat.* 1307–13, 401.
[55] *Walsall Records*, 36–7, 77; *S.H.C.* 1911, 317; *Cal. Pat.* 1313–17, 33. Somery was still described as lord in 1316: *Feud. Aids*, v. 14.
[56] *Ex. e Rot. Fin.* ii. 28–9.
[57] *Cal. Inq. Misc.* i, p. 418; Shaw, *Staffs.* i, app. to Gen. Hist. p. xvii.
[58] *V.C.H. Warws.* iv. 40; *S.H.C.* vi (1), 148, 174; *Feud. Aids*, v. 9.
[59] *V.C.H. Warws.* iv. 40 n.

l'Archer. The share had been settled on Alice at her betrothal to the brother of a Ralph Basset, and although the two were not married Alice nevertheless claimed the moiety. Her mother, however, was able to uphold her own claim.[60] Margery died in 1302 or 1303 and was succeeded by her son Thomas,[61] who had been knighted by 1304.[62] He was known by the surname le Rous, taken from his mother's maiden name; Margery herself was frequently called by the surname la Rousse, perhaps because of her break with her first husband.[63] In 1335 the king released Thomas for life from payment of the rent due upon his moiety.[64] Alice l'Archer successfully revived her claim in 1338.[65] In the same year, however, Thomas had granted his share to Lord Basset,[66] whose grandson and heir was Thomas's godson,[67] and in 1339 Alice waived her claim in Basset's favour.[68]

Both moieties were thus united in the hands of the Bassets of Drayton. Ralph, Lord Basset, died in 1343. His heir Ralph was a minor, and by a grant of 1336 the custody passed to Thomas de Beauchamp, earl of Warwick, whose daughter Joan married the heir, probably in 1339.[69] Ralph took possession in 1355.[70] Under a settlement of 1339 the manor passed on his death in 1390 to his brother-in-law Thomas de Beauchamp the younger, earl of Warwick.[71] The earl's estates were confiscated in 1397, and in the same year the manor was granted to John Beaufort, marquess of Dorset.[72] The grant was renewed in May 1399,[73] but Warwick was restored later that year and was holding Walsall at his death in 1401.[74] In 1400 the king granted Beaufort the fee-farm rent from Walsall manor; the rent was held by his son John, duke of Somerset, at his death in 1444 and later by Somerset's son-in-law Sir Henry Stafford. In 1485 Margaret, countess of Richmond, to whom the rent had been assigned, settled it on her husband Thomas Stanley, earl of Derby, for life.[75]

The manor descended from 1401 to 1525 with the manor of Sutton-in-Coldfield in Sutton Coldfield (Warws.), passing to the Crown in 1492 on the death of Anne, countess of Warwick.[76] In 1525 it was granted to the king's natural son Henry, duke of Richmond (d. 1536),[77] and in 1541 to Sir John Dudley, later earl of Warwick and duke of Northumberland.[78] The manor, which was leased out by the Crown mainly to royal officials, was described in the leases from 1506 as the manor of the foreign, perhaps because in 1501 the borough was leased to the mayor, bailiffs, and burgesses.[79]

On Northumberland's attainder and forfeiture in 1553 Walsall passed back to the Crown. In 1557 it was sold to Richard Wilbraham of Woodhey in Faddiley (Ches.), master of the queen's jewels and already the tenant, his brother Thomas, and Richard's heirs.[80] Richard died in 1558, a few weeks after Thomas, and was succeeded by his son Thomas, a minor.[81] Thomas died in 1610, and Walsall passed to his son Sir Richard, created a baronet in 1621. Richard died in 1643 and was succeeded by his son Thomas, who died in 1660 with his son, another Thomas, as his heir.[82] In 1686 Thomas and his wife Elizabeth settled the manor, subject to their own life-interest, on their younger daughter Mary, wife of Richard Newport, later earl of Bradford. Thomas died in 1692 and Elizabeth in 1705. Walsall passed to Mary and on her death in 1737 to her son Thomas, earl of Bradford, an imbecile. When he died in 1762 his property passed to his sister Diana, countess of Mountrath, and his nephew Henry Bridgeman. They divided the property in 1763, and Walsall went to Lady Mountrath. She died in 1766, leaving Walsall to her son Charles, earl of Mountrath. On his death in 1802 it passed to his cousin Orlando Bridgeman, Baron Bradford and from 1815 earl of Bradford. The manor then descended with the earldom.[83] In 1945 the greater part of Lord Bradford's Walsall estate, then consisting mainly of freehold ground-rents, was sold, and by 1974 little remained.[84]

There was a manor-house by the later 14th century south of the present Moat Road about a mile west of the town. The first buildings there were erected on what had been cultivated land[85] and may have dated from John's reign when William le Rous created a park in that area.[86] He was described

60 *S.H.C.* vi (1), 214–15.
61 *Cal. Close*, 1302–7, 23, 145; *S.H.C.* xi. 89; xv. 38.
62 B.M. Cott. MS. Nero C. xii, ff. 143v.–144.
63 In 1262 a case of novel disseisin was brought by Ric. de Alazun and Margery his wife, but in 1270 Margery la Rousse brought another against her husband and Wm. de Morteyn: W.S.L., S. MS. 332 (i), pp. 319, 500.
64 *Cal. Pat.* 1334–8, 131.
65 *S.H.C.* xi. 85, 89.
66 *Walsall Records*, 58–61.
67 *S.H.C.* 1913, 156.
68 *Walsall Records*, 63–75; *Cal. Pat.* 1338–40, 238; 1340–3, 176.
69 *S.H.C.* 1913, 97–9; *Complete Peerage*, ii. 2–3 (wrongly dating to 1338 the document of 1339 which appears to be a marriage settlement); *Walsall Records*, 52–4 (the document of 1339, wrongly described in the margin as of 1340); *S.H.C.* xv. 40; *Cal. Close*, 1343–6, 248. Dugdale, *Baronage*, i. 380, followed by several later writers, gives Joan as the wife of the Ralph who d. 1343.
70 *S.H.C.* 1913, 155–7; *Complete Peerage*, ii. 3–6; C 136/65 no. 9; W. A. Shaw, *Knights of Eng.* i. 3, 9.
71 *Cal. Close*, 1389–92, 204; *Walsall Records*, 52–4; *S.H.C.* xv. 34.
72 *Complete Peerage*, xii (2), 377; *Cal. Pat.* 1396–9, 186, 211.
73 Westminster Abbey Muniments, 6045.
74 *Complete Peerage*, xii (2), 377; C 137/27 no. 38.
75 *Cal. Pat.* 1399–1401, 404; C 137/80 no. 44; *Cal. Close*, 1405–9, 141; C 139/121 no. 19; *S.H.C.* N.S. iv. 165, 167; *Complete Peerage*, x. 826–7; *Rot. Parl.* (Rec. Com.), vi. 311.
76 C 139/94 no. 54; C 139/96 no. 3; C 139/123 no. 43; *S.H.C.* xi. 249–50; *Rot. Parl.* (Rec. Com.), vi. 100; *Cal. Pat.* 1476–85, 68, 137, 161, 487; 1485–94, 4, 55, 175, 298; *Cal. Close*, 1485–1500, p. 90; *V.C.H. Warws.* iv. 233.
77 *L. & P. Hen. VIII*, iv (1), p. 673; *Complete Peerage*, x. 830.
78 *L. & P. Hen. VIII*, xvi, p. 330.
79 D.L. 29/641/10415–20; *Cal. Pat.* 1494–1509, 475; *L. & P. Hen. VIII*, i (1), pp. 120, 454; ibid. iv (1), p. 57; B.M. Harl. MS. 606, f. 7; C1/1319 no. 7; C1/1389 no. 41; E 326/12378; below p. 213.
80 *Cal. Pat.* 1553–4, 83; 1555–7, 449.
81 C 142/124 no. 176; G. Ormerod, *Hist. of County Palatine and City of Chester* (1882 edn.), iii. 379.
82 Ormerod, *County Palatine and City of Chester*, iii. 378–80.
83 Ibid. 380; *V.C.H. Staffs.* iv. 172–3; *S.H.C.* i. 376–8; *S.H.C.* N.S. ii. 144–5, 193, 267–8, 279; *Complete Peerage*, ii. 274–7.
84 S.R.O., D. 1287/box 8, Walsall sales 1945; ex inf. Mr. G. C. Trentham of Fleetwood & Co. of Birmingham (1974).
85 Ex inf. (1974) Mr. and Mrs. S. Wrathmell, who have excavated the site for the Walsall Local Hist. Soc.
86 See p. 184.

as of Walsall in the later 1220s.[87] On the division of the manor between his daughters in 1247 a house probably passed to Emecina with the park and fishpond.[88] The house was, however, first mentioned in 1275, and Margery, the younger daughter, acknowledged, apparently in 1276, that it belonged to Emecina's son William de Morteyn.[89] He was holding it at his death in 1283,[90] and it presumably passed with his moiety of the manor to his nephew Roger de Morteyn and subsequently to Ralph, Lord Basset, when he secured the Morteyn moiety. Basset, whose principal seat was Drayton, apparently kept Walsall manor-house in use. He may have established his son and daughter-in-law there, since Ralph, his grandson and eventual heir, was said to have been born at Walsall in 1333.[91]

Excavation on part of the site has revealed at least two early phases of building, followed by the construction of a moat and further rebuilding. At some date between the first occupation of the site and the formation of the moat part of the site was used for metal-working:[92] perhaps an unmoated lodge or manor-house was temporarily converted to industrial use before being rebuilt on a more substantial scale. No precise dates for those developments have been established, but apparently by the 1380s the moated house was the lord's Walsall residence. It was presumably there that Lady Neville and two of her children lived in 1385 and 1386, when they were staying at Walsall. Meanwhile the owner of the house, Ralph Basset the younger, Lord Basset, was preparing to build 'a new castle' at Walsall,[93] but it seems that in fact no new house was built. Instead the existing 'manor-house within the moat of the park' was repaired and extended: in 1388–9 the roof of the hall was repaired, a wooden belfry was made for the chapel, a small room with a privy was built next to the knights' chamber, a new drawbridge was made over the moat, and the great gates were reinforced with iron. Basset presumably stayed in the house during his three short visits to Walsall in 1389.[94] After his death in 1390 there is no evidence that the owners ever stayed there. In the later 1390s, however, the house was repaired and a new chamber built.[95] The chapel was apparently disused by 1417,[96] and the house seems to have been abandoned by the later 1430s. Only the moat was thereafter of any value: in the late 1430s a 20-year lease of rights in 'the fishery called le Mote in the park of Walsall manor' was granted to the bailiff of the foreign.[97] The house had disappeared by 1576.[98]

In 1763 the moated site was in the tenure of a Mr. Holmes, probably Roger Holmes the town clerk, and two houses stood there.[99] The site was leased out as building-land in 1865,[1] and by 1885 the north side of the moat had been filled in and buildings had been erected on part of it.[2] In 1974 most of the remainder survived and still contained water.

The bounds of Walsall manor were those of the ancient parish.[3] Several sub-manors, however, emerged.

A carucate of land at *BESCOT* was held by the king in 1086 but was then waste.[4] By the later 13th century Bescot was part of the manor of Walsall, but it had become a separate manor by the mid 14th century. Overlordship remained with the lords of Walsall at least until 1610.[5] William Hillary held land in Bescot in 1271.[6] About 1300 Roger de Morteyn granted him further land in Bescot and Walsall, including all the waste in Bescot which Roger had previously reserved to himself.[7] Those lands formed the demesne of the manor of Bescot, which William's son Sir Roger Hillary held at his death in 1356 at a rent of 2*d.* a year. Sir Roger was succeeded by his son, another Sir Roger.[8] In 1384 he settled the manor on himself and his wife Margaret, with reversion to Sir John Rochford, son of his sister Joan and her second husband.[9] Sir Roger died in 1400,[10] but Margaret was still living in the manor-house in 1411.[11]

In that year, however, Sir Roger's trustees granted the manor to William Mountfort of Coleshill (Warws.), great-grandson of Joan Hillary by her first husband John de Clinton.[12] In 1425 Bescot was settled by trustees on Baldwin Mountfort,[13] possibly William's eldest son, who was later knighted.[14] In 1451, however, William settled the manor successively on his third son Robert and his second son Edmund.[15] In doing so he disinherited Sir Baldwin, who was similarly deprived of estates in Warwickshire.[16] William Mountfort died in 1452.[17] Sir Baldwin evidently secured Bescot, for in 1453 William's widow Joan sued him for dower there.[18] Robert Mountfort, however, retained a claim to the Bescot estate, which in 1479 he settled in trust.[19] Nevertheless, by 1469 Sir Baldwin had been succeeded at Bescot by his son Sir Simon,[20] who was attainted of treason in 1495.[21] Sir Simon's son and heir Thomas petitioned for reversal of the attainder in 1503, and the king was then empowered by Parliament to reverse it.[22] Reversal, however, was not obtained until 1534, and Bescot was evidently included among the estates then granted to Thomas's

[87] *S.H.C.* iv (1), 75; vi (1), 33; *Pipe R.* 1230 (P.R.S. N.S. iv), 212.
[88] See p. 184.
[89] *S.H.C.* vi (1), 56; *Cal. Close,* 1272–9, 339.
[90] *S.H.C.* 1911, 188.   [91] Ibid. 1913, 155–7.
[92] Ex inf. Mr. and Mrs. Wrathmell.
[93] S.R.O., D. 641/1/2/32.
[94] B.M. Eg. Roll 8467.
[95] Ibid. 8474–5.
[96] Ibid. 8501.
[97] Ibid. 8532.
[98] S.R.O., D. 1287/1/2, survey of Walsall manor, 1576, m. 1.
[99] Ibid. /8/2.
[1] S.R.O., D. 1362/57, p. 161.
[2] O.S. Map 6″, Staffs. LXIII. SW. (1889 edn.).
[3] See p. 143 n. 11.
[4] *V.C.H. Staffs.* iv. 38, no. 6 (which wrongly gives the Bresmundescote of the original as Bremundescote).

[5] C 142/321 no. 84.
[6] *S.H.C.* iv (i), 183.
[7] B.M. Harl. MS. 2131, f. 11.
[8] *Cal. Inq. p.m.* x, p. 280.
[9] B.M. Harl. MS. 2131, f. 14; C 137/36 no. 36.
[10] C 137/36 no. 36.
[11] *S.H.C.* xvi. 89.
[12] B.M. Harl. MS. 2131, f. 16; Dugdale, *Warws.* ii. 1007–8.
[13] B.M. Harl. MS. 2131, ff. 19–20.
[14] *V.C.H. Warws.* iv. 50.
[15] *S.H.C.* xi. 247.
[16] *V.C.H. Warws.* iv. 50.
[17] C 139/150 no. 33.
[18] *S.H.C.* N.S. iii. 212.
[19] B.M. Harl. MS. 2131, ff. 24–5.
[20] *S.H.C.* N.S. iv. 160.
[21] *Rot. Parl.* vi. 503; 11 Hen. VII, c. 64.
[22] 19 Hen. VII, c. 28.

son Simon.[23] Simon was succeeded between 1535 and 1548 by his son Francis (d. 1592).[24] On his death the manor passed successively to his son William (d. 1610), his grandson Sir Edward (d. 1632),[25] and his great-grandson Simon.[26] By 1648 Simon's lands had been sequestered for recusancy.[27] In 1652 he and his creditor Walter Hillary obtained a lease for seven years of two-thirds of the estate, the remaining third having been leased for a year to George Hill, mayor in 1654–5.[28] Simon had evidently recovered the manor by 1663,[29] and he died in 1664.[30] He was succeeded by his brother Edward,[31] who died in 1672, leaving a son Simon (d. c. 1672) and a daughter Elizabeth, both minors. Under a settlement of 1671 the manor passed to Edward's widow Elizabeth (d. c. 1675).[32]

The estate then passed into the hands of trustees, the survivor of whom gave possession c. 1681 to Thomas Harris, guardian of Edward Mountfort's daughter Elizabeth. By 1684 Elizabeth had brought Bescot in marriage to Harris's son Thomas.[33] After his death she married Jonas Slaney.[34] He had died by 1727, and in 1728 Elizabeth settled the manor on Jonas Slaney the younger of Dawley (Salop.), reserving £2,000 and a rent-charge to Dorothy, wife of Nicholas Parker of Bloxwich. On Elizabeth's death Dorothy entered the estate, but in 1739 the property was secured to Slaney.[35] He died in 1762 or early in 1763 leaving as heir his son Jonas, who lived at Bescot at some time before 1768 but by then had moved to Bristol. He had returned to Bescot by 1772 and was vicar of Rushall by 1778.[36] As a result of financial difficulties he conveyed the estate in 1781 to trustees, after settling 105 a. on his wife Mary. In 1791 they sold the hall and 80 a. to Richard Wilkes, who had been living at the hall since 1788.[37] Mary Slaney still held her share of the estate in 1796, but by 1825 it had passed to William Spurrier, who still owned it in 1843. It was then a compact farm east of Wednesbury Road.[38]

In 1794 Wilkes sold his property at Bescot to Richmond Aston, a Tipton banker.[39] Aston died in 1796,[40] and his widow lived at the hall until at least 1800.[41] She still owned the estate in 1817.[42] By 1820 the property had passed to Richmond Aston's trustees, who then sold it to Edward, Stephen, and John Crowther.[43] From at least 1817 they had held 152 a. of the estate, which Jonas Slaney's trustees had evidently sold to Dorothy Crowther by 1796.[44] By 1843 John Crowther was sole owner. The estate then consisted of a compact block of 204 a. at Bescot, houses, gardens, and a croft at Bloxwich, and 3 a. of meadow at Shelfield.[45] In 1852 Crowther left the property to William Crowther, a relative.[46] The Crowthers did not live at Bescot and the hall was occupied by a succession of tenants.[47]

William Crowther died in 1865. The estate then passed to trustees and in October 1871 was split up and sold. Richard Bagnall, who was living at the hall in April, agreed to buy it and c. 24 a. there but subsequently sold the option to James Slater, who bought the property in 1872.[48] Slater died in 1901 and the estate passed to trustees; among them was his widow Elizabeth, who lived at Bescot until her death in 1922.[49] The estate, consisting of 48 a., was then offered for sale by the trustees,[50] but without success. The house remained unoccupied for a short time, but in the mid 1920s it was the home of Pitt Bonarjee, minister of Wednesbury Congregational church.[51] It was demolished in 1929–30.[52] The trustees sold the estate in small parcels from 1925 to 1939.[53]

The original manor-house was moated. Along much of the north-west side the ditch was double.[54] It stood in what is now Pleck Park between the park entrance from Bescot Drive and the M6 motorway, which crosses the south-west corner of the moat. In 1972 the site was marked by a group of trees, the moat having been almost obliterated. The house existed by 1311 when William Hillary was besieged there by Thomas le Rous and over fifty others,[55] and in 1345 Roger Hillary was licensed to crenellate.[56] In at least the later 14th century it contained a chapel.[57] By 1666 the house was a substantial

[23] *L. & P. Hen. VIII*, vii, p. 175; S.R.O., D. 260/M/T/1/47.
[24] S.R.O., D. 260/M/T/1/47; /M/F/1/5, f. 29; /M/F/1/8, Walsall foreign rental.
[25] S.R.O., D. 260/M/F/1/5, ff. 29, 144; C 142/321 no. 84.
[26] *S.H.C.* v (2), 219.
[27] *Cal. Cttee. for Compounding*, i. 90.
[28] Ibid. iv. 2745–6.   [29] *S.H.C.* v (2), 219.
[30] Ibid. 219 n.; Willmore, *Walsall*, 285.
[31] *S.H.C.* 1923, 126; *S.H.C.* v (2), 218–19.
[32] C 5/164/12; L.J.R.O., B/V/7/Aldridge, recording burial of Edw. Mumford of Bescot 25 Mar. 1672.
[33] C 5/164/12.
[34] Shaw, *Staffs.* ii. 81. Slaney was the executor of Humphrey Persehouse, who was living at the hall in 1692 and died in 1698: S.R.O., D. 260/M/T/1/74; W.S.L. 45/56, folder 28, no. 14; and see below pp. 233, 273.
[35] S.R.O., D. 260/M/T/2/74.
[36] *Aris's Birmingham Gaz.* 21 Mar. 1763, 1 Feb. 1768; W.S.L. 67/20/22, abstract of title of Jas. Fisher, pp. 7, 8, 14; F. W. Willmore, *Records of Rushall* (Walsall, 1892), 97; Willmore, *Walsall*, 447.
[37] Willmore, *Rushall*, 81–2; Willmore, *Walsall*, 447; Shaw, *Staffs.* ii. 81; Walsall Council House, Bescot deeds, bdle. 2, deeds of 24 Nov. 1791 and 25 Mar. 1817; S.R.O., Q/RTg/1/1, 1788–9, no. 67; 1789–90, no. 109; 1790–1, no. 104.
[38] S.R.O., D. 1041, indentures of 9 May 1796, 17 Dec. 1825; W.S.L., S. MS. 417/Walsall, *sub* Spurrier.
[39] Walsall Council House, Bescot deeds, bdle. 2, deeds of 3–4 Apr. 1794.
[40] *Staffs. Advertiser*, 12 Mar. 1796.
[41] Shaw, *Staffs.* ii, app. p. 15.
[42] Walsall Council House, Bescot deeds, bdle. 2, deed of 9 Apr. 1817.
[43] Willmore, *Walsall*, 447.
[44] Walsall Council House, Bescot deeds, bdle. 2, deeds of 5 May 1796, 25 Mar. 1817; S.R.O., D. 1041, copy indenture 20 Apr. 1796.
[45] W.S.L., S. MS. 417/Walsall, nos. 453, 455, 1422–56, 2921.
[46] Willmore, *Walsall*, 447.
[47] Pigot, *Com. Dir. Birm.* (1829), 90; W.S.L. 67/14/22; Ede, *Wednesbury*, 238; J. Roscoe, *Book of the Grand Junction Railway* (1839), 47; Willmore, *Walsall*, 286; W.S.L., S. MS. 417/Walsall; S.R.O., D. 595/12, probate of will of H. Barnett, 1st and 2nd codicils.
[48] Walsall Council House, Bescot deeds, abstract of title 1964; R.G. 10/2962 f. 22. For Bagnall see F. W. Hackwood, *Hist. of Tipton in Staffs.* (Dudley, 1891), 44–5.
[49] *Staffs. Advertiser*, 4 Jan. 1901; *Walsall Red Book* (1923), 420.
[50] W.S.L., Sale Cat. D/1/47.
[51] *Kelly's Dir. Staffs.* (1924); *Walsall Red Book* (1925; 1927); A. G. Matthews, *Congregational Churches of Staffs.* 266.
[52] Blay, 'Street Names of Walsall', 104.
[53] Walsall Council House, Bescot deeds.
[54] *V.C.H. Staffs.* i. 368; O.S. Map 1/2,500, Staffs. LXIII. 14 (1918 edn.).
[55] *S.H.C.* ix (1), 31.
[56] *Cal. Pat. 1343–5*, 48.
[57] *S.H.C.* n.s. viii. 6; L.J.R.O., B/A/1/6, f. 125v.

building taxable on fourteen hearths, and fourteen rooms are mentioned in 1672.[58] In the 18th century it was demolished and rebuilt on a new site north-east of the moat on what is now the west side of Bescot Drive. The old site was laid out as a garden connected with the new house by a bridge over the moat.[59] The bridge survived the demolition of the hall but was ruinous by 1937;[60] it has since been removed.

The Georgian house was a brick building of two storeys and an attic, with stone quoins and balus-traded parapet. It was considerably enlarged by Richmond Aston, who added a third full storey, a one-storeyed wing on the north-west side, and a semicircular porch with Tuscan columns.[61] In the 19th century a second storey was added to the wing, and an annexe, including a basement and a conservatory surmounted by a balustrade, was built at the rear of the house. In 1922 there were 35 rooms.[62]

BLOXWICH was originally part of the manor of Walsall.[63] In the later 16th century a separate manor is mentioned[64] which is identifiable with the holdings acquired in Bloxwich by the Hillary family in the 14th century. There is, however, no evidence of manorial jurisdiction and the estate did not continue to be called a manor. It was held of the lords of Walsall manor until at least 1617.[65]

About 1300 Roger de Morteyn gave John son of Nicholas Wodemon of Bloxwich a plot of waste in Walsall, probably in Bloxwich. John gave all his lands in Bloxwich to William Hillary. By 1377 they had passed to Sir Roger Hillary of Bescot. Roger de Morteyn also gave a house and land in Bloxwich to John de Bloxwich, clerk, and 2 a. of waste there to Thomas, son of Robert de Ruycroft of 'Hulton' (probably Hilton in St. Peter's, Wolverhampton). Those holdings too later passed to Sir Roger Hillary. Margery le Rous (d. 1302–3) held as part of her moiety of the manor of Walsall a piece of waste in Bloxwich called Northwood Heath. Her son Thomas granted it to a Walter Marchis, and in 1315–16 Emme le Marchis and Thomas her son gave half of it to William Hillary. Thomas le Rous in 1330 granted the whole tenement to Robert Hillary, rector of Sutton Coldfield (Warws.). It too was later held by Sir Roger Hillary.[66]

All these tenements may have formed part of an estate in Bloxwich inherited by Sir Roger from his father Sir Roger in 1356.[67] After the younger Sir Roger's death in 1400[68] the estate descended with the manor of Goscote; after 1510 the rights were shared between the coparceners of Goscote, half descending with Lord Berners's share and the rest with that of Lady Sheffield. When Lord Sheffield sold his share to John Skeffington in 1565 it was

described as a moiety of the manor of Bloxwich.[69] Skeffington died in 1604 and his Bloxwich estate, no longer called a manor, passed to his son William, who was created a baronet in 1627 and died in 1635. William's son and heir John died in 1651 and was succeeded by his eldest son William (d. 1652). The rights to the Skeffington estate in Bloxwich then passed to his cousin John, son of his uncle Sir Richard Skeffington.[70]

At some time before 1632 Sir William Skeffington and his son John sold part of the estate to Simon Woodward and George Smyth of Great Bloxwich.[71] John mortgaged other property there in 1637 to a Katherine Barford. In 1638 she assigned the mortgage to her son-in-law Thomas Brome of Fisherwick in St. Michael's, Lichfield, in trust for her unmarried daughters. Brome sold it in 1648 to Theodore Colley of London. Meanwhile in 1642 John Skeffington had mortgaged a further 72 a. in Bloxwich to Colley and in 1648 granted him a lease for 93 years of all his holdings there. In 1660 Colley sold the lease to Edmond Lathwell of London and William Pretty of Fazeley in Tamworth. John Skeffington resigned his rights the following year. Lathwell disposed of his share of the estate by selling it in small parcels between 1661 and 1665 to John Slaney, William Bayley, Zacharias Greene, and Nicholas Parker, all of Bloxwich.[72]

A manor-house at Bloxwich occurs in 1564, when it was occupied by John Baylye.[73] At some time before 1637 the Skeffingtons leased it to a Joan Cowley, and it became known as Cowley's Farm. It passed in 1660 to Edmond Lathwell, who at some time between 1661 and 1665 sold it to Zacharias Greene.[74]

The manor of *GOSCOTE* is identifiable with the property in that hamlet held of the manor of Walsall by the Hillary family in the 14th century. The lords of Walsall manor remained overlords until at least 1604.[75]

Sir Roger Hillary of Bescot was receiving 20s. rent from free tenants at Goscote in 1356.[76] The estate descended with Bescot until 1411, when William Mountfort obtained seisin.[77] In 1411 or 1412, however, the estates of the younger Sir Roger Hillary (d. 1400) were divided and Goscote was assigned to Robert and Joan Roos, Margery, widow of Frederick Tylney, and John Gibthorp. Joan and Margery were Hillary's great-nieces and John was their nephew.[78] Later Goscote was apparently assigned to the Rooses and from 1423 presumably descended with Stretton on Fosse (Warws.) to Robert Whittlebury, who held it in 1498. Robert died in 1506, leaving the estate settled on his wife Anne for life; she, however, sold it in 1508 to Edmund Dudley.[79] After Dudley's forfeiture in 1510 the estate, then

[58] *S.H.C.* 1923, 126; L.J.R.O., will of Edw. Mountfort (proved 18 June 1672), inventory.
[59] Shaw, *Staffs.* ii. 81 and plate facing p. 82, reproduced facing p. 176 below; W.S.L., S. MS. 417/Walsall, no. 1454.
[60] W.C.L., photograph 266.
[61] Shaw, *Staffs.* ii, plate facing p. 82.
[62] W.S.L., Sale Cat. D/1/47, pp. 2, 6, and plans.
[63] *V.C.H. Staffs.* iv. 38, no. 7; *S.H.C.* v (1), 178.
[64] Sims, *Cal. of Deeds,* p. 32 (1559); S.R.O., D. 260/M/T /2/7, deeds of 5 Nov. 1565. The manor mentioned in E 150/1027 no. 2 in 1517 may be Bloxwich.
[65] S.R.O., D. 260/M/F/1/8, ct. of recog. and survey, 1617, p. 26.
[66] B.M. Harl. MS. 2131, ff. 110–14; *S.H.C.* xiii. 145; above pp. 170–1.
[67] *Cal. Inq. p.m.* x, p. 280.   [68] See p. 171.

[69] See below and p. 174; S.R.O., D. 260/M/T/2/7, deeds of 5 Nov. 1565.
[70] C 142/680 no. 12; S.R.O., D. 260/M/T/2/7; J. Nichols, *Hist. and Antiquities of the Town and County of Leicester,* iii (1), 449.
[71] Sims, *Cal. of Deeds,* p. 62.
[72] S.R.O., D. 260/M/T/2/7.
[73] Ibid., deed of 5 Nov. 1565 (endorsement of 11 Dec.).
[74] S.R.O., D. 260/M/T/2/7.
[75] *S.H.C.* 1913, 167–8; C 137/36 no. 36; C 142/680 no. 12.   [76] *S.H.C.* 1913, 167–8.
[77] B.M. Harl. MS. 2131, f. 16v.
[78] B.M. Harl. MS. 506, p. 332; *S.H.C.* xvii. 135; *Lincs. Pedigrees,* iii (Harl. Soc. iii), 829.
[79] *V.C.H. Warws.* v. 154; E 150/1018 no. 1; *Cal. Inq. p.m. Hen. VII,* iii, p. 198; *Cal. Close, 1500–9,* p. 343.

described as the manor of Goscote, passed to John, Lord Berners, and Ellen, wife of Sir Robert Sheffield. They were the heirs respectively of Margery Tylney and John Gibthorp.[80] In 1520 Berners sold his share to Sir John Skeffington of London.[81] It then descended with the manor of Shelfield.[82]

By 1516 Sir Robert Sheffield (d. 1517) was holding the other share of the manor by the courtesy.[83] His son Sir Robert obtained possession in 1518 and was succeeded on his death in 1531 by his son Edmund (d. 1549), created Baron Sheffield in 1547. Edmund's son and heir John, Lord Sheffield, sold the property (described as a moiety of the manor) to John Skeffington in 1565.[84] The two halves were thus reunited, and when Skeffington died in 1604 he was holding the whole manor.[85] He was succeeded by his son William, who in 1631 sold it to John Birch of Goscote.[86]

Birch's property had been sequestered for recusancy by 1648.[87] He died c. 1651 and his right to the manor passed to his widow Mary (or Joan), also a recusant, who died in 1652. She was succeeded by John Birch's nephew, another John, who immediately sold the right to Francis Gregg of Clement's Inn, London. Between 1652 and 1654 Gregg attempted to have the sequestration reversed, apparently without success.[88] John Birch recovered the manor after the Restoration and was living at Goscote in 1666.[89] In 1674 he settled the estate on his son Henry,[90] who conveyed it to his son Charles in 1703.[91] Charles was still in possession in 1710,[92] but by 1745 it had passed to his widow Anne and his son Thomas. Anne was dead by 1763, leaving Thomas as sole lord of the manor.[93] In 1776 he sold it to Thomas Huxley of Rushall Hall.[94]

Huxley died in 1790 and was succeeded by his daughter Dorothy.[95] In 1794 she sold the manor to Joseph Bradley and Francis Edwards of Leominster (Herefs.) and Elijah Waring of Tipton, who had entered into a partnership to mine and work iron and coal at Goscote.[96] The full purchase price was not paid, however, until 1810 when Dorothy's cousin and heir Thomas Green of Liverpool reconveyed the manor to Edwards and Bradley.[97] In the same year they dissolved their partnership and Bradley conveyed his share in the manor to Edwards in trust for the sale of the whole.[98] In 1816

the estate passed to a trustee for Dr. Samuel Hughes.[99] Joseph Smith, a Rushall corn-miller, bought it in 1819,[1] and in 1843 he owned 117 a. in Goscote.[2] By will of 1858 Smith left the property to his son Joseph Crowther Smith of Wolverhampton, who died in 1886. The property then passed to trustees for his niece Harriet Cooke of Aldridge.[3] She and her trustees sold 45 a. to R. T. Bradley in 1925,[4] and he conveyed it to the corporation in 1933.[5] Part of the estate passed with the Goscote sewage farm to the Upper Tame Main Drainage Authority in 1966; the corporation still held most of the remainder in 1973.[6]

The lords of the manor were absentees until the 17th century, and there seems to have been no manor-house before that period. In 1649, however, John Birch held a house and garden in Goscote, perhaps formerly a part of his original tenement there. He sold them with the manor to Francis Gregg in 1652.[7] The house was still part of the estate in 1819 and apparently stood in Goscote Lane on the site of the present Barley Mow inn.[8] The inn, though dating largely from the 19th and 20th centuries, incorporates remains of an earlier building.

By 1810 the estate also included Goscote Lodge Farm between Slacky Lane and the present Hildick's Crescent. Joseph Bradley was living there in 1810 and Joseph Smith in 1834 and probably in 1854; in 1843, however, it was occupied by a tenant. It descended with the estate and was demolished in the earlier 1940s.[9]

In 1557 George Hawe held a lease of what was called half the manor of *HAY HEAD*. The other half was apparently held by his brother Nicholas, to whom George left his share on his death in 1558.[10] In 1560 Nicholas left the lease to Thomas Wollaston and John Curteys, his brothers-in-law.[11] The manor is probably identifiable with Hay Head farm, which formed part of Walsall manor demesne between at least 1763 and 1843 and was let to tenants.[12] By 1860 it had passed to the Revd. Thomas Burrowes Adams. In 1861 he conveyed it to Samuel Priestley, an Aldridge lime-master, who sold it to Robert Myers Wood in 1864. Wood was living there by 1868 and sold it to James Rooker Mason in 1871. Mason died in 1877 and the estate passed to his trustees, who conveyed it in 1903 to

[80] E 150/1018 no. 1; Act of Restitution of John Dudley, 3 Hen. VIII, c. 19. In 1506, however, it was called the manor of Walsall: *Cal. Inq. p.m. Hen. VII*, iii, p. 198.
[81] *S.H.C.* xi. 262 (not describing it as a moiety).
[82] Wards 9/129 f. 169; N.R.A., Chilham Castle, Kent, Massereene (Staffs.) deeds, 29; below p. 279.
[83] C 54/383 no. 7; E 150/1027 no. 2.
[84] C 142/53 no. 20; /92 no. 90; *Complete Peerage*, xi. 661–2; S.R.O., D. 260/M/T/2/7, deed of 5 Nov. 1565.
[85] C 142/680 no. 12.
[86] See p. 173; C.P. 25(2)/485/6 Chas. I Hil.; S.R.O., D. 1375/box 11, abstract of title to Goscote manor, 1815, ff. 1–2.
[87] *Cal. Cttee. for Compounding*, i. 89.
[88] W.S.L., S. MS. 339(i), pp. 361–83.
[89] S.R.O., D. 260/M/F/1/5, f. 158.
[90] S.R.O., D. 1375/box 11, abstract of title, 1815, ff. 4–5.
[91] Ibid. f. 5; C.P. 25(2)/965/2 Anne Trin. no. 539; C.P. 43/481 rot. 14d.
[92] Abstract of title, 1815, ff. 6–7.
[93] Ibid. ff. 7–8; S.R.O., Q/SO 4, f. 266v.
[94] Abstract of title 1815, ff. 8–9.
[95] Ibid. ff. 11–13; *Aris's Birmingham Gaz.* 1 Mar. 1790.
[96] Abstract of title 1815, ff. 13–14.
[97] Ibid. ff. 14–17. Waring had left the firm in 1809.

[98] Ibid. ff. 25–6, 21d.–23d.
[99] W.C.L., ACJ XII/25; C.P. 25(2)/1416/57 Geo. III East. (missing 1972).
[1] W.C.L., ACJ XII/25.
[2] W.S.L., S. MS. 417/Walsall *sub* Smith, Joseph.
[3] Walsall Council House, deeds bdle. 614, abstract of title of Harriet Cooke, 1925.
[4] Ibid., supplemental abstract of title of R. T. Bradley, 1933.
[5] Ibid., deed of 29 Dec. 1933.
[6] Ex inf. the town clerk (1973).
[7] W.S.L., S. MS. 339(i), pp. 379, 383.
[8] W.C.L., ACJ XII/25; S.R.O., D. 351/M/B/209.
[9] S.R.O., D. 1375/box 11, abstract of title 1815, ff. 25–6, 21d.; White, *Dir. Staffs.* (1834); *P.O. Dir. Staffs.* (1854); W.S.L., S. MS. 417/Walsall, no. 694; Walsall Corporation files (showing renewal of lease in 1941); O.S. Map 6″, SK 00 SW. (1956 edn., revised 1945).
[10] Fink, *Queen Mary's Grammar Sch.* 132. Geo.'s will also calls Walsall Park a manor.
[11] S.R.O., D. 260/M/F/1/5, f. 72; Fink, *Queen Mary's Grammar Sch.* plate facing p. 144.
[12] S.R.O., D. 1287/8/2; /18/26, business corresp. 1835–7, P. Potter to Lord Bradford, 26 Feb. 1835; W.S.L., S. MS. 417/Walsall, nos. 1824–9, 1855–61, 1863, 1865–6, 1868–70, 1954.

Mary, wife of Dr. Tom Longmore of Walsall. In 1937 she sold it to the corporation, which still held it in 1974. The farm continued to be occupied by tenants in the late 19th and the 20th centuries.[13] There was no farm-house at Hay Head in 1763, but one had been built by the late 1770s.[14] The present farm-house dates from after the Second World War.

OTHER ESTATES. Daffodil Farm, Wood End, stood south of Sutton Road near the present Fallowfield Road. It seems to have belonged to the Hurst family in the 14th century. In 1333 William atte Hurst held land at Wood End which later formed part of the estate; he was still living in 1338.[15] In 1388 John atte Hurst conveyed his property there to trustees, who in 1404 granted it to his widow Isabel. John's son William was apparently in possession by 1408.[16] In 1434 he leased most of the estate to his son John, retaining part of the house and outbuildings and some land.[17] William was still alive in 1438 but by 1446 had been succeeded by another son, Thomas.[18] By 1479 the estate had passed to Edmund Hurst, who was still in possession in 1493.[19] It had apparently descended by 1504 to his nephew Geoffrey Hurst, who died between 1514 and 1527.[20]

The estate was later held by Henry Hurst but had passed to John Floude of London and his wife Alice by 1546 when they leased it to Rowland Charles, a spurrier. The house was then called Hurst's House.[21] John was dead by 1556 when Alice leased the property to Robert Conyworth, a London merchant taylor.[22] By 1576 it had been bought by John Conyworth. He still held it in 1612, but by 1614 the estate had passed to his son-in-law Thomas Ashton of Sheldon (Warws.). In 1621 Ashton's daughter Anne and her husband Gamaliel Purefey of Wolvershill in Bulkington (Warws.) held the property; the house was then known as Hurst House or Wood End House.[23] The Purefeys sold the estate to William Scott in 1624, and he made a settlement of it in 1629.[24] A William Scott was living at Wood End between at least 1661 and 1672,[25] and between at least 1719 and 1722 the estate was held by Richard Scott, a Walsall ironmonger.[26] By 1784

it had passed to a Mr. Goodall,[27] and the house was known by 1816 as Daffodilly House.[28] In 1843 the estate was owned by Frances Hewett and consisted of 76 a. let to Robert Parsons. The house was then called Daffydowndilly House.[29] John Shannon (d. 1875), a Walsall clothing manufacturer, was apparently the owner in the later 19th century; in 1894 his trustees held the property.[30] It later passed to his son E. J. Shannon (d. 1913) and descended with Wood End farm until 1957.[31] From c. 1900 it was known as Daffodil farm.[32] The estate was broken up from 1957; most of it was sold in lots to John Maclean & Sons Ltd. between 1957 and 1959 as building land. The corporation bought 5 a. in 1968, and the remainder, a small plot in Skip Lane, was sold to K. M. Gilmore of Sutton Coldfield (Warws.) in 1970.[33]

In 1434 Hurst's House was apparently timber-framed and had a detached kitchen.[34] By the mid 16th century it was moated.[35] It was taxable on five hearths in 1666.[36] The house in 1819 consisted of a rectangular range with a north wing, a projecting block in the centre, and a further wing at the south-east corner. A pool at the north-west corner may have been the remains of the moat.[37] By 1885 the house had been rebuilt.[38] It had been demolished by 1959.[39]

Gillity Greaves, a farm-house at Wood End, stood at the south end of the present Allington Close. In 1525 the farm was held by Richard Hill and was then known as 'Gyllot in greves'.[40] By 1548 the property, including a house, belonged to Thomas Webbe; a Thomas Webbe held it in 1576.[41] On his death his property was divided between his heirs Joan Ball and Thomas Nicholls.[42] Nicholls still held his share in 1616.[43] In 1628 Joan Ball settled her moiety on her son John, retaining a life-interest.[44] The farm later passed to John Scott, who occupied it between at least 1753 and 1766,[45] and then successively to Thomas Paviour, to John Brown, and by 1770 to Simon Burrowes.[46] Burrowes died in 1785. His estates apparently passed to Joanna, daughter of Thomas Burrowes and wife of Francis Goodall. She died in 1790, and the property was then shared between her daughter Joanna Freer, Elizabeth Delight (probably another

[13] Walsall Council House, deeds bdle. 805; *P.O. Dir. Staffs.* (1868; 1872; 1876); *Kelly's Dir. Staffs.* (1880 and later edns.).
[14] S.R.O., D. 1287/8/2; /6/14, sketch-map.
[15] B.R.L. 608897, 608901, 608930.
[16] Ibid. 608916, 608923, 608926.
[17] Ibid. 608930.   [18] Ibid. 608932–4.
[19] Ibid. 608940; Sims, *Cal. of Deeds*, pp. 22, 26.
[20] B.R.L. 608940; S.R.O., D. 260/M/T/7/3, deed of 31 July 1504; *S.H.C.* 1928, 244, 261.
[21] B.R.L. 608942; S.R.O., D. 260/M/F/1/8, Walsall foreign rental.   [22] B.R.L. 608943.
[23] S.R.O., D. 1287/1/2, survey of Walsall manor, 1576, m. 10; B.R.L. 427777, 431962, 431964, 434077. Yet John Conyworth was still said to hold it in 1617: S.R.O., D. 260/M/F/1/8, ct. of recog. and survey, 1617, p. 31.
[24] *S.H.C.* n.s. x (1), 58; Shaw, *Staffs.* ii. 104.
[25] W.T.C. II/13/49; *S.H.C.* 1923, 128; B.R.L. 329000.
[26] B.R.L., Homer 261; S.R.O., D.(W.)1753/5 and 6.
[27] Fink, *Queen Mary's Grammar Sch.* end-papers.
[28] B.M. O.S.D. 212.
[29] W.S.L., S. MS. 417/Walsall, nos. 1842–8, 1885–94.
[30] Deeds in poss. of Pearman Smith & Sons Ltd., Walsall, deed of 31 Oct. 1894, map. For Shannon see pp. 204–5.
[31] Deeds in poss. of Pearman Smith & Sons., deed of 30 Apr. 1917; below p. 179.

[32] O.S. Map 6", Staffs. LXIII. SE. (1903 and later edns.); deeds in poss. of Pearman Smith & Sons, deed of 30 Apr. 1917.
[33] Deeds in poss. of Pearman Smith & Sons, deed of 31 Aug. 1957, endorsements; agreement of 3 Feb. 1970.
[34] B.R.L. 608930.
[35] Ibid. 608942–3.
[36] *S.H.C.* 1923, 128.
[37] S.R.O., D. 351/M/B/209, no. 1833.
[38] O.S. Map 6", Staffs. LXIII. SE. (1890 edn.); 1/2,500, Staffs. LXIII. 12 (1914 edn.).
[39] O.S. Map 6", SP 09 NW. (1972 edn., revised 1959).
[40] S.R.O., D. 260/M/T/1/1a, deed of 15 June 1525. There have been various spellings of the name. 'Greves' means woods, while 'Gyllot' may be a personal name or may mean 'hussy': *O.E.D.*; *Eng. P.N. Elements* (E.P.N.S.), i. 207.
[41] S.R.O., D. 260/M/F/1/8, Walsall foreign rental; D. 1287/1/2, survey of Walsall manor, 1576, m. 3.
[42] S.R.O., D. 260/M/F/1/8, ct. of recog. and survey, 1617, p. 19.
[43] Ibid./1/5, ff. 135v.–136.
[44] Ibid. f. 147v.
[45] *Aris's Birmingham Gaz.* 17 Dec. 1753, 14 Apr. 1766.
[46] S.R.O., D. 1287/1/8, chief rents of Walsall manor, 1768–70, p. 15.

daughter), and a third coheir. Elizabeth was dead by 1825, and in 1826 her heirs and those of Joanna Freer agreed that the property should be divided.[47] By 1843 Gillity Greaves had passed to Fanny Goodall, who was presumably the third coheir or her successor. Samuel Wood, then the tenant, later bought the property and was succeeded by John Wood.[48] In 1918 it was bought by George and Charles Frederick Griffin; Charles died the same year, and in March 1919 George sold it to Edward Holt, who resold it to G. H. Stanley in July.[49] Stanley apparently continued to own and occupy the farm until 1939.[50] The area has since been covered with houses,[51] and the site of the farmhouse is a playground and open space.

Goscote Hall on the corner of Slacky and Goscote Lanes formed part of an estate owned by the Price family in the mid 18th century.[52] In 1756 it was held by Elizabeth Beckett, widow of Thomas Price of Goscote, and their son John Price. In 1788 John settled the hall and farm on his brother Thomas Price of Shareshill, who died in 1826 leaving the estate to Anne Cale, widow of Benjamin Cale, a London japanner. In 1827 she settled it on her son John, who in 1862 granted it to his son Benjamin George Cale; it then consisted of 149 a. In 1876 Benjamin sold the estate to Elias Crapper, a Walsall lime-master, who died in 1885. In 1889 his trustees sold it to John and William Starkey, coal-masters of Pelsall. As a result of mortgage transfers it passed in 1902 to Edward Davies of Whittington Hall and F. W. Smith of Walsall, who sold it to the corporation in 1905. The corporation transferred 24 a. with Goscote hospital to the Ministry of Health in 1948, and part of the rest with Goscote sewage farm to the Upper Tame Main Drainage Authority in 1966. The hall had been demolished by 1966, but the corporation still owned the site in 1973.

Sir William Skeffington (d. 1635) sold to John Cowley land in Bloxwich which apparently included the site of the Hills in Bealey's Lane.[53] Cowley lived in Bloxwich between at least 1636 and 1642.[54] In 1682 the property belonged to his daughter Winefrid Pretty of Great Barr in Aldridge.[55] By 1694 she had been succeeded by her son Thomas,[56] who sold the estate in 1697 to his brother-in-law John Hunt of Birmingham.[57] The property, known as Hills farm

in 1766, had passed by 1781 to John Bealey of Bloxwich.[58] A John Bealey was living in Bloxwich in 1829,[59] but by 1832 he had been succeeded by Joseph Bealey, who was living at the house, then known as the Hills.[60] In 1843 the estate consisted of 109 a. occupied by Bealey and other land let to tenants.[61] Joseph was succeeded between 1850 and 1854 by his son John Edward Bealey (d. 1889), who left the estate to his nephew Joseph Bealey Strongitharm, subject to the right of Eliza Farnall (d. 1893) to occupy the house for life.[62] Strongitharm lived at the Hills between at least 1896 and 1907.[63] In 1907 he settled the estate in trust for sale; the Hills Estate Co. bought it in 1918.[64] The company sold it in 1935 to the corporation, which assigned 25 a. as part of the King George V Playing-fields in 1938 and sold more for building in 1959. About 1946 it let the house and 120 a. to a tenant, who was still farming there in 1973.[65] The Hills is a three-storeyed brick building of c. 1800, with mid-19th-century extensions including an Italianate stuccoed front.

Having appropriated Walsall church in the mid 13th century[66] Halesowen abbey retained the rectory until its dissolution in 1538. In 1255 the church was said to be worth 40 marks a year[67] and in 1291 £12.[68] By 1535 the rectory was farmed for £10.[69] In 1538 the Crown granted it with the advowson to Sir John Dudley, later earl of Warwick and duke of Northumberland,[70] who leased the rectorial tithes to William Taillour, ex-abbot of Halesowen, for life.[71] The Crown resumed possession of the rectory on Dudley's attainder in 1553 and granted it in 1590 to Robert Balthrop of London and John Welles.[72] Later in 1590 Balthrop sold it to Edward Leigh of Rushall; a barn was included.[73] The rectory then remained with the Leighs until the earlier 18th century.[74] In 1718 William Leigh's brother Edward and his widow Esther sold the portion of the rectorial tithes known as the borough tithes to John Dolphin of Stafford and Shenstone. Those tithes arose from the southern part of the foreign but were called the borough tithes because they were then rated to the borough; the borough itself was apparently tithe-free. Dolphin (d. 1724) was succeeded by his son John, of Shenstone (d. 1756). His heir was his nephew John Dolphin of Shenstone (d. 1782), who was succeeded by his son Thomas

[47] S.R.O., 364/M/2, deed of 21 Jan. 1828; tablets to [Si]mon Burrowes and Joanna Goodall in S. aisle of St. Matthew's Church.
[48] W.S.L., S. MS. 417/Walsall, no. 1820; S.R.O., D. 1287, box 7, bdle. 101.
[49] S.R.O., D. 1287, box 7, bdles. 101, 881.
[50] Ibid. bdle. 101; Walsall Red Book (1939).
[51] See pp. 183–4.
[52] For this para. see Walsall Council House, deeds bdles. 165 and 165 (old).
[53] Homeshaw, Bloxwich, 131; W.C.L., box 5, no. 5; box 6, no. 4.
[54] W.C.L., box 5, no. 5; box 6, no. 2.
[55] S.R.O., D. 260/M/T/2/46, deed of 10 July 1682.
[56] W.C.L., box 8, nos. 6 and 8.
[57] Ibid. box 5, no. 6; box 8, nos. 4 and 6; box 9, no. 2.
[58] Ibid. box 9, no. 7; Aris's Birmingham Gaz. 12 May 1766.
[59] Pigot, Com. Dir. Birm. (1829), 90.
[60] Staffs. Advertiser, 22 Dec. 1832.
[61] W.S.L., S. MS. 417/Walsall, nos. 211–12, 224–8, 234, 266, 450–1, 616–17, 619.
[62] Staffs. Advertiser, 1 Nov. 1834; P.O. Dir. Staffs. (1850; 1854; 1860); Walsall Council House, deeds bdle. 682, deeds of 23 May 1865, 2 Mar. 1918.
[63] Kelly's Dir. Staffs. (1896); Walsall Red Book (1908).

[64] Walsall Council House, deeds bdle. 682, deed of 2 Mar. 1918.
[65] Ibid., abstract of title 1958; Homeshaw, Bloxwich, 206–7 and plate facing p. 209; Walsall Observer, 16 June 1973.   [66] See p. 226.
[67] Shaw, Staffs. i, app. to Gen. Hist. p. xvii.
[68] Tax. Eccl. (Rec. Com.), 243.
[69] Valor Eccl. (Rec. Com.), iii. 207.
[70] L. & P. Hen. VIII, xiii (2), p. 191.
[71] E 210/9919. The deed of surrender to the king is dated 9 June 1538 and the grant by the king to Dudley 1 Sept.; Dudley's grant to Taillour, however, is dated 14 June.
[72] Cal. Pat. 1569–72, p. 2; C 66/1360 mm. 29–31; Shaw, Staffs. ii. 64.
[73] Shaw, Staffs. ii. 64–5, stating that it was Edw.'s son Hen. who bought the rectory. Edw., however, made a settlement of it in 1596 at the time of Hen.'s marriage, reserving a life-interest to himself and his wife, with reversion to Hen.: B.M. Add. MS. 6704, ff. 88–9; S.H.C. xviii (1), 9–10.
[74] B.M. Add. MS. 6704, ff. 88–90v., 93v.–94; S.H.C. n.s. vi (1), 59; C 5/296/50; C.P. 25(2)/723/15 Chas. II Mich.; /726/35 Chas. II Mich.; 966/East. 8 Anne; C.P. 43/523 rot. 161; S.R.O., D. 1041, abstract of title of T. V. Dolphin to tithes of Walsall.

The Terrace from the south-east *c.* 1835

Bescot Hall from the south-west before the alterations of *c.* 1795

WALSALL

The White Hart, Caldmore, in 1845

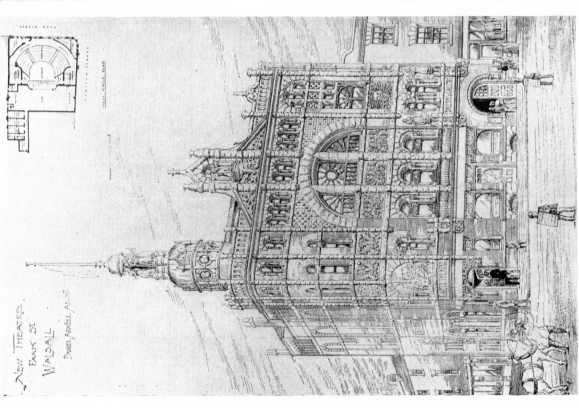

The Guildhall in 1867

The theatre opened in Park Street in 1890

WALSALL

Vernon Dolphin. Under an Act of 1795 Thomas sold the tithes in thirty-two lots; those from the property of the lord of the manor were settled in trust to meet half the repairs of the chancel of St. Matthew's.[75] The tithes from the rest of the foreign had passed by 1719 from the Leighs to William Persehouse of Reynold's Hall[76] and descended with the Reynold's Hall estate.[77] By c. 1830 the two largest shares of the tithes were held by Lord Bradford and John Walhouse, who were jointly responsible for the repair of the chancel.[78] By 1843 part of the tithes, including Lord Bradford's share, had been commuted. The rest were commuted that year for a rent-charge of £445, of which £330 was assigned to Lord Hatherton and the remainder to 139 other tithe owners.[79]

In the 15th century William Reynold held a large estate in Walsall. It included a house near the present Arboretum Road known by 1575 as Reynold's Hall.[80] Reynold was dead by 1488 and was succeeded by his granddaughter Elizabeth Pearte of Darlaston. She married William Flaxall and then William Walker of Darlaston, who in 1500 did fealty for the estate. By c. 1528 she had been succeeded by her son Richard Walker, who still held the estate in 1546 when his daughter Elizabeth married John Persehouse.[81] Walker was dead by 1551,[82] and Elizabeth died in or soon after 1552.[83] John Persehouse continued to hold the estate by the courtesy, and from 1561 to 1590 he redeemed the rights of the collateral heirs of Richard Walker.[84] He died in 1605 and was succeeded by John, his eldest son by his second wife.[85] The younger John died in 1636,[86] and the property passed to his son Richard, whose estates were sequestered for his delinquency in 1648.[87] He died in 1650 and his rights passed to his son John, who had obtained a discharge in 1649 but was still seeking confirmation of his title in 1652.[88] John was in possession by 1660 and died in 1667 or 1668, leaving as heir a son John, a minor (d. 1713).[89] The property passed successively to his sons John (d. between 1724 and 1735) and William (d. 1749) and William's son Richard (d. 1771).[90]

Richard Persehouse left the property in trust for his godson John Walhouse, son of Moreton Walhouse of Hatherton in St. Peter's, Wolverhampton.[91] His copyhold lands in Walsall, however, passed to his sister Elizabeth and her husband Robert Burgis of Offenham (Worcs.); in 1778 they agreed to sell them to the trustees.[92] John Walhouse died in 1835, leaving his Staffordshire estates to his nephew Edward John Littleton, created Baron Hatherton in 1835. The Reynold's Hall estate then descended with the barony until the early 20th century.[93] Most of it was apparently sold c. 1909; the Hatherton estate trustees still held ground-rents in Walsall in 1926 but in 1951 owned no property there.[94]

By 1588 Reynold's Hall included hall, parlour, kitchen, and outbuildings. In 1588–9 a further three-storeyed and jettied timber-framed block with a short range joining it to the old hall was built. It included kitchen, larder-house, and boulting-house on the ground floor, two chambers above with dormer-windows, and a cock-loft with three 'clerestories'. A porch was built at either end, with a study over the one facing the town. The old kitchen, apparently also timber-framed, was rebuilt and extended, and a new timber-framed barn, gatehouse, and brick and timber dovecot were constructed.[95] The house included at least 30 rooms in 1639,[96] and in 1749 20 rooms were mentioned.[97] It was still occupied in 1784 but had been demolished by 1800.[98]

Reynold's Hall Farm, south of the former hall and east of Persehouse Street, existed by 1819.[99] It occurs as Reynold's Hall in 1864 and Reynold's Hall Farm from 1882. It was occupied by tenants in the mid and later 19th century and was demolished in 1897 for the building of Foden Road.[1]

Apparently in the later 14th century John March held land or pasture, known as the Wastes, between the town and the park; it passed after his death to William de Walsall and Roger de Mollesley. By 1388 it had been bought by Lord Basset (d. 1390), who left it in trust for the endowment of a chantry in Lichfield cathedral.[2] Instead, however, the property,

[75] Act for vesting the settled estates of John Dolphin in trustees, 35 Geo. III, c. 52 (Priv. Act); S.R.O., D. 1041; Walsall Council House, Bescot deeds, bdle. 2, deed of 5 May 1796. For the Dolphins see H. Sanders, *Hist. and Antiquities of Shenstone* (1794), 135–8. For the name 'borough tithes' see W.T.C. II/50/25. For the apparent exemption from tithes of the borough township in 1843 see L.J.R.O., B/A/15/Walsall.

[76] S.R.O., D. 260/M/T/1/122a. The borough tithes seem to have been mortgaged to Persehouse by 1718: D. 1041, abstract of title of T. V. Dolphin to tithes of Walsall.

[77] S.R.O., D. 260/M/T/2/73, articles of agreement 9 Nov. 1726; ibid./M/T/1/122; ibid./M/T/4/71; W.T.C. II/50/36; see below.

[78] *Rep. Com. Eccl. Revenues* [67], pp. 504–5, H.C. (1835), xxii; White, *Dir. Staffs.* (1834; 1851); docs. at St. Matthew's, Walsall, Churchwardens' Accts. 1841–75, p. 9; Glew, *Walsall*, 25.

[79] L.J.R.O., B/A/15/Walsall (of which W.S.L., S. MS. 417/Walsall, is a partial transcript).

[80] S.R.O., D. 260/M/T/1/11b, deed of 12 Apr. 1575; Northants. R.O., I.L. 3192.

[81] C 1/683 no. 17; /686 no. 13; S.R.O., D. 260/M/F/1/5, ff. 51, 72v., 77; /M/T/1/11a, deeds of 17 Jan. and 3 Feb. 1545/6.

[82] D. 260/M/T/1/11a, deed of 20 Sept. 1551.

[83] Ibid. deed of 27 June 1552; /11b, letters patent of 6 May 1567.

[84] Ibid./11b, *passim*.

[85] Ibid./M/F/1/5, ff. 43, 72.

[86] *S.H.C.* v (2), 235; W.S.L. 45/56, folder 28, no. 12.

[87] S.R.O., D. 260/M/T/1/117; *Cal. Cttee. for Compounding*, iii. 1799–1800.

[88] *S.H.C.* v (2), 233–5; *Cal. Cttee. for Compounding*, iii. 1799–1800.

[89] W.T.C. II/13/49; D. 260/M/F/1/5, f. 152 (stating that John died in 1667); C 93/32/6 (giving the date of death as 25 Dec. 1668); W.S.L. 45/56, folder 27, no. 11.

[90] S.R.O., D. 260/M/T/1/120f, deeds of 8 June 1711 and 26 June 1719; /M/E/425/4, leases of 28 Feb. 1721/2 and 14 Feb. 1734/5; /M/T/1/122, will proved 24 Apr. 1749; /M/T/1/123, depositions of 28 Oct. 1773; W.S.L. 45/56, folder 27, no. 12; Shaw, *Staffs.* ii. 74; *Aris's Birmingham Gaz.* 16 Dec. 1771.

[91] D. 260/M/T/1/123, will of Ric. Persehouse.

[92] Ibid., articles of agreement 9 Mar. 1778.

[93] Ibid./3/8, will proved 17 June 1835; *Complete Peerage*, vi. 394–6.

[94] D. 260/M/E/173, Walsall rental 1908 (cancelled 1909); ex inf. Mr. E. Huntbach of Hand, Morgan & Owen, Stafford (1973). [95] D. 260/M/F/1/5, ff. iv.–16v.

[96] Ibid. ff. 174v.–176.

[97] *Aris's Birmingham Gaz.* 22 May 1749.

[98] *Bailey's Brit. Dir.* (1784), 468; Shaw, *Staffs.* ii. 75.

[99] S.R.O., D. 351/M/B/209, no. 1276.

[1] W.S.L., S. MS. 417/Walsall, no. 1967; *Kelly's Dir. Staffs.* (1884); S.R.O., D. 260/M/E/173, Walsall Estate Rentals, statements Mich. 1882, Mich. 1897; /174, 28 June 1864, p. 3; O.S. Map 6", Staffs. LXIII. NE. (1889 edn.); above p. 152.

[2] B.M. Eg. Roll 8467; *Cal. Pat.* 1401–5, 347; *Cat. Anct. D.* v, A 11372; above p. 170.

with a pasture called Bentleyland in the park, pasture in Walsall called the Coningre, a carucate and pasture at Clayhanger, and other pasture in Walsall, passed to Thomas, earl of Stafford (d. 1392).[3] The estate then descended with the Stafford earldom. In 1403 it was assigned to the queen during the minority of Humphrey, earl of Stafford.[4] The Staffords' title, however, was disputed by the earls of Warwick as heirs to Lord Basset's possessions in Walsall.[5] By 1403 Richard, earl of Warwick (d. 1439), was leasing Bentleyland from Lord Stafford[6] and by 1408 had apparently abandoned his claim to the Wastes.[7] On the other hand he seems by 1409 to have made good the claim to the Clayhanger property and the Coningre,[8] though Stafford's heirs continued to claim them until at least 1535.[9] The earls of Warwick continued to lease Bentleyland from the earl of Stafford until at least 1435,[10] although by 1441 they had ceased to pay the rent and the pasture had been re-absorbed into Walsall park.[11] The Wastes was held by the Staffords until the forfeiture of Edward, duke of Buckingham, in 1521.[12] In 1526 the Crown leased it to Robert (later Sir Robert) Acton for 21 years, and in 1528 granted it to him in tail male.[13] In 1531 the reversion was granted to Henry, Lord Stafford.[14] Acton sold his life interest in 1547 to John Dudley, earl of Warwick, later duke of Northumberland.[15] The property then descended with the manor of Walsall, Lord Stafford receiving compensation for the reversion in 1558.[16]

The house at Caldmore Green which is now the White Hart inn is said to have belonged to the Hawe family in the 17th century.[17] They had already acquired property in Walsall from the Flaxall family in the earlier 16th century. Thomas Flaxall in the late 15th or early 16th century had held a house and land in Walsall, which descended to his son Roger and then to his four daughters, Joan, wife of John Hawe, Elizabeth, wife of Richard Avery, Agnes, wife of Robert Wykes or Wilkes, and Eleanor, a spinster. The daughters held it jointly at some time before 1529, but John Hawe later bought the rights of his sisters-in-law. He was dead by 1548; his widow Joan died in 1558, leaving the property to their son Nicholas (d. 1560). It then apparently passed to Nicholas's nephew George, who also inherited land in Walsall from Nicholas and his brother George (d. 1558).[18] He died in 1605 and was succeeded by his son, another George.[19]

George Hawe acquired a house and land in Caldmore and further property in Walsall by his marriage to Mary, daughter of John Hall of Caldmore (d. 1622). George was living in Caldmore by 1635.[20] During the Civil War he moved to Lichfield; his property was sequestered because of his delinquency but was granted in 1644 to Mary, who had compounded for it. The estate had again been confiscated by 1646 and was still under sequestration in 1648. It later passed to George Hawe's eldest son George, a parliamentarian (d. 1660),[21] his grandson George (d. 1679), his great-grandson John (d. 1721), and his great-great-grandson, another John, who died apparently in 1755, leaving his property to his daughter Mary. In 1764 she married Thomas Parker of Park Hall in Caverswall (d. 1797). The property passed to his son Robert (d. 1806), who left it to his brother Thomas Hawe Parker.[22] Thomas sold most of it in lots in 1814.[23] If the identification of the house with the White Hart is correct, it was presumably included in the sale, as it was an inn by 1818.[24] After numerous changes of ownership it passed in 1966 to Ansells Brewery Ltd.,[25] the owner in 1973.

The White Hart inn dates from the later 17th century and was presumably built by George Hawe (d. 1679), who is said to have improved the estate.[26] It was probably preceded by a timber-framed house, the timbers of which were reused in the present roof. The present house, of two storeys and attics, is of brick with moulded-brick dressings. It includes a principal range with gabled projections at the rear forming a double-depth plan, and a cross-wing and projecting block at the east end. A porch in the angle of the main range and the wing marks the original entrance. All four fronts are surmounted by shaped gables and have brick-mullioned windows; two canted bay-windows, rising through two storeys, on the south front of the main range probably lit the hall, the parlour, and the principal bedrooms. On the north front are three gables; the two easternmost are original, and there are canted bays, apparently original, below them. The third gable marks the position of the stair. About 1884 the interior of the house was replanned, much of the brickwork was restored, a new front door was inserted, and a bay-window was added to the cross-wing.[27] The inn has since been twice extended, first at the north-west corner when the north-west gable was rebuilt, and later at the north-east corner.

[3] Willmore, *Walsall*, 75; C 136/76 m. 59; B.M. Eg. Rolls 8468–9.

[4] *Cal. Pat.* 1401–5, 328, 347; *Cal. Close*, 1402–5, 237.

[5] *Complete Peerage*, xii. 179–84; B.M. Eg. Rolls 8469 sqq.; S.R.O., D. 641/1/2/53.

[6] B.M. Eg. Rolls 8480, 8482.   [7] Ibid. 8488.

[8] Ibid. 8488–9; *Cal. Close*, 1405–9, 186.

[9] S.R.O., D. 641/1/2/108. In 1576 Clayhanger was part of the demesne lands of Walsall manor: S.R.O., D. 1287/1/2, survey of Walsall manor, 1576, m. 1.

[10] B.M. Eg. Roll 8525; S.R.O., D. 641/1/2/53.

[11] B.M. Eg. Rolls 8530 sqq. Yet the rent was recorded in the Stafford estate accounts without allowance for non-payment until 1484: S.R.O., D. 641/1/2/54–76.

[12] Willmore, *Walsall*, 75; S.R.O., D. 641/1/2/53 sqq.; *L. & P. Hen. VIII*, iv (1), p. 991.

[13] *L. & P. Hen. VIII*, iv (1), p. 991; iv (2), p. 1896.

[14] Ibid. v, p. 176.   [15] *Cal. Pat.* 1560–3, 150–1.

[16] Ibid. 1557–8, 254; 1560–3, 150; Wards 7/45/110; S.R.O., D. 1287/8/2, map.

[17] A. E. Everitt, 'The Old Houses in our Neighbourhood', *T.B.A.S.* 1871, 11.

[18] *S.H.C.* 1931, 151; C 1/381 no. 57; C 3/94/12; S.R.O., D. 260/M/F/1/8, Walsall foreign rental; Fink, *Queen Mary's Grammar Sch.* plate facing p. 144.

[19] C 142/298 no. 88.

[20] S.R.O., D. 260/M/F/1/5, f. 115v.; /M/T/2/7/8.

[21] *S.H.C.* 4th ser. i. 191; W.S.L., S. MS. 339 (iii), pp. 381–9; *Cal. Cttee. for Compounding*, i. 89; Willmore, *Walsall*, 290.

[22] Shaw, *Staffs.* ii. 74; W.S.L. 45/56, folder 31, Persehouse v. Hawe, pp. 1–6; Act for setting aside settlements made by John Hawe, 3 Anne, c. 66 (Priv. Act); *Staffs. Advertiser*, 9 Dec. 1797; W.S.L., D. 1798/291a, abstract of title of T. H. Parker, 1814 (wrongly giving the date of the Act as 1703); W.T.C. II/50/27/41; *Gent. Mag.* xxxiv. 250.

[23] *Staffs. Advertiser*, 8 Jan. 1814; W.S.L., D. 1798/290–291a.

[24] Parson and Bradshaw, *Dir. Staffs.* (1818).

[25] Deeds at Ansells Brewery, Aston Cross, Birmingham.

[26] Shaw, *Staffs.* ii. 74.

[27] *Building News*, 12 Dec. 1884; O.S. Map 1/500, Staffs. LXIII. 10. 25 (1886 edn.); *Walsall Red Book* (1912), plate facing p. 224; plate facing p. 177 above.

In the 15th century the house on Sutton Road later known as Wood End Farm and land at Wood End were held by William Shelfield. The estate passed to his daughter Eleanor and her husband William Burgess, a Leicester carpenter, who in 1493 granted it to the chaplain of John Flaxall's chantry.[28] In 1554 it was included in the endowments of Walsall grammar school, which held it until 1894. The governors then sold it to E. J. Shannon, a Walsall clothing manufacturer (d. 1913). His executors sold it in 1917 to the tenant, T. W. Downes.[29] Downes died in 1949; the farm passed to his widow Evelyn and on her death in 1956 to their children, Thomas, Gilbert, and Joan Downes. In 1959 Thomas and Gilbert released their rights to Joan, who still owned the property in 1973.[30]

The 15th-century farm-house apparently stood within a moat c. 100 yd. west of Sutton Road.[31] Three sides of the moat survived until the later 1960s when the ditches were filled in;[32] traces were still visible in 1973. By 1784 the house had been rebuilt on a site east of the moat.[33] The present house, a brick building nearer the road, dates from 1836.[34]

The other endowments in Walsall granted to the grammar school in 1554 consisted of former chantry lands in Bloxwich, Caldmore, Harden, and the borough.[35] The governors acquired further property in Little Bloxwich in 1657.[36] They sold their Walsall estate in parcels from c. 1921.[37]

In 1549 the Crown sold land called 'Yeld feldes' in Little Bloxwich and other property there to speculators. It had belonged to the chantry in Walsall church founded by John de Beverley and William Coleson, who had given houses and land in the parish as part of the endowment in 1365.[38] The estate passed to John Bowes (d. 1551) and then to his son John, who sold it in 1559 to Francis Cockayne.[39] Cockayne was living at Bloxwich at his death in 1568 or 1569 and left his property to his wife Mary for her life.[40] She died there in 1582; one of her executors was Gilbert Wakering,[41] who apparently acquired some of the estate.[42] In 1586 he was confirmed in possession of two houses and land in Walsall and Bloxwich by William Pirton and his wife Dorothy, daughter and heir of Francis Cockayne.[43] In 1587 Wakering bought further property in Bloxwich from Edmund, Lord Sheffield, and

from Richard Middlemore and in 1590 acquired meadow and pasture there from John Stone.[44] By 1593 he was living at Bloxwich in a house known by 1596 as Yieldfields.[45] He acquired further land in Bloxwich and Goscote in 1598 and 1600 from James and Edward Noell.[46] He was knighted in 1604 and died in 1616.[47] The estate passed successively to his nephew John Wakering[48] and to John's son Dionysius,[49] whose daughter and heir Mary married Francis St. John of Longthorpe (Northants.). St. John held the estate in 1675. By 1770 it had passed to Sir Robert Bernard of Huntingdon, son of St. John's daughter Mary; it was then 210 a. in extent.[50] Bernard had sold it to Henry Vernon of Hilton in St. Peter's, Wolverhampton, by 1776.[51] The Vernon family remained owners until 1936 or 1937 when they sold the estate to the tenant, Mrs. M. E. Yates. In 1958 she settled it on her children Walter and Geoffrey Yates and Mrs. P. Whitehouse; they still held it in 1973. It then included c. 400 a. in Walsall and a farm in Newtown in Essington (in Bushbury).[52]

The present Yieldfields Hall dates largely from the 18th century. It is a red-brick double-depth building with three storeys and cellars. There is a central entrance hall approached from the south front and leading to a staircase at the rear; it is flanked by two rooms on either side. Seventeenth-century panelling on the first floor and some reused timbers in the cellars were probably taken from the earlier house. In the earlier 19th century a two-storeyed kitchen block was added on the north side of the house, and the front range was extended eastwards c. 1900.[53]

From 1599 Henry Stone, mayor of Walsall in 1604–5, bought several properties in the parish.[54] By 1617 his holdings included five burgages and several part-burgages in the borough, and a house and land in the foreign.[55] The house was apparently in Birmingham Street.[56] In 1624 he bought another house, a windmill, and lands in Walsall and Great Bloxwich.[57] By his death in 1642 he also held land in Cannock, Yardley (Worcs.), and Castle Bromwich (Warws.). Under his will his property passed to his nephew Henry Stone of Plymouth, who was required to occupy his house in Walsall.[58] The younger Henry, a prominent parliamentarian, died in 1689.[59] He left his property to his second son

[28] Sims, Cal. of Deeds, p. 26.
[29] Cal.Pat. 1553–4, 285; deeds in possession of Pearman Smith & Sons Ltd., Walsall, deeds of 31 Oct. 1894 and 30 Apr. 1917.
[30] Ex inf. Mr. J. A. Walker of Pearman Smith & Sons, Miss J. M. Downes, and Mr. G. W. Downes (1973).
[31] Sims, Cal. of Deeds, p. 26; V.C.H. Staffs. i. 368.
[32] Ex inf. Mr. Downes.
[33] Fink, Queen Mary's Grammar Sch. front end-paper.
[34] Ibid. 249.
[35] Cal. Pat. 1553–4, 205.
[36] 9th Rep. Com. Char. H.C. 258, p. 566 (1823), ix.
[37] Fink, Queen Mary's Grammar Sch. 239.
[38] Cal. Pat. 1364–7, 165; 1549–51, 125–6; below p. 228.
[39] C 142/97 no. 68; S.H.C. xiii. 209.
[40] S.H.C. 1938, 195; Prob. 11/56 (P.C.C. 45 Martyn).
[41] L.J.R.O., will proved 17 Aug. 1582.
[42] Stained glass of the 16th century over a doorway in the house includes the arms of Cockayne and his wife and those of Wakering: Homeshaw, Bloxwich, 97–8. For Wakering see V.C.H. Staffs. v. 59, 62.
[43] S.H.C. xv. 171. For Dorothy see Prob. 11/56 (P.C.C. 45 Martyn); /61 (P.C.C. 44 Bakon), f. 346.
[44] S.H.C. xv. 177–8; xvi. 98.

[45] S.R.O., D.(W.)1721/3/90; D. 260/M/F/1/5, f. 39v.
[46] S.H.C. xvi. 181, 198.
[47] W. A. Shaw, Knights of Eng. ii. 129; C 142/401 no. 116.
[48] C 142/401 no. 116; Prob. 11/129 (P.C.C. Weldon 6); S.R.O., D. 260/M/F/1/8, ct. of recog. and survey, 1617, p. 23.
[49] Visitations of Essex, i (Harl. Soc. xiii), 513–14; Homeshaw, Bloxwich, 100, stating that he lived at Yieldfields in 1649.
[50] B.A.A., C. 370, pp. 1–2; W.S.L., S. MS. 453; Burke, Ext. & Dorm. Baronetcies (1838), 59, 562; Visitations of Essex, ii (Harl. Soc. xiv), 613–14; Visitations of Northants. 1681 (Harl. Soc. lxxvii), 163.
[51] W.S.L., S. MS. 453; Homeshaw, Bloxwich, 102–3.
[52] Homeshaw, Bloxwich, 103; ex inf. Mrs. P. Whitehouse (1973).
[53] Ex inf. Mrs. Whitehouse.
[54] S.H.C. xvi. 189, 197, 208, 219; n.s. iii. 47, 63.
[55] S.R.O., D. 260/M/F/1/8, ct. of recog. and survey, 1617, pp. 8, 9, 12–14, 24.
[56] Willmore, Walsall, 306.
[57] S.H.C. n.s. x (1), 49.
[58] C 5/184/33.
[59] Ibid.; above p. 145.

Samuel, after whose death it was to pass successively to his third son Henry and his grandson Samuel Bury of Plymouth.[60] He thereby disinherited his grandson Henry Stone of Plymouth, son of his eldest son John.[61] Samuel Stone was still alive in 1698 but had died by 1700.[62] After proceedings in Chancery the estate seems to have been divided between his daughters, Sarah, Elizabeth, and Anne, Samuel Bury, and their cousin Henry Stone.[63] Some or all of the Walsall property, including land at Bloxwich, passed to a Mary Stone, who sold it in 1706 to Jonas Slaney. It was later owned by Matthew Stubbs, whose descendants held it in the early 1750s. Most of the property was evidently sold in lots in the late 18th century.[64]

Henry Stone the younger was living in Birmingham Street in 1662 when he rebuilt a house there, presumably that left to him by Henry Stone the elder. By the late 18th century it had become the Wheatsheaf inn and was demolished c. 1813.[65]

In or before 1272 William de Morteyn granted Halesowen abbey land in Walsall said to be 2½ a. in 1275 and 3 a. in 1291.[66] The abbey had acquired further property in the parish by the Dissolution.[67]

Dean Yotton's chantry, founded in 1513 in Lichfield cathedral, was said in 1535 to hold land in Walsall, though the property was apparently not recorded at the suppression.[68] By the mid 1540s St. Mary's guild at Lichfield held property in Little Bloxwich, and St. Mary's chantry at Wombourn held land at Wood End.[69]

ECONOMIC HISTORY. AGRICULTURE. By at least the later 12th century most of Walsall parish lay within Cannock forest. Only the area south and east of the Holbrook was excluded.[70] There was evidently arable cultivation about the time of the Conquest: some former arable at Bescot was waste in 1086.[71] Presumably there was arable farming by the time the manor was granted to Herbert le Rous in 1159,[72] and the area of cultivation was gradually extended by assarting. Herbert was evidently making assarts at Walsall in 1160.[73] In the earlier 13th century William le Rous's charter to the burgesses reserved his right to approve the waste.[74] In 1286 eleven tenants were presented for purpres-

tures, mostly of 1-acre plots.[75] In the late 13th and early 14th centuries the lords made grants of waste for inclosure in parcels of up to 40 a. in Bescot, Bloxwich, and Birchills.[76] By the later Middle Ages a mixed pattern of common-field farming and cultivation in severalty had emerged.

As in other parishes in Cannock forest[77] there were several groups of small and irregular common fields, associated with the centres of settlement at Walsall, Great and Little Bloxwich, and Harden. The Walsall fields lay on the north, east, and south sides of the town. Wisemore, which was bounded by Park Street, Ford Brook, Walsall Brook, and probably by the present Stafford Street, occurs between 1409 and 1689.[78] Further east were Walsall field and the 'field behind the town', both mentioned in 1349.[79] They may at first have been distinct fields, but they formed one field by 1567.[80] The combined field extended from Rushall Street westward beyond the Holbrook,[81] presumably to Ford Brook. Middley, which is mentioned from the late 13th century, was another name for that part of it east of the Holbrook.[82] The field was still open in 1636.[83]

Other fields lay north-east of the town. A common field called Holbrook occurs between 1319 and 1681; it was sometimes termed Walsall Holbrook to distinguish it from Holbrook in Rushall.[84] It presumably existed by the late 13th century, since Hungerfurlong, later part of it, is mentioned at that time.[85] The Holbrook was evidently the northern boundary of the field, which extended from the Rushall road almost to the Sutton road near its junction with the modern Broadway.[86] South of Holbrook field lay Churchgreave field, which existed by the late 13th century and remained open until at least 1735.[87] Chuckery Road probably marks the boundary of Holbrook and Churchgreave fields; the latter extended west at least as far as the present Eldon Street, south to the line of Kinnerley Street, and east probably to the line of Prince's Avenue.[88] West of it lay two small areas of common field. The Lee occurs as a common field in 1324 and 1438, though in 1409 and 1430 it was said to be part of Churchgreave field.[89] It may have been the field called Lordeslegh or Lordesheye mentioned in 1399 and 1410.[90] Paddock was apparently treated as a separate common field in the late 16th century.[91]

[60] W.S.L. 45/56, folder 73, will proved 1690.
[61] C 5/184/33.   [62] C 5/283/31; 285/72.
[63] C 5/283/31; Willmore, Walsall, 306.
[64] 9th Rep. Com. Char. H.C. 258, pp. 588–90 (1823), ix; Shaw, Staffs. ii. 74.
[65] W.T.C. II/13/49; Willmore, Walsall, 306; Walsall Observer, 2 Dec. 1966; Shaw, Staffs. ii. 74.
[66] Cal. Inq. p.m. iv, p. 348; Tax. Eccl. (Rec. Com.), 251.
[67] Valor Eccl. (Rec. Com.), iii. 206; S.H.C. xii (1), 186; Sims, Cal. of Deeds, pp. 47–9.
[68] Valor Eccl. iii. 140; S.H.C. 1915, 159; L. & P. Hen. VIII, i (2), p. 934.
[69] S.R.O., D. 260/M/F/1/8, Walsall foreign rental; S.H.C. 1915, 171, 354–5.
[70] S.H.C. v (1), 166–7, 172, 175, 178; V.C.H. Staffs. ii. 336, 338.
[71] V.C.H. Staffs. iv. 38, no. 6.
[72] See p. 169.   [73] S.H.C. i. 29–31.
[74] See p. 212; W.T.C. I/1.   [75] S.H.C. v (1), 172.
[76] B.M. Harl. MS. 2131, ff. 11–14; S.H.C. x (1), 6–7; xiii. 145–6; Walsall Records, 33, 49; S.R.O., D. 239/M/2758; D. 593/A/2/22/35.
[77] V.C.H. Staffs. v. 126–7; Trans. Lich. & S. Staffs. Arch. Soc. iii. 28–39.
[78] B.M. Eg. Roll 8489; W.S.L. 344/34, 346/34, 348/34; S.R.O., D. 260/M/F/1/5, f. 124.

[79] W.S.L., D. 1798/84, deed of 20 Apr. 1349.
[80] S.R.O., D. 260/M/T/1/49, deed of 20 Aug. 1567.
[81] Ibid., deed of 15 Mar. 1616/17; /M/T/1/39, deed of 8 Apr. 1587; L.J.R.O., B/V/6/Walsall, 1636.
[82] Sims, Cal. of Deeds, p. 3; D. 260/M/T/1/1b, deed of 24 Nov. 1567; /M/T/1/49, deeds of 24 June 1587, 15 Mar. 1616/17.   [83] L.J.R.O., B/V/6/Walsall, 1636.
[84] W.S.L., D. 1798/84, deeds of 2 Apr. 1319, 26 Feb. 1374/5; S.R.O., D. 260/M/T/1/73, deed of 25 Mar. 1681.
[85] Sims, Cal. of Deeds, p. 3; S.R.O., D. 1287/1/2, survey of Walsall manor, 1576, m. 2; D. 260/M/T/1/73, deed of 25 Mar. 1681.
[86] W.S.L., D. 1798/84, deed of 2 Apr. 1319; W.S.L., S. MS. 417/Walsall, nos. 1929, 1954, 1971; B.M. Eg. Roll 8498; S.R.O., D. 1287/8/2, map.
[87] Sims, Cal. of Deeds, p. 3; S.R.O., D. 260/M/E/425/4, lease of 12 Feb. 1734/5. The spelling of the name varies.
[88] S.R.O., D. 1287/8/2, map; W.S.L., D. 1798/100, deed of 6 Dec. 1476; S. MS. 417/Walsall, nos. 1878, 1944–5, 1947; O.S. Map 6", Staffs. LXIII. SE. (1890 and later edns.).
[89] Walsall Records, 48; W.S.L., D. 1798/83, deeds of 12 June 1376, 22 Dec. 1438; S.R.O., D. 260/M/F/1/5, f. 79.
[90] B.M. Eg. Rolls 8477, 8489.
[91] W.T.C. I/140.

The two principal fields south of the town were Vicar's field, mentioned from 1323, and Windmill field, mentioned from 1341.[92] They seem at first to have been distinct but were united by 1570; they were apparently divided again at some time between 1604 and 1637 and reunited at some time between 1679 and 1731.[93] In 1735 Windmill field was said to have come to be known as Furfield, but it was again called Windmill or Vicar's field in 1756 and Windmill field in 1766.[94] The boundaries of the fields are uncertain. References to land in Vicar's field from the late 16th to the 18th century appear to show that it extended from the Wednesbury to the Birmingham road, but the combined field may have been meant.[95] There were several smaller common fields in the south of the parish. Lee field next to Windmill field occurs between 1502 and 1619.[96] Mill Furlong, which lay between Tasker Street, Wednesbury Road, and Long Meadow, was a common field from at least 1502 and apparently to the 18th century.[97] A field called Stockinge is mentioned in 1348; it was apparently in Palfrey and presumably resulted from assarting.[98] A field called Armescote occurs between 1310 and 1332; it apparently lay south of the town mill.[99]

There were also common fields in the Birchills area. Synderhulleffeld, which is mentioned in 1333, may be identifiable with Synderhill, an inclosed pasture in Green Lane mentioned from 1565.[1] A common field called Long field near Birchills is mentioned in 1733.[2]

At Great Bloxwich there were eight common fields. Chapel field is mentioned from 1576 and was also known as Windmill field in the 18th century.[3] In 1763 it was bounded by the present High Street, Field Road, and Lichfield Road.[4] South-east of it lay Comwall field, which existed by c. 1300. It was also called Comberfield in 1652 and Big field in 1763, when it extended from High Street approximately to the present Ryle Street and from Field Road to Valley Road.[5] Another field lay between Blakenall Lane and the modern Guild Avenue; it extended almost to High Street on the south-west

and perhaps to Blakenall Heath on the north-east. It occurs as Brondardes field in 1544 and Brundards field in 1818.[6] Woodwall or Woodall field occurs between 1576 and 1818; it lay on the west side of High Street and Green Lane, but its other boundaries are uncertain.[7] Cockstall field is mentioned from 1579 and was still open in 1783 but had been inclosed by 1818. It evidently lay west of Bloxwich village and north of the present Central Drive.[8] Another field lay between Sneyd Brook and Mossley Lane. It occurs as Maltesleye c. 1300 and Mosley or Moseley from 1665. It was still open in 1783 but had been inclosed by 1818.[9] Two small common fields, Barnhall, which occurs between 1371 and 1696, and Litchkin or Clitchkin, mentioned in 1665 and 1696, probably resulted from collective or subdivided assarts. Barnhall lay on the parish boundary west of Broad Lane, and Litchkin adjoined it on the south.[10]

Several fields were associated with Little Bloxwich. Hoods field occurs between 1567 and 1693. By 1770 it seems to have been divided into Hodge, Low Hodge, and Little Hodge fields. It lay north of Comwall field, probably between Selman's Hill, High Street, and Lichfield Road; a close in the area was called Hooch Field in 1843.[11] Harehill field occurs in 1770; it lay between Hooch Field and Stoney Lane. Lydiatt field is mentioned from 1617. It lay immediately north of Comwall field; Lichfield Road was probably the northern boundary.[12] Mill field, which occurs from 1576, was on the west of Little Bloxwich village between Lichfield Road and Stoney Lane; part of it was still open in 1763 and was then called Little Mill field.[13] Hill and Long fields are mentioned from 1567. Their position is uncertain, but Hill field probably lay between Broad Lane, Bealey's Lane, and the parish boundary, and Long field south of it on the site of Long Field farm.[14] A common field called Turnoresland at Little Bloxwich is mentioned in 1351 and 1617; its site is unknown.[15]

Harden also had its common fields. Harden field occurs from 1513; it was also called Cadmans field

[92] W.S.L., D. 1798/84, deeds of 27 Nov. 1323, 2 Feb. 1340/1.

[93] Sims, *Cal. of Deeds*, pp. 36, 49; S.R.O., D. 260/M/T/1/69, deed of 15 Apr. 1637; /M/T/1/102t, deed of 22 Oct. 1679; /M/T/1/83, deed of 29 Apr. 1731.

[94] L.J.R.O., B/A/27(i), pp. 419–21; S.R.O., D. 260/M/E/425/4, leases of 12 Feb. 1734/5 and 8 July 1766.

[95] S.R.O., D. 260/M/T/1/81, deed of 6 Apr. 1581; /83, deed of 29 Apr. 1731; W.S.L., M. 442; Sims, *Cal. of Deeds*, pp. 46–7; L.J.R.O., B/V/6/Walsall, 1693 and 1701.

[96] S.R.O., D. 593/A/2/22/17, /19, /43; D. 260/M/F/1/8, ct. of recog. and survey, 1617, p. 30; D. 260/M/T/1/52.

[97] S.R.O., D. 593/A/2/22/17, /19, /43; D. 1287/6/14, deed of 19 Oct. 1618; D. 1287/8/2, map; W.S.L., S. MS. 417/Walsall, nos. 1382–5; L.J.R.O., B/V/6/Walsall, where it occurs as arable in successive copies of glebe terriers to 1786. By 1775, however, it was lammas land: below p. 182. For Long Meadow see ibid.

[98] Sims, *Cal. of Deeds*, p. 7; S.R.O., D. 260/M/T/1/1a, deed of 28 Mar. 1513. The name means 'a clearing of stumps': *Eng. Place-name Elements* (E.P.N.S.), ii. 156.

[99] *Walsall Records*, 29, 50; W.S.L., D. 1798/84, deed of 27 Nov. 1323.

[1] B.R.L. 608897; Sims, *Cal. of Deeds*, p. 34; S.R.O., D. 1287/8/2, map.   [2] W.S.L. 44/26/41.

[3] S.R.O., D. 1287/1/2, survey of Walsall manor, 1576, m. 3; W.S.L. 67/2/22; Homeshaw, *Bloxwich*, 132.

[4] S.R.O., D. 1287/8/2, map.

[5] Ibid.; D. 593/A/2/22/35; D. 1287/1/2, survey of Walsall manor, 1576, m. 3; W.C.L., box 25, no. 24; W.S.L., S. MS. 417/Walsall, no. 24. The spelling of Comwall varies.

[6] W.C.L., box 25, no. 22; S.R.O., D. 1287/8/2, map; W.S.L., S. MS. 417/Walsall, nos. 835, 839; *S.H.C.* 1931, 82–3. The spelling of the name varies considerably.

[7] S.R.O., D. 1287/1/2, survey of Walsall manor, 1576, m. 3; D. 1287/8/2, map; *S.H.C.* 1931, 82–3.

[8] S.R.O., D. 260/M/F/1/5, ff. 90v.–91v.; /M/T/2/12, deeds of 15 Mar. 1630/1 and 20 Oct. 1676; W.S.L. 35/1/48; S. MS. 417/Walsall, nos. 334–7. For the inclosure of 1818 see below.

[9] B.M. Harl. MS. 2131, ff. 12v.–13; S.R.O., D. 260/M/T/2/7, deed of 10 Apr. 1665; D. 351/M/B/209; W.C.L., box 6, no. 4; W.S.L. 35/1/48; S. MS. 453; S. MS. 417/Walsall, nos. 292, 295, 320.

[10] S.R.O., D. 239/M/3006; D. 798/1/1/33; D. 260/M/T/2/46, deed of 30 Mar. 1611; /T/2/7, deed of 10 Apr. 1665; W.T.C. II/251/11; W.S.L., S. MS. 417/Walsall, nos. 285–6, 298; Pearce, *Walsall*, 223; Willmore, *Walsall*, 441.

[11] W.S.L. 81/10/41; S.R.O., D. 260/M/F/1/8, ct. of recog. and survey, 1617, pp. 23, 25, 29; /M/T/2/34, deed of 16 Nov. 1686; L.J.R.O., B/V/6/Walsall, 1693; W.S.L., S. MS. 453; S. MS. 417/Walsall, no. 150.

[12] S.R.O., D. 260/M/F/1/8, ct. of recog. and survey, 1617, p. 23; L.J.R.O., B/V/6/Bloxwich, 1701; W.S.L., S. MS. 453 (Lidget and Harehill fields); S. MS. 417/Walsall, nos. 146, 546; *S.H.C.* 1931, 82–3.

[13] S.R.O., D. 1287/1/2, survey of Walsall manor, 1576, m. 3; /8/2, map.

[14] W.S.L. 81/10/41; S. MS. 453; S. MS. 417/Walsall, nos. 264, 267, 270, 281–2.

[15] Belvoir Castle MSS. no. 5141; S.R.O., D. 260/M/F/1/8, ct. of recog. and survey, 1617, p. 29.

in 1694, and part was apparently still open in 1726.[16] Two other fields occur as 'le fryssys' and 'le furfield' in 1513 and as Great and Little Fursons in 1617. Great Fursons was still open in 1627.[17] The location of those fields is unknown. Brundards field was evidently shared between Harden and Great Bloxwich.[18] A Mill field in Harden occurs in 1576, but it may have been the Little Bloxwich field of that name.[19]

Though there was inclosed arable in the parish by the early 14th century,[20] it may have resulted from assarting rather than incroachment on the common fields. Nevertheless inclosure of the fields had evidently begun before the mid 16th century: in the early 17th century John Persehouse recorded that the Lee had been inclosed immemorially.[21] He had himself inclosed land in Walsall field *c.* 1587 and in Holbrook field *c.* 1591.[22] Under an agreement with the freeholders of Walsall in 1594 he was to throw the latest inclosures open but might retain others in Walsall field, Holbrook, and Churchgreave field; further inclosure was forbidden.[23] It continued nevertheless: in 1653 an inclosure, probably in Holbrook, made by John's grandson was thrown down by rioters. A dispute ensued between Persehouse and the corporation but the result is not clear.[24] An inclosure in Windmill field occurs in 1722 and one in Churchgreave field in 1735;[25] in 1756 the new burial ground in Bath Street was described as recently inclosed out of Windmill field.[26] All the open fields of Walsall township had been inclosed by 1819.[27] At Bloxwich inclosures in Chapel field and Hoods field are mentioned in 1686 and in Harden field in 1726.[28] In 1818 the remaining open-field area, 190 a. in Chapel, Comwall, Lydiatt, Brundards, and Woodwall fields, was inclosed by agreement.[29]

There were several common meadows in the parish. Long Meadow, which lay south of the town east of Walsall Brook as far as Tasker Street, occurs from 1405. Most of it belonged to the lord of the manor by 1763.[30] By 1805 it formed part of lammas lands thrown open as common pasture in August.[31] Mill Furlong was also lammas land by 1775.[32] In 1410–11 the jurors of the manor court presented that Wisemore meadow, held by four tenants in severalty, was thrown open as common pasture when Wisemore field lay fallow.[33] Common meadows at Great Bloxwich included Leamore meadow by 1420,[34] Harden Mores by 1638,[35] and Wall meadow, which was east of Bloxwich Road, by 1642.[36] Nutt meadow, Hallow meadow, and Ford meadow, all evidently in Little Bloxwich, occur in 1617.[37] There were also parcels of meadow in the common fields. Meadow land in Walsall field is mentioned from 1349; it lay on either side of the Holbrook.[38] There was also meadow in Wisemore, Holbrook, and Vicar's fields.[39] From at least the 14th century, however, some meadow land was held in severalty.[40]

In the earlier 13th century William le Rous granted common pasture in the waste to the burgesses.[41] There was evidently intercommoning between Walsall and neighbouring forest parishes. Thus in 1281 Margery le Rous had common in Stonnall in Shenstone by right of her land in Walsall, and in 1307 William Hillary had like rights in Essington in Bushbury, as did Lord Bradford and his Bloxwich freeholders as late as 1809. Conversely, in 1304 the abbot of Osney (Oxon.) had common in Walsall belonging to his freehold in Stonnall.[42] The inhabitants of Walsall and other parishes retained common rights in Bentley Hay until the 17th century; Walsall abandoned its right in 1638.[43] In the 14th century assarting caused disputes about common rights in the parish,[44] and pasture was stinted by 1425.[45]

By the later 14th century encroachment on the waste was leading to its dismemberment and the emergence of individual commons, some of which later disappeared. 'Hendemere' Green in Bloxwich is mentioned in 1372,[46] and Stocking Green near Palfrey occurs in 1513.[47] Blakenall Heath existed by 1544[48] and Goscote Heath by 1568.[49] By 1617 the waste had been reduced to six principal commons: Wallington, Blakenall, Short, and Dead Man's Heaths, Birchills, and the Pleck.[50] By 1763 the commons had been reduced to four in Bloxwich and

[16] S.R.O., D. 260/M/T/1/1a, deed of 28 Mar. 1513; /T/2/49, will of Thos. Baker; L.J.R.O., B/V/6/Bloxwich, 1694.

[17] D. 260/M/T/1/1a, deed of 28 Mar. 1513; /M/F/1/8, ct. of recog. and survey, 1617, p. 30; W.C.L., box 25, no. 12.

[18] W.C.L., box 24, no. 3; S.R.O., D. 260/M/F/1/8, ct. of recog. and survey, 1617, p. 30.

[19] S.R.O., D. 1287/1/2, survey of Walsall manor, 1576, m. 10.

[20] *Walsall Records*, 34; W.S.L., D. 1798/84, deed of 16 May 1323.

[21] W.S.L., D. 1798/83, deed of 22 Dec. 1438, endorsement.

[22] S.R.O., D. 260/M/T/1/102c; /M/F/1/5, f. 24v.

[23] W.T.C. I/140.

[24] *Cal. S.P. Dom.* 1653–4, 180; Homeshaw, *Walsall*, 41–2.

[25] S.R.O., D.(W.)18/1/1, marriage settlement of Thos. Turnpenny and Mary Woodhouse; D. 260/M/E/425/4, lease of 12 Feb. 1734/5.

[26] L.J.R.O., B/A/27(i), pp. 419–21.

[27] S.R.O., D. 351/M/B/209.

[28] S.R.O., D. 260/M/T/2/34; /49, will of Thos. Baker, dated 31 Jan. 1726.

[29] *S.H.C.* 1931, 82–3. A map of 1819 (S.R.O., D. 351/M/B/209) shows no other open-field area in Bloxwich.

[30] Sims, *Cal. of Deeds*, p. 13; L.J.R.O., B/V/6/Walsall, 1682 and 1693; S.R.O., D. 1287/8/2.

[31] S.R.O., D. 1287/1/37, valuation of Walsall estate, 1805.

[32] Ibid. 1/2, survey of Walsall, 1775.

[33] S.R.O., D. 260/M/F/1/5, f. 172.

[34] Sims, *Cal. of Deeds*, p. 14.

[35] W.C.L., box 6, no. 4.

[36] Ibid. no. 2; L.J.R.O., B/V/6/Bloxwich, 1694.

[37] S.R.O., D. 260/M/F/1/8, ct. of recog. and survey, 1617, p. 28.

[38] W.S.L., D. 1798/84, deeds of 20 Apr. 1349, 22 Jan. 1475/6; S.R.O., D. 260/M/T/1/1b, deed of 24 Nov. 1567; /49, deed of 15 Mar. 1616/17; L.J.R.O., B/V/6/Walsall, 1636.

[39] S.R.O., D. 260/M/T/1/1b, deed of 7 June 1563; /M/F/1/5, f. 107; Sims, *Cal. of Deeds*, p. 38.

[40] W.S.L., D. 1798/84, deeds of 16 May 1323, 2 June 1370. [41] Sims, *Cal. of Deeds*, p. 1.

[42] *S.H.C.* v (1), 149–50; vii (1), 124, 189; S.R.O., D. 1287/18/24/business corresp. 1807–9, Hen. Bowman to Lord Bradford, 11 July 1809; D. 1287/box 7/manorial accts. etc., mins. of evid. in support of Lord Bradford's claim, 30 Mar. 1809.

[43] E 134/35 and 36 Eliz. I Mich./19; W.T.C. II/8/1 and 2; below p. 271.

[44] *S.H.C.* vii (1), 124; x (1), 6–7; xiii. 145–6.

[45] S.R.O., D. 260/M/F/1/5, f. 171.

[46] S.R.O., D. 239/M/3006.

[47] D. 260/M/T/1/1a, deed of 28 Mar. 1513.

[48] W.C.L., box 25, no. 14. [49] Ibid. box 24, no. 26.

[50] S.R.O., D. 260/M/F/1/8, ct. of recog. and survey, 1617, p. 34. The acreages of Short and Dead Man's Heaths given there are smaller than in a survey of 1805: W.C.L., box 21, no. 10.

Blakenall with an area of *c.* 37 a.[51] In 1805 they
were little smaller[52] but by 1843 had shrunk to less
than 25 a.; three other small plots of waste, *c.* 2½ a.
altogether, survived in the south of the parish beside Park Brook.[53]

Encroachments on the waste in the 17th and 18th
centuries were sometimes for industrial purposes,
particularly brick-making.[54] More were inclosures
for cultivation, but most were occasioned by cottage-
building. Recent cottage-building on Short Heath
is mentioned in 1576,[55] and on the waste at Townend, Great Bloxwich, and Little Bloxwich in 1617.[56]
The lord of the manor in 1677 drew £5 6s. 4d. rent
from cottages and inclosures on the waste.[57] In 1763
209 tenants of the manor occupied 211 separate encroachments in Walsall and Bloxwich, totalling 42 a.;
most were cottages.[58] A survey of 1805 lists some
300 encroachments, mostly at Townend, on the
Bloxwich commons, and along the roads from Walsall to Bloxwich. The improved value of the inclosed land was noted, and evidently as a result of
the survey the rents had been tripled by 1810.
The rental continued to rise until 1840, but from
1842 the cottages were sold off.[59]

Labour services on the demesne were still owed
by the customary tenants in the late 14th century.
Each tenant had to plough one day at the winter
and Lenten sowings, to mow one day a year, and to
harvest the lord's corn for three days. The services,
no longer exacted in kind, were assessed on 20½
tenements. In 1385–6 services were commuted for
the duration of the tenancy on 11½ tenements and
on an annual basis on the rest. From 1401, however,
the tenants refused to pay the rents in lieu of services; although the assessment was evidently reduced in 1440–1, the strike continued.[60]

There was a three-course rotation on the demesne
by 1343,[61] and probably in the common fields too:
in 1410–11 Wisemore field was said to lie fallow
every third year.[62] In the 16th and 17th centuries
crops grown in the open fields included rye, wheat,
mongcorn (mixed corn), barley, oats, and dredge.[63]
Hemp and flax were also grown in both Walsall and
Bloxwich, and a hempleck in Rushall Street is mentioned in 1597.[64] A former flax oven in Chapel field,
Bloxwich, was used as a Methodist chapel in the
late 18th century.[65] Lands in Walsall advertised for
sale in 1813 included Flaxoven Croft and Flaxoven

Piece.[66] Hops, peas, apples,[67] and plums[68] were
grown in the earlier 17th century.

Animal husbandry may have been significant at
an early date. In 1178–9 the sheriff was allowed 32s.
for restocking the manor farm.[69] In the later
1380s the lord bought bullocks to fatten in the park
over the summer; 55 were purchased in 1388–9.[70]
In 1417 twelve fat oxen were sent from Walsall to
Worcester for the lord's household in France.[71]
There is evidence of cattle-keeping in the later 15th
century,[72] and in the 16th and earlier 17th centuries
it was probably a more important source of wealth
than arable farming. Most farmers kept cattle, including dairy and beef animals and oxen. The herd
was often worth several times the value of the crops
on a holding. In 1605 John Persehouse of Reynold's
Hall had at least 64 cattle.[73] Many farmers also kept
sheep; few had more than 40, but John Persehouse
in 1599 had over 150 wethers, hog-sheep, ewes, and
lambs.[74] He let pasture to outsiders for stock-
fattening[75] but also sent his own sheep outside the
parish for summer pasturing.[76] Pigs and poultry
were frequently kept; in 1588 Persehouse commissioned a large timber-framed hen-house and
swine-cote.[77] There is evidence of bee-keeping in
the early 17th century.

By 1801 agriculture was already of secondary importance owing to urbanization, but it still employed 1,073 people living in the foreign and 44
people in the borough, or some 17 per cent of all
workers in the parish.[78] By 1921 the work-force had
fallen to 366, less than one per cent of those employed in the county borough,[79] and by 1966 only
90 people were employed in agriculture.[80] Yet
much of the parish remained farm-land. In 1842
39 per cent was meadow and pasture and 42 per
cent arable.[81] In 1951 3,047 a. (35 per cent) of
8,780 a. in the borough was farm-land.[82] Walsall
farming was probably affected by the trend towards
milk production for the urban market: in 1851 besides 12 farmers there were 6 cow-keepers, mostly
in or near the town.[83]

In the early 1950s mixed farming was practised;
stock included cattle, horses, sheep, and poultry.
There were 19 milk producers.[84] Farming continued
to decline in the 1950s and 1960s, especially in the
Wood End area where Daffodil farm, Gillity
Greaves, and Daisy Bank farm were all broken up

[51] S.R.O., D. 1287/8/2.
[52] W.C.L., box 21, no. 10.
[53] W.S.L., S. MS. 417/Walsall, nos. 174, 265, 497, 642, 1290–1, 1293.
[54] S.R.O., D. 260/M/F/1/8, ct. of recog. and survey, 1617, p. 6; D. 1287/1/8, Roger Holmes's acct. 1766–71, 28 June 1768, 9 Sept. 1769.
[55] D. 1287/1/2, survey of Walsall manor, 1576, m. 13.
[56] D. 260/M/F/1/8, ct. of recog. and survey, 1617, pp. 5–6.
[57] D. 1287/1/2, rent roll of Walsall manor, 1677.
[58] Ibid./8/2.
[59] Ibid./1/37, Walsall cottages 1805 and Walsall cottage rents 1810 sqq.; D. 1287/Colliery Box no. 2, estate corresp. 1843–53, cottage sales 1842–8.
[60] S.R.O., D. 641/1/2/32; B.M. Eg. Rolls 8477, 8493, 8514, 8530–41.
[61] S.H.C. 1913, 98.
[62] S.R.O., D. 260/M/F/1/5, f. 172.
[63] Except where otherwise indicated, statements about 16th- and 17th-century farming in this and the next para. are based on a sample of probate inventories in L.J.R.O.
[64] S.R.O., D. 260/M/T/1/30, deed of 8 Apr. 1597.
[65] See p. 245.
[66] W.S.L., D. 1798/290, list of lands in Walsall belonging

to T. H. Parker to be sold 24 Jan. 1813.
[67] S.R.O., D. 260/M/F/1/5, f. 82.
[68] C 3/334/37.
[69] S.H.C. i. 93; above p. 169.
[70] S.R.O., D. 641/1/2/32; B.M. Eg. Roll 8467.
[71] B.M. Eg. Roll 8501.
[72] S.H.C. n.s. iii. 133; n.s. iv. 98–9.
[73] S.R.O., D. 260/M/F/1/5, f. 76v.
[74] Ibid. f. 59v.
[75] Ibid. f. 76.
[76] Ibid. ff. 36v., 59v., 80, 86.
[77] Ibid. ff. 4v., 5v.; Joan Thirsk, 'Horn and Thorn in Staffs.' N. Staffs. Jnl. of Field Studies, ix. 7.
[78] Census, 1801.
[79] Census, 1921.
[80] Sample Census, 1966, Economic Activity County Leaflet: Staffs., 5.
[81] L.J.R.O., B/A/15/Walsall, p. 46.
[82] Walsall Observer, 3 July 1953.
[83] R. Sturgess, 'Response of Agriculture in Staffs. to the Price Changes of the 19th century' (Univ. of Manchester Ph.D. thesis, 1965), 362; White, Dir. Staffs. (1851).
[84] I. Davies, 'Agriculture of W. Midland Conurbation' (Birmingham Univ. M.A. thesis, 1953), 294 and map 29.

for housing development.[85] In 1973 Hay Head and Wood End farms survived; the latter included 90 a. of land principally devoted to sheep.[86] Of four farms covering c. 570 a. in the north of the borough one ran sheep and another kept beef cattle and goats; the rest combined wheat and barley with dairying and beef-fattening.[87]

In 1086 there was woodland at Bloxwich three furlongs by one.[88] Much of the medieval woodland in the parish, however, was presumably at Walsall Wood.[89] The wood of Birchills is mentioned in the early 14th century.[90] In 1523 Sir John Sutton leased woods in Walsall to William Stone, a Bloxwich lorimer, granting him licence to fell the trees.[91] The demands of the iron industry encouraged felling. About 1618 John Persehouse sold 103 cords of wood to Thomas Parkes, a Wednesbury ironmaster,[92] and in 1770 19 cords and a foot of cordwood from Lord Mountrath's estate were bought by John Wright, an ironmaster.[93] By the early 19th century the only large wood in Walsall was Reed's Wood. In 1805 it was stated to be inclosed and open every seven years alternately; when open it was a common. By 1839 it was being worked as a coal mine. The common rights were extinguished in the mid 1880s when the area was laid out as a park.[94] In 1843 there was only 12 a. of woodland in Walsall, most of it plantations at Hay Head.[95]

Roger de Morteyn was granted free warren in his demesne at Walsall in 1284,[96] and the lords of the manor retained the right until at least the 17th century.[97] By 1677 the right of warren had been let, but the tenant was then unknown.[98] In 1344 Sir Roger Hillary was granted free warren in his lands at Walsall and Goscote.[99]

The lords of the manor held several fisheries in the parish. The great fishpond of Walsall is mentioned in 1248, when Emecina and Geoffrey de Bakepuse apparently surrendered their right in it to Margery le Rous, and Isabel, widow of William le Rous, in return for a lease.[1] It seems to have been held by William de Morteyn from at least 1275 to his death in 1283.[2] It may have been the fishpond of Walsall mill mentioned in 1332[3] and presumably lying north of the mill-dam. The fishery of the town mill was held by a tenant in 1385–6.[4] Fishing rights from the town bridge to the New Mill were granted c. 1300 by Margery le Rous to Sir Roger de Morteyn.[5] A new fishpool was made at the New Mill c. 1370; in 1391–2 the fishing rights were sold for the year.[6] In 1398–9 the lord was also leasing out the fishery at Sir Roger Hillary's rebuilt mill there.[7] In 1305 Sir Roger de Morteyn granted Sir Thomas le Rous his share of a fishpond called the Ladypool, which was apparently in the Caldmore area.[8] The moat in the park was let as a fishery to Nicholas Flaxall c. 1436.[9] William Wylkes and Stephen Couper held a private fishery in Great Bloxwich in 1484,[10] and in 1843 the lake south of Greenslade Road was a fishpool owned by Joseph Curtis.[11]

PARK. William le Rous created a park at Walsall in John's reign.[12] It apparently passed to his daughter Emecina and thereafter descended with her share of the manor.[13] The land was apparently still imparked in 1541 but had been disparked by 1553.[14] It was let as a unit until at least 1576[15] but by 1617 had been divided into closes leased to 20 tenants.[16]

The original extent is not known. In the earlier 13th century lands in Bentley in St. Peter's, Wolverhampton, were included.[17] In the 15th century the boundaries of the Walsall sector were probably Park Brook, the Wolverhampton and Darlaston roads, and the present Pleck Road. To the north the park included the manor-house and moat, while James Bridge lay on or near the southern boundary. The land in Bentley, which probably lay between Park Brook, Wolverhampton Road, and Bentley Mill Lane, was by then hedged off from that in Walsall. Closes covering the areas on both sides of the brook were known as the 'park lands' in 1763; they included just under 400 a., though the park in 1576 and 1617 was said to contain c. 210 a.[18] A new gate on the north side of the park was made in 1452–3, and 'the park gate' is mentioned in 1617.[19]

A herd of deer was apparently maintained in the park from at least the late 13th century.[20] In 1385–6 foals and fillies from Lord Basset's stud at Drayton were depastured there.[21] The pasture was leased

[85] Above pp. 154, 176; O.S. Map 6″, SP 09 NW. (1955 edn.).
[86] Ex inf. Mr. G. W. Downes of Wood End Farm (1973).
[87] *Walsall Observer*, 13 July 1973; ex inf. Mrs. A. Roe of the Hills and Mrs. P. Whitehouse of Yieldfields Hall (1973) and Miss Turner of Poplars Farm, Fishley (1974).
[88] *V.C.H. Staffs.* iv. 38.
[89] See p. 279.
[90] *S.H.C.* 1910, 199.
[91] S.R.O., D. 593/A/2/20/11.
[92] S.R.O., D. 260/M/F/1/5, f. 110v.
[93] S.R.O., D. 1287/1/8, Roger Holmes's acct. 1766–71, casual profits, 17 Feb. 1770.
[94] Ibid./1/37, valuation of Walsall estate, 1805; S.R.O., D. 1287/18/26, business corresp. 1838–9, P. Potter to Lord Bradford, 4 Dec. 1839; *Walsall Red Book* (1886), 30; above p. 160.
[95] W.S.L., S. MS. 417/Walsall, nos. 1374, 1860, 1862, 1864, 1867, 1874, 1883, 1900.
[96] *Cal. Chart. R. 1257–1300*, 272.
[97] *S.H.C.* N.S. vi (1), 39.
[98] S.R.O., D. 1287/1/8, rent roll of Walsall manor, 1677.
[99] *Cal. Chart. R. 1341–1417*, 31.
[1] *Walsall Records*, 1; *S.H.C.* xv. 38.
[2] *S.H.C.* vi (1), 56; 1911, 187–8.
[3] *Walsall Records*, 50.
[4] S.R.O., D. 641/1/2/32.
[5] *Walsall Records*, 35.

[6] S.R.O., D. 641/1/2/32; B.M. Eg. Roll 8469.
[7] B.M. Eg. Roll 8477.
[8] *Walsall Records*, 28, 30–1, stating that it was 'towards the grange of Calewenhull'. For Calewenhull see W.S.L., D. 1798/84, deed of 27 Nov. 1323; B.M. Harl. MS. 2131, f. 11v. [9] B.M. Eg. Rolls 8532, 8541.
[10] *S.H.C.* N.S. vi (1), 155.
[11] W.S.L., S. MS. 417/Walsall, no. 1776.
[12] Shaw, *Staffs.* i, app. to Gen. Hist. p. xvii; Sims, *Cal. of Deeds*, p. 3.
[13] *Walsall Records*, 1; *Cal. Close, 1272–9*, 339; *S.H.C.* 1911, 188; *Cal. Pat. 1281–92*, 514; *1324–7*, 291.
[14] See p. 145; *L. & P. Hen. VIII*, xvi, p. 330; *Cal. Pat. 1553–4*, 83.
[15] Fink, *Queen Mary's Grammar Sch.* 133; S.R.O., D. 260/M/F/1/5, f. 72; D. 1287/1/2, survey of Walsall manor, 1576, m. 1.
[16] S.R.O., D. 260/M/F/1/8, ct. of recog. and survey, 1617, pp. 1–2.
[17] *Walsall Records*, 23.
[18] B.M. Eg. Rolls 8517, 8520, 8522; S.R.O., D. 1287/1/2, survey of Walsall manor, 1576, m. 1; D. 260/M/F/1/8, ct. of recog. and survey, 1617, pp. 1–2; D. 1287/8/2.
[19] B.M. Eg. Roll 8536; S.R.O., D. 260/M/F/1/8, ct. of recog. and survey, 1617, p. 16.
[20] *Cal. Pat. 1281–92*, 514; B.M. Eg. Rolls 8516, 8525 sqq.; Willmore, *Walsall*, 90.
[21] S.R.O., D. 641/1/2/32.

from 1392–3, though in leases of 1416 and 1423 the lord reserved part of it as grazing for beasts taken as heriots and waifs.[22] In 1385–6 part of the park was inclosed to protect the timber, which was used to remake Walsall pillory in 1396–7 and the park fences in the 15th century. The area was still well wooded in 1576.[23]

MILLS. The water corn-mill most commonly known as the Town mill,[24] but also called Walsall mill, the Ford mill, the Port mill, the Old Mill, and the Malt Mill,[25] stood on Walsall Brook to the north of what is now the Bridge.[26] It was part of Walsall manor by 1247. Margery le Rous claimed a share in it in 1276, and her son Thomas held it, or a share in it, in 1317.[27] Lord Basset held it at his death in 1343.[28] In 1701 Dame Elizabeth Wilbraham, her daughter, and her son-in-law granted a 500-year lease of it to Walsall corporation at a nominal rent; it was ruinous, and the corporation agreed to repair it and to apply any profits to the poor.[29] Repairs were made and the corporation began to receive small sums of money for grinding.[30] By 1763 the building had been demolished or converted to other uses.[31]

A 'new mill' which existed c. 1300 was destroyed by floods between 1343 and 1355. It was then part of Walsall manor.[32] In 1394 Sir Roger Hillary of Bescot rebuilt it and took a lease of it from the earl of Warwick.[33] The New Mill was still worked in 1576, apparently as a corn-mill,[34] but by 1617 it was disused and the mill-pool was a meadow. It was then stated that the mill had formerly been used as a smithy.[35] It probably stood on Walsall Brook, perhaps in the area north of Wallows Lane known as the Old Mill Grounds in 1763.[36]

A fulling-mill existed c. 1300,[37] presumably at

Caldmore where in 1355 there was a fulling-mill on Walsall Brook west of the site of the later New Mills.[38] It was worked by tenants of the lord of Walsall manor until at least 1460,[39] although with one long vacancy (1403–26) and at least two shorter ones.[40] In 1479 it was again vacant, and it was probably not used again.[41]

A water-mill called Meadow mill occurs as part of Walsall manor in 1576. It was then held with part of Long Meadow, which extended along Walsall Brook south of the town bridge. Meadow mill presumably stood on that stretch of the brook, possibly at the southern end of the meadow.[42]

Between 1601 and 1603 John Wollaston of Walsall built a pair of over-shot water corn-mills under one roof on a site east of the Wednesbury road between the present Countess Street and Bescot Crescent. It was powered by a new fleam drawn from Walsall Brook at the town bridge and rejoining it west of the mills.[43] In 1603 Thomas Wilbraham granted Wollaston a long lease,[44] and what became known as the New Mills were worked as corn mills by tenants of the lord of the manor until the mid 1890s.[45] They were rebuilt in 1788–9.[46] A miller's house adjoining them was built between 1740 and 1757.[47] The mills were demolished in the earlier 1920s.[48]

A water-mill called Coal Pool mill was leased in 1692 by Margery and Isabel Horton to Thomas Hildick the younger, a Walsall whitesmith.[49] It was presumably the forge or mill which in the later 18th century stood on a stream just south of the Wyrley and Essington Canal in the triangle formed by the canal, Harden Road, and Goscote Lane.[50] A Robert Hildick had a mill, evidently at Coal Pool, in 1793.[51] Coal Pool mill may still have been worked in 1834, when Henry Hildick, an edge-tool manufacturer,

[22] B.M. Eg. Rolls 8470, 8478, 8493, 8495, 8501, 8509, 8532, 8536, 8541; D.L. 29/641/10411–17.
[23] B.M. Eg. Rolls 8474, 8536, 8541; S.R.O., D. 641/1/2/32; D. 1287/1/2, survey of Walsall manor, 1576, m. 1.
[24] See e.g. S.R.O., D. 641/1/2/32 (1385–6); B.M. Eg. Roll 8540 (1455–6); S.R.O., D. 1287/1/2, survey of Walsall manor, 1576, m. 3; W.S.L. 348/34 (1689).
[25] Walsall mill: *Walsall Records*, 50 (1332). Ford Mill: see e.g. W.S.L., D. 1798/84, deed of 27 Nov. 1384; B.M. Eg. Roll 8540. Port Mill: B.M. Cott. MS. Nero C. xii, f. 155 (1395–6). Old Mill: see e.g. W.T.C. II/13/36 (1648–9), /61 (1674–5). Malt Mill: see e.g. S.R.O., D. 1287/1/8 (1677); W.T.C. II/251/15 (1701).
[26] Willmore, *Walsall*, 63; S.R.O., D. 1287/8/2, map.
[27] *Cal. Close*, 1272–9, 339; *Walsall Records*, 35, where the editor wrongly dates the deed 1318.
[28] *S.H.C.* 1913, 98.
[29] W.T.C. II/251/15.
[30] W.T.C. II/13/73 and 99.
[31] S.R.O., D. 1287/8/2, survey, p. 14; W.T.C. II/208; *Statement of Accts.* 68.
[32] *Walsall Records*, 35; S.R.O., D. 641/1/2/32, stating (in 1386) that it was destroyed 'in the time of the earl of Warwick'. For Warwick's custody of Walsall manor 1343–55 see above p. 170.
[33] B.M. Eg. Rolls 8471–2.
[34] S.R.O., D. 1287/1/2, survey of Walsall manor, 1576, m. 1, referring to the New Mill merely as a 'molendinum aquaticum'.
[35] S.R.O., D. 260/M/F/1/8, ct. of recog. and survey, 1617, m. 2.
[36] It was not on the site of the later New Mills, for in 1617 John Wollaston held both the New Mills and the site of the New Mill: ibid. The grant c. 1300 of a fishery from Walsall town bridge to the 'new mill' (*Walsall Records*, 35) suggests that it stood on Walsall Brook. For the Old Mill Grounds see S.R.O., D. 1287/8/2, map.
[37] B.M. Harl. MS. 2131, f. 11v.

[38] W.S.L., D. 1798/22, deed of 24 Apr. 1355; S.R.O., D. 260/M/F/1/5, f. 75, mentioning (in 1603) Walkmill bridge near the site of the New Mills.
[39] S.R.O., D. 641/1/2/32; B.M. Eg. Rolls 8467, 8471, 8477, 8496 (misnumbered), 8516–17, 8520, 8522, 8525, 8530, 8532, 8534, 8536, 8540–1.
[40] For the 1403–26 vacancy see B.M. Eg. Rolls 8480, 8501, 8514. At the end of it the building was in ruins and the pool silted up. There were short vacancies in the earlier 1390s (ibid. 8470) and some time between 1445 and 1452 (ibid. 8534, 8536).
[41] D.L. 29/641/10411–18.
[42] S.R.O., D. 1287/1/2, survey of Walsall manor, 1576, m. 1; ibid./8/2.
[43] Ibid./6/14, indenture of 8 June 1603 referring to agreement of 15 Mar. 1600/1; ibid., indenture of 10 Oct. 1625 reciting indenture of 15 June 1603. For the site see e.g. S.R.O., D. 1287/8/2; W.S.L., S. MS. 417/Walsall, sub Lord Bradford (proprietor), Wm. Jones (occupier); O.S. Map 1/2,500, Staffs. LXIII. 10 (1917 edn.).
[44] S.R.O., D. 1287/6/14, indenture of 10 Oct. 1625.
[45] For tenancy see e.g. ibid./1/8; ibid./1/37; ibid./1/47; ibid./22/5; ibid./22/8; ibid./box 7/agreement between Hen. Boys and Walsall corporation, 1891. The mills closed c. 1895: *Walsall Red Book* (1895), 57; (1896), 57.
[46] S.R.O., D. 1287/22/5, Walsall rental, 1788–9. Willmore, *Walsall*, 63, gives no authority for his statement that 'the existing structure' was built c. 1740.
[47] S.R.O., D. 1287/6/14, abstract of Wm. Woolrich's title to messuage and buildings in Walsall, 1797; *Walsall Advertiser*, 8 June 1901, recording 'rude paintings on the walls of the Mill House dated 1757', by then partially destroyed.
[48] Local inf. (1973). [49] W.S.L., M. 445.
[50] Yates, *Map of Staffs.* (edns. of 1775 and 1799).
[51] S.R.O., D. 1287/22/5, 'Draft of the clause to preserve Walsall mill waters, 1793'. See also S.R.O., Q/RUm/9, and book of reference nos. 8, 10, 11.

was living at Coal Pool.[52] It had gone out of use by 1843;[53] what may have been the remains of the mill-pool were visible in the earlier 1880s but had disappeared by 1901.[54]

A water-mill existed at Goscote in 1693[55] and is probably to be identified with a mill which stood on Ford Brook in the later 18th century.[56] A water corn-mill called Goscote mill, presumably that on Ford Brook, belonged in 1746 to John Price. In 1804 a share in it was sold by two of his heirs to Joseph Bradley of Goscote.[57]

A windmill owned in 1305 by Sir Roger de Morteyn probably stood south of Walsall in Windmill field. In 1306 Sir Roger granted it to Henry de Prestwode and his son John, and in 1318 John sold his life-interest in it to Ralph, Lord Basset.[58] It may have been the windmill which was held of the lord of Walsall from 1385 to 1393,[59] destroyed by a gale in 1393,[60] and not rebuilt.[61] Between 1612 and 1619 John Persehouse built a windmill near Walsall; it was working in 1621.[62] The site is unknown but may have been in Windmill field, where Persehouse held land.[63] If so, the windmill may have been one of the two which stood between Walsall and Caldmore in 1682;[64] the other was presumably that built in Windmill field c. 1672 by John Blackham, a Walsall baker, and sold in 1675 to Sir Thomas Wilbraham.[65] One of the two mills disappeared between 1732 and 1735.[66] The survivor stood on a site west of the present Highgate Road,[67] where in 1973 the brick tower of a windmill remained. It was apparently that worked as a corn-mill by Thomas Jennings in the 1830s and by James Griffiths in the early 1860s; it went out of use between 1864 and 1868.[68] In the later 1920s it was converted into an observatory.[69] Another windmill, about half a mile east-north-east of that in Highgate Road, was built between 1769 and 1799[70] and still stood in 1816.[71]

A windmill conveyed to Henry Stone by the Whitall family in 1624 may have been in Bloxwich.[72] There were two windmills between Great and Little Bloxwich in 1682.[73] By 1693 there was one, in Chapel field,[74] standing south of Lichfield Road c. ¼ mile east of High Street; it was still in use in 1816 but had disappeared by 1819.[75]

A map of 1682 depicts two windmills in the area between Goscote, Shelfield, and Pelsall.[76] They are not, however, mentioned in the 1693 glebe terrier nor in later ones to 1735.[77] Subsequent terriers show that a windmill was built in Goscote field between 1735 and 1744 and still stood in 1786.[78] Maps of 1775 and 1799 show a windmill c. 100 yds. west of Goscote Lane;[79] it had disappeared by 1816.[80]

Between 1801 and 1804 Thomas Brown began to work a steam corn-mill, apparently the first in Walsall, on the Wyrley and Essington Canal at Birchills.[81] It ceased working between 1851 and 1860.[82] Other 19th-century steam corn-mills included Bloxwich mills or Pratt's mill (so called from the family who worked it until the early 20th century), built in 1812 where the Bloxwich road crosses the Wyrley and Essington Canal and still in use in 1940;[83] the Crown mill in Wolverhampton Street, worked between the 1860s and the 1890s;[84] and the Britannia mills in Stafford Street, worked in the 1880s and 1890s.[85] The Albion Flour Mill in Wolverhampton Street was built in 1849, probably for Thomas Caloe, miller there from at least 1851 until the 1890s.[86] By 1900 Smith Bros. (Walsall) Ltd. had taken it over, and the firm was still milling there in 1973.[87]

In 1395–6, after the lessee of the Town mill had complained that the burgesses were not bringing their corn and malt to be ground there, the burgesses successfully defended their right to grind where they wished.[88] Their quittance presumably dated from William le Rous's renunciation in his charter of all secular demands except tallage and pannage.[89] In

52 White, *Dir. Staffs.* (1834).
53 W.S.L., S. MS. 417/Walsall, *sub* Jackson, Chas.
54 O.S. Map 6″, Staffs. LXIII. NE. (edns. of 1889 and 1903).
55 L.J.R.O., B/V/6/Walsall, 1693, calling it 'new erected'. The description cannot be relied on: all later terriers repeat the phrase, which may have been copied from an earlier terrier now lost.
56 Yates, *Map of Staffs.* (edns. of 1775 and 1799).
57 W.C.L., ACJ XII/31. What became of the other shares is not clear.
58 *Walsall Records*, 28–9, 39; W.S.L., D. 1798/84, deed of 2 Feb. 1340/1.
59 S.R.O., D. 641/1/2/32; B.M. Eg. Rolls 8467, 8469–70 (with attached inquest of 19 Jan. 1390/1).
60 B.M. Eg. Rolls 8471–2.
61 See e.g. ibid. 8501; D.L. 29/641/10411. The windmill site in Windmill field held in 1617 by John Wollaston (S.R.O., D. 260/M/F/1/8, ct. of recog. and survey, 1617, m. 2) may have been that of the medieval mill.
62 S.R.O., D. 260/M/E/425/12; ibid./M/F/1/5, ff. 114v.–115; ibid./M/E/425/1, lease of 1621.
63 Ibid./M/F/1/8, ct. of recog. and survey, 1617, m. 15.
64 Plot, *Staffs.* map dated 1682.
65 S.R.O., D. 1287/6/14, indenture of 4 June 1675, citing lease of 1672 allowing Blackham to dismantle and remove mill when lease expires.
66 L.J.R.O., B/V/6/Walsall, 1732 and 1735. J. Smith, *New Map of Staffs.* (1747), shows 2 windmills, as does E. Bowen, *Improved Map of Staffs.* [1749], but both are probably based on the 1682 map.
67 Yates, *Map of Staffs.* (1775).
68 White, *Dir. Staffs.* (1834); Pigot, *Nat. Com. Dir.* (1835), 465; *P.O. Dir. Staffs.* (1860; 1864). It does not occur ibid. (1868).
69 Woodall, *Walsall Milestones*, 7.

70 It is not on Yates, *Map of Staffs.* (1775 edn., based on survey of 1769–75) but is shown ibid. (1799 edn.).
71 B.M. O.S.D. 212.
72 *S.H.C.* n.s. x (1), 49. For the Whitalls' Bloxwich connexions see Homeshaw, *Bloxwich*, 52, 89, 101.
73 Plot, *Staffs.* map dated 1682.
74 L.J.R.O., B/V/6/Walsall, 1693. Smith, *New Map of Staffs.* (1747), shows 2 windmills at Bloxwich, and Bowen, *Improved Map of Staffs.* [1749], 2 between Bloxwich and Little Bloxwich, but both are probably based on the 1682 map.
75 Yates, *Map of Staffs.* (edns. of 1775 and 1799); B.M. O.S.D. 212; Walsall Council House, deeds bdle. 682 (old), deed of 13 Aug. 1816. It is not shown on S.R.O., D. 351/M/B/209.
76 Plot, *Staffs.* map dated 1682.
77 L.J.R.O., B/V/6/Walsall, 1693, 1701, 1732, 1735.
78 Ibid. 1735, 1744, 1786.
79 Yates, *Map of Staffs.* (edns. of 1775 and 1799).
80 B.M. O.S.D. 212.
81 W.S.L. 35/7/48, 35/8/48.
82 White, *Dir. Staffs.* (1851); *P.O. Dir. Staffs.* (1860).
83 Pearce, *Walsall*, 163; White, *Dir. Staffs.* (1834; 1851); *P.O. Dir. Staffs.* (1860 and later edns. to 1876); *Kelly's Dir. Staffs.* (1880 and later edns. to 1940).
84 *P.O. Dir. Staffs.* (1868; 1872; 1876); *Kelly's Dir. Staffs.* (1880 and later edns. to 1896).
85 *Kelly's Dir. Staffs.* (1888; 1892).
86 Inscription on S. front; White, *Dir. Staffs.* (1851); *P.O. Dir. Staffs.* (1860 and later edns. to 1876); *Kelly's Dir. Staffs.* (1880 and later edns. to 1896).
87 *Kelly's Dir. Staffs.* (1900 and later edns. to 1940); ex inf. Smith Bros. (Walsall) Ltd. (1973).
88 B.M. Cott. MS. Nero C. xii, f. 155.
89 *British Borough Charters 1042–1216*, ed. A. Ballard, 43, 49, 60, 92. For the charter see below p. 212.

1317 Sir Thomas le Rous insisted on 20 years' suit of mill when he granted a life tenancy, but no other such demand has been found.[90] In 1612 Sir Richard Wilbraham stated that his manorial tenants owed suit of mill.[91] He does not seem, however, to have tried to enforce the claim nor was the matter raised when between 1610 and 1620 he disputed his rights as lord with the burgesses.[92]

MARKETS AND FAIRS. In 1220 the Crown granted William le Rous a Monday market at Walsall.[93] The grant was to last during Henry III's minority only, but it was never thereafter challenged and was confirmed in 1399.[94] In 1417 the market day was changed to Tuesday.[95] By 1845 there was also a market on Saturday evenings,[96] and between 1855 and 1889 Saturday became the principal market day.[97] Tuesday and Saturday remained the market days in 1973. By 1927 there was also a Saturday market at Bloxwich. It was discontinued in 1942, revived in 1951, and still held in 1973.[98]

A market-place in Walsall is mentioned in 1309.[99] The centre of the market seems originally to have been the top of High Street, but by the early 19th century trading was spreading into Digbeth on busy market days.[1] In 1816, to ease the congestion in High Street, a separate pig-market was opened in a long yard stretching north from High Street. It was extended in 1834–5.[2] Nevertheless the market spread for a time into other streets. The Walsall Improvement and Market Amendment Act of 1850 allowed the sale of cattle at the Bridge and in all the streets leading out of it except Digbeth, while reserving High Street and Digbeth for the retail market.[3] In 1889 cattle were still sometimes sold in Bridge and Bradford Streets on market days.[4] In 1973 Walsall market was held in the open in High Street. Bloxwich market was also so held, at the junction of Elmore Green Road and Station Street.

There was a market cross by 1386.[5] By the 16th century it stood at the top of High Street and shortly before 1589 was replaced by a market house (the High Cross, or High Cross House), built by the town council on the same site.[6] In 1692 the corporation rebuilt the house on the same site.[7] By the 1760s its position, in the centre of the road and close to the turning into Rushall Street, had made it an obstruction to traffic. It was demolished in 1800.[8]

In 1809 the corporation replaced it by a smaller house a few yards further up hill, adjoining the steps leading to St. Matthew's Church and out of the line of traffic.[9] It was intended for the sale of poultry, eggs, butter, and similar produce, but by the 1830s it was little used, except on wet days. By 1851 it had become merely a store for market stalls. It was demolished in 1852.[10]

From at least the 1750s the market trade was mainly in pigs, poultry, butter, garden produce, and crockery.[11] With the end of the Napoleonic wars the trade in pigs was much increased. The navy no longer needed large quantities of Irish bacon for victualling, and live pigs were shipped from Ireland for general sale; by 1817 Walsall was one of the chief inland markets dealing in them.[12] It was probably because of the pig trade that in 1818 Walsall was considered the second market town in the county.[13] It was claimed in 1855 that as many as 2,000 pigs had sometimes been brought to market in a day. By then, however, the coming of railways had diverted most of the trade to Birmingham and Wolverhampton.[14] In 1845 the corporation built shambles in part of the pig-market and also provided standings there for retailers. The intention was avowedly to ease the congestion in High Street during the Saturday evening market, but the reduction in the area allotted to pig-pens suggests that the heyday of the trade had passed.[15] By 1889 the pig-market was little used, and few cattle were sold on market days.[16] Such livestock trade as survived probably ended in the 1890s. Grain was sold wholesale at the Tuesday market until at least 1906. In 1835 prices were quoted for wheat, oats, beans, barley, and peas, but by the later 19th century wheat alone seems to have been marketed.[17] The market's general retail trade, however, flourished. There had been a decline in the 1820s and early 1830s,[18] but by 1889 the market was regarded as an improving one as the population of the town grew.[19] It was a general retail market in 1973.

The 1220 grant included a fair on St. Matthew's day (21 September) and its eve, and in 1399 another was added on the Nativity of St. John the Baptist (24 June) and its eve.[20] In 1417 the two fairs were replaced by one on the feast of St. John before the Latin Gate (6 May) and another on St. Simon and St. Jude's day (28 October).[21] The 1627 charter

[90] Walsall Records, 35, where the editor wrongly dates the deed 1318.
[91] S.R.O., D. 260/M/E/425/12.
[92] See p. 214.
[93] C 60/12 m. 4.
[94] Westminster Abbey Muniments, 6045.
[95] Cal. Chart. R. 1341–1417, 485.
[96] Staffs. Advertiser, 24 May 1845.
[97] Glew, Walsall, 16; Rep. Com. Market Rights and Tolls, vol. viii [C. 6268-II], p. 164 (1890–1), xxxviii.
[98] Markets and Fairs in Eng. and Wales: Part II, Midland Markets (Min. of Agric. and Fisheries, Econ. Ser. No. 14, 1927), 140; Staffs. Life, Sept. 1951, 16–17.
[99] W.T.C. I/9.
[1] S.R.O., D. 1287/10/2/Walsall market rights etc., rep. of the King v. Jos. Cotterell, Staffs. Lent Assizes, 1817, f. 5.
[2] Ibid. ff. 3, 7; Statement of Accts. 195, 199.
[3] 13 Vic. c. xv (Local and Personal), s. 20.
[4] Rep. Com. Market Rights and Tolls, vol. viii, 164.
[5] S.R.O., D. 641/1/2/32.
[6] Sims, Cal. of Deeds, pp. 42–3.
[7] W.T.C. II/13/66; W.C.L., photograph 137, showing inscription formerly on building. For the site see J. Snape, Plan of Town of Walsall (1782).

[8] C.J. xxx. 832; Shaw, Staffs. ii. 74; Homeshaw, Walsall, 111. Willmore, Walsall, 193–4, gives 1802 for date of demolition.
[9] Pearce, Walsall, 128; T. Mason, Plan of Town of Walsall, 1824 (in W.C.L.).
[10] Walsall Note Book, 162–3 (copy in W.C.L.); White, Dir. Staffs. (1834; 1851); Glew, Walsall, 16; plate facing p. 224 below. For the corporation's scheme in 1847 to build a market hall on the bowling-green behind the Dragon see Glew, Walsall, 15–16.
[11] S.R.O., D. 1287/10/2/Walsall market rights etc., the King v. Jos. Cotterell, f. 12.
[12] Ibid. f. 2.
[13] Parson and Bradshaw, Dir. Staffs. (1818), p. clxxiii.
[14] Glew, Walsall, 17.
[15] Staffs. Advertiser, 24 May 1845.
[16] Rep. Com. Market Rights and Tolls, vol. viii, 164.
[17] Grain prices at Walsall market are quoted in Staffs. Advertiser, 26 Sept. and 3 Oct. 1835 and then fairly regularly from the 1860s until the issue of 6 Jan. 1906.
[18] Walsall Note Book, 162–3.
[19] Rep. Com. Market Rights and Tolls, vol. viii, 164.
[20] W.S.L., S. MS. 327, p. 7; Westminster Abbey Muniments, 6045.
[21] Cal. Chart. R. 1341–1417, 485.

granted two fairs, with a court of piepowder, one on St. Matthias's day (24 February) and the other on the Tuesday before Michaelmas.[22] By 1792 a pleasure fair, held by prescription on Whit Tuesday, had been added to the two charter fairs.[23] The February fair was last held in 1896 and was then abolished at the corporation's request. The fair held on the Tuesday before Michaelmas was transferred to the Tuesday in August Bank Holiday week in 1898 and became solely a pleasure fair.[24]

The fairs, like the markets, were held in High Street and Digbeth, spreading in the 19th century to the Bridge and the streets leading off it.[25] Trade was in livestock, dairy produce, and vegetables. In the late 1620s and early 1630s a few horses were being sold, with vendors and purchasers coming mainly from south and central Staffordshire, Warwickshire, Worcestershire, and Derbyshire.[26] By 1742 the horse fair was important enough for the corporation to fix its site in Digbeth.[27] In the early 19th century horses and cattle were sold at the charter fairs and at the Whit Tuesday pleasure fair. The fair held on the Tuesday before Michaelmas was also noted for sales of cheese and onions.[28] It was popularly known as the Onion Fair, and cheese and onion sales still flourished at it c. 1870, though they had ceased by 1889. The February fair, popularly known as the Orange Fair, was also in decline by 1889.[29] Cattle and horses, however, continued to be sold, at least at the Onion Fair, and from 1898 the corporation licensed their sale on the Tuesday before Michaelmas to suit farmers and dealers who had previously gone to the Onion Fair. The horses were sold in Midland Road, the cattle in the pig-market.[30] The sales were apparently held until the late 1920s.[31]

The medieval grants of markets and fairs were made to the lord of the manor, and in the 1490s the borough bailiff was still accounting annually to the lord for market toll.[32] Clerks of the market and flesh-tasters continued to be appointed at the court leet until the mid 19th century, and as late as 1806 the leet promulgated by-laws to regulate trading.[33] Nevertheless in the 17th century control had in fact passed to the corporation. The 1627 charter granted it the markets and fairs and the court of piepowder.[34] It was paying the clerks of the market by the 1630s;[35] it built the market houses;[36] it provided weights and

measures.[37] In the late 18th and early 19th centuries the bellman collected toll from stall-holders in the name of the lord of the manor; but he did so with the corporation's consent, and it was the corporation which permitted him to keep the money he collected.[38] Its ownership apparently went unchallenged until 1816, when, having opened its new pig-market, it forbade burgesses to exercise their privilege of erecting pig-pens in High Street on market days. When Joseph Cotterell disobeyed the order, asserting that it was void because the market belonged to the lord of the manor, the corporation prosecuted him and won its case, both at Stafford assizes and on appeal. Lord Bradford did not intervene and his manorial steward, Joseph Stubbs, who was also town clerk, gave evidence on the corporation's behalf.[39] Authority to collect market tolls was transferred to the improvement commissioners by the Walsall Improvement and Market Act of 1848 but reverted to the corporation under the Amendment Act of 1850.[40] The corporation still owned and managed the markets and fairs in 1973. Under the 1969 Walsall Corporation Act the markets and fairs became statutory.[41]

The mayor walked the fairs by at least the 1640s. In 1647 it was decreed that the twenty-four capital burgesses should walk with him, wearing their gowns;[42] the musicians whom the corporation paid in the 1640s for coming to play at the fairs[43] presumably also took part in the ceremony, for until c. 1832 a band formed part of the procession.[44] In the 17th century men carrying the carved clubs traditionally known as Bayard's Colts acted as escorts; that practice was, however, gradually abandoned and seems to have been dead by the early 19th century.[45] In the 1850s and 1860s 'the little civic procession' consisted of the mayor, the other members of the town council, and the borough officials, escorted by police; they walked from the guildhall to the church steps, where the fair was proclaimed, proceeded down High Street to the Bridge, where the proclamation was repeated, and then returned to the guildhall.[46] The custom was abolished in the early 1870s.[47]

COAL-MINING. Most of Walsall lies within the exposed sections of the South Staffordshire and Cannock Chase coalfields. The Bentley Faults, the

[22] Pearce, *Walsall*, 89–90.
[23] *Rep. Com. Market Rights and Tolls*, vol. i [C. 5550], p. 203 (1888), liii; *vol. viii*, 164.
[24] *Walsall Red Book* (1899), 132; *Walsall Council Mins. 1897–8*, 190–1, 418–19; *1898–9*, 230.
[25] W.C.L., TS. account of Walsall fairs; *Rep. Com. Market Rights and Tolls, vol. viii*, 164.
[26] W.T.C. II/40.
[27] Ibid. /146.
[28] Parson and Bradshaw, *Dir. Staffs.* (1818), p. ccxxxix.
[29] W.C.L., TS. account of Walsall fairs; *Rep. Com. Market Rights and Tolls, vol. viii*, 167.
[30] *Walsall Council Mins. 1897–8*, 418–19; *1898–9*, 230. For a complaint about the selling of horses and cattle in the streets at fair times see *Staffs. Advertiser*, 1 Oct. 1892.
[31] An annual horse and cattle market on that date is listed in *Walsall Red Book* up to and including the 1929 edn. It is not, however, mentioned in the account of Walsall markets given in *Markets and Fairs in Eng. and Wales: Part II, Midland Markets*, 140.
[32] D.L. 29/641/10414–18.
[33] See pp. 209–10.
[34] Pearce, *Walsall*, 89–91. The charter stipulated, however, that none of its provisions was to prejudice the rights of the lord of the manor: ibid. 92–3.

[35] W.T.C. II/13/20–2.
[36] See p. 187.
[37] E.g. W.T.C. II/13/8, 33, 70, 90.
[38] S.R.O., D. 1287/10/2/Walsall market rights etc., the King v. Jos. Cotterell, ff. 13–14.
[39] Homeshaw, *Walsall*, 128; S.R.O., D. 1287/10/2/Walsall market rights etc., the King v. Jos. Cotterell; 'The King v. Cotterill', *The English Reports*, cvi. 25–30.
[40] 11 & 12 Vic. c. 161 (Local and Personal); 13 Vic. c. 15 (Local and Personal).
[41] Walsall Corp. Act 1969, c. 58 (Local); *Markets Year Book* (1971–2); *Walsall Observer*, 9 Mar. 1973.
[42] W.T.C. II/235; J. Turner, *Glimpses of Walsall History* (Walsall, 1927), 10, 18–19.
[43] W.T.C. II/13/30–1, 34.
[44] *Walsall Red Book* (1882), 86.
[45] Ibid. 85–6, recording abandonment of practice but not giving date of last appearance of clubmen. Shaw, *Staffs.* ii. 73, implies that the clubs were no longer in use when he wrote. For the clubs see below p. 220.
[46] *Walsall Red Book* (1882), 86; plate facing p. 224 below.
[47] *Walsall Red Book* (1882), 86, states that it was abolished in 1870. Newspaper reports of the 1870 and 1871 Onion Fairs state, however, that they were walked with the usual ceremonies: *Staffs. Advertiser*, 1 Oct. 1870, 30 Sept. 1871.

boundary between the fields, cross it from Reedswood to Ryecroft. The coal lay close to the surface on both sides of the faults, outcropping at Coal Pool, at Reedswood, and in Corporation Street (formerly Coal Pit Lane). It was absent only in the Silurian inlier south and east of the town.[48] Several seams have been worked in both mining sectors, usually in conjunction with ironstone and fireclay.

Coal was evidently being mined in Walsall by the early 14th century. The lords of the divided manor agreed c. 1300 to share the profits of coal and ironstone mines, and in leases of land at Birchills in 1326 and 1327 Sir Thomas le Rous reserved the right to license coal-mining.[49] Before 1385 the lords of the manor had apparently mined coal for sale, but no profits were obtained from that year until at least 1460.[50] The manorial accounts for 1490–1 include a payment for prospecting for a mine in the park.[51] About 1540 Walsall was supplying coal to Sutton Coldfield (Warws.),[52] and in 1557 the farmer of Walsall manor was renting coal-mines there.[53] Colliers in the parish are mentioned from 1578.[54] In 1597 the council leased a coal-mine at Great Bloxwich to George Whitall, who was to provide the inhabitants of Walsall with coal of two qualities,[55] and another pit occurs at Bloxwich in 1628.[56] In 1774 a mine at Great Bloxwich, next to the Walsall–Stafford turnpike road, was advertised for sale; the coal was at a depth of 111 ft.[57] Henry Whateley in 1775 obtained a mining lease in Comwall and Leamore fields, also in Great Bloxwich.[58] From the 17th century mines were worked elsewhere in the parish. There was a coal-pit at Birchills in 1612,[59] and coal was evidently mined south of the town by 1613.[60] By 1764 Jonas Slaney was working coal at Little Bloxwich.[61] The presence of minerals at Goscote was known by 1776, and a colliery was opened there c. 1794.[62]

Most parts of the exposed field in Walsall had thus been worked by the late 18th century. The Wyrley and Essington Canal, built in the 1790s partly to facilitate the transport of coal[63] and passing close to the mines of Bloxwich, Birchills, and Goscote, encouraged the expansion both of coal-mining

and of ironstone-mining, iron-working, and brick-making which were often associated with it. In 1806 a railway was built from the canal to a new colliery, ironworks, and brickworks at Birchills.[64] There were 6 collieries in the parish in 1834, of which 3 were at Birchills and 3 at Bloxwich.[65] By 1843 there were at least 8 pits, 4 at Birchills, one at Bloxwich, one at James Bridge, and one at Bentley Moor.[66] Several mines at Bloxwich were advertised for sale during the following years.[67] There were some 19 collieries in 1853; most of the newer ones were in Bloxwich. Three had attached ironworks with blast-furnaces, and Green Lanes Colliery had a brickworks.[68] The growth of population in the foreign between 1851 and 1861 was attributed partly to the extension of coal-mining,[69] and the number of pits continued to increase rapidly until the mid 1860s.[70]

By the later 1860s, however, the coal industry in Walsall had begun to decline. The centre of production had continued to move from the Birchills area to Bloxwich and the north of the parish, where a colliery at Fishley began working c. 1865. Of some 40 collieries in 1868, only 29 were working.[71] In the next fifteen years the number declined rapidly; 13 closed between 1873 and 1883, and in 1882 there were only 8 collieries working.[72] By 1916 there were only 3 pits working in Bloxwich and none further south.[73] The abandonment of the Broad Lane No. 2 Pit in 1925 marked the end of mining; attempts to resume it in the later 1920s and the 1930s failed.[74] Coal was worked open-cast, however, in Reedswood Park in the later 1940s.[75]

IRONSTONE-MINING. The Coal Measures around Walsall include several beds of ironstone, both between and below the coal seams; they are nearest the surface south and south-east of the town.[76] Mining had evidently begun by c. 1300 when the lords of the divided manor agreed to share the profits.[77] In the late 1380s and the 1390s the lord had mines in Windmill field and in 'Godeforthfeld', probably in Caldmore.[78] In 1537–8 Thomas Acton was leasing mines in the foreign from the Crown,[79] and in 1539 Thomas Rugeway of Shipley (Salop.) let two mines

48 V.C.H. Staffs. i. 16; ii. 70–1; G. Barrow and others, Memoirs of Geol. Surv., Geol. of Country around Lichfield, 23, 67, 91–3, 102–4, 110–11; Geol. Surv. Map 6″, Staffs. LVII. SW., SE. (1922 edn.); LXIII (1922 edn.); F. W. Willmore, Transcript of First Reg. Bk. of Par. Ch. of St. Matthew, Walsall, 1570–1649 (Walsall, 1890), 172 n.; Homeshaw, Bloxwich, 201; Guide to Walsall, 1889, 91.
49 Walsall Records, 35, 49.
50 S.R.O., D. 641/1/2/32; B.M. Eg. Rolls 8467 sqq.
51 D.L. 429/641/10415.
52 Leland, Itin. ed. Toulmin Smith, v. 23.
53 B.M. Harl. MS. 606, f. 6v.
54 Willmore, First Reg. of Ch. of St. Matthew, 47, 50, 52, 108, 151–2, 182.
55 Sims, Cal. of Deeds, pp. 45–6.
56 Willmore, First Reg. of Ch. of St. Matthew, 224.
57 Homeshaw, Bloxwich, 134.
58 Fink, Queen Mary's Grammar Sch. 243.
59 Willmore, First Reg. of Ch. of St. Matthew, 196.
60 S.R.O., D. 260/M/F/1/5, f. 109v.
61 Homeshaw, Bloxwich, 135.
62 W.C.L., ACJ XII/12, /19.
63 See p. 168; Homeshaw, Bloxwich, 124.
64 J. Farey, General View of Agric. of Derbs. iii. 453.
65 White, Dir. Staffs. (1834).
66 W.S.L., S. MS. 417/Walsall, nos. 357, 1044, 1074, 1083, 1086, 1167, 1184, 1191–2, 1282; P.O. Dir. Staffs. (1845).
67 Staffs. Advertiser, 29 Apr. 1848, 28 Sept. 1850, 20 and 27 May 1854; Midland Counties Herald, 27 Jan. 1853,

6 and 27 Apr., 11 and 18 May, 22 June, 6 July 1854; S.R.O., D. 1287/particulars of . . . copyhold property at Little Bloxwich . . . with mines of coal . . . which will be sold . . . on . . . 22 Oct. 1850.
68 R. Hunt, Memoirs of Geol. Surv., Mineral Statistics of U.K. for 1853 and 1854, 42, 104, listing 2 Walsall pits under Darlaston and some pits outside the parish under Walsall; W.S.L. 35/21/48.
69 Census, 1861.
70 Hunt, Mineral Statistics 1864, 162; 1865, 277–8; 1866, 162–3; 1867, 179–80.
71 Ibid. 1865, 277; 1868, 180–1.
72 Reps. Inspectors of Mines for 1882 [C. 3621], pp. 596–600, H.C. (1883), xix; Summaries of Reps. Inspectors of Mines and Mineral Statistics for 1883 [C. 4058], pp. 259–71, H.C. (1884), xix.
73 List of Mines . . . for 1916 (H.M.S.O., 1917), 268, 275.
74 Ibid. 1925, 328; 1928, 313; 1936, 269, 271; 1937, 270–2.
75 41st Ann. Rep. Walsall Educ. Cttee. (1944–5), 26 (copy in W.C.L.); Geol. Surv. Map 6″, Staffs. LXIII. NW. (prov. edn. with geol. inf. 1952 and 1955).
76 G. Barrow and others, Memoirs of Geol. Surv., Geol. of Country around Lichfield, 94, 208–11; Geol. Surv. Map 6″, Staffs. LXIII. SE. (1922 edn.).
77 Walsall Records, 35.
78 B.M. Eg. Rolls 8467–70, 8476. For 'Godfordesland' in Caldmore see Walsall Records, 75–6.
79 S.C. 6/Hen. VIII/ 7049.

at 'Stubcross' near Walsall to John Hodgettis and John Stone of Walsall.[80] About the same time the chantry priest of St. Mary under the rood was mining ironstone in chantry land,[81] and Leland c. 1540 remarked on the ironstone mines of the town.[82]

In the later 16th and early 17th centuries the ore was extensively mined to supply works elsewhere. Walsall ironstone was used in Lord Paget's blast furnace in Cannock forest from the start of operations in 1561; between August 1561 and December 1563 2,068 loads of the stone were carried to the furnace.[83] In 1576 his son was leasing 8 open-cast mines in Walsall, and 23 more were opened between 1577 and 1585. In most cases royalties were paid to the owners or tenants of the properties in return for mining rights, but some owners evidently dug the stone themselves. The pits were worked for periods varying from a few months to at least nine years.[84] Only a few sites are identifiable. Those leased from the lord of the manor included a mine in the park, worked in 1577–8,[85] and others in the Rough and Plain Wastes, probably between the park and Walsall Brook and worked from at least 1576 to 1582.[86] A mine in Marsh field, leased from one Brasier from 1577 to 1581, was probably in the Marsh Street area.[87] Several pits were leased from Walter Leveson of Lilleshall (Salop.); they included a mine in Pinfold leasow next to the pinfold at Bloxwich worked from at least 1576 to 1581,[88] one in Rough leasow adjoining the present Corporation Street worked from at least 1576 to 1580,[89] and another at Palfrey Green worked from 1581 to 1584.[90] Paget also mined at Caldmore between 1578 and 1580,[91] at 'Walsytch' (probably in Caldmore) in 1580,[92] in Windmill field between 1578 and 1582,[93] and in Monks field (probably in the Pleck area) in 1576–7.[94] Fulke Greville, who took over Paget's ironworks in 1589, also obtained ore from Walsall.[95] In 1571 Sir Francis Willoughby was negotiating for Walsall ore for his ironworks at Middleton (Warws.) and used it in his new furnace there in 1592. In 1595 Percival Willoughby leased an ironstone mine at Brockhurst on the Wednesbury boundary.[96] In 1590 John Worthington of Walsall sold ironstone for the Friar Park smithy in West Bromwich,[97] and in 1591 Hugh Lyddiatt of Walsall leased mining rights to Thomas Parkes, a Wednesbury ironmaster.[98] In 1651 John

Persehouse leased mines in the Caldmore area to John Jennens, a Birmingham ironmonger, requiring him to use the ore in his furnace at Aston (Warws.)[99] In the late 17th century Walsall and Rushall ores were the source of 'tough iron' used for the best wares.[1]

In the 19th century ironstone was still widely mined in the parish, but production moved away from the outcrop to the deeper seams, which were worked in conjunction with coal; most collieries thus mined ironstone. The Broad Lane colliery was probably the last to do so.[2] Lord Hatherton, however, let out separate ironstone mines at Sargent's Hill in 1865 and at Five Ways in 1869.[3]

LIMESTONE. The Silurian rocks around Walsall include three productive beds of limestone. The lowest, the Barr or Woolhope Limestone, outcrops along the eastern boundary of the parish from Hay Head to Gillity Greaves. The Upper and Lower Wenlock Limestones are found nearer the town centre; the more valuable bed, the Lower Limestone, outcrops around Church Hill and in the Arboretum area and is close to the surface at Townend Bank. Further west the Upper and Lower Limestones were reached by shafts through the overlying Coal Measures. The Lower Limestone extends into Rushall, where several limeworks often stated to be in Walsall were in fact situated.[4]

Walsall limestone was used for building by the late 16th century: in 1594 John Persehouse of Reynold's Hall granted a lease of a lime-pit, reserving some of the building stone for himself.[5] By the 15th century the stone was also burnt for lime. In 1417–18 fourteen cart-loads of burnt limestone were bought at Walsall to repair a mill at Warwick, and in the 1460s the stone was burnt for use in the rebuilding of Walsall church. Lime-burners are mentioned in a list of trades c. 1494.[6] By the earlier 16th century Walsall supplied lime to Sutton Coldfield (Warws.)[7] and in 1569 to Grafton Manor (Worcs.);[8] it was apparently used at the ironworks at Middleton (Warws.) in 1593.[9] In 1675 it was used in work at Seighford church.[10] From at least 1763 it was sent to Freeford for agricultural use.[11] In the earlier 19th century the Barr Limestone provided engineering cement and the stucco with which many houses in Walsall were faced, while the Wenlock

[80] S.R.O., D. 593/A/2/20/12.
[81] C 1/1008/52.
[82] See p. 145.
[83] V.C.H. Staffs. ii. 110; S.R.O., D.(W.)1734/3/4/35/1; /3/3/223.
[84] S.R.O., D.(W.) 1734/3/3/211–15, passim; E 101/546/16 nos. 1 and 2; Hist. MSS. Com. 69, Middleton, p. 494.
[85] S.R.O., D.(W.)1734/3/3/211, f. 39; /212, f. 33v.
[86] Ibid./211, ff. 2v.–3; /215, pp. 15, 68; D. 1287/8/2, map; above p. 177.
[87] D.(W.)1734/3/3/211, f. 39; /214, f. 38; D. 1287/8/2, map.
[88] D.(W.)1734/3/3/211, f. 3; /213, ff. 52v., 59v.–60; /214, f. 24.
[89] Ibid./211, f. 2v.; /213, f. 52v.; D. 593/J/22/5; above p. 189.
[90] D.(W.)1734/3/3/214, ff. 40, 54; E 101/546/16 no. 1, 1 Aug. 1584.
[91] D.(W.)1734/3/3/212, f. 20v.; /213, f. 44.
[92] Ibid./213, ff. 23v., 40; D. 260/M/F/1/5, f. 13v.
[93] D.(W.)1734/3/3/212, f. 45; /215, p. 68.
[94] Ibid./211, ff. 2v., 47; D. 593/A/2/20/33.
[95] V.C.H. Staffs. ii. 111; S.H.C. 1931, 250; D. 260/M/F/1/5, f. 24v.

[96] R. A. Pelham, 'Establishment of the Willoughby ironworks in North Warws. in the 16th cent.' Univ. of Birmingham Hist. Jnl. iv (1), 19, 23–9 (wrongly identifying Hay Head limestone as ironstone).
[97] C 3/295/94.
[98] S.R.O., D. 260/M/F/1/5, f. 24v.
[99] S.R.O., D. 260/M/E/425/1, indenture of 26 Sept. 1651.   [1] Plot, Staffs. 161.
[2] See p. 189; Walsall Council House, deeds bdle. 682, lease of 31 Mar. 1919.
[3] S.R.O., D. 260/M/E/430/8 and 9.
[4] G. Barrow and others, Memoirs of Geol. Surv., Geol. of Country around Lichfield, 9–20; R. I. Murchison, Silurian System (1839), ii. 488; H. E. Green, 'The Foundations of Walsall: an account of the limestone ind. of the district' (TS. in possession of Mr. Green), 42, 50; V.C.H. Staffs. ii. 192–7.
[5] S.R.O., D. 260/M/F/1/5, f. 36v.
[6] B.M. Eg. Roll 8503; S.H.C. 1928, 189–93, 224.
[7] Leland, Itin. ed. Toulmin Smith, v. 23.
[8] Green, 'Foundations of Walsall', 13.
[9] Nott. Univ. Libr., Middleton MSS. 5/165/51, pp. 11–16.   [10] W.S.L., M. 600, p. 123.
[11] S.R.O., D. 661/21/6/1, ff. 3v., 6, 9, 14.

Limestone was in demand as a flux in iron-smelting.[12]

The Barr Limestone was apparently being worked by the 15th century. In 1443 a lease of land at Holt Croft, probably near Gillity Greaves, reserved a limestone mine there.[13] A lime-pit on Daffodil farm was worked at some time before 1546.[14] The limestone quarries at Hay Head were the chief source of Barr Limestone in Walsall and were worked by 1593.[15] A mine at Laundhill near by was in production between at least 1617 and 1677.[16] Lord Mountrath had a works in the Dingle (partly in Aldridge) from at least 1767, and probably by the mid 1770s Thomas Hoo owned another adjoining it on the south.[17] About 1800 the Hay Head quarries were disused, but by 1808 John Wilkinson, evidently the Bilston ironmaster, had begun to work them again. In 1813 the quarries were occupied by James Brindley.[18] The former Mountrath sector had been abandoned by 1843; Hoo's was then owned by Sir Edward Dolman Scott and by T. E. Foley of Stoke Edith (Herefs.) and was let to William Tolley.[19] In 1850 Foley's widow re-let the works to Charles Roberts and Henry Eberhardt of Stourbridge (Worcs.). Their partnership was dissolved in 1853 and an agreement of 1854 gave Roberts sole rights.[20] He advertised the lease for sale later in the year, but the works had been abandoned by 1865.[21] In 1790 a works was opened on Wood End farm near Daisy Bank; it was in production until at least 1822, but nothing further is known of it.[22]

The earliest workings in the Wenlock Limestone were probably in the outcrop around Church Hill. Old limestone workings were known under Peal Street in 1889, and one below High Street was discovered in 1910.[23] The area east of Ablewell Street was called Lime Pit Bank by the 1760s, and a limestone quarry west of the street was being worked in 1782.[24]

By the late 18th century large-scale working of the Lower Limestone had moved northwards to the present Arboretum area; Hatherton Lake there is a flooded quarry. Mines worked by the Persehouse family from at least 1733 were probably on that site.[25] Open-cast quarrying there was developed by John Walhouse, who succeeded Richard Persehouse in 1771, and by the end of the century he had demolished Reynold's Hall to reach the limestone underneath.[26] In 1801 the works was said to be let to a 'Mr. Griffiths';[27] this may refer to the Joseph Griffin who occupied it between at least 1813 and 1825.[28] A mineral railway was built in 1823 to carry limestone from the works to a wharf on the Walsall Canal.[29] In 1826 Walhouse re-let the works, then known as the Butts Limeworks, to George Strongitharm of Daw End in Rushall, Samuel Wagstaff of West Bromwich, and William Harrison of Walsall. By that time it extended into Rushall. A further lease was granted in 1834 to Harrison only, but the works had apparently been abandoned by 1843.[30] The pits were flooded by 1845 when the mayor, J. H. Harvey, was drowned while swimming there.[31]

By then operations had begun further west in the concealed veins, which were worked by the pillar-and-stall method.[32] In 1813 there was a mine south of Wolverhampton Street owned by Lord Bradford and let to Thomas Price of Bescot Hall.[33] The workings were apparently underground; they had been closed by 1838. By then John Strongitharm had opened another mine adjoining them on the south-east.[34] It had closed by 1843.[35] A third mine immediately east of that of 1813 on both sides of Wolverhampton Street was worked by 1823; in 1838 it belonged to the Daw End Lime Co. and was advertised for sale in 1862.[36] A mine with shafts in Marsh Street and on the site of the railway station was worked presumably before 1849.[37] In 1851 John Brewer and in 1860 John Whitgreave each apparently had a limeworks in Wolverhampton Street.[38]

From the Wolverhampton Street area mining spread gradually northwards. In 1824 John Walhouse bought Shaw's Leasowes north of the present Shaw Street and granted mining rights there to the lessees of his Butts Limeworks in 1826. By 1832 William Harrison had built a tramway to the Birchills branch canal, and production had apparently begun by 1834.[39] In 1845 11,348 tons of limestone and 5,076 tons of lime were produced.[40]

[12] *Trans. Birm. Enterprise Club*, v. 19; Pearce, *Walsall*, 134–5; White, *Dir. Staffs.* (1834). The Barr Limestone, though a chemically superior flux, was apparently not used as one: *Birm. and Mid. Hardware Dist.* 53, 61.
[13] W.S.L., D. 1798/84, deed of 2 Feb. 1442/3. For the site see S.R.O., D. 260/M/T/1/1a, deed of 15 June 1515.
[14] B.R.L. 608942.
[15] Nott. Univ. Libr., Middleton MSS. 5/165/51, pp. 11–16.
[16] S.R.O., D. 260/M/F/1/8, ct. of recog. and survey, 1617, p. 3; D. 1287/1/8, Walsall rental 1677. For Laundhill see D. 1287/1/2, survey of Walsall manor, 1576, m. 12.
[17] D. 1287/1/8, Roger Holmes's acct. 1766–71, 2 June 1767; D. 1287/16/14, pencil sketch map.
[18] J. Farey, *General View of Agric. of Derbs.* iii. 454–6; Pearce, *Walsall*, 135; Fink, *Queen Mary's Grammar Sch.* 247.
[19] W.S.L., S. MS. 417/Walsall, nos. 1852, 1862, 1864.
[20] S.R.O., D. 695/1/30/39, lease of 24 May 1850; /41, draft agreement Feb. and agreement 3 July 1854.
[21] D. 695/4/25/1: *Birm. and Mid. Hardware Dist.* 51.
[22] Fink, *Queen Mary's Grammar Sch.* 239, 241, 247–8.
[23] Green, 'Foundations of Walsall', 43, 51.
[24] See p. 153; J. Snape, *Plan of Town of Walsall* (1782).
[25] S.R.O., D. 260/M/E/425/11; D. 661/21/6/1, ff. 6, 14.
[26] Shaw, *Staffs.* ii. 75; above p. 177.
[27] R. Warner, *Tour through the Northern Counties of England and the Borders of Scotland* (1802), i. 103.
[28] Pearce, *Walsall*, 156; Parson and Bradshaw, *Dir.*

Staffs. (1818); B.R.L., Gough 316/44c; S.R.O., D. 260/M/E/427/1, lease of 25 Mar. 1826.
[29] D. 260/M/T/3/7; T. Mason, Plan of Town of Walsall, 1824 (in W.C.L.).
[30] D. 260/M/E/427/1, leases of 25 Mar. 1826 and 25 Mar. 1834; W.S.L., S. MS. 417/Rushall, nos. 269, 270a; /Walsall, nos. 2227–41.
[31] W. R. Foster, 'Hist. of Walsall Arboretum' (TS. in possession of Mr. Foster), 7–8.
[32] *Trans. Birm. Enterprise Club*, v. 18; County Boro. of Walsall, *Proposed Primary Highway Network: Report Drawings*, 1972, plan 11.
[33] Pearce, *Walsall*, 134.
[34] S.R.O., D. 1287/18/26, business corresp. 1838–9, Peter Potter to Lord Bradford, 10 Apr. 1838 and plan attached.
[35] W.S.L., S. MS. 417/Walsall, no. 1368.
[36] *Staffs. Advertiser*, 28 Mar. 1862; D. 1287/18/26, business corresp. 1838–9, Potter to Bradford, 10 Apr. 1838, plan.
[37] County Boro. of Walsall, *Proposed Primary Highway Network: Report Drawings*, 1972, plan 11; above p. 168.
[38] White, *Dir. Staffs.* (1851); P.O. *Dir. Staffs.* (1860).
[39] S.R.O., D. 260/M/T/3/3, deed of 25 Mar. 1824; /M/E/427/1, leases of 25 Mar. 1826 and 25 Mar. 1834; /430/2, draft lease of 25 Mar. 1842; J. Phillips and W. F. Hutchings, *Map of Staffs.* (1832).
[40] S.R.O., D. 260/M/E/186, p. 67.

Harrison was succeeded between 1851 and 1860 by Edward Strongitharm, who worked the pits till at least 1861.[41]

Two underground mines[42] were sunk in the 1840s north of the town centre. One on the corner of Birchills and Green Lane, later known as the Birchills Limeworks, was opened in the earlier 1840s and was worked by James Smallman until at least 1851.[43] By 1861 he had been succeeded by Mary Newton & Co.[44] By 1873 the mine was worked by Thomas Matthews, but between 1888 and 1892 it passed to Brewer & Marriott. It closed c. 1892.[45] In 1843 Lord Hatherton leased a mine between Hatherton Street and Wisemore Lane, later known as the Hatherton Limeworks, to Emanuel Benton and Job Hollowood. It was in production by 1845, and in 1847 12,063 tons of limestone were raised and 1,494 tons of lime made. In 1854 the lease was sold to Elias Crapper (d. 1885), whose company held it until at least 1888. The Portland Street Limeworks north of the Hatherton works had been established by John Brewer by 1860; between 1868 and 1872 it was taken over by Crapper and later merged with the Hatherton works, though both names were retained. About 1889 the works passed to Brewer & Marriott; Marriott was probably J. J. Marriott, one of Crapper's legatees. It was taken over c. 1895 by G. L. Lavender, who closed it in 1903.[46] It was the last limeworks in Walsall.[47]

BRICK-MAKING. Brick clays, including the Etruria Marls of the Upper Coal Measures and clays of the Silurian Wenlock Shales, have been available for working in most parts of the parish.[48] Though there is evidence of brick-making at Bescot in 1617, at Wood End during much of the 18th century, at Hampton Lane (probably the present Wolverhampton Street) by 1768, and at Wallington Heath by 1769, those works may have been small and short-lived.[49] In 1777, however, a brickworks at Wallington Heath was evidently producing 180,000 bricks a year.[50] In the earlier 19th century the industry became firmly established. In 1813 there were 3 works in the parish, one (in existence by 1806) at Birchills Colliery, one on the Birmingham road, and

one belonging to Samuel Wood, who made bricks, tiles, sough tiles, and quarries.[51] By 1829 the number of works had reached 6, and by 1834 there were eight. Three works in 1834 were near the town centre, and there were others at the Parks, at James Bridge, and at Wisemore.[52] The industry expanded until at least the late 1850s, with yards widely distributed throughout the parish. The largest, R. Thomas's works at Bloxwich, produced 1,200,000 bricks in 1858 and was then among the five largest in South Staffordshire. At least one yard, at Goscote, made pipes and tiles as well as bricks.[53] Bricks continued to be made until at least the Second World War. In the late 1930s there were still five firms making bricks in the county borough,[54] but by 1951 all had closed.[55]

METAL-WORKING. *The primary metal industries.* Despite the importance of Walsall ironstone early iron-smelting in the parish seems to have been small-scale and intermittent, perhaps because water-power was limited. About 1300 Roger de Morteyn granted Adam the bloomer an acre of waste at Bloxwich.[56] The name 'Synderhulleffeld', which occurs in 1333, may indicate early iron-smelting in the Birchills area.[57] In the late 1380s and 1390s Robert Grubbere was apparently working a bloomsmithy, buying the ore from the lord of the manor and reselling the metal to him. In 1390–1 the lord also bought 42 blooms of iron from Warin de Walton of Walsall and William Hoggettes.[58] There was probably a bloomsmithy near the Tame at some time before 1528, when Martin Pemerton sold Bloomsmithy meadow 'beneath Tame Shrugges' to Roger Westcote.[59] It may have been on Full Brook near Palfrey Green, where Smithy leasow is mentioned in 1617; the remains of a bloomsmithy in that area were found when Brockhurst sewage farm was built in the early 1880s.[60] In the later 1570s Richard Worthington, William Gorwey, and John Stone of Walsall felled trees in Bentley Hay to provide charcoal for their 'smithmills',[61] possibly Meadow mill which Worthington was leasing in 1576 and which probably stood on Walsall Brook near Long Meadow.[62] Another bloomsmithy was

[41] Ibid./188, p. 5; White, *Dir. Staffs.* (1851); *P.O. Dir. Staffs.* (1860).
[42] Barrow and others, *Geol. Country around Lichfield*, 20.
[43] *P.O. Dir. Staffs.* (1845); White, *Dir. Staffs.* (1851); W.S.L., S. MS. 417/Walsall, nos. 1140, 1143; O.S. Map 6", Staffs. LXIII. NW. (1889 edn.).
[44] Harrison, Harrod & Co. *Dir. Staffs.* (1861).
[45] S.R.O., D. 695/4/25/2, bill from Matthews to Saunders & Bennett, 1873; S.R.O., D. 1287/1/47, Walsall accts. 1880–1, p. 19; *List of Mines . . . in . . . 1888* (H.M.S.O., 1889), 149; *Kelly's Dir. Staffs.* (1892). It disappears from *List of Mines* after the edn. for 1892.
[46] S.R.O., D. 260/M/E/430/2, leases of 29 Sept. 1843, 25 Sept. 1855; M/E/186, pp. 66–8; /418; *P.O. Dir. Staffs.* (1860; 1868; 1872); *List of Mines, 1888*, 149; *1903*, 338; *Walsall Red Book* (1889; 1895); *Kelly's Dir. Staffs.* (1892); O.S. Map 6", Staffs. LXIII. NE., NW. (1889 edn.); County Boro. of Walsall, *Proposed Primary Highway Network: Report Drawings, 1972*, plan 11; above p. 176.
[47] None is given in *List of Mines, 1904* and later edns.
[48] G. Barrow and others, *Memoirs of Geol. Surv., Geol. of Country around Lichfield*, 115, 206–7; *Records of the School of Mines*, i (2), 211–12.
[49] S.R.O., D. 260/M/F/1/8, ct. of recog. and survey, 1617, p. 6; S.R.O., D.260/M/E/425/4, leases of 28 Feb. 1721/2, 12 and 14 Feb. 1734/5; *Sketchley's and Adams's . . . Univ. Dir. Birmingham . . .* (1770); S.R.O., D. 1287/1/8, Roger

Holmes's acct. 1766–71, casual profits, 28 June 1768 and 9 Sept. 1769.
[50] D. 1287/1/8, Walsall demesne rental 1771–6, casual profits, 24 Mar. 1777.
[51] Pearce, *Walsall*, 141; above p. 189.
[52] Pigot, *Com. Dir. Birm.* (1829), 91; White, *Dir. Staffs.* (1834).
[53] R. Hunt, *Memoirs of Geol. Surv., Mineral Statistics of U.K. for 1858*, ii. 80–6.
[54] *Kelly's Dir Staffs.* (1940).
[55] None within the Walsall boundary is listed in Walsall and District Chamber of Commerce, *Dir. of Walsall Manufacturers and Buyers Guide to Commodities* (1951 edn.).
[56] S.R.O., D. 593/A/2/22/35.
[57] See p. 181.
[58] B.M. Eg. Rolls 8467–70.
[59] S.R.O., D. 593/A/2/20/47. For the later descent of the property see ibid./38 and 41; /J/22/5, Walsall rental (n.d. but between 1533 and 1569); D. 260/M/F/1/5, ff. 18, 21v.; /M/T/1/16; /M/F/1/8, ct. of recog. and survey, 1617, p. 21.
[60] D. 260/M/F/1/8, ct. of recog. and survey, 1617, p. 30; Willmore, *Walsall*, 242; below p. 221.
[61] E 134/35 and 36 Eliz. I Mich./19; *V.C.H. Staffs.* ii. 109.
[62] S.R.O., D. 1287/1/2, survey of Walsall manor, 1576, m. 1; above p. 185.

apparently working in the mid 16th century; it may have been at the New Mill, where there was a ruined bloomsmithy and forge in 1617.[63]

The first recorded blast-furnace in Walsall was built at Birchills, on the site of the present Beechdale estate, apparently between 1802 and 1806. By 1813 the works was owned by Stubbs & James and included a colliery. A second furnace had been built by 1823, but both were then out of blast and remained so until at least 1830. The works is probably identifiable with the Old Birchills furnaces at Birchills Colliery operated by Williams Bros. (otherwise Philip Williams & Sons) from c. 1849 to 1856 when it was apparently taken over by F. C. Perry. It had closed by 1858.[64]

In the late 1840s a second works, the New Birchills on the east side of Green Lane and the north bank of the Wyrley and Essington Canal, was opened by George Jones of Shackerley in Donington (Salop.), a former partner of Philip Williams.[65] It too was associated with a colliery. There were two furnaces by 1848 and five by 1853. By 1851 the works employed 400 men and the make was some 20,000 tons of pig a year. George Jones was succeeded in the mid 1850s by his son John, who sold the works in 1867. At that time it was an integrated concern using coal and iron ore from the site and making finished iron from pig; there were 28 puddling furnaces, a foundry, and mills for the production of sheet and hoop iron. The works was split up after the sale. The finished-iron plant had passed by 1872 to two new companies, Bunch, Jones & Co. and the Birchills Hall Iron Co. (from the mid 1880s the Bloxwich Iron & Steel Co.). The blast-furnaces were acquired by the Birchills Estate Co., which sold them in 1874 to the Castle Coal & Iron Co. There were then only four furnaces; the Castle company rebuilt two and demolished the rest. Pig was produced until 1878, but the company could make no profit and in 1880 leased the works to E. C. and W. A. Peake. They made 53,000 tons of pig in the next three years but lost much money and had to give up the lease in 1883. The works then ceased production altogether. It was sold to T. W. Ward of Sheffield in 1890 but had been demolished by 1901.

In 1851 Thomas and Charles Highway, lessees of the Green Lanes Colliery on the west side of Green Lane opposite the New Birchills works, opened an ironworks there.[66] It was known as the Green Lanes Furnaces. One furnace was built in 1851 and a second had been finished by 1853. In 1861 they were held by Isaac Highway, but c. 1867 they were taken over by the Walsall Iron Co., owned by John Jones & Sons. The firm failed in 1882 but was reconstituted as Jones Bros. and evidently continued to work the plant until 1894. In that year the works was bought by John Russell & Co. Ltd., a Walsall firm of wrought-iron and tube manufacturers. Russells was succeeded between 1904 and 1908 by Birchills Furnaces Ltd., which continued to operate the furnaces until at least 1917. By 1920 the firm had stopped making pig-iron but was still working a foundry, which closed c. 1925. The furnaces had been demolished by 1938.

In 1845 Lord Hatherton leased land for a colliery and ironworks adjoining the canal north of Leamore Lane, Bloxwich, to Richard Fryer of the Wergs, Tettenhall.[67] The lease passed to his son W. F. Fryer in 1846. Two furnaces were built apparently in the early 1850s. At some time between 1868 and 1871 Fryer leased the works, known as the Hatherton Furnaces, to George and Richard Thomas of Bloxwich. From the early 1880s until 1923 they operated a forge and rolling-mill at Birchills in conjunction with the furnaces. In the mid 1920s the firm became G. & R. Thomas Ltd.; it was liquidated in 1935 and the assets were acquired by A. J. While. In 1960 the company was taken over by the Staveley Coal & Iron Co. Ltd., and c. 1968 it passed to Staveley Industries Ltd. The furnaces, the last in Walsall, were blown out in 1948, but the firm continued to refine iron until 1965, thereafter concentrating on the production of castings. In 1974 G. & R. Thomas Ltd. formed part of the Alloy Castings Division of Bradley & Foster Ltd., a subsidiary of Staveley Industries Ltd. The works then produced electrically melted alloy castings and medium jobbing grey-iron castings.

In the 1850s and 1860s a number of works for the manufacture of bar and sheet iron and rolled sections were established. The first seems to have been that in Pleck Road owned in 1851 by Sinkinson & Lancaster; by 1856 the firm was Brayford & Lancaster and had a second works at Birchills.[68] By 1873 there were seven works in the Birchills district, Pleck Road, and Bridgeman Street; the largest, Edward Russell's Cyclops Ironworks in Pleck Road, had 22 puddling furnaces and 3 rolling-mills.[69] Although the smelting industry was already in difficulties, the wrought-iron trade apparently continued to prosper. In the late 1880s there were eight works, producing 1,250 tons a week of rounds, squares, flats, and horse-shoe and sheet-iron.[70] The Bloxwich Iron &

[63] S.R.O., D. 593/J/22/5, Walsall rental; above p. 185. Willmore, *Walsall*, 242, identifies the Brockhurst smithy with that at the New Mill. *V.C.H. Staffs.* ii. 113, states wrongly that there was a bloomsmithy at Bescot working in 1600, apparently referring to the New Mill.

[64] J. Farey, *General View of Agric. of Derbs.* iii. 453; Pearce, *Walsall*, 134–5; H. Scrivenor, *Hist. of Iron Trade* (1854), 96–8, 133; J. Phillips and W. F. Hutchings, *Map of Staffs.* (1832); A. Birch, *Econ. Hist. of Brit. Iron and Steel Ind. 1784–1879*, 390; *P.O. Dir. Staffs.* (1850; 1854); R. Hunt, *Memoirs of Geol. Surv., Mineral Statistics of U.K. for 1853 and 1854*, 42; *V.C.H. Staffs.* ii. 128. It is listed in Hunt, *Mineral Statistics 1858*, 89, but not ibid. *1859*.

[65] For this para. see B. Poole, *Statistics of Brit. Commerce* (1852), 203; Birch, *Brit. Iron and Steel Ind.* 390; *P.O. Dir. Staffs.* (1850; 1854; 1872); White, *Dir. Staffs.* (1851); Hunt, *Mineral Statistics 1853–4*, 42; *1857*, 76; S.R.O., D. 695/4/25/2–4; O.S. Map 6″, Staffs. LXIII. NW. (edns. of 1889 and 1903).

[66] For this para. see W.S.L. 35/21/48, /22/48, /23/48; Hunt, *Mineral Statistics 1853–4*, 42; *1867*, 74; *1868*, 81; *P.O. Dir. Staffs.* (1854; 1872); Harrison, Harrod & Co. *Dir. Staffs.* (1861); S. Griffiths, *Griffiths's Guide to Iron Trade of Gt. Brit.* (1873), 255; *Kelly's Dir. Staffs.* (1880 and later edns. to 1908); *Walsall Observer*, 10 Nov. 1894; *Walsall Red Book* (1910 and later edns. to 1925); *Walsall Blue Book* (1920); O.S. Map 1/2,500, Staffs. LXIII. 6 (1915 edn.; prov. edn. with addns. of 1938).

[67] This para. is based on S.R.O., D. 260/M/E/430/2, counterpart lease of 7 June 1845 and endorsements; Hunt, *Mineral Statistics 1855*, 46; *P.O. Dir. Staffs.* (1868; 1872); *Kelly's Dir. Staffs.* (1884; 1928); *Iron and Steel Works of the World* (1969 edn.); inf. from Mr. C. G. While of G. & R. Thomas Ltd. (1974).

[68] *Robinson's Walsall Dir.* (1851); Hunt, *Mineral Statistics 1856*, 66.

[69] Griffiths, *Iron Trade*, 269; *P.O. Dir. Staffs.* (1872).

[70] *Guide to Walsall* (1889), 65.

Steel Co. also made Bessemer steel and tubes at the Birchills Hall works.[71] From the 1890s, however, the number of firms fell, presumably owing to the increased use of mild steel and the consequent decline in demand for the wrought iron of the Black Country.[72] The Bloxwich Iron & Steel Co. was liquidated in 1895.[73] The New Side and the Cormorant ironworks at Pleck had merged by 1896, and by 1900 the number of firms had fallen to five.[74] By the early 1920s there were only four firms, and two of them closed between 1928 and 1932.[75] At the end of the Second World War two firms survived. One, W. M. Lester & Sons Ltd., evidently closed between 1947 and 1952; the other, the Walsall District Iron Co. Ltd., was still making rolled metal in Birchills Street in 1970 but closed c. 1972.[76]

Although the use of non-ferrous metals in finished products has a long history in Walsall, they were not smelted or refined there on a large scale until the 20th century, when first zinc and later copper and aluminium smelters were established. The Delaville Spelter Works in Willenhall Lane, Bloxwich, was begun in 1902 by the New Delaville Spelter Co. Ltd., a consortium headed by A. C. Griffiths of Birmingham.[77] One distillation furnace was completed in 1902 and a second in 1907. By 1918 there were eight furnaces smelting zinc ash and two sweater furnaces for recovering zinc from hard spelter; zinc oxide was also produced. In 1929 the works also began to make zinc dust. About that time the company became the Delaville Spelter Co. Ltd., and was taken over by the Imperial Smelting Corporation in 1933. In 1935 the zinc oxide furnace was closed; metallic zinc was smelted intermittently until 1945, but the plant was then scrapped. During and after the Second World War, however, zinc dust production expanded, and in 1941 a plant was installed to make Mazak zinc alloy for die-casting. By 1970 a million tons of alloy had been produced. In the early 1950s the company also transferred production of high purity zinc anodes for electroplating from its works at Avonmouth (in Bristol), and in 1957 the Bloxwich works began making special anodes to protect steel against sea-water corrosion. In 1974 the works made zinc dust, zinc alloy, and anodes. As a result of company reorganizations it was then occupied by I.S.C. Alloys Ltd., owned by Australian Mining and Smelting Ltd., a subsidiary of Rio-Tinto Zinc Corporation Ltd. The Mazak alloy plant, however, was owned by Mazak Ltd., a subsidiary of Imperial Smelting formed in 1966.

In 1919 the Wolverhampton Metal Co. Ltd. of Wednesfield in St. Peter's, Wolverhampton, bought a factory at James Bridge as a copper-smelting works for its subsidiary, James Bridge Copper Works Ltd. Owing to financial difficulties copper production was intermittent until c. 1930, but it has been continuous from that time. In 1967 Wolverhampton Metal was taken over by I.M.I. and became I.M.I. Refinery Holdings Ltd. As a result of extensions to the plant from the mid 1960s the refinery was in 1974 the largest works in Britain producing copper from scrap and residues. The principal products were electrolytic copper cathodes and shapes; other metals refined as by-products included nickel, zinc, tin, lead, gold, silver, platinum, and palladium.[78] In 1949 a site in Goscote Lane was acquired for a copper refinery by Mercury Securities Ltd. Its subsidiary, Elkington Ltd., moved there from Birmingham in 1950. In 1954 a factory for hot-brass pressings was also established on the site but was sold in 1955 to the Delta Metal Group. The copper refinery was retained as Elkington Copper Refiners Ltd. The works was extended in 1966, and in 1968 a tin-recovery plant was added. The chief product has been copper cathodes, which were still made in 1974, but copper alloy ingots were also cast there until 1968.[79] About 1948 J. Frankel (Aluminium) Ltd. began to refine aluminium on the site of the former Globe Ironworks in Charles Street. In 1974 it was producing aluminium alloy ingots from scrap for use by foundries, rolling-mills, and steelworks.[80]

The lighter metal trades. Since at least the 15th century the principal industry of Walsall has been metal-working, particularly the manufacture of small articles in iron and brass. The most important products have been the metal parts of saddlery, but the parish has also been a centre of the buckle, lock, awl-blade, nail, chain, and pewter and brass hollow-ware trades. In the late 19th and the 20th centuries there has been even greater variety.

Robert Grubbere had a forge in the borough in 1362–3.[81] In 1394–5 Richard Marchal of Walsall sold nails to the borough bailiff for the earl of Warwick's household. His smithy on the church hill was still working in 1404–5, when there was also a smithy in Rushall Street belonging to William Marshall.[82] In 1410 William Mercer was granted waste in Bloxwich to build a smithy.[83] Several other smiths occur later in the 15th century.[84] By the mid 15th century some iron-workers were specializing in horse furniture. John Sporior, admitted a burgess in 1377, may have been a spurrier.[85] Three Walsall lorimers occur in 1435,[86] and thereafter the trade is often mentioned. About 1540 Leland noted that there were many smiths and bit-makers in the town.[87] By then horse furniture was also made in the foreign. A Bloxwich lorimer occurs in 1523,[88] and John Baily of Bloxwich was working as a lorimer

[71] *Kelly's Dir. Staffs.* (1888).
[72] *V.C.H. Staffs.* ii. 127.
[73] *Walsall Red Book* (1895), 182; (1896), 188.
[74] *Kelly's Dir. Staffs.* (1896; 1900).
[75] Cope, *Dir. Staffs.* (1921); *Kelly's Dir. Staffs.* (1928; 1932).
[76] *Kelly's Dir. Merchants, Manufacturers, and Shippers* (1947; 1952); *P.O. Telephone Dir. Sect. 451: 1970*; ex inf. (1974) John Stokes Ltd., who took over the Walsall District Iron Co.'s premises.
[77] This para. is based on inf. from Mr. L. T. Evans of I.S.C. Alloys Ltd. (1974); E. J. Cocks and B. Walters, *Hist. of Zinc Smelting Ind. in Brit.* 56, 93–4, 125, 135–6, 139–40, 149; *Kelly's Dir. Staffs.* (1928; 1932).

[78] Ex inf. Mr. F. W. James of I.M.I. Refinery Holdings Ltd. (1974).
[79] *Birmingham Post*, 4 July 1966; *Metal Bulletin*, 22 Nov. 1968; ex inf. Mr. H. Rowbotham of Elkington Copper Refiners Ltd. (1974).
[80] *Non-ferrous Metalworks of the World* (1967); ex inf. Mr. H. L. Roberts of J. Frankel (Aluminium) Ltd. (1974).
[81] *S.H.C.* xiv (1), 115–16.
[82] B.M. Eg. Rolls 8472, 8481.
[83] S.R.O., D. 260/M/F/1/5, f. 172.
[84] B.R.L. 428413; B.M. Eg. Roll 8453; *S.H.C.* n.s. iv. 143.
[85] W.T.C. II/238, m. 1.
[86] *S.H.C.* n.s. iii. 130.
[87] See p. 145.
[88] See p. 184.

when he died in 1561.[89] In 1608 there were lorimers at both Great and Little Bloxwich.[90] A lorimer at Wood End occurs in 1615, and a spurrier at Harden in 1636.[91] The Smith family of Caldmore were spur-makers by the earlier 18th century.[92]

By the mid 16th century Walsall horse furniture reached a wide market. Richard Hopkes of Walsall in 1542 recorded debts for stirrups, 'odd bits', fine bits, and snaffles sold at Exeter and Bristol. He was also owed money, presumably for hardware, by saddlers and others of Devonshire, Somerset, Dorset, and the West Riding of Yorkshire.[93] He may have been a chapman selling lorimers' wares but not making them himself. Nicholas Jackson of Walsall (d. 1560) was almost certainly a chapman: at his death nearly half his possessions consisted of bits, stirrups, spurs, and buckles, but there were no smith's tools.[94] By the early 17th century the wares of smaller producers were normally sold to such chapmen travelling to London and elsewhere.[95]

By the late 17th century the horse-furniture trade was highly specialized and each article usually included parts made by several different craftsmen. Products then included several designs of spur, 5 types of snaffle with 6 varieties of end, 6 types of bit, 4 sorts of stirrup, and other ironwork including curbs, chains, bolts, rings, swivels, saddle-bars, and plates.[96] The industry continued to prosper in the 18th century. A list of trades in 1770 includes 19 spur and spur-rowel makers, 11 stirrup-makers, 5 bit-makers, 18 snaffle-makers, and 10 saddlers' ironmongers. Most of the craftsmen were working in the borough, but there were 2 stirrup-makers at Windmill, 2 spurriers and 2 snaffle-makers at Caldmore, 2 spurriers at Whitehall, 4 snaffle-makers and 3 stirrup-makers at Birchills, and a snaffle-maker in Bloxwich Lane.[97] By 1784 there were 17 saddlers' ironmongers in the town.[98]

In the late 17th century horse furniture was still the staple trade,[99] but in the 18th century buckle-making became the chief source of industrial employment. It probably arose out of the horse-furniture trade, as buckles were required for spurs, bridles, and saddle-straps. Buckles were already being made in the 16th century. In 1542 Richard Hopkes was trading in them,[1] and in 1551 a buckle-maker was admitted a burgess.[2] In the late 17th century saddlery buckles were the chief product but shoe and garter buckles were also made, usually by other craftsmen. Most were probably of iron, but some were of brass.[3] By the early 18th century there

were many buckle-makers. In 1715 22 buckle-makers, a buckle-tongue maker, and a chape-maker were among those charged with burning down the meeting-house in Bank Court.[4] By 1750 buckle-making was apparently the chief trade,[5] and by 1770 there were 278 workshops, including those of makers, forgers, and filers of chapes and tongues. Most were in the borough but there were 24 at Windmill, 11 at Caldmore, 4 at Doveridge, 16 at Birchills, several in Bloxwich Lane, and one at Park Brook.[6] Buckles were exported to France, Spain, Holland, and Germany.[7] In the 1790s, however, rising prices of raw materials due to the war, and the fashion for shoe-strings, greatly reduced the demand for buckles. In 1792 a deputation of Walsall buckle-makers persuaded the Prince Regent to enforce the wearing of shoe-buckles at Court, but the regulation had no lasting effect. By c. 1800 many buckle-makers were unemployed or learning new trades.[8]

As has been mentioned, nails were made in the borough in the late 14th century. Nailing as a specialist trade was found from the 17th century: three Walsall nailers occur in 1603, and Bloxwich nailers are mentioned from 1606.[9] By 1673 nails were among Walsall's main products.[10] The trade became concentrated in the foreign. In 1767 there was only one nailer in the borough and none occurs in subsequent 18th-century lists; in the 1790s, however, nailing was 'very considerable' in the foreign, employing many women and children 'making the finer and lighter sorts, which they do very well'.[11]

Walsall locksmiths are mentioned in 1597 and 1614.[12] Samuel Wilks of Bloxwich (d. 1764) was a locksmith.[13] In 1767 there were four locksmiths in the borough, and in 1770 there were also one at Caldmore and one at Birchills.[14] Other iron-working trades were also established by the later 18th century. Cast-iron pots were made in the 1680s.[15] A Walsall file-cutter occurs in 1753, and in 1767 there were two file-makers and a file-cutter in the borough. One file-maker, John Heptinstall, continued to work in the town until at least the 1790s.[16] Thomas Ross was making awl blades at Windmill in 1767, and by 1770 Matthew Ross (also at Windmill) and Joseph Ross at Whitehall were also making them.[17] Bloxwich, however, was evidently the main source of awl blades from the 1760s.[18] Thomas Elwell was making steel trusses at Walsall by 1754,[19] and from at least 1765 until his death in 1793 William Elwell had an iron-foundry in the town.[20] There were also two die-sinkers and

[89] L.J.R.O., will proved 12 June 1561.
[90] *S.H.C.* 1948–9, 70, 83.
[91] Sims, *Cal. of Deeds*, p. 54; W.C.L., box 24, no. 20.
[92] W.S.L., S. MS. 333/32, p. 3.
[93] L.J.R.O., will proved 1543.
[94] Ibid., will proved 23 Aug. 1560, inventory.
[95] *V.C.H. Staffs.* ii. 236.
[96] Plot, *Staffs.* 376.
[97] *Sketchley's and Adams's . . . Univ. Dir. Birmingham . . .* (1770), excluding the Bloxwich area.
[98] *Bailey's Brit. Dir.* (1784), 467–9.
[99] R. Blome, *Britannia* (1673), 206; Plot, *Staffs.* 376–7.
[1] L.J.R.O., will proved 1543.
[2] W.T.C. II/238, m. 10.
[3] Plot, *Staffs.* 377.
[4] Assizes 4/18, pp. 237–8.
[5] *Walsall Records*, 27 (2nd nos.).
[6] *Sketchley's and Adams's . . . Univ. Dir. Birmingham . . .* (1770).
[7] *Narrative of the Eventful Life of Thomas Jackson . . . Written by Himself* (Birmingham, 1847), 2.

[8] Ibid. 2, 124; Willmore, *Walsall*, 382; Shaw, *Staffs.* ii. 75–6.
[9] *S.H.C.* 1940, 21, 296; B.R.L. 464643.
[10] Blome, *Britannia*, 206.   [11] Shaw, *Staffs.* ii. 75.
[12] *S.H.C.* 1932, 306; L.J.R.O., will of Ric. Heyes, proved 1 Mar. 1613/14, inventory.
[13] Homeshaw, *Bloxwich*, plate facing p. 113.
[14] *Sketchley's Birmingham . . . Dir.* (1767); *Sketchley's and Adams's . . . Univ. Dir. Birmingham . . .* (1770).
[15] Plot, *Staffs.* 377.
[16] *Aris's Birmingham Gaz.* 26 Nov. 1753; *Sketchley's Birmingham . . . Dir.* (1767); *Univ. Brit. Dir.* iv. 667.
[17] *Sketchley's Birmingham . . . Dir.* (1767); *Sketchley's and Adams's . . . Univ. Dir. Birmingham . . .* (1770).
[18] *Birm. and Mid. Hardware Dist.* 128.
[19] *Aris's Birmingham Gaz.* 21 Oct. 1754.
[20] S.R.O., D. 1287/6/14, lease of lands in Walsall and Bentley, 1 May 1765; *Bailey's Brit. Dir.* (1784), 468; *Univ. Brit. Dir.* iv. 667; C. J. L. Elwell, *The Iron Elwells* (Ilfracombe, 1964), 37, 39.

stampers in 1767,[21] and one die-sinker in the later 1790s.[22]

Pewter and brassware were also made at Walsall by the late Middle Ages. A John Brasier, presumably a brazier, was admitted a burgess in 1377,[23] and Richard Marche was working as a brazier in the earlier 15th century.[24] Braziers are mentioned in a list of tradesmen of 1494.[25] Pewtering may have been established by 1400: the father of Thomas Fylkes, a citizen and pewterer of London in 1415, was living at Walsall by 1399.[26] Richard Woodward of Walsall was described as a pewterer in 1438–9,[27] and from the mid 16th century pewterers and braziers occur frequently. Some craftsmen worked in both metals.[28] A bell-founder is mentioned in 1462, and there were two in the earlier 17th century.[29] In the late 16th and earlier 17th centuries, however, most craftsmen were making household utensils: pots, pans, kettles, warming-pans, and ladles of brass, and spoons, saucers, plates and dishes, candlesticks, salt-cellars, bottles, measures, and chamber-pots of fine or ley pewter.[30] Most of the pewterers and braziers worked in the borough, but there was a pewterer in Caldmore probably in the late 16th century.[31] The pewter trade probably declined from the mid 17th century: later-17th-century observers make no mention of it, and by 1767 there was only one pewterer in the town.[32] The brass trade, however, continued to flourish. Mention is made in 1664 of the casting of brasses at Walsall for window casements,[33] and in the 1680s not only brass but also copper hollow-ware was made. The copper-smiths also produced bosses, pendants, stars, labels, coach-nails, and studs.[34] A brazier and four copper-smiths became capital burgesses between 1700 and 1720.[35] In the later 18th century, however, the copper and brass hollow-ware trades probably declined. There was only one brazier in 1770, in the 'market place' (presumably High Street), and there were only two in the town in the later 1790s.[36] Buckles, on the other hand, were often made of brass; a brass-locksmith occurs in 1770 and a brass-cock founder in 1771.[37] In the late 18th century Walsall metal goods still required much brass, and the corporation in 1783 supported a petition to the Commons against the export of raw brass.[38]

Tinning was established in Walsall by the late 17th century; both horse furniture and brass, copper, and iron hollow-ware were often tinned.[39] The brazier mentioned in 1770 and one of the two braziers of the later 1790s were also tinners.[40] Two whitesmiths and two saddle-tree platers occur in 1767, and two other platers, one of whom made bits, in 1784.[41] Japanned buckles were made by 1770, and by the 1790s some buckles were plated with silver.[42]

The demands of war in the late 18th and early 19th centuries led to a rapid increase in the number of horse-furniture workshops. In 1813 there were 37 general bit-makers, 11 coach-bit makers, 20 snaffle- and bradoon-makers, 2 pelham-makers, 22 stirrup-makers, 3 spur-makers, 2 spur-rowel makers, 11 curb-makers, 6 martingale-hook and spring-saddle-bar makers, and 15 saddlers' ironmongers. Most of the bit-makers worked in and around Bloxwich. The other trades centred on the borough, but there were several curb- and stirrup-makers at Bloxwich, Birchills, and Townend.[43] The number of works making saddlers' ironmongery expanded very rapidly until the 1830s. There were at least 153 firms producing it in 1829, and by 1834 there were 144 bit-makers alone. Expansion took place mainly within the existing centres: bit-making remained chiefly concentrated in Bloxwich and spur- and curb-making in the borough, but by 1834 many bit and stirrup workshops had been established in Green Lane, Blue Lane, Stafford Street, Wisemore, and Ryecroft Street.[44] After 1834, despite a steady rise in demand, few additional workshops were established. In the earlier 1860s there were some 250 firms making saddlers' ironmongery; a few occupied factories but most worked in single shops. The trade employed about 1,000 people. Most firms apparently still specialized in one or two items but some made a larger range.[45]

In the later 19th century the relative importance of Bloxwich in the bit and stirrup trades declined. In 1872 only 47 bit-makers and 9 stirrup-makers are recorded in Bloxwich and Blakenall, while in Walsall in 1873 there were 57 bit-makers and 27 stirrup-makers; most were either in the area around Stafford Street and Littleton Street or in Caldmore. There were also 22 spur-makers in 1873; most were in the Caldmore area but there were workshops in New, Goodall, Lichfield, and Bradford Streets. Allied trades included 6 Devonshire-slipper manufacturers and 7 spring-saddle-bar makers.[46] The change in the distribution of the works was probably due to the introduction of malleable-iron horse furniture; bits and stirrups could be cast rather than forged. Malleable iron-founding is said to have

21 *Sketchley's Birmingham . . . Dir.* (1767).
22 *Univ. Brit. Dir.* iv. 667.
23 W.T.C. II/238, m. 1.
24 *Cal. Pat.* 1446–52, 293, describing him as late of Walsall.
25 *S.H.C.* 1928, 224.
26 W.S.L. D. 1798/96, deed of 17 May 1415; *Cal. Pat.* 1396–9, 496.
27 D. 1798/84, deed of 23 Feb. 1438/9.
28 L.J.R.O., wills of Ric. and Eliz. Parker (proved 8 May 1534 and 16 Jan. 1541/2), Wm. Nicholls (17 Jan. 1578/9), Thos. Jennings (3 Apr. 1616), Rob. Ebb (1 May 1637), inventories.
29 *Cal. Pat.* 1461–7, 172; T. S. Jennings, *Hist. of Staffs. Bells* (priv. print. n.d. but *c.* 1968), 62; W.T.C. II/13/34.
30 L.J.R.O., wills of Wm. Nicholls, Thos. Jennings, Rob. Ebb, inventories; will and inventory of John Nicholls (2 Aug. 1629); admin. of John Seney, granted 8 Oct. 1630, inventory.
31 Ibid., will of Joshua Nicolls, proved 31 Mar. 1615.
32 *Sketchley's Birmingham . . . Dir.* (1767).
33 Hist. MSS. Com. 24, *Rutland*, iv, p. 543.
34 Plot, *Staffs.* 377.   35 Homeshaw, *Walsall*, 160–1.
36 *Aris's Birmingham Gaz.* 18 Sept. 1780; *Sketchley's and Adams's . . . Univ. Dir. Birmingham . . .* (1770); *Univ. Brit. Dir.* iv. 667–8.
37 *Sketchley's and Adams's . . . Univ. Dir. Birmingham . . .* (1770); W.S.L., M. 957.
38 H. Hamilton, *Eng. Brass and Copper Inds. to 1800*, 224.   39 Plot, *Staffs.* 377.
40 *Sketchley's and Adams's . . . Univ. Dir. Birmingham . . .* (1770); *Univ. Brit. Dir.* iv. 668.
41 *Sketchley's Birmingham . . . Dir.* (1767); *Bailey's Brit. Dir.* (1784), 468.
42 *Sketchley's and Adams's . . . Univ. Dir. Birmingham . . .* (1770); *Univ. Brit. Dir.* iv. 665.
43 Pearce, *Walsall*, 148–69.
44 Pigot, *Com. Dir. Birm.* (1829), 90–4; White, *Dir. Staffs.* (1834).
45 *3rd Rep. Com. Child. Emp.* [3414-i], p. 5, H.C. (1864), xxii; *Birm. and Mid. Hardware Dist.* 126, 130.
46 *P.O. Dir. Staffs.* (1872); *Walsall Red Book* (1873).

begun in Walsall *c.* 1811,[47] but at first it seems to have made little impact on saddler's ironmongery. By 1834 there were six malleable iron-founders making horse furniture, and by 1851 thirteen.[48] In the earlier 1860s, however, it was estimated that there were about 25 to 30 malleable iron-founders; they cast bits and snaffles and sold them to the small finishers.[49] The number was probably exaggerated,[50] but in 1873 there were 17 iron-founders making horse furniture in Walsall; most of them were in the town centre and in Caldmore, in the Bridgeman Street area, and round Stafford Street.[51]

The spread of malleable iron-founding, and in the late 19th century of nickel casting, evidently encouraged the concentration of horse-furniture production in larger units, and in the late 19th century workshops rapidly fell in number. A list of 1900 records only 28 bit-makers, of whom 10 were at Blakenall Heath, 5 at Bloxwich, one at Harden, and most of the rest either in the Hatherton Street area or Caldmore; 11 stirrup-makers and stirrup-iron manufacturers, of whom 2 were at Bloxwich, 3 at Caldmore, and the rest near the town centre; and 2 spring-bar makers in Pool and Short Acre Streets.[52] While the number of works fell, their average size increased. In 1889 it was estimated that there were 50 bit-makers alone with over 450 workers, and 30 stirrup-makers with 250 workers. By 1905 there were 50 employers with nearly 1,000 workers.[53] One of the larger firms, Matthew Harvey & Co. Ltd., extended its works between 1896 and 1900 by adding a long range in Bath Street to the original premises in Windmill Street. By 1914 the firm employed 600 workers and made a variety of metal castings and leather goods as well as horse furniture.[54]

In the earlier 20th century the horse-furniture trade suffered a decline interrupted briefly by the First World War.[55] By 1939 there were only 14 firms making bits, spurs, and stirrups.[56] During and after the Second World War there were several mergers of the larger firms. In 1943 John Dewsbury & Sons Ltd., of Littleton Street West, was taken over by James Cotterell & Sons Ltd., which also absorbed A. S. Smith & Sons Ltd. of Charles Street in 1959.[57] In 1953 Matthew Harvey & Co. Ltd. took over F. Eglington of Bridgeman Street.[58] In 1974 there were four large firms specializing in saddlery hardware. Cotterells, which had left Littleton Street West for Bridgeman Street in 1973, made saddlery hardware and leather-goods fittings. Harveys at the Glebeland Works in Bath Street produced steel and nickel bits, spurs, and stirrups,

brass and iron buckles, coach fittings, and many other small metal articles.[59] Stanley Bros. (Walsall) made bits, spurs, stirrups, and buckles at its works in Intown Row, and S. B. & N. Ltd. in Brockhurst Crescent produced stainless-steel saddlery hardware and castings. There were five smaller specialist lorimers in Caldmore and Bloxwich,[60] and Samuel Price, buckle-makers in Tantarra Street, also made saddlery hardware.[61]

A number of other trades allied to horse-furniture also flourished in the 19th century. By 1813 chains and all kinds of ironwork used in cart harness were made in Walsall.[62] There were seven manufacturers of hames and harness irons with works in Blue Lane, Stafford Street, Wisemore Lane, Intown Row, Ablewell Street, George Street, and Prospect Row.[63] The number of firms making cart gear and allied products reached 16 in 1851, and by 1873 there were 11 cart-gear makers and another 22 firms making hames and harness-irons. Down to 1860 most firms remained in the centre, but by 1873 there were several works in Blue Lane, Green Lane, Littleton Street West, and Wisemore, and odd firms in Bath Street and Pleck Road.[64] The number of works had fallen again by 1900,[65] but presumably because of the war the number of firms making cart gear had increased to 33 by 1921; some of them were also horse-furniture manufacturers.[66] By 1939, however, 20 firms had ceased production.[67] In the 1950s and 1960s most of the remaining firms gave up cart gear, but three were still producing it in 1974.[68]

The manufacture of spring-hooks and swivels, items used in both saddlery and cart gear, also developed in the 19th century.[69] In 1813 Hughes & Newton were making 'new driving spring-hooks' in Park Street. There were 5 firms making spring-hooks and swivels by 1834 and 18 by 1873. In 1914 there were 14 firms; several of them also made saddlery hardware, chains, cart gear, and buckles. After the First World War it appears that spring-hook making was usually combined with the manufacture of those products.

By 1813 the coach-harness, coach-brassware, and coach-ironmongery trades were well established in the borough. There were 3 firms of coach-brass founders, 4 coach-harness makers including one at Townend, and a coach founder.[70] By 1829 there were 12 coach and harness-furniture manufacturers; most were working near the centre, but there was one in Windmill Street and one in Stafford Street.[71] A coach-builder in Freer Street occurs in 1835.[72] By 1841 there were 2 carriage-lamp makers in Park Street and Lichfield Street.[73] The trade

[47] Allen, *Ind. Dev. Birm.* 36.
[48] White, *Dir. Staffs.* (1834; 1851).
[49] *3rd Rep. Com. Child. Emp.* 31.
[50] *P.O. Dir. Staffs.* (1860) lists only 20 iron-founders.
[51] *Walsall Red Book* (1873).
[52] *Kelly's Dir. Staffs.* (1900).
[53] *Guide to Walsall* (1889), 57–8; *Walsall Past and Present* (1905), 8.
[54] *Kelly's Dir. Staffs.* (1896; 1900); *Walsall Red Book* (1914), pp. xxix sqq.
[55] e.g. *Kelly's Dir. Staffs.* (1912); Cope, *Dir. Staffs.* (1921).
[56] *Walsall Red Book* (1939); ex inf. S. B. & N. Ltd. (1974).
[57] *Walsall Observer*, 17 Aug. 1973.
[58] Ex inf. Mr. C. M. Harvey of Matthew Harvey & Co. Ltd. (1974).
[59] *Walsall Observer*, 17 Aug. 1973; ex inf. Mr. Harvey.

[60] Ex inf. the firms (1974).
[61] *Walsall Chamber of Commerce & Ind. Dir. 1974/5.*
[62] Pearce, *Walsall*, 145.
[63] White, *Dir. Staffs.* (1834).
[64] *Robinson's Walsall Dir.* (1851); *P.O. Dir. Staffs.* (1860); *Walsall Red Book* (1873).
[65] *Kelly's Dir. Staffs.* (1900).
[66] Cope, *Dir. Staffs.* (1921).
[67] *Walsall Red Book* (1939).
[68] Ex inf. Walsall Locks & Cart Gear Ltd. and Peter Bull & Sons (Walsall) Ltd. (1974).
[69] For this para. see Pearce, *Walsall*, 157; White, *Dir. Staffs.* (1834); *Walsall Red Book* (1873; 1914; 1939); Cope, *Dir. Staffs.* (1921).
[70] Pearce, *Walsall*, 146, 172–3.
[71] Pigot, *Com. Dir. Birm.* (1829), 92.
[72] Pigot, *Nat. Com. Dir.* (1835), 467.
[73] Pigot, *Nat. Com. Dir.* (1841), Staffs. p. 82.

continued to expand: in 1900 there were 9 coach and carriage builders and 5 coach-ironmongers; most firms were near the centre, but there were also 2 carriage-lamp makers in Lichfield Street and one in Bath Street.[74] In the earlier 20th century several of the coach-furniture firms began making fittings and bodies for motor-cars,[75] and light cars were produced by Crescent Motors Ltd. in Pleck Road from c. 1911 to c. 1913.[76] In 1970 there were still four firms building car and coach bodies, with works in Garden, Frederick, Bath, and Hillary Streets. Seven firms made car accessories.[77]

From c. 1830 Walsall metal-workers also benefited from the developing market for ornamental harness furniture, mainly horse-brasses. In 1834 there were 36 firms of brass-founders and harness-furniture manufacturers and many others making plated harness furniture, including bits and stirrups. Most of the foundries were in the town centre, but there were 4 in Windmill Street, one at Doveridge, one in Caldmore Terrace, and one in Wolverhampton Road.[78] In the mid 1860s it was estimated that 1,000 workers were employed in plating and 500 in brass-founding, both mainly associated with harness furniture;[79] by 1873 98 firms apparently produced harness furniture.[80] In the later 19th century the number fell; a list of 1900 records only 24, in the same areas as before.[81] Though ornamental harness-furniture making continued into the 20th century, most of the manufacturers were primarily producers of bits, spurs, stirrups, buckles, and other small metal articles.

Allied with harness furniture were the chasing, embossing, and engraving trades. Samuel Barber was working as a chaser in Rushall Street in 1767 and William Thacker in 1834,[82] but there was little growth until the mid 19th century. In 1851 there were 3 engravers and 3 chasers,[83] and by 1873 there were 15 firms of chasers and embossers.[84] From the late 19th century the number of establishments fell again. By 1939 there were only three embossers, H. Gill in Caldmore Road, E. F. Sharpe in Freer Street, and T. Higgins in Sandwell Street; Gill and Sharpe were also heraldic chasers.[85] Both Gill and Sharpe had apparently abandoned the trade by 1953, when Sharpe was making locks.[86]

A list of 1818 records 44 platers in the parish, of whom 31 were in the borough, 11 at Windmill, one in Doveridge Place, and one in Stafford Street.[87] By 1829 the trade had spread to Bloxwich where there were 6 platers out of a total of 42 in the parish; most of the rest were in the town centre, but there were 9 in the streets to the north, 2 at Windmill, and one at Caldmore. At least six plated lorimers' ware and

at least three plated buckles.[88] As already seen, the development of ornamental harness furniture encouraged the expansion of plating, and in the mid 19th century electro-plating was introduced.[89] In 1873 there were at least four firms of electro-platers and gilders besides the harness-furniture platers.[90] From the late 19th century fewer firms specialized in plating, which was more often carried on in conjunction with other work: it was stated in 1905 that almost every manufacturer of small metal goods had his own plating plant.[91] In 1970, however, there were at least twelve specialist electro-platers and metal finishers in Walsall, besides the chromium-plating works of the Verichrome Plating Co. in Wallows Lane.[92]

As already seen, harness chains were made in the late 17th century. In 1770 there was a dog-chain maker in New Street and a watch-chain maker in Hole End.[93] In 1813 there were six dog-chain makers in the Caldmore area and in Rushall Street, Lime Pit Bank, and Stafford Street, and in Ablewell Street a maker of curb-chains, military-overall chains, dog couples, and greyhound starters.[94] Thereafter the trade grew rapidly. The chief products were curb and harness chains and cart chains wrought by the hame-makers. The number of chain-making firms probably reached a peak in the 1840s. There were 69 in 1841, but by 1851 the number had apparently fallen to 52, of which 2 were in Caldmore, one in Bloxwich, one in Blakenall, and the rest in the town, most of them at the north end.[95] In the late 19th century chains were probably being made by saddlers'-ironmongery and cart-gear manufacturers, but the number of specialist chain-makers seems to have fallen. In 1900 there were 20 hame- and chain-makers and a further 10 specialist chain-makers; two firms made chain cables.[96] Chain-making remained closely connected with cart gear and horse furniture in the 20th century. In 1921 there were 30 chain-makers, but most were primarily makers of cart gear, horse furniture, or buckles.[97] That was still true of the 8 firms making chains in 1953; only one was a specialist chain-maker.[98] Chain-making nevertheless survived the decline of the cart-gear trade and in 1974 3 firms specialized in light chains (including dog and harness chains) and 2 in industrial chains.[99]

Although the slump in the buckle trade in the late 18th century reduced it to secondary importance there were still 21 buckle-makers in 1813; hat, knee, brace, and saddlery buckles were produced. Some buckle-makers also made spoons, locks, or coach brassware. One was in Birchills, two in Caldmore, one at Doveridge, one in Fullbrook

[74] Kelly's Dir. Staffs. (1900).
[75] Walsall Red Book (1929).
[76] G. R. Doyle and G. N. Georgano, The World's Automobiles 1862–1962, 56; G. R. Doyle, The World's Automobiles (1959 edn.), 57; Kelly's Dir. Staffs. (1912); above p. 114.
[77] P.O. Telephone Dir. Sect. 451: 1970.
[78] White, Dir. Staffs. (1834).
[79] Birm. and Mid. Hardware Dist. 127–8.
[80] Walsall Red Book (1873).
[81] Kelly's Dir. Staffs. (1900).
[82] Sketchley's Birmingham ... Dir. (1767); White, Dir. Staffs. (1834).
[83] White, Dir. Staffs. (1851).
[84] Walsall Red Book (1873).   [85] Ibid. (1939).
[86] Kelly's Dir. Merchants, Manufacturers, and Shippers (1953).

[87] Parson and Bradshaw, Dir. Staffs. (1818).
[88] Pigot, Com. Dir. Birm. (1829), 93.
[89] Birm. and Mid. Hardware Dist. 127; Walsall Past and Present (1905), 15.
[90] Walsall Red Book (1873).
[91] Walsall Past and Present (1905), 15.
[92] P.O. Telephone Dir. Sect. 451: 1970.
[93] Sketchley's and Adams's ... Univ. Dir. Birmingham ... (1770).
[94] Pearce, Walsall, 152, 163, 169.
[95] Pigot, Nat. Com. Dir. (1841), Staffs. p. 82; White, Dir. Staffs. (1851).
[96] Kelly's Dir. Staffs. (1900).
[97] Cope, Dir. Staffs. (1921).
[98] Kelly's Dir. Merchants, Manufacturers, and Shippers (1953).
[99] Ex inf. the firms (1974).

Road, and the rest in the borough.[1] After the French wars the trade expanded again. There were 32 buckle-makers in 1818 and 39 in 1829.[2] In 1834 49 buckle-makers, 16 buckle-tongue makers, and 15 buckle-platers are recorded, and by 1841 there were 61 buckle-makers, 11 tongue-makers, and 15 buckle-platers. In 1834 9 malleable-iron founders were casting buckles. Most buckle workshops remained near the centre but in 1841 there were 4 at Caldmore, 4 in Little London, and 8 at the north end of the town; a buckle-maker at Harden occurs in 1834.[3] From the mid 19th century the number of firms gradually declined: 43 buckle-makers and 12 tongue-makers are recorded in 1851 and 22 buckle-makers and 7 tongue-makers in 1900. The trade also became less concentrated in the centre. In 1900 there were three works in Wisemore and others in Cecil Street, Hatherton Street, John Street, and Birchills, and in Caldmore and Pleck. One buckle-tongue maker worked in Bloxwich.[4] The fall in the number of works in the later 19th century was probably related to an increasing scale of production. Output evidently expanded, and c. 1905 the trade employed between 2,000 and 3,000 people; mechanization was widespread and some metal buckles were produced automatically.[5] In the early 20th century more works were established: there were 34 buckle-makers and 5 buckle-tongue makers in 1921. Several firms also made horse furniture, cart gear, and small castings.[6] The number of buckle-makers again fell, however, to 25 in 1939 (including those making leather-covered buckles) and 12 in 1947.[7] There was some recovery after the Second World War, and in 1962 16 buckle manufacturers are recorded.[8] Automated buckle machines were introduced from the later 1960s, increasing production but reducing the number of firms. In 1974 there were some 11 firms making both cast and pressed buckles; two of them were primarily saddlery-hardware manufacturers, another two also produced presswork, and one also made plastic badges and fittings.[9] The works were scattered throughout the borough.

As has been seen, awl blades were made in the parish in the later 18th century. By 1813 the trade was concentrated in the Bloxwich area and remained so until the 20th century. There were 14 workshops there in 1813, with one at Whitehall near Caldmore.[10] The expansion of local saddlery in the early 19th century evidently stimulated the production of awl blades.[11] By 1834 there were 41 workshops; 4 were in Maw Green, Little London, and Caldmore, one in Stafford Street, one at Harden, and the rest at Great Bloxwich, Short Heath, and Wallington Heath. Some workshops also made shoe tacks.[12] Thereafter the number of awl-blade makers fell, at first probably because of concentration of manufacture. In 1841 there were 37 firms with 241 workers[13] and in the earlier 1860s 27 firms with 200 workers and 50 apprentices.[14] In the later 19th and early 20th centuries, however, the introduction of stitching machinery in the saddlery trade reduced the demand for awl blades, and many firms went out of business. By 1904 there were only 10 in the county borough, of which 8 were in Bloxwich.[15] Between 1912 and 1921 the trade revived, presumably owing to the war; in 1921 there were 13 firms, but the industry again declined thereafter.[16] There were still 8 firms in 1953, of which 5 were in Bloxwich,[17] but in 1974 the only surviving manufacturer was Thomas Somerfield & Sons Ltd. in Clarendon Street, Bloxwich, a subsidiary of the Needle Industries Group.[18]

File-making continued in Walsall into the 20th century. By 1813 John Heptinstall's works in Ablewell Street had been taken over by William Parker, who was making files on a large scale for home and oversea markets.[19] By 1818 there was a second file-maker, in Rushall Street.[20] There were usually from three to five firms during the 19th century. Until the late 19th century most file-makers worked in the town centre but workshops occur in Homebridge Forge Lane (Butts Lane) in 1851, in Green Lane between at least 1860 and 1910, and in Short Acre Street in 1873 and 1900. By 1900 the centre of production had moved northwards: besides the Green Lane and Short Acre Street works there were others in North Street, Algernon Street, and Littleton Street West.[21] In the 20th century specialist file-making declined. By 1941 there was only one manufacturer, W. H. Malpus in Algernon Street. His works evidently closed between 1953 and 1962.[22]

'Every description' of cast- and wrought-iron nails was still made in Walsall in 1813, but in 1818 only one nail-maker, in New Street, is recorded.[23] Nailing continued on a small scale in Bloxwich: 3 nail and tack makers are recorded there in 1841 and 4 nailers in 1860.[24] From the earlier 19th century, however, until at least 1939 there were usually two or three firms making saddle-nails.[25]

Lock-making remained an important Walsall industry in the 19th and early 20th centuries. In 1813

[1] Pearce, *Walsall*, 145, 150–70.
[2] Parson and Bradshaw, *Dir. Staffs.* (1818); Pigot, *Com. Dir. Birm.* (1829), 91.
[3] White, *Dir. Staffs.* (1834); Pigot, *Nat. Com. Dir.* (1841), Staffs. pp. 81–2.
[4] White, *Dir. Staffs.* (1851); *Kelly's Dir. Staffs.* (1900).
[5] *Walsall Past and Present* (1905), 8–9.
[6] Cope, *Dir. Staffs.* (1921).
[7] *Walsall Red Book* (1939); *Kelly's Dir. Merchants, Manufacturers, and Shippers* (1947).
[8] *Barrett's County Boro. of Walsall Dir.* (1962–3).
[9] Ex inf. the firms (1974).
[10] Pearce, *Walsall*, 154–70.
[11] *Birm. and Mid. Hardware Dist.* 127.
[12] White, *Dir. Staffs.* (1834).
[13] Pigot, *Nat. Com. Dir.* (1841), Staffs. p. 80; *V.C.H. Staffs.* ii. 135.
[14] *3rd Rep. Com. Child. Emp.* 5, 30.
[15] *Kelly's Dir. Staffs.* (1904); *Walsall Past and Present* 1905), 7.

[16] Cope, *Dir. Staffs.* (1921); *Walsall Red Book* (1939).
[17] *Kelly's Dir. Merchants, Manufacturers, and Shippers* (1953).
[18] Ex inf. Thos. Somerfield & Sons Ltd. (1974).
[19] Pearce, *Walsall*, 147.
[20] Parson and Bradshaw, *Dir. Staffs.* (1818).
[21] Pigot, *Com. Dir. Birm.* (1829), 92; White, *Dir. Staffs.* (1834; 1851); *P.O. Dir. Staffs.* (1860); *Walsall Red Book* (1873; 1884); *Kelly's Dir. Staffs.* (1900).
[22] *Kelly's Dir. Merchants, Manufacturers, and Shippers* (1941). It is listed ibid. (1953), but not in *Barrett's County Boro. of Walsall Dir.* (1962–3).
[23] Pearce, *Walsall*, 144; Parson and Bradshaw, *Dir. Staffs.* (1818).
[24] Pigot, *Nat. Com. Dir.* (1841), Staffs. p. 84; *P.O. Dir. Staffs.* (1860).
[25] White, *Dir. Staffs.* (1834; 1851); *P.O. Dir. Staffs.* (1860); Cope, *Dir. Staffs.* (1921); *Walsall Red Book* (1929; 1939).

there were 21 locksmiths and lock-makers, of whom 2 also made buckles and other hardware. Four works were in Little Bloxwich, 4 in Short Heath, one in Birchills, 2 in Stafford Street, one in Paddock Lane, and the rest in the town centre.[26] During the next 20 years the trade grew rapidly. In 1834 there were 16 workshops in the north of the parish and 36 in Walsall and the Birchills area; the chief products were cabinet, pad, and rim locks. There were also 10 key-makers.[27] In the mid and later 19th century works became fewer and larger. There were 21 lock-makers in Walsall and 16 in Bloxwich and Blakenall in 1851, but only 10 lock-makers in Bloxwich in 1872 and 14 in Walsall in 1873.[28] Yet the work force doubled between the mid 1850s and the mid 1860s. Padlocks accounted for most of the extra production.[29] In the late 19th century the lock trade became less significant. In 1900 there were 14 firms; 6 were in Bloxwich, 2 in Hollyhedge Lane, and the others in Wolverhampton, Pargeter, Burrowes, and Stafford Streets, Upper Hall Lane, and Bath Street.[30] In 1905 the industry employed between 300 and 400 people.[31] The number of firms rose again to 20 in 1931[32] but later declined. In 1974 only some 4 firms remained, producing vehicle locks, padlocks, bank locks, and home-security locks.[33]

Iron-founding has been an important Walsall industry since the early 19th century, and light castings have predominated. There were 2 iron-founders in 1813, 7 in 1829, and 24 in 1834; most of the foundries were in the town centre. The increase was probably due to the introduction of malleable iron. As has been seen, many firms made malleable-iron horse furniture, and cast-iron buckles were also produced. In 1834 8 iron-founders were casting buckles and 5 builders' ironmongery.[34] The number of foundries varied little between the 1830s and the early 1890s. In 1892 there were 23 iron-founders and casters, 17 of whom worked in malleable iron. There were 3 works in Birchills, one in Blue Lane East, one in Green Lane, 2 in Stafford Street, and 6 at the south end of the town; the rest were in the centre.[35] From the 1890s, however, many new foundries were established. In 1896 there were 29 founders and 2 casters, and in 1921 57 founders; 53 of them made malleable-iron castings. Though the distribution of the foundries had not greatly changed by 1921, there were more in outlying areas, including one in Bloxwich.[36] From the 1920s the number of foundries fell, and in 1971 23 remained, including some making castings for the firm's own use. The biggest concentration of works in 1971 was north and west of the town centre, in Hatherton Street,

Stafford Street, Northcote Street, Croft Street, Old Birchills, Thomas Street, Wolverhampton Road, Pleck Road, and Frederick Street. There were others in Lower Rushall Street, Chuckery Road, Selborne Street, and Bath Street and in Leamore and Bloxwich.[37]

Until the late 19th century iron-founding remained closely connected with the saddlery-hardware and buckle trades. In 1873 most of the iron-founders were making buckles or malleable-iron horse furniture.[38] Although malleable iron has remained predominant, the types of casting produced have become increasingly diverse. The development of the cycle and motor trades created a new demand for malleable-iron castings. In 1905 12 malleable-iron founders were making motor and cycle fittings.[39] Builders' ironmongery was also an important product. In 1905 there were 3 or 4 large works, one of which employed nearly 200 hands, and in 1939 6 firms, of which 3 were iron-founders, were specializing in builders' hardware.[40] By 1930 several firms were also making castings for the electrical, engineering, shipbuilding, agricultural, textile, and other trades.[41] Such variety remained in the early 1970s.[42]

A number of firms specialized in other metal articles in the 19th century. In 1813 there were clock- and watch-makers and a pump-maker in the town and an edge-tool maker at Coal Pool.[43] A snuffer-maker, a wire-drawer, and a steel-toy maker occur in 1818; there were four snuffer-makers in 1834 and 2 in 1860.[44] Two die-sinkers and 6 stampers occur in 1834.[45] Tinning continued in the 19th century, and a small tin-plate industry also developed. There were 5 tin-plate workers in the borough in 1818, 2 tinned-spoon makers in 1834, and 3 'polishers and tinners' and 3 'braziers and tinners' in 1851.[46] In 1929 there were still 5 tin-plate workers and 2 tinners. Most works remained in the town centre, but there was one in Green Lane and another in Church Street, Bloxwich.[47] Although as has been seen brass-founding was closely connected with the harness-furniture trade in the 19th century, in 1905 the manufacture of brass gas-fittings, brass and gun-metal steam and water valves and fittings, and brass and gun-metal castings was said to have been established for some years.[48] Steel pens were made by Charles Windle and H. C. Blyth in Birmingham Road from the earlier 1840s to at least the mid 1860s.[49]

In the mid 1870s a galvanized-iron works was opened in Pleck Road by the Staffordshire Galvanizing & Corrugated Iron Co. The firm became Walker Bros. c. 1879 and took over the adjoining Victoria Ironworks between 1888 and 1892.

[26] Pearce, *Walsall*, 149–73.
[27] White, *Dir. Staffs.* (1834).
[28] *Robinson's Walsall Dir.* (1851); *P.O. Dir. Staffs.* (1872); *Walsall Red Book* (1873).
[29] *Birm. and Mid. Hardware Dist.* 87–8, 127.
[30] *Kelly's Dir. Staffs.* (1900).
[31] *Walsall Past and Present* (1905), 14.
[32] *Walsall Red Book* (1931).
[33] Ex inf. the Bloxwich Lock & Stamping Co. Ltd., D. Lycett & Son, and W. J. Goodwin & Son Ltd. (1974); *Walsall Chamber of Commerce & Ind. Dir. 1974/5*.
[34] Pearce, *Walsall*, 152, 162; Parson and Bradshaw, *Dir. Staffs.* (1818); Pigot, *Com. Dir. Birm.* (1829), 92; White, *Dir. Staffs.* (1834).   [35] *Kelly's Dir. Staffs.* (1892).
[36] Ibid. (1896); Cope, *Dir. Staffs.* (1921).
[37] *Walsall Red Book* (1929; 1939); *Foundry Dir. and Reg. of Forges* (1971–2).

[38] *Walsall Red Book* (1873).
[39] *Walsall Past and Present* (1905), 14–15.
[40] Ibid. 9; *Walsall Red Book* (1939).
[41] *County Boro. of Walsall Official Handbook* (6th edn.), 35.
[42] *Foundry Dir. and Reg. of Forges* (1971–2).
[43] Pearce, *Walsall*, 151, 157, 168.
[44] Parson and Bradshaw, *Dir. Staffs.* (1818); White, *Dir. Staffs.* (1834); *P.O. Dir. Staffs.* (1860).
[45] White, *Dir. Staffs.* (1834).
[46] Parson and Bradshaw, *Dir. Staffs.* (1818); White, *Dir. Staffs.* (1834; 1851).
[47] *Walsall Red Book* (1929).
[48] *Walsall Past and Present* (1905), 12.
[49] *P.O. Dir. Staffs.* (1845; 1860); Allen, *Ind. Dev. Birm.* 60. They occur in *P.O. Dir. Staffs.* (1868) as patentees of metallic pens but not as manufacturers.

Galvanized sheet production was abandoned after the Second World War; in 1974 Walkers was galvanizing steelwork for a variety of trades.[50] About 1883 Johnson Bros. & Co. Ltd. opened the Wisemore Works in Littleton Street West for the production of iron fencing and gates. The firm moved to Marlow Street *c.* 1920 and closed in the early 1970s.[51] In 1900 there were 11 firms making bicycles and 2 others producing cycle fittings and accessories.[52]

As has been seen, some of the firms making horse furniture, buckles, and other traditional wares have extended their range to include many other products; others abandoned the traditional industries altogether for new trades. Joseph Withers & Sons Ltd. was manufacturing harness in Wisemore in 1928. By 1932, having changed its style to Withers (Walsall) Ltd. and moved to Bath Street, it was making non-ferrous castings and fittings for hollowware, bathrooms, and motor-cars. The firm was still in business in 1962 but had ceased production by 1970.[53] The firm of J. & J. Wiggin Ltd. was making bridle-bits at Bloxwich from 1893 and took over the former mission hall in Revival Street, Bloxwich, in the early 20th century. The works was rebuilt after a fire in 1928 and the firm began making stainless-steel tableware. Bit-making was abandoned *c.* 1933, and by 1939 about half the output of the works consisted of tableware. After the Second World War it became the principal product, and in 1963 the firm's style was changed to Old Hall Tableware Ltd. In the early 1970s the range of products included over 1,500 articles in stainless steel, crystal, and cast iron.[54] Such diversification has been the chief characteristic of the Walsall metal trades in the 20th century. In 1970 there were many metalworking firms specializing in a wide variety of products, and there were also several firms engaged in fabrication, metal-finishing, and welding. Many works were still in the centre and in areas of 19th-century development, but others were established on industrial estates elsewhere in the borough.[55]

Metal tubes. About 1830 Walsall became a centre of wrought-iron gas-tube production. By the mid 1860s the industry employed 1,500 workers, and tubular products such as chandeliers and bedsteads were also made.[56] Welded steel tubes were being produced by 1905, and in 1906 the manufacture of

seamless tubes was introduced.[57] In the 1940s the government concentrated welded-tube production at Corby (Northants.) and the four surviving Walsall firms turned to tube manipulation and the production of tube fittings.[58] Seamless tubes were still made in the 1970s.

The first firm to be established was that of Edward and William Dixon, who were making cocks and gas apparatus in Birmingham Street in 1829.[59] The firm began making gas tubes apparently in 1830.[60] It moved *c.* 1834 to the premises in Ablewell Street known by 1860 as the Alpha Tube Works.[61] After several changes in the partnership the firm was trading as Lambert Bros. by 1868.[62] It moved *c.* 1910 to a works (also known as the Alpha Tube Works) on the Wyrley and Essington Canal in Green Lane; *c.* 1911 the style became Lambert Bros. (Walsall) Ltd.[63] In 1930 the Green Lane works was producing wrought-iron and mild-steel tubes, cast-iron cocks, valves, lamp columns, and manhole covers.[64]

Several other works were set up in the mid 19th century. In 1855 Edward Russell opened the large Alma Tube Works on land leased from Lord Bradford at the corner of Rollingmill and Wharf Streets.[65] By 1860 it had passed to John Russell & Co. of Wednesbury.[66] The company continued to occupy the works until 1929 when Stewarts & Lloyds took over Russells and closed it.[67] In 1860 another firm, Brown & Chesterton, was making tubes in Station Street, but by 1873 it was concentrating on gas-fittings and chandeliers.[68] Three more works opened in the 1870s.[69] George Gill, manager of the Alma works in 1872, and a Mr. Hildick had by 1876 established the Walsall Tube Works on the north side of the Cyclops Ironworks in Pleck Road.[70] Gill left the partnership *c.* 1879 and the firm became Hildick, Mills & Hildick.[71] The style changed to Hildick & Hildick in 1884.[72] About 1876 A. C. and J. G. Russell, trading as Russell Bros., opened the Bradford Tube Works in Upper Brook Street.[73] The firm became Russell Bros. (Walsall) Ltd. at some time between 1917 and 1920.[74] About 1880 George Gill had joined with T. A. Russell to establish the Cyclops Tube Works on that part of the Cyclops Ironworks site flanking Wharf Street.[75] The firm became Gill & Russell Ltd. in 1911.[76]

[50] *P.O. Dir. Staffs.* (1876); *Walsall Red Book* (1878); *Kelly's Dir. Staffs.* (1880; 1888; 1892); ex inf. Walker Bros. Ltd. (1974).
[51] *Walsall Red Book* (1884); S.R.O., 410/M/B/2; O.S. Map 1/500, Staffs. LXIII. 6. 20 (1886 edn.); *Walsall Blue Book* (1920); *Walsall Blue & Red Book* (1921); ex inf. the occupiers of the Marlow Street works (1974).
[52] *Kelly's Dir. Staffs.* (1900).
[53] Ibid. (1928; 1932); *Walsall Red Book* (1928–31); *Barrett's County Boro. of Walsall Dir.* (1962–3). Withers occurs as a retailer only in *P.O. Telephone Dir. Sect. 451: 1970.*
[54] See p. 248; *Walsall Observer*, 19 Sept. 1971; Homeshaw, *Bloxwich*, 169; M. Wiggin, *Memoirs of a Maverick*, 6–8; *County Boro. of Walsall Official Town Guide* [1972], 94; ex inf. Old Hall Tableware Ltd. (1974).
[55] *P.O. Telephone Dir. Sect. 451: 1970.*
[56] *Birm. and Mid. Hardware Dist.* 127.
[57] *Walsall Past and Present* (1905), 19; *County Boro. of Walsall Official Handbook* (6th edn.), 59.
[58] Ex inf. Tipper Bros. of Bilston and Gill & Russell Ltd. (1974). [59] Pigot, *Com. Dir. Birm.* (1829), 94.
[60] *Jones's Mercantile Dir. Iron Dist.* . . . (1865), 502; White, *Dir. Staffs.* (1834), listing Cowley, Dixon & Hill.
[61] Pigot, *Nat. Com. Dir.* (1835), 464; *P.O. Dir. Staffs.* (1860).

[62] Pigot, *Nat. Com. Dir.* (1841), Staffs. p. 83; *P.O. Dir. Staffs.* (1845; 1854; 1860; 1868); White, *Dir. Staffs.* (1851).
[63] *Walsall Red Book* (1910; 1911; 1912); O.S. Map 6", Staffs. LXIII. NW. (1920 edn.).
[64] *County Boro. of Walsall Official Handbook* (6th edn.), 58.
[65] W.C.L., box 22, no. 17; S.R.O., D. 1362/57, p. 113; Glew, *Walsall*, 30.
[66] *P.O. Dir. Staffs.* (1860).
[67] *V.C.H. Staffs.* ii. 274.
[68] *P.O. Dir. Staffs.* (1860); *Walsall Red Book* (1873).
[69] In addition O.S. Map 6", Staffs. LXIII. NW. (1889 edn., surv. 1884–5) shows a works off Birch St.; it is not shown on the 1903 edn.
[70] *P.O. Dir. Staffs.* (1872; 1876); O.S. Map 1/2,500, Staffs. LXIII. 10 (1917 edn.).
[71] *Walsall Red Book* (1878; 1880).
[72] Ibid. (1884; 1885).
[73] *P.O. Dir. Staffs.* (1876); S.R.O., D. 1362/57, p. 203.
[74] *Walsall Red Book* (1917); *Walsall Blue and Red Book* (1921).
[75] *Walsall Red Book* (1880), erratum slip on p. 55; S.R.O., D. 1287/box 7/Cyclops Ironworks, indenture of 23 Dec. and declaration of W. H. Duignan, 24 Dec. 1891.
[76] *Walsall Red Book* (1912).

The largest of the Walsall tube-making firms, the Talbot-Stead Tube Co. Ltd., was founded in 1906 by W. J. (later Sir William) Talbot and Geoffrey Stead, who opened a works on the east side of Green Lane. The firm concentrated on seamless steel tubes; it supplied a quarter of the boiler tubes made for the Royal Navy during the First World War and those used in the liner *Queen Mary*.[77] At its peak in 1960 the factory employed 2,250 workers. It amalgamated in 1931 with Tube Investments Ltd., and in 1962 became T.I. Stainless Tubes Ltd. In 1972 the company decided to close the works and the site, then covering 48 a., was sold. In 1973, however, T.I. Chesterfield Ltd. took a lease of 17 a. of it again to continue limited production of stainless-steel tubes.[78]

Three of the four former welded-tube makers closed their Walsall works in the 1960s, but in 1974 Gill & Russell were still in business as tube manipulators and tube-fittings manufacturers at the Cyclops works. Other firms in the tube-manipulation trade then included Frank Charlton Ltd. in Eldon Street and Lyndene (Bloxwich) Co. Ltd. in Blue Lane West.[79]

Engineering. In the 19th and 20th centuries several engineering firms were established in Walsall. The earliest works was on the north side of Goscote Lane; Joseph Bradley and Elijah Waring opened coal and ironstone mines there *c.* 1794 and were working a foundry by the early 1800s. Their partnership was dissolved in 1809, and by 1829 the foundry was worked by Perks & Otway.[80] By 1834 Perks had been replaced by Henry Wennington; the partners were then steam-engine builders and millwrights as well as founders.[81] By 1841 they were also general machinists.[82] The works passed in the earlier 1840s to W. V. Wennington, who was succeeded in the earlier 1850s by the Goscote Foundry Co., managed by H. B. Wright.[83] By 1860 the works was occupied by E. T. Wright, a steam-engine builder and boiler-maker, who exhibited a patent diagonal-seam steam boiler at the London International Exhibition of 1862.[84] By 1868 the firm's style had changed to Wright Bros. & Co. Ltd.[85] The works apparently closed between 1876 and 1880.[86]

From the mid 19th century other firms were established. Besides the Goscote works there were 4 engineers and machinists in 1851, 3 in 1860, and

4 in 1873, when there were also 3 firms of boiler-makers including a second at Goscote.[87] From the late 19th century the industry expanded more rapidly, and in 1970 there were 42 firms of general engineers in Walsall and 14 in Bloxwich, besides 7 other firms engaged in precision, 3 in mechanical, one in hydraulic, 2 in structural, and 7 in heating, ventilating, and hot-water engineering. At least 2 other firms made mechanical handling equipment, one lifting gear, 2 press-tools, and 7 engineering patterns; there were engineering factories and work-shops in most parts of the borough.[88]

THE LEATHER TRADES. Walsall has been a noted centre both of leather manufacture and of the production of saddlery and other leather goods. There was a tanning industry by the mid 15th century. Walsall barkers occur from 1440[89] and tanners from the 16th century.[90] John Lyddiatt, a tanner, was mayor three times between 1584 and 1607.[91] Early tanneries seem to have been in the borough: in Digbeth in 1636 and in Rushall Street in 1658.[92] A Walsall currier occurs in 1752, and in 1767 there were 3 curriers and 2 tanners in the town.[93] In 1813 there were 7 curriers and 3 tanners, all in the borough; and by 1818 4 tanners and 7 curriers, one of whom was working in Caldmore.[94]

The development of the saddlery trade brought about further expansion of currying in the 1820s and 1830s. There were 8 curriers in 1829 and 1834 and 9 in 1841.[95] Tanning, however, declined; though there were still two tanneries in 1824 on the corner of Park Street and Bridge Street and in Rushall Street,[96] none is recorded between 1829 and 1841.[97] By 1843, however, Joseph Bagnall was leasing one in Lichfield Street.[98] Both tanning and currying apparently expanded in the 1840s, and in 1851 there were at least two tanneries in Lower Rushall Street and Hatherton Street. One tanning firm, Cozens & Greatrex, also curried and japanned leather; 14 firms of curriers and leather-sellers had established works near the centre of the town.[99] Production grew between 1849 and 1865, and Walsall became the chief centre of leather manufacture in South Staffordshire.[1] Yet the number of firms did not increase. There were 3 tanneries in 1872, all in Hatherton Street, where Ford Brook provided a supply of water; there were also 11 curriers, 2 of whom were working in Caldmore and the rest near

[77] *County Boro. of Walsall Official Handbook* (6th edn.), 59–60; Quaestor, *I met them in the Midlands* (1937), 157; Cason, *Blakenall Heath*, 42; O.S. Map 6″, Staffs. LXIII. NW. (1920 edn.).
[78] *Express & Star*, 22 Dec. 1972; *Walsall Observer*, 6 July 1973; ex inf. T. I. Chesterfield Ltd. and S.T.D. Services Ltd. (1974).
[79] Ex inf. Gill & Russell Ltd. (1974); *Walsall Chamber of Commerce and Ind. Dir.* (1974–5).
[80] W.C.L., ACJ XII/19; W.S.L. 8/4/46; Pigot, *Com. Dir. Birm.* (1829), 92.   [81] White, *Dir. Staffs.* (1834).
[82] Pigot, *Nat. Com. Dir.* (1841), Staffs. p. 84.
[83] Ibid.; *P.O. Dir. Staffs.* (1845; 1854); White, *Dir. Staffs.* (1851).
[84] *P.O. Dir. Staffs.* (1860); *V.C.H. Staffs.* ii. 168.
[85] *P.O. Dir. Staffs.* (1868).
[86] It occurs ibid. (1876) but not in *Kelly's Dir. Staffs.* (1880).
[87] White, *Dir. Staffs.* (1851); *P.O. Dir. Staffs.* (1860; 1872; 1876); *Walsall Red Book* (1873).
[88] *P.O. Telephone Dir. Sect. 451: 1970.*
[89] *S.H.C.* n.s. iii. 154; n.s. iv. 177; *Cal. Pat.* 1441–6, 206; S.R.O., D. 593/A/2/22/22.

[90] C 1/816/19; F. W. Willmore, *Transcript of First Reg. Bk. of Par. Ch. of St. Matthew, Walsall, 1570–1649* (Walsall, 1890), 162, 169, 171, 188; W.S.L., S.D. 337/34, 340/34, 347/34, 349/34.
[91] Homeshaw, *Walsall*, 153; below p. 269.
[92] W.S.L. 115/10/41, deed of 20 Jan. 1635/6; S.R.O., D. 260/M/T/1/102q.
[93] *Aris's Birmingham Gaz.* 11 May 1752; *V.C.H. Staffs.* ii. 235.
[94] Pearce, *Walsall*, 149–50, 152, 155–7, 162, 165, 172; Parson and Bradshaw, *Dir. Staffs.* (1818).
[95] Pigot, *Com. Dir. Birm.* (1829), 93; White, *Dir. Staffs.* (1834); Pigot, *Nat. Com. Dir.* (1841), Staffs. p. 83.
[96] W.C.L., A.G. 138; C. 4 (T. Mason, Plan of Town of Walsall, 1824).
[97] Mason, Plan of Town of Walsall (1832; printed as back end-paper in Fink, *Queen Mary's Grammar Sch.*), shows 2 tanneries, but these are merely copied from his earlier map.
[98] W.S.L., S. MS. 417/Walsall, no. 2213.
[99] White, *Dir. Staffs.* (1851).
[1] *Birm. and Mid. Hardware Dist.* 128; Allen, *Ind. Dev. Birm.* 69.

the town centre.[2] The number of curriers had risen again by 1876, when there were 26, and by 1880 new firms were established at the north end of the town in Short Acre Street, Stafford Street, and Lower Forster Street.[3]

The late-19th-century depression in the Walsall saddlery trade[4] had little adverse effect on the leather manufacturers, who were turning their attention to carriage, bag, and fancy leather, and special leathers for export. The number of firms grew between 1880 and 1900. There were 5 tanneries in 1889 employing nearly 100 men, and 7 tanneries by 1900. All the tanning firms were also curriers; there were about 20 other curriers in 1889 and 31 in 1896. The tanneries were situated in Hatherton Street, Darwall Street, Park Street, Portland Street, and Warewell Street; most were thus near running water. The currying trade too was still concentrated near the town centre, though several works had been established east of Ablewell Street and south-west of the station.[5]

In the early 20th century there was further diversification. By 1905 leather was prepared for boots and shoes, cycles, and motor-cars, and pigskins were being worked; the trade then employed between 500 and 600 workers.[6] In 1916 Boak Walsall Ltd. at its works in Bridgeman Street, Navigation Street, and Midland Road was making leather for many trades, including fancy leathers from calf, sheep, and goat skins.[7] Most firms, however, continued to tan and curry cow-hides, which were less used by local leather-goods firms.[8] There were 8 tanners and 27 curriers in 1910, and 8 tanners and 33 curriers in 1930.[9] From the 1930s the number of firms engaged in leather manufacture declined. In 1939 there were 5 tanners and 30 curriers, and by the early 1960s there were only 12 tanners and curriers.[10] It seems that the change was caused by the concentration of the industry in larger units, which had begun before the First World War; 630 people were still employed in leather manufacture in 1960.[11] Tanning declined in the 1960s,[12] but in 1970 there were still 14 firms engaged in leather production. Many of the works were in or near Park Street and north of Townend Bank, but there were three factories in Ryecroft, three north-east of Ablewell Street, and one in Caldmore.[13]

Although finished leather goods were being made in Walsall by the 16th century,[14] manufacture was apparently slight until the later 18th century when a saddlery and harness trade appeared.[15] It was at first chiefly concerned with bridle-cutting, but by the mid 19th century many saddlers were established in the town.[16] Saddlery and harness remained the chief finished-leather manufactures until c. 1900. They have since declined in importance, though saddlery expanded in the 1950s and 1960s owing to the revived fashion for riding.[17]

In 1834 most saddlery and harness workshops were in the borough, though there were six in Stafford Street and one in Windmill Street.[18] Throughout the later 19th century the distribution of workshops followed the growth of the urban area around the old town, though there were still many in the town centre.[19] In 1970 there were at least 26 saddlers and harness-makers in Walsall occupying at least 35 works, all of which lay in areas built up by the end of the 19th century; most were near the town centre. There were also two firms in Bloxwich.[20]

The development of saddlery and harness in Walsall stimulated the manufacture of other leather articles from the later 18th century. In 1752 a Walsall saddler also made upholstery, and by 1834 four firms were producing it.[21] The bridle-cutters supplied straps for the army during the Napoleonic Wars.[22] Leather ancillaries for riders and travellers were produced by the saddlers and harness-makers throughout most of the 19th century. By the 1870s they also made purses and cigar-cases.[23] In 1876 two firms made dog-collars and three specialized in fancy-leather goods; one firm of bridle-cutters also worked in fancy leather.[24] The depression in the saddlery trade in the late 19th century accelerated the development of the fancy and light leather-goods industry as an independent trade, and the diversity of products increased. By 1886 some firms were making bicycle-saddles[25] and by 1904 there were three fancy-leather workers, nine leather-goods manufacturers (including six producing fancy goods), and several firms making purses, straps, and dog-collars.[26] Fancy-leather articles made at the beginning of the 20th century included watch-guards, garters, blotters, and a variety of small containers.[27] In 1910 42 firms were making leather goods, and there were 73 by 1915 and 92 by 1920.[28] In 1922 67 firms were making general leather goods and 40 fancy goods; purses were the chief product

[2] P.O. Dir. Staffs. (1872).
[3] E. Tonkinson, 'The Walsall and Midlands Leather Trades' (Birm. Univ. M. Com. thesis, 1947), chap. iv (copy in W.C.L.); Kelly's Dir. Staffs. (1880).
[4] V.C.H. Staffs. ii. 237.
[5] Guide to Walsall, (1889), 59; Kelly's Dir. Staffs. (1896; 1900).
[6] Walsall Past and Present (1905), 18.
[7] R. G. A. Bolton, 'Geog. Study of Growth and Present Day Pattern of Leather Ind. and Allied Trades in Walsall' (St. Peter's College, Birmingham, Geog. Dept. thesis, 1970), 64 (copy in W.C.L.).
[8] Allen, Ind. Dev. Birm. 398.
[9] Tonkinson, 'Walsall Leather Trades', chap. iv.
[10] Ibid.; Barrett's County Boro. of Walsall Dir. (1962–3), 63.
[11] Allen, Ind. Dev. Birm. 321; Bolton, 'Growth of Leather Ind.' 155.
[12] Bolton, 'Growth of Leather Ind.' 119.
[13] Ibid. 133; P.O. Telephone Dir. Sect. 451: 1970.
[14] Shoemakers are mentioned from c. 1494, a jerkin-maker in 1577, and a glover in 1596 and 1601: S.H.C. 1928, 224; Willmore, First Reg. of Ch. of St. Matthew, 28, 43, 51, 150, 163, 172, 175, 197.

[15] V.C.H. Staffs. ii. 236. For a fuller account of the Walsall saddlery and harness trades see ibid. 236–8.
[16] Sketchley's Birmingham...Dir.(1767); Pearce, Walsall, 146–7; White, Dir. Staffs. (1834; 1851); V.C.H. Staffs. ii. 236. For a bridle-cutter in 1660 see S.R.O., D. 260/M/T/1/102t. The V.C.H. wrongly gives the number of saddle-makers in 1834 as 26; there were in fact five: White, Dir. Staffs. (1834).
[17] Bolton, 'Growth of Leather Ind.' 81, 146.
[18] White, Dir. Staffs. (1834).
[19] Ibid. (1851); P.O. Dir. Staffs. (1860 and later edns.); Kelly's Dir. Staffs. (1880 and later edns. to 1900).
[20] P.O. Telephone Dir. Sect. 451: 1970; Bolton, 'Growth of Leather Ind.' 138.
[21] Aris's Birmingham Gaz. 13 Nov. 1752; White, Dir. Staffs. (1834).
[22] Pearce, Walsall, 146.
[23] Tonkinson, 'Walsall Leather Trades', ch. viii; Walsall Past and Present (1905), 12.
[24] P.O. Dir. Staffs. (1876).
[25] Allen, Ind. Dev. Birm. 224.
[26] Kelly's Dir. Staffs. (1904).
[27] Walsall Past and Present (1905), 12.
[28] Tonkinson, 'Walsall Leather Trades', ch. iv.

of 26 firms, pocket-books of 19, ladies' fancy bags of 9, watch-guards of 5, and footballs of four. Two firms chiefly made gloves and one razor strops. Thirteen firms made dog-collars, of which Walsall was then the chief centre of manufacture in Britain.[29] The leather-goods industry continued to prosper in the 1920s and 1930s, though during the Second World War many leather-goods firms seem to have reverted to saddlery.[30]

During the earlier 20th century the cutting-out process was mechanized,[31] and several large firms emerged. In 1914 Matthew Harvey & Co. Ltd. had 600 employees at its factory in Bath Street, which made castings and metal horse furniture as well as leather goods.[32] Of 106 leather-goods firms existing c. 1950 10 employed more than 100 workers and 18 between 50 and 100, but most employed fewer than twenty-five.[33]

In the 1950s the Walsall leather-goods industry suffered from the competition of artificial substitutes; the number of firms had fallen to 70 by 1961 and the number of workers also declined.[34] There was an increased demand for fancy goods in the 1960s, however, and in 1970 there were at least 42 leather-goods firms with 92 works in Walsall and a further 7 firms in Bloxwich.[35] In 1973 half the British production of fancy-leather goods was concentrated in the borough.[36]

The change of emphasis in the late 19th and early 20th centuries from saddlery to other leather goods had little effect on the siting of the industry. Although two works were established in Bloxwich by 1928, the rest remained concentrated near the centre of the town in a zone extending from Mill Street to South Street and from Wolverhampton Road to Walsingham Street.[37] That was still true in 1970; a group of 17 works then lay immediately west of the railway station in Station Street, Marsh Street, Bridgeman Street, Navigation Street, and Frederick Street, but the rest were widely scattered throughout the zone.[38] Many firms still occupied late-19th-century buildings, while those which had replaced their works usually rebuilt on or near their old sites.[39]

The manufacture of whip-thongs emerged as a separate branch of the Walsall leather trade in the later 18th century. The earliest known maker was Thomas Penrose, who was in business in Gorton's Yard, by 1770,[40] and thereafter directories regularly

list a few whip and whip-thong makers in the town: there were, for example, 4 in 1818, 7 in 1851, 3 in 1900, 4 in 1929, and 3 in 1940.[41] Most firms apparently lasted no more than a generation. The name Carver, however, was connected with the trade from 1776[42] until c. 1940,[43] and in 1887 Edward Goddard established in Station Street the firm which, as Edward Goddard Ltd., of the Reliance Works, Farringdon Street, was in 1974 the town's only whip manufacturer.[44]

CLOTH AND CLOTHING. There was a fulling-mill at Walsall c. 1300,[45] and cloth was made in the parish by the mid 15th century. A Bloxwich weaver occurs in 1449, and a Walsall weaver in 1494;[46] in the early 16th century weavers formed part of a college of tradesmen whose admission fees helped to provide a light in the parish church.[47] In 1620 the corporation made an agreement with William Staunton to teach twenty or thirty children 'spinning, twisting, doubling, and quilling' worsted, woollen, and linen yarn.[48] Staunton was working as a clothier when he died in 1639.[49] There were still weavers at Bloxwich and perhaps elsewhere in the foreign in the 16th and 17th centuries.[50] It is probable, however, that the town was more important in marketing and tailoring. Walsall mercers occur from 1471.[51] An ordinance of c. 1494 for the maintenance of play garments belonging to the church gave one-third of the responsibility to a group including the mercers, drapers, shearmen, and tailors of the town.[52] Guilds of clothiers and tailors occur in 1502, and the mercers, drapers, tailors, and shearmen formed part of the early-16th-century college of tradesmen.[53] In 1595 a Walsall weaver was punished by forfeiture for practising as a mercer, and in 1616 a Walsall draper was trading with Coventry, Shrewsbury, Tamworth, and Yorkshire.[54] In 1770 there were 6 mercers and a woollen manufacturer, and in 1834 7 linen and woollen drapers and 7 travelling drapers.[55]

In the late 19th century Walsall became a centre of industrialized clothing manufacture.[56] The industry was founded by John Shannon, a Scots draper who started business in Walsall in 1826. In 1845 he leased land in George Street from Lord Bradford and opened a shop there. He was mayor in 1850–1. In the earlier 1870s he set up a workshop in George Street with 20 workpeople to make mens'

[29] *Kelly's Dir. Leather Trades* (1922).
[30] Tonkinson, 'Walsall Leather Trades', ch. xi; *V.C.H. Staffs.* ii. 238.
[31] Tonkinson, 'Walsall Leather Trades', ch. xi.
[32] *Walsall Red Book* (1914), pp. xxix sqq.
[33] Walsall Junior Chamber of Commerce, *Industrial Survey of Walsall* (Walsall, 1949–50), 5 (copy in W.C.L.).
[34] *Express & Star*, 28 Sept. 1955; *V.C.H. Staffs.* ii. 238; Bolton, 'Growth of Leather Ind.' 155.
[35] *P.O. Telephone Dir. Sect. 451: 1970*; Bolton, 'Growth of Leather Ind.' 140.
[36] *Walsall Observer*, 20 July 1973.
[37] *Kelly's Dir. Staffs.* (1928).
[38] Bolton, 'Growth of Leather Ind.' 140.
[39] Ibid. 98–124.
[40] *Sketchley's and Adams's . . . Univ. Dir. Birmingham . . .* (1770).
[41] Parson and Bradshaw, *Dir. Staffs.* (1818); White, *Dir. Staffs.* (1851); *Kelly's Dir. Staffs.* (1900; 1940); *Walsall Red Book* (1929), 646.
[42] *Walsall Observer*, 29 Sept. 1967.
[43] Joseph Carver Ltd.: *Kelly's Dir. Staffs.* (1940).

[44] Ex inf. Mr. J. E. Darby of Edward Goddard Ltd. (1974).   [45] See p. 185.
[46] S.R.O., D. 593/B/1/7/5/3; /A/2/22/22.
[47] See p. 229.   [48] W.T.C. II/34.
[49] L.J.R.O., admin. of 17 Aug. 1640, inventory.
[50] *Cal. Pat.* 1554–5, 353; L.J.R.O., wills of Thos. Clarke (proved 10 June 1625) and John Atherley (5 Jan. 1636/7), inventories; S.R.O., D. 260/M/F/1/5, f. 177; W.T.C. II/13/66.   [51] S.R.O., D. 593/A/2/22/4, 12, 14, 15.
[52] *S.H.C.* 1928, 224.
[53] Sims, *Cal. of Deeds*, p. 26; below p. 229.
[54] *S.H.C.* 1932, 100; L.J.R.O., admin. of Thos. Webbe, 24 July 1616, inventory.
[55] *Sketchley's and Adams's . . . Univ. Dir. Birmingham . . .* (1770); White, *Dir. Staffs.* (1834).
[56] This para. is based on TS. notes supplied by Mr. R. H. Mears of John Shannon & Son Ltd. (1973); S.R.O., D. 1362/57, pp. 40–1; *P.O. Dir. Staffs.* (1845; 1872; 1876); *Walsall Red Book* (1890), 86; (1891), 153; *Guide to Walsall* (1889), 65; *Walsall Past and Present* (1905), 10–11; O.S. Map 1/500, Staffs. LXIII. 11. 11 (1886 edn.); 1/2,500, Staffs. LXIII. 11 (1903 edn., revised 1901); plaque over main entrance to factory.

clothing for the local market. He died in 1875 and was succeeded by his son Edmund John, who greatly expanded the business. It became incorporated as John Shannon & Son Ltd. *c.* 1890. The factory was rebuilt in 1887, and by 1901 large extensions had been built on the north, south, and west sides. In 1887 179,860 garments were made, and in 1899 706,580. There were evidently some 600 employees in 1887, over 1,000 by 1889, and over 2,000 by 1905.

A second firm, Stammers, was established in Dudley Street in 1904; in 1906 it became a limited company as a subsidiary of Foster Bros. Clothing Co. Ltd. of Birmingham and moved to New Street. By 1908 there were three firms; in 1916 four firms, including Shannons, made men's and boys' outerwear and ladies' costumes and a fifth made men's shirts and women's overalls, pinafores, and skirts. The trade in 1916 employed over 3,000 workers.[57] The number of firms continued to rise in the earlier 1920s: there were 5 clothing firms and 2 blouse manufacturers in 1921 and 11 clothiers in 1926.[58] Nevertheless the trade was depressed by 1923, and in 1926 Shannons was liquidated after the resignation of the managing director, John C. Shannon, who had succeeded Edmund, his father, in 1913.[59] Though Shannons was later reconstructed, there was no further expansion in the number of firms. Until the 1920s the industry was concentrated in the town centre, but of the ten works in 1940 one was in Leamore Lane and one in Hillary Street, Pleck.[60] There were still ten clothing manufacturers in 1963[61] but only six by 1973. In that year Shannons still occupied the late-19th-century premises in George Street, and Stammers Ltd. the factory in New Street, which had been extended *c.* 1925; both firms made men's and boys' outerwear. Three other firms, F. E. Towe Ltd. in Station Street, F. Milward & Son Ltd. in Caldmore Road, and T. Bednall & Co. Ltd. in Mountrath Street, made suitings in 1973; Towes also specialized in riding wear and Milwards in uniforms. Mark Cohen & Co. Ltd., a Birmingham firm which established a branch in Whittimere Street in 1927 and moved all its operations there in 1958, made girls' light clothing. The trade in 1973 employed some 600 people, of whom about 450 worked for Shannons and Stammers.[62]

ROPE- AND TENT-MAKING. Two rope-makers occur in Walsall in the 16th century, William Alport in 1545 and John Alport in 1583.[63] No more is known of the trade until the 19th century, when a few firms in Walsall and Bloxwich made rope, dressed flax, and spun twine. Much of the work was for the saddlery trade, although in the early 20th century rope for collieries and ironworks was also being produced.[64] Some 12 firms occur during the 19th century, but only 3 or 4 were active at the same time and the only ones to survive for long were those owned by members of the Hallsworth and Hawley families.

Edward Hallsworth was making rope in George Street in 1813 and 1818 and in Park Street in 1822 and 1835.[65] Joshua Hallsworth had his own business in Dudley Street between at least 1818 and 1845.[66] In 1843 he held a rope-walk off what is now Selborne Street as a tenant of Lord Bradford.[67] He was evidently succeeded by Ann (or Hannah) Hallsworth, who was making rope in Dudley Street in the early 1850s.[68] John Hallsworth had taken over the business by 1860[69] and continued to make rope in Dudley Street until *c.* 1875.[70]

John Hawley established a rope-making concern in 1837.[71] The business was in George Street in 1841, but by 1845 Hawley had moved it to Goodall Street, where in 1861 he was making rope, line, twine, sacking, oilcloth, marquees, and rick-cloths.[72] The firm became John Hawley & Son *c.* 1879, John Hawley & Co. *c.* 1884, and John Hawley & Co. (Walsall) Ltd. *c.* 1919.[73] It had opened additional works in Tantarra Street by 1869[74] and another in Selborne Street by 1880.[75] In 1928 it moved its entire operations to the Goodall Works in Bloxwich Road.[76] Rope was made there until 1948, but the firm's main interest had by then become tentmaking, and in the 1970s it made only tents and camping equipment. In 1974 it became Hawley-Goodall (Walsall) Ltd.[77]

John James Hawley, John Hawley's eldest son, opened a business in Park Street in 1860, making rope, cordage, and canvas products for the saddlery and agricultural trades.[78] Rope-walks were subsequently set up in Lichfield Road and Cartbridge Lane. In 1909 Hawleys moved to its new Speciality Works in Lichfield Road. The works included a rope-walk and seaming, weaving, and tarpaulin

[57] Ex inf. (1973) Mr. J. M. Martin of Walsall, formerly managing director of Stammers; *Kelly's Dir. Staffs.* (1908; 1916); Walsall Chamber of Commerce, *Walsall Comm. Year Book* (1916), 101, 172–3, 245–7.

[58] Cope, *Dir. Staffs.* (1921); *Walsall Red Book* (1926).

[59] *Staffs. Advertiser*, 29 Dec. 1923; TS. notes supplied by Mr. Mears; *Shannons Mag.* (copy in W.C.L.); above p. 175.

[60] *Kelly's Dir. Staffs.* (1940).

[61] *Barrett's County Boro. of Walsall Dir.* (1962–3).

[62] Ex inf. Mr. Mears and Mr. Martin (1973) and Mr. K. Towe, Mr. A. W. J. Bednall, Mr. F. C. Milward, and Mr. M. Cohen (1974); *Walsall Observer*, 14 Dec. 1973.

[63] W.T.C. II/238, m. 9; Sims, *Cal. of Deeds*, p. 39.

[64] *Walsall Past and Present* (1905), 15.

[65] Pearce, *Walsall*, 156; Parson and Bradshaw, *Dir. Staffs.* (1818); Pigot, *New Com. Dir.* (1822–3), 490; Pigot, *Nat. Com. Dir.* (1835), 466. He was presumably the Edw. Hallsworth of Park St. whose death at a very advanced age was reported in *Staffs. Advertiser*, 14 July 1838.

[66] Parson and Bradshaw, *Dir. Staffs.* (1818); *P.O. Dir. Staffs.* (1845). He was presumably the Joshua Hallsworth who died 7 Oct. 1845 aged 52: *Reg. of Inscriptions, Bath*

Street Burial Ground, Walsall (Walsall, n.d.), 21 (copy in W.C.L.).

[67] W.S.L., S. MS. 417/Walsall, no. 2186. The tenant's name is given as Joseph Allsworth, but Hallsworth is evidently the man in question.

[68] Slater, *Nat. Com. Dir.* (1850), Staffs. p. 112, giving Hannah; White, *Dir. Staffs.* (1851), giving Ann.

[69] *P.O. Dir. Staffs.* (1860).

[70] He occurs in *Walsall Red Book* (1876), 99, but not in later edns. or in *P.O. Dir. Staffs.* (1876).

[71] See e.g. advert. in *Walsall Red Book* (1878), p. xxix.

[72] Pigot, *Nat. Com. Dir.* (1841), Staffs. p. 85; *P.O. Dir. Staffs.* (1845); unpaginated advert. in Harrison, Harrod & Co. *Dir. Staffs.* (1861).

[73] *Walsall Red Book* (1880), 57; (1885), 103; *Walsall Blue Book* (1920), 456.

[74] White, *Dir. Birmingham* (1869). Hawley leased building land in Upper Tantarra St. from Lord Bradford in 1857: S.R.O., D. 1362/57, p. 129.

[75] *Kelly's Dir. Staffs.* (1880).

[76] Cason, *Blakenall Heath*, 42.

[77] Ex inf. the firm (1974).

[78] This para. is based on '*Borough*' *Guide to Walsall* (n.d. but 1909), 57; *Walsall Chamber of Commerce & Ind. Dir. 1974/5*, 24; inf. from Mr. J. A. Hawley (1974).

rooms; the firm produced rope, twine, tents, sacks, and cart- and rick-sheets, and also cordage and waterproof goods for the saddlery trade. It became John James Hawley (Speciality Works) Ltd. in 1917. In 1974 it was the largest British maker of horse clothing and of saddlery cordage products, such as halters and reins; the rope for those was also made at the works. Other products included tents, camping equipment, and garden furniture.

BRUSH-MAKING. The manufacture of brushes was established in Walsall by the mid 1760s, when there were at least three workshops. Joseph Nightingale, a former Walsall brush-maker, occurs in 1765, and by 1770 a Joseph Nightingale was working in Chapel Street. Hannah Reynolds was making brushes in 1766, and by 1770 George Reynolds had a workshop in Church Street. Simon Burrowes made brushes in Rushall Street by 1767, and by 1770 he was specializing in bone brushes.[79] The number of firms had increased to 5 by the 1790s and 10 by 1818.[80] In 1834 there were still 10 workshops, three of which made bone and ivory brushes.[81] The trade had progressed enough by 1841 for C. S. Forster, in a speech nominating a parliamentary candidate, to wish that the world's dust might be swept by Walsall brushes.[82] By 1851 there were 12 manufacturers working near the town centre and one in Bloxwich.[83] In the mid 1860s the trade employed c. 100 workmen; products included paint-brushes, shoe-brushes, brushes for clothes, hats, and hair, and others for various household purposes.[84]

In the late 19th century the industry was mechanized; production grew, and by 1889 several hundred workers were employed. Factories were evidently enlarged, though some established themselves outside the town centre. There were 11 firms in 1872, of which one was in Palfrey, one in High Street, Bloxwich, and the rest in the centre of Walsall. The Excelsior Works in Harrison Street, Bloxwich, was built in 1888, and in 1900 there were 3 firms in Bloxwich and 13 in Walsall, most of them near the town centre. In the early 20th century some firms made as many as 5,000 different kinds of brush, and during the South African War the town exported 20,000 brushes a week for the army.[85] By 1912 the number of firms had fallen, and the industry had moved northwards; there were 4 works in Bloxwich, 2 in Green Lane, and 2 in Stafford Street, though 4 firms remained in the town centre.[86] In the next ten years one firm, Vale & Bradnack, took over two others, and by 1921 the number of

firms had fallen to nine.[87] In the early 1920s the industry apparently suffered a depression, and by 1928 there were only five brushworks in the county borough; all but one of the Bloxwich works had closed.[88] By 1940 one more firm had evidently ceased production but two new works had been established in Holtshill Lane and High Street, Bloxwich.[89] Four brushworks survived in 1951,[90] but by the early 1960s there were only three, Vale Bros. in Green Lane, Bradnack & Son at the Defiance Works in Birmingham Road, and Busst & Marlow in Lower Rushall Street.[91] Busst & Marlow closed in the early 1970s.[92] In 1965 the Green Lane works of Vale Bros. was acquired by the corporation; at the same time Vales took over Bradnack & Son, becoming Vale Bros. Ltd. and moving to the Defiance Works, which was extended. At the same time it discontinued the production of general brushware and concentrated on animal-grooming brushes. In 1973 Vales still specialized in grooming brushes, most of which were exported; they were produced both mechanically and by hand, much of the hand-made brushware being entrusted to outworkers.[93] The only other brushmaking firm in the borough in 1973 was J. Brierley & Sons Ltd., which moved from Birmingham to the Forest Works in Forest Lane in 1967 and made a wide range of industrial brushes and personal giftware.[94]

BREWING AND DISTILLING. Although until the 1890s there seems to have been no wholesale brewing in Walsall several trades ancillary to it were well represented in the 18th and 19th centuries. There were, for example, 15 maltsters in the town in 1780,[95] 12 in 1818,[96] and 16 in 1851, with another at Bloxwich.[97] There were hop-dealers in the town in 1767 and 1770.[98] In the 1790s Joseph and Stephen Barber of Walsall were selling barley and hops to a brewer at Warrington (Lancs.).[99]

The first recorded wholesale breweries in Walsall were the Town Brewery in Short Acre Street, opened c. 1892,[1] and Highgate Brewery in Lodge (now Sandymount) Road, opened in 1898.[2] The former, owned from the mid 1890s by the Lord family, was still working in 1939 but had been closed by 1956.[3] Highgate Brewery, established by the Fletcher family, was sold in 1939 to Mitchells & Butlers of Smethwick. In 1974 it was the only brewery still open in the town and produced its own brand of mild beer.[4] The White Horse Brewery, Wolverhampton Street, the longest-lived of four or five other more ephemeral breweries around the

[79] Aris's Birmingham Gaz. 17 June 1765, 17 Mar. 1766; Sketchley's Birmingham . . . Dir. (1767); Sketchley's and Adams's . . . Univ. Dir. Birmingham . . . (1770).
[80] Univ. Brit. Dir. iv. 666–9; Parson and Bradshaw, Dir. Staffs. (1818).
[81] White, Dir. Staffs.(1834). [82] Willmore, Walsall, 417.
[83] Robinson's Walsall Dir. (1851).
[84] Birm. and Mid. Hardware Dist. 129, 131.
[85] Guide to Walsall (1889), 61–2; Walsall Past and Present (1905), 8; P.O. Dir. Staffs. (1872); Kelly's Dir. Staffs. (1900); plaque on Excelsior Works.
[86] Kelly's Dir. Staffs. (1912).
[87] Ex inf. Mr. D. R. Vale of Vale Bros. Ltd. (1973); Cope, Dir. Staffs. (1921).
[88] Staffs. Advertiser, 29 Dec. 1923; Kelly's Dir. Staffs. (1928).
[89] Kelly's Dir. Staffs. (1940).
[90] Walsall and District Chamber of Commerce, Dir. of Walsall Manufacturers and Buyers Guide to Commodities (1951 edn.).
[91] Barrett's County Boro. of Walsall Dir. (1962–3); ex inf. Mr. Vale.
[92] It occurs in P.O. Telephone Dir. Sect. 451: 1970 but not in Sect. 552: 1972. [93] Ex inf. Mr. Vale.
[94] Ex inf. J. Brierley & Sons Ltd. (1973).
[95] Pearson and Rollason, Birmingham . . . Dir. (1780). Two were also bakers.
[96] Parson and Bradshaw, Dir. Staffs. (1818).
[97] White, Dir. Staffs. (1851). The Bloxwich maltster was also an inn-keeper.
[98] Sketchley's Birmingham . . . Dir. (1767); Sketchley's and Adams's . . . Univ. Dir. Birmingham . . . (1770).
[99] T. S. Ashton, An Eighteenth-Century Industrialist, 72, 75.
[1] Walsall Red Book (1893), 105.
[2] Walsall Observer, 31 Dec. 1966.
[3] Walsall Red Book (1896), 88; (1939), 653. The brewery does not occur in Barrett's Walsall Dir. [1956].
[4] Walsall Observer, 31 Dec. 1966, 13 and 27 Oct. 1972, 10 Aug. 1973.

town centre, was opened *c.* 1923 and was still open shortly after the Second World War.[5] At Bloxwich the Bloxwich Brewery Co. was established in High Street *c.* 1898[6] and survived until the early 1920s;[7] the Crown Brewery, attached to the Crown hotel, Leamore Lane, was opened *c.* 1911 and closed in 1953.[8]

At least four distillers called Scott, all probably of the same family, were active in Walsall in the 18th and early 19th centuries. John and Richard Scott, distillers and chapmen, were declared bankrupt in 1754.[9] Thomas Scott was distilling by 1759.[10] By 1767 his business was in Ablewell Street, where it remained.[11] He was still active *c.* 1796.[12] The firm was Mary Scott & Co. in 1818 and Scott & Barber in 1822. In 1829 it was owned by Richard Barber. By then distilling was apparently the less important side of a retail wine and spirit business.[13] Three other distillers occur in later-18th-century directories: the most successful seems to have been Richard Burrowes, at work in Rushall Street by 1767 and still in business *c.* 1796.[14]

CHEMICALS. Several works made chemicals and allied products in the late 19th and the 20th centuries, but most were small and short-lived. A glue and gelatine works was established by Henry Townsend in Hatherton Street *c.* 1870. In 1872 the concern was bought by a group of local men trading as Townsend & Co. Ltd.; they built a new works in Green Lane on the Wyrley and Essington Canal and renamed the firm the Walsall Glue Co.[15] In 1916 the works was producing fine skin glues and gelatine.[16] It apparently closed between 1962 and 1971.[17] In 1972 Apollo Chemicals Ltd. began manufacturing industrial adhesives and coatings on the Walsall Factory Estate in West Bromwich Road.[18]

Manure was apparently made in Bloxwich *c.* 1872 by the Patent Urban Manure Co. Ltd. and the Urban Phospho-Manure Co. Ltd., both managed by J. T. Hall.[19] Busst & Marlow, a Lower Rushall Street firm of ivory and bone turners and brush-makers, also made bone and chemical manure between at least 1921 and 1939.[20] The Walsall Varnish Manufacturing Co. opened a varnish works in Wisemore in the late 1890s; it closed between 1904 and 1908.[21] The Walsall Polish Manufacturing Co. made boot, shoe, floor, furniture, and metal polishes and harness oil at the Sultan Works, Lichfield Street, from

c. 1926 to *c.* 1932.[22] An acid-processing works in Bescot Crescent was established by a Birmingham firm, Robinson Chemicals Ltd., in 1954; the company returned to Birmingham in 1974.[23]

ORGAN-BUILDING. About 1862 Maria Nicholson and her son Charles Henry Nicholson moved their family's organ-building business to Walsall from Rochdale (Lancs.), where it had been founded in 1816. In 1869 Nicholson & Son had a works off Ablewell Street.[24] The works had been moved to the corner of Bradford and Newport Streets by 1872.[25] In 1874 the firm became Nicholson & Lord, and *c.* 1877 it moved its works to Vicarage Place.[26] About 1922 it became Nicholson & Lord (Walsall) Ltd.[27] It merged with W. Hawkins & Son, another Walsall organ-building concern, in the late 1920s, but the firms soon parted again. Nicholson & Lord, by then in decline, ceased to build organs *c.* 1932 and thereafter only repaired. It gave up its factory some time during the Second World War and ceased trading in the late 1940s.[28] At its height it had exported organs to Ireland, France, Russia, Argentina, Australia, and New Zealand; about 1914 its factory was the largest organ-building works in the Midlands and the firm made all the components for its instruments.[29]

A John Dresser was building organs at Walsall in the 1870s.[30] W. Hawkins & Son was established in 1913 with a works in Paddock Lane. It moved to John Street in 1935 and to Walsall Wood in 1946.[31] A fourth firm of organ-builders, Stanton & Son, was founded *c.* 1923 with its works in Corporation Street. A. H. Stanton, one of the partners, continued the business under his own name from *c.* 1932 until its closure *c.* 1951.[32]

Ernest Holt began making organ parts in Hope Street in 1890. He moved to Wolverhampton Street *c.* 1892, to Lower Forster Street in 1896, and back to Wolverhampton Street in 1906. After his death in 1930 the firm was continued under his name by his sons E. E. and Sidney Holt until 1966. The firm built three organs between 1910 and 1925; its main business was always, however, the manufacture of consoles and other parts.[33]

ELECTRICAL INDUSTRIES. By 1884 the Walsall Electrical Co. was producing electrical apparatus and fittings, bells, switches, and indicators at a works at

[5] *Walsall Red Book* (1924), 555, as G. S. Twist, 92 Wolverhampton St.; *Walsall Observer*, 10 Aug. 1973.
[6] *Walsall Red Book* (1899), 219.
[7] It is listed ibid. (1923), 565, but not in the 1924 edn.
[8] *Walsall Red Book* (1912), 445; Homeshaw, *Bloxwich*, i, 181, 209.
[9] *Aris's Birmingham Gaz.* 11 Feb., 1 Apr. 1754; *Lond. Gaz.* 19–23 Feb. 1754.   [10] B.R.L. 337233.
[11] *Sketchley's Birmingham . . . Dir.* (1767). For his purchase of additional property there in 1774 see B.R.L. 337368.
[12] *Univ. Brit. Dir.* iv. 668.
[13] Parson and Bradshaw, *Dir. Staffs.* (1818); Pigot, *New Com. Dir.* (1822–3), 490; Pigot, *Com. Dir. Birmingham* (1829), 94.
[14] *Sketchley's Birmingham . . . Dir.* (1767); *Univ. Brit. Dir.* iv. 667.
[15] *Staffs. Advertiser*, 20 July 1872; *P.O. Dir. Staffs.* (1872; 1876); O.S. Map 6", Staffs. LXIII. NW. (1889 edn.).
[16] Walsall Chamber of Commerce, *Walsall Comm. Year Book* (1916), 174.
[17] It occurs in *Barrett's County Boro. of Walsall Dir.* (1962–3), but not in *P.O. Telephone Dir. Sect. 227: 1971*.

[18] Ex inf. Apollo Chemicals Ltd. (1974).
[19] *P.O. Dir. Staffs.* (1872).
[20] Cope, *Dir. Staffs.* (1921); *Walsall Red Book* (1939).
[21] *Kelly's Dir. Staffs.* (1900; 1904; 1908).
[22] *Walsall Red Book* (1927; 1932); *County Boro. of Walsall Official Handbook* (6th edn.), 74.
[23] Ex inf. Robinson Chemicals Ltd. (1974).
[24] *Staffs. Advertiser*, 20 Sept. 1862, advert.; White, *Dir. Birmingham* (1869), 854, and adverts. p. 96; *County Boro. of Walsall Official Handbook* (6th edn.), 75.
[25] *P.O. Dir. Staffs.* (1872); *Walsall Red Book* (1873), 50, and adverts. p. xvi.
[26] *Walsall Advertiser*, 26 Dec. 1874; *Walsall Red Book* (1878), 67.   [27] *Walsall Red Book* (1923), 521.
[28] Ex inf. Mr. H. Benyon of W. Hawkins & Son, Walsall Wood (1974).
[29] Printed brochure listing organs built by Nicholson & Lord (n.d. but *c.* 1914; photocopy in W.C.L.).
[30] *Walsall Red Book* (1873), 60; (1878), 51.
[31] Ex inf. Mr. Benyon; *Walsall Observer*, 5 July 1974; below p. 282.
[32] *Walsall Red Book* (1924), 529; (1933), 532; ex inf. Mr. Benyon.
[33] Ex inf. Mr. E. E. Holt (1974).

the Bridge.[34] The works was transferred to Butts Mill in 1885, though an office was retained at the Bridge. In the late 1880s the firm made lamp holders, voltmeters, batteries, and apparatus for collieries, fire-brigades, and scientific experiments. From the later 1880s to the early 1900s light-bulb holders, switches, electroliers, reflectors, and lamps for use in houses and ships were produced at the Selborne Works in Selborne Street, at first by Bayley Bros. and later by the Edison & Swan United Electric Light Co. Ltd.[35] By 1905 there were seven or eight firms with 200 employees making electrical apparatus, including dynamos, motors, switchboards, arc-lamps, and measuring instruments.[36]

The electrical trade continued to expand rapidly in the early 20th century. By 1921 there were 15 firms of electrical engineers and 8 firms making conduits and fittings. There were also three firms making instruments and switches: the Walsall Electrical Co. Ltd. produced both, the Central Manufacturing Co. specialized in instruments, and J. A. Crabtree Ltd., newly founded in Upper Rushall Street, in switches.[37] Crabtrees had moved to Lincoln Road by 1928.[38] By the early 1970s its works occupied most of the area enclosed by Lincoln Road, Beacon Street, Broadway North, Walhouse Road, and Calder Avenue; wiring accessories, motor control gear, and circuit-breakers were its chief products.[39] Electrical conduits and fittings have remained an important branch of manufacture in the borough. In 1929 there were 8 firms, and in 1970 4 firms in Walsall and 3 in Bloxwich made conduits, while another 2 in Walsall made light fittings and fixtures. In the earlier 1970s there were also several firms making switch and control gear, instruments, domestic appliances, transformers, and electronic apparatus.[40]

OTHER INDUSTRIES. Walsall has also been a centre for making optical glass and mirrors. The best-known firm was that founded by Moses Eyland, who was making spectacles in Lower Rushall Street by 1813; by 1818 he combined the trade with that of saddler's ironmonger. By 1822 the firm had become Moses Eyland & Sons. By 1834 it was grinding lenses and producing some 3,000 pairs of spectacles a week.[41] In 1889 it was grinding glass and rock-crystal lenses for its spectacles on a large scale as well as making buckles and engaging in gilding and electro-plating. Tariff barriers killed the export trade in spectacles, and early in the 20th century Eylands abandoned glass-working.[42] Mirrors

and fancy glass-ware were made at the Selborne Works, Selborne Street, by Bayley Bros. from c. 1878. In the late 1890s the works was taken over by the Edison & Swan United Electric Light Co. Ltd. It was closed between 1900 and 1904.[43]

Packing-cases have been made in Walsall from the 19th century. Of 6 coopers in 1834 2 made packing-cases, James Rooker Mason in High Street and Mary Silleter in the Square.[44] In 1900 there were 4 packing-case firms, in Goodall, Whittimere, and Lichfield Streets and Midland Road.[45] By 1929 there were 8 firms.[46] In 1962 only one of them, T. Ginder & Son Ltd. in Whittimere Street, survived, but Packing Supplies (Walsall) Ltd. in Teddesley Street and the Walsall Packing Case Co. in Cecil Street were also producing packing-cases.[47] All three firms were still in business in 1971.[48] Paper and card-board boxes have been made since at least 1900. Six firms are known to have produced them in the 20th century, and four were still in the trade in the early 1970s.[49]

A works making artificial teeth was established in Bradford Street c. 1892 by G. W. Whateley, a dentist.[50] In the early 20th century the industry grew rapidly. By 1905 Walsall exported false teeth to most parts of the world,[51] and by 1916 there were apparently 14 firms in the trade.[52] At that time the Birmingham Dental Supply and Manufacturing Co. Ltd. made diatonic, tube, crown, and platinum pin teeth at the Manor Works in Fieldgate.[53] It was the sole firm in the business by 1921 and went into liquidation in 1929.[54]

The firm of E. Perkins & Co. Ltd., established as engineers in Selborne Street in 1915, had begun producing plastic mouldings by 1924.[55] Between 1928 and 1932 a second firm, Plastics Products Co., began making bakelite mouldings at a works in Midland Road.[56] It moved to Wednesbury between 1945 and 1947.[57] Several other firms entered the trade in the 1940s, and in 1953 there were six plastic-mouldings manufacturers.[58] In 1970 there were some 8 firms making plastic goods; at least 3 of them specialized in mouldings.[59]

LOCAL GOVERNMENT. The division of Walsall manor between two lords from 1247 until 1338 seems to have had little effect on administration, although in the 15th century the tenants were still divided for the purpose of certain customary payments into those of the Rous fee and those of the

---

[34] Kelly's Dir. Staffs. (1884).
[35] Ibid. (1888); Guide to Walsall (1889), 62–5; and see below.
[36] Walsall Past and Present (1905), 11.
[37] Cope, Dir. Staffs. (1921).
[38] Walsall Red Book (1928).
[39] County Boro. of Walsall Official Town Guide [1972], 80, 92.
[40] Walsall Red Book (1939); P.O. Telephone Dir. Sect. 451: 1970; Walsall Chamber of Commerce & Ind. Dir. 1974/5.
[41] Pearce, Walsall, 154; Parson and Bradshaw, Dir. Staffs. (1818); Pigot, New Com. Dir. (1822–3), 489; White, Dir. Staffs. (1834), 416 n.
[42] Guide to Walsall (1889), 63; Walsall Past and Present (1905), 17–18, 120, noting the firm's diversification into other work but still listing spectacles-making among its interests; Kelly's Dir. Staffs. (1908), listing Eylands as buckle-manufacturers only.
[43] Walsall Red Book (1879), advts. p. xi; Guide to Walsall (1889), 63–4; Kelly's Dir. Staffs. (1900; 1904).

[44] White, Dir. Staffs. (1834).
[45] Kelly's Dir. Staffs. (1900).
[46] Walsall Red Book (1929).
[47] Barrett's County Boro. of Walsall Dir. (1962–3).
[48] P.O. Telephone Dir. Sect. 227: 1971.
[49] Ibid.; Kelly's Dir. Staffs. (1900 and later edns. to 1932); Cope, Dir. Staffs. (1921); Walsall Red Book (1929).
[50] Walsall Red Book (1893), 109.
[51] Walsall Past and Present (1905), 18.
[52] Kelly's Dir. Staffs. (1916).
[53] Walsall Chamber of Commerce, Walsall Comm. Year Book (1916), 3.
[54] Cope, Dir. Staffs. (1921); Walsall Observer, 27 Sept. 1974.
[55] County Boro. of Walsall Official Town Guide [1972], 76, 94.
[56] Kelly's Dir. Staffs. (1928; 1932).
[57] Kelly's Dir. Merchants, Manufacturers, and Shippers (1945; 1947).
[58] Ibid. (1941; 1947; 1953).
[59] P.O. Telephone Dir. Sect. 451: 1970.

Morteyn fee.[60] The important division was that between borough and foreign; with the creation of a borough, apparently in the 13th century, the rest of the manor became known as the foreign. The borough became gradually more and more independent, a process doubtless helped by the lack of a resident lord of the manor from 1390. There seems, however, to have been no formal boundary fixed between the borough and foreign townships before 1814.

MANORIAL GOVERNMENT. The lord was holding a court in the earlier 13th century and was enforcing the assize of bread and ale.[61] By the mid 13th century the lords held view of frankpledge;[62] in the earlier 14th century their twice-yearly courts leet[63] were probably held jointly.[64] There were separate three-weekly courts baron for the borough and for the foreign by the 1380s and separate courts leet for each by the earlier 15th century.[65] In 1491–2 the courts leet for the borough and those for the foreign were held on the same day;[66] probably that was the usual practice. They were held jointly by the early 19th century, and probably as early as the 1570s.[67] The courts sat in the guildhall at least in the 17th and early 18th centuries.[68] From at least the 1820s the leet was held at the George hotel.[69]

By 1834 the courts leet had been reduced to annual events.[70] They still sat annually in the mid 1860s,[71] but no later evidence of sittings has been found.[72] By the early 19th century the leet did little apart from appointing officials.[73] In 1806 it promulgated some market by-laws,[74] but no later examples of such activity have been found.

The court baron was probably in decay by the later 18th century. In 1620 the lord had abandoned his claim to heriots from the freeholders and copyholders of the borough and foreign; in the later 18th century the copyholders paid no fines or heriots but merely acknowledgements of a few pence each a year.[75] The inclosure of most of the common fields in the parish by the 18th century[76] removed another source of business. By the later 19th century the

forms of manorial conveyancing, which required a meeting of the court baron, were employed if the steward was asked by the parties concerned to use them; but the court was simply a meeting of the parties at the steward's office. It continued to be held in that way until at least 1919.[77] In 1915 it was stated that the lord received no income or dues from the manor.[78]

By the 1380s, and presumably from the reunion of the manor in 1338, there was a single steward. In the late 14th and the 15th centuries Walsall was under the steward responsible for overseeing the Staffordshire manors of the Bassets and their successors as lords of Walsall, the earls of Warwick.[79] Subsequently the stewardship of Walsall seems to have become an honorific post: it was held in 1478 by John, Lord Dudley, and his son Edmund Dudley jointly, and in 1496 by Sir Humphrey Stanley, a knight of the body.[80] In 1585 the steward was a rising lawyer, Roger (later Sir Roger) Wilbraham, a relative of the lord; the courts were being held by his deputy, who was a local man, George Clarkson.[81] In 1616 John Persehouse of Reynold's Hall was steward.[82] By at least the 1730s the town clerk was acting as steward, and the two posts were regularly combined until the 19th century.[83] From the later 1830s the stewards were members of the Potter family, the solicitors who acted as Lord Bradford's Walsall agents.[84]

The lord's bailiff is mentioned in the earlier 13th century.[85] By the 1380s the bailiff of the manor was a paid permanent official responsible, under the steward, for the administration of the entire manor; the accounts which he rendered covered both the borough and the foreign.[86] The 1309 borough charter mentioned borough bailiffs as well.[87] It is not clear whether there was then more than one at any one time; by the later 14th century there was a single borough bailiff, apparently subordinate to the bailiff of the manor. He received no fee from the lord and held office for only a year.

The system was reorganized in 1397, probably by the officials of the marquess of Dorset, the new lord.

[60] e.g. B.M. Eg. Roll 8514. For the division of the manor see above pp. 169–70. Absence of court rolls leaves many details of the manorial administration obscure. In the 1880s rolls for 1672–1742 still survived: Willmore, *Walsall*, 101. The only other manorial jurisdiction known to have been exercised within the ancient parish was that of the lords of Shelfield, for which see below p. 281.

[61] *S.H.C.* vi (1), 174.

[62] Shaw, *Staffs.* i, app. to Gen. Hist. p. xvii.

[63] W.S.L., D. 1798/84, deeds of 23 Apr. 1303 and 23 June 1308; /86, Thos. le Rous to John le Harpour, n.d.; *Walsall Records*, 32, 34, 41.

[64] *S.H.C.* ix (1), 28.

[65] S.R.O., D. 641/1/2/32; B.M. Eg. Roll 8469; below p. 210.   [66] D.L. 29/641/10416.

[67] Pearce, *Walsall*, 183; S.R.O., D. 1287/1/2, survey of Walsall manor, 1576, m. 6.

[68] W.T.C. II/251/2 and 19; below p. 218.

[69] See e.g. *Staffs. Advertiser*, 27 Oct. 1821, 18 Nov. 1837, 2 Nov. 1844, 12 Nov. 1853.

[70] White, *Dir. Staffs.* (1834).

[71] S.R.O., D. 1287/1/37, Walsall estate accts. 1864, p. 18; ibid. 1865, p. 17; *Staffs. Advertiser* (S. Staffs. edn.), 10 Nov. 1866.

[72] It is recorded in *Kelly's Dir. Staffs.* up to and including 1924 edn., but payments for leet business had disappeared from the Walsall rentals and accounts of the lord of the manor by 1880 (see e.g. S.R.O., D. 1287/1/47). The accounts for 1866–79 have not been traced.

[73] For reports of leet business see e.g. n. 69 above.

[74] Pearce, *Walsall*, 191–2.

[75] See p. 214; Shaw, *Staffs.* ii. 73.

[76] See p. 182.

[77] See e.g. S.R.O., D. 1287/box 7, deeds nos. 593 and 881 and unnumbered bdle. relating to surrender of copyhold property by H. Nickols and others, 1899.

[78] Ibid./box 6, valuation of Walsall estate, 1915.

[79] S.R.O., D. 641/1/2/32 (1385–6); B.M. Eg. Rolls 8467–8542 (a broken series 1388–1460).

[80] *Cal. Pat.* 1476–85, 137; S.C. 1/51/109. Stanley was also high steward of the boro.: below p. 213.

[81] S.R.O., D. 260/M/T/1/11b, copy of ct. roll 12 Apr. and 3 May 1585. For Wilbraham see G. Ormerod, *Hist. of County Palatine and City of Chester* (1882 edn.), iii. 440, 515; *Visitation of Cheshire, 1613* (Harl. Soc. lix), 259–60; *Camd. Misc.* x (Camd. 3rd ser. iv), 'Jnl. of Sir Roger Wilbraham', pp. v–viii.

[82] S.R.O., D. 260/M/F/1/5, f. 136. For Persehouse see above p. 177.

[83] Homeshaw, *Walsall*, 87; W.S.L. 333/32, p. 75; Pearce, *Walsall*, 108, 183, 191.

[84] See e.g. *Staffs. Advertiser*, 9 Nov. 1839; Walsall Council House, deeds bdle. 127, abstract of title 1898, pp. 14, 19; S.R.O., D. 1287/18/31, business corresp. 1873, P. Potter to Lord Bradford, 16 Oct. 1873; refs. in n. 77 above.

[85] W.T.C. I/1.

[86] For the rest of this para. see, unless otherwise stated, S.R.O., D. 641/1/2/32; B.M. Eg. Rolls 8467–73.

[87] See p. 213.

The bailiff of the manor was thenceforth known as the bailiff of the foreign.[88] He normally acted as parker also.[89] Responsibility for income from the borough (mainly rents, perquisites of court, and market tolls) and expenditure within it was transferred to the borough bailiff, who began to account separately.[90] He continued to serve without fee, receiving no money from the lord except for his expenses, and, as before, held office for only a year.[91] From at least 1424 he was elected at the lord's borough court leet;[92] his election at the Michaelmas court is mentioned in the earlier 16th century.[93] Both borough and foreign bailiffs occur in 1585,[94] but the subsequent history of the offices is obscure. By the late 18th century there was a single bailiff of the manor, who was also known as the crier of the court leet and was apparently appointed for life or years; the post still existed in 1830.[95]

The leet appointed constables for the borough and for the foreign. The borough constable occurs in 1377,[96] the foreign constable in 1458;[97] in the early 16th century the former was apparently assisted by serjeants, also appointed by the leet.[98] Two constables were still appointed in 1866; by the late 1820s they were known as head constables, there being several deputy constables by then for both borough and foreign.[99] Goscote by at least the end of the 16th century was outside the foreign constablewick, forming a separate constablewick with Rushall.[1]

Other officials appointed by the leet were ale-tasters, flesh-tasters, leather-sealers, and pinners. Two ale-tasters were appointed at the court for the borough in 1424,[2] and the office of ale-taster for the foreign is mentioned in 1647.[3] From at least 1677 until at least 1853 the leet appointed two ale-tasters or clerks of the market for the borough; from 1737 they were known simply as clerks of the market. From 1816 they and the flesh-tasters apparently performed market duties as borough officials, although the leet continued to appoint them.[4] A thirdborough

or ale-taster was appointed for the foreign in 1725, but the office had lapsed by the earlier 19th century. Two flesh-tasters were appointed for the borough from at least 1677 until 1844,[5] when the number was increased to three; three were still appointed in 1853. Two leather-sealers were appointed for the borough from at least 1677 until 1808, when a change in the law rendered the office obsolete. A pinner was appointed for the borough from at least 1677; the office still existed in the later 1850s, though it became difficult to fill.[6] A pinner was appointed for the foreign in 1725. In the early 19th century two pinners were being appointed, for Bloxwich and for Walsall Wood and Shelfield.[7] By 1839 the number had been increased to three, with separate Walsall Wood and Shelfield pinners,[8] and by 1853 there were four pinners for the foreign.

In 1293 the lords of the manor claimed the right to gallows, pillory, and tumbrel.[9] In 1396–7 a felon was tried before the steward and hanged,[10] and the existence in 1617 of a pasture called Gallows Leasow probably in the Bloxwich area gives some indication of the site of a gallows.[11] The lord remade the borough pillory in 1396–7 and provided a pillory for the foreign in 1414–15 and again in 1490–1.[12] A cucking-stool ('gumstole') was made for the foreign in 1414–15 and another in 1488–9.[13] New stocks were made for the foreign in 1487–8; they were probably at Bloxwich, where there were stocks in 1567 apparently near the church.[14] The lord paid for the repair of a pinfold in the foreign in 1490–1.[15]

PARISH GOVERNMENT. By the earlier 17th century the parish was divided into borough and foreign townships. Each raised its own rates, had its own vestry meeting, and relieved its own poor. The borough vestry normally met at the parish church and the foreign vestry probably at Bloxwich chapel. There was also a parish vestry, meeting at the church.[16]

By the 18th century the borough churchwardens met the general parochial expenses in the first

[88] B.M. Eg. Roll 8474 (1396–7) is the first account rendered for the foreign alone. Dorset received the income for the last 3 months of the year covered by the account, which includes the expenses of his officials who came to Walsall to check and revise the rental. The new title may have been used before: ibid. 8469.

[89] See e.g. B.M. Eg. Rolls 8471, 8536 sqq.; Rot. Parl. (Rec. Com.), vi. 373–5; C1/1389/41. From at least 1485 the office was that of keeper of the park.

[90] B.M. Eg. R. 8476 (1398–9) is the first account for the boro. alone. Earlier the boro. bailiff had occasionally made cash payments to the lord's receiver: ibid. 8470–1.

[91] Boro. bailiff's accounts among ibid. 8476–8542.

[92] S.R.O., D. 260/M/F/1/5, f. 171, giving list of officials appointed at a foreign court 3 Hen. VI. This 17th-cent. transcript from a now missing court roll apparently misidentifies the court, which must be that of the boro. Rob. More, the man elected bailiff, served as bailiff of the boro. 3–4 Hen. VI (B.M. Eg. Roll 8512); among official selected with him was a portreeve; other business included presentments of non-burgess brewers.

[93] Willmore, Walsall, 165. For the dating see p. 213.

[94] S.R.O., D. 260/M/T/1/11b, copy of ct. roll, 12 Apr. and 3 May 1585.

[95] S.R.O., D. 1287/10/2, Walsall market rights etc., case and opinion respecting ownership of Walsall market, pp. 3, 9–10; Walsall Note Book, 41, 67, 93–4 (copy in W.C.L.).   [96] See p. 213.

[97] S.R.O., D. 260/M/F/1/5, f. 171.

[98] Willmore, Walsall, 165.

[99] Staffs. Advertiser (S. Staffs. edn.), 10 Nov. 1866. The term 'head constable' is used in a report of the leet in Staffs. Advertiser, 7 Nov. 1829 and in newspaper reports in later years.

[1] S.H.C. xv. 213; 1923, 138; 1935, 121; 4th ser. i. 331, 333.

[2] S.R.O., D. 260/M/F/1/5, f. 171; above n. 92.

[3] W.S.L. 469/32.

[4] For the remainder of the para. see, unless otherwise stated, S.R.O., D. 1287/10/2, Walsall market rights etc., case and opinion respecting ownership of Walsall market, pp. 2 sqq.; ibid., case as to appointment of certain officers of the market, pp. 2–5; Pearce, Walsall, 184–5; Staffs. Advertiser, 12 Nov. 1853.

[5] Staffs. Advertiser, 2 Nov. 1844.

[6] Ibid. 1 Dec. 1860.

[7] Pearce, Walsall, 185, noting appointment in 1812 of pinners for Great Bloxwich and for Walsall Wood; Staffs. Advertiser, 7 Nov. 1818, reporting appointment of pinners for Bloxwich and for Walsall Wood and Shelfield.

[8] Staffs. Advertiser, 9 Nov. 1839.

[9] S.H.C. vi (1), 270.

[10] B.M. Eg. Roll 8474.

[11] S.R.O., D. 260/M/F/1/8, ct. of recog. and survey, 1617, p. 20.

[12] B.M. Eg. Rolls 8474, 8498; D.L. 29/641/10415.

[13] B.M. Eg. Roll 8498; D.L. 29/641/10413.

[14] D.L. 29/641/10412; S.H.C. 1938, 142; Homeshaw, Bloxwich, 156.

[15] D.L. 29/641/10415.

[16] W.T.C. II/50/1 (statement of the position in 1648); docs. at St. Matthew's, Vestry Bks. from 1681, containing records of parish and borough meetings. For the few minutes of the foreign vestry known to survive see W.T.C. II/155/2 and 3; docs. at All Saints', Bloxwich, Out-poor Bk., mins. of meetings of the inhabitants of the foreign to choose a minister 1803 (at the chapel) and 1825 (at the chapel, adjourned to the King's Arms).

instance and claimed back half from the foreign.[17] The foreign wardens, however, did not always pay. In 1760 a parish vestry agreed that the borough wardens should try to recover the foreign share and promised to meet their expenses in so doing.[18] In 1796, 1809, and 1821 disputes arose over the foreign's contribution towards the cost of work on the parish church.[19] In 1830 the parish vestry approved a general church-rate instead of the usual separate rates. The foreign wardens refused to pay, and the borough vestry began legal proceedings against them.[20] Church-rates were also causing hostility between local dissenters and Anglicans by 1837, but shortly afterwards they ceased to be collected in Walsall.[21]

Poor-rates were another source of contention. Walsall's method of raising them was unusual. They were levied not according to the location of land but according to the occupier's residence. Thus if a man held land in the foreign but lived in the borough he paid rates to the borough overseers and vice versa. Outsiders paid to the borough. Neither borough nor foreign liked the system. The borough ratepayers would have preferred a general rate throughout the parish: the borough suffered more unemployment than the foreign and so had more poor to support; the ratepayers claimed in 1754 to be paying three times as much in the £ as the foreigners. The foreign ratepayers wanted to keep the two divisions but to rate by land and not place of residence since there was more rateable land in the foreign.[22] Various disputes arose, and in 1677 the borough and foreign concluded an agreement recognizing the independence of each but attempting to modify the rating system.[23] Despite further disputes[24] the old system apparently continued until the late 1740s. In 1752 the Walsall justices appointed four overseers for the whole parish. The borough ratepayers welcomed the justices' action, but the foreigners resisted. One of their retiring overseers, Samuel Wilks, went to prison rather than surrender his books to the justices, and three other foreigners secured a mandamus in 1753 ordering the justices to appoint overseers for the foreign. The justices refused. Despite another King's Bench judgement for the foreign in 1754, the justices continued their stand, and in 1755 no poor-rate was levied. At the beginning of 1756, however, the justices gave way, the previous system was reinstated,

and separate overseers were appointed.[25] Disputes continued[26] and culminated in 1812 when the overseers of the foreign rated 64 borough residents who held property in the foreign. In 1813 the King's Bench declared the old rating practice illegal and enforced rating by land. It also ordered a boundary to be agreed between borough and foreign, and one was duly fixed in 1814.[27]

Churchwardens occur from 1405.[28] Since at least the earlier 17th century there have been separate wardens of the borough and of the foreign. It is not clear when that distinction began to be made; earlier variations in the numbers of recorded wardens may reflect the inclusion or omission of the foreign wardens. In 1462 there were two wardens of All Saints', but from 1466 to at least 1530 three usually held office. They were also known as the wardens of the high altar. By the early 16th century there were additional wardens of the other altars and chapels.[29] Two churchwardens occur in 1553, besides a chapelwarden at Bloxwich.[30] In the later 16th and early 17th centuries the recorded number of churchwardens varied from two to four.[31] The foreign wardens are first mentioned in 1634, when they were responsible for Bloxwich chapel. Earlier chapelwardens there may in fact have been wardens of the foreign.[32] Two wardens of the borough and one of the foreign signed the hearth-tax returns in 1666.[33] Since at least 1693 there have been four wardens, two for the borough and two for the foreign.[34] The vicar appointed one borough and one foreign warden by at least 1763.[35] Despite the reduction in the size of St. Matthew's parish from the 19th century four wardens continue to be appointed by the vicar and the parishioners.[36] Under the borough ordinances of the early 16th century the churchwardens, like the other wardens at the parish church, had to account yearly before the mayor on St. Catherine's day (25 November); by the earlier 18th century, however, they were accounting to the vestry.[37]

A vestry clerk occurs by 1769.[38] By the earlier 1820s he was salaried,[39] and in 1824 he was also paid to collect church-rates and keep the churchwardens' accounts. His successor in 1825 was also surveyor and assessor of rateable property, superintendent of church repairs, and clerk to the select vestry.[40] There was a parish clerk by 1588[41] and a sexton by 1653.[42] A bellman of the church occurs in 1515.[43] In 1771

[17] W.T.C. II/50/25; Vestry Bk. 1681–1793, pp. 93, 147 sqq.

[18] Vestry Bk. 1681–1793, pp. 93–5, 108–9; Pearce, *Walsall*, 94.

[19] Vestry Bk. 1794–1854, pp. 11, 50, 174, 231–2, 258, 271–2, 285–6, 299–300, 309.

[20] Willmore, *Walsall*, 394–5, without stating the outcome; Vestry Bk. 1794–1854, pp. 320 sqq.; *Walsall Note Book*, 80, 92, 95–8, 121–3 (copy in W.C.L.); White, *Dir. Staffs.* (1834).

[21] S.R.O., D. 1287/18/26, business corresp. 1835–7, P. Potter to Lord Bradford, 21 Mar. 1837; Glew, *Walsall*, 71 n.

[22] Homeshaw, *Walsall*, 59–60; W.T.C. II/50/1 and 25; W.T.C. II/59; Shaw, *Staffs.* ii. 73.

[23] Homeshaw, *Walsall*, 60–2; W.T.C. II/13/62.

[24] Homeshaw, *Walsall*, 62; W.T.C. II/13/66 and 68.

[25] Homeshaw, *Walsall*, 97–9.

[26] W.T.C. II/50/34–6.

[27] Homeshaw, *Walsall*, 127; Vestry Bk. 1794–1854, pp. 63–4; Pearce, *Walsall*, 228–34; H. Jacob, *Plan of Boundary Line between Township of Boro. and Township of Foreign of Walsall* (Birmingham, 1816; copy in W.C.L.).

[28] Sims, *Cal. of Deeds*, p. 13.

[29] *S.H.C.* 1928, 178–9, 189; below p. 228.

[30] *S.H.C.* 1915, 298; below p. 235.

[31] L.J.R.O., B/V/1/4–5, /7–8, /13, /16, /20–1, /23–4, /28, /32, /37, /57, *sub* Walsall.

[32] See p. 235.

[33] *S.H.C.* 1923, 131, 146.

[34] L.J.R.O., B/V/6/Walsall, 1693.

[35] Docs. at St. Mathew's, Vestry Bk. 1681–1793; 1794–1854.

[36] Ex inf. Mr. L. Harper, vicar's warden (1972).

[37] Willmore, *Walsall*, 168, 172; Vestry Bk. 1681–1793, p. 23; below p. 213.

[38] Vestry Bk. 1681–1793, note attached to p. 150.

[39] Docs. at St. Matthew's, Churchwardens' Accts. 1794–1841, f. 72v.

[40] Vestry Bk. 1794–1854, pp. 222, 242–3. For the clerk's functions as overseer of the poor see below p. 212.

[41] S.R.O., D. 260/M/F/1/5, f. 3v.; F. W. Willmore, *Transcript of First Reg. Bk. of Par. Ch. of St. Matthew, Walsall, 1570–1649* (Walsall, 1890), 162.

[42] W.T.C. II/13/41.

[43] *S.H.C.* 1928, 250.

the vestry voted him a salary as dog-whipper.[44] There were two dog-whippers by 1797 and three by 1801; from that date they were known as beadles.[45] From at least 1865 there has been a tower-keeper.[46]

The constables appointed by the manor court were accounting to the vestry by the late 17th century.[47] There was a lock-up at Bloxwich which in 1836 the parish assigned to the borough police.[48]

By the mid 18th century two or more highway surveyors were appointed for the borough and two or more for the foreign.[49] By the 17th century the corporation maintained the streets of the town.[50] By 1768 the rest of the parish was divided into four highway districts, each with two surveyors; the borough township formed one district and there were three for the foreign—the area covered by Wood End, Townend, and Caldmore, the Bloxwich area, and the Walsall Wood area. By 1834 a fifth district covering Coal Pool and Goscote had been formed out of the Bloxwich district.[51] The borough vestry, besides appointing the two surveyors for the borough township under the Highway Act of 1835, appointed a salaried assistant surveyor in 1838 who was also to collect the highway rate.[52] The Bloxwich district had a board of surveyors by 1856.[53] All roads passed under the control of the corporation when it became an urban sanitary authority under the Public Health Act of 1872.[54]

By the earlier 17th century there were four overseers of the poor, two each for the borough and the foreign.[55] In the 17th century the mayor administered much of the relief.[56] There appears to have been an assistant overseer for the borough in 1781,[57] and from 1789 until 1802 there was a third overseer for the borough, who was also vestry clerk.[58] In 1802 he was appointed assistant overseer and was paid a salary.[59] In 1799–1800 there were three overseers of the foreign, one of them being also 'governor of the poor'.[60] In 1822, under the Sturgess Bourne Act, a select vestry was set up for the borough.[61]

By the earlier 17th century the main form of relief was weekly doles of 3d. to 8d.[62] The corporation helped the poor to pay their rent and provided medical care.[63] It subscribed to Stafford General Infirmary from its opening in 1766 and to Birmingham General Hospital by 1803.[64] In 1812 the vestry arranged for the vaccination of poor children.[65]

Poorhouses, apparently situated in the Ditch,

were maintained by the corporation between at least 1648 and 1723.[66] In 1717 the corporation acquired for the poor three houses near the top of Hill Street charged with a payment to the organist at the parish church.[67] A vestry meeting agreed in 1727 that a workhouse should be built, and by 1732 the corporation had either converted or rebuilt the Hill Street houses as a borough workhouse, which was leased to the vestry.[68] By 1752 there was a workhouse for the foreign on Chapel (later Elmore) Green in Bloxwich.[69] In the mid 1770s the borough workhouse had accommodation for 130 and that at Bloxwich for seventy.[70] The borough workhouse was enlarged in 1799, but in 1813 it was stated to be 'very inconveniently situated on account of the difficulty of conveyance to it'.[71]

In 1733 and again in 1740 the parish vestry appointed a committee to be governors of the new borough workhouse.[72] By the early 1750s there was one governor.[73] The borough vestry appointed a full-time paid governor in 1761.[74]

The Walsall poor-law union was formed in 1836, covering the parishes of Walsall, Aldridge, Darlaston, and Rushall and the townships of Bentley and Pelsall in St. Peter's, Wolverhampton. The borough elected four of the nineteen guardians and the foreign six.[75] The union workhouse in Pleck Road was built in 1838;[76] its remaining buildings form part of Manor Hospital.

THE BOROUGH. A borough had been established at Walsall by the earlier 13th century when the lord of the manor, William le Rous (d. 1247), granted the burgesses quittance from every service, custom, and secular demand except tallage. In the same charter he granted them extensive pasture rights but reserved pannage. He limited fines for breaches of the assize of bread and ale to 6d. a time for the first three offences. The burgesses were to pay an annual rent of 12d. for every burgage, and when a burgage was offered for sale the lord had the right to buy it at 12d. below the highest offer received. The burgesses paid 12 marks for the charter, which probably dates from c. 1235.[77]

In 1309 Sir Roger de Morteyn and Sir Thomas le Rous, the lords of the divided manor, extended the privileges.[78] The new charter discharged the burgesses from tallage and pannage, further reduced

[44] Vestry Bk. 1681–1793, p. 136.
[45] Churchwardens' Accts. 1794–1841, ff. 3v., 7v. sqq.
[46] Inscription on clock in tower; ex inf. Mr. L. Harper.
[47] Vestry Bk. 1681–1793.
[48] See p. 224.
[49] W.T.C. II/50/9/2, p. 10; II/149.
[50] W.T.C. II/13; II/31/5 and 6; II/39/1 and 2.
[51] Pearce, Walsall, 221–4; Homeshaw, Walsall, 100, 114; Shaw, Staffs. ii. 73; White, Dir. Staffs. (1834).
[52] Vestry Bk. 1794–1854, pp. 426–7, 450, 154 (2nd nos.).
[53] W.T.C., Mins. of Bloxwich Board of Surveyors, 1856–72.   [54] Willmore, Walsall, 195.
[55] W.T.C. II/50/1.   [56] W.T.C. II/13.
[57] Vestry Bk. 1681–1793, p. 239.
[58] Pearce, Walsall, 101–2; Vestry Bk. 1794–1854, p. 128.
[59] Vestry Bk. 1794–1854, pp. 26, 40–1, 46–7, 79–80, 89, 188, 191.
[60] Docs. at All Saints', Bloxwich, Out-poor Bk.; Pearce, Walsall, 102.
[61] Vestry Bk. 1794–1854, pp. 130, 188 sqq.
[62] W.T.C. II/38, /49.
[63] W.T.C. II/13, /52, /85, /235 (10 Sept. 1662).
[64] Homeshaw, Walsall, 166, 170; S.R.O., D. 685/12/1; D. 1287/12/3, printed ann. reps. on state of the General

Hospital near Birmingham; 1st Rep. Com. Mun. Corps. H.C. 116, App. p. 2051 (1835), xxv.
[65] Vestry Bk. 1794–1854, p. 68.
[66] W.T.C. II/31/12; II/13/59, 66, 69–70, 75, 83.
[67] Pearce, Walsall, 126; below p. 233.
[68] Vestry Bk. 1681–1793, pp. 36, 46, f. 107 (reverse).
[69] Homeshaw, Bloxwich, 92; W.T.C. II/50/9/3, p. 20.
[70] Rep. Cttee. Returns made by Overseers of Poor, 1777, H.C. ser. i, p. 458 (1803), ix.
[71] Pearce, Walsall, 125–6.
[72] Vestry Bk. 1681–1793, pp. 47–8.
[73] W.T.C. II/50/9/3, p. 19.
[74] Vestry Bk. 1681–1793, p. 95.
[75] 3rd Ann. Rep. Poor Law Com. H.C. 546 (1), p. 164 (1837), xxxi.
[76] White, Dir. Staffs. (1851).
[77] W.T.C. I/1 (printed in sections in A. Ballard, Brit. Boro. Charters 1042–1216, 43, 49, 66, 69, 92, 158, 239). The date c. 1235 has been suggested by Mr. K. F. Brown, formerly archivist at Walsall Central Libr., who is preparing an article on this and the 1309 charter for the Transactions of the South Staffordshire Archaeological and Historical Society.
[78] W.T.C. I/9.

fines for breach of the assize of ale, and excused such fines altogether between Christmas Eve and Candlemas and during the fairs. Disputes between burgesses which could not be settled otherwise were to be settled in the court (presumably the manor court) by two men of the court. The burgesses were to be impleaded for offences committed in the town before the bailiffs of the borough and no one else, and only the bailiffs could distrain them. If the burgesses' cattle were impounded for trespassing on the lord's corn or pasture, the damage was to be assessed by two men from the town and two from the foreign and by the lord's bailiff; if they could not agree it was to be assessed in the lord's court by two free men of the court. Free passage was granted for manure, wood, and other necessities along certain streets. Anyone taking a burgage had first to come to an agreement about the liberties of the town with its community (*communitas*).

The references to the bailiffs of the town and to the community show that by 1309 the borough enjoyed some form of self-government. By 1377 there existed an assembly (*consilium*) of burgesses, a mayor, a constable, and a bailiff. That year an assembly ordained that a burgess should be admitted only if those officers and twelve other burgesses were present. The same assembly also ordained that anyone revealing the counsel of the burgesses should be fined.[79] Such assemblies continued to meet at varying intervals of years to admit new burgesses. By the mid 15th century, however, the mayor alone seems to have been responsible for admissions: the assemblies then met to receive from him the list of burgesses whom he had admitted and his account of admission fees, or burgess silver.[80] Such accounting became annual from at least the late 1490s.[81] The portreeve who occurs in the later 1390s as annually appointed and responsible to the borough bailiff for the market toll was presumably the mayor; he occurs again in 1424 as elected at the manor court.[82] There was a steward by the late 15th century: Sir Humphrey Stanley, admitted a burgess in 1461, had been appointed steward of the town by the king by 1485 and occurs as high steward at the beginning of the 16th century.[83] In 1501, when the Crown held the manor, the borough was leased to the mayor, bailiff, and burgesses for 50 years.[84]

The group of twelve burgesses mentioned in 1377 may have been the forerunner of the council, called the Twenty-five at first but subsequently the Twenty-four.[85] An ordinance made c. 1500 by the high steward, mayor, and Twenty-five imposed a fine on any member of the Twenty-five who failed to attend meetings; thenceforth the divulging of council business was to result not only in a fine but in expulsion. A dispute between members was to be settled by members who were not involved, and failure to abide by their decision was to lead to expulsion. A further ordinance, apparently made in 1501–2, stipulated annual accounting by the retiring mayor before the new mayor on St. Clement's day (23 November). It also provided that anyone 'misordering' himself against the steward, under-steward, mayor, bailiff, the other officers, or any of the Twenty-five was to submit to correction by the mayor, officers, and Twenty-five or else be expelled from the town.[86]

A more comprehensive set of ordinances was drawn up apparently between 1510 and 1520.[87] They mention the appointment of mayor, bailiff, constable, and serjeants at the Michaelmas meeting of the manor court and show that the council of Twenty-four was a self-perpetuating body, not elected by the burgesses at large.[88] They provided for a meeting of all burgesses, presumably once a year, to swear obedience to the mayor and officers and to assist in the good government of the town. Absentees were to be fined, and persistent absentees were to lose their burgess status, regaining it only on payment of a 10s. fine. There was a repetition of the earlier regulations governing the conduct of members of the council (although reinstatement of anyone expelled was permitted on payment of a fine) and the punishment of those who resisted the officers. Fines were levied not by the mayor but by the bailiff. Retiring mayors were to account on St. Clement's day[89] before the mayor and at least five of the Twenty-four. If the new mayor was negligent in the matter he was to be fined, as was the retiring mayor if he was not ready with his accounts.

To be admitted a burgess a candidate had to pay a fee and swear loyalty to the town and its officers. Fees varied from 6s. 8d. to 2s. in 1377, but normally they were either a full fee of 6s. 8d. or a half fee of 3s. 4d.[90] It is not usually stated what governed the amount paid. Residence was a factor: one of the candidates in 1377 lived in Rushall and had to pay 6s. 8d. because he neither lived in the manor of Walsall nor held land there.[91] Occasionally in the early 17th century a burgess's son and heir was admitted free,[92] while in the 16th century at least a man who married a burgess or a burgess's daughter and heir was admitted for 3s. 4d.[93] Women, however, were rarely admitted; a spinster was admitted in 1568 and a widow in 1593, both for 3s. 4d.[94] Bachelors paid 3s. 4d. by the later 16th century.[95]

---

[79] W.T.C. II/238, m. 1.
[80] Ibid. mm. 1d., 2d.
[81] Ibid. mm. 4 sqq.
[82] B.M. Eg. Rolls 8474 sqq.; above p. 210 n. 92.
[83] Willmore, *Walsall*, 171–4; *Rot. Parl.* vi. 373; W.T.C. II/238, m. 2d.; Sims, *Cal. of Deeds*, p. 26. He was also steward of the manor: see above p. 209.
[84] W.T.C. I/49 (a 17th-cent. copy wrongly dating the original to 1438: Willmore, *Walsall*, 86–7).
[85] The three burgesses who head the 1426 list of admissions are each described as 'cap' (W.T.C. II/238, m. 3), perhaps an abbreviation of 'capitalis'.
[86] W.T.C. II/238, mm. 3d.–2d., 4d., mostly summarized in Willmore, *Walsall*, 171–2.
[87] W.T.C. I/46*, transcribed in Glew, *Walsall*, 101–7, and Willmore, *Walsall*, 165–9. The dating is indicated by references to Lord Berners and Sir Rob. Sheffield as patrons of certain Walsall chantries; as lords of Goscote

and Shelfield manors they shared the advowson of Sir Roger Hillary's chantries, not earlier than 1510 and not later than 1520: see above pp. 173–4 and references in nn. 80–1 and below pp. 228, 279 and references in nn. 62–4. The statute against unlawful games mentioned in the 7th ordinance is that of 1503, not 1542.
[88] W.T.C. I/163.
[89] For the few instances of mayoral accounting on St. Catherine's day (25 Nov.) see W.T.C. II/238, mm. 5, 6.
[90] Ibid. *passim*; Willmore, *Walsall*, 167.
[91] W.T.C. II/238, m. 1.
[92] Ibid. mm. 13d., 14d. For the admission of Ric. Wever in 1480–1 'per descensum . . . Henrici Marchall', himself admitted in 1402, see ibid. m. 1.
[93] Ibid. mm. 5d., 12d.
[94] Ibid. mm. 15, 12d.
[95] Ibid. mm. 11 sqq.

The performance of a special service could lead to a reduction.[96] The ordinances of *c.* 1510–20 laid down that burgesses should pay half their fine at the time of admission and the other half when the mayor admitting them went out of office. Any burgess who had not paid his fine by the time the retiring mayor rendered his account was to lose his burgess status and to be readmitted only on payment of a fine.[97] There are several instances of the enforcement of the ordinances in the later 16th and early 17th centuries.[98] Burgesses continued to be admitted until at least 1619,[99] but the charter of incorporation of 1627 made no provision for common burgesses.

In the course of the 15th century the guild of St. John the Baptist became closely involved in the government of the town.[1] By 1426 the guildhall had become the meeting-place of the assembly of burgesses and thereafter continued as the town hall.[2] On three occasions in the later 15th century the retiring mayor is described as accounting for the burgess silver before the guildsmen, and in the earlier 1540s the masters of the guild attended accounting sessions.[3] The guild in turn was subject to some control by the town authorities.[4] In addition, from at least 1502 the wardens of the craft guilds were fined if they failed to account to the mayor on St. Clement's day or St. Catherine's day (25 November).[5]

Although the development of the borough was at the expense of the manorial jurisdiction, the lord of Walsall retained some control through the manor court where, as already mentioned, the mayor and other officers were appointed each Michaelmas. No friction is recorded before the 1520s. Indeed in 1512–13 Robert Rushton, the bailiff of the foreign and one of the two lessees of the manor, was admitted a burgess.[6] Trouble came after the manor was leased to William Gower and Robert Acton, officials of the king's chamber, in 1524. Within about a year Acton was complaining in Star Chamber that leading townsmen were withholding lands, rents, and services, felling timber in the park, and hunting there, and that when he had objected they had threatened him.[7]

Relations with the Wilbraham family, who secured the manor in the 1550s, seem to have been good at first. At Michaelmas 1579 the retiring mayor presided at the manor court.[8] In 1589 Thomas Wilbraham leased the High Cross to the town out of 'love' for the inhabitants, and in 1594 and 1595 he acted as intermediary in transactions between John Persehouse of Reynold's Hall and the borough.[9] In 1610, however, his son Sir Richard was claiming heriots, reliefs, and fines from property in the borough, even though a survey of 1576 had stressed that

burgages were exempt from heriots. The dispute lasted ten years. In 1620 Sir Richard compounded with the freeholders and copyholders of the borough and foreign, acknowledging that the burgage holders owed him only 12*d.* a year for each burgage and suit of court, with no heriots.[10]

Initially all or most of the borough's income probably came from fines and admission fees. Two keepers of the treasure were elected at the assembly of burgesses in 1426, and money was handed over to them 'from the treasure in the box'.[11] The early-16th-century ordinances laid down that after the retiring mayor had paid over the burgess fees 'and all other duties' to his successor, the money and the burgess roll were to be placed in the burgess box and the box put away 'in the treasure coffer' until the next accounting.[12] The box or the coffer is probably the box mentioned in 1524 by Robert Acton in the course of his dispute with the borough as 'a common box called Bayard's Box, in the which be great sums of money purposely for the same box gathered to maintain their evil doings'.[13] One of them may be identifiable with the town chest, which occurs from the 1650s as the repository of corporation muniments.[14]

In time landed property became a more important source of income. The town estate, which in 1626 produced rents of £38 from Bascote in Long Itchington (Warws.) and £29 from Walsall and Rushall,[15] can be traced back to 1441 when Thomas Mollesley of Walsall leased Bascote manor to ten feoffees, to two of whom he granted it in 1451. It was later alleged that the land was granted to the use of the town of Walsall. Although no such limitation is recorded the estate was charged later in 1451 with the payment of Mollesley's Dole in Walsall. One of the feoffees, William Lyle, was sole lord from 1452 to at least 1466, but whether or not as a trustee is not clear: from 1468 feoffees for St. John's guild were lords, and a claim to the estate by Lyle's son John failed in 1514. The feoffees remained in possession after the suppression of the guild, and in 1556 the mayor and 'his brethren' were said to be lords of Bascote manor.[16] Since it was concealed guild property their title was insecure, and the Crown granted all or part of the estate to speculators in 1564.[17] Although the grant was not effective it eventually obliged the town feoffees to take steps from 1586 to 1592 to secure their possession. These measures created a second set of feoffees, but a new feoffment of 1607 included representatives of both groups.[18]

By then the feoffees also held property in Walsall and Rushall, of which the nucleus was chantry land and land belonging to St. John's guild, some of it

---

[96] Ibid. mm. 2, 4d. (the latter badly rubbed but copied in W.T.C. II/16).

[97] Willmore, *Walsall*, 167. The penalty for non-payment of the entrance fine had already been laid down in the ordinance of 1501–2: ibid. 172.

[98] W.T.C. II/238, mm. 14, 15, 10d., 11d., 12d., 13d., 14d.

[99] The last date on the Burgess Roll (ibid. m. 15d.).

[1] For the guild see p. 229.

[2] See p. 218.

[3] W.T.C. II/238, mm. 2, 8, 9.

[4] W.T.C. I/67; Willmore, *Walsall*, 169; below p. 229.

[5] W.T.C. I/83.

[6] W.T.C. II/238, m. 5d.; *L. & P. Hen. VIII*, i (1), p. 454.

[7] W.T.C. II/48.

[8] Sims, *Cal. of Deeds*, p. 39.

[9] W.T.C. I/140 and II/15; above p. 187.

[10] W.T.C. I/163–7; /197; /261, arts. 7, 8, 28–9, 31. For the 1576 manorial survey see S.R.O., D. 1287/1/2.

[11] W.T.C. II/238, m. 3.

[12] Willmore, *Walsall*, 167, 172.

[13] W.T.C. II/48.

[14] W.T.C. II/13/41, 43, 60, 62–3, 65; *Charter of Corp. of Walsall*, 42.   [15] W.T.C. II/31/4.

[16] Sims, *Cal. of Deeds*, pp. 17–21, 24–5, 27, 29, 31–3, 35–7, 39; *9th Rep. Com. Char.* H.C. 258, pp. 573–4 (1823), ix; W.T.C. I/67; I/71; I/87*, mm. 1, 4–5; II/2/1; II/234; Dugdale, *Warws.* (2nd edn.), i. 347; *Monastic and Other Estates in the County of Warwick, 1546–1547* (Dugdale Soc. ii), 95; below p. 266.

[17] *Cal. Pat.* 1563–6, pp. 62–6.

[18] Sims, *Cal. of Deeds*, pp. 41–5, 47, 50; *1st Rep. Com. Mun. Corps.* H.C. 116, App. III, p. 2049 (1835), xxv; W.T.C. II/9/3.

appropriated by the town council after the suppression and some acquired in 1565. Other property had been bought in 1556, 1602, and 1605, and more was bought in 1614.[19] Much of the local property had been sold by c. 1660.[20] The Bascote estate was sold in stages between 1840 and 1918; the last manorial court there held by the corporation was in 1888.[21]

Between at least 1619 and 1685 the rents of the estate were received by the high warden, apparently the successor of the guild wardens; he then paid them to the mayor. It is not clear whether high wardens continued to be appointed thereafter; the mayor may have received the rents directly.[22]

In the early 17th century the borough claimed to be a corporation by prescription,[23] but probably the dispute with Sir Richard Wilbraham suggested the need for a new charter.[24] By will proved in 1627 Nicholas Parker of Bloxwich left £100 for the purchase of one,[25] and later that year a charter was granted incorporating the borough and foreign.[26]

The charter appointed a mayor and twenty-four capital burgesses. The mayor was thereafter to be elected from among the Twenty-four every Michaelmas, and the Twenty-four were to be self-perpetuating. The mayor was to be fined if he refused the office, and he could be removed by the Twenty-four for misconduct. Provision was made for a deputy mayor.[27] The only qualification for election as a capital burgess was residence in the borough or foreign. Capital burgesses had life-tenure but could be expelled for misconduct. They and the mayor were exempted from jury service outside the borough and foreign unless they held lands outside. There were to be a recorder and a town clerk, chosen by the mayor and Twenty-four, sworn by the mayor, and holding office during the corporation's pleasure. The mayor was empowered to appoint and swear two serjeants-at-mace. A commission of the peace was granted, with the mayor, his immediate predecessor, the recorder, and the two senior capital burgesses acting as justices. A court of record was established consisting of the mayor, the recorder, and the town clerk. The corporation was empowered to buy and dispose of property worth up to £20 a year. Two fairs a year with a court of piepowder were granted and previous market rights confirmed. The rights of the lord of the manor were safeguarded, while the jurisdiction of the county justices was preserved in cases of felony.

The main constitutional feature of the corporation's history in the mid 17th century was the set of fifteen ordinances of 1647.[28] Five dealt with the election of the mayor and with the penalties to be imposed on a mayor who refused to serve or failed to present his accounts on St. Clement's day. A retiring mayor forced to serve a second term by his successor's refusal to serve was to be allowed to keep the fine due without accounting for it as compensation for the 'trouble and charge' involved in a second term. The other ten ordinances dealt with penalties to be imposed on members of the Twenty-four who were absent from meetings and the walking of the fairs, who divulged the secrets of the corporation, or who failed to serve on the jury at quarter sessions when required.

The charter was exemplified in 1661.[29] Commissioners appointed under the Corporation Act of 1661 visited Walsall three times in 1662 'to purge the corporation' and replaced the recorder and fourteen capital burgesses. Nine of the burgesses had been mayor; among them was the parliamentarian Henry Stone, described in 1662–3 as a 'violent Presbyterian'.[30] None the less there remained a group in the corporation described in royalist circles as disaffected in contrast with 'the loyal party'; by July 1663 it was trying to secure a new charter which would free Walsall completely from the authority of the county justices.[31] In 1668, however, when the Privy Council ordered the strict application everywhere of the 1661 Act, the town clerk gave an assurance that all was well in Walsall.[32] The feoffees of the town lands, however, did not come within the jurisdiction of the commissioners, and many of the purged members of the corporation remained feoffees and so in control of most of the corporation's income; friction duly resulted.[33] The purge of 1662 left the foreign with a predominance among the capital burgesses. By 1676 the borough was again dominant, and in 1678 eighteen of the Twenty-four were living in High Street, Rushall Street, Newgate Street, and Church Hill. The rivalry of borough and foreign, however, cut across party lines in that there was a strong Tory element among the borough burgesses as well as among those of the foreign.[34] The only constitutional change of the period came in 1676 when an ordinance was passed by the council providing that the mayor needed the consent of the Twenty-four to spend more than £5 (except on necessary poor-relief) and to lease lands.[35]

In 1680 John Cumberlege, the retiring mayor, dispersed the Michaelmas meeting of the capital burgesses before a successor was chosen.[36] The meeting had been a heated and protracted affair because of disputes over the borough charities, and Cumberlege was stated to have had to leave because of illness. He thus remained mayor, but he failed to act during the ensuing year. In the summer of 1681, therefore, the attorney-general brought a writ of

[19] W.T.C. II/234; Sims, Cal. of Deeds, pp. 32–4, 41, 43, 47–51, 53.
[20] Charter of Corp. of Walsall, 52.
[21] Lee, Walsall, 13.
[22] W.T.C. II/13; II/31/1; Statement of Accts. passim.
[23] W.T.C. I/163.
[24] The preamble to the 1627 charter mentioned 'certain doubts and questions' that could arise about the liberties of the borough and foreign: see references in n. 26 below.
[25] W.T.C. II/162/1, f. [8]; below pp. 270–1. For the expenses incurred in securing the charter see Willmore, Walsall, 186–8.
[26] W.T.C. I/208, summarized in Boro. of Walsall: Abstract of First Consolidated Charter (pub. for tercentenary; copy in W.C.L.).
[27] For the existence of a deputy mayor in 1561 see

W.T.C. II/238, m. 9d. For deputy mayors 1649–1832 see W.T.C. II/55.
[28] W.T.C. II/235. The ordinances, two of which were subsequently cancelled, are printed by J. Turner, Glimpses of Walsall Hist. (Walsall, 1927), 10–11.
[29] W.T.C. II/75, printed in Charter of Corp. of Walsall.
[30] Homeshaw, Walsall, 37, 42–3, 45–8; S.H.C. 4th ser. ii. 30; above p. 145. The reference to purging is from the account of Thos. Osburne, mayor 1661–2: W.T.C. II/13/50.
[31] Cal. S.P. Dom. 1663–4, 197, 211.
[32] Homeshaw, Walsall, 51–2.
[33] Ibid. 54–8, 63, 65.
[34] Ibid. 48, 68–9, 75. For the rivalry see above p. 210.
[35] W.T.C. II/235.
[36] For the next 3 paras. see, unless otherwise stated, Homeshaw, Walsall, 64–81.

Quo Warranto against Walsall, and by November the corporation had offered the king its submission and petitioned for a new charter or the renewal of the old. The attorney-general then advised the Privy Council that the charter was forfeit and recommended the grant of a new charter once the old had been officially surrendered. The inhabitants of the foreign petitioned against incorporation with the borough in the new charter, which, they claimed, just a few of the borough inhabitants were trying to secure. Another petition from the foreign requested incorporation with the borough but with at least an equal number of magistrates. The petitioners pointed out that several charitable gifts belonged to the borough and foreign jointly and claimed that unless the foreign had a voice in the corporation its numerous poor were unlikely to see much of the charities. They accused the borough of wanting a new charter mainly because the magistrates of the town themselves held the charity lands at very low rents. They also took the opportunity to stress the disaffection of the borough and the strength of nonconformity there in contrast to the loyalty and good quality of the gentlemen of the foreign.

The charter was surrendered, and early in 1683 negotiations for a new one were in an advanced stage. Various people then brought their influence to bear against a new grant, notably Thomas Lane of Bentley in St. Peter's, Wolverhampton, Sir Francis Lawley of Spoonhill in Much Wenlock (Salop.) and Canwell,[37] one of the 1662 commissioners, and John Persehouse of Reynold's Hall. In addition 500 to 600 inhabitants of the foreign petitioned the king against the granting of a charter. The Privy Council heard both sides in May 1684, and the king then ordered the Law Officers to find out the views of the substantial inhabitants. They reported in December that well over two-thirds of the ratepayers of Walsall parish were opposed to a new charter. The king thereupon ordered that none should be granted.

The previous October, presumably to secure the town lands in anticipation of such a decision, the three senior feoffees had made a new feoffment to seventeen others to the use of the three. By the beginning of 1685 Sir Francis Lawley and John Persehouse were leading an attack on the governors of the grammar school and the feoffees of the town lands, accusing them of misusing their revenues. In January 1685 the two parties on the former corporation entered into an agreement to abandon all strife.[38] The cost incurred by one of the parties in the recent attempt to renew the charter was to be met out of the revenue from the town lands, and the cost of meeting the new attack and of any future attempt to secure a new charter was to come from the same source. One of the capital burgesses was appointed treasurer or receiver of the rent. Finally, in 1688 James II restored the charter, which remained in force until 1835.

Troubles next arose rather from indifference.[39] In 1704 an ordinance was made stipulating that any tenant of town lands who refused to accept election as a capital burgess was to be ejected. There were only twelve burgesses (including the mayor) in September 1731. Only eight were present at the election of the nine new burgesses on the 28th, although the retiring mayor had sent the serjeants-at-mace to fetch the missing members. The nine included William Persehouse, the first of his family to be a capital burgess since 1650; the next day he was elected mayor. A dispute with the town clerk followed, and a court order of 1733 vindicating the clerk and removing the new burgesses of 1731 directed that the number of burgesses was to be filled up; in the event the order was not fully carried out. In 1804 there were only fourteen members of the corporation, and it was not until its last years that the corporation was up to strength.[40] There seems also to have been some reluctance to serve as mayor, an office which could prove expensive. In 1741 an ordinance provided that anyone who served more than one term was to receive an allowance for the two entertainments due at Michaelmas and on 5 November.[41] It in fact became common for a mayor to serve more than one term, though not usually consecutively. Administration seems to have been slack. In 1696 it had been found necessary to pass an ordinance requiring the mayor to hold quarter sessions under pain of a fine. William Persehouse stated in 1733 that Matthew Stubbs, the town clerk, was lazy and obstructive and that the recorder was non-resident and had not attended the court of record for years.

An ordinance of 1702 ordered the annual appointment of a treasurer from among the capital burgesses to handle all expenditure except the sums of up to £5 which the mayor was allowed to spend. Fines were authorized for refusal to act and failure to account. The ordinance was repealed in 1704, and although re-enacted in 1707 it seems to have been ignored.[42] By the early 1770s there was financial confusion, but some improvement followed, perhaps as a result of the admission of eight new burgesses in 1773.[43] Mayor's accounts were kept systematically from that year under the supervision of the town clerk, who also became the salaried receiver of rents from the town lands in 1789 and in effect acted as treasurer. The mayor no longer accounted on St. Clement's day; indeed for a time it was the practice to audit two years' accounts together, often some time after the period concerned. From 1795, however, the mayor accounted annually at a special meeting of the council in September.[44] A more lucrative leasing policy was adopted for the town lands, and the annual rental of £230 in 1773–4 had reached over £500 by 1803–4 and nearly £840 in 1833–4.[45] Most of the corporation's income came from its estates, and it levied no rate.[46] In the earlier 19th century, however, its right to apply the income from the Warwickshire property for general corporation purposes was persistently, though unsuccessfully, challenged.[47]

[37] *S.H.C.* 1920 and 1922, 135, 157; Shaw, *Staffs.* ii, p. *21; W.T.C. II/112.

[38] W.T.C. II/111/1 (reproduced in Homeshaw, *Walsall*, plate facing p. 64) and 2.

[39] For this para. see, unless otherwise stated, Homeshaw, *Walsall*, 83–91, 155–7, 161–2.

[40] Ibid. 85, 115; White, *Dir. Staffs.* (1834).

[41] W.T.C. II/55.

[42] Ibid./235; Homeshaw, *Walsall*, 84–5.

[43] Homeshaw, *Walsall*, 105–8; W.T.C. II/152.

[44] Homeshaw, *Walsall*, 108–9, 113; *1st Rep. Com. Mun. Corps.* H.C. 116, App. III, p. 2051 (1835), xxv.

[45] Homeshaw, *Walsall*, 110–11, 122–3, 165, 168.

[46] Ibid. 147, 165, 168.

[47] Ibid. 123–31; *1st Rep. Com. Mun. Corps.* App. III, 2048–51.

Several of the corporation's responsibilities passed to the improvement commissioners established under an Act of 1824. They consisted of the mayor and capital burgesses, the recorder, the town clerk, the vicar of Walsall, the headmaster of the grammar school, the steward of the manor of Walsall, the churchwardens, and the overseers of the poor, all *ex officio*, and 46 others with a property qualification of £1,000, nominated by the Act. The body was self-perpetuating. The area for which the commissioners were responsible was the borough and the built-up parts of the foreign adjoining it.[48] In fact they were unable to raise enough money to carry out their work, even after levying the maximum permitted rate in 1826. As a result the corporation became involved in expenditure which should have been met by the commissioners.[49]

The corporation in its last years was not unenlightened. Its shortcomings, as the *Report* of the Municipal Corporations Commission pointed out,[50] lay rather in the poor public relations of a self-elected body.

On the publication of the commission's report in 1835 the mayor resigned and supported the cause of reform. There was also a local petition to the House of Commons in favour of reform.[51] Under the 1835 Municipal Corporations Act the borough and foreign were replaced by a new borough divided into three wards, Bridge, St. George's, and Foreign, with six aldermen and eighteen elected councillors.[52] The detached portion of the foreign comprising Walsall Wood and Shelfield was not included in the new borough.[53] At the second council meeting, on 1 January 1836, the previous mayor was chosen mayor and a new town clerk and a treasurer were appointed. Council meetings became public towards the end of 1836.[54] A borough rate was levied for the first time in 1839.[55] The 1835 Act transferred the powers of the improvement commissioners to the new corporation, but the Walsall Improvement and Market Act of 1848 (amended in 1850) created a new body of commissioners consisting of the mayor and council and three elected members from the part of Rushall parish adjoining the town; their area of responsibility was the built-up part of the borough and the adjoining part of Rushall covering Ryecroft, the Butts, and the Lichfield road area as far as the later Buchanan Road.[56] The corporation took over the commissioners' sanitary powers in 1872 and their remaining powers in 1876. The part of Rushall in the commissioners' district, 94 a. in extent, was added to the borough in 1876; it had been part of the parliamentary borough from 1868.[57] The court of record established in 1627 ceased to sit in 1847 when a county court district centred on Walsall was formed.[58]

Walsall became a county borough in 1889.[59] In 1890 a further 617 a. were added from Rushall, covering the Coal Pool Lane and Mellish Road areas and the area south of Aldridge Road; the district was already part of the parliamentary borough, with which the county borough then became coextensive. The three wards were replaced by eight (Bridge, Birchills, Bloxwich, Caldmore, Hatherton, Leamore, Paddock, and Pleck), with eight aldermen and twenty-four councillors.[60] In 1931, when the borough was again enlarged, two new wards were created, Harden and Palfrey, and the size of the council was increased to 10 aldermen and 30 councillors.[61] An eleventh ward was created in 1959 by the division of Bloxwich into East and West, increasing the membership of the council to 11 aldermen and 33 councillors.[62]

In 1966, as part of the reorganization of local government in the West Midlands, the borough of Walsall was extended to include most of the urban districts of Darlaston and Willenhall and parts of the county boroughs of West Bromwich and Wolverhampton, of the boroughs of Bilston and Wednesbury, of the urban districts of Aldridge, Coseley, and Wednesfield, and of the parish of Essington. Parts of Walsall were transferred to West Bromwich, the new urban district of Aldridge-Brownhills, and Cannock urban district.[63] In 1974 the county borough became part of the metropolitan district of Walsall,[64] which was granted borough status by letters patent of 1973.[65] In 1972 Walsall became the seat of a crown court.[66]

Before 1910 party issues did not normally obtrude in Walsall municipal politics and there were not many contested elections.[67] The Liberals, however, had had a majority on the council for a long time, and in the local elections of 1910 there was a marked rivalry between Liberals and Unionists. A Socialist had been elected to the council in 1888 and held his seat for three years; otherwise the few early working-class representatives were in alliance with the Liberals. In 1912, however, several seats were contested by the Labour party, and in 1913 the first Labour councillor was elected, in Pleck ward; a second Labour member was returned unopposed in 1914. Labour greatly strengthened its representation in the years between the two World Wars, but that led the Conservatives and Liberals to develop an anti-Labour alliance; the Labour party was also weakened by internal dissensions. The first woman to be elected was the secretary of the Walsall Women's Unionist Association, who won a seat in Paddock ward in 1911.

Labour won control of the council in 1945. Its

[48] Homeshaw, *Walsall*, 133–5; 5 Geo. IV, c. 68 (Local and Personal).
[49] Homeshaw, *Walsall*, 147–8; below p. 224.
[50] *1st Rep. Com. Mun. Corps.* App. III, 2053.
[51] Homeshaw, *Walsall*, 148.
[52] 5 & 6 Wm. IV, c. 76; Homeshaw, *Walsall*, 148–9.
[53] See p. 143.
[54] Homeshaw, *Walsall*, 149.
[55] W.T.C., Council Mins. 1835–48, 8 Feb. 1839.
[56] 11 & 12 Vic. c. 161 (Local and Personal); 13 Vic. c. 15 (Local and Personal); White, *Dir. Staffs.* (1851).
[57] Willmore, *Walsall*, 195–6; *Staffs. Advertiser*, 7 Sept. 1872; Walsall Gas Purchase and Boro. Extension Act, 1876, 39 & 40 Vic. c. 119 (Local); *Walsall Red Book* (1877), 76–8; Lee, *Walsall*, 33; O.S. Map 6″, Staffs. LXIII. NE. (1889 edn.); below p. 225.
[58] *Lond. Gaz.* 10 Mar. 1847, p. 1012; Glew, *Walsall*, 8.

[59] Local Govt. Act, 1888, 51 & 52 Vic. c. 41.
[60] Walsall Corp. Act, 1890, 53 & 54 Vic. c. 130 (Local); Lee, *Walsall*, 33; O.S. Map 6″, Staffs. LXIII. NE. (1903 edn.).
[61] K. J. Dean, *Town & Westminster* (Walsall, 1972), 220–1; above p. 143.
[62] *County Boro. of Walsall: Council Year Book 1959–60*, 117–18, 160.
[63] West Midlands Order 1965, S.I. 1965, no. 2139, pp. 6, 8, and maps; *County Boro. of Walsall: Council Year Book 1966–67*, 131–8, 158, 164–5.
[64] Local Govt. Act 1972, c. 70; The Metropolitan Districts (Names) Order 1973, S.I. 1973, no. 137.
[65] In W.T.C.
[66] *Walsall Observer*, 4 Feb. 1972.
[67] For this para. see Dean, *Town & Westminster*, 5, 201 sqq.

majority, however, was narrow, and when it lost a seat in a by-election later the same year the council became evenly divided between Labour and Independents.[68] The Independents won control in 1947, retaining it until 1954.[69] They won it back in 1956 and lost it again for a year in 1958.[70] The Labour and anti-Labour groups became evenly balanced in 1962, and Labour took control in 1963, retaining it by a narrow majority on the enlarged council of 1966.[71]

By the 15th century the hall of St. John's guild in High Street was used as the town hall. The assembly of burgesses met there by 1426, and the mayor presented his accounts there later in the century.[72] After the suppression of the guild the building was appropriated by the borough.[73] Between at least 1652 and 1837 the premises were leased out, with the exception of the hall itself and other rooms used for corporation business.[74] From at least 1769 the rest of the property was used as the Green Dragon inn (known as the Dragon by the end of the 18th century).[75] The hall was used for a variety of functions. It remained the normal meeting-place of the corporation in the 17th and 18th centuries.[76] By at least the later 17th century the borough and manor courts were held in the guildhall.[77] It was apparently used for mayoral banquets by the earlier 16th century, and in 1566 it was stated that marriages and church-ales were customarily kept there.[78]

The medieval building included a hall and probably one or two cross-wings. Reused timbers of the 15th or earlier 16th century survived in 1973 in the roof of the 18th-century west wing; they suggest that the latter was preceded by a timber-framed wing of the same width, with a chamber of two or more bays open to the roof. The wing was probably two-storeyed; a buttery mentioned in the mid 16th century was presumably on the ground floor.[79] The first floor was apparently reconstructed in the later 16th or earlier 17th century: moulded ceiling beams of that period survived in the building in 1973. There was a kitchen by 1483[80] and a parlour and court solar by 1631.[81] The solar was probably the room in Walsall called the court chamber where the manor court was held by 1621.[82] It was probably over the parlour where by 1661 there was a chamber used for council business.[83] The chamber and parlour may have been in a cross-wing at the east end of the hall. A room called 'the chequer', presumably the treasury, was repaired in 1639–40.[84]

A new room was built over the hall in 1768–9,[85] and there was also a second parlour next to the hall by 1769.[86] The lessee of the Green Dragon was then required to rebuild the inn within five years with a sashed front, a parapet, and a stone cornice.[87] The whole complex is said to have been rebuilt *c.* 1773. By the end of the 18th century the guildhall was of brick with two wings and a recessed front on High Street approached by a flight of steps. The hall itself was in the centre block; the east wing contained the mayor's parlour, and the west wing formed part of the Dragon inn. Courts were then held in the hall, and the corporation met in the mayor's parlour. The plan was asymmetrical and probably followed that of the earlier building.[88] A bay window was added to the front of the west wing apparently at some time between 1783 and 1817.[89]

In 1865–7 the centre block and east wing were demolished and replaced by a brick and stone building of two storeys and a basement. It was designed by G. B. Nichols of West Bromwich in an Italianate style and contained a council chamber, a mayor's parlour, a court wing, corporation offices, cells, and stores.[90] Between 1884 and 1888 the offices were transferred to a building on the corner of Bridge and Goodall Streets acquired by the corporation from the Birmingham and Staffordshire Gas Light Co. in 1876.[91]

The Council House in Lichfield Street was built in 1902–5. It is a building of Hollington stone designed in a Baroque style by J. S. Gibson of London and includes a hall, a council chamber, committee rooms, and offices.[92] It is surmounted by a tower containing a carillon bought under the will of J. A. Leckie (d. 1938) and hung in 1953.[93] An organ was placed in the hall in 1908.[94] New civic offices were begun in Darwall Street in 1973.[95]

The guildhall continued as a magistrates' court,[96] but in 1973 work began on a court building in Stafford Street to replace it.[97] The Dragon inn ceased to be used as an hotel between 1908 and 1912[98] and in 1973 was occupied by the offices of the clerk to the justices.

By the 1850s the county court met in the assembly-room in Goodall Street behind the guildhall. The offices of the court occupied part of the ground-floor of the former library building on the corner of Lichfield and Leicester Streets by 1855. The court itself moved into the building in the 1860s, and a large extension, including a court-room, was opened at the rear in 1869.[99]

[68] Ibid. 233; Woodall, *Walsall Milestones*, 40.
[69] *Walsall Observer*, 8 Nov. 1947, 14 May 1954.
[70] Ibid. 19 May 1956, 15 May 1959.
[71] Ibid. 11 and 18 May 1962, 17 May 1963, 14 May 1965, 25 Mar. 1966.
[72] W.T.C. II/238, mm. 2, 1d.
[73] E 133/1/61.
[74] W.T.C. II/1/6 and 10; II/251/2, 19, 27, 36, 45.
[75] W.T.C. II/251/27, 36, 45; Shaw, *Staffs.* ii. 73.
[76] *Charter of Corp. of Walsall*, 5; W.T.C. II/13, *passim*.
[77] W.T.C. II/251/2; and see below.
[78] E 133/1/61 ff. 12–13.
[79] W.T.C. I/261, art. 38.   [80] W.C.T. I/67.
[81] W.T.C. II/31/6.
[82] S.R.O., D. 360/M/T/1/55–6, 68.
[83] W.T.C. II/251/2 and 19.
[84] W.T.C. II/13/28.
[85] W.T.C. II/13/89.
[86] W.T.C. II/251/27.
[87] Ibid.
[88] Glew, *Walsall*, 36–7; Shaw, *Staffs.* ii. 73; T. Mason,

Plan of Part of the High Street, Walsall (1817; in W.C.L.).
[89] J. Snape, *Plan of Town of Walsall* (1782); Mason, *Plan of Part of the High Street*.
[90] *Staffs. Advertiser*, 5 Jan. 1867; plate facing p. 177 above.
[91] *Kelly's Dir. Staffs.* (1884; 1888); *Guide to Walsall* (1889), 47; O.S. Map 1/500, Staffs. LXIII. 2. 1 (1885 edn.).
[92] *The Builder*, 13 Oct. 1900; *Boro. of Walsall: Souvenir of Opening of Town Hall, 27 Sept. 1905* (copy in W.C.L.); inscription at main entrance; plate facing p. 97 above.
[93] Plaque at base of tower. For Leckie see p. 275.
[94] *County Boro. of Walsall: Council Year Book 1971–72*, 182.   [95] *Walsall Observer*, 13 July 1973.
[96] *Kelly's Dir. Staffs.* (1908 and later edns.).
[97] *Express & Star*, 8 Nov. 1973.
[98] *Kelly's Dir. Staffs.* (1908; 1912).
[99] Glew, *Walsall*, 52; Harrison, Harrod & Co. *Dir. Staffs.* (1861), showing the court in Goodall St.; *P.O. Dir. Staffs.* (1868), showing the court in Lichfield St.; *Staffs. Advertiser*, 17 Apr. 1869.

There was a gaol at Walsall by 1498.[1] By 1589 the High Cross in High Street was used as a place of punishment; it is probably identifiable with the house of correction which was leased to the county in the 17th century.[2] There was a town cage in the 17th century.[3] The charter of 1627 granted the corporation the right to a gaol in the borough with the mayor or his nominee as the keeper.[4] It was situated in the successive town halls.[5] Early in the 19th century it consisted of two rooms and three dungeons; it was cold and damp and had no court, sewer, or water. The gaoler received fees instead of a salary.[6] The gaol was rebuilt in 1815, and immediately afterwards a house was built for the gaoler.[7] Still part of the guildhall, the gaol consisted of six cells round a small yard below street level and was described in 1833 as damp and lacking space for exercise. The mayor as keeper was then appointing a salaried deputy gaoler, usually one of the serjeants-at-mace; by 1836 the police superintendent was acting as deputy.[8] In 1836 the county magistrates agreed to house prisoners from Walsall in Stafford gaol upon contract, and the agreement took effect in 1837.[9] The gaol was replaced by a lock-up which formed part of the police station built in Goodall Street in 1843.[10] Prisoners serving sentences of a week or less were being kept there in 1861, when it was recommended that they too should be taken to Stafford.[11] In 1864 the borough council successfully petitioned for the removal of Walsall gaol from the schedule of prisons closed under the Act of 1865.[12] A gaoler was still being appointed in 1872,[13] but no further evidence has been found that Walsall gaol was used other than as a lock-up after 1861.

What were probably the borough stocks are mentioned in 1534,[14] and by 1662 they were kept at the High Cross.[15] There were foot-stocks at the bottom of the steps up to St. Matthew's in the earlier 19th century.[16] Stocks stood in front of the guildhall from 1847 to 1854.[17] Foot-stocks are preserved in the Arboretum. A new pillory was paid for by the mayor in 1704.[18] A borough whipping-stock and a cucking-stool occur in the 17th century.[19] A scold's bridle, or

branks, was bought by the mayor in 1617–18 and was apparently replaced by another in 1654–5.[20] Plot noted the Walsall bridle with another at Newcastle-under-Lyme as 'an instrument scarce heard of, much less seen'.[21] A bridle is preserved in the borough museum.[22]

A pound at Walsall occurs in 1361–2,[23] and there was one in the foreign by 1490–1.[24] Although the pinners were manorial officials,[25] responsibility for pounds in both the borough and the foreign evidently rested with the corporation by the 17th century. In 1612 the mayor accounted for the making of a pound at Townend, presumably on the east side of Stafford Street where one stood in the later 18th and earlier 19th centuries. About the end of 1861 it was replaced by a new pound in Freer Street by the pig market.[26] There was also a pound at Bloxwich by 1639 when the mayor accounted for the cost of making a pinfold there.[27] It presumably stood at the south-east end of the village where the street-name Pinfold survives. There was still a pound at Bloxwich in 1849.[28]

The copper matrix of the first known common seal[29] is round, $1\frac{5}{8}''$, and bears a shield of arms: quarterly, France Modern and England, ensigned with a coronet of five fleurs-de-lis. The arms are flanked by two lions addorsed sejant guardant with tails flory interlaced in base. Legend, black-letter: SIGILLUM COMMUNE MAIORIS ET COMMUNITATIS VILLE DOMINI REGIS DE WALSALE. It presumably dates from between 1487 and 1553,[30] and it was still in use in 1865.[31] By 1867 a new cast-iron seal-press with the same device and legend had been adopted, differing from the old seal in minor details of design.[32] It was still in use in 1973.

The insignia include two maces made in 1627–8 under the terms of the 1627 charter. Each is silver, parcel gilt, $21\frac{1}{4}''$ long. The mace-heads are surmounted by coronets and bear the badges of Charles II, which were engraved in 1660. It seems probable that the maces had been altered during the Interregnum and that the arms of Charles II

[1] S.H.C. n.s. x (1), 80; S.H.C. 1912, 3.
[2] Sims, Walsall Records, p. 43; S.H.C. 1934 (2), 24–5; W.T.C. II/1/5; II/13/6; II/31/8; S.R.O., Q/SO 7, f. 10v. For the High Cross see also above p. 187.
[3] S.R.O., Q/SR, T. 1617, no. 46; ibid. M. 1618, no. 20; W.T.C. II/13/38, 41, 51; II/23/24.
[4] Charter of Corp. of Walsall, 22–3.
[5] W.T.C. II/23/32; II/251/2 and 19; Homeshaw, Walsall, 83, 131; J. Snape, Plan of Town of Walsall (1782).
[6] Gent. Mag. lxxvi (2), 1124.
[7] Statement of Accts. 75–97, passim; Homeshaw, Walsall, 129, 132; 1st Rep. Com. Mun. Corps. H.C. 116, App. III, pp. 2047, 2051 (1835), xxv.
[8] W.T.C., Watch Cttee. Mins. 1836–52, 15 and 19 Jan. 1836.
[9] Staffs. Advertiser, 22 Oct. 1836; S.R.O., Q/FAm 6/1, county treasurer's acct. for quarter ending 14 Oct. 1837.
[10] Glew, Walsall, 37; W.T.C., General Cttees. 1842–50, 30 Aug. 1842, 5 June, 18 July 1843, 14 July 1844.
[11] 26th Rep. Inspectors of Prisons, Midland Dist. [2898], p. 110, H.C. (1861), xxix.
[12] Staffs. Advertiser, 11 June 1864; Bill for . . . Discontinuance of certain Gaols [Bill 93], H.C. (1864), ii; Prison Act, 1865, 28 & 29 Vic. c. 126.
[13] Staffs. Advertiser, 16 Nov. 1872.
[14] S.H.C. 1910, 36.
[15] Glew, Walsall, 121 (from W.C.L., box 9, no. 4).
[16] Walsall Observer, 12 Aug. 1966.
[17] Glew, Walsall, 36. There seem to have been stocks at the guildhall in 1843: Staffs. Advertiser, 10 June 1843.

[18] W.T.C. II/13/75.
[19] W.T.C. II/13/10, 40, 62; II/23/27; Glew, Walsall, 121.
[20] W.T.C. II/13/6 and 43.
[21] Plot, Staffs. 389.
[22] One of the two bridles now in Lichfield Mus. was presented by a Walsall man: Midland Mag. 114.
[23] S.H.C. xiv (1), 115–16.
[24] See p. 210.
[25] See p. 210.
[26] W.T.C. II/13/4; S.R.O., D. 260/M/F/1/8, ct. of recog. and survey, 1617, p. 5; D. 1287/8/2, map; Snape, Plan of Walsall (1782); W.C.L., A.G. 146; W.T.C., Streets Cttee. Mins. 1849–51, 7 Mar. 1850, 4 Nov. 1851; W.C.L., Council Mins. 1848–66, 9 Nov. 1861; O.S. Map 1/500, Staffs. LXIII. 11. 1 (1885 edn., surv. 1885). For the maintenance of the pound in the 17th cent. see W.T.C. II/13; II/23/24; II/31/9 and 11; II/50/37.
[27] W.T.C. II/13/27. The sum, however, was only 13s. 4d.; the cost of making the borough pound in 1611–12 was £3 5s. 6d. (II/13/4).
[28] Staffs. Advertiser, 10 Feb. 1849, advert. for sale of houses near the pinfold.
[29] In W.T.C.
[30] The seal cannot be earlier than the resumption of the manor by the Crown in 1487, or later than the accession of Mary I: Homeshaw, Walsall, 16; Willmore, Walsall, 181–2; Cat. Anct. D. v, A 11056; above p. 170.
[31] Walsall Council House, deeds bdle. 682, deed of 28 May 1865.
[32] W.T.C. II/252, Bascote agreement, 27 Aug. 1867.

replaced the state arms of that period.[33] The mayor's chain is of gold and was presented by the council in 1875.[34] The gilt badge bears the device of the common seal with the legend BURGUM DE WALSALL CHARTIS VETERUM REGUM FUNDATUM.

A set of twelve clubs with carved heads, two halberds, two pole-axes, and a bill were displayed at the guildhall by the end of the 18th century.[35] In 1969 they were transferred to the central library. They have been traditionally identified with Bayard's Colts, clubs mentioned in the earlier 16th century as kept in the town hall and carried about the town on ceremonial occasions. The bill dates from the 15th or 16th century and the pole-axes from the 16th century; the halberds are of the 17th and 18th centuries respectively. Most of the clubs seem to date from the 17th century or later, and one of the heads is dated 1712. It has also been suggested that the clubs are mummers' staves.

Lists of mayors, town clerks, and recorders to 1835 are printed by E. J. Homeshaw, *The Corporation of the Borough and Foreign of Walsall* (Walsall, 1960).[36] A complete list of mayors from 1835 to 1974 is given in *Metropolitan Borough of Walsall: Council Year Book 1974–75*.[37] Town clerks both before and since 1835 are listed on a board in the ante-room of the council chamber.

PUBLIC SERVICES. As early as 1309 the charter granted by the lords of the manor to the burgesses of Walsall stipulated that the market-place should be kept clean.[38] By the 17th century the authorities were giving regular attention to the demands of public health. The corporation paid for the sweeping of the streets in the town.[39] Thoroughgoing measures were taken when plague threatened in 1636 and 1637. In November 1636 the Walsall justices issued orders to prevent it from spreading to their area. The constable of the borough was to appoint four warders every day from 'the better sort' of inhabitants to watch the various entrances to the town and keep out any traveller unable to prove that he had not come from an infected place. Similarly the constable of the foreign was to appoint two warders, one to act at Great Bloxwich and the other wherever the constable directed. Innkeepers and victuallers were not to lodge anyone unable to prove freedom from contact with infection. Carriers living in the borough and travelling to London were not to bring their horses and loads into the town, and warders were to be appointed to keep them out or else conduct them through the town with a minimum of danger;

the constable was to ensure that carriers returning home stayed in their houses and received no visitors.[40] Similar orders were made for the borough in June 1637, and in July a Walsall shoemaker was prosecuted for fetching leather from an infected street in Birmingham.[41] At the same time a woman from plague-stricken Birmingham was paid to leave Walsall.[42] Orders of the same sort were made in August 1665 after it had been discovered that carriers were bringing people and goods from infected areas, being able to make large profits thereby; also a man had died in Walsall of the plague that month. The measures were evidently effective. In November it was noted in the parish register that there were few burials during the months when many thousands died of the plague in London.[43]

The growth of the town produced the usual sanitary problems. The main problem by the early 1840s was inadequate drainage, which resulted in accumulation of filth and stagnant water in the courts and alleys. Such public sewers as there were discharged into Walsall Brook. The town authorities employed two scavengers, who emptied the cesspools and about once a week cleaned the streets. The standard of housing was claimed to be superior to that of many industrial towns; there were few back-to-back houses and no cellar dwellings. The general health of the town was considered good; typhus and ague were rare, although pulmonary disease was common.[44] There were outbreaks of cholera in 1832 and 1849.[45]

The improvement commissioners established in 1848 laid down a system of sewerage in the 1850s; it covered only the central part of the town, however, leaving Bloxwich and the other outlying districts without sewers.[46] Though the new sewerage meant that the brook ceased to be a drain in the town centre, by the mid 1860s it was polluted instead by the refuse from tanneries and skin-dressing establishments. At that time too drainage was still a problem in the numerous courts, and one writer blamed the landlords for leaving so many of them without tap-water although a piped supply was then available. Nuisances were also caused by pig-keeping and by failure to empty soil-pits, at any rate at seasons when farmers were too busy to collect night-soil for manure. Typhoid fever was endemic. Although some of the bad areas to the north of the town centre had been improved after the 1849 cholera outbreak, the writer considered that the problems would be solved only when the inspector of nuisances, whose authority was limited, had been replaced by 'a thoroughly independent medical officer of health'.[47]

[33] Ll. Jewitt and W. H. St. John Hope, *Corp. Plate and Insignia of Office of Cities and Corporate Towns of Eng. and Wales*, ii. 323–4; W.T.C. II/13/48–9.

[34] Inscription on reverse of badge.

[35] This para. is based on *Folklore*, lxxxi. 266–7 (giving the date of the head as 1714); Shaw, *Staffs*. ii. 73; Glew, *Walsall*, 37, 109, 121 (the last being from W.C.L., box 9, no. 4); Willmore, *Walsall*, 91; W.C.L., Bayard's Colts corresp. file, letters to boro. librarian of 8 Aug., 16 Sept., 28 Oct. 1969; inf. from the boro. librarian (1973); above p. 145.

[36] pp. 180–1. Corrections to the list of mayors are available at W.C.L.   [37] pp. 185–6.

[38] W.T.C. I/9; above p. 212.   [39] W.T.C. II/13.

[40] J. Turner, *Glimpses of Walsall Hist.* (Walsall, 1927), 4–6 (from W.T.C. II/23/3).

[41] Ibid. 6–7 (from W.T.C. II/23/5 and 7); Glew, *Walsall*, 119 (from W.C.L., box 33, no. 14).

[42] W.T.C. II/13/25.

[43] Glew, *Walsall*, 119–20 (from W.C.L., box 33, no. 16); Willmore, *Walsall*, 278–9; below p. 223.

[44] *2nd Rep. Com. State of Large Towns and Populous Districts* [602], App. pp. 32–4, H.C. (1845), xviii. For mention in 1774 of a water-course running through tenements in Ablewell St. and removing waste see B.R.L. 337368.

[45] Willmore, *Walsall*, 421; Fink, *Queen Mary's Grammar Sch.* 449–50.

[46] *Birmingham Daily Post*, 19 June 1866, p. 5; Walsall Improvement and Market Act, 1848, 11 & 12 Vic. c. 161 (Local and Personal), s. 30; W.T.C., Streets Cttee. Mins. 1849–51, 13 Aug. 1850, 4 Jan. 1851; W.C.L., 2 posters relating to proposed new sewerage; S.R.O., D. 1287/ Colliery Box no. 2, misc. corresp. 1845–57, J. Potter to Bailey, Shaw & Co., 26 July 1855.

[47] *Birmingham Daily Post*, 19 June 1866, p. 5.

In 1871 a medical officer was appointed.[48] At the time of the smallpox epidemic of 1872 the poor-law medical officer listed the local causes favouring the spread of an epidemic as defective sewerage and overcrowding in courts badly supplied with water, the great number of unvaccinated children, and the difficulty of isolating infectious cases.[49] The medical officer of health in his first report in 1871 also noted the widespread keeping of pigs in crowded parts of the town as an evil.[50]

In 1882 the corporation bought Brockhurst farm on the Wednesbury boundary and in 1884 opened a sewage farm there.[51] A new works was completed there in 1894 and another in 1914 with extensions in 1925. Two smaller works for the outlying parts of the borough had been opened by the beginning of the 20th century. One lay just over the north-eastern boundary south of Willenhall Lane and had been closed by the mid 1950s. The other was situated on the north-western boundary at Goscote; it was extended c. 1960 and again in the early 1970s. In 1966 control of the Brockhurst and Goscote works passed to the Upper Tame Main Drainage Authority.

In 1882 the Walsall Health Society was established to spread knowledge of 'the Laws of Health' throughout the town and neighbourhood. The means proposed were lectures and classes, a library, publications, ambulance corps, and annual prizes.[52]

Under the 1824 Improvement Act many old buildings were removed to make room for new streets.[53] In the early 1850s dilapidated houses around the church were demolished as part of a general opening-up of the area.[54] In 1876 the corporation, as the urban sanitary authority, adopted the Artizans and Labourers Dwellings Improvement Act of 1875 and proceeded with the rebuilding of the slum area around Townend Bank, 'peopled by the lowest and most depraved of the community'; 120 houses, with a population of 592, were demolished and replaced by new houses north of Blue Lane West. Other slum areas noted at that time were Peal Street, Church Street, Rushall Street, and Ryecroft Park (otherwise Ryecroft Street), but the medical officer of health considered that the Townend Bank area had the worst 'conglomeration of abominations' in the town.[55] By 1914 the corporation was considering a housing scheme, but it was not until after the Housing Act of 1919 that it in fact began to build. The first council house to be completed was in Blakenall Lane in 1920, and by

1939 nearly 8,000 council houses, flats, and bungalows had been built. Walsall was also the first borough in the country to provide small holdings for ex-servicemen after the First World War. In 1930 an extensive slum-clearance scheme was adopted, and by 1939 2,193 of the 3,030 unfit houses had been demolished and 10,912 people had been rehoused from unfit property. Building was resumed after the Second World War, and the 10,000th council house was opened in 1950 in Primley Avenue.[56] In the early 1950s the council started to build outside the borough with the extension of the Little Bloxwich estate into Pelsall.[57] By 1966 the council owned over 18,500 dwellings, including several estates of multi-storey flats.[58] Slum clearance too continued after the war.[59] Reclamation of derelict land was also undertaken. By 1953 580 a. of the 1,000 derelict acres existing in 1945 had been reclaimed and 2,200 houses and a number of schools and factories had been built there. Forty-four acres of low-lying ground had been reclaimed by controlled tipping.[60]

A well called Able Well, evidently near the junction of Ablewell and Rushall Streets, occurs in 1398–9; it probably existed at the beginning of the 14th century.[61] Official attention was being given to the town's water-supply by the 1630s. In 1637 the mayor paid a man 'for opening the pipes to let the water to the well in Rushall Street'.[62] It may have been Able Well, which was repaired in 1637–8, or the Ware Well, which was repaired in 1640–1 and was apparently situated near the junction of Lower Rushall Street and Ablewell Street where the name survives in Warewell Street.[63] A pump in Park Street was either installed or repaired in 1637–8.[64] In 1652–3 repairs were carried out to Heynes Well, presumably identifiable with Haynes's soft-water pump which stood at the south end of Ablewell Street in 1782.[65] Repairs were carried out to a pump 'under the hill', presumably at or near the top of High Street, in 1654–5.[66] A cistern mentioned in 1651[67] may have had some connexion with the water-supply known as the town service which occurs in 1652–3; repairs were carried out then to the town service well and money was also spent on sinking a well and bringing water from it to the town service. The supply may have come from the springs on Vicarage Moor on the south-west of the town where new spouts were set up in 1663–4.[68]

In the later 1670s a new system of supply was

[48] *Walsall Free Press*, 9 Sept. 1871.
[49] Jo Manton, *Sister Dora*, 284.
[50] *Walsall Free Press*, 9 Sept. 1871.
[51] This para. is based on *Kelly's Dir. Staffs.* (1888 and later edns. to 1916); Local Govt. Board's Provisional Orders Confirmation (Acton, etc.) Act, 1881, 44 & 45 Vic. c. 172 (Local); Blay, 'Street Names of Walsall', 32–3; *Walsall Red Book* (1895), 81; *County Boro. of Walsall: Council Year Book 1971–72*, 182; inf. from the boro. surveyor (1973); *Express & Star*, 9 Dec. 1965; O.S. Map 6", Staffs. LXIII. NW., NE. (1903 edn., revised 1900–1); SW. (edns. of 1889, 1904, 1920). For the sewage works opened near by at Bescot in 1888 by Wednesbury corporation see Ede, *Wednesbury*, 337, 367.
[52] *Walsall Health Soc.: Inaugural Rep. Apr. 1882* (copy in W.C.L.). [53] White, *Dir. Staffs.* (1834).
[54] Willmore, *Walsall*, 427.
[55] *Staffs. Advertiser*, 30 Dec. 1876, p. 4; ibid. 24 Mar. 1877, p. 7; 38 & 39 Vic. c. 36; Local Govt. Board's Provisional Orders Confirmation (Artizans and Labourers Dwellings) Act, 1877, 40 & 41 Vic. c. 241 (Local); W.C.L., box 50, no. 1; W.C.L., photographs 64 and 67; *1st Rep.*

Com. Housing of Working Classes [C. 4402–I], pp. 702–3, H.C. (1884–5), xxx; *Guide to Walsall* (1889), 39–40; above pp. 160–1. For Ryecroft Park see Blay, 'Street Names of Walsall', 153.
[56] County Boro. of Walsall, *Souvenir Programme of Official Opening of the 10,000th Council House* (copy in W.C.L.); ex inf. the boro. housing manager (1973); *Walsall Red Book* (1931), 65. For the small holdings see Lee, *Walsall*, 54; above p. 161.
[57] *Walsall Observer*, 2 Jan. 1953.
[58] Ex inf. the boro. housing manager.
[59] *10,000th Council House.*
[60] *Walsall Observer*, 3 July 1953.
[61] B.M. Eg. Rolls 8476, 8525. 'Abelwellsych' occurs in 1309: above p. 147.   [62] W.T.C. II/13/25.
[63] W.T.C. II/13/30; II/31/9; W.S.L. 351/34. Both wells were repaired in 1670: W.T.C. II/13/57.
[64] W.T.C. II/13/26; II/31/9.
[65] W.T.C. II/13/41; *Sketchley's Birmingham . . . Dir.* (1767), 97; J. Snape, *Plan of Town of Walsall* (1782).
[66] W.T.C. II/13/43.   [67] Ibid. /13/39.
[68] Ibid. /13/41–2, 53–4, 71, 76, 78.

constructed from Vicarage Moor. In 1676 the corporation commissioned a 'head of water house' there, with pipes to a cistern in High Street containing at least fourteen hogsheads of water and covered by a conduit-house. All or most of the work seems to have been carried out by 1677. The conduit was inscribed in gold letters and adorned with the town arms.[69] By 1782 the Vicarage Moor supply served High Street, Digbeth, Park Street, Rushall Street, and the northern end of Ablewell Street.[70] By 1830, however, the supply had become contaminated with gas, which was killing off frogs in the conduit.[71] In the mean time, at the beginning of the 19th century, the corporation had brought a supply of soft water to the town.[72] Under the Improvement Act of 1824 the public supply passed under the control of the improvement commissioners.[73]

It was claimed in the early 1840s that the town had an abundant supply of wholesome water; the Park Street area was an exception, its supply having been drained away by the near-by mines. There were eight or ten public pumps in the town, and there was a pump in most of the courts; the better-class houses each had their own pump.[74] By 1852 the drawing off of water by the mines had become more widespread and water was generally scarce.[75] Walsall came within the area supplied by the South Staffordshire Water Works Co., which opened its first works in 1858 at Lichfield with a reservoir at Moat Hill in Walsall south of Wolverhampton Road. It was not until 1875, however, that all the higher parts of the borough could be supplied.[76]

There was an alum well in the Moat Hill area. In 1855 it was stated to contain a strong chalybeate water and formerly to have been a place of much resort, although lately fallen into disuse.[77] Its memory is preserved in Alumwell Road running south from Wolverhampton Road. About 1680 Plot noted that the well water at the house of the mayor, John Cumberlege, was aluminous.[78]

Washing-places maintained by the corporation occur from 1640-1.[79] One at the Bridge is mentioned in 1689-90 when a washing-stock was set up there,[80] and by 1782 there was a wash-house south of the Bridge.[81]

In the early 1840s Walsall had no open bathing-place or public baths. It was an offence to bathe in the canal and also in the old limestone pits of the neighbourhood, which were dangerous; the brook and the mill-stream were too shallow, and in summer the former was usually stagnant as well.[82] In 1850 Thomas Gamson opened the Vicarage Water Baths in Dudley Street on a site facing the present Bath Street, which took its name from them. They were supplied with spring water and consisted of a swimming-bath and shower- and slipper-baths.[83] There were baths in Littleton Street West between at least the late 1860s and the mid 1890s, owned by Elias Crapper and after his death in 1885 by James Crapper.[84] In 1896 the corporation opened baths in what is now Tower Street, with Bailey & McConnal of Walsall as the architects. They were demolished in 1959 and the Gala Baths opened on the site in 1961.[85] There was an open-air swimming bath in the Arboretum from 1912 to 1956; a children's lido was opened there in 1953.[86] An open-air swimming bath was built at Bloxwich by the corporation in 1922 in what is now Field Close, and the following year slipper-baths were added. The establishment was converted into covered baths in 1932.[87] By 1931 there was an open-air pool in Reedswood Park, which was modernized in 1964; there is also a children's pool there.[88]

A Self-supporting, Charitable, and Parochial Dispensary was established in 1829, but after the formation of the poor-law union in 1836 it was closed because of the improved medical relief offered by the union.[89] There was a cholera hospital at Town-end Bank in the 1830s,[90] but for general hospital treatment Walsall had to depend on Birmingham and Stafford until 1863.[91] In that year Walsall Cottage Hospital was opened in a converted shop in Bridge Street, with members of the Sisterhood of the Good Samaritan from Coatham in Kirkleatham (Yorks. N.R.) providing the nursing.[92] It was at this hospital that Sister Dora (Dorothy Pattison) worked from 1865 until 1878.[93] The hospital moved to the Mount, a villa in Wednesbury Road, in 1868.[94] A disastrous explosion at the Green Lanes Furnaces of the Walsall Iron Co. in 1875 drew attention to the inadequacy of the building, and in 1878 a new hospital was opened on the site of the Mount; it was designed by Henman, Harrison & Perrott of London.[95] It was initially an accident hospital, and it was not until 1894 that medical cases were admitted.[96] In that year the name was changed to

[69] Ibid. /13/62-4; II/98; II/103; II/126; II/133.
[70] Snape, *Plan of Walsall* (1782). Homeshaw, *Walsall*, 115, mentions the erection of a pump at Hill Top in 1778.
[71] *Walsall Note Book*, 123, 156, 194-5 (copy in W.C.L.).
[72] *Further Rep. Cttee. of Inquiry into Public Charities and Donations belonging to Town and Parish of Walsall* (Walsall, 1806), 12 (copy in W.C.L.); Homeshaw, *Walsall*, 125.
[73] 5 Geo. IV, c. 68 (Local and Personal), s. 104.
[74] *2nd Rep. Com. State of Large Towns*, App. p. 33.
[75] S.R.O., D. 1287/15/1, bdle. marked 'Roads . . . 19th cent.', P. Potter to Lord Bradford, 16 Dec. 1852.
[76] F. Feeny, *S. Staffs. Water Works Co.: Descriptive Sketch of the Company and Works* (Birmingham, 1880), 17-19, 22-3, 32 (copy in W.S.L. Pamphs. *sub* Public Utilities); K. J. Dean and P. Liddle, *Urban Growth of Walsall, 1763-1966* (Walsall, 1967), 19-20.
[77] Glew, *Walsall*, 5; W.S.L., S. MS. 417/Walsall, no. 1256, Alumwell field.   [78] Plot, *Staffs.* 106.
[79] W.T.C. II/13/30, 43, 48, 57, 64.
[80] Ibid. /13/65.
[81] Snape, *Plan of Walsall* (1782).
[82] *2nd Rep. Com. State of Large Towns*, App. p. 33; above p. 191.
[83] White, *Dir. Staffs.* (1851); Glew, *Walsall*, 32. They no longer existed in 1889: *Guide to Walsall* (1889), 51.

[84] *P.O. Dir. Staffs.* (1868); *Kelly's Dir. Staffs.* (1888; 1892); ibid. (1896), giving only Andrew McKean, manager; above p. 176.
[85] *Walsall Red Book* (1897), 152; *Official Opening of Walsall Gala Baths* (copy in W.C.L.).
[86] *Walsall Observer*, 17 and 24 Aug. 1973.
[87] Homeshaw, *Bloxwich*, 207-8; Lee, *Walsall*, 55; *Official Opening of Walsall Gala Baths*.
[88] *Walsall Red Book* (1931), 84; *Metropolitan Boro. of Walsall Official Town Guide* [1974], 60.
[89] *Prospectus of Walsall Self-supporting Charitable & Parochial Dispensary, established 1829* (copy in S.R.O., D. 1287/12/3); *Walsall Note Book*, 24, 146; *2nd Rep. Com. State of Large Towns*, App. p. 34. For medical attention provided earlier for the poor see above p. 212.
[90] Manton, *Sister Dora*, 269.
[91] Walsall Hospital Management Cttee. *Walsall Hospitals 1863-1963*, 11 (copy in W.C.L.); above p. 212.
[92] *Walsall Hospitals*, 11 and plate facing p. 17.
[93] See p. 145.
[94] *Walsall Hospitals*, 13.
[95] Ibid. 22, 24; *Walsall Red Book* (1877), 89-90; *Walsall Cottage Hospital Ann. Rep. 1878*, 5-6 (copy in S.R.O., D. 1287/box 7); plate facing p. 225 below.
[96] *Walsall Hospitals*, 30.

Walsall and District Hospital; it became Walsall General Hospital in 1918 and Walsall General (Sister Dora) Hospital in 1954.[97]

Public agitation as a result of the smallpox epidemic of 1868 led the corporation to build an isolation hospital in Deadman's Lane (then changed to Hospital Street). It was opened in 1872 when Walsall was already suffering from another smallpox epidemic. During a new outbreak in 1875, however, it was not until Sister Dora took charge that people were willing to use the hospital, and it seems that only in that way was a further epidemic avoided.[98] It was reused during a smallpox epidemic in the 1890s and again during a diphtheria epidemic in 1924-5.[99] Meanwhile in 1900 a smallpox hospital was opened in Sneyd Lane, Bloxwich; it was retained until 1948.[1] The diphtheria epidemic emphasized the need for better accommodation, and in 1929-30 the council built an isolation hospital at Goscote; a tuberculosis sanatorium was opened there in 1933, and the hospital was again enlarged in 1936. From 1949 it dealt only with chest cases and with preconvalescent cases from other Walsall hospitals. The building of a geriatric unit was begun in 1973.[2]

The poor-law guardians opened an infirmary, designed by H. E. Lavender of Walsall, at the workhouse in Pleck Road in 1896. It was taken over by the corporation in 1930 as a general hospital and named Manor Hospital. The workhouse itself, which was renamed Beacon Lodge, became St. John's Hospital after the Walsall Hospital Management Committee was set up in 1948; it was subsequently developed as the geriatric unit of Manor Hospital.[3]

Bloxwich Maternity Home dates from 1929. It occupies the house on the corner of High and Reeves Streets previously called the Manor House and bought by the corporation from the Foster family in 1927.[4]

In 1751 the feoffees of the corporation lands and revenues conveyed 2¼ a. on the east side of the lane later called Bath Street to trustees for a burial ground. It was consecrated in 1756.[5] Its maintenance was a parish responsibility.[6] An inquiry in 1854 or 1855 revealed not only gross overcrowding but its use as 'a playground for children, a pasture for sheep, and a resort for dissolute characters, who actually converted the tombstones into gaming tables'.[7] It was closed in 1857 except for interments

in vaults and brick graves, and completely in 1954.[8] It was subsequently laid out as a public garden.

By the mid 1850s too the graveyard at St. Matthew's was full and that at St. Peter's was waterlogged.[9] In 1857 the town council, having been constituted a burial board, opened a 13-acre cemetery, with separate chapels for Anglicans and Nonconformists, south-west of what is now the junction of Queen and Rollingmill Streets.[10] It became overcrowded, and in 1894 the corporation opened another cemetery of 28 a. at Ryecroft. Separate chapels were provided for Anglicans, Roman Catholics, and Nonconformists, but as a result of Nonconformist pressure there was no religious distinction in any part of the burial ground.[11] By 1972 it covered 40 a. and was nearing its capacity.[12] A crematorium was established there in 1955.[13] With the opening of Ryecroft, Queen Street cemetery was closed for general burials.[14] It was closed completely in 1969, and in 1972 work began on its conversion into a public garden known as Sister Dora Garden; Sister Dora's grave was to be preserved.[15]

The corporation bought 6 a. in Field Road, Bloxwich, in 1873 and laid out part of it as a cemetery which was opened in 1875.[16] By 1972 it covered 16½ a.[17]

In the later Middle Ages the chief police officer of the borough seems to have been the bailiff. There is reference in 1455 to his staff 'used from of old for the keeping of the peace'.[18] He was apparently responsible for the enforcement of early-16th-century ordinances against unlawful games and late 'sitters up'.[19] A borough constable occurs by 1377 and a foreign constable by 1458.[20] Serjeants were appointed in the borough court at Michaelmas by the early 16th century,[21] and two serjeants-at-mace were established by the 1627 charter.[22] In 1618 watchmen are mentioned.[23] During the plague threat of 1665 the watch was used to control access to the town at night, a separate system of warders being used during the day.[24]

Policing arrangements proved inadequate during Jacobite riots in 1715, 1750, and 1751 and during riots caused by economic distress later in the century; even the presence of troops in 1750 and 1751 was ineffective.[25] Supplementary measures were therefore taken. Deputy constables were sworn during food riots in 1766.[26] In 1767 the foreign vestry

[97] Walsall Red Book (1895), 186; ex inf. the group secretary, Walsall Hospital Management Cttee. (1973).
[98] Manton, Sister Dora, 283 sqq., 359-60; Robinson's Map of Walsall (pub. with Walsall Red Book, 1876).
[99] W. S. Swayne, Parson's Pleasure, 146-51; Lee, Walsall, 50. It is shown as disused on O.S. Map 6", Staffs. LXIII. NW. (1903 edn., revision of 1900-1).
[1] Kelly's Dir. Staffs. (1908); Walsall Red Book (1900), 202; ex inf. the group secretary, Walsall Hospital Management Cttee.
[2] Lee, Walsall, 50; Walsall Red Book (1931), 64; (1934), 34; (1937), 36; Walsall Observer, 8 June 1973; ex inf. the group secretary.
[3] Walsall Hospitals, 9, 43-4, 50-1; Walsall Observer, 26 Oct. 1973.
[4] Walsall Hospitals, 45; Lee, Walsall, 55; Walsall Council House, deeds bdle. 323.
[5] L.J.R.O., B/A/27(i), pp. 419-21.
[6] Docs. at St. Matthew's, Vestry Mins. 1681-1793, p.217; Churchwardens' Accts. 1794-1841, ff. 4v., 32v., 48-9.
[7] Glew, Walsall, 26-7; Staffs. Advertiser, 18 Mar. 1854, p. 7.
[8] Reg. of Inscriptions, Bath St. Burial Ground, Walsall (Walsall, n.d.), title-page; Walsall Corp. Act 1954, 2 & 3 Eliz. II, c. 43 (Local), s. 67.

[9] Glew, Walsall, 27-8; Staffs. Advertiser, 18 Mar. 1854, p. 7.
[10] Lich. Dioc. Regy., B/A/2(i)/Q, pp. 1-8; Staffs. Advertiser, 11 and 25 July 1857.
[11] Lich. Dioc. Regy., B/A/2(i)/U, pp. 491-4; W.C.L., newspaper cutting on Ryecroft cemetery; Walsall Red Book (1892), 162, 166; (1895), 186; Swayne, Parson's Pleasure, 145-6.
[12] Walsall County Boro. Structure Plan: Rep. of Survey 1972: Public Utilities, 61.
[13] Metropolitan Boro. of Walsall Official Town Guide [1974], 64.
[14] Kelly's Dir. Staffs. (1896).
[15] Walsall Observer, 23 Feb., 10 Aug. 1973; Walsall Corp. Act 1969, 17 & 18 Eliz. II, c. 58 (Local), s. 76.
[16] Lich. Dioc. Regy., B/A/2(i)/S, pp. 35-48, 67-70.
[17] Walsall County Boro. Structure Plan: Rep. of Survey 1972: Public Utilities, 61.
[18] B.M. Eg. Roll 8539.
[19] Willmore, Walsall, 167, 172; above p. 213.
[20] See pp. 210, 213.   [21] See p. 210.
[22] See p. 215.
[23] S.R.O., Q/SR, M. 1618, no. 20.
[24] Willmore, Walsall, 279 (from W.C.L., box 33, no. 16).
[25] Homeshaw, Walsall, 92-6.   [26] Ibid. 95.

agreed that the cost of prosecutions for thefts committed within the foreign should be met out of the poor-rate; offenders had too often not been prosecuted by their victims because of the expense involved.[27] An association for the prosecution of felons was formed for the parish in 1771[28] and another for the Bloxwich area in 1814.[29] In the winter of 1811 a patrol was formed for the town, apparently an attempt to revive the watch. The town was divided into six districts, each with a watch-house; the cost of equipment was met by the constable out of the poor-rate.[30] In October 1812 the court leet appointed sixteen deputy constables for the borough and eighteen for the foreign.[31] The Improvement Act of 1824 provided for a night watch, and watchmen were appointed in 1825 and 1826. They were discontinued, however, because the rate permitted was inadequate. The inhabitants of the main street in the town then raised a subscription to maintain a watch, but that scheme too was soon abandoned.[32] In December 1831, with the district in a disturbed state owing to a miners' strike, 600 special constables were enrolled. During the election of 1832 more were enrolled and troops were brought in on election day. In addition a permanent police force was established consisting of a superintendent and three officers. The corporation fitted up a building next to the churchyard as both a police station and a fire-engine house, but it was 'of a very inferior description', the cells in particular being unwholesome.[33] In 1836 the parish lock-up at Bloxwich was handed over to the police.[34] In the same year the watch committee ordered the appointment of extra police to serve on Sundays.[35] A new central police station was built in Goodall Street adjoining the guildhall in 1843.[36] It was replaced by a station in Green Lane in 1966.[37] Bloxwich police station was apparently at Short Heath in 1861 and in Harrison Street by the 1870s; a station was built as part of the public buildings in Station Street in 1882–4.[38] In 1966 the control of the borough force passed to the West Midlands Police Authority.[39]

The parish was maintaining a fire-engine by the later 18th century. At one time it was kept in the west porch of St. Matthew's, but by the 1790s an engine-house had been built near the lich-gate.[40] The Improvement Act of 1824 authorized the commissioners to provide a fire-engine.[41] The parish, however, continued to maintain its own 'engines',[42] and it was the corporation which in 1832 fitted up the fire-engine house by the churchyard.[43] In the early 1840s there were two engines in the town, one belonging to the Norwich Union Fire Office and kept in Lichfield Street, the other belonging to the Birmingham Fire Office and kept in premises on the corner of Bridge Street and the Bridge.[44] It was presumably because of such alternative arrangements that in 1840 the vestry had resolved to sell 'the parish engines' and engine-house; the building was demolished during the improvement of the area in 1852 and 1853.[45] The corporation formed a fire brigade in 1879, with its main station at the borough offices in Goodall Street and sub-stations at the police stations in Stafford Street and at Bloxwich; in 1888 the brigade was placed under the control of the chief constable. A central fire station was opened in 1930 in a converted tannery in Darwall Street.[46] It was replaced by a new station in Blue Lane West opened in 1974.[47]

In 1826 the improvement commissioners opened a gas-works on a site later covered by Arboretum Road. Designs for a roof 55 ft. long and 29 ft. in span, with members of cast and wrought iron, were prepared by J. U. Rastrick, the civil engineer, in 1825.[48] By 1848 the works could not meet the growing demand for gas, and under the Improvement Act of that year a new works was built by the commissioners in Wolverhampton Street in 1850.[49] In 1876 the corporation took over the interests of the commissioners and in 1877 those of the Birmingham and Staffordshire Gas Light Co. in the borough.[50] In 1877 it opened a works at Pleck.[51] The manufacture of gas was transferred to the new works, but the Wolverhampton Street works was still used as a storing station in 1895.[52] The commissioners leased the first works out at a large rent which enabled them to keep the improvement rates low, and in 1882 the council announced that the profits from the gasworks were such that there was no need for a borough rate.[53] With nationalization in 1949 the undertaking

[27] W.T.C. II/155(b, c).
[28] Ibid. (a); *Aris's Birmingham Gaz.* 7 Oct. 1782.
[29] Homeshaw, *Bloxwich*, 150–2.
[30] Pearce, *Walsall*, 186–91; W.C.L., printed forms requesting attendance of members of the patrol.
[31] Pearce, *Walsall*, 183–5.
[32] *1st Rep. Com. Mun. Corps.* H.C. 116, App. III, p. 2047 (1835), xxv.
[33] Ibid. 2047–8, 2051, 2053; Homeshaw, *Walsall*, 132, 135–6.
[34] W.T.C., Watch Cttee. Mins. 1836–52, 2 Feb. 1836.
[35] Ibid. 2 Mar., 21 June 1836.
[36] Glew, *Walsall*, 37; W.T.C., General Cttees. 1842–50, 11 July 1843.
[37] *Walsall Observer*, 28 Oct. 1966.
[38] R.G. 9/2012 no. 56; Homeshaw, *Bloxwich*, 171; *Staffs. Advertiser*, 16 Nov. 1872, 30 Dec. 1882; below p. 252.
[39] West Midlands Police (Amalgamation) Order 1966, S.I. 1966, no. 62.
[40] Docs. at St. Matthew's, Churchwardens' Accts. 1794–1841, ff. 5v., 7; *Gent. Mag.* lxix (2), 763; Pearce, *Walsall*, 165.
[41] 5 Geo. IV, c. 68 (Local and Personal), s. 61.
[42] Churchwardens' Accts. 1794–1841, f. 88; docs. at St. Matthew's, Vestry Bk. 1794–1854, pp. 310, 351.
[43] See above.
[44] *2nd Rep. Com. State of Large Towns*, App. p. 33; *P.O.*

Dir. Staffs. (1845); Glew, *Walsall*, 48; W.C.L., Meikle Coll., 'Middle of the Midlands', chap. 7.
[45] Churchwardens' Accts. 1794–1841, f. 137; W.T.C., Streets Cttee. Mins. 1849–51, loose sheets of 23 Aug. and 1 Sept. 1852; above p. 149.
[46] *Walsall Red Book* (1880), 11; (1882), 30; (1889), 23; *County Boro. of Walsall Official Town Guide* [1972], 73–4; W.C.L., fire brigade papers; inscription on ceremonial hatchet of 1930 in W.C.L. For the tannery see R. G. A. Bolton, 'Geog. Study of Growth and Present Day Pattern of Leather Ind. and Allied Trades in Walsall' (St. Peter's College, Birmingham, Geog. Dept. thesis, 1970), 72, 75 (copy in W.C.L.).
[47] *Walsall Observer*, 8 Feb. 1974.
[48] Willmore, *Walsall*, 196–7. Details about Rastrick's designs have been provided by W.C.L. from inf. supplied by Mr. N. Mutton of the City of Birmingham Polytechnic out of Rastrick's notebook 1822–5 in the Goldsmiths' Libr., Univ. of London.
[49] White, *Dir. Staffs.* (1851); above p. 217.
[50] *Walsall Red Book* (1877), 76, 78, 80–4; Walsall Gas Purchase and Boro. Extension Act, 1876, 39 & 40 Vic. c. 119 (Local).
[51] Willmore, *Walsall*, 197.
[52] 'Walsall Electric Lighting', *The Electrical Engineer*, 20 Dec. 1895 (copy in W.C.L.).
[53] White, *Dir. Staffs.* (1834); *Walsall Red Book* (1883), 118.

The mayor and corporation walking the fair at the Bridge in 1859

High Street in 1845, with St. Matthew's Church in the background and, to the right of the steps, the market house of 1809

WALSALL

WALSALL: SISTER DORA AT THE GREEN LANES FURNACES AFTER THE 1875 EXPLOSION

WEST BROMWICH: FORMER RYLAND MEMORIAL SCHOOL OF ART
opened in 1902

passed into the control of the West Midlands Gas Board.[54]

Under powers acquired in 1890 the corporation launched an electricity undertaking in 1895, with a generating station on part of the gas-works site in Wolverhampton Street.[55] A new power station was built at Birchills in 1914–16.[56] It was transferred to the West Midlands Joint Electricity Authority in 1927 and quickly extended; the corporation, however, continued to distribute current.[57] In 1948 the undertaking passed into the control of the Midlands Electricity Board. A new power station was opened at Birchills in 1949.[58]

In his will of 1550 Richard Stone left money for the repair of 'foul ways about Walsall'.[59] In 1552 or 1553 one of the bells at the church was broken and was sold with the consent of the parishioners 'to the amendment of divers bridges and highways about their town which were very noisome to the king's people passing that way'.[60] Walsall was one of five places ordered by quarter sessions in 1587 to repair thier common ways.[61] The bequests of William Parker (d. 1616) included £150 for the repair of the roads in Walsall, Bloxwich, and Rushall, the inhabitants of each place having the right to decide how their £50 should be spent.[62] Soon after the grant of the charter in 1627 the new corporation tried to secure exemption from county rates for the maintenance of bridges, having twelve of its own to repair. The county quarter sessions granted exemption in 1664 on the ground that the corporation was 'at very great charges' in repairing bridges and highways within the borough and foreign.[63]

With the opening of the railway a 'light van' was introduced to convey passengers between the station and the George.[64] In 1884 the South Staffordshire and Birmingham District Steam Tramways Co. Ltd. introduced tram services from Wednesbury and Darlaston to Pleck and thence through Walsall to Mellish Road; there was also a service from Walsall to Bloxwich, and a depot was built at Birchills.[65] The routes were electrified in 1892, Walsall being one of the first towns in the country to have electric trams; the public service was opened at the beginning of 1893. The undertaking passed under the control of the British Electric Traction Co. Ltd. in 1897 and of Walsall corporation in 1901; it continued to be leased to an operating company until 1903. The Bloxwich line was extended to the end of High Street in 1902, and in 1904 new lines were opened from the centre of Walsall to Willenhall, to Walsall

Wood, and along Birmingham Road to the borough boundary. Motor buses were introduced by the corporation from 1915, the first being from Bloxwich to Hednesford in Cannock. In 1928 buses began to replace trams, and the last tram ran in 1933, on the Bloxwich route. The central bus station in St. Paul's Street on the site of the former Blue Coat School was opened in 1935; offices were opened there in 1937. Trolley buses were introduced in 1931, from Townend Bank to Willenhall, and a full service throughout the borough came into operation in 1933. The Birchills tram depot was converted for the new form of transport. Trolley buses were withdrawn in favour of motor buses in stages between 1965 and 1970. The corporation transport undertaking passed to the West Midlands Passenger Transport Executive in 1969.

By 1767 there was a post office in Digbeth, and by 1780 it was in Rushall Street. About 1800 it moved to the Bridge. There were several more moves during the 19th century before a general post office was opened on the corner of Darwall and Leicester Streets in 1879. The present general post office on the opposite side of Darwall Street was opened in 1928.[66] Bloxwich was on the route of a horse-mail between Walsall, Cannock, and Penkridge established in 1829.[67] There was a post office at Bloxwich by 1851; the post office opened in High Street in 1898 was replaced in 1972 by one in New Street.[68]

Parks and libraries are treated elsewhere.[69]

PARLIAMENTARY HISTORY. Walsall became a parliamentary borough returning one member by the Reform Act of 1832. Walsall Wood and Shelfield were excluded from the constituency, the boundary of which was otherwise that of the parish.[70] In 1868 the boundary was extended to include those parts of Rushall which were added to the administrative borough in 1876 and 1890.[71] In 1955 the constituency was divided into two seats, Walsall North and Walsall South, and new areas were added. Brownhills urban district, including Walsall Wood, was transferred from Cannock constituency to Walsall North, and Aldridge urban district from Lichfield and Tamworth constituency to Walsall South.[72] Under an Order of 1970 Brownhills and Aldridge were detached from the Walsall constituencies to form the new constituency of Aldridge-Brownhills; Willenhall (in St. Peter's, Wolverhampton) was added to Walsall North, and Darlaston to Walsall South.[73]

[54] Boro. of Walsall: Council Year Book 1950–1951, 137.
[55] The Electrical Engineer, 20 Dec. 1895; Electric Lighting Orders Confirmation (No. 3) Act, 1883, 46 & 47 Vic. c. 215 (Local); Electric Lighting Orders Confirmation Act, 1890, 53 & 54 Vic. c. 186 (Local).
[56] Souvenir of Official Opening of Birchills Electricity Generating Station, October 31st, 1916 (copy in W.C.L.).
[57] Walsall Red Book (1929), 82; (1939), 64.
[58] Boro. of Walsall: Council Year Book 1950–1951, 138.
[59] W.S.L. 45/56, folder 74.
[60] Annals of Dioc. of Lichfield, iv. 73 (copy in W.S.L. Pamphs. sub Lichfield).
[61] S.H.C. 1929, 168.
[62] S.R.O., D. 260/M/T/2/53, p. 45. For other bequests by Parker see below pp. 234, 255, 269.
[63] W.T.C.II/83/3 and 5.   [64] See p. 168.
[65] For the rest of this para. see J. S. Webb, Black Country Tramways, i (Bloxwich, priv. print. 1974), 23–8, 37–48, 114, 120–2; County Boro. of Walsall, Jubilee of Transport Undertaking 1904–1954 (copy in W.C.L.); West Midlands

Passenger Transport Executive, Walsall's Trolleybuses: Souvenir Brochure 1931–1970 (copy in W.C.L.); The West Midlands Passenger Transport Area (Transfer of Undertakings) Order 1969, S.I. 1969, no. 1175; Walsall Observer, 10 Aug. 1935, 25 Sept. 1937.
[66] F. G. Holloway, 'The Postal Hist. of Walsall' (TS. in W.C.L.); Walsall Observer, 28 Jan. 1928; Willmore, Walsall, 402–3; Glew, Walsall, 49; Kelly's Dir. Staffs. (1880); Walsall Red Book (1929), 67.
[67] Staffs. Advertiser, 31 Oct. 1829.
[68] White, Dir. Staffs. (1851); Walsall Observer, 10 Nov. 1972.   [69] See pp. 152, 157, 159–60, 163, 251–2.
[70] V.C.H. Staffs. i. 272; S. Lewis, Topog. Dict. Eng. (1835), v, plate lxxxiii.
[71] The Boundary Act, 1868, 31 & 32 Vic. c. 46, first sched.; above p. 217.
[72] The Parliamentary Constituencies (South East Staffs.) Order, 1955, S.I. 1955, no. 170.
[73] The Parliamentary Constituencies (England) Order 1970, S.I. 1970, no. 1674, pp. 1, 28, 66–7.

The Order took effect at the general election of February 1974.

Walsall's first member was C. S. Forster, a Tory and a local banker and former mayor. He held the seat until 1837, when it was captured by a Liberal who retired in 1841. In the by-election of February 1841 J. N. Gladstone, brother of W. E. Gladstone, gained the seat for the Conservatives. He narrowly defeated a candidate sponsored by the Anti-Corn Law League, which was intervening for the first time in a parliamentary election. In June, however, the league's candidate recovered the seat for the Liberals.[74] In 1847 there were two Liberal candidates, Charles Forster, son of C. S. Forster, and the Hon. E. R. Littleton (later Baron Hatherton). Forster's supporters alleged that if Littleton were elected Walsall would become a pocket borough.[75] Littleton nevertheless won the seat, which he held for five years.[76] In 1852 Forster was returned unopposed, and he remained member for Walsall until his death in 1891; he was created a baronet in 1874.[77] There were Liberal members from 1891 to 1892, 1893 to 1895, 1900 to 1910, and 1922 to 1924. Conservatives represented the town in the intervening years and from 1924 to 1929 when the first Labour member was returned. In 1931 J. A. Leckie, who stood as a National Liberal, gained the seat. On his death in 1938 another National Liberal was elected and served until 1945.[78] A Labour member held the borough from 1945 to 1955. When the constituency was divided he was elected member for Walsall North, while Walsall South was taken by a Conservative. Both members held their seats until 1974.[79] In the general elections of February and October that year Labour members were returned for both the Walsall seats and for the new Aldridge-Brownhills seat.[80]

CHURCHES. There was a church at Walsall by 1200. It had dependent chapels at Wednesbury and Rushall for all or most of the Middle Ages,[81] and a third was founded at Bloxwich apparently in the early 15th century. It was not until the 19th century, however, that further new churches were built within the parish.

Walsall church was recorded in 1200 when the Crown gave it to the bishop and his successors.[82] It is likely to have been lost in 1208, when John seized the lands of the clergy; also the bishop died

that year. It does not seem to have been restored when John reached his settlement with the pope in 1213, the see of Coventry being still vacant.[83] The Crown presented a rector in 1210 or 1211[84] and was patron in 1227.[85] About 1220 William le Rous granted the church to the Premonstratensian abbey of Halesowen (Worcs.) to enable it to meet the demands of hospitality; the grant was confirmed by the bishop and in 1221 by the prior of Coventry, subject to the appointment of a vicar and saving the rights of the existing rector.[86] In 1223 le Rous acknowledged the Crown's patronage and denied that he had claimed to be patron himself.[87] The king confirmed the grant in 1233, and in 1235 the pope licensed the abbey to take possession of the church on its next vacancy, subject to the ordination of a vicarage.[88] In 1245, however, the Crown again presented a rector[89] and a month later granted the patronage to Halesowen.[90] The abbot began to arrange for appropriation but early in 1247 asked the bishop to return the documents since the king had not intended appropriation.[91] In June 1247 the Crown once more presented.[92] The abbot acceded to the presentation but reserved his future rights of patronage,[93] which the Crown confirmed in October.[94]

In 1248, at the king's instance, the bishop decreed the appropriation of Walsall church to Halesowen, subject to the ordination of a vicarage and to the payment of a pension of £4 to Lichfield cathedral, which claimed rights in the church.[95] The pension was confirmed in 1255,[96] but in 1278, after a dispute, the abbey was released from payment.[97] In 1489 Halesowen was paying 40s. a year from Walsall church and Wednesbury chapel to support two choristers at Lichfield cathedral, an arrangement dating apparently from the early 14th century.[98]

The patronage of the vicarage remained with Halesowen until the Reformation. As Premonstratensians the canons could appoint one of their own number to serve the church and did so regularly.[99] With the surrender of the abbey in 1538 the advowson passed to the Crown,[1] which granted it the same year to Sir John Dudley, subsequently earl of Warwick and duke of Northumberland.[2] On his forfeiture in 1553 the advowson passed back to the Crown, which sold it with the manor of Walsall to Richard Wilbraham and his brother Thomas in 1557.[3] The patronage then descended with the manor until 1945; in that year Lord Bradford transferred it to the bishop of Lichfield, who remains the

[74] Willmore, *Walsall*, 410–17; Homeshaw, *Walsall*, 157; N. McCord, *The Anti-Corn Law League 1838–1846*, 83, 85–6, 88–9, 95.
[75] *Staffs. Advertiser*, 24 and 31 July 1847; Willmore, *Walsall*, 410.
[76] Willmore, *Walsall*, 417–18.
[77] K. J. Dean, *Town & Westminster* (Walsall, 1972), 3; Willmore, *Walsall*, 418.
[78] Dean, *Town & Westminster*, 169, 247.
[79] Ibid. 253; *Who's Who* (1972), 810, 3381.
[80] *The Times*, 2 Mar., 12 Oct. 1974.
[81] Ede, *Wednesbury*, 54 sqq.; Shaw, *Staffs.* ii. 67–8; *Cal. Papal L.* xii. 493–9.
[82] *Rot. Chart.* (Rec. Com.), 49–50.
[83] See *V.C.H. Staffs.* iii. 11.
[84] *S.H.C.* iv (1), 24–5.
[85] Ibid. 70.
[86] Dudley Central Libr. 16/1.
[87] *S.H.C.* iv (1), 24–5.
[88] *Cal. Chart. R.* 1226–57, 182; *Cal. Papal Regs.* i. 147.

[89] *Cal. Pat.* 1232–47, 454.
[90] *Walsall Records*, 24–5.
[91] Bodl. MS. Ashmole 1527, f. 93v.
[92] *Cal. Pat.* 1232–47, 503.
[93] Bodl. MS. Ashmole 1527, f. 94.
[94] B.R.L. 351064.
[95] *S.H.C.* 1924, p. 344. The appropriation was to take effect on the resignation or death of the rector, Master Vincent; he had in fact resigned a few months before: Bodl. MS. Ashmole 1547, f. 94.
[96] *S.H.C.* 1924, p. 11.
[97] Ibid. pp. 81–2.
[98] *V.C.H. Worcs.* ii. 164.
[99] F. W. Willmore, *Transcript of First Reg. Bk. of Par. Ch. of St. Matthew, Walsall, 1570–1649* (Walsall, 1890), pp. xxv–xxvii; B.R.L. 351089; *S.H.C.* n.s. viii. 122; D. Knowles, *Religious Orders in Eng.* ii. 139–40.
[1] *S.H.C.* xii (1), 186.
[2] *L. & P. Hen. VIII*, xiii (2), p. 191.
[3] *Cal. Pat.* 1555–7, 449; B.M. Harl. MS. 606, f. 7.

patron.[4] In 1569 and 1575, however, it was exercised by the lessee of the rectory, George Clarkson.[5] In 1796 Lord Mountrath granted Philip Pratt the elder the right of presentation for eight years in order to secure the living to Philip Pratt the younger, nephew of Mountrath's friend Mr. Preston; by 1803 the right had passed to the younger Philip, who then presented himself.[6]

At the appropriation of the church to Halesowen in 1248 the bishop had provided for the institution of a vicarage worth 13 marks. The churchyard (*area*) and the buildings were to be divided between the canons and the vicar, and the vicar was to meet the bishop's and the archdeacon's customary charges. In return for assuming full responsibility for the chapels at Wednesbury and Rushall the vicar was to have all obventions from the chapels except sheaves of corn; if the revenue was not sufficient to enable him to carry out the duties he was to receive further provision from the revenues of Walsall church. The abbot and the vicar were to bear all other charges proportionately.[7] In 1535 the vicar was receiving £10 19s. 10d. a year net from glebe, tithes, and offerings. Among the charges on his income was the payment of 17s. 4d. to 11 'presbyteris et pauperibus' in Walsall for the soul of John Harper.[8] In 1553 the vicar leased out the vicarage house.[9] The vicarage was said to be worth £50 in 1604. In 1646, however, its value was given as £30 and the Committee for Plundered Ministers ordered an augmentation of up to £50 a year out of the sequestered tithes of Wednesfield, Hatherton, Featherstone, and Bentley, all in St. Peter's, Wolverhampton. Apparently an increase of £30 was granted.[10] In 1773 the vicar stated that the annual value of the living was variously reported as £300, £200, and £130, but he believed that even £130 'is rather more than I have hitherto made of it'.[11] In 1830 the income was given as some £180 from tithes, £150 from glebe, between £80 and £100 from surplice fees, and £20 from Easter dues and other small payments.[12] By 1693 many of the vicar's tithes were paid in cash,[13] and under the commutation of 1843 he was assigned a rent-charge of £300 in place of the vicarial tithes. The glebe then consisted of 17 a. of meadow and pasture, mostly to the south-west of the town; except for the vicarage house it had all been leased out.[14] The endowments of the vicarage in 1851 were listed as land worth £210, tithes worth £300, and glebe worth £60, and there were fees of £100.[15] In the late 1850s the vicar wished to let

glebe-land on 99-year building leases, and he complained to the Ecclesiastical Commissioners about the expense involved in letting church property, which put him at a great disadvantage compared with other property owners in the same area.[16] It was not in fact until the late 19th century that the glebe was developed for building.[17] By 1972 much of it had recently been sold, and the remainder, in the area of Vicarage Place, Caldmore Road, and Glebe Street, was let.[18]

The ancient site of the vicarage house was south of Vicarage Place.[19] The house was rebuilt in the early 19th century but was described in 1881 as unsuitable. It was replaced by the Terrace, an early-19th-century house in Hanch Place acquired in 1881 from the vicar, William Allen, who had bought it privately in 1876.[20] By 1972 the former house was occupied as the Mount Catholic Club. The Terrace was sold to the trustees of the Blue Coat school in 1931, and Westmount in Highgate Road was bought that year in its place.[21] Ardleigh in Jesson Road, the present vicarage house, was bought in 1965 and the Highgate Road house sold in 1966.[22]

By the early 16th century there was a deacon serving the church, appointed by the mayor and council.[23] Thereafter curates are regularly mentioned until the mid 17th century and again from the mid 18th century.[24] In 1548 the chantry commissioners appointed Thomas Dobson, one of the chantry priests, as curate, but in 1549 the surveyor of crown lands in Staffordshire described him as unfit for the post. The surveyor considered all the chantry priests equally unsuitable, describing them and the vicar as ignorant and superstitious, and he recommended that a preacher should be endowed in place of the curate. Dobson, however, was still curate in 1553.[25] Robert Wilson, who was vicar from 1575 to 1609, occurs as reader in 1561.[26] The curates who occur in 1604 and 1610 were graduates and preachers, the first being also master of the grammar school; in 1648 the curate was again master of the school.[27] In 1773 the vicar, who was resident, stated that the curate was supported by subscription, read prayers daily, and preached an afternoon sermon, presumably on Sundays.[28] In the earlier 19th century the curates were styled lecturers.[29] By the late 1820s the curate was paid a stipend by the vicar.[30] There were two curates by 1856, and c. 1886 the number was increased to three. There were still three in the early 1970s.[31]

There were several chapels and side altars in the

[4] Lich. Dioc. Regy., Reg. of Transfers of Patronage, p. 93; *Lond. Gaz.* 1 Nov. 1946, pp. 5360–1; Lich. Dioc. Regy., B/A/1/42, pp. 457–8; above p. 170.

[5] L.J.R.O., B/A/1/15, ff. 64, 67.

[6] S.R.O., D. 1287/22/5, heads of deeds relating to next presentation to vicarage of Walsall; Willmore, *Walsall*, 138; L.J.R.O., B/A/1/28, pp. 31, 38.

[7] *Walsall Records*, 26.

[8] *Valor Eccl.* (Rec. Com.), iii. 149.

[9] C 3/122/2; C 3/129/17.   [10] *S.H.C.* 1915, 303.

[11] L.J.R.O., B/V/5/1772–3.

[12] L.J.R.O., A/V/1/2, no. 47.

[13] L.J.R.O., B/V/6/Walsall, 1693.

[14] W.S.L., S. MS. 417/Walsall.

[15] H.O. 129/380/3/2.

[16] S.R.O., D. 260/M/F/5/115.   [17] See p. 156.

[18] Ex inf. Mr. D. W. F. Harrison of Fox & Harrison, Walsall (1972).

[19] L.J.R.O., B/V/6/Walsall, 1636; J. Snape, *Plan of Town of Walsall* (1782); W.S.L., S. MS. 417/Walsall, no. 2061. For Vicar's field in that area by 1323 see above p. 181.

[20] Deeds in possession of the trustees of the Blue Coat School, conveyances of 4 Sept. 1876 and 18 July 1881.

[21] Lich. Dioc. Regy., B/A/2(i)/W, pp. 281, 412.

[22] Ibid./X, pp. 701–2; docs. at St. Matthew's, Churchwardens' Chest, Church Commissioners to the vicar, 5 Aug. 1966.

[23] Req. 2/10/223. The document is damaged, but it appears that the wage was paid by the vicar and the mayor and council.

[24] *S.H.C.* 1915, 298; L.J.R.O., B/V/1/8 and 62; Pearce, *Walsall*, 103–4.   [25] *S.H.C.* 1915, 298, 303.

[26] L.J.R.O., B/V/1/5; *S.H.C.* 1915, 298, 303.

[27] *S.H.C.* 1915, 298, 303–4; Fink, *Queen Mary's Grammar Sch.* 415.   [28] L.J.R.O., B/V/5/1772–3.

[29] Pearce, *Walsall*, 104; docs. at St. Matthew's, Churchwardens' Accts. 1794–1841, f. 21, p. 187 (1st nos.); Homeshaw, *Bloxwich*, 263; Homeshaw, *Walsall*, 126–7.

[30] *Rep. Com. Eccl. Revenues* [67], p. 505, H.C. (1835), xxii.

[31] Lich. Dioc. Ch. Cal. (1857; 1887); Lich. Dioc. Dir. (1973).

church by the late Middle Ages. An altar of St. John the Baptist existed by 1365 and a chapel by 1520.[32] There was an altar of St. Mary by 1391.[33] By 1452 a second altar of St. Mary had been established, under the rood,[34] and by 1462–3 the first altar had its own chapel.[35] By 1488 there was an altar of St. Nicholas, which later had a chapel, apparently by 1534.[36] A chapel of St. Clement had been established by 1468[37] and a chapel of St. Catherine by 1502.[38] Six chapels were mentioned in 1534; the sixth may have been a chapel round the altar of St. Mary under the rood.[39] Each altar, including the high altar, had its own endowment, which was in the care of altar wardens.[40] From 1502 St. Catherine's chapel was maintained out of the admission fees paid by members of the college of mercers, tailors, drapers, shearmen, weavers, coopers, and barbers[41] as well as from its earlier endowments. In 1510 Agnes Cooke gave a silver girdle in honour of St. Catherine.[42]

From the 14th century onwards several chantries were founded. In 1365 John de Beverley and William Coleson gave land in Walsall and Rushall worth 5 marks a year to support a chaplain celebrating mass daily; further endowments, including land in Bentley in St. Peter's, Wolverhampton, were later given by Thomas Beaumont and Henry Vernon.[43] In 1391 Sir Roger Hillary obtained licence to give land in Walsall, Shelfield, and Rushall to support one chaplain celebrating daily; at the suppression the endowment included a priest's chamber.[44] By 1535 Hillary was credited with the foundation of two chantries, and his second chantry was also mentioned in 1549. It had apparently been augmented in 1411 by Thomas Thykness and others with land in West Bromwich; at the suppression it held land there and in Walsall, Shelfield, and Aldridge.[45] In 1390 Sir Thomas Aston of Haywood in Colwich was licensed to endow a chantry, with one chaplain, for the guild of St. John the Baptist.[46] The endowment, not completed until 1404, consisted of land and rent worth 10 marks a year in Walsall, Rushall, Great Barr in Aldridge, Rugeley, Essington in Bushbury, King's Bromley, Finchpath in West Bromwich, Norton Canes, and Stonnall and Little Aston in Shenstone.[47] Also in 1404 Aston endowed a second chantry with land and rent worth a further 10 marks yearly for the souls of guildsmen killed at the battle of Shrewsbury in 1403. In 1535 it held land in Walsall, Rushall, Shenstone, and Essington.[48] In 1448

Thomas Mollesley and Henry Flaxall gave land worth 18 marks a year, apparently in Shustoke (Warws.), to endow a chantry of two chaplains. The priests were to pray for the king and queen, the marquess of Suffolk and his wife, the duke of Warwick, and the guildsmen of St. John the Baptist.[49] In the reign of Henry VI a chantry was founded by William Spernor. The endowment in 1535 consisted of land in Walsall, Shelfield, and Rushall. At the suppression there was one chaplain, who had a chamber provided.[50] In 1478 John Flaxall gave land worth 8 marks to endow a chantry, with a priest who was to say mass for the founder, his father, the king and queen, and all who supported the chantry. In 1493 Eleanor and William Burgess gave Wood End farm to the chantry; in 1535 it also held land in Perry Barr in Handsworth.[51] By 1527 a further chantry, with one priest, had been founded by the mayor and burgesses or by St. John's guild; by 1535 the endowment included land in Walsall, West Bromwich, Rushall, Tipton, and Codsall.[52] By the suppression there was also a chantry with one chaplain which had been recently founded by the guild.[53]

None of the chantries had its own chapel. The priests of those founded by Beverley and Coleson, Aston, Spernor, and the mayor and burgesses celebrated at the altar of St. John the Baptist.[54] Hillary's chantry of 1391 was founded at St. Mary's altar, and by the suppression both the chantries credited to him were attached to it.[55] John Flaxall founded his chantry at the altar of St. Mary under the rood.[56] The chantry of Mollesley and Henry Flaxall was founded at the altar of St. John the Baptist but was attached to St. Mary under the rood by the suppression.[57] All the chantries were apparently under the supervision either of the guild of St. John the Baptist or of Our Lady's Guild by the early 16th century. The borough ordinances of c. 1510–20 provided that when any of the chantries fell vacant the officials of the relevant guild were to ensure that the patrons quickly appointed priests 'able in conyng of pryksonge' and of good life, 'neither disars ne cardars'.[58]

Fourteen obits are recorded in the chantry certificates of 1548, most, if not all, founded in the 15th and 16th centuries. Two others founded in 1536 were not mentioned there. Of the fourteen all but one provided for donations to the poor on the obit days.[59] Another obit was founded in 1558 by George Hawe.[60]

[32] *Walsall Records*, 5–6; S.R.O., D. 260/M/F/1/5, ff. 49v.–50.
[33] *Walsall Records*, 7.
[34] W.T.C. I/54*.
[35] *S.H.C.* 1928, 190. In 1527 it is referred to as on the N. side of the church (ibid. 261) but by 1550 it was in the S. aisle (W.S.L. 45/56, folder 74, will of Ric. Stone proved 1550; Shaw, *Staffs.* ii. 78).
[36] *S.H.C.* 1928, 220; W.S.L. 45/56, folder 74, will of Ric. Stone proved 1550; L.J.R.O., will of Ric. Parker proved 8 May 1534.
[37] *S.H.C.* 1928, 206.
[38] Willmore, *Walsall*, 262.
[39] L.J.R.O., will of Ric. Parker.
[40] See e.g. *S.H.C.* 1928, 178–82, 213, 219, 244, 251, 261; W.T.C. I/67; above p. 211.
[41] W.T.C. I/83.
[42] *S.H.C.* 1928, 238.
[43] *Walsall Records*, 5–6; *Cal. Pat.* 1364–7, 160; *S.H.C.* n.s. viii. 109; *S.H.C.* 1915, 299; *Valor Eccl.* (Rec. Com.), iii. 151. *S.H.C.* 1928, 183, identifies Vernon's chantry with William Spernor's (see below) without citing evidence.
[44] *Walsall Records*, 7–8; *Cal. Pat.* 1549–51, 46.

[45] *Valor Eccl.* iii. 151; *Cal. Pat.* 1549–51, 13, 95–6; above p. 26.
[46] *Cal. Pat.* 1388–92, 370.
[47] Ibid. 1401–5, 350; *Walsall Records*, 17–18.
[48] *Walsall Records*, 21; *Valor Eccl.* iii. 151.
[49] *Cal. Pat.* 1446–52, 150; *Valor Eccl.* iii. 151; S.R.O., D. 260/M/F/1/5, f. 72v.
[50] *S.H.C.* 1915, 299; *Valor Eccl.* iii. 151; *Cal. Pat.* 1549–51, 96.
[51] *Cal. Pat.* 1476–85, 96; *Valor Eccl.* iii. 151; above p. 179.
[52] *S.H.C.* 1915, 299; *Cal. Pat.* 1549–51, 95, 125–6; 1553, 218, 233; 1553–4, 205.
[53] *S.H.C.* 1915, 301.
[54] Ibid. 299; *Cal. Pat.* 1364–7, 160.
[55] *Walsall Records*, 7; *S.H.C.* 1915, 300.
[56] *Cal. Pat.* 1476–85, 96.
[57] Ibid. 1446–52, 150; *S.H.C.* 1915, 300.
[58] Willmore, *Walsall*, 168.
[59] *S.H.C.* 1915, 301; Sims, *Cal. of Deeds*, pp. 22, 27; S.R.O., D. 260/M/F/1/5, ff. 55–56v.; L.J.R.O., wills of Thos. Kempson (proved 30 May 1536) and Rob. Doore (proved 23 Jan. 1543/4).
[60] Fink, *Queen Mary's Grammar Sch.*, plate facing p. 145.

There was a light at St. Nicholas's altar in 1488,[61] a light of St. John in 1494-5,[62] and a light of St. Mary in 1505.[63] In the early 16th century a light of St. Anne was maintained from part of the admission fees of the college of mercers, tailors, drapers, shearmen, weavers, coopers, and barbers.[64]

Between 1549 and 1553 most of the endowments of the chantries, obits, and lights were sold to speculators, mainly Londoners.[65] Some lands, however, remained in 1554 to form part of the endowments of Walsall grammar school.[66] It seems that chantry lands were also appropriated by the corporation and subsequently sold.[67] Sales by the Crown of small parcels of concealed lands continued until at least 1589.[68]

The guild of St. John the Baptist, for men and women, had been founded by 1390.[69] By the 16th century its endowments included lands in Walsall and Bloxwich, Rushall, Great Barr in Aldridge, Bentley in St. Peter's, Wolverhampton, Bradley, and Wheaton Aston in Lapley.[70] It seems also to have been receiving the issues of the manor of Bascote in Long Itchington (Warws.).[71] By 1426 the guild possessed a hall, which was also used as the town hall.[72] Many members lived outside the parish, including local notables such as the abbots of Halesowen and of Merevale (Warws.). Persons of more than local importance were rarely admitted. In 1482-3, however, new members included the Prince of Wales, Lord Rivers, Sir Richard Grey, Sir Thomas Stanley, Lord Lisle, and the bishop of Worcester. In the early 16th century there were over 300 members, of whom about 130 were Walsall inhabitants.[73] At the beginning of the 15th century the guild was under a master and two wardens.[74] By the later 15th century, however, there were normally only two officers, called masters. They were chosen each year after the guild's feast and presented their accounts to the mayor, usually in August.[75] There were seven chaplains, presumably also chantry priests, attached to the guild by 1520.[76]

The guild of St. Mary or Our Lady existed by 1471. Its endowment included property in the borough. The ordinances of c. 1510-20 mention its wardens and four chantries attached to it.[77]

The two guilds seem to have been amalgamated in 1520. In that year St. John's guild was refounded and incorporated. The guild was thenceforth to be attached to both St. John's and St. Mary's chapels. Two masters or wardens were to be elected annually on 1 August in St. John's guildhall. They were licensed to acquire lands in mortmain and to make ordinances. The guild was to maintain seven chaplains, who were to perform divine office daily for the king, the queen, and the guildsmen and for their souls after death.[78] The guild was suppressed under the Act of 1547. The Crown sold small parcels of guild property in 1549, 1553, 1572, and 1590, but most of it passed to the feoffees of the town lands.[79]

In the 14th century Walsall was one of several parishes taking part in an annual procession to Lichfield in Whitsun week to make offerings at the cathedral. In 1357 the parishes involved were forbidden to carry banners as they had hitherto, because rivalry between them had led to brawling; instead they were to carry crosses only.[80] Another Whitsun custom was the brewing of ale to be sold for the upkeep of the church. In 1536-7 it was stated that by ancient usage the churchwardens had a monopoly of public brewing from the Sunday before Whitsun until the feast of Corpus Christi.[81] By the early 17th century the vicar provided bread and wine at Easter during his incumbency in return for a lump sum payment of 50s. by the parishioners.[82]

In 1604 the vicar was described as 'no preacher',[83] but his successor was considered by John Persehouse to be 'a good preacher of God's word'.[84] Royal endowment of a preacher in Walsall had already been suggested in 1549,[85] and payments for sermons were made by the mayor in the earlier 17th century.[86] There were also several gifts and bequests for sermons in the parish church. In or shortly before 1618 William Wheate of Coventry left £20 to endow four annual sermons; the vicar received £8 in 1823 but payment had lapsed by 1855.[87] By will proved in 1627 John Parker of London, a native of Bloxwich, left 20s. yearly for four more sermons; the vicar received 80p in 1972.[88] Henry Stone gave £3 a year in 1639 for a lecture or sermon to be preached on the first Tuesday of each month; the vicar received £2·78 in 1972.[89] Walsall was one of the places that benefited from a double lecture founded by John Machin of Seabridge in Stoke-upon-Trent and given from 1653 to 1660.[90]

There is some evidence of Puritanism in the parish in the earlier 17th century. In 1615 the churchwardens were alleged to have permitted a silenced minister to preach.[91] Three parishioners were presented in 1625 for receiving communion seated,[92] and in 1635 two others were said to have worn their hats during service.[93] Thomas Byrdall, assistant curate by the later 1630s and vicar by 1644, signed

[61] S.H.C. 1928, 220.
[62] Ibid. 225.
[63] Ibid. 231.
[64] W.T.C. I/83.
[65] Cal. Pat. 1548-9, 392; 1549-51, 13, 95-6, 125-6, 131, 254; 1550-3, 108, 442; 1553, 131, 218-19, 233.
[66] See p. 179.
[67] Willmore, Walsall, 445.
[68] Cal. Pat. 1558-60, 89; 1560-3, 406-7; 1563-6, p. 99; 1569-72, pp. 227, 348; W.C.L., box 16, no. 3.
[69] Cal. Pat. 1388-92, 370.
[70] Sims, Cal. of Deeds, pp. 14, 19-20, 29, 31; Cal. Pat. 1569-72, p. 348; C 1/644 no. 43.
[71] See p. 214.
[72] See p. 218.
[73] W.T.C. I/67, /89.
[74] Cal. Pat. 1401-5, 420.
[75] W.T.C. I/67.
[76] S.R.O., D. 260/M/F/1/5, f. 49v.
[77] B.M. Eg. Roll 8543; Willmore, Walsall, 169.
[78] S.R.O., D. 260/M/F/1/5, ff. 49v.-50.

[79] Cal. Pat. 1549-51, 13; 1553, 219, 233; 1569-72, p. 348; C 66/1351 m. 28; above pp. 214-15.
[80] L.J.R.O., B/A/1/3, f. 140v.
[81] C 1/816 no. 19.
[82] W.C.L., box 13, no. 12.
[83] S.H.C. 1915, 303.
[84] S.R.O., D. 260/M/F/1/5, f. 99.
[85] See p. 227.
[86] W.T.C. II/13/5, 14, and 21.
[87] 9th Rep. Com. Char. H.C. 258, p. 592 (1823), ix; Glew, Walsall, 202.
[88] S.R.O., D. 260/M/T/2/55, pp. 70-1, 161-2; L.J.R.O., B/V/6/Walsall, 1693; ex inf. Mr. L. Harper, vicar's warden (1973); below p. 270.
[89] W.T.C., Charity Box, docs. relating to Hen. Stone's Char., deed of 10 Apr. 1639; ex inf. Mr. Harper.
[90] A. G. Matthews, Congregational Churches of Staffs. 30-1.
[91] L.J.R.O., B/V/1/31, f. 35.
[92] B/V/1/47.
[93] B/V/1/55.

the Testimony in 1648, and in 1654 he was appointed assistant to the commissioners for the removal of scandalous ministers.[94] By 1661 he was preaching weekly, and his sermons were described as 'powerful' and 'practical'.[95] He denounced his parishioners for the drunkenness, swearing, sabbath-breaking, cursing, lying, oppression, and fornication which abounded in the town—'such wild grapes, such stinking fruit growing on you'.[96] Had he not died in 1662 he would almost certainly have been ejected under the Act of Uniformity of that year, like the curate of Bloxwich.[97]

By the later 18th century church attendance had declined. In 1646 there had been 1,000 communicants;[98] in 1773, however, only 70 regularly received communion, though the number rose to 120 on exceptional occasions. At that time communion services were held on the first Sunday of every month, on the three great festivals, and on Good Friday. The vicar catechized in Lent and four times in the year.[99]

A revival took place under George Fisk, vicar from 1837 to 1845 and the author of several tracts against popery.[1] In 1831 it had been alleged that services were thinly attended; sabbath-breaking prevailed in the town, and less than a fifth of the population attended church or chapel on any Sunday.[2] Fisk's sermons show that he was anxious to remedy the situation, and he took steps to promote church attendance.[3] Within three months of his arrival his preaching so packed the church that the galleries were in danger of collapse and had to be repaired,[4] and he was later described as 'a very stormy preacher', who made 'many of the ladies very nervous'.[5] He instituted evening lectures on Sundays and Thursdays, and in 1838 he established a District Visiting Society.[6] Religious societies for young men and women were also founded, and monthly instruction was given to them.[7] In 1838 three Sunday services were held and an evening service on Thursday. The three Sunday services were still held in 1851; about 1,000 people were then said to attend morning service.[8]

The incumbencies of William Allen (1871–82) and Robert Hodgson (1883–92) were another period of vigorous activity. A mission was opened in Bott Lane in 1871, probably the predecessor of St. Luke's,

Selborne Street.[9] Parochial missions were held in 1873, 1876, 1880, 1886, and 1887.[10] The clergy were active in a Gospel Temperance (Blue Ribbon Army) Mission in 1882; between 9,000 and 10,000 people took the pledge.[11] In 1885 open-air services were held in St. Luke's mission district and were well attended.[12] A warehouse in George Street was converted into a parish room in 1876. In 1886 a church house was built on the corner of Temple and Church Streets; it was replaced in 1961 by a new building in St. Matthew's Close.[13] A branch of the Church of England Working Men's Society was founded in 1877.[14] A men's guild was established c. 1886 and guilds for boys and girls c. 1892.[15] A weekly offertory was established in 1872 and provided the stipends of the curates. It was administered by a finance committee, which also acted as a parochial council. Pewrents were abolished in 1880.[16] Easter communions numbered 297 in 1883 and 765 in 1887.[17]

From the early 19th century several new churches and missions were opened from St. Matthew's. The incumbencies of Fisk and Allen in particular were marked by the establishment of new centres and the assignment of parishes to existing ones. The first mission was established at Walsall Wood in the earlier 1820s.[18] St. Peter's, Stafford Street, was begun in 1839.[19] There was a mission in the Lime Pit Bank area in 1840.[20] Bloxwich became a separate parish in 1842.[21] Pleck mission, later St. John's, was opened in 1854,[22] and Caldmore mission, later St. Michael's, in 1866.[23] A mission room was opened in Bott Lane in 1871, enlarged in 1876, and apparently replaced by the mission church of St. Luke, Selborne Street, in 1879.[24] St. George's, Persehouse Street, was begun in 1873,[25] and St. Paul's chapel was assigned a parish out of St. Matthew's in 1875.[26] There was a mission room in Adam's Row, Digbeth, c. 1896.[27] The conventional district of St. Gabriel's, Fullbrook, established in 1936, included part of St. Matthew's parish.[28] In 1959 services were begun at the Red House inn, Sutton Road, and the mission church of St. Martin, on the corner of Sutton and Daffodil Roads, was consecrated in 1960.[29]

The church of *ST. MATTHEW* has been so called since at least the late 18th century, but from at least 1391 it had been known as All Saints'.[30] It consists of a chancel with undercroft, north organ

[94] B/V/1/62; *S.H.C.* 1915, 298, 303.
[95] T. Byrdall, *The Profit of Godliness* (1666).
[96] Ibid. 222.
[97] A. G. Matthews, *Calamy Revised*, 97.
[98] *S.H.C.* 1915, 303.   [99] L.J.R.O., B/V/5/1772–3.
[1] R. Simms, *Bibliotheca Staffordiensis*, 168.
[2] *Walsall Note Book*, 256 (copy in W.C.L.).
[3] G. Fisk, *Duty and Necessity of attending Public Worship* (Walsall, 1838; copy in W.S.L. Sermons).
[4] S.R.O., D. 1287/18/26, business corresp. 1846–7, P. Potter to Lord Bradford, 3 Aug. 1837; docs. at St. Matthew's, Churchwardens' Accts. 1794–1841, f. 123.
[5] *2nd Rep. Com. Child. Emp. App. Pt. II* [432], p. q68, H.C. (1843), xv.
[6] Willmore, *Walsall*, 139; G. Fisk, *Past Mercies* (Walsall, 1838), p. iv (copy in W.S.L. Sermons); Fisk, *The Solemn Enquiry* (Walsall, 1839), p. iii (copy in W.S.L. Sermons).
[7] Fisk, *Public Worship*, 2.
[8] Ibid.; H.O. 129/380/3/2.
[9] See below.
[10] *Lich. Dioc. Mag.* Sept. 1880, 9; 1883, 29; 1886, 208; 1888, 15.
[11] Ibid. 1882, 123–4; *Walsall Red Book* (1883), 117; *Staffs. Advertiser*, 8 and 22 July 1882.
[12] *Lich. Dioc. Mag.* 1885, 142.

[13] Ibid. 1883, 29; 1887, 35; *Birmingham Daily Gaz.* 17 Aug. 1886; *Walsall Observer*, 14 Dec. 1973. For a view of the 1886 building see *Walsall Red Book* (1904).
[14] *Lich. Dioc. Mag.* 1889, 71.
[15] *Walsall Red Book* (1887), 45; (1893), 147.
[16] *Lich. Dioc. Mag.* 1883, 29; *Staffs. Advertiser*, 21 Oct., 16 Dec. 1871.
[17] *Lich. Dioc. Mag.* 1883, 29, 42; 1887, 95.
[18] See p. 281.
[19] See p. 236.
[20] *Staffs. Gaz.* 28 Nov., 5 Dec. 1840.
[21] See p. 234.
[22] See p. 237.
[23] See p. 238.
[24] *Walsall Red Book* (1879), 38; *Lich. Dioc. Mag.* 1883, 29; *Lich. Dioc. Ch. Cal.* (1877), 78; O.S. Map 1/500, Staffs. LXIII. 11. 2 (1886 edn.); below p. 233.
[25] See p. 239.
[26] See p. 236.
[27] *Lich. Dioc. Ch. Cal.* (1897), 107.
[28] See p. 239.
[29] P. J. Norris, *Parish Church of St. Matthew, Walsall* [1972 edn.], 23; *Birmingham Post*, 11 Oct. 1960; below p. 233.
[30] *Walsall Records*, 7; Shaw, *Staffs.* ii. 76; Pitt, *Staffs.* 146.

chamber, and vestries, an aisled, clerestoried, and galleried nave with north and south transepts and a north-west staircase block, and a south-west tower with a spire. The undercroft consists of a vaulted transverse passage open to the churchyard, an outer or eastern crypt, and an inner or western crypt. The present appearance of the church is largely the product of 19th-century restoration and rebuilding.

The earliest surviving part is the late-13th-century inner crypt, which has two bays of quadripartite vaulting arranged transversely. Its east wall, in which

1467; William Wotton then held the post until at least 1471.[32] Stone was brought from Sutton Coldfield (Warws.), Brewood, and Hamstead in Handsworth.[33]

As a result of the rebuilding the chancel was lengthened by three bays, with a rib-vaulted passage over a footpath below the east bay and an undercroft below the second and third bays.[34] The new undercroft, like the old, was probably intended as a vestry as it was entered by steps from the sanctuary. It contained a fireplace in the south wall. The nave was

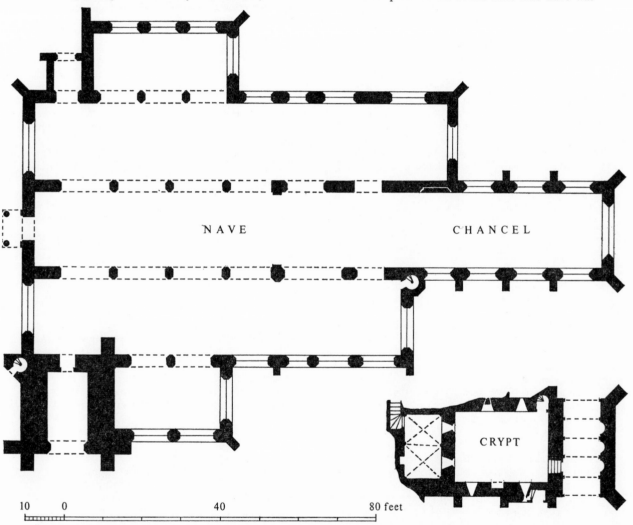

NAVE   CHANCEL

CRYPT

10   0   40   80 feet

THE CHURCH OF ST. MATTHEW IN 1819

there are two lancets, represents the limit of the chancel at that time. The crypt itself, however, was probably built when an earlier chancel was being enlarged. It was entered by a stair from the north side of the sanctuary and was probably intended as a vestry.

The medieval church was largely rebuilt in the later 15th century. The 'new work' on those parts for which the parishioners were responsible began in 1462 and continued until 1474.[31] John Nightingale was apparently master mason from 1462 to

extended eastwards into the former chancel, and in 1463 the rood screen was moved. The 'old chancel' thus became the responsibility of the parishioners; work on it was finished c. 1467.[35] The extent to which the aisles and chapels of the nave represented a rebuilding or an enlargement of earlier features is not clear. The breadth of the aisles suggests that they were widened, and their length was increased by the incorporation of former chancel chapels. The south aisle was evidently at its present width by 1465 since the tower was built outside it.[36] Of the two

[31] S.H.C. 1928, 189–212.
[32] Ibid. 189–94, 200–1, 203–4, 206, 209.
[33] Ibid. 190, 195, 201.
[34] For this para. see, unless otherwise stated, L.J.R.O., B/C/5/1821, Walsall, ground- and first-floor plans; Shaw,

Staffs. ii. 78 and plates on p. 70 and facing p. 73; Gent. Mag. lxviii (2), plate facing p. 837; Pearce, Walsall, frontispiece. The tracery and certain other details in the plates appear to be inaccurate.
[35] S.H.C. 1928, 193, 201.   [36] See p. 232.

outer chapels the northern one, St. Clement's, was probably built in the 1460s as it is mentioned in 1468.[37] The south chapel, St. Catherine's, may have been built between 1462 and 1474 or may have been a later addition. The rebuilt nave had a clerestory, and the nave, aisles, and side-chapels had low-pitched roofs. The walls were finished with stone parapets; that over the west end of the nave was embattled. The north aisle was later extended and the adjoining chancel window blocked up.

Payments are recorded for work on the tower from 1465.[38] It had four stages, the lowest serving as a porch, and was apparently surmounted by a stone spire.

The church underwent little structural change between the 15th and the 19th centuries. A porch was repaired in 1496.[39] In 1669 John Brown, described as 'of Wincott, Warwickshire', agreed to rebuild the spire.[40] It was again replaced in 1777, and it was apparently then that the tower was reduced in height by half a stage.[41] In the 18th century the 15th-century tracery in the east window of the chancel was replaced by casements.[42] In the late 18th century a Tuscan portico replaced the west porch.[43]

By the early 19th century the church was much decayed, and owing to the irregular disposition of the pews and galleries it could not accommodate the growing congregation. Accordingly Francis Goodwin of London was appointed to reconstruct it, and the work took place between 1819 and 1821.[44] The Church Building Society made a grant towards the cost, and a brief was issued in 1820.[45]

The new work, in a mainly Perpendicular style, follows the external plan of the old church exactly.[46] The walls of the nave, aisles, and side-chapels were repaired and cased in Bath stone. The old openings were blocked and new windows with cast-iron tracery made. The tracery of the larger windows is identical with that of the east window of Christ Church, West Bromwich, also Goodwin's work.[47] The chancel arch and the nave arcades were demolished and replaced by new arcades of five bays with cast-iron piers and responds on bases of Gornal stone; the spandrels of the arches are of brick. The clerestory was rebuilt in Bath stone and the nave roof was reconstructed. A flat ceiling ornamented by a timber and plaster fan-vault with turned and plastered pendants was inserted. The side-chapels were converted into transepts by the provision of new gabled roofs at right-angles to that of the nave. The west portico was demolished and the west doorway remodelled in a Gothic style, two new porches were

added immediately east of the north and south transepts, and the north-west porch was rebuilt. The tower was cased in Bath stone and the window openings were altered to provide three-stage external elevations. The buttresses, pinnacles, battlements, string-courses, and labels outside the church, except for those of the chancel, were entirely renewed.

The chancel was restored in 1879–80 by Ewan Christian of London.[48] The stone window tracery was restored to conform with that of the blocked 15th-century north-west window, the inside of which was again exposed. The chancel arch was rebuilt in sandstone, and two windows in a Perpendicular style were inserted in the gable wall above it. An organ chamber and a vestry were added on the north side of the chancel; the sedilia and south doorway also date from that time. Remains of earlier sedilia and of a south doorway had been found during the restoration. A 15th-century piscina was also restored. A staircase block was added to the east wall of the south transept. New choir vestries were dedicated in 1908.[49] The spire was restored about the same time and the upper part rebuilt in 1951.[50]

Seats in the church were being let by the later 15th century.[51] Bequests for new seats were made in the 17th century,[52] and by 1819 the nave and aisles were lined with irregular rows of box pews.[53] In 1639 Henry Stone of Walsall gave £3 a year to repair a gallery which he had erected for poor people; in 1972 £2·75 was paid towards the maintenance of the fabric.[54] Several private galleries were erected in the 18th century; by 1819 there were irregular galleries on the four sides of the nave[55] and a gallery in the chancel. In the reconstruction of 1819–21 the old pews and galleries in the nave and aisles were removed and replaced by new ones of regular design, and further galleries were erected in the side-chapels; the accommodation was thus greatly increased. At the same time the chancel gallery was removed.[56] At the restoration of 1879–80 the pews were replaced by chairs and the east gallery and the galleries over the side-chapels were removed.[57]

During the reconstruction of 1819–21 the pulpit was replaced by a three-decker, itself replaced by a stone pulpit at the restoration of 1879–80.[58] The octagonal alabaster font dates largely from the early 15th century; the rim and the lead lining of the bowl were added in 1712. Panels on the sides of the bowl enclose demi-angels bearing shields with coats of arms, including those of the Staffords and Beauchamps.[59] The medieval rood-screen, rebuilt in

[37] See p. 228. [38] *S.H.C.* 1928, 195 sqq.
[39] Ibid. 227.
[40] W.T.C. II/87. 'Wincott' may be Wilnecote (in Warws. part of Tamworth) or Wincot in Quinton (Warws., formerly Glos.).
[41] Willmore, *Walsall*, 148; docs. at St. Matthew's, Vestry Bk. 1681–1793, p. 210, f. 122 (reverse nos.).
[42] *Gent. Mag.* lxviii (2), plate facing p. 837.
[43] Ibid. lxix (2), 763–4.
[44] L.J.R.O., B/C/5/1821, Walsall, petition for faculty; Vestry Bk. 1794–1854, p. 117; Churchwardens' Accts. 1794–1841, f. 48v.; plaque in outer crypt.
[45] Churchwardens' Accts. 1794–1841, ff. 64v.–67; B.M. Ch. Br. lvi. 5.
[46] For this para. see L.J.R.O., B/C/5/1821, Walsall, plans; docs. at St. Matthew's, contracts of 22 Oct. 1819 and 30 Sept. 1820; ibid., accts. of contractor, 1820–3.
[47] See p. 55.
[48] L.J.R.O., B/C/5/1877, Walsall; Willmore, *Walsall*, 152–3; *Walsall Observer*, 5 July 1879; *Lich. Dioc. Mag.*

Sept. 1880, 9. For Lord Bradford's contribution towards the cost see S.R.O., D. 1287/1/47, Walsall accts. 1880–1, p. 33. [49] *Lich. Dioc. Mag.* 1908, 175.
[50] Photograph in *Walsall Red Book* (1909); P. J. Norris, *Parish Church of St. Matthew, Walsall* [1972 edn.], 9, stating that it was rebuilt in 1951; there is, however, a graffito dated 1877 near the base of the spire.
[51] *S.H.C.* 1928, 206, 232–3.
[52] *Charter of Corp. of Walsall*, 46.
[53] L.J.R.O., B/C/5/1821, Walsall, ground-floor plan.
[54] W.T.C., Charity Box, docs. relating to Hen. Stone's Char., deed of 10 Apr. 1639; ex inf. Mr. L. Harper, vicar's warden (1973).
[55] L.J.R.O., B/C/5/1734, Walsall; /1738, Walsall; /1751, Walsall; /1753, Walsall; /1821, Walsall, first-floor plan.
[56] Ibid./1821, Walsall. [57] *Lich. Dioc. Mag.* Sept. 1880, 9.
[58] L.J.R.O., B/C/5/1821, Walsall; W.S.L. 33/44, no. 45.
[59] S. A. Jeavons, 'The Fonts of Staffs.' *T.B.A.S.* lxviii. 19; inscription in bowl; *Gent. Mag.* lxii (2), 902–3; lxxiii (2), 828.

1463, was presumably removed at the Reformation. The present screen dates from 1915.[60] The woodwork in St. Clement's chapel dates from 1920 when the chapel was furnished as a war memorial.[61] The mutilated effigy of Sir Roger Hillary (d. 1400) is an oolitic-limestone figure of an armed knight reclining on one elbow and formerly lay on a tomb-chest.[62]

The chancel contains 15th-century stalls. There are nine seats on each side with poppy-heads, moulded arm-rests, and carved misericords; four stalls have disappeared since the end of the 18th century.[63] There was a choir by 1485, with chantry priests among its members.[64] 'Organs' were mentioned in 1473.[65] The organ which in 1605 stood in a loft on the north side of the old chancel was demolished in 1642.[66] In 1697 a new organ was built by Bernard (Father) Smith and placed in a gallery at the east end of the nave. It was replaced in 1773 by one built by Samuel Green of London.[67] An organ chamber was built on the north side of the chancel during the restoration of 1879–80.[68] By will proved in 1625 Robert Parker left £4 to be paid annually by the Merchant Taylors' Company of London to the organist and £1 to the organ-blower. The organ was to be played every Sunday morning and afternoon.[69] Payment was discontinued when the organ was destroyed in 1642, but it was resumed in 1701; £4 was still paid to the organist in 1972.[70] In 1717 Thomas Harris of Worcester conveyed houses and land in Walsall and £30 in money to the corporation to provide a further £4 a year for the organist. The grant was in satisfaction of £80 which had been given for the purpose by the Merchant Taylors' Company to Harris's uncle.[71] From 1813 the corporation increased the payment to £10.[72] Harris's gift was lost as a result of legal disputes in the 1840s.[73] From 1738 the vestry, which by then appointed the organist, paid an additional stipend.[74]

There was a chiming clock in the tower by 1466.[75] It was repaired by the corporation in the 17th century.[76] In 1795 it was replaced by a new clock with dial-plates,[77] itself replaced in 1865.[78]

In 1553 there were four bells, a sacring bell, and a sanctus bell; a fifth bell had been broken and sold.[79] By 1656, however, there were again at least five bells.[80] A new bell was cast in 1674, and the 'great bell' was recast by Joseph Smith of Edgbaston (Warws.) in 1731.[81] There were eight by 1775, when they were recast by Thomas Rudhall of Gloucester. The sixth bell was recast by Thomas Mears of London in 1809. A treble and second bell were added in 1863.[82] In 1928–9 all ten bells were recast by Taylor & Co. of Loughborough (Leics.) and the present (i) and (ii) added.[83]

The church goods in 1553 included a silver chalice and paten, parcel gilt; a gilt copper cross, two lead cruets, a tin pax, and two brass candlesticks.[84] In 1972 the plate included two silver chalices with patens, dated 1636; a silver chalice and paten given in 1882 with a parcel gilt cup on a silver base; a silver chalice and paten, parcel gilt, given in memory of Beatrice Wallace in 1962; and another parcel gilt chalice and paten. There were also a silver salver given by Jonas Slaney in 1698 and a silver flagon given by Humphrey Persehouse also in 1698;[85] a second silver flagon surmounted by a cross; and three glass flagons mounted in silver, of which one was given in 1904.

The registers date from 1570 and are complete.[86] The churchyard is mentioned in 1248.[87] By the early 1690s it was ½ a. in extent and had a lich-gate.[88] The present lich-gate dates from 1927.[89]

The mission church of St. Luke, Selborne Street, was designed by H. E. Lavender of Walsall. It is of red brick with stone and blue-brick dressings and consists of nave, narthex, and a chancel added in 1934; there is a bell in a bellcot at the west end.[90] The mission church of St. Martin on the corner of Sutton and Daffodil Roads was designed by Shipley & Foster of Walsall.[91] It has a framework of reinforced-concrete crucks with brick infilling.

A chapel of ease to Walsall parish church was founded at Bloxwich apparently by Margaret, widow of Sir Roger Hillary of Bescot, in the early 15th century. In 1413 the inhabitants of Bloxwich were granted a licence to hold services there.[92] It seems that there was no resident priest until 1515 when a chantry was founded in the chapel by Richard Hurst and John and Richard Stooke. The chaplain

[60] S.H.C. 1928, 193; J. Hope Urwin, *Walsall Parish Church: a Short Hist. and Description*, 'Nave' (copy in W.S.L. pamphs. *sub* Walsall).
[61] Norris, *Church of St. Matthew*, 7.
[62] J. Turner, *The Effigy of Sir Roger Hillary* (Walsall, 1930), 5–7 (copy in W.C.L.); Bodl. MS. Dugdale 11, f. 154v.; *Gent. Mag.* lxix (2), 763; docs. at St. Matthew's, Churchwardens' Accts. 1794–1841, f. 52v.
[63] S. A. Jeavons, 'Medieval Woodwork in S. Staffs.' *T.B.A.S.* lxvii. 49; Shaw, *Staffs.* ii. 78.
[64] Hist. MSS. Com. 24, *12th Rep. IV, Rutland*, i, p. 9.
[65] S.H.C. 1928, 218.
[66] W.T.C. I/261, art. 24; *Gent. Mag.* lxx (1), 124; S.R.O., D. 260/M/F/1/5, f. 129v.
[67] *Gent. Mag.* lxx (1), 124; C 78/1774 no. 7.
[68] F. W. Willmore, *The Organs in St. Matthew's Parish Church, Walsall* (Walsall, 1892), 14 (copy in W.C.L.); *Lich. Dioc. Mag.* Sept. 1880, 9.
[69] S.R.O., D. 260/M/T/2/54, pp. 30–1.
[70] W.T.C. I/261, art. 24; Willmore, *Organs in St. Matthew's*, 7; Sims, *Cal. of Deeds*, p. 67; C 78/1774 no. 7; ex inf. Mr. Harper; below p. 270.
[71] *9th Rep. Com. Char.* H.C. 258, p. 584 (1823), ix.
[72] Homeshaw, *Walsall*, 126, 170.
[73] Glew, *Walsall*, 180.
[74] Docs. at St. Matthew's, Vestry Bk. 1681–1793, pp. 61, 209; 1794–1854, p. 69.
[75] S.H.C. 1928, 195, 206.
[76] W.T.C. II/13.

[77] Vestry Bk. 1794–1854, p. 4; *Gent. Mag.* lxviii (2), plate facing p. 837.
[78] Inscription on clock.
[79] *Annals of Dioc. of Lichfield*, iv. 73 (copy in W.S.L. Pamphs. *sub* Lichfield); above p. 225.
[80] W.T.C. II/41, Boro. Churchwarden's Acct. 1656–7 and Churchwardens' Accts. 1674–5.
[81] Vestry Bk. 1681–1793, p. 43.
[82] Docs. at St. Matthew's, record of buildings etc., 1916, Bells; *Staffs. Advertiser*, 2 Jan. 1864.
[83] A. E. Garbett, 'Church Bells of Staffs.' *Trans. Old Stafford Soc.* 1952–3, 11; *Walsall Red Book* (1931), 63.
[84] S.H.C. 1915, 297.
[85] S. A. Jeavons, 'Church Plate in the Archdeaconry of Stafford' *T.B.A.S.* lxxiii. 21; W.S.L. 45/56, folder 28, no. 14.
[86] They are printed to 1649 by F. W. Willmore, *Transcript of First Reg. Bk. of Par. Ch. of St. Matthew, Walsall, 1570–1649* (Walsall, 1890).
[87] See p. 227.
[88] L.J.R.O., B/V/6/Walsall, 1693; S.R.O., D. 260/M/T/1/74.
[89] Inscription on lich-gate.
[90] *Staffs. Advertiser*, 25 Oct. 1879; inscription on chancel arch of St. Luke's.
[91] Ex inf. Mr. Harper.
[92] L.J.R.O., B/A/1/7, f. 151v. Margaret too was named in the licence, but she seems to have died in 1411: above p. 171. But see also n. 93 below.

was to say mass for the souls of the founders, the king, the queen, and others.[93] The chapel and its graveyard were confiscated at the suppression of the chantries, and the Crown sold them in 1549 to speculators;[94] in 1551 they were owned by John Bowes, whose son John sold them to William Gorwey and William Fynney in 1570.[95] Nevertheless in the later 16th century services presumably continued to be held in the chapel, since it was served by its own curate from at least 1561.[96] It remained dependent on St. Matthew's until the 19th century but secured burial rights in 1733.[97] In 1842 a parish was formed out of St. Matthew's.[98] The living, styled a perpetual curacy from at least 1803, became a vicarage in 1868.[99]

It is not clear who presented the curates in the 16th century. By will proved in 1616, however, William Parker of London, a native of Bloxwich, left land to the Merchant Taylors' Company, London, to provide an annual stipend of £20 for the minister. The patronage subsequently became determined by his will, although its terms were insufficiently specific. It stipulated that the minister was to have been educated at Merchant Taylors' School, London, and St. John's College, Oxford, and to be licensed by the bishop. If no curate so qualified could be found the inhabitants were to choose a suitable person, but otherwise the will did not state who was to present.[1] In consequence the inhabitants seem usually to have acted as patrons. In 1710, however, the Merchant Taylors claimed the right to choose any applicant from the school and the college, and by the early 19th century St. John's College had put forward a claim to present which it waived at the vacancy of 1803 for that turn.[2] Upon the next vacancy in 1825 the inhabitants proceeded to an election, but the vicar of Walsall, at the instigation of one of the candidates, claimed the right to present.[3] The dispute continued until 1826. By then the Merchant Taylors' Company was also claiming the patronage.[4] A compromise could not be reached and the bishop presented.[5] From 1865 the right of presentation has been held by the parishioners, though it was exercised on their behalf in 1936 by the parochial church council, and in 1942 and 1946 by the churchwardens and the secretary of the council.[6] The company, however, retained a nominal claim to the patronage until at least 1960.[7]

The pre-Reformation endowments of the chapel were those of the chantry and consisted of land in Bloxwich, Essington in Bushbury, and Tipton, worth 8 marks a year in 1515.[8] Some of the chantry lands were sold by the Crown to speculators between 1549 and 1553, and land in Tipton formerly belonging to the chantry was given by Mary I as part of the endowment of Walsall grammar school in 1554.[9] The Crown sold some remaining lands of the chantry in 1590 to an Edward Wingate.[10] In 1549 the Crown sold pasture in Harden and Bloxwich forming part of the endowment of a light, probably the light before the rood mentioned in 1548.[11]

There seems to have been no permanent endowment attached to the living between the suppression and William Parker's benefaction of 1616, though in 1604 the curate was receiving a stipend of £3 a year.[12] From 1616 the principal source of income was the annual stipend of £20 from the Merchant Taylors' Company. It was discontinued in 1643 but was evidently recovered in 1649.[13] The stipend was augmented by Queen Anne's Bounty in 1810, 1811, 1818, 1819, and 1823.[14] The gross income of the curacy in 1830 was estimated at £130, which included £90 from the Bounty, £18 from leases of the glebe, £20 from the Merchant Taylors, and £5 from fees.[15]

There was a priest's house in 1546, but by 1551 it was owned like the chapel by John Bowes.[16] It is probably identifiable with the curate's house which had been turned into an ale-house by 1613. William Parker left £20 for its restoration for the minister.[17] About the same time Sir Gilbert Wakering of Yieldfields Hall laid out money for its repair.[18] In 1830 the incumbent's house was a small brick building, probably on the north side of the churchyard where it stood in 1845.[19] The present house on the same site dates from the 19th century. The glebe lands attached to the chapel in 1682 consisted of a meadow, a croft, and a house and croft, all of which were let; the area was estimated at 4 a.[20] Those parcels may have been chantry lands concealed at the suppression, as in 1694 they were said to have been reputedly given for reading mass in the chapel.[21] In 1841 there were four small pieces of glebe land, 6 a. in extent, which were leased out.[22] Part of the glebe was sold in 1874,[23] and none remained in 1972.[24]

In 1604 the curate was described as 'no preacher'.[25] By will proved in 1627 John Parker of London, brother of William, left £2 for four sermons a year to be preached in the chapel; in 1973 £1·60 was paid to the vicar in respect of this foundation.[26] The

[93] *L. & P. Hen. VIII*, ii (1), p. 67. In 1536 and 1546 the foundation was ascribed to Sir Roger Hillary, but in 1548 to Hurst, John Stooke, and others: *S.H.C.* 1915, 302.
[94] *Cal. Pat.* 1549–51, 126.
[95] C 142/97 no. 68; S.R.O., D. 260/M/T/2/46.
[96] L.J.R.O., B/V/1/5, /7, /8, /13, /21, /23, /24, /32; Homeshaw, *Bloxwich*, 63.   [97] See p. 236.
[98] *Lond. Gaz.* 19 Aug. 1842, pp. 2243–5.
[99] L.J.R.O., B/A/1/28, p. 38; *Lich. Dioc. Ch. Cal.* (1869).
[1] H. B. Wilson, *Hist. of Merchant-Taylors' Sch.* i (1812), 416; below p. 269.
[2] Wilson, *Merchant-Taylors' Sch.* i. 418–19; L.J.R.O., B/A/1/28, p. 38.
[3] Docs. at All Saints', Out Poor Bk., entries at end of volume; Fink, *Queen Mary's Grammar Sch.* 445.
[4] W.S.L., M. 37.
[5] White, *Dir. Staffs.* (1834); L.J.R.O., B/A/1/29, p. 116.
[6] Lich. Dioc. Regy., B/A/1/40, p. 311; /41, pp. 73, 247; *Lich. Dioc. Dir.* (1972).
[7] Ex inf. the vicar (1972).
[8] *L. & P. Hen. VIII*, ii (1), p. 67.
[9] *Cal. Pat.* 1549–51, 126, 363; 1553, 219; 1553–4, 205.

[10] C 66/1351 m. 28.
[11] *Cal. Pat.* 1549–51, 125; *S.H.C.* 1915, 302.
[12] 'A Puritan Survey of the Church in Staffs. in 1604', ed. A. Peel, *E.H.R.* xxvi. 350.
[13] Homeshaw, *Bloxwich*, 87; Sims, *Cal. of Deeds*, p. 67; W.T.C. I/261, art. 24.
[14] C. Hodgson, *Account of Augmentation of Small Livings by Governors of the Bounty of Queen Anne* (1845 edn.), p. ccxcvii.   [15] L.J.R.O., A/V/1/2, no. 28.
[16] *S.H.C.* 1915, 302; C 142/97 no. 68.
[17] Wilson, *Merchant-Taylors' Sch.* i. 417–18.
[18] Homeshaw, *Bloxwich*, 100.
[19] L.J.R.O., A/V/1/2, no. 28; Lich. Dioc. Regy., B/A/2(i)/N, p. 341 (plan of churchyard).
[20] L.J.R.O., B/V/6/Walsall, 1682.
[21] Ibid./Bloxwich, 1693/4.
[22] Ibid./Bloxwich, 1841.
[23] Lich. Dioc. Regy., B/A/1/33, p. 294.
[24] Ex inf. the vicar (1972).
[25] *S.H.C.* 1915, 304.
[26] S.R.O., D. 260/M/T/2/55, pp. 71, 160–2; ex inf. Mr. L. Harper, vicar's warden of St. Matthew's (1973).

curate was ejected in 1662.[27] Communion services were held throughout the 18th century,[28] and in 1773 it was stated that prayers were read there on saints' and holy days.[29] In 1830 two services were held on Sundays and communion was celebrated monthly; there were usually 15 to 20 communicants.[30] There was an assistant curate at Bloxwich at the end of the 18th century; the minister, James Davenport, was evidently an absentee after he obtained the living of Stratford-upon-Avon (Warws.) in 1787.[31] An additional curate occurs in 1851, and by 1860 grants had been secured to maintain a permanent assistant curate.[32]

A mission was licensed in a schoolroom at Blakenall Heath in 1843,[33] and another schoolroom mission elsewhere in the parish in 1875.[34] The mission chapel of St. John the Evangelist, Sneyd Lane, was built in 1885–6. It was replaced in 1959 by St. Thomas's mission church in Cresswell Crescent,[35] a dual-purpose brick building with offices attached; there is a house for the curate-in-charge east of the church. Pinfold mission room was opened c. 1887. It was replaced in 1905 by a mission room in Old Lane, a brick building in a lancet Gothic style with a bell under a canopy at the west end.[36] The vicar began to hold services at the Saddler's Arms on the Lower Farm Estate in 1963 pending the opening of a church, and the mission church of the Holy Ascension, a dual-purpose building in Sanstone Road, was opened in 1968.[37]

A chapelwarden of Bloxwich occurs in 1553.[38] From at least 1561 there were two wardens.[39] They were evidently the wardens of the foreign of Walsall, who were sometimes called chapelwardens[40] and in 1634 and again in 1767 accounted for expenses at Bloxwich chapel.[41] Indeed in 1813 it was stated that there was no chapelwarden at Bloxwich, the foreign wardens generally acting.[42] There have been two independent churchwardens of Bloxwich from at least 1849, and presumably from 1842.[43] By c. 1730 there was a chapel clerk, appointed in the early 19th century at least by the minister.[44]

The church of *ALL SAINTS* was originally dedicated to St. Thomas of Canterbury but was rededicated in 1875.[45] It stands on the west side of Bloxwich High Street between Elmore Green Road and Elmore Row. It probably retained much of its medieval structure until the 18th century, but little

is known of its early design or development. There was a tower by the mid 16th century;[46] it was replaced in 1702–3 by one of brick with stone dressings.[47] The chapel apparently consisted in 1763 simply of a three-bay nave and tower.[48]

In 1790 the vestry decided to rebuild the chapel and to repair and alter the tower. Work on the new building was far advanced by 1792, but it seems not to have been completed until after 1794.[49] Built of brick in a classical style apparently to the designs of Samuel Whitehouse, it consisted of sanctuary and nave. The old tower, flanked by two new porches, was retained at the west end; the north porch served as a vestry and the south porch contained a staircase.[50] The money collected was not sufficient to repair the tower, but an appeal for further funds was launched in 1802.[51] The chapel was enlarged in 1833 by the addition of an apsidal chancel in a style similar to that of the nave. It had a vestry at the north-west corner and a staircase on the south side.[52]

In 1874 it was decided to enlarge and reconstruct the old church, 'plain almost to ugliness', as a Gothic building.[53] The new work, which is of brick with stone dressings, was designed by Davies & Middleton of Dudley and Birmingham and completed in 1877. The apsidal chancel was demolished and replaced by a longer structure with north vestries and south organ chamber. The plan of the old nave was retained, but the north and south walls were restored and new Gothic windows inserted in the old embrasures. Arcades of Codsall stone were intruded to support a clerestory, with exposed internal brickwork, rising above the level of the old roof. The west tower was rebuilt and heightened, and the western porches were partly reconstructed.[54] A south porch was built in the mid 1880s.[55]

The fittings of the old chapel were evidently removed during the rebuilding of the 1790s: Stebbing Shaw, at any rate, found 'nothing worthy notice'.[56] The old pews were replaced by new seating designed by Benjamin Wyatt. A three-decker pulpit was erected at the east end of the nave. There were galleries on the north, south, and west sides.[57] A fourth gallery across the chancel arch was inserted evidently in 1833; it was taken down in 1875. Also in 1875 the pews were replaced by free seating and a new stone pulpit, font, and reredos were provided.[58]

[27] A. G. Matthews, *Calamy Revised*, 489.
[28] Docs. at St. Matthew's, Walsall, Vestry Bk. 1681–1793, *passim* (accounts for sacrament wine).
[29] L.J.R.O., B/V/5/1772–3.
[30] Ibid., A/V/1/2, no. 28.
[31] Shaw, *Staffs.* ii. 81; *Gent. Mag.* N.S. xvi. 439.
[32] White, *Dir. Staffs.* (1851); *Lich. Dioc. Ch. Cal.* (1861), 141.
[33] See p. 237.
[34] Lich. Dioc. Regy., B/A/1/33, p. 334.
[35] *Lich. Dioc. Mag.* 1885, 163; 1886, 50; *Walsall Observer*, 8 May 1959.
[36] *Walsall Red Book* (1888), 126; (1905), 241; (1906), 234.
[37] *Walsall Observer*, 15 Nov. 1963; ex inf. the vicar (1972).
[38] *S.H.C.* 1915, 302.
[39] L.J.R.O., B/V/1/5, /7, /8, /21, /23, /32, /57.
[40] L.J.R.O., B/V/6/Bloxwich, 1693/4; docs. at St. Matthew's, Churchwardens' Accts. 1794–1841, f. 45v.; W.T.C. II/204 (b).
[41] W.T.C. II/41; docs. at St. Matthew's, Vestry Bk. 1681–1793, p. 143; Homeshaw, *Bloxwich*, 94.
[42] Pearce, *Walsall*, 195.
[43] L.J.R.O., B/V/6/Bloxwich, 1849.

[44] Docs. at All Saints', register 1772–1812, 9 July 1772; L.J.R.O., A/V/1/2, no. 28.
[45] W.T.C. I/54*; *Staffs. Advertiser*, 6 Nov. 1875.
[46] *S.H.C.* 1915, 302.
[47] Homeshaw, *Bloxwich*, 89–91.
[48] S.R.O., D. 1287/8/2, map.
[49] L.J.R.O., B/C/5/1792, Bloxwich; Shaw, *Staffs.* ii. 81.
[50] B/C/5/1792, Bloxwich.
[51] W.T.C. II/204 (b); S.R.O. 781; *Staffs. Advertiser*, 6 Nov. 1875.
[52] W.S.L., T. P. Wood 43; W.S.L., Staffs. Views, ii, pp. 92 (reproduced facing p. 81 above), 93a; photograph in possession of vicar; White, *Dir. Staffs.* (1834); L.J.R.O., B/C/5/1874, Bloxwich.
[53] *Staffs. Advertiser*, 6 Nov. 1875; B/C/5/1874, Bloxwich.
[54] B/C/5/1874, Bloxwich; *Staffs. Advertiser*, 21 Apr. 1877.
[55] *Kelly's Dir. Staffs.* (1884; 1888).
[56] Shaw, *Staffs.* ii. 81.
[57] L.J.R.O., B/C/5/1792, Bloxwich; A/V/1/2, no. 28; Homeshaw, *Bloxwich*, 168; photograph in possession of vicar.
[58] Homeshaw, *Bloxwich*, 168; *Staffs. Advertiser*, 6 Nov. 1875, 21 Apr. 1877; L.J.R.O., B/C/5/1874, Bloxwich.

In 1546 the chapel possessed 5 oz. of gilt plate.[59] In 1841 the plate consisted of a silver cup and a small silver salver.[60] The plate in 1972 included a silver flagon, chalice, and paten presented by J. E. Bealey in 1877[61] but dating from the 18th century;[62] a silver chalice and paten, parcel gilt, given by the communicants in 1898;[63] a silver credence paten presented in 1899; a stepped silver paten of the same period; a silver ciborium presented by H. Cheadle and his wife, parents of R. Cheadle, vicar 1960–72; a silver wafer box; and a silver alms-basin given c. 1945.[64]

There were two bells in the tower in 1548.[65] The bells were apparently recast in 1752,[66] but by 1830 there was only one bell, cast by Thomas Mears and installed in 1823.[67] A peal was planned in 1875 for the rebuilt church, and seven new bells cast by Mears & Stainbank of London were dedicated in 1887.[68] The second bell was presented by the congregation of Bloxwich Wesleyan chapel. The old bell of 1823 was retained as the tenor; the ring of eight bells thus created remained in 1972.[69]

The registers date from 1733; until 1843 they include only baptisms and burials.

In 1591 a chapelyard of 1 a., presumably the medieval graveyard, was still held by William Fynney and William Gorwey.[70] John Parker left money to repair the chapelyard in 1627.[71] From the Reformation, however, the inhabitants buried their dead at Walsall, but in 1733 ¾ a. adjoining the church was consecrated as a graveyard for Bloxwich.[72] It was enlarged in 1845[73] and restored and levelled in 1957.[74] The lich-gate dates from 1936.[75] Immediately south of the church is a preaching-cross with a plain octagonal shaft and moulded capital surmounted by a ball.

In 1797 the governors of Walsall grammar school were statutorily empowered to build a chapel at Walsall, dedicated to *ST. PAUL*, for the use of the school and the public.[76] About 1820 land was bought north of Bridge Street,[77] and a chapel there was consecrated in 1826.[78] The pews were appropriated to the governors, who leased them out.[79] The minister

was the headmaster of the grammar school; his stipend was £50 a year, and he was assigned a house.[80] In 1830 it was stated that the chapelwarden was always chosen from the school governors.[81] In 1874 the chapel was sold by the school to the townspeople for £1,000,[82] and in 1875 it was assigned a parish out of the parishes of St. Matthew and St. Peter.[83] The patronage of the vicarage passed to the vicar of Walsall, who still holds it.[84] The benefice was united with that of St. George's in 1964.[85] As headmaster of the grammar school the minister lived in a house forming part of the school buildings, at first in Park Street and from 1850 in Lichfield Street.[86] After the reorganization of 1874–5 the vicar lived in St. Paul's Close until 1886 when a vicarage house was built east of the church in Darwall Street.[87] It was sold in 1957 and a house in Buchanan Road was bought.[88]

There was a mission room at Shaw's Leasowes from c. 1876 to c. 1882.[89] A second mission room in School Street was opened in 1877 and closed in the early 1960s.[90]

The first church of St. Paul, approached from the newly built St. Paul's Street, was designed by Francis Goodwin. It was a classical building in stuccoed brick, consisting of nave and west tower;[91] a chancel was added in 1852.[92] In 1892–3 it was replaced by the present church, a larger building of Codsall sandstone designed by J. L. Pearson in a predominantly Decorated style. It consists of chancel, shallow north and south transepts, north-east vestry, aisled and clerestoried nave, and north and south porches. The chancel ends in an apse and has an apsidal south chapel and a double north aisle surmounted by an organ loft. The lower part of the walls is lined with oak panelling throughout. The vestry, though part of the original design, was added only in 1901. A tower and spire above the south porch were planned but not built.[93]

The church of *ST. PETER*, Stafford Street, was begun in 1839 on a site given by Lord Hatherton; it was consecrated in 1841.[94] Meanwhile in 1840 the vicar of St. Matthew's was licensed to hold services in a new schoolroom in John Street.[95] The living

[59] *S.H.C.* 1915, 302.
[60] L.J.R.O., B/V/6/Bloxwich, 1841.
[61] Inscriptions on plate.
[62] Ex inf. the vicar (1972), citing silversmith's rep.
[63] Inscriptions on chalice and paten.
[64] Docs. at All Saints', schedule of plate; ex inf. the vicar (1972).
[65] *S.H.C.* 1915, 302.
[66] W.C.L., box 13, no. 9.
[67] L.J.R.O., A/V/1/2, no. 28; C. Lynam, *Church Bells of the County of Stafford* (1889), 5.
[68] *Staffs. Advertiser*, 6 Nov. 1875; *Lich. Dioc. Mag.* 1887, 23.
[69] Docs. at All Saints' Vicarage, schedule of bells.
[70] *S.H.C.* 1930, 97; above p. 234.
[71] S.R.O., D. 260/M/T/2/55, pp. 71–2.
[72] L.J.R.O., B/A/27(i), pp. 217–18; Homeshaw, *Bloxwich*, 92.
[73] Lich. Dioc. Regy., B/A/2(i)/N, pp. 346–50.
[74] Order of service for dedication of restored churchyard, 1957 (copy in possession of vicar).
[75] *Walsall Red Book* (1937), 36.
[76] 37 Geo. III, c. 70 (Priv. Act); S.R.O., D. 1287/22/5, T. Hodgkins to J. Bradfield, 3 Feb. 1796.
[77] Fink, *Queen Mary's Grammar Sch.* 292; Lich. Dioc. Regy., B/A/2(i)/H, pp. 101–23; White, *Dir. Staffs.* (1834).
[78] Fink, *Queen Mary's Grammar Sch.* 257; *Staffs. Advertiser*, 30 Sept. 1826; *Rep. Com. Eccl. Revenues* [67], pp. 506–7, H.C. (1835), xxii.

[79] 37 Geo. III, c. 70 (Priv. Act); Fink, *Queen Mary's Grammar Sch.* 240.
[80] 37 Geo. III, c. 70 (Priv. Act); *Rep. Com. Eccl. Revenues*, 504–7.
[81] L.J.R.O., A/V/1/3, no. 32; Fink, *Queen Mary's Grammar Sch.* 299.
[82] Lich. Dioc. Regy., B/A/2(i)/R, p. 677; *Walsall Red Book* (1875), 64.
[83] Lich. Dioc. Regy., B/A/1/33, p. 347; *Lond. Gaz.* 14 May 1875, pp. 2575–6.
[84] B/A/1/33, p. 347; *Lich. Dioc. Dir.* (1968).
[85] See p. 239.
[86] Fink, *Queen Mary's Grammar Sch.* 275–6, 307; Pigot, *Com. Dir. Birm.* (1829), 90; *P.O. Dir. Staffs.* (1872).
[87] *Lich. Dioc. Mag.* 1886, 91.
[88] Lich. Dioc. Regy., B/A/2(i)/T, p. 59; /X, pp. 330–1.
[89] *Lich. Dioc. Ch. Cal.* (1877), 173; (1883), 195.
[90] *Walsall Red Book* (1893), 148. It disappears from *Lich. Dioc. Dir.* after the edn. of 1962.
[91] Fink, *Queen Mary's Grammar Sch.* 294–5 and plate facing p. 289; W.S.L. 33/44, no. 51; above p. 147.
[92] Lich. Dioc. Regy., B/A/2(i)/AO, pp. 500–5.
[93] *Lich. Dioc. Mag.* 1893, 180–1; *Staffs. Advertiser*, 24 Sept. 1892; ibid. 4 Jan. 1902, p. 6. For the Flemish reredos transferred from St. Mark's see below p. 239.
[94] *Staffs. Advertiser*, 21 Sept. 1839, 17 Apr. 1841, 20 July 1844; S.R.O., D. 260/M/F/5/115.
[95] *Staffs. Advertiser*, 2 and 9 May 1840.

was endowed with £2,000 capital raised by subscription, notably from Lord Bradford.[96] In 1845 a parish was assigned out of St. Matthew's.[97] The living, at first a perpetual curacy and a vicarage from 1868, has remained in the gift of the vicar of St. Matthew's.[98] The vicarage house in Bloxwich Road was built soon after the completion of the church; Lord Bradford sold the site below its market price.[99]

The following missions have been opened from St. Peter's: Birchills in 1855;[1] John Street Mission Room, opened c. 1886, closed in the early 1960s,[2] and subsequently used as a garage; St. Chad's Mission Room, Green Lane, built in 1896–7 and closed in the late 1940s.[3]

St. Peter's was designed in a lancet Gothic style by Isaac Highway of Walsall[4] and stands in a churchyard formerly surrounded by streets on four sides; the orientation is reversed. The church consists of chancel with 'south' vestry and organ chamber and 'north' chapel, nave, and 'west' tower flanked by porches. The nave and tower are of brown brick with stone dressings; the east end, added in 1910,[5] is of red brick. There were originally galleries on three sides of the nave, but those on the north and south were removed in 1938.[6] Box pews forming part of the original fittings were removed in 1868.[7]

CHRIST CHURCH, Blakenall Heath, originated in a mission licensed in 1843 at the newly built National school there.[8] In 1865 a church was started on a site in Bloxwich Road, Leamore,[9] but in the same year the foundations were moved to a site on Blakenall Heath given by Lord Bradford. The church was opened in 1870 and consecrated in 1872.[10] In 1873 a parish was assigned out of Bloxwich.[11] The Ecclesiastical Commissioners in 1874 endowed the living with £200 a year.[12] The vicarage has remained in the gift of the vicar of Bloxwich.[13] The original vicarage house north of the church was built in the 1870s; it was rebuilt on the same site in 1968.[14]

Several missions have been opened from Christ Church. St. Paul's, Little Bloxwich, was built in 1876 and closed in the 1960s.[15] St. John's, Leamore, was opened in 1883, rebuilt in 1931, and demolished in 1967.[16] St. Mary's, Coal Pool, was opened in 1892, closed in 1965, and demolished in 1970.[17] St. Chad's, a dual-purpose building in Edison Road on the Beechdale estate, was dedicated in 1958; from 1970, however, services were held in the near-by

Roman Catholic church of St. Catherine and both congregations used St. Chad's for social functions.[18] St. Aidan's, Hawbush Road, a blue-brick building with a steeply pitched roof, was opened in 1964.[19]

Christ Church is built of local limestone with Bath stone dressings and was designed in an Early English style by a Mr. Naden (probably Thomas Naden) of Birmingham.[20] It consists of chancel, north vestry, south organ chamber, north and south transepts, aisled and clerestoried nave, south porch, and west tower. The tower was included in the original design but was completed only in 1882 with funds provided by J. E. Bealey of the Hills, Bloxwich. There are five bells, also presented by Bealey.[21]

The church of *ST. JOHN THE EVANGELIST*, Pleck, originated in a mission begun in 1854 when a curate was established by Charles Bagnall to serve the district and also to act as chaplain to the collieries of John Bagnall & Sons. Lord Bradford gave a site in Pleck Road for a church and school. The school was built in 1855, and services were held there until the completion of St. John's in 1858. The living was endowed with £1,000.[22] In 1860 a parish was assigned out of St. Matthew's.[23] In 1861 Queen Anne's Bounty granted £200.[24] The vicar of St. Matthew's has remained the patron of the living, at first a perpetual curacy and a vicarage from 1868.[25] A vicarage house adjoining the church was built in 1861 and replaced by a new house on the same site in 1969.[26]

About 1898 a mission room was opened in Queen Street. It was replaced in 1902 by the iron mission church of St. James in Rollingmill Street, which was closed c. 1930; it was sold in 1933 to the Church Mission to the Deaf and Dumb, which retained it until c. 1945.[27]

The church of St. John was designed in a Decorated style by Griffin & Weller of Wolverhampton.[28] It is of limestone rubble with dressings of Codsall sandstone and consists of chancel, north vestry, south organ chamber, north and south transepts, and aisled nave with north porch and south choir vestry. The latter was apparently added in 1908.[29] The north transept has been used as a Lady chapel since 1959.[30] There is a south-eastern bell-turret containing a bell.

The church of *ST. ANDREW*, Birchills Street, originated in a mission established from St. Peter's

---

[96] Lich. Dioc. Regy., B/A/2(i)/L, p. 670; White, *Dir. Staffs.* (1851); *Staffs. Advertiser*, 11 Nov. 1843.
[97] *Lond. Gaz.* 12 Aug. 1845, pp. 2422–3.
[98] Lich. Dioc. Regy., B/A/1/30, p. 257; *Lich. Dioc. Dir.* (1972).
[99] *Staffs. Advertiser*, 17 Apr. 1841, 20 July 1844; S.R.O., D. 1287/12/3, P. Potter to Lord Bradford, 21 Feb. 1849.
[1] See below and p. 238.
[2] *Walsall Red Book* (1887), 47; *Lich. Dioc. Dir.* (1962).
[3] *Walsall Red Book* (1897), 197; *Lich. Dioc. Mag.* 1897, 10; *Lich. Dioc. Dir.* (1946; 1948–9).
[4] *Staffs. Advertiser*, 21 Sept. 1839.
[5] *Walsall Red Book* (1911), 156, 162; *Lich. Dioc. Mag.* 1911, 13.   [6] *Lich. Dioc. Dir.* (1939–40), 195.
[7] *Walsall Red Book* (1875), 66.
[8] Nat. Soc. files/Blakenall Heath, 14 Feb. 1843; Lich. Dioc. Regy., B/A/1/30, p. 227.
[9] *Staffs. Advertiser*, 14 Oct. 1854; Cason, *Blakenall Heath*, 12.
[10] Cason, *Blakenall Heath*, 12; *Staffs. Advertiser*, 25 May 1872.
[11] *Lond. Gaz.* 6 May 1873, pp. 2267–8.
[12] Lich. Dioc. Regy., B/A/2(i)/R, p. 675.
[13] Ibid., B/A/1/33, p. 268; /37, p. 259; /39, pp. 47, 322–3; /42, p. 427; *Lich. Dioc. Dir.* (1972).

[14] *Kelly's Dir. Staffs.* (1876); Cason, *Blakenall Heath*, 65.   [15] Cason, *Blakenall Heath*, 17, 55.
[16] Ibid. 22, 43, 55.   [17] Ibid. 24, 55.
[18] Ibid. 57, 70.   [19] Ibid. 59.
[20] *Staffs. Advertiser*, 25 May 1872; *P.O. Dir. Staffs.* (1860), 257; *Kelly's Dir. Birm.* (1888), 594.
[21] *Lich. Dioc. Mag.* 1882, 182; Cason, *Blakenall Heath*, 21.
[22] *Staffs. Advertiser*, 18 Apr. 1857; *Walsall Red Book* (1875), 69; Lich. Dioc. Regy., B/A/2(i)/Q, pp. 163–6.
[23] *Lond. Gaz.* 30 Oct. 1860, pp. 3905–6.
[24] C. Hodgson, *Account of Augmentation of Small Livings by Governors of Bounty of Queen Anne: Supplement* (1864), p. lxviii.
[25] Lich. Dioc. Regy., B/A/2(i)/Q, pp. 166–8; B/A/1/42, p. 459; *Lich. Dioc. Ch. Cal.* (1869); *Lich. Dioc. Dir.* (1972).
[26] *Walsall Red Book* (1875), 69; Lich. Dioc. Regy., B/A/2(i)/Y, p. 83; ex inf. the vicar (1972).
[27] *Walsall Red Book* (1899), 167; (1903), 232; (1931), 94; *Lich. Dioc. Ch. Cal.* (1902; 1903); Lich. Dioc. Regy., B/A/1/36, pp. 234–5; Char. Com. files; G.R.O., Worship Reg. no. 61631.
[28] *Staffs. Advertiser*, 18 Apr. 1857, 31 July 1858.
[29] Inscription on foundation-stone.
[30] Inscription in transept.

in 1855 in the newly built Birchills National school in Hollyhedge Lane to counteract the influence of Roman Catholicism in the area.[31] A chancel was added in 1877.[32] A mission district was assigned in 1883 and a curate appointed.[33] St. Andrew's was begun in 1884 on a site given by Lord Bradford, but completion was delayed by lack of funds. It was finally consecrated in 1887.[34] A parish was assigned out of St. Peter's in 1889.[35] Under an agreement of 1887 the first nomination to the vicarage was made by the vicar of St. Peter's and subsequent incumbents were presented by the bishop of Lichfield, who is still the patron.[36] In 1895 the Ecclesiastical Commissioners endowed the living with £150 a year from the Common Fund.[37] The vicar at first lived in Hollyhedge Lane and later in Cairns Street.[38] A site for a vicarage house south of the church was acquired in 1915;[39] the house is a red-brick building in a Queen Anne style.

The church of St. Andrew, of red brick with stone dressings, was designed by J. E. K. Cutts of London in a lancet Gothic style.[40] It consists of chancel with north chapel, south organ chamber, and east vestries, aisled and clerestoried nave, and west baptistery flanked by porches. There is a timber bell turret, containing one bell, over the junction of chancel and nave. Most of the internal brickwork of the church is exposed, and the arcades have stone piers.

The church of *ST. MICHAEL AND ALL ANGELS* originated in a mission which the vicar of Walsall established in the Caldmore district in 1866. Services were held at first in a cottage near Caldmore Green and from 1867 in the Caldmore church schools. The present church in Bath Road was built by a committee in 1870–1 as part of a scheme for subdividing St. Matthew's parish. The site was given by Thomas Marlow of Aldridge.[41] In 1872 a parish was assigned out of St. Matthew's.[42] The Ecclesiastical Commissioners endowed the benefice in 1873 with £200 a year out of the Common Fund. The vicarage has remained in the gift of the bishop of Lichfield.[43] The vicarage house west of the church was built in 1913 by Elizabeth Laing, sister of the vicar, J. F. Laing, who continued to live there after his retirement in 1921. It was conveyed to the Ecclesiastical Commissioners for permanent use as a vicarage house in 1932.[44]

The mission church of St. Mary and All Saints, Palfrey, was opened from St. Michael's in 1893.[45]

St. Michael's was designed by J. R. Veall of Wolverhampton in an Early English style.[46] It is built of red sandstone with Bath stone dressings and consists of an apsidal chancel with north-east vestry and north and south chapels, aisled nave, and west porch surmounted by vestries. The aisles were part of the original design but were not built immediately for lack of funds; the north aisle was added in 1878 and the south aisle in 1880.[47] The south chapel was built by J. F. Laing at some time between 1880 and 1884.[48] He added the north chapel and vestry in the mid 1920s in memory of Elizabeth.[49] The west porch and vestry were added apparently in 1896.[50] There is a bell on the west gable wall of the nave. The church was gutted by fire in 1964, restored, and reconsecrated in 1967.[51]

In 1871 a mission chapel dedicated to *ST. MARK* was built in Butts Road within the parish of St. Michael, Rushall.[52] A conventional district was established in 1920 with a curate-in-charge.[53] The building was consecrated in 1925,[54] and a parish of St. Mark was then formed from Rushall and from the Walsall parishes of St. George, St. Paul, and St. Peter.[55] The vicarage was in the gift of the bishop of Lichfield and the vicar of Rushall jointly from 1925,[56] but on its voidance in 1970 the rights of the patrons were suspended.[57] From 1971 to 1973 the vicar of St. Paul's acted as priest-in-charge; the church was closed in 1973[58] and demolished in 1974. A house in the Butts was acquired for the vicar *c.* 1935.[59] In 1950 a house in Westbourne Road was purchased as the vicarage house; it was sold in 1971.[60]

St. Stephen's mission church, Ryecroft, was dedicated in 1890.[61] It was at first attached to St. Michael's, Rushall, but was transferred to St. Mark's when the parish was formed.[62] It had been closed by 1946 and was then leased to the Walsall branch of the British Limbless Ex-Servicemen's Association, which bought it in 1950.[63]

The church of St. Mark, designed in a plain Gothic style by Robert Griffiths of Stafford, the county surveyor,[64] was of red brick with blue-brick dressings. It consisted of sanctuary, north organ chamber, nave, and a west vestry added in 1949.[65] Over the west end of the church was a bellcot con-

[31] *Staffs. Advertiser*, 20 Oct. 1855; Nat. Soc. files/Walsall/St. Peter (Birchills), handbill 1854; *Lich. Dioc. Mag.* 1886, 210. [32] *Walsall Observer*, 2 June 1877.
[33] *Lich. Dioc. Mag.* 1888, 10.
[34] Lich. Dioc. Regy., B/A/2(i)/T, pp. 159–60; *Lich. Dioc. Mag.* 1884, 189; *Staffs. Advertiser*, 3 Dec. 1887.
[35] *Lond. Gaz.* 22 Feb. 1889, pp. 1017–18.
[36] Lich. Dioc. Regy., B/A/2(i)/T, pp. 155–8; B/A/1/35, p. 150; *Lich. Dioc. Dir.* (1972).
[37] B/A/2(i)/U, p. 77.
[38] *Kelly's Dir. Staffs.* (1888), 362; (1904), 430.
[39] B/A/2(i)/V, p. 500; *Kelly's Dir. Staffs.* (1916), 464.
[40] *Staffs. Advertiser*, 3 Dec. 1887.
[41] *Walsall Free Press*, 31 Aug., 7 Sept. 1867; *Staffs. Advertiser*, 15 Apr. 1871; *Walsall Red Book* (1875), 74; Lich. Dioc. Regy., B/A/2(i)/R, pp. 529–32; *Staffs. Advertiser*, 5 June 1875.
[42] *Lond. Gaz.* 22 Mar. 1872, pp. 1554–5.
[43] Lich. Dioc. Regy., B/A/2(i)/R, p. 532; B/A/1/42, p. 166; *Lich. Dioc. Dir.* (1972).
[44] Inscriptions on vicarage and in church; I. K. Lowe, *St. Michael & All Angels Church, Caldmore: 100 Years* [1971], 9 (copy in W.S.L. Pamphs. *sub* Walsall); Lich. Dioc. Regy., B/V/2(i)/W, p. 435.
[45] See p. 239.

[46] *Staffs. Advertiser*, 15 Apr. 1871; *New Dist. of St. Michael & All Angels, Caldmore* (n.d. but *c.* 1872; copy in S.R.O., D. 1287/12/4, subscriptions 1870–9).
[47] *Staffs. Advertiser*, 15 Apr. 1871; *Lich. Dioc. Ch. Cal.* (1878), 194; *Lich. Dioc. Yr. Bk.* (1880), 21; *Kelly's Dir. Staffs.* (1880). [48] *Kelly's Dir. Staffs.* (1880; 1884).
[49] Ibid. (1924; 1928); inscription in church.
[50] Lowe, *St. Michael & All Angels*, 6.
[51] Inscription in porch.
[52] *Staffs. Advertiser*, 29 Apr. 1871; *Walsall Red Book* (1872), 35.
[53] Lich. Dioc. Regy., B/A/1/38, pp. 103–4.
[54] Ibid., B/A/2(i)/W, pp. 186–91.
[55] *Lond. Gaz.* 29 Dec. 1925, pp. 8637–8.
[56] Lich. Dioc. Regy., B/A/2(i)/W, p. 188; B/A/1/42, pp. 270–1. [57] Notice on door of church (1972).
[58] Ex inf. the priest-in-charge (1972); *Express & Star*, 1 May 1973. [59] *Lich. Dioc. Ch. Cal.* (1936), 35.
[60] Lich. Dioc. Regy., B/A/2(i)/X, pp. 191–2; ex inf. the priest-in-charge. [61] *Walsall Red Book* (1891), 65.
[62] Ibid. (1938), 76.
[63] Ex inf. the priest-in-charge.
[64] *Walsall Observer*, 29 Apr. 1871. For Griffiths see *P.O. Dir. Staffs.* (1872), *sub* Stafford.
[65] Ex inf. the priest-in-charge.

taining a bell. The church contained a Flemish carved wooden reredos probably of the 16th century, which was brought from St. Mary's, Wolverhampton, in 1948; it was transferred to St. Paul's in 1973.[66]

The church of *ST. GEORGE*, Persehouse Street, was built in 1873–5 as part of a scheme for dividing St. Matthew's parish.[67] Lord Hatherton gave the site.[68] In 1878 a parish was assigned out of St. Matthew's and the vicarage was endowed with £200 a year.[69] It was originally intended that the patronage should be exercised alternately by the vicar of St. Matthew's and by a committee of three laymen,[70] but in fact the incumbents were nominated by the vicar of St. Matthew's.[71] A vicarage house in that part of Persehouse Street now called Arboretum Road was dedicated in 1892; Lord Hatherton gave the site.[72] In 1964 the benefice was united with that of St. Paul's, and St. George's was demolished.[73]

St. George's was designed by Robert Griffiths of Stafford in a Geometric style. It originally consisted of a chancel, with south organ chamber and north vestries, and an aisled nave; a side chapel was added in 1911. A tower and spire were planned but never built. The building was of coursed limestone rubble with facings of Codsall and Penkridge sandstone. The inside walls were faced in brick with Bath stone dressings; the piers of the arcade were of York stone.[74]

A mission church of *ST. MARY AND ALL SAINTS* in Sun Street, Palfrey, was built in 1893 and a conventional district assigned from the parish of St. Michael and All Angels.[75] The church, however, soon proved too small for the needs of the district, whose population was estimated at 5,000 in 1897.[76] A larger church was built on the corner of Sun and Dale Streets in 1901–2; Thomas Marlow gave the site.[77] The living was endowed with £1,000.[78] In 1902 a parish was assigned out of St. Michael's.[79] The vicarage has remained in the gift of the bishop of Lichfield.[80] The vicarage house east of the church was built in 1909.[81]

The church of St. Mary and All Saints was designed by J. E. K. and J. P. Cutts of London[82] in a mixed Tudor style. It is of red brick and consists of a chancel, with north chapel, organ chamber,

north-east vestry, and south chapel, an aisled and clerestoried nave, and north and south porches. There is a bellcot with one bell. The former mission church, still used as a parish hall, is built of corrugated iron in a severe Gothic style.

The church of *ST. GABRIEL*, Fullbrook, originated in a mission founded in 1936 when a conventional district was formed out of the parishes of St. Matthew, Walsall, St. Michael, Caldmore, St. Mary, Palfrey, and St. Paul, Wood Green, Wednesbury. A curate-in-charge was appointed by the bishop of Lichfield and received a stipend of £300.[83] Services were at first held in the mission church of the Good Shepherd at Delves Green, transferred from St. Paul's parish.[84] In 1938 a site in Walstead Road was acquired for the new church, which was consecrated in 1939. The cost of erection was met largely by a bequest from J. F. Laing, vicar of St. Michael's 1877–1921.[85] Late in 1939 the district became a parish.[86] The living, at first a perpetual curacy and from 1969 a vicarage, has remained in the gift of the bishop of Lichfield.[87] The incumbent's house was in Broadway; the present house south-east of the church was built in 1956.[88]

The mission church of the Annunciation on the Yew Tree estate, West Bromwich, was opened from St. Gabriel's in 1958.[89]

St. Gabriel's was designed by Lavender & Twentyman of Wolverhampton.[90] It is a red-brick building in a modern style and consists of chancel surmounted by tower, north Lady chapel, nave, and west baptistery; there is a gallery over the baptistery. At the west end the church is joined by a covered way to a hall, opened in 1971.[91]

ROMAN CATHOLICISM. Among the numerous recusants who occur in Walsall from the early 1580s[92] were several prominent local families. Members of the Birch family of Goscote were presented as recusants until at least 1668; John Birch was sequestered for recusancy by 1648.[93] The wives of William Mountfort of Bescot Hall and of his son and heir Sir Edward were both stated to be recusants in 1605 and 1607, and Sir Edward was returned as a 'half recusant' in 1607.[94] Simon Mountfort had

[66] Ex inf. the priest-in-charge; *Kelly's Dir. Staffs.* (1888), 428; *Walsall Observer*, 2 Nov. 1973.
[67] Lich. Dioc. Regy., B/A/2(i)/S, pp. 70–4; *Walsall Red Book* (1875), 72; *Staffs. Advertiser*, 5 June 1875. For schemes for a church in the Lichfield Street area in 1857 and one in Holtshill Lane in 1866 see S.R.O., D. 1287/18/29, business corresp. 1857, P. Potter to Lord Bradford, 9 Apr. 1857; D. 260/M/E/174, 23 Oct. 1866.
[68] Lich. Dioc. Regy., B/A/2(i)/R, p. 697.
[69] *Lond. Gaz.* 26 Feb. 1878, pp. 954–5; 5 July 1878, p. 3972.
[70] *Staffs. Advertiser*, 5 June 1875.
[71] Lich. Dioc. Regy., B/A/1/34, p. 54; /37, p. 300; /39, p. 87.
[72] *Lich. Dioc. Mag.* 1892, p. 53; S.R.O., D. 260/M/E/173, statement for Mich. 1891; *Kelly's Dir. Staffs.* (1904), 427; (1912), 438.
[73] *Lond. Gaz.* 3 Apr. 1964, p. 2898; *Walsall Observer*, 3 Jan. 1964.
[74] *Staffs. Advertiser*, 29 Nov. 1873, 5 June 1875; *Walsall Red Book* (1912), 202.
[75] *Walsall Red Book* (1894), 149, 173; *Lich. Dioc. Ch. Cal.* (1894), 135.
[76] *Lich. Dioc. Mag.* 1897, 42.
[77] Lich. Dioc. Regy., B/A/2(i)/U, p. 550; *Lich. Dioc. Mag.* 1903, 23; inscription on foundation-stone.
[78] Lich. Dioc. Regy., B/A/1/36, p. 304.

[79] *Lond. Gaz.* 30 Dec. 1902, pp. 8977–8.
[80] Lich. Dioc. Regy., B/A/1/36, pp. 305–6; *Lich. Dioc. Dir.* (1972).
[81] Inscription on foundation-stone.
[82] *Walsall Observer*, 20 Dec. 1902.
[83] Lich. Dioc. Regy., B/A/1/40, pp. 209–11. By 1939 the district also included part of the parish of St. John, Pleck: B/A/2(i)/W, p. 651.
[84] B/A/1/40, pp. 212–14.
[85] B/A/2(i)/W, pp. 646, 651–5.
[86] *Lond. Gaz.* 1 Dec. 1939, pp. 8031–2.
[87] B/A/2(i)/W, p. 673; *Lich. Dioc. Dir.* (1972).
[88] Ex inf. the vicar (1972).   [89] See p. 60.
[90] *Walsall Observer*, 11 Feb. 1939.
[91] Ex inf. the vicar.
[92] See e.g. *S.H.C.* 1929, 37, 39, 42; *C.R.S.* xviii. 303–5, 307, 309; *C.R.S.* lx. 112; *S.H.C.* 1915, 298; *Staffs. Cath. Hist.* iv. 28–9; ibid. v. 28; L.J.R.O., B/V/1; Glew, *Walsall*, 117–18; *S.H.C.* 4th ser. ii. 88.
[93] *S.H.C.* 1929, 37; *C.R.S.* xviii. 297, 299–300; liii. 176; lvii. 145, 151; lx. 112; lxi. 86, 218; *Staffs. Cath. Hist.* iv. 28; L.J.R.O., B/V/1/33 sqq. to /75; *S.H.C.* 4th ser. ii. 88; above p. 174. Dorothy Birch, widow, occurs among the Roman Catholics of Walsall in 1705 and 1706: *Staffs. Cath. Hist.* xiii. 46.
[94] Hist. MSS. Com. 9, *Cecil*, xvii, pp. 623, 643; *Staffs. Cath. Hist.* iv. 28–9.

been sequestered for recusancy by 1648, and his son Edward was maintaining a priest at Bescot Hall in 1671.[95] Edward Purcell and his wife were returned as recusants in the foreign in 1630, and members of the family continued to appear among the recusants of the parish until at least 1668; by then the family lived at Yieldfields Hall.[96] Thirty-two recusants were returned in 1657,[97] and in 1676 there were stated to be 40 papists.[98] Thirty-two papists were listed in 1705.[99] In 1767 110, including children, were returned, all either farmers or 'common trading people and labourers'.[1] John Bradford, the Independent minister at Walsall in the later 1780s, claimed that he found there 'as much papists as those at Rome'.[2] In 1786, however, the constables returned only 19, of whom 16 were in the foreign.[3]

A priest named Timothy Hayes was apparently working in Walsall at the time of his arrest in 1605.[4] There was probably a mass-centre at Bescot Hall by 1671: in that year Edward Mountfort and his wife were maintaining a 'Romish priest' there named Francis Dormer alias Johnson. Dormer was executed at Worcester in 1678 and was stated to have left £1,500 out of the Bescot estate for superstitious uses, evidently as a trustee of Edward Mountfort.[5] The Purcells too seem to have maintained priests,[6] and in 1701 Thomas Purcell of Wolverhampton gave £160 to the Roman Catholic clergy to be used after his death to support a mass-centre at Yieldfields Hall. A priest was to spend two nights there every month and say a mass for Thomas's soul and another for his wife's; he was also to instruct 'all the poor Catholics . . . in the neighbourhood' and administer the sacraments to them. Thomas nominated a Philip Higgins as the first priest if he was available; otherwise the appointment was left to the vicar apostolic of the Midland District.[7] In 1773 a non-resident priest named Taylor was serving Yieldfields,[8] and from c. 1786 the centre was the responsibility of John Perry, the newly appointed out-priest at Wolverhampton, who said mass there one Sunday a month. The occupants of Yieldfields ceased to be Roman Catholics c. 1800, but mass continued to be said in a small room at the top of the house.[9] By the 18th century Walsall Roman Catholics also attended the centre at Oscott in Handsworth, where there was a resident priest.[10]

About 1800 a Revd. James Gordon left money to support a mission in the neighbourhood, and Perry bought a house and shop in Harden Lane (now Harden Road), Bloxwich. The shop was lengthened and converted into a chapel, and Perry appointed an émigré priest as his resident assistant. He was succeeded in 1804 by another émigré, who was followed in 1807 by Francis Martyn. By then the number of communicants, which c. 1800 never exceeded 20, had reached about 50, and in 1808 there were 90 Easter communicants. The chapel became too small for the growing congregation and was enlarged in 1808 to hold about 300. The dedication was to St. Thomas the Apostle.[11] By will proved in 1819 Perry left the property to the vicar apostolic of the Midland District.[12] The congregation exceeded 300 by 1819, and Martyn then opened a centre in Walsall itself.[13] In 1851 the average Sunday mass attendance at St. Thomas's was 145, but the congregation was very scattered, some living 6 miles away.[14] The church was replaced by St. Peter's in Bloxwich in 1869, but the building still stood in 1974 when it was known as Cromwell Cottage and was occupied by a women's hairdressing business.

In 1819 the assembly room at the Dragon in High Street, Walsall, having been leased and fitted up as a chapel, was opened by Martyn as a mass-centre.[15] It soon proved too small, and in 1825 Martyn began to build a chapel on the Mount. The site was given by Joseph Cox and his wife, who also sold the land to the north for use as a burial ground. Joseph Bagnall of Spring Hill, a Walsall tanner and a member of the congregation, was a notable contributor towards the cost of the chapel, and the 16th earl of Shrewsbury came to the rescue when the expense proved much greater than had been estimated. The chapel, dedicated to St. Mary and designed in a Grecian style by Joseph Ireland, was opened in 1827.[16] The presbytery to the south was built at the same time, and Martyn moved there from St. Thomas's, which had a separate priest from 1829.[17] St. Mary's was consecrated in 1891.[18] Communicants numbered some 400 in the earlier 1830s,[19] and Sunday mass attendance averaged 700 in 1850–1. Half of those attended a mass at 8 a.m. held 'for poor people who from want of proper clothes do not like to appear out of doors at a later period of the

[95] See p. 172 and below.
[96] S.R.O., D. 1287/9/10, return of Staffs. papists by bp. of Coventry and Lichfield Mar. 1629/30; L.J.R.O., B/V/1/52, 55, 71, 75; S.H.C. 4th ser. ii. 88; W.T.C. II/13/49, dole acct.; S.H.C. v (2), 246–7; S.H.C. 1923, 126.
[97] S.H.C. 4th ser. ii. 88.   [98] See p. 145.
[99] Staffs. Cath. Hist. xiii. 46. The following year 29 were returned: ibid. 46–7.   [1] Ibid. vii. 25–9.
[2] Willmore, Walsall, 381; A. Willis, Hist. of Bridge St. Chapel, Walsall (Walsall, 1893), 10; A. G. Matthews, Congregational Churches of Staffs. 139.
[3] W.T.C. II/178/9.
[4] Cal. S.P. Dom. 1603–10, 268. Two of the Gunpowder Plot conspirators were taken at Walsall in Nov. 1605: Hist. MSS. Com. 9, Cecil, xvii, p. 503.
[5] C 5/164/12.   [6] Homeshaw, Bloxwich, 102.
[7] B.A.A., A. 416. The priest was also to say two monthly masses for Thomas's parents and for the souls in Purgatory at some other time.
[8] Staffs. Cath. Hist. vii. 29.
[9] 'Catholic Chapels in Staffs.' Cath. Mag. v (1834; printed in Staffs. Cath. Hist. xiv), 307–8; Homeshaw, Bloxwich, 104; W.T.C. II/182, II/183/3. For the second priest at Wolverhampton, established under the will of Bp. Bonaventure Giffard (d. 1734) with the duty of serving

the surrounding area, and also for Perry see Cath. Mag. v. 383–4; V.C.H. Staffs. iii. 110, 112 n. The tenants in the later 18th century were the Partridges, who were Roman Catholics: W.S.L., S. MS. 453; W.T.C. II/178/9 sqq.
[10] Cath. Mag. v. 310; B. W. Kelly, Hist. Notes on Eng. Cath. Missions, 410; C.R.S. xiii. 290–1; V.C.H. Warws. vii. 399.
[11] Cath. Mag. v. 308. This gives the 1804 priest as L. Bertrand, but he signs the register in 1805 as G. S. Bertrand (B.A.A., R. 83, p. 1). Before 1805 the Sedgley Roman Catholic register was used for the mission: ibid., note on title-page. For the situation of the chapel see W.S.L., S. MS. 417/Walsall, no. 843.
[12] B.A.A., C. 370.
[13] Cath. Mag. v. 308–9.
[14] H.O. 129/380/3/2 (printed in Staffs. Cath. Hist. viii. 32).
[15] Cath. Mag. v. 311; Laity's Dir. (1820); S.H.C. 4th ser. iii. 142.
[16] Cath. Mag. v. 311–12. For Bagnall see White, Dir. Staffs. (1834), 430.
[17] Laity's Dir. (1827), 26; Pigot, Com. Dir. Birm. (1829), 90; St. Peter's Cath. Church, Bloxwich, list of priests (Walsall, 1956; copy in W.C.L.).
[18] Walsall Red Book (1892), 161.
[19] Cath. Mag. v. 312.

Canal junction south of Wolverhampton Street, with Albion Flour Mill in the background

Lower Rushall Street, showing houses adapted as workshops

WALSALL

WALSALL: ST. PATRICK'S ROMAN CATHOLIC CHURCH opened in 1966

WEST BROMWICH: BRATT STREET SCHOOL
opened in 1858

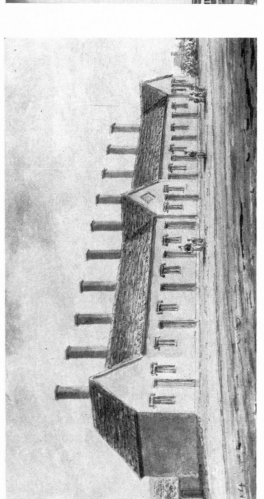

WALSALL: MOLLESLEY'S ALMS-HOUSES IN 1845

WEST BROMWICH: CARTER'S GREEN WESLEYAN METHODIST CHAPEL
opened in 1876

day'.[20] In 1967 mass was being said in the hall attached to St. Martin's Anglican church in Sutton Road; by 1974 it was being said in the church.[21] The Roman Catholic population of St. Mary's parish in 1973 was 2,100.[22] There was a community of Sisters of Charity of St. Paul in the parish c. 1853–63.[23]

St. Patrick's Church on the north side of Blue Lane East, a building of 1855–6 in a Gothic style, was founded from St. Mary's to serve the large Irish population in that part of the town.[24] A church was built on a site to the west on the corner of Green Lane and Blue Lane East in 1965–6; designed in a modern style on a basic V-shape by B. V. James of Harrison & Cox, Birmingham, it is of brown brick with dressings of blue brick and concrete. The earlier church was demolished and a new school built on the site.[25] The presbytery on the south side of Blue Lane East was built in 1909–10 with accommodation for five priests.[26] A chapel of ease dedicated to St. Catherine Labouré was built in 1961–3 on the Beechdale estate; since 1970 it has been shared with the Anglicans, whose former mission church of St. Chad has been shared for social functions. Designed by J. T. Lynch of Brierley Hill, St. Catherine's is an octagonal building of brown brick surmounted by a flèche.[27] The Roman Catholic population of St. Patrick's parish in 1973 was 2,250.[28] The Sisters of Charity of St. Paul opened St. Patrick's convent in Arboretum Road in 1927.[29]

St. Peter's Church in High Street, Bloxwich, was opened in 1869 on land given by Charles Beech. Of brick and Bath stone, it was designed by Bucknall & Donnelly of Birmingham in a Gothic style with apsidal sanctuary and aisled and clerestoried nave. It was extended and renovated between 1952 and 1954, with Jennings, Homer & Lynch of Brierley Hill as architects; the main addition was a westward extension to High Street with a façade of two towers. The presbytery, which was built at the same time as the church, adjoins it on the south-east.[30] The Roman Catholic population of St. Peter's parish in 1973 was 1,700.[31] In 1904 the Sisters of Charity of St. Paul of Chartres bought Wallington House and some 20 a.; they opened a secondary school at the convent in 1905 and erected school buildings in 1909. The school was closed in 1964 and the nuns left.[32]

In 1958 a priest was appointed to a newly formed parish for the Harden area, and at first he used Edgar Stammers school in Harden Road for Sunday mass. The church of St. Thomas of Canterbury in Dartmouth Avenue was built in 1959–60. Designed by Jennings, Homer & Lynch of Brierley Hill, it is of brick and is cruciform in plan with an apsidal east end and a south-west tower. A presbytery, completed in 1959, adjoins it.[33] The Roman Catholic population of St. Thomas's parish in 1973 was 834.[34]

PROTESTANT NONCONFORMITY. ASSEMBLIES OF GOD. The Assemblies of God registered premises in Stafford Street in 1943; the registration was cancelled in 1945.[35] They registered Glad Tidings Hall in Broadway North in 1944, and that registration too was cancelled in 1945.[36] They registered the Bible Pattern Church in Lower Hall Lane as Glad Tidings Hall in 1945 and replaced it with the newly built Glad Tidings Hall Pentecostal Church in Corporation Street West, which was registered in 1958.[37] In 1967 the Assemblies also reopened the former Bethel Gospel Church in Stokes Street, Bloxwich, as Bethel Pentecostal Church.[38] In 1970 the former Catholic Apostolic Church in Brace Street was being used by West Indian members of the Church of the Assemblies of God.[39]

BAPTISTS. There was a Baptist congregation at Walsall in 1651 when Robert Stotesbury and Thomas Cumberlidge signed on its behalf the letter addressed to Cromwell by Baptist groups in the Midlands.[40] Cumberlidge was a tinker who had served in Henry Stone's Parliamentarian troop during the Civil War and was a ring-leader in the anti-inclosure riots at Walsall in 1653.[41] There was at least one Anabaptist in the parish in 1663,[42] and the vicar reported one in 1773.[43]

The house in New Street registered by the occupier, Robert Benton, in 1826[44] was presumably for Baptists since a room in Benton's house in New Street was used by a group of five for Particular Baptist preaching for a few Sundays in 1831. It was then replaced by the larger assembly room at the Black Boy inn in New Street. The group consisted at least in part of seceders from Bridge Street Congregational church who had long held Baptist views. There was a resident pastor from 1832, and a chapel with a school was built on the corner of

[20] Staffs. Cath. Hist. viii. 32.
[21] Walsall Observer, 14 Apr. 1967; ex inf. the parish priest of St. Mary's (1974).
[22] Cath. Dir. of Archdioc. of Birm. (1974).
[23] Cath. Dir. (1854; 1863), showing them in charge of the girls' school; G. Hudson, Mother Geneviève Dupuis, 150.
[24] Glew, Walsall, 30; Cath. Dir. of Province of Birm. (1915), 56; above p. 238.
[25] Cath. Dir. of Archdioc. of Birm. (1969), 230; Express & Star, 10 June, 3 Oct. 1966; Walsall Observer, 3 June 1966; plate on facing page.
[26] Cath. Dir. of Province of Birm. (1915), 57.
[27] Cath. Dir. of Archdioc. of Birm. (1964), 204; Walsall Observer, 17 May 1963; G.R.O., Worship Reg. no. 69547; above p. 237.
[28] Cath. Dir. of Archdioc. of Birm. (1974).
[29] Ex inf. the sister superior (1974); above p. 152.
[30] St. Peter's Catholic Church, Bloxwich (Walsall, 1956; copy in W.C.L.); Staffs. Advertiser, 18 Sept. 1869.
[31] Cath. Dir. of Archdioc. of Birm. (1974).
[32] Cath. Dir. of Province of Birm. (1913), 108; Homeshaw, Bloxwich, 154; D. E. Parry and K. F. Jones, Bloxwich in History (Bloxwich, 1941), 20 (copy in W.C.L.); Evening Mail, 29 Apr. 1964.
[33] Cath. Dir. of Archdioc. of Birm. (1960), 198; (1961), 198–9.
[34] Ibid. (1974).
[35] G.R.O., Worship Reg. no. 60656.
[36] Ibid. no. 60913.
[37] Ibid. nos. 61193, 66802.
[38] Express & Star, 4 Dec. 1967.
[39] St. Michael & All Angels, Caldmore, Par. Mag. June 1970 (copy in W.C.L.).
[40] A. G. Matthews, Congregational Churches of Staffs. 36.
[41] Homeshaw, Walsall, 41; above pp. 145, 182.
[42] L.J.R.O., B/V/1/71. Two others, including Stotesbury, were included but deleted.
[43] L.J.R.O., B/V/5/1772–3.
[44] S.H.C. 4th ser. iii. 67 (wrongly giving the year as 1825)

Goodall and Freer Streets in 1833.[45] A branch Sunday school was started at Short Acre to the north of the town in 1836, and a schoolroom was built there in 1840; another was opened in Newhall Street about the same time. Both still existed in 1855.[46] The chapel was enlarged in 1849 and two schoolrooms were built.[47] On Census Sunday 1851 there was a congregation of 123 in the morning and 215 in the evening, numbers said to be unusually low.[48] There was also an attendance of 20 at an afternoon service that day at the Short Acre schoolroom.[49] Goodall Street was closed in 1918; the building was sold and has been demolished. The congregation worshipped at the Temperance Hall until 1919 when a new church was opened on the corner of the Crescent and Lumley Road. It is of wood and asbestos; a brick Sunday-school building was added at the rear in 1934.[50] In 1971 the church had 14 members.[51]

A small group of Particular Baptists, apparently seceders from Goodall Street, worshipped from 1840 in a room in the town and in 1845 acquired the former Primitive Methodist chapel on the corner of Lower Hall Lane and Newport Street. Attendance on Census Sunday 1851 was 45 in the morning, 22 in the afternoon, and 65 in the evening; there was no Sunday school. The chapel was replaced by the Strict Baptist chapel in Midland Road begun in 1909 and opened in 1910; it is of brick with terracotta dressings on the façade.[52]

In 1845 the minister of Goodall Street and several others separated from that church, worshipping first in the assembly-room attached to the Dragon and then in the club-room of the Black Boy and also in a room attached to the Green Man in Dudley Street. In 1846 they began work on Ebenezer, a brick chapel on the corner of Stafford Street and Littleton Street West; it was opened in 1847.[53] In 1851 it was described as a General Baptist church, and on Census Sunday it had a congregation of 55 in the morning and 150 in the evening. There was then a Sunday school.[54] A gallery was erected in 1859. In 1869 the building was enlarged and a classical façade added; the single-storey school at the rear was rebuilt with two storeys.[55] In 1971 there were 113 members and 104 children and young people.[56] Ebenezer was replaced by a new church in Green Lane in 1972; designed in a modern style by Charles Brown, it is built of dark brick and includes classrooms and ancillary facilities.[57] By 1973 the old church was occupied by the Church of God at Walsall.

Work was begun on a chapel in Vicarage Walk, Caldmore, in 1878 under the auspices of Ebenezer. It was opened in 1879, and the congregation became an independent church in 1881.[58] Designed in an Italian style by W. F. Markwick of Walsall, it is of brick with dressings of stone and moulded plaster. Initially it contained two schoolrooms; the adjoining schools were built in 1883–4.[59] In 1971 Vicarage Walk had a membership of 107 with 70 children and young people.[60] By the earlier 1880s Vicarage Walk was running the mission established in Dudley Street by Thomas Gameson c. 1872; his sons A. and C. H. Gameson continued to support it after his death in 1887, and it still existed c. 1916.[61]

The church in Bell Lane in the part of the Delves added to Walsall in 1931 was registered in 1951.[62] In 1971 there were 68 members and 98 children and young people.[63]

A new Baptist congregation was worshipping in the Temperance Hall in 1867,[64] and there was a temporary Baptist church at the assembly-room of the Royal Oak in Ablewell Street in the early 1870s.[65]

BETHEL GOSPEL CHURCH. The Bethel Gospel Church began to hold services in Bloxwich in 1930, using the drill hall and then various warehouses. A church was opened in Stokes Street in 1932 and continued in use until c. 1964. It was reopened by the Assemblies of God in 1967.[66]

BIBLE PATTERN CHURCH. The Bible Pattern Church Fellowship registered the Tabernacle in Lower Hall Lane in January 1944. By October 1945 it had been taken over by the Assemblies of God.[67]

BRETHREN. A building in Bridge Street was registered for Plymouth Brethren in 1863.[68] By 1871 they had moved to a meeting-room in Burrowes Street, still used in the later 1930s but closed by 1964.[69] Caldmore Gospel Hall in West Bromwich Street was registered for Brethren in 1921;[70] the building had been extended by 1973. A meeting-room off Wolverhampton Road was registered for Brethren in 1936; the registration was cancelled in 1939.[71] A meeting-room in Lower Hall Lane was registered for Brethren in 1955; it was replaced by a meeting-room in Sandymount Road, registered in 1967.[72] Stephenson Hall in Stephenson Square on the Beechdale estate was registered for Plymouth Brethren in 1957.[73]

[45] B. A. Millard, *Goodall St. Chapel, Walsall, 1833–1908*, 3–6 (copy in W.C.L.); T. G. Wilkins, *The Founding of the Baptist Cause in Walsall*, 4–5 (copy in W.C.L.); *Vicarage Walk Bazaar Gaz.* no. 1 (copy in W.C.L.); A. Willis, *Hist. of Bridge St. Chapel, Walsall* (Walsall, 1893), 16.
[46] Millard, *Goodall St. Chapel*, 8; Glew, *Walsall*, 35; H.O. 129/380/3/1.
[47] Millard, *Goodall St. Chapel*, 9.
[48] H.O. 129/380/3/2. For the reason see above p. 131.
[49] H.O. 129/380/3/1.
[50] Ex inf. Mrs. E. Henshaw, correspondent (1974).
[51] *Baptist Handbook* (1972), 180.
[52] R. F. Chambers, *Strict Baptist Chapels of Eng.* iv. 9; Wilkins, *Baptist Cause in Walsall*, 15–16; H.O. 129/380/3/2; O.S. Map 1/500, Staffs. LXIII. 10. 10 (1886 edn.). The Midland Rd. chapel is dated 1909.
[53] Wilkins, *Baptist Cause in Walsall*, 7; *Vicarage Walk Bazaar Gaz.* no. 1.   [54] H.O. 129/380/3/1.
[55] Wilkins, *Baptist Cause in Walsall*, 13–14, 19; *Walsall Red Book* (1939), 77.
[56] *Baptist Handbook* (1972), 180.

[57] *Walsall Observer*, 13 and 27 Oct. 1972; *Express & Star*, 23 Oct. 1972.
[58] *Vicarage Walk Bazaar Gaz.* no. 1.
[59] *Walsall Red Book* (1880), 123–4; (1884), 151; (1885), 56.   [60] *Baptist Handbook* (1972), 180.
[61] *Walsall Red Book* (1884), 142; (1917), 45. It is not mentioned in later edns.
[62] G.R.O., Worship Reg. no. 62964.
[63] *Baptist Handbook* (1972), 180.
[64] *Walsall Free Press*, 12 and 26 Jan., 9 Mar. 1867.
[65] *Walsall Red Book* (1872), 38.
[66] *Express & Star*, 26 Apr. 1966; *Walsall Red Book* (1932), 82; above p. 241.
[67] Worship Reg. no. 60695; above p. 241.
[68] Worship Reg. no. 15821 (cancelled 1876 on certificate of supt. registrar).
[69] R.G. 10/2962 no. 119; Worship Reg. no. 23014 (cancelled 1964 on revision of official list); *Walsall Red Book* (1939), 83.
[70] Worship Reg. no. 48125.   [71] Ibid. no. 56578.
[72] Ibid. nos. 65266, 70877.   [73] Ibid. no. 66403.

The Delves Gospel Hall, a wooden building in Talke Road in the area added to Walsall in 1931, was registered for Brethren in 1955. A new brick hall in front of it was registered in 1958, but the old building continued to be used as a Sunday school.[74]

CATHOLIC APOSTOLIC CHURCH. A Catholic Apostolic Church on the corner of White and Brace Streets was consecrated in 1876. It ceased to be used as such c. 1928.[75] It was used by the congregation of St. Michael's, Caldmore, during the restoration of St. Michael's from 1964,[76] and in 1970 it was occupied by the Assemblies of God.[77] In 1973 it was used by Toc H.

CHRISTADELPHIANS. The Christadelphians began to hold meetings at Walsall about the early 1880s, using the Temperance Hall and later the Athenaeum Buildings and the Central Hall. In 1910 they took over the chapel in Lower Hall Lane vacated by the Strict Baptists.[78] A room in Tudor House, Bridge Street, was registered as a Christadelphian meeting-room in 1936 and replaced by a hall in premises in Upper Bridge Street, registered in 1940.[79]

CHRISTIAN SCIENTISTS. The Christian Scientists registered premises in Denmark Road (now Broadway North) in 1933. The society no longer existed in 1954.[80]

CONGREGATIONALISTS (INDEPENDENTS), LATER UNITED REFORMED CHURCH. In 1763 twenty-eight members of the Presbyterian meeting and the two deacons seceded because of the minister's Unitarianism and built an Independent meeting-house in Dudley Street, the first in Staffordshire. In time two side galleries were erected in addition to the existing one, and a vestry was built. Several of the ministers after 1783 belonged to the Countess of Huntingdon's Connexion.[81] A new and larger chapel was opened on the south side of Bridge Street in 1791, with Captain Jonathan Scott as one of those officiating at the opening service. The trust deed insisted on its Independent affiliation.[82] Meanwhile in 1787 a second and apparently rival meeting was started in the club-room of the Castle inn in what is now George Street by a former minister of Dudley Street. It lasted until 1795 when Thomas Grove became minister at Bridge Street and the seceders returned.[83] A Sunday school, the first in Walsall, was started in connexion with Dudley Street in 1789. It was at first held in a room in Freer's Yard, High Street, belonging to one of the deacons, but it

soon moved to larger premises, a warehouse in the Square. It remained there until schools were built adjoining the Bridge Street chapel in 1818.[84] At the beginning of Grove's pastorate there were 57 members enrolled; by the end (1817) there were 285, with Bridge Street the leading Congregational church in Staffordshire and Grove the leading minister.[85] In 1850–1 the average Sunday morning congregation was 500.[86] New Sunday schools were built in 1879–80.[87] A new façade was added to the chapel in 1903 with statues of Richard Baxter and Isaac Watts.[88]

In 1857 there was a secession from Bridge Street after the minister had tried to investigate charges against one of the deacons, Jerome Clapp Jerome, father of the writer Jerome K. Jerome. The seceders worshipped first in the club-room at the New Inn, Park Street, and then in the assembly-rooms in Goodall Street.[89] In 1858 they began building a chapel, Ephratah, in Wednesbury Road which was opened in 1859.[90] It was enlarged in 1901 and partly rebuilt after bomb damage in 1916.[91] It was of brick with stone dressings and crocketed pinnacles; there were towers on the north-west and south-west and a projecting porch between them. Classrooms, a schoolroom, and a lecture room were attached.[92] It was designed by Jerome, who modelled it on the Congregational church at Bideford (Devon), having formerly been minister at the near-by Appledore.[93]

Both Bridge Street and Wednesbury Road congregations declined between the World Wars, and in 1945 they united. Wednesbury Road became the Walsall Congregational Church and Bridge Street was sold, although the building was used for a time as offices and survived until 1966.[94] By 1970 the Wednesbury Road church was in disrepair and the congregation—in 1971 52 members and 20 children—was no longer concentrated near by; the meeting-rooms, however, were much used as a result of the church's local social work, notably among the many immigrants. In 1973 the building was demolished and work was started on the Glebe Centre on the same site, incorporating a sanctuary, meeting-rooms, a reading room, and a gymnasium.[95]

In 1819 Thomas Butteaux, the Independent minister at Cannock, registered a house in Bloxwich. He registered another house there in 1820.[96] The cause apparently did not flourish, and it was not until 1882 that another Congregational centre was founded in the northern part of the borough. The former Methodist Free church on the corner of Blakenall Lane and Booth Street was then opened as a Congregational church under the auspices of Bridge Street. A new church and schools on the

[74] Ibid. nos. 65135, 67024.
[75] *Walsall Red Book* (1877), 63; O.S. Map 1/500, Staffs. LXIII. 10. 20 (1886 edn.). It last appears in the *Red Book* in the edn. of 1929 (p. 97).
[76] *St. Michael and All Angels, Caldmore, Par. Mag.* une 1970 (copy in W.C.L.).
[77] See p. 241.
[78] *Walsall Red Book* (1912), 80.
[79] Worship Reg. nos. 56511, 59481.
[80] Ibid. no. 54393 (cancelled 1954 on revision of official list).
[81] A. Willis, *Hist. of Bridge St. Chapel, Walsall* (Walsall, 1893), 3–4; A. G. Matthews, *Congregational Churches of Staffs.* 139. The trust deed was dated Mar. 1764.
[82] Willis, *Bridge St. Chapel*, 5–7.
[83] Ibid. 10, 13; Matthews, *Cong. Churches*, 146, 264.
[84] Willis, *Bridge St. Chapel*, 11, 15.
[85] Ibid. 14; Matthews, *Cong. Churches*, 142.
[86] H.O. 129/380/3/2.

[87] *Walsall Red Book* (1880), 107; (1881), 109.
[88] Matthews, *Cong. Churches*, 245.
[89] Willis, *Bridge St. Chapel*, 18. This states that 20 members seceded with Jerome; *Walsall Red Book* (1880), 125 (followed by Willmore, *Walsall*, 428), states that 60 communicants withdrew.
[90] *Walsall Red Book* (1880), 125.
[91] Ibid. (1939), 78; W.C.L., photograph 362.
[92] *Walsall Red Book* (1880), 125 and plate facing p. 126.
[93] Blay, 'Street Names of Walsall', 109.
[94] Kathleen U. Whitfield, *Short Hist. of Congregationalism in Walsall* (copy in W.C.L.); *Walsall Observer*, 25 Feb. 1966. The E. end of the Bridge St. building still stood in 1974.
[95] *Express & Star*, 8 Jan., 20 May 1970; *Walsall Observer*, 12 May, 30 June 1972, 25 May, 29 June 1973, 29 Mar. 1974; *Cong. Year Book* (1972), 183.
[96] *S.H.C.* 4th ser. iii. 49.

corner of Chantry Avenue and Blakenall Lane were begun in 1933 and opened in 1936. The building, designed by F., A., and W. M. Smith, church members, is in a Gothic style. Of brick with stone dressings, it is faced with stucco and has a rusticated base; there is a loggia on the south side. The site includes a garden of rest and a manse.[97] In 1971 the church had 72 members and 36 children.[98] The former chapel became a feeding centre for school-children in 1939. It was used by the Harden and District Community Association by the early 1950s and was taken over for commercial purposes in 1955.[99] It had been demolished by 1974.

By the later 1830s two members of Bridge Street were conducting Sunday services in a house at Ryecroft. In 1838 the Independent Sabbath School of Ryecroft and Birchills was formed under the auspices of Bridge Street, and its building, extended in 1857, was also used for Sunday services. In 1851, however, these were stated to be only occasional; the average congregation was 80. A church was erected on the corner of North and Mill Streets in 1860; designed by J. C. Jerome, it is of brick with stone dressings and has lancet windows. For some years it was a branch of Wednesbury Road.[1] By 1971 it shared a minister with Blakenall. There were then 37 members and 25 children.[2] By 1972 the building had become too decayed to be repaired and it was closed; services were transferred to members' homes.[3]

Broadway Congregational church on the corner of Broadway North and Gillity Avenue was begun in 1958 and opened in 1959. In 1971 it had 93 members and 90 children.[4]

ELIM FOURSQUARE GOSPEL ALLIANCE. Elim Hall in Caxton Chambers, Darwall Street, was registered in 1939. It was replaced by Elim Church of the Foursquare Gospel in Broadway North, registered in 1941; the registration was cancelled in 1944.[5]

FREE CHURCH OF ENGLAND. St. Jude's Church in Bott Lane was opened in 1886 to meet the needs of Evangelical churchmen. It was replaced by a new church in Eldon Street, registered in 1897. In 1909 the congregation joined the Free Church of England.[6] Sunday schools were opened in Bott Lane in 1913, and in 1931 new schools were opened on a site in Eldon Street to the south of the church.[7]

FRIENDS. In 1773 the vicar of Walsall reported one Quaker in the parish.[8] A meeting consisting of eighteen people from Walsall and district was started at a house in Leigh Road in 1932. It was recognized

as a regular part of the Warwickshire Monthly Meeting in 1942. The Friends met in various places and by 1973 worshipped each Sunday at the Social Service Centre in Whittimere Street. There were then twenty members.[9]

INDEPENDENTS, see CONGREGATIONALISTS.

JEHOVAH'S WITNESSES. The Witnesses had a meeting-room at no. 126 Lichfield Street by 1936 when it was registered for the International Bible Students' Association; it had ceased to be used by 1954.[10] The Kingdom Hall housed in the former Primitive Methodist church in Victor Street was registered in 1958.[11]

A Kingdom Hall at no. 79 High Street, Bloxwich, was registered in 1944 but had ceased to be used by 1954.[12] A hall was registered at no. 152 Lichfield Road, Bloxwich, in 1963 and was replaced by a hall at Sandbank, registered in 1973.[13]

LATTER-DAY SAINTS. In 1855 the Mormons registered a lecture room in Wisemore; it had ceased to be used by 1876.[14] A Walsall church was established in 1961. By 1968 it had 250 members and met at the Blind Institute in Hatherton Road, where it still met in 1974.[15]

METHODISTS. *Wesleyan.* In May 1743 Charles Wesley preached from the steps of Walsall market house to a crowd of 'fierce Ephesian beasts . . . who roared and shouted and threw stones incessantly'. The Walsall mob continued to play a part in the anti-Methodist outbreaks of the district which persisted into 1744. John Wesley himself was a victim in September 1743 when a mob, having taken him from Wednesbury to Bentley in an unsuccessful attempt to bring him before a magistrate, took him to Reynold's Hall in an equally unsuccessful attempt to bring him before William Persehouse. He was then seized by the Walsall mob and dragged into the town. There he managed to preach and was eventually escorted back to Wednesbury.[16]

Wesley came from Wednesbury to Walsall in 1764, and although trouble was expected he secured an attentive hearing. He preached in the open since the house where the Methodists met, apparently in New Street, was too small for the numbers on that occasion.[17] A room in Dudley Street was hired for meetings in 1770; in 1790 the loft over the stables at the Castle inn in what is now George Street became the meeting-place.[18] In 1773 the vicar reported a Methodist meeting-house, duly licensed; as with the Presbyterians the congregation, although including some

[97] Brochure for opening of new church hall and schools, June 1936 (copy in W.C.L.); *Walsall Red Book* (1934), 34; (1939), 77. The church was intended to be a hall used only temporarily for worship, there being plans for a church on the site. [98] *Cong. Year Book* (1972), 183.
[99] *36th Ann. Rep. Walsall Educ. Cttee.* (1939–40), 11 (copy in W.C.L.); *51st Ann. Rep.* (1954–5), 32.
[1] Matthews, *Cong. Churches*, 229; Willis, *Bridge St. Chapel*, 17; H.O. 129/380/4/2; *Walsall Red Book* (1912), 82. [2] *Cong. Year Book* (1972), 183.
[3] *Walsall Observer*, 28 July 1972.
[4] Stone on church dated 1958; *Cong. Year Book* (1972), 183. [5] G.R.O., Worship Reg. nos. 58553, 59706.
[6] *Walsall Red Book* (1888), 139; (1913), 76; Worship Reg. no. 35940.
[7] *Walsall Red Book* (1914), 211; (1932), 49.
[8] L.J.R.O., B/V/5/1772–3.

[9] Ex inf. the secretary (1973).
[10] Worship Reg. no. 56665 (cancelled 1954 on revision of official list). [11] Ibid. no. 67007.
[12] Ibid. no. 60714 (cancelled on 1954 revision).
[13] Ibid. nos. 69258, 73402.
[14] Ibid. no. 6796 (cancelled 1876 on certificate of supt. registrar).
[15] *Walsall Observer*, 8 Nov. 1968, 12 May 1972.
[16] *Journal of the Rev. Charles Wesley, M.A.* (1849), i. 307, 347–8; *Works of John Wesley*, i. 437–8, 453–4; viii. 212; xi. 80; Willmore, *Walsall*, 360–4.
[17] *Works of Wesley*, iii. 163; D. E. Parry, *Notes on Bloxwich and Bloxwich Methodism* (copy in W.C.L.).
[18] Parry, *Bloxwich Methodism*. Willmore, *Walsall*, 365, states that the house mentioned by Wesley as too small was a room at the Castle and that later the Methodists moved to a larger room over the stables at the Dragon.

'substantial people', consisted mainly 'of those of the inferior class', and he thought that there had been no recent increase in numbers.[19]

In 1801 the Wesleyans built a chapel in Bedlam Court on the south side of High Street.[20] A Sunday school was started in 1807.[21] The chapel was replaced by one in Ablewell Street begun in 1828 and opened in 1829; it was designed in a Grecian style by John Fallows of Birmingham. There was a minister's house adjoining and a Sunday school under the chapel. A vestry was added in 1834 and a girls' schoolroom was later built behind the chapel.[22] The first chapel was converted into cottages which still stood in 1929.[23] In 1835 Ablewell Street became the head of the new Walsall circuit, formed out of Wednesbury circuit.[24] Attendances at the chapel on Census Sunday 1851 were 260 in the morning, 112 in the afternoon, and 358 in the evening.[25] A new chapel was built on an adjoining site in 1859; of red brick with Bath stone dressings, it was designed by William and Samuel Horton of Wednesbury. In 1887 it was described as the largest place of worship in the town.[26] The former chapel was converted into a day and Sunday school; new Sunday schools were built in 1910.[27] The cause declined in the early 20th century, and the Conference of 1928 created a Walsall mission. The chapel was reconstructed in 1929 and reopened in 1930 as the Central Hall. Membership rose from 176 in 1928 to 371 in 1932.[28] In 1972 further reconstruction began. The gallery level was filled in and in 1973 opened as the church; the well of the hall was then still being converted into a conference centre with other parts of the building as ancillary rooms.[29]

At Bloxwich in the late 18th century, possibly from 1781, Methodists were meeting in a flax oven on Bullock's Fold in Chapel field in the north-eastern part of the village. The building was leased as a chapel from 1795.[30] A new Wesleyan chapel was built to the south in what is now Park Road in 1832.[31] Its predecessor remained in use as a Sunday school but had been replaced before 1856 when a school at the back of the 1832 chapel was enlarged.[32] Attendances at the chapel on Census Sunday 1851 were 160 in the morning and 390 in the evening.[33] It was replaced in 1865 by a new chapel on the corner of High Street and what is now Victoria Avenue; designed by S. and J. Loxton of Wednesbury, it was

in a Gothic style with a south-west tower and turret. The 1832 building then became the Sunday school and by 1877 was being used as a temperance hall; it later became a cinema, and by 1973 it was used by Midland Aeroquipment Ltd. A manse was built in Victoria Avenue behind the new chapel in 1874. New Sunday schools were built beside the manse in 1910.[34] The High Street chapel had been closed by 1963,[35] and the former Methodist Free church in New Street replaced it until 1966 when St. John's Methodist church was opened in Victoria Avenue to the east of the schools. It is a building of brick and concrete designed in a modern style by Hulme, Upright & Partners of Tunstall, Stoke-on-Trent.[36]

A Wesleyan meeting-place was established at Pleck in a cottage in Narrow Lane apparently c. 1827.[37] The society moved to a cottage in Wellington Street in 1830, and in 1840 a chapel was opened in Chapel Street (later St. Quentin Street and now obliterated) off Old Pleck Road. On Census Sunday 1851 there was a congregation of 13 in the afternoon and 37 in the evening, although average attendances were claimed of 30 and 45 respectively.[38] A new chapel was opened on the corner of Regent (later Caledon) and Oxford Streets in 1861; a Sunday school was opened opposite in 1865. A church was built on the corner of Bescot and Wednesbury Roads in 1899–1901. Designed in a Perpendicular style by C. W. D. Joynson of Joynson Bros., Darlaston,[39] it is of brick with terracotta dressings and consists of nave, transepts, and apsidal east end; there is a north-west tower with a spire, and at the south-west corner is a turret. The Caledon Street chapel was taken over by the Primitive Methodists. A Sunday school and church rooms were built in Bescot Road in 1914–15.

By 1837 a site for a Wesleyan chapel had been bought under the auspices of Ablewell Street.[40] It was presumably in Stafford Street where a Sunday school had been started by 1839 and where Centenary chapel was opened in 1840. A new Sunday school was built in 1841. Attendances at the chapel on Census Sunday 1851 were 121 in the morning, 151 in the afternoon, and 170 in the evening.[41] The school was enlarged in 1854 and 1858. The chapel was extended in 1860 and again in 1889 when a new façade with a balustraded portico was built. It became the head of a new circuit in 1863 when Walsall circuit was

[19] L.J.R.O., B/V/5/1772–3.
[20] Pearce, *Walsall*, 114. For the name of the court see Blay, 'Street Names of Walsall', 15; Willmore, *Walsall*, 365; Glew, *Walsall*, 45.
[21] Parry, *Bloxwich Methodism*.
[22] Ibid.; *Staffs. Advertiser*, 30 Aug. 1828; *S.H.C.* 4th ser. iii. 74; H.O. 129/380/3/2; H. M. Colvin, *Biog. Dict. Eng. Architects 1660–1840*, 203.
[23] Blay, 'Street Names of Walsall', 16.
[24] *Hall's Circuits and Ministers* (1897 edn.), 314; Parry, *Bloxwich Methodism* (giving 1832 as date of new circuit).
[25] H.O. 129/380/3/2.
[26] *Staffs. Advertiser*, 5 Nov. 1859, 25 June 1887; *P.O. Dir. Staffs.* (1860), sub Wednesbury (for the Hortons).
[27] See p. 259; *Walsall Red Book* (1912), 176.
[28] L. Davison, *Story of Methodism in Walsall*, 5, 7 (copy in W.C.L.); *News from Walsall*, Apr. 1932 (copy in W.C.L.); *Walsall Red Book* (1930), 63, 66.
[29] *Walsall Observer*, 28 July 1972, 19 Oct. 1973.
[30] Homeshaw, *Bloxwich*, 144–5, 147.
[31] *Staffs. Advertiser*, 27 Oct. 1832, p. [4]. It was not registered until 1837: *S.H.C.* 4th ser. iii. 152. For a view of 1847 see Homeshaw, *Bloxwich*, plate facing p. 129.
[32] Homeshaw, *Bloxwich*, 145; Parry, *Bloxwich Methodism*.

[33] H.O. 129/380/2/2.
[34] Homeshaw, *Bloxwich*, 145–8, with a photograph of the 1865 church facing p. 129; *Staffs. Advertiser*, 22 Oct. 1864; Parry, *Bloxwich Methodism*; *Walsall Red Book* (1877), 75; (1911), 155; *Express & Star*, 9 Oct. 1973; below p. 251.
[35] Its registration was cancelled in July 1963: G.R.O., Worship Reg. no. 17826.
[36] Ibid. nos. 16700, 70737; *Walsall Observer*, 9 Dec. 1966. The other Methodist church in Bloxwich, Pinfold, was sold in 1964: see p. 247.
[37] For this para. see, unless otherwise stated, the pamphlet pub. for the jubilee celebrations in 1951 (copy in W.C.L.).
[38] H.O. 129/380/3/1. For the reason for the low attendance on Census Sunday see above p. 131.
[39] Jubilee pamph.; *Walsall Red Book* (1912), 88.
[40] S.R.O., D. 1287/18/26/business corresp. 1835–7, Peter Potter to Lord Bradford, 11 May 1837. The Mr. Miller, a Wesleyan minister, there mentioned as appealing to Lord Bradford for a donation towards the cost of the chapel was presumably Jas. Miller, minister at Ablewell St. (Pigot, *Nat. Com. Dir.* (1841), Staffs. p. 79).
[41] Parry, *Bloxwich Methodism*; H.O. 129/380/3/1.

divided into Wesley and Centenary circuits.[42] The chapel had ceased to be used by the Methodists by 1940 when it was registered as Walsall Town Mission.[43]

A Wesleyan chapel was opened at the Coal Pool end of Coal Pool Lane in 1852.[44] A new chapel was erected on the same site in 1896.[45] It is of brick in a plain style.

The Wesleyans were holding afternoon services at Palfrey by 1857, apparently in the Millerchip family's house in Dale Street.[46] A chapel was opened in Dale Street, apparently in 1863, under the auspices of Ablewell Street, but with the opening of a chapel in Corporation Street in 1876 services at Dale Street were reduced. There was, however, a Sunday school by 1868, and a new school was built in 1887. Dale Street then had a membership of 24, which had risen to 55 by 1888. The chapel was rebuilt in 1909–10; of brick with stone dressings, it was designed in a Gothic style by Hickton & Farmer of Walsall. It was closed in 1974.

A Wesleyan chapel was built at Leamore on the west side of Broadstone (now Bloxwich Road) in 1862–3 to the design of Mr. Loxton of Wednesbury; an extension designed by S. and J. Loxton of Wednesbury was begun in 1864. There was then a flourishing Sunday school. The site was taken over by the corporation in 1963 and the building demolished.[47] A new church was opened on the corner of Bloxwich Road and Carl Street in 1965.[48] Designed by J. M. Warnock,[49] it is of brick with a central spire and includes a hall.

A school-chapel was opened in Queen Street under the auspices of Centenary chapel in 1864. A chapel was built on the corner of Bridgeman and Queen Streets in 1867 and was used until c. 1931. It then seems to have been taken over by the Bethel Evangelistic Society.[50]

There was a Wesleyan meeting-place in Corporation Street, Caldmore, by the beginning of 1876.[51] Trinity chapel in Corporation Street was begun later that year and opened in 1877. Designed in a Gothic style by Samuel Loxton of Walsall, it was of brick with Hollington stone dressings and consisted of nave and transepts with a north-west tower and spire. A Sunday school was built at the rear.[52] The spire was blown down in 1894.[53] New Sunday schools

were begun in 1906.[54] The church (now Caldmore Methodist church) was rebuilt on the same site in 1957–8 to serve both the Trinity and Victor Street societies.[55] Designed in a modern style by C. C. Gray of Walsall,[56] it is of brick with stone and concrete dressings.

A Wesleyan chapel was opened on the corner of Butts and Lichfield Roads in 1883; Sunday schools were built on an adjoining site in 1887.[57] Mellish Road church on the same site was built in 1909–10; W. M. Lester was the principal subscriber.[58] Designed in a Perpendicular style by Hickton & Farmer of Walsall,[59] it is of brick and stone and consists of an aisled and clerestoried nave, transepts, and a south-east tower and spire; there is an extensive basement approached from Butts Road. The Sunday schools in Butts Road adjoining the church were built in 1935.[60]

A Wesleyan school-chapel, now Reedswood Methodist church, was opened in Edward Street in 1903.[61]

In 1973 there were nine Methodist churches in the area of the pre-1966 borough.[62] The Central Hall in Ablewell Street and Coal Pool made up Walsall Mission circuit, formed in 1928. Mellish Road, Bloxwich Road, Caldmore, and Dale Street were in Walsall Methodist circuit. St. John's and Reedswood were in Bloxwich circuit, formed out of Walsall Centenary circuit in 1932. Pleck was in Darlaston circuit, formed out of Wednesbury circuit in 1931.

New Connexion. New Connexion Methodists had taken a lease of land in Teddesley Street by 1858 as the site for a chapel. By 1860 they had built a school-room which was also used for services. It still existed in the early 1870s.[63]

Primitive. The Primitive Methodists registered a room in George Street in 1830.[64] A chapel was built on the corner of Lower Hall Lane and Newport Street in 1832–3.[65] It was taken over by Particular Baptists in 1845,[66] and in 1850 the Primitive Methodists moved into the former Ragged School at Townend Bank. The average Sunday morning congregation was 50 by 1851, and there was also a Sunday school.[67] By 1876 the Primitive Methodists had built Mount Zion chapel on a site at the corner of Blue Lane West and Margaret Street, the building lease of which had been granted in 1871.[68] A Sun-

[42] Parry, *Bloxwich Methodism*; *Hall's Circuits and Ministers* (1897 edn.), 315.
[43] See p. 249.
[44] *Walsall Red Book* (1939), 78.
[45] Date on church.
[46] For this para. see *The Methodist Church, Dale St., Palfrey, Walsall* (duplicated pamph. for 1960 jubilee; copy in W.C.L.); *Walsall Observer*, 6 Dec. 1974.
[47] *Staffs. Advertiser*, 22 Nov. 1862, 6 Aug. 1864; *Walsall Observer*, 25 Oct. 1963, 13 Mar. 1964; O.S. Map 1/2,500, Staffs. LXIII. 2 (1886 edn.). The 1862 architect is given as Mr. Loxton by *Staffs. Advertiser*; for Sam. Loxton see Harrison, Harrod & Co. *Dir. Staffs.* (1861), 161.
[48] Plaque in entrance hall.
[49] Ibid.
[50] Parry, *Bloxwich Methodism*; G.R.O., Worship Reg. no. 16228 (cancelled Feb. 1932); below p. 249. It last appears in *Walsall Red Book* in the edn. of 1931 (p. 101).
[51] *The Methodist Church, Dale St., Palfrey.*
[52] *Walsall Observer*, 26 May, 2 June 1877; *Walsall Red Book* (1880), 120–2.
[53] *Walsall Red Book* (1895), 183.
[54] Ibid. (1907), 249.
[55] Memorial stones laid by the former societies; below p. 247.
[56] Date on memorial stones; ex inf. Mr. C. C. Gray (1973).

[57] *Walsall Red Book* (1884), 149; F. W. Willmore, *Records of Rushall* (Walsall, 1892), 118; O.S. Map 1/2,500, Staffs. LXIII. 7 (1902 edn.).
[58] *Walsall Red Book* (1910), 157; (1911), 154; *Walsall Observer*, 8 May 1970.
[59] *Walsall Red Book* (1935), 52.
[60] *Walsall Observer*, 28 May 1910.
[61] *Walsall Advertiser*, 17 Jan. 1903; G.R.O., Worship Reg. no. 39415. It was recertified in 1936 and 1946 (nos. 56855, 61543).
[62] This para. is based on circuit plans of 1973 at W.C.L. and inf. on the dates of circuits supplied by Mr. G. Beard, Quarterly Meeting Secretary, Smethwick Circuit (1971).
[63] S.R.O., D. 260/M/E/174, 22 Mar. 1864; *P.O. Dir. Staffs.* (1860; 1872). It does not occur ibid. (1876).
[64] *S.H.C.* 4th ser. iii. 152.
[65] S.R.O., D. 1287/box 7, abstract of title 1923. It was not registered until 1836: W.C.L., QSM 1/272; *S.H.C.* 4th ser. iii. 152, wrongly gives 1830.
[66] See p. 242.
[67] H.O. 129/380/3/1; White, *Dir. Staffs.* (1851).
[68] *Robinson's Map of Walsall* (pub. with *Walsall Red Book*, 1876); W.S.L., D. 1798/551, no. 390. An application was made to Lord Hatherton in 1864 for a lease of land in Blue Lane for a chapel (S.R.O., D. 260/M/E/174, 2 Aug. 1864), but no denomination is given.

day school was opened behind in Margaret Street in 1877.[69] The registration of the chapel was cancelled in 1960,[70] and it had been demolished by 1973.

A Primitive Methodist chapel was built in High Street, Bloxwich, near the junction with Pinfold in 1842. The Sunday congregation in 1850–1 averaged 100 in the morning and 160 in the evening, and there was also a Sunday school.[71] The chapel was rebuilt in 1895–6,[72] and a new school was begun in 1902.[73] As Pinfold Methodist church it was sold with the school and the site in 1964, being one of the three Bloxwich Methodist churches which were replaced in 1966 by St. John's in Victoria Avenue.[74] By 1973 the buildings had been demolished and the site formed part of a garage.

A chapel was built in North Street, Ryecroft, in 1845. By 1850–1 there was an average Sunday congregation of 120 in the afternoon and 160 in the evening, and there was also a Sunday school.[75] It was replaced by a chapel and Sunday school built in Stafford Street in 1904–5.[76] The chapel, in a Gothic style, is of red brick with terracotta dressings and has a north-west tower and spire. It was closed c. 1965[77] and was used as a warehouse by the early 1970s.

A Primitive Methodist chapel used also as a schoolroom was opened in 1850 in the street now called Old Birchills by a group that had met in a cottage at Bentley in St. Peter's, Wolverhampton. By 1851 the Sunday congregation averaged 30 afternoon and evening. Further work on the building was carried out c. 1880 and in 1897. In 1904 a new chapel was opened on the corner of Dalkeith Street and Old Birchills nearly opposite the old building, which remained in use as a Sunday school.[78] The 1904 chapel was burnt down in 1946 and the congregation joined Reedswood Methodist church.[79]

A Primitive Methodist chapel was built in Darlaston Road, Pleck, c. 1860.[80] In 1901 the congregation took over the vacated Wesleyan chapel in Caledon Street instead, retaining it until c. 1963.[81] It was subsequently demolished, but the Darlaston Road chapel, a Gothic building of red brick with white-brick dressings, became a Sikh temple in 1965.[82] A chapel was built in Chapel Street, Blakenall Heath, c. 1866. It was converted into shops c. 1920 after standing empty for two years.[83] A chapel was built

in Victor Street, Caldmore, in 1884.[84] By 1957 the congregation had united with that of Trinity, Corporation Street, and the Victor Street chapel was taken over by Jehovah's Witnesses.[85]

Methodist Free Church. The Methodist Free Church opened a chapel in Whittimere Street in 1862. It was still in use in 1880 but closed soon afterwards.[86]

The Free Church built a chapel in Bloxwich in 1864–5 in what came to be called Revival Street.[87] It was replaced by a chapel in New Street begun in 1894. Schools and a club were opened in 1930. New Street was closed with the opening of St. John's Methodist church in Victoria Avenue in 1966.[88] A building of brick with stone dressings in a Gothic style, it was apparently used as a warehouse in the early 1970s.

The Free Church registered a preaching-room in Birchills Street in 1866. It had ceased to be used by 1896.[89]

The Free Church registered a school-chapel at Blakenall in 1868.[90] A chapel was built on the corner of Blakenall Lane and Booth Street in 1871. It was closed a few years later and in 1882 was taken over by the Congregationalists.[91]

PRESBYTERIANS, LATER UNITED REFORMED CHURCH. Presbyterianism was strong in Walsall in the later 17th century. Besides supporters among the clergy and members of the corporation,[92] Sir Thomas Wilbraham of Weston-under-Lizard, lord of Walsall manor and patron of the living, was thought in 1662–3 to be a Presbyterian,[93] while Edward Leigh of the near-by Rushall Hall was considered 'a dangerous Presbyterian'.[94] John Reynolds, minister at Wolverhampton 1658–60, was presented at the county quarter sessions with seven inhabitants of Walsall for holding a conventicle there in May 1663,[95] and in July four ejected ministers were reported to be living in Walsall.[96] In 1669 there were at least seven ejected ministers there, all Presbyterians; they preached at the houses of Mrs. Pearson, Mr. Fowler, and Mr. Eaves, and their followers were estimated at over 300.[97] In 1672 the houses of Edward Eaves, George Fowler, and Elizabeth Deakin were licensed for Presbyterian worship and Richard Bell, an ejected minister, was licensed as a

[69] *Walsall Red Book* (1878), 109; O.S. Map 1/500, Staffs. LXIII. 6. 25 (1885 edn.).
[70] G.R.O., Worship Reg. no. 35735.
[71] H.O. 129/380/2/2; S.R.O., D. 260/M/E/430/3; /M/T 6/93, agreement of 2 Mar. 1847; Lich. Dioc. Regy., B/A/2(i)/L, p. 55; O.S. Map 1/2,500, LXIII. 2 (1886 edn.).
[72] *Walsall Red Book* (1896), 189; (1897), 191.
[73] *Staffs. Advertiser*, 3 Jan. 1903, p. 6.
[74] *Walsall Observer*, 26 Feb. 1964; above p. 245.
[75] H.O. 129/380/4/2; O.S. Map 1/500, Staffs. LXIII. 6. 15 (1886 edn.), showing the school at the rear.
[76] *Walsall Red Book* (1905), 240, 243; (1906), 238.
[77] The registration (Worship Reg. no. 41168) was cancelled in Oct. 1965.
[78] *Walsall Observer*, 16 Nov. 1973; *Walsall Red Book* (1912), 84; H.O. 129/380/3/1; O.S. Map 1/2,500, Staffs. LXIII. 6 (1902 edn.).
[79] *Walsall Observer*, 31 Aug. 1973.
[80] It was registered in Dec. 1860: Worship Reg. no. 11143.
[81] Ibid. no. 38449 (cancelled Jan. 1964); above p. 245.
[82] See p. 249.
[83] Cason, *Blakenall Heath*, 11, 35.
[84] *Walsall Red Book* (1885), 57–8.
[85] See pp. 244, 246. The registration was cancelled in Jan. 1957: Worship Reg. no. 28113.

[86] *Staffs. Advertiser*, 13 Dec. 1862; *Kelly's Dir. Staffs.* (1880). It does not occur ibid. (1884).
[87] *Staffs. Advertiser*, 9 July 1864 (laying of foundation-stone); Worship Reg. no. 16700 (registration May 1865); O.S. Map 6″, Staffs. LVII. SW. (1887 edn.). In 1864 the address was given as Church Street. The Free Church also registered Bloxwich Music Hall later in 1865; the registration was cancelled in 1896 on the revision of the official list: Worship Reg. no. 16522.
[88] Worship Reg. no. 70737; *Walsall Red Book* (1895), 188; (1931), 65.
[89] Worship Reg. no. 17265 (cancelled 1896 on revision of list).
[90] Ibid. no. 18393.
[91] Ibid. no. 20245; *Staffs. Advertiser*, 8 July 1871; S.R.O., D. 260/M/E/174, 23–31 Jan., 21–28 Feb., 7–14 Mar. 1871; brochure for opening of new church hall and schools at Blakenall, June 1936 (copy in W.C.L.); above p. 243.
[92] See pp. 215, 229–30, 235.
[93] *S.H.C.* 4th ser. ii. 32; *V.C.H. Staffs.* iii. 119.
[94] *S.H.C.* 4th ser. ii. 36; *S.H.C.* 1920 & 1922, 78–82.
[95] A. G. Matthews, *Calamy Revised*, 409.
[96] *Cal. S.P. Dom.* 1663–4, 211.
[97] Matthews, *Calamy Revised*, 60, 135, 196, 267, 350, 370–1, 461; A. G. Matthews, *Congregational Churches of Staffs.* 90.

Presbyterian teacher.[98] The number of nonconformists was given as 200 in 1676,[99] all or most of them presumably Presbyterians.

It was stated in 1681 that a meeting-house had been built where conventicles were kept, undisturbed by the mayors and frequented by most of the magistrates.[1] Richard Hilton, one of the Presbyterian ministers at Walsall in 1669, was maintaining a lecture there in 1690, but he received 'little assistance though many able men in the town'.[2] His house there was licensed for worship in 1693.[3] A 'great room' known as 'the chapel' and adjoining George Fowler's house was leased to Fowler by his father Simon, of Cheadle, in 1707,[4] and that was presumably the meeting-house in Bank (later Fox's and Cox's) Court on the north side of High Street that was burnt by a mob in 1715.[5]

The meeting-house was restored with financial help from the government,[6] and in 1717 there were 400 hearers.[7] In 1737 a house in Upper Rushall Street occupied by the minister was settled in trust by Thomas Walker and licensed as a meeting-house a few days later.[8] In 1773 the vicar reported a Presbyterian meeting-house supported, like that of the Methodists, by some 'substantial people' but mainly by 'those of the inferior class'; he thought that numbers had changed little in recent years.[9] In fact the meeting-house had by then passed under Unitarian influence. Hostility to such influence was probably the cause of a secession in 1751. A new meeting-house was begun in that year at Hill Top, but the uncompleted structure was soon destroyed by a mob.[10] There was another secession in 1763 which resulted in the building of an Independent meeting-house.[11]

Presbyterianism was revived in Walsall in 1876 when services were begun in the Exchange Rooms in High Street by a group of 23 seceders from Bridge Street Congregational chapel; a Sunday school was also started. The cause was recognized as a preaching station the same year and as a fully constituted congregation in 1877. In that year the services were transferred to the Temperance Hall in Freer Street.

A church was built on the corner of Hatherton Road and Darwall Street in 1881-2.[12] Designed by Cotton & McConnal[13] in a Gothic style, it is of brick with stone dressings; there is a north-east tower, which originally had a spire but had lost it by the early 1970s. The schools at the rear were enlarged in 1904.[14] Since 1972 it has been Hatherton United Reformed Church.

QUAKERS, see FRIENDS.

SALVATION ARMY. The Walsall corps of the Salvation Army was formed in 1882 and opened a barracks at the skating rink in Hatherton Street in 1883. It had ceased to be used by 1896.[15] A barracks and schools in Green Lane were opened in 1902.[16] A Salvation Army hall in premises in West Bromwich Street was registered in 1934; the registration was cancelled in 1951.[17]

In 1863 William (later General) Booth was living with his wife and son at no. 5 Hatherton Street and ran a mission in the town, forming the Hallelujah Band of reformed reprobates.[18] The activities of the band in Bloxwich in 1865 led to the building of a hall in what came to be called Revival Street.[19] By 1898 the hall was known as the Revival Chapel and was used by the Salvation Army.[20] A barracks in Clarendon Street, Bloxwich, was registered in 1901,[21] and about that time the chapel was taken over by J. & J. Wiggin, who turned it into a factory.[22] The barracks was replaced by the Gospel Mission Hall in Pinfold, registered for the Salvation Army in 1907; it had ceased to be used by 1964.[23]

SEVENTH-DAY ADVENTISTS. Advent Church in Stafford Street was registered in 1945. It had ceased to be used by 1954.[24]

SPIRITUALISTS. Walsall Spiritualist Church was founded in 1877,[25] and a room in Exchange Buildings in High Street was registered for it in 1879.[26] The room was replaced by Central Hall in Bradford Street, begun in 1889 and opened in 1890.[27] This

[98] *Cal. S.P. Dom.* 1671-2, 326, 529; Matthews, *Cong. Churches*, 92.
[99] See p. 145.
[1] *Cal. S.P. Dom.* 1680-1, 555. And see ibid. 1683, Jan. to June, 31, for a similar complaint.
[2] *Freedom after Ejection*, ed. A. Gordon, 96, 284. He was also Presbyterian minister at West Bromwich: see above p. 67.
[3] L.J.R.O., B/A/12(ii).
[4] W.S.L. 337/34 and 349/34.
[5] Assizes 4/18, pp. 232-3, 237-8, 250. For its site see Glew, *Walsall*, 58; A. Willis, *Hist. of Bridge St. Chapel, Walsall* (Walsall, 1893), 3; Willmore, *Walsall*, 351; Blay, 'Street Names of Walsall', 54.
[6] *Cal. Treas. Bks.* Jan.-Dec. 1717, 186.
[7] Matthews, *Cong. Churches*, 129.
[8] G. E. Evans, *Midland Churches: a Hist. of the Congregations on the Roll of the Midland Christian Union* (Dudley, 1899), 215; Willis, *Bridge St. Chapel*, 3 (describing the licence as evidence of a secession), 8.
[9] L.J.R.O., B/V/5/1772-3.
[10] Matthews, *Cong. Churches*, 145; L.J.R.O., B/A/2(i)/ABCD, p. 354; Homeshaw, *Walsall*, 94; *General Advertiser*, 26 July 1751.
[11] See p. 243.
[12] *Presbyterianism in Walsall: the Fifty Years, 1876-1926*, 6-9 (copy in W.C.L.); Willis, *Bridge St. Chapel*, 19; *Walsall Red Book* (1879), 41.
[13] *Presbyterianism in Walsall*, 8.
[14] Inscription on building.

[15] Ede, *Wednesbury*, 317; *Walsall Red Book* (1884), 147; (1885), 54, 56. The registration of 1883 was cancelled on the revision of the official list in 1896: G.R.O., Worship Reg. no. 27540.
[16] *Walsall Red Book* (1903), 235; *Staffs. Advertiser*, 3 Jan. 1903, p. 5.
[17] Worship Reg. no. 55268.
[18] *Walsall Observer*, 20 Nov. 1970; Blay, 'Street Names of Walsall', 25; *Walsall Red Book* (1914), 202.
[19] D. E. Parry and K. F. Jones, *Bloxwich in History* (Bloxwich, 1941), 23 (copy in W.C.L.).
[20] W.C.L., Town Clerk's Misc., box 84. Part of the hall was let to a brewery and another part was unused.
[21] Worship Reg. no. 38755.
[22] *Walsall Observer*, 19 Sept. 1971; Homeshaw, *Bloxwich*, 169; M. Wiggin, *Memoirs of a Maverick*, 7-8; above p. 201.
[23] Worship Reg. no. 42217 (cancelled 1964 on revision of official list).
[24] Ibid. no. 60994 (cancelled 1954 on revision of official list).
[25] *Walsall Observer*, 16 Feb. 1973, notice of services.
[26] Worship Reg. no. 24739.
[27] *Walsall Red Book* (1891), 63, 69. It was not registered until 1894 when the registration of the previous building was cancelled: Worship Reg. no. 34444. For the reopening of Central Hall as a permanent Spiritualist church in 1932 see *Walsall Red Book* (1933), illus.; Worship Reg. no. 54495. The building, which extends back to Midland Rd., was used as commercial premises in 1973.

was in turn replaced by a church on the corner of Vicarage Place and Caldmore Road built in 1957.[28]

Bloxwich National Spiritualist Church was formed in 1921[29] and had a church in Wolverhampton Road.[30] A new church was built in Revival Street in 1938.[31]

UNITARIANS. The meeting-house in Bank Court off High Street turned from Presbyterianism to Unitarianism in the later 18th century.[32] It was replaced in 1827 by Christ's Chapel in Stafford Street,[33] a small classical building of brick with a stuccoed façade. A Sunday school was established in the late 18th century.[34] In 1883 the *Religious Reformer*, the monthly paper of the Walsall Unitarian Free Church, noted that Unitarianism was making slow progress locally: 'Unitarianism in Walsall is like Protestantism in Spain, or Christianity in Turkey; . . . tradition, prejudice, popularity, interest, and fashion are all against it.'[35]

UNITED REFORMED CHURCH, *see* CONGREGATIONALISTS; PRESBYTERIANS.

OTHER GROUPS. The Free Church registered a church in James Street (now Leckie Road), Ryecroft, in 1866. It had been closed by 1896.[36]

A Primitive Christian meeting-room in Freer Street was registered in 1866. It had been closed by 1896.[37]

The Town Mission Hall in North Street, Ryecroft, was registered in 1909. The mission moved to the former Wesleyan chapel on the corner of Stafford and John Streets, registered as Walsall Town Mission in 1940.[38] The building was no longer in use in 1973.

Services were being held in a meeting-room in Lower Hall Lane c. 1911 and continued until at least 1916.[39]

Bethel Temple in Queen Street was opened by the Bethel Evangelistic Society in 1932 but had become undenominational by 1933.[40] It evidently occupied the former Wesleyan chapel on the corner of Bridgeman Street. The building no longer stood in 1973.

Beulah Pentecostal Mission in premises in Wednesbury Road was registered in 1935 but was no longer in existence in 1954.[41]

Birchills Labour Church in premises in Holly-hedge Lane was registered in 1936 but was no longer in existence in 1954.[42]

The New Testament Church of God registered a building behind no. 88 Wednesbury Road in 1967.[43]

Bethany Church of God registered two rooms at no. 57 Wednesbury Road in 1972.[44] A board over the door in 1973 read: 'Bethany Church of God, "Zionist", kept by the Power of God.'

The Church of God at Walsall was in occupation of the former Ebenezer Baptist church in Stafford Street in 1973.

NON-CHRISTIAN RELIGIONS. The Guru Nanak Sikh temple in West Bromwich Street was registered in 1964 and rebuilt on the same site in 1971–2. Designed by G. Wright of Bloxwich, the new temple is of brick with concrete dressings. It consists of two floors, with a kitchen and hall on the ground-floor and the sanctuary on the first-floor approached by separate staircases for men and women. While the temple was being rebuilt the Sikhs met in the Congregational church in Wednesbury Road.[45] The Nanak Sar temple in the former Primitive Methodist chapel in Darlaston Road was registered in 1965.[46]

The Muslim Prayer House at no. 56 South Street was registered in 1966,[47] a mosque at no. 102 Wednesbury Road in 1969,[48] and the Pakistan Welfare Society Mosque at no. 97 Rutter Street in 1971.[49]

SOCIAL LIFE. By 1612 a wake was held at Walsall late in September.[50] It may thus have originated in festivities at the St. Matthew's day fair, but it coincided with the Michaelmas fair from 1627.[51] It was discontinued in 1895.[52] A wake has been held at Bloxwich from at least 1769, when the inhabitants fixed the date as the Sunday nearest to 16 August.[53] In the 19th and 20th centuries, however, the wake has often continued for up to three days in the week following.[54] In the late 18th century it took place on 'the village green',[55] presumably Short Heath. By 1911 it was restricted to that part of the former heath between High Street and Park Road. In that year, however, Patrick Collins, the amusement caterer, bought land behind his home, Lime Tree House in High Street, for use as a fair ground.[56] The wake

---

[28] A stone on the church is dated 1957. It was registered in June 1958: Worship Reg. no. 66762.

[29] One of the stones on the present church was laid by Sam Wiggin, described as 'first president of this Church 1921'.

[30] It occurs in *Kelly's Dir. Staffs.* (1928; 1932).

[31] The foundation-stone is dated 22 Oct. 1938. The church was registered in Jan. 1939: Worship Reg. 58513.

[32] See p. 248.

[33] *S.H.C.* 4th ser. iii. 152; Glew, *Walsall*, 58; date on building.

[34] See p. 257.

[35] *Religious Reformer*, Oct. 1883, 2 (copy in W.C.L.).

[36] Worship Reg. no. 17178 (cancelled 1896 on revision of official list).

[37] Ibid. no. 17255 (cancelled 1896 on revision of official list).

[38] Ibid. nos. 43581, 59511.

[39] *Walsall Red Book* (1912), 83; (1917), 145.

[40] Worship Reg. nos. 53569, 54722; *Walsall Red Book* (1934), 67.

[41] Worship Reg. no. 56111 (cancelled 1954 on revision of official list).

[42] Ibid. no. 56826 (cancelled 1954 on revision of official list).

[43] Ibid. no. 70819.

[44] Ibid. no. 72875.

[45] G.R.O., Worship Reg. nos. 69713, 73375; *Walsall Observer*, 31 Dec. 1971, 12 Apr. 1972; *Express & Star*, 17 Apr. 1972.

[46] Worship Reg. no. 70251.

[47] Ibid. no. 70536.

[48] Ibid. no. 71735.

[49] Ibid. no. 72746.

[50] F. W. Willmore, *Transcript of First Reg. Bk. of Par. Ch. of St. Matthew, Walsall, 1570–1649* (Walsall, 1890), 196.

[51] *Walsall Red Book* (1889), 157; S.R.O., D. 1287/18/24/ business corresp. 1803–5, R. Jesson to Lord Bradford, 11 Sept. 1804. For the fair see above pp. 187–8.

[52] *Walsall Observer Centenary Supplement*, 25 Oct. 1968.

[53] *Aris's Birmingham Gaz.* 24 July 1769.

[54] *Staffs. Advertiser*, 20 Aug. 1853, 25 Aug. 1858, 22 Aug. 1863, 25 Aug. 1866; *Evening Mail*, 21 Aug. 1968.

[55] Homeshaw, *Bloxwich*, 220.

[56] Ibid. 218.

was held there until the land was sold in 1970.[57] Since then it has taken place on temporary sites.[58]

A traditional custom at Walsall was the throwing of apples, nuts, and hot copper coins from the guild-hall windows to the assembled populace on St. Clement's day (23 November), when the mayor accounted. The distribution was followed by bob-apple, bite-apple, and other games. It was abolished in 1860.[59]

A bull-ring at Walsall is mentioned in 1618. In 1804 it was claimed that there had been no bull-baiting for more than 20 years. Bull-baiting took place at Bloxwich wake until the sport was banned by law in 1835.[60] Bear-baiting was probably another traditional sport: a bearward occurs in 1590, and a place called the bear-garden, evidently on Church Hill, is mentioned in 1750.[61] In 1702 there was a house in the town known as the Cock House, per-haps a cock-pit, and in the early 19th century mains were fought in a cock-pit behind the New Inn, Park Street, during Walsall races.[62] Cock-fighting appar-ently remained popular at Bloxwich until the late 19th century, and there were centres in Field Street and at the Barley Mow, Goscote.[63] In 1855 police raided a cock-fight at the Brickmakers' Arms, Birchills.[64]

In 1599 John Persehouse the elder leased land in Holbrook field called 'bowling leys' to Roger Com-berlege, reserving the right for himself and his friends to play bowls there.[65] The Persehouse family also had a bowling-green in Walsall field by 1693; it apparently descended with the Reynold's Hall estate.[66] In 1629 Edward Leigh of Rushall was im-prisoned by the mayor for playing bowls on 'an open green' at Bloxwich.[67] There was a bowling-green at the Green Dragon in High Street by 1769, and by 1782 another in Birmingham Street, adjoin-ing the Wheatsheaf. Both were still in use in 1813, when there was a third green at the Dog and Par-tridge, Windmill Street.[68]

There were race-meetings at Walsall from 1777 to 1871 and from 1873 to 1876 on a course in Long Meadow between the brook and the mill fleam. Until 1869 they were held in the same week as the Michaelmas fair, and it was stated in 1804 that they had been instituted as a substitute for bull-baiting at the wakes. In 1870 and 1871, however, they took place in October, and from 1873 in August. A grand

stand designed by Benjamin Wyatt of Sutton Cold-field (Warws.) was built at the north-east end of the course in 1809 and demolished in 1879.[69] Occasional meetings have been held in the town in the 20th cen-tury: in 1942 one took place on a course near Mellish Road.[70] Races were held at Bloxwich by 1841. They coincided with the wakes, and plays and shows were put on at a temporary theatre on the course. The site of the original course is unknown; in 1866 the races were run in a field at Blakenall Heath, but they have also been held on the site of the present Leamore playing-fields.[71]

Mystery plays were performed in Walsall in the late 15th century: in 1494 the council ordained that groups of tradesmen should contribute to the repair and maintenance of the play garments.[72] In the late 16th and early 17th centuries visiting companies, including the Queen's, the King's, and the Prince's, put on plays in the guildhall,[73] where plays were still performed in the 1750s.[74] In 1766 William Siddons, later husband of Sarah Siddons, gave a performance of *Douglas* at a malt-house in Lime Pit Bank.[75] The assembly-room at the Dragon was used as a tempor-ary theatre from at least 1787 to 1803. In 1802, how-ever, J. B. Watson, an owner of theatres in several provincial towns, petitioned the mayor and justices for permission to build a permanent theatre in Walsall. A theatre in the Square was built by sub-scription in 1803; Watson apparently owned the business by 1813.[76] Performances were still being held there in 1841, but in 1845 the proprietors were evicted for arrears of rent. By the mid 1850s the building was occupied by shops or offices.[77]

After the closure of the theatre performances were given by travelling companies, and an amateur group, the Walsall Dramatic Club, was founded in 1865.[78] There was, however, no permanent theatre for some years. An Agricultural Hall built in Dar-wall Street in 1868 was used as a theatre from at least 1869. Between 1881 and 1883 the building was altered for use as a permanent theatre; it was known from c. 1886 as St. George's Hall, from c. 1891 as St. George's Hall and Theatre, and from c. 1895 as St. George's Theatre. It was again renovated in 1899 and was renamed the Imperial Theatre. In 1908 it became Walsall's first cinema. It was closed c. 1968 and in 1974 was a bingo hall.[79] By 1873 Charles Crooke was holding theatrical performances in the Alexandra Concert Hall, his former beer and wine

[57] *Walsall Observer*, 3 July 1970; *Express & Star*, 1 Feb. 1971.
[58] *Walsall Observer*, 10 Aug. 1973.
[59] Glew, *Walsall*, 37; *Walsall Red Book* (1882), 83–5; Willmore, *Walsall*, 428–9; above p. 213.
[60] S.R.O., Q/SR, M. 1618, no. 20; D. 1287/18/24, busi-ness corresp. 1803–5, J. Curtis to Lord Bradford, 15 Oct. 1804; Homeshaw, *Bloxwich*, 220; D. E. Parry and K. F. Jones, *Bloxwich in History* (Bloxwich, 1941), 18 (copy in W.C.L.); Act to consolidate and amend the several laws relating to the cruel and improper treatment of animals, 5 & 6 Wm. IV, c. 59.
[61] Willmore, *First Reg. of Ch. of St. Matthew*, 31; *Walsall Records*, 8 (2nd nos.).
[62] W.S.L. 896/36; Pearce, *Walsall*, 133; *Milward's List of Walsall Races* [1817] (copy in W.C.L.).
[63] Cason, *Blakenall Heath*, 25.
[64] *Staffs. Advertiser*, 2 June 1855.
[65] S.R.O., D. 260/M/F/1/5, f. 60v.
[66] L.J.R.O., B/V/6/Walsall, 1693–1796; above p. 177.
[67] Sims, *Cal. of Deeds*, p. 60.
[68] W.T.C. II/251/27; J. Snape, *Plan of Town of Walsall* (1782); Pearce, *Walsall*, 133; W.C.L., C. 4.
[69] *V.C.H. Staffs.* ii. 366–7; *Walsall Red Book* (1877),

67; Pearce, *Walsall*, frontispiece and p. 130; *Staffs. Adver-tiser*, 2 Oct. 1869, 8 Oct. 1870, 7 Oct. 1871, 23 Aug. 1873; S.R.O., D. 1287/18/24/business corresp. 1803–5, R. Jesson to Lord Bradford, 11 Sept. 1804.
[70] *Walsall Observer*, 8 Aug. 1942.
[71] *Staffs. Gaz.* 19 Aug. 1841; *Staffs. Advertiser*, 12 Aug. 1843, 20 Aug. 1853, 25 Aug. 1858, 25 Aug. 1866; W. F. Blay, *Story of Walsall Turnpike Roads and Tollgates* (Wal-sall, 1932), 11 (copy in W.C.L.).
[72] *S.H.C.* 1928, 224–5.
[73] W.T.C. II/13/1, 4, 7, 10–11; II/31/1–2, 7.
[74] *Aris's Birmingham Gaz.* 2, 9, and 16 Feb. 1756.
[75] Shaw, *Staffs.* ii. 75 and app. p. 15.
[76] *Aris's Birmingham Gaz.* 17 Sept. 1787; Pearce, *Wal-sall*, 132; W.T.C. II/204/3.
[77] Advertisement of 7 June 1841 (in W.C.L.); *Walsall Observer*, 4 Mar. 1966; Glew, *Walsall*, 38.
[78] *Staffs. Advertiser*, 25 Mar. 1865, 8 Dec. 1866; *Walsall News*, 27 Oct. 1866.
[79] *Kelly's Dir. Staffs.* (1880 and later edns. to 1940); *Staffs. Advertiser*, 22 May 1869; *Walsall Red Book* (1884), 148; (1886), 44; (1891), 44; (1895), 157; (1900), 201; O.S. Map 1/500, Staffs. LXIII. 11. 1 (1885 edn.); *Walsall Observer*, 1 Mar. 1968.

shop on the corner of Park and Station Streets. By 1879 it was a variety theatre called the Alexandra Theatre; it was later known as the Gaiety Theatre. It was rebuilt as the Grand Theatre in 1890 to the design of Daniel Arkell of Birmingham and became a variety theatre again in 1899. It was converted into a cinema in 1931 and was burnt down in 1939.[80] Her Majesty's Theatre at Townend Bank was opened in 1900 and became a variety theatre in 1905. It was converted into a cinema in 1933 and was demolished in 1937. In 1938 the Savoy cinema, later the A.B.C., was opened on the site.[81]

Although the Imperial Theatre became a cinema in 1908, the first purpose-built cinema in the borough was the Electric Picture Palace in the Square, opened in 1910.[82] Two cinemas were soon afterwards opened in Bloxwich, the Central Picture Palace in the former Wesleyan chapel in Park Road by 1912, and the Electric Picture Theatre (or Palace) in High Street by 1913.[83] There were 6 cinemas in the county borough by 1925 and 9 by 1939; by 1962 only 5 remained.[84] By 1973 there was only one cinema, the A.B.C. at Townend Bank, which was converted to a triple cinema in that year.[85]

The guildhall was probably the chief centre for public assemblies until the 18th century. Not only were plays performed there, but by the 1750s concerts and variety shows also.[86] A new assembly-room at the Castle inn is mentioned in 1768, and in 1793 one was built at the George. By 1787 there was also an assembly-room at the Dragon.[87] In 1851 it was enlarged and provided with ante-rooms and a new front in Goodall Street, of brick with stone dressings in a classical style.[88] The assembly-room at the George closed between 1892 and 1896.[89] The rooms in Goodall Street closed c. 1895;[90] in 1974 they were used as a probation office. In 1866 the Walsall Temperance Association began building a hall in Freer Street, designed by Loxton Brothers of Wednesbury. Opened in 1867, it was used for public meetings, lectures, and concerts, and in 1931 it became a cinema. It was demolished in 1965.[91] A public hall was built by subscription at the junction of High Street and Wolverhampton Road, Bloxwich, in 1857; it is of brick with stone dressings, in a classical style. It was used for music, plays, lectures, and other entertainment, and as a drill hall. By 1941 it was a labour exchange.[92] In 1974 it was the gym-

nasium of the neighbouring Bloxwich Church of England school.

In the 1640s the corporation paid for music at the fairs, and in the 1750s concerts were held in the guildhall.[93] The Walsall Harmonic Society was established apparently c. 1819. In 1830 and 1831 it held concerts of vocal and instrumental music at the Blue Coat School in Digbeth, but nothing further is known of it.[94] A choral society was founded c. 1841, but it was dissolved in 1853. A Philharmonic Society for the pursuit of both vocal and instrumental music was established in 1863, and a Choral Union c. 1870. They amalgamated in 1880 as the Walsall Philharmonic Union. In 1889 the union was affiliated to the Science and Art Institute in Bradford Place and was renamed the Walsall Institute Philharmonic Union; it resumed its earlier style c. 1904. At some time between 1917 and 1920 it became the Walsall Philharmonic Society. It was disbanded c. 1936.[95] Several other musical societies were founded from the 1880s onwards but most were short-lived.[96]

The first public library in Walsall was a subscription library established in 1800 by Thomas Bowen, the Unitarian minister, in his house in Rushall Street. By 1813 it had been moved to a room at Valentine & Throsby's stationery shop in High Street.[97] A permanent library was built in Lichfield Street in 1830–1. It is a stuccoed building of Greek Doric design, fronted by a tetrastyle portico.[98] It originally contained a large hall, divided into news and reading rooms and surrounded by a first-floor gallery. It soon became dilapidated, and in 1847 was sold to C. F. Darwall, clerk to the magistrates. It was in use as a savings bank in 1851, but between 1853 and 1855 Darwall adapted it to contain the county court offices and a lecture hall on the ground-floor and a freemasons' hall on the first floor.[99] After the sale to Darwall the library and news-room were transferred to J. R. Robinson's printing works at the Bridge; they remained there until 1875 when the library was dissolved and the books were presented to the free library.[1] A second subscription library was established in 1898 and dissolved in 1903.[2]

Walsall adopted the Free Libraries Act in 1857, and a library building was opened in Goodall Street in 1859. Designed by Nichols & Morgan, it is of brick in a Renaissance style.[3] In 1872 it was

[80] P.O. Dir. Staffs. (1872); Staffs. Advertiser, 29 Nov. 1873, 15 Nov. 1879; O.S. Map 1/500, Staffs. LXIII. 10. 5 (1886 edn.); Kelly's Dir. Staffs. (1892); Building News, 17 Nov. 1893; Walsall Red Book (1900), 205; Walsall Observer, 6 Jan. 1967; Walsall Observer Centenary Supplement, 25 Oct. 1968. For a view of the Grand Theatre see plate facing p. 177 above.
[81] Walsall Red Book (1900), 204; (1906), 248; Kelly's Dir. Staffs. (1928); Birmingham Mail, 19 May 1936; W.C.L., Newscuttings, vii, p. 119.
[82] Walsall Red Book (1911), 152.
[83] Ibid. (1912), 327; (1913), 179; Staffs. Advertiser, 27 Sept. 1913; Walsall Observer, 1 Mar. 1968.
[84] Walsall Red Book (1925), 153; (1939), 95; Barrett's County Boro. of Walsall Dir. (1962–3).
[85] Walsall Observer, 21 Sept., 23 Nov. 1973.
[86] Aris's Birmingham Gaz. 19 Aug. 1751, 18 Sept. 1752.
[87] Ibid. 28 Mar. 1768, 17 Sept. 1787; Pearce, Walsall, 131–2.
[88] Plaque on building; Staffs. Advertiser, 20 Dec. 1851.
[89] Kelly's Dir. Staffs. (1892; 1896).
[90] It occurs in Walsall Red Book (1895), 146, but not ibid. (1896), 157, or in later edns.
[91] Ibid. (1877), 58–72; (1932), 49; Staffs. Advertiser,

12 May 1866, 2 Feb. 1867; Walsall Observer Centenary Supplement, 25 Oct. 1968.
[92] Parry and Jones, Bloxwich, 22–3; Kelly's Dir. Staffs. (1892); Walsall Red Book (1905), 232.
[93] W.T.C. II/13/30–1, 34; and see above.
[94] Staffs. Advertiser, 4 Dec. 1830 (12th concert), 12 Nov. 1831 (13th concert).
[95] Staffs. Gaz. 20 Jan. 1842; G. Gill and H. D. Clark, Walsall Philharmonic Union 1863–1913 . . ., 5, 7, 17, 25 (copy in W.C.L.); Walsall Red Book (1872), 27; (1876), 47–8; (1881), 107; (1905), 229; (1917), 193; Walsall Blue Book (1920), 115. The Philharmonic Soc. last appears in Walsall Red Book in the edn. of 1936, p. 100.
[96] Walsall Red Book (1883 and later edns.).
[97] Pearce, Walsall, 114; H. Warnock, 'Short Sketch of the Origin and Progress of Nonconformity in Walsall', 3 (TS. in W.C.L.).
[98] Walsall Note Book, 50, 67, 161 (copy in W.C.L.); plate facing p. 97 above.
[99] White, Dir. Staffs. (1851); Staffs. Advertiser, 9 July 1853; Glew, Walsall, 51–2.
[1] White, Dir. Staffs. (1851); Willmore, Walsall, 392–3.
[2] Walsall Advertiser, 17 Jan. 1903.
[3] T. Kelly, Hist. of Public Libraries in Gt. Brit. 1845–1965, 455; Walsall Red Book (1917), 75; Pevsner, Staffs. 294.

converted into a news-room, and a library and reading room was built over it.[4] The building was extended in 1887, and in 1890 the upper room was converted to contain an art gallery, museum, and reference library.[5] It was replaced in 1906 by the present library in Lichfield Street, built with funds given by Andrew Carnegie.[6] The new building is of brick with stone dressings and was designed in a Baroque style by J. S. Gibson of London.[7] Open access was introduced in 1931.[8] In 1965 an extension was built and named the E. M. Flint Gallery after the chairman of the borough's library and art gallery committee; it included an art gallery and rooms for lectures and exhibitions.[9] In 1967–8 a museum of leathercraft was established there with items lent by the Museum of Leathercraft in London, which transferred its entire collection to Walsall in 1971.[10] In 1974 the first-floor of the original building was reorganized as a gallery housing the Garman-Ryan art collection, given by Lady (Kathleen) Epstein in 1973.[11] The first branch library in Walsall was established in Harrison Street, Bloxwich, in 1872.[12] It later moved to the public buildings in Station Street built in 1882–4.[13] Separate accommodation for the library was provided in 1948 in a temporary structure in Pinfold.[14] The present library in Elmore Row was opened in 1960; an extension containing a hall used as a theatre and lecture room was opened in 1964.[15]

From the earlier 19th century several monthly magazines were established in Walsall, but all have been short-lived. The first was the *Walsall Note Book*, which appeared from July 1830 to June 1831. Founded by J. L. Chavasse, it included articles and letters on local affairs, local history, religion, and scientific subjects, short stories, and verses.[16] Later periodicals of a similar type included the *Walsall Monthly Magazine and Journal of Popular Literature* (1855–6);[17] the *Walsall Observer and Repository of Local Literature* (1862–3);[18] and the *Midland Magazine* (1880).[19] The *Walsall Whip and South Stafford-shire Charivari* (1881–2) was a Liberal political and satirical magazine. Two other monthly magazines, the *Walsall Tatler* (1909) and the *Walsall Enterprise* (1927–8), included gossip and articles on local affairs and women's fashions; the *Enterprise* also ran articles on sport.[20]

The earliest known Walsall newspaper was a weekly *Walsall Courier and South Staffordshire Gazette*, established in 1855; its publishers, Newey & Foster of New Street, claimed that it would be 'equally suited for all classes . . . really a Walsall family newspaper'.[21] It was evidently short-lived. A weekly *Walsall Guardian and District Advertiser* was established in 1856 and was continued, with various modifications to its title, until 1869. It was apparently never printed in Walsall, and in its later issues contained little or no Walsall news.[22] Another weekly, the Liberal *Walsall Free Press and South Staffordshire Advertiser*, ran from 1856 until 1903, when it was incorporated into the *Walsall Observer*.[23]

The *Walsall Advertiser and Newspaper* was established in 1857 by J. R. Robinson, a Walsall printer and bookseller. It started as a free advertising-sheet containing a little local news. In 1892 it was enlarged, began to provide normal news coverage, and became a penny newspaper. The title became simply the *Walsall Advertiser*. In 1916 it was renamed the *Walsall Pioneer and District News*. Its politics had been Unionist since its transformation in 1892, but from 1916 it became more closely identified with Conservative policies. In 1922 it too was incorporated into the *Walsall Observer*.[24] W. H. Tomkins, a Walsall printer and bookbinder, ran a weekly *Walsall Herald* from January 1861 until January 1862.[25] A Liberal weekly, the *Walsall News and General District Advertiser*, was established in 1865 by the brothers John and William Griffin, who printed and published it until May 1867. It was then continued in other hands until 1872.[26] F. W. Willmore mentions a *Walsall Standard* among the news-

---

[4] *Staffs. Advertiser*, 8 June, 12 Oct. 1872.

[5] *Walsall Observer*, 20 Dec. 1924.

[6] *Staffs. Advertiser*, 29 Dec. 1906. For the later use of the old library as an art school see below p. 265.

[7] *Programme and Souvenir of Opening of New Free Library, Lichfield Street, Walsall, 24 July 1906* (copy in W.C.L.).

[8] Ex inf. the director of libraries and museum services (1975).

[9] *Opening of the Extension to the Central Library and E. M. Flint Art Gallery* (copy in W.C.L.).

[10] *County Boro. of Walsall: Public Libraries and Art Gallery: 109th Ann. Rep. 1967–68* (copy in W.C.L.); *Walsall Observer*, 5 Feb. 1971.

[11] *Walsall Observer*, 29 July 1973, 12 July 1974.

[12] Homeshaw, *Bloxwich*, 171; *Walsall Observer*, 20 Dec. 1924.

[13] *Staffs. Advertiser*, 30 Dec. 1882; *Walsall Red Book* (1885), 58.

[14] Homeshaw, *Bloxwich*, 213.

[15] *Express & Star*, 30 Sept. 1960; *Programme of Inaugural Play of Bloxwich Drama and Lecture Room 10–16 Sept. 1964* (copy in W.C.L.); 'County Boro. of Walsall: Public Libraries Service . . . 1966', 2 (TS. in W.C.L.).

[16] *Walsall Note Book* (copy in W.C.L.); Willmore, *Walsall*, 403. For Chavasse see Fink, *Queen Mary's Grammar Sch.* 345.

[17] Willmore, *Walsall*, 428; *Walsall Monthly Mag.* i (7), Feb. 1856 (copy in W.C.L.). A *Walsall Miscellany* established in the 1850s (Willmore, *Walsall*, 427) may also have been a magazine.

[18] Set in W.C.L.   [19] Set in W.C.L.

[20] Sets in W.C.L.

[21] Willmore, *Walsall*, 427, dating it c. 1853; undated handbill (copy in W.C.L.) advertising first issue of *Walsall Courier*, to appear on Saturday 26 May. In 1855 26 May fell on a Saturday; the handbill also contains what is apparently a reference to the abolition, in 1855, of newspaper stamp-duty. No copy of the newspaper has been traced.

[22] Files of the newspaper in B.M. Newspaper Libr. It became the *Walsall Guardian and Mercantile Advertiser* for the issue of 19 July 1856 and the *Walsall Guardian and Midland Counties Advertiser* on 26 July 1856. By Jan. 1869 it was the *Walsall Guardian, Birmingham, Lichfield, Stafford, and Midland Counties Advertiser*. The last issue in the B.M. Newspaper Libr. is that of 28 Sept. 1869; the newspaper evidently did not survive much longer.

[23] Files of the newspaper in W.C.L.

[24] Files of the newspaper in W.C.L. From 24 Apr. 1920 it was the *Walsall Pioneer and South Staffordshire News*. For its politics see *Walsall Advertiser and Newspaper*, 4 June 1892, announcing transformation of paper from next issue; K. J. Dean, *Town & Westminster* (Walsall, 1972), 240.

[25] Files of the newspaper in B.M. Newspaper Libr. It was entitled the *Walsall Herald* for issues of 5 Jan. to 6 Apr. 1861, became the *Walsall Herald and District Intelligencer* on 13 Apr. 1861 and the *Walsall Herald and Willenhall and Bloxwich Advertiser* on 29 June 1861.

[26] Files of the newspaper in B.M. Newspaper Libr. There are issues for 1868–72 in W.C.L. The last issue in the B.M. Newspaper Libr. is that of 30 Mar. 1872; the newspaper evidently did not survive much longer. For its politics see issues of 16 Sept. 1865 and 17 Oct. 1868.

papers founded in the 1850s and 1860s, naming the editor.[27]

The weekly *Walsall Observer and South Staffordshire Chronicle* was established in 1868, under a slightly different title, by John and William Griffin.[28] It has absorbed three rivals and in 1954 became again (as it had briefly been in the 1920s) the town's only newspaper. In 1974 the head offices and printing works of its proprietors, the West Midlands Press Ltd., were in Leamore Lane, Bloxwich.

The *Walsall Recorder*, a half-penny weekly which stated that politically it stood for 'Liberalism and Labour', was established in April 1906 and ran until April 1907.[29] The weekly *Walsall Times and South Staffordshire Advertiser* was established in 1925 by E. F. Cope, proprietor of a Walsall printing firm. He intended to break the monopoly then enjoyed by the *Walsall Observer*, and continued the paper until his death in 1954. Later that year the *Times* was incorporated into the *Observer*.[30]

In 1836 a Walsall Literary Society was founded.[31] Nothing further is known of it, but in 1841 the Walsall Philosophical Institution was established in connexion with the library. It continued until 1875.[32] A Walsall Lecture Institute was founded *c.* 1868,[33] and in 1876 there was a Literary Institute which met weekly in the Borough Club in Freer Street; it had about 60 members.[34] Both foundations were apparently short-lived. A new Literary Institute was founded in 1884, holding weekly lectures in the Temperance Hall. It opened a reading room in Bridge Street in 1889; the room was moved to Lichfield Street in 1891 and was closed in 1896. In 1910 the institute was disbanded. It was revived from 1928 to 1934.[35]

Walsall Cricket Club existed by 1833; at first it used a ground at the Chuckery, but it moved to one at Windmill in 1847 and remained there until *c.* 1850. During those years the Chuckery ground was occupied by another club, the Tradesmen's. During the 1850 and 1851 seasons both clubs apparently stopped playing, but in 1852 the Walsall Cricket Club was re-formed and took a new lease of the Chuckery ground. It remained there until 1909 when a new ground was opened at Gorway. The club still occupied it in 1974.[36] An Independent Cricket Club was founded at Bloxwich *c.* 1848; it may have been the Bloxwich Cricket Club which existed by 1863 and

by 1911 had a ground in Stafford Road. It was disbanded during the First World War but was re-established *c.* 1928 with a ground in Lichfield Road. It became Bloxwich Stafford Road Sports Club *c.* 1935.[37]

Walsall's first football club was established in 1873 in connexion with Walsall Cricket Club. By 1882 there were 30 clubs. The most important were Walsall Swifts, founded in 1877, and Walsall Town, founded in 1879. In the 1880s the two clubs had adjoining grounds at the Chuckery. In 1888 they amalgamated as Walsall Town-Swifts, becoming Walsall Football Club in 1896. The united club moved from the Chuckery to a ground at Maw Green in 1893 and to one in Hillary Street in 1896. It returned temporarily to Maw Green in 1900 but since 1903 has played on the Hillary Street ground, known since at least 1931 as Fellows Park after H. L. Fellows, then chairman.[38] The principal Bloxwich club was Bloxwich Strollers, which existed by 1893. By 1895 it was playing on a ground in Little Bloxwich Lane. About 1901, however, it moved to a field behind the Red Lion, Leamore, the club's headquarters from at least 1910. The ground was taken over by Bloxwich Football Club *c.* 1933. The Strollers was disbanded *c.* 1934 but was revived after the Second World War.[39]

The first known friendly societies in Walsall were formed in the 1760s, and the first known societies in Bloxwich in the 1770s.[40] By 1803 there were 10 societies in the borough and 13 in the foreign, with a total membership of 1,864.[41] In 1813 there were some 30 or 40 societies in borough and foreign, with a total membership of 1,786. They included gift clubs, benefit societies attached to chapels, and six lodges of national orders such as Odd Fellows and Loyal Britons; it was claimed that Walsall had more friendly societies than any other town in Staffordshire.[42] The primacy, if true, was not maintained. In 1876 there were 36 registered societies in Walsall[43] and 13 in Bloxwich.[44] Most had been established in the 1860s and 1870s; none of the 18th-century societies, and only 4 of those founded before 1830, had survived. Among the Walsall societies in 1876 were 12 lodges and one juvenile branch of Odd Fellows, 8 courts and one juvenile society of the Ancient Order of Foresters, a division of the Sons of Temperance, and a sanctuary of the Ancient Order

[27] Willmore, *Walsall*, 427. No copy has been traced.
[28] The original title was *Walsall Observer and General District Advertiser*. For the following para. see *Walsall Observer*, 31 Dec. 1965, 20 Oct. 1972; *Walsall Observer Centenary Supplement*, 25 Oct. 1968. There are files of the newspaper in W.C.L.
[29] Files of the newspaper in B.M. Newspaper Libr. There are copies of the 1906 issues in W.C.L.
[30] *Walsall Times*, 17 Jan. 1925, 20 Mar. and 12 June 1954. There are files of the newspaper in W.C.L.
[31] *Staffs. Advertiser*, 11 June 1836.
[32] See p. 264.
[33] *Staffs. Advertiser*, 17 Apr. 1889.
[34] *Walsall Red Book* (1876), 52.
[35] Ibid. (1886), 40; (1890), 120; (1891), 137; (1897), 198; (1911), 84; (1935), 34; W.C.L., Walsall Literary Institute Mins. 1928–34, 16 July 1928.
[36] *V.C.H. Staffs.* ii. 368; B. Evans and J. B. Griffin, *Hist. of Walsall Cricket Club* (Walsall, 1904), 11, 13, 81–5; E. J. A. Cook, *The Gorway Story: the Later Hist. of Walsall Cricket Club* (Walsall, 1959), 12–13, 15; *Metropolitan Boro. of Walsall Official Town Guide* [1974], 57.
[37] *Staffs. Advertiser*, 19 Aug. 1848, 11 Apr. 1863; *Walsall Red Book* (1912), 183; (1917), 226; (1928), 125; (1935), 90.
[38] *Walsall Red Book* (1882), 52, 101; (1931), 126; *V.C.H. Staffs.* ii. 371, 373; W. B. Rowlinson, *1888–1955: Walsall Football Club: the Walsall Observer Handbook*, 3, 7 (copy in W.C.L.); O.S. Map 6", Staffs. LXIII. SE. (1903 edn.).
[39] *Walsall Red Book* (1893), 188; (1895), 207; (1901), 216; (1910), 336; (1933), 90; Homeshaw, *Bloxwich*, 208–9; Cason, *Blakenall Heath*, 37.
[40] Pearce, *Walsall*, 218–20.
[41] *Abstract of Returns relative to Expence and Maintenance of Poor*, H.C. 175, p. 469 (1803–4), xiii. Shaw, *Staffs.* ii. 73 and app. p. 15, estimated *c.* 1800 that *c.* 750 men and women were members of friendly societies in Walsall and that a few years earlier *c.* 1,200 had belonged.
[42] *Abstract of Answers and Returns relating to Expense and Maintenance of Poor in Eng.* p. 419, H.C. (1818), xix, giving membership but not number of societies; Pearce, *Walsall*, 218–21, listing lodges, benefit clubs, and gift societies. Pearce's statement (p. 219) that there were 19 benefit clubs and 10 gift societies, in addition to the 6 lodges, appears to conflict with the list he gives.
[43] *Rep. Chief Registrar of Friendly Societies, 1876*, App. P, H.C. 429-1, pp. 411–12 (1877), lxxvii.
[44] Ibid. pp. 176, 393.

of Shepherds. The Bloxwich societies included 2 lodges and 2 independent societies of Odd Fellows, 2 courts of Foresters, a lodge of Free Gardeners, and 2 lodges of Benevolent Brothers.

EDUCATION. There was a school at Walsall by 1377, when Robert the schoolmaster was admitted as a burgess.[45] In the 1490s a Walsall chantry priest, John Staple, kept a school where he taught poor children free.[46] The school was not attached to his chantry, and there is no evidence that any of the chantry priests kept school in the 1540s. The chantry commissioners in fact suggested that a school which existed at Shenstone should be transferred to Walsall, one of the six Staffordshire towns which they considered suitable sites for free schools. The proposal came to nothing, but a grammar school was eventually established in the town by royal charter in 1554.[47] At Bloxwich the minister kept a school in his house in the mid 16th century; in 1613, however, the house was a tavern, and the school had apparently been discontinued.[48] It was succeeded by an endowed English school for Bloxwich and the surrounding hamlets, established in 1617. Between 1656 and 1662 Walsall corporation maintained a school for poor children, possibly a precursor of a Blue Coat charity school which existed in the town by the earlier 18th century. A dissenting charity school was endowed by George Fowler by his will of 1699.[49]

Several Sunday schools had been established in Walsall and Bloxwich by 1813, the first in 1789 in connexion with Dudley Street Independent chapel.[50] In 1819 there were in the parish, besides the endowed schools, 5 schools taught by masters, with 96 boys and 21 girls; 25 schools taught by mistresses, with 178 boys and 322 girls; an unspecified number of boarding schools for boys, with 58 pupils; and four Sunday schools, with 843 pupils. It was stated that the Walsall poor had sufficient schools but that the Bloxwich poor were short of them.[51] In 1833 more than 1,200 children attended day schools in the parish and there were over 1,700 pupils at Sunday schools.[52]

A survey of elementary education in the town in 1870 showed that there were 5,755 children at day schools, 462 at night schools, and 14 'half-timers'.

It was considered that over 2,000 extra school places were needed.[53] A school board was formed in 1871,[54] and it was then discovered that in fact over 4,000 extra places were required.[55] A by-law making school attendance compulsory was passed in 1872, but for many years Walsall had the worst attendance record of any of the Black Country boroughs. It was not until c. 1900, after the formation of a school attendance committee, that the position improved.[56]

In 1903 Walsall, as a county borough, took responsibility for all stages of public education. In 1929–32 schools were reorganized on the basis of the Hadow Report.[57] In 1947 a bilateral secondary school was established; by 1973 comprehensive secondary education was general except at the town's two voluntary aided grammar schools, Queen Mary's Schools, whose future was then undecided.[58]

In 1894 the board established a pupil-teachers' centre. The governors of Queen Mary's Schools were empowered to set up a pupil-teachers' centre in 1904; all pupil-teacher training was given at Queen Mary's Schools from 1906 until its abolition c. 1920.[59] In 1968 the borough opened an education development centre to provide courses and other in-service training for teachers employed by the borough.[60]

Special education for handicapped children began in 1894 when, under the 1893 Elementary Education (Blind and Deaf Children) Act,[61] the board began to pay for children to attend the deaf, dumb, and blind institutes at Edgbaston, Birmingham.[62] The borough opened a special open-air school for delicate or anaemic children, one of the first in the country, in Reedswood Park in 1919.[63] The Open Air School, from 1951–2 Reedswood Park Day Special School,[64] moved to temporary premises in Willenhall in 1968[65] and to purpose-built premises in Skip Lane in 1970, when it became Three Crowns Special School.[66]

The Midland Truant (later Beacon) School at Lichfield, an industrial school for boys, was built in 1893 by Walsall and the boroughs of Burton-upon-Trent and West Bromwich.[67] The industrial-school system was abolished in the early 1920s; Walsall then took sole responsibility for Beacon School and reopened it as a residential school for mentally defective children in 1926.[68] It was co-educational until 1940–1, when it began to admit only boys.[69]

[45] W.T.C. II/238, m. 1.
[46] Fink, *Queen Mary's Grammar Sch.* 33–4.
[47] Ibid. 50–8, 61–4.
[48] H. B. Wilson, *Hist. of Merchant-Taylors' Sch.* i(1812), 418 n.; above p. 234.
[49] See pp. 255–7.
[50] Pearce, *Walsall*, 117, 127; above p. 243.
[51] *Digest of Returns to Sel. Cttee. on Educ. of Poor*, H.C. 224, p. 869 (1819), ix (2).
[52] *Educ. Enquiry Abstract*, H.C. 62, p. 890 (1835), xlii.
[53] P. Liddle, 'Development of Elementary Education in Walsall between 1862 and 1902' (London Univ. M.A. (Educ.) thesis, 1967), 48–9; *Walsall Free Press*, 17 Dec. 1870. Attendance figures included children at the workhouse schools but not those at the grammar school or the 15 private-adventure schools charging more than 9d. a week.
[54] Willmore, *Walsall*, 437; *Staffs. Advertiser*, 21 and 28 Jan., 4 Feb. 1871; Liddle, 'Elementary Education', 49–53.
[55] Liddle, 'Elementary Education', 57–8; *Staffs. Advertiser*, 15 July 1871.
[56] *Staffs. Advertiser*, 10 Feb. 1872; Liddle, 'Elementary Education', 74, 76–92.
[57] *1st Rep. Walsall Educ. Cttee.* (1904), *passim*; *26th Ann.*

Rep. Walsall Educ. Cttee. (1929–30), 5; *28th Ann. Rep.* (1931–2), 7. There is a complete set of the reps. in W.C.L.
[58] *44th Ann. Rep.* (1947–8), 7; Walsall Educ. Cttee. *Secondary Educ. in Walsall* (Walsall, 1973), 1–5 (copy in W.C.L.).
[59] Liddle, 'Elementary Education', 67, 197, 217–20, and photographs facing pp. 67 and 217; Fink, *Queen Mary's Grammar Sch.* 322, 362.
[60] *64th Ann. Rep.* (1967–8), 31. And see *65th Ann. Rep.* (1968–9), 2; *67th Ann. Rep.* (1970–1), 2; *68th Ann. Rep.* (1971–2), 20.   [61] 56 & 57 Vic. c. 42.
[62] Liddle, 'Elementary Education', 189.
[63] *16th Ann. Rep.* (1918–19), 42; *17th Ann. Rep.* (1920–1), 24; *Walsall Observer*, 10 Nov. 1972.
[64] *48th Ann. Rep.* (1951–2), 11.
[65] *64th Ann. Rep.* (1967–8), 18; *65th Ann. Rep.* (1968–9), 21.
[66] *66th Ann. Rep.* (1969–70), 21, 23; *Walsall Observer*, 10 Nov. 1972.
[67] *Kelly's Dir. Staffs.* (1896; 1912), *sub* Lichfield. For a description of the school c. 1900 see P. Dean, 'The Midland Truant School', *Windsor Mag.* xiii. 719–23.
[68] *20th Ann. Rep.* (1923–4), 8; *22nd Ann. Rep.* (1925–6), 7; *Staffs. Advertiser*, 6 Mar. 1926.
[69] *37th Ann. Rep.* (1940–1), 4.

After extensive rebuilding, completed in 1971, it became co-educational again in 1972.[70] In 1959 the corporation opened the non-residential Castle Special School in Odell Road, Bloxwich.[71] A training centre in Brewer Street for mentally handicapped children, managed by the Department of Health and Social Security, was handed over to the borough in 1971 and renamed Mary Elliot Special School.[72]

The education committee maintained a day nursery from c. 1917 until the early 1920s;[73] shortly after it was opened there was an attempt, apparently unsuccessful, to develop it into a nursery school.[74] From 1930–1 nursery classes were formed in some infants' schools; there were seven such classes by 1934.[75] During the Second World War the council established three nursery schools, Coal Pool, Fullbrook, and Sandbank.[76] Two more nursery schools, Little Bloxwich and Blakenall (later Valley), had been opened by 1973.[77] In 1969–71 12 nursery classes had been added to primary schools.[78]

A camp site for Walsall schoolchildren was bought in 1926 at Streetly in Shenstone by a voluntary body, the Walsall School Children's Holiday Camp Trust.[79] The site was sold in 1960, and in 1969 the trust bought a house and small estate at Llangollen (Denb.). It was subsequently developed by the trust in partnership with Walsall corporation as Bryntysilio Outdoor Education Centre, the trust providing holiday courses there for deprived children and the corporation using it as an outdoor education centre for secondary-school children.[80]

Several charities provide scholarships and grants for Walsall children and young people. They include the Fishley Educational and Apprenticing Foundation, the C. C. Walker Charity, and the Blanch Wollaston Walsall Charity.[81]

Queen Mary's Schools. Queen Mary's Grammar School was founded in 1554 and endowed with former chantry lands in Walsall, Tipton, and Norton Canes.[82] It was housed in a building on Church Hill adjoining the churchyard.

From 1793 the governors maintained a separate elementary school for 40 boys in Chatterton's Fold off Park Street.[83] In 1802 another elementary school for 40 boys was opened in Park Street; it was expanded to 50 boys in 1803. From 1806 until 1814 a master at Bloxwich was paid to teach writing and arithmetic to 25 boys there.[84] In 1815 the grammar school moved to a house in Park Street. The elementary schools in Chatterton's Fold and Park Street were merged and reopened as a Lancasterian school in the former grammar-school building. An

infants' school was set up in Park Street in 1831. In 1833 there were 35 boys and 35 girls at the infants' school; it was financed partly by the governors and partly by weekly payments from the children.[85]

In 1837 the grammar school was subdivided into a grammar school, which remained in Park Street, and a commercial school, which took over the premises of the Lancasterian school. The grammar school left Park Street in 1847 and was housed in the grand stand at Walsall race-course until 1850, when it and the commercial school moved into newly erected buildings in Lichfield Street. In 1873 it was renamed the high school and the commercial school became the lower school. The two schools were reunited in 1893 to form a single high school, renamed Queen Mary's Grammar School in 1909.

In 1893 the governors opened Queen Mary's High School for Girls in buildings in Upper Forster Street adjoining the boys' buildings in Lichfield Street. In 1918 they leased Moss Close, a house in Mellish Road, as a junior department for the grammar school, buying it in 1926. In 1924 Mayfield, a house in Sutton Road, was bought; it became a preparatory school for the girls' high school and a mixed kindergarten. The estate attached to Mayfield had already been bought in 1913 and 1921.

In 1947 the grammar school and the girls' high school, by then direct-grant schools, took instead voluntary aided status.[86] Mayfield became an independent preparatory school, though managed by the Queen Mary's Schools governors. It remained such in 1973.[87] The first stage of a new boys' grammar school was opened on the Mayfield estate in 1961. Moss Close was then closed and the junior boys moved to the Lichfield Street buildings.[88] The second stage was opened in 1965; the grammar school then vacated the Lichfield Street buildings, which were taken over by the girls' high school.

Bloxwich Church of England Junior and Infants' School. By will proved in 1616 William Parker, a London merchant taylor and a native of Bloxwich, left land to the Merchant Taylors' Company to provide a stipend of £20 for the minister of Bloxwich chapel. A condition of the bequest was that the minister should, without charge, teach the boys of Great and Little Bloxwich, Walsall, and Harden, 'and others that dwell in odd houses in Walsall parish' to read English, both printed and handwritten. The school was to be held in either the chapel or the minister's house.[89] In 1617 a newly appointed minister subscribed also as master of Bloxwich school.[90]

The minister was still the schoolmaster in the

[70] *68th Ann. Rep.* (1971–2), 27–9.
[71] *56th Ann. Rep.* (1959–60), 1.
[72] *67th Ann. Rep.* (1970–1), 11, 23; Walsall Educ. Dept., TS. List of Schools, Mar. 1973.
[73] *14th Ann. Rep.* (1916–17), unpaginated; *19th Ann. Rep.* (1922–3), 7.   [74] *15th Ann. Rep.* (1917–18), 19–20.
[75] *27th Ann. Rep.* (1930–1), 16–18; *30th Ann. Rep.* (1933–4), 10.
[76] *42nd Ann. Rep.* (1945–6), 4; TS. List of Schools, Mar. 1973.
[77] TS. List of Schools, Mar. 1973; *Walsall Observer*, 20 Dec. 1973.   [78] *67th Ann. Rep.* (1970–1), 3, 5, 11.
[79] *23rd Ann. Rep.* (1926–7), 16; *Staffs. Advertiser*, 4 June 1927; Dept. of Educ. and Science, reg. of educ. charities (1971).
[80] *Evening Mail*, 31 Jan. 1969; *66th Ann. Rep.* (1969–70), 55–6; *68th Ann. Rep.* (1971–2), 64–5; *Walsall Observer*, 22 Sept. 1972, 27 July 1973.

[81] Dept. of Educ. and Science, educ. char. reg. (1971); below pp. 269, 272–3.
[82] For what follows see, unless otherwise stated, Fink, *Queen Mary's Grammar Sch.* A fuller account of the school is reserved for a future volume of the Staffordshire *History*.
[83] For Chatterton's Fold see Blay, 'Street Names of Walsall', 156; J. Snape, *Plan of Town of Walsall* (1782).
[84] See p. 256. The governors also supported teachers in Walsall Wood and Shelfield: below p. 283.
[85] *Educ. Enquiry Abstract*, 890.
[86] *43rd Ann. Rep.* (1946–7), 14.
[87] *Walsall Observer*, 6 July 1973.
[88] For the rest of this para. see programme of official opening of new buildings 25 May 1966 (copy in W.C.L.).
[89] H. B. Wilson, *Hist. of Merchant-Taylors' Sch.* i (1812), 415–18, printing part of Parker's will; above p. 234.
[90] L.J.R.O., B/A/4/17, 2 Dec. 1617.

early 18th century.[91] By the early 19th century, however, he no longer taught but paid £8 of the £20 stipend to a master who taught 15 poor boys to read.[92] Between 1806 and 1814 the governors of Walsall grammar school also paid the master £25 a year to teach 25 boys writing and arithmetic.[93] In 1819 the payment was being continued by the parish.[94] The chapel clerk was the master in the early 19th century. He lived in the non-resident minister's house rent-free and apparently taught the children there;[95] the 'day school in the chapel yard' mentioned in 1813[96] was presumably the minister's house. In 1826, however, John Baylie, the newly appointed minister, decided to occupy the house. Then homeless, the school declined into a Sunday school, meeting in public house club-rooms.[97]

Baylie re-established the school in 1828 as a National school for boys and girls, built on a site given by Lord Bradford at what is now the northern end of High Street, Bloxwich. Fees of 1d. or 2d. a week were charged, but part of the income from Parker's bequest was used to provide free education at the school for 15 boys.[98] In 1833 108 boys and 70 girls attended on weekdays and 140 boys and 80 girls on Sundays. In 1844–5, with the aid of grants from government and the National Society, a classroom and an infants' schoolroom were added. A teacher's house was built in 1846.[99] In 1857 the basic weekly fee was 2d. for boys and girls and 1d. for infants. There was an additional fee of 2d. a week for older girls and for boys who attended an extra class held between 4 p.m. and 5 p.m.[1]

In 1862 the schools were rebuilt on the same site.[2] They were enlarged c. 1900.[3] In 1931, after further additions and alterations to the buildings, the schools, by then known as Bloxwich Church of England Schools, were reorganized as senior mixed and junior mixed and infants' schools. The senior mixed school became a secondary modern school after the 1944 Education Act. Both schools took voluntary controlled status in 1948.[4] In 1974 the secondary school was closed and its buildings were taken over by the junior and infants' school.[5]

Blue Coat Church of England Schools. Between

1656 and 1662 the corporation paid a man to teach poor children.[6] The payments may mark the establishment of the town's Blue Coat charity school;[7] if so, the school must have been supported by private donations after 1662, for the corporation seems to have made no further payments. No Walsall charity school is mentioned in a list published in 1709.[8]

By will dated 1723 the Revd. John Whittingham, headmaster of Walsall grammar school 1666–88, bequeathed £200 to the corporation after the extinction of life interests, to the use of the charity school, if it existed.[9] By the later 18th century the corporation was paying £10 a year to the Blue Coat school, the interest on the bequest.[10] Three smaller bequests had brought the school's endowment to £245 by 1773.[11] Jacob Smith of Walsall (d. 1800) bequeathed a further £100 in the form of a 25-year annuity of £4,[12] and by 1804 the school also received rent of £2 10s. yearly from land at Dudley (Worcs.) given by a John Taylor.[13] By then, however, most of the school's income came from collections and subscriptions. From at least 1765 collections in aid of the school were taken at an annual charity sermon preached at St. Matthew's on Wake Sunday, and by 1773 there were also subscribers.[14] In 1804 the school's income was some £123, of which about £20 came from the collections and about £60 from subscribers.[15]

By the later 18th century the school consisted of 24 boys and 16 girls. According to rules drawn up in 1779 they were to be elected by subscribers at the age of seven and must leave school at twelve. Boys were taught the elements and girls the elements, knitting, and sewing. 'Blue coat' clothing, traditionally worn at such schools, was provided annually.[16]

In 1776 the mayor granted the Blue Coat schoolmaster the use of the 'cross chamber' for a schoolroom. It was presumably the room in the market house in which the school was held in the 1790s.[17] The market house was demolished in 1800 and the school moved to premises in Digbeth, adjoining the George. The building consisted of a single schoolroom with a teacher's house attached, but in 1818–19 a second storey was added to the school to house a

[91] Ibid./13, 10 Jan. 1709/10.
[92] Pearce, *Walsall*, 117. *9th Rep. Com. Char.* H.C. 258, p. 605 (1823), ix, states that the master taught reading free to as many poor boys from the chapelry as were sent to him; but the number of free places was certainly 15 in the 1850s: see below.
[93] Fink, *Queen Mary's Grammar Sch.* 268; Pearce, *Walsall*, 117.
[94] *Digest of Returns to Sel. Cttee. on Educ. of Poor*, H.C. 224, p. 869 (1819), ix (2).
[95] Ibid.; *9th Rep. Com. Char.* 605.
[96] Pearce, *Walsall*, 117.
[97] Nat. Soc. files.
[98] Ibid.; S.R.O., D. 812/Bloxwich Nat. Schools; Pigot, *Nat. Com. Dir.* (1841), Staffs. p. 79.
[99] *Educ. Enquiry Abstract*, 890; Nat. Soc. files; S.R.O., D.812/Bloxwich Nat. Schools.
[1] Ed. 7/112/Walsall/4.
[2] A. C. Gregory, *One Hundred Years: the Story of Bloxwich Church of England Schools 1861–1961* (Walsall, 1961), 2–4 (copy in W.C.L.); S.R.O., D. 812/Bloxwich Nat. Schools.
[3] Nat. Soc. files.
[4] Gregory, *One Hundred Years*, 2, 8, 12, 14–15; *27th Ann. Rep. Walsall Educ. Cttee.* (1930–1), 10, 38; *28th Ann. Rep.* (1931–2), 9, 38.
[5] Ex inf. the headmaster (1974).

[6] W.T.C. II/13/45–50.
[7] Fink, *Queen Mary's Grammar Sch.* 161–2.
[8] *Account of Charity Schools lately erected in Great Britain and Ireland: with the benefactions thereto . . .* (8th edn., 1709).
[9] *9th Rep. Com. Char.* 572; Shaw, *Staffs.* ii. 80. For Whittingham see Fink, *Queen Mary's Grammar Sch.* 219–23, 227.
[10] *Abstract of Rets. of Charitable Donations, 1786–8*, H.C. 511, pp. 1132–3 (1816), xvi (2).
[11] L.J.R.O., B/V/5/1772–3, Walsall, mentioning total benefactions of £245. They were evidently those of Whittingham, John Harrison (£5), John Barber (£20), and John Hawe (£20): Shaw, *Staffs.* ii. 80–1.
[12] W.C.L., box 14, no. 7.
[13] S.R.O., D. 1287/18/24, business corresp. 1803–5, J. Curtis to H. Bowman, 15 Oct. 1804; *9th Rep. Com. Char.* 572.
[14] D. G. S. Watson, TS. hist. of Walsall Blue Coat schools, p. 7 (in possession of Mr. Watson, Blue Coat Secondary Sch. 1974); L.J.R.O., B/V/5/1772–3, Walsall; Shaw, *Staffs.* ii. 74.
[15] S.R.O., D. 1287/18/24, business corresp. 1803–5, Curtis to Bowman, 15 Oct. 1804.
[16] L.J.R.O., B/V/5/1772–3, Walsall; Watson, TS. hist. p. 8.
[17] W.T.C. II/170; Shaw, *Staffs.* ii. 74.

Sunday school.[18] Henceforth there was accommodation for 140 boys and 160 girls.[19] In 1819 free education was provided for 25 boys and 25 girls (24 boys and 16 girls being given blue-coat uniform), and there were 100 fee-paying children.[20]

By the mid 1820s the Digbeth building was unsafe and the school was meeting in borrowed rooms. As a first step towards its reinvigoration a National school was established in connexion with it in 1825.[21] In 1826 the two schools were formally united as Walsall Blue Coat and National School, which in 1827 moved back into the Digbeth building, repaired and enlarged to accommodate 228 boys and 228 girls.[22] In 1830 25 boys and 25 girls were taught free and 20 of each sex were also clothed; the remaining 125 boys and 108 girls paid 1d. a week.[23]

In 1859 the school moved to a larger building in St. Paul's Close designed in the Early English style by Henry Cooper of London. It was claimed to be the handsomest school building in the county and comprised schools for both sexes and houses for a master and a mistress. There was a large domestic science room for the girls, with a wash-house where laundering could be taught. The money for the site and the building came from gifts, subscriptions, the sale of the old school and of the school's land at Dudley, and a grant from government.[24] From 1884 the school took the older pupils from St. Matthew's Church of England School, and in 1906 the St. Matthew's School building became officially the Blue Coat infants' school.[25] After the 1891 Elementary Education Act the Blue Coat managers abolished school fees for infants, though continuing to charge them for older children.[26]

The St. Paul's Close building was closed in 1933; it was bought by the corporation and its site became the town's central bus station. Senior pupils were moved to a new building in Springhill Road, juniors to the former St. Matthew's vicarage in Hanch Place.[27] The infants' school moved into the Bath Street council school building after that school was closed in 1940.[28] In the reorganization after 1944 the senior school became secondary modern. In 1953 the governors decided to retain voluntary aided status and to provide new buildings for the secondary school. In 1965 the secondary school moved to Birmingham Street, the junior school to Springhill Road, and the infants' school to Hanch Place. From 1972 the secondary school was expanded to form a larger comprehensive school with its own sixth form.

The building of the former Chuckery council school was used as an annexe, and in 1973–4 additional buildings were being completed in Birmingham Street opposite those of 1965.[29]

The Dissenting Charity School. By will dated 1699 George Fowler devised land in Windmill Field, Walsall, upon trust, the income to be used for teaching poor children of the town of Walsall.[30] Fowler was a prominent Walsall Presbyterian,[31] and the feoffees of 'the dissenting charity school' who held land in Windmill Field in the 1760s and 1770s[32] presumably belonged to the town's Presbyterian meeting-house. From the late 18th century the charity was applied to a Sunday school established at the meeting-house, which had by then turned to Unitarianism. In the early 19th century some 30 children were taught reading and writing without charge. In 1823 writing lessons were given on weekday evenings in addition to the instruction on Sundays.[33] In 1855 the school held morning and afternoon sessions on Sundays and afternoon and evening sessions on Thursdays. Some 70 children attended on Sundays.[34]

Pleck Church of England School, otherwise Pleck and Bescot National School or St. John's National School. A National school was established at Pleck in 1825. It was then estimated that there were at Pleck 60 children aged between 7 and 13 who needed cheap or free schooling; the schoolroom which was built on the waste that year with the aid of a grant from the National Society was designed for fifty. It was proposed that they should pay fees of 2d. a week.[35] The school was put in the charge of a mistress.[36] In 1855 the population of Pleck was increasing rapidly and the 'small, ill-conditioned room' had become inadequate. A new school with a teacher's house attached was built on a site in Pleck Road given by Lord Bradford. Building grants were made by government and the National Society; local contributors included working men living in Pleck. The 1825 building was possibly retained as an infants' schoolroom.[37] Services were held in the new building until the opening of St. John's Church in 1858.[38] The new school was apparently opened in January 1856, and by September there were 54 boys and 46 girls on the books, all paying pence. The master conducted an evening school in connexion with the day school; it was held twice weekly, and attended by men and boys working in local collieries.[39] The building was enlarged in 1867, with the aid of a

---

[18] Shaw, *Staffs.* ii, App. p. 15; S.R.O., D. 1287/18/24, business corresp. 1803–5, Curtis to Bowman, 15 Oct. 1804; Walsall Char. Sch. accts. 1813–40 (in custody of Hon. Treasurer, Walsall Blue Coat Church of England Schools, 1973). For the demolition of the market house see above p. 187.

[19] Nat. Soc. files/Walsall/St. Matthew.

[20] *Digest of Returns to Sel. Cttee. on Educ. of Poor,* 869.

[21] Nat. Soc. files/Walsall/St. Matthew, applic. for grant 6 Mar. 1827, stating that the schoolrooms have not been used for many months and giving date of union with the Society as Oct. 1825.

[22] Ibid.; Watson, TS. hist. p. 9; S.R.O., D. 812/Blue Coat Nat. Sch., Walsall.

[23] S.R.O., D. 1287/12/1, Walsall and Wigan schools, list of subscribers to Walsall Blue Coat and Nat. Sch. 11 June 1830.

[24] *Staffs. Advertiser,* 30 Apr. 1859 (containing description of buildings), 14 May 1859; S.R.O., D. 812/Blue Coat Nat. Sch., Walsall.

[25] *Walsall Observer,* 15 May 1953; below p. 259.

[26] Nat. Soc. files/Walsall/Blue Coat Secondary Sch.

[27] *Walsall Observer,* 15 May 1953; Watson, TS. hist. pp. 9–10; above p. 227.

[28] Watson, TS. hist. pp. 10, 44A; below p. 260.

[29] *Walsall Observer,* 15 May 1953; Watson, TS. hist. pp. 10, 44A; below p. 261.

[30] Glew, *Walsall,* 182.

[31] See p. 247.

[32] S.R.O., D. 1287/1/8, rentals of chief and cottage rents of Walsall manor, 1765–7, 1768–70, 1771–4.

[33] Pearce, *Walsall,* 113; *9th Rep. Com. Char.* 572; above p. 248. The statement in *Digest of Returns to Sel. Cttee. on Educ. of Poor,* 869, that there were 230 children at the school appears to be an exaggeration.

[34] Glew, *Walsall,* 58, 182–3, 217.

[35] Nat. Soc. files/Walsall/Pleck and Bescot; /St. Matthew, letter of 17 Oct. 1825.

[36] White, *Dir. Staffs.* (1834; 1851).

[37] Nat. Soc. files; *Walsall Red Book* (1875), 69–70; S.R.O., D. 812/Pleck and Bescot Nat. Sch.

[38] See p. 237.

[39] Ed. 7/112/Walsall/18.

government grant, to provide separate schoolrooms for boys and girls.[40] In 1930 the building was remodelled and became an infant's school only.[41] It was closed in 1962.[42]

St. Peter's Roman Catholic Junior and Infants' School, formerly St. Thomas's Roman Catholic School. From 1825 a Roman Catholic day school was held in a small room next to the chapel of St. Thomas the Apostle in Harden Lane (now Harden Road), Bloxwich.[43] A schoolroom was built adjoining the chapel c. 1830. In 1833 some 56 pupils attended on weekdays and some 76 on Sundays. It seems that normally only reading was taught. Children whose parents could afford it were charged 1d. a week; there were extra fees of 1d. a week for writing and 1d. for arithmetic.[44] St. Thomas's was replaced by a new church, St. Peter's, opened in High Street, Bloxwich, in 1869;[45] the school was replaced in 1870, when a school was opened in Harrison Street, behind the new church. In 1871 it had 65 pupils on the books, all paying pence.[46] Numbers increased rapidly and three extensions had been built before 1899, when a new building was added; the 1870 building became the infants' department.[47] Senior pupils left in 1963 when Francis Martyn Roman Catholic High School was opened.[48] The school moved in 1972 to new buildings in Lichfield Road, Bloxwich.[49]

St. Mary's Roman Catholic Junior and Infants' School. In 1831 or 1832 a day and Sunday school for boys and girls was established in Vicarage Place in connexion with St. Mary's chapel. In 1833 80 pupils attended on weekdays and a few more on Sundays. Children whose parents could afford it paid 2d. a week.[50] In 1834 it was described as a charity school with an orphanage attached.[51] By 1855 the building had been enlarged and there was a day school under the care of the Sisters of Charity of St. Paul with an average attendance of some 150; there was a community of the Sisters in St. Mary's parish c. 1853–63.[52] In 1861 there were 50 boys, 71 girls, and 48 infants, all paying pence.[53] A new infants' department known as St. Joseph's Infants' School was opened in Glebe Street in 1912, the earlier building being extended and becoming a mixed department.[54] Senior pupils left in 1963 when Francis Martyn Roman Catholic High School was opened.[55] The Vicarage Place building was damaged by fire in 1967 and the school was housed in the former Bath Street council school until 1970, when a new St. Mary's School was opened in Jesson Road.[56]

St. Peter's Church of England Junior and Infants' School. In 1840 a building for a day and Sunday school for boys and girls was opened on a site in John Street given by Thomas Fowler. Some 130 children attended the day school on the first morning.[57] The money to build it was raised locally by a group of trustees headed by the vicar of St. Matthew's. When the parish of St. Peter was formed in 1845 the incumbent became manager of the school. In 1846 it was united with the National Society. There was then an average week-day attendance of 80 boys and 100 girls, and a further 80 boys and 30 girls attended on Sundays. The boys' curriculum consisted of the elements and religious instruction; they paid 1d. a week, or 3d. a week if they wrote on paper instead of slates. By 1849 there was also an infants' school held in a small temporary schoolroom.[58] It was replaced later in 1849 by a schoolroom for infants, also in John Street; the National Society contributed towards its cost and the cost of a house for two teachers, built at the same time. The infants' schoolroom was enlarged in 1866.[59]

In 1870 the girls were moved from John Street to buildings in Whitehouse Street erected with the aid of grants from government and the National Society. An infants' school was opened there in January 1871, and in February there was an average attendance of 120 girls and 90 infants.[60] In 1914 the boys were transferred from John Street to new buildings in Marlow Street.[61] In 1933 Marlow Street became a junior mixed school and Whitehouse Street an infants' department. Whitehouse Street was closed in 1955 and the infants joined the juniors in Marlow Street.[62]

Christ Church Church of England Junior and Infants' School, Blakenall Heath. In 1843 John Baylie, minister of Bloxwich, opened a National school for infants at Blakenall Heath, a branch of the National school at Bloxwich. Lord Bradford gave the site, and there were grants from government, the National Society, and the archidiaconal board of education. Queen Adelaide contributed to the building fund.[63] The building was also used as a mission church.[64] In 1846–7 a mistress, with some volunteer helpers on Sundays, taught 40 boys and 44 girls on Sundays and weekdays and 20 more boys on Sundays only.[65] The buildings were repaired and enlarged in 1861 and older children admitted; the first qualified mistress was appointed in 1863.[66] When Christ Church, Blakenall Heath, was opened

[40] *Walsall Red Book* (1875), 71; S.R.O., D. 812/Pleck and Bescot Nat. Sch.
[41] *26th Ann. Rep. Walsall Educ. Cttee.* (1929–30), 13; *27th Ann. Rep.* (1930–1), 7, 38.
[42] W.C.L., Pleck C. of E. Infants' Sch. log bk. 1947–62, p. 256.
[43] *St. Peter's Catholic Church, Bloxwich* (Walsall, 1956), chap. 6 (copy in W.C.L.); White, *Dir. Staffs.* (1851).
[44] *St. Peter's Catholic Church*, chap. 6, stating that it was built by J. Dunne, priest-in-charge 1829–31; *Educ. Enquiry Abstract*, 890, stating that sch. commenced in 1829. It may be the 'Walsall Roman Catholic School' which was built in 1830: Ed. 7/113/Walsall/20.
[45] See p. 241. [46] Ed. 7/112/Walsall/5.
[47] *St. Peter's Catholic Church*, chap. 6; *Walsall Red Book* (1900), 202, 207. [48] *Evening Mail*, 16 May 1964.
[49] *Walsall Observer*, 22 June 1973.
[50] *Educ. Enquiry Abstract*, 890; Ed. 7/112/Walsall/20; O.S. Map 1/500, Staffs. LXIII. 10. 15 (1885 edn.).
[51] *Catholic Mag.* v. 312.
[52] Glew, *Walsall*, 29–30; above p. 241.
[53] Ed. 7/112/Walsall/20.
[54] Ibid.; inscription on foundation-stone; *Walsall Red Book* (1912), 216; (1913), 201.
[55] *Evening Mail*, 16 May 1964.
[56] *Walsall Observer*, 13 Jan. 1967; *Express & Star*, 15 July 1970.
[57] Nat. Soc. files; *Staffs. Gaz.* 2 May 1840; *Staffs. Advertiser*, 20 July 1844. [58] Nat. Soc. files.
[59] Ibid.; S.R.O., D. 1287/12/3, P. Potter to Lord Bradford, 21 Feb. 1849.
[60] Ed. 7/112/Walsall/23; Nat. Soc. files; *Staffs. Advertiser*, 15 Oct. 1870; S.R.O., D. 812/St. Peter's Girls' and Infants' Nat. Schools, Walsall.
[61] Ed. 7/112/Walsall/23; Nat. Soc. files.
[62] Ex inf. the headmistress (1974).
[63] Nat. Soc. files/Bloxwich; ibid./Blakenall Heath. The building may have been completed late in 1842, but it was not opened until Apr. 1843. [64] Nat. Soc. files.
[65] National Society, *Church Schools Enquiry, 1846–7* (priv. print 1849).
[66] Ed. 7/112/Walsall/3; Cason, *Blakenall Heath*, 10.

in 1870 the school ceased to be used for worship. Responsibility for it passed to the new parish formed in 1873.[67] The buildings were altered and improved in 1928 and it subsequently became a junior mixed and infants' school.[68] It took voluntary controlled status in 1951.[69] It moved to new buildings off Harden Road, Blakenall Heath, in 1971.[70]

St. Paul's School, Shaw's Leasowes. There was an Anglican Sunday school at Shaw's Leasowes in 1840, and a day school connected with St. Paul's Church had been established by 1845 in a building there owned by the grammar school governors.[71] In 1846–7 a mistress taught 65 boys and 25 girls, and the school was supported by subscriptions and pence.[72] Control later passed, apparently in 1851, to the managers of St. Peter's National schools, who rented the building from the governors. In 1857 there were 60 children on the books.[73] The school had been closed by 1860.[74]

Wesleyan School, Bloxwich. A Wesleyan Methodist day school for boys and girls, with a master and mistress, had been established at Short Heath, Bloxwich, by 1845. It seems to have been closed soon after 1850.[75]

Ablewell Street Wesley School or Walsall Wesleyan Day School, later Ablewell Street Council School. A Wesleyan Methodist day school was opened in 1845 in a newly erected building in Forster Street. The managers stated in 1847 that it was open to children of all denominations.[76] When the Wesleyans built a new chapel in Ablewell Street in 1859 the old Ablewell Street chapel was converted into a day and Sunday school, presumably to replace the Forster Street building; the ground floor became an infants' school and a first floor was inserted to accommodate older children. The new school building was opened 1860 with two teachers and an average attendance of 80 boys, 50 girls, and 95 infants.[77] Ablewell Street became a council school in 1922.[78] It was reorganized to form a junior and infants' school in 1930 and was closed in 1931.[79]

Ragged School. A ragged school was established in Pig Lane in the late 1840s by a group which included the vicar of Walsall's wife and E. T. (later Sir Edward) Holden. It may be the Walsall Ragged Sunday school which existed in 1848. In 1849 or 1850 it was moved to a newly erected building at Townend Bank. It was closed in 1850 because, Holden subsequently explained, 'the smell of the children was such as to impair the health of the teachers', and later that year the building became a Primitive Methodist chapel.[80]

St. Matthew's Church of England School. An infants' school was opened in 1853 on a site given by Lord Bradford adjoining the east end of St. Matthew's Church; access was from Hill Street. Building grants were received from government, the National Society, and the diocesan board of education. There was accommodation for 150 in a single schoolroom, and a teacher's house was attached.[81] In 1855 there were 100 infants on the books, paying 2*d.* a week.[82] Subsequently older children were also admitted. From 1884 the school was run in conjunction with the Blue Coat schools and in 1906 the building became the Blue Coat infants' school.[83]

St. Andrew's Church of England Junior and Infants' School, formerly Birchills National School or St. Peter's (Birchills) School. In 1855 the managers of St. Peter's National schools opened a branch school in Hollyhedge Lane, Birchills. The school and a teacher's house stood on a site given by Lord Bradford and were built with the aid of grants from government and the National Society. The school was used as a mission church until St. Andrew's was consecrated in 1887.[84] In 1857 there was an average daily attendance of 80 children, paying weekly fees of 2*d.*, 3*d.*, or 4*d.*; the teacher conducted an evening school thrice weekly.[85] Birchills became an infants' school c. 1870;[86] older pupils were again admitted in the later 1880s.[87] It was handed over to the new parish of St. Andrew in 1890, but continued to be known as St. Peter's (Birchills) School until after the Second World War.[88] The buildings were enlarged in the 1890s.[89] It became a junior mixed and infants' school in the early 1930s.[90]

St. Patrick's Roman Catholic Junior and Infants' School. A day school was established in 1859 in a newly built schoolroom behind St. Patrick's Church in Blue Lane East. There was an average attendance in 1861 of 170, some of whom were apparently taught free.[91] A separate room for infants was added in 1864 and a new infants' school opened in 1902.[92] The school buildings were improved in 1929–30.[93]

[67] See p. 237; Nat. Soc. files.
[68] *25th Ann. Rep. Walsall Educ. Cttee.* (1928–9), 7, 9; *27th Ann. Rep.* (1930–1), 38.
[69] Cason, *Blakenall Heath*, 51.
[70] *Walsall Observer*, 16 July 1971.
[71] *Staffs. Gaz.* 24 Oct. 1840; *P.O. Dir. Staffs.* (1845); Ed. 7/113/Walsall/Shaw's Leasowes. The directory and *P.O. Dir. Staffs.* (1854) describe it as a National school, but there appears to be no evidence that it was united with the National Society.
[72] National Society, *Church Schools Enquiry, 1846–7.*
[73] Ed. 7/113/Walsall/Shaw's Leasowes. It was still connected with St. Paul's in 1849: Nat. Soc. files/Walsall/St. Peter (Girls and Infants).
[74] It does not occur in *P.O. Dir. Staffs.* (1860) or later directories.
[75] *P.O. Dir. Staffs.* (1845); Slater, *Nat. Com. Dir.* (1850), Staffs. p. 106. It does not occur in *P.O. Dir. Staffs.* (1850) or later directories.
[76] *Staffs. Advertiser*, 2 Aug. 1845; Ed. 7/112/Walsall/1.
[77] Ed. 7/112/Walsall/1; *Guide to Walsall* (1889), 46; L. Davison, *Story of Methodism in Walsall*, 5 (copy in W.C.L.); S.R.O., D. 812/Wesleyan Chapel Sch., Walsall.
[78] *Walsall Educ. Cttee. Mins. 1922–23* (copy in W.C.L.), 21–2, 30, 134; *19th Ann. Rep. Walsall Educ. Cttee.* (1922–3), 7.

[79] *26th Ann. Rep.* (1929–30), 45; *27th Ann. Rep.* (1930–1), 43; *28th Ann. Rep.* (1931–2), 37, 39.
[80] Slater, *Nat. Com. Dir.* (1850), Staffs. p. 106; *Walsall Free Press*, 15 July 1871; *Staffs. Advertiser*, 30 Dec. 1848; above p. 246.
[81] Glew, *Walsall*, 16, 25; S.R.O., D. 812/St. Matthew's Church of England Sch.; Nat. Soc. files.
[82] Ed. 7/113/Walsall/St. Matthew's Infant. Sch.
[83] *Walsall Observer*, 15 May 1953; *3rd Rep. Walsall Educ. Cttee.* (1906), 16. For the later history of the school see above p. 257.
[84] *Staffs. Advertiser*, 20 Oct. 1855; Nat. Soc. files; above pp. 237–8.   [85] Ed. 7/112/Walsall/24.
[86] It was described as a mixed school in 1869 (Nat. Soc. files) but as an infants' school in *P.O. Dir. Staffs.* (1872).
[87] It was still an infants' school in 1884 but had become a mixed and infants' school by 1888: *Kelly's Dir. Staffs.* (1884; 1888).
[88] Nat. Soc. files; *Ann. Reps. Walsall Educ. Cttee.*
[89] *Kelly's Dir. Staffs.* (1900); Nat. Soc. files.
[90] *28th Ann. Rep. Walsall Educ. Cttee.* (1931–2), 7.
[91] Ed. 7/112/Walsall/22; O.S. Map 1/500, Staffs. LXIII. 6. 20 (1886 edn.).
[92] Ed. 7/112/Walsall/22; *Walsall Red Book* (1902), 215; (1903), 228.
[93] *26th Ann. Rep. Walsall Educ. Cttee.* (1929–30), 13.

Senior pupils left in 1963 when Francis Martyn Roman Catholic High School was opened.[94] The school moved into new buildings in Blue Lane East in 1967.[95]

Caldmore Church of England School. In 1866 the vicar of Walsall appealed for funds to build a school and teacher's house at Caldmore. A government grant was also obtained.[96] The school, for boys, girls, and infants, with a teacher's house attached, was opened in 1867 on the corner of Caldmore Road and St. Michael Street.[97] When the new parish of St. Michael and All Angels was formed in 1872 the school was handed over to it.[98] In 1907 the infants' department was closed.[99] In the early 1930s Caldmore, by then a mixed school, became first a mixed and infant's school and then a junior mixed and infants' school.[1] It was closed in 1959.[2]

Wednesbury Road Congregational School, later Wednesbury Road Board School. There were British and infants' schools in connexion with the Congregational chapel in Wednesbury Road by 1869.[3] Larger day and Sunday schools were opened adjoining them in 1871.[4] By 1876 there were 476 pupils; but the managers could not afford to maintain the school, and in 1880 the building was leased to the board.[5] It continued as a board school until 1884, when Palfrey Board Schools were opened; it was again used as a temporary board and council school from 1902 to 1905.[6]

Whittimere Street School. In 1869 the trustees of the Methodist Free Church in Whittimere Street established a day school in their Sunday-school building. In 1872 there were 41 boys, 56 girls, and 27 infants on the books, with an average attendance of about 85. Fees ranged from 2d. to 6d. a week. The day school may have continued until the chapel closed in the early 1880s.[7]

Centenary Wesleyan School, later Centenary Council School. In 1870 a day school was established at Centenary Wesleyan Methodist chapel, Stafford Street; it occupied the Sunday-school rooms adjoining the chapel. A few days after it was opened there were 70 pupils, all paying pence.[8] In 1873 the school moved into new buildings in John Street with accommodation for 300 children.[9] It was transferred to the borough in 1930. The buildings were re-

modelled, and the school was reopened later in 1930 as a senior and junior council school for boys.[10] It was closed in 1934.[11]

OTHER PUBLIC ELEMENTARY SCHOOLS IN EXISTENCE BEFORE 1871. These included infants' schools in Church Street and at Townend Bank in 1834;[12] another infants' school which had been established in the Windmill area by c. 1847 and still existed there in 1851;[13] and a British school in Bridge Street, opened in the early 1850s.[14]

SCHOOLS OPENED SINCE 1871.

Abbey Junior and Infants' School, Glastonbury Crescent, Mossley, was opened in 1964.[15]

Alumwell Comprehensive School, *see* Wilfred Clarke School.

Alumwell Junior and Infants' Schools, Primley Avenue, consist of an infants' school opened as a junior and infants' school in 1951, and a junior school added in 1954.[16]

Bath Street School was opened in 1875 as a board school for boys, girls, and infants.[17] It was a mixed and infants' school in 1902[18] and became a junior mixed and infants' school in 1931.[19] It was closed in 1940, the population in its area having been reduced by slum clearance.[20] The buildings were subsequently used by the Blue Coat Infants' School and St. Mary's Roman Catholic School.[21]

Beechdale Infants' School, Remington Road, was opened in 1955.[22]

Beechdale Junior School, Remington Road, was opened in 1959.[23]

Bentley Drive Junior and Infants' School was opened in 1967. It was Walsall's first open-plan school and was one of the earliest in the country to be built for team-teaching.[24]

Blakenall Heath Junior and Infants' Schools, Blakenall Lane, consist of a junior school opened as a junior and infants' school in 1928, and an infants' school added in 1931.[25]

Busill Jones Junior and Infants' Schools, Ashley Road, Bloxwich, consist of an infants' school opened as a junior and infants' school in 1950, and a junior school added in 1953.[26]

[94] *Evening Mail*, 16 May 1964.
[95] Ex inf. the headmistress (1974).
[96] *Staffs. Advertiser* (S. Staffs. edn.), 28 Apr. 1866.
[97] Ed. 7/112/Walsall/10; S.R.O., D. 812/Caldmore Nat. Sch.; *Robinson's Map of Walsall* (pub. with *Walsall Red Book*, 1876).
[98] *Staffs. Advertiser*, 6 Apr. 1872. The school building was used for divine worship from 1867 until the building of the church of St. Michael and All Angels: above p. 238.
[99] *4th Rep. Walsall Educ. Cttee.* (1907), 24.
[1] *26th Ann. Rep. Walsall Educ. Cttee.* (1929–30), 46; *27th Ann. Rep.* (1930–1), 44; *31st Ann. Rep.* (1934–5), 36; *32nd Ann. Rep.* (1935–6), 36.
[2] *55th Ann. Rep.* (1958–9), 7.
[3] White, *Dir. Birmingham* (1869).
[4] *Staffs. Advertiser*, 19 Aug. 1871.
[5] P. Liddle, 'Development of Elementary Education in Walsall between 1862 and 1902' (London Univ. M.A. (Educ.) thesis, 1967), 29; Ed. 7/113/Walsall/29.
[6] Ed. 7/112/Walsall/17; /113/Walsall/29; *3rd Rep. Walsall Educ. Cttee.* (1906), 12.
[7] Ed. 7/113/Walsall/Whittimere St. Sch.; above p. 247.
[8] Ed. 7/112/Walsall/11.
[9] *Staffs. Advertiser* (S. Staffs. edn.), 5 Apr., 12 July 1873.
[10] W.C.L., Centenary Wesleyan Sch. log bk. 1925–30,

pp. 37, 39; *26th Ann. Rep. Walsall Educ. Cttee.* (1929–30), 12–13. [11] *31st Ann. Rep.* (1934–5), 6–7.
[12] White, *Dir. Staffs.* (1834).
[13] *Staffs. Almanack for 1848*, 43 (Stafford; copy in W.S.L., Salt Pamphs. 4); White, *Dir. Staffs.* (1851). It may have developed from an Anglican Sunday sch. which existed in the area in 1840: *Staffs. Advertiser*, 28 Nov. 1840.
[14] White, *Dir. Staffs.* (1851); *P.O. Dir. Staffs.* (1854).
[15] *Walsall County Boro. Structure Plan: Rep. of Survey 1972: Education*, table 2.
[16] *47th Ann. Rep.* (1950–1), 6, 8; *51st Ann. Rep.* (1954–5), 3. [17] Ed. 7/112/Walsall/2.
[18] *2nd Rep. Walsall Educ. Cttee.* (1905), App. pp. 4–5.
[19] W.C.L., Bath St. Sch. log bk. 1925–40, p. 128.
[20] Ibid. p. 228; *Walsall Observer*, 1 June 1940.
[21] Above pp. 257–8.
[22] *52nd Ann. Rep.* (1955–6), 3, referring to it as the infant department of Gipsy Lane Primary Sch. The Beechdale housing estate served by the school was originally known as Gipsy Lane: above p. 165.
[23] *56th Ann. Rep.* (1959–60), 1.
[24] *Walsall Observer*, 24 Nov. 1967.
[25] *25th Ann. Rep.* (1928–9), 8–9; *27th Ann. Rep.* (1930–1), 9; *28th Ann. Rep.* (1931–2), 8.
[26] *46th Ann. Rep.* (1949–50), 7–8, 28; ex inf. the headmaster, Busill Jones Junior Sch. (1974).

Butts Junior and Infants' School, Butts Road, originated as a National school in Butts Road, opened in 1868 and standing in that part of Rushall which was added to Walsall in 1876.[27] Later in 1876 the building was leased to the board and reopened as a board school. In 1880 it was replaced by a new board school for boys, girls, and infants, standing on the corner of Butts Road and Cecil Street. The new school was enlarged in 1882 and became a junior and infants' school in 1933–4.[28]

Chuckery Junior and Infants' Schools, Lincoln Road, were what remained in 1973 of a group of council schools built on a site between Lincoln Road, Tong Street, and Chuckery Road.[29] The first was opened in Tong Street in 1905 to house senior and junior mixed schools. New junior and infants' schools were added in 1931 and remained in use as such in 1973. When they were opened the former junior mixed school became a senior school for girls and the former senior mixed school a senior school for boys.[30] The two senior schools became secondary modern in 1945. In 1959 they were formed into a single mixed secondary modern school, which was closed in 1972. Its building became an annexe of the Blue Coat secondary school.

Croft Street Junior and Infants' School, Birchills, was opened in 1894 as a mixed and infants' board school and was enlarged in 1899.[31] In 1923 the mixed department was divided into separate boys' and girls' departments, and in 1929 it was again divided into junior mixed and senior girls' departments.[32] The senior girls' department became a secondary modern school for girls in the reorganization after 1944[33] and was closed in 1965.[34]

Delves Infants' School, Bell Lane, was opened in 1937.[35]

Delves Junior School, Bell Lane, was opened in 1972.[36]

Edgar Stammers Junior and Infants' Schools, Harden Road, consist of an infants' school opened as a junior and infants' school in 1949, and a junior school added in 1951.[37]

Edward Shelley Schools, Scarborough Road, Pleck, were opened in 1930 as a junior school and a selective central school which specialized in technical education.[38] In the reorganization after 1944 the central school became a technical high school.[39] The junior school closed in 1958 and the technical high school absorbed Walsall Secondary Technical

School.[40] The technical high school became part of the new Wilfred Clarke comprehensive school in 1971,[41] and in 1973 the Scarborough Road building was used as an annexe to the comprehensive school.[42] *And see* Walsall Secondary Technical School.

Elmore Green Junior and Infants' School, Elmore Row, Bloxwich, originated as a mixed and infants' board school opened at Elmore Green in 1882.[43] In 1902–3 lack of space at the school compelled the transfer of the younger boys to temporary premises in High Street, Bloxwich;[44] a building for a junior mixed school was added at Elmore Green in 1904.[45] In 1906 the schools were reorganized into junior mixed and infants' and upper-standard schools.[46] The latter was recognized by government as a higher elementary school in 1908 and as a selective central school in 1922–3.[47] It offered commercial and academic courses;[48] in the reorganization after 1944 it became Elmore Green High School, offering grammar, commercial, and technical courses.[49] In 1958 its pupils and staff moved to new premises in Lichfield Road, Bloxwich, to form the nucleus of the comprehensive T. P. Riley School.[50] In 1973 its Elmore Green buildings were being used as an annexe to T. P. Riley School.

Field Street School, *see* Richard C. Thomas Schools.

Forest Comprehensive School was opened in 1973 in the buildings formerly occupied by W. R. Wheway School. It also shared an annexe in Field Road with Manor Farm School.[51]

Francis Martyn Roman Catholic High School, Dartmouth Avenue, Coal Pool, a voluntary aided secondary modern school, was opened in 1963.[52] Its buildings became an annexe of St. Thomas More Roman Catholic comprehensive school, Willenhall, in 1973.[53]

Frank F. Harrison School, Leamore Lane, was opened in 1965 as a comprehensive secondary school. Its buildings were extended in 1968 and 1971.[54]

Green Rock Junior and Infants' School, Mersey Road, Goscote, was opened in 1950.[55]

Harden Junior and Infants' Schools, Goldsmith Road, consist of an infants' school opened as a junior and infants' school in 1938, and a junior school added in 1939.[56]

Hatherton Lane Infants' School, Bloxwich Lane, Beechdale, was opened in 1956.[57]

[27] Ed. 7/112/Walsall/9; F. W. Willmore, *Records of Rushall* (Walsall, 1892), 99, 118.
[28] *Staffs. Advertiser*, 28 Feb. 1880; Willmore, *Rushall*, 119; *30th Ann. Rep.* (1933–4), 7.
[29] For this para see, unless otherwise stated, D. Bolton, *Hist. of Chuckery Secondary School, Tong Street, 1904–1972* (Walsall, 1972; copy in W.C.L.).
[30] *28th Ann. Rep.* (1931–2), 8.
[31] Ed. 7/112/Walsall/13; *Walsall Red Book* (1895), 180; *Kelly's Dir. Staffs.* (1900), giving date of building (1893), not that of opening.
[32] *20th Ann. Rep.* (1923–4), 23; *26th Ann. Rep.* (1929–30), 45.
[33] *Walsall Educ. Development Plan* (1952), 14 (copy in W.C.L.).
[34] *61st Ann. Rep.* (1964–5), 15.
[35] *34th Ann. Rep.* (1937–8), 38–9.
[36] *Express & Star*, 14 July 1973.
[37] *47th Ann. Rep.* (1950–1), 3, 6, 8.
[38] *26th Ann. Rep.* (1929–30), 10, 12; *28th Ann. Rep.* (1931–2), 10.
[39] *44th Ann. Rep.* (1947–8), 15.
[40] *54th Ann. Rep.* (1957–8), 5; below p. 263.
[41] *67th Ann. Rep.* (1970–1), 11.

[42] Walsall Educ. Dept., TS. List of Schools, Mar. 1973.
[43] Ed. 7/112/Walsall/6.
[44] Ed. 7/113/Walsall/High St. Temporary Sch., Bloxwich; Walsall Educ. Cttee. *His Majesty's Inspector's Reps. . . . for 1903*, 13, 25 (copy in W.C.L.).
[45] Ed. 7/112/Walsall/6; *1st Rep. Walsall Educ. Cttee.* (1904), 10.
[46] *3rd Rep.* (1906), 17; *4th Rep.* (1907), 2; *5th Ann. Rep.* (1908), 25.
[47] *19th Ann. Rep.* (1922–3), 24.
[48] *28th Ann. Rep.* (1931–2), 10.
[49] *45th Ann. Rep.* (1948–9), 14.
[50] Walsall Educ. Cttee. *Educ. in Walsall* (Walsall, 1960; copy in W.C.L.).
[51] Ex inf. the deputy headmaster (1974).
[52] *Catholic Pictorial*, 24 May 1964.
[53] Ex inf. the school (1974).
[54] *61st Ann. Rep.* (1964–5), 15–16; *Express & Star*, 10 Mar. 1972.
[55] *46th Ann. Rep.* (1949–50), 7; TS. List of Schools, Mar. 1973.
[56] *35th Ann. Rep.* (1938–9), 8, 36; TS. List of Schools, Mar. 1973.
[57] *53rd Ann. Rep.* (1956–7), 2, 5.

Hatherton Lane Junior School, Bloxwich Lane, Beechdale, was opened in 1960.[58]

Hillary Street Junior and Infants' Schools, Pleck, originated as a mixed and infants' board school opened in Hillary Street in 1893.[59] A higher elementary school was added in 1906 and remained one of Walsall's two central schools until Edward Shelley Schools were opened in 1930.[60] It then became a senior mixed school, was transformed into a mixed secondary modern school in the reorganization after 1944,[61] and was closed when Wilfred Clarke School opened in 1971.[62] The mixed department, which had become a junior mixed school in 1929, and the infants' school were still open in 1973.[63]

Joseph Leckie School, Walstead Road West, the Delves, was opened in 1939 as two senior schools, for boys and for girls, in a single building.[64] In 1947 they were combined to form a bilateral secondary school taking both selective and non-selective pupils. It was the first such school in the country and represented Walsall's first move towards comprehensive secondary education.[65] Extensive new buildings were added in 1972 and the school then became fully comprehensive.[66]

Leamore Junior and Infants' School, Bloxwich Road, was opened in 1873 as a board school for boys, girls, and infants.[67] The boys' department was closed in 1916 because of the wartime shortage of teachers. In 1919 the girls were moved into the vacant department, the infants to the girls' department, and a domestic-science centre was opened in the infants' department. When a domestic-science centre was opened at Field Street School in 1925 that at Leamore was closed, and Leamore became a mixed (from 1929 a junior mixed) and infants' school.[68]

Little Bloxwich Church of England Junior and Infants' School, Grenfell Road, Little Bloxwich, originated in 1873 or possibly earlier as a day and Sunday school run as a branch of the Blakenall Heath National school. There was no school building; the day school met in a small room in a public house, the Sunday school in the same room until 1875 and then in a villager's kitchen.[69] A National school building was opened in Pelsall Lane in 1877; a leading promoter of the enterprise was J. E. Bealey of the Hills, Bloxwich.[70] The managers were those of the Blakenall Heath National school. They allowed the first mistress to run a private-adventure school in the building, presumably because they could not afford to pay her a salary; it was not until 1878 that, with a new mistress, they took full control. There was then an average attendance of some 50 children, all paying pence.[71] The school was reconstructed and enlarged in the 1930s when it became a junior and infants' school. It took voluntary controlled status in 1951. In 1971 it moved to its present buildings.[72]

Lower Farm Junior and Infants' School, off Buxton Road, Bloxwich, was opened in 1968.[73]

Manor Farm School was opened as a comprehensive secondary school in 1973 in the buildings in Field Road, Bloxwich, formerly used by Richard C. Thomas School.[74]

Mossley Infants' School, Mossley Lane, Bloxwich, was opened in 1959.[75]

Mossley Junior School, Tintern Crescent, Bloxwich, was opened in 1962.[76]

North Walsall Junior and Infants' Schools, Derby Street, originated as a council school with senior mixed, junior mixed, and infants' departments, opened in 1904 on a site bounded by Derby, Kent, Essex, and Hereford Streets.[77] The senior department was recognized as a higher elementary school in 1906, becoming a senior school for boys in 1929 and a secondary modern school for boys in the reorganization after 1944.[78] It was closed in 1965.[79]

Palfrey Junior and Infants' Schools, Milton Street and Sun Street, were opened in 1884 as a board school for boys, girls, and infants. The boys' department was housed in a building in Sun Street and the girls' and infants' departments in a building in Milton Street; the school's playgrounds lay between the two streets.[80] A senior mixed school was added in Milton Street in 1906.[81] In 1929 the boys' and girls' departments were reorganized as junior departments and the senior school became a senior school for boys.[82] The latter was closed in 1939 on the opening of Joseph Leckie School. The junior girls' department moved into its building, the infants moved into what had been the junior girls' department, and both departments shared the infants' building.[83] The junior departments were reorganized as a junior mixed school in 1956. In 1957 the infants' school moved into the Sun Street building and the junior school took over the entire Milton Street building.[84]

Park Hall Junior and Infants' School, Park Hall Road, was opened in 1970.[85] Junior and infants' classes had been held elsewhere since 1969.[86]

[58] Ex inf. the headmaster (1974).
[59] Ed. 7/112/Walsall/14.
[60] 3rd Rep. Walsall Educ. Cttee. (1906), 12–13; 24th Ann. Rep. (1927–8), 11–12; above p. 261.
[61] 27th Ann. Rep. (1930–1), 44; Walsall Educ. Development Plan (1952), 9.
[62] 67th Ann. Rep. (1970–1), 11.
[63] 26th Ann. Rep. (1929–30), 45; TS. List of Schools, Mar. 1973.
[64] 35th Ann. Rep. (1938–9), 8; 36th Ann. Rep. (1939–40), 9.
[65] 43rd Ann. Rep. (1946–7), 4; 44th Ann. Rep. (1947–8), 15; Walsall Observer, 10 Mar. 1972.
[66] Walsall Observer, 10 Mar. 1972, 16 Mar. 1973.
[67] Ed. 7/112/Walsall/7.
[68] 21st Ann. Rep. (1924–5), 21; 26th Ann. Rep. (1929–30), 45.
[69] Nat. Soc. files; Staffs. Advertiser (S. Staffs. edn.), 8 Nov. 1873.
[70] Ed. 7/112/Walsall/15; Walsall Red Book (1878), 103; Cason, Blakenall Heath, 12, 17.
[71] Ed. 7/112/Walsall/15.
[72] Nat. Soc. files; Cason Blakenall Heath, 45, 51; 27th Ann. Rep. (1930–1), 44; 34th Ann. Rep. (1937–8), 38; Walsall Observer, 16 July 1971.
[73] Express & Star, 10 Jan. 1968.
[74] Walsall Educ. Cttee. Secondary Educ. in Walsall (1973), 20–1 (copy in W.C.L.); Walsall Observer, 26 Oct. 1973.
[75] 56th Ann. Rep. (1959–60), 1.
[76] Ex inf. the school (1974).
[77] 1st Rep. Walsall Educ. Cttee. (1904), 10.
[78] 3rd Rep. (1906), 6, 16; 4th Rep. (1907), 24; 26th Ann. Rep. (1929–30), 45; Walsall Educ. Development Plan (1952), 14.
[79] 61st Ann. Rep. (1964–5), 15.
[80] Ed. 7/112/Walsall/17; Staffs. Advertiser (S. Staffs. edn.), 14 June 1884.
[81] Ed. 7/112/Walsall/17; 3rd Rep. Walsall Educ. Cttee. (1906), 12.
[82] 26th Ann. Rep. (1929–30), 45.
[83] Ex inf. Mr. V. S. Aston, headmaster of Palfrey Junior Sch. (1974).
[84] 52nd Ann. Rep. (1955–6), 5; 53rd Ann. Rep. (1956–7), 5.
[85] Evening Mail, 8 June 1970.
[86] 65th Ann. Rep. (1968–9), 7.

Priory Junior and Infants' School, Odell Road, Bloxwich, was opened in 1972.[87]

Richard C. Thomas School, Bloxwich, was opened in 1912 as the mixed Field Street council school. It became a senior school in 1929.[88] In 1932 a senior school for girls was built on the Field Street site, the earlier building became a senior school for boys, and the two were named Richard C. Thomas Schools.[89] They became secondary modern schools in the reorganization after 1944 and were merged to form a single mixed secondary modern school in 1960.[90] It was reorganized as Manor Farm comprehensive school in 1973.[91]

Tantarra Street School was opened as a board school for boys, girls, and infants in 1873. It was a mixed and infants' school by 1902 and was closed in 1931 on the opening of new junior and infants' schools at the Chuckery.[92]

A technical day school for boys was opened in 1891 at the Science and Art Institute in Bradford Place with 52 pupils.[93] The institute was taken over in 1897 by the borough, which continued the school. In 1905–6 there were 150 pupils and the school had been recognized by the Board of Education as a secondary school. The Board, however, demanded alterations to the building and more staff and equipment as the price of continued recognition. The council refused to meet the demands and closed the school in 1906.[94]

T. P. Riley School, Lichfield Road, Bloxwich, a comprehensive secondary school, was opened in 1958 and subsequently extended. In 1973 it was using the buildings of the former Elmore Green High School as an annexe.[95]

Walsall Secondary Art School originated in 1912, when a junior full-time art department, the first in any English art school, was opened at the municipal School of Art.[96] Pupils, selected by examination from the town's elementary schools, were admitted at 14 (later 13), and took two- or three-year courses in which art and craft work was mingled with general education.[97] In the reorganization after 1944 the department was recognized as a secondary school.[98] It was closed in 1954.[99]

Walsall Secondary Technical School originated in a junior full-time commercial course established at the Technical College in 1937 and a junior engineering course established there in the early 1940s. In the reorganization after 1944 they were recognized as secondary schools.[1] In 1948 they were amalgamated to form a single school, which ranked as a department of the college and was in the charge of a college lecturer. Pupils selected by examination were transferred to it from secondary modern schools at 13 and took two-year technical or commercial courses.[2] In the early 1950s most classes were held in the college's Bradford Place building.[3] Responsibility for the school was transferred in 1956 to the headmaster of Edward Shelley High School and the length of the courses was extended to three years.[4] The school was merged with Edward Shelley High School in 1958, when the closure of Edward Shelley Junior School made it possible for the Bradford Place pupils to be transferred to Scarborough Road.[5]

Whitehall Junior and Infants' Schools, West Bromwich Road and Weston Street, originated as a board school for boys, girls, and infants, opened in West Bromwich Road in 1899.[6] The infants were moved to a separate building in Weston Street in 1903.[7] In 1929 the boys' and girls' departments in West Bromwich Road were reorganized as a senior school for girls and a junior mixed school.[8] The school buildings were extended in 1932.[9] The senior school for girls was closed in 1939 on the opening of Joseph Leckie School.[10]

Wilfred Clarke School, Primley Avenue, a purpose-built comprehensive secondary school, was opened in 1971. It was the first school in Walsall to be designed for use as a community centre out of school hours.[11] It was renamed Alumwell Comprehensive School in 1974.[12]

Wisemore Board School, for boys, girls, and infants, was opened in 1873.[13] The boys' department was closed in 1930[14] and the school itself in 1937.[15]

Wolverhampton Road Board School, for boys, girls, and infants, was opened in 1883.[16] A new building for the infants was opened on the opposite side of the road in 1901.[17] A senior mixed school in a new building was added in 1906.[18] In 1929 the schools were divided into four departments, senior boys, senior girls, junior mixed, and infants.[19] The

[87] Walsall Observer, 27 Oct. 1972.
[88] 9th Ann. Rep. (1911–12), 5; Kelly's Dir. Staffs. (1916); 26th Ann. Rep. (1929–30), 45.
[89] 27th Ann. Rep. (1930–1), 9; 28th Ann. Rep. (1931–2), 8, 38.
[90] Walsall Educ. Development Plan (1952), 10; ex inf. the secretary, Manor Farm Sch. (1974).   [91] See p. 262.
[92] Ed. 7/112/Walsall/25; Walsall Educ. Cttee. His Majesty's Inspector's Reps. . . . for 1903, 25; 25th Ann. Rep. (1928–9), 9; 27th Ann. Rep. (1930–1), 5.
[93] Liddle, 'Elementary Education', 251–2. For the institute see below p. 265.
[94] 3rd Rep. Walsall Educ. Cttee. (1906), 4–6.
[95] 55th Ann. Rep. (1958–9), 1; Educ. in Walsall (1960); TS. List of Schools, Mar. 1973.
[96] 50th Ann. Rep. (1953–4), 19.
[97] 22nd Ann. Rep. (1925–6), 13; 36th Ann. Rep. (1939–40), 20.
[98] Walsall Educ. Development Plan (1952), 12.
[99] 50th Ann. Rep. (1953–4), 18–19.
[1] W.T.C., Walsall Higher Educ. Sub-cttee. Min. Bk. 9, p. 240; 35th Ann. Rep. (1938–9), 26; 40th Ann. Rep. (1943–4), 17; Walsall Educ. Development Plan (1952), 12.
[2] 45th Ann. Rep. (1948–9), 17–19; 46th Ann. Rep. (1949–50), 20–1.
[3] 50th Ann. Rep. (1953–4), 18; 51st Ann. Rep. (1954–5), 17.

[4] 52nd Ann. Rep. (1955–6), 5, 14.
[5] 54th Ann. Rep. (1957–8), 5–6.
[6] Ed. 7/112/Walsall/26; Walsall Red Book (1900), 204.
[7] 1st Rep. Walsall Educ. Cttee. (1904), 10.
[8] 26th Ann. Rep. (1929–30), 45.
[9] 28th Ann. Rep. (1931–2), 8–9.
[10] Ex inf. Mr. V. S. Aston, headmaster of Palfrey Junior Sch. (1974).
[11] 67th Ann. Rep. (1970–1), 2, 11; Secondary Educ. in Walsall, 26–7; Walsall Observer, 8 June 1973.
[12] Walsall Observer, 15 Mar. 1974.
[13] Ed. 7/112/Walsall/27; Staffs. Advertiser (S. Staffs. edn.), 26 Apr. 1873.
[14] 26th Ann. Rep. (1929–30), 12–13; 27th Ann. Rep. (1930–1), 7.
[15] 34th Ann. Rep. (1937–8), 38–9, describing it as a junior mixed and infants' sch. 32nd Ann. Rep. (1935–6), 36, had described it as a girls' and infants' sch., 33rd Ann. Rep. (1936–7), 38, as a junior girls' and infants' sch.
[16] Ed. 7/112/Walsall/28.
[17] W.C.L., Wolverhampton Rd. Infants' Sch. log bk. 1904–64, pp. 248–9 and note on fly-leaf.
[18] Ed. 7/112/Walsall/28; 3rd Rep. Walsall Educ. Cttee. (1906), 12–13.
[19] 26th Ann. Rep. (1929–30), 45; 27th Ann. Rep. (1930–1), 44.

senior departments became a secondary modern school in the reorganization after 1944.[20] The junior and infants' departments were closed in 1967 and the secondary modern school in 1971.[21]

W. R. Wheway School, Hawbush Road, Leamore, a mixed secondary modern school, was opened in 1954, brought into full use in 1955, and extended in 1971–2.[22] It was reorganized as Forest Comprehensive School in 1973.[23]

SCIENTIFIC AND LITERARY INSTITUTIONS, FURTHER AND HIGHER EDUCATION. A mechanics' institute, with a library and reading room, was established in Freer Street in 1839 under the presidency of Richard James, a merchant and factor. The annual subscription was 10s.[24] Although it was avowedly non-political and non-sectarian it had been promoted by Francis Finch, the Radical M.P. for the borough; Peter Potter, Lord Bradford's agent, feared that it had been founded 'entirely for factious and party purposes' and alleged that one of the secretaries was 'an avowed and proselytising infidel'.[25] The secretary in question, Joseph Hickin, a leading Walsall Radical, had been a prominent member of the Walsall Political Union and later became chief clerk and organizer of the Anti-Corn Law League's headquarters.[26] The Tories used their influence to undermine the institute, forbidding their employees to attend; by 1841 its membership, originally over 100, had dwindled to 35 and it was in debt.[27] It survived, however.[28] By 1845 it had moved to Lower Rushall Street, where it remained in 1850.[29] In 1851 the 38 members had a library of 119 volumes and there were occasional lectures. The subscription had apparently been raised to a guinea or 10s. 6d. a year.[30] The institute was evidently disbanded shortly afterwards.[31] An attempt to found another mechanics' institute began in 1857 but was transformed into a campaign, eventually successful, to establish a free library.[32]

In 1841 the Walsall Library, founded in 1800, became Walsall Library and Philosophical Institution. A museum and a laboratory were opened and

lectures and discussions organized. The aim, to promote literature, science, and the arts 'on Christian principles', suggests a conscious rivalry with the mechanics' institute, but the £1 annual subscription limited membership to the more prosperous. In 1844 the managers attempted to attract a wider membership by offering clerks, shopmen, and apprentices a 7s. 6d. subscription and evening classes in geography, history, arithmetic, and ethics.[33] The effort was, however, unsuccessful; despite the attraction of two courses of lectures a year there were only 64 members in 1851, and the institution appears to have remained a middle-class body until it closed in 1875.[34]

A working men's college was established in 1860 in union with a similar college founded at Wolverhampton in 1857. Seventy students attended its first series of classes.[35] It evidently did not survive the decline of the Wolverhampton college, which closed in 1865.

Other institutions included the Bridge Street Mutual Improvement Society, which from c. 1860 met at the schoolroom of Bridge Street Congregational chapel under the presidency of the minister;[36] a Walsall Wesleyan Mutual Improvement Society, which existed by 1861;[37] the Walsall Church of England Institute, established in 1863;[38] and the Butts Working Men's Institute, formed by 1873.[39] Free lectures for working men were begun in 1861 in connexion with the public library.[40] Several Sunday morning adult schools were founded in the 1880s.[41]

Technical education in the town apparently began with the establishment in 1854 of Walsall School of Design and Ornamental Art. It was founded by W. Smith, a local sculptor, and was at first poorly attended; it may, however, have survived until at least 1865.[42] About 1861 drawing was taught at an evening class held in the schoolroom of Goodall Street Baptist chapel. The teachers were unpaid and the pupils' fees of 1d. an evening were spent on materials.[43] The minister of the chapel, A. A. Cole, was chiefly responsible for the formation of the class

[20] Walsall Educ. Development Plan (1952), 14.
[21] 63rd Ann. Rep. (1966–7), 5; 67th Ann. Rep. (1970–1), 11.
[22] 51st Ann. Rep. (1954–5), 3; 52nd Ann. Rep. (1955–6), 3; 68th Ann. Rep. (1971–2), 5.
[23] See p. 261.
[24] Rules and regulations of the Walsall Mechanics' Institution, established January 1839 (Walsall, n.d.; copy in S.R.O., Q/RSe). For James's occupation see e.g. White, Dir. Staffs. (1851).
[25] S.R.O., D. 1287/18/26, business corresp. 1838–9, Potter to Bradford, 25 Feb. 1839.
[26] Willmore, Walsall, 405–6; N. McCord, The Anti-Corn Law League, 109, 133, 173. The institute's Rules and regulations prints a list of officers.
[27] Glew, Walsall, 40–2.
[28] It is wrongly stated ibid. 41 that it was dissolved 12 Nov. 1841. It was not until 1843 that it submitted its rules to quarter sessions for approval, and Wm. Langham, then secretary, was still secretary c. 1850: notes on copy of institute's Rules and regulations in S.R.O., Q/RSe; J. W. Hudson, Hist. of Adult Education (1851), 230.
[29] S.R.O., D. 260/M/T/6/46, deed of 25 Mar. 1847 with enclosed agreement for sale of 30 Dec. 1845; Slater, Nat. Com. Dir. (1850), Staffs. p. 105.
[30] Census, 1851, Tables relating to Schools, &c. 236. Hudson, Adult Educ. 230, gives subscriptions as 2s. 6d., 2s., or 1s. 6d. a quarter and states that there were 800 volumes in the library.
[31] White, Dir. Staffs. (1851), states that the town has no mechanics' institute.
[32] Staffs. Advertiser, 9 and 30 May 1857; S.R.O., D. 1287/18/29, business corresp. 1857, Potter to Bradford 12 and 28 May, 30 June 1857; above p. 251.
[33] G. Fisk, A Lecture . . . before the Members of the Walsall Library and Philosophical Institution (Walsall, 1844), 3–6 (copy in W.S.L. Pamphs. sub Walsall); Walsall Library and Philosophical Institution, Catalogue of Books and Abstract of Rules (Walsall, 1846), 3–4 (copy in W.S.L. Pamphs. sub Walsall). It may be identifiable with the mutual instruction class fostered by some of the Tories which the secretary of the mechanics' institute mentioned in 1841: Glew, Walsall, 40.
[34] Census, 1851, Tables relating to Schools, &c. 236, giving subscription as 5s. a year; Glew, Walsall, 47; Staffs. Advertiser, 9 May 1857; Willmore, Walsall, 392–3.
[35] Staffs. Advertiser, 22 Sept. 1860, 2 Feb. 1861. For the Wolverhampton college see J. Jones, Historical Sketch of Art and Literary Institutions of Wolverhampton, 1794–1897 (priv. print. 1897), 64–74 (copy in W.S.L.).
[36] A. Willis, Hist. of Bridge Street Chapel, Walsall (Walsall, 1893), 17–18; Staffs. Advertiser, 27 Oct. 1860, 26 Jan., 8 June 1861.
[37] Staffs. Advertiser, 22 June 1861.
[38] Ibid. 17 Oct. 1863.
[39] Ibid. (S. Staffs. edn.), 22 Nov. 1873.
[40] Staffs. Advertiser, 6 Apr. 1861.
[41] See e.g. Walsall Red Book (1884), 146; ibid. (1885), 57, 59.
[42] Glew, Walsall, 42–5; Staffs. Advertiser, 20 May 1865.
[43] Guide to Walsall (1889), 37.

and later became prominent as a promoter of technical education in Walsall.[44]

Schools were established in connexion with the Science and Art Department in 1869: the Walsall Artizans' Art Class in Bridgeman Place and the Ablewell Street Science Institution in the schoolroom of the Ablewell Street Methodist chapel.[45] In 1871 the art class took rooms over the railway station.[46] The schools tended to duplicate each other's work: some science was taught at the art school, some drawing at Ablewell Street. In 1872, therefore, they united to form the Walsall Science and Art Institute. The M.P. for the borough, Charles Forster, had worked for the merger and became the institute's first president.[47] The rooms over the railway station and the Ablewell Street schoolroom continued to be used.[48]

In 1874 the institute's managers disbanded the art classes. A separate school of art was immediately established in Bridge Street by a group which disagreed with the managers' action; it too was held in connexion with the Science and Art Department. By 1876 there were some 140 pupils and a branch had been established at Bloxwich.[49] In 1879 it was reunited with the institute.[50]

By 1884 annual enrolments at the institute had risen to some 600; accommodation was inadequate and the institute was threatened with the loss of its government grant.[51] A site in Bradford Place for an institute building had already been presented in 1882 by Lord Bradford. In 1887 the mayor successfully appealed for funds to erect and equip such a building, to be the town's memorial to Queen Victoria's golden jubilee.[52] It was opened in 1888, a three-storey building of red brick with terracotta dressings, designed in a free Gothic style by Dunn & Hipkiss of Birmingham.[53] In 1888–9 some 1,600 students enrolled for classes in art, literature, music, science, and technology.[54]

Walsall adopted the Technical Instruction Act in 1890 and the corporation's technical instruction committee became members of the institute's committee of management. In 1897 the institute was handed over to the corporation and became the Walsall Municipal Institute.[55] From 1908, when the art school moved into separate premises in Goodall Street,[56] the institute concentrated on providing scientific, technical, and commercial education. In 1927 it was renamed Walsall Technical College.[57] By at least the early 1930s the Bradford Place building had become too small for the college's work and additional premises were being used elsewhere in the town.[58] By 1937–8 enrolments had risen to 1,315.[59] From 1937 until 1956 there was a full-time junior department.[60]

In 1938 the corporation and the county council agreed to replace the college by a jointly-run technical college on a site provided by the corporation in Wisemore.[61] Owing to the war building did not start until 1949, and the first instalment of the new Walsall and Staffordshire Technical College buildings in St. Paul's Street, a workshop block, was not fully taken into use until 1952.[62] A laboratory wing was added in 1956. From 1957 the college, until then jointly administered by the Walsall and Staffordshire education committees, had its own governors, consisting of representatives from the corporation, the county council, and Birmingham University.[63] A further wing, containing an assembly hall, classrooms, and offices, was completed in 1959 and the Bradford Place building was then vacated; a workshop bay was added at Wisemore in 1960.[64] Most of the college's daytime work was subsequently conducted in the new building, and from 1969, with the opening of another block containing classrooms, refectory, and students' common room, all the day classes were held at Wisemore.[65] In 1974, following local government reorganization, the county council withdrew from the joint administration of the college, which was renamed Walsall College of Technology.[66] The main college buildings, designed by Hickton, Madeley & Salt in association with the county architect,[67] consist of two blocks in a modern style.

In 1908 the Municipal School of Art moved from Bradford Place to a building in Goodall Street formerly occupied by the public library.[68] It was known as the Municipal Technical School of Art between the two World Wars,[69] subsequently as the Municipal School of Art and Crafts, from 1967 as Walsall School of Art and Crafts, and from 1974 as Walsall College of Art.[70] A junior full-time department existed from 1912 to 1954.[71] Premises adjoining the Goodall Street building were acquired and brought

[44] Woodall, *Walsall Milestones*, 54. By 1888 Cole was chairman of the Walsall Science and Art Institute: *Staffs. Advertiser*, 29 Sept. 1888.

[45] D. C. Carless, 'Hist. of Technical Education in Walsall during the 19th century' (TS. in W.C.L.), 75; *Guide to Walsall* (1889), 37.

[46] *Walsall Free Press*, 5 Aug. 1871; *Staffs. Advertiser*, 5 Aug. 1871.

[47] *Staffs. Advertiser*, 9 Nov. 1872; *Guide to Walsall* (1889), 37.

[48] Carless, 'Hist. of Technical Education', 81; *Institute Chronicle* (Dec. 1913), 10 (magazine of Walsall Municipal Institute; copy in W.C.L.).

[49] *2nd Ann. Rep. Walsall Government School of Art, 1875–6* (copy in W.C.L.); *Staffs. Advertiser*, 19 Feb. 1876.

[50] *Staffs. Advertiser*, 6 Sept. 1879, 10 Jan. 1880.

[51] *Institute Chronicle* (Dec. 1913), 10–11; *Staffs. Advertiser*, 29 Sept. 1888.

[52] *Staffs. Advertiser*, 30 Dec. 1882; *Guide to Walsall* (1889), 35.

[53] *Guide to Walsall* (1889), 37–8; *Staffs. Advertiser*, 25 June 1887, 29 Sept. 1888, giving descriptions of exterior and interior.

[54] *Guide to Walsall* (1889), 38.

[55] Carless, 'Hist. of Technical Education', 84–6; *Walsall Council Mins.* (1896–7), 328–9 (copy in W.C.L.).

[56] See below.

[57] *23rd Ann. Rep. Walsall Educ. Cttee.* (1926–7), 25.

[58] See e.g. *30th Ann. Rep.* (1933–4), 25.

[59] *34th Ann. Rep.* (1937–8), 28.   [60] See p. 263.

[61] *34th Ann. Rep.* (1937–8), 7, 27; Walsall and Staffs. Technical College, Prospectus, 1963–4, 3 (copy in W.C.L.).

[62] *45th Ann. Rep.* (1948–9), 20; *48th Ann. Rep.* (1951–2), 3–4, 23–4; programme of official opening, 18 Oct. 1962 (copy in W.C.L.).

[63] *52nd Ann. Rep.* (1955–6), 19; *53rd Ann. Rep.* (1956–7), 19.

[64] *53rd Ann. Rep.* (1956–7), 19; programme of official opening, 1962; see below.

[65] Programme of official opening, 1962; *66th Ann. Rep.* (1969–70), 31–2.

[66] *Express & Star*, 12 Apr. 1974; ex inf. the principal, Walsall College of Technology (1974).

[67] Programme of official opening, 1962; *Walsall Observer*, 6 Jan. 1967.

[68] *5th Ann. Rep.* (1908), 14–15.

[69] *16th Ann. Rep.* (1918–19), 11; *22nd Ann. Rep.* (1925–6), 13; W.T.C., Walsall Higher Educ. Sub-cttee. Min. Bk. 9, pp. 118, 153, 206, 263.

[70] *43rd Ann. Rep.* (1946–7), 20; ex inf. the principal, Walsall College of Art (1974).

[71] See p. 263.

into use in 1927–8; they were demolished and an annexe built on the site in 1929–30.[72] The former institute building in Bradford Place became an annexe of the school of art in 1959, when it was vacated by the technical college.[73] The school of art began day-release courses in fancy leathergoods manufacture, a leading Walsall industry, c. 1944, and in 1974 it was one of only three centres for leathergoods training in Great Britain.[74]

The West Midlands College of Education, for training men and women teachers, was opened at Gorway in 1963 as a college of Birmingham University School of Education.[75] It is maintained by Walsall education committee; its governing body, appointed by that committee, includes representatives nominated by Birmingham, Sandwell, and Wolverhampton corporations. In 1974 the college became the first establishment of its kind to have all its courses approved by the Council for National Academic Awards. There were then some 1,200 students.

The college stands on a site of c. 48 a. at the junction of Broadway and Birmingham Road which includes the former Gorway House estate;[76] it is approached from Gorway Road. Its first buildings included student residences and a four-storey teaching block raised on supports. Subsequent additions have included a drama studio, a tutorial block, and a study block (1968); a library (1971); and two student hostels, a dining hall, a medical centre, staff and teaching accommodation, a physical-education complex, and a music centre (1972).[77] All were designed by Richard Sheppard, Robson & Partners.[78]

PRIVATE SCHOOLS. A boarding school for boys existed in Rushall Street by 1766, and Thomas Bowen, minister of the Unitarian chapel and author of an English grammar, kept an academy in the same street in the early 19th century.[79] There were other, more specialized, teachers in the town: a writing-master c. 1756 and a drawing-master who established a school in 1780.[80] A Mrs. Hawkins kept a Roman Catholic academy at Bloxwich from c. 1816 to c. 1819, members of the Arrowsmith family kept another in King Street, Walsall, from 1820 to c. 1822, and a Mrs. Pemberton opened another at Bloxwich c. 1822.[81]

Directories list 18 or more academies in 1841 and 13 in 1868.[82] Only the more respectable schools were listed, and in 1870 Walsall had 15 private-adventure schools with fees of more than 9d. a week.[83] Even so, it was claimed in 1855 that there was only one private school of any note in the town, George Bayley's Ablewell House Academy, established c. 1843 in a house on the corner of Ablewell Street and Lower Rushall Street.[84] In the mid 1860s only 150 middle-class boys attended private schools, a figure considered by a government inspector to be 'unusually small' for a town of Walsall's size, and there were only two middle-class girls' schools, with 37 day pupils.[85]

Dame schools and the poorer sort of private-adventure schools appear to have flourished throughout the 19th century without, in general, leaving much trace. Thomas Jackson, who kept a cheap private-adventure school at his house between 1828 and 1832, taught the sons of colliers and brickmakers. He later recalled that he 'had to cultivate ignorance of the grossest kind, and stupidity in its natural state . . . all [were] as ignorant as the young animals of the field; no kind of decency taught them at home, they were naturally hardened in impudence'.[86] By 1870 there were 30 dame schools and cheap private-adventure schools in the town, with over 1,000 pupils.[87] They survived the establishment of the first board schools and continued to find custom among parents who were unwilling to comply with the board's stricter attendance regulations; they were, however, adversely affected when, in 1891, most board and voluntary schools abolished school fees.[88]

CHARITIES FOR THE POOR. *Mollesley's Dole and Corporation Alms-houses.* By deed of 1451 William Lyle of Moxhull in Wishaw (Warws.) gave Halesowen abbey (Worcs.) a rent-charge of 9 marks from the manor of Bascote in Long Itchington (Warws.), which had been conveyed to Lyle and a William Magot by Thomas Mollesley of Walsall the same year. The monks were to distribute 8 marks at Walsall on Mollesley's obit day for his soul and that of his wife Margery, retaining the ninth for themselves. The distribution, which was apparently not restricted to the poor, was to be supervised by the vicar and churchwardens of Walsall, the chaplains of St. John's guild, and all trustworthy men of the church there.[89] In 1477–8 £4 was lent from the funds of the guild to maintain the dole.[90] After the Dissolution the town council, which had acquired the revenues of Bascote manor, continued to pay the dole voluntarily. In 1538–9 £7 10s. 9d. was distributed.[91]

[72] *24th Ann. Rep.* (1927–8), 27; *25th Ann. Rep.* (1928–9), 36; *26th Ann. Rep.* (1929–30), 40.
[73] Ex inf. the principal, Walsall College of Technology.
[74] Ex inf. the principal, Walsall College of Art.
[75] For this para. see *County Boro. of Walsall Official Town Guide* [1972], 30, 32; *Walsall Observer*, 15 Mar. 1974; ex inf. the college (1974).
[76] *County Boro. of Walsall Official Town Guide* [1972], 30; above p. 155.
[77] *64th Ann. Rep.* (1967–8), 33; *68th Ann. Rep.* (1971–2), 47–8; *West Midlands College of Education, Phase III Extensions* (brochure produced for official opening of extensions, 22 Sept. 1972, with enclosed programme containing plan of college buildings; copy at the college).
[78] For a description of the buildings see Pevsner, *Staffs.* 296 and pl. 104.
[79] *Aris's Birmingham Gaz.* 7 July 1766; Pearce, *Walsall*, 113–14.
[80] W.T.C. II/50/10/11; *Aris's Birmingham Gaz.* 25 Sept. 1780.
[81] *Laity's Dir.* (1817 and subseq. edns. to 1823).

[82] Pigot, *Nat. Com. Dir.* (1841), Staffs. p. 80; *P.O. Dir. Staffs.* (1868).
[83] *Walsall Free Press*, 17 Dec. 1870.
[84] Glew, *Walsall*, 34; advert. in *Staffs. Advertiser*, 24 Dec. 1853.
[85] *Rep. Schools Enquiry Com. vol. viii* [3966-VII], p. 239, H.C. (1867–8), xxviii (7). Boys did not go to the grammar school instead; the 'more genteel' people of Walsall seldom used it: ibid. *vol. xv* [3966-XIV], p. 471, H.C. (1867–8), xxviii (12).
[86] *Narrative of the Eventful Life of Thomas Jackson . . . Written by Himself* (Birmingham, 1847), 136–9, 145.
[87] *Walsall Free Press*, 17 Dec. 1870.
[88] P. Liddle, 'Development of Elementary Education in Walsall between 1862 and 1902' (London Univ. M.A. (Educ.) thesis, 1967), 41, 44.
[89] *9th Rep. Com. Char.* H.C. 258, p. 573 (1823), ix. The foundation deed is in W.C.L., box 4, no. 10.
[90] W.T.C. I/67.
[91] *Charter of Corp. of Walsall*, 41–2; Plot, *Staffs.* 314–15; *9th Rep. Com. Char.* 573–5; above p. 214.

It is not clear how the dole was distributed in the 15th century. By the 17th century, and probably by the 16th, a house-by-house distribution was made on Twelfth Night of a penny for every resident or visitor in Walsall and Rushall parishes. The cost of the dole thus increased with the population; in 1648 and again in 1650 the mayor tried to reduce the expense by a more stringent application.[92] About 1769 the corporation attempted to stop the dole, but riots forced its continuance.[93] In the early 19th century it was paid on 1 January; the cost in 1823 was £61 5s. 7d.[94] From 1817 an amercement of 1d. imposed on householders who did not attend the court leet of the manor was offset against their share of the dole.[95]

The corporation, warned by the charity commissioners that the charity should be applied to a better purpose, suspended the dole in 1824 and abandoned it in 1825. It then built a range of eleven one-room alms-houses in Bath Street for needy widows chosen by the mayor, five from the borough, five from the foreign, and one from Rushall. Each inmate received 2s. a week from corporation funds, a sum still paid in 1854.[96] By 1859 the payment had been increased to 3s.[97] The Walsall Corporation Act of 1890 required the council to maintain the alms-houses and to pay the 3s. allowance.[98] In 1937 it was decided not to fill future vacancies because the alms-houses were unfit to live in.[99] The last inmate died c. 1950. The old buildings were demolished in 1952 and replaced in 1955 by seven bungalows in Heather Close, Bloxwich, and four in Sandbank, Bloxwich.[1] The weekly allowance was resumed in 1955 and was still paid in 1972. The bungalows were then occupied by aged widows and spinsters.[2]

Harper's Alms-houses. William Harper (d. 1508), lord of Rushall, settled in trust four alms-houses in Walsall which he had built to provide lodging for poor men visiting the town. The trust was dependent on regulations to be made by Harper, but he died without having framed them. The property descended to his son John, who reconveyed it with an endowment of two kine and land in Walsall. His will of 1519 stipulated that since the alms-houses were said to have attracted many idle people to the town, there were thenceforth to be four permanent inmates, who were to pray for the souls of the founders, their wives, and others. The inmates were to be chosen by the vicar of Walsall or his deputy, with the consent of the lord of Rushall. The vicar was to make gifts to the inmates out of the income.[3] Further endowments were received later. By 1548 6d. a year was being paid to the alms-houses out of the endowment of Ellen Rawlinson's obit in Aldridge church.

George Hawe by will proved in 1558 left land at Townend; annuities were afterwards given to the inmates by William Ridware and John and Thomas Wollaston.[4] The land of the original endowment was being sold in the later 19th century, and none remained in 1959.[5] The income in 1972 was £54 from stock and from land in Walsall bought in 1880. Weekly allowances of £0·20 were paid to each inmate.[6]

By the late 18th century there were only two dwellings. They were demolished c. 1793 and replaced by a set of six one-room dwellings in Dudley Street, all occupied by women in the early 19th century.[7] The alms-houses were rebuilt in 1878 as four dwellings on the corner of Bath and Dudley Streets. Designed by H. E. Lavender, they form a red-brick terrace of one storey with a basement. Each house has two rooms, and there is a communal outside lavatory.[8] In 1972 there were four almswomen.

Wollaston's Alms-house. By will proved in 1634 John Wollaston, a former mayor, left a house in Hall Lane as a rent-free home for 'some poor body'. By 1823, and probably much earlier, the charity had lapsed.[9]

Persehouse's Alms-houses. By will proved in 1636 John Persehouse of Reynold's Hall left a house and two shops under it 'at the stair head' near the churchyard to be used as an alms-house for three poor men or three poor widows of the borough and foreign, to be chosen by his heirs. In default nomination was to pass to the vicar and the borough and foreign overseers with the advice of the mayor. Persehouse left the inmates annuities of 3s. 4d. each to be paid by his heirs in two instalments out of the rent from land near Walsall park.[10] They were paid until at least 1670, but nothing is known of their subsequent history.[11]

The alms-houses, however, continued to be used in the 18th century. Late in the century the inmates were chosen from poor people previously employed in the lime-works belonging to John Walhouse, who held the Persehouse estate. Towards the end of the century the alms-houses were demolished during improvements to the area and the inmates were transferred to Harper's alms-houses.[12] The charity then seems to have lapsed.

Victor Street Alms-houses. By deed of 1868 Edward Marsh and Harriet Lyon of Walsall settled twelve cottages on the corner of Bescot and Victor Streets in trust for the use of poor and infirm persons of good character, living in the Walsall area and regularly attending a Protestant place of worship. By deed of 1886 Marsh gave £2,500 as an endowment. By will dated 1898 he left two further sums

[92] Plot, *Staffs.* 314; W.T.C. II/31/1 and 8; Homeshaw, *Walsall*, 5; E 133/1/61 f. 10.
[93] Homeshaw, *Walsall*, 106; Shaw, *Staffs.* ii. 78.
[94] *9th Rep. Com. Char.* 573; Homeshaw, *Walsall*, 170.
[95] S.R.O., D. 1287/10/2, Walsall market rights etc.
[96] Fink, *Queen Mary's Grammar Sch.* 443; J. Cotterell, *A Letter, &c.* (Walsall, 1825), 12 (copy in W.C.L.); *9th Rep. Com. Char.* 576; White, *Dir. Staffs.* (1834); W.T.C. II/216; Glew, *Walsall*, 210; plate facing p. 241 above.
[97] *Statement of Accts. of Treasurer of Boro. of Walsall, 1859–60*, 2 (copy in W.C.L.).
[98] Walsall Corp. Act, 1890, 53 & 54 Vic. c. 130 (Local), s. 136 (3).
[99] Walsall Council House, Char. Cttee. Mins. 1917–51, pp. 77, 82–3; *County Boro. of Walsall: Rep. of Town Clerk on . . . Chars.* (Walsall, 1945), 2 (copy in W.C.L.).
[1] Char. Cttee. Mins. 1917–51, p. 37; Char. Com. files.

[2] Char. Cttee. Mins. 1952–72, pp. 33 sqq.
[3] W.T.C. II/27; *Cal. Inq. p.m. Hen. VII*, iii, pp. 278–9.
[4] *S.H.C.* 1915, 6; Fink, *Queen Mary's Grammar Sch.* plate facing p. 145; below pp. 268, 271–2.
[5] Char. Com. files; docs. at St. Matthew's, record of buildings etc., 1959.
[6] Char. Com. files; ex inf. Mr. L. Harper, vicar's warden (1973).
[7] *9th Rep. Com. Char.* 580.
[8] Char. Com. files; *Walsall Observer*, 25 May 1973.
[9] L.J.R.O., will proved 28 Aug. 1634; *9th Rep. Com. Char.* 597.
[10] W.S.L. 45/56, folder 28, no. 12, p. 10; *9th Rep. Com. Char.* 593.
[11] *Charter of Corp. of Walsall*, 49; C 93/32/6.
[12] *9th Rep. Com. Char.* 593; *Gent. Mag.* lxix (2), 763–4; above pp. 177, 191.

of £1,000 each to be added to the endowment fund after his sisters' death.[13] The cottages were sold in 1960 and subsequently demolished. A Scheme of 1972 united the two trusts and permitted the trustees to pay the income, then about £400, to infirm and aged persons living in or near Walsall who regularly attended a Protestant place of worship, or to charities benefiting them.[14]

Cox's Charity. By deed of 1885 Samuel Cox of Walsall settled in trust thirteen alms-houses for aged and infirm persons in the former barracks in Bullock's Row. He also gave six houses in Balls Street, the rents of which were to maintain the alms-houses. In 1900 the alms-houses were condemned as uninhabitable and were demolished. The income was apparently not spent again until at least 1937, when a Scheme authorized weekly allowances of between 1s. 6d. and 5s. for poor persons living in the borough and normally to be over sixty. In 1938 the houses in Balls Street were demolished, the site was sold, and the proceeds were invested in stock. Payments were suspended in 1941 for the duration of the war but resumed in 1952, when the income was devoted to providing home helps for old-age pensioners.[15] Under a Scheme of 1960 the name of the charity was changed from Cox's Alms-houses Trust to the Charity of Samuel Cox; the income was to be used for either weekly allowances or Christmas presents.[16] From 1962 it was paid in cash.[17] The income in 1972 was £41; it was distributed in £0·75 doles at Christmas among aged poor living within the boundaries of the pre-1966 borough.[18]

Crump's Alms-houses. By deed of 1886 John Farrington Crump, a Walsall solicitor, settled in trust three newly built alms-houses in Eldon Street. After the death of Crump and his wife £500 was to be added as an endowment. The inmates were to be sober and industrious Anglicans, married or single but preferably women, over 60, and resident in the parliamentary borough for at least five years.[19] By will proved in 1972 Ann Elizabeth Brook of Walsall left £1,000 to the charity for general purposes; it was used to augment the endowment fund.[20] The alms-houses, of brick in a baroque style, consist of three bed-sitting rooms and a communal scullery and lavatory.

The Henry Boys Alms-houses. By deed of 1887 Henry Boys, a Walsall brick manufacturer, settled in trust twelve alms-houses on the corner of Wednesbury Road and Tasker Street with an endowment of £4,000. There were to be 24 inmates, aged over 60, sober, and industrious; each house was to be occupied by a married couple or by two single persons of the same sex. No clergyman of any sect was to be a trustee.[21] By his will proved in 1894 Boys left

a further endowment of £4,000.[22] The alms-houses, designed by F. E. F. Bailey of Walsall, are of red brick from Boys's own yard with stone dressings and terracotta decoration.[23] They are of one storey throughout and consist of a principal range facing Wednesbury Road with short flanking wings. Each alms-house contains four rooms and a rear block which was originally a coal-house and outside lavatory but was converted in 1972–3 into a bathroom.[24]

Marsh's Alms-houses. By deed of 1894 Edward Marsh, founder of the Victor Street Alms-houses, endowed with £1,500 six one-room alms-houses which he was building in Bath Road for six aged or infirm Protestants. In 1972 the alms-houses were vacant.[25] They were converted in 1972–3 into three flats for poor people.

Obit and Intercessory Charities. In 1535 it was stated that the poor had a share in 17s. 4d. distributed yearly by the vicar for the soul of John Harper,[26] but nothing further is known of the payment. Thirteen annuities to the poor from endowed obits, altogether worth about £2 15s., were recorded in 1548 and presumably suppressed.[27] By will proved in 1558 George Hawe left an annuity of 6s. 8d. from lands in Walsall to be distributed to the poor on his obit day. His brother Nicholas by will dated 1560 left an 8s. rent-charge from that and other property to the poor, who were to pray for his soul and those of his parents, his brethren, and all Christians.[28] Nothing further is known of those two foundations.

Ridware's Charity. By deed of 1569 William Ridware, rector of Swynnerton and formerly a chantry priest at Walsall,[29] settled land in Essington in Bushbury in trust for the yearly payment after his death of 6s. 8d. to the most aged, poor, and impotent people in Great and Little Bloxwich and 2s. to the poor in the alms-houses at Walsall.[30] In 1804 the land was said to be held by Henry Vernon, who had withheld payment for some years.[31] By 1823 the property could no longer be identified,[32] and nothing further is known of the charity.

Thomas Webbe's Charity. By deed of 1602 Thomas Webbe, probably a former mayor, settled a rent-charge of 20s. from land in Shelfield in trust for yearly distribution to the poor of the town (evidently the borough). By 1823 the rent-charge had been reduced to 18s., which was augmented from Syvern's Charity and spent on gowns for poor women in the borough.[33] It was redeemed in 1958. The income in 1972 was £0·90 from stock. It was applied with Wilcox's Charity and the borough and foreign shares of John Parker's Charity and Robert Parker's General Charity; £0·25 tickets were sent at Christmas to the vicars of the parish churches of Walsall Deanery for distribution.[34]

---

[13] Char. Com. files.
[14] Char. Com. Scheme, 21 Nov. 1972; ex inf. the sec. to the trustees (1973).
[15] *Rep. Town Clerk on Chars.* 6–7; Blay, 'Street Names of Walsall', 11; Walsall Council House, mins. of Cox's Alms-house Trustees, pp. 3378–3419.
[16] Char. Com. Scheme, 26 July 1960.
[17] Trustees' Mins. p. 3426.
[18] Ex inf. the mayor's sec. (1972).
[19] Trust deed in possession of the clerk to the trustees (1973).   [20] Ex inf. the clerk (1973).
[21] W.T.C., box labelled Hen. Boys Charities, copy deed of settlement, 26 May 1887. A tablet on the alms-houses gives the date of building and endowment as 1886.
[22] Box labelled Hen. Boys Charities, copy will dated 5 Aug. 1893. For date of probate see W.T.C., box labelled

Hen. Boys Almshouses, draft appointment of trustees (1926).
[23] *Guide to Walsall* (1889), 33; *Staffs. Advertiser,* 25 June 1887.   [24] Ex inf. occupants (1973).
[25] Char. Com. files; inscrip. on alms-houses.
[26] *Valor Eccl.* (Rec. Com.), iii. 149.
[27] *S.H.C.* 1915, 301.
[28] Fink, *Queen Mary's Grammar Sch.* plate facing p. 145; S.R.O., D. 260/M/F/1/5, f. 72; above p. 228.
[29] E 133/1/61 f. 1.   [30] W.S.L., D. 1790/D/1.
[31] *Rep. Cttee. appointed at Vestry Meeting . . . to investigate . . . Public Charities* (Walsall, 1804), 27–8 (copy in W.C.L.).   [32] *9th Rep. Com. Char.* 607.
[33] *9th Rep. Com. Char.* 594; *Rep. Cttee. Public Chars.* (1804), 13; Homeshaw, *Walsall,* 153.
[34] Char. Com. files; ex inf. Mr. L. Harper (1973).

The Boltons' Charity. By deed of 1608 John Bolton, probably a former mayor, and his wife Alice gave a rent-charge of 10s. from land in Walsall to be distributed on Good Friday to 30 poor widows of the borough.[35] The owners of the land paid the rent-charge intermittently until 1660 when John Persehouse refused to do so. Thereafter the rent-charge seems to have been irrecoverable, and by 1823 the land was unidentifiable.[36]

Gorway's Charity. By will proved in 1611 Thomas Gorway, a Walsall butcher and probably a former mayor, left a rent-charge of £2 from lands in Rushall and West Bromwich for annual distribution to the poor of the town and parish of Walsall, 'without affection'.[37] By c. 1660 half was paid to the borough and half to the foreign.[38] The payment to the foreign was discontinued in 1811 but had been resumed by 1849.[39] In 1854 the borough share was distributed to 60 poor widows.[40] The charity has since lapsed.

Lyddiatt's Charity. By will proved in 1614 John Lyddiatt, a Walsall tanner and former mayor, left £10 to be lent yearly to poor men dwelling in Walsall.[41] About 1670 the charity was said to be applied regularly.[42] Its existence was recorded in 1786,[43] but there is no evidence that the money was being lent at any time in the 18th century. Nothing further is known of the charity.

The Fishley Charity. By will proved in 1616 William Parker of London, a native of Bloxwich, left £200 for a stock to provide work for the poor of Walsall parish.[44] In 1621 the money seems to have been applied in loans,[45] and in 1627 in premiums for apprentices also.[46] The fund passed into the control of the Stone family. In 1657, under an agreement with the corporation, Henry Stone invested the capital, augmented by £100 out of parish funds, in property in Bloxwich, including land at Fishley, to provide an income for apprenticing poor children in both borough and foreign.[47] The management of the charity passed to the corporation in 1669–70 when £10 13s. was spent on premiums.[48] By the early 19th century the apprentices were chosen by the overseers of the poor, who applied to the corporation for the premiums. These, however, were too small to secure respectable situations for the children, and much of the income remained unapplied.[49] A Chancery order of 1837 transferred the charity,

with the Bentley Hay Charity and Richard Stone's Charity, to a body of trustees; they were thereafter known as the Municipal Charities.[50]

A Scheme of 1864 directed that half the apprentices were to come from the borough and half from the foreign. No child was to be apprenticed to a publican or to work more than 10½ hours a day, six days a week.[51] A succession of Schemes from 1883 to 1909 diverted an increasing proportion of the income to education, and under a Scheme of 1970 the charity was renamed the Fishley Educational and Apprenticing Foundation; part of the income was to provide outfits or money for young people entering a profession, and the rest was to be used for education.[52] By 1945 part of the funds had been invested in stock and in property in Brixton in Lambeth (Surr.) and Hornsey (Mdx.).[53] The income in 1971–2 was £3,337 from those investments and the rent of Fishley farm in Walsall; £975 was spent on apprenticeships.[54]

Shaw's Charity. By will proved in 1617 Michael Shaw of Walsall left a rent-charge of 40s. from land in Walsall to be paid yearly to the poor of the parish.[55] In the early 19th century it was distributed in 6d. bread tickets.[56] It is last known to have been applied in 1855.[57]

Wheate's Charity. Besides his bequest for sermons William Wheate of Coventry at some time before 1618 left £20 to be lent to ten poor men in sums of 40s. for three years at a time. The charity still existed c. 1660, but nothing further is known of it.[58]

Hall's Charity. By deed of 1618 John Hall of Caldmore gave a rent-charge of £4 from land in Walsall to provide 28 loaves of white bread to be distributed weekly to the vicar, the parish clerk, and 25 poor. If the rent-charge proved inadequate the deficit was to be made up from the profits of the land.[59] Between at least 1657 and 1669 the dole appears to have been given in a house-to-house distribution of money.[60] The expenditure had increased to £5 12s. by 1804 and was then devoted to bread.[61] About 1814 Thomas Hawe Parker, the owner of the land, raised the payment to £10.[62] A Scheme of 1859 reduced the amount given in bread to £5, diverting £5 to St. Peter's National school and any surplus to the Blue Coat school.[63] In 1972 £5 from the charity was paid into the vicar's sick and poor fund.[64]

[35] *Charter of Corp. of Walsall*, 45; C 93/32/6; Homeshaw, *Walsall*, 153.

[36] C 93/32/6; W.T.C. II/89/5; *9th Rep. Com. Char.* 594; below p. 271.

[37] L.J.R.O., will proved 21 Dec. 1611; Homeshaw, *Walsall*, 153.

[38] *Charter of Corp. of Walsall*, 49–50. The charity and other material printed ibid. 41–60 is from W.T.C. II/53/3, dated 1729; internal evidence shows it to be a copy of notes made between 1658 and 1661 and probably in 1660.

[39] *9th Rep. Com. Char.* 592; L.J.R.O., B/V/6/Bloxwich, 1849.

[40] Glew, *Walsall*, 195.

[41] L.J.R.O., will proved 19 Jan. 1613/14; Homeshaw, *Walsall*, 153.

[42] W.T.C. II/129.

[43] *Abstract of Returns of Charitable Donations, 1786–8*, H.C. 511, pp. 1132–3 (1816), xvi (2).

[44] S.R.O., D. 260/M/T/2/53, p. 47.

[45] W.T.C. II/37/1.

[46] W.T.C. II/13/13.

[47] W.T.C. II/67; II/69; *Charter of Corp. of Walsall*, 54; *9th Rep. Com. Char.* 577 (wrongly stating that Hen. Stone the elder was Hen. Stone the younger's father).

[48] W.T.C. II/13/57 sqq.

[49] *Rep. Cttee. Public Chars.* (1804), 10–11; *9th Rep. Com.*

Char. 578; *1st Rep. Com. Mun. Corps.* H.C. 116, App. III, p. 2051 (1835), xxv; *Statement of Accts.* 137–57, 210 sqq.

[50] Glew, *Walsall*, 140, 177–81.

[51] Char. Com. Scheme, 13 May 1864.

[52] *Schemes for the Administration of . . . the Walsall Municipal Charities . . .* (Walsall, 1915), 13–14, 32–4 (copy in Char. Com. files); Dept. of Educ. and Science Scheme, 13 July 1970.

[53] *Rep. Town Clerk on Chars.* 18–19.

[54] Corp. char. accts. 1972 (copy at Walsall Council House).   [55] W.T.C. II/29.

[56] *Rep. Cttee. Public Chars.* (1804), 15; *9th Rep. Com. Char.* 595.

[57] Glew, *Walsall*, 193–4.

[58] *Charter of Corp. of Walsall*, 47; above n. 38.

[59] *9th Rep. Com. Char.* 585–6; S.R.O., D. 260/M/F/1/5, f. 115v.

[60] W.T.C. II/60.

[61] *Rep. Cttee. Public Chars.* (1804), 19; *9th Rep. Com. Char.* 586.

[62] *9th Rep. Com. Char.* 586; docs. at St. Matthew's, Churchwardens' Accts. 1794–1841, ff. 128v.–129; Glew, *Walsall*, 143.

[63] Chancery Scheme, 23 Feb. 1859 (copy in Char. Com. files).

[64] Ex inf. Mr. L. Harper (1973).

Curteys's Charity. By deed of 1618, in performance of her husband's will proved in 1617, Ellen, relict of John Curteys of Walsall, settled a rentcharge of £1 6s. 8d. from land in Caldmore in trust for the poor of the borough, to be distributed twice yearly.[65] The charity still existed in 1823 but had lapsed by 1854.[66]

Dee's Charities. By deed of 1620 John Dee, a Walsall baker, gave the rent from land in Walsall for distribution annually to 60 poor of Walsall, apparently the borough. The vicar and constable were to have 1s. each for distributing it. The rent was then 22s., but by 1823, although it had increased, the dole had been reduced to 21s. The Charity Commissioners recommended that the whole rent be paid, but by 1854 only 20s. was being distributed.[67] Nothing further is known of the charity.

At an unknown date Dee also left an annuity of 6s. 8d. from a house in Newgate Street to the poor of the borough. By c. 1660 the money was no longer paid.[68]

Robert Parker's General Charity. By will proved in 1625 Robert Parker, a London merchant taylor and brother of William Parker, left £400 to the Merchant Taylors' Company to buy land in Staffordshire worth £20 a year for the poor of Walsall, Rushall, and Pelsall in St. Peter's, Wolverhampton. The company was to pay one-third to Great Bloxwich, one-third to Little Bloxwich, Goscote, Harden, Coal Pool, 'Rushall End', Daw End, Pelsall, Shelfield, Wood End, and Caldmore, and one-third to the borough.[69] After proceedings against the company the corporation enforced payment in 1631.[70] The capital was apparently absorbed into the company's funds, but it normally paid the dole in full in the 17th century.[71] At some time between 1733 and 1769 a deduction was made for land tax, but the full sum was again paid by 1822. By then the shares payable to both borough and foreign were united with those from John Parker's Charity in one fund. The borough share of the fund was applied in 1823 with Thomas Webbe's Charity to buy gowns for poor women; the foreign share was given in money to the poor at Bloxwich.[72] When Bloxwich became a separate parish in 1842 the foreign share was divided between the churchwardens of Bloxwich and those of the foreign.[73] In 1972 the borough share and the reduced foreign share were applied with Thomas Webbe's Charity; £10 6s. 8d. was paid to Bloxwich and applied with the Bloxwich Dole, King's, Whateley's, Crowther's, and Picken's Charities and the foreign share of Nicholas Parker's Charity in £1 tickets distributed yearly.[74]

Robert Parker's Charity to Great Bloxwich. Robert Parker also left £4 from the rent of land in Bloxwich for the aged poor of Great Bloxwich and the rest for the repair of Bloxwich chapel. After proceedings in Chancery the land was settled in trust in 1627.[75] By 1804 the payment to the poor had been increased to £7.[76] In the early 19th century it was applied with the Bloxwich share of Robert Parker's General Charity.[77] In 1838 the land was leased for mining at a minimum rent of £140 with royalties, a suit in Chancery was brought to establish trustees for the proceeds, and the whole income from 1838 to 1849 was lost in consequence.[78] Trustees had been appointed by 1849.[79] A Scheme of 1886 allotted £30 to the repair of Bloxwich church; pensions of at least 6s. a week were to be paid to two poor persons resident in the former chapelry for not less than four years. Any surplus was to be given to other deserving poor.[80] By 1945 the surplus was distributed yearly in 5s. vouchers; the pensioners received 6s. a week.[81] The trustees sold most of the land c. 1970. The income in 1972 was about £1,700, chiefly interest from stock. No distribution had been made since 1970, and plans were being considered for the erection of alms-houses.[82]

Robert Parker's Organ Charity. When the organs in Walsall church were destroyed in 1642 the annuity of £5 left by Robert Parker to the organist and organ-blower ceased.[83] After proceedings in Chancery a decree of 1649 required the annuity to be paid to provide bread for the poor, one-third to the borough and two-thirds to the foreign. The arrears were to be divided likewise.[84] About 1660 the Merchant Taylors' Company suspended payment. From 1701, after a further suit, the charity was again paid to the organist.[85]

John Parker's Charity (the Langthorne Dole). By will proved in 1627 John Parker of London, brother of William and Robert, left a rent-charge of £20 from the manor of Langthorne in Bedale (Yorks. N.R.) for sermons at Walsall, Rushall, and Bloxwich, repairs to Bloxwich chapel, and a yearly house-by-house distribution to the poorest inhabitants of Walsall, Rushall, Bloxwich, and Harden in specified proportions.[86] Payment did not begin until 1637.[87] From that time £14 13s. 4d. of the income was divided between the poor of the borough, the poor of Bloxwich, Harden, Goscote, and Coal Pool, and the poor of the rest of the foreign and Rushall.[88] In 1655 it was being given with the doles of Robert Parker and Henry Stone the elder.[89] By 1736 deductions were made for land tax, fixed at £4 by 1823.[90] Since at least 1822 the dole has been applied with Robert Parker's General Charity.[91] The rent-charge, then £16, was redeemed in 1922; in 1972 the same income was received from stock.[92]

Nicholas Parker's Charities. By will proved in 1627

[65] W.T.C. I/192; L.J.R.O., will of John Curteys, proved 23 Jan. 1616/17.
[66] *9th Rep. Com. Char.* 596–7; Glew, *Walsall*, 141.
[67] W.T.C. I/198; *9th Rep. Com. Char.* 596; Glew, *Walsall*, 195. [68] *Charter of Corp. of Walsall*, 45.
[69] S.R.O., D. 260/M/T/2/54, pp. 16–18, 36–8; C 3/418/34. Parker believed that Rushall and Pelsall were in Walsall.
[70] C 3/418/34; Sims, *Cal. of Deeds*, p. 61.
[71] *9th Rep. Com. Char.* 582; W.T.C. II/59;/60;/63/1;/97.
[72] W.T.C. II/162; *9th Rep. Com. Char.* 582–5; docs. at St. Matthew's, Churchwardens' Accts. 1794–1841, 2nd leaf. [73] L.J.R.O., B/V/6/Bloxwich, 1841, 1849.
[74] Ex inf. (1973) Mr. L. Harper and Mr. W. J. Bridge, churchwarden of Bloxwich in 1971.
[75] C 3/418/34; W.T.C. II/162, ff. 9v.–12; *9th Rep. Com. Char.* 605.

[76] *Rep. Cttee. Public Chars.* (1804), 5.
[77] *9th Rep. Com. Char.* 606.
[78] Glew, *Walsall*, 167–8.
[79] L.J.R.O., B/V/6/Bloxwich, 1849.
[80] Char. Com. Scheme, 12 Nov. 1886.
[81] *Rep. Town Clerk on Chars.* 15.
[82] Ex inf. the clerk to the trustees and Mr. W. J. Bridge, a trustee (1973). [83] See p. 233.
[84] W.T.C. I/261, arts. 24, 26; II/54.
[85] W.T.C. II/63/4; II/93; above p. 233.
[86] S.R.O., D. 260/M/T/2/55, pp. 68–9, 160–2.
[87] Sims, *Cal. of Deeds*, pp. 59–60; W.T.C. II/45–7.
[88] W.T.C. II/46/4; *Charter of Corp. of Walsall*, 51.
[89] W.T.C. II/60.
[90] W.T.C. II/162, f. [7]; *9th Rep. Com. Char.* 582.
[91] See above. [92] Ex inf. Mr. L. Harper (1973).

Nicholas Parker of Great Bloxwich, brother of William, Robert, and John, left a rent-charge of £4 from lands in Walsall and Rushall; 20s. was to be given to the poor of Rushall, 20s. to the poor of Great and Little Bloxwich and Harden, and £2 to Walsall church to reduce the church-rates paid by the poor.[93] The last charity was withheld in 1651, had been resumed by the mid 18th century, and ceased in 1762. The dole to the poor of the foreign was paid until c. 1760.[94] The charity is probably identifiable with Parker's Dole, recorded in 1767 and then said to be worth £2. It had not, however, been paid for many years and had been lost by 1804.[95]

Nicholas Parker also left the poor of Walsall a rent-charge of 40s. from a pasture in Walsall called Peakers.[96] By 1767 the charity was known as Peaker's Dole.[97] In 1823 half was used by the borough churchwardens for general purposes and half by the foreign churchwardens in gifts to the poor.[98] The foreign share was paid to Bloxwich by 1849.[99] The rent-charge was still paid in 1972; the borough share was paid into the vicar's sick and poor fund and the foreign share applied with the Bloxwich share of Robert Parker's General Charity.[1]

Charity of John Wollaston the elder. By will proved in 1634 John Wollaston, a former mayor, left the rent of a house in the churchyard to the poor of the borough; 2s. was to be given to the four inmates of Harper's alms-houses and the rest distributed to the poor. The charity existed in 1670, but nothing further is known of it.[2]

John Persehouse's Charity. By will proved in 1636 John Persehouse left a rent-charge of 40s. from land near Walsall park to be distributed twice yearly to the poor of the borough and foreign.[3] In 1657 the dole was distributed with the gifts of John Hall and Henry Stone the elder.[4] The rent was withheld in 1660, and payment seems never to have been resumed.[5]

Bentley Hay Charity. By deed of 1638 Thomas Lane of Bentley in St. Peter's, Wolverhampton, agreed to pay £20 a year out of the profits of Bentley Hay to the poor of Walsall borough if the inhabitants of the parish waived their claim to common in the hay.[6] By Exchequer decree of 1640 the moneys were divided equally between the borough and the foreign.[7] The rent-charge to the foreign lapsed soon after,[8] but that to the borough continued to be paid until at least 1667. Lane's grandson subsequently

refused to pay it[9] but redeemed it in 1702 for £220.[10] Of that sum £141 1s. 6d. was spent on property in Walsall, which was settled in trust.[11] The rest appears to have been used to buy three alms-houses for ten poor families, but nothing further is known of them.[12] The rents of the estate were distributed yearly in gowns to poor widows.[13]

By the early 19th century the charity lands were administered with the corporation's estates,[14] but from 1822 they were separately managed. In 1837 control passed to the trustees of the Municipal Charities, who distributed the gowns.[15] A Scheme of 1864 required the income to be applied in gifts of clothes, coats, or provisions to poor not receiving relief.[16] By 1945 tickets were being used for the distribution; the greater part of the property had by then been sold and the proceeds invested in stock.[17] A remaining rent-charge was redeemed in 1970.[18] Under a Scheme of that year the charity was amalgamated with Richard Stone's; the income was to be spent in cash grants to needy persons in the county borough.[19] In 1972 the income of the joint charity was £206 from stock; £160 was distributed to aged poor in Christmas gift tokens of £0·75.[20]

Henry Stone the elder's Charities. By deed of 1639 Henry Stone the elder of Walsall, a former mayor, settled a rent-charge of £34 14s. from land in Walsall, Castle Bromwich (Warws.), and Yardley (Worcs.). The trustees were to spend £13 in a house-by-house distribution twice yearly to poor householders of the borough and foreign; a further £7 10s. was to be spent on coats for 12 poor men of the borough and gowns for 12 poor women, and £4 4s. a year was to be given to them in bread each Sunday. The trustees were to keep £2 for an annual dinner, give £1 to the preaching minister of Cannock, and pay the remainder to Walsall church for repairs and sermons.[21]

In the 1640s and 1650s Henry Stone the younger was augmenting the dole to poor householders, £13 6s. 8d. being usually paid.[22] In 1659 it was said to be distributed together with John Persehouse's.[23] Stone also paid the other charges regularly and renewed the trust in 1686.[24] In 1706 the rent-charge on the Castle Bromwich and Yardley lands was apparently reduced by £2. By 1777 a further deduction was made for land tax. At some time between 1753 and 1788 the rent-charge, amounting to £7, on part of the Walsall property ceased to be paid. The

[93] W.T.C. II/162, f. [8]; II/129; *9th Rep. Com. Char.* 584–5.
[94] C 93/32/6; W.T.C. II/162, f. [7v.].
[95] Docs. at St. Matthew's, Vestry Bk. 1681–1793, p. 142; *Rep. Cttee. Public Chars.* (1804), 13. In the mid 17th century Rob. Parker's General Charity was called Parker's Dole: W.T.C. II/59.
[96] W.T.C. II/132; *Charter of Corp. of Walsall*, 50–1.
[97] Docs. at St. Matthew's, Vestry Bk. 1681–1793, p. 142. The description of the charity there conflicts with another of the same date in W.T.C. II/162, f. [7v.].
[98] *9th Rep. Com. Char.* 585.
[99] L.J.R.O., B/V/6/Bloxwich, 1849.
[1] Ex inf. Mr. L. Harper and Mr. W. J. Bridge (1973).
[2] L.J.R.O., will proved 28 Aug. 1634; Homeshaw, *Walsall*, 153; *9th Rep. Com. Char.* 597, giving an incorrect pedigree of the Wollastons. For the family see J. Nichols, *Hist. and Antiquities of Town and County of Leicester*, iv (2), 541.
[3] W.S.L. 45/56, folder 28, no. 12, p. 10.
[4] W.T.C. II/60.
[5] W.T.C. II/89/3 and 5; C 93/32/6; *9th Rep. Com. Char.* 593.

[6] W.T.C. II/8/5.
[7] W.T.C. II/8/6.
[8] *S.H.C.* 1910, 177.
[9] Ibid. 195; W.T.C. II/8/11.
[10] W.T.C. II/8/7, 11, 14–16; *9th Rep. Com. Char.* 601.
[11] *9th Rep. Com. Char.* 601.
[12] *Rep. Cttee. Public Chars.* (1804), 29.
[13] *9th Rep. Com. Char.* 602.
[14] Ibid. 601–3; *Statement of Accts.* 1–125.
[15] *Statements of Accts.* 126; Glew, *Walsall*, 140–1; above p. 269.
[16] Char. Com. Scheme, 13 May 1864.
[17] *Rep. Town Clerk on Chars.* 19–20.
[18] Char. Com. files. For its origin see S.R.O., Q/RSc 1, pp. 44–7.
[19] Char. Com. Scheme, 1 Oct. 1970.
[20] Corp. char. accts. 1972.
[21] W.T.C., Char. Box, docs. relating to Hen. Stone's Char., deed of 10 Apr. 1639; Homeshaw, *Walsall*, 153; above p. 229.
[22] W.T.C. II/51.
[23] W.T.C. II/63/2.
[24] W.T.C. II/51; W.T.C., Char. Box, docs. relating to Hen. Stone's Char., deed of 4 Oct. 1686.

weekly distribution of bread was abandoned in 1801. By 1823 the trustees received only £24 4s., though that was augmented by £5 from Henry Stone the younger's Charity. In the early 19th century c. £12 was usually spent on coats for 18 poor men and women and half-crowns were given to the poor at Christmas.[25]

The distribution of bread had been resumed by 1838, when loaves were given weekly.[26] Between at least 1841 and 1849 £4 17s. 6d. was paid to the poor of Bloxwich.[27] In 1875 £7 of the rent-charge was redeemed, and the remainder had likewise been converted to stock by 1910.[28] A Scheme of the latter year separated the donations to the church and Cannock from those to the poor, which were united with Henry Stone the younger's Charity as the Stone Eleemosynary Charity. The income was to be spent on clothes, bedding, fuel, tools, or medical aid. The annual dinner was abolished.[29] In 1971–2 the income was £28; food- and clothing-vouchers worth £29 were given to poor people in the pre-1966 borough.[30]

By his will dated 1634 Henry Stone the elder left £50 to be lent to poor tradesmen in sums of £2 to £5 for two years at a time.[31] The charity had lapsed by 1804.[32]

Richard Stone's Charity. By will proved in 1640 Richard Stone of Walsall, a former mayor, left a rent-charge of 20s. from land in Bentley in St. Peter's, Wolverhampton, to the mayor of Walsall to be given in cloth to two poor men at Christmas. He also left the mayor 26s. charged on further land in Bentley; 20s. was to provide cloth for two poor women of the borough yearly, and the corporation was to keep the rest.[33] By the early 19th century both rent-charges were being used with the rents of the Bentley Hay Charity for clothing.[34] In 1837 control passed to the Municipal Charities trustees.[35] A Scheme of 1864 restricted the application to the provision of coats for old men.[36] By 1945, however, the income was again being combined with that of the Bentley Hay Charity and was used to purchase tickets.[37] The rent-charges were redeemed in 1970, and the charity was amalgamated with the Bentley Hay Charity by a Scheme of that year.[38]

Haynes's Charity. In her will Cicely Haynes (d. 1650) left a rent-charge of 10s. a year from land in Wolverhampton to be paid to 30 poor widows of Walsall borough on St. Andrew's day (30 November). It ceased to be paid in 1775.[39]

Thomas Wollaston's Charities. In his will Thomas Wollaston (d. 1657), a former mayor, left the rent

of a house below Walsall churchyard to the poor. After the deduction of the chief rent 2s. was to be paid to the four inmates of Harper's alms-houses and the rest distributed to the poor of the borough. He also left 10s. rent, from a cottage at Townend which he held on a 99-year lease, to be paid yearly to 30 poor widows of the borough. The charities existed in 1670, but nothing further is known of them.[40]

Richard Stone of Caldmore's Charity. Probably before 1660 Richard Stone of Caldmore gave 6s. 8d. from land at Palfrey for bread for the poor at Christmas.[41] The rent-charge was paid until c. 1784 but thereafter lapsed.[42]

William Webbe's Charity. By deed of 1670 William Webbe of London settled in trust two houses in Walsall 'under the hill . . . and near the pump'. The rent was to be spent upon the poor of the borough and foreign. The charity existed in 1692, but nothing further is known of it.[43]

Charity of John Wollaston the younger. By will dated 1670 John Wollaston, a former mayor, left the rent of his house in Walsall to be distributed to the poor of the borough on Good Friday at the discretion of his heirs.[44] Nothing further is known of the charity.

Blanch Wollaston's Charity. By will proved in 1678 Blanch Wollaston of Walsall, widow of John Wollaston the younger, left land in Great Barr in Aldridge and a house in Walsall for the poor. From the Barr property 10s. was to be given yearly to 20 poor widows of the borough; the rest, with the rent of the house, was to be spent in apprenticing children in the borough. Out of her personal estate land was to be bought to augment the charity; £5 of the income was to be given to the poor of Bickenhill (Warws.) and the rest united with her Walsall apprenticing fund.[45] The charity was not payable until after her son's death and did not take effect until 1692 at the earliest.[46] The augmentation was effected by the purchase of land in Aldridge in 1698.[47] By 1823 40 widows were receiving £4 each yearly, and in the previous ten years 74 children had been apprenticed.[48] In the mid 1850s much of the income was unused because apprenticing was restricted to borough children, but only in 1871 were the trustees authorized to draw upon the whole parish.[49]

By a Scheme of 1910 separate charities were established for Walsall and Bickenhill. The trustees were to give £10 of the Walsall charity's income to poor widows in the borough; the rest was to be spent

[25] *9th Rep. Com. Char.* 587–92.
[26] Docs. at St. Matthew's, Churchwardens' Accts. 1794–1841, f. 128v.
[27] L.J.R.O., B/V/6/Bloxwich, 1841 and 1849.
[28] W.T.C., Char. Box, misc. docs., papers relating to redemption of rent-charge, Hen. Stone's Char., 1875; Char. Com. Scheme, 23 Mar. 1910.
[29] Char. Com. Scheme, 23 Mar. 1910.
[30] Corp. char. accts. 1972; circular of 23 Oct. 1972, town clerk to trustees (copy in possession of the mayor's sec. 1972). [31] *Charter of Corp. of Walsall*, 47.
[32] *Rep. Cttee. Public Chars.* (1804), 8.
[33] L.J.R.O., will proved 7 Mar. 1639/40; W.T.C. II/131; Homeshaw, *Walsall*, 153.
[34] *9th Rep. Com. Char.* 603.   [35] See p. 269.
[36] Char. Com. Scheme, 13 May 1864.
[37] *Rep. Town Clerk on Chars.* 18.
[38] Char. Com. files; above p. 271.
[39] *Charter of Corp. of Walsall*, 47; *Wolverhampton Par. Reg.* (Staffs. Par. Reg. Soc. 1932), i. 202; *4th Rep. Com. Char.* H.C. 312, p. 365 (1820), v.

[40] *Charter of Corp. of Walsall*, 48; *9th Rep. Com. Char.* 597; Homeshaw, *Walsall*, 43, 153; above p. 271 n. 2.
[41] *9th Rep. Com. Char.* 604; *Charter of Corp. of Walsall*, 45, identifying Stone with Ric. Stone of Walsall. The latter's will, however, does not mention the bequest: L.J.R.O., will proved 7 Mar. 1639/40. For the date see above p. 269 n. 38.
[42] *Rep. Cttee. Public Chars.* (1804), 14; *9th Rep. Com. Char.* 604; Glew, *Walsall*, 191.
[43] W.T.C. II/120.
[44] W.T.C. II/148 (calling him John Wolverston); *9th Rep. Com. Char.* 598; Homeshaw, *Walsall*, 154; above p. 271 n. 2.
[45] L.J.R.O., will proved 3 May 1678; W.T.C. II/102/2; *9th Rep. Com. Char.* 598.
[46] W.T.C. II/102/2 and 3.
[47] *9th Rep. Com. Char.* 598–9.
[48] Ibid. 600–1.
[49] Glew, *Walsall*, 141, 161–2, 179; W.T.C., Char. Box, letter to trustees of Blanch Wollaston's Char. 22 June 1871.

on apprenticing and on outfits for young people entering a trade.[50] A further Scheme of 1933 restricted the application to minors.[51] By 1945 the widows received clothing tickets at Christmas. By 1947 the payments for apprenticeships had been replaced by more general vocational assistance.[52]

Land at Great Barr was sold in 1896 and land at Aldridge in 1935.[53] The income in 1971–2 was £590 from the remainder of the estates in Barr and Aldridge and from stock; £82 was spent on Christmas gifts to widows in the pre-1966 borough and £100 on a student's grant.[54]

Syvern's Charity. By will proved in 1684 William Syvern, a Walsall shoemaker, left £5 a year to the poor of the town.[55] The capital was converted into a rent-charge of £5 on property in Birmingham. By 1804 payment was confined to the borough. Each year £1 14s. 8d. was spent on bread; eight loaves were distributed each Sunday. The balance was applied with Thomas Webbe's Charity.[56] In 1972 the rent-charge was paid into the vicar's sick and poor fund.[57]

Roger Hinton's Charity. By will dated 1685 Roger Hinton of Rickerscote in Castle Church devised rent-charges from lands in Rickerscote and Burton, also in Castle Church, to the poor of several Staffordshire parishes and townships, including one of £5 to Walsall. The annuities were at first withheld, but under a Chancery decree the estate was settled in 1692 upon the trusts of Hinton's will; the trustees were also to divide the surplus revenue after payment of the rent-charges between the places in five equal portions.[58] By the early 19th century the sum payable to Walsall was spent on gowns and coats for poor people in winter. It had increased to £23 18s. 11d. by 1821.[59] Under a Scheme of 1909 at least £10 of the clear yearly income of the estate was to be paid to Walsall; it could be spent on medical aid, fuel, food, clothing, or other assistance.[60] Since then the Walsall income, £67 in 1971–2, has usually been applied in gifts of tickets to poor living in the pre-1966 borough.[61]

Henry Stone the younger's Charity. By will proved in 1690 Henry Stone the younger of Walsall settled in trust a rent-charge of £5 from his estates in Staffordshire and Warwickshire. The money was to provide coats for five poor men of the borough and gowns for five poor widows on Christmas day. By 1777, despite an exemption clause in the will, the annuity was charged on the property in Castle Bromwich (Warws.) and Yardley (Worcs.) already encumbered with Henry Stone the elder's Charity.

By the early 19th century it was administered with that charity, and the two were formally united in 1910 as the Stone Eleemosynary Charity.[62]

Robert Moseley's Charity. By will proved in 1697 Robert Moseley of Walsall left a rent-charge of £2 1s. from land in Bushbury to the vicar of Walsall and the churchwardens of the borough. They were to distribute 40s. yearly to the poor of the borough, retaining 1s. themselves.[63] It is not known that the rent-charge was ever paid.[64]

Humphrey Persehouse's Charity. By will proved in 1698 Humphrey Persehouse left a rent-charge of £5 from land in Great Bloxwich to be paid yearly to the poor, £2 to the borough and £3 to the foreign.[65] The dole to the borough may have been paid in the earlier 18th century; that to the foreign was still paid c. 1770.[66] The charity had been lost by 1804.[67]

Murrey's Charity. By will proved in 1710 Samuel Murrey of Walsall left land in Darlaston to sixteen poor men of the foreign, who were each to receive 6d. yearly from the profits.[68] The charity may have existed in the later 18th century,[69] but nothing further is known of it.

Robinson's Charity. By will proved in 1724 Richard Robinson, a Bushbury nailer, left a rent-charge of 40s. from a cottage apparently in Bushbury to be distributed to the poor of Great and Little Bloxwich twice yearly. It had ceased to be paid by the mid 18th century.[70]

King's Charity. By will proved in 1729 William King of Great Bloxwich gave land there to the poor widows of Great Bloxwich. The charity was to take effect after his wife's death. The income in 1736 was £2.[71] By 1804, however, the charity had been in abeyance for some years, as the land had been mortgaged for securing a debt 'for Burton ale'.[72] By 1823 the owner of the property was applying about £2 a year in small gifts to the poor, but by 1849 a £2 rent-charge was distributed by the minister.[73] In 1864 by order of the Master of the Rolls the rent-charge was redeemed and the capital invested in stock. The income was to be applied in bread, coals, clothing, or fuel for the poor of Bloxwich parish, preferably widows.[74] By 1965 the stock had been united with that of Crowther's Charity. The joint income in 1971 was £53 and was applied with the Bloxwich share of Robert Parker's General Charity.[75]

Mills's Charity. By will proved in 1754 Bridget Mills of Walsall left £100, the interest on which, after the death of her nieces, was to be distributed yearly among 100 poor of the borough.[76] The charity

[50] Char. Com. Scheme, 23 Mar. 1910.
[51] Char. Com. Scheme, 4 Apr. 1933.
[52] *Rep. Town Clerk on Chars.* 11–12; Walsall Council House, mins. of trustees of Blanch Wollaston and Hen. Stone Chars. 1947–, *passim*.
[53] Char. Com. Orders, 19 Aug. 1896, 8 June and 8 Nov. 1935.   [54] Corp. char. accts. 1972.
[55] L.J.R.O., will proved 27 Nov. 1684; *Charter of Corp. of Walsall*, 61.
[56] *Rep. Cttee. Public Chars.* (1804), 8; *9th Rep. Com. Char.* 594.
[57] Ex inf. Mr. L. Harper (1973).
[58] *7th Rep. Com. Char.* H.C. 129, pp. 418–19 (1822), x; W.T.C. II/113/2; *V.C.H. Staffs.* v. 99.
[59] *9th Rep. Com. Char.* 601.
[60] Char. Com. Scheme, 16 Feb. 1909.
[61] Walsall Council House, mins. of trustees of Hinton's Char., *passim*; Corp. char. accts. 1972.
[62] W.S.L. 45/56, folder 73, will, pp. 6–7; *9th Rep. Com.*

Char. 603–4; Char. Com. Scheme, 23 Mar. 1910; above p. 271.
[63] L.J.R.O., will proved 3 July 1697.
[64] *Char. Dons.* 1786–8, 1132–3.
[65] W.S.L. 45/56, folder 28, no. 14.
[66] W.T.C. II/162 [ff. 7, 12v.].
[67] *Rep. Cttee. Public Chars.* (1804), 20; *9th Rep. Com. Char.* 593–4.
[68] L.J.R.O., will proved 3 Mar. 1709/10.
[69] W.T.C. II/162 [f. 3].
[70] W.T.C. II/162 [f. 6]; *9th Rep. Com. Char.* 607.
[71] L.J.R.O., will proved 12 Dec. 1729 (giving the land to 'the poor widow'); W.T.C. II/162 [ff. 6v., 7].
[72] *Rep. Cttee. Public Chars.* (1804), 12.
[73] *9th Rep. Com. Char.* 606; L.J.R.O., B/V/6/Bloxwich, 1849.
[74] Char. Com. files.
[75] Ibid.; ex inf. Mr. W. J. Bridge (1973).
[76] L.J.R.O., will proved 8 July 1754.

had become payable by 1804; the income in the early 19th century was £5, which was given in flannel by 1838–9.[77] In 1972 the income, £3 from stock, was paid into the vicar's sick and poor fund.[78]

Whateley's Charity. By will dated 1799 Henry Whateley left a rent-charge of £6 from land at Coal Pool for annual payments of £4 4s. to old and infirm men and women of the foreign not receiving pay from the overseers and £1 1s. to the curate of Bloxwich for a sermon; the distributors were to retain 15s. for refreshment afterwards.[79] The annuity was still paid in 1971 and was applied with the Bloxwich share of Robert Parker's General Charity.[80]

Wilcox's Charity. Before 1804 John Wilcox gave 16s. a year to be distributed to the poor of the borough. By 1804 it was charged on land in Darlaston. It was agreed in 1823 to set aside ½ a. of the property for the poor. It was sold in 1845 and the proceeds were invested in stock.[81] In 1972 the income, £4, was applied with Thomas Webbe's Charity.[82]

The Bloxwich Dole. By 1819 a rent-charge of £2 11s. out of a farm in Little Bloxwich was being given yearly to the poor of the foreign.[83] Payment was interrupted from 1820 but had been resumed by 1841.[84] The rent-charge was redeemed in 1893 and invested in stock.[85] In 1971 the income, £2·55, was applied with the Bloxwich share of Robert Parker's General Charity.[86]

Crowther's Charity. By will proved in 1857 John Crowther of Wednesbury left £2,000 to be invested in stock. The income was to be spent on coats, gowns, and blankets distributed to poor parishioners of Bloxwich, preference being given to regular church-goers. By 1965 the stock had been united with that of King's Charity, and the two funds are applied together.[87]

Ricketts's Charity. By will proved in 1866 George Ricketts, a Walsall whip-thong maker, left £100 out of his residuary estate for charitable purposes within St. Peter's parish. In 1972 the income, about £2·50 derived from stock, was paid to needy people there.[88]

Bealey's Charities. By will proved in 1890 J. E. Bealey of the Hills, Bloxwich, left £200 to provide bread for distribution weekly to poor widows of the district of Christ Church, Blakenall Heath, and £100 for bread for poor widows and other needy persons living near Little Bloxwich mission church. A Scheme of 1937 permitted both charities to be applied in cash.[89] By 1972 the two funds had been amalgamated with Farnall's Charity; the income in that year, £5 from stock, was paid to needy persons in Christ Church parish.[90]

Hill's Charities. By will proved in 1892 William

Henry Hill of Walsall left £300, payable after his wife's death, for yearly gifts of food and clothing to the poor of St. Michael's parish, Caldmore, and £300 to St. Matthew's parish on like trusts. The charity took effect in 1903.[91] The income of the Caldmore charity in 1972, £10 from stock, was given in cash and food at Christmas.[92] The St. Matthew's income, £19, was paid into the vicar's sick and poor fund.[93]

The Henry Boys' Charities. By will proved in 1894 Henry Boys left £1,250 for yearly gifts of Witney blankets to poor widows over 50, £1,250 to provide boots for poor, infirm, and unemployable men over 50, and £1,000 for a yearly gift of shoes to equal numbers of orphan boys and girls aged between 6 and 12. Life-long residents of Walsall were to be preferred.[94] The income in 1972 was £90; £56 was spent on boots and shoes distributed to old men and orphans in the pre-1966 borough, and £48 on blankets given to widows there.[95]

Farnall's Charity. By will proved in 1894 Eliza Farnall of the Hills, Bloxwich, left £100 for yearly gifts of flannel to poor widows living near Little Bloxwich mission church.[96] By 1972 the capital had been united with that of Bealey's Charities and the incomes were applied jointly.

The Sarah Janet Kirkpatrick Trust. By will proved in 1894 Sarah Janet Kirkpatrick of Walsall settled £500 to benefit poor women.[97] From 1921 to 1952 the income was paid to the Sutton Coldfield Home of Rest for Women and Girls, and between 1922 and 1935 to the Wolverhampton Hospital for Women also. Since 1952 it has been divided between the Walsall Tuberculosis After Care Committee and the Walsall Civic Guild of Help (now the Walsall Guild of Social Service and Citizens' Advice Bureau).[98] The income in 1972 was £24.[99]

Trees Dole. By will proved in 1896 James Trees of Walsall left £300 to be distributed in winter clothing yearly to the poor of St. George's parish, half for men and half for women.[1] A Scheme of 1966 divided the interest equally between St. Matthew's and St. Paul's parishes for gifts in money or in kind to poor residents in the former parish of St. George. In 1972 the income, £7, was paid into the sick and poor funds of the two parishes.[2]

Brace's Charity. By will proved in 1911 Eliza Brace of Walsall left £500 to pay the travel and subsistence expenses of poor patients from the borough and foreign staying in convalescent homes. A Scheme of 1934 restricted the application to poor mothers in St. Matthew's parish but permitted expenditure for other medical purposes or for gifts of money or clothing. The income in 1972 was £15,

---

[77] *Rep. Cttee. Public Chars.* (1804), 12; *9th Rep. Com. Char.* 605; docs. at St. Matthew's, Churchwardens' Accts. 1794–1841, ff. 128v.–129.
[78] Ex inf. Mr. L. Harper (1973).
[79] *9th Rep. Com. Char.* 607.
[80] Char. Com. files; ex inf. Mr. W. J. Bridge (1973).
[81] *Rep. Cttee. Public Chars.* (1804), 21; *9th Rep. Com. Char.* 604; Glew, *Walsall*, 192.
[82] Ex inf. Mr. L. Harper (1973).
[83] *9th Rep. Com. Char.* 606.
[84] Ibid.; L.J.R.O., B/V/6/Bloxwich, 1841.
[85] Char. Com. files.
[86] Ex inf. Mr. W. J. Bridge (1973).
[87] Char. Com. files.
[88] Char. Com. files; ex inf. the vicar of St. Peter's (1973).
[89] Char. Com. files; L.J.R.O., Copies of Wills, vol. lxxxv, f. 54.

[90] Ex inf. the vicar of Christ Church (1973).
[91] Char. Com. files.
[92] Ex inf. the vicar of St. Michael's (1973).
[93] Ex inf. Mr. L. Harper (1973).
[94] See references in p. 268 n. 22.
[95] Corp. char. accts. 1972.
[96] Char. Com. files.
[97] W.T.C., box labelled Sir Edwin and Lady Smith's Char., will of S. J. Kirkpatrick; Walsall Council House, mins. of Cox's Alms-house Trustees, p. 3379; *Boro. of Walsall: Council Mins. 1920–21*, 719.
[98] Walsall Council House, mins. of Char. Cttee. 1917–51, pp. 11 sqq.; 1952–72, pp. 6, 15, 49, 198.
[99] Corp. char. accts. 1972.
[1] L.J.R.O., Copies of Wills, vol. ci, f. 53v.
[2] Char. Com. Scheme, 8 Mar. 1966; Char. Com. files; ex inf. the treasurer of St. Matthew's (1973).

which was spent on convalescent holidays for poor women.[3]

Sir Edwin and Lady Smith's Gifts. In 1917 Sir Edwin Thomas Smith of Marryatville, South Australia, a native of Walsall, gave £1,000 to provide clothing, boots, bedding, fuel, or similar articles at Christmas for poor of the borough over 50.[4] The income was distributed in kind from 1917 to 1952 and from 1953 in tickets.[5] The income in 1971–2 was £35; £53 was distributed within the area of the pre-1966 borough.[6]

Archer's Charity. By will proved in 1918 Joseph Allen Archer, a Walsall leather-goods manufacturer, left £500 for a yearly distribution after his wife's death of boots among poor children in the borough. The charity had come into effect by 1926. The income in 1971–2 was £17 from stock; £26 was spent on boots and shoes in the pre-1966 borough.[7]

Blyth's Charity. By will proved in 1919 William Edward Blyth left £25 for the poor of St. Matthew's parish. In 1972 the income, £0·93 from stock, was paid into the vicar's sick and poor fund.[8]

Windle's Charity. By will proved in 1920 Mary Jesson Windle of Walsall left £100 to the sick and poor fund of St. Matthew's parish. The income in 1972 was £5 from stock.[9]

The Isabel Jones Trust. By will proved in 1933 Thomas Halbert Jones of Walsall left £500 in memory of his daughter for poor Walsall children. The trustees decided to spend the income on boots, clothing, spectacles, and milk for needy school children under 17. In 1971–2 the income was £18 from stock; £30 was spent on needy children.[10]

The J. A. Leckie Trust Gift. By will proved in 1938 J. A. Leckie of Sutton Coldfield (Warws.), M.P. for Walsall 1931–8 and mayor 1926–7, left a share of his residual estate to the Walsall Victoria Nursing Institution. In 1956 his trustees decided that the money, then amounting to £1,000, should be administered under a resolution of the town council's charities committee that it be invested and the income distributed to aged poor living in the borough. The fund was first so applied in 1958.[11] The income in 1971–2 was £51·75 from stock; £61·50 was spent on £0·75 tickets distributed at Christmas within the area of the pre-1966 borough.[12]

Hopkins Charity. The charity, applied in St. Matthew's parish, is said to have been founded in 1940, but the donor and instrument are unknown. Two funds were established, one for bread for the poor and the other for 10s. gifts to them at Christmas. In 1972 the income of the bread charity was £10·96 and that of the gift charity £6·54 from stock; both were paid into the vicar's sick and poor fund.[13]

The Annie Elizabeth Bull Charity. By will proved in 1943 Frederick Bull, a Walsall spring-hook and chain manufacturer, left £2,600 in memory of his wife for Christmas distributions in cash, food, or clothing among poor over 65 and resident in the county borough for at least ten years.[14] In 1971–2 the income was £90; £78 was spent on £0·75 tickets distributed in the pre-1966 borough.[15]

The Alice Hanlon Charity. By will proved in 1950 Alice Hanlon, sister of Frederick Bull, left £2,330 on trusts identical with those of the foregoing.[16] The income in 1971–2 was £117, which was distributed in £0·75 tickets.[17]

The Mayor's Old People's Christmas Gift Fund. In 1958 £2,100, raised by public appeal in 1957 by D. Cartwright, then mayor, was settled by the corporation to provide Christmas gifts in cash to men over 65 and women over 60 living in the borough.[18] In 1971–2 the income was £129 from stock and was distributed in the pre-1966 borough.[19]

Picken's Charity. By will proved in 1963 John Picken of Bloxwich, a retired colliery-timber sawyer, left £100 for the general charitable purposes of Bloxwich church. In 1971 the income amounted to £10 from stock, which was applied with the Bloxwich share of Robert Parker's General Charity.[20]

WALSALL WOOD

The area that became the civil parish of Walsall Wood was originally a detached part of the foreign of Walsall.[1] It was 1,551 a. in extent[2] and lay on either side of the Walsall–Lichfield road to the north-east of the main area. In 1894 it became a civil parish within the urban district of Brownhills,[3] which in 1966 became part of the urban district of Aldridge-Brownhills, itself taken into the metropolitan district of Walsall from 1974. The present article covers the history of Walsall Wood to 1974, except for the modern development of the northern extremity. That development is part of the growth of Brownhills (in Norton Canes and Ogley Hay) and is reserved for treatment in a future volume.

Walsall Wood was bounded on the west by Ford (or Clayhanger) Brook and on the south-east by its

[3] Char. Com. files; Char. Com. Schemes, 7 Feb. 1913 and 29 May 1934; ex inf. the organizing sec. of the Walsall Guild of Social Service and Citizens' Advice Bureau (1973).

[4] *Rep. Town Clerk on Chars.* 10–11.

[5] Walsall Council House, mins. of Char. Cttee. 1917–51, *passim*; 1952–72, pp. 5, 15 sqq.

[6] Corp. char. accts. 1972; circular of 23 Oct. 1972, town clerk to council (copy in possession of the mayor's sec. 1972).

[7] Char. Com. files; Walsall Council House, mins. of trustees of Archer's Char., 1–2; *Rep. Town Clerk on Chars.* 1; W.T.C., box labelled Archer's Charity; Corp. char. accts. 1972; ex inf. the mayor's sec.

[8] Char. Com. files; ex inf. Mr. L. Harper (1973).

[9] Char. Com. files; ex inf. Mr. L. Harper (1973).

[10] Char. Com. files; *Rep. Town Clerk on Chars.* 9; Walsall Council House, mins. of Char. Cttee. 1917–51, pp. 62 sqq.; 1952–72, *passim*; Corp. char. accts. 1972.

[11] Char. Com. files; Walsall Council House, mins. of Char. Cttee. 1952–72, pp. 46, 64.

[12] Corp. char. accts. 1972.

[13] Ex inf. Mr. L. Harper (1973).

[14] Char. Com. files.

[15] Corp. char. accts. 1972; circular of 23 Oct. 1972, town clerk to council (copy in possession of the mayor's sec. 1972).

[16] Char. Com. files; Walsall Council House, mins. of Char. Cttee. 1917–51, p. 144.

[17] Corp. char. accts. 1972; circular of 23 Oct. 1972, town clerk to council.

[18] *Walsall Observer*, 27 Sept. 1957; *County Boro. of Walsall: Mins. of Procs. of Council, May 1957 to May 1958*, lvii, p. 565.

[19] Corp. char. accts. 1972.

[20] Char. Com. files; ex inf. Mr. W. J. Bridge (1973).

[1] This article was written mainly in 1973–4.

[2] O.S. Map 6″, Staffs. LVII. SE. (1903 edn.).

[3] *Census*, 1901.

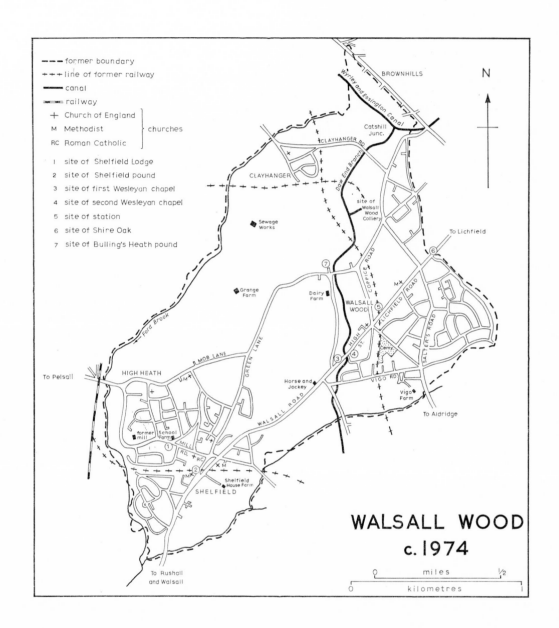

- - - former boundary
+ + + line of former railway
──── canal
railway
+ Church of England
M Methodist   } churches
RC Roman Catholic

1 site of Shelfield Lodge
2 site of Shelfield pound
3 site of first Wesleyan chapel
4 site of second Wesleyan chapel
5 site of station
6 site of Shire Oak
7 site of Bulling's Heath pound

N

BROWNHILLS

Wyrley and Essington Canal

Catshill
Junc.

CLAYHANGER RD.

Daw End Branch

CLAYHANGER

site of
Walsall
Wood
Colliery

To Lichfield

Sewage
Works

COPPICE ROAD

Grange
Farm

Dairy
Farm

WALSALL
WOOD

LICHFIELD ROAD

SALTER'S ROAD

Cemy.

Ford Brook

GREEN LANE

MOB LANE

HIGH HEATH

Horse and
Jockey

VIGO RD.

Vigo
Farm

To Pelsall

WALSALL ROAD

To Aldridge

former
mill

School
Farm

MILL RD.

RC

Shelfield
House Farm

SHELFIELD

To Rushall
and Walsall

WALSALL WOOD
c. 1974

0   miles   ½

0   kilometres   1

276

tributary Shelfield (or Shavers End) Brook and by Langley Brook.[4] The north-eastern boundary ran up Commonside[5] close to the Vigo Fault and along the southern side of Brownhills High Street, crossing it to form the northern tip of the area. Where the north-eastern boundary crosses the Walsall–Lichfield road, it was marked by a tree called Shire Oak; the tree was mentioned in 1533, and its remains were removed in the mid 1890s.[6] The area is situated on the Coal Measures, and the soil is chiefly marl and clay, with alluvium along the brooks.[7] The level of the ground rises from some 420 ft. at the confluence of Ford and Shelfield Brooks on the south-west to some 540 ft. at the site of the former Shire Oak.[8]

The area is occupied by three main settlements, Shelfield, Walsall Wood, and Clayhanger, each of them still physically separate. There is in fact much open country, notably in the north-west, consisting chiefly of farm-land and reclaimed land. As the name Walsall Wood suggests, the area was once a well-wooded part of Cannock forest. Much of it remained common or waste until the 19th century, but by c. 1600 encroachment had produced scattered settlement.[9] In 1619 there were 237 recipients of Mollesley's Dole and in 1661 387.[10] The population was given as 900 in 1837 and then consisted chiefly of nailers and chain-makers.[11] By 1851 it had reached 1,142, chiefly miners, although no mining had yet started in Walsall Wood itself.[12] By the 1850s the area was becoming more prosperous. In 1825 the population of Walsall Wood hamlet was said to consist entirely of paupers, and in 1845 the incumbent stated that he had 'only one person of independent property in the place'. In 1857, however, he surveyed the changes since 1825 and claimed that 'a new place is formed. A church has been built. . . . The mud and thatched cottages disappear. The old ragged inhabitants of a wild district drop off.'[13] The population had risen to 1,930 by 1861 as a result of the extension of mining in the neighbourhood and the opening of brickyards.[14] There was a notable rise during the decade 1871–81, from 2,077 to 3,242, attributed partly to the building of the railway; in addition Walsall Wood Colliery was opened then. By 1891 the population had reached 4,582 and consisted of shopkeepers, colliers, brick-makers, and a few small farmers. By 1901 it had risen to 6,492, an increase again attributed mainly to the development

of coal-mining and brick-making. Having reached 7,116 in 1911 and 8,351 in 1921, it had dropped to 7,597 by 1931. It was 8,805 in 1951. In 1961 the population of the slightly smaller area (1,520 a.) covered by the two new wards of Walsall Wood and of Shelfield and High Heath was 11,519.

Shelfield was at first the main settlement. It probably existed before the Conquest since Domesday Book recorded a hide of land there; in 1086, however, the hide was waste.[15] Shelfield was an inhabited area by the earlier 13th century[16] and was called a hamlet in 1276.[17] It had its own common fields.[18] Its centre was at the junction of Mill Road, Field Lane, and Birch Lane;[19] Shelfield Lodge on the south side of Mill Road (demolished in 1961) was an 18th-century house incorporating the remains of a late-medieval hall house.[20] Mill Road continued north on the line of the present Ford Brook Road to join the road running from High Heath to Pelsall.[21] There was settlement at High Heath by 1576 when a cottage there was described as a recent encroachment.[22] By 1763 there were also cottages at Shelfield (later Birches) Green on the Walsall–Lichfield road, at Irondish to the north where the present New Street meets the main road, along Green Lane which runs north from the green, and at Coal-heath to the south on the main road.[23] By 1775 there was a house at Shaver's End on the main road near the southern boundary, a site later occupied by Shelfield Farm (in 1974 commercial premises).[24] A house at the south-east corner of Birches Green on the site of the present Shelfield House Farm existed by the early 19th century and possibly by 1775.[25] Houses were built in the later 19th century in the triangle formed by Lichfield Road, New Street, and Spring Road[26] and towards the end of the century at High Heath along what is now the Coronation Road stretch of Mob Lane.[27] There is some housing of the period between the two World Wars, and after the Second World War Shelfield expanded greatly, with housing estates, both council and private, being built over the whole area between Mill Road, High Heath, Green Lane, and Ford Brook Lane, in the area south of Mill Road, and at Coalheath.

The village of Walsall Wood had become the main settlement by the early 19th century. The name was in use by 1200 when the wood of Walsall

[4] Shelfield and Langley Brooks were named as the bounds on the SE. in 1576 and 1617: S.R.O., D. 1287/1/2, survey of Walsall manor, 1576, m. 12; Willmore, *Walsall*, 440. The names Clayhanger and Shavers End Brooks were used in the late 18th and early 19th centuries: Pearce, *Walsall*, 224–5.

[5] It was probably not the path over the heath to Catshill mentioned in 1576: S.R.O., D. 1287/1/2, survey of Walsall manor, 1576, m. 12; below p. 278.

[6] S.R.O., D. 1287/8/2, map; W.S.L., S. MS. 417/Walsall, map; *S.H.C.* 1910, 35; *Walsall Observer*, 9 May 1896.

[7] Geol. Surv. Map 1″, solid and drift, sheet 154 (3rd edn.); *Kelly's Dir. Staffs.* (1940).

[8] O.S. Map 6″, Staffs. LVII. SE. and LXIII. NE. (prov. edn.).

[9] See pp. 279–80.

[10] W.T.C. II/31/1; II/13/49. The figures may have included visitors: above pp. 266–7.

[11] White, *Dir. Staffs.* (1834); Lich. Dioc. Regy., B/A/2(i)/K, p. 552.

[12] White, *Dir. Staffs.* (1851), 636; *Census*, 1861; below p. 281.

[13] Nat. Soc. files, Walsall Wood, 30 July 1825, 21 Feb. 1845, 6 Nov. 1857.

[14] The rest of this para. is based on *Census*. The occupational details for 1891 are taken from Nat. Soc. files, Walsall Wood (Clayhanger), 20 Oct. 1891. Most of the brick-and tile-making in the area has been just over the boundary in Aldridge: below p. 280.

[15] See p. 279.

[16] A Ric. of Shelfield occurs then: *Walsall Records*, 24; *S.H.C.* 1911, 146.

[17] *S.H.C.* vi (1), 80.   [18] See p. 279.

[19] See e.g. Yates, *Map of Staffs.* (1775); B.M. O.S.D. 212.

[20] S. R. Jones, 'Shelfield Lodge Farm, Aldridge, Staffs.' *Trans. S. Staffs. Arch. Soc.* x.

[21] Yates, *Map of Staffs.* (1775).   [22] See p. 280.

[23] S.R.O., D. 1287/8/2.

[24] Yates, *Map of Staffs.* (1775); O.S. Map 6″, Staffs. LXIII. NE. (1889 edn.).

[25] Yates, *Map of Staffs.* (1775); B.M. O.S.D. 212; S.R.O., D. 351/M/B/209; W.S.L., S. MS. 417/Walsall.

[26] O.S. Map 6″, Staffs. LVII. SE. (1903 edn.). A Wesleyan chapel was opened there in 1864, a school in 1878, and an Anglican mission church in 1895: see pp. 282–3.

[27] S.R.O., Q/RDc 106; O.S. Map 6″, Staffs. LVII. SE. (1903 edn.); datestone of 1894 in Spring Lane. For the mission church of c. 1886 see p. 282.

was a distinct part of Cannock forest.[28] Squatting on the extensive commons was in progress by the later 16th century.[29] By 1763 there was a hamlet along the Walsall–Lichfield road, and there was also settlement at Bullings Heath at the junction of Green Lane and the present Hall Lane, at Goblins Pit further south in Green Lane, around the common to the south of the main road, and at Shire Oak. By 1805 the southern common was known as Holly Bank Common and the settlement on its south side as Vigo. In 1763 there was also settlement on the edge of Walsall Wood Common north of the main road: at Paul's Coppice (so named by 1805) on the west of the common and at Catshill on the north by the Chester road. A way ran over the common to Catshill, evidently approximating to the line of the present Brownhills Road and Lindon Road.[30] Coppice Road running up the west side of the common from Walsall Wood village existed by the earlier 19th century.[31] An Anglican mission was established in the earlier 1820s and a school was opened in 1825.[32] At the inclosure of 1876 roads were laid out, to some extent following or replacing existing ways: Holly Bank Road (now King Street and Beechtree Road) and the present Queen Street and Vigo Road along the south-western edge of Holly Bank Common, and the present Coppice Road, Camden Street, Lindon Road, Friezland Lane, and Brownhills Road over Walsall Wood Common.[33] In the later 1870s too Walsall Wood Colliery was opened at Paul's Coppice.[34] Development followed, particularly from the end of the century.[35] There are three large housing estates: on the west side of Salter's Road and dating from the period between the two World Wars, on the east side of the road and built since the Second World War, and around Friezland Lane and also dating from the post-war period. Houses have also been built on the north side of Queen Street and Vigo Road since the war, and building was still in progress in 1974. Since the war several small factories have been built around the junction of Hall Lane and High Street, and in 1974 an industrial estate was being built over the site of Walsall Wood Colliery.

Clayhanger in the north occurs as arable, pasture, and woodland in the later 14th and early 15th centuries; it was an extensive area of pasture in 1576.[36] By 1763 there was settlement on the west side of Clayhanger Common, which occupied the north of the area, and the present Clayhanger Road ran over the common by the early 19th century.[37] By the

earlier 19th century the small village of Clayhanger was developing along what are now Bridge and Church Streets. A mission centre was opened c. 1872, and High Street was laid out as Caddick Street at the inclosure of 1876.[38] By 1878 the population was over 400.[39] A few houses (demolished by 1974) were built in Bridge Street between the railway and the canal about the end of the century,[40] and more were built in the village itself between the two World Wars. Since the Second World War a housing estate has been laid out to the south of High Street, and there has been some rebuilding on the sites of 19th-century houses.

Walsall Wood lies on the road from Walsall to Lichfield, turnpiked in 1766 as far as Muckley Corner on Watling Street.[41] A little beyond the boundary at Shire Oak the road crosses the old London–Chester road,[42] which as Brownhills High Street runs through the northern tip of the former parish. Shelfield bridge over Shelfield Brook, which occurs in 1576 and 1617,[43] presumably stood on the site of the bridge that carries the Lichfield road over that brook south of Shelfield. The lane leading from Shelfield to Aldridge, mentioned in 1324,[44] presumably followed the line of the present Spring Road and Stubbers Green Road. The road from Aldridge to Hednesford in Cannock via Walsall Wood is mentioned in the early 18th century, passing through the area apparently along the line of the present Northgate, Salter's Road, Brownhills Road, and Lindon Road to the Chester road at Catshill.[45]

The Wyrley and Essington Canal, opened in 1797, crosses the northern extremity of the area. About 1800 the Daw End branch was built from Catshill Junction south through Walsall Wood village to the Hay Head limestone quarries in Walsall.[46]

A railway was completed from Aldridge through Walsall Wood to Norton Canes in 1882, and a station was opened in High Street, Walsall Wood, when a passenger service was introduced in 1884. That service was withdrawn in 1930, and in 1962 the station was closed for freight also.[47] The Leighswood mineral branch was opened through the Shelfield area in 1872 from the South Staffordshire line at Pelsall to Leighswood Colliery in Aldridge; it was disused by the 1960s.[48] There was also a mineral line from the South Staffordshire line to Walsall Wood Colliery.[49]

Wakes were held, sometimes at Walsall Wood and sometimes at Shelfield, on the last Monday of Octo-

[28] See p. 279.
[29] See pp. 279–80.
[30] S.R.O., D. 1287/8/2; Yates, *Map of Staffs.* (1775); and see below. For the names Holly Bank, Vigo, and Paul's Coppice in 1805 see W.C.L., box 21, no. 10. Catshill occurs as Cattes Lowe alias Cattes Hill in 1576: S.R.O., D. 1287/1/2, survey of Walsall manor, 1576, m. 13.
[31] B.M. O.S.D. 212; O.S. Map 1″, sheet 62 NW. (1834 edn.).
[32] See pp. 281, 283. For dissenters there in 1813 see p. 282.
[33] S.R.O., Q/RDc 106.
[34] See p.281 .
[35] O.S. Map 6″, Staffs. LVII. SE. (1887 and later edns.); datestones of 1890–1905; S.R.O., C/E/1/B/7/12, p. 10; above p. 277. A house in Paul's Coppice (formerly New St.) is inscribed 'By the Sweat of a Miner's Brow 1895'.
[36] *Walsall Records*, 78; S.R.O., D. 641/1/2/32; above p. 178 and below p. 279.
[37] S.R.O., D. 1287/8/2; B.M. O.S.D. 212.
[38] O.S. Map 1″, sheet 62 NW. (1834 edn.); S.R.O., Q/RDc 106; below p. 282.

[39] Nat. Soc. files, Walsall Wood, 29 Oct. 1878.
[40] O.S. Map 6″, Staffs. LVII. NE. (1903 edn.).
[41] See p. 165.
[42] For the London–Chester road see *V.C.H. Staffs.* ii. 277.
[43] S.R.O., D. 1287/1/2, survey of Walsall manor, 1576, m. 7; Willmore, *Walsall*, 440.
[44] B.M. Harl. MS. 2131, f. 13v.; S.R.O., D. 1287/1/2, survey of Walsall manor, 1576, m. 12, mentioning the road from Shelfield to Stubbers Green; Yates, *Map of Staffs.* (1775).
[45] S.R.O., Q/SO 11, T. 1708; Yates, *Map of Staffs.* (1775); Willmore, *Walsall*, 375.
[46] See p. 168.
[47] C. R. Clinker, *Railways of the West Midlands, a Chronology 1808–1954*, 38–9, 40, 42–3, 60; *V.C.H. Staffs.* ii. 322; O.S. Map 6″, Staffs. LVII. SE. (1887 edn.); ex inf. British Railways, London Midland Region (1972).
[48] Clinker, *Railways of W. Midlands*, 39.
[49] O.S. Map 6″, Staffs. LVII. SE. (1887 edn., surveyed 1882).

ber or the first in November between at least 1894 and 1913.[50] Walsall Wood's only cinema, the Electric Picture Palace in Brookland Road, had been opened by 1924; it still existed in 1940 but had been demolished by 1974.[51] A recreation centre at Oak Park, Lichfield Road, was completed in 1973. It includes a swimming pool, three football pitches, three tennis courts, two bowling-greens, and facilities for other games.[52]

A friendly society at Walsall Wood was registered in 1833. By 1876 there were six societies, including three lodges of Odd Fellows.[53]

MANOR AND OTHER ESTATES.
In 1086 the king held a hide of waste land at Shelfield apparently as part of the manor of Walsall.[54] In 1300 the vill was still held by the lords of Walsall.[55] A separate manor of *SHELFIELD* is first mentioned in 1556. It originated in the property acquired by John le Rous in the early 14th century. In 1312 John and his wife Joan were granted land and rent in Shelfield by Florence de Verney and her husband Philip.[56] In the same year Sir Thomas le Rous, one of the joint lords of Walsall, granted John other rents and services there.[57] By 1317 John was holding courts at Shelfield.[58] In 1344 he conveyed all his property there to Sir Roger Hillary,[59] whose family had held other lands in Shelfield since at least 1278.[60] After Roger's death in 1356 his Shelfield estate descended with the manor of Goscote in Walsall until at least 1411.[61]

Soon afterwards, however, it was assigned to Margery Tylney, and it apparently descended through her son Frederick (or Philip) and her grandson Sir Frederick (d. before 1447) to her great-granddaughter Elizabeth Tylney (d. 1497). Elizabeth's second husband, Thomas Howard (d. 1524), earl of Surrey and from 1514 duke of Norfolk, was holding the estate by the courtesy from at least 1508.[62] In 1520 Elizabeth's heir, John Bourchier, Lord Berners, her son by her first husband,[63] conveyed it to the trustees of Sir John Skeffington of London.[64] Norfolk had resigned his life-interest by 1521.[65] Skeffington died in 1525,[66] leaving as heir his son William (d. 1551). When William's son John obtained possession of the estate on coming of age in 1556, it was described as the manor of Shelfield.[67] He died in 1604 and was succeeded by his son William (created

a baronet in 1627),[68] who in 1632 sold the manor to William Glascote.[69] In 1634–5 Glascote sold it to Sir Richard Wilbraham, lord of Walsall,[70] and Shelfield manor was then presumably absorbed into Walsall manor.

St. Peter's chantry in Lichfield cathedral, founded by 1253, had property in Shelfield at the suppression, including a house and land granted to Walsall grammar school in 1554 and known by 1915 as School farm. The school governors acquired further property at Walsall Wood in 1844 and sold both estates in 1944.[71] School Farm, a brick building of the mid 19th century, still stood in 1973, but by then houses had been built over most of the farm-land.

ECONOMIC HISTORY.
Shelfield formed part of Cannock forest by the later 12th century, and the wood of Walsall was mentioned in 1199–1200.[72] The woodland was still extensive in the late 16th and early 17th centuries.[73] By 1843, however, 21 a. at Paul's Coppice and 6 a. at Goblins Pit were all that remained.[74]

Early clearance was presumably around the settlement at Shelfield. In 1086 a hide of arable there was waste.[75] By 1317 there were three common fields. Town field lay on either side of the present Field Lane and was bounded by Mill Lane, Ford Brook Lane, Coronation Road, Spring Lane, and Birch Lane. Another field, called Wadgreve or Wadgrene in 1317, Watgreave or Thorneyfield in 1766, and Thorn field by 1784, lay north of High Heath. A third, Rodbardesfeld, is probably identifiable with the 18th-century Pool field, which lay west of the heath and north of Coronation Road. All three fields were apparently still open in 1766 but had been inclosed by 1819.[76] The common fields, however, were small, and by the later Middle Ages most farm-land was probably held in severalty. In the late 16th and early 17th centuries farming was mainly pastoral, with stock consisting of cattle, sheep, and some pigs. Rye, oats, and barley were grown.[77]

By 1576 much of the waste round Shelfield had evidently been inclosed; it then consisted of three commons, Shelfield Green (later Birches Green), Colliers Ford Heath (probably the later Coalheath), and High Heath. At Clayhanger 160 a. of 'sterile ground' was held in severalty; the rest of the Walsall Wood area was one large common. Squatting on the

50 St. Francis R.C. Primary Sch., [Shelfield, log bk. 1893-1958, pp. 35, 73, 184, 214, 284.
51 *Kelly's Dir. Staffs.* (1924; 1940); O.S. Map 1/2,500, Staffs. LVII. 16 (prov. edn., revised 1938).
52 *Walsall Observer*, 7 Dec. 1973, 15 Feb. 1974.
53 S.R.O., Q/RSf; *Rep. Chief Registrar of Friendly Societies, 1876, App. P*, H.C. 429–1, pp. 411–12 (1877), lxxvii.
54 *V.C.H. Staffs.* iv. 38, no. 7; Homeshaw, *Walsall*, 7.
55 *S.H.C.* v (1), 178.   56 *S.H.C.* 1911, 77.
57 *Walsall Records*, 41.
58 B.M. Harl. MS. 2131, f. 13.
59 Ibid. f. 12.
60 Ibid. f. 13v.
61 See p. 173 and references there cited.
62 B.M. Harl. MS. 506, p. 332; *Cal. Pat.* 1446–52, 43; *Complete Peerage*, ix. 614–15; E 150/1018 no. 1; *Visitations of Norfolk* (Harl. Soc. xxxii), 288–9; *Cal. Inq. p.m. Hen. VII*, iii, p. 279.
63 *Complete Peerage*, ii. 153–4.
64 N.R.A., Chilham Castle, Kent, Massereene (Staffs.) deeds, 24; S.R.O., D. 260/M/T/2/6.
65 *S.H.C.* xi. 262–3.
66 C 142/49 no. 44.
67 Massereene (Staffs.) deeds, 29.
68 C 142/680 no. 12.
69 Shaw, *Staffs.* ii. 81, states that the sale took place in 1641. The fine, however, is dated 1632 (C.P. 25(2)/485/8 Chas. I East.).
70 Shaw, *Staffs.* ii. 81.
71 *Cal. Pat.* 1553–4, 205; *S.H.C.* 1915, 157; O.S. Map 6", Staffs. LVII. SE. (1921 edn., revised 1915); Fink, *Queen Mary's Grammar Sch.* 245, 247.
72 *S.H.C.* ii (1), 94; v (1), 178.
73 S.R.O., D. 1287/1/2, survey of Walsall manor, 1576, m. 13; D. 260/M/F/1/8, ct. of recog. and survey, 1617, p. 34.
74 W.S.L., S. MS. 417/Walsall, nos. 2617, 2667.
75 *V.C.H. Staffs.* iv. 38, no. 7.
76 B.M. Harl. MS. 2131, f. 13 (a 17th-cent. MS. giving Wadgrene, perhaps in error); Fink, *Queen Mary's Grammar Sch.* 245 and front end-paper; S.R.O., D. 351/M/B/ 209; W.S.L., S. MS. 417/Walsall, nos. 2689–90, 2702–5, 2711–18, 2732–48, 2750–7.
77 L.J.R.O., wills of Thos. Fletcher (proved 7 Jan. 1582/3), Wm. Bettes (8 June 1608), John Byrche (3 Mar. 1612/13), inventories; admins. of Rob. and Wm. Launder (30 May 1617 and 25 Jan. 1627/8), inventories.

waste, however, had already begun. A house and 4 a. at Walsall Wood and a cottage on High Heath were recent encroachments.[78] In 1617 a shop and 8 cottages stood on the waste; 6 cottages had been built recently.[79] By 1763 there were 124 encroachments at Walsall Wood, 11 at Coalheath, 10 at Green Lane, Shelfield, and Irondish, and one at High Heath. The waste, however, was still extensive. The southern commons, High Heath, Shelfield Green, Coalheath, and Moss Pit Green to the west of Shelfield, covered 37 a.; Walsall Wood and Clayhanger Commons formed a single stretch of waste of 504 a.[80] The part of Walsall Wood Common south of Lichfield Road was known by 1805 as Holly Bank Common. There were then some 218 encroachments; 25 were at or near Shelfield and the rest in the north, 99 being on Walsall Wood Common.[81] By 1843 the northern waste, though still continuous, had been further reduced; Clayhanger, Walsall Wood, and Holly Bank Commons covered c. 365 a.[82] In 1876 the surviving commons, altogether 350 a., were inclosed under an Act of 1865, partly for agriculture and partly for new roads and houses.[83]

The area of farm-land was greatly reduced to make way for housing after the Second World War. By 1974 four farms remained. Grange farm west of Green Lane consisted of 177 a. used for dairying and corn-growing. Dairy farm in Hall Lane, c. 70 a., produced beef, barley, and potatoes. Shelfield House farm consisted of 63 a.; 8 a. was under barley and the rest was used for dairy cattle, pigs, and poultry. Vigo farm was a 12-acre small holding.[84]

A windmill was built at Shelfield between 1744 and 1786, but its location is unknown.[85] By 1816 there was a windmill on the north side of Mill Lane, Shelfield, on the site of the present Shelfield mill; it was presumably the windmill occupied in 1814 by William Bacon.[86] It had been rebuilt as a steam corn-mill by the early 1880s and was worked as such until the mid 1930s. In 1973 the building was used as a factory by the Grafton Heater Co. (1960) Ltd. and the Pelsall Tool and Engineering Co. Ltd.; until a fire in 1953 part of the windmill had survived within the later structure.[87]

The existence of a croft in Shelfield called Bloomers Parrok in 1402[88] may indicate early iron-smelting. A bloomsmithy stood on Shelfield Brook west of the later Shelfield Farm in 1576,[89] but nothing further is known of it. There is evidence of

light metal-working in Shelfield and Walsall Wood from the early 18th century. In 1715 two Shelfield buckle-makers and a stirrup-maker were mentioned.[90] A button-maker of Walsall Wood occurs in 1729,[91] and a maker of tinned stirrups in 1813.[92] Chain-makers occur throughout the 19th century, mostly specializing in heavy chains. There was one chain-maker in 1813,[93] and from at least 1834 to the later 1840s Henry Homer was making chains in Shelfield.[94] At Walsall Wood there were five chain-makers in 1834, all members of the Jackson family, which continued to dominate the local trade until the 20th century. William Jackson, who abandoned the business at the beginning of the 20th century, was the last chain-maker in the area. A hame-maker occurs in 1860. Nailing was also practised by the earlier 19th century. There were 5 nail-makers in 1860, and 4 nailers were assigned land when the commons were inclosed in 1876. The last nail-maker, Abraham Harrison, gave up the trade between 1892 and 1896. Between 1904 and 1908 John Grainger began making boilers in Shelfield; the business closed between 1932 and 1936.[95] There was an iron-foundry in Beech Tree Road for some time before 1952 when it was taken over by Stephen F. Butler & Co. Ltd., who converted it for use as an aluminium foundry. Butlers moved to Lindon Road in 1958 and to Brownhills in 1964.[96] Several other metal-working firms set up factories in Walsall Wood and Shelfield after the Second World War, and at least 16 were still in business in 1974. Products included presswork, tools, rivets, wheelbarrows, refrigerator equipment, aluminium castings, dies, punches and drills, metal windows, and steel fabrications.[97]

The abundant Etruria Marl at Walsall Wood has been used for brickmaking from at least the 18th century, though the largest works in the area have been just over the parish boundary in Aldridge. Bricks were made on the manorial waste at Shire Oak in 1775.[98] By 1843 there was a brickyard east of Birches Green at Shelfield owned by John Stokes,[99] and in 1858 one Brawn made bricks, tiles, sewage pipes, and drain-pipes at a works in Shelfield.[1] The Walsall Wood Colliery Co. opened a brickworks at Paul's Coppice in the late 1870s,[2] which apparently closed at some time between 1916 and 1937;[3] most of the buildings had been demolished by 1938.[4] By 1882 Clayhanger Brickworks had

[78] S.R.O., D. 1287/1/2, survey of Walsall manor, 1576, m. 13.

[79] S.R.O., D. 260/M/F/1/8, ct. of recog. and survey, 1617, p. 6.   [80] S.R.O., D. 1287/8/2.

[81] D. 1287/1/37, Walsall cottages 1805; W.C.L., box 21, no. 10.

[82] W.S.L., S. MS. 417/Walsall, nos. 2559, 2577, 2709, 2731, 2800, 2842, 3002, 3068.

[83] S.R.O., Q/RDc 106; 29 & 30 Vic. c. 29 (Local and Personal).   [84] Ex inf. the farmers (1974).

[85] It is not mentioned in L.J.R.O., B/V/6/Walsall, 1744, but occurs ibid. 1786. It is not shown on Yates, Map of Staffs. (edns. of 1775 and 1799).

[86] B.M. O.S.D. 212; Homeshaw, Bloxwich, 152. A Wm. Bacon was miller at Shelfield in the 1860s: P.O. Dir. Staffs. (1860; 1864; 1868).

[87] Kelly's Dir. Staffs. (1884); Walsall Observer, 24 Apr. 1953; ex inf. Mr. G. Allsopp, Shelfield Mill House (1973).

[88] W.S.L., D. 1798/94.

[89] S.R.O., D. 1287/1/2, survey of Walsall manor, 1576, m. 10.

[90] Assizes 4/18, p. 237.

[91] Lond. Gaz. 7–10 June 1729.

[92] Pearce, Walsall, 169.   [93] Ibid. 158.

[94] White, Dir. Staffs. (1834); P.O. Dir. Staffs. (1845). He is not listed in White, Dir. Staffs. (1851).

[95] White, Dir. Staffs. (1834; 1851); P.O. Dir. Staffs. (1845 and later edns.); Kelly's Dir. Staffs. (1884 and later edns. to 1936); S.R.O., Q/RDc 106.

[96] Ex inf. Butler Foundries Ltd., Brownhills (1974).

[97] Walsall Chamber of Commerce & Ind. Dir. 1974/5; Kelly's Dir. Merchants, Manufacturers, and Shippers (1947; 1952; 1953); Kelly's Dir. Manufacturers and Merchants (1966); P.O. Telephone Dir. Sect. 227: 1971.

[98] S.R.O., D. 1287/1/2, survey of Walsall, 1775.

[99] W.S.L., S. MS. 417/Walsall, no. 2927.

[1] R. Hunt, Memoirs of Geol. Surv., Mineral Statistics of U.K. for 1858, ii (1860), 83. The works of Joberns & Arrowsmith listed ibid. 85 as at Walsall Wood was presumably on its later site in Aldridge.

[2] Kelly's Dir. Staffs. (1880); O.S. Map 6″, Staffs. LVII. SE. (1887 edn.).

[3] It occurs in List of Quarries . . . for 1916 (H.M.S.O. 1917), 526, but not in Kelly's Dir. Building Trades (1937).

[4] O.S. Map 6″, Staffs. LVII. SE. (1921 edn., revised 1915; prov. edn., revised 1938).

been opened on a site adjoining the Wyrley and Essington Canal; it evidently made red bricks. It was advertised for sale in 1896, but was disused in 1901. Though it seems to have been in production again c. 1904 it had evidently closed by 1910.[5]

Walsall Wood overlies that part of the concealed Cannock Chase coalfield which is bounded by the Vigo and Clayhanger Faults.[6] The existence of coal there was suggested in 1777, and in 1841 Lord Bradford's agent urged that trial shafts should be sunk.[7] Mining did not begin, however, until the 1870s. In 1873 Lord Bradford granted a lease to a consortium and sinkings were begun at Paul's Coppice close to the Daw End branch canal. The lease was assigned to the Walsall Wood Colliery Co. in 1876.[8] The Deep Coal was reached in 1877 at 1,677 feet, the shaft being the deepest in the Cannock Chase coalfield.[9] Production began in 1879.[10] In 1899 the colliery was producing up to 4,000 tons a week,[11] and c. 1955 it employed 660 men underground, working three seams.[12] It was closed in 1964.[13] In 1974 the buildings were occupied by Brownhills Motor Sales Ltd. and by Effluent Dispersal Ltd. which used the workings for waste disposal; the rest of the site was being developed as an industrial estate.

Since the Second World War several light industries have been established in Walsall Wood and Shelfield. In 1974 there were a clothing factory and a factory producing timber-framed buildings in Coppice Road; two leather-goods works and an electrical washer and gasket factory in Hall Lane; an organ-building works in Walsall Road; and an electrical-appliance works at Shelfield Mill.

LOCAL GOVERNMENT AND PUBLIC SERVICES. The lord of Shelfield manor was holding two courts a year by 1317,[14] and in 1632 he was said to possess view of frankpledge.[15] Otherwise the evidence shows Walsall Wood and Shelfield as part of Walsall manor.[16] In the earlier 19th century pinners for Walsall Wood and Shelfield were appointed at Walsall manor court.[17] There was a pound at Bullings Heath, Walsall Wood, at the east end of Green Lane, in the earlier 1840s.[18] A small plot at the south-west corner of the green at Shelfield was assigned to the lord of Walsall manor under the inclosure award of 1876 for use as a public pound. A pound still stood there in 1901.[19]

For parochial purposes the area was a detached part of the township of Walsall foreign until the 19th century. It formed one of the highway districts into which the foreign was divided by 1768.[20] It was not, however, included with the rest of the foreign in the new borough of Walsall in 1835. Its exclusion led to problems in the administration of the poor law, and the Walsall Improvement and Market Act of 1848 extended the powers of the borough justices to the area for poor-law purposes.[21] In 1894 it became part of the urban district of Brownhills.[22]

A sewage works had been built by 1882 to the north of Green Lane near the canal bridge. It passed to the Brownhills urban district council and in 1966 to the Upper Tame Main Drainage Authority.[23] A gasworks (now demolished) had been built by 1872 on the Wyrley and Essington Canal near Catshill Junction by the Brownhills Gas Co. Ltd., later the Ogley Hay and Brownhills Gas Co. Ltd.[24] There was a police station at Walsall Wood by 1868[25] and a post office by 1880.[26] From 1904 trams ran to Walsall Wood from the centre of Walsall. Buses were introduced in 1927 as part of a service from Walsall to Lichfield and replaced the trams in 1928.[27]

CHURCH. The church of *ST. JOHN*, Walsall Wood, originated in a mission established by the earlier 1820s. Services were at first held in cottages, but in 1825 the vicar of St. Matthew's was licensed to hold them in a schoolroom.[28] In 1836 1½ a. on the north side of the present High Street was acquired from Lord Bradford as the site for the church, which was consecrated in 1837.[29] The living was endowed with £500 raised by subscription and augmented by £20 yearly out of Walsall vicarage.[30] In 1845 a new parish of St. John was formed out of St. Matthew's parish.[31] The living, at first a perpetual curacy and from 1868 a vicarage, has remained in the gift of the vicar of St. Matthew's.[32] The minister's house originally lay west of the church on the site of the present St. John's Close.[33] It was replaced by a new

[5] Ibid. (1887 edn., surv. 1882; 1903 edn., revised 1901); S.R.O., D. 682/22; *List of Quarries, 1904*, 405. It does not occur in *List of Quarries, 1910*.

[6] *V.C.H. Staffs.* ii. 71–2; G. Barrow and others, *Memoirs of Geol. Surv., Geol. of Country around Lichfield*, 16, 94–6, 165; Geol. Surv. Map 6", Staffs. LVII. SE. (1921 edn.).

[7] S.R.O., D. 1287/6/14, R. Holmes to J. Bradfield, 13 Aug. 1777; D. 1287/18/26, business corresp. 1840–2, P. Potter to Lord Bradford, 4 Aug. 1841 and plan.

[8] Ibid./18/31, business corresp. 1873, Potter to Bradford, 13 Oct. 1873; D. 570/6, lease of 29 May 1937; *Walsall Observer*, 3 Oct. 1873.

[9] Ex inf. N.C.B. (1973); Barrow and others, *Geol. Country around Lichfield*, 45; S.R.O., D. 1287/18/31, business corresp. 1877, Potter to Bradford, 5 Dec. 1877.

[10] D. 1287/18/31, business corresp. 1878, Potter to Bradford, 5 May 1878; ex inf. N.C.B.

[11] S.R.O., D. 570/6, Walsall Wood pit costs 1898–9.

[12] Colliery Guardian, *Guide to the Coalfields* (1956), 325.

[13] *Walsall Observer*, 7 Feb. 1964; ex inf. N.C.B.

[14] B.M. Harl. MS. 2131, f. 13.

[15] C.P. 25 (2)/485/8 Chas. I East.

[16] The whole area was included in the bounds of Walsall manor in 1576 and 1617: S.R.O., D. 1287/1/2, survey of Walsall manor, 1576, m. 10; Willmore, *Walsall*, 440.

[17] See p. 210.

[18] W.S.L., S. MS. 417/Walsall, map.

[19] S.R.O., Q/RDc 106; O.S. Map 6", Staffs. LVII. SE. (1903 edn., revised 1901). [20] See p. 212.

[21] 11 & 12 Vic. c. 161 (Local and Personal), s. 61. The area was also excluded from the Walsall parliamentary borough of 1832: see p. 225.

[22] See p. 275.

[23] O.S. Map 6", Staffs. LVII. SE. (edns. of 1887 and 1903); *Express & Star*, 9 Dec. 1965.

[24] O.S. Map 6", Staffs. LVII. SE. (edns. of 1887 and 1921); *P.O. Dir. Staffs.* (1872). It is last mentioned in *Kelly's Dir. Staffs.* in 1932.

[25] *P.O. Dir. Staffs.* (1868).

[26] *Kelly's Dir. Staffs.* (1880).

[27] County Boro. of Walsall, *Jubilee of Transport Undertaking 1904–1954* (copy in W.C.L.); W.P.L., announcement of beginning of bus service 18 Apr. 1927.

[28] Sunday-sch. centenary leaflet, 1880 (framed copy in St. John's vestry); Lich. Dioc. Regy., B/A/1/29, p. 89.

[29] Lich. Dioc. Regy., B/A/2(i)/K, pp. 549–51, 556–60; *Staffs. Advertiser*, 26 Aug. 1837.

[30] Lich. Dioc. Regy., B/A/2(i)/K, pp. 553–4; /L, p. 1.

[31] *Lond. Gaz.* 12 Aug. 1845, pp. 2422–3.

[32] Lich. Dioc. Regy., B/A/1/30, p. 96; *Lich. Dioc. Ch. Cal.* (1869), 104; *Lich. Dioc. Dir.* (1972).

[33] W.S.L., S. MS. 417/Walsall, no. 3040.

house north of the church in 1967 and demolished in 1968.[34]

Several missions have been opened from St. John's. A mission centre was established at Clay-hanger c. 1872.[35] The mission church of Holy Trinity there was opened in 1879; designed by D. Shenton Hill of Birmingham, it is a brick building with rendered walls and has a bell in a bellcot.[36] Christ Church, High Heath, was opened c. 1886 and is built of rendered brick in a mixed Gothic and Renaissance style; it was closed in 1973.[37] St. Mark's, School Street, Shelfield, was opened in 1895 and closed in 1964. It was replaced in 1965 by a new mission church of St. Mark in Green Lane, with a house near by for an assistant curate.[38]

The church of St. John was designed by a Mr. Highway of Walsall (probably Isaac Highway) in a plain Gothic style.[39] It originally consisted of a nave and west tower in blue brick; of that building only the tower and west wall of the nave remain. A south aisle of red brick and a sanctuary were added in 1886, and a north aisle designed by H. E. Lavender of Walsall was built to match in 1895; there is a vestry at the end of each aisle.[40] The rebuilt nave has an arcade of five bays with cast-iron piers and foliage capitals. The original graveyard was c. ½ a. in extent; under the inclosure award of 1876 4 a. in what is now Brookland Road was assigned to the parish as a burial ground for all denominations in Walsall Wood.[41]

ROMAN CATHOLICISM.

ROMAN CATHOLICISM. A mass-centre was opened from St. Patrick's, Walsall, in 1891 in the clubroom of the Four Crosses inn at Shelfield.[42] A school-chapel dedicated to St. Peter and St. Paul was opened in 1893 on the corner of Mill Road and Broad Lane on a site given by Peter Aspinall of the Four Crosses; designed by S. Loxton of Walsall and Cannock, it is of brick. A parish, which at first included Aldridge, was formed in 1909; a resident priest was appointed and occupied a house adjoining the church. The Franciscans took over the parish in 1924. They left in 1966, and Shelfield passed back into the care of the archdiocese of Birmingham. In 1932 the church of St. Francis was opened on the opposite side of Mill Road to the earlier buildings, part of the cost being met by a gift of £3,000 from R. Holden. In 1974 the former chapel and house were

being used respectively as a parish hall and a social club. The Roman Catholic population of St. Francis's parish in 1974 was 1,025.

PROTESTANT NONCONFORMITY.

PROTESTANT NONCONFORMITY. A barn at Shelfield Lodge and the clubroom at the Horse and Jockey inn at Walsall Wood were registered in 1813 for unspecified dissenting worship.[43] About the early 1820s Benjamin Wheeley and other Wesleyan Methodists from Walsall began to hold a school on Sunday mornings in a barn at Walsall Wood, with a service in the afternoon.[44] By 1851 the congregation at the afternoon services averaged 25, but there was still no proper chapel.[45] There was a chapel in Walsall Road to the south-west of the canal bridge by 1882, and probably by 1878; it is a Gothic building of brick. It was replaced c. 1902 by a chapel further north on the opposite side of the road; it had been closed by 1959 and was subsequently demolished. The earlier chapel became a Sunday school and since 1946 has been occupied by W. Hawkins & Son, organ-builders.[46]

By 1851 Wesleyans were meeting in temporary premises at Shelfield, and on Census Sunday that year there was an evening congregation of 25.[47] In 1864 a chapel was built on the corner of Lichfield and Spring Roads;[48] it is a Gothic building of brick with a cement façade. It was replaced in 1906–7 by a chapel built to the south.[49] Designed by T. W. Sanders of Walsall,[50] it is of brick and has an ornamental façade with stone dressings. The earlier chapel became a hall.

Ebenezer Primitive Methodist chapel in Lichfield Road towards the northern end of Walsall Wood was built in 1863.[51] In 1891 a new chapel, of red brick in a baroque style, was built on the same site.[52] The adjacent school is dated 1908. A Primitive Methodist chapel was built at High Heath on the corner of Mob Lane (now Coronation Road) and Broad Lane (now Broad Way) in 1893.[53] It is of red brick with blue-brick dressings. A Primitive Methodist chapel was built in Four Crosses Road, Shelfield, in 1906.[54] Now Shelfield Centenary Methodist church, it is a brick building with applied half-timbering.

The Church of the Latter-day Saints registered a building near the Horse and Jockey in 1855; they had ceased to use it by 1876.[55] There was a chapel of

[34] Ex inf. the vicar (1972); *Evening Mail*, 28 Nov. 1968.
[35] *Lich. Dioc. Ch. Cal.* (1873), 183; Nat. Soc. files, Walsall Wood, 29 Oct. 1878, describing the mission as 'a cottage service'.
[36] Sunday-sch. centenary leaflet, 1880.
[37] *Lich. Dioc. Yr. Bk.* (1886), 22; *Lich. Dioc. Ch. Cal.* (1887), 113; *Walsall Observer*, 11 May 1973.
[38] Lich. Dioc. Regy., B/A/1/35, p. 400; ex inf. the vicar (1972).
[39] *Staffs. Advertiser*, 26 Aug. 1837; plate facing p. 81 above. For Isaac Highway see Pigot, *Nat. Com. Dir.* (1841), Staffs. p. 82.
[40] *Lich. Dioc. Mag.* 1886, 101; 1895, 189; Pevsner, *Staffs.* 297 (which, however, confuses N. and S. aisles).
[41] Lich. Dioc. Regy., B/A/2(i)/K, p. 553; /S, pp. 566, 573–7; /W, p. 599; S.R.O., Q/RDc 106; S.R.O., D. 1287/18/30/business corresp. 1866, J. Potter to Lord Bradford, 25 Sept. 1866.
[42] This para. is based on *Cath. Dir. of Archdioc. of Birm.* (1965), 197; *Staffs. Advertiser* (S. Staffs. edn.), 22 Apr. 1893; tablet to members of the Aspinall family, formerly in the school-church and now in St. Francis R.C. Primary Sch., Shelfield; inf. from the parish priest (1974).
[43] *S.H.C.* 4th ser. iii. 30.

[44] D. E. Parry, *Notes on Bloxwich and Bloxwich Methodism* (copy in W.C.L.).   [45] H.O. 129/380/4/1.
[46] O.S. Map 6", Staffs. LVII. SE. (1887 edn., surv. 1882); O.S. Map 1/2,500, Staffs. LVII. 16 (1919 edn.); G.R.O., Worship Reg. no. 4272 (registration of 1854, replaced 1898 by no. 36723, cancelled Oct. 1959); ibid. no. 38907 (registration of 1902, cancelled July 1959); Nat. Soc. files, Walsall Wood, letter from vicar 29 Oct. 1878; *Evening Mail*, 11 June 1970.
[47] H.O. 129/380/4/1. The building was listed as not used exclusively for worship.
[48] Date on the building.
[49] *Staffs. Advertiser*, 29 Dec. 1906, p. 6; 28 Dec. 1907, p. 7; date of 1906 on the church.
[50] Inscription on memorial stone laid by him.
[51] Inscription on a stone from the first chapel reset in the south boundary wall.
[52] Date on the church.
[53] Date on the church. It was registered in Dec. 1893: Worship Reg. no. 34166.
[54] Date on the church. It was registered in June 1907: Worship Reg. no. 42490.
[55] Worship Reg. no. 6942 (cancelled 1876 on certificate of supt. registrar).

unknown denomination at the west end of Beech Tree Road between at least 1878 and 1883.[56]

The Christian Brethren registered the Gospel Hall in Clayhanger Road in 1927 and the House of Prayer in Coppice Road in 1934.[57]

EDUCATION. From 1804 until 1826 the governors of Walsall grammar school paid two schoolmistresses to teach children in Walsall Wood to read. Both taught in Walsall Wood village until 1806, when one of them apparently moved to Shelfield.[58] The vicar of Walsall started a Sunday school at Walsall Wood in 1825[59] and set about establishing a day school. Land was leased from Lord Bradford at a nominal rent, and later in 1825 a schoolroom for 50 boys and 50 girls was built. The National Society made a building grant. The vicar intended that the children should be taught free and relied for funds upon subscriptions and help from the governors of Walsall grammar school. The school did not in fact open until 1829, when the governors of the grammar school began to pay the salary of a schoolmaster. In 1833 68 boys and 68 girls attended on weekdays and 80 boys and 84 girls on Sundays. The governors of the grammar school stopped paying the master's salary in 1841, but in 1844 they joined Lord Bradford in settling the school site in trust; the minister of St. John's, Walsall Wood, then became manager.[60] In 1845 a teacher's house was built with the aid of grants from government and the National Society. By 1857, however, the schoolroom was in disrepair and the school was threatened with the loss of its annual government grant. In 1859 a larger school with a teacher's house was opened in Lichfield Road on a site given by Lord Bradford. The old school and teacher's house were sold and the money applied to the new buildings.[61] An infants' school was added in 1882.[62] In 1885 men from the village who attended Sunday morning classes in reading and writing at the schools built a new classroom for the 1859 schoolhouse and altered and added to the infants' school.[63] The mixed school was again enlarged in 1898.[64] The schools were reorganized into junior and infants' schools in 1932 and were merged into a single school in 1974.[65]

Walsall Wood did not come under the jurisdiction of Walsall school board; it was instead one of four areas grouped together in 1876 under a new Norton-under-Cannock United District school board.[66] Responsibility for education passed in 1903 to the county council and in 1974 to the metropolitan borough of Walsall.

SCHOOLS OPENED SINCE 1876. Castlefort Junior and Infants' School, Castlefort Road, Walsall Wood, was opened in 1960 as Holly Lane Junior and Infants' School. It was renamed in 1961.[67]

High Heath Church of England School was opened c. 1886 as a National school in connexion with the mission church of Christ Church, High Heath. It was closed in 1932.[68]

Holy Trinity Church of England Infants' School, Clayhanger, was opened in 1880 as a National school for girls and infants. It was housed in a schoolroom beside Holy Trinity Church.[69] It later became a school for infants only. In 1968 it was moved to a new building on an adjoining site.[70]

St. Francis Roman Catholic Junior and Infants' School, formerly St. Peter and St. Paul Roman Catholic School, was opened in 1893 for boys, girls, and infants in the Roman Catholic school-chapel on the corner of Mill Road and Broad Lane, Shelfield.[71] In 1938 the school, renamed after the patron saint of the new church, became a junior and infants' school only.[72] New buildings in Mill Road to replace the old school were opened in three stages between 1961 and 1969.[73]

Shelfield Infants' School, School Street, Shelfield, is housed in the premises of the former Shelfield Board School. The board school was opened in 1878 as a mixed and infants' school and was enlarged in 1885 and 1895.[74] A new building for the infants was opened in 1909.[75] In 1932 senior pupils were transferred to new buildings in Coalheath Lane, Shelfield, and the School Street buildings became a junior mixed and infants' school. In 1961 the juniors were also moved to the Coalheath Lane buildings.[76]

Shelfield Junior and Infants' School, Coalheath Lane, Shelfield, was established in 1961 as a junior mixed school with pupils from School Street. It became a junior mixed and infants' school in 1964.[77]

Shelfield School, Mob Lane, High Heath, a comprehensive secondary school, was opened in 1932 in Coalheath Lane, Shelfield, as Shelfield Senior School. It became Shelfield Secondary Modern School in 1945. In 1960 it was moved to new buildings in Mob Lane. It became a comprehensive school in 1971 and was renamed Shelfield School.[78]

Shire Oak School, Lichfield Road, Walsall Wood, a comprehensive secondary school, was formed in 1970 by merging Shire Oak Grammar School, opened in 1961, with Walsall Wood Secondary Modern School, which had been moved to new buildings adjoining those of the grammar school in 1966.[79]

Walsall Wood Junior and Infants' School, Brown-

[56] Nat. Soc. files, Walsall Wood, letter from vicar 29 Oct. 1878; O.S. Map 1/2,500, Staffs. LVII. 16 (1884 edn., surv. 1883). [57] Worship Reg. nos. 50707, 55041.
[58] Fink, *Queen Mary's Grammar Sch.* 267–8.
[59] Ibid. 443–4.
[60] Nat. Soc. files; *Educ. Enquiry Abstract*, H.C. 62, p. 890 (1835), xlii; Fink, *Queen Mary's Grammar Sch.* 268.
[61] Nat. Soc. files; S.R.O., D. 812/Walsall Wood National School, plans dated 1857; *P.O. Dir. Staffs.* (1860).
[62] Nat. Soc. files.
[63] Ibid.; *Lich. Dioc. Mag.* 1885, 122.
[64] *Kelly's Dir. Staffs.* (1900).
[65] Nat. Soc. files; *Walsall Observer*, 25 Jan. 1974.
[66] S.R.O., C/E/1/B/7, pp. 1, 11.
[67] Ex inf. the headmaster (1974).
[68] Nat. Soc. files; *Staffs. County Council Educ. Cttee. Mins.* (1932–3), p. 39 (copy in S.R.O.).

[69] Log bk. 1880–1921, p. 1 (at the school, 1974); Nat. Soc. files.
[70] Ex inf. the headmistress (1974).
[71] Log bk. 1893–1958, p. 2 (at the school, 1974); above p. 282.
[72] Log bk. 1893–1958, p. 422.
[73] Ex inf. the headmaster (1974).
[74] *Kelly's Dir. Staffs.* (1900).
[75] An inscription on the building gives the date 1908, but it was not opened until Jan. 1909: G. Balfour, *Ten Years of Staffs. Education, 1903–1913* (Stafford, 1913), 126 (copy in W.S.L.).
[76] S.R.O., Survey of log bks. and other sch. recs. (1965), *sub* Shelfield.
[77] Ibid.
[78] Ibid.; ex inf. the deputy head teacher (1974).
[79] Ex inf. the headmaster (1974).

hills Road, Walsall Wood, was opened in 1903 as the mixed and infants' Walsall Wood Board School. A new infants' school was erected in 1906, and the original building was enlarged in 1912.[80] In 1932 the school was reorganized to form a senior school and a mixed and infants' school. The former became a secondary modern school in 1945, moved to new buildings in Lichfield Road, Walsall Wood, in 1966, and merged with Shire Oak Grammar School to form Shire Oak School in 1970.[81]

In 1974 there were two special schools in the area: High Heath, in Green Lane, Shelfield (1965), and Aldridge (later renamed Oakwood), in Druids Walk, Walsall Wood (1971).[82]

[80] S.R.O., C/E/1/B/7/12, p. 247; Balfour, *Ten Years of Staffs. Educ.* 126; inscription on building.

[81] S.R.O., Survey of log bks. (1965), *sub* Brownhills.
[82] Ex inf. the head teachers (1974).

INDEX